366 FATLINER WEIRDIES 2

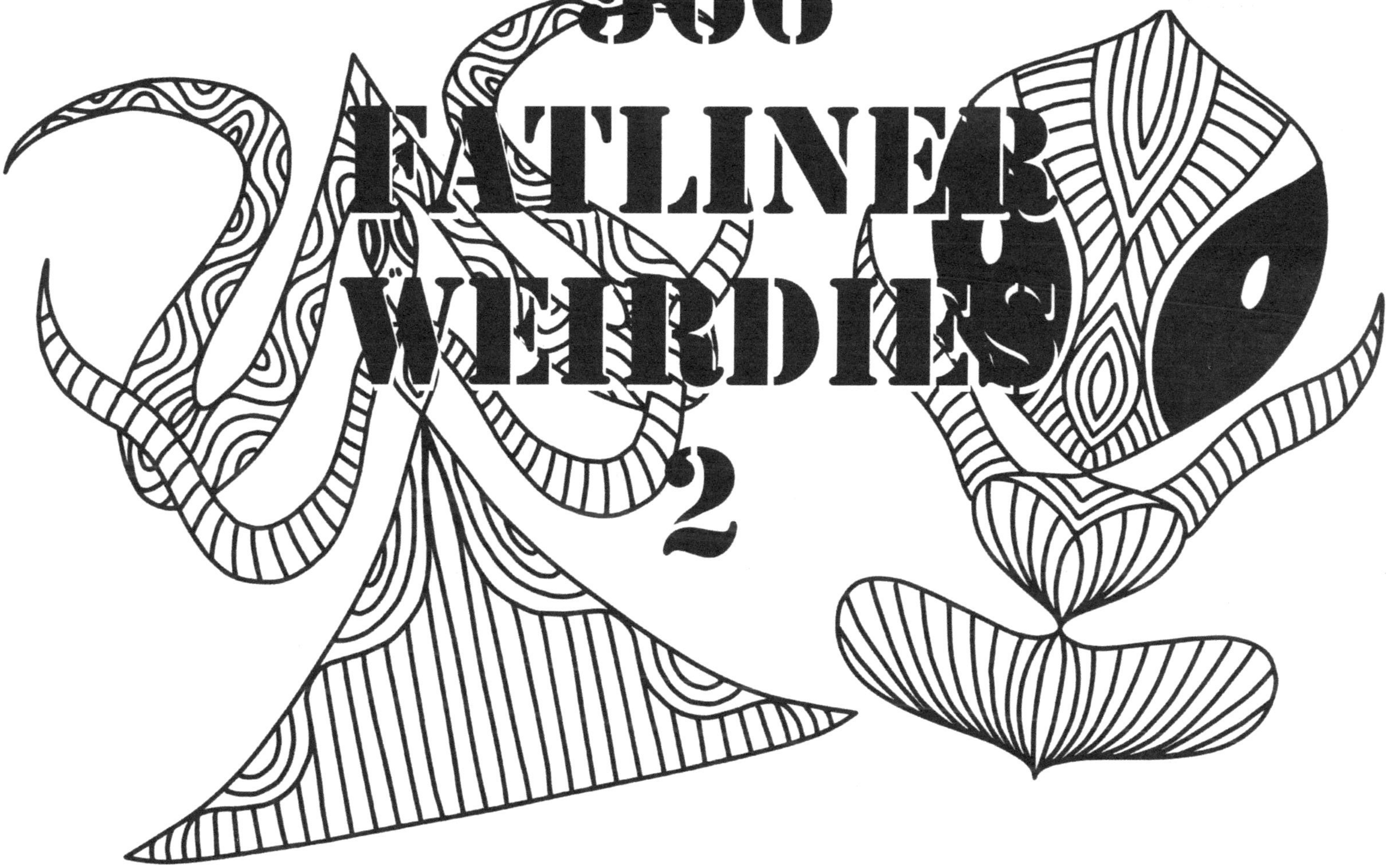

I0498910

Share your colored versions with us ! We love seeing your results
and hearing from you
we are social !

The Official FB book page, stay on top of what we have in the works !
www.facebook.com/AMVWART
The Community group, share your colored pages, meet the artists, enjoy exclusive freebies, take part in community Charity books and so much more......
www.facebook.com/groups/fansandfriendsamvwart
www.facebook.com/groups/ColorAWeirdieADay
Follow us on Twitter.... @GlobalDoodlegem
We are on Instagram too
@globaldoodlegems for instagram
...and if you are not social like that we have a blog
globaldoodlegems.wordpress.com

Copyright © 2019 Global Doodle Gems
All rights are reserved by Global Doodle Gems.
Duplication of pages for personal use are allowed. You are invited to color the pages then scan/post your coloured versions to social networks, mentioning the book title and author/artist (Global Doodle Gems).
All artwork and images are protected by copyright laws. This book or any portion thereof may not, otherwise, be reproduced and/or distributed or transmitted without the express written permission of the artist/publisher of Global Doodle Gems.
All of us from the Global Doodle Gems wish you a colortastic time and look forward to seeing your wonderful color results online !

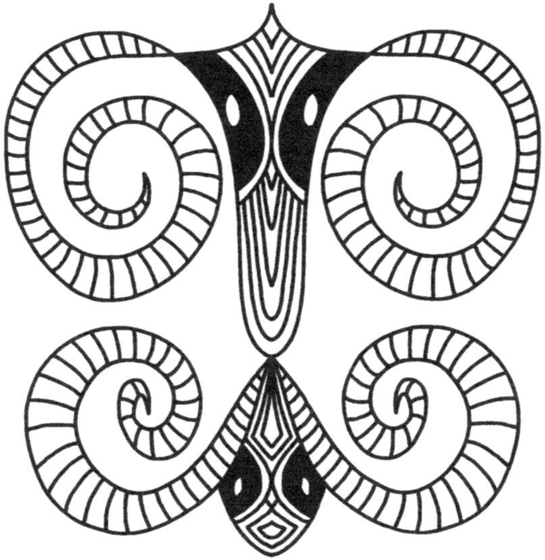
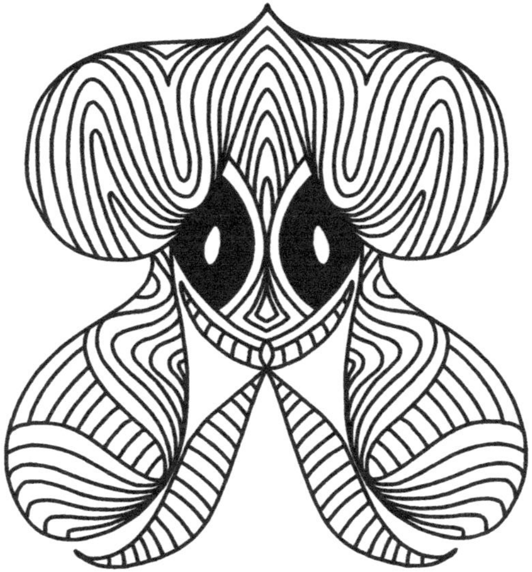

Fatliner Weirdies Volume 2

My second set of Fatliner Weirdies from Fatliner Weirdies The Templates 1

"This book is dedicated to the love of my life, my daughter Victoria Panthera. I make these books in hopes that your life as an adult will be everything you want It to be! I love you more than words can say!"

Maria Wedel

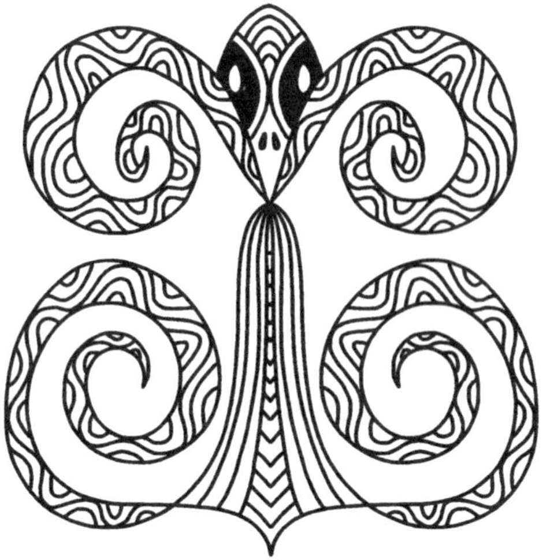

FATLINER WEIRDIES
VOLUME 1

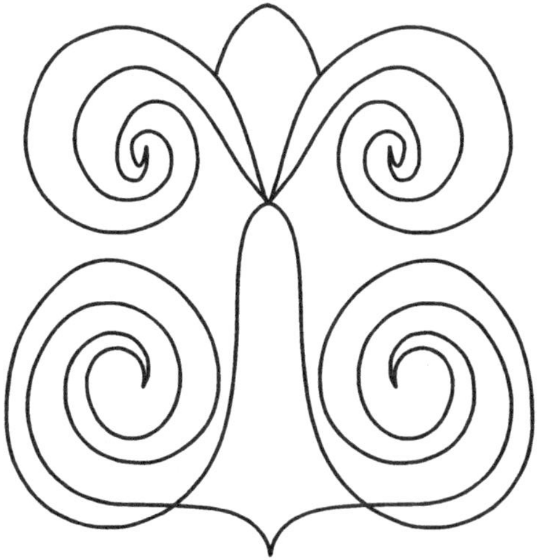

FATLINER WEIRDIES
THE TEMPLATES 1

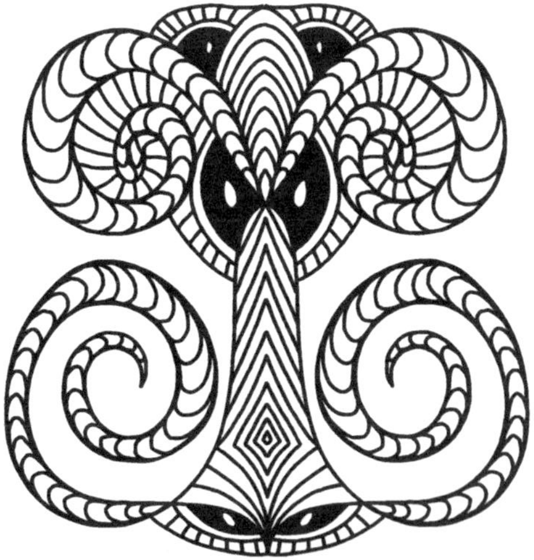

FATLINER WEIRDIES
VOLUME 3

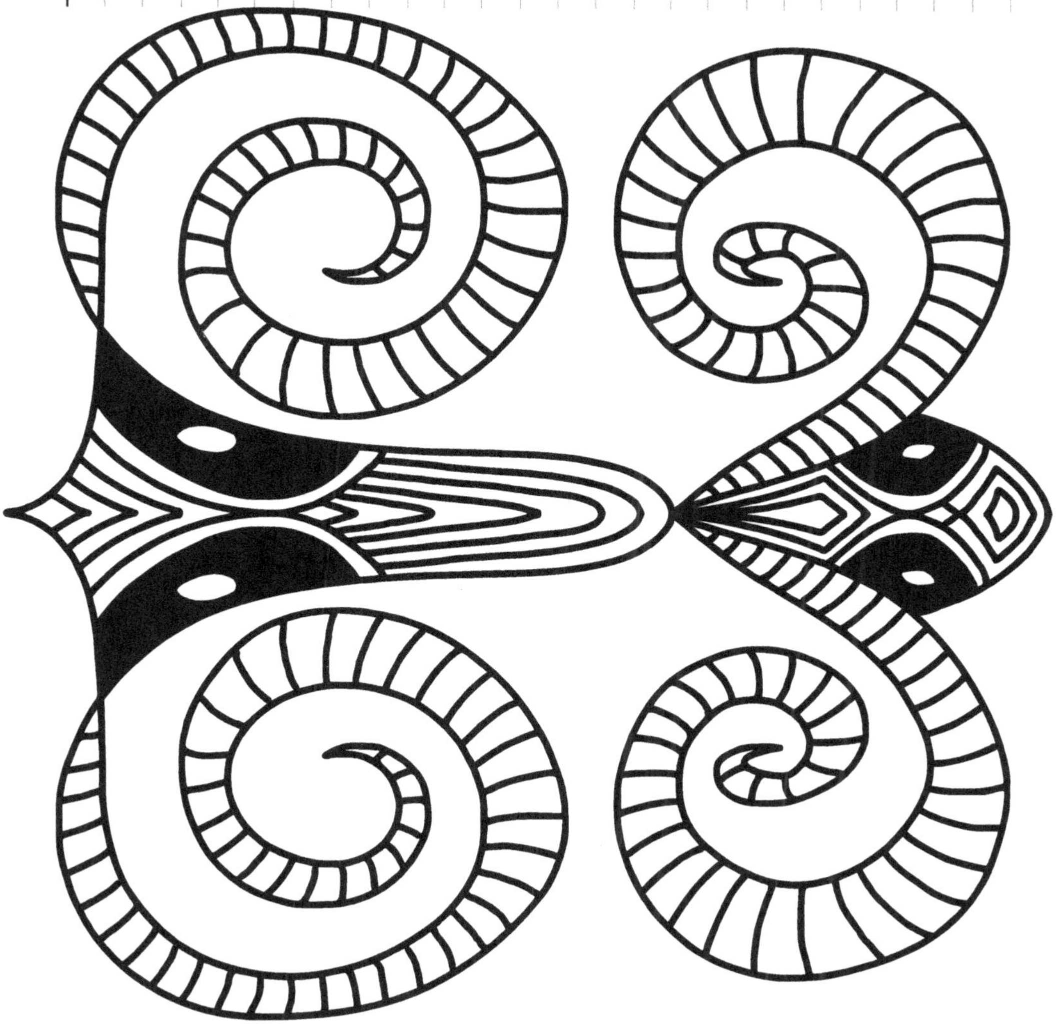

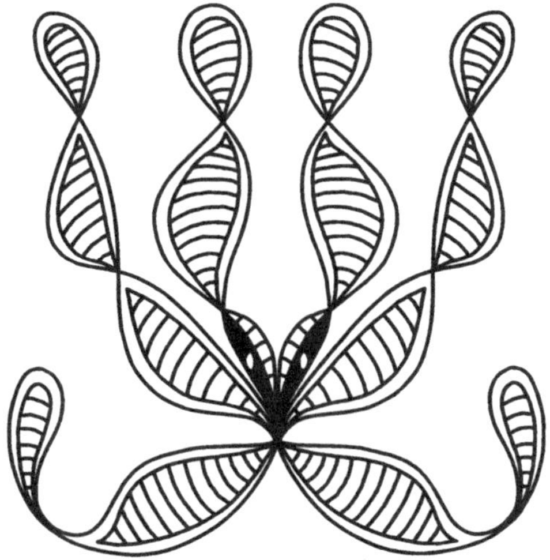

FATLINER WEIRDIES
VOLUME 1

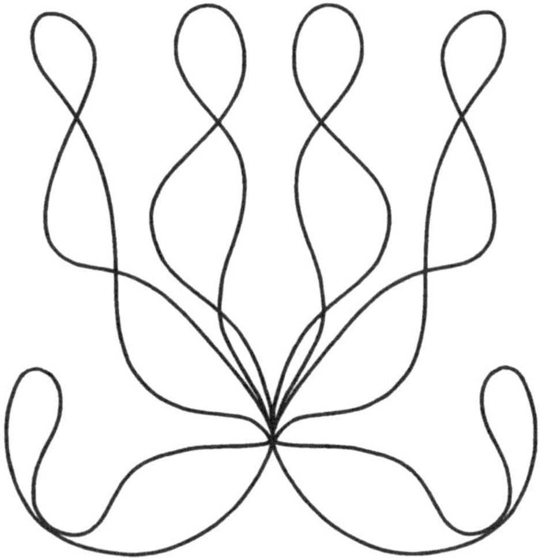

FATLINER WEIRDIES
THE TEMPLATES 1

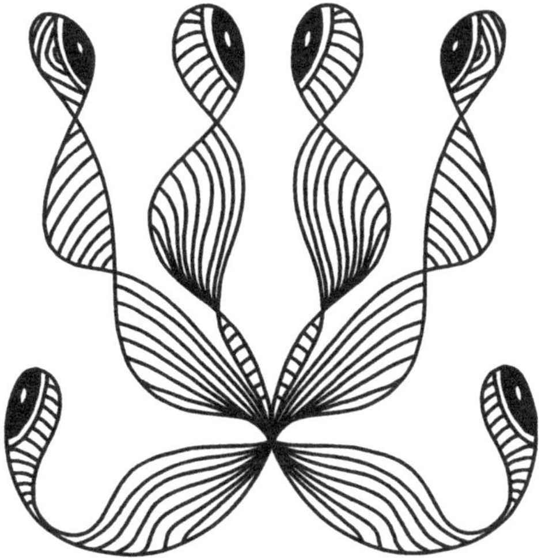

FATLINER WEIRDIES
VOLUME 3

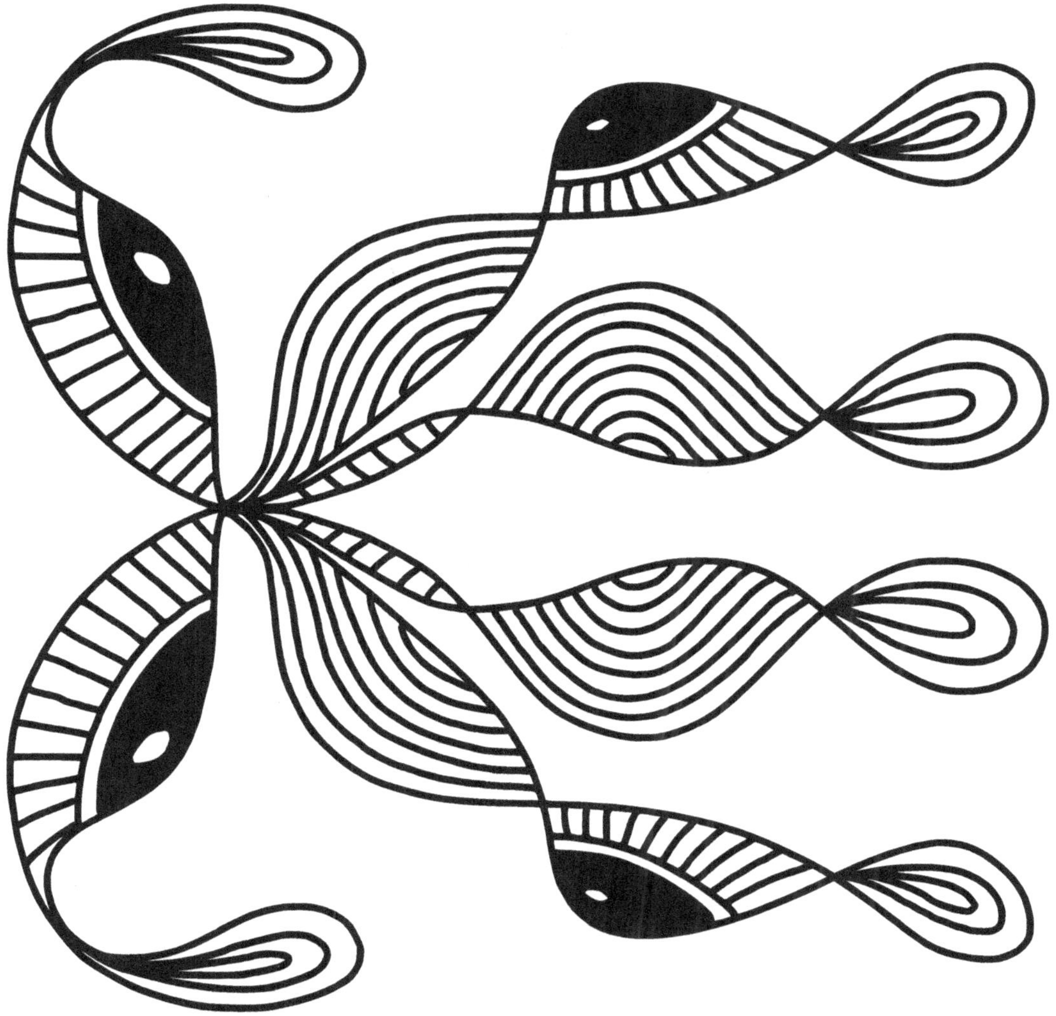

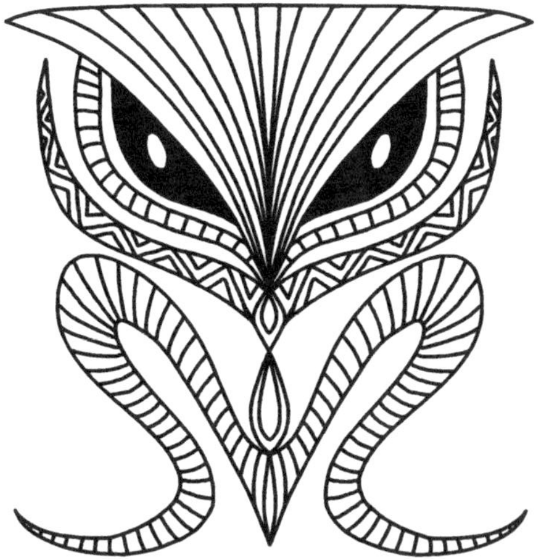

FATLINER WEIRDIES
VOLUME 1

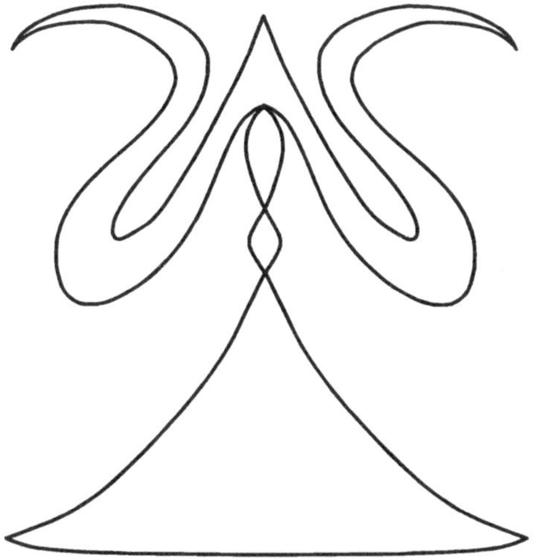

FATLINER WEIRDIES
THE TEMPLATES 1

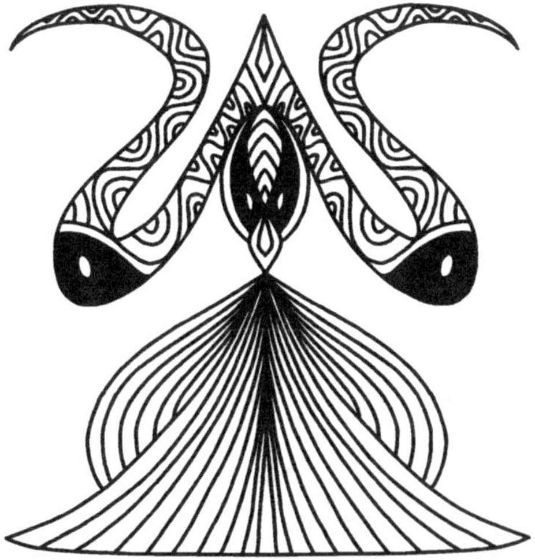

FATLINER WEIRDIES
VOLUME 3

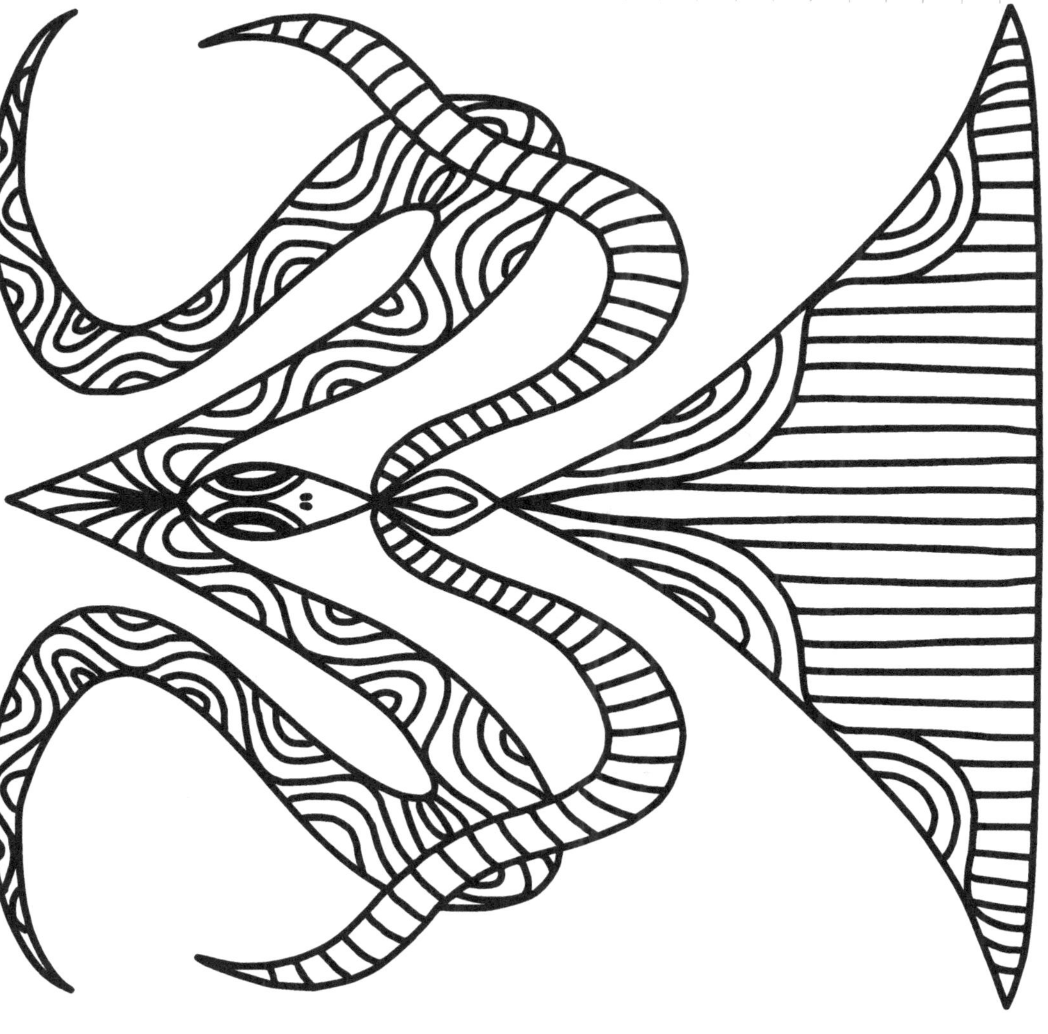

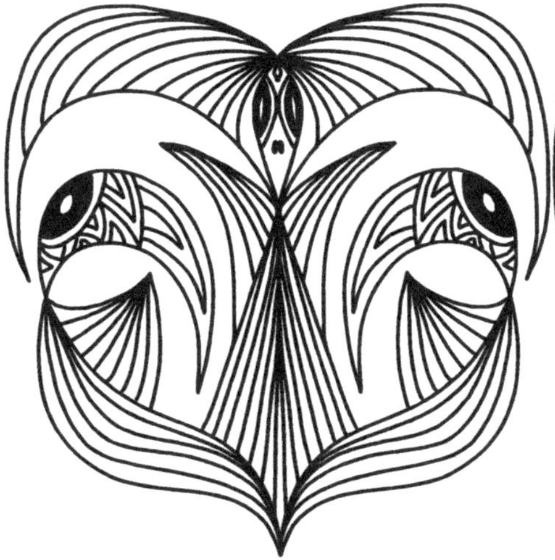

FATLINER WEIRDIES
VOLUME 1

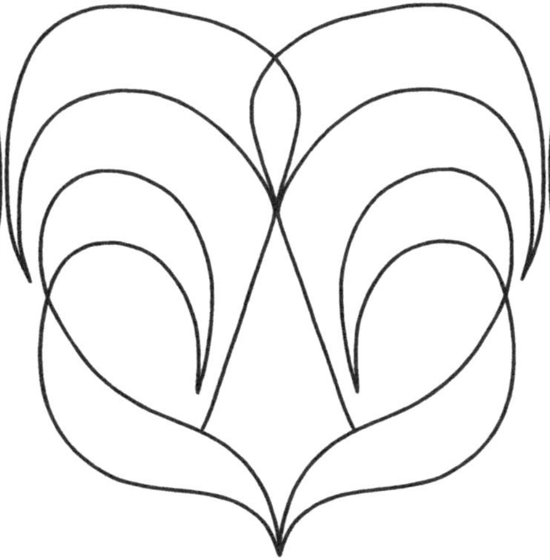

FATLINER WEIRDIES
THE TEMPLATES 1

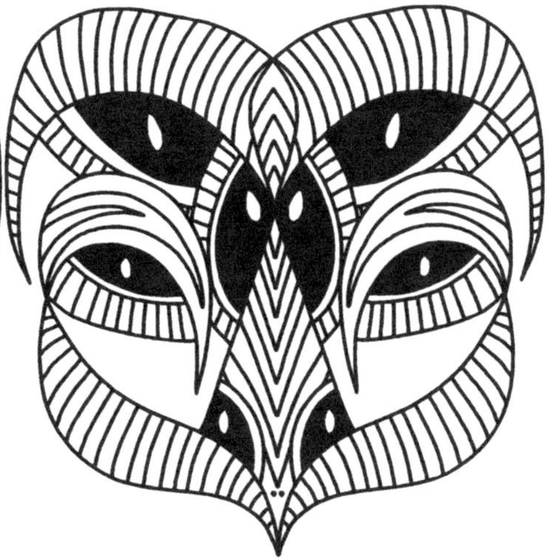

FATLINER WEIRDIES
VOLUME 3

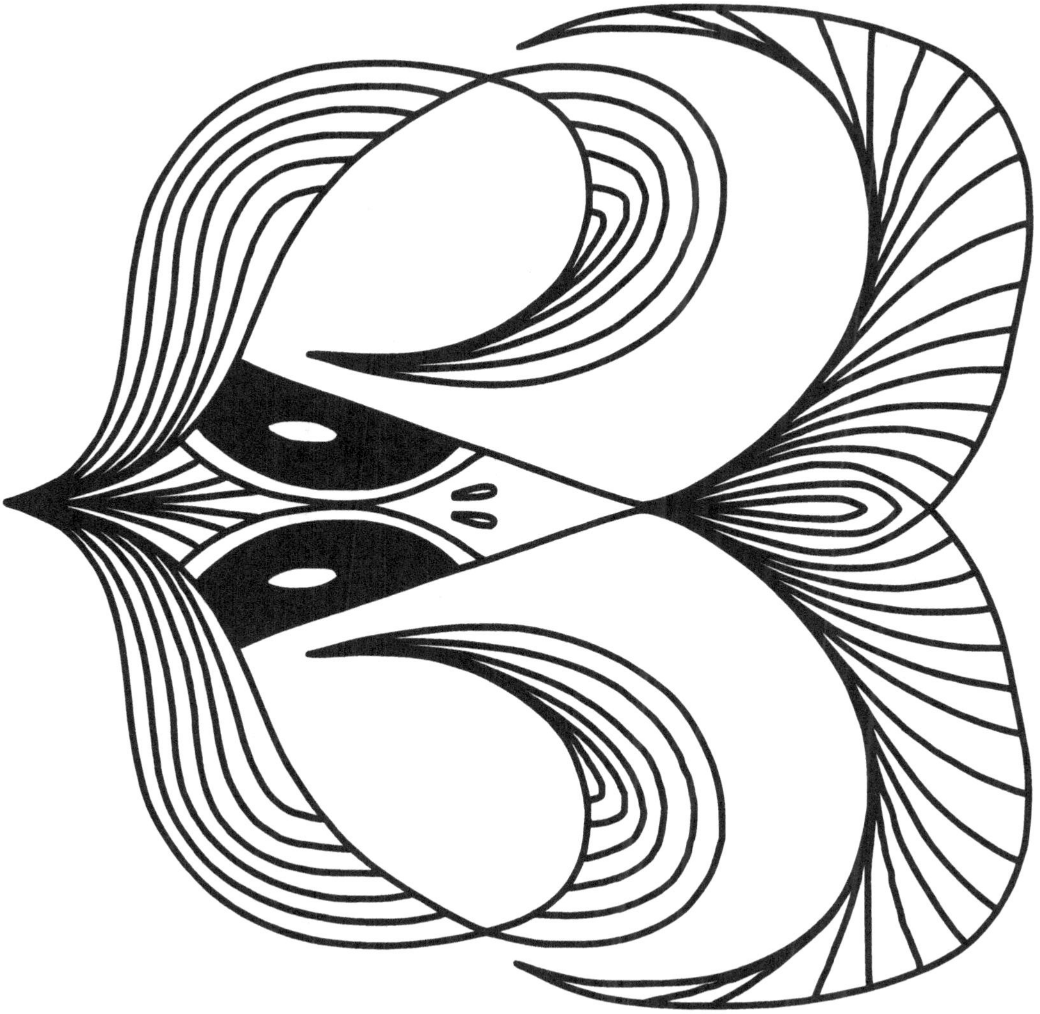

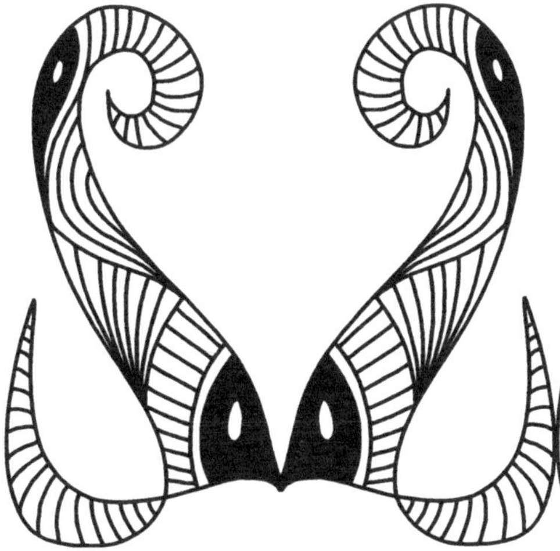

FATLINER WEIRDIES
VOLUME 1

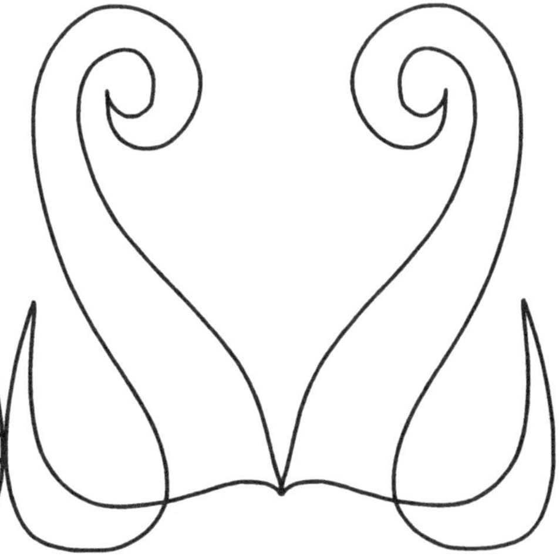

FATLINER WEIRDIES
THE TEMPLATES 1

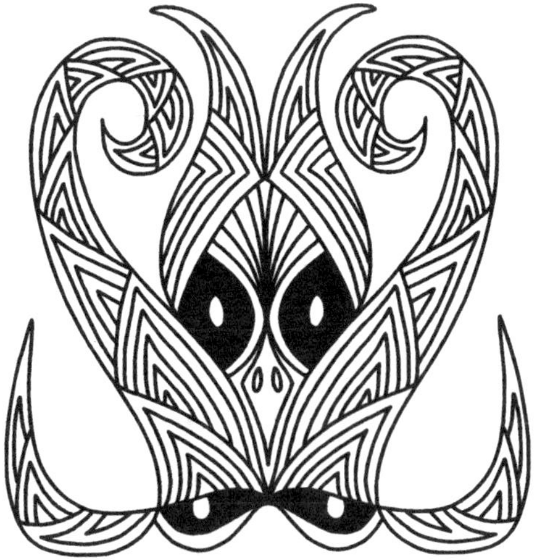

FATLINER WEIRDIES
VOLUME 3

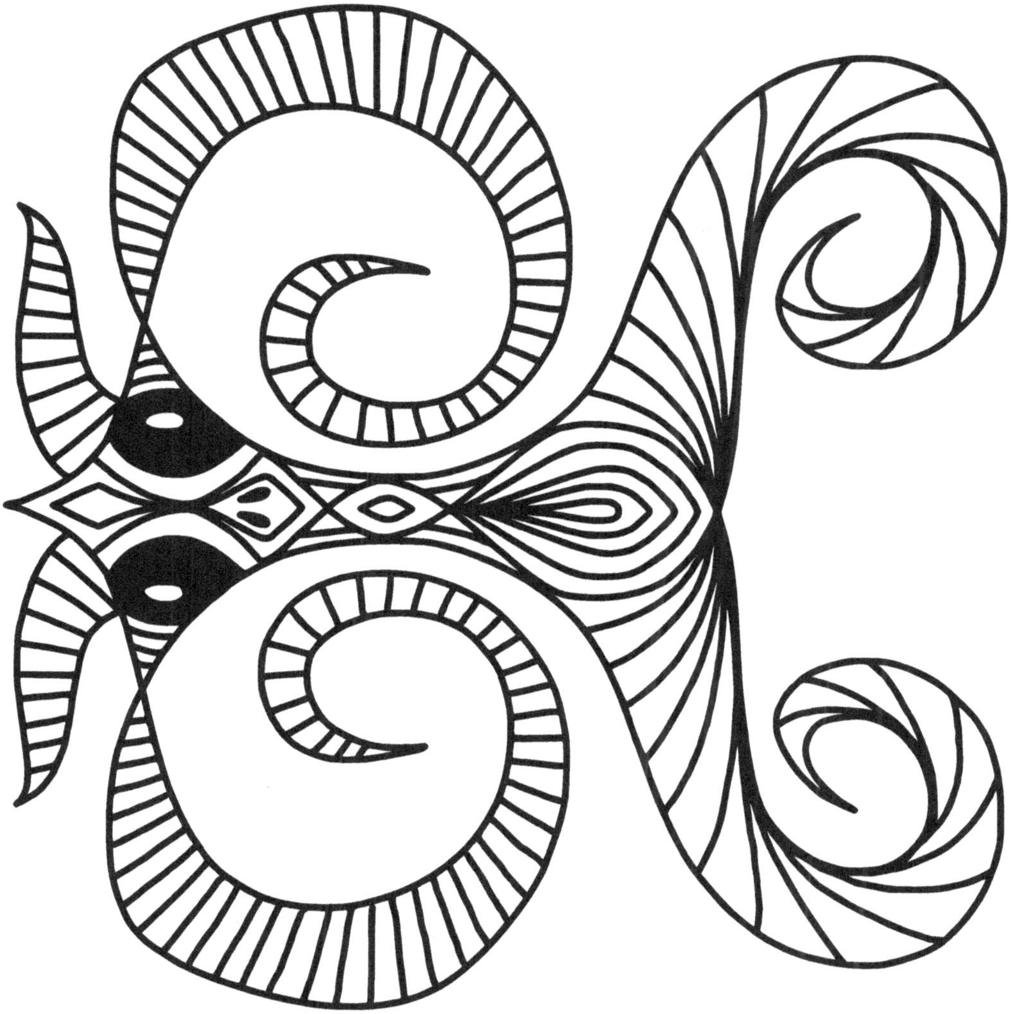

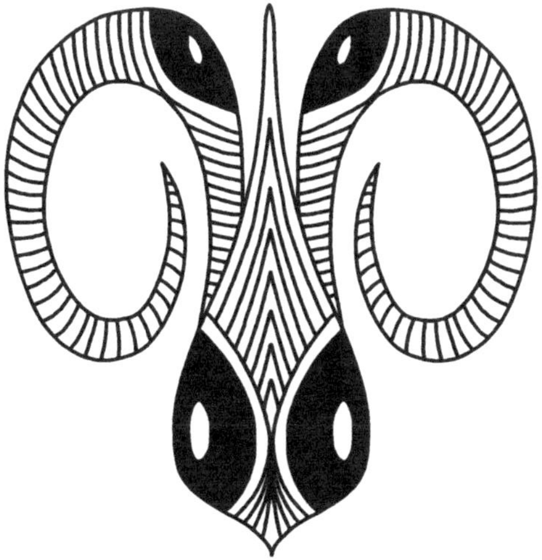

FATLINER WEIRDIES
VOLUME 1

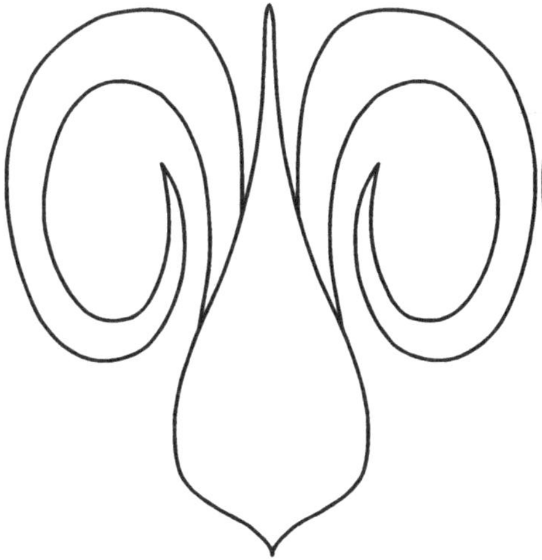

FATLINER WEIRDIES
THE TEMPLATES 1

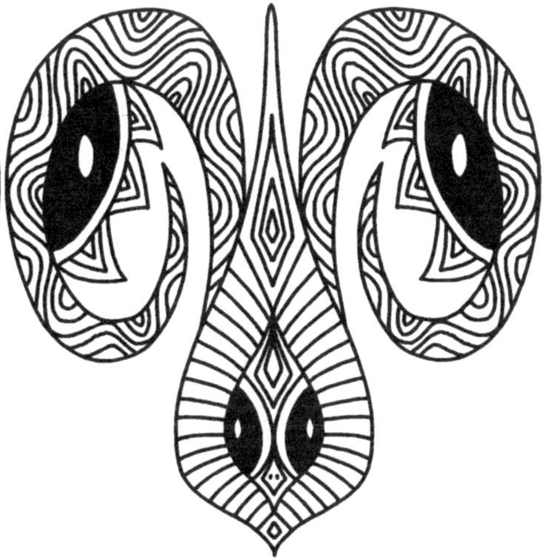

FATLINER WEIRDIES
VOLUME 3

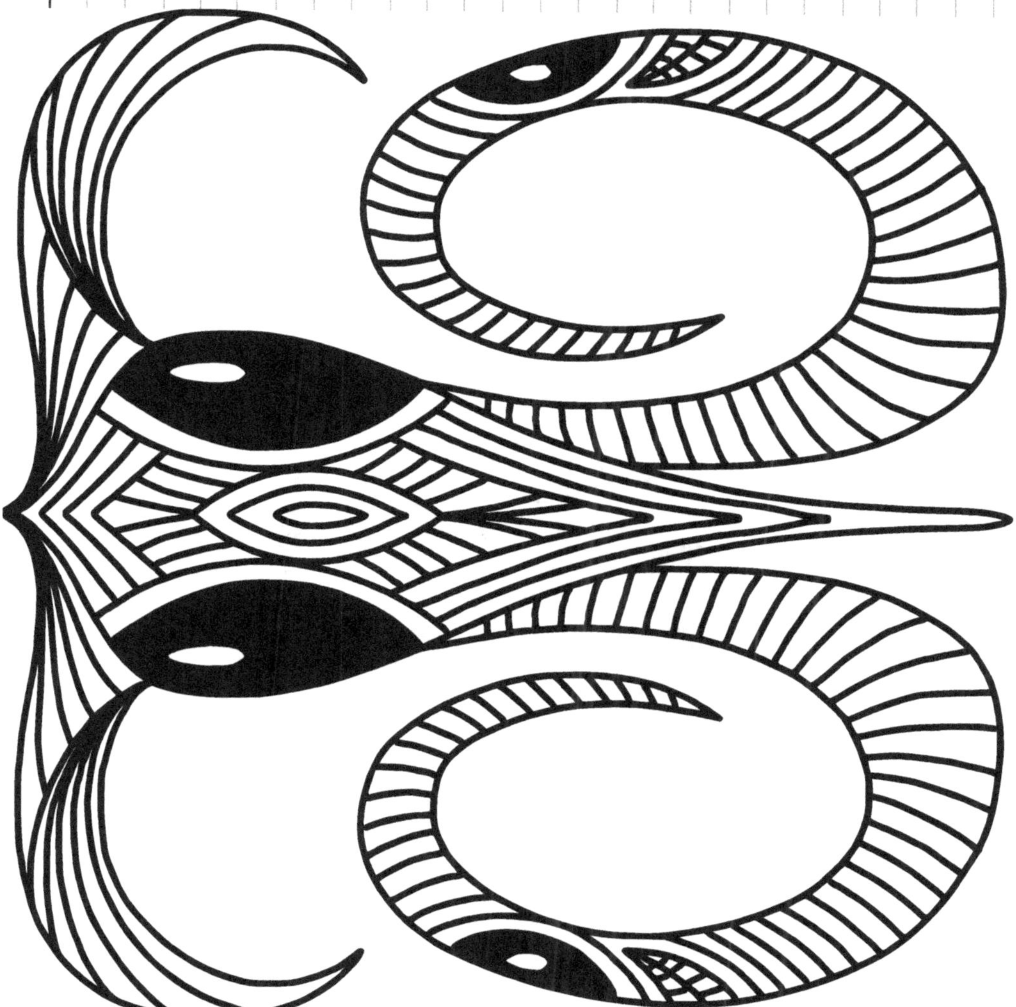

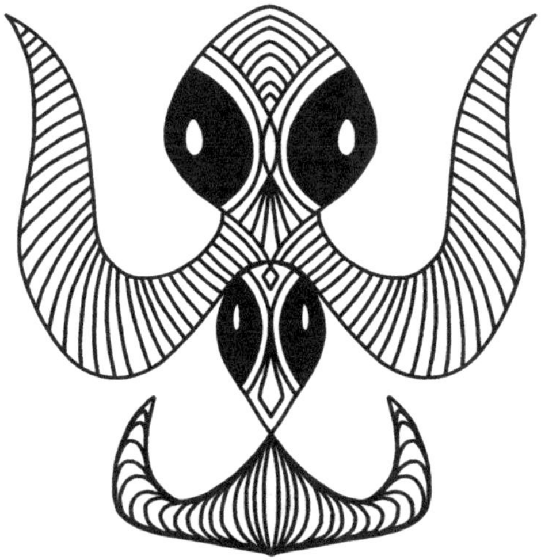

FATLINER WEIRDIES
VOLUME 1

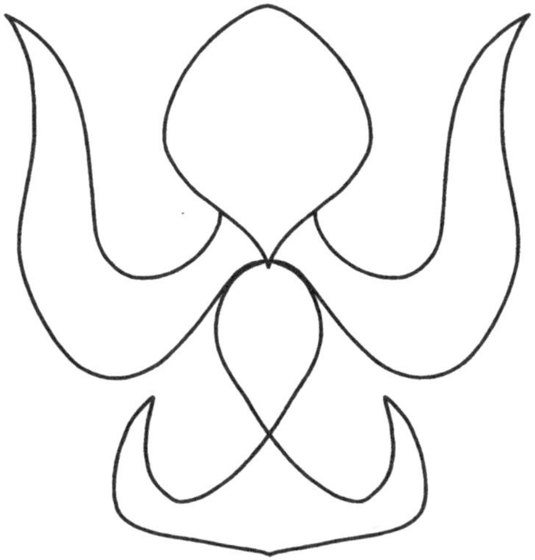

FATLINER WEIRDIES
THE TEMPLATES 1

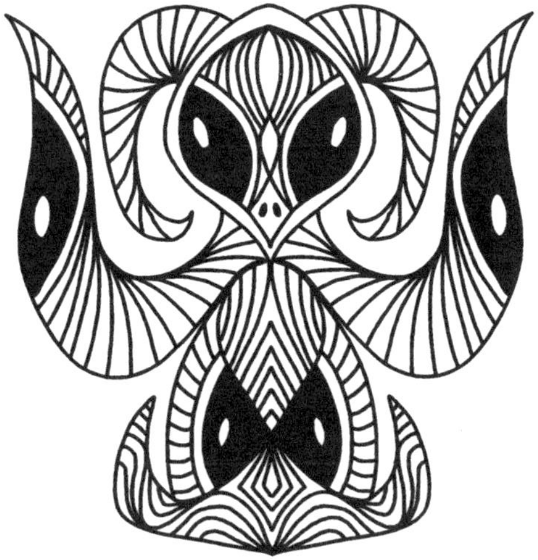

FATLINER WEIRDIES
VOLUME 3

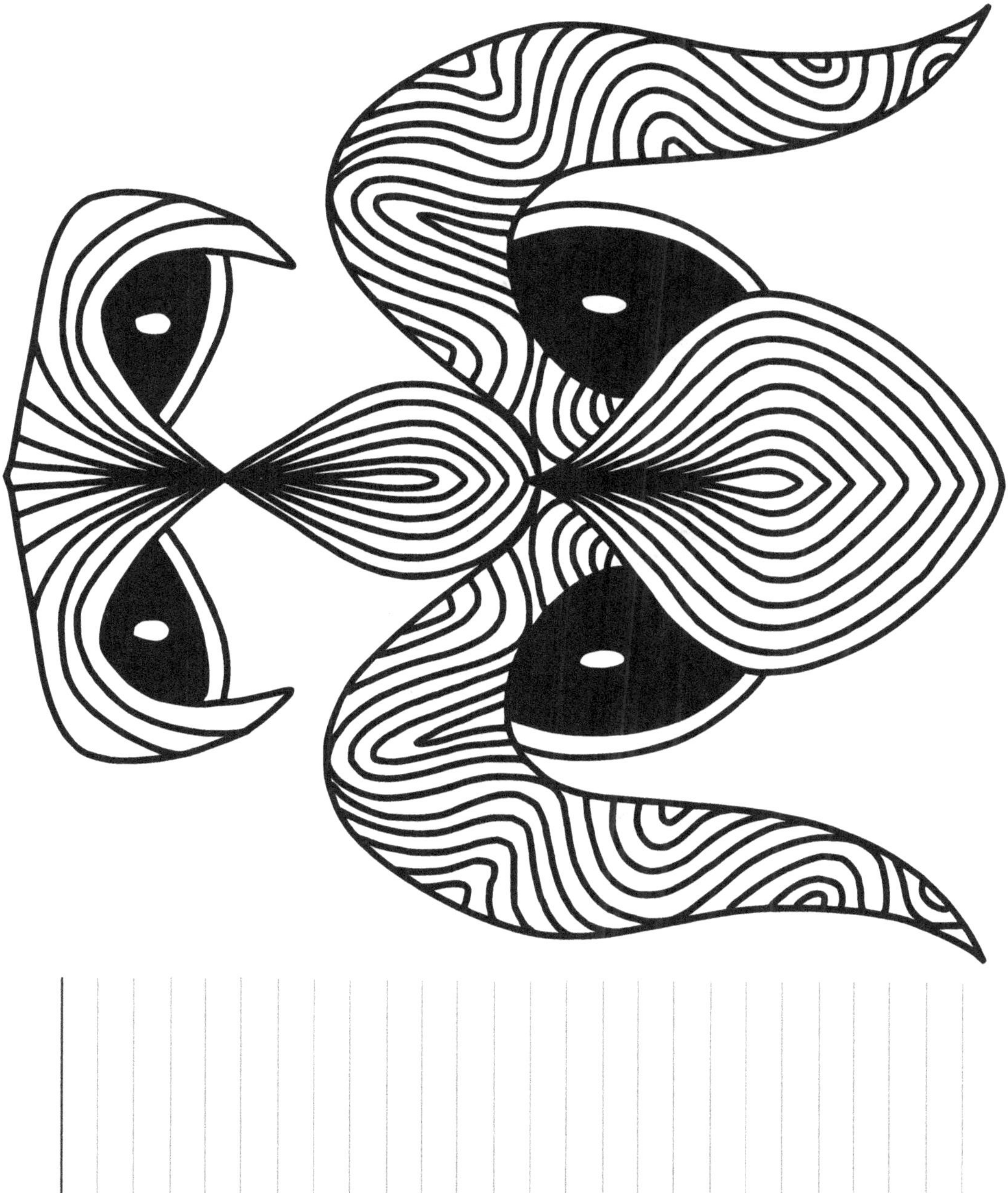

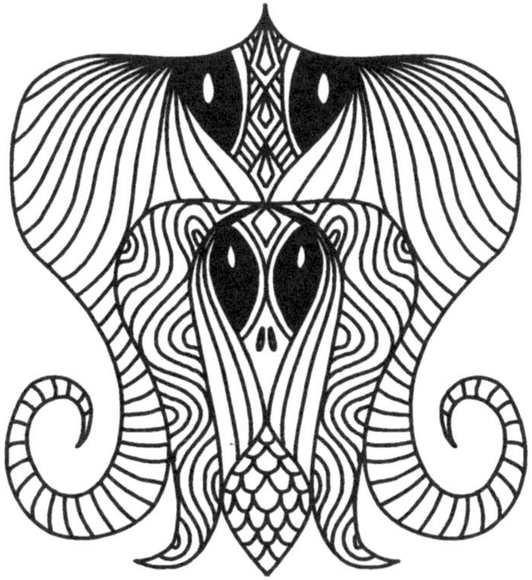

FATLINER WEIRDIES
VOLUME 1

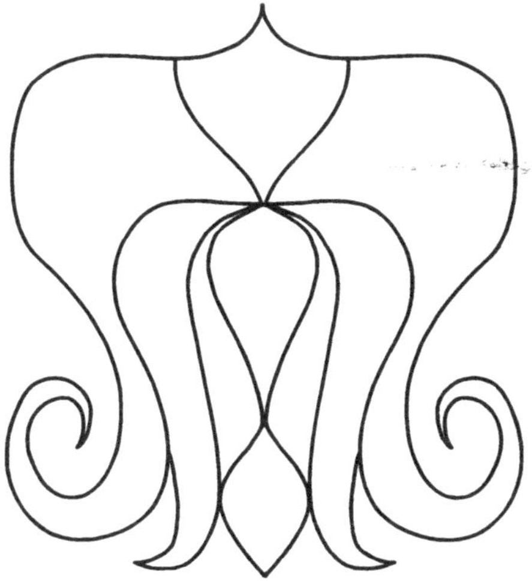

FATLINER WEIRDIES
THE TEMPLATES 1

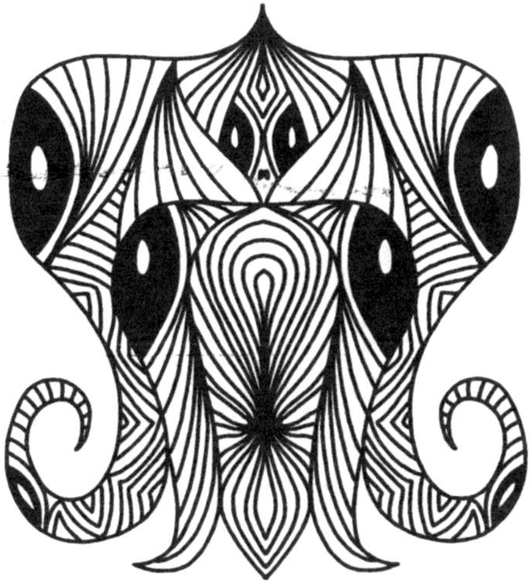

FATLINER WEIRDIES
VOLUME 3

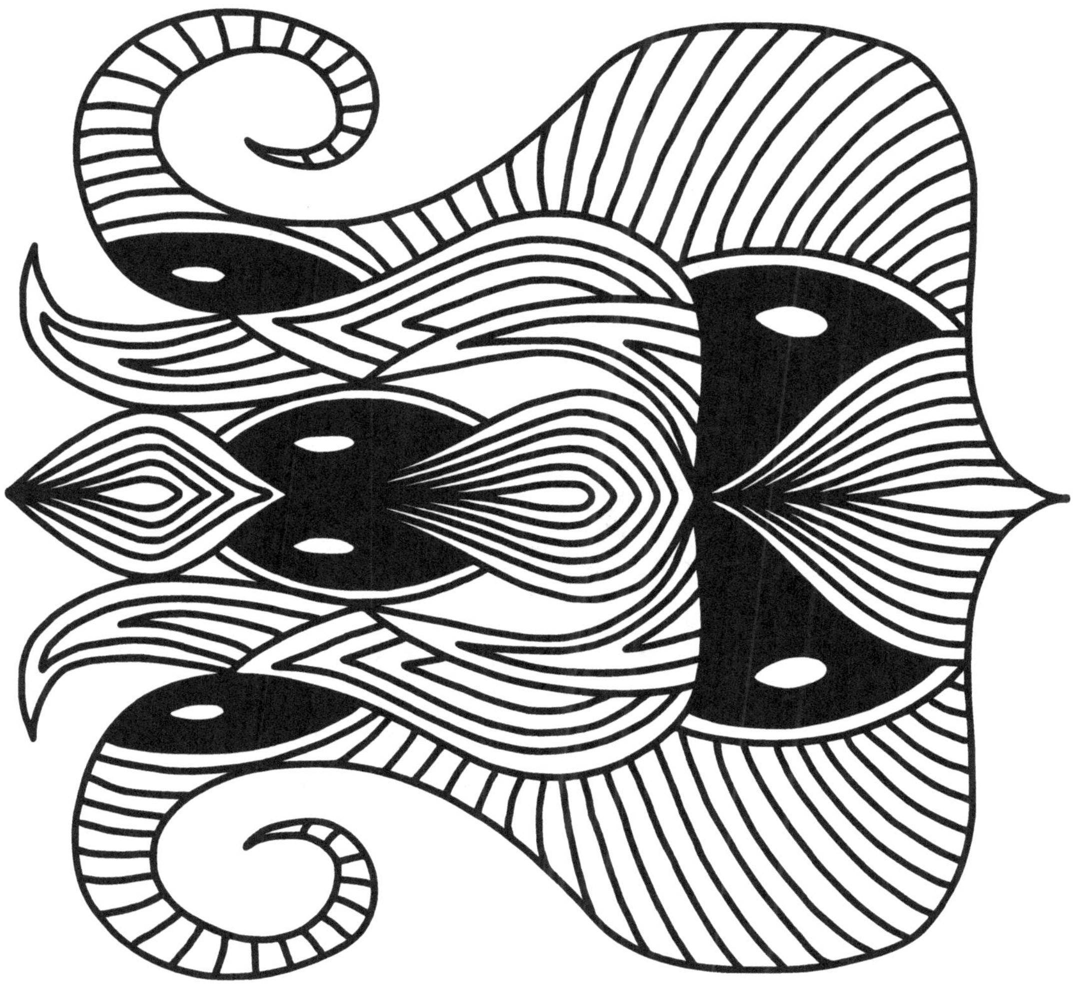

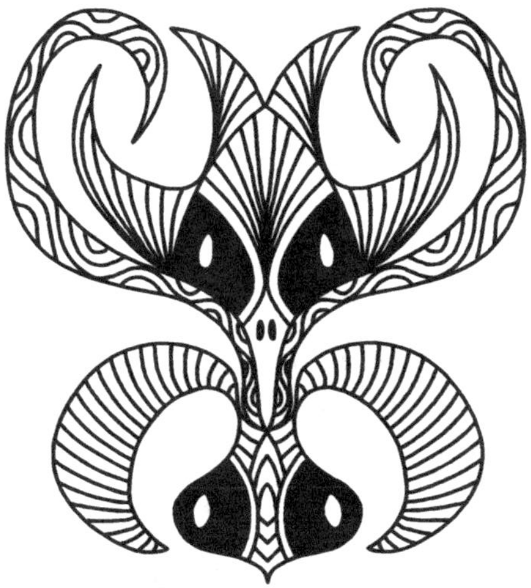

FATLINER WEIRDIES
VOLUME 1

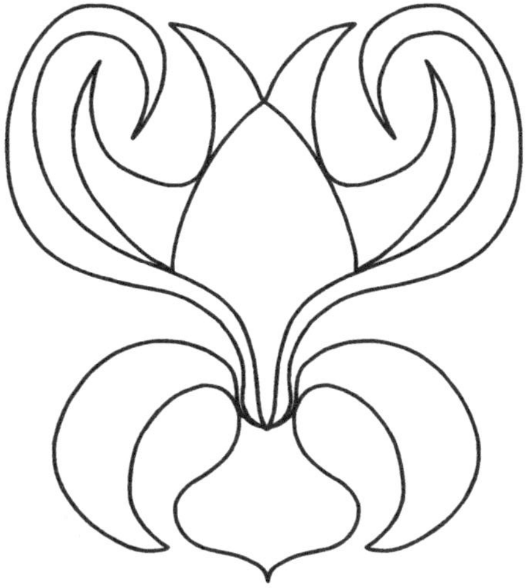

FATLINER WEIRDIES
THE TEMPLATES 1

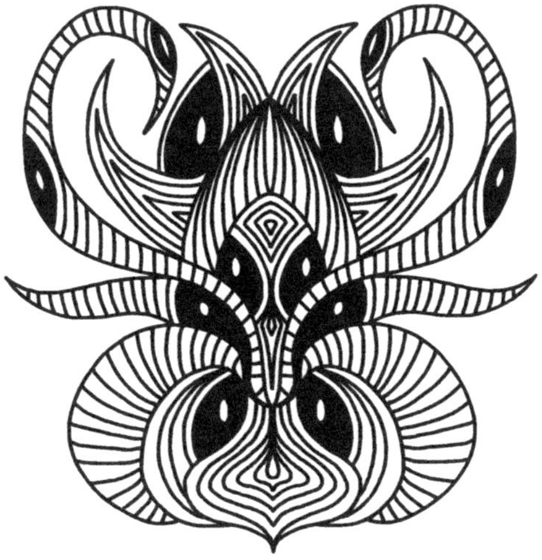

FATLINER WEIRDIES
VOLUME 3

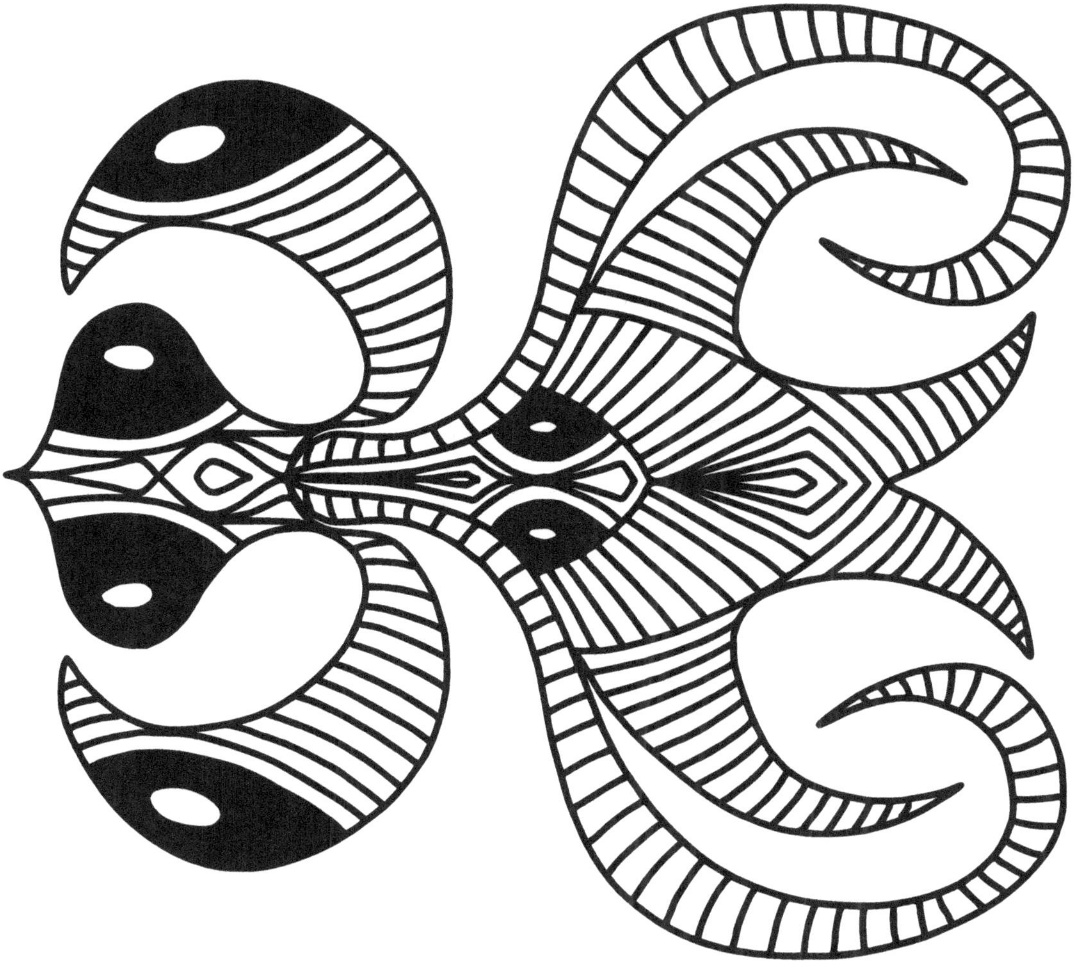

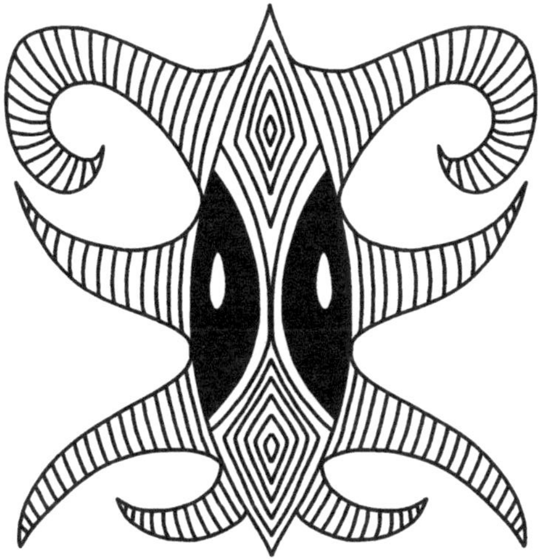

FATLINER WEIRDIES
VOLUME 1

FATLINER WEIRDIES
THE TEMPLATES 1

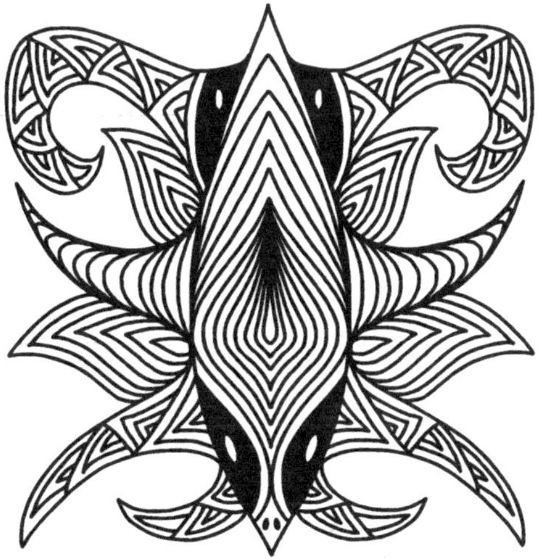

FATLINER WEIRDIES
VOLUME 3

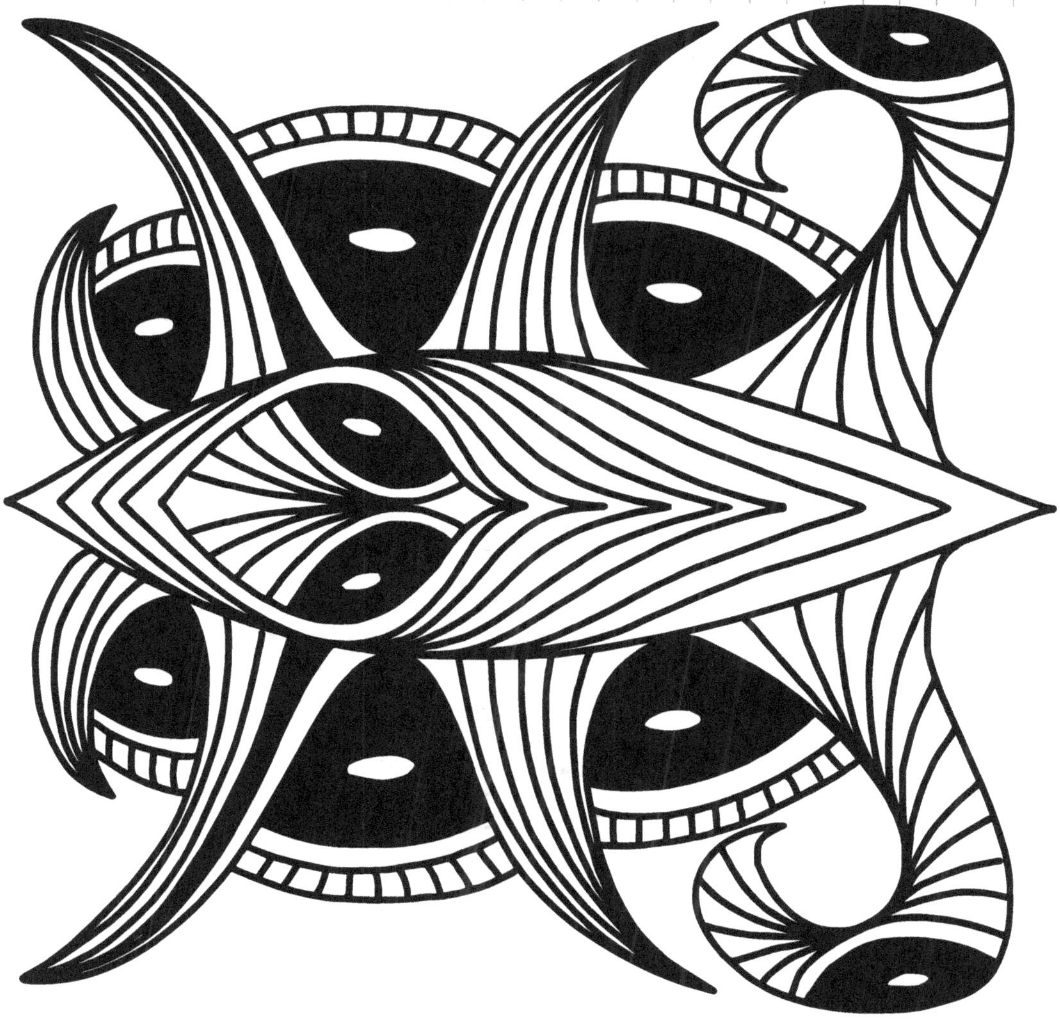

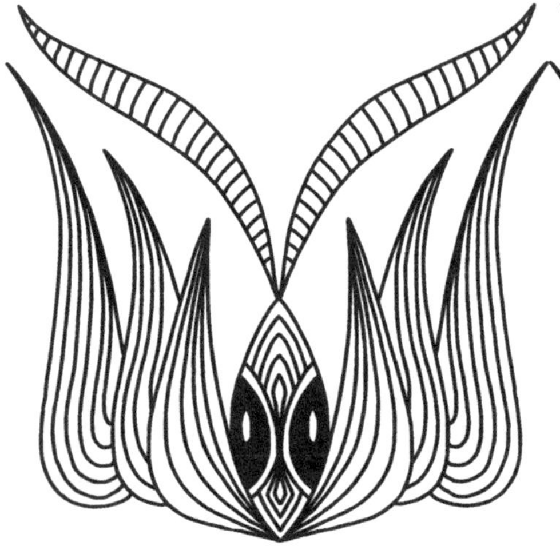

FATLINER WEIRDIES
VOLUME 1

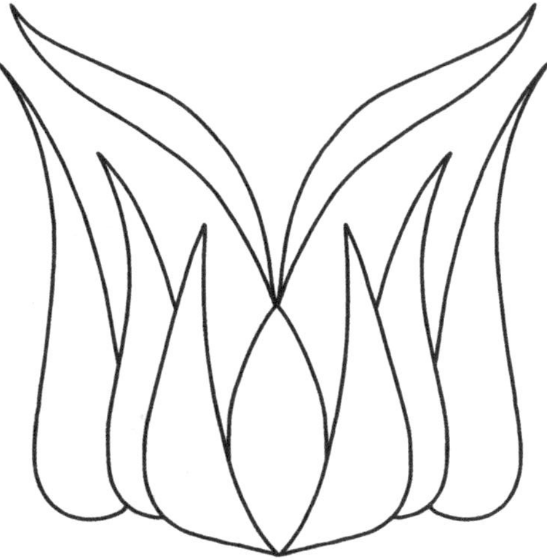

FATLINER WEIRDIES
THE TEMPLATES 1

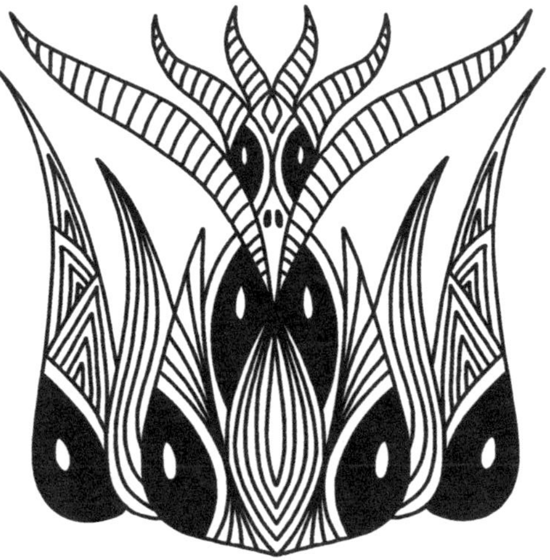

FATLINER WEIRDIES
VOLUME 3

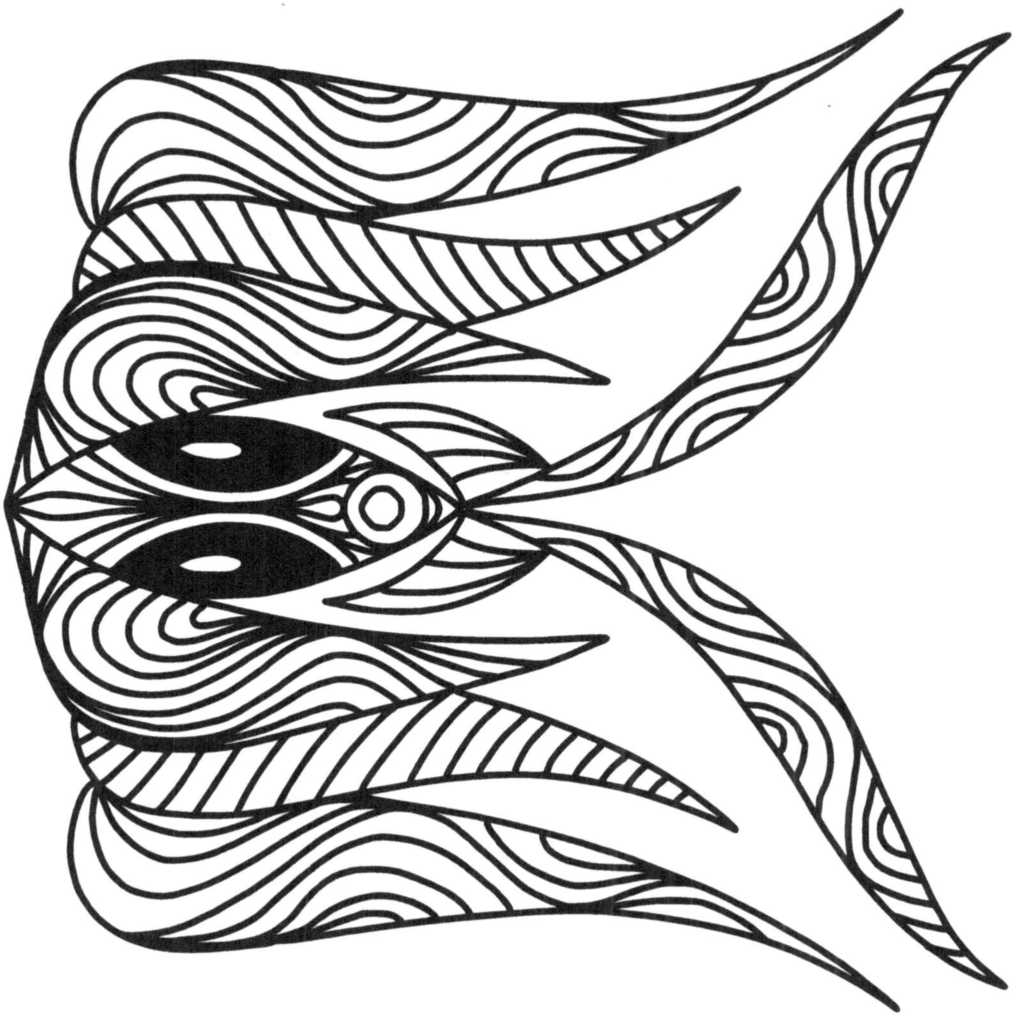

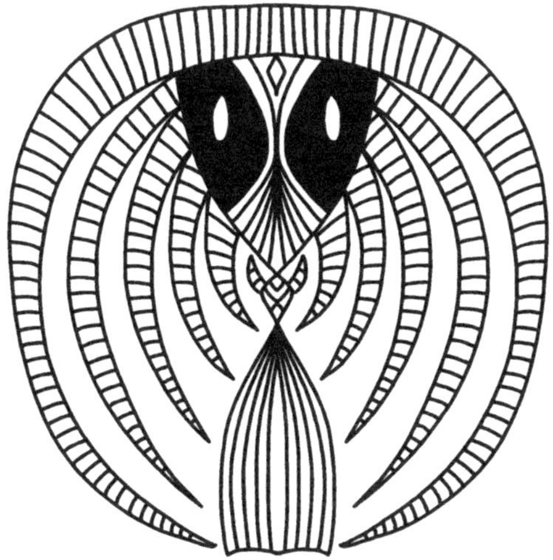

FATLINER WEIRDIES
VOLUME 1

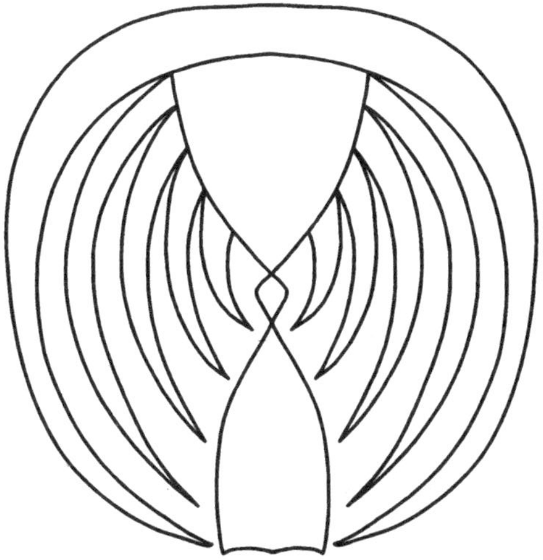

FATLINER WEIRDIES
THE TEMPLATES 1

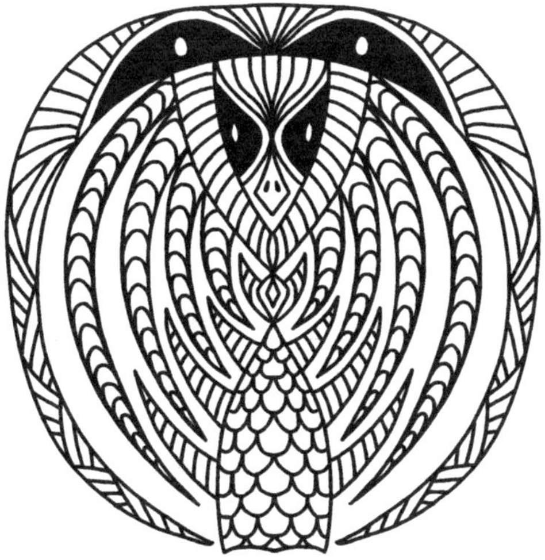

FATLINER WEIRDIES
VOLUME 3

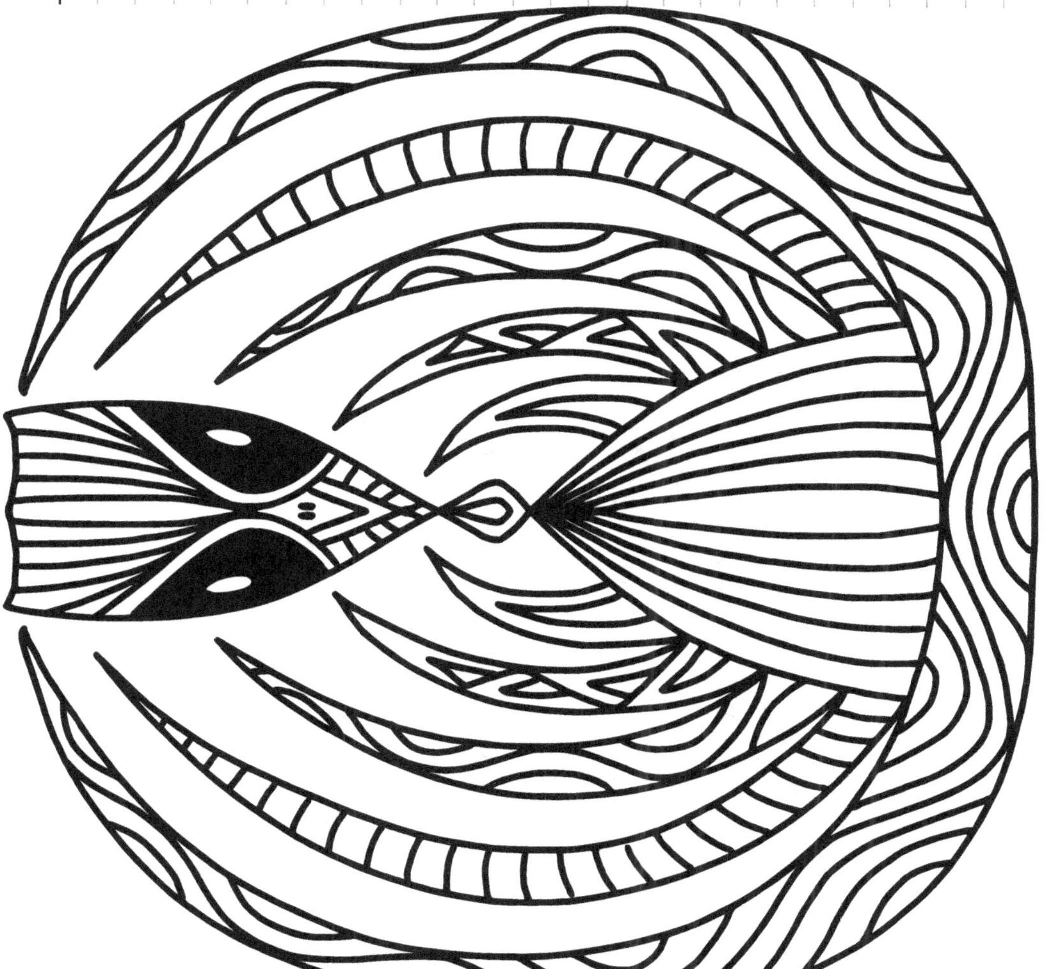

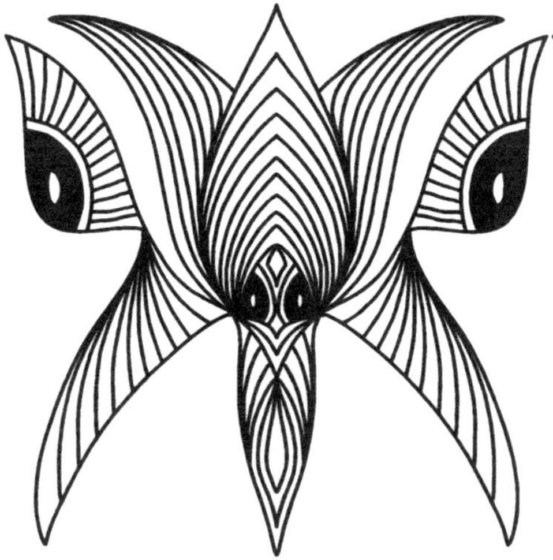

FATLINER WEIRDIES
VOLUME 1

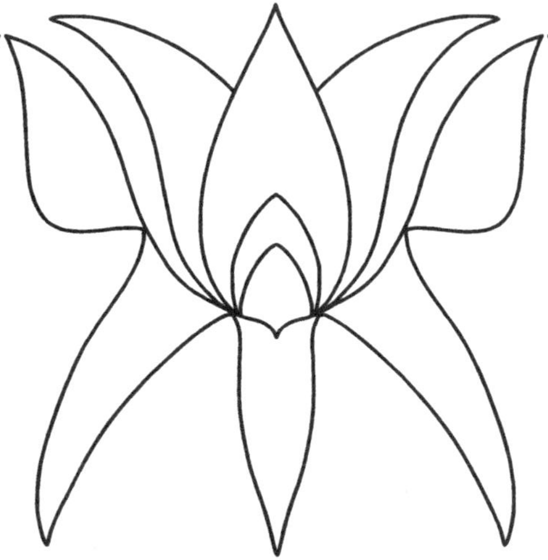

FATLINER WEIRDIES
THE TEMPLATES 1

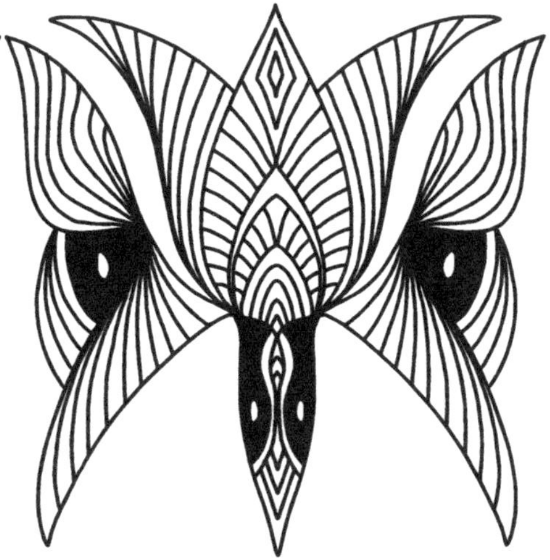

FATLINER WEIRDIES
VOLUME 3

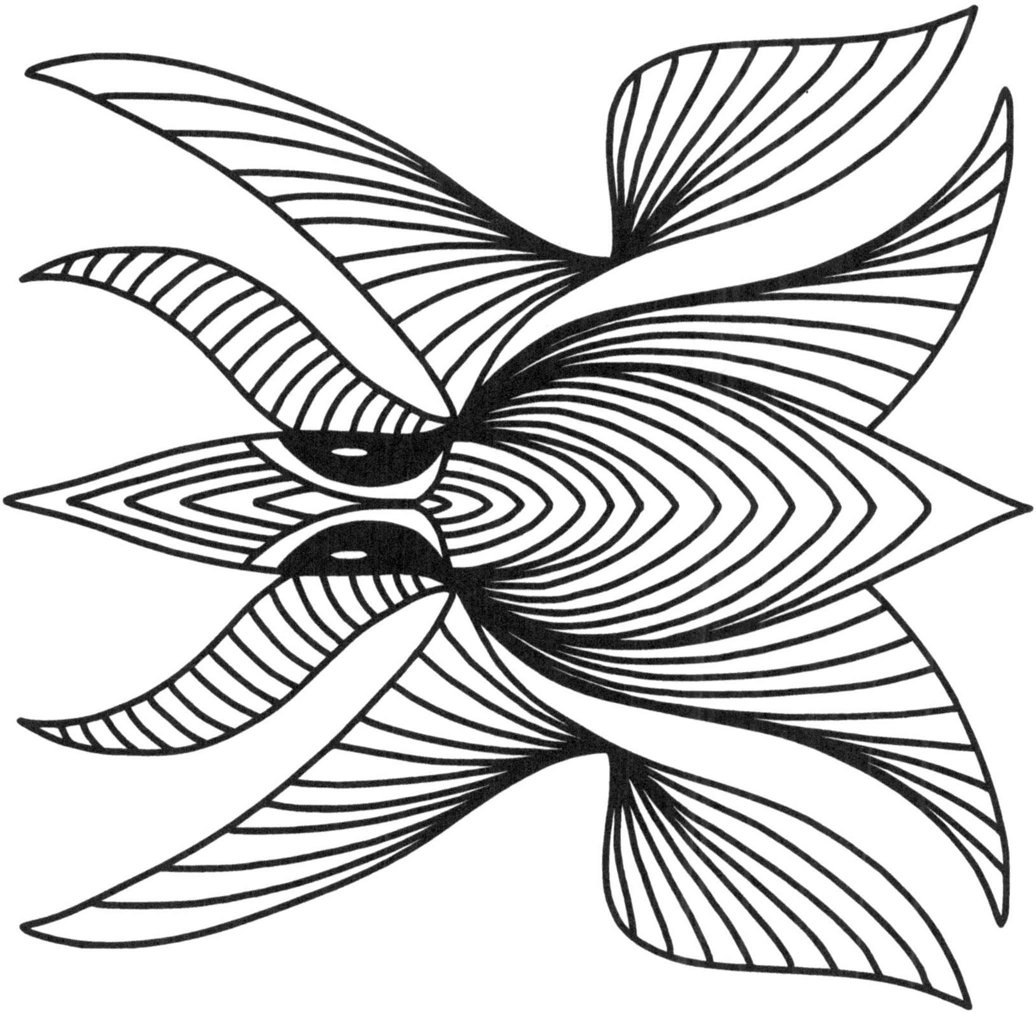

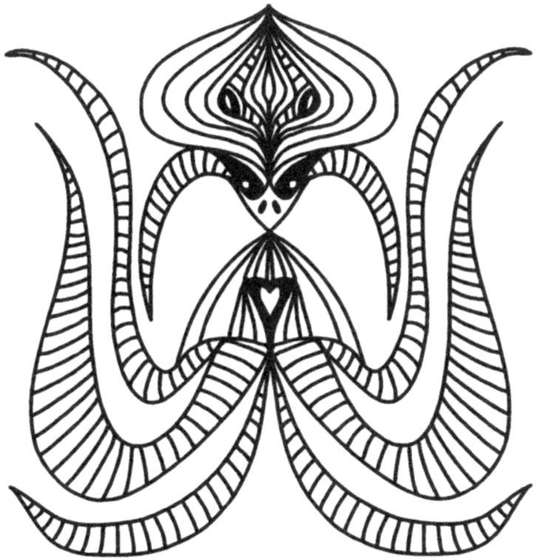

FATLINER WEIRDIES
VOLUME 1

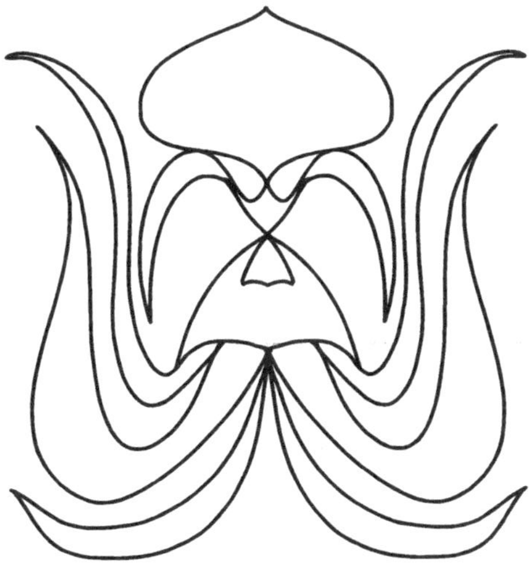

FATLINER WEIRDIES
THE TEMPLATES 1

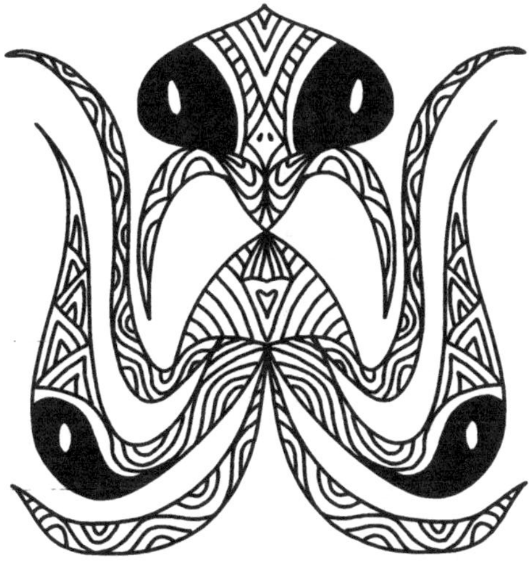

FATLINER WEIRDIES
VOLUME 3

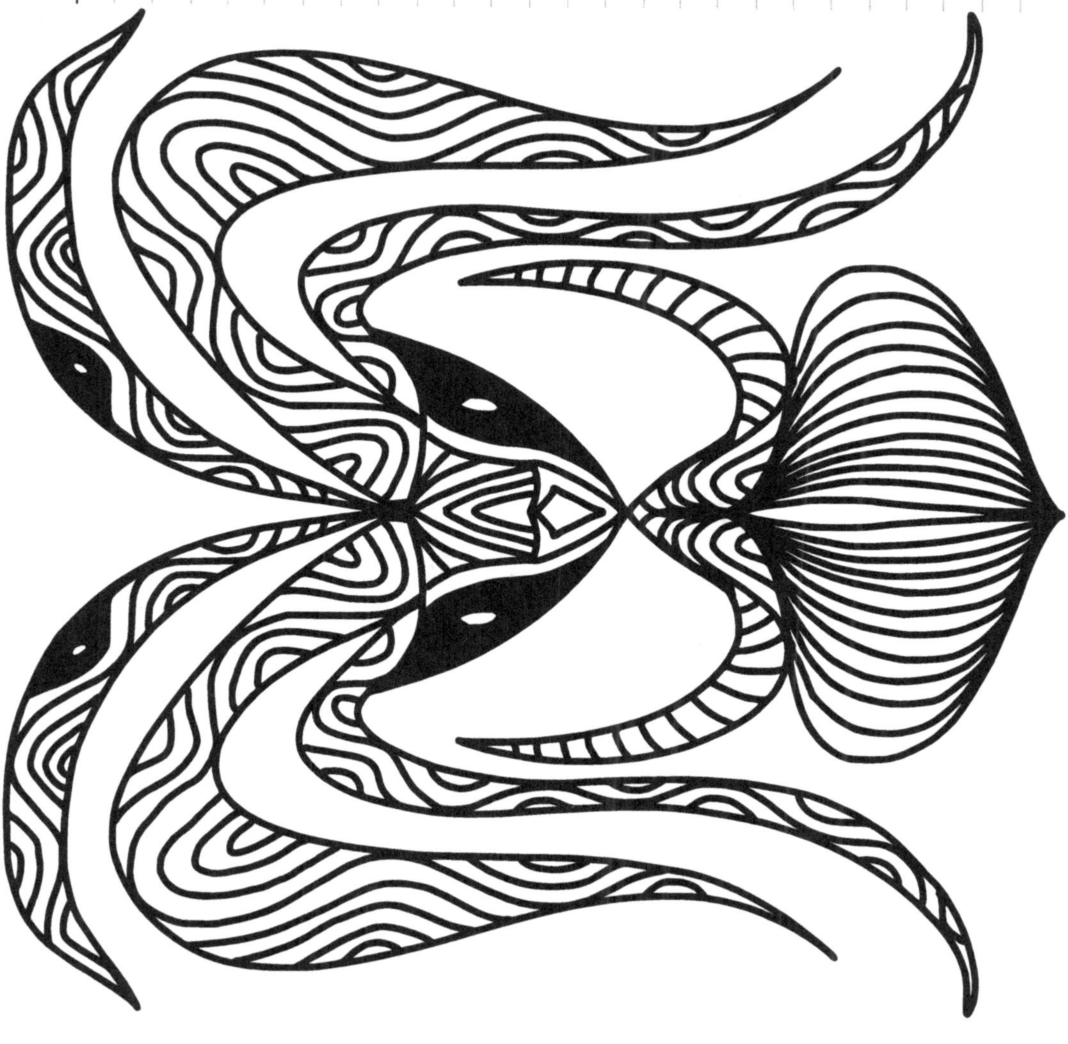

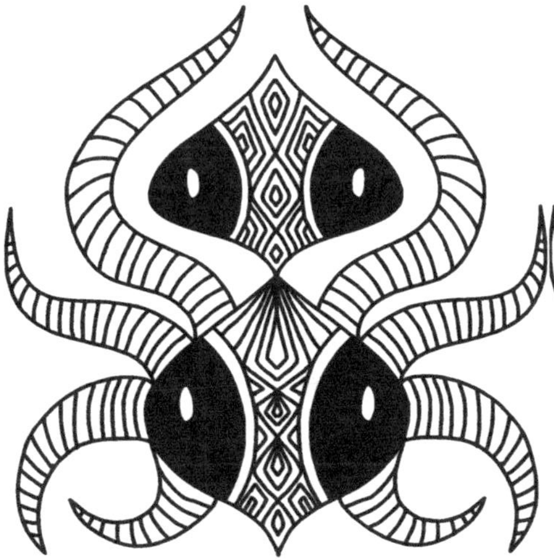

FATLINER WEIRDIES
VOLUME 1

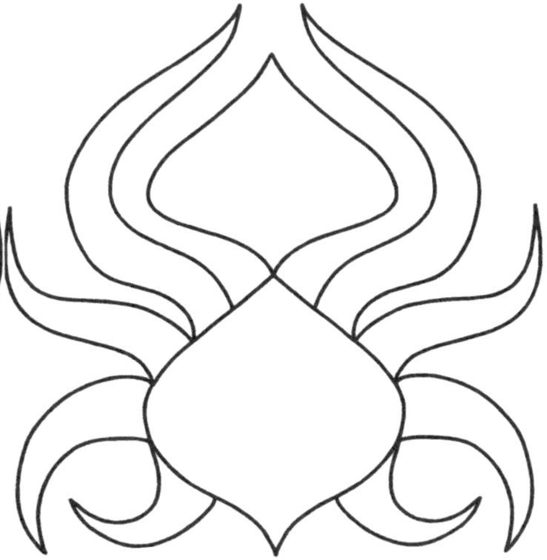

FATLINER WEIRDIES
THE TEMPLATES 1

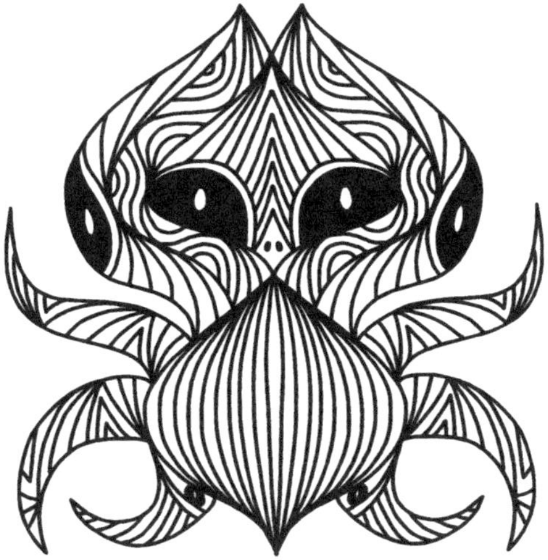

FATLINER WEIRDIES
VOLUME 3

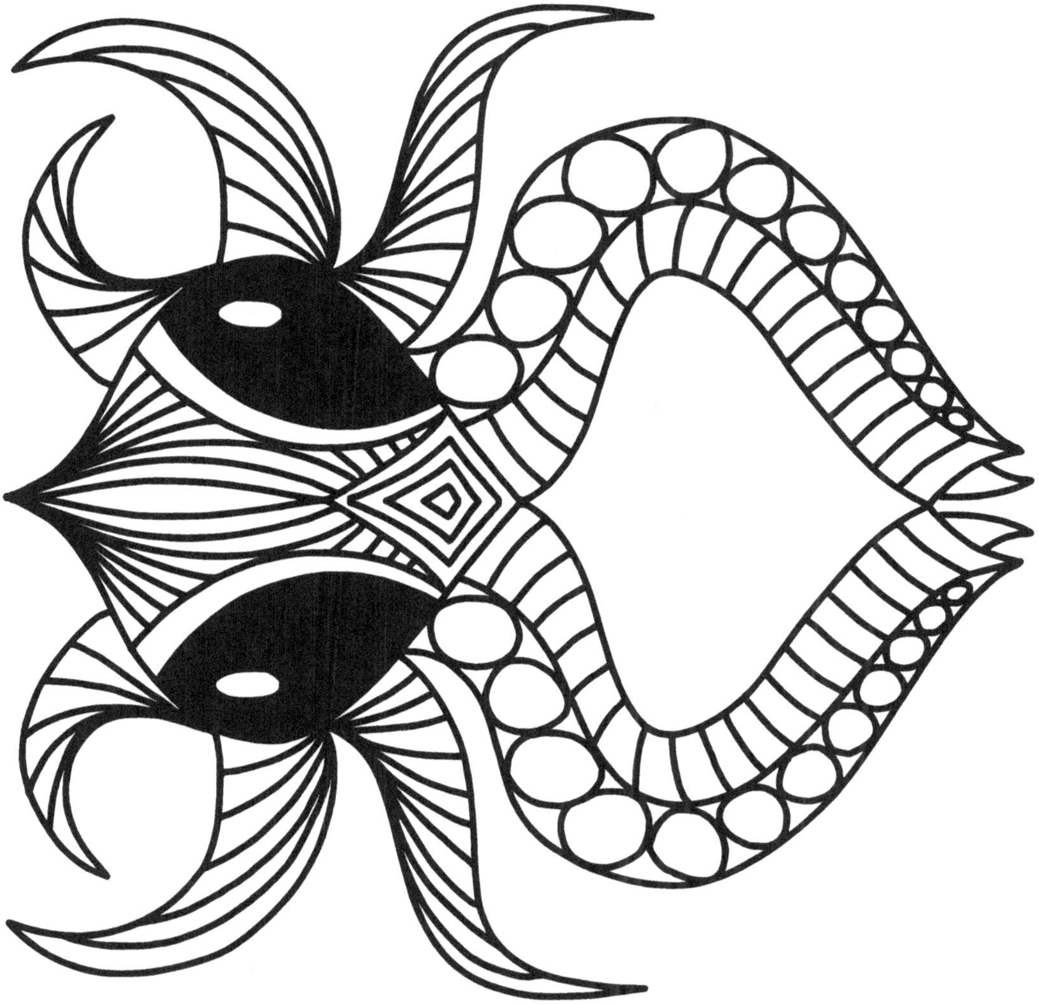

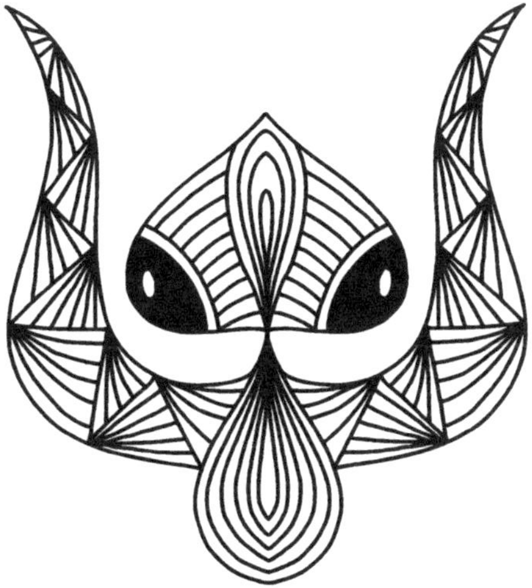

FATLINER WEIRDIES
VOLUME 1

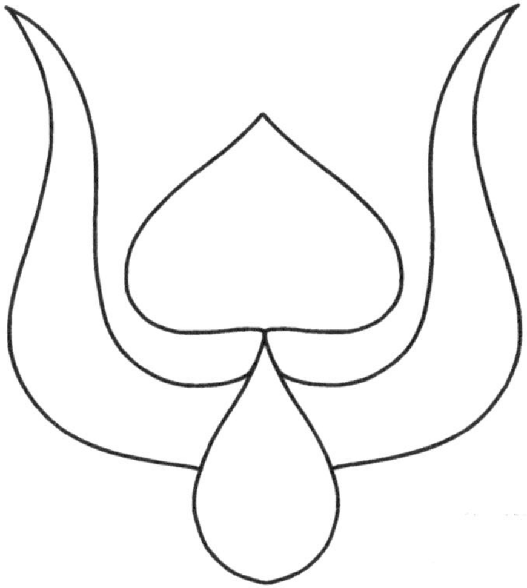

FATLINER WEIRDIES
THE TEMPLATES 1

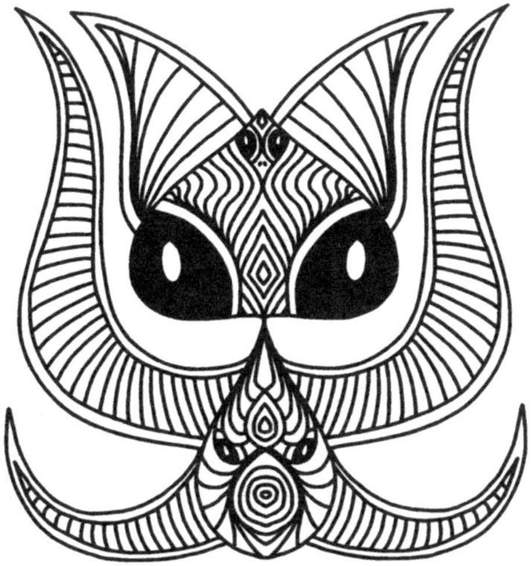

FATLINER WEIRDIES
VOLUME 3

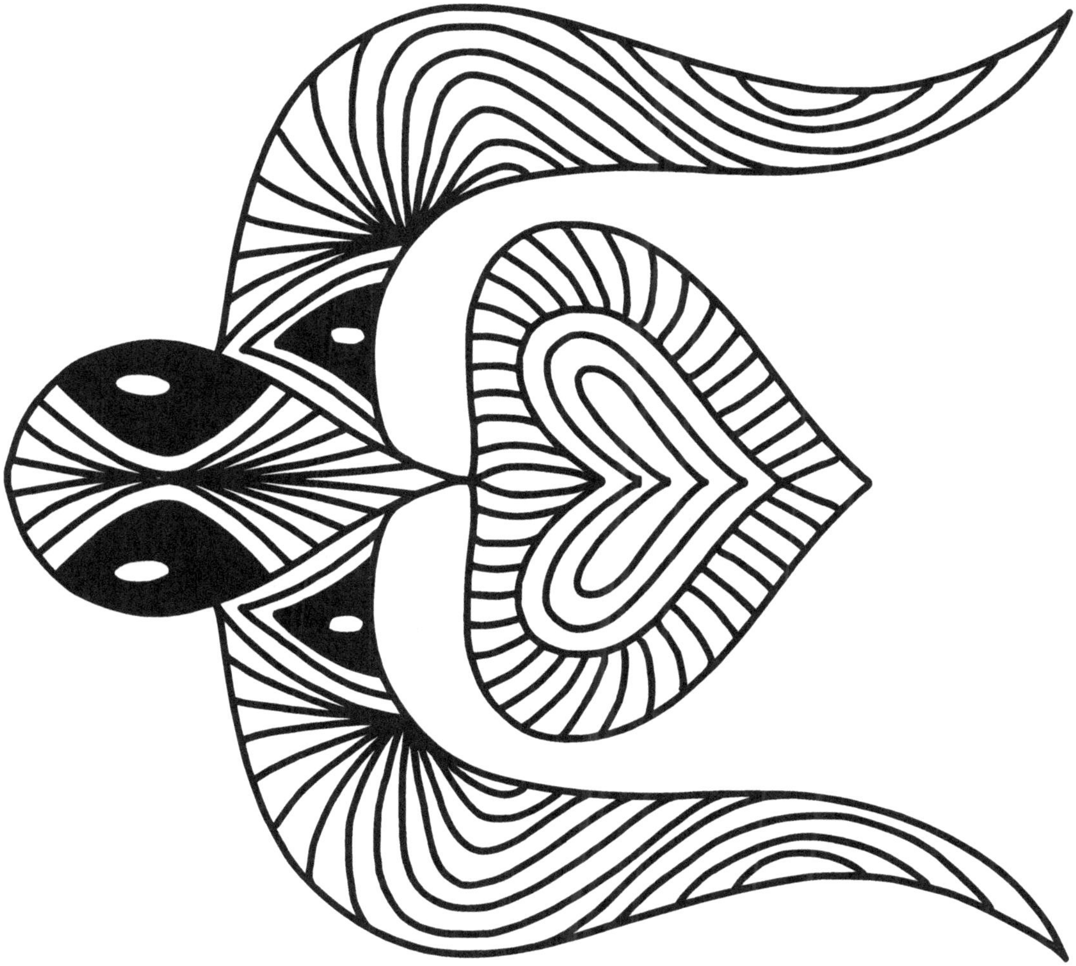

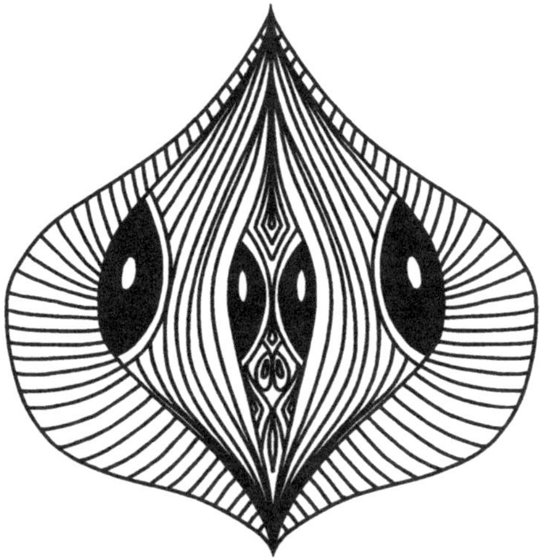

FATLINER WEIRDIES
VOLUME 1

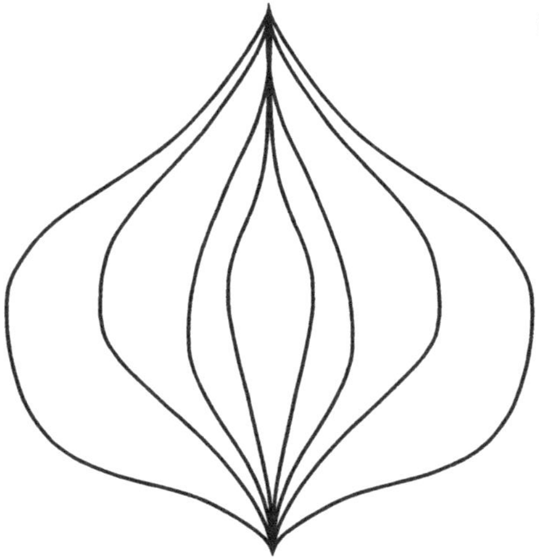

FATLINER WEIRDIES
THE TEMPLATES 1

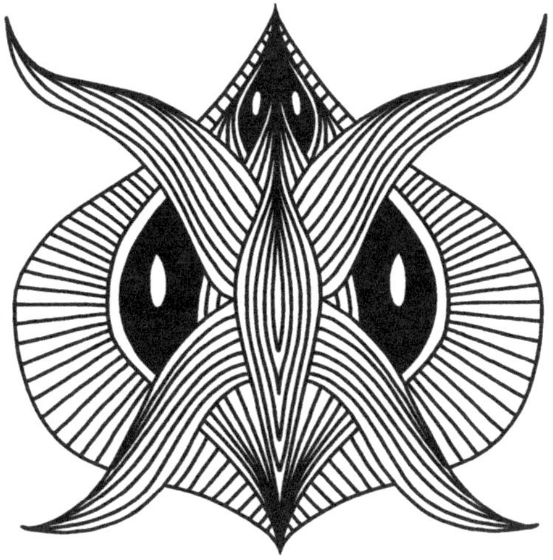

FATLINER WEIRDIES
VOLUME 3

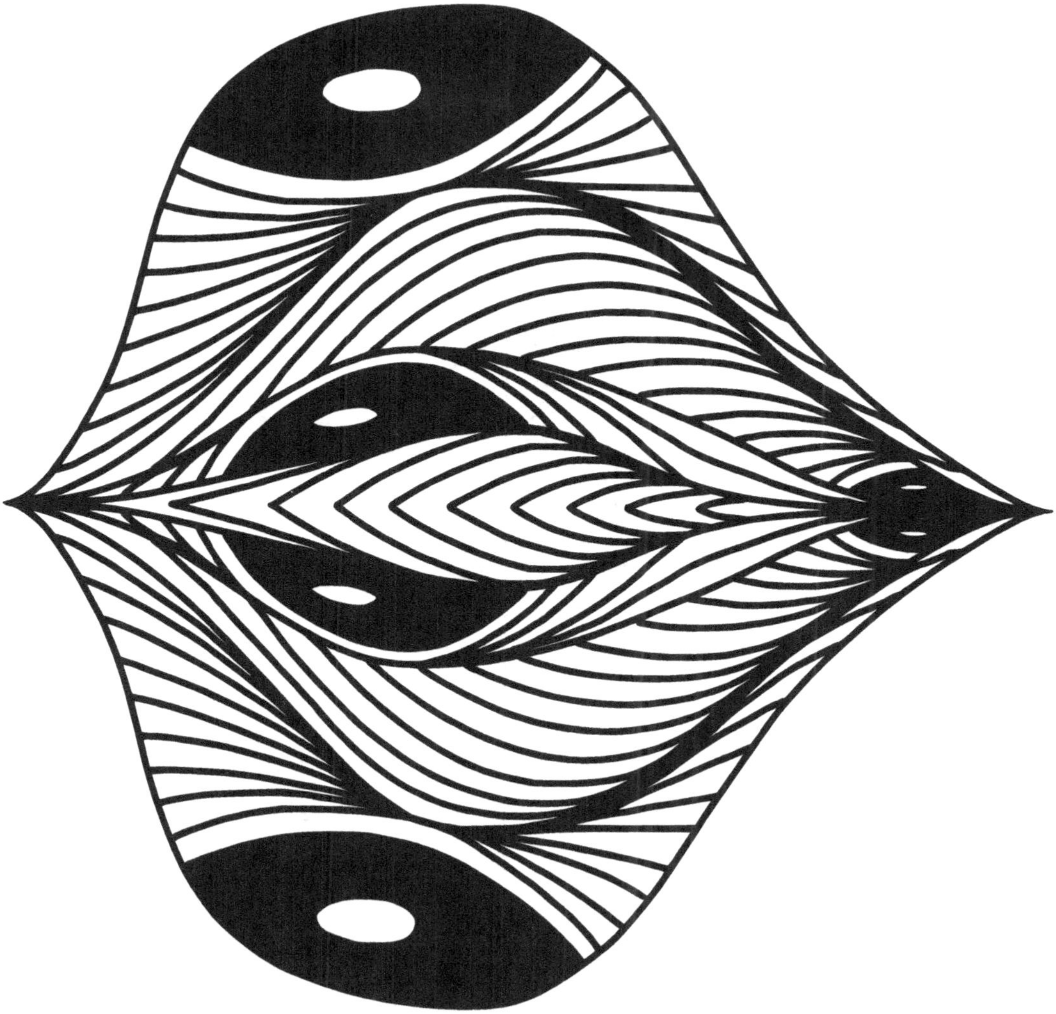

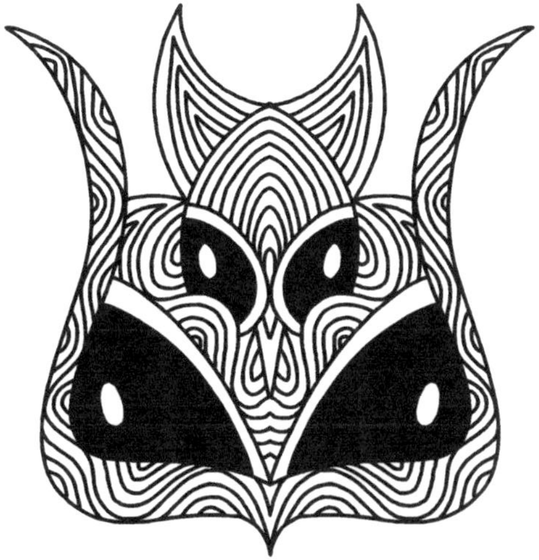

FATLINER WEIRDIES
VOLUME 1

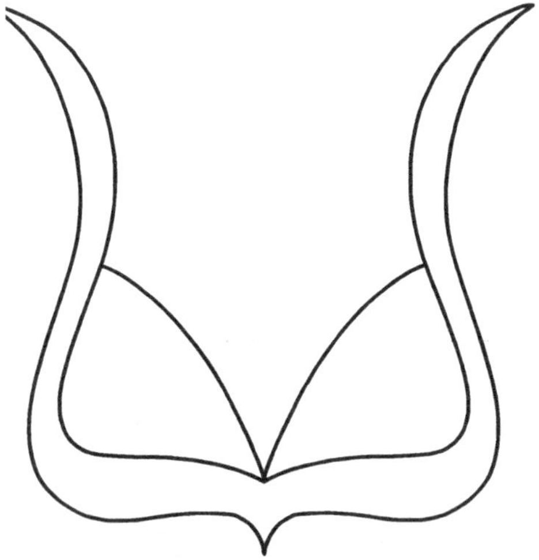

FATLINER WEIRDIES
THE TEMPLATES 1

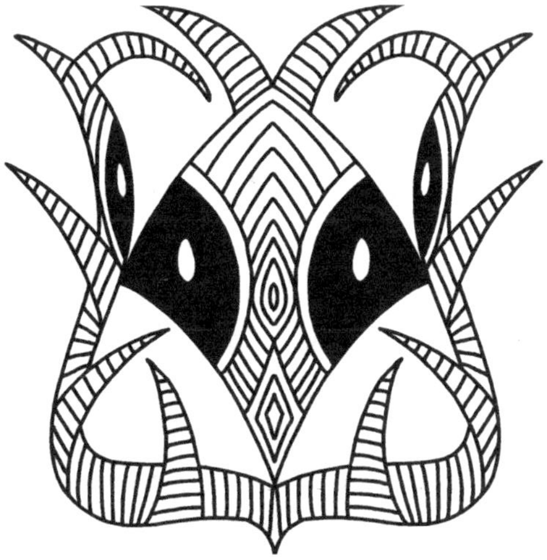

FATLINER WEIRDIES
VOLUME 3

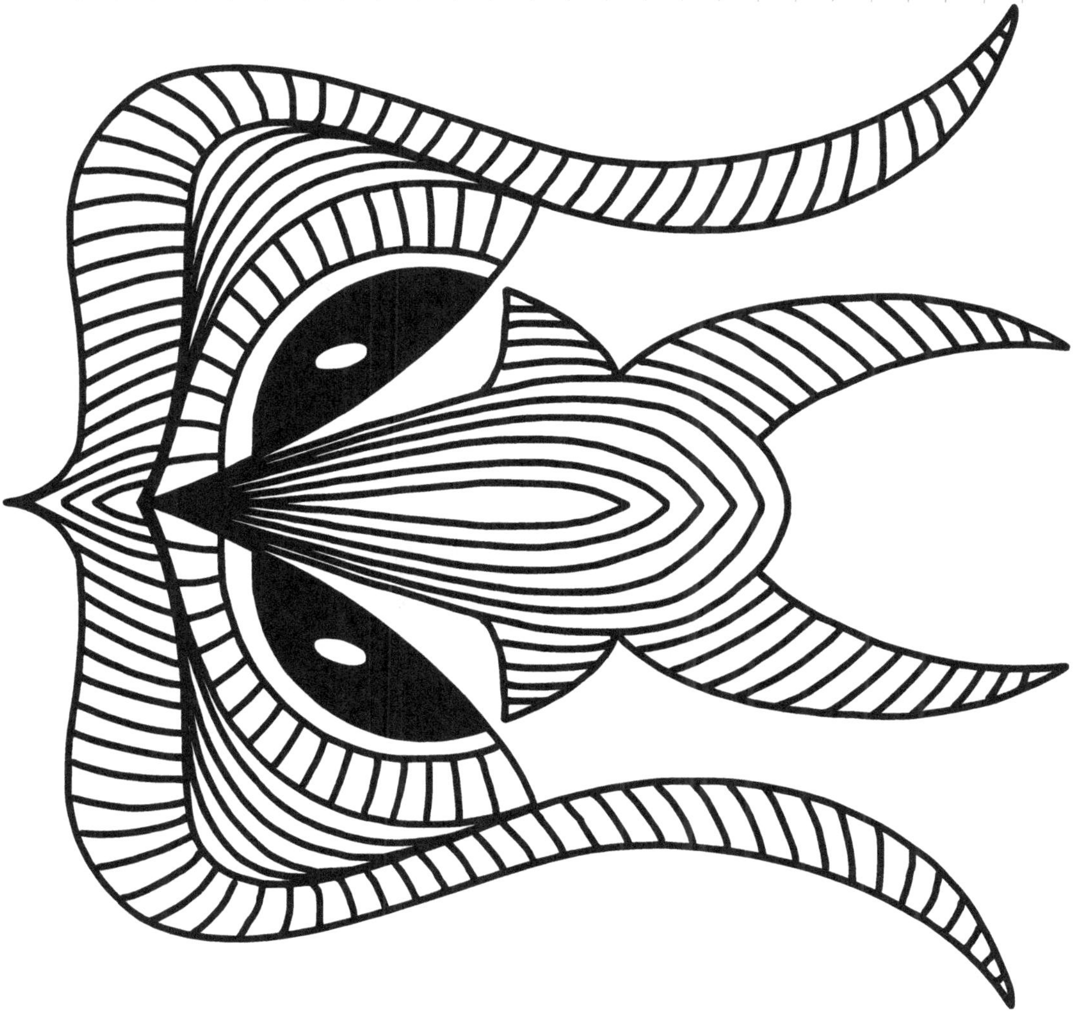

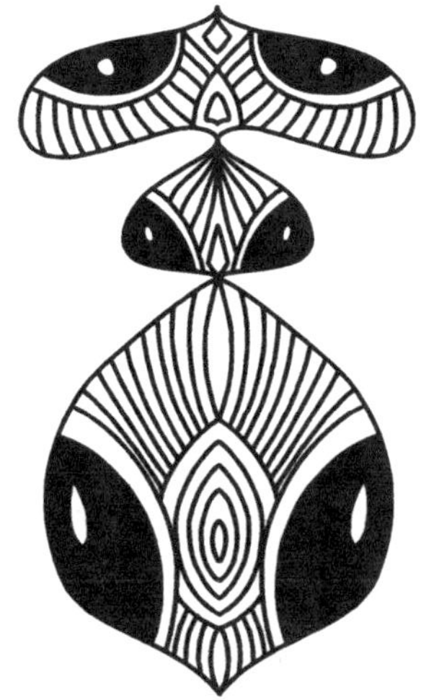

FATLINER WEIRDIES
VOLUME 1

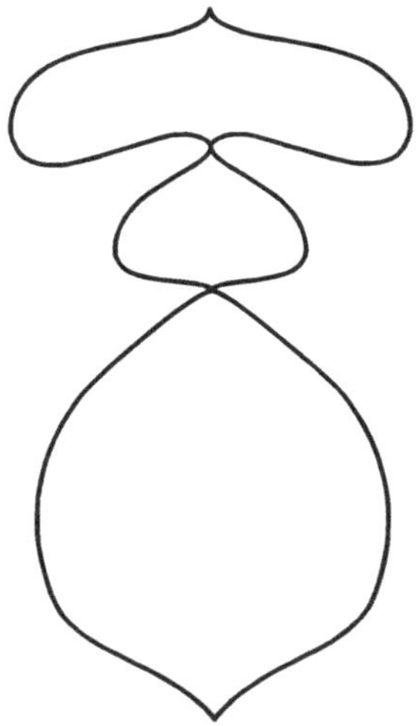

FATLINER WEIRDIES
THE TEMPLATES 1

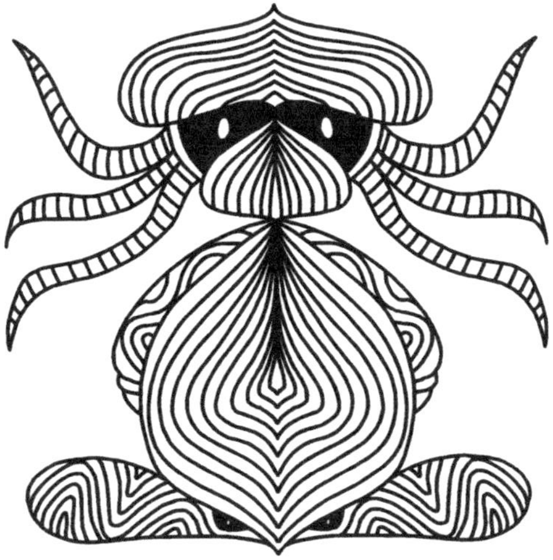

FATLINER WEIRDIES
VOLUME 3

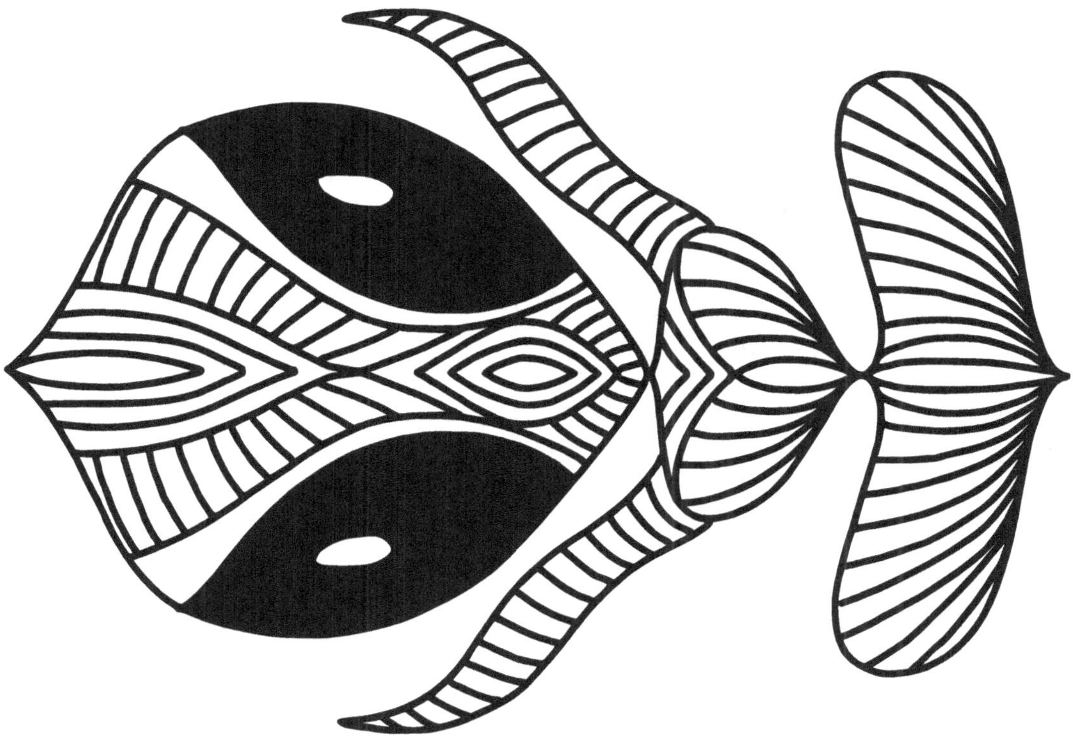

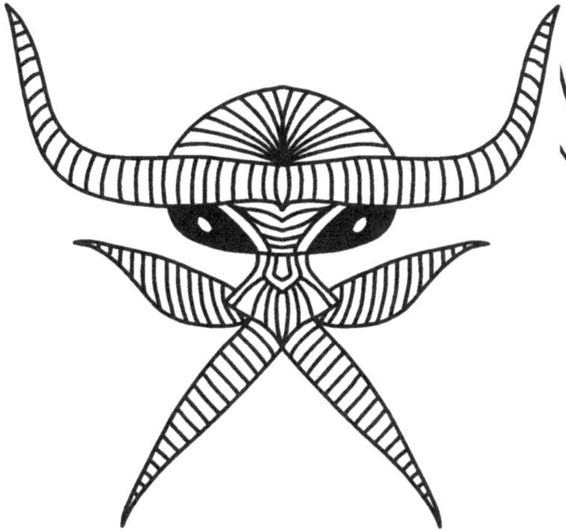

FATLINER WEIRDIES
VOLUME 1

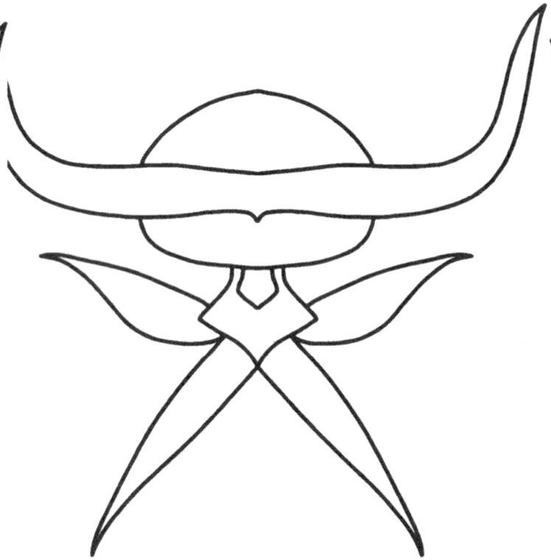

FATLINER WEIRDIES
THE TEMPLATES 1

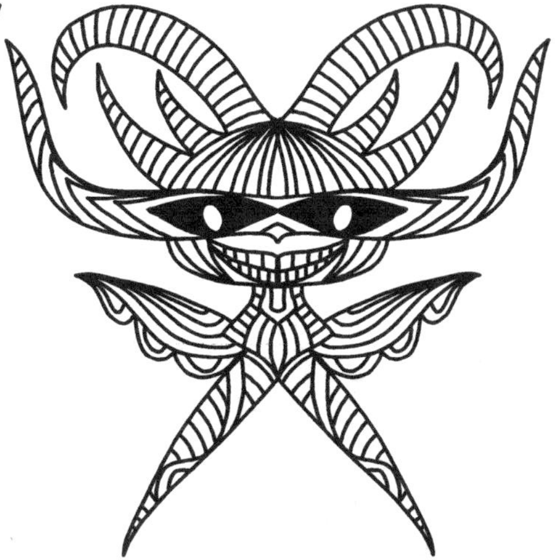

FATLINER WEIRDIES
VOLUME 3

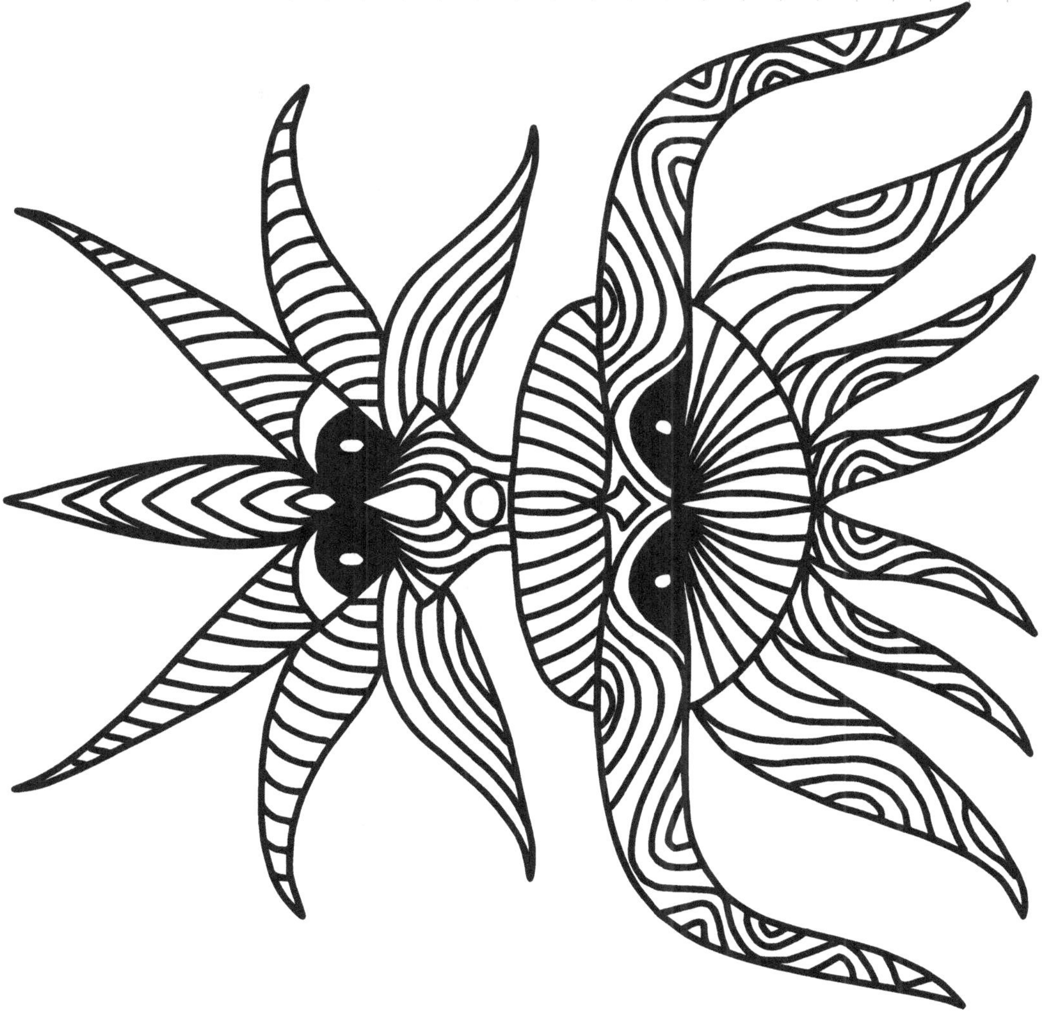

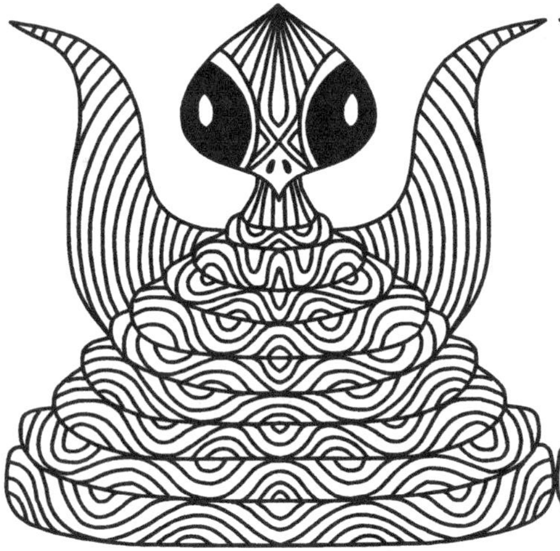

FATLINER WEIRDIES
VOLUME 1

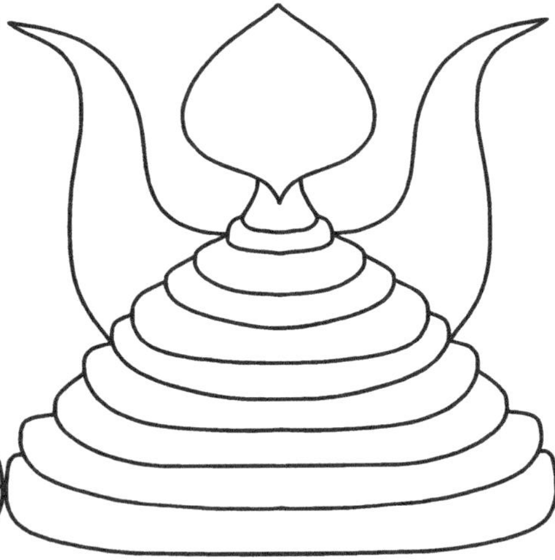

FATLINER WEIRDIES
THE TEMPLATES 1

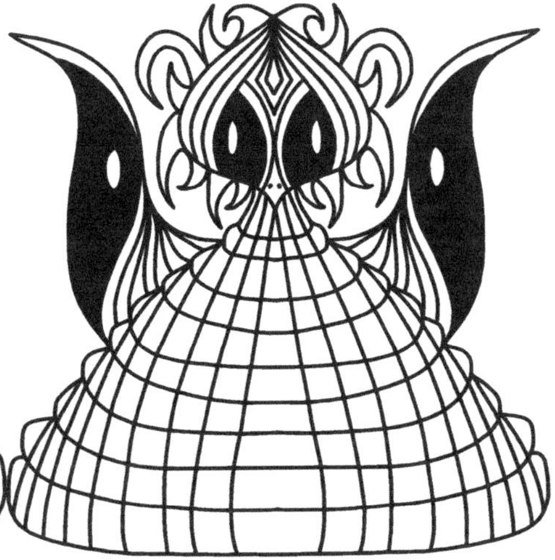

FATLINER WEIRDIES
VOLUME 3

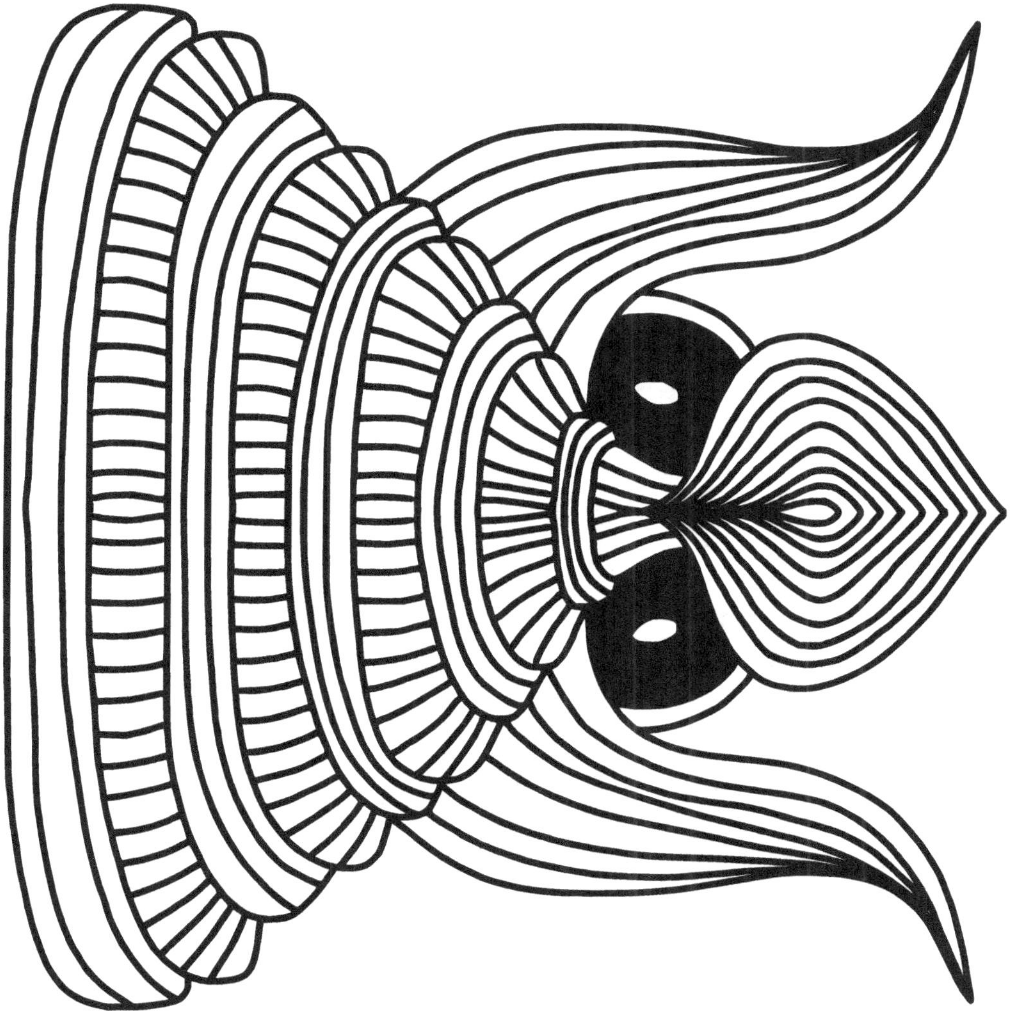

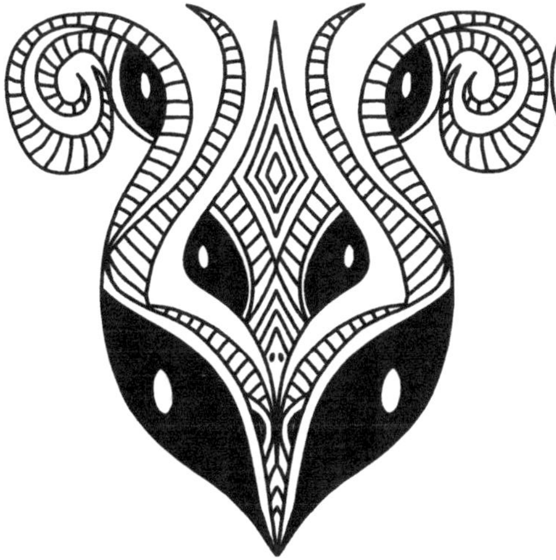

FATLINER WEIRDIES
VOLUME 1

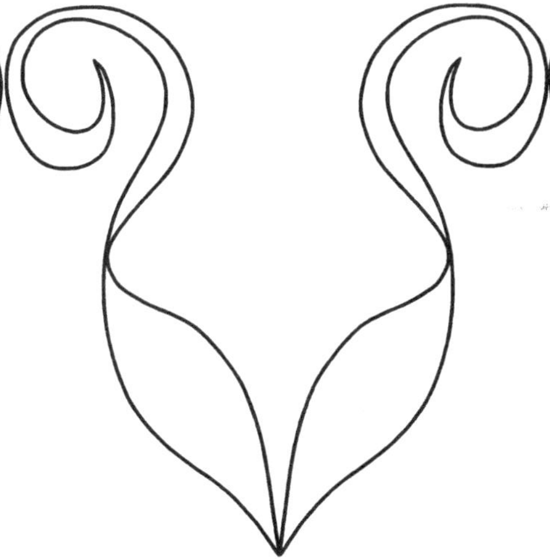

FATLINER WEIRDIES
THE TEMPLATES 1

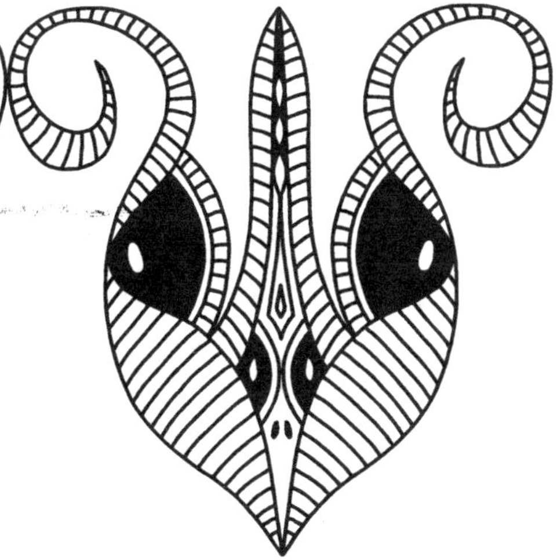

FATLINER WEIRDIES
VOLUME 3

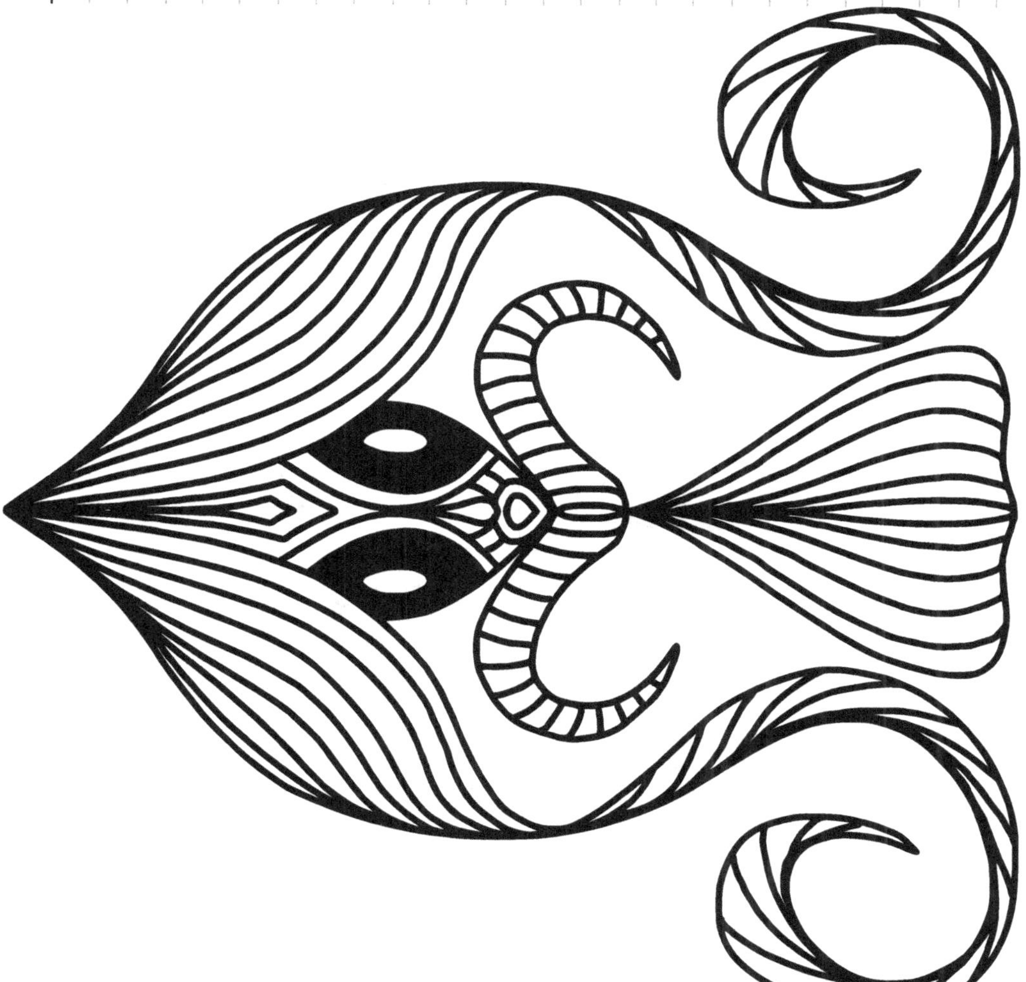

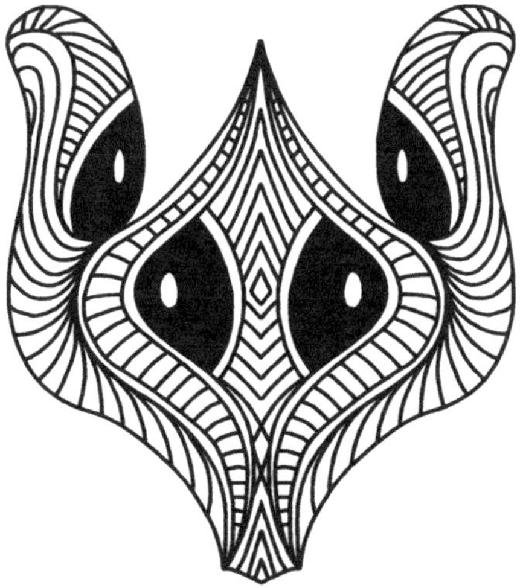

FATLINER WEIRDIES
VOLUME 1

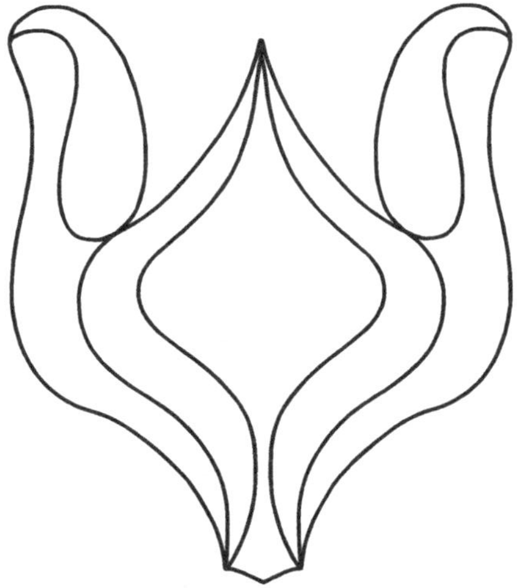

FATLINER WEIRDIES
THE TEMPLATES 1

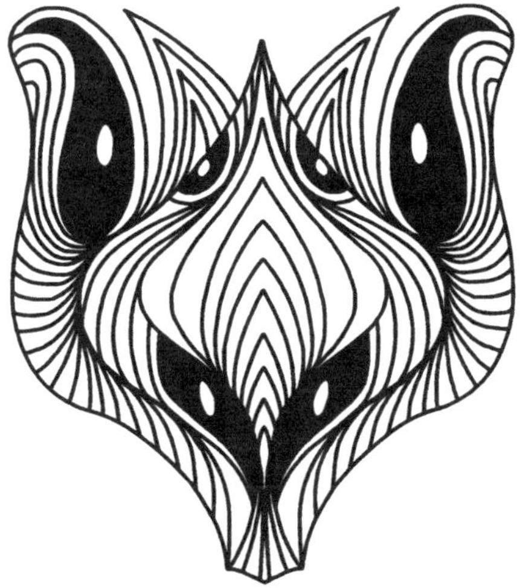

FATLINER WEIRDIES
VOLUME 3

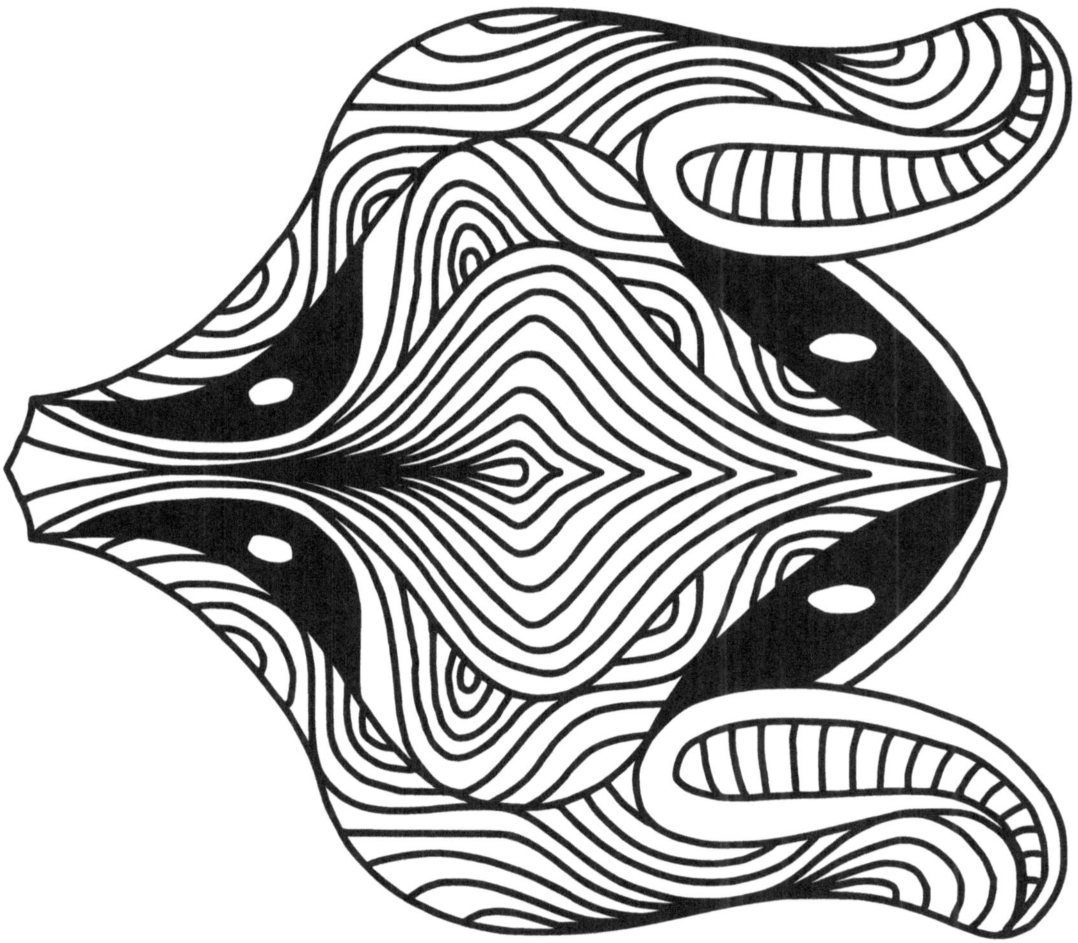

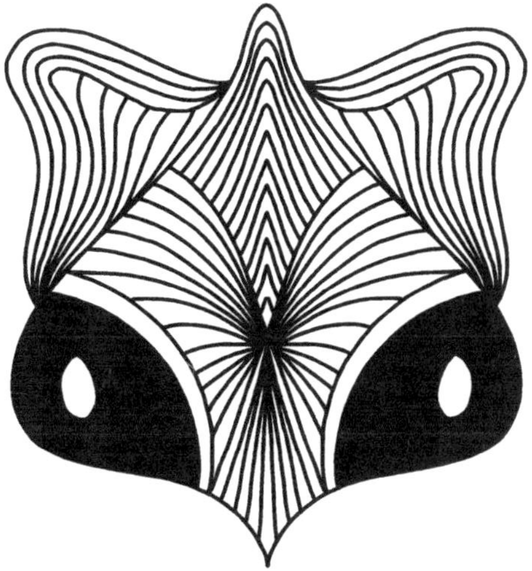

FATLINER WEIRDIES
VOLUME 1

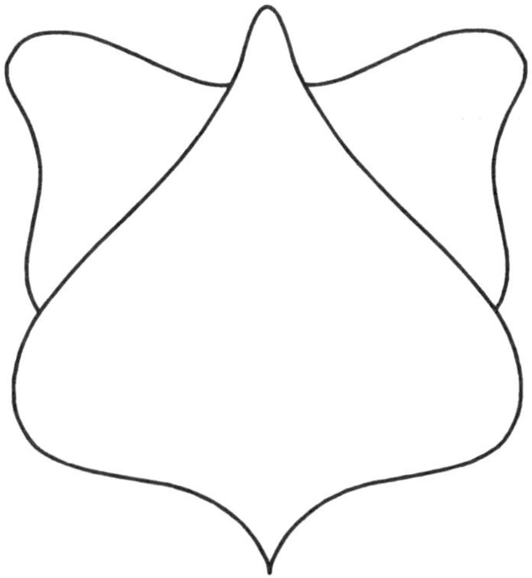

FATLINER WEIRDIES
THE TEMPLATES 1

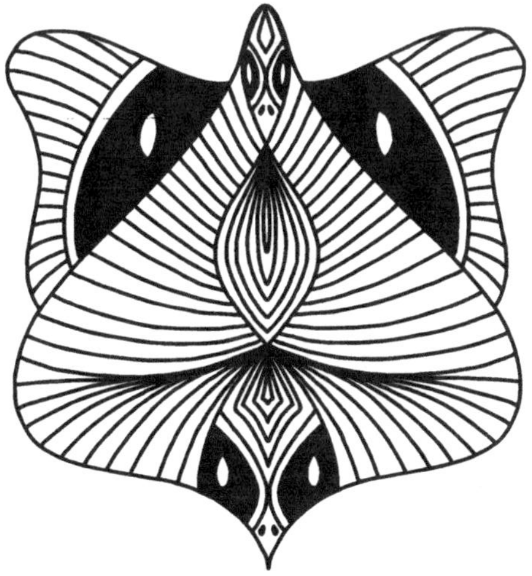

FATLINER WEIRDIES
VOLUME 3

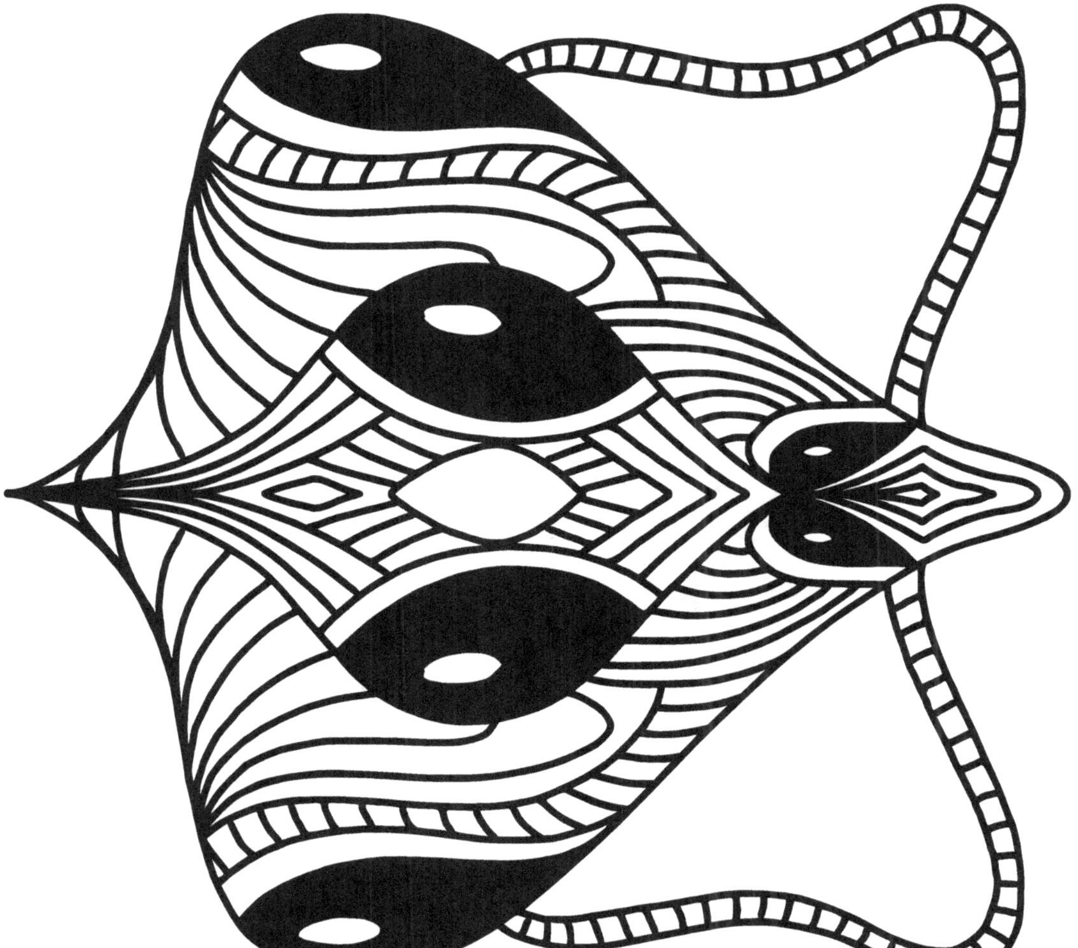

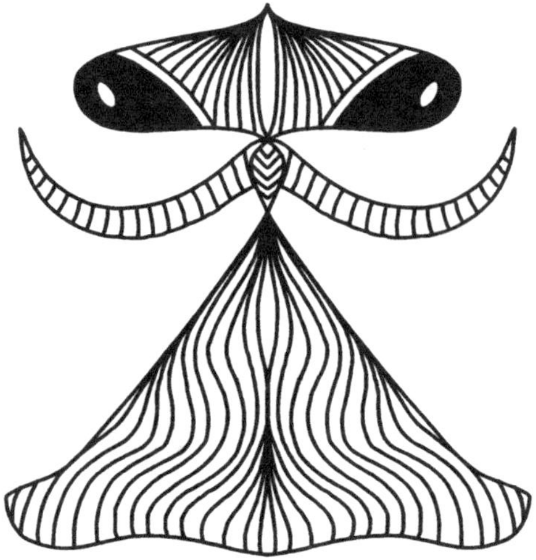

FATLINER WEIRDIES
VOLUME 1

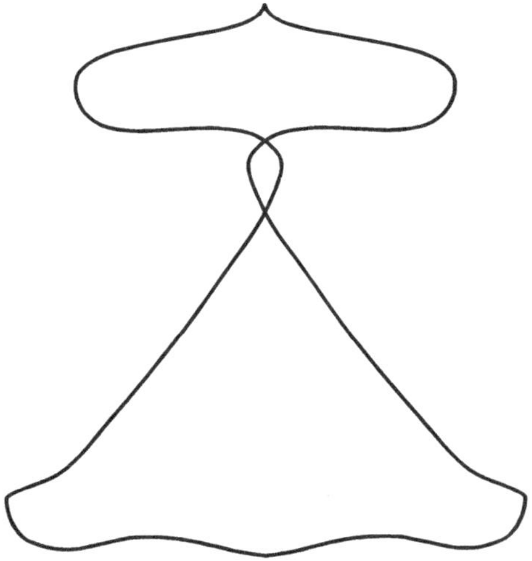

FATLINER WEIRDIES
THE TEMPLATES 1

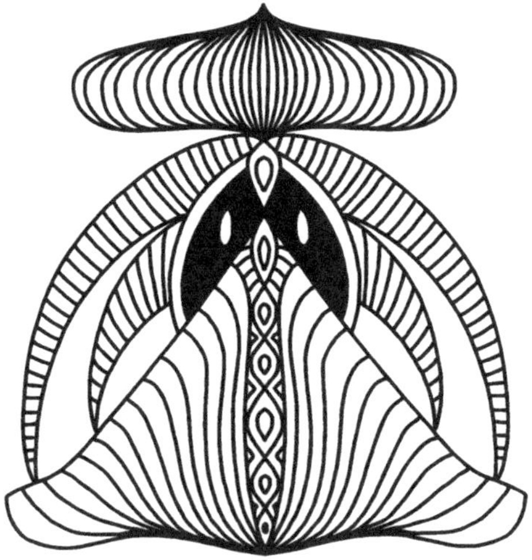

FATLINER WEIRDIES
VOLUME 3

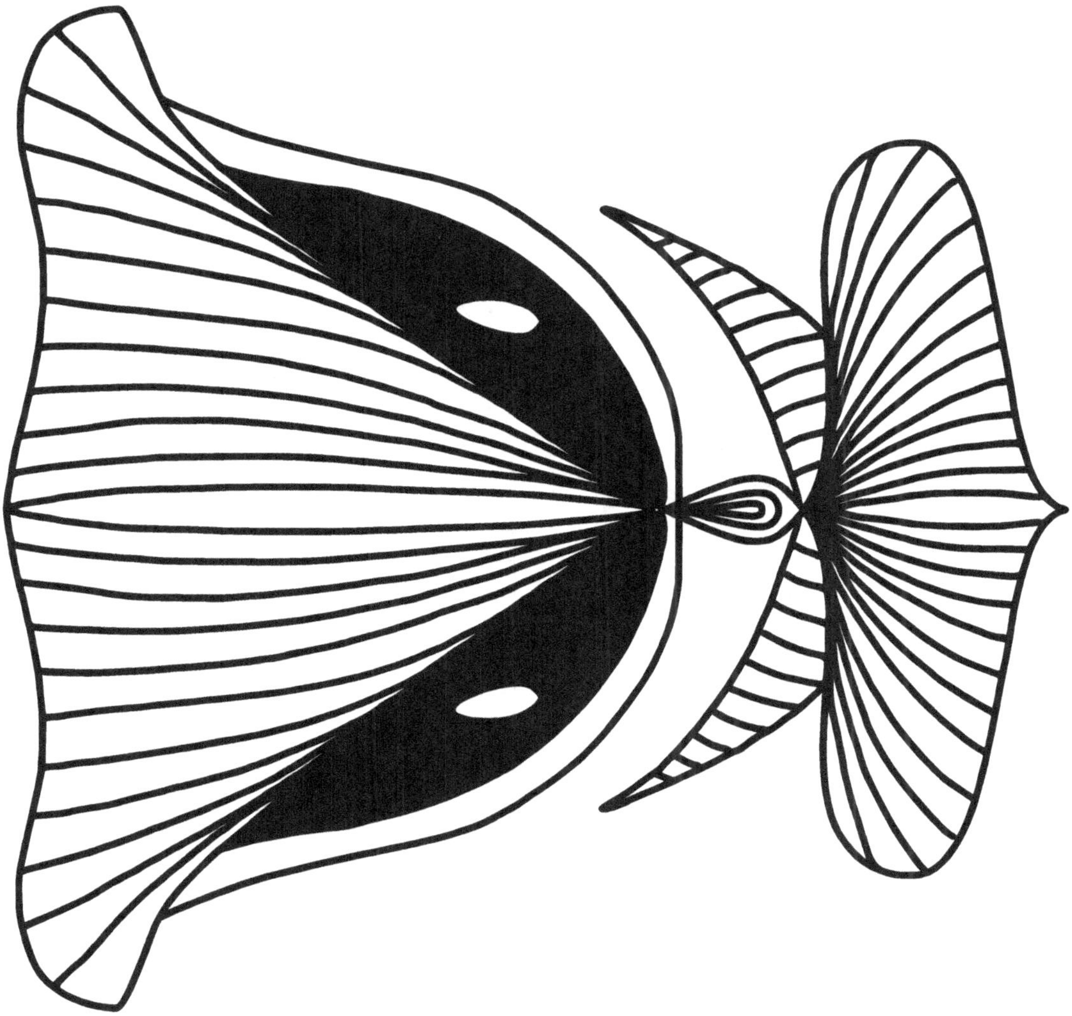

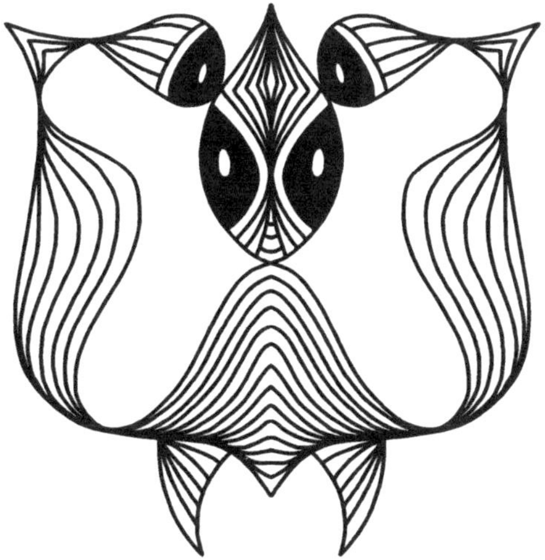

FATLINER WEIRDIES
VOLUME 1

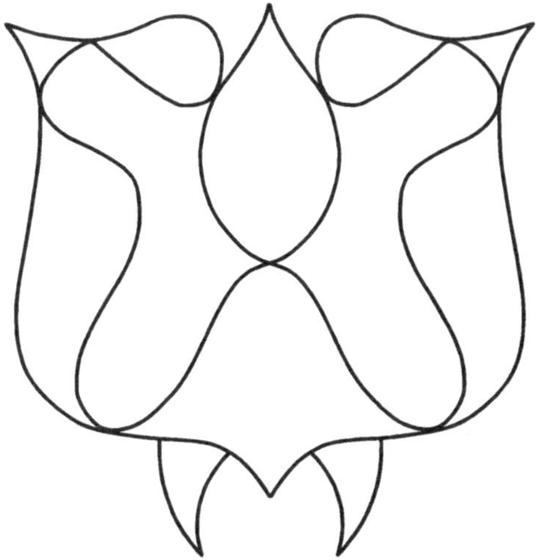

FATLINER WEIRDIES
THE TEMPLATES 1

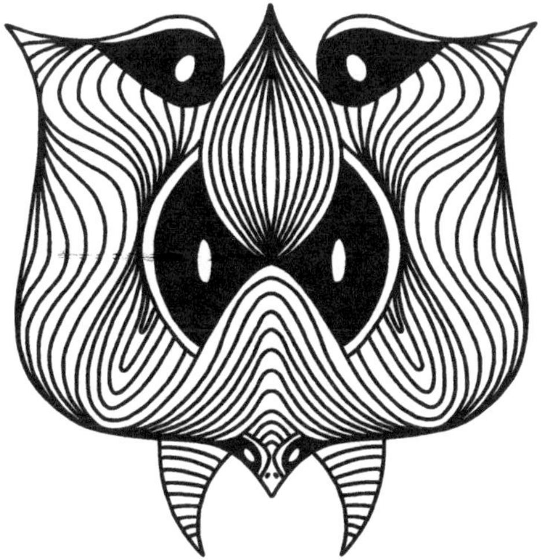

FATLINER WEIRDIES
VOLUME 3

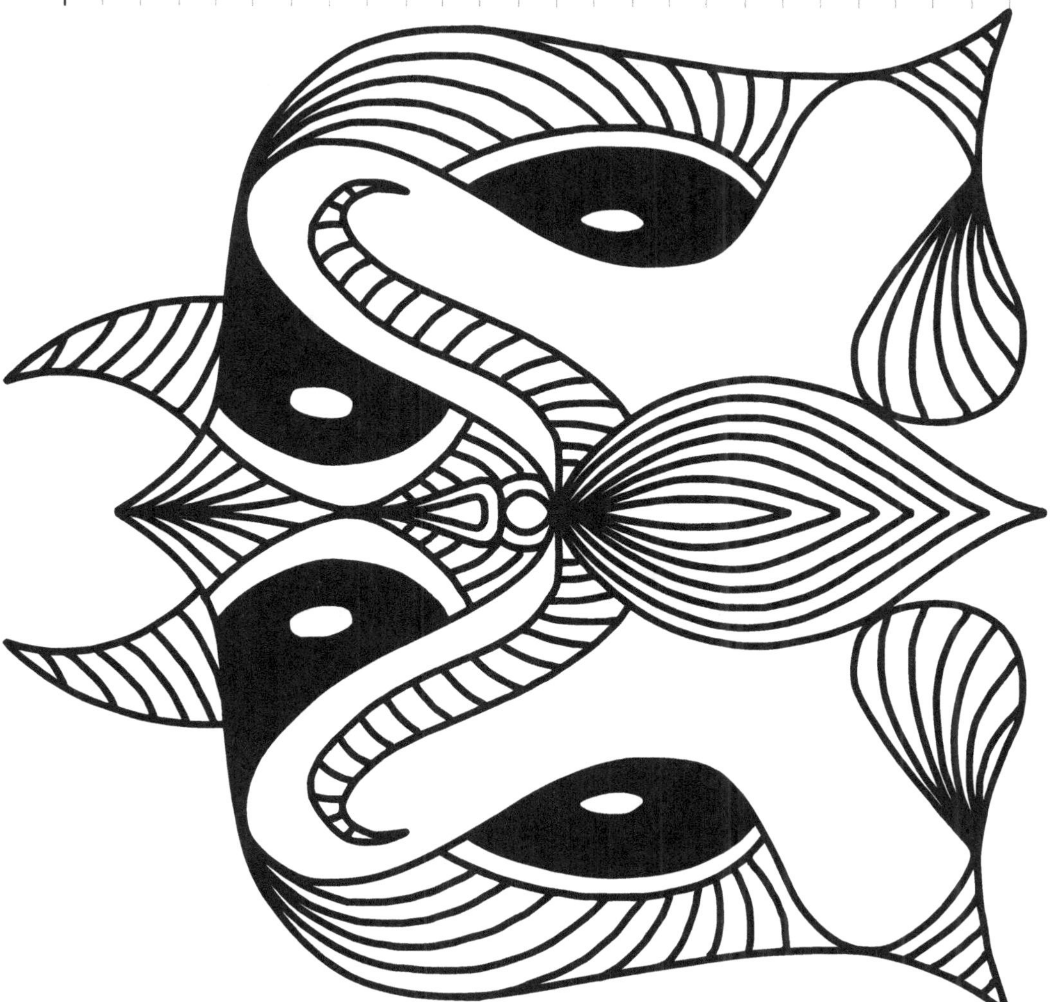

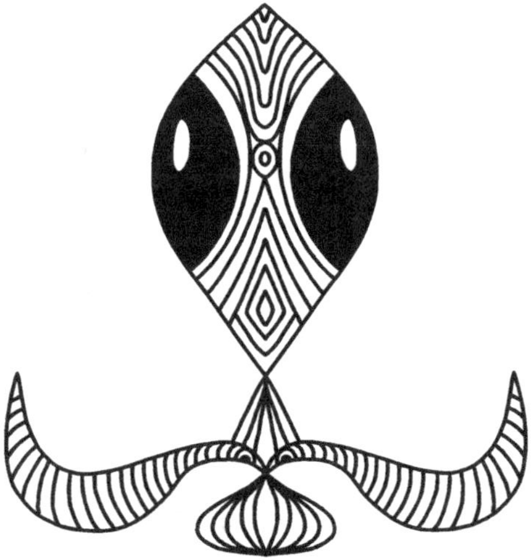

FATLINER WEIRDIES
VOLUME 1

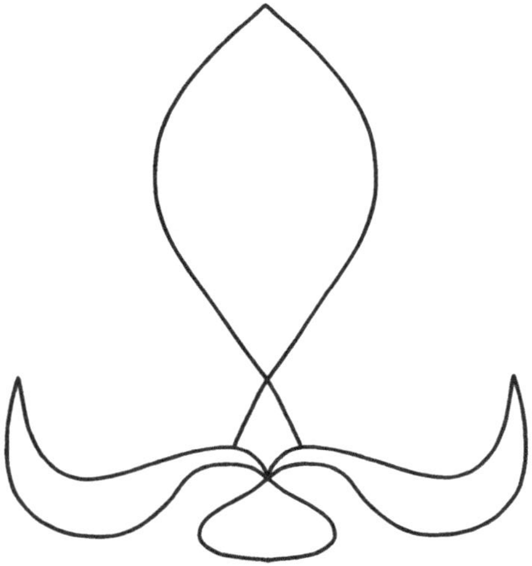

FATLINER WEIRDIES
THE TEMPLATES 1

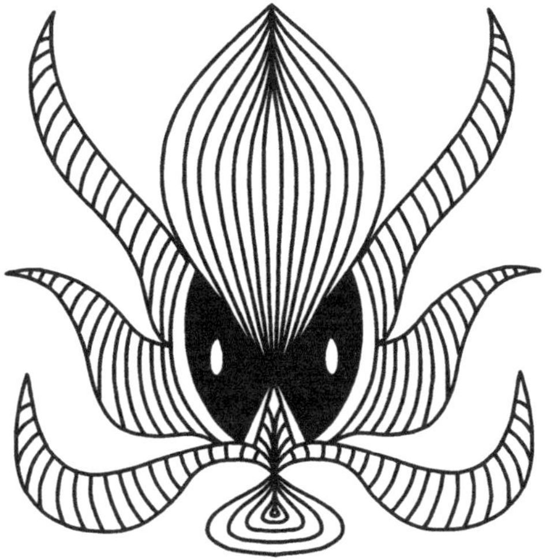

FATLINER WEIRDIES
VOLUME 3

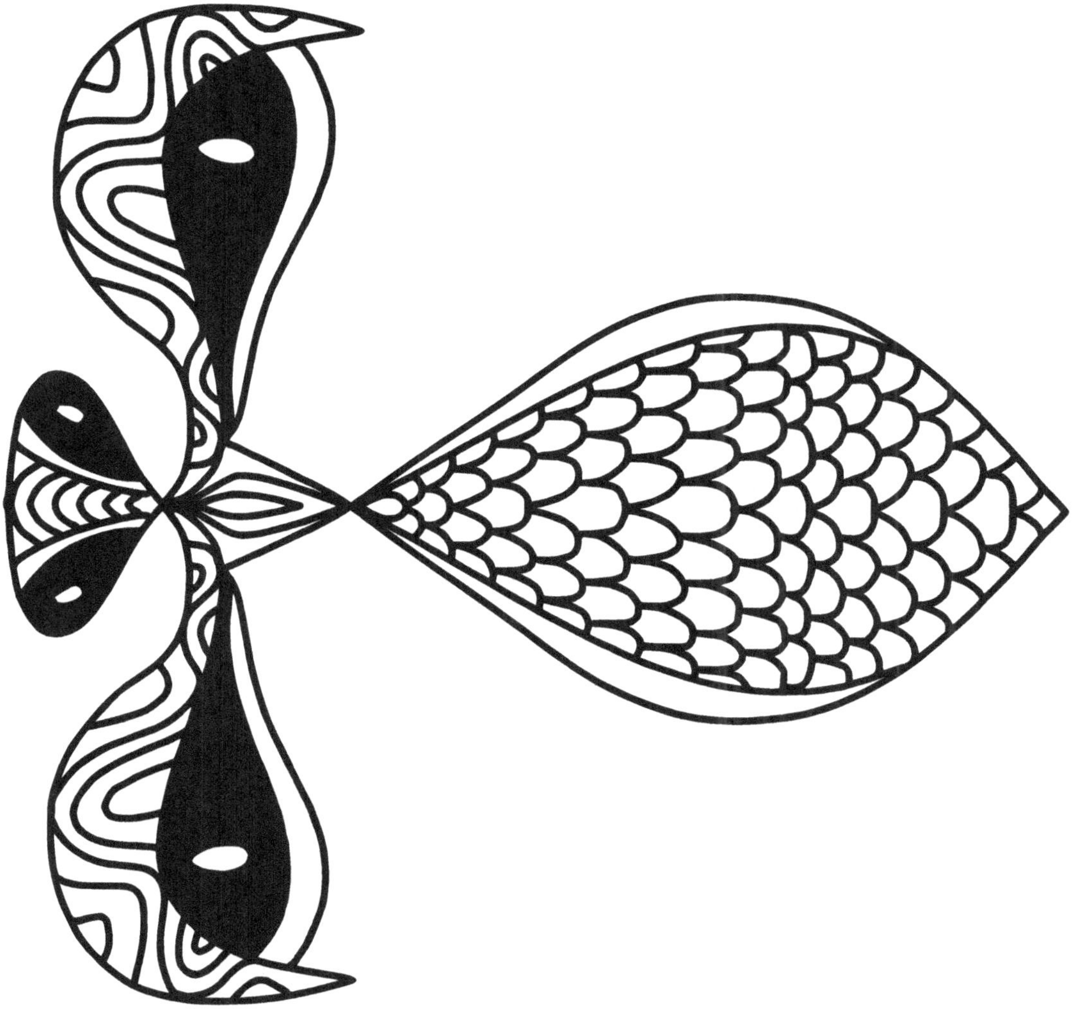

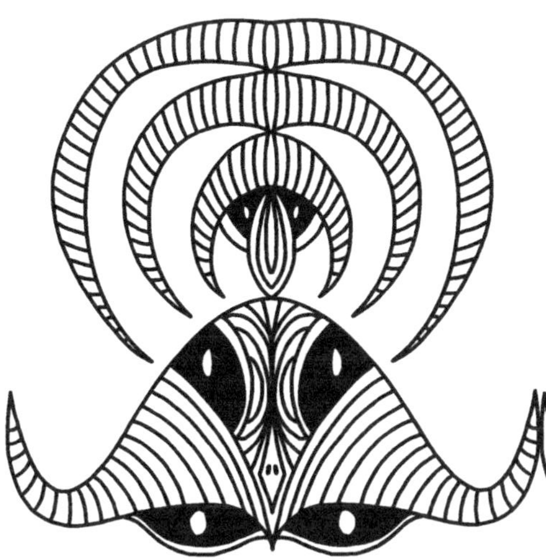
FATLINER WEIRDIES
VOLUME 1

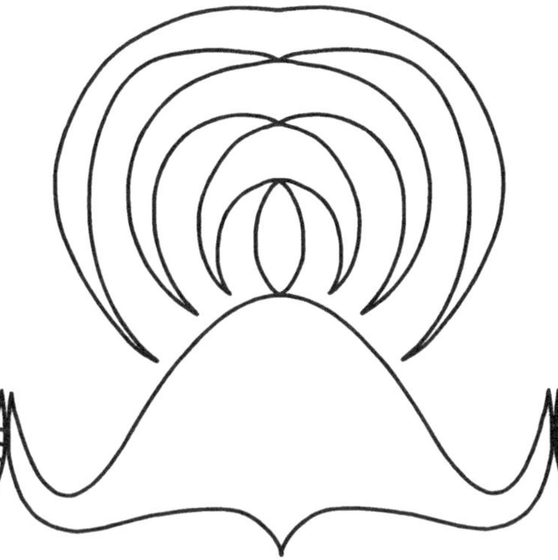
FATLINER WEIRDIES
THE TEMPLATES 1

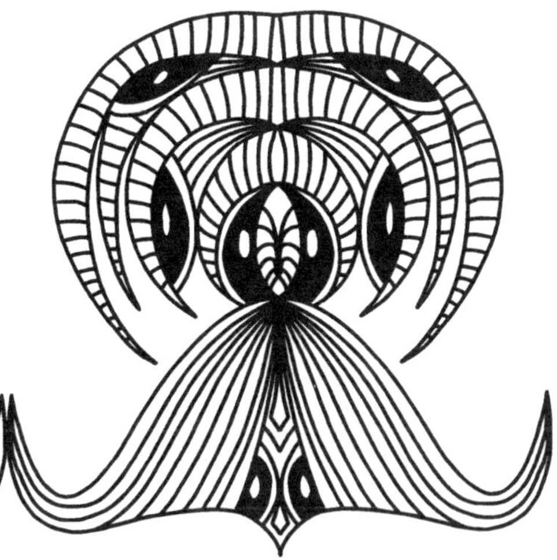
FATLINER WEIRDIES
VOLUME 3

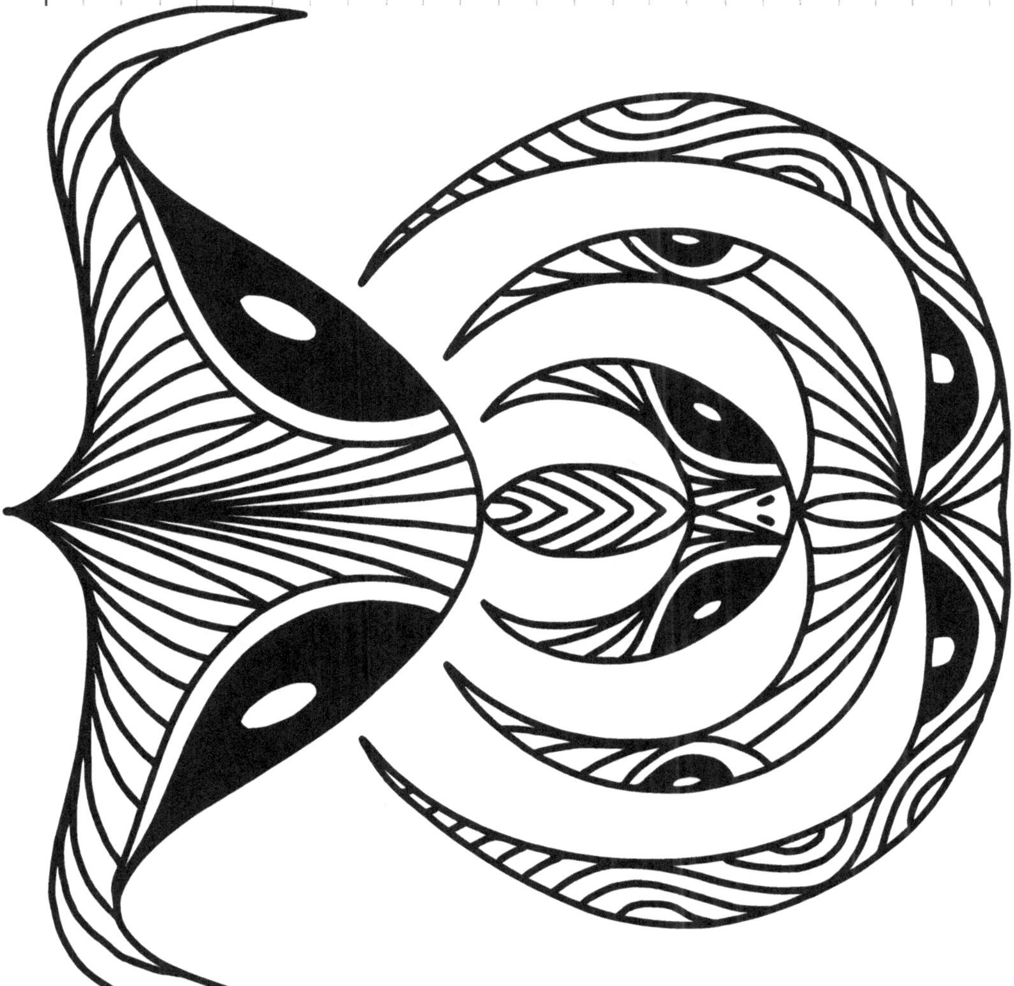

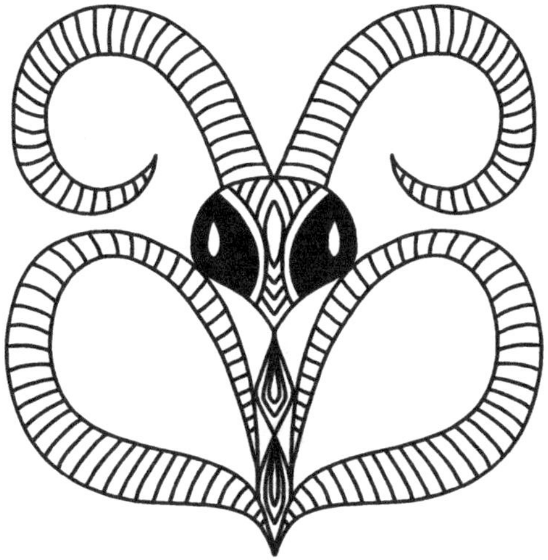

FATLINER WEIRDIES
VOLUME 1

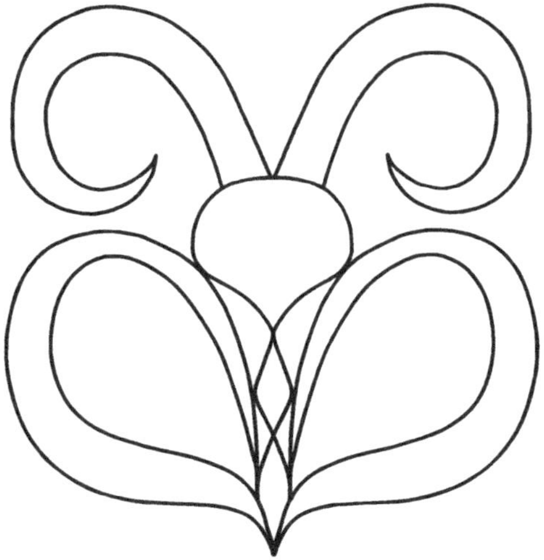

FATLINER WEIRDIES
THE TEMPLATES 1

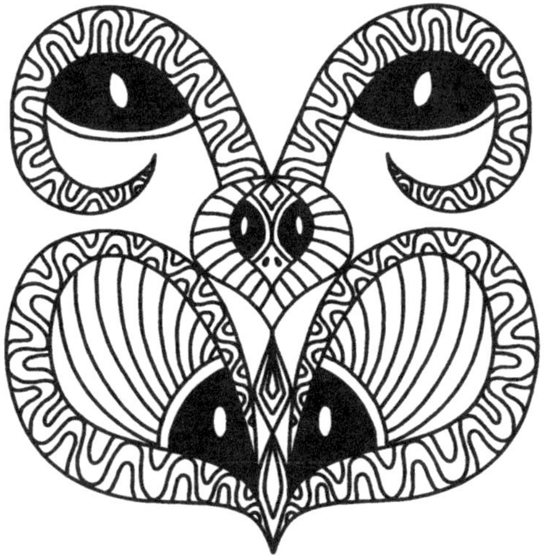

FATLINER WEIRDIES
VOLUME 3

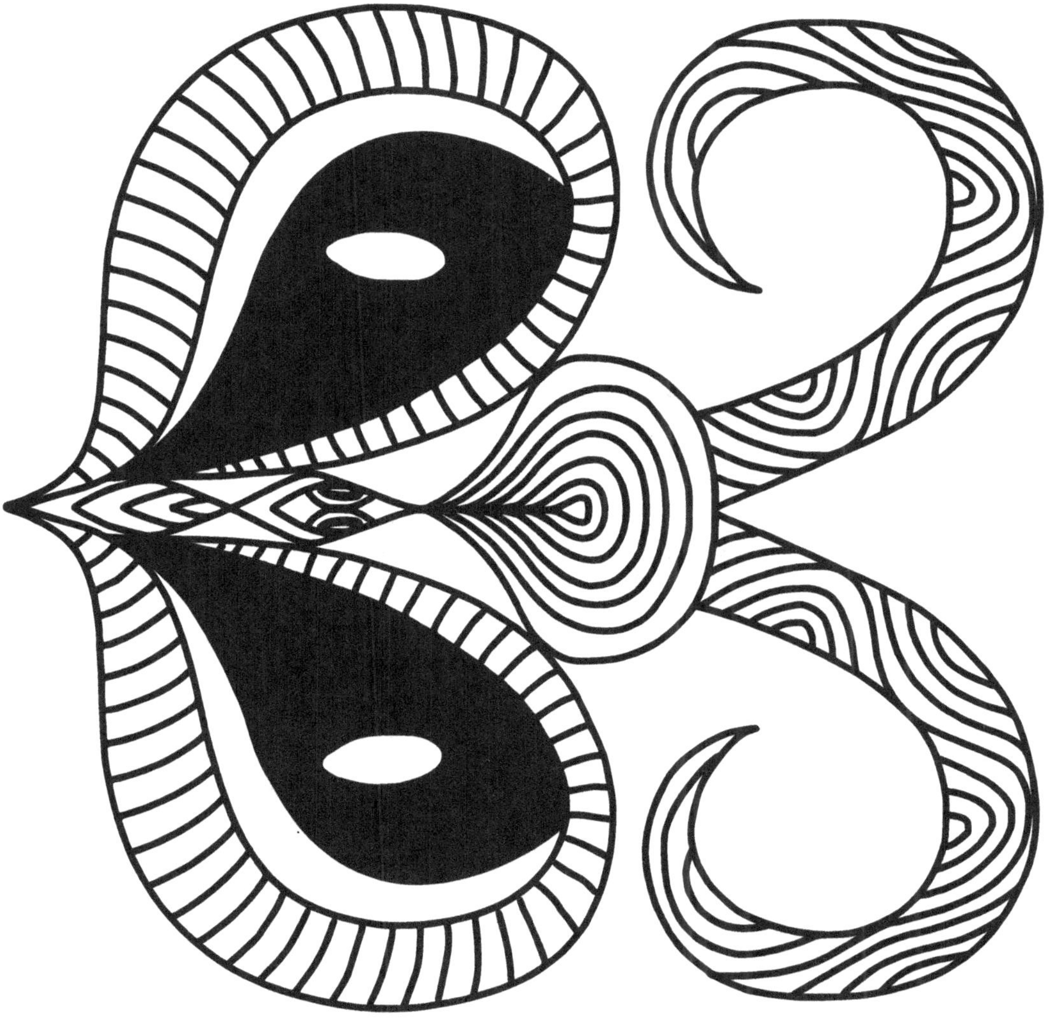

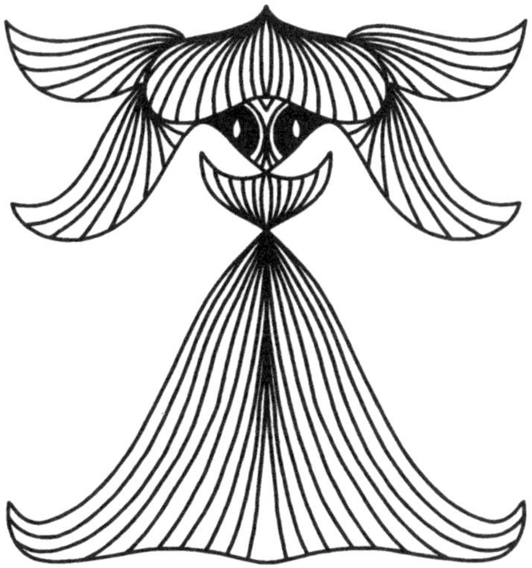
FATLINER WEIRDIES
VOLUME 1

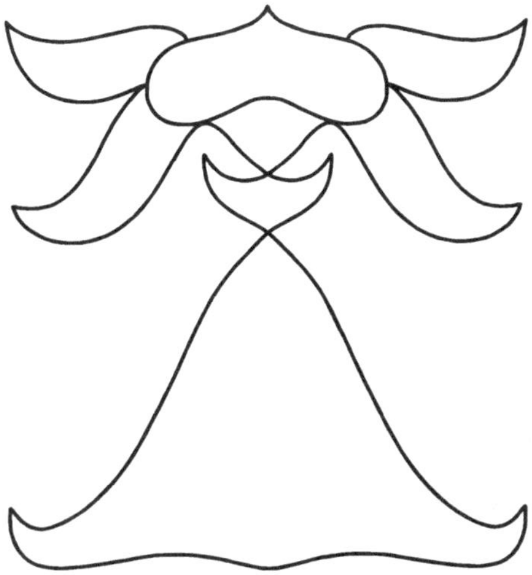
FATLINER WEIRDIES
THE TEMPLATES 1

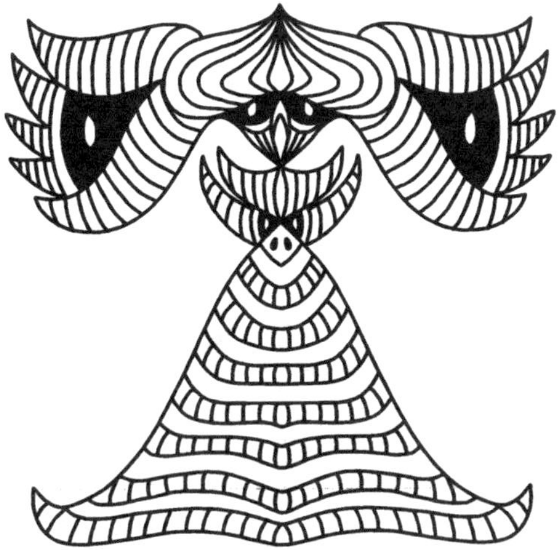
FATLINER WEIRDIES
VOLUME 3

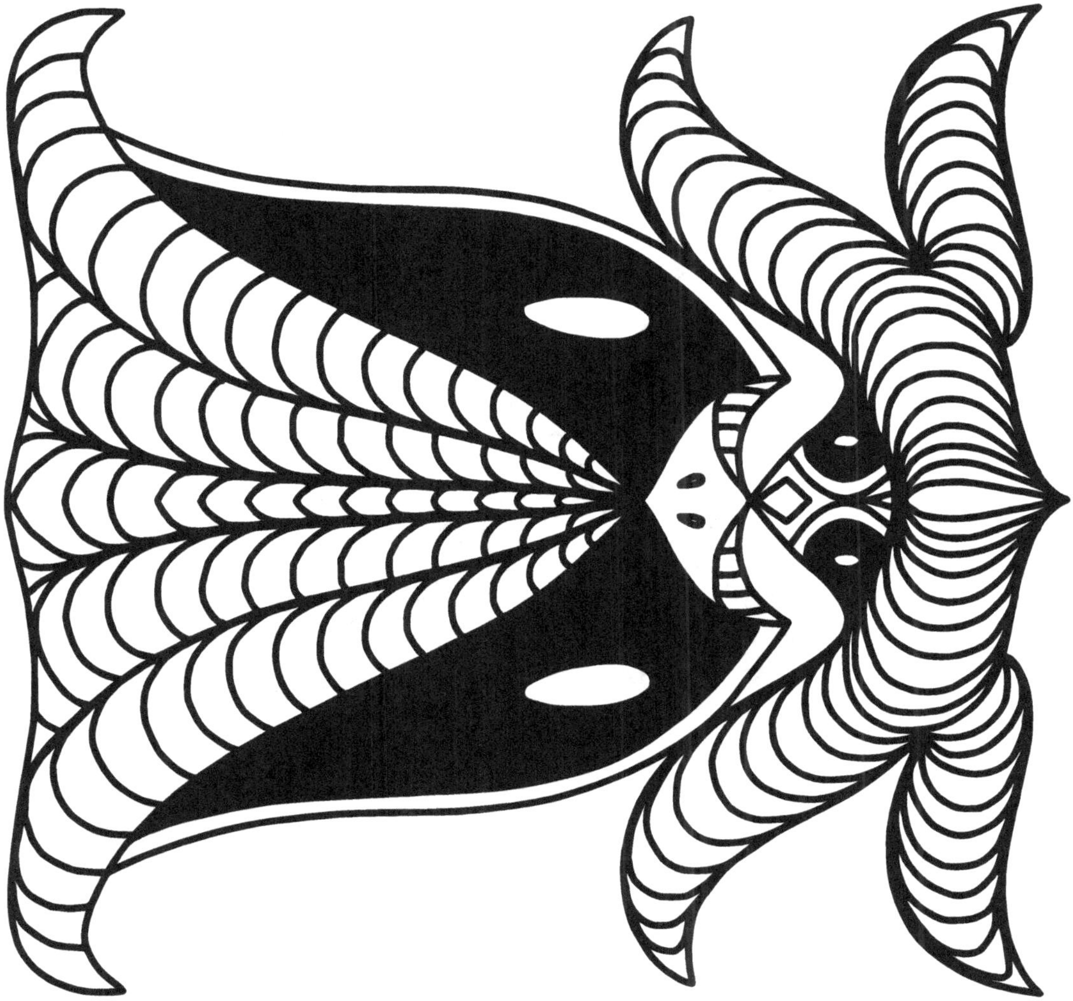

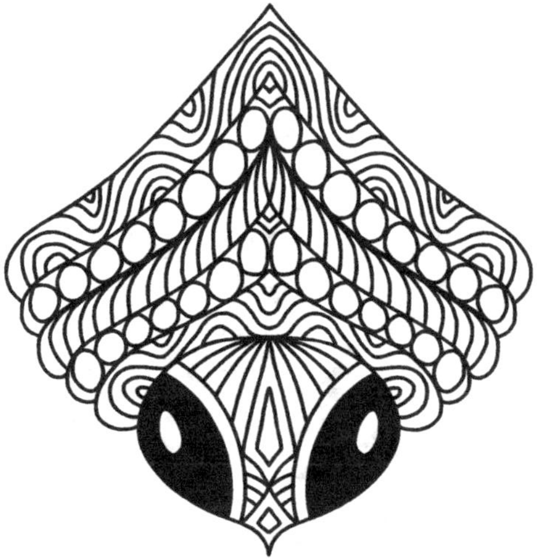

FATLINER WEIRDIES
VOLUME 1

FATLINER WEIRDIES
THE TEMPLATES 1

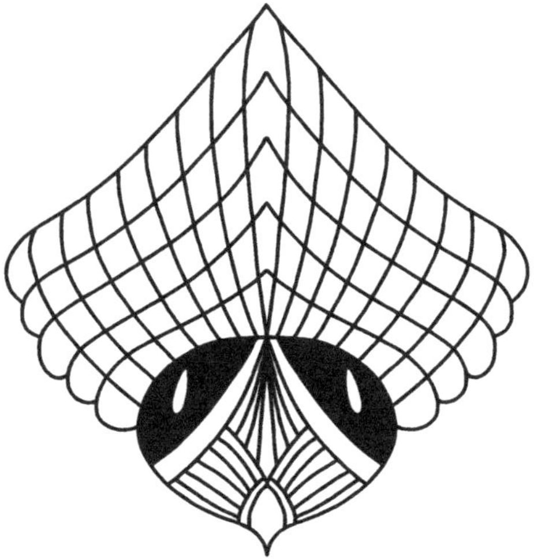

FATLINER WEIRDIES
VOLUME 3

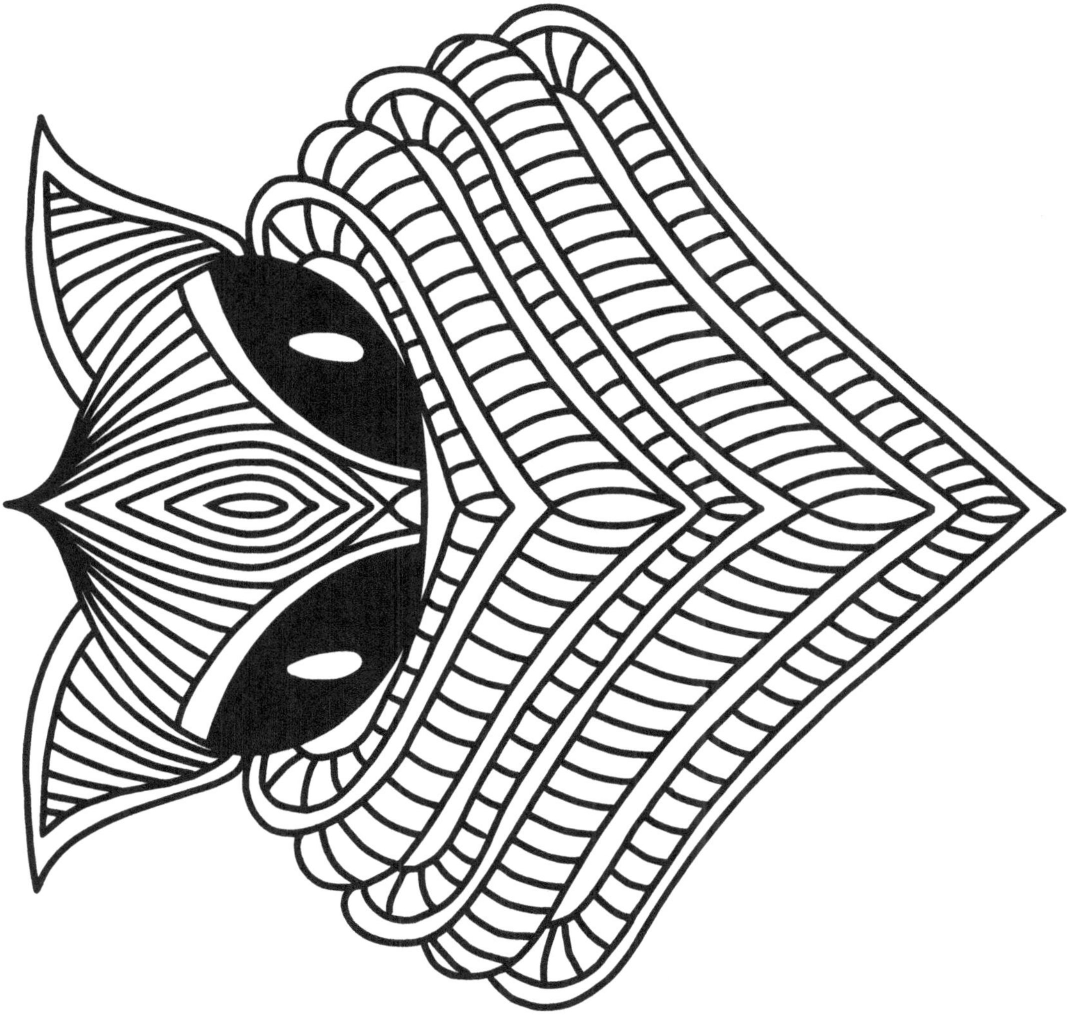

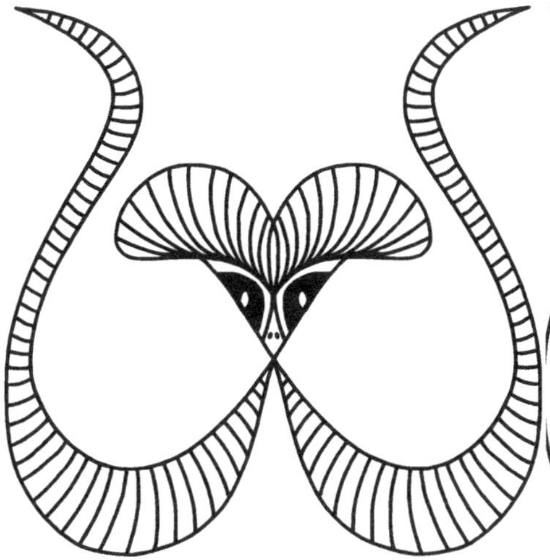

FATLINER WEIRDIES
VOLUME 1

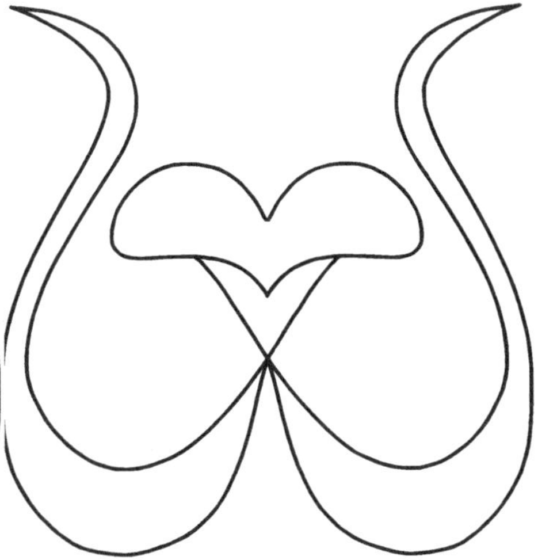

FATLINER WEIRDIES
THE TEMPLATES 1

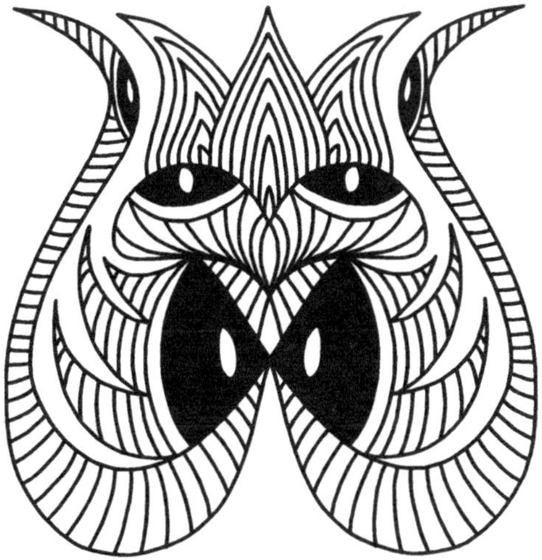

FATLINER WEIRDIES
VOLUME 3

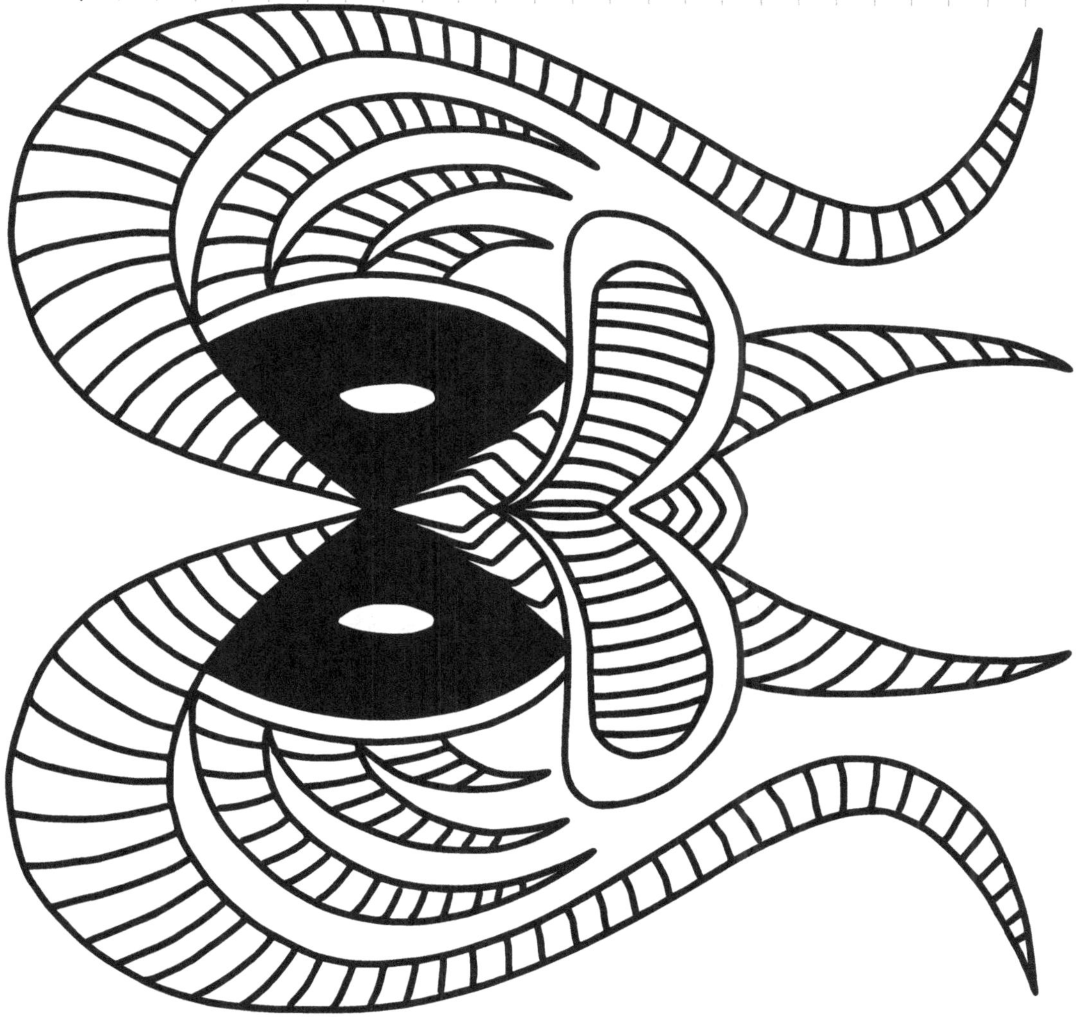

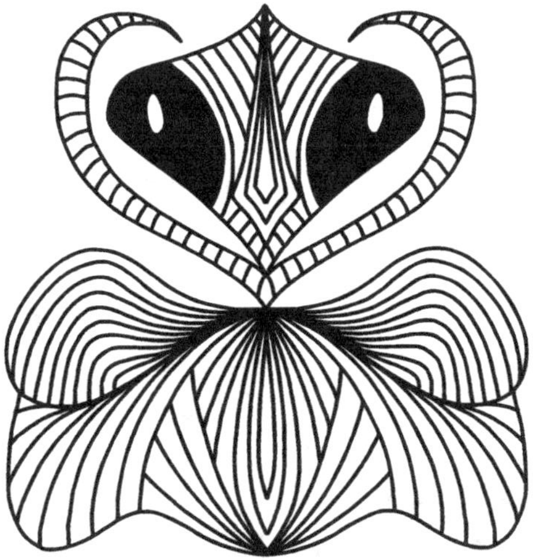
FATLINER WEIRDIES
VOLUME 1

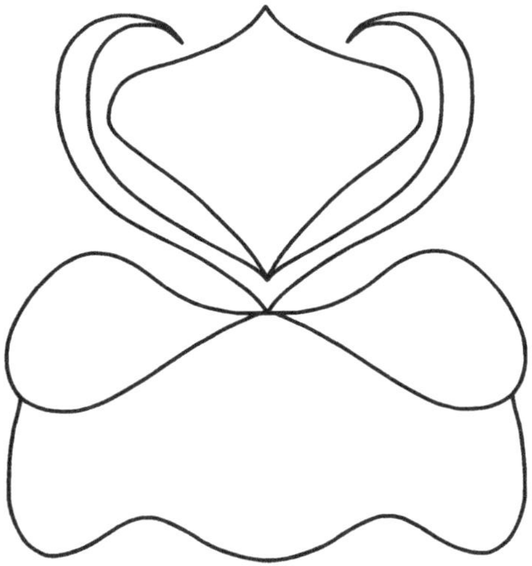
FATLINER WEIRDIES
THE TEMPLATES 1

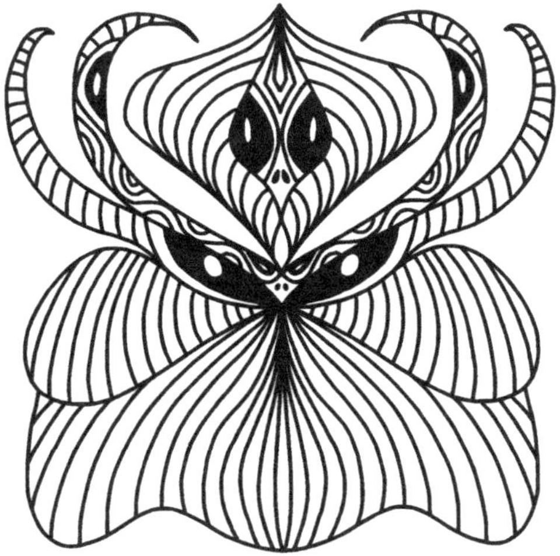
FATLINER WEIRDIES
VOLUME 3

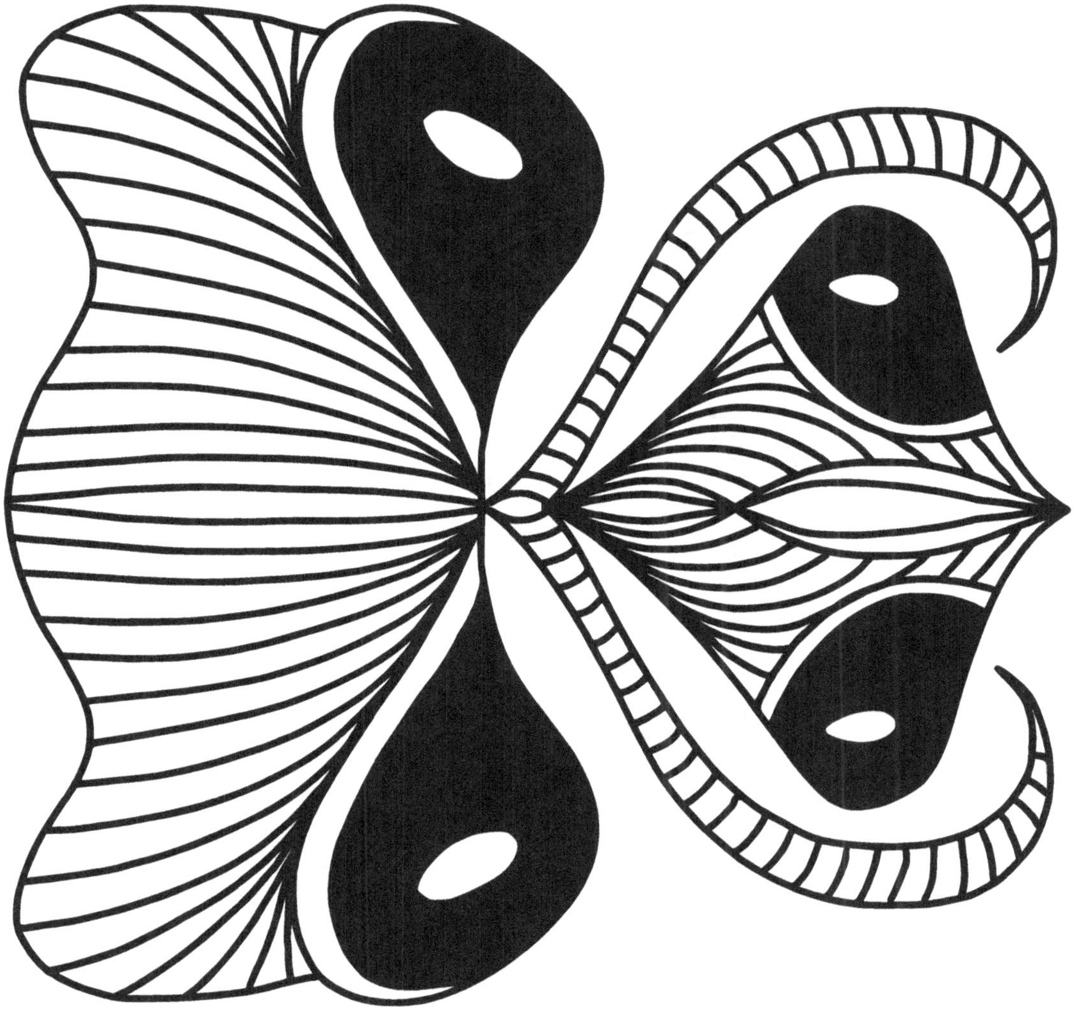

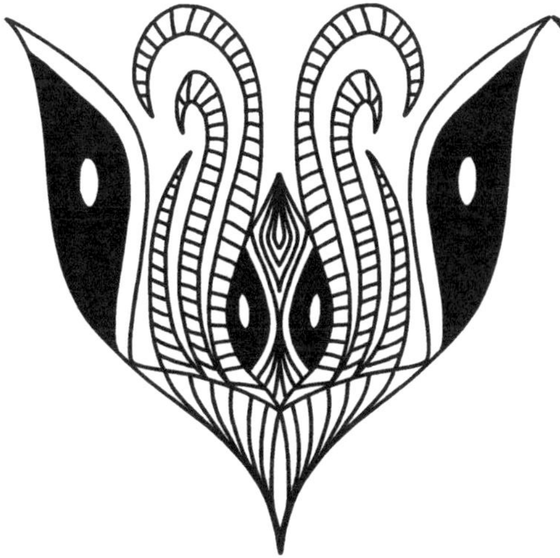

FATLINER WEIRDIES
VOLUME 1

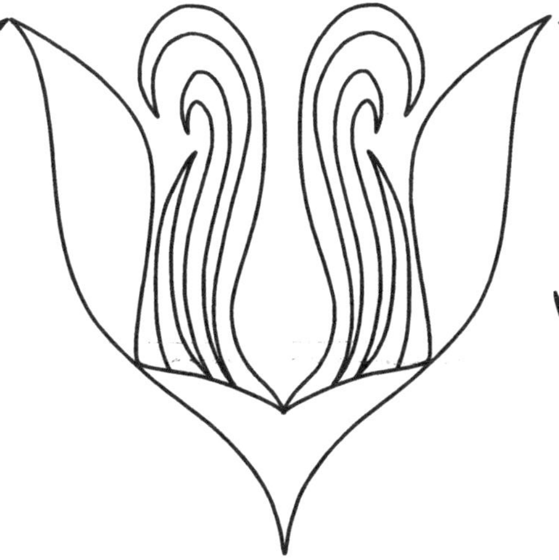

FATLINER WEIRDIES
THE TEMPLATES 1

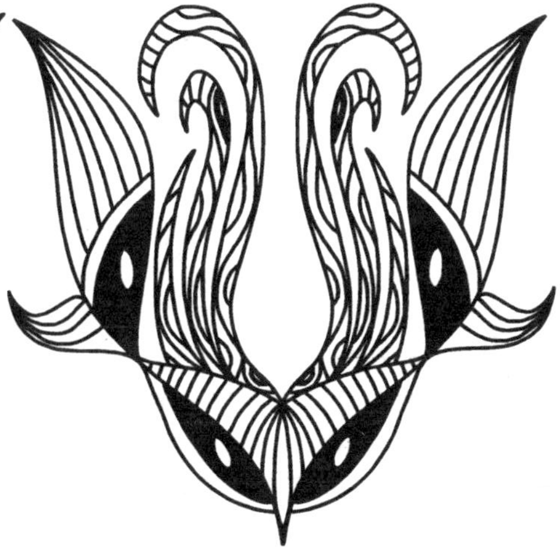

FATLINER WEIRDIES
VOLUME 3

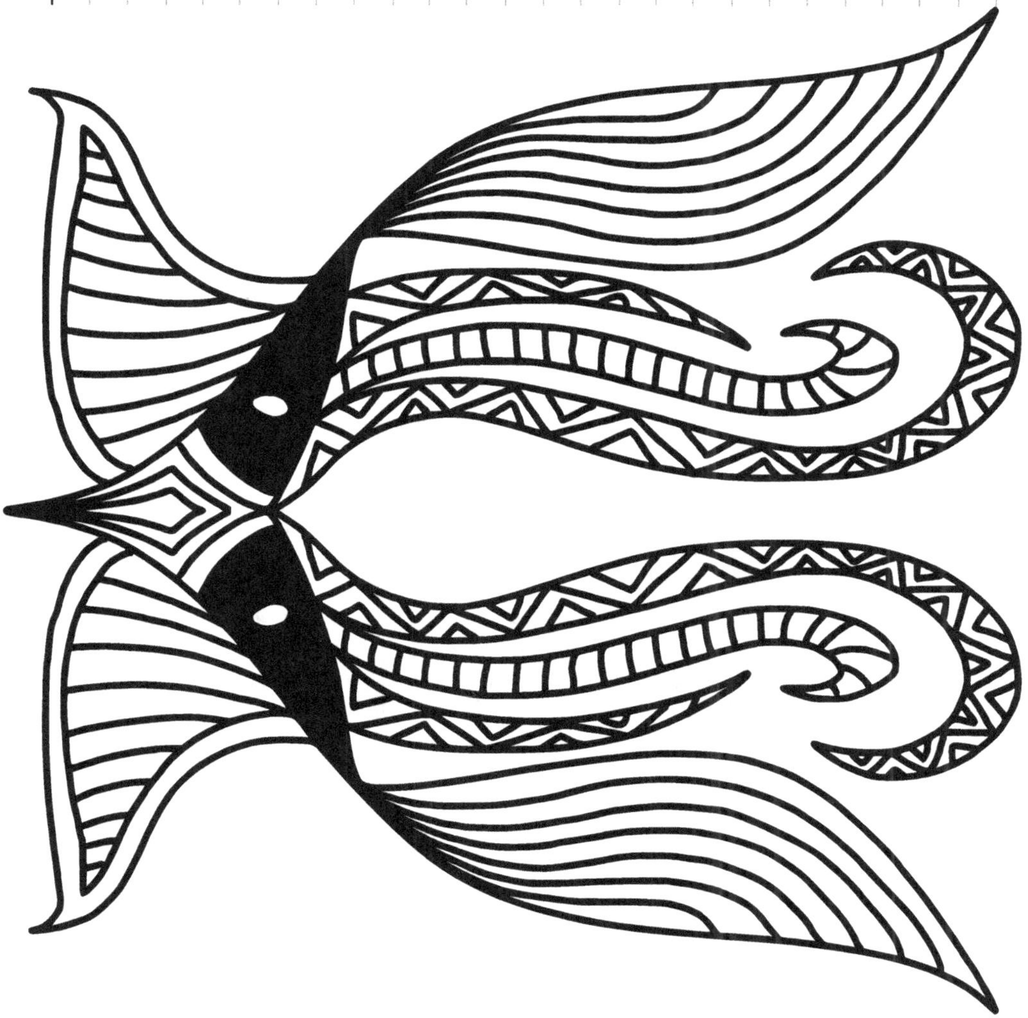

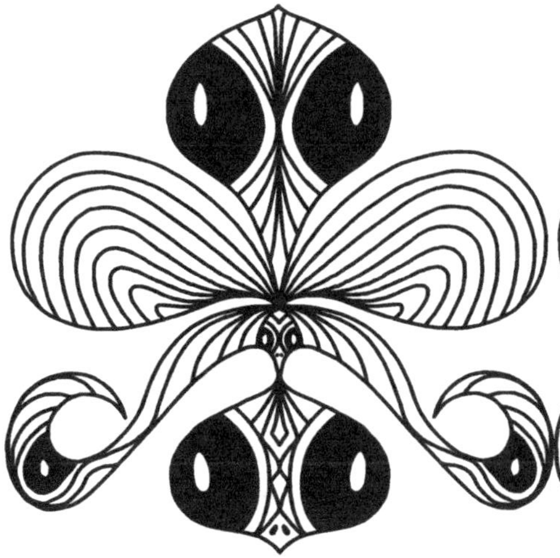

FATLINER WEIRDIES
VOLUME 1

FATLINER WEIRDIES
THE TEMPLATES 1

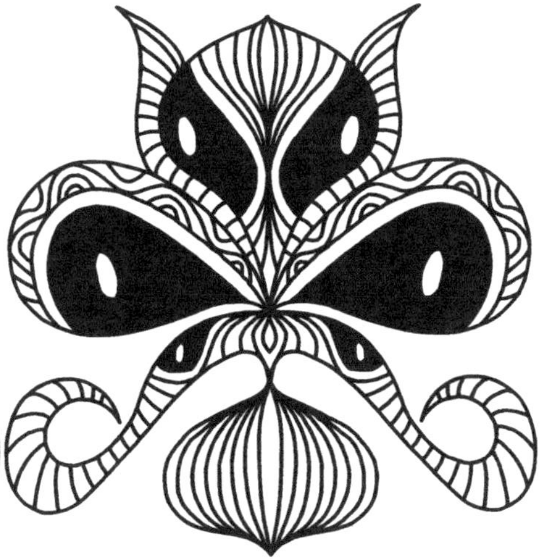

FATLINER WEIRDIES
VOLUME 3

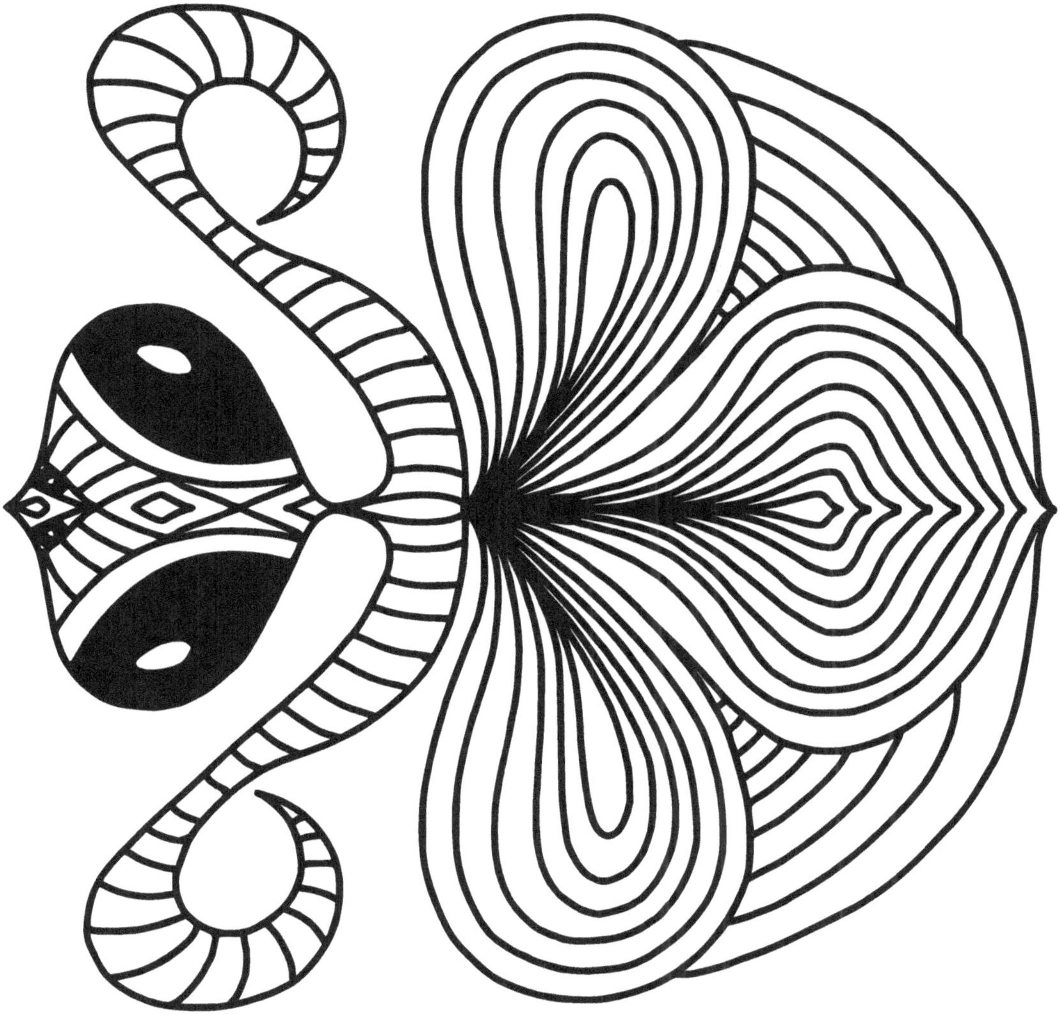

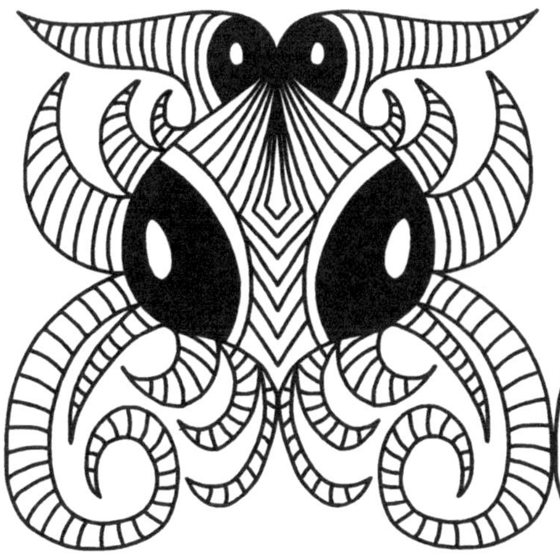

FATLINER WEIRDIES
VOLUME 1

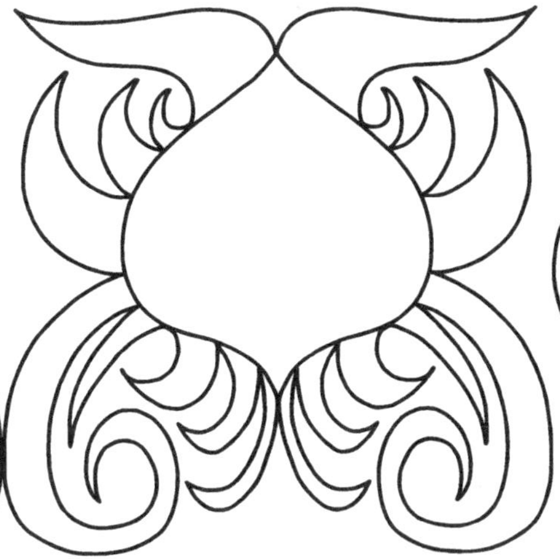

FATLINER WEIRDIES
THE TEMPLATES 1

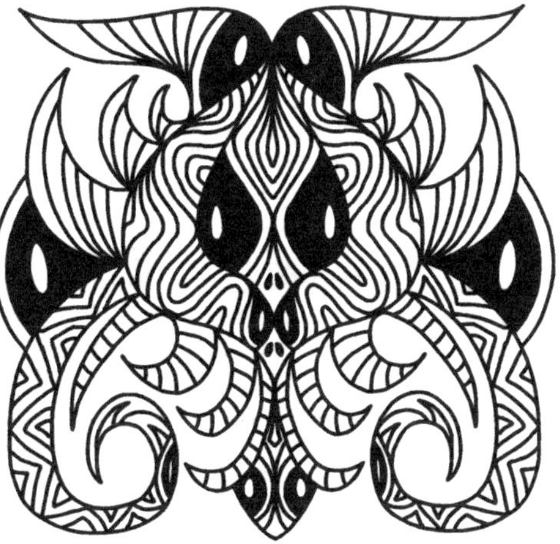

FATLINER WEIRDIES
VOLUME 3

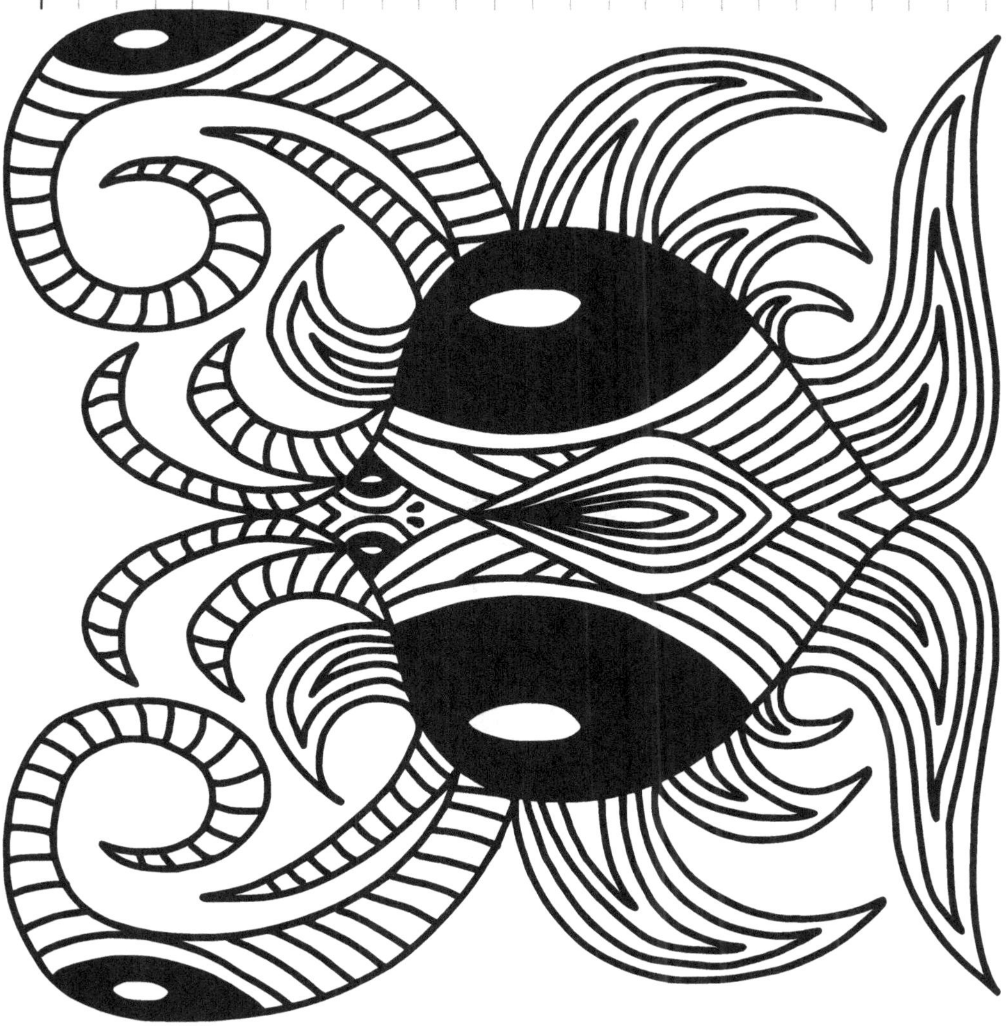

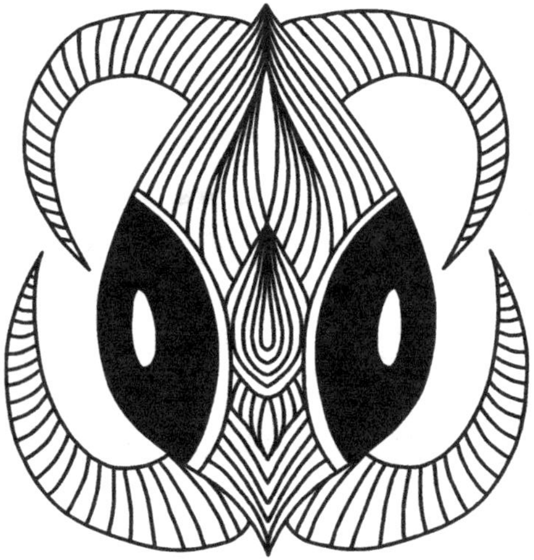

FATLINER WEIRDIES
VOLUME 1

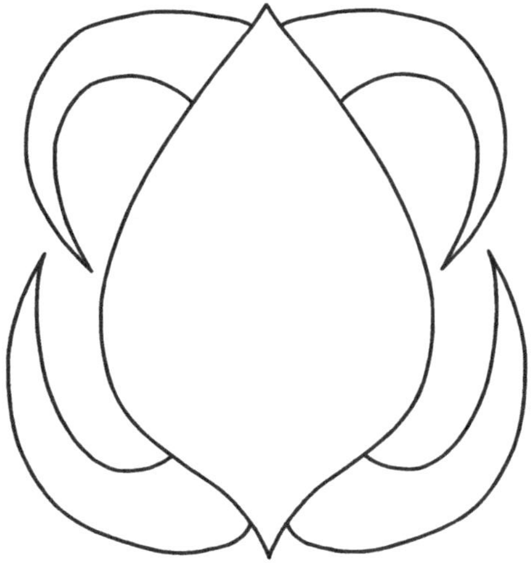

FATLINER WEIRDIES
THE TEMPLATES 1

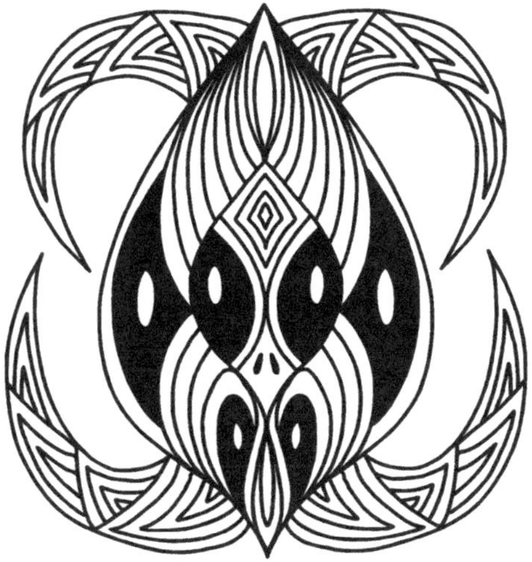

FATLINER WEIRDIES
VOLUME 3

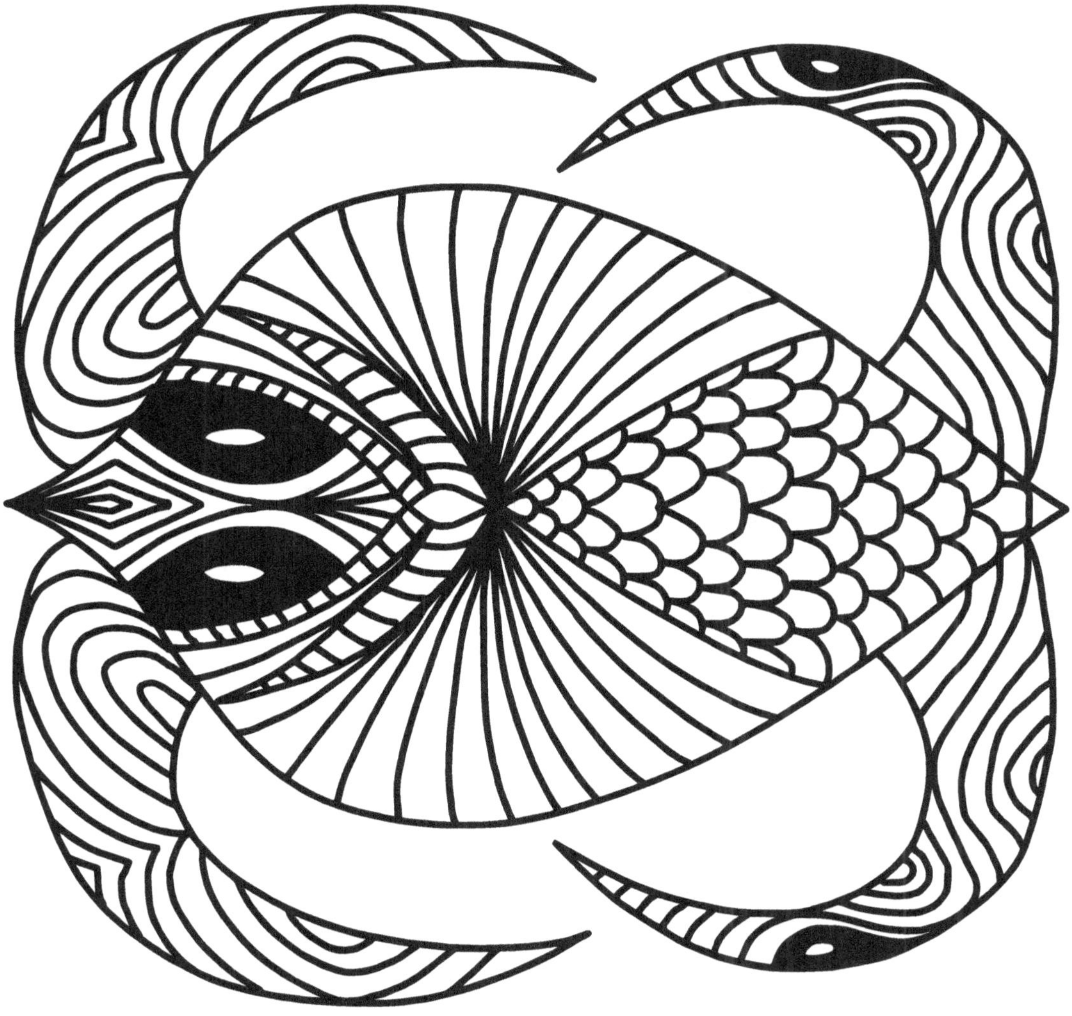

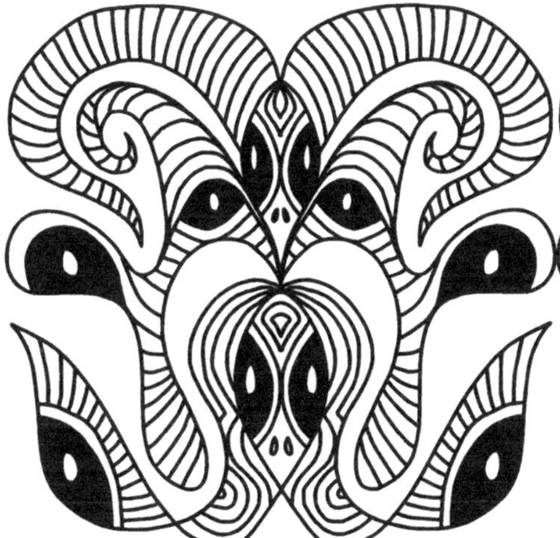

FATLINER WEIRDIES
VOLUME 1

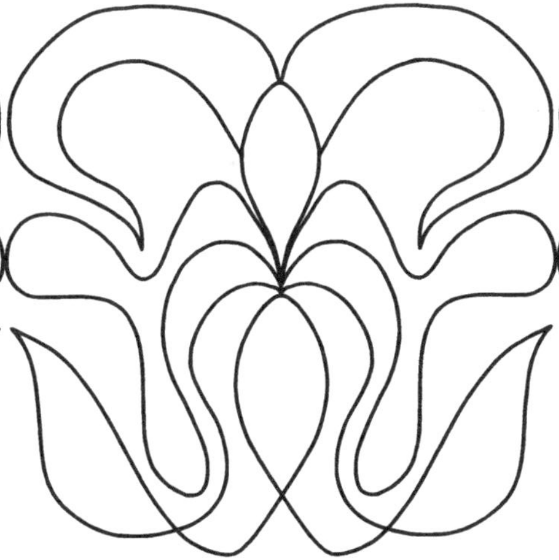

FATLINER WEIRDIES
THE TEMPLATES 1

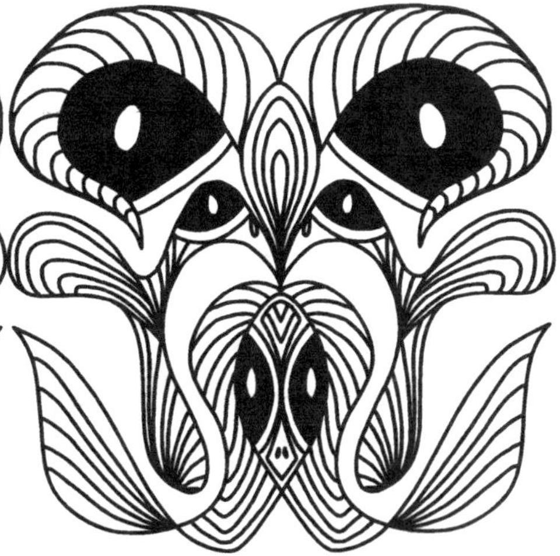

FATLINER WEIRDIES
VOLUME 3

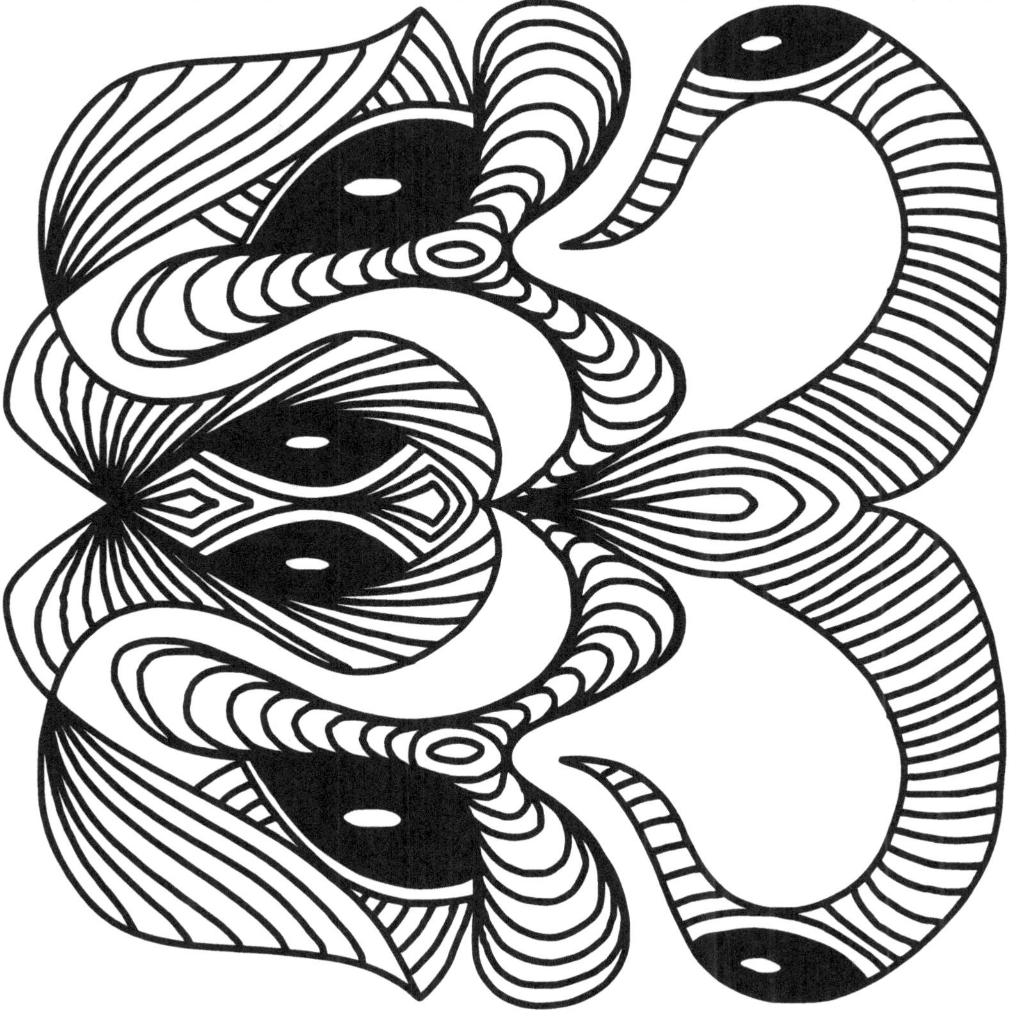

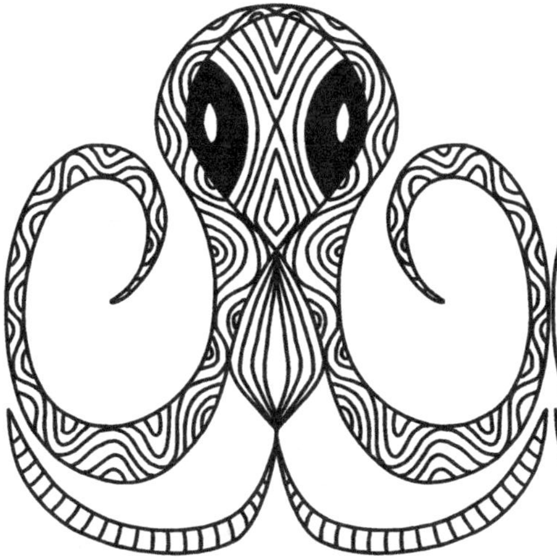

FATLINER WEIRDIES
VOLUME 1

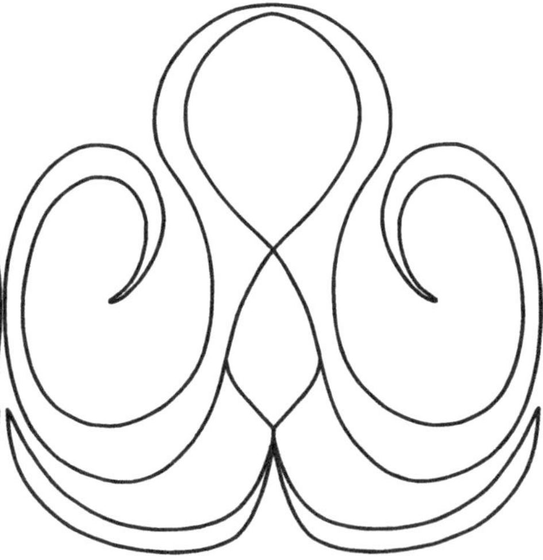

FATLINER WEIRDIES
THE TEMPLATES 1

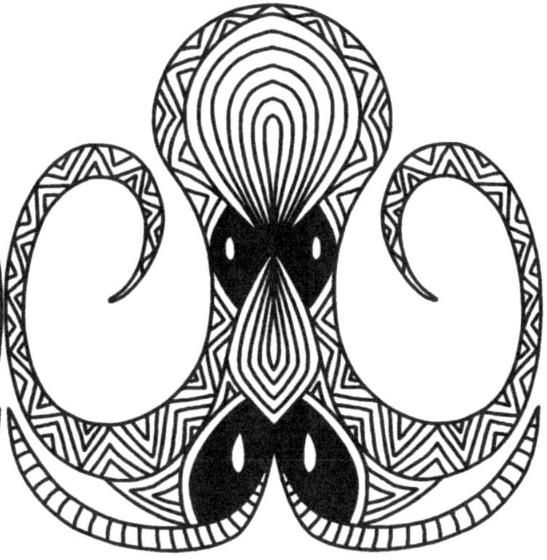

FATLINER WEIRDIES
VOLUME 3

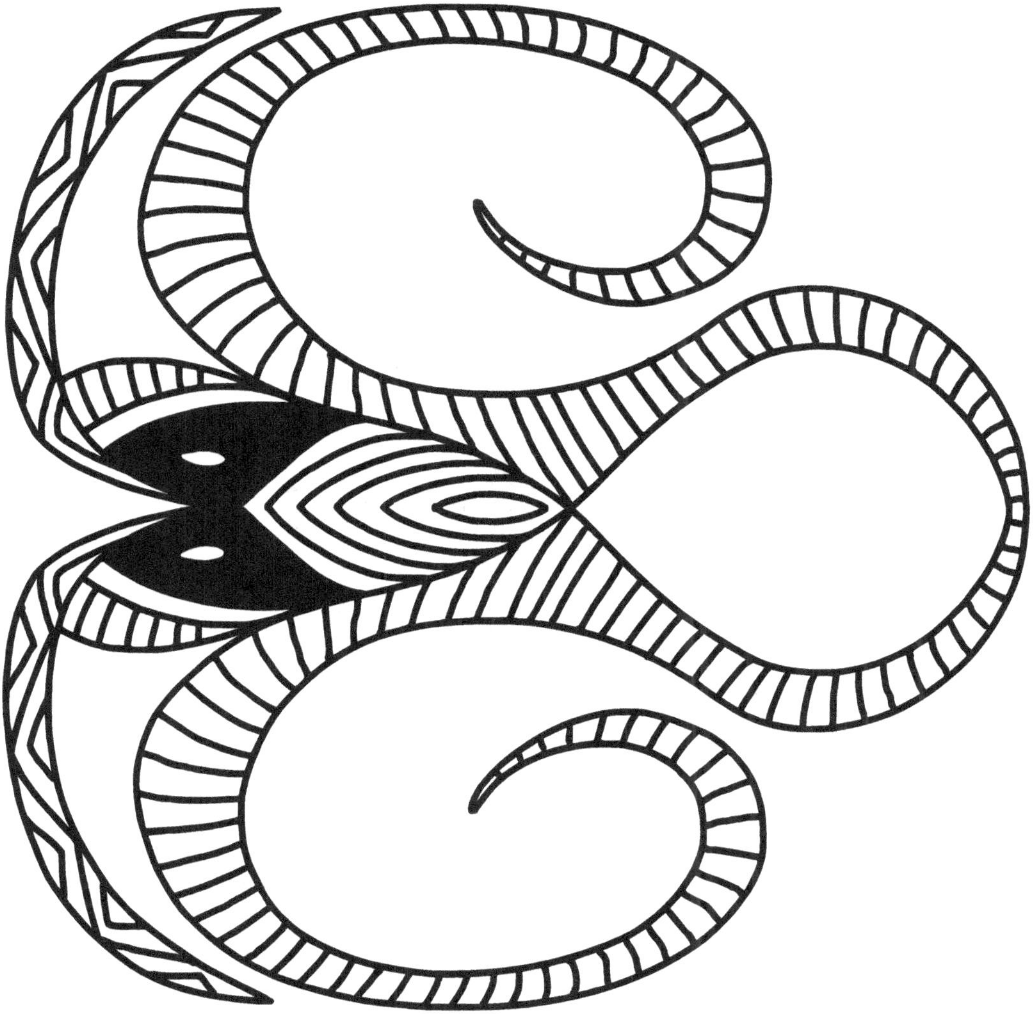

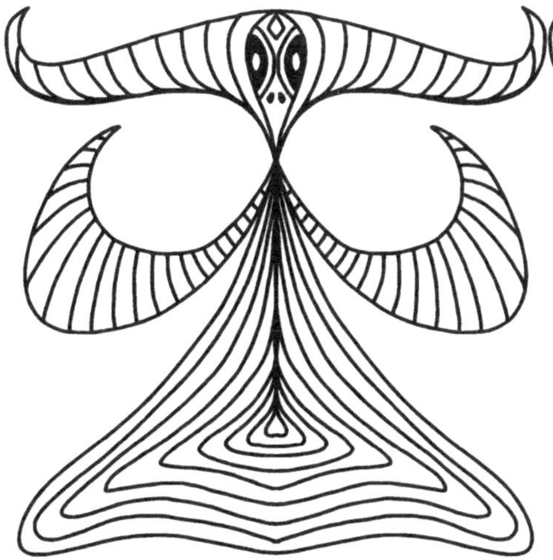

FATLINER WEIRDIES
VOLUME 1

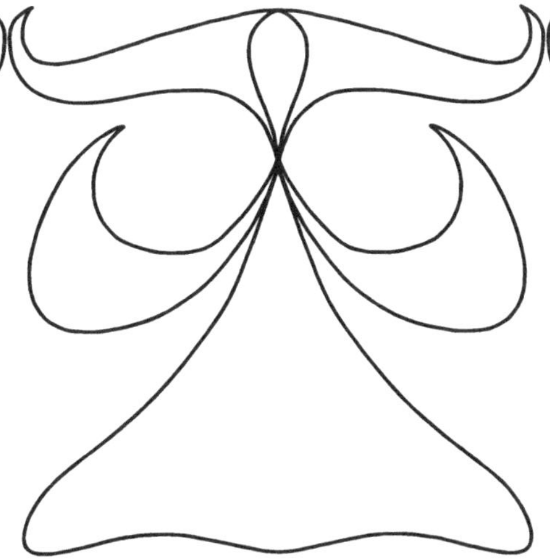

FATLINER WEIRDIES
THE TEMPLATES 1

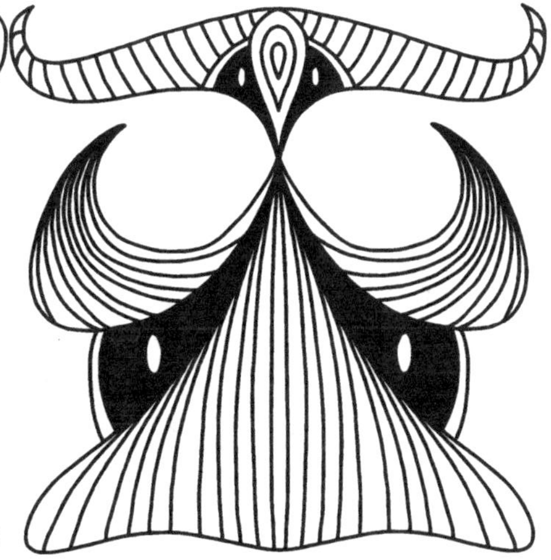

FATLINER WEIRDIES
VOLUME 3

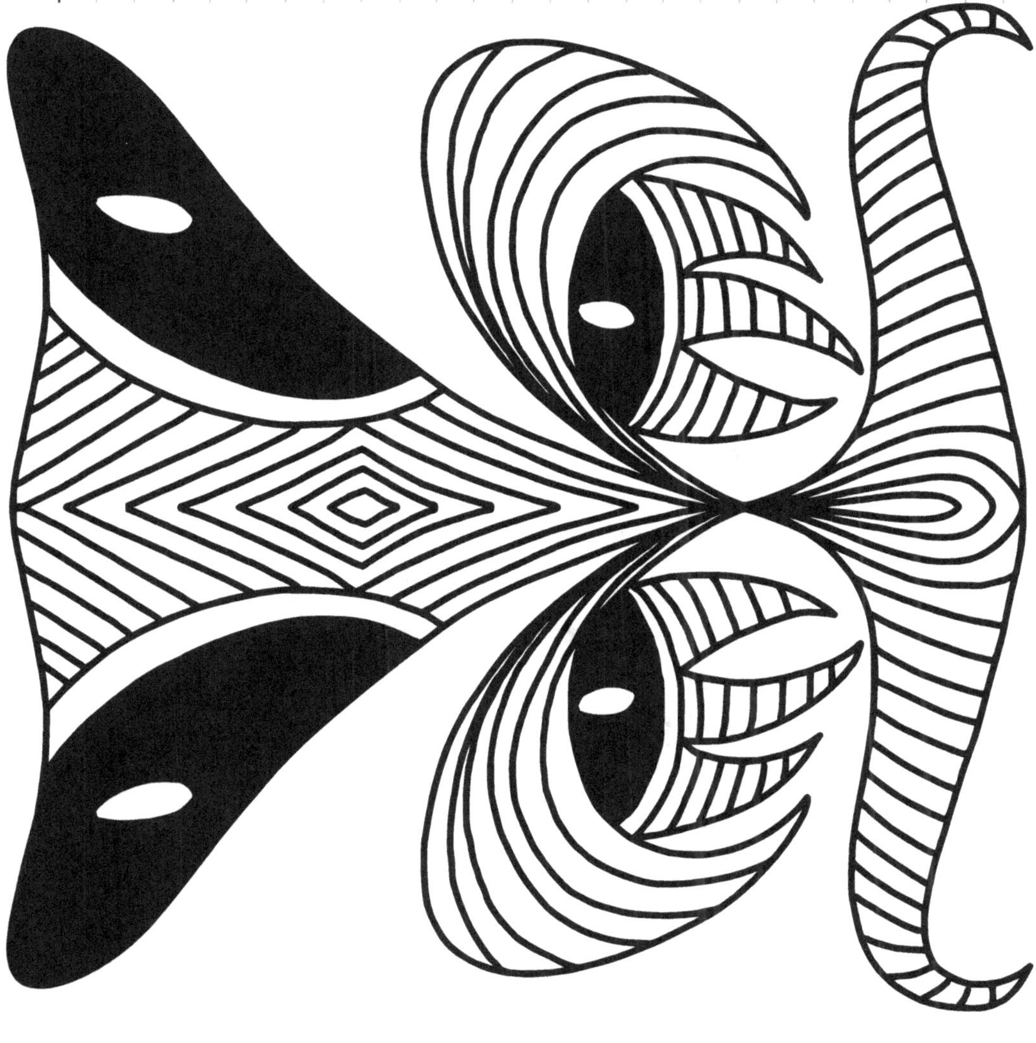

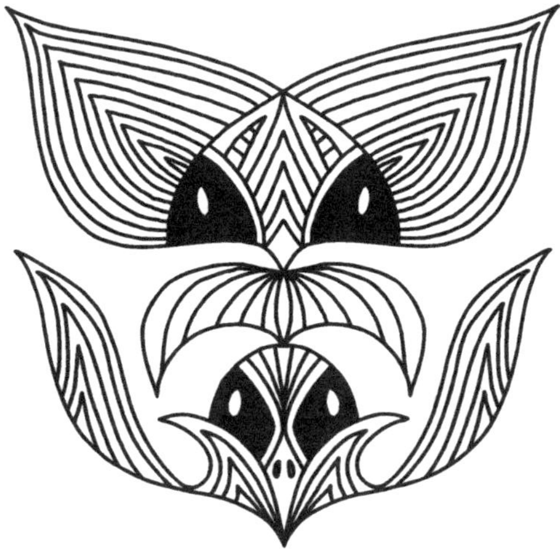

FATLINER WEIRDIES
VOLUME 1

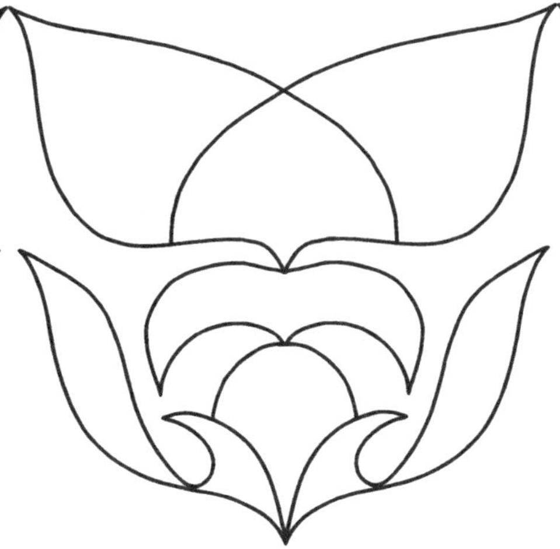

FATLINER WEIRDIES
THE TEMPLATES 1

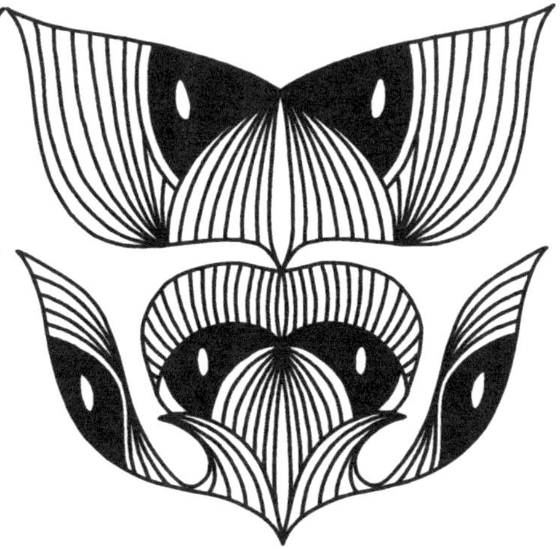

FATLINER WEIRDIES
VOLUME 3

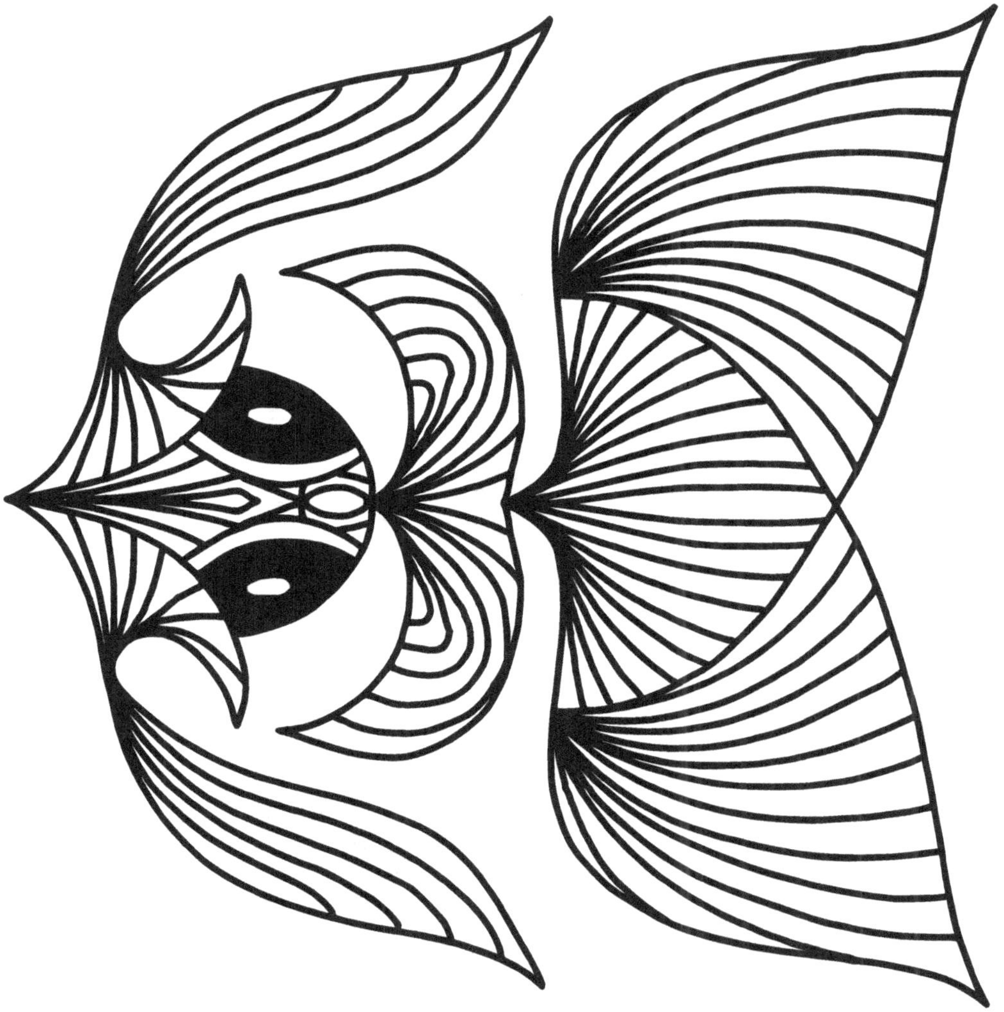

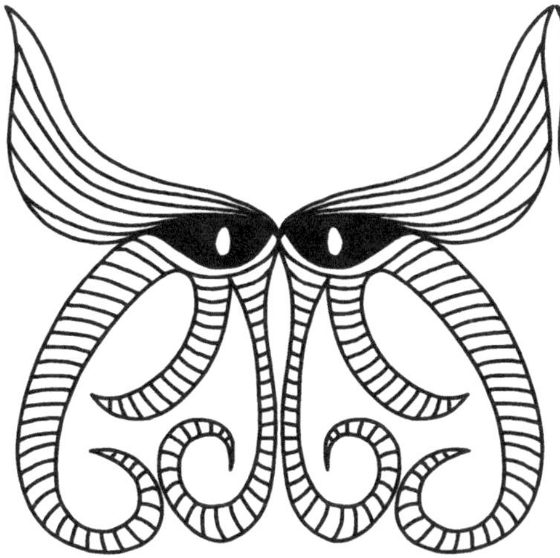

FATLINER WEIRDIES
VOLUME 1

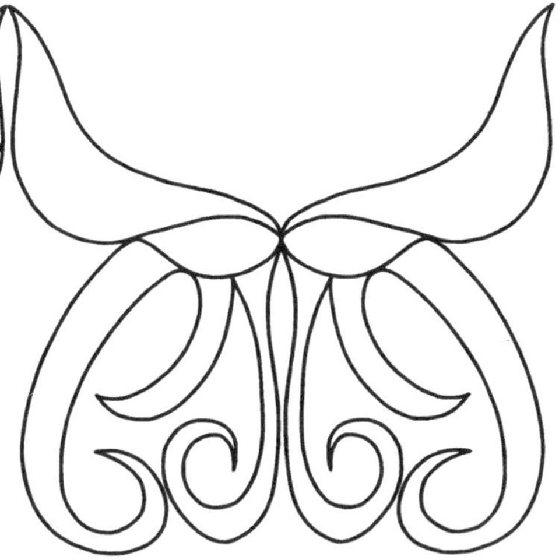

FATLINER WEIRDIES
THE TEMPLATES 1

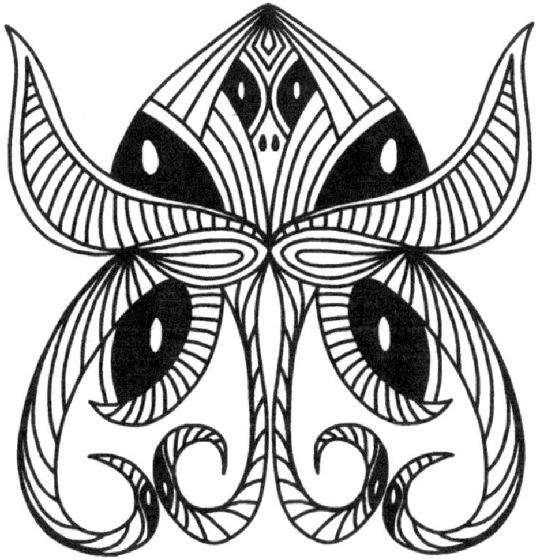

FATLINER WEIRDIES
VOLUME 3

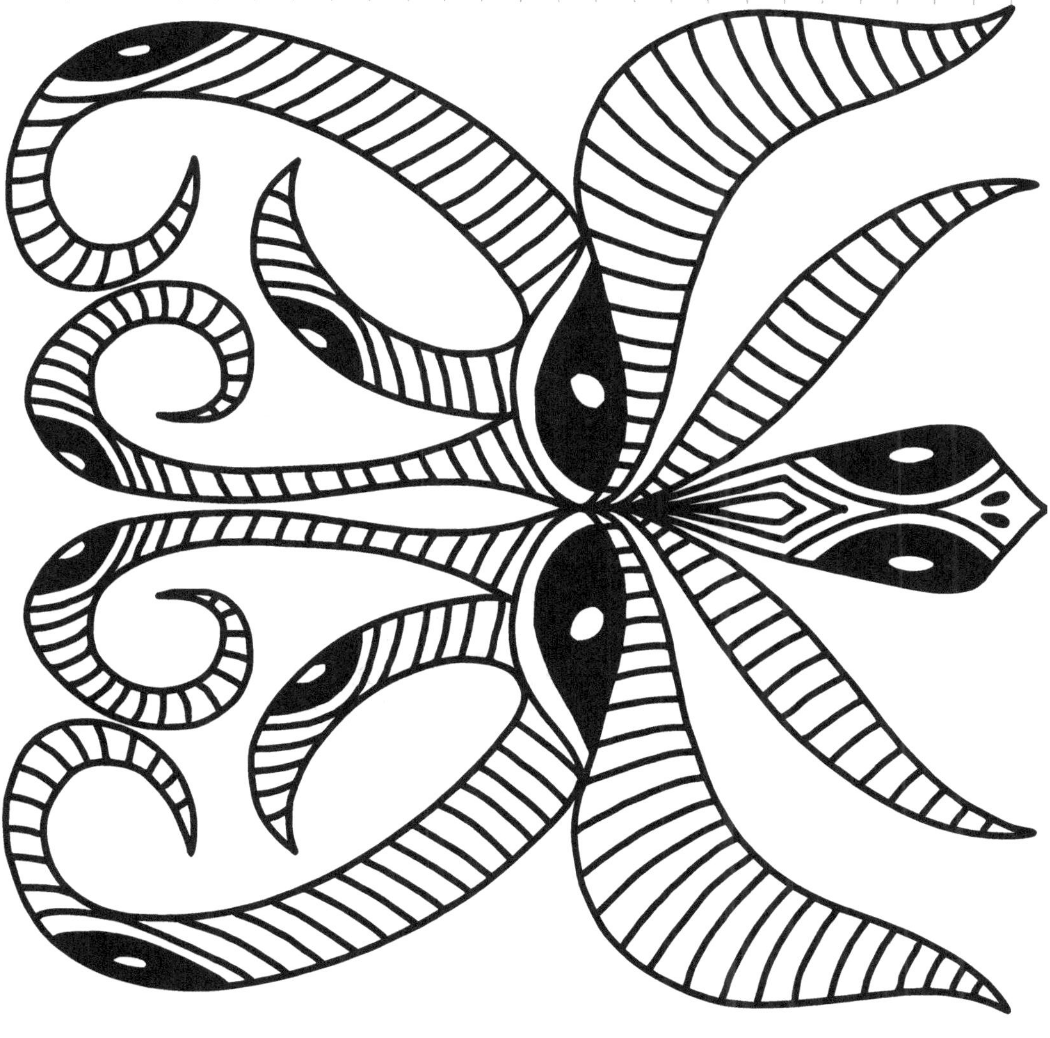

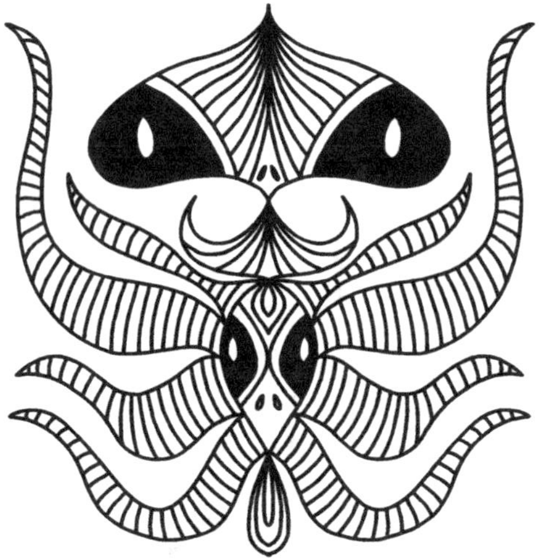

FATLINER WEIRDIES
VOLUME 1

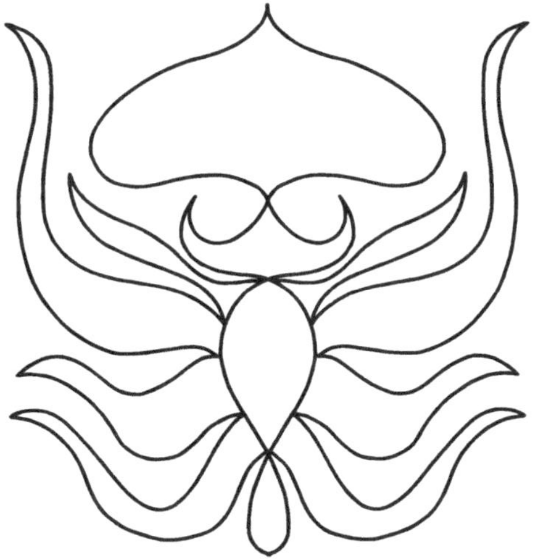

FATLINER WEIRDIES
THE TEMPLATES 1

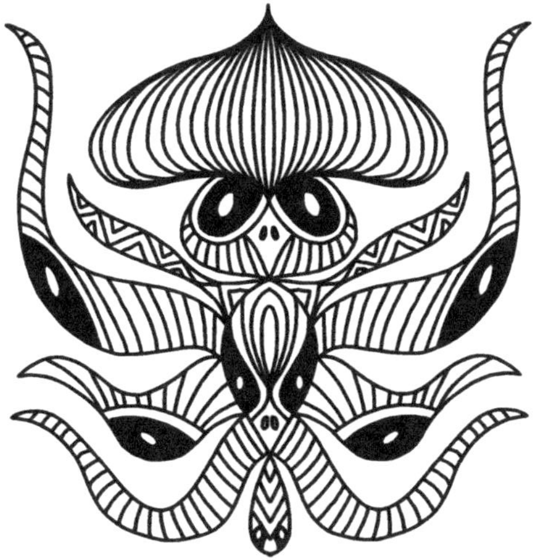

FATLINER WEIRDIES
VOLUME 3

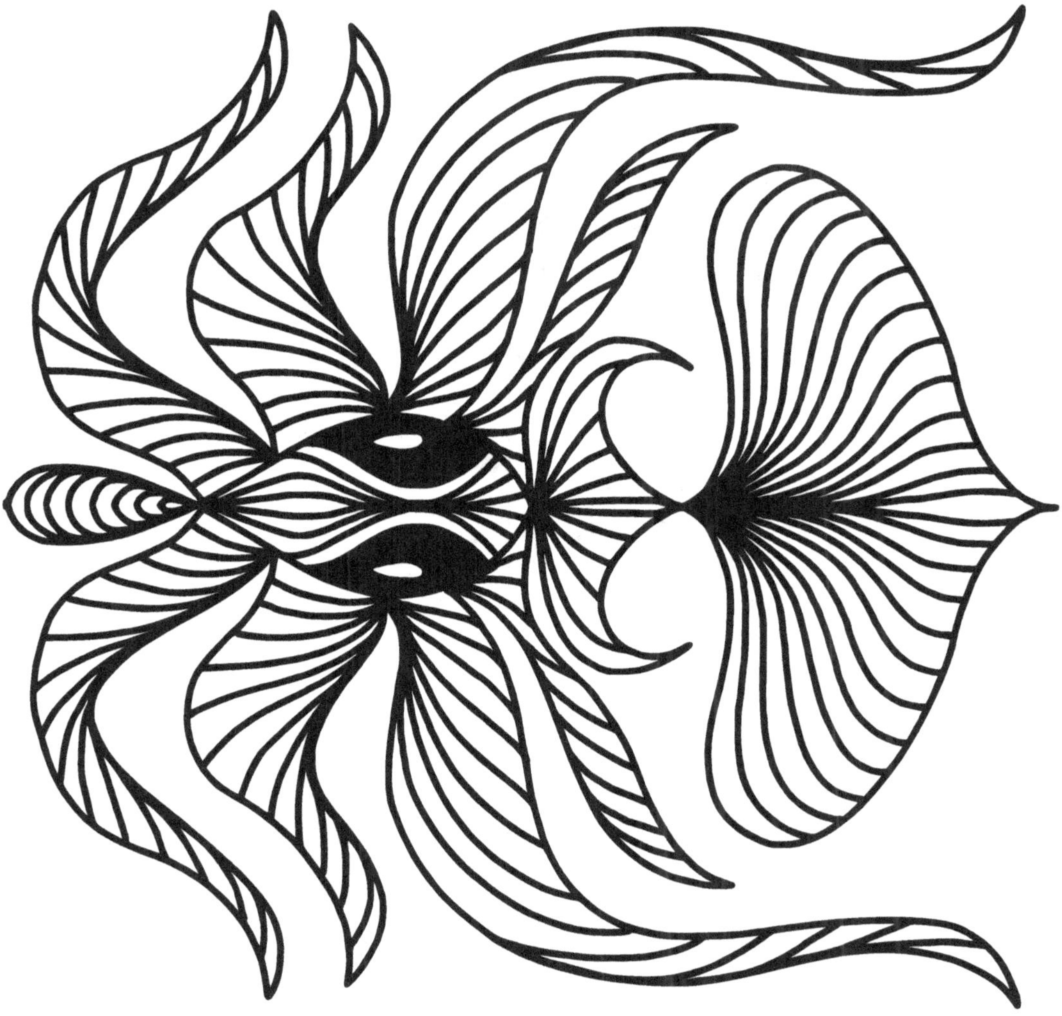

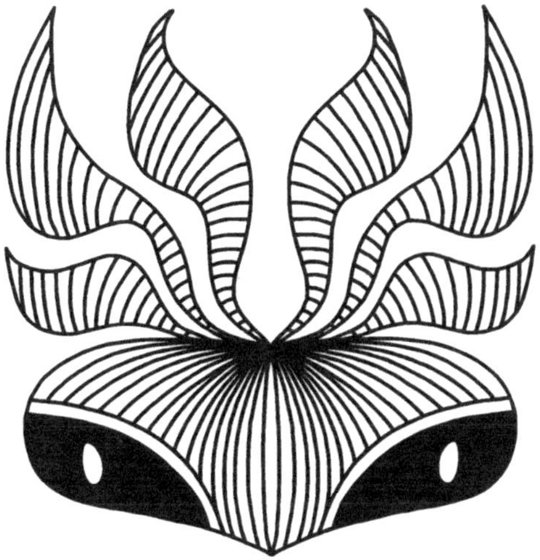

FATLINER WEIRDIES
VOLUME 1

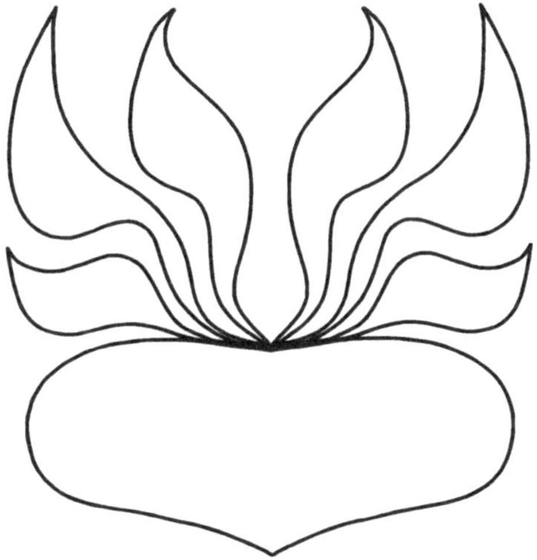

FATLINER WEIRDIES
THE TEMPLATES 1

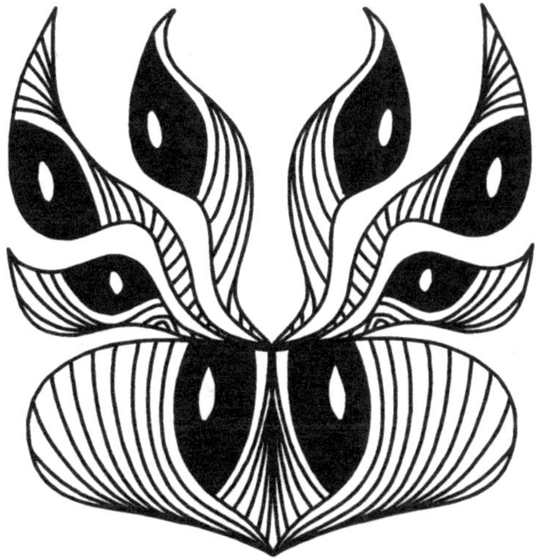

FATLINER WEIRDIES
VOLUME 3

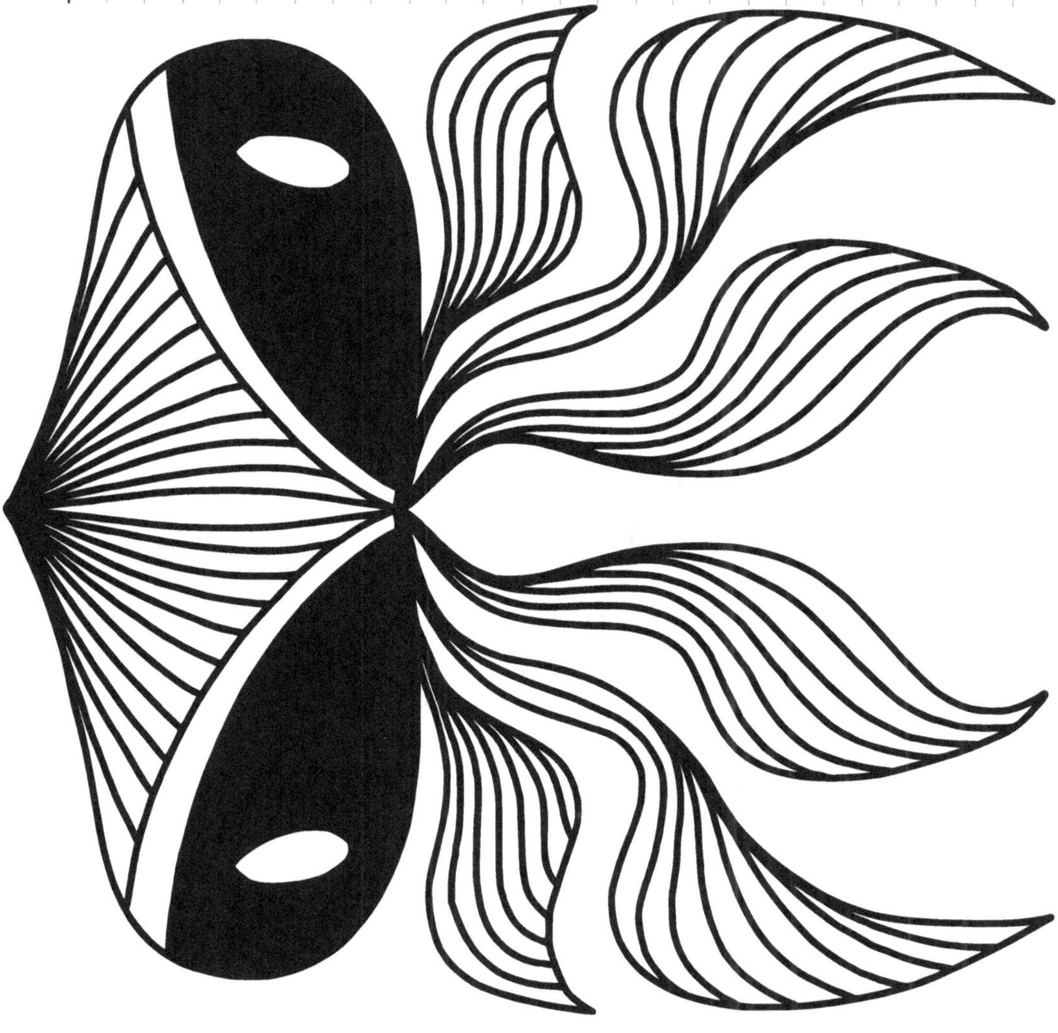

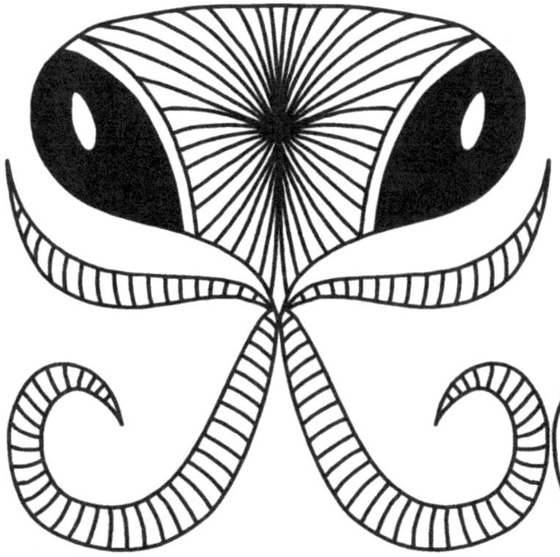

FATLINER WEIRDIES
VOLUME 1

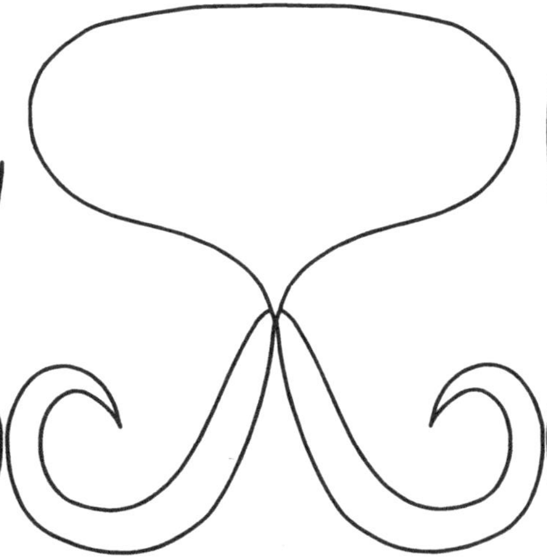

FATLINER WEIRDIES
THE TEMPLATES 1

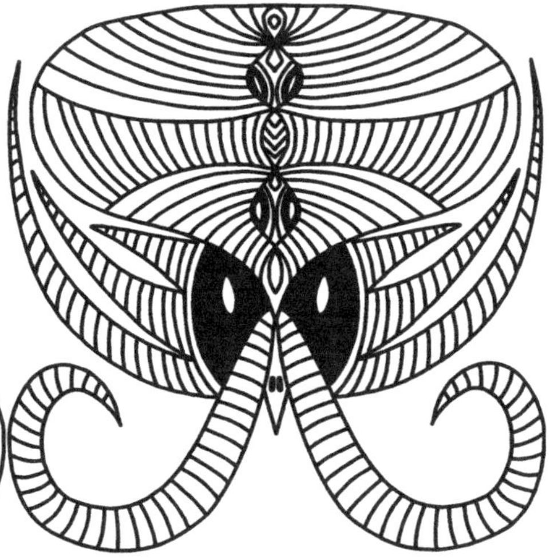

FATLINER WEIRDIES
VOLUME 3

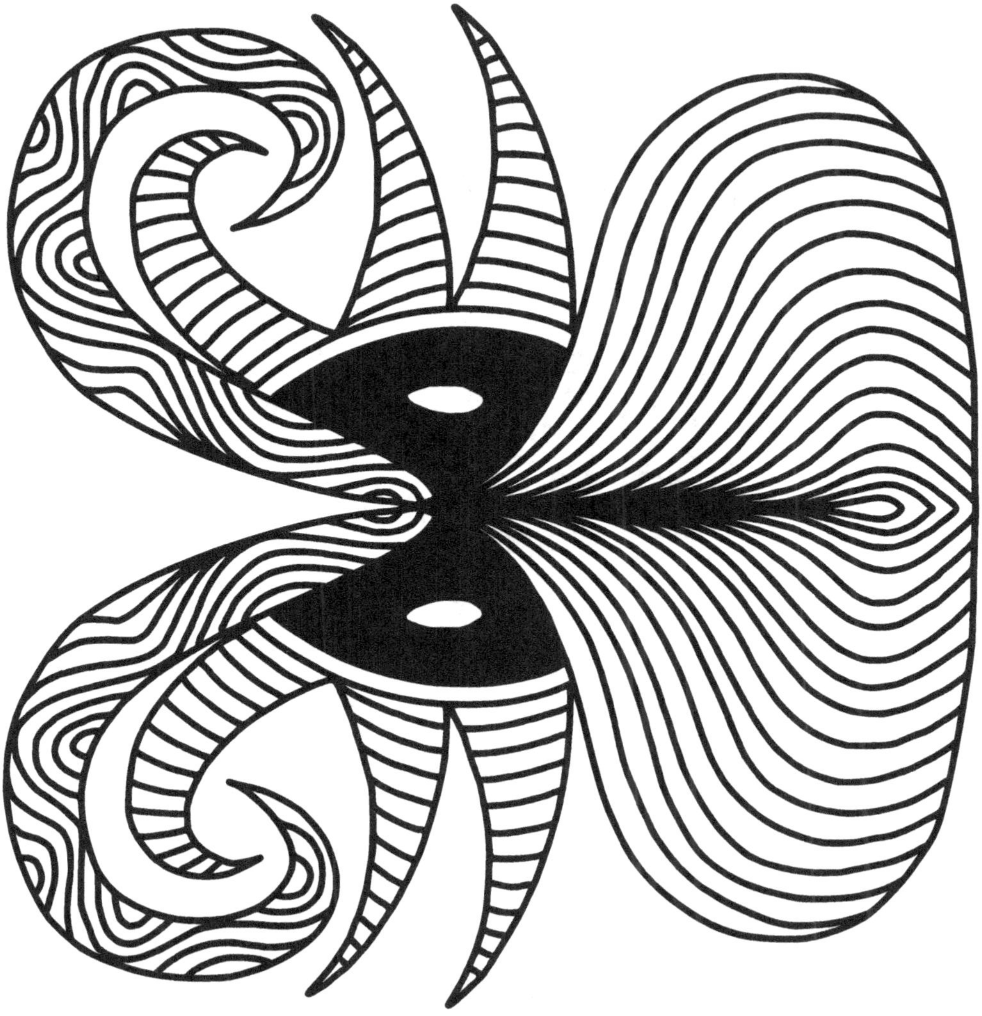

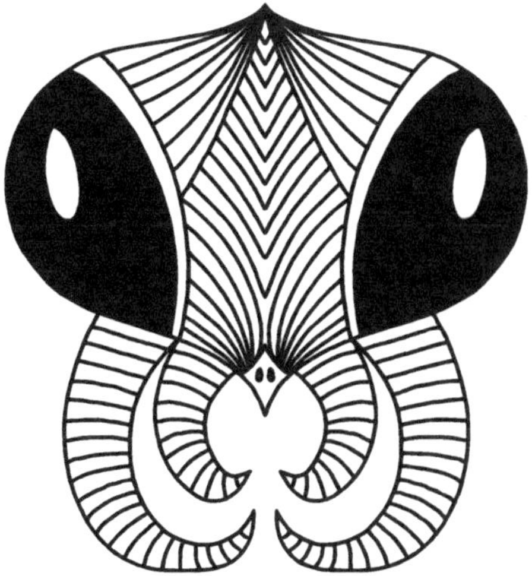

FATLINER WEIRDIES
VOLUME 1

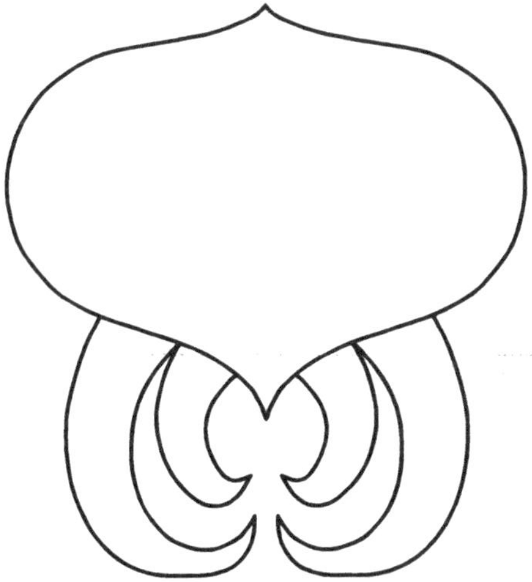

FATLINER WEIRDIES
THE TEMPLATES 1

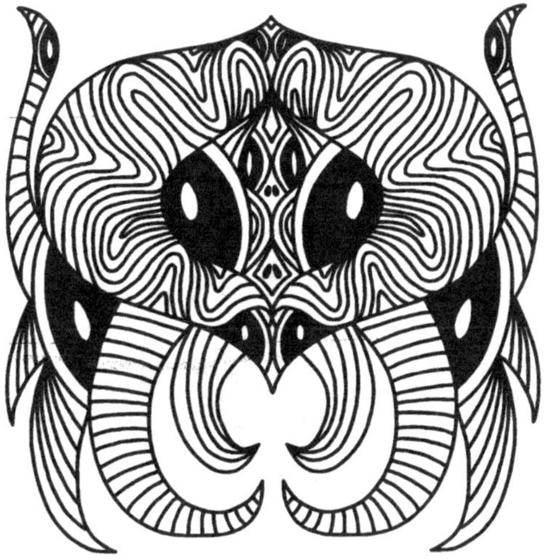

FATLINER WEIRDIES
VOLUME 3

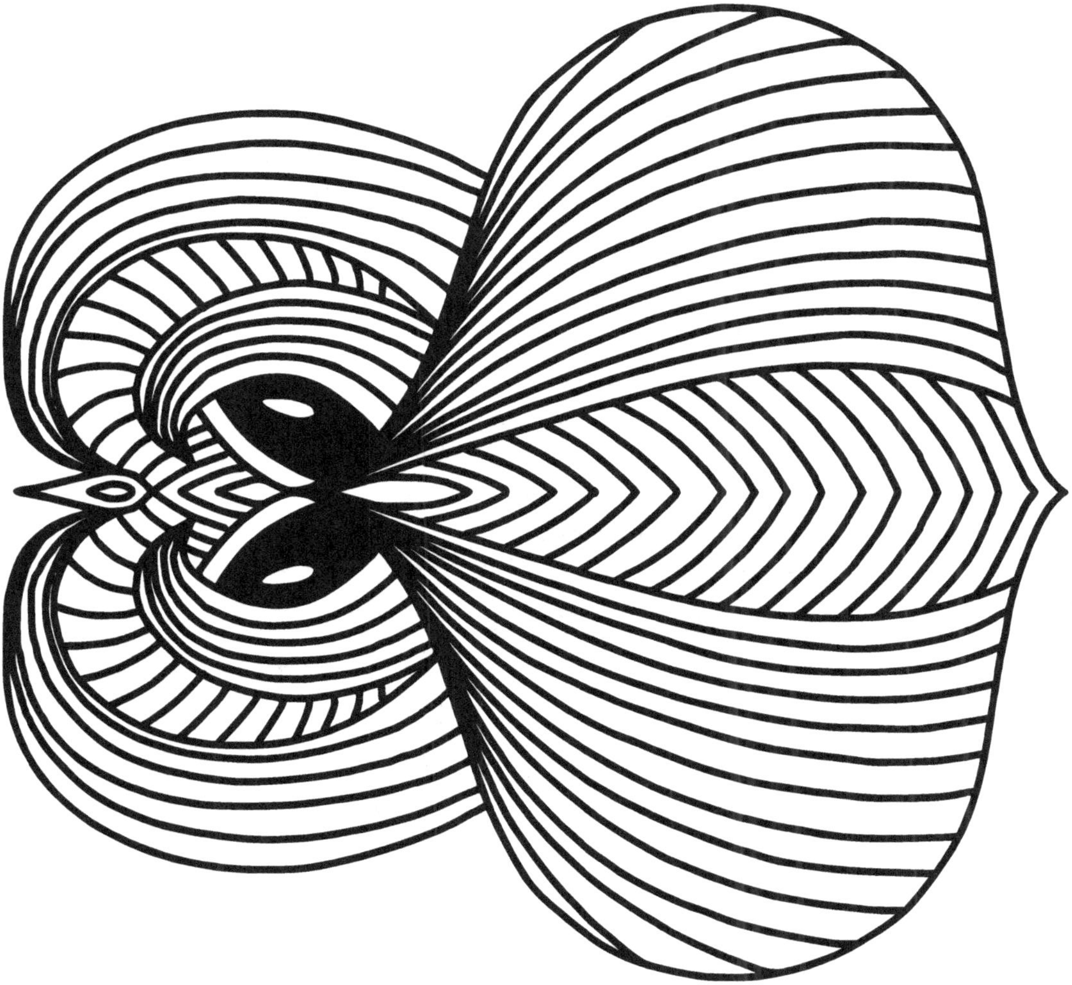

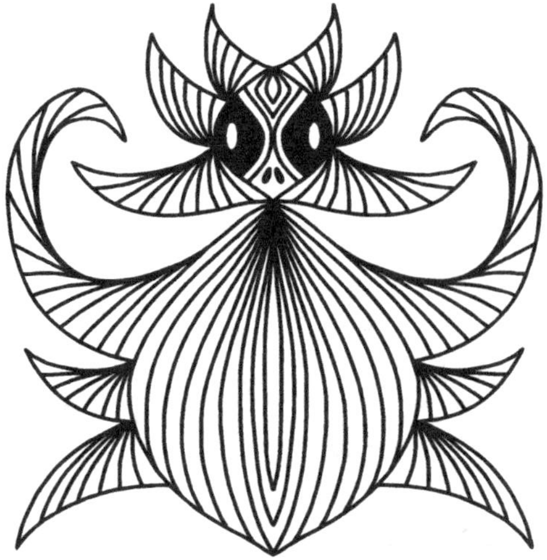

FATLINER WEIRDIES
VOLUME 1

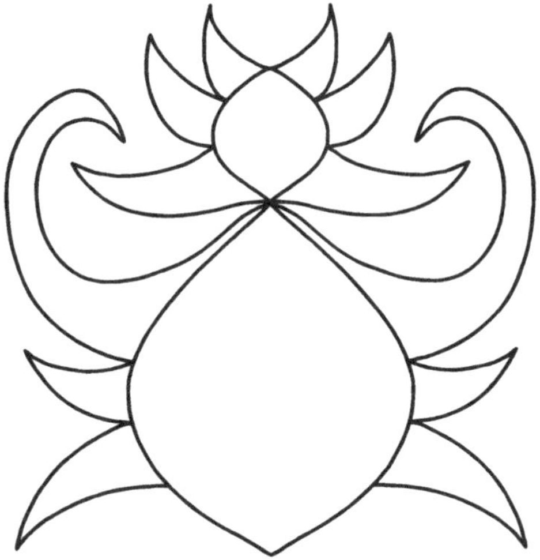

FATLINER WEIRDIES
THE TEMPLATES 1

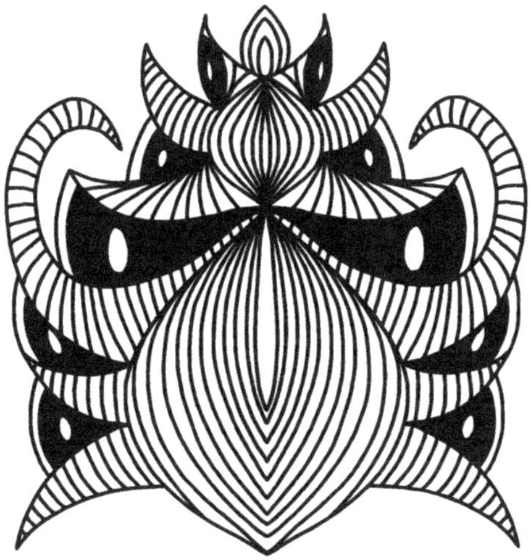

FATLINER WEIRDIES
VOLUME 3

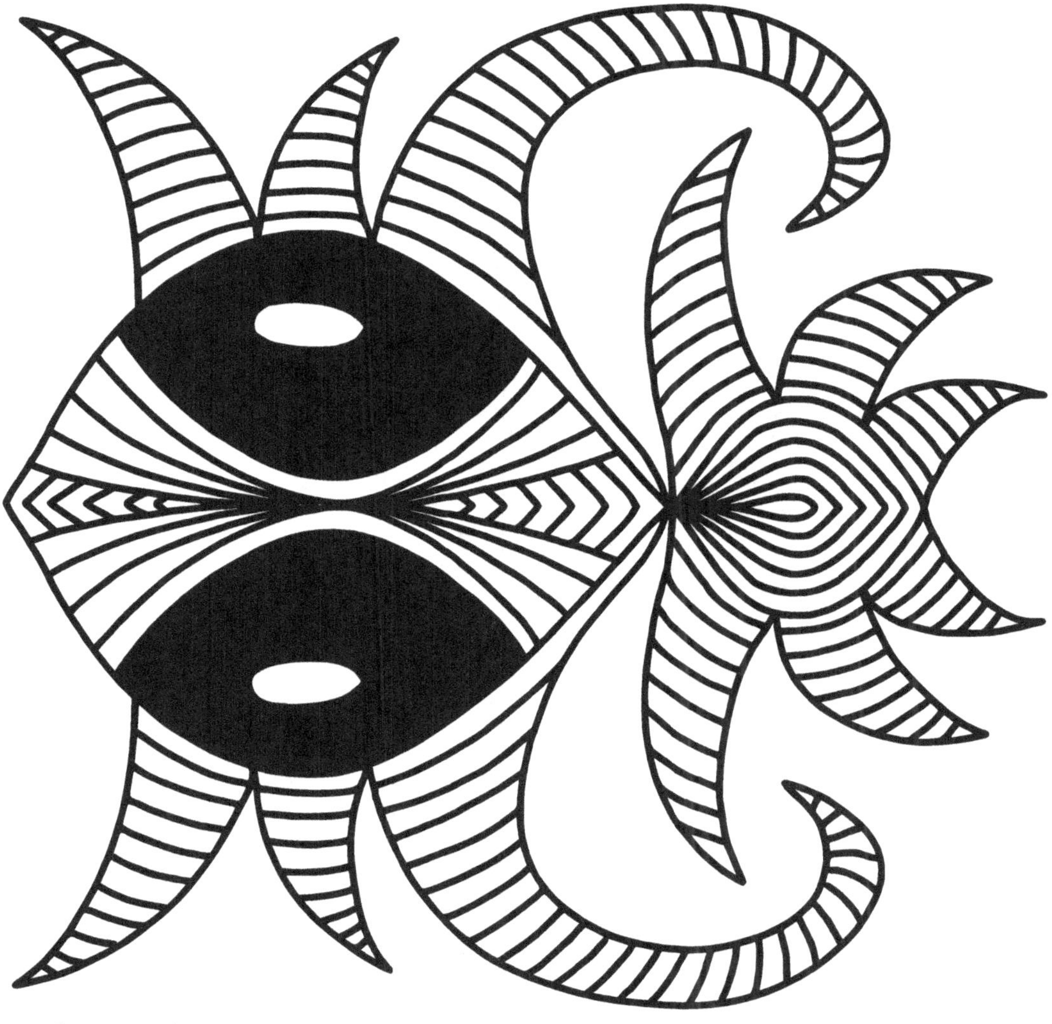

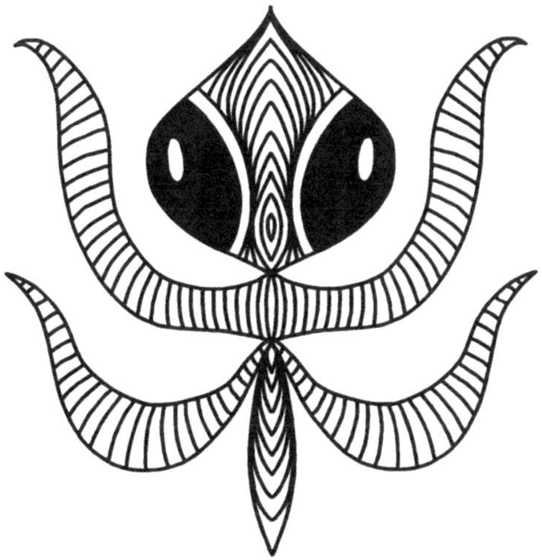

FATLINER WEIRDIES
VOLUME 1

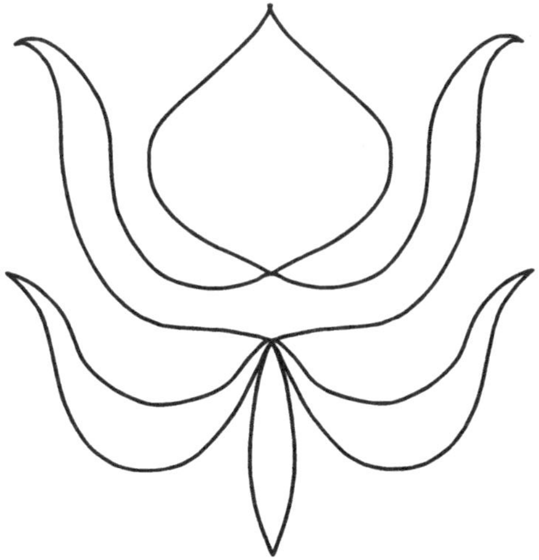

FATLINER WEIRDIES
THE TEMPLATES 1

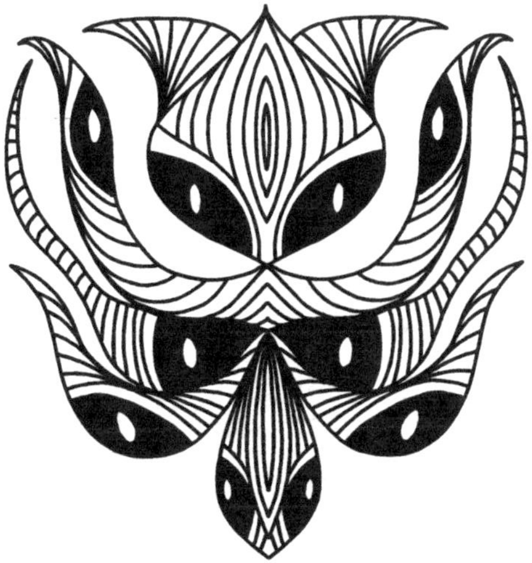

FATLINER WEIRDIES
VOLUME 3

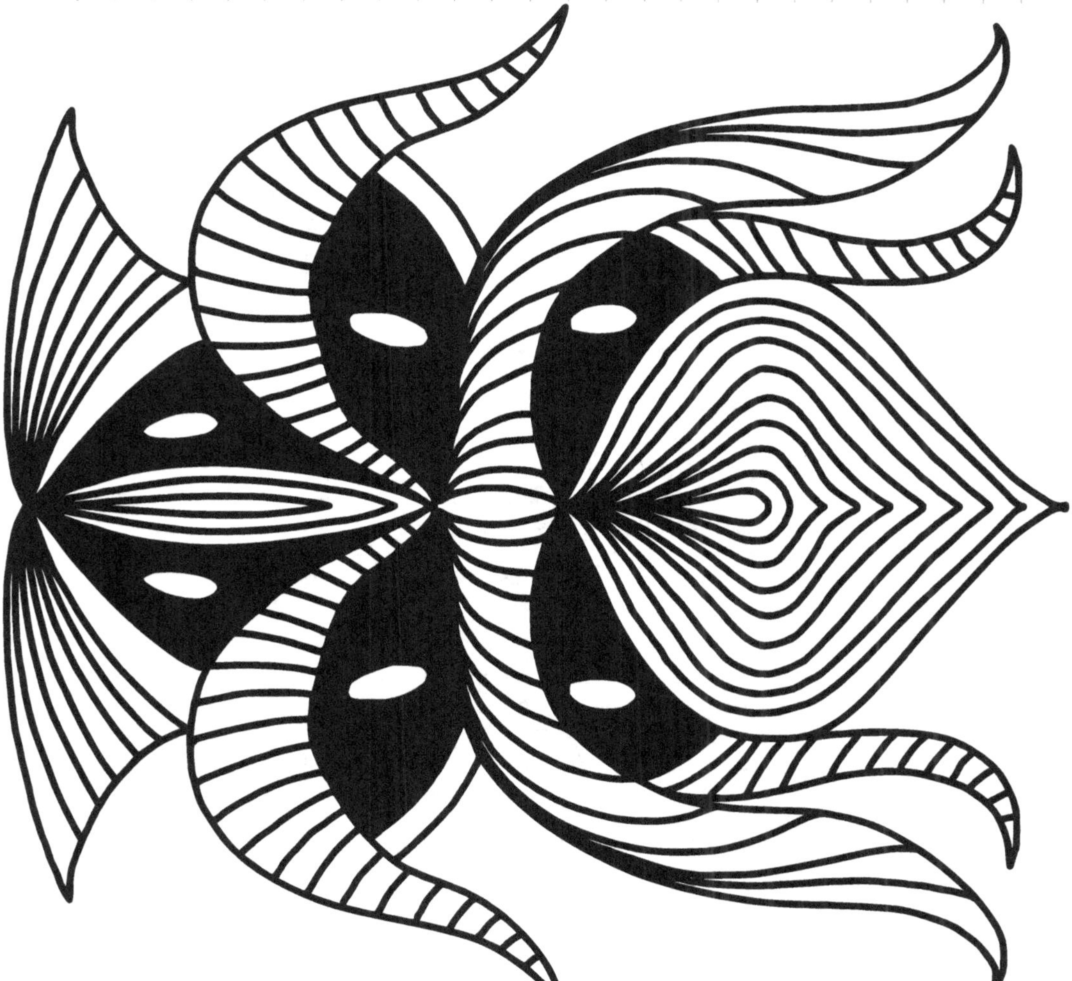

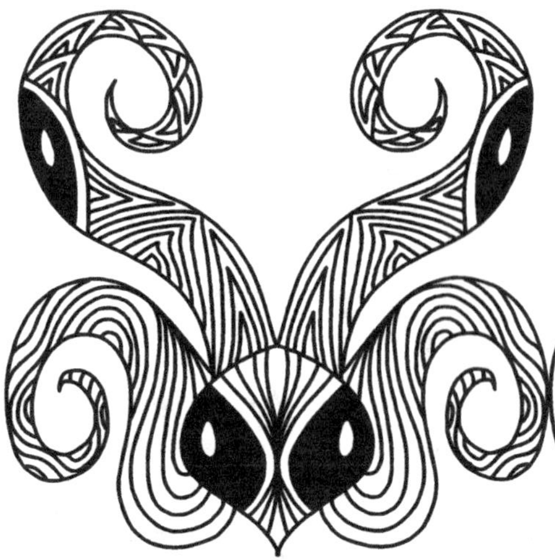

FATLINER WEIRDIES
VOLUME 1

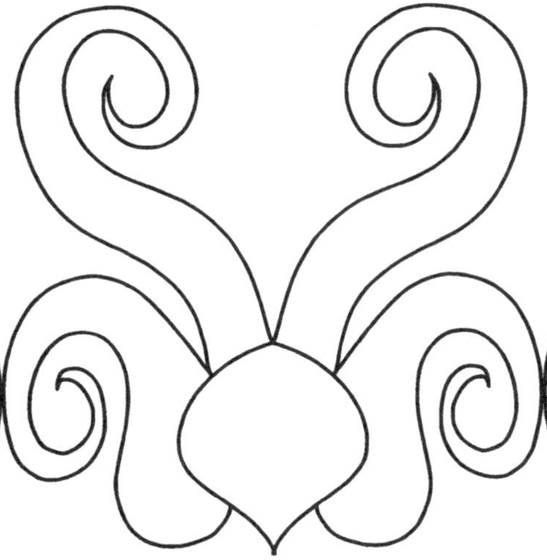

FATLINER WEIRDIES
THE TEMPLATES 1

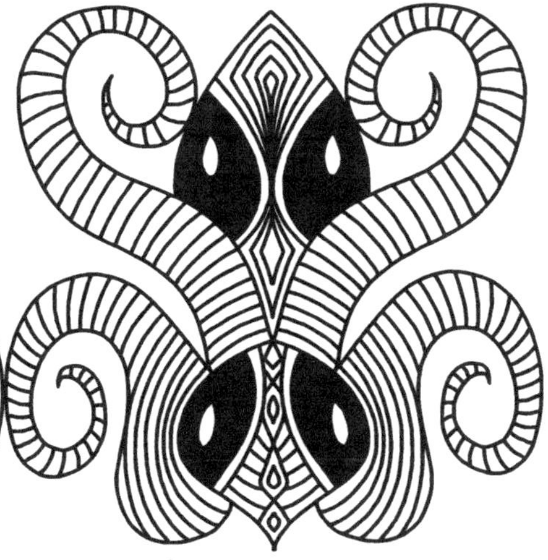

FATLINER WEIRDIES
VOLUME 3

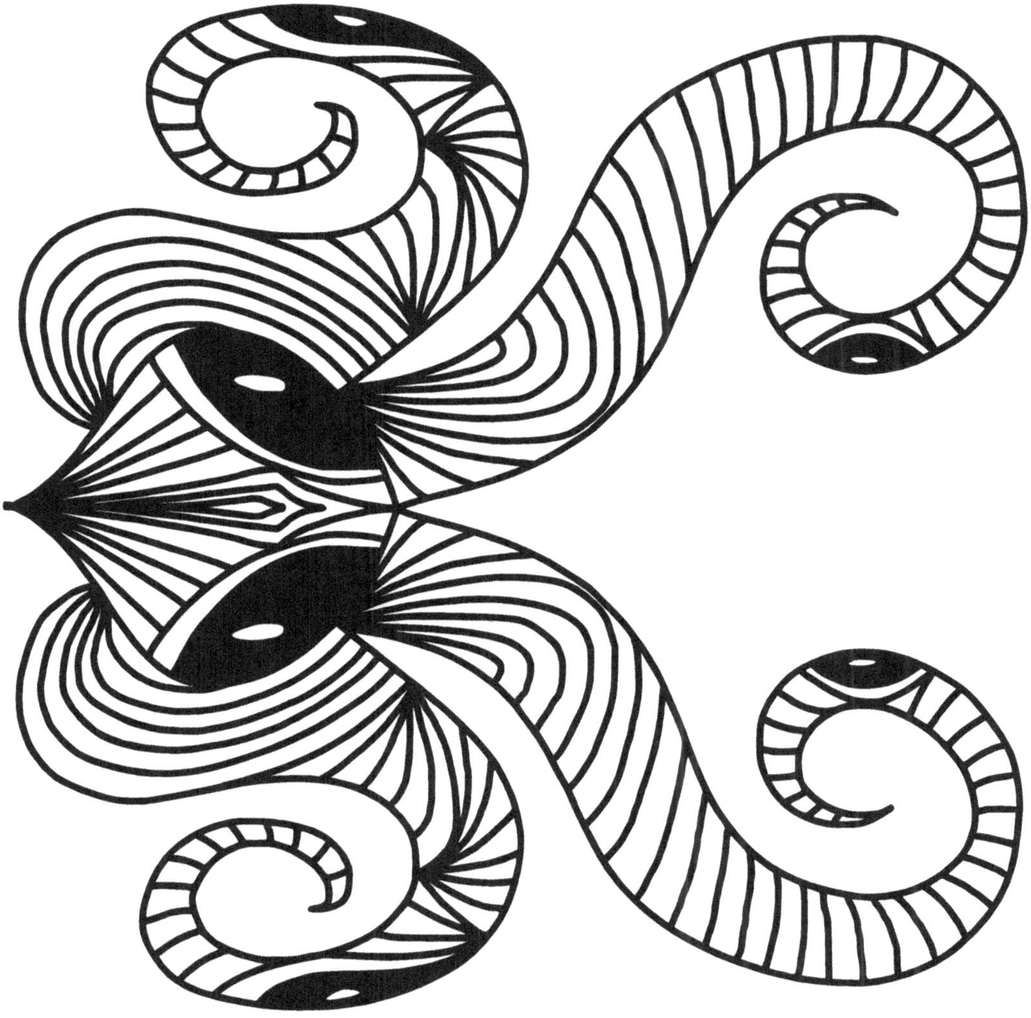

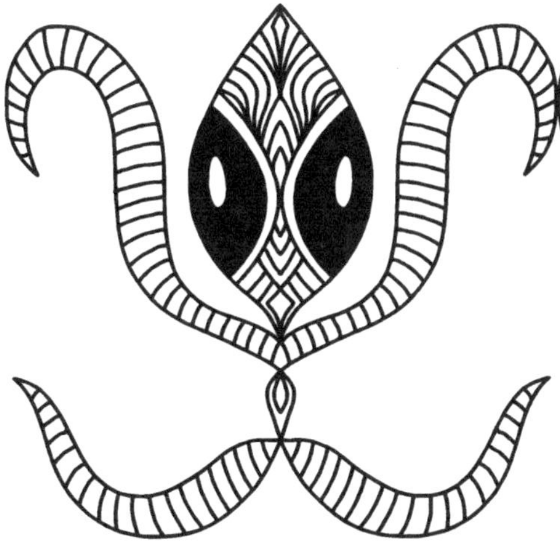

FATLINER WEIRDIES
VOLUME 1

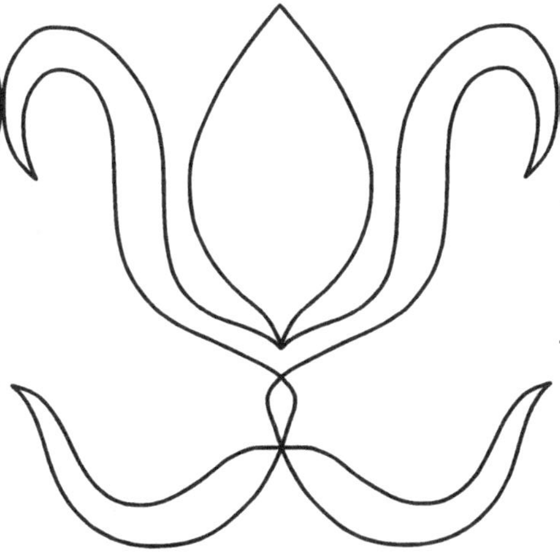

FATLINER WEIRDIES
THE TEMPLATES 1

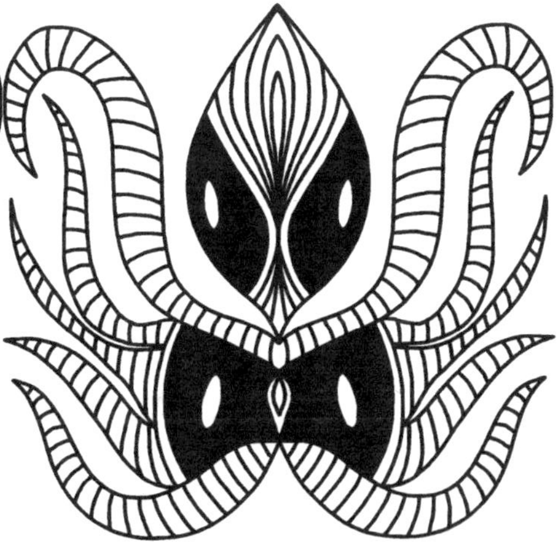

FATLINER WEIRDIES
VOLUME 3

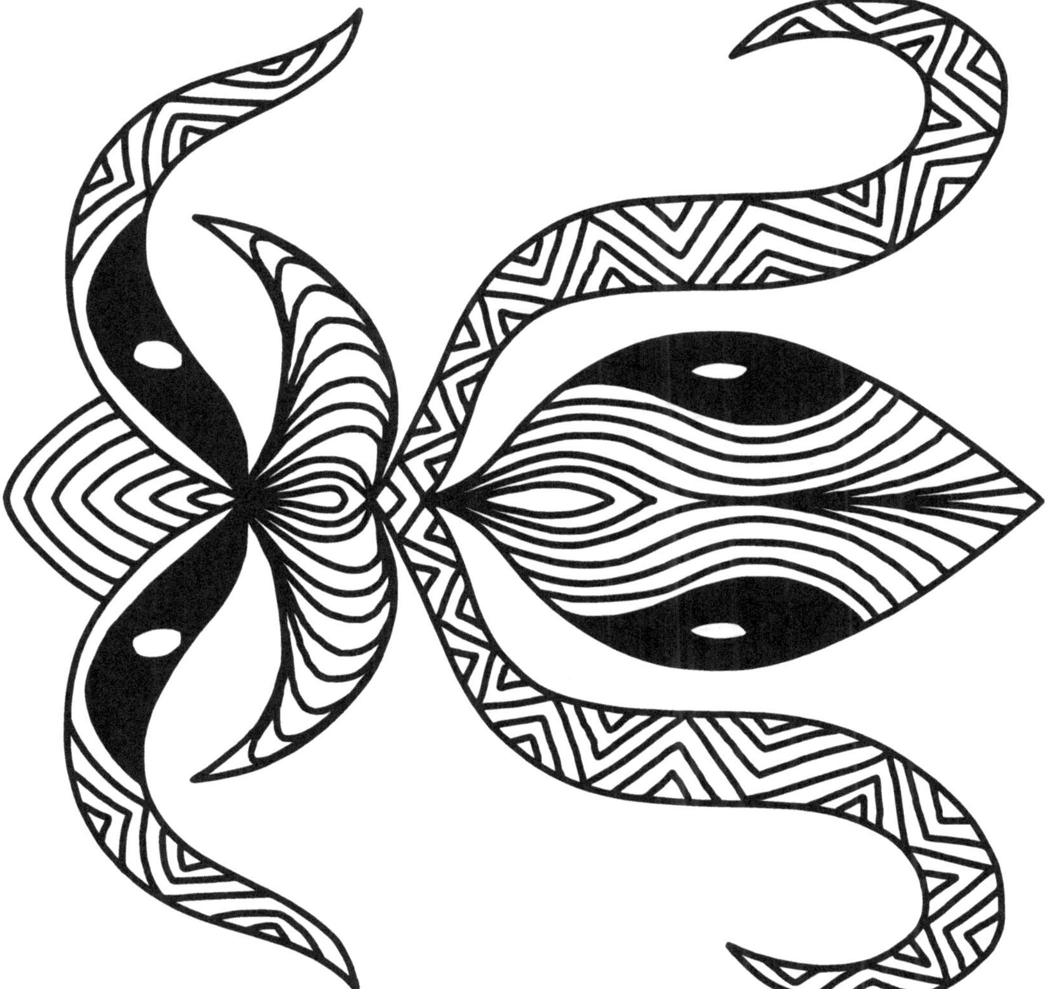

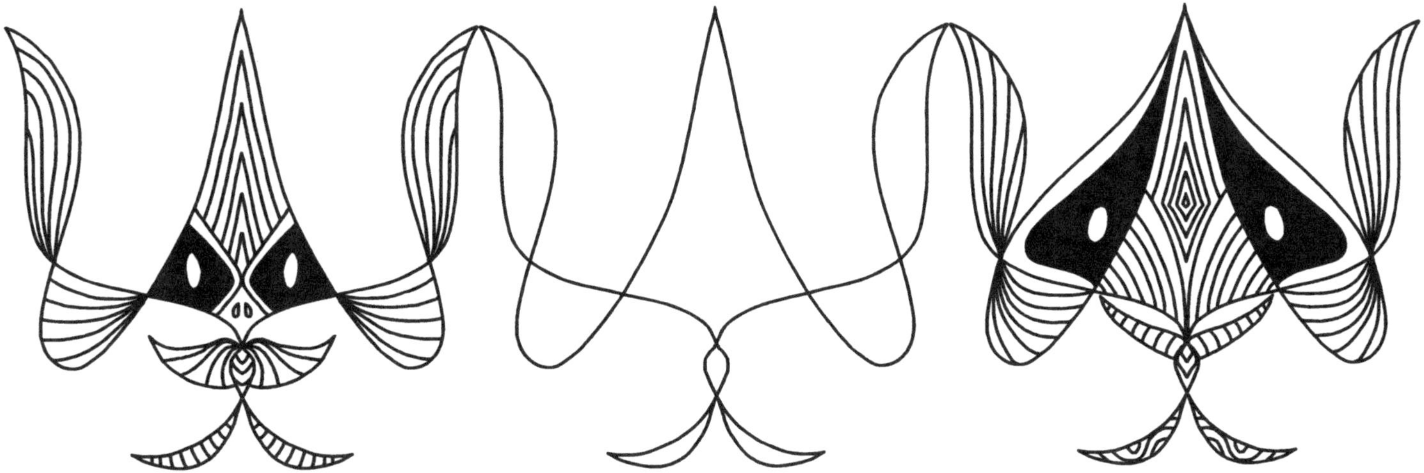

FATLINER WEIRDIES
VOLUME 1

FATLINER WEIRDIES
THE TEMPLATES 1

FATLINER WEIRDIES
VOLUME 3

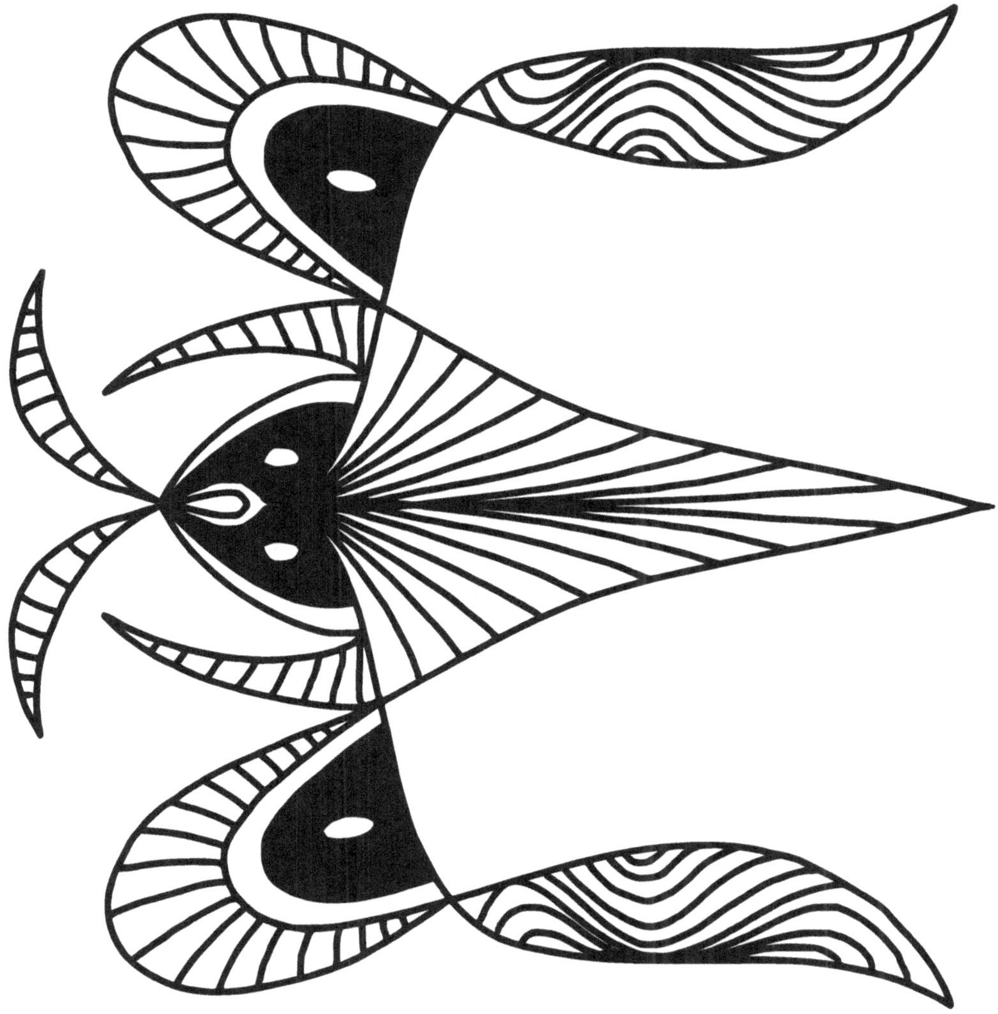

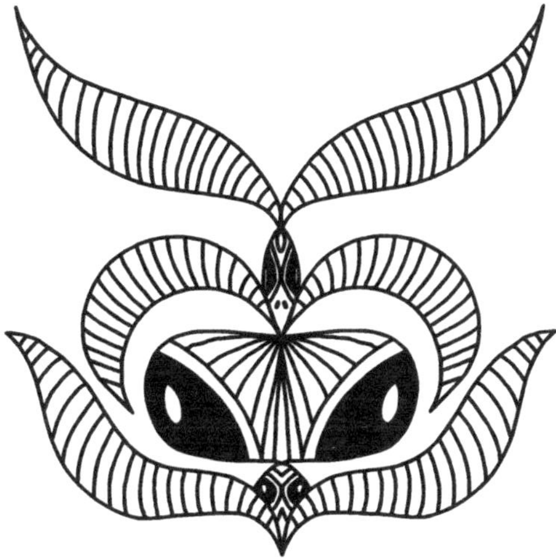

FATLINER WEIRDIES
VOLUME 1

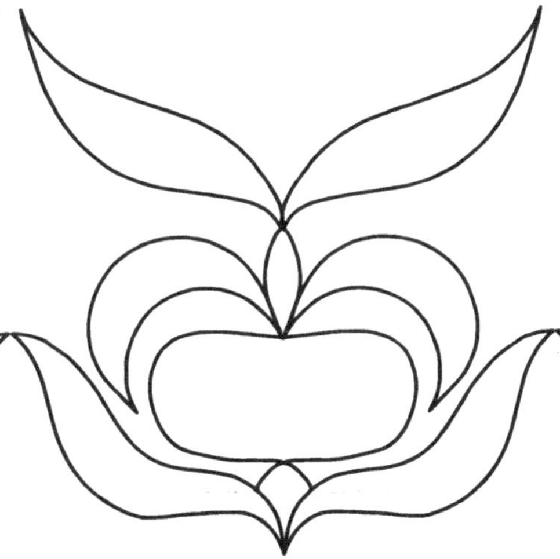

FATLINER WEIRDIES
THE TEMPLATES 1

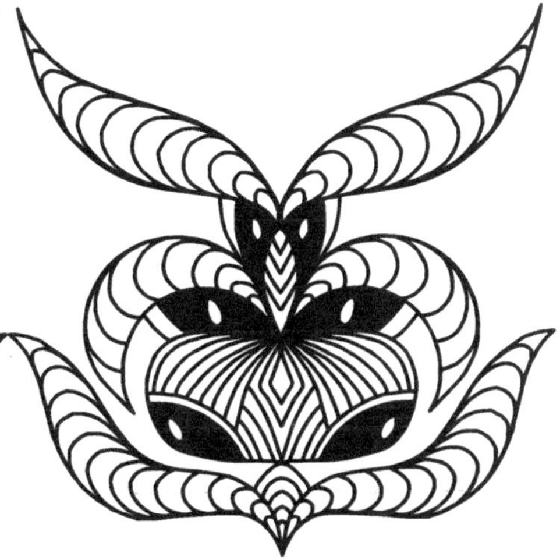

FATLINER WEIRDIES
VOLUME 3

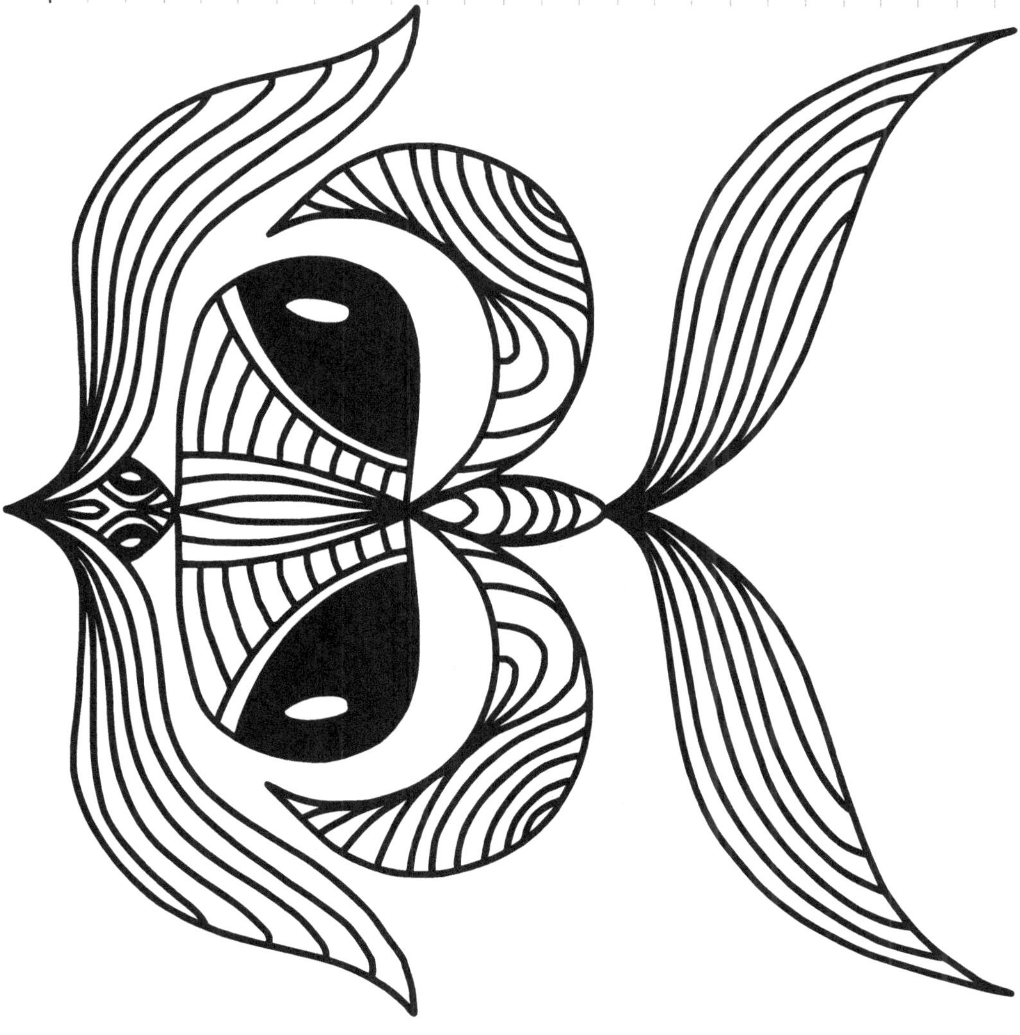

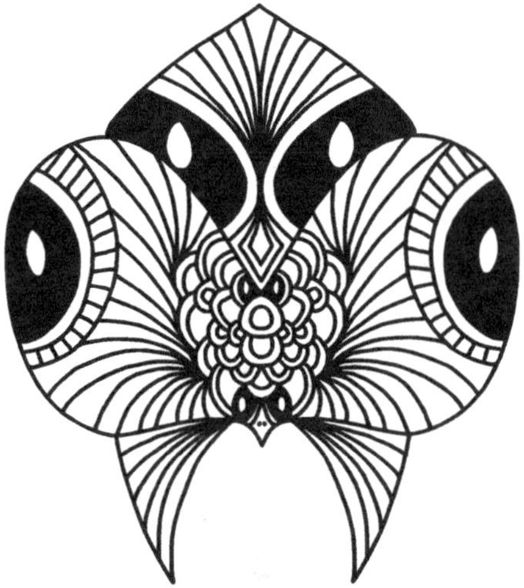

FATLINER WEIRDIES
VOLUME 1

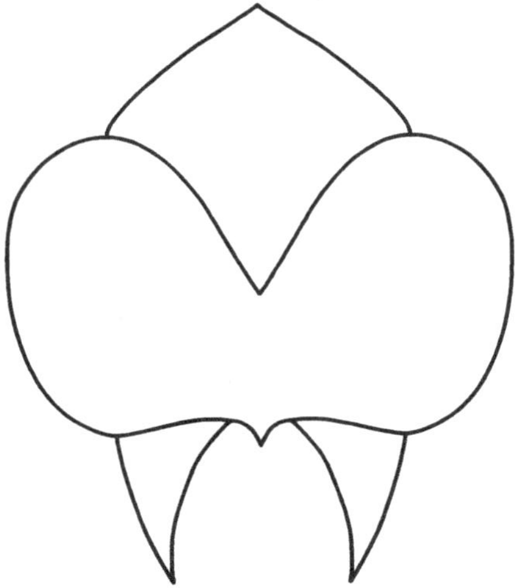

FATLINER WEIRDIES
THE TEMPLATES 1

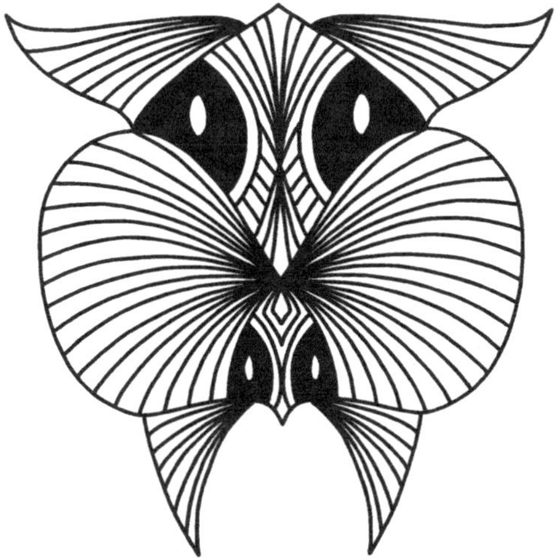

FATLINER WEIRDIES
VOLUME 3

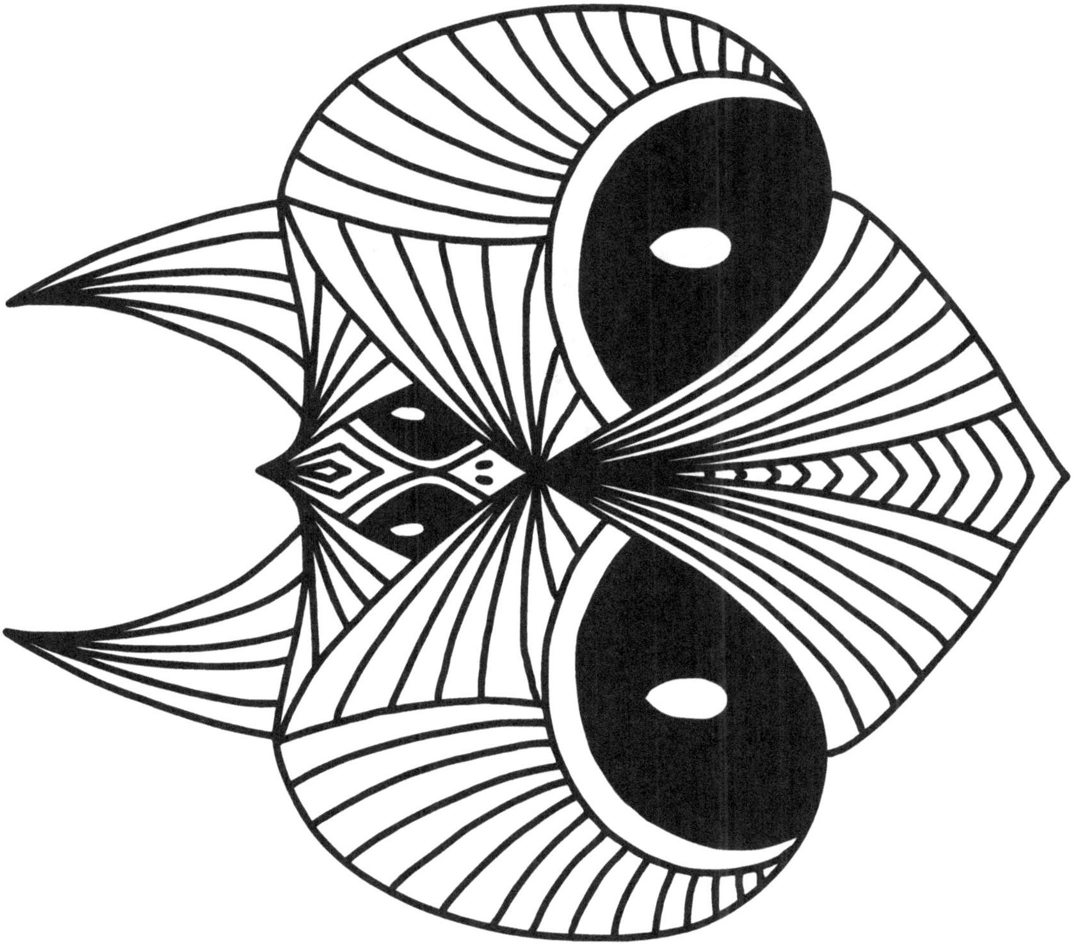

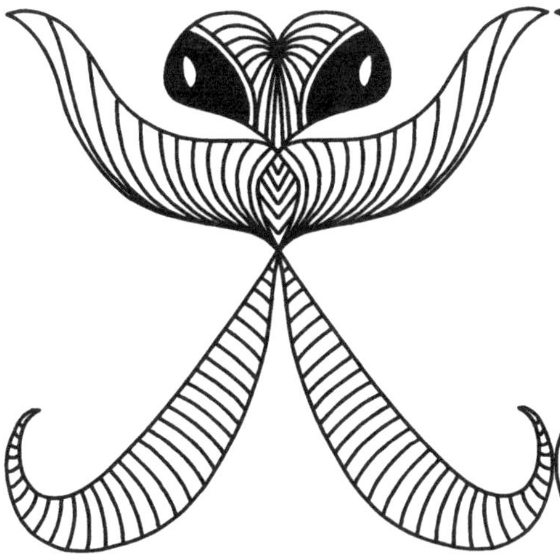

FATLINER WEIRDIES
VOLUME 1

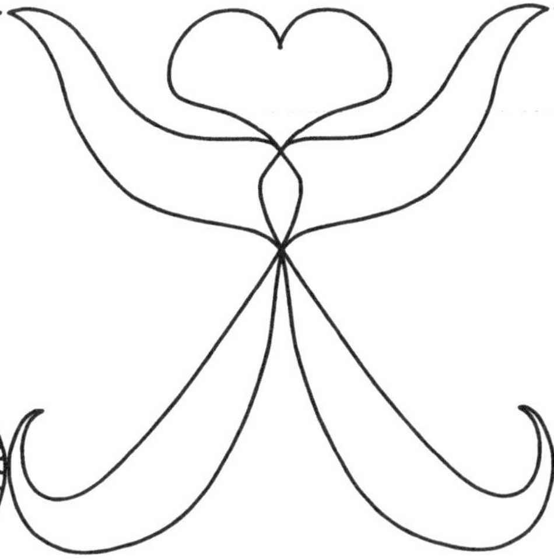

FATLINER WEIRDIES
THE TEMPLATES 1

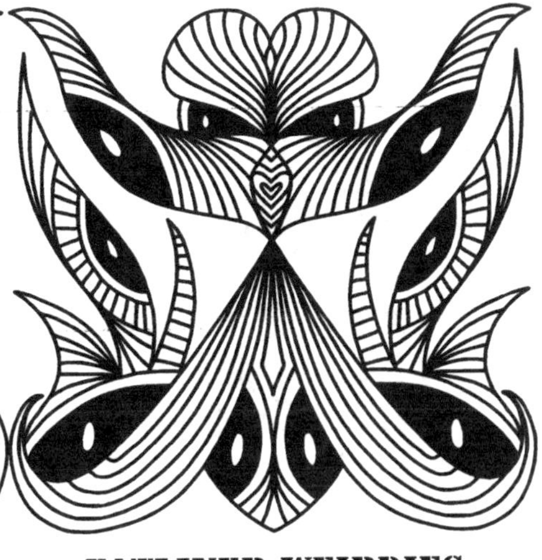

FATLINER WEIRDIES
VOLUME 3

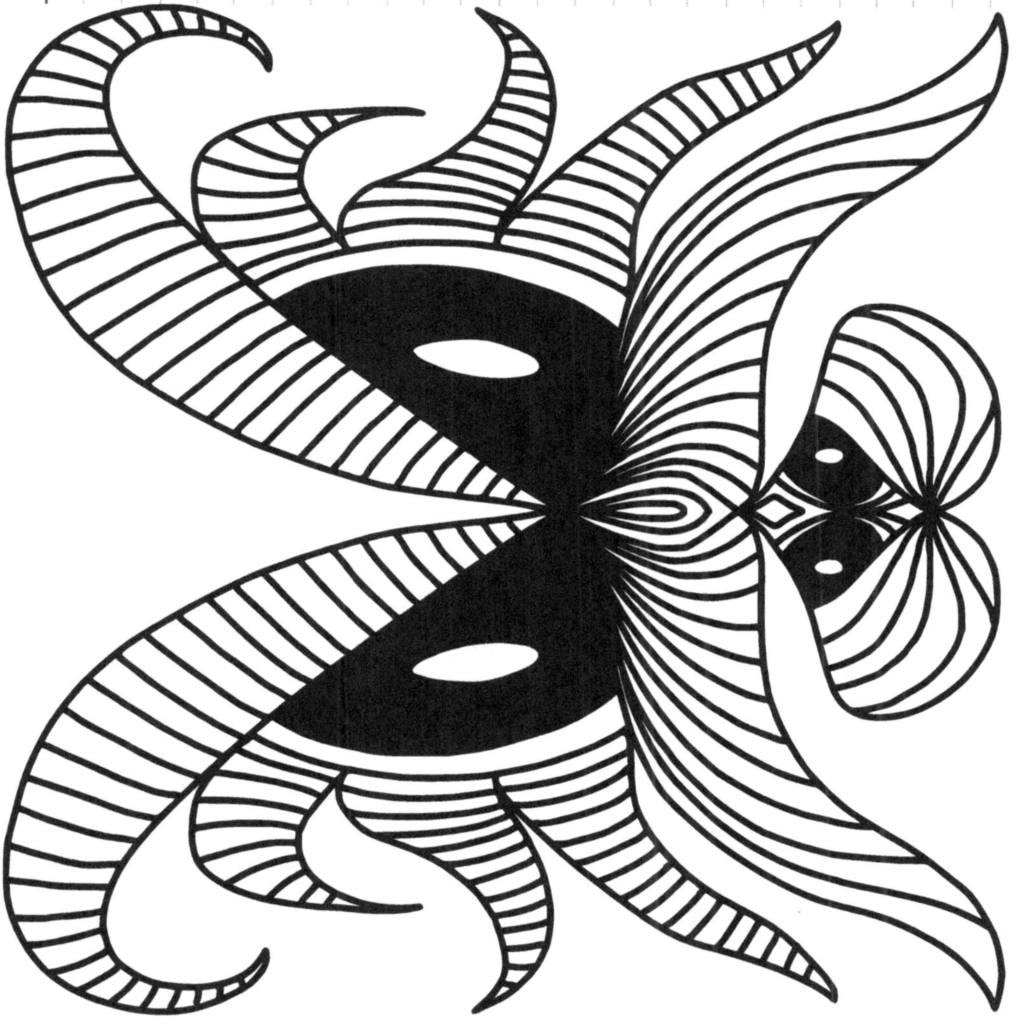

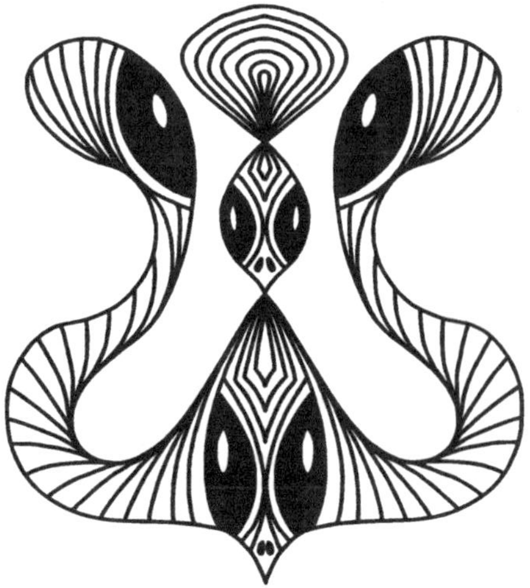

FATLINER WEIRDIES
VOLUME 1

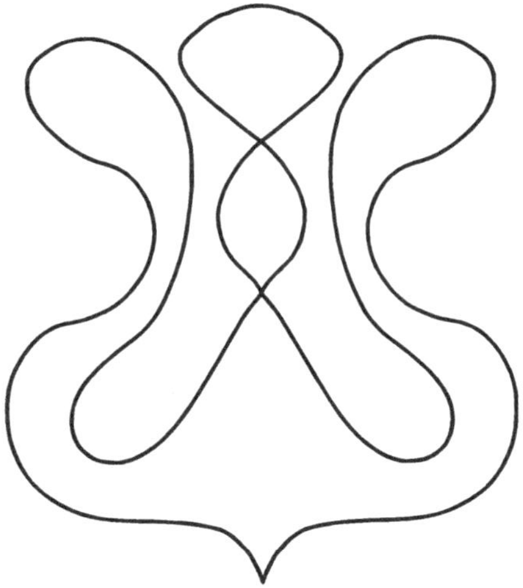

FATLINER WEIRDIES
THE TEMPLATES 1

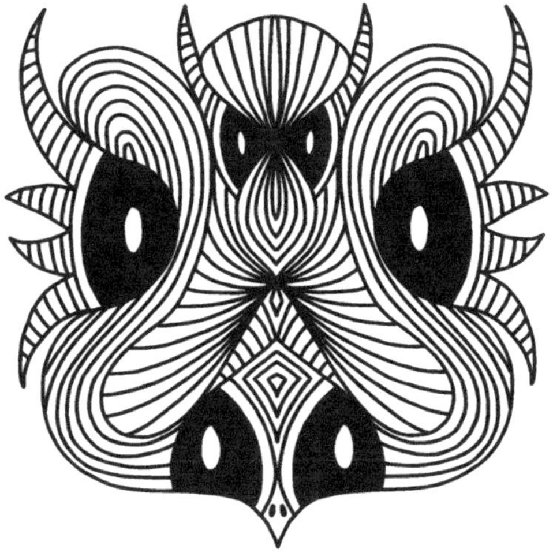

FATLINER WEIRDIES
VOLUME 3

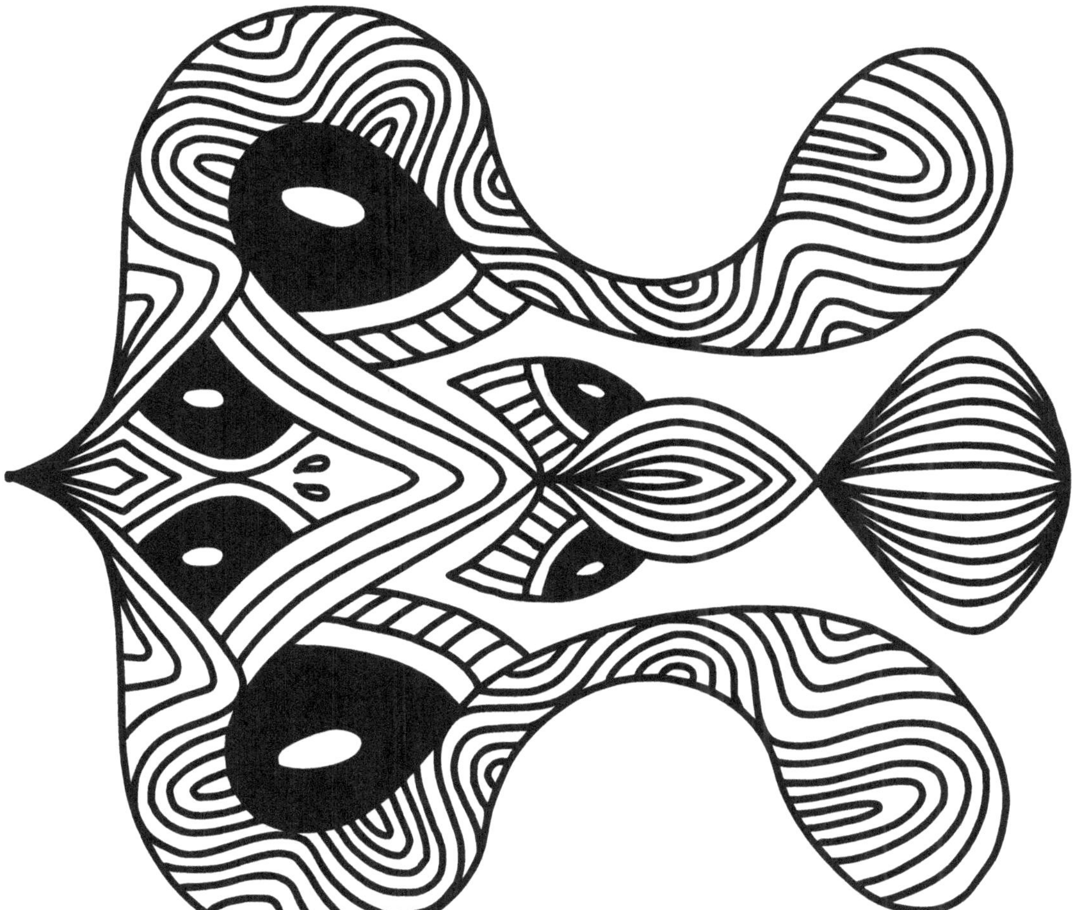

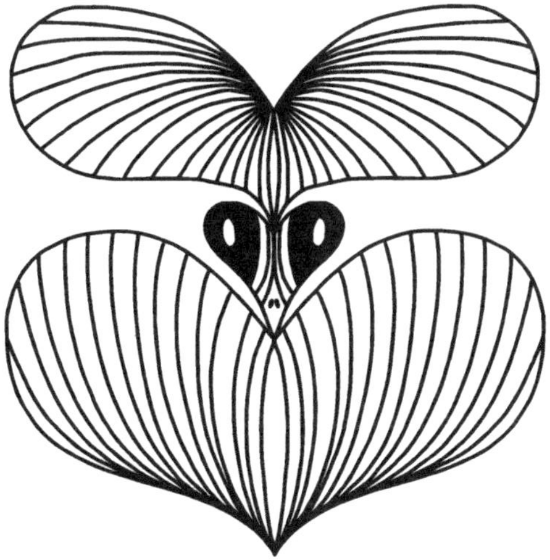

FATLINER WEIRDIES
VOLUME 1

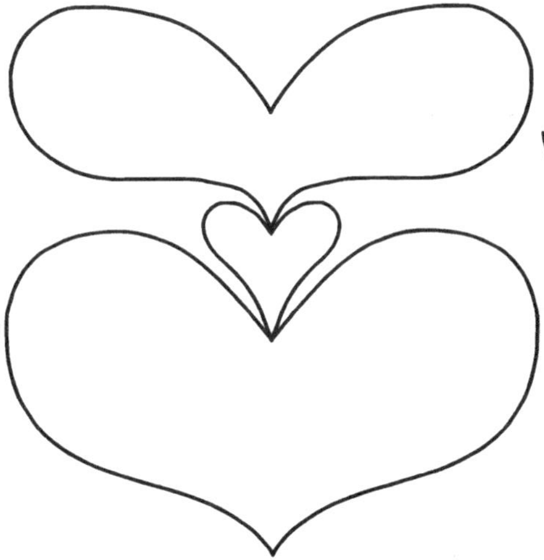

FATLINER WEIRDIES
THE TEMPLATES 1

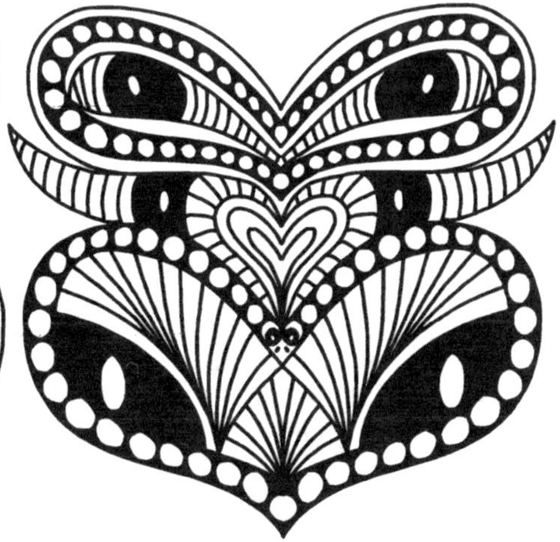

FATLINER WEIRDIES
VOLUME 3

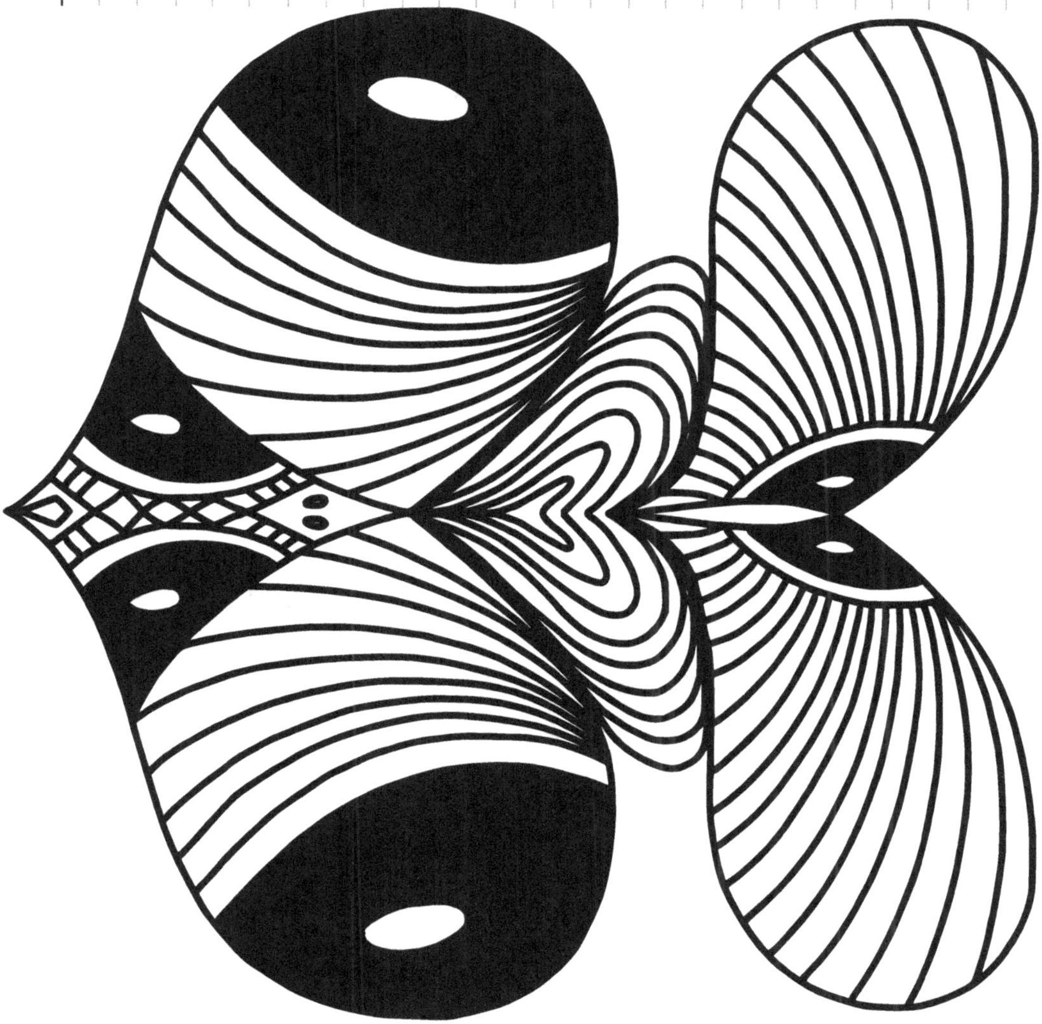

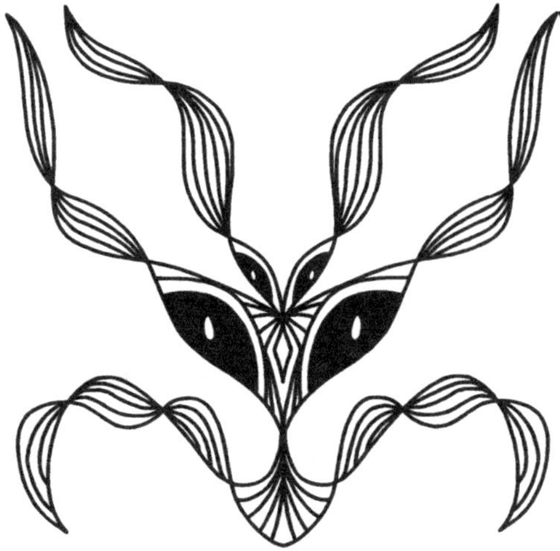

FATLINER WEIRDIES
VOLUME 1

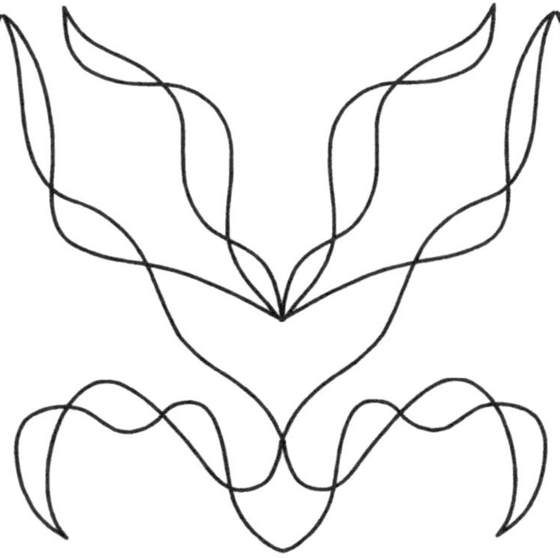

FATLINER WEIRDIES
THE TEMPLATES 1

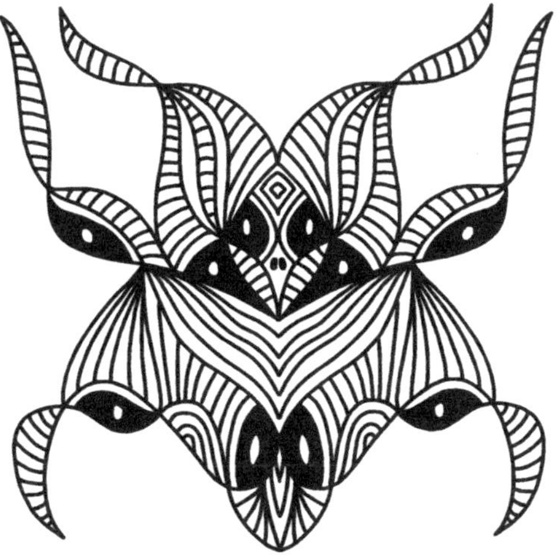

FATLINER WEIRDIES
VOLUME 3

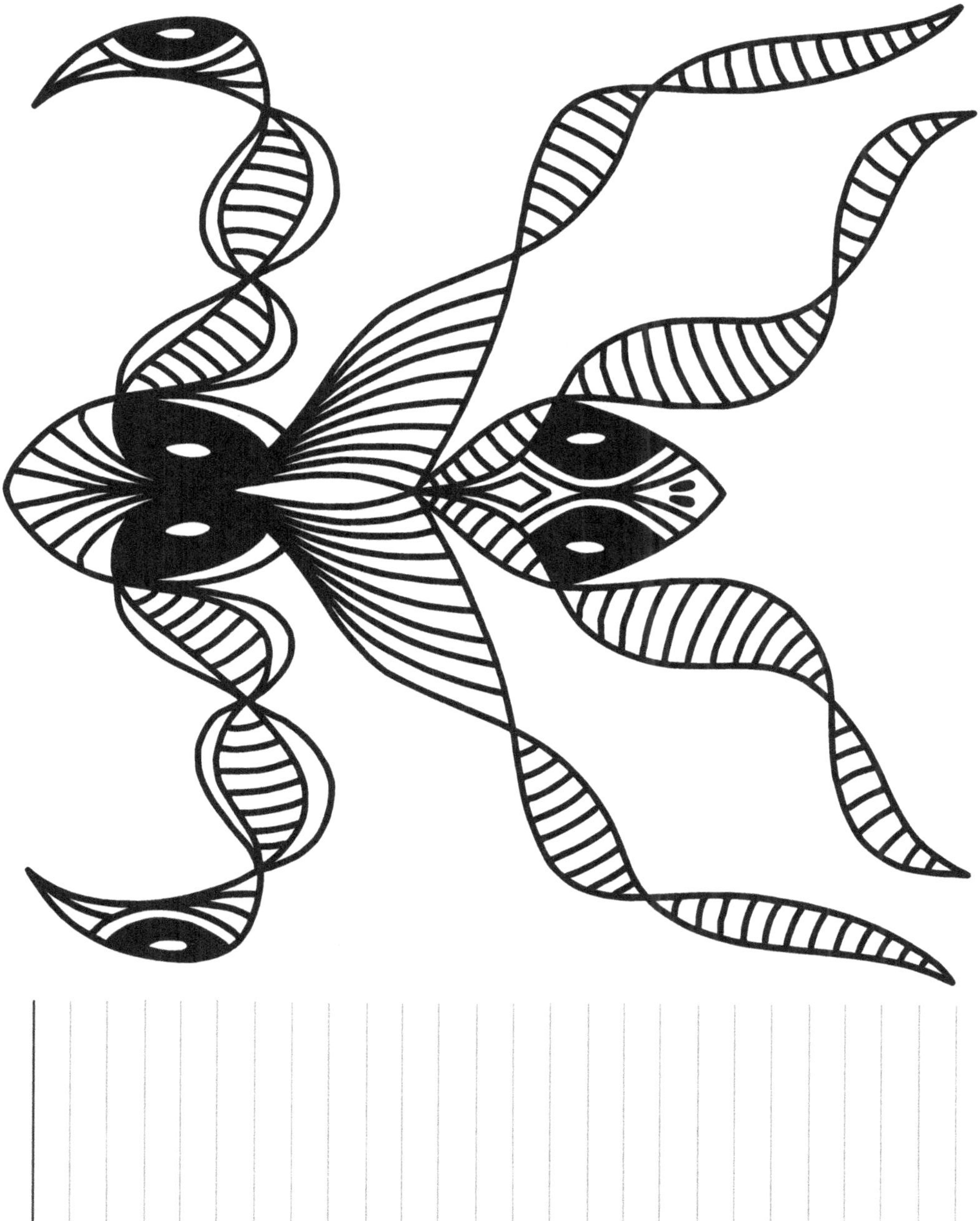

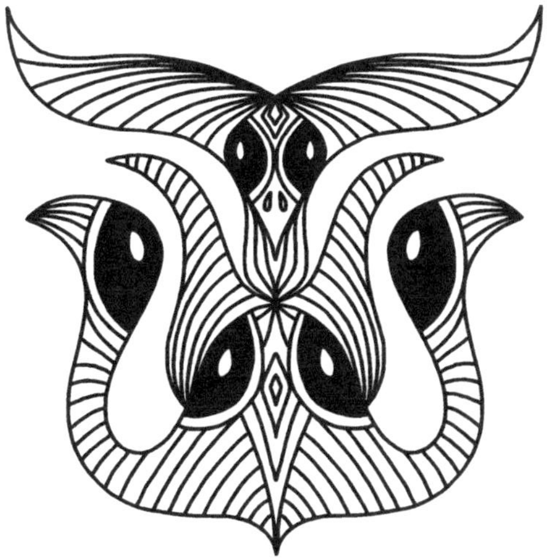

FATLINER WEIRDIES
VOLUME 1

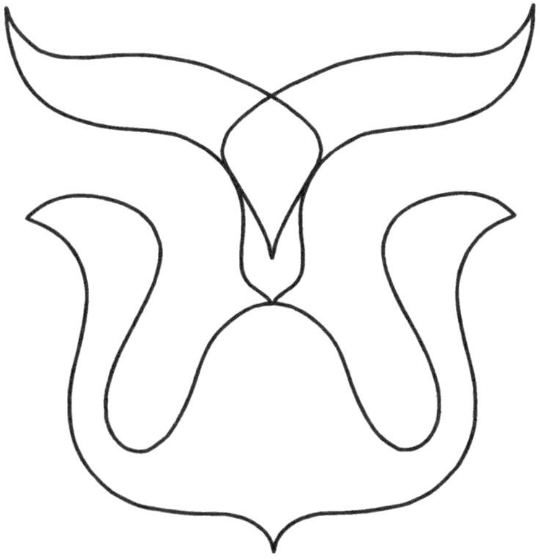

FATLINER WEIRDIES
THE TEMPLATES 1

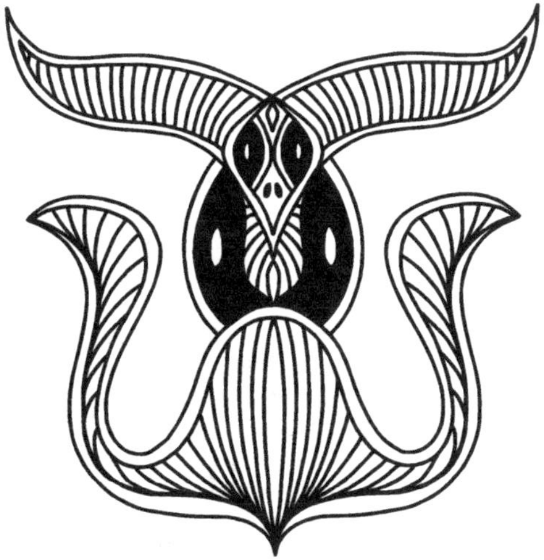

FATLINER WEIRDIES
VOLUME 3

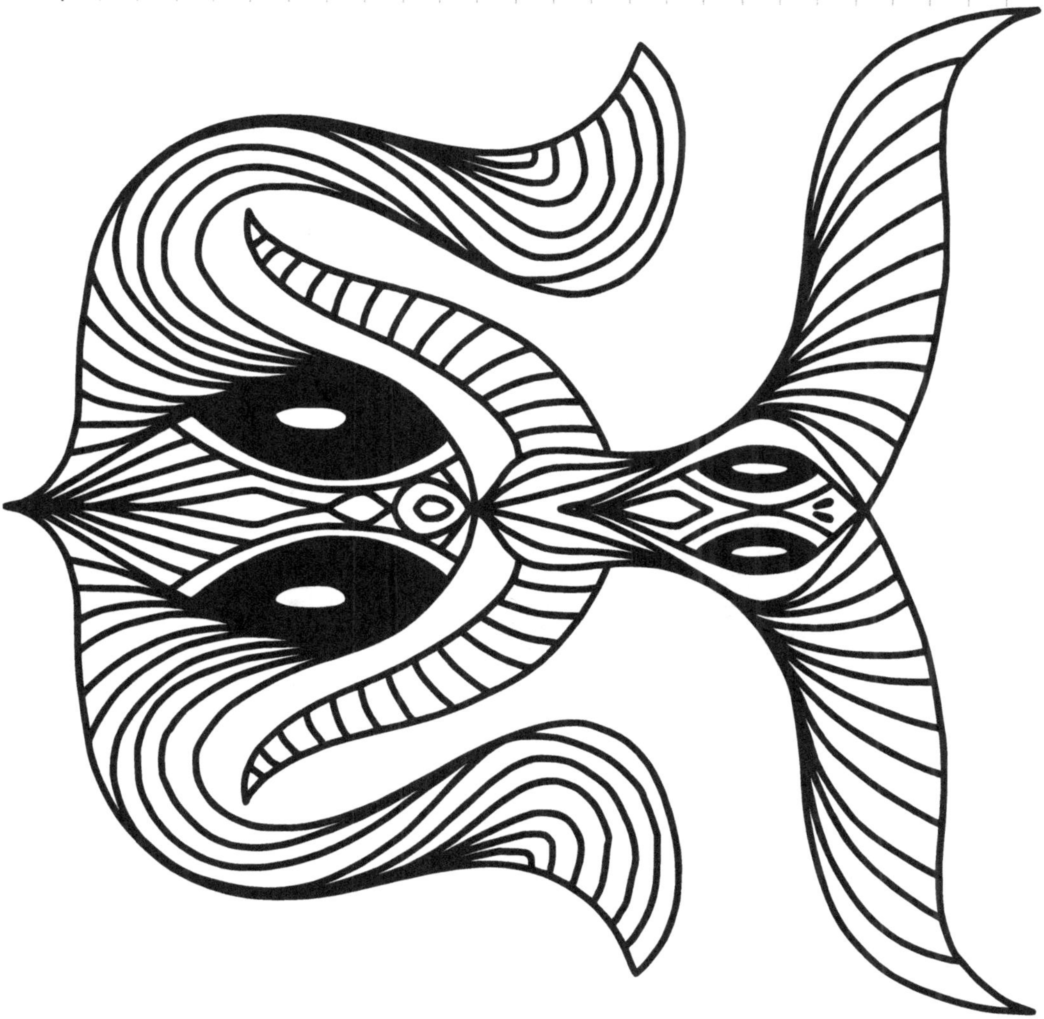

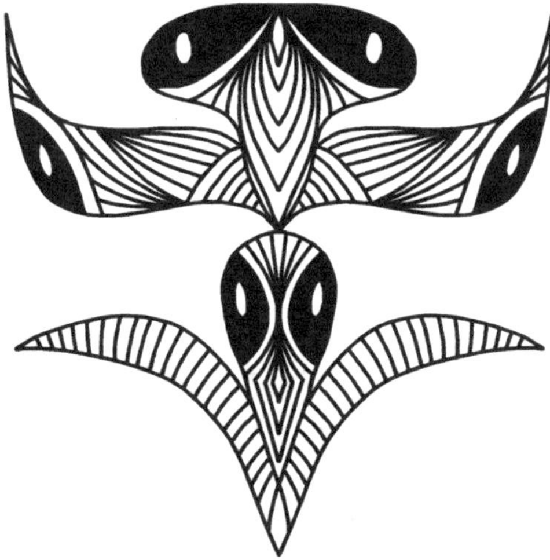

FATLINER WEIRDIES
VOLUME 1

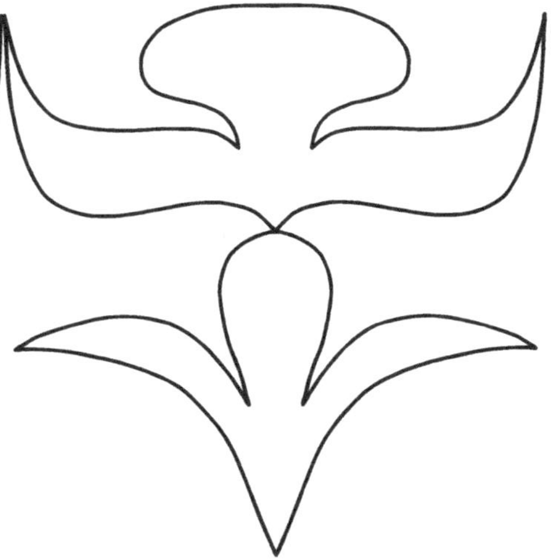

FATLINER WEIRDIES
THE TEMPLATES 1

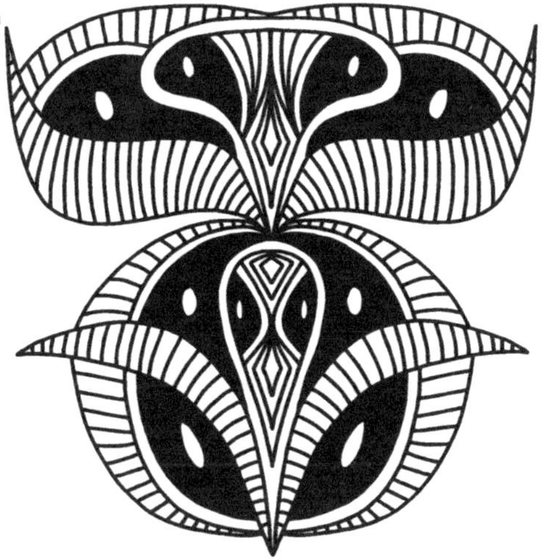

FATLINER WEIRDIES
VOLUME 3

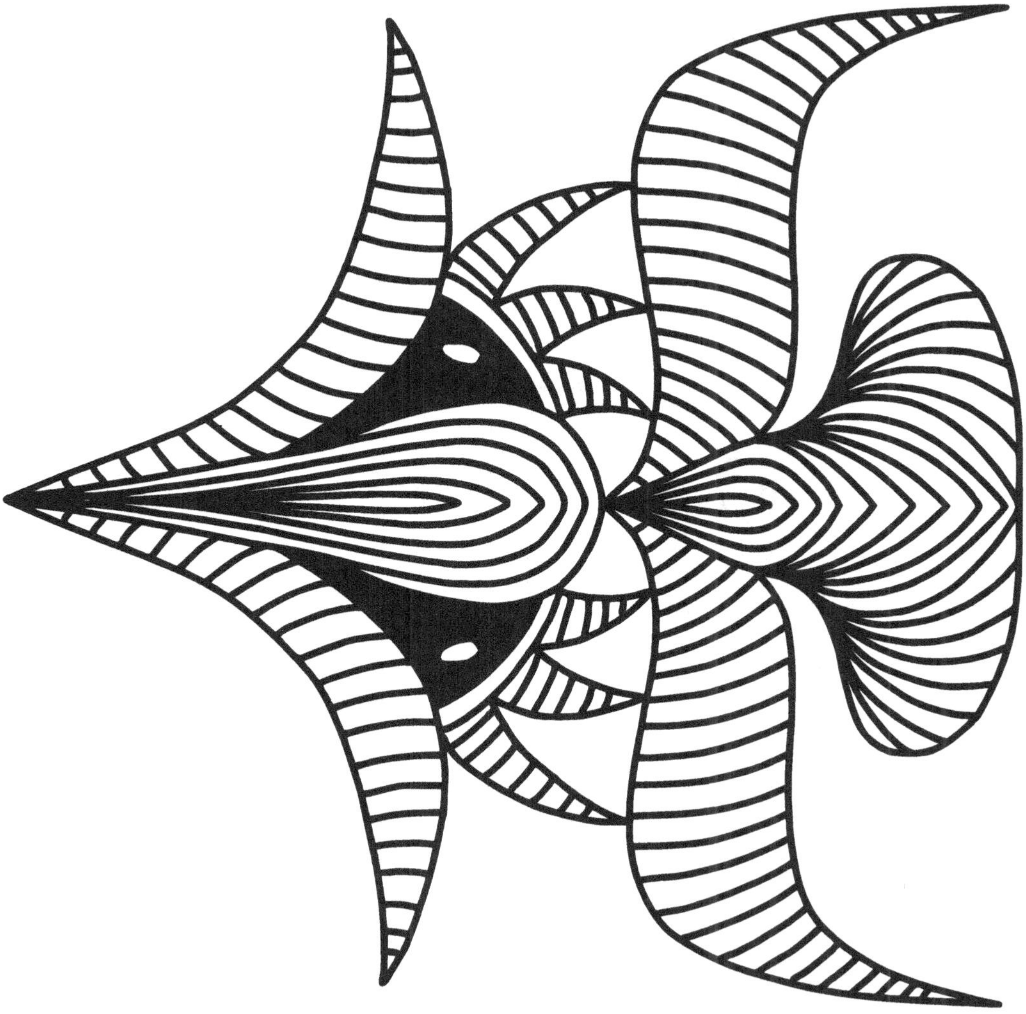

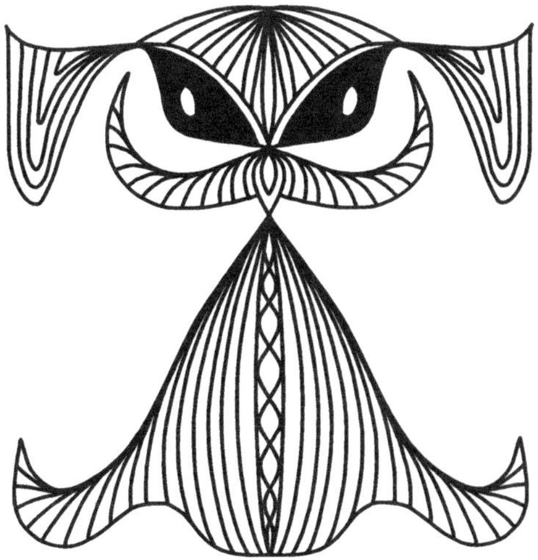

FATLINER WEIRDIES
VOLUME 1

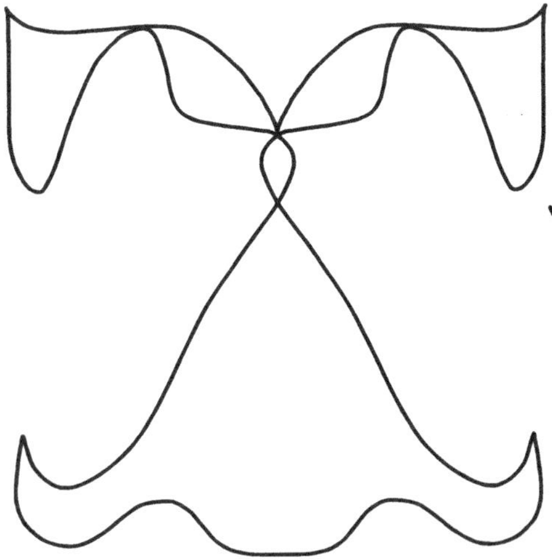

FATLINER WEIRDIES
THE TEMPLATES 1

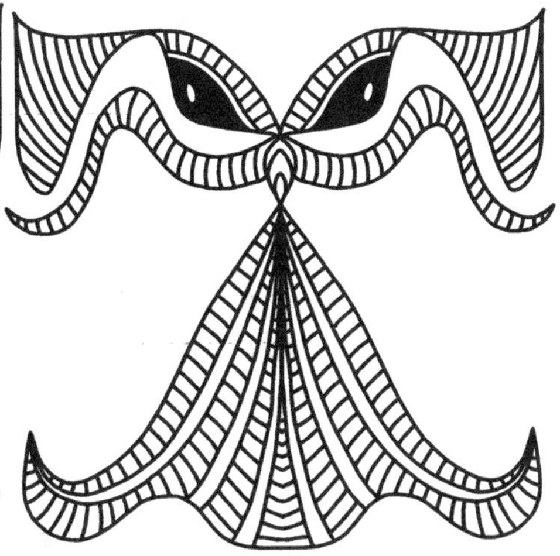

FATLINER WEIRDIES
VOLUME 3

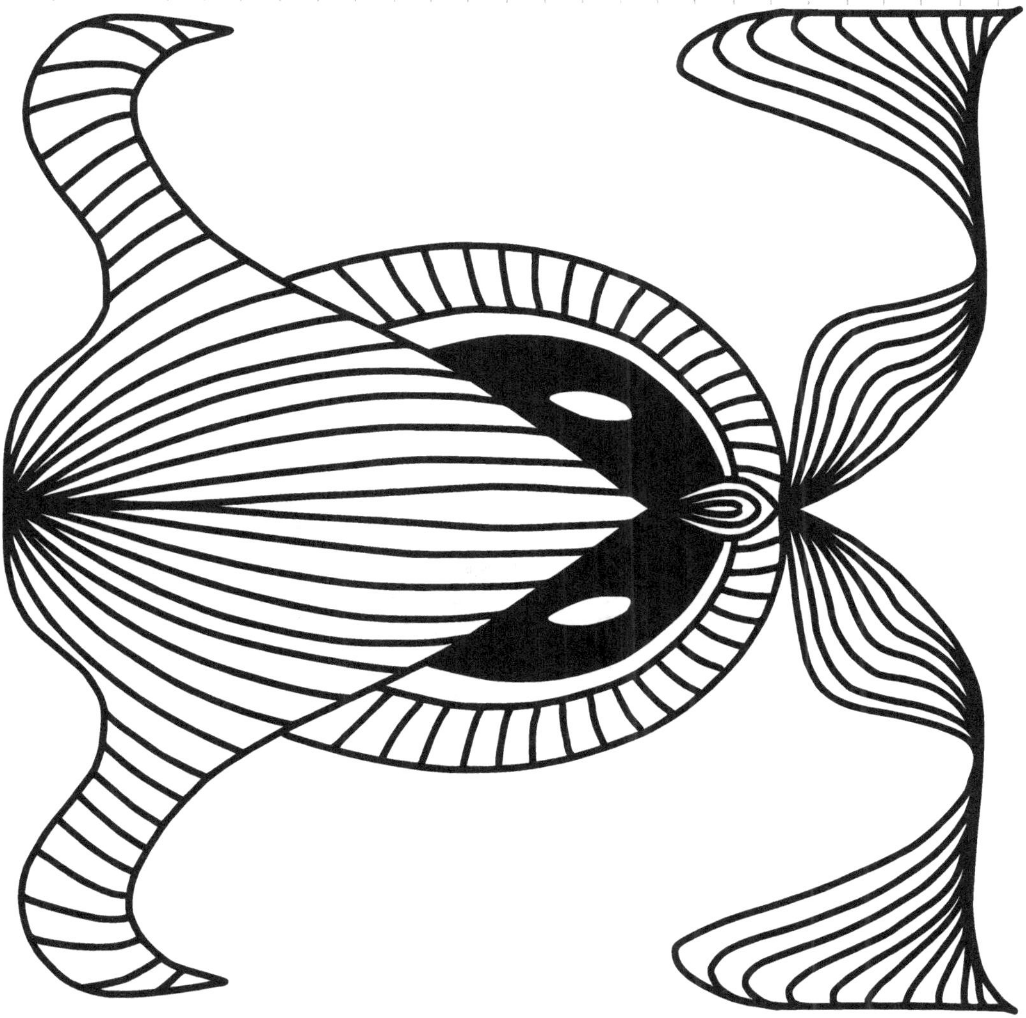

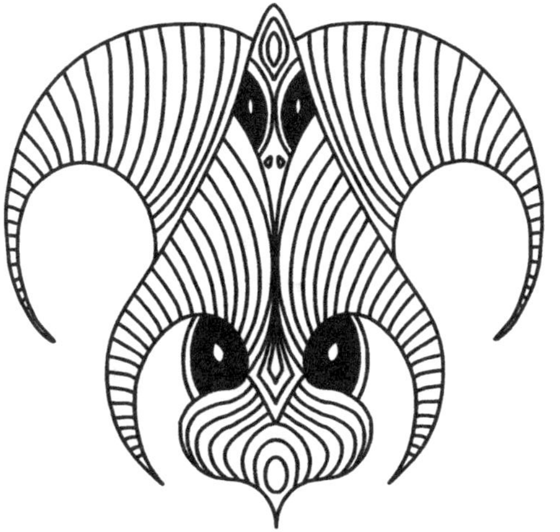

FATLINER WEIRDIES
VOLUME 1

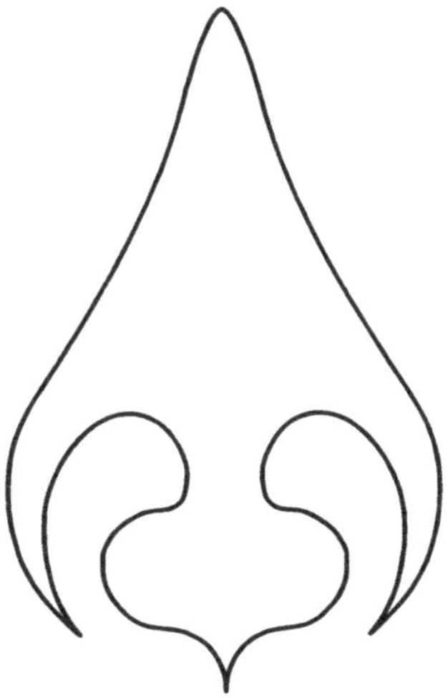

FATLINER WEIRDIES
THE TEMPLATES 1

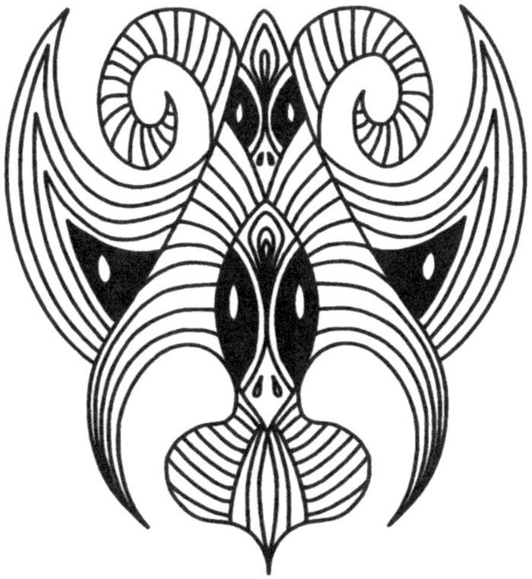

FATLINER WEIRDIES
VOLUME 3

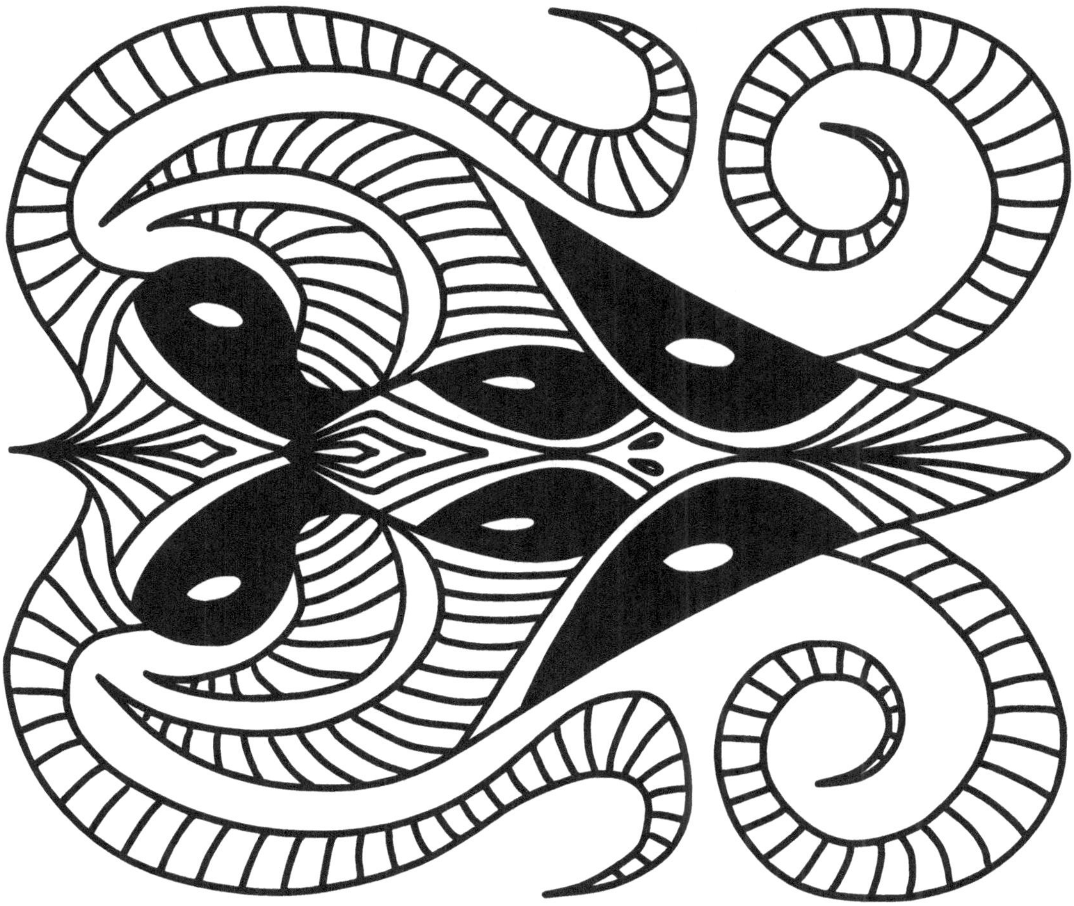

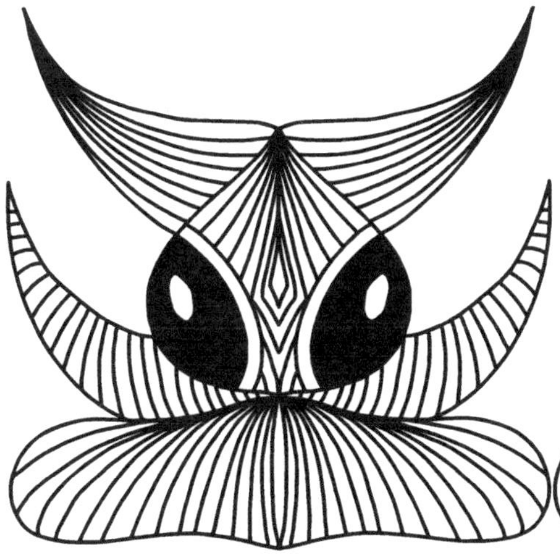

FATLINER WEIRDIES
VOLUME 1

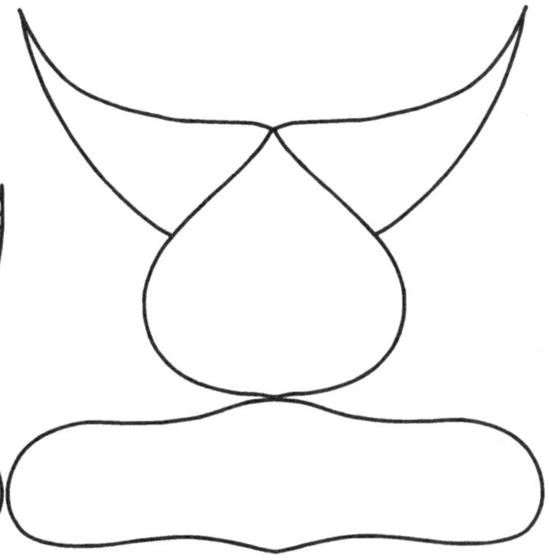

FATLINER WEIRDIES
THE TEMPLATES 1

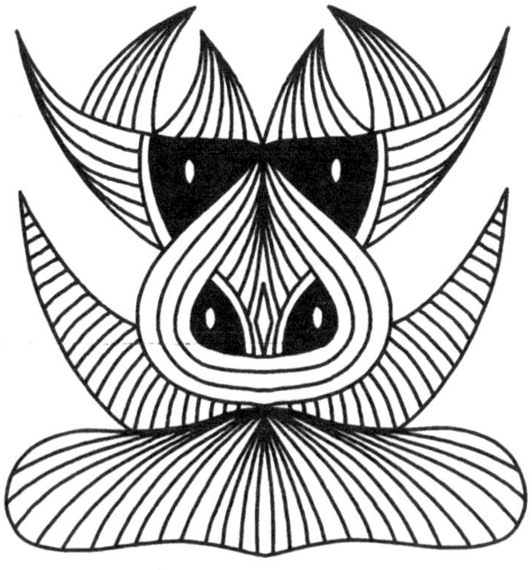

FATLINER WEIRDIES
VOLUME 3

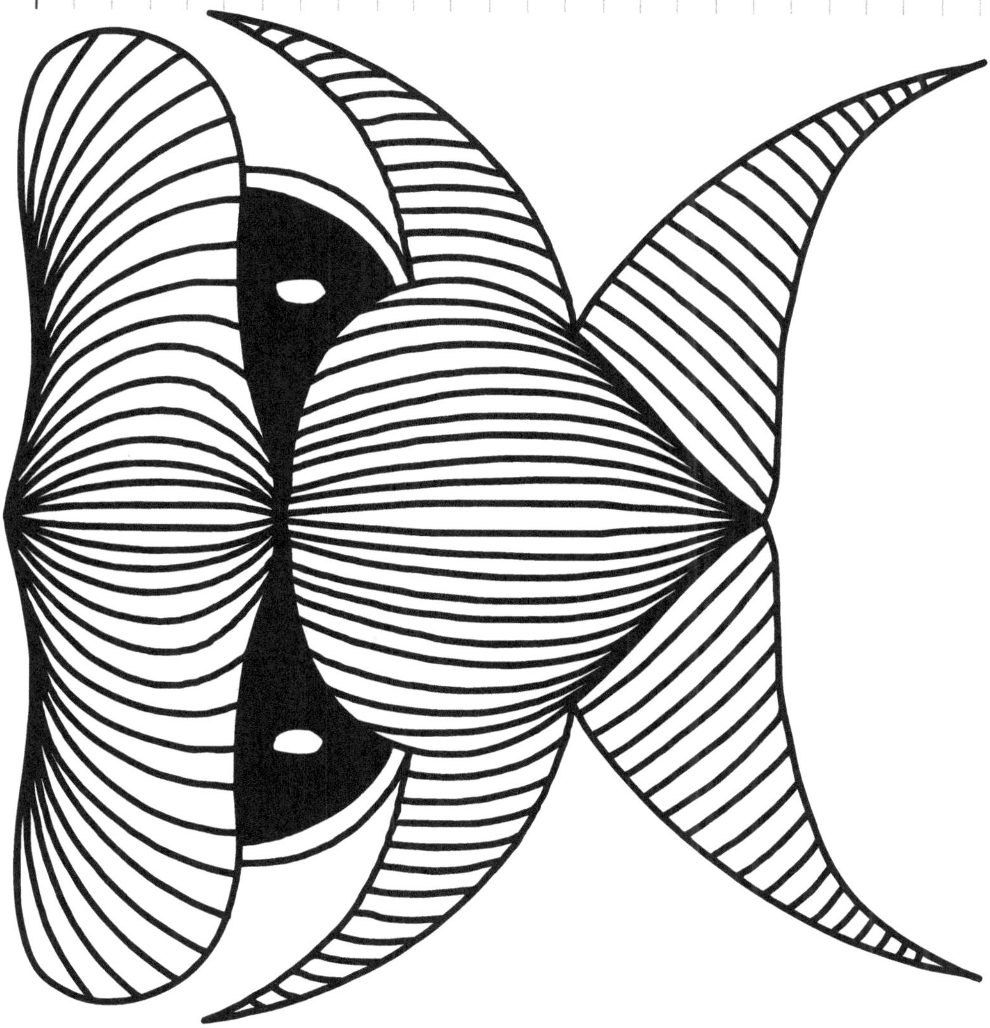

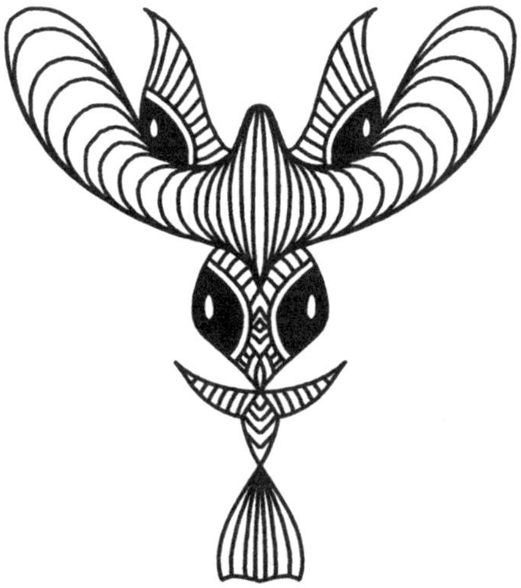

FATLINER WEIRDIES
VOLUME 1

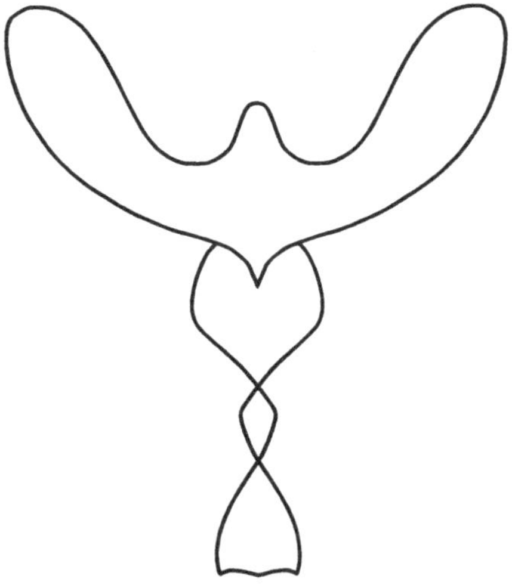

FATLINER WEIRDIES
THE TEMPLATES 1

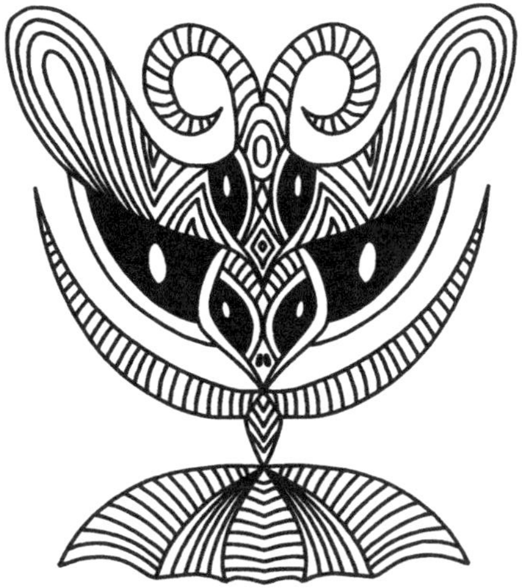

FATLINER WEIRDIES
VOLUME 3

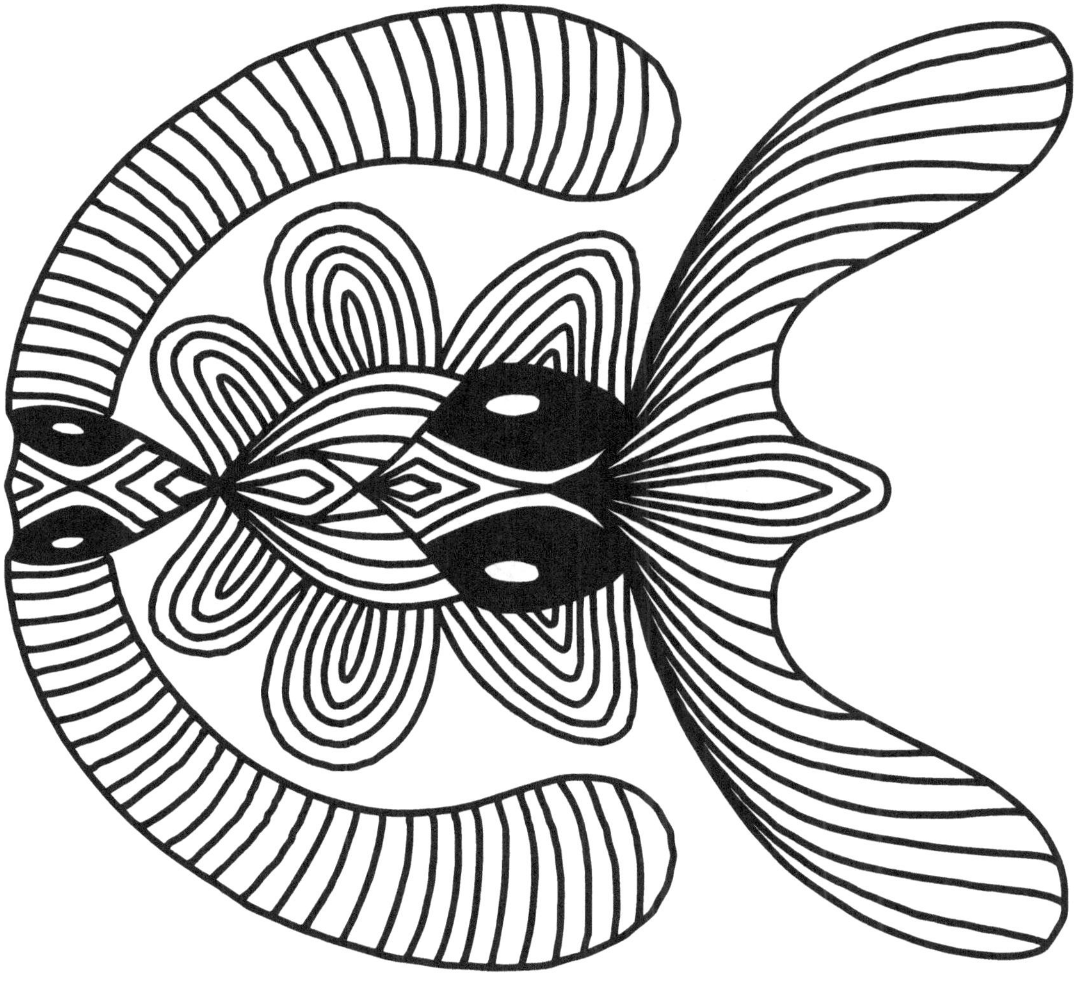

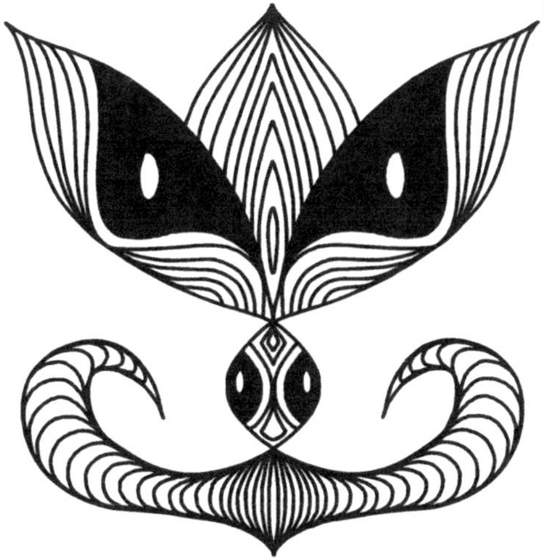

FATLINER WEIRDIES
VOLUME 1

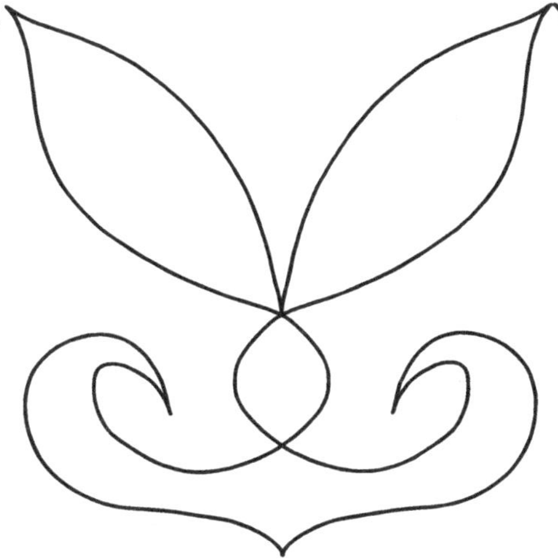

FATLINER WEIRDIES
THE TEMPLATES 1

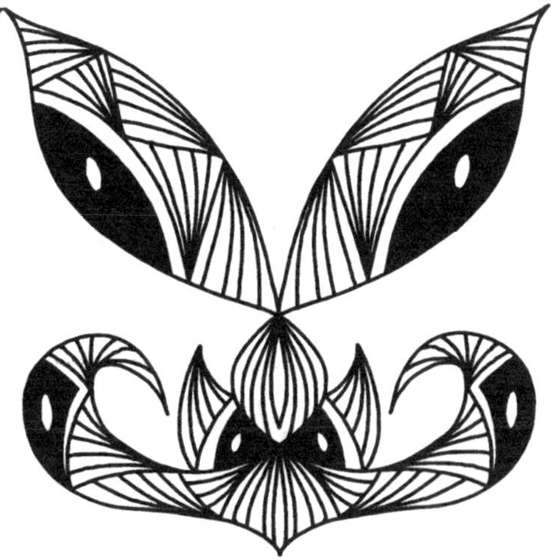

FATLINER WEIRDIES
VOLUME 3

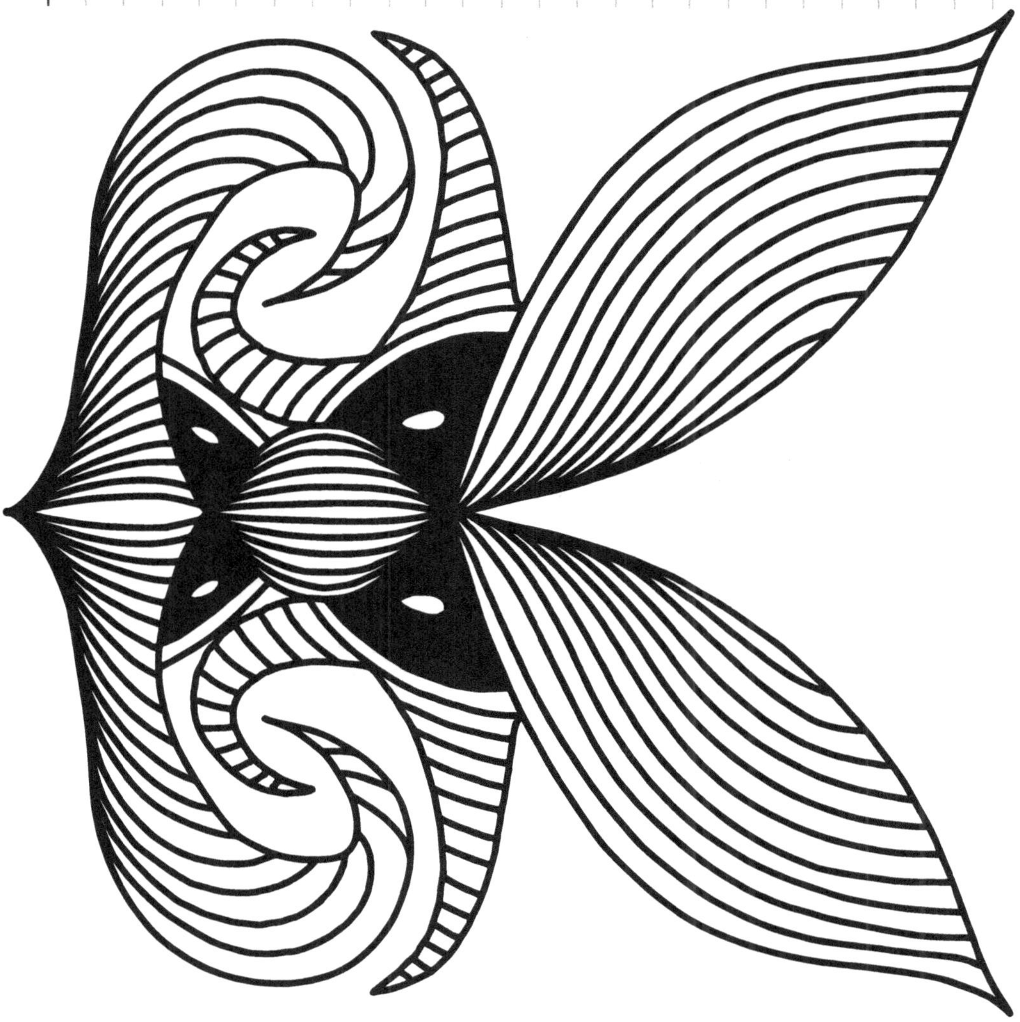

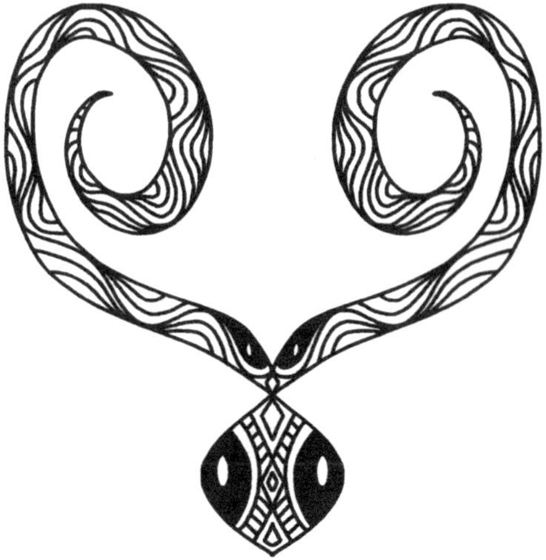

FATLINER WEIRDIES
VOLUME 1

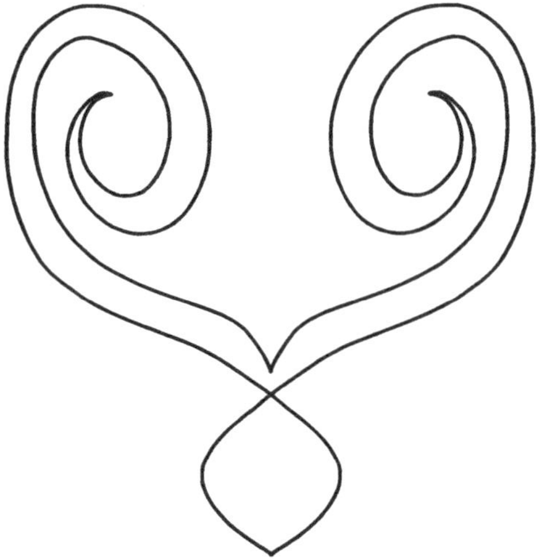

FATLINER WEIRDIES
THE TEMPLATES 1

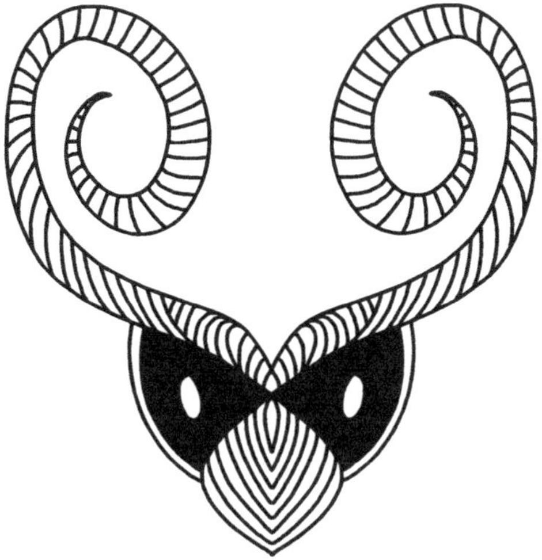

FATLINER WEIRDIES
VOLUME 3

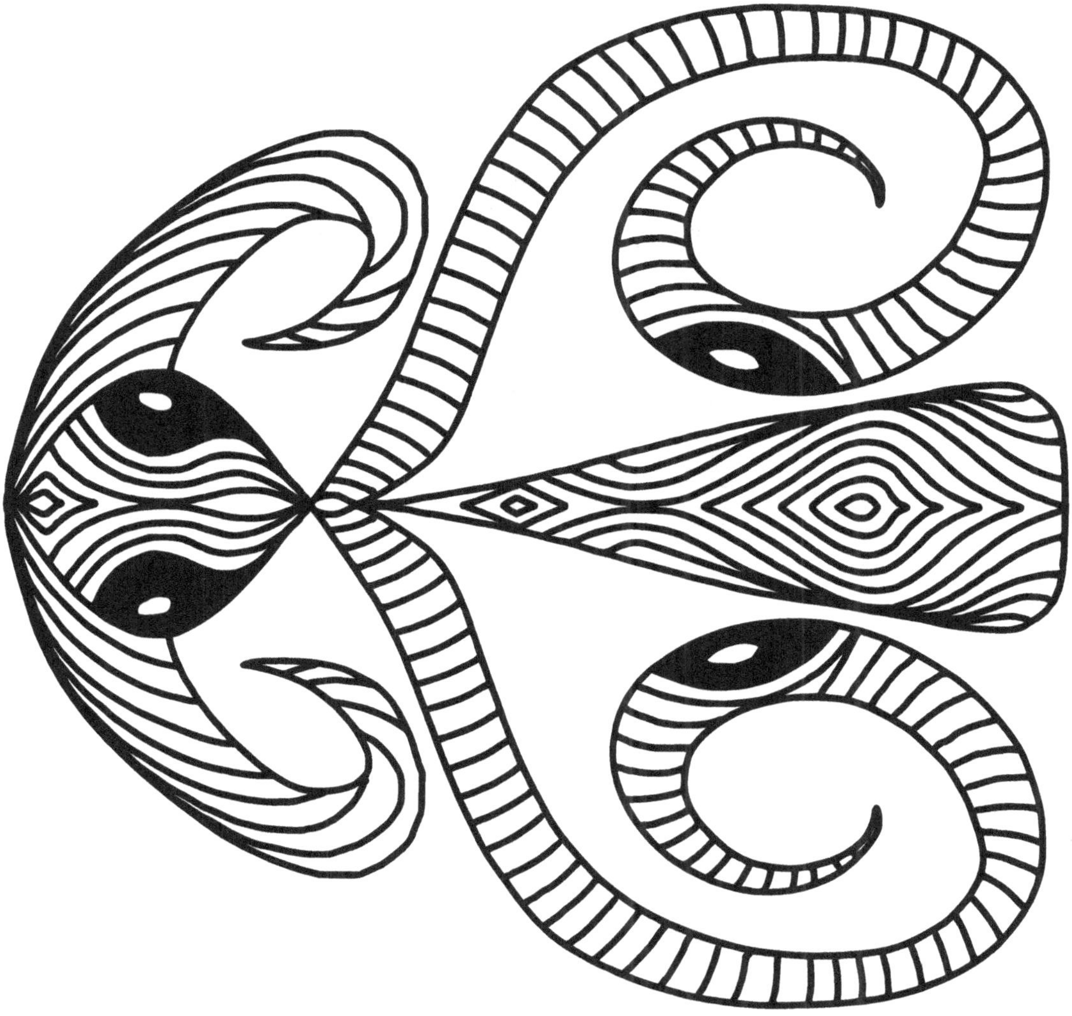

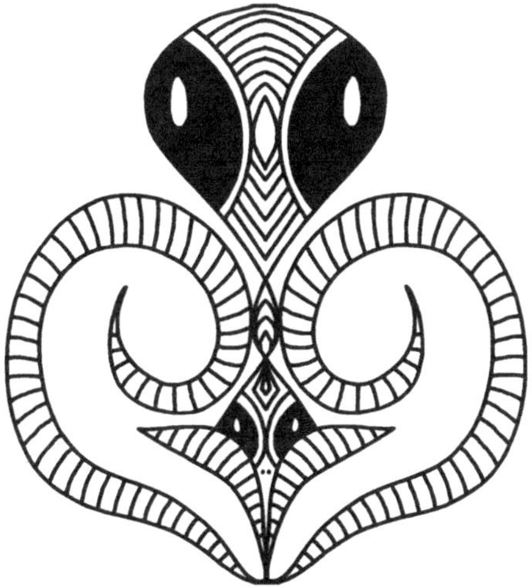

FATLINER WEIRDIES
VOLUME 1

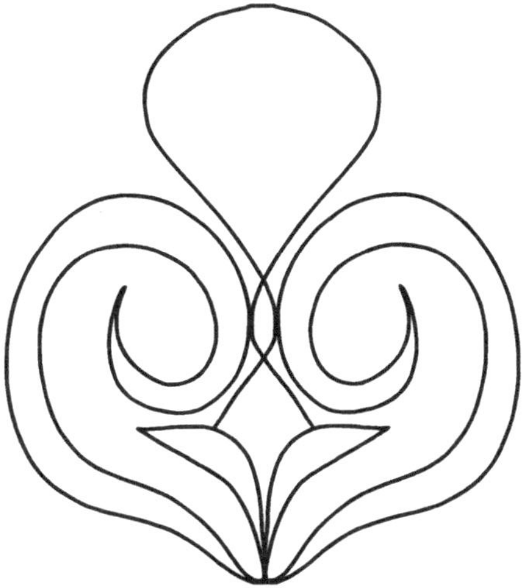

FATLINER WEIRDIES
THE TEMPLATES 1

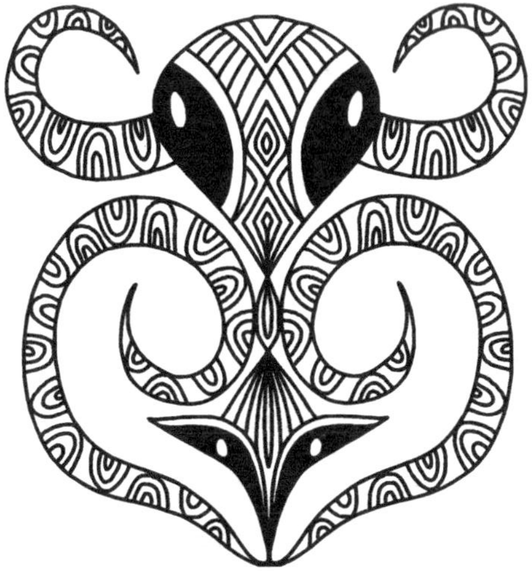

FATLINER WEIRDIES
VOLUME 3

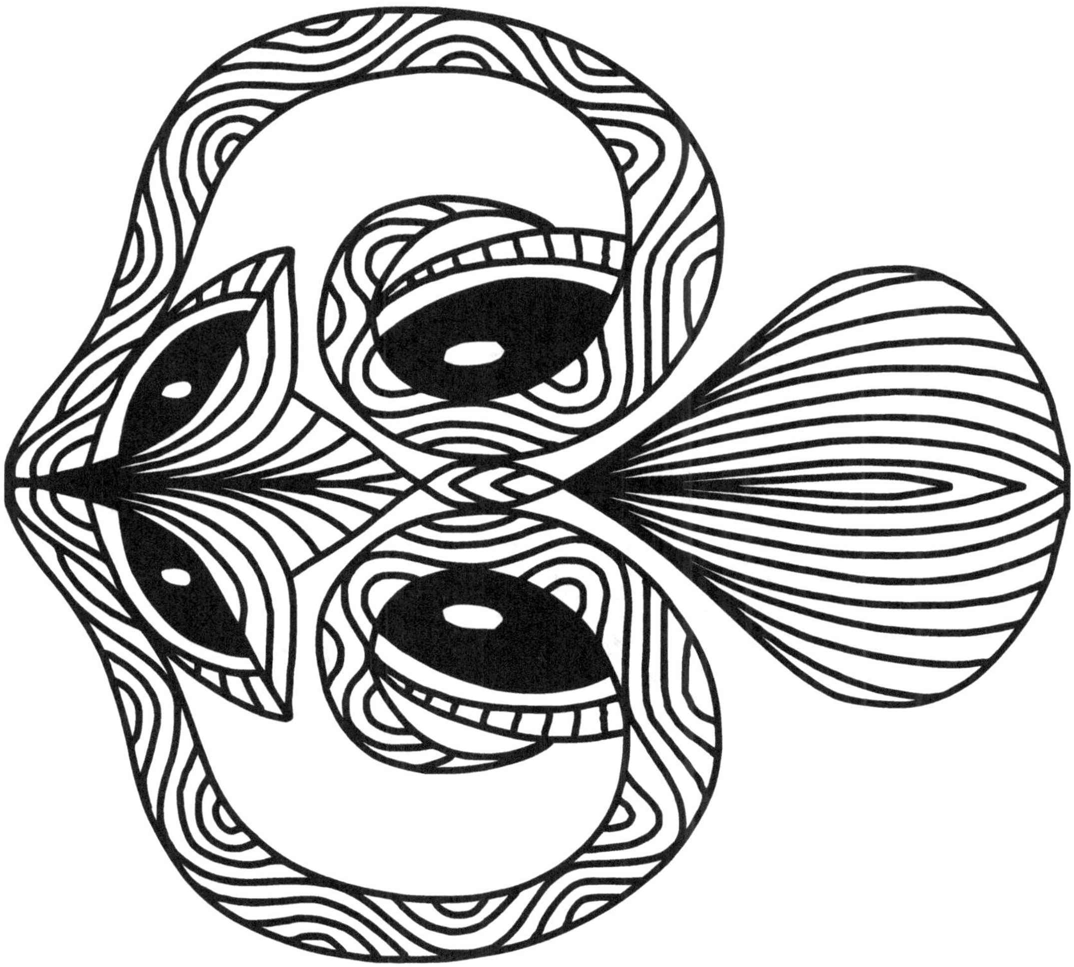

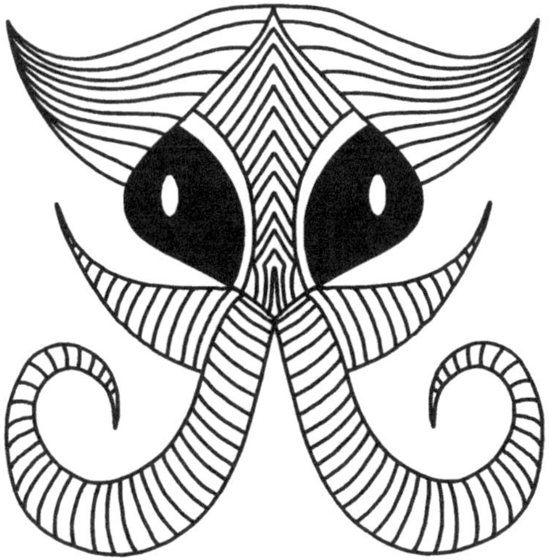

FATLINER WEIRDIES
VOLUME 1

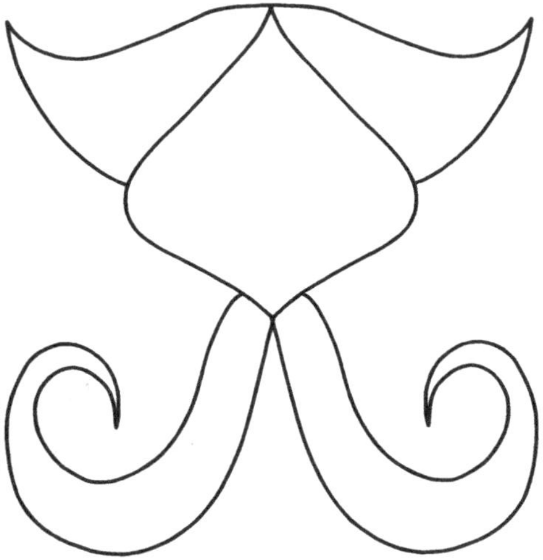

FATLINER WEIRDIES
THE TEMPLATES 1

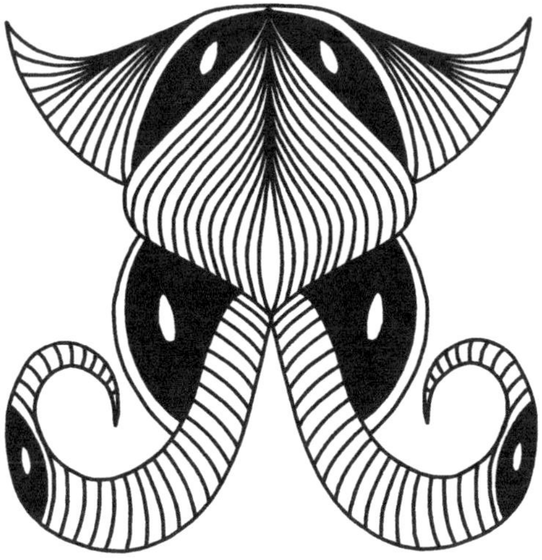

FATLINER WEIRDIES
VOLUME 3

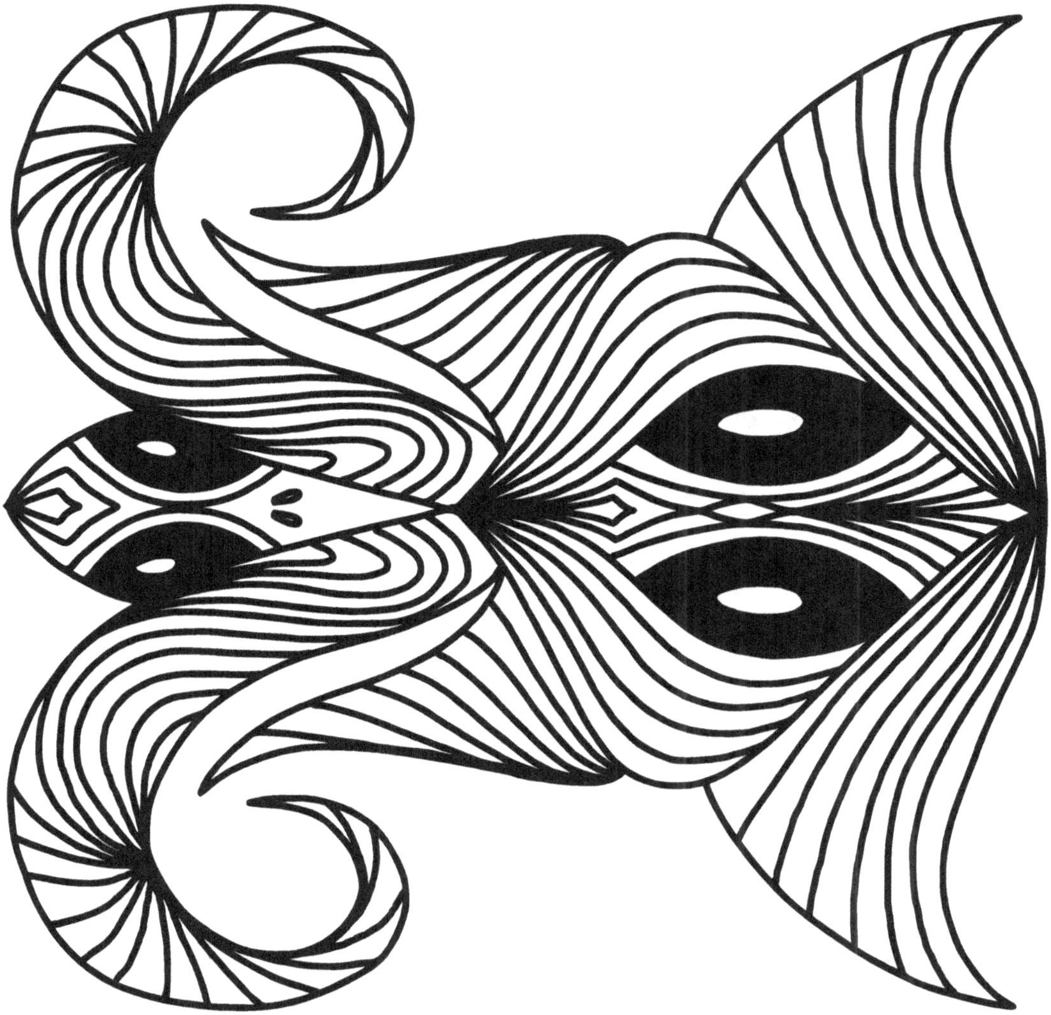

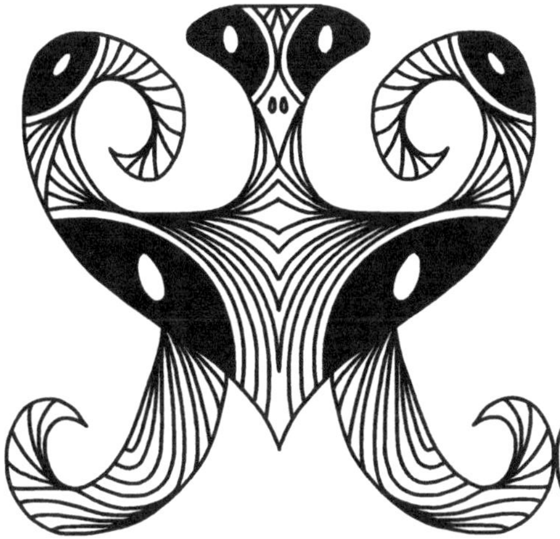

FATLINER WEIRDIES
VOLUME 1

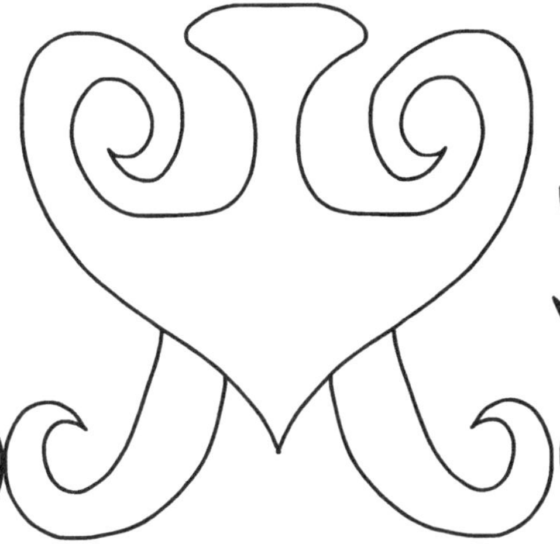

FATLINER WEIRDIES
THE TEMPLATES 1

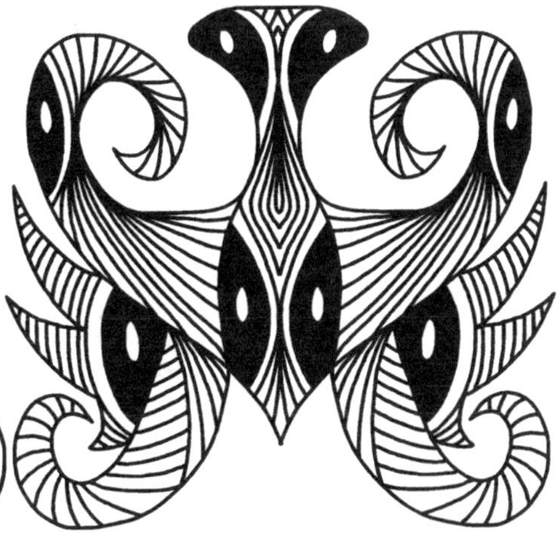

FATLINER WEIRDIES
VOLUME 3

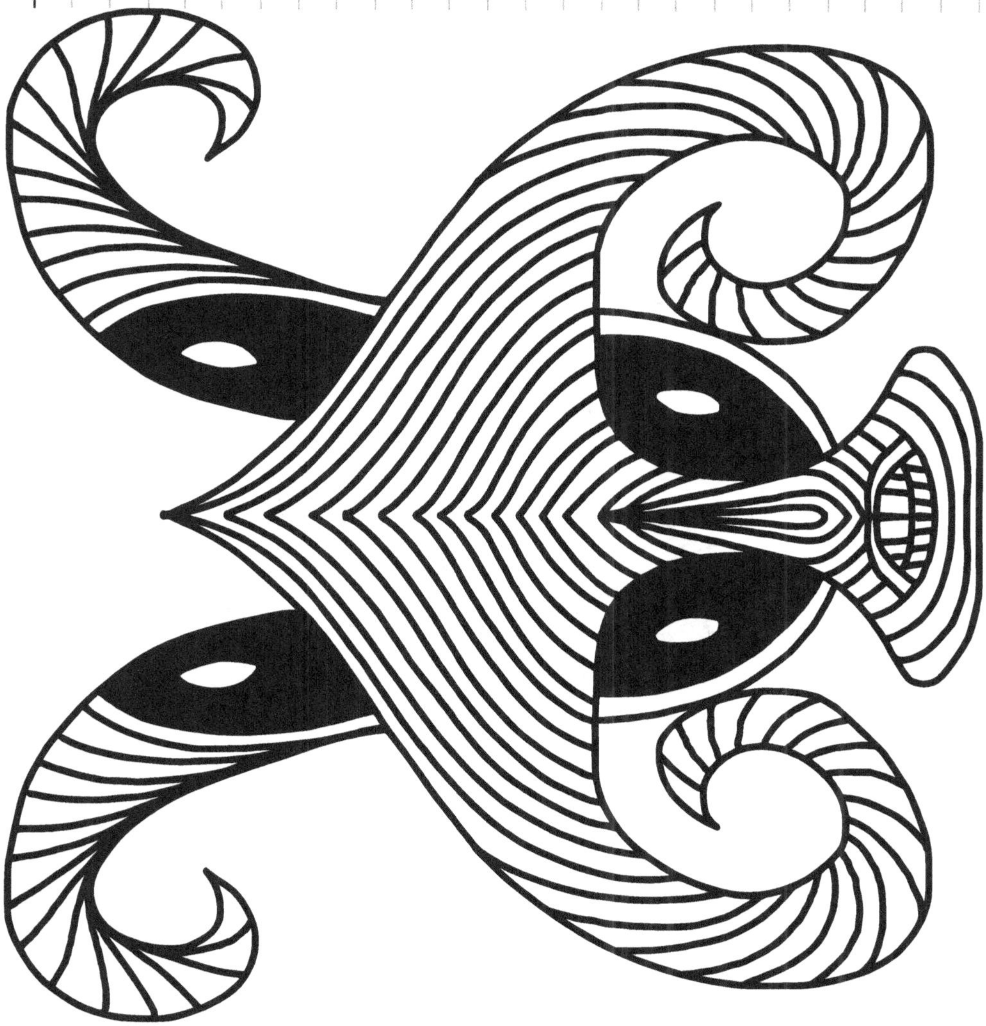

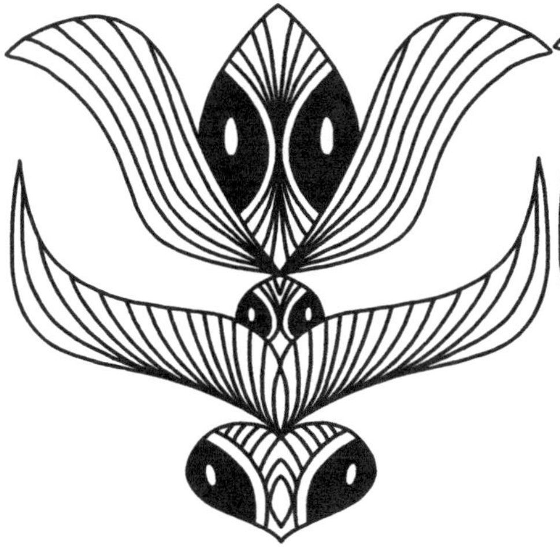

FATLINER WEIRDIES
VOLUME 1

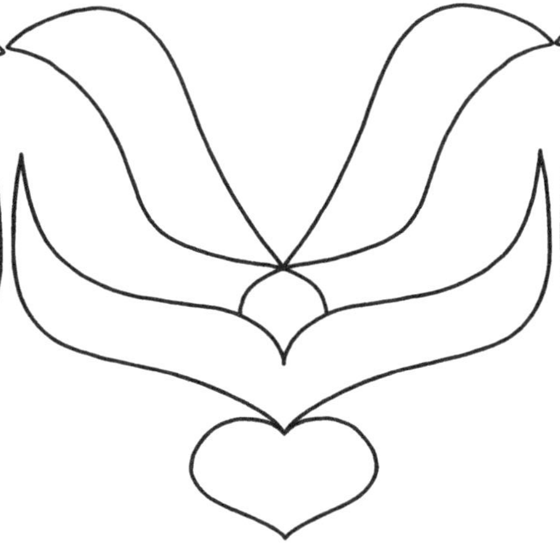

FATLINER WEIRDIES
THE TEMPLATES 1

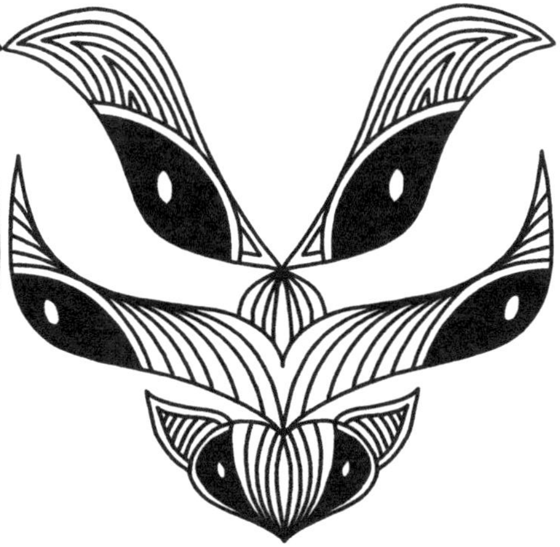

FATLINER WEIRDIES
VOLUME 3

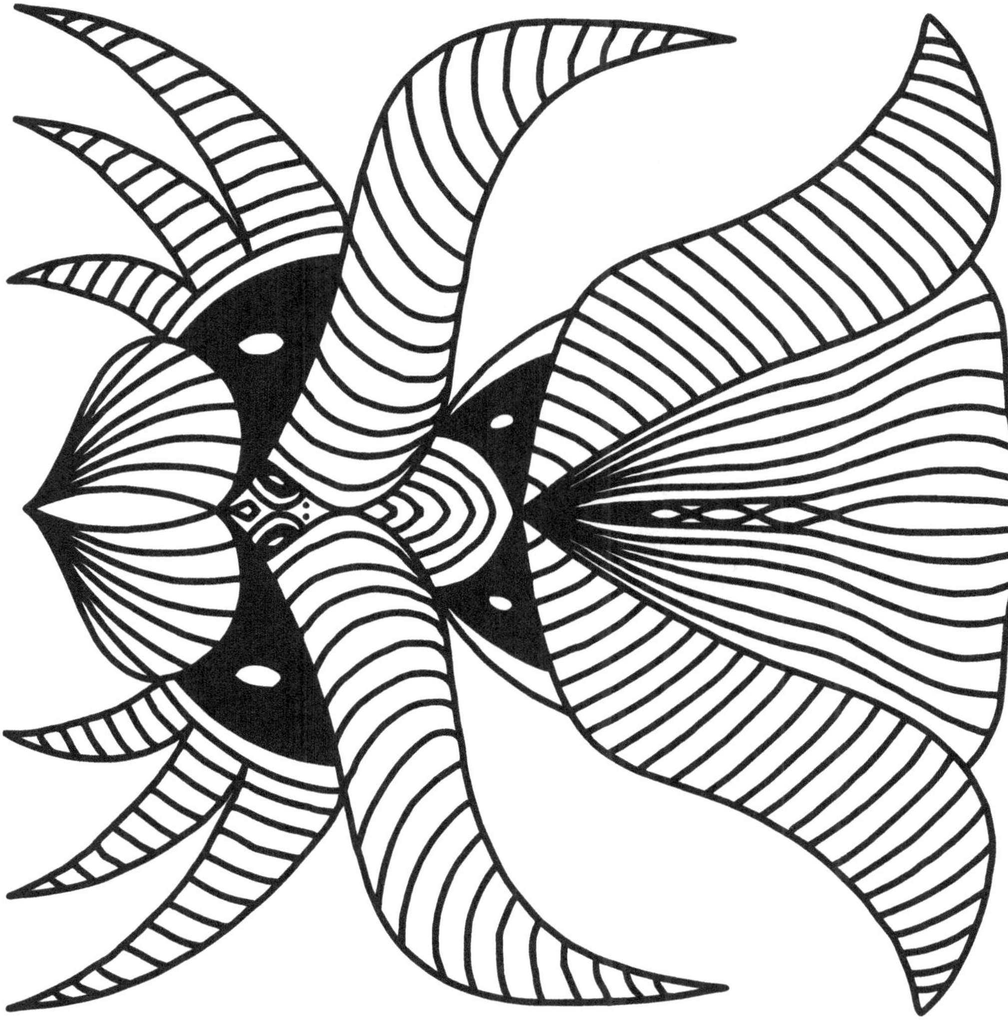

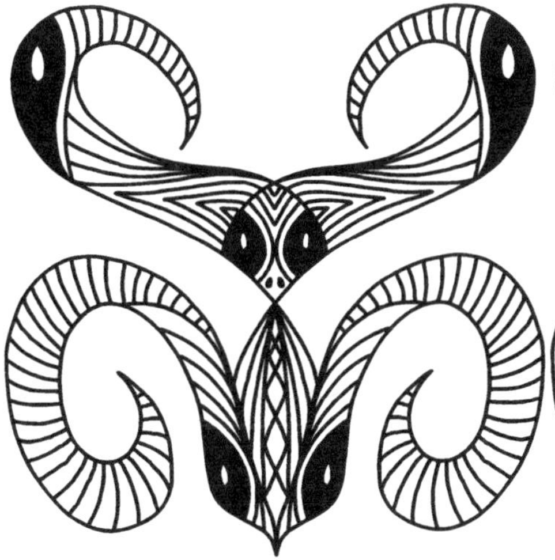

FATLINER WEIRDIES
VOLUME 1

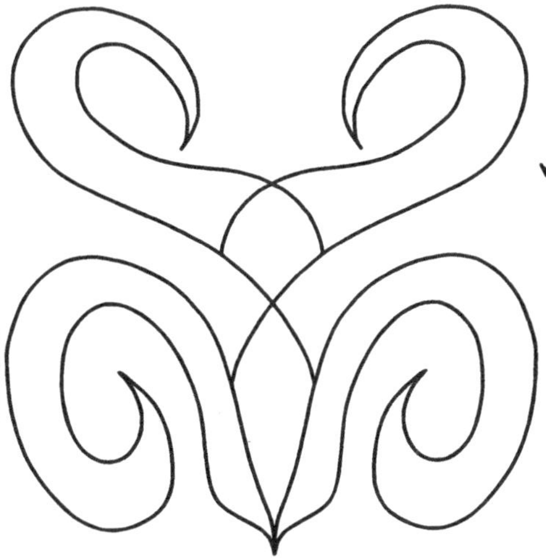

FATLINER WEIRDIES
THE TEMPLATES 1

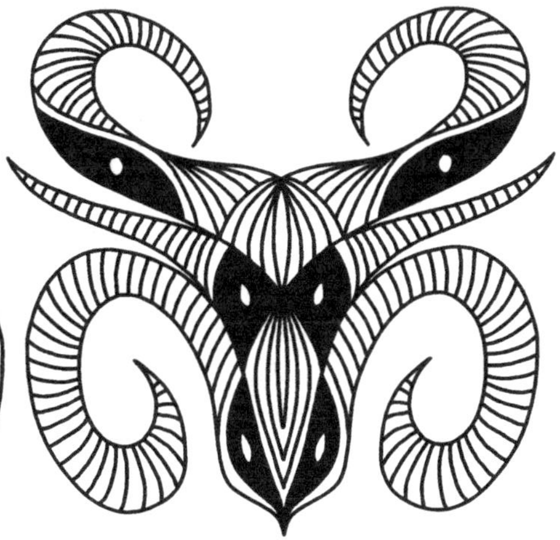

FATLINER WEIRDIES
VOLUME 3

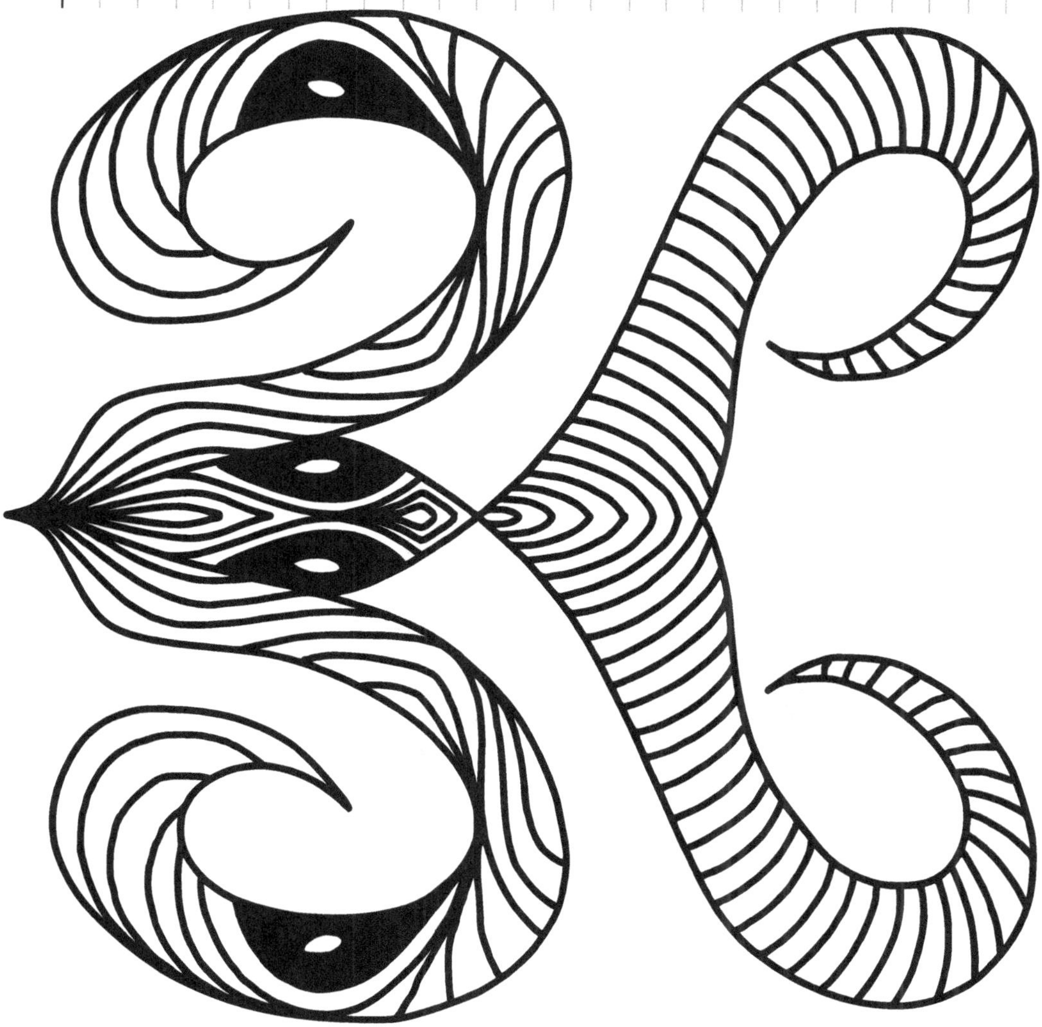

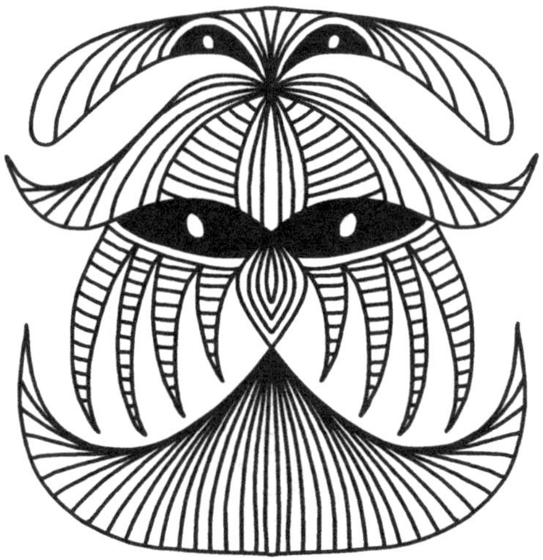

FATLINER WEIRDIES
VOLUME 1

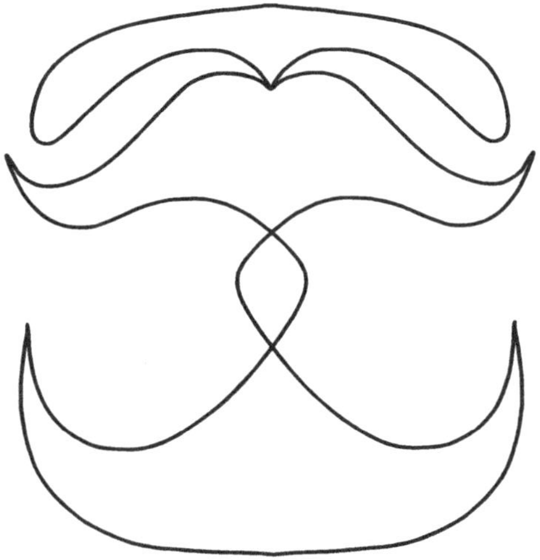

FATLINER WEIRDIES
THE TEMPLATES 1

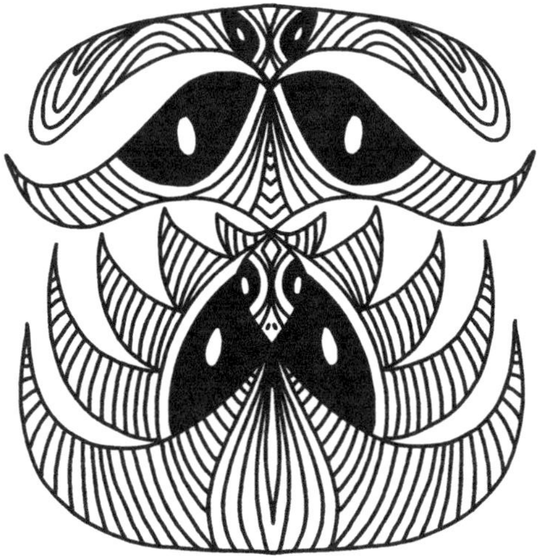

FATLINER WEIRDIES
VOLUME 3

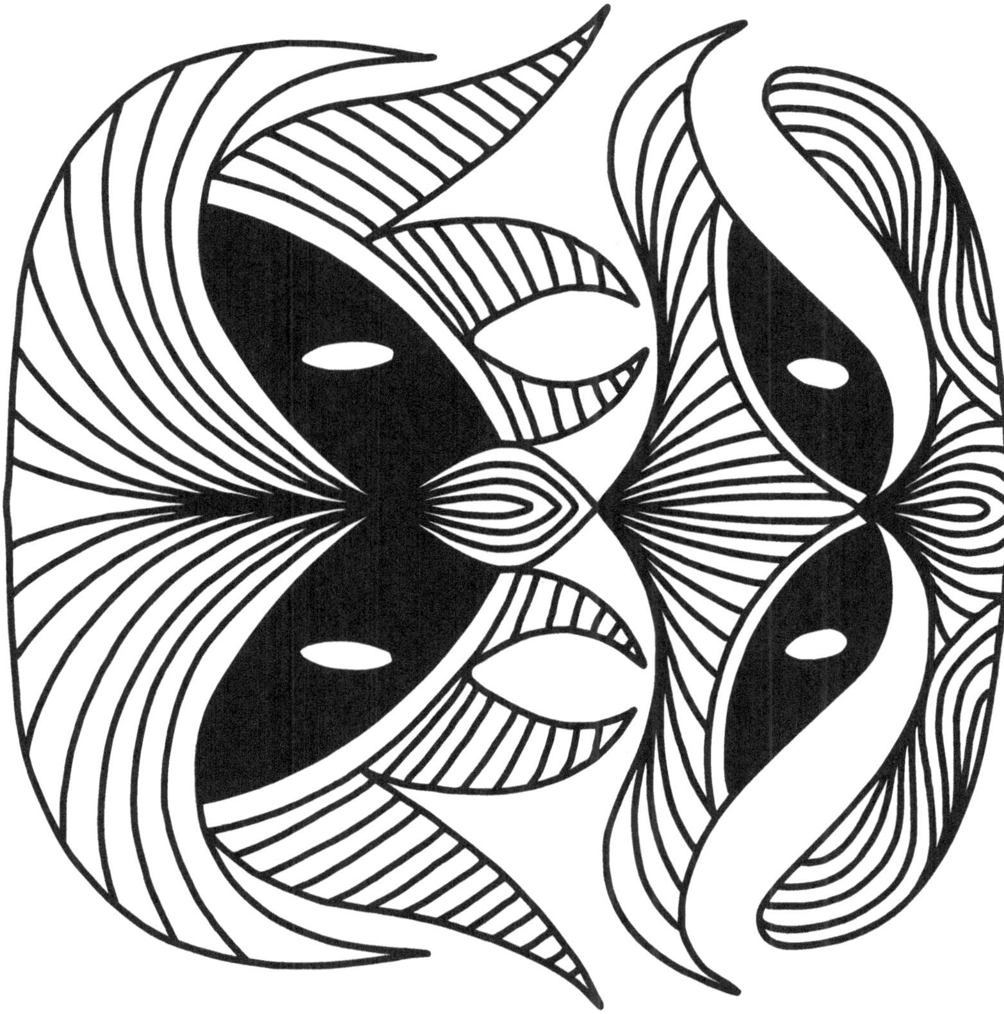

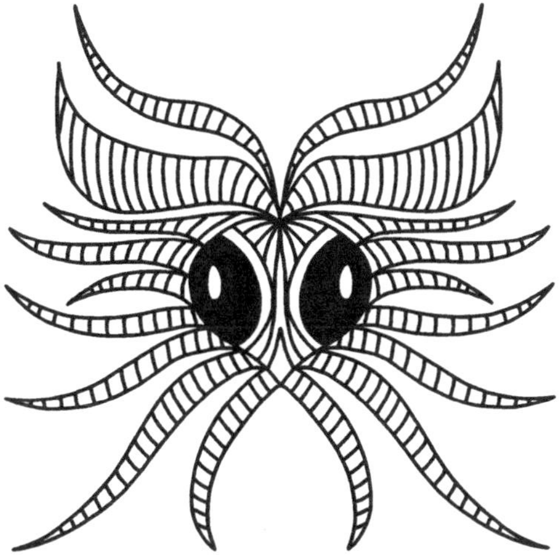

FATLINER WEIRDIES
VOLUME 1

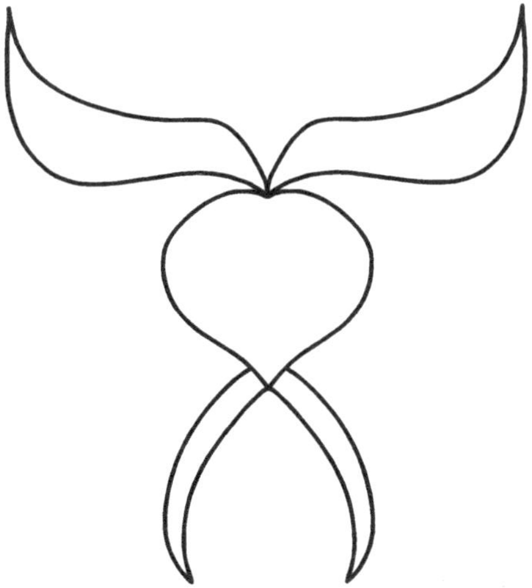

FATLINER WEIRDIES
THE TEMPLATES 1

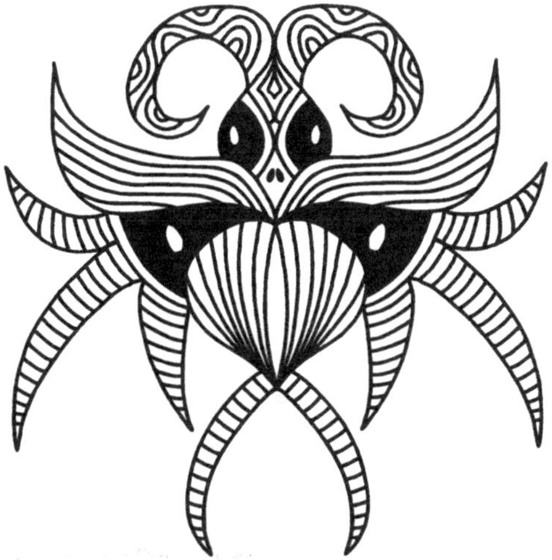

FATLINER WEIRDIES
VOLUME 3

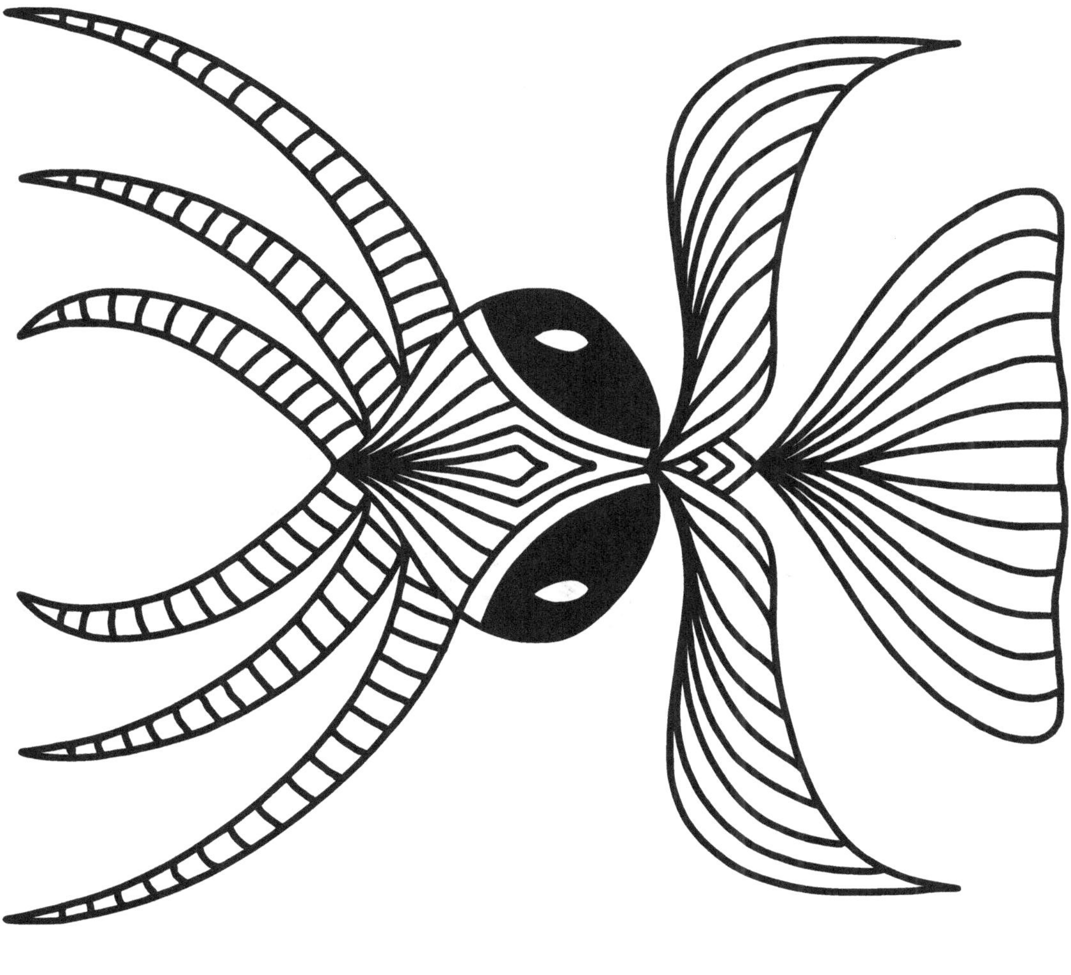

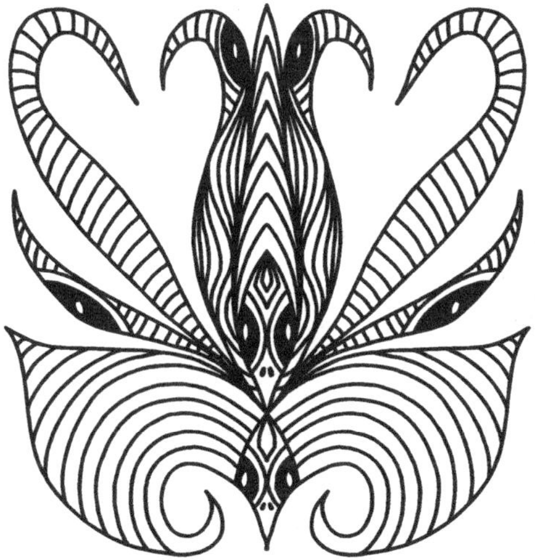

FATLINER WEIRDIES
VOLUME 1

FATLINER WEIRDIES
THE TEMPLATES 1

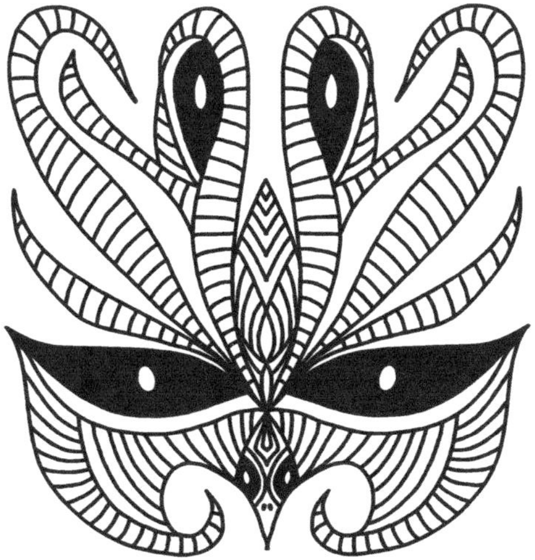

FATLINER WEIRDIES
VOLUME 3

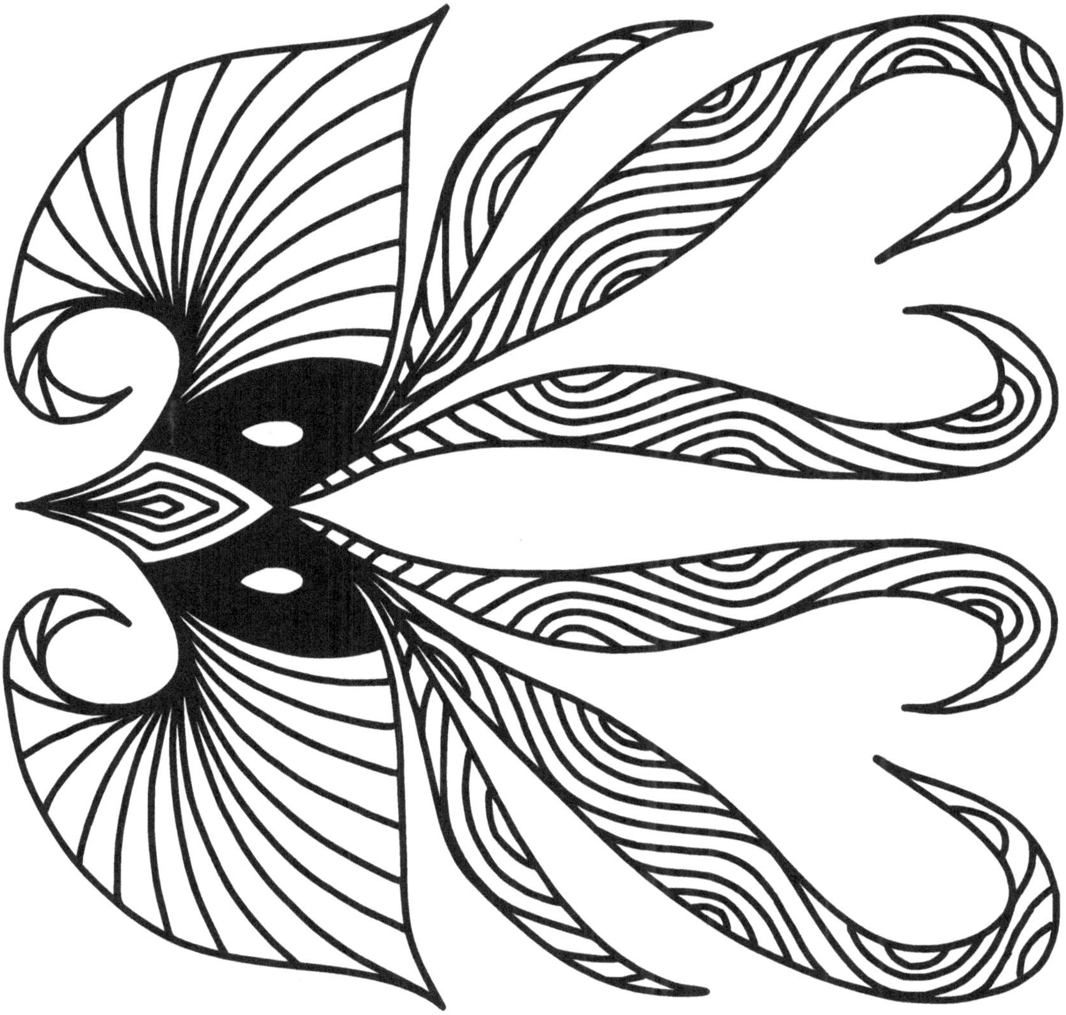

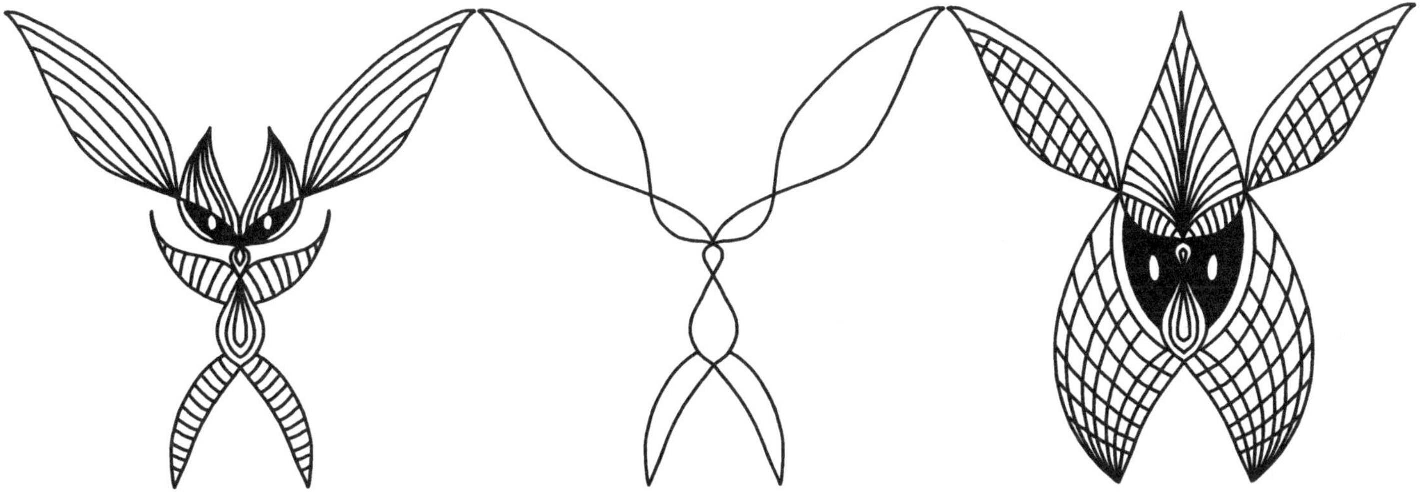

FATLINER WEIRDIES
VOLUME 1

FATLINER WEIRDIES
THE TEMPLATES 1

FATLINER WEIRDIES
VOLUME 3

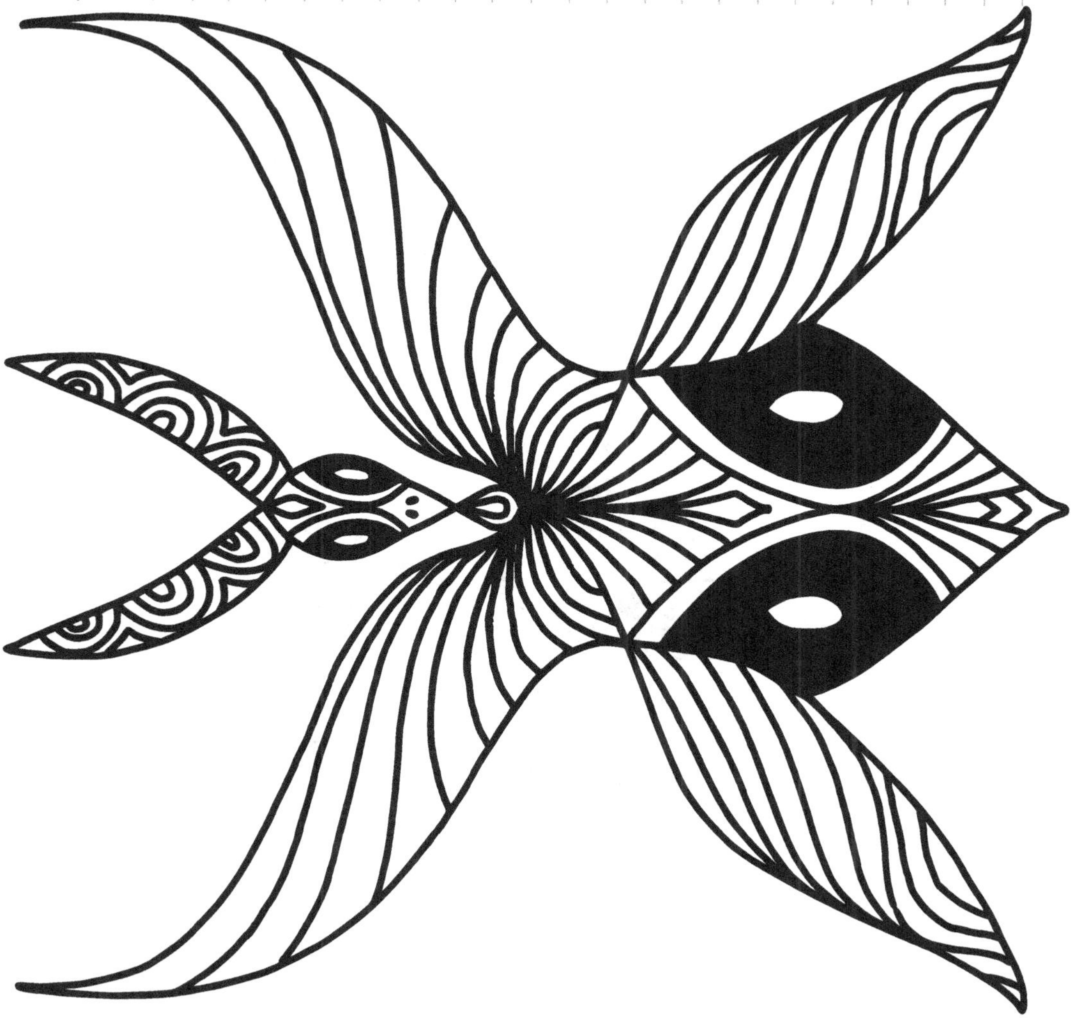

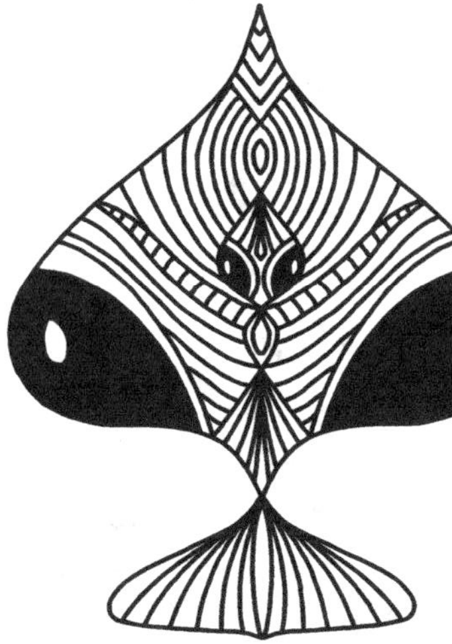

FATLINER WEIRDIES
VOLUME 1

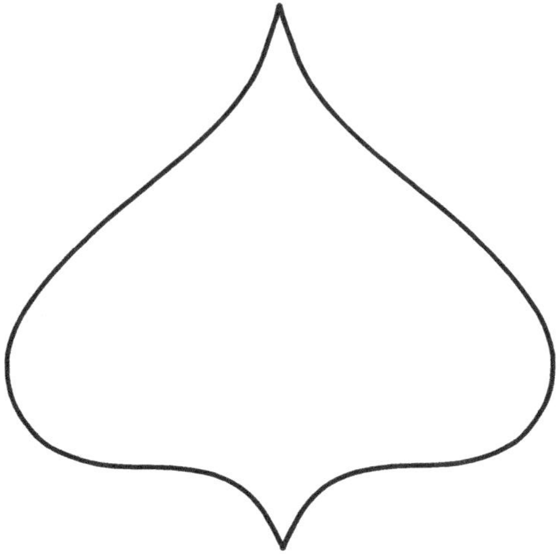

FATLINER WEIRDIES
THE TEMPLATES 1

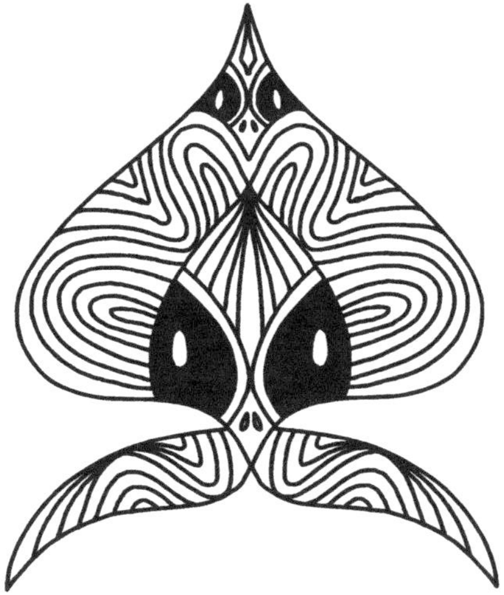

FATLINER WEIRDIES
VOLUME 3

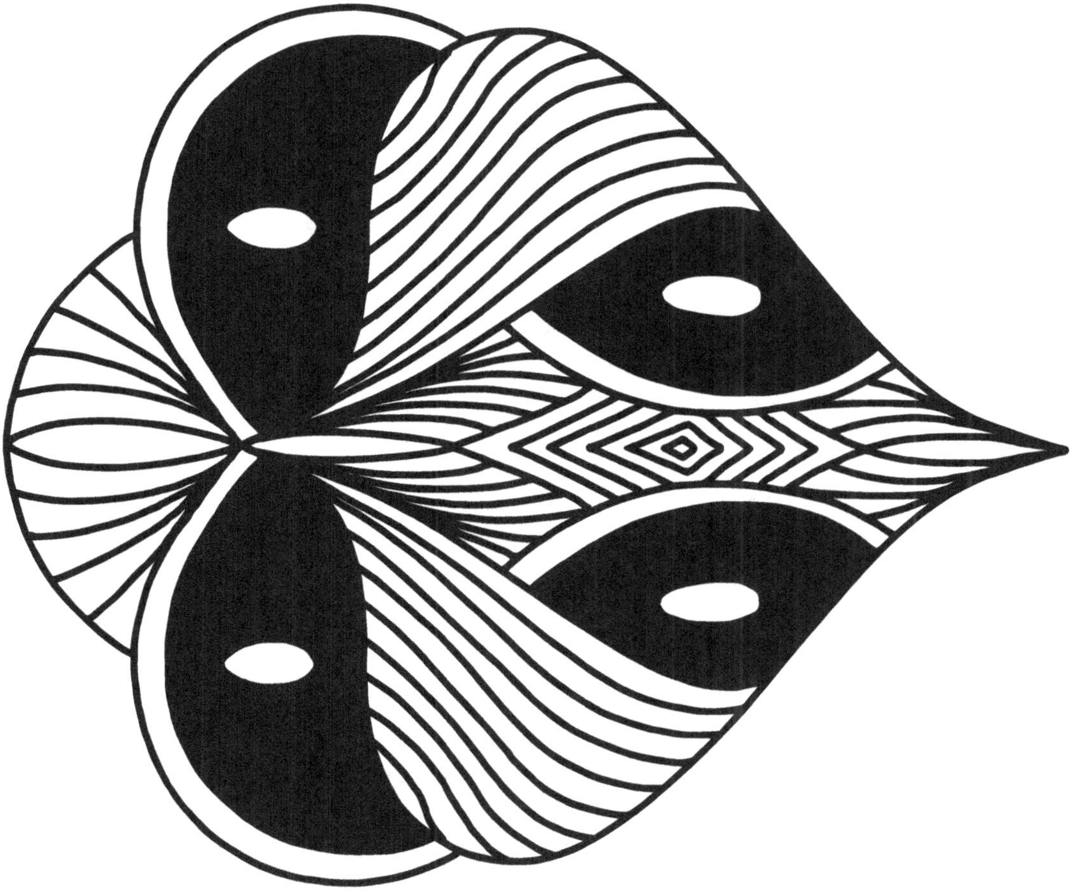

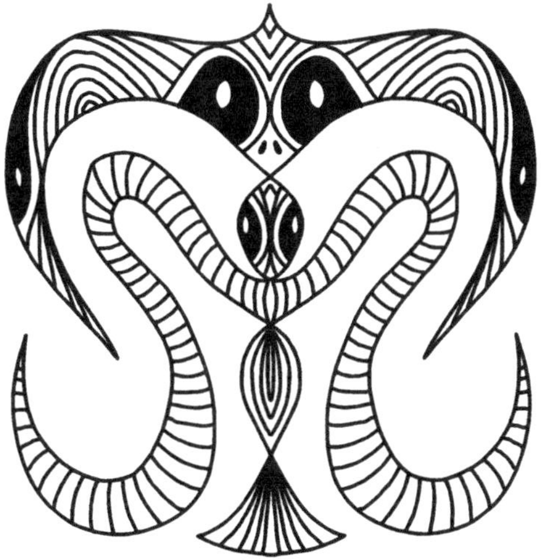

FATLINER WEIRDIES
VOLUME 1

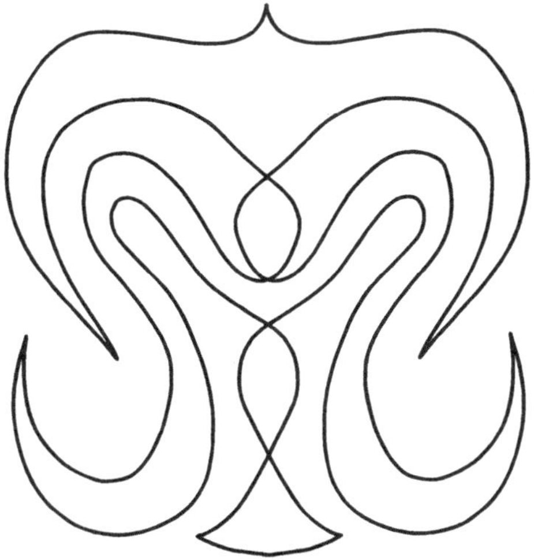

FATLINER WEIRDIES
THE TEMPLATES 1

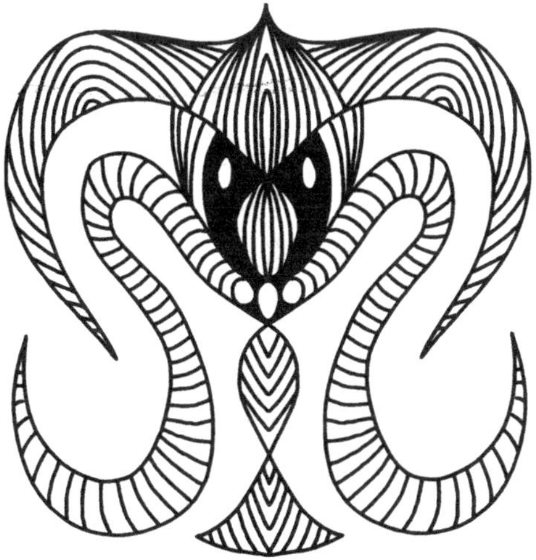

FATLINER WEIRDIES
VOLUME 3

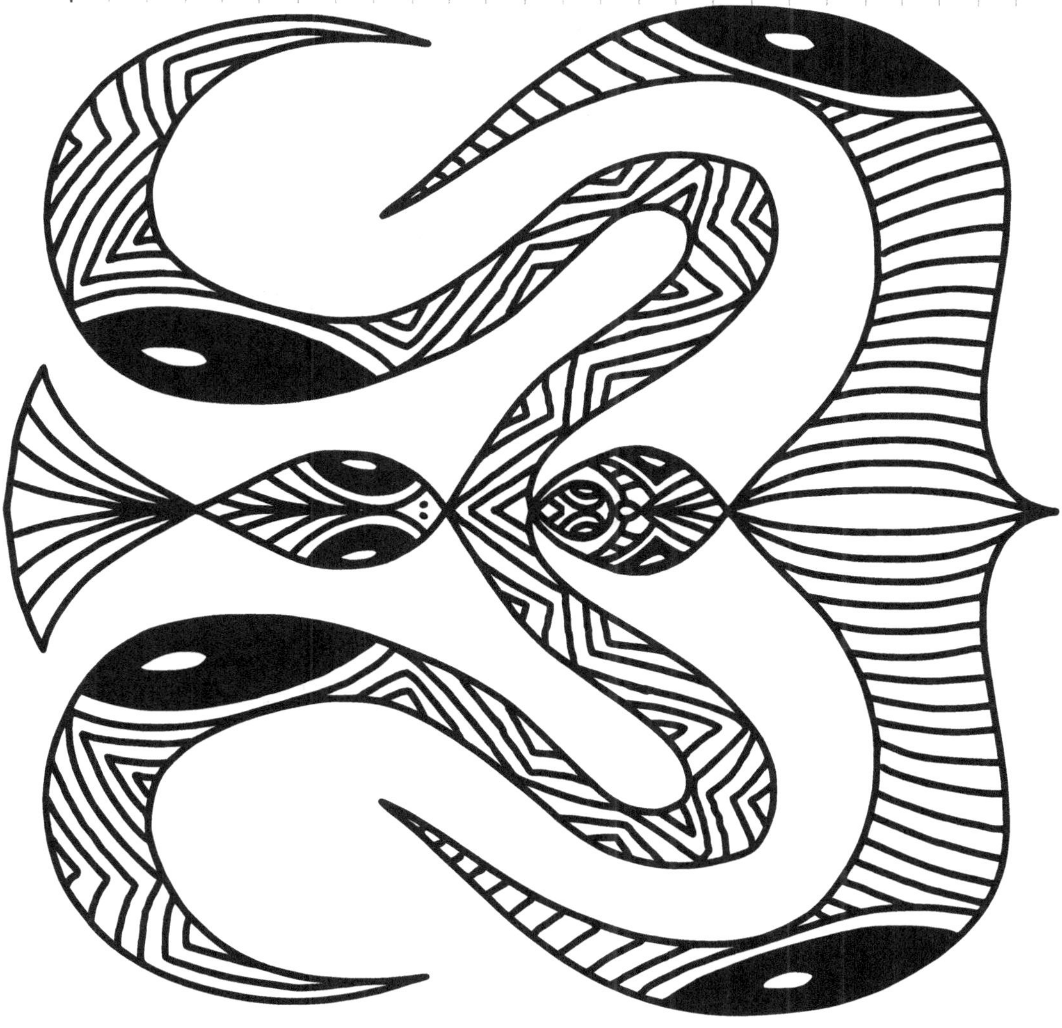

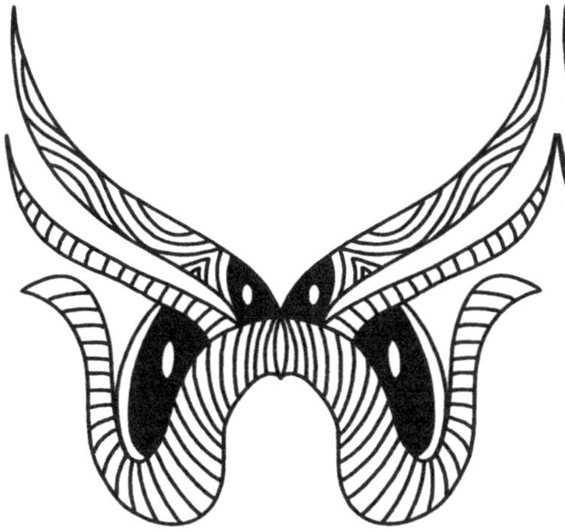

FATLINER WEIRDIES
VOLUME 1

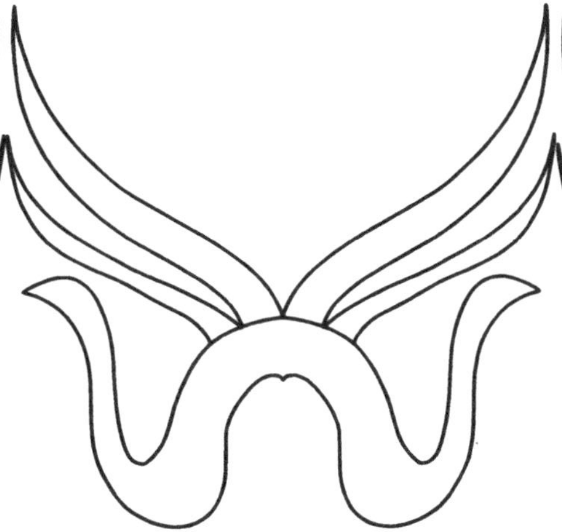

FATLINER WEIRDIES
THE TEMPLATES 1

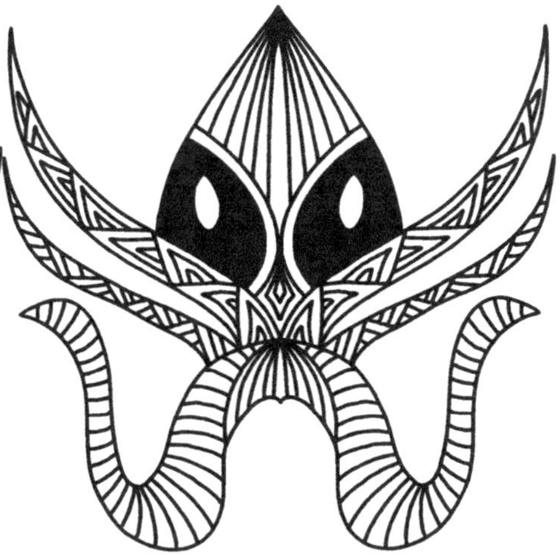

FATLINER WEIRDIES
VOLUME 3

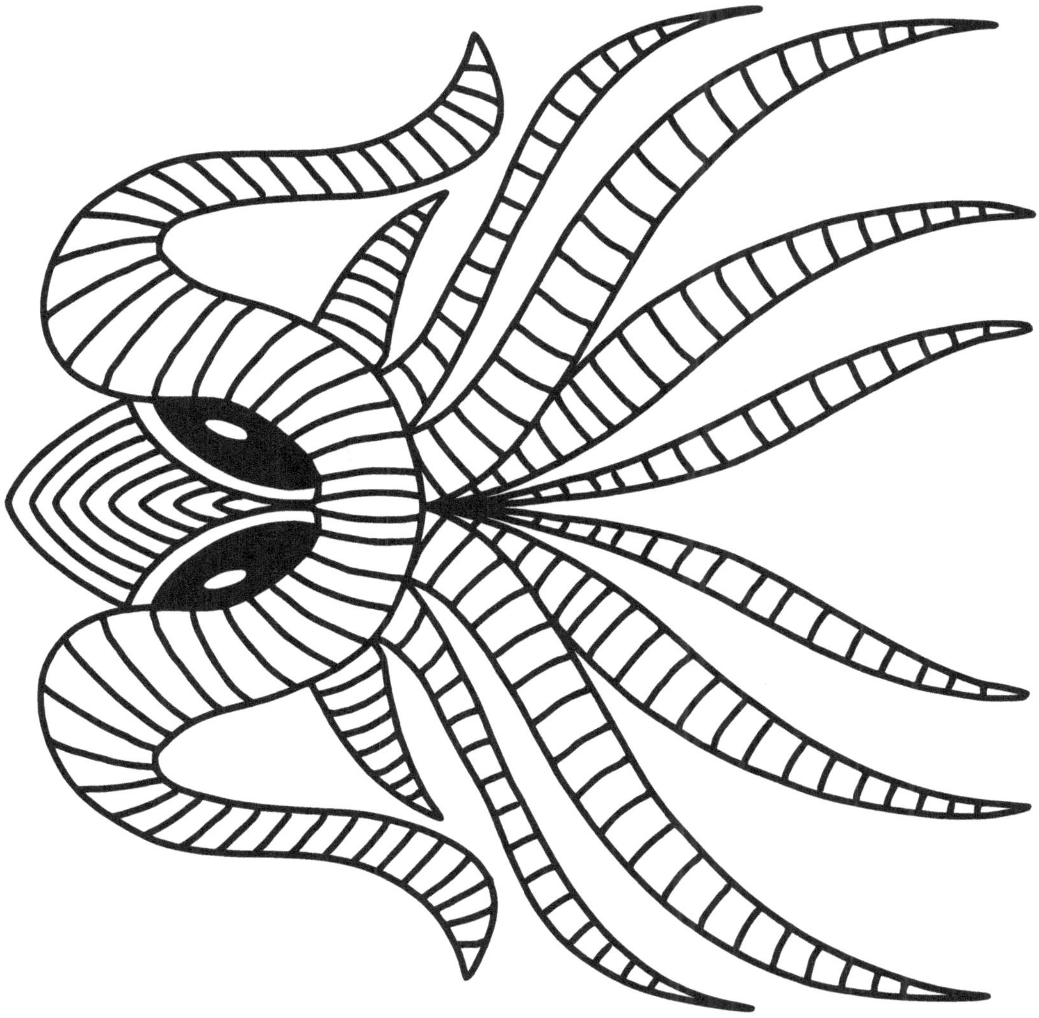

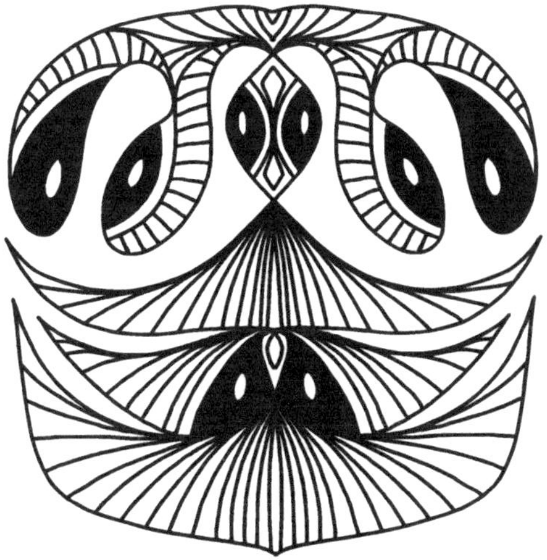

FATLINER WEIRDIES
VOLUME 1

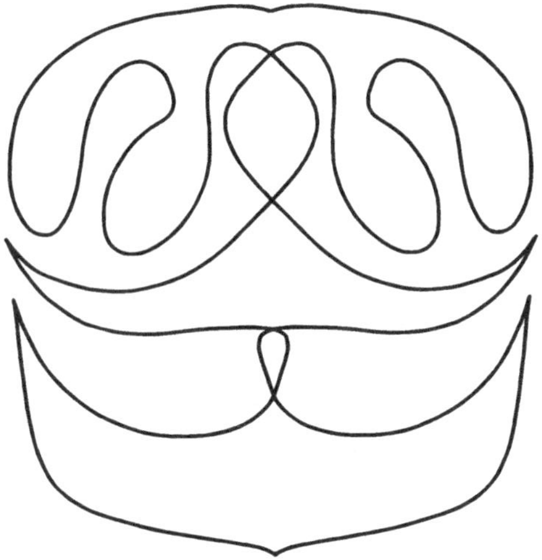

FATLINER WEIRDIES
THE TEMPLATES 1

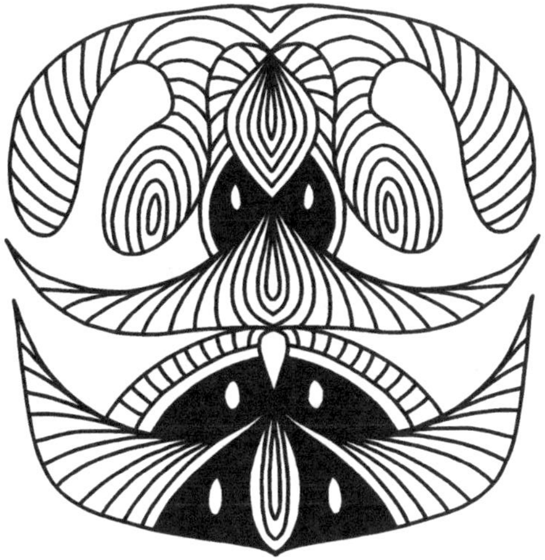

FATLINER WEIRDIES
VOLUME 3

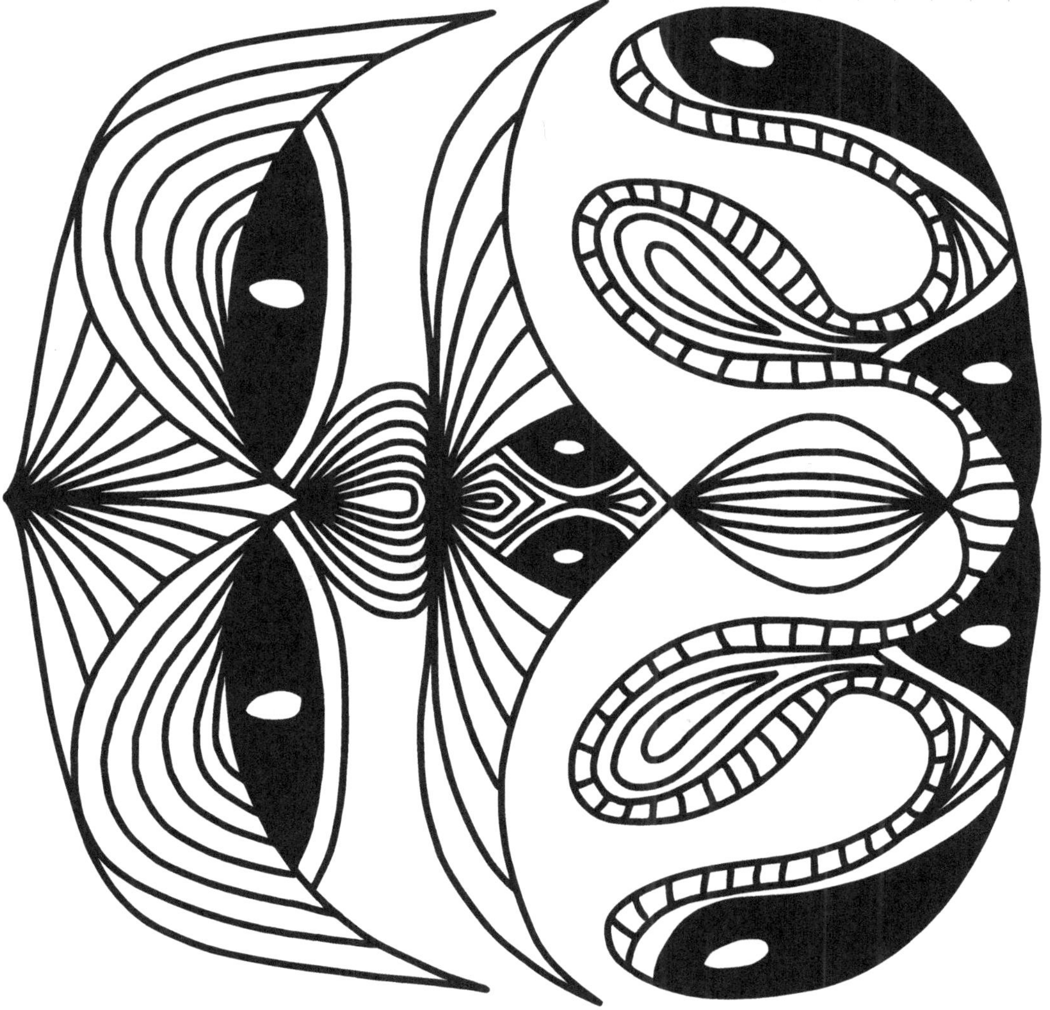

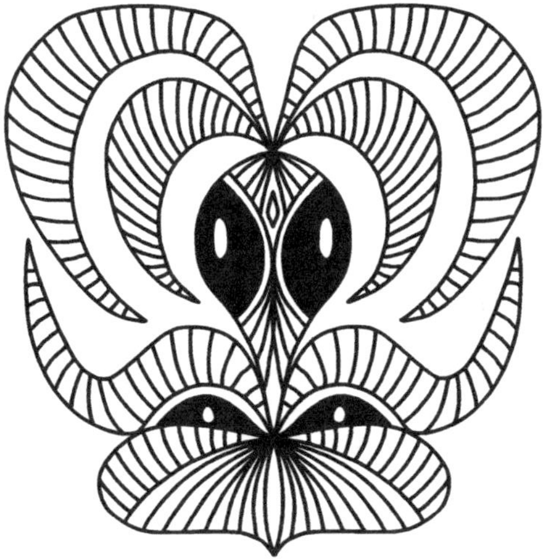

FATLINER WEIRDIES
VOLUME 1

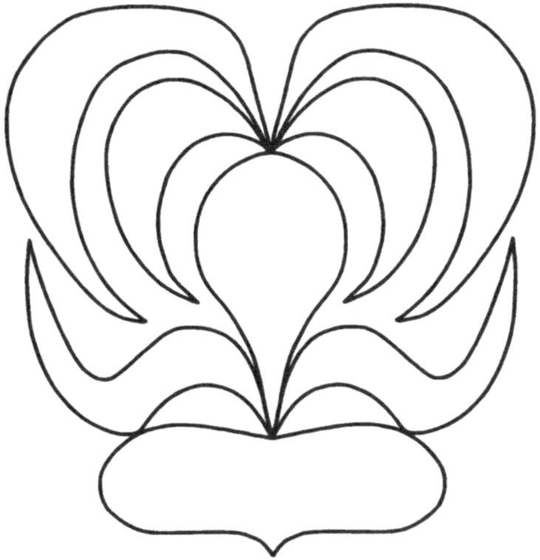

FATLINER WEIRDIES
THE TEMPLATES 1

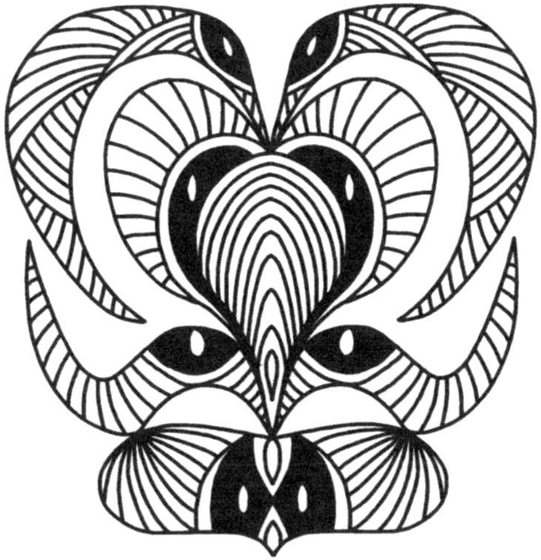

FATLINER WEIRDIES
VOLUME 3

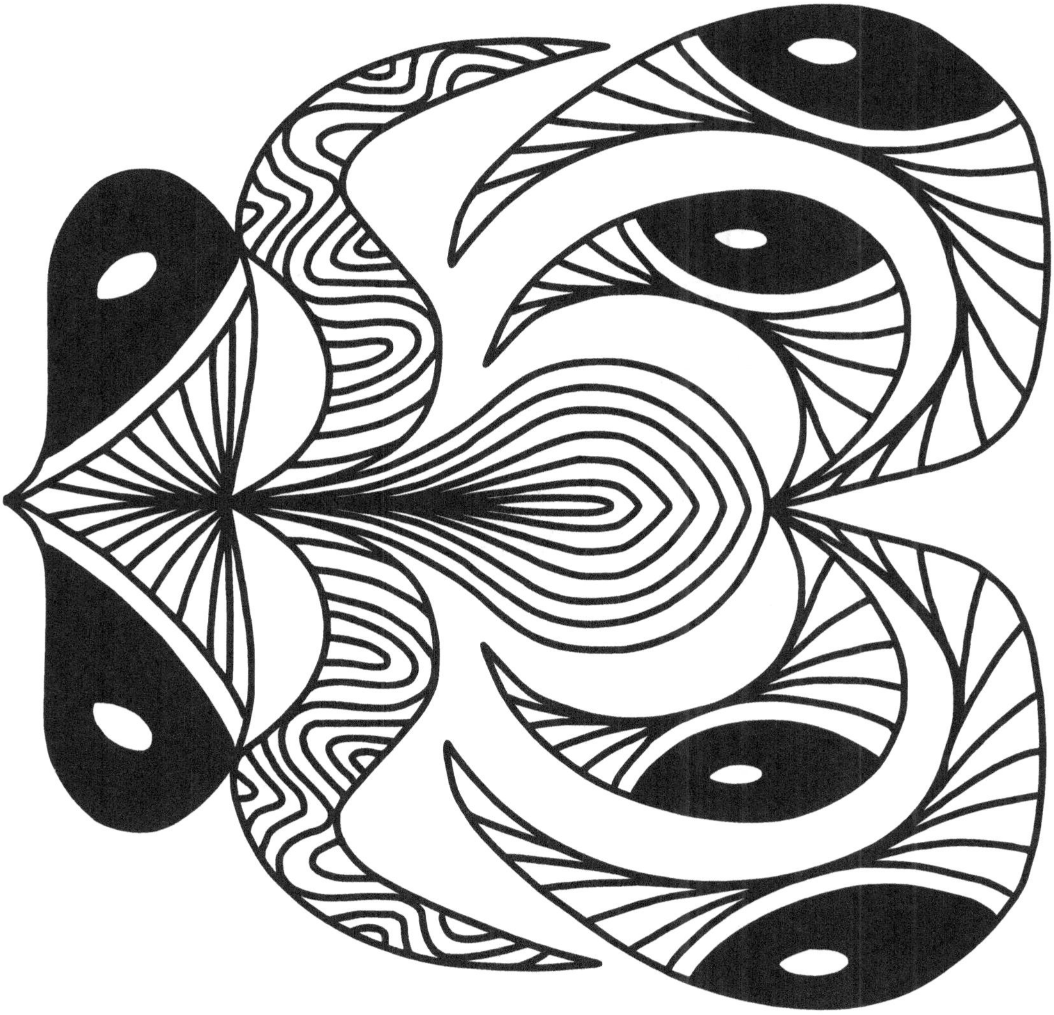

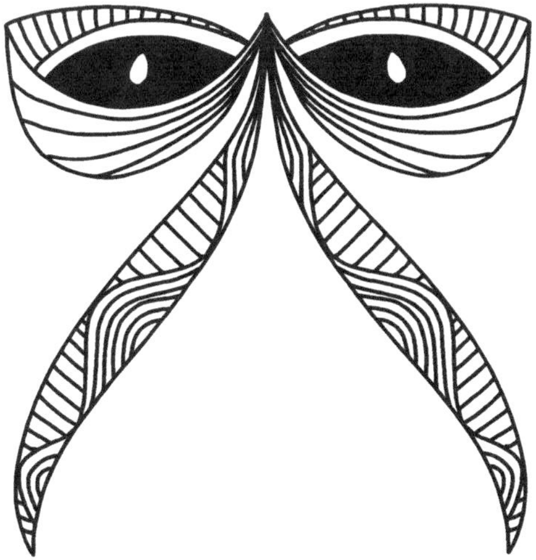

FATLINER WEIRDIES
VOLUME 1

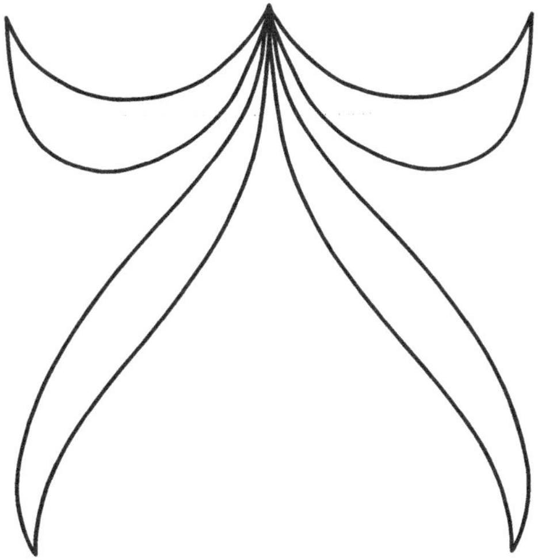

FATLINER WEIRDIES
THE TEMPLATES 1

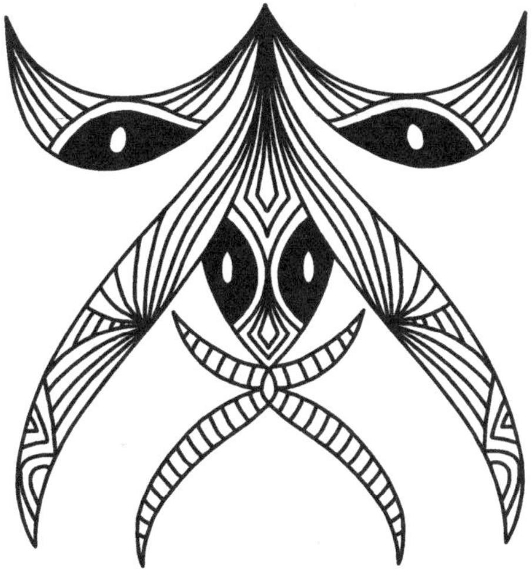

FATLINER WEIRDIES
VOLUME 3

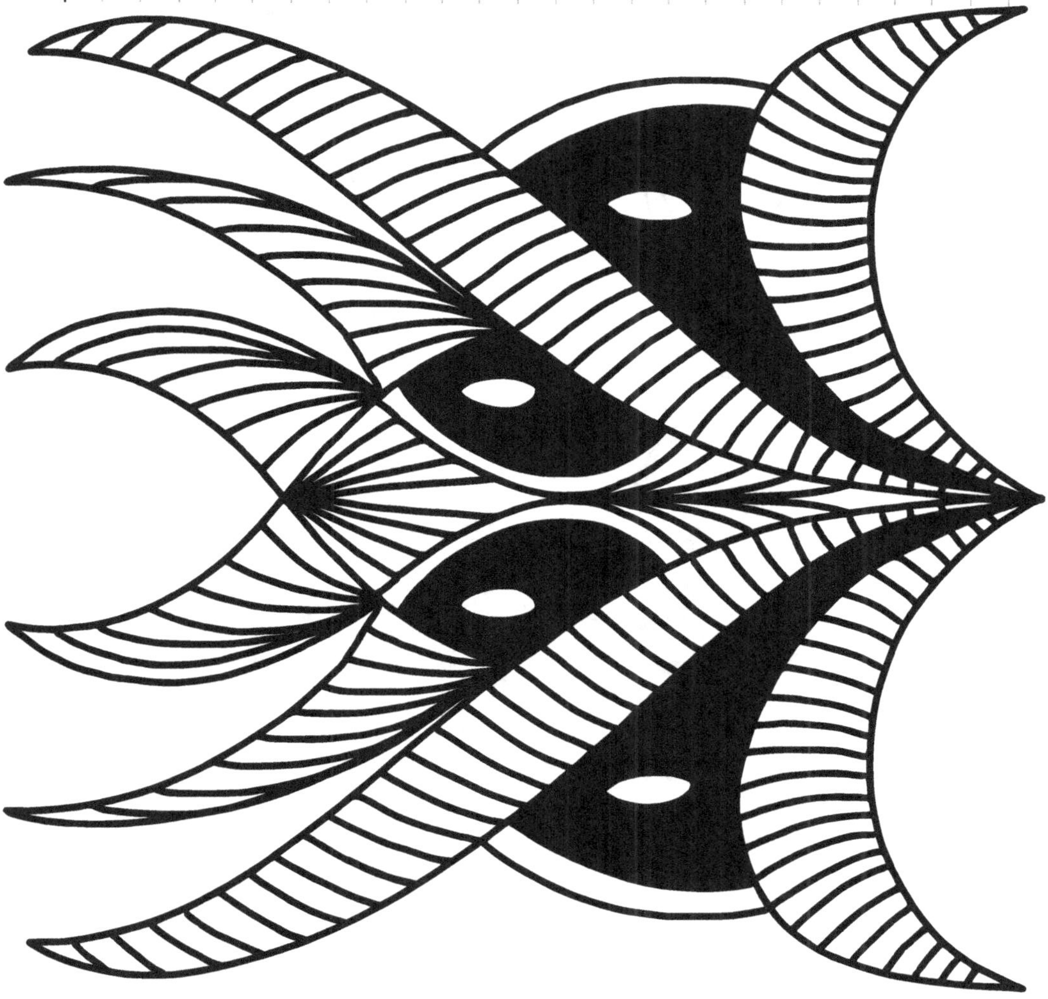

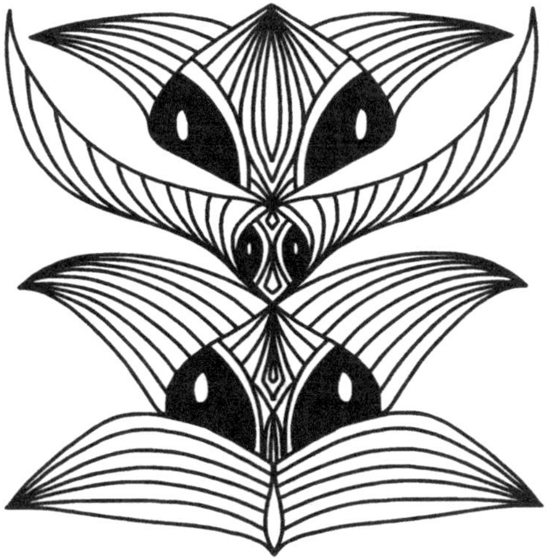

FATLINER WEIRDIES
VOLUME 1

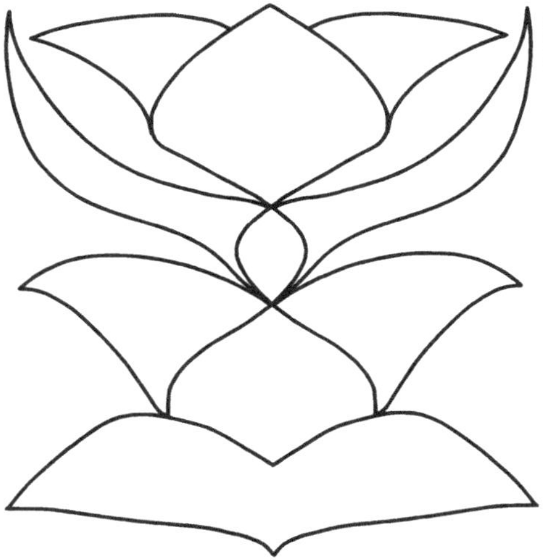

FATLINER WEIRDIES
THE TEMPLATES 1

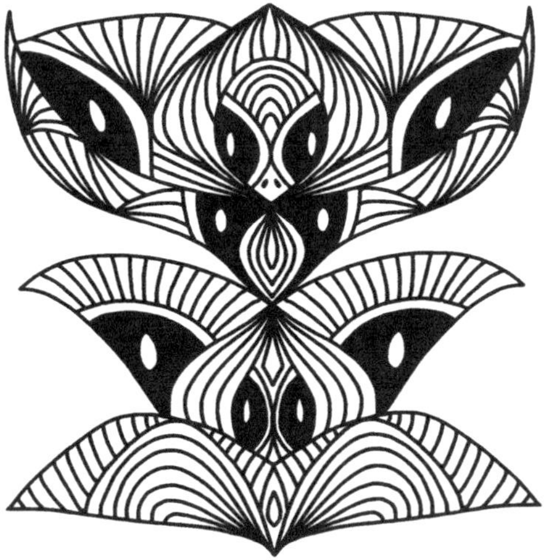

FATLINER WEIRDIES
VOLUME 3

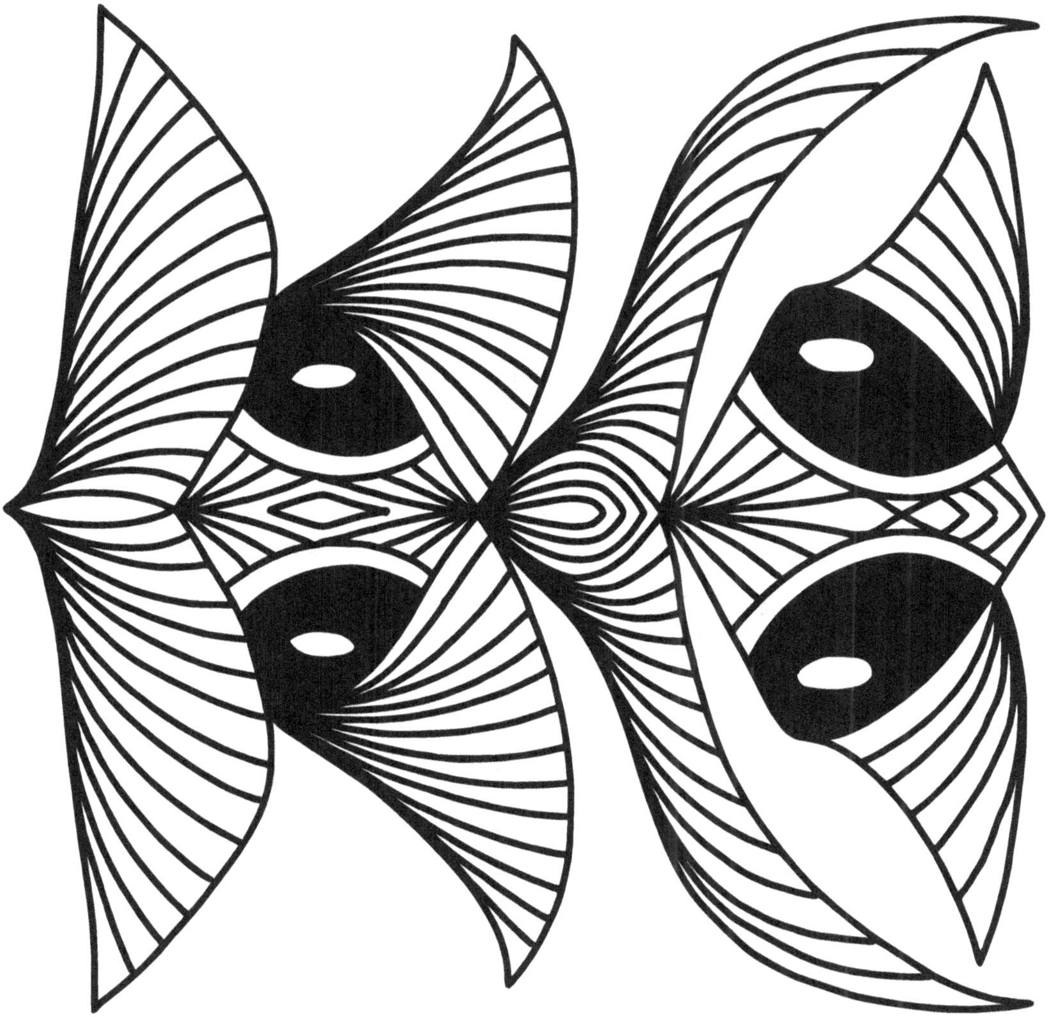

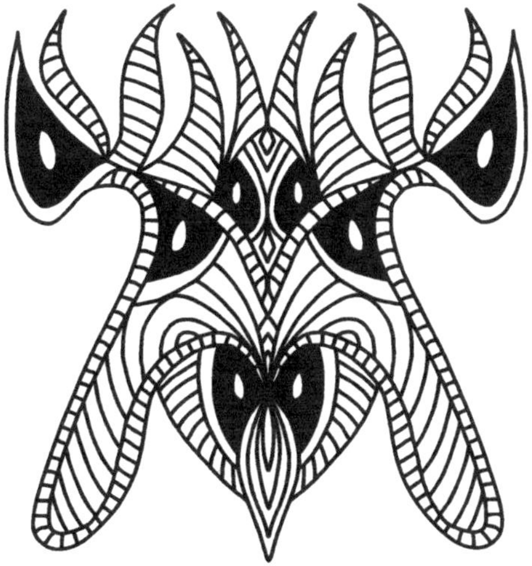

FATLINER WEIRDIES
VOLUME 1

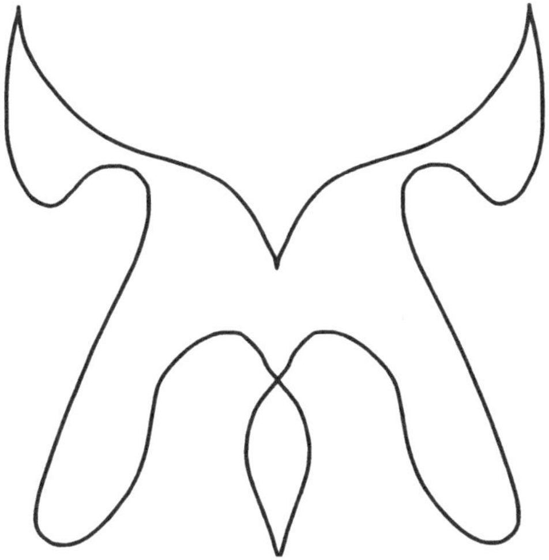

FATLINER WEIRDIES
THE TEMPLATES 1

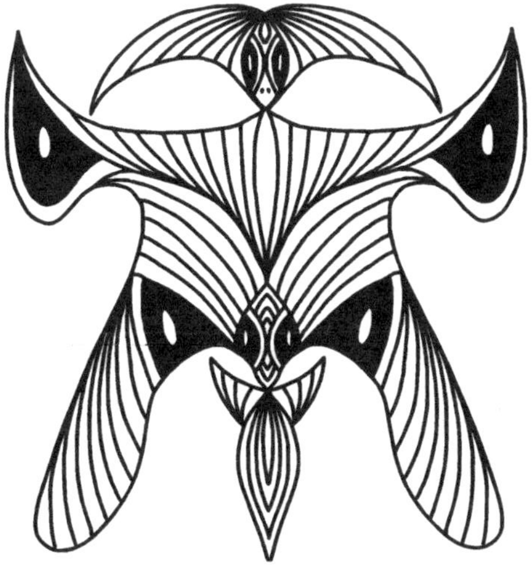

FATLINER WEIRDIES
VOLUME 3

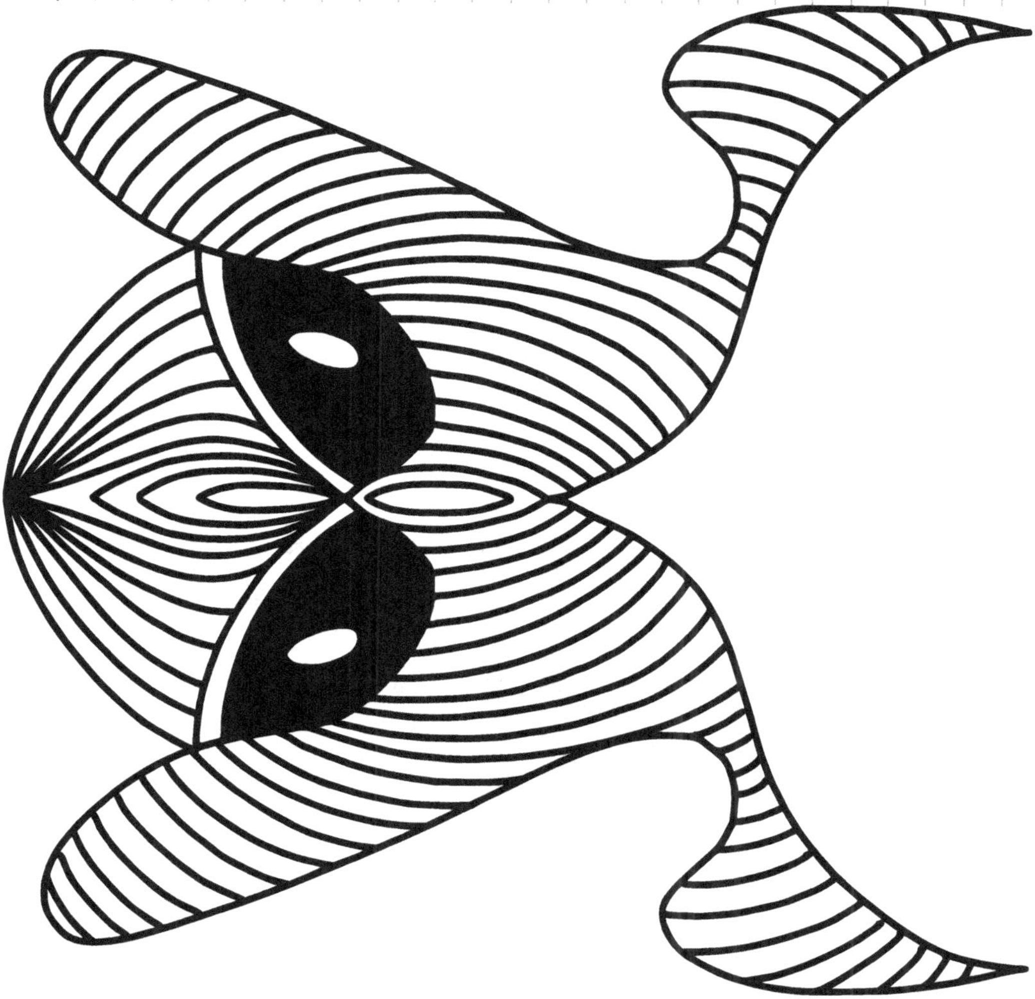

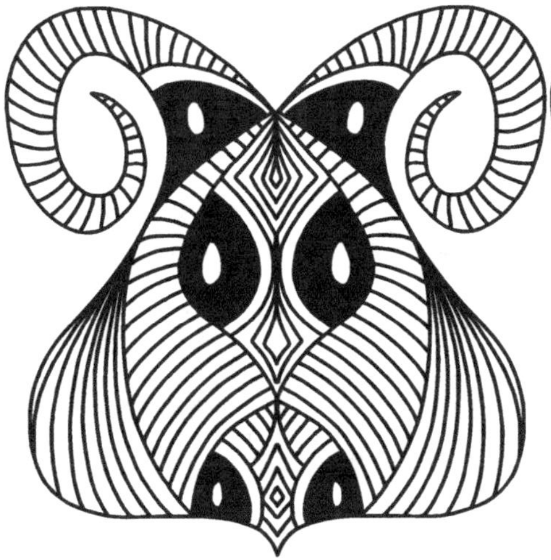

FATLINER WEIRDIES
VOLUME 1

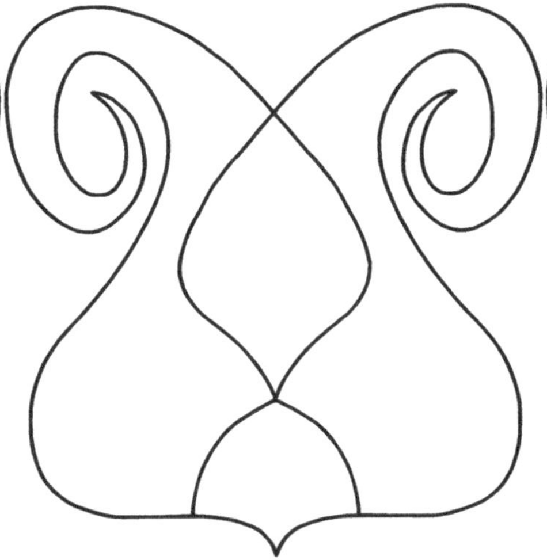

FATLINER WEIRDIES
THE TEMPLATES 1

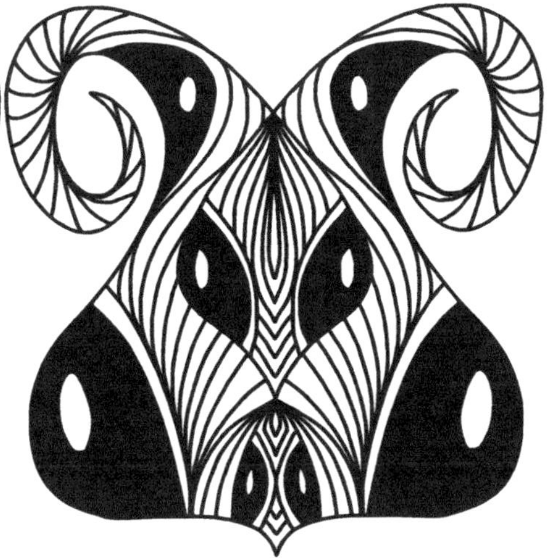

FATLINER WEIRDIES
VOLUME 3

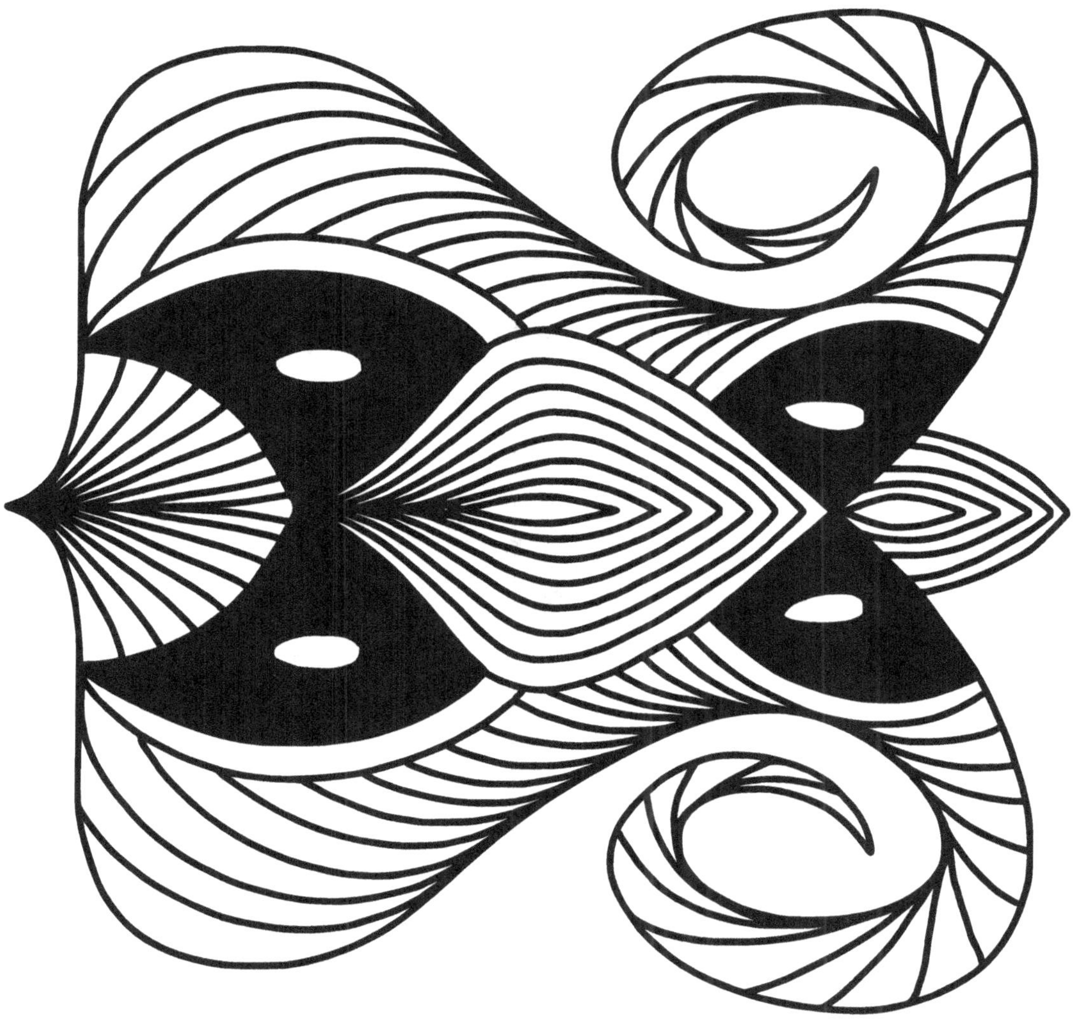

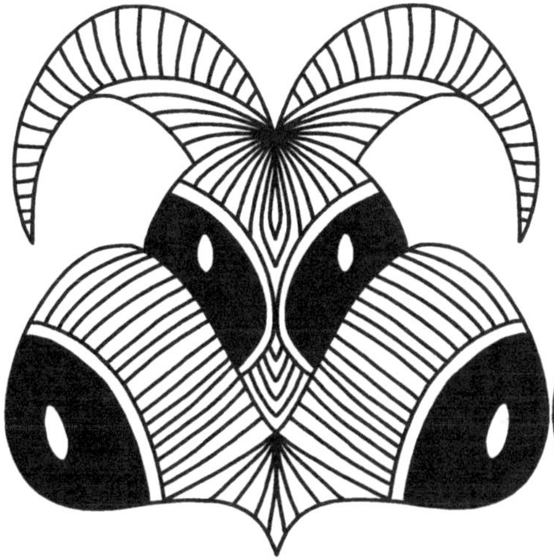

FATLINER WEIRDIES
VOLUME 1

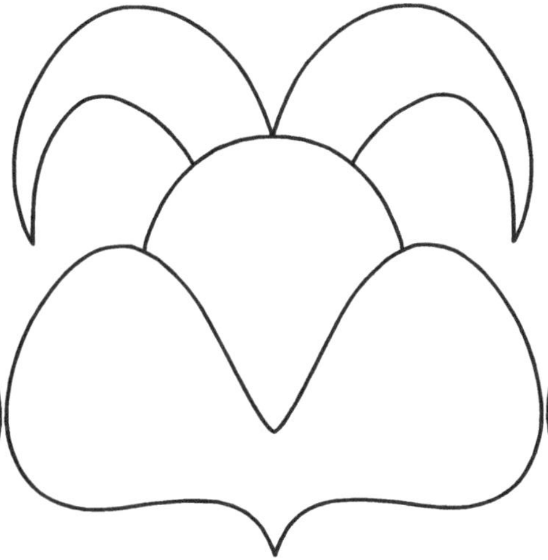

FATLINER WEIRDIES
THE TEMPLATES 1

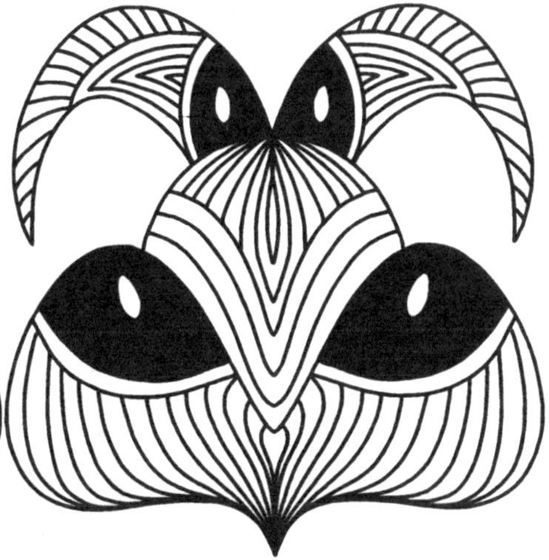

FATLINER WEIRDIES
VOLUME 3

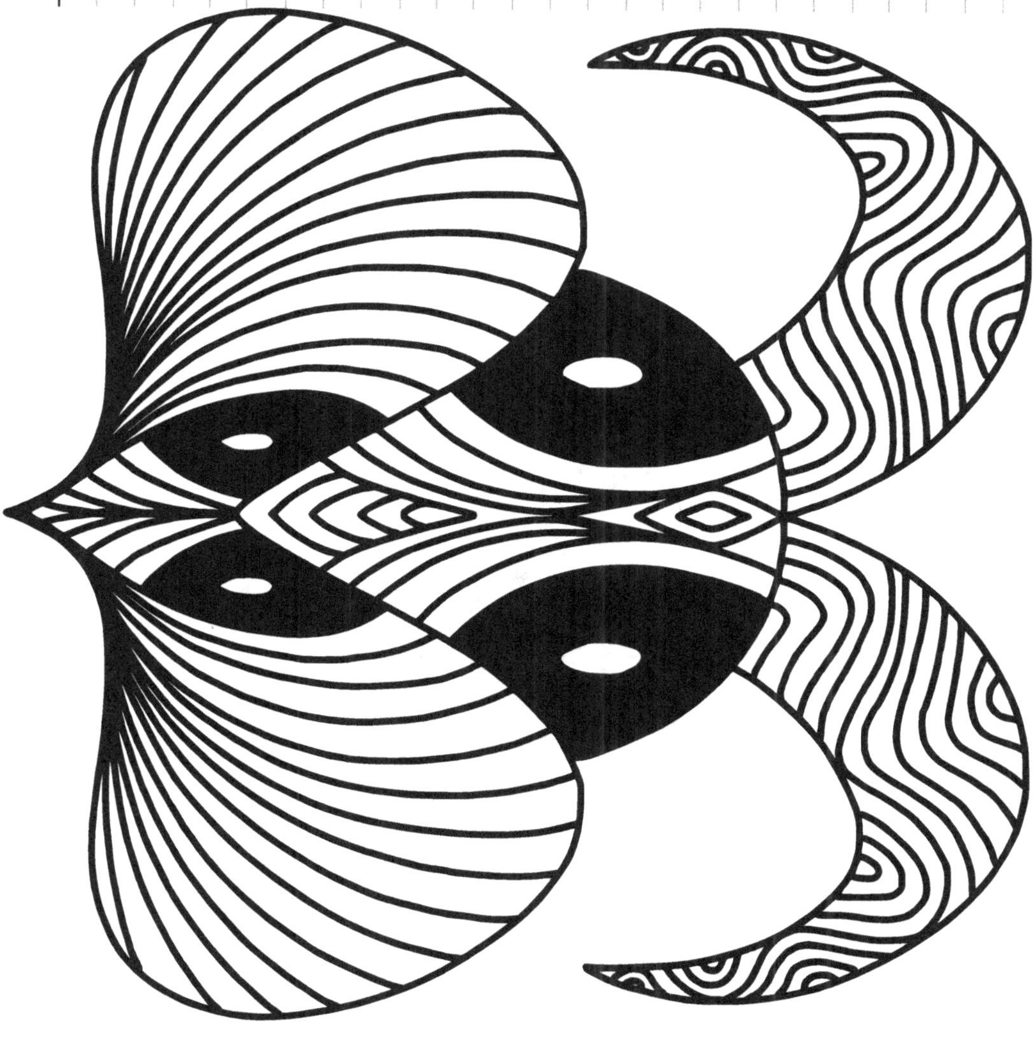

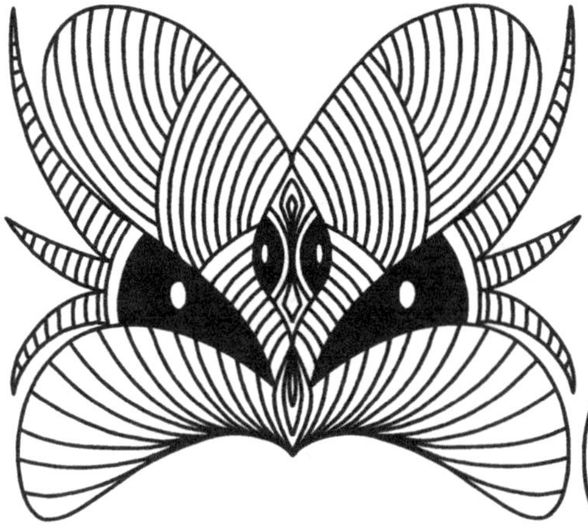

FATLINER WEIRDIES
VOLUME 1

FATLINER WEIRDIES
THE TEMPLATES 1

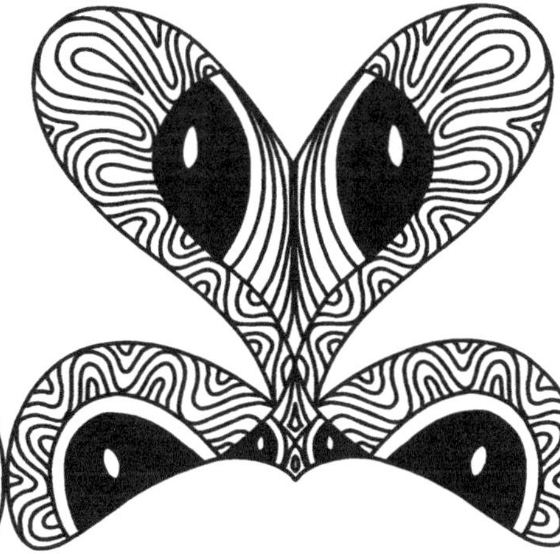

FATLINER WEIRDIES
VOLUME 3

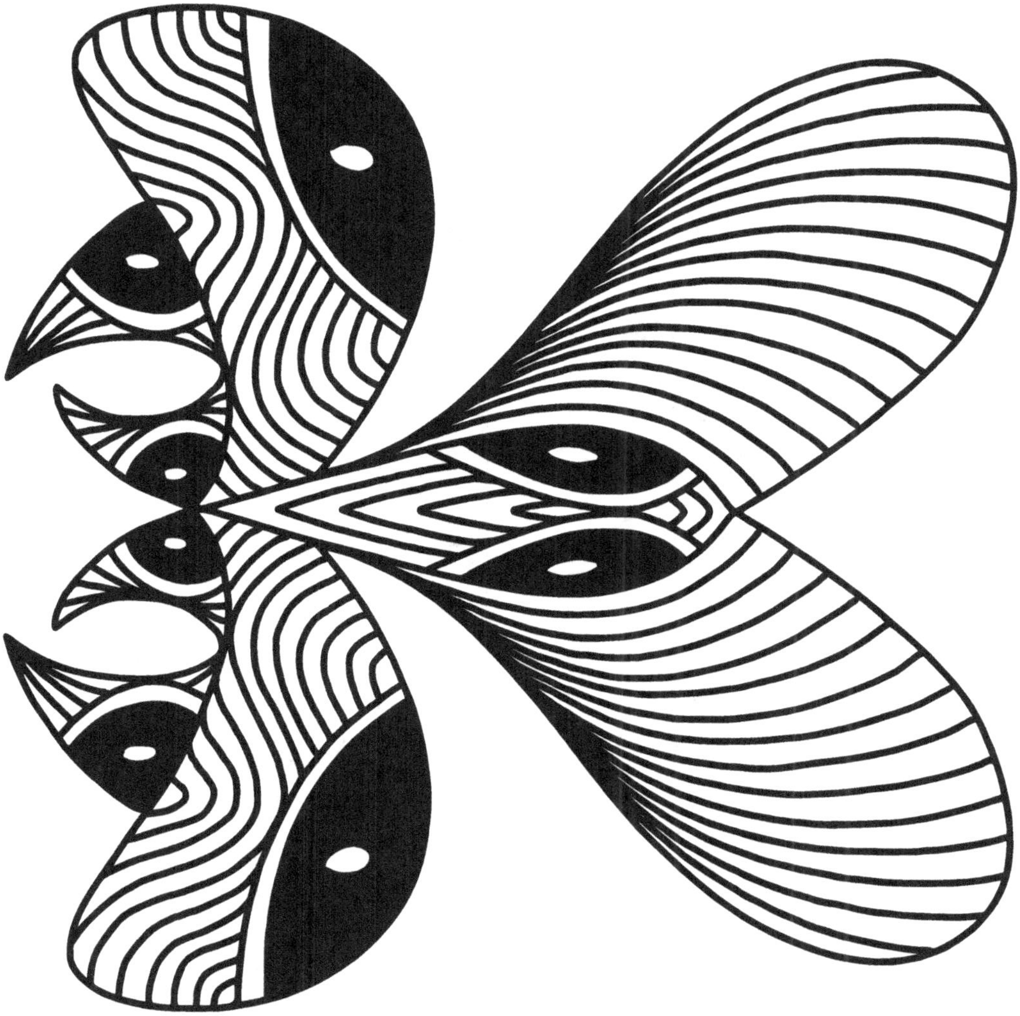

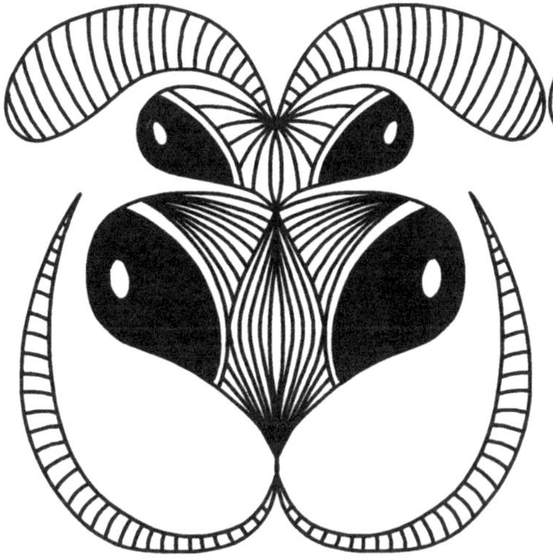

FATLINER WEIRDIES
VOLUME 1

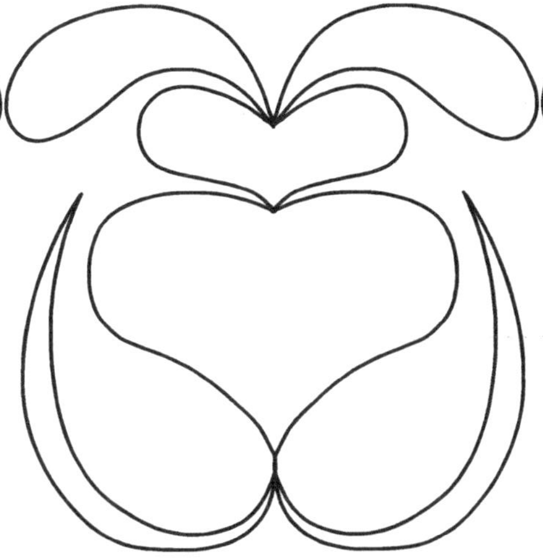

FATLINER WEIRDIES
THE TEMPLATES 1

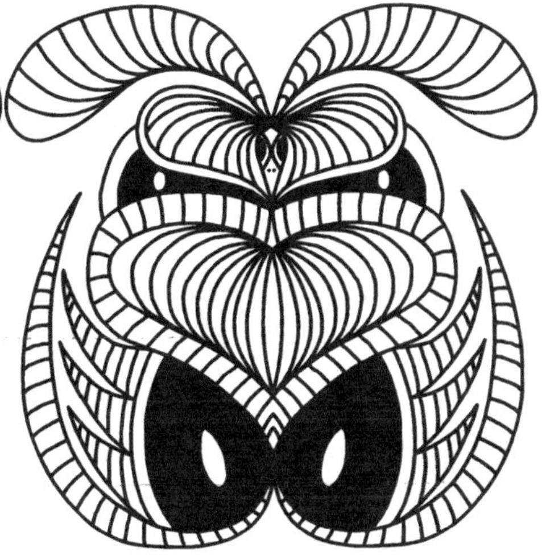

FATLINER WEIRDIES
VOLUME 3

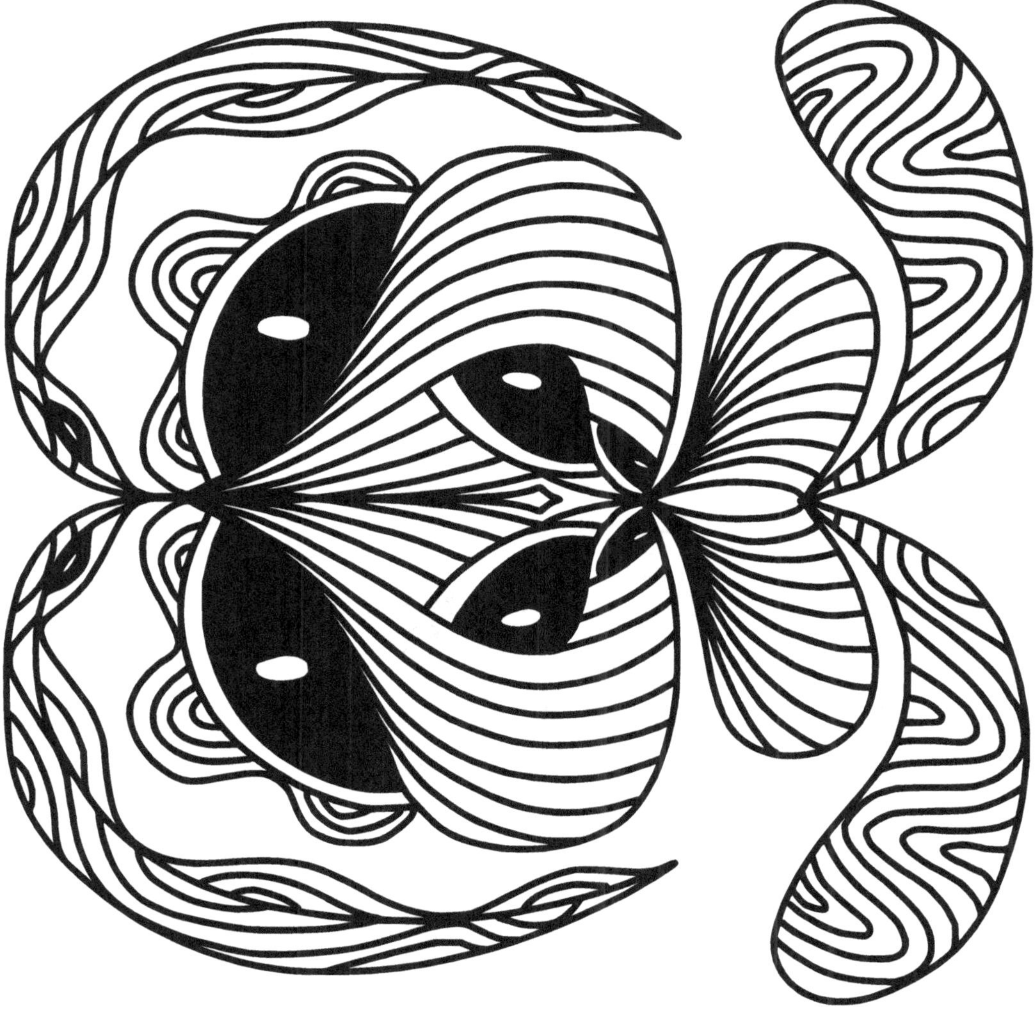

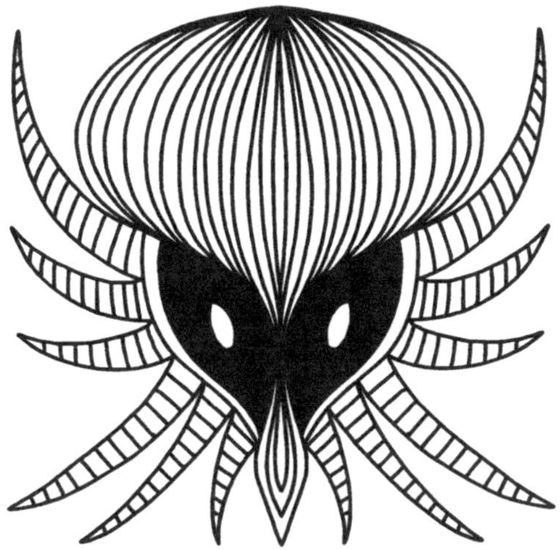

FATLINER WEIRDIES
VOLUME 1

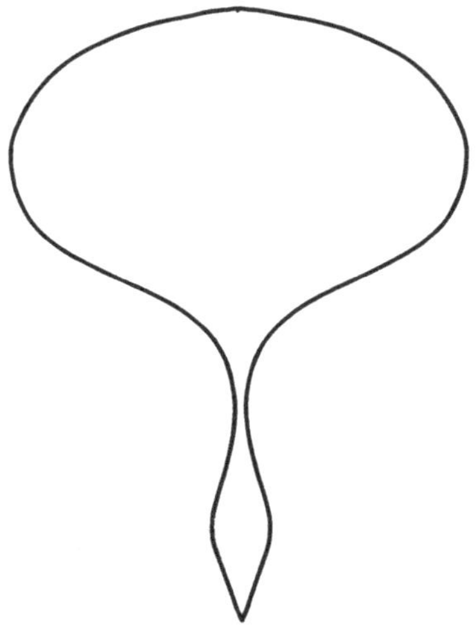

FATLINER WEIRDIES
THE TEMPLATES 1

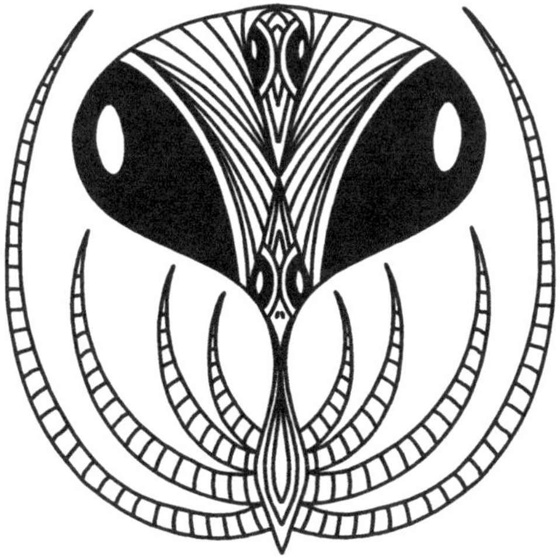

FATLINER WEIRDIES
VOLUME 3

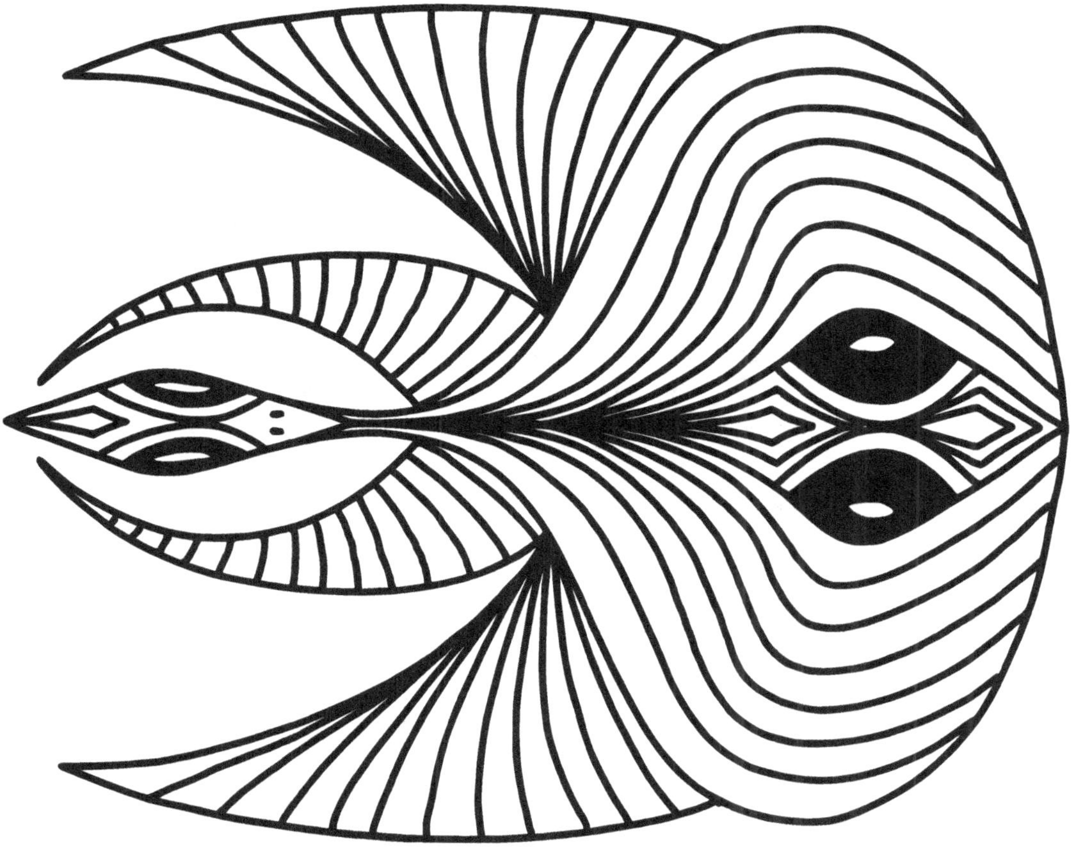

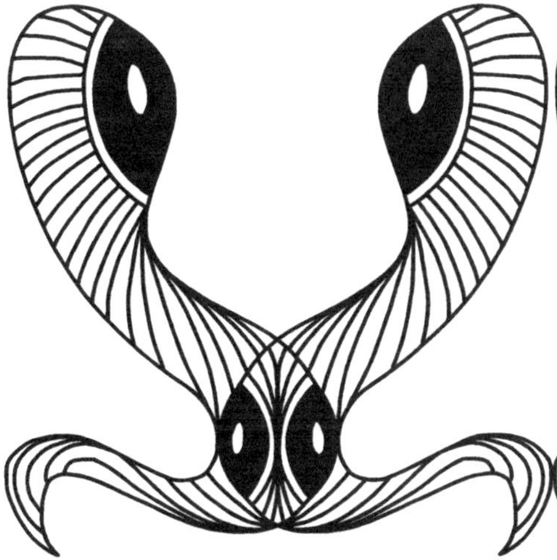

FATLINER WEIRDIES
VOLUME 1

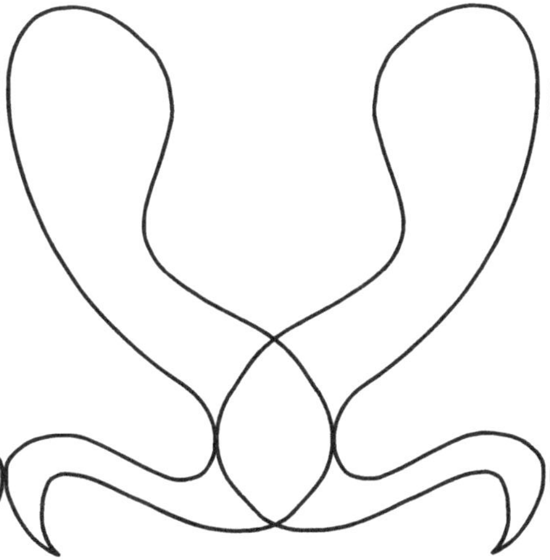

FATLINER WEIRDIES
THE TEMPLATES 1

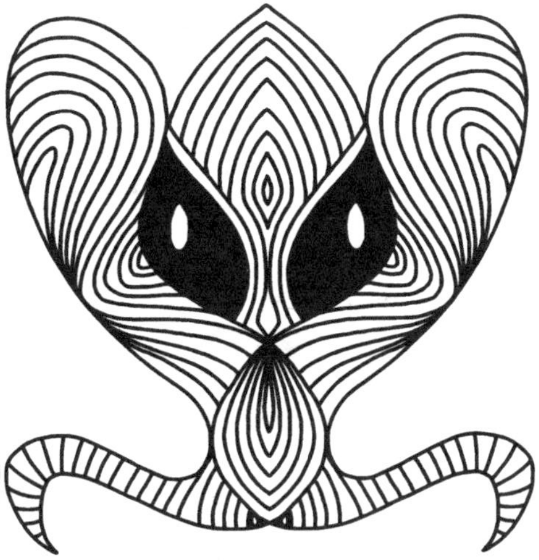

FATLINER WEIRDIES
VOLUME 3

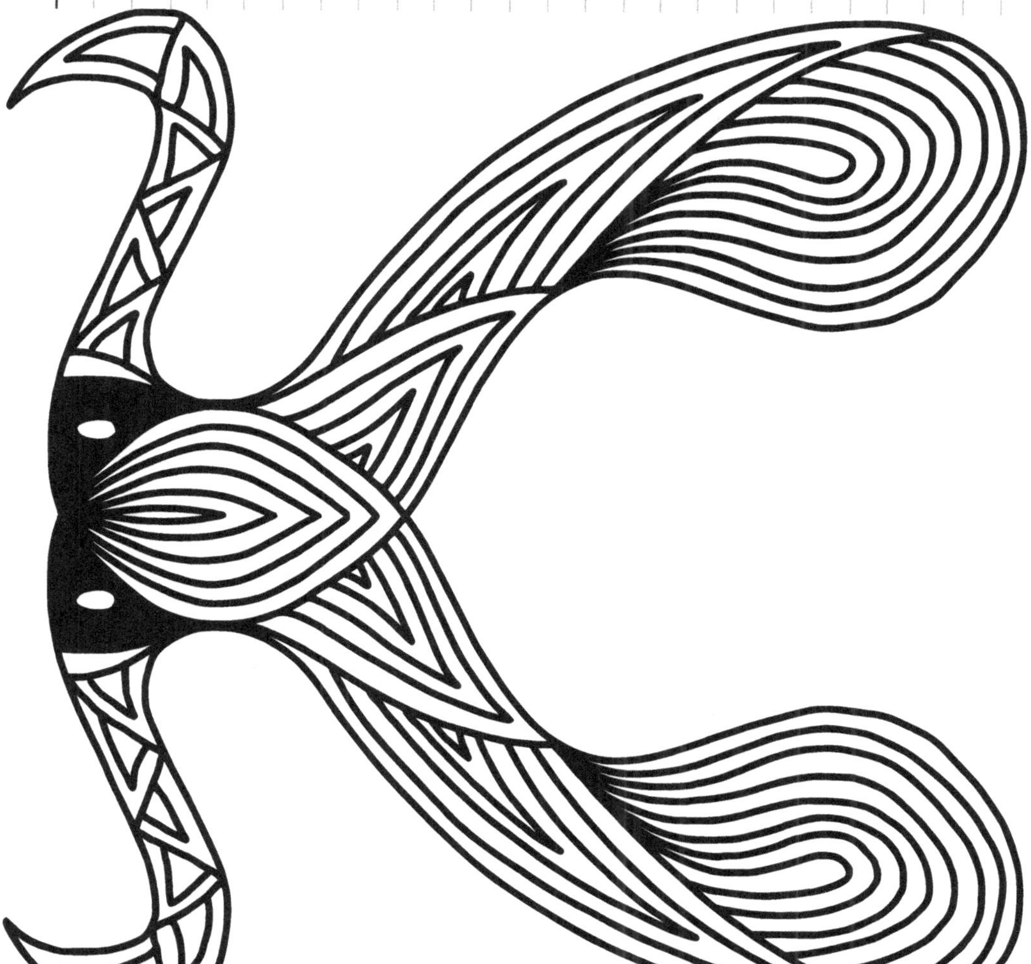

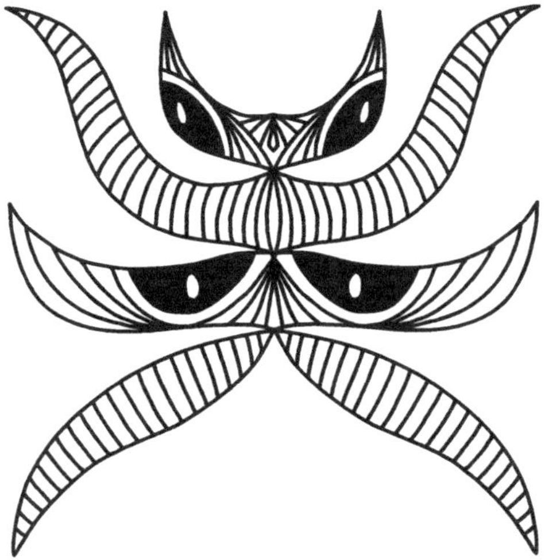

FATLINER WEIRDIES
VOLUME 1

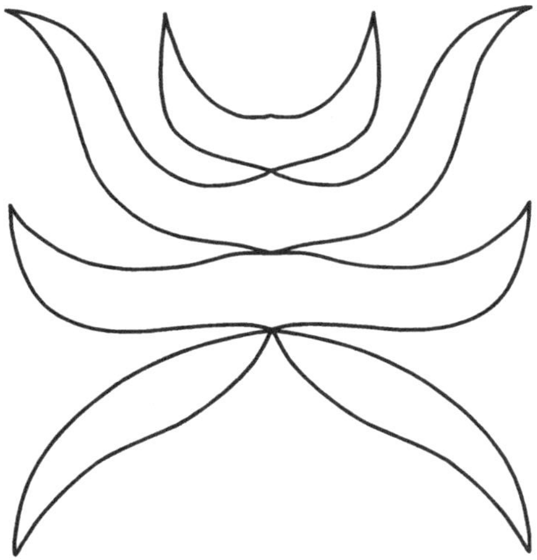

FATLINER WEIRDIES
THE TEMPLATES 1

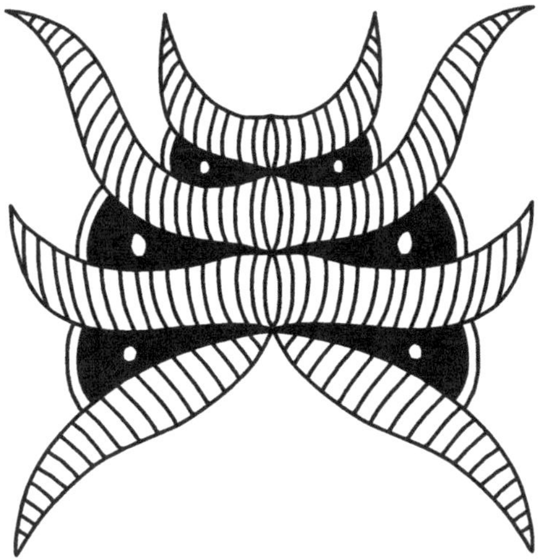

FATLINER WEIRDIES
VOLUME 3

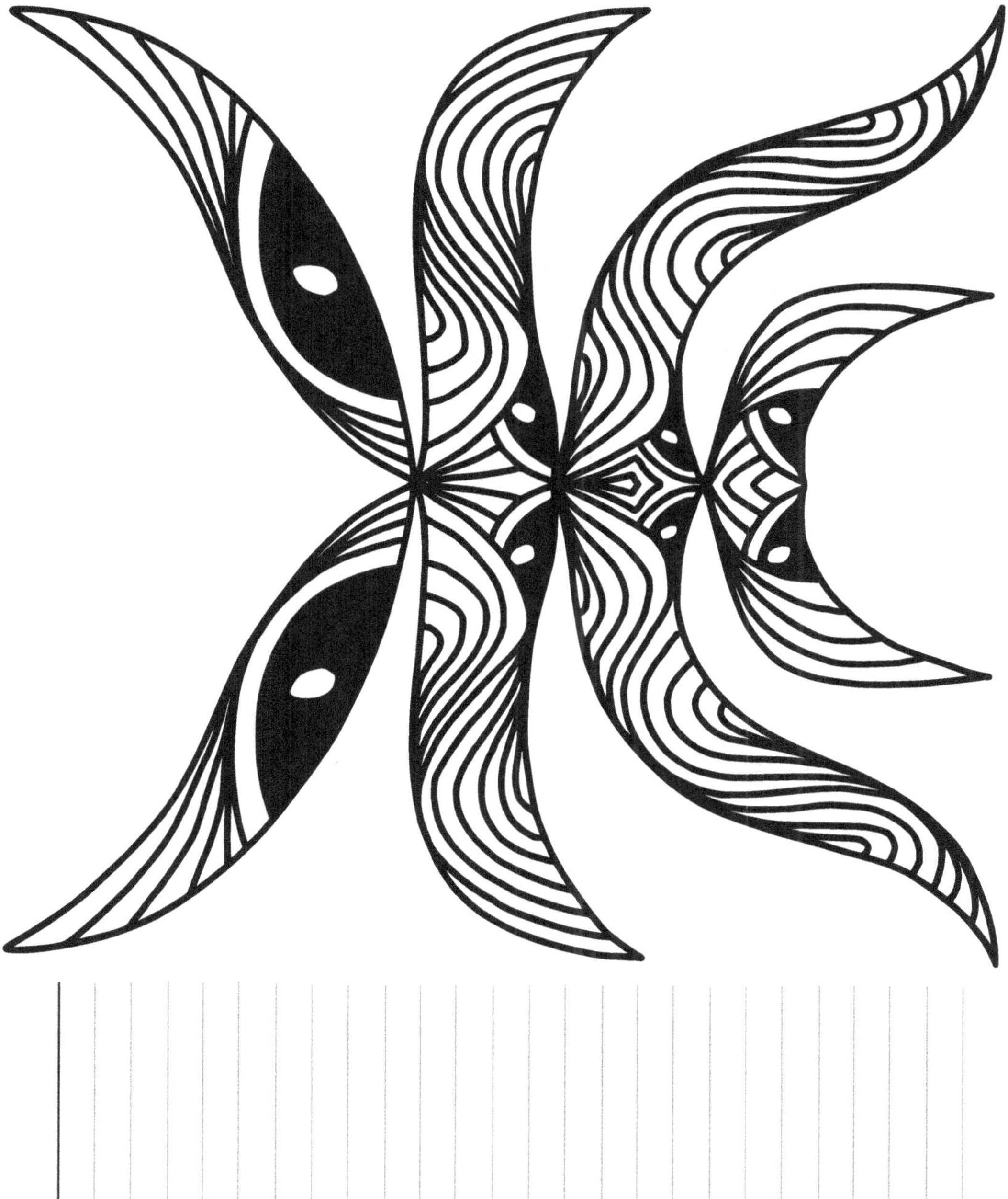

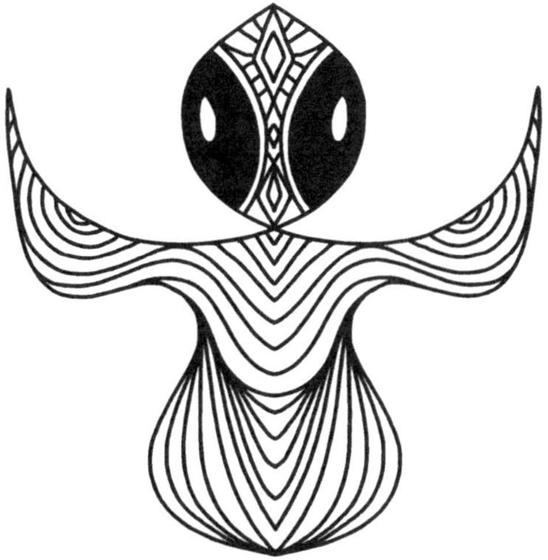

FATLINER WEIRDIES
VOLUME 1

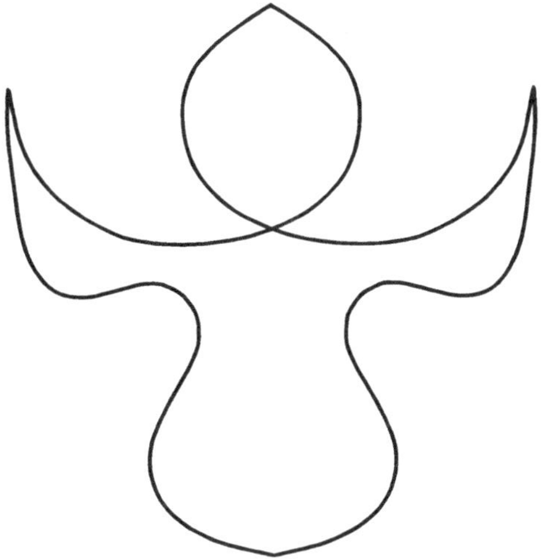

FATLINER WEIRDIES
THE TEMPLATES 1

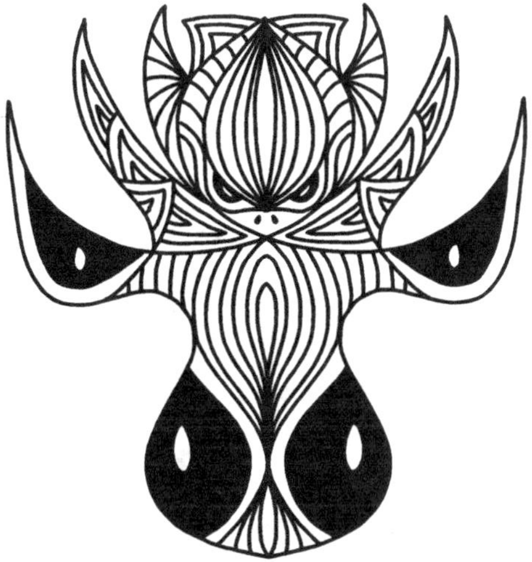

FATLINER WEIRDIES
VOLUME 3

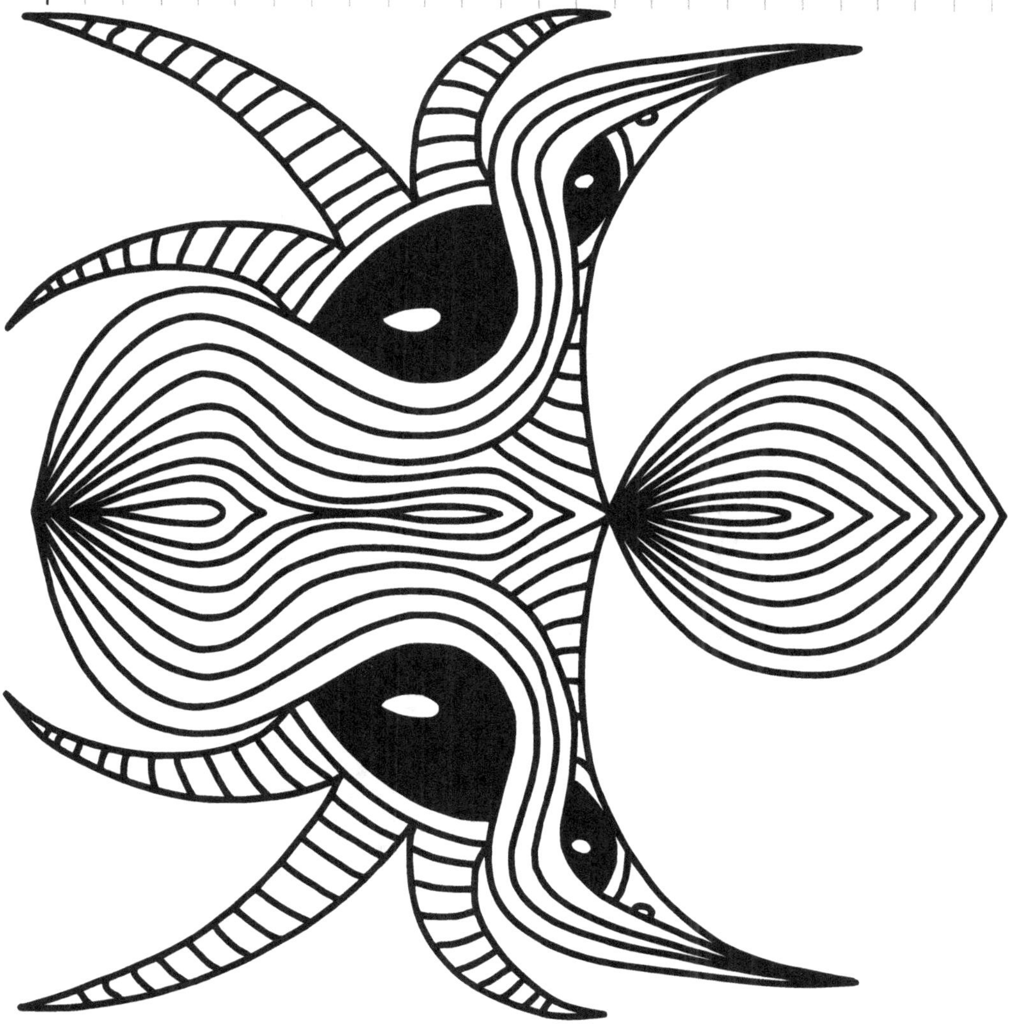

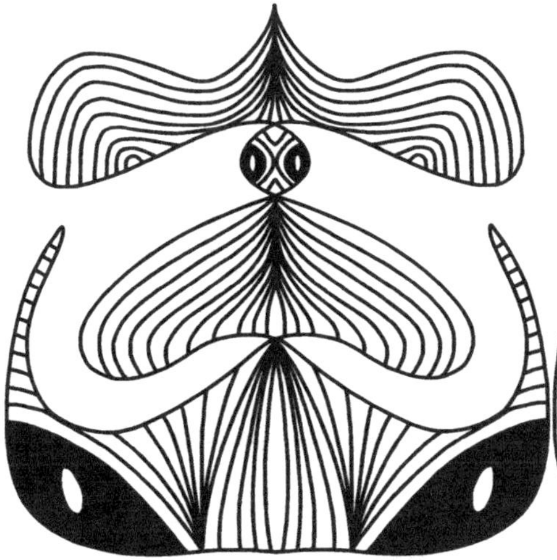

FATLINER WEIRDIES
VOLUME 1

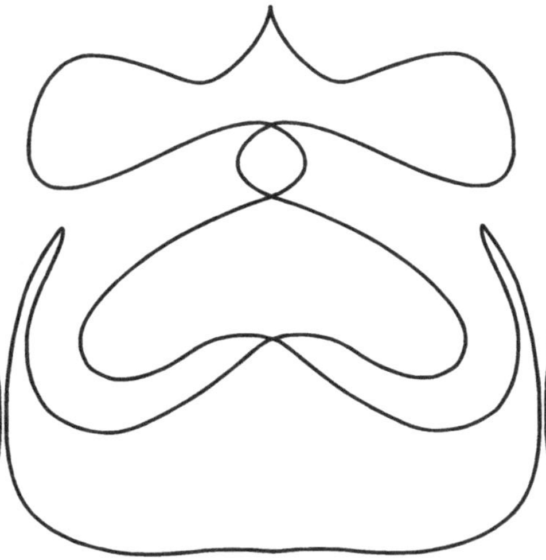

FATLINER WEIRDIES
THE TEMPLATES 1

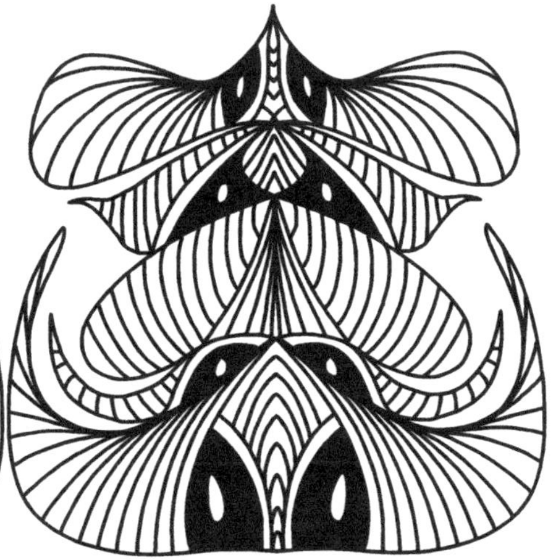

FATLINER WEIRDIES
VOLUME 3

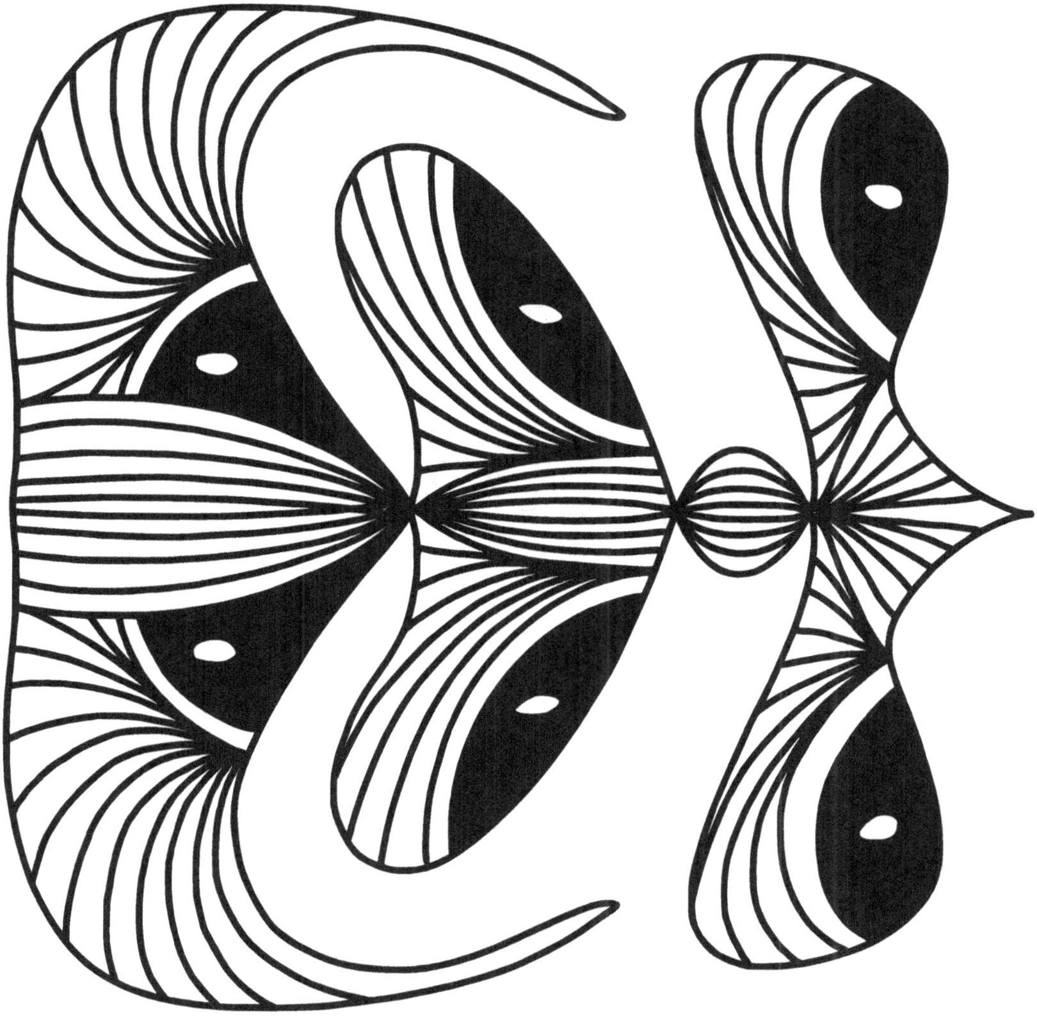

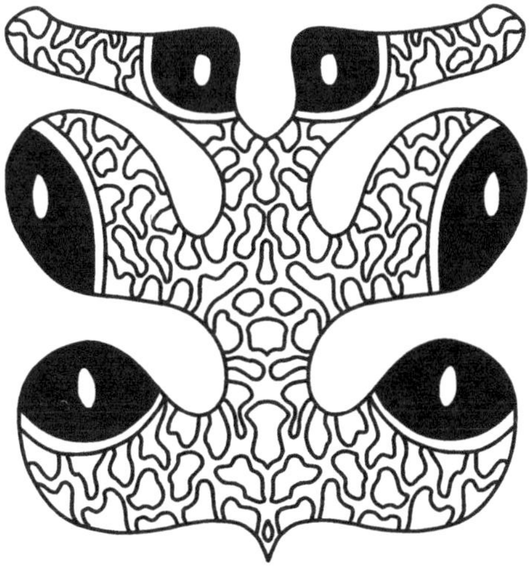

FATLINER WEIRDIES
VOLUME 1

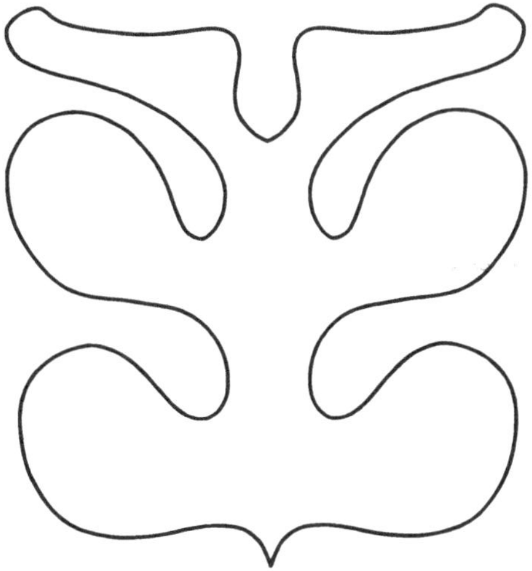

FATLINER WEIRDIES
THE TEMPLATES 1

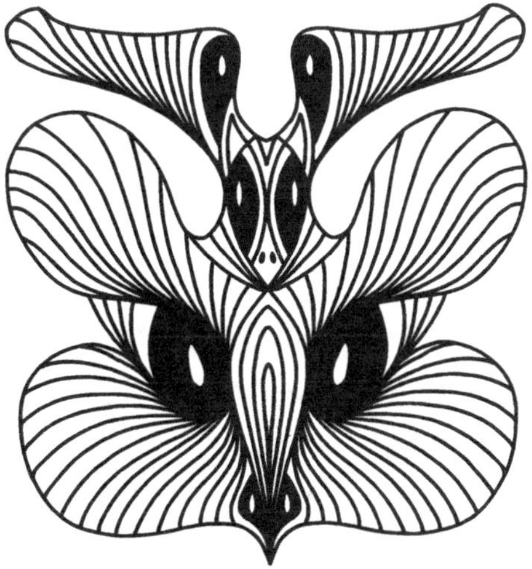

FATLINER WEIRDIES
VOLUME 3

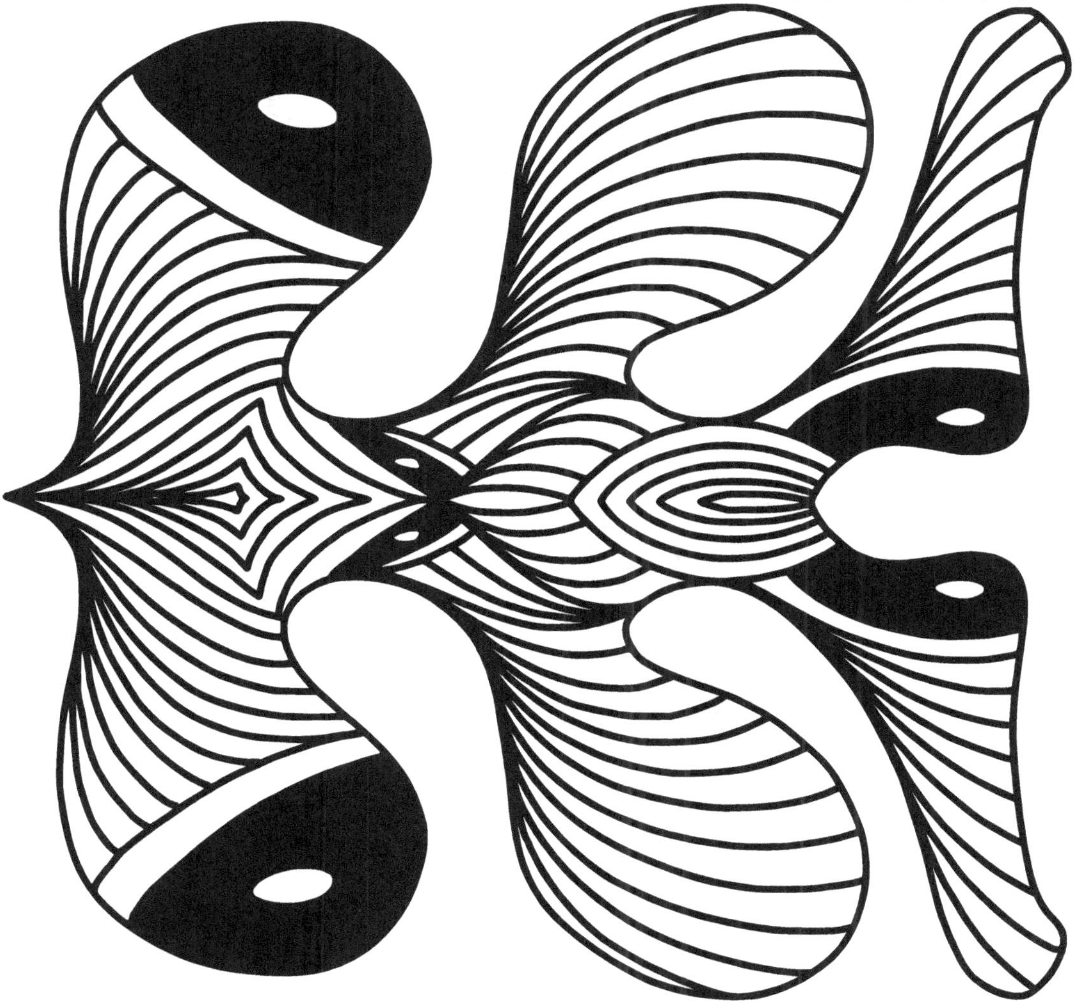

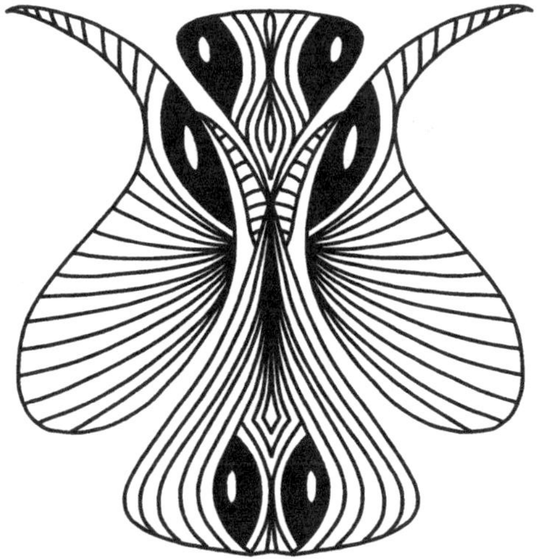

FATLINER WEIRDIES
VOLUME 1

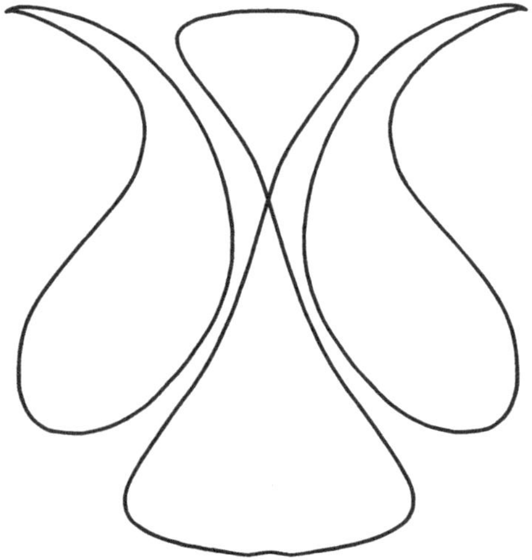

FATLINER WEIRDIES
THE TEMPLATES 1

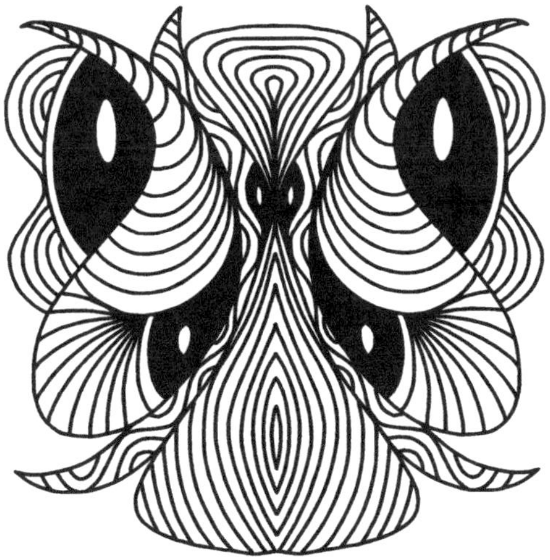

FATLINER WEIRDIES
VOLUME 3

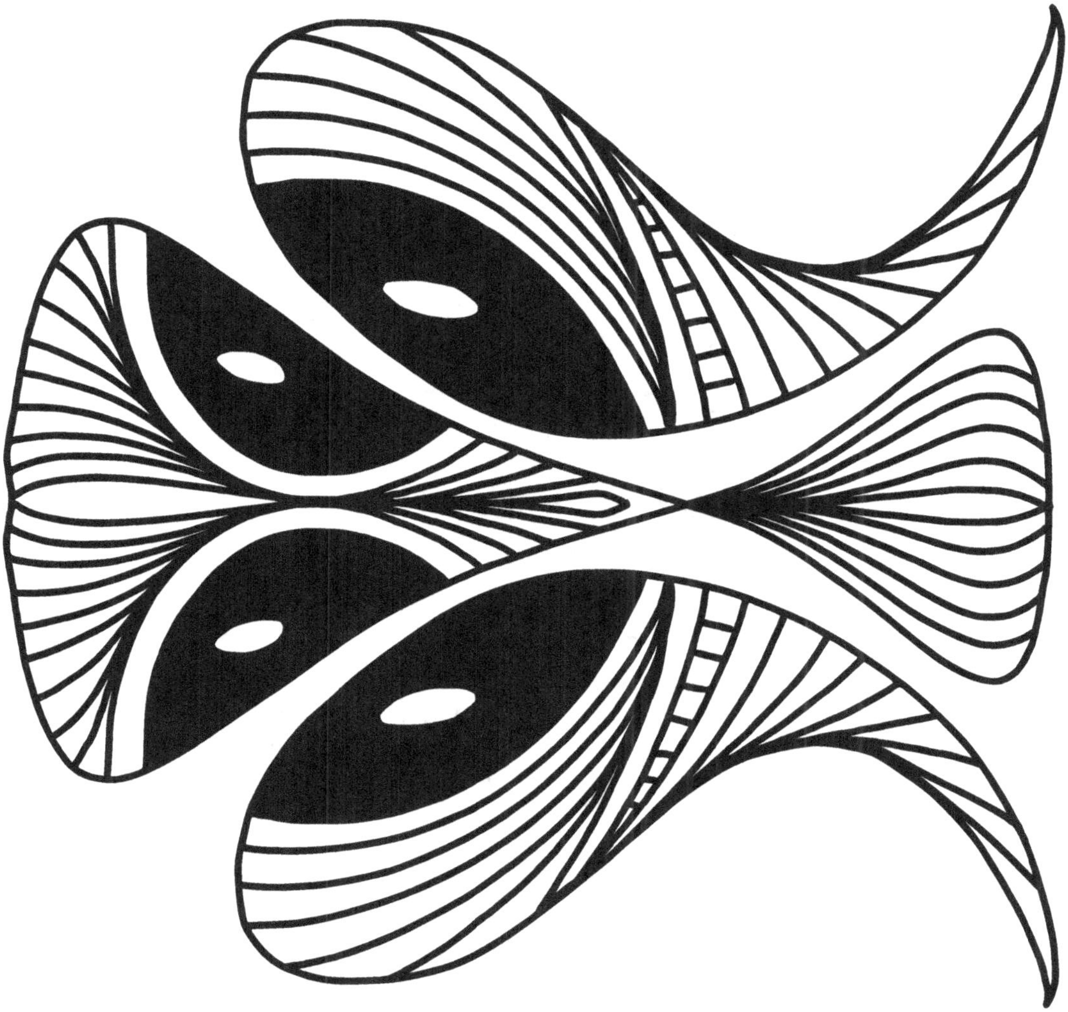

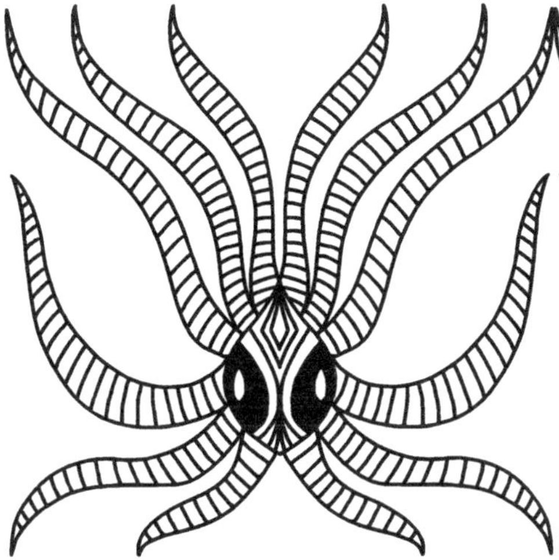

FATLINER WEIRDIES
VOLUME 1

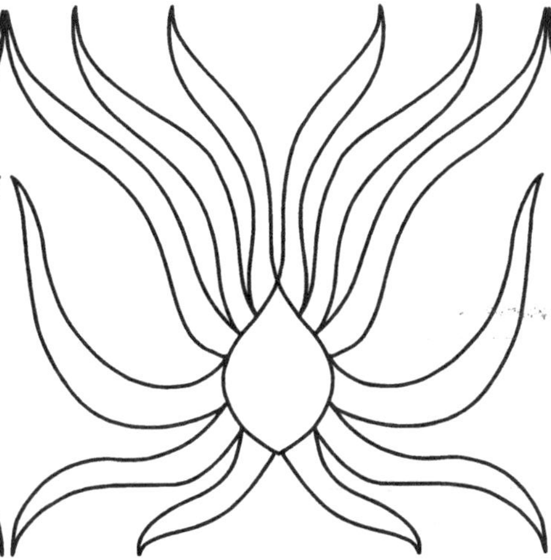

FATLINER WEIRDIES
THE TEMPLATES 1

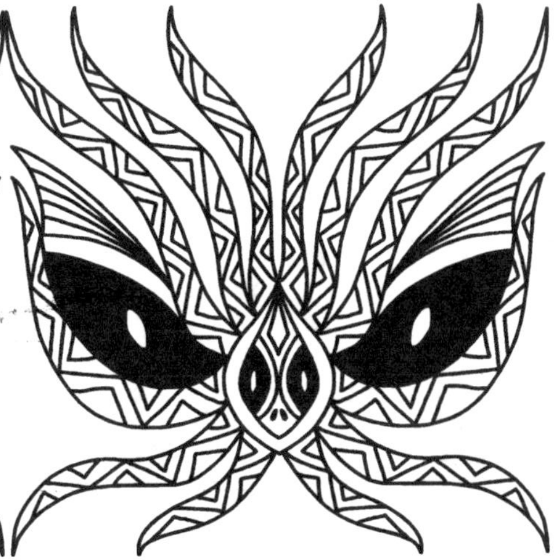

FATLINER WEIRDIES
VOLUME 3

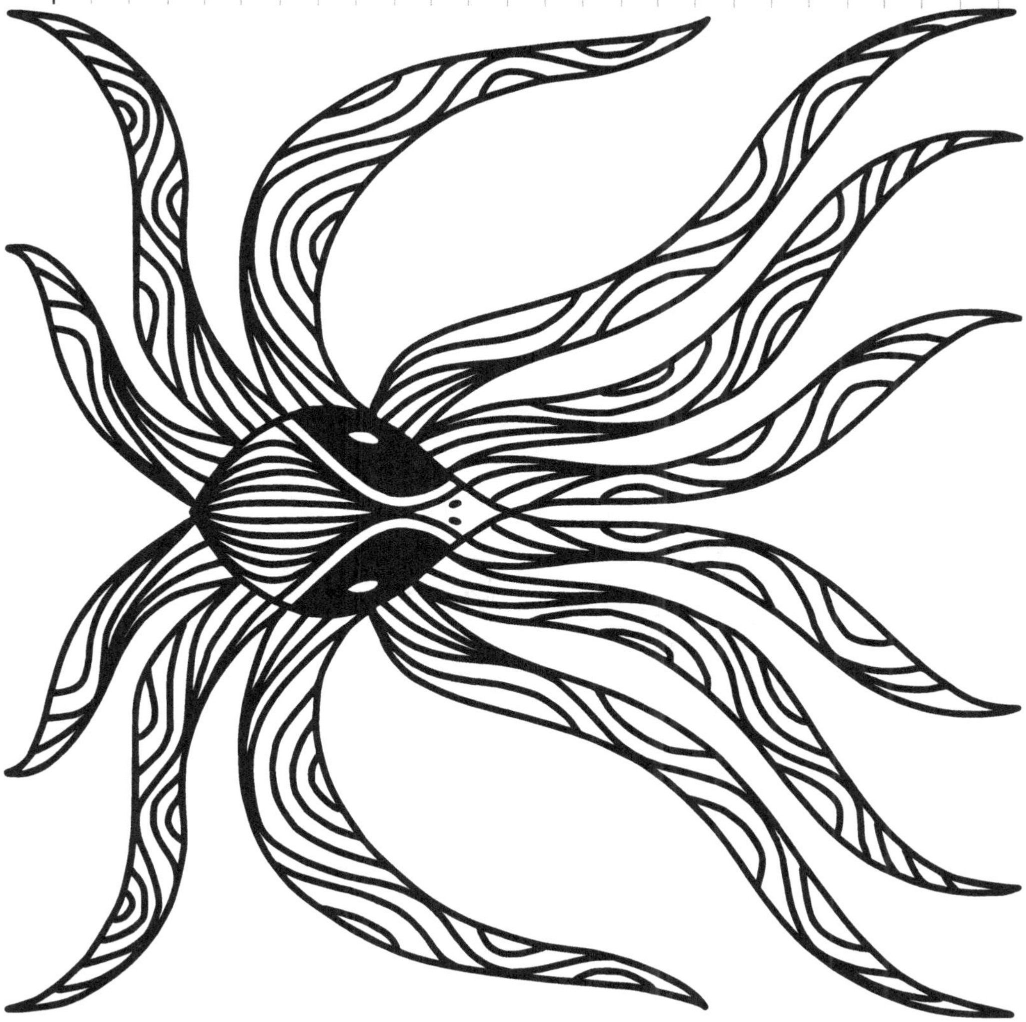

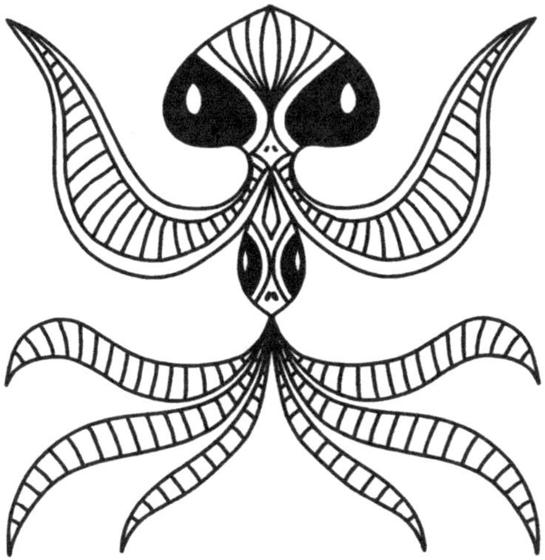
FATLINER WEIRDIES
VOLUME 1

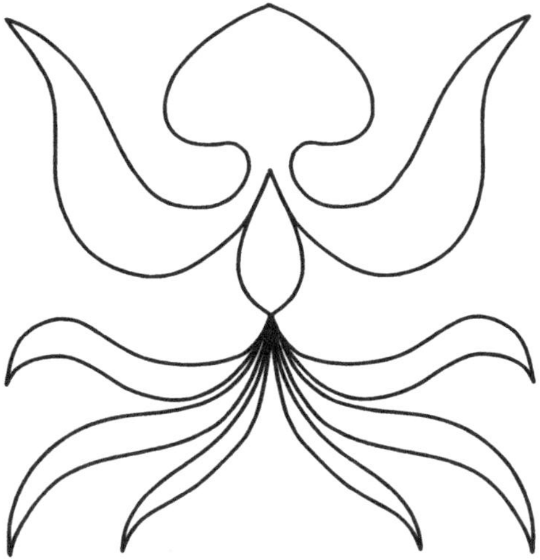
FATLINER WEIRDIES
THE TEMPLATES 1

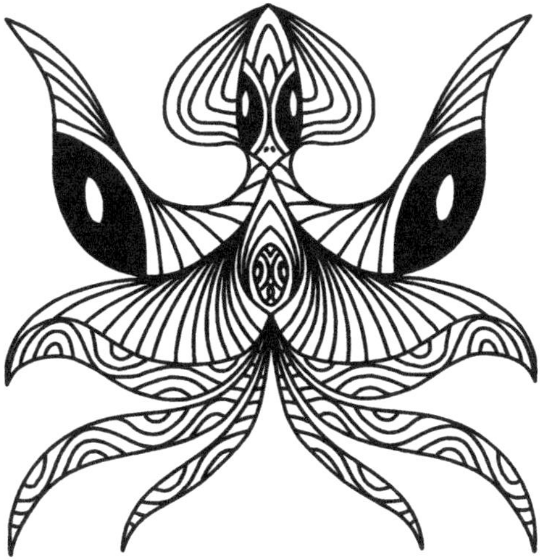
FATLINER WEIRDIES
VOLUME 3

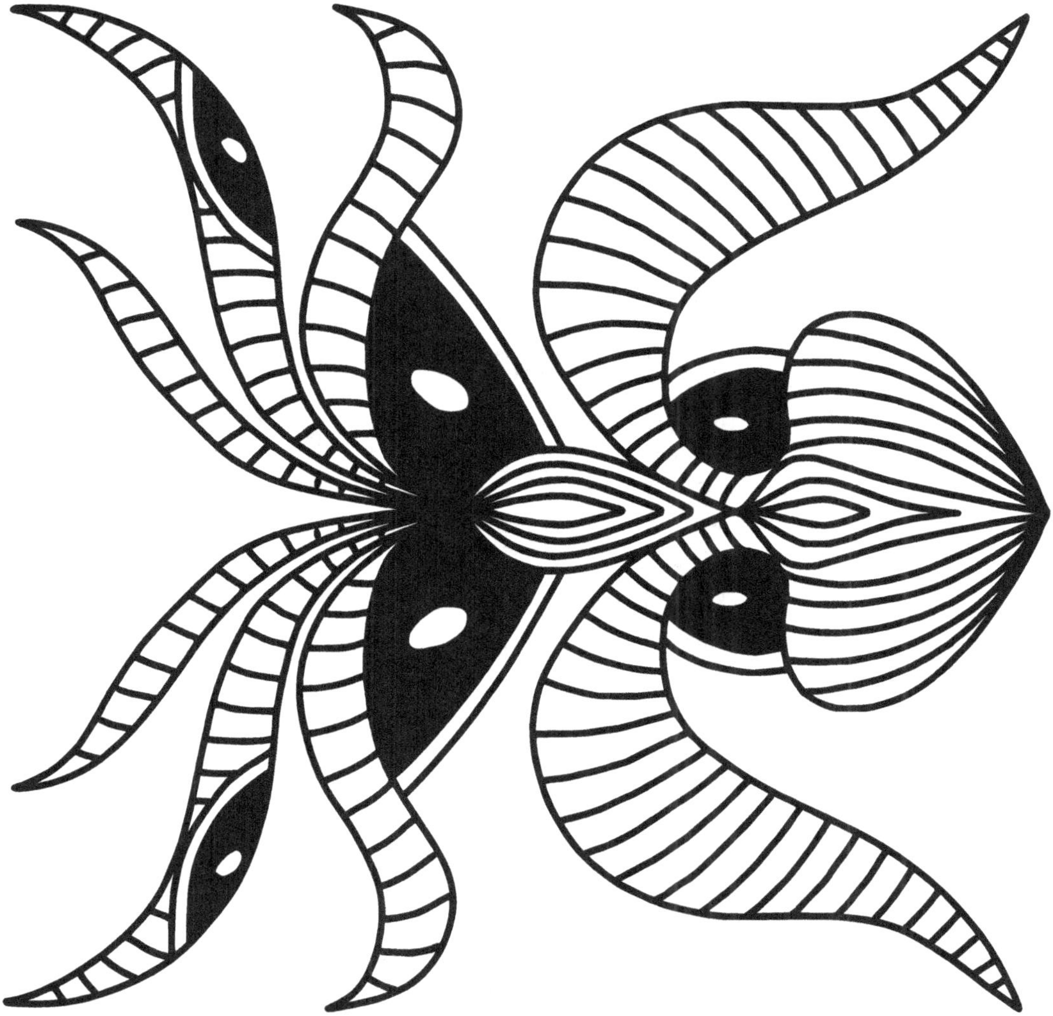

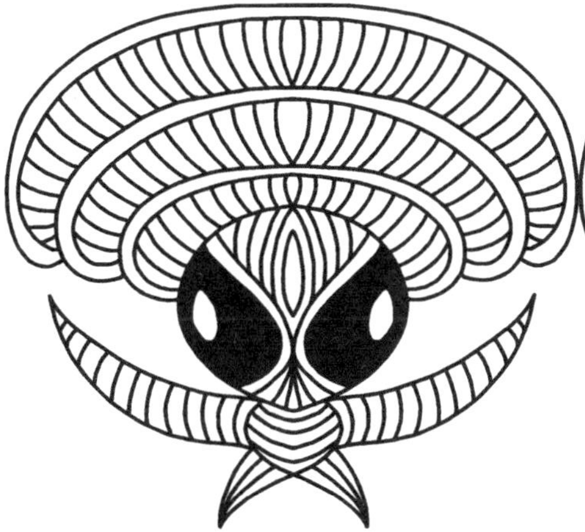

FATLINER WEIRDIES
VOLUME 1

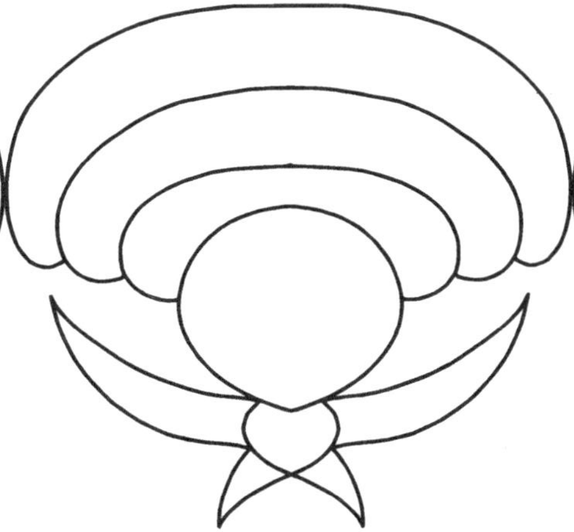

FATLINER WEIRDIES
THE TEMPLATES 1

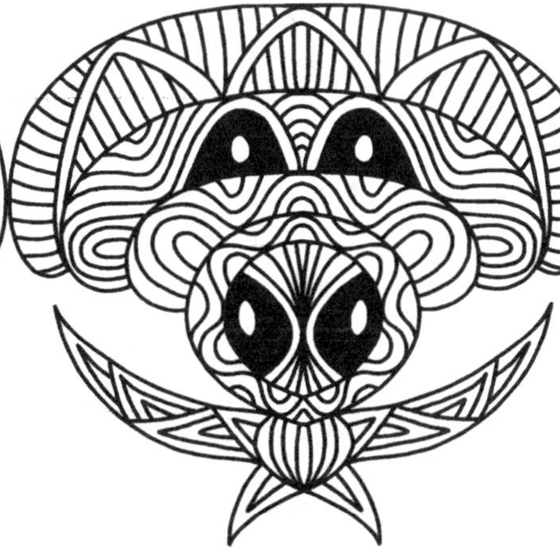

FATLINER WEIRDIES
VOLUME 3

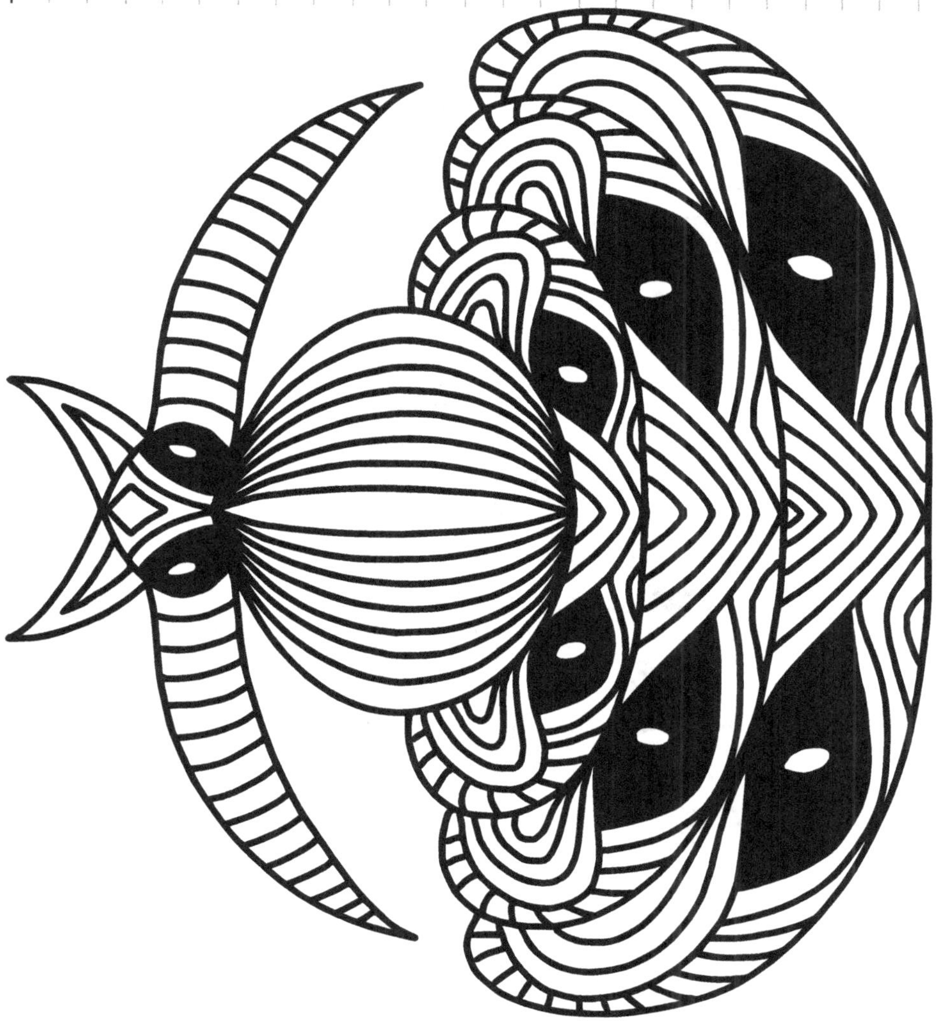

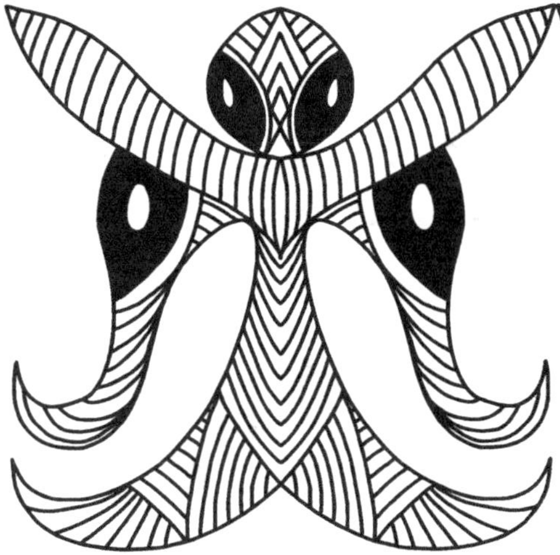

FATLINER WEIRDIES
VOLUME 1

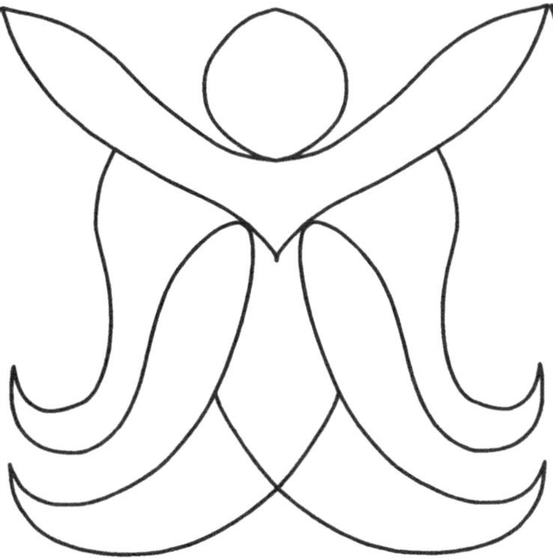

FATLINER WEIRDIES
THE TEMPLATES 1

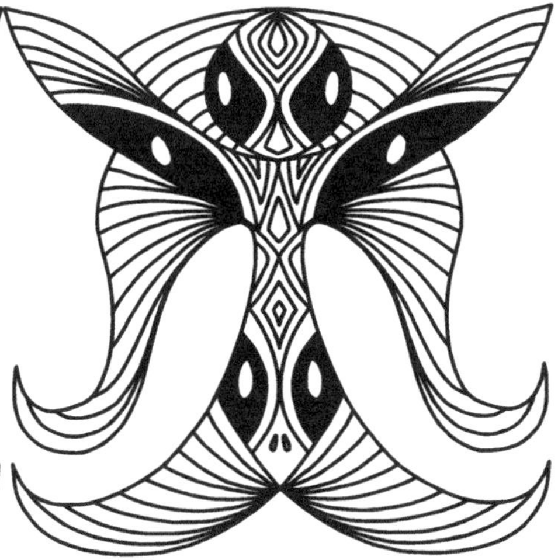

FATLINER WEIRDIES
VOLUME 3

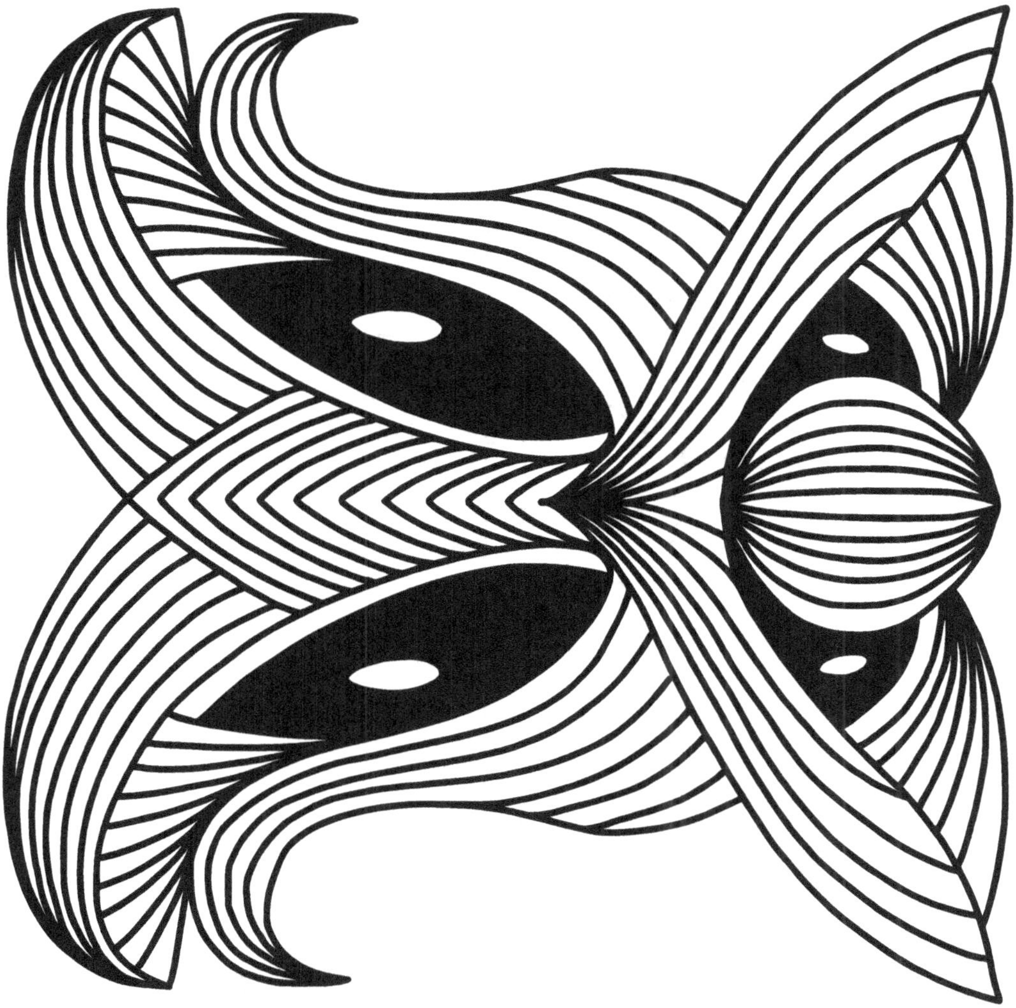

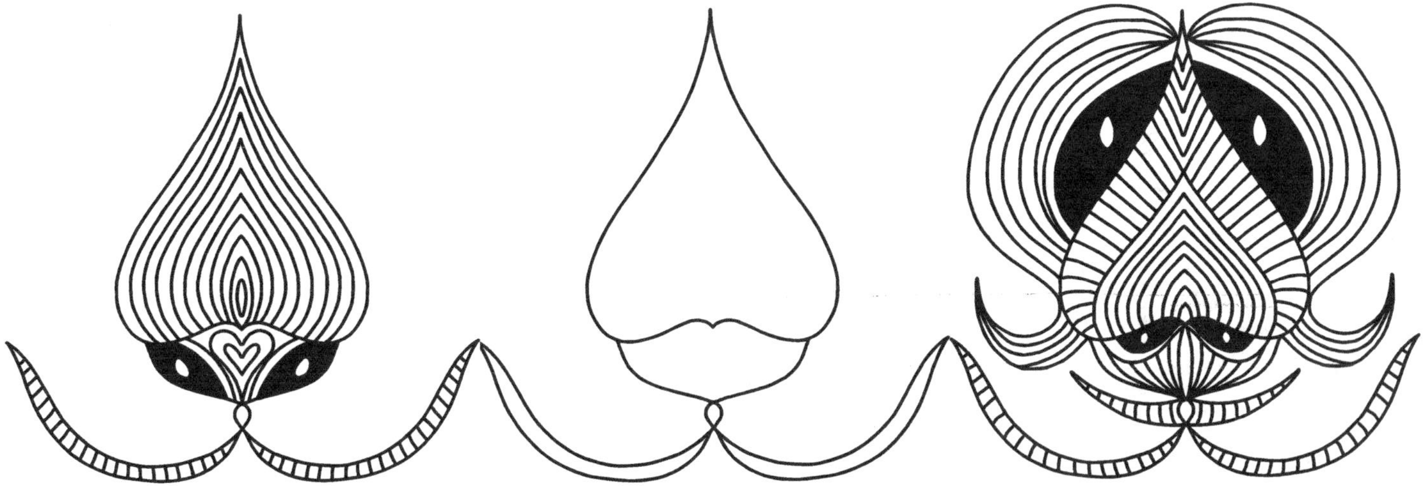

FATLINER WEIRDIES
VOLUME 1

FATLINER WEIRDIES
THE TEMPLATES 1

FATLINER WEIRDIES
VOLUME 3

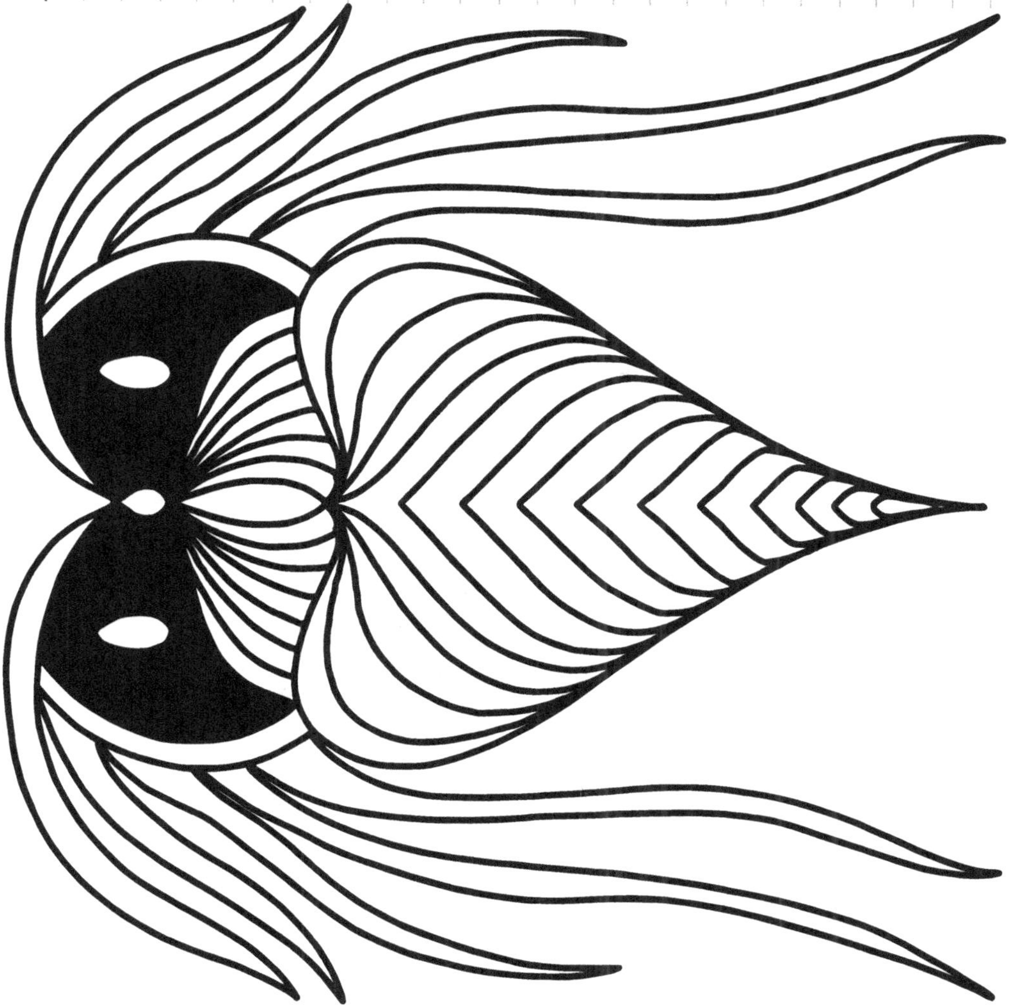

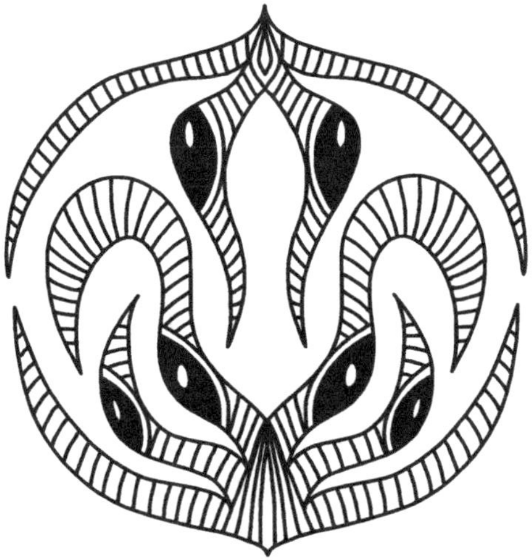
FATLINER WEIRDIES
VOLUME 1

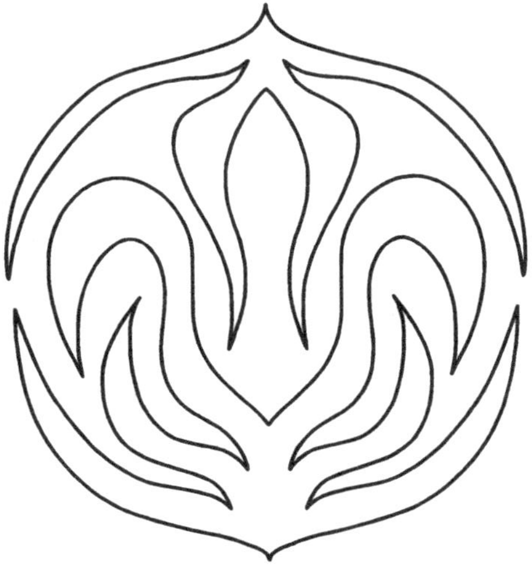
FATLINER WEIRDIES
THE TEMPLATES 1

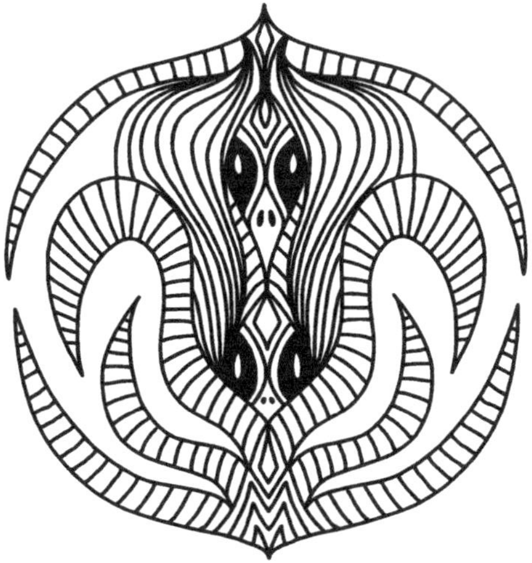
FATLINER WEIRDIES
VOLUME 3

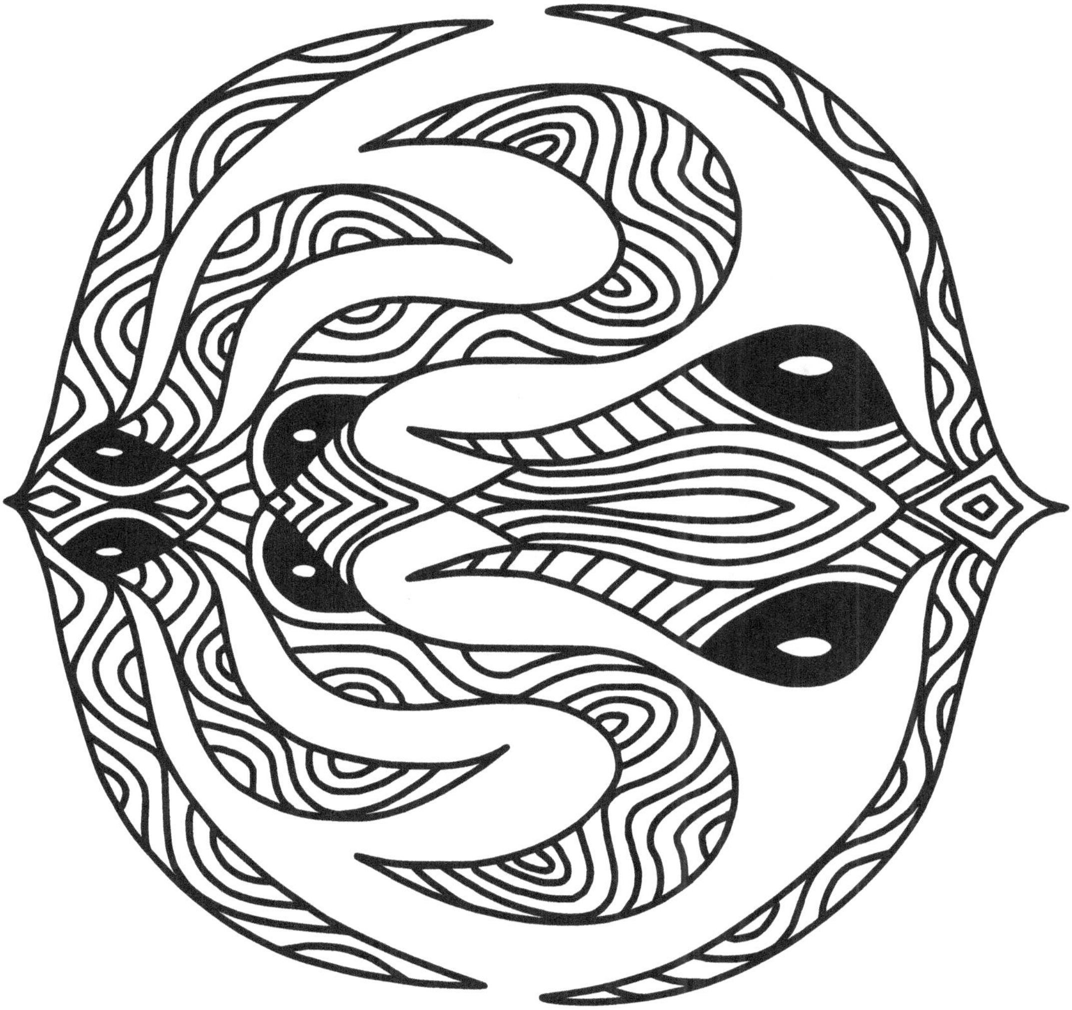

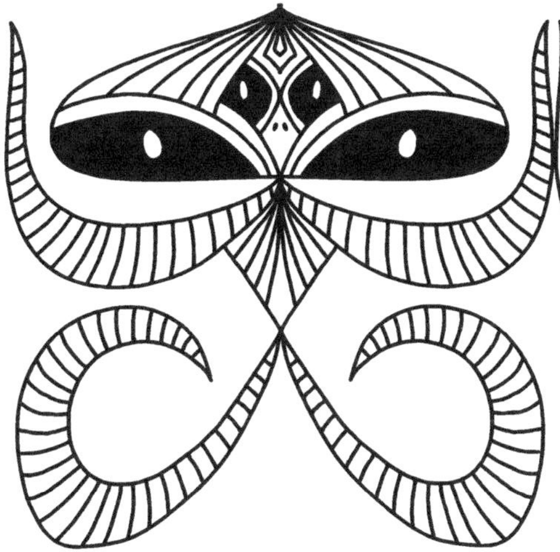

FATLINER WEIRDIES
VOLUME 1

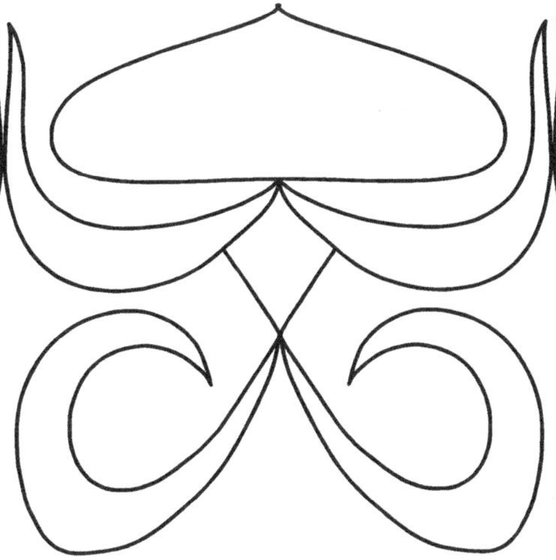

FATLINER WEIRDIES
THE TEMPLATES 1

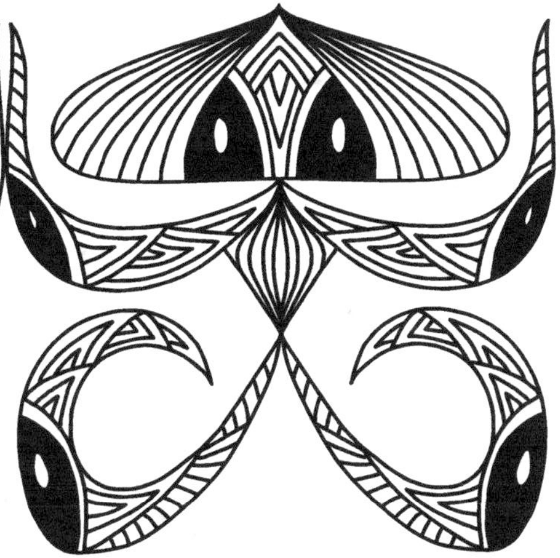

FATLINER WEIRDIES
VOLUME 3

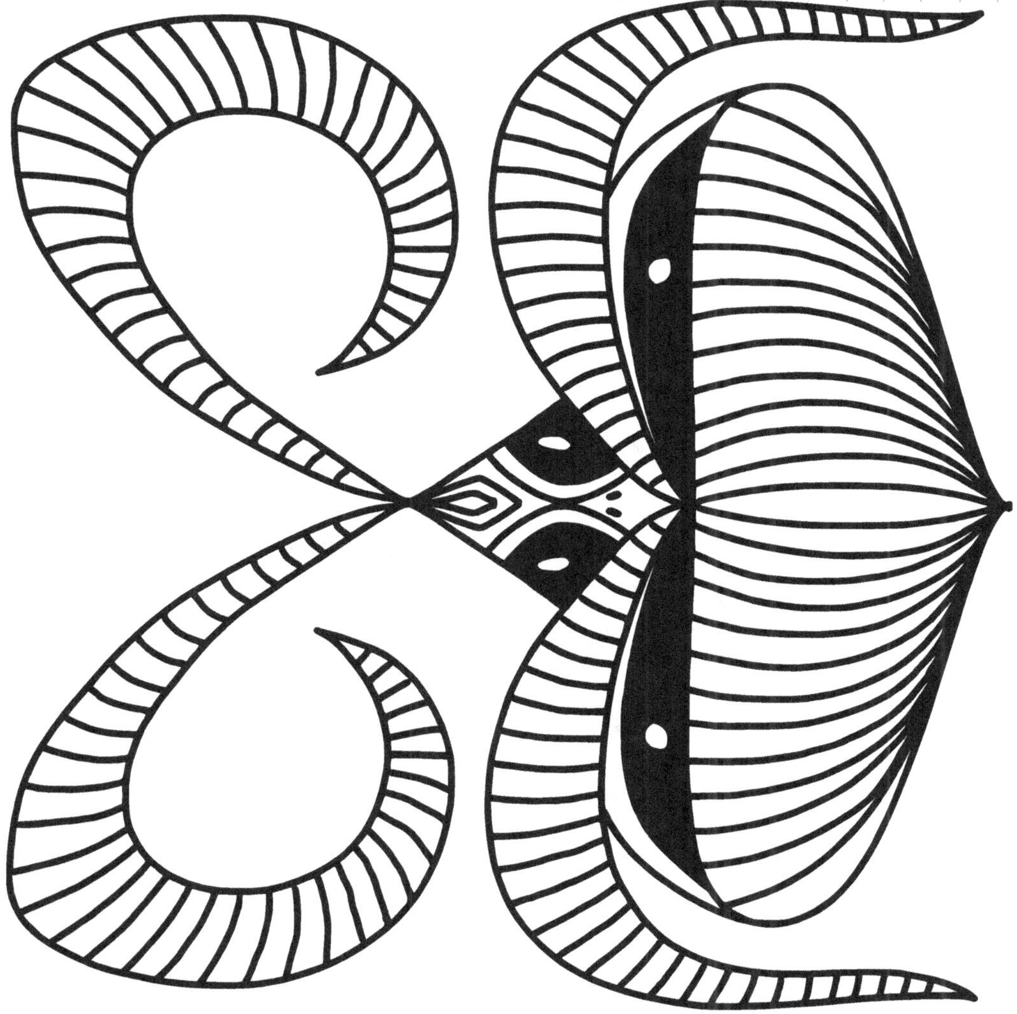

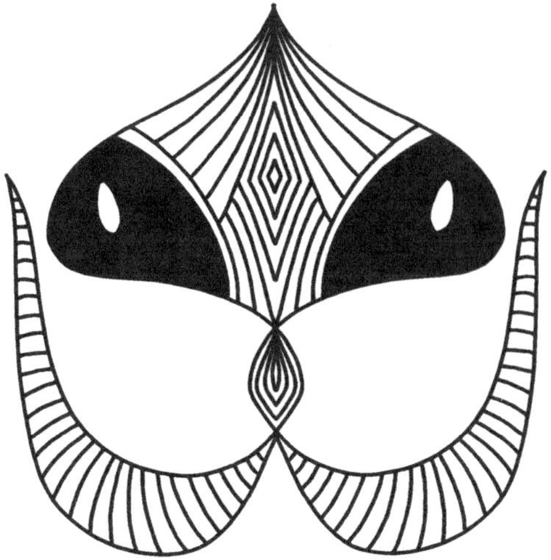

FATLINER WEIRDIES
VOLUME 1

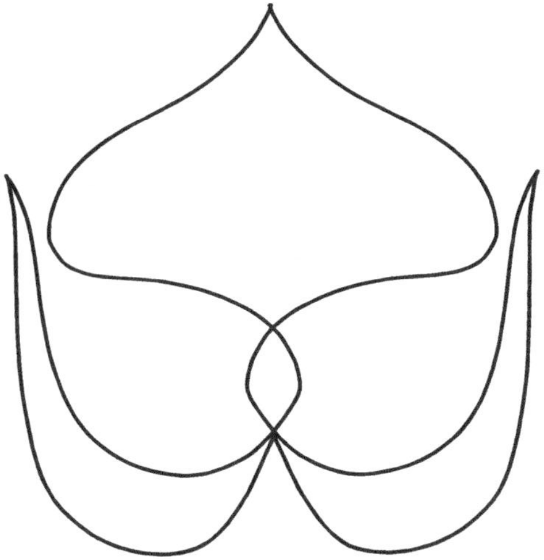

FATLINER WEIRDIES
THE TEMPLATES 1

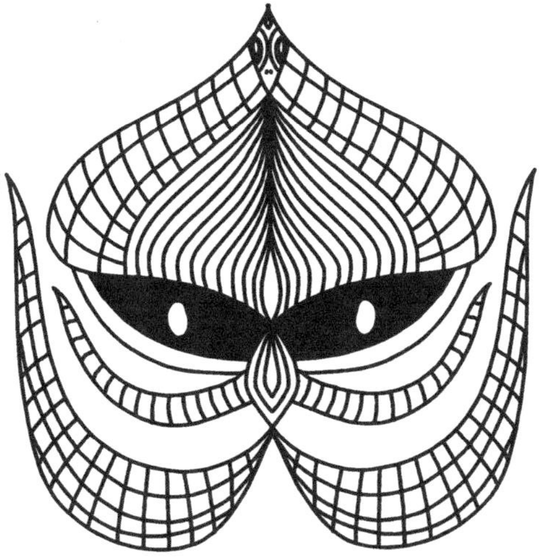

FATLINER WEIRDIES
VOLUME 3

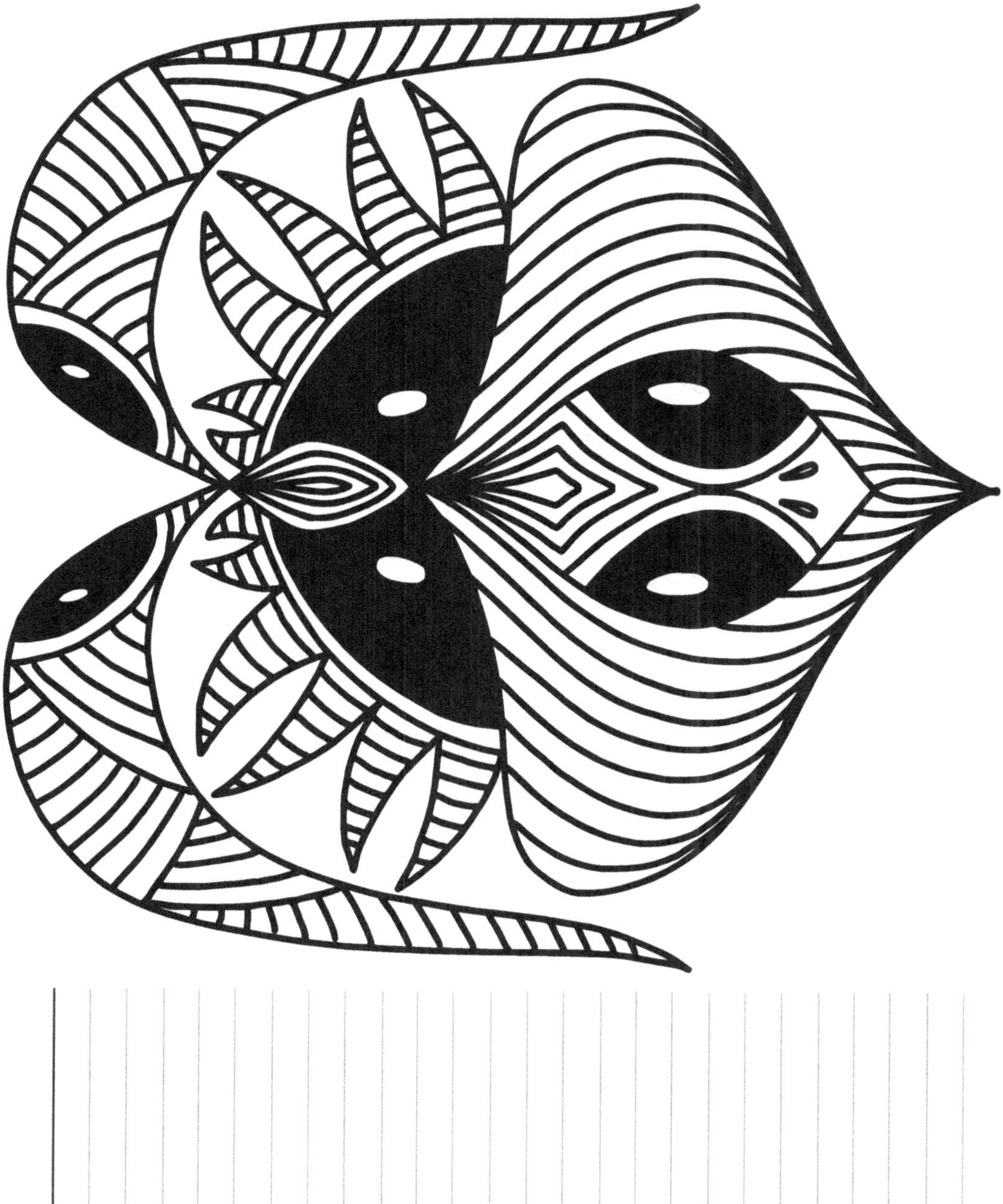

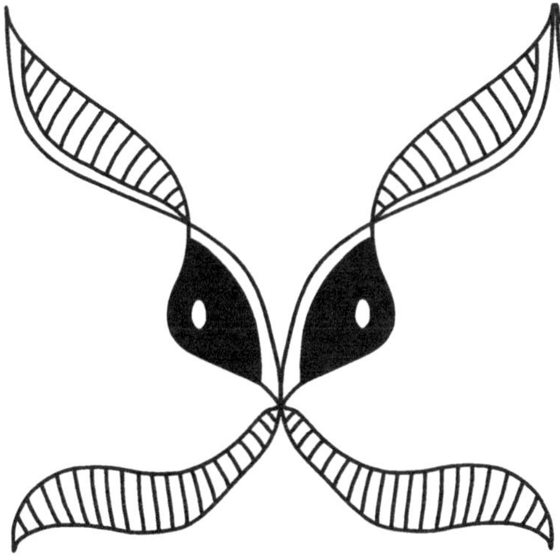

FATLINER WEIRDIES
VOLUME 1

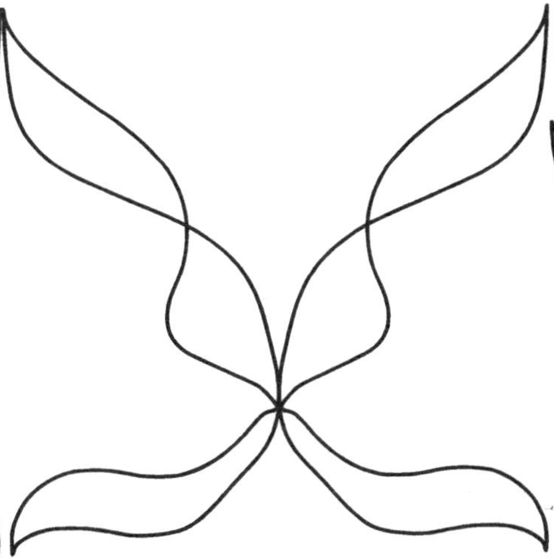

FATLINER WEIRDIES
THE TEMPLATES 1

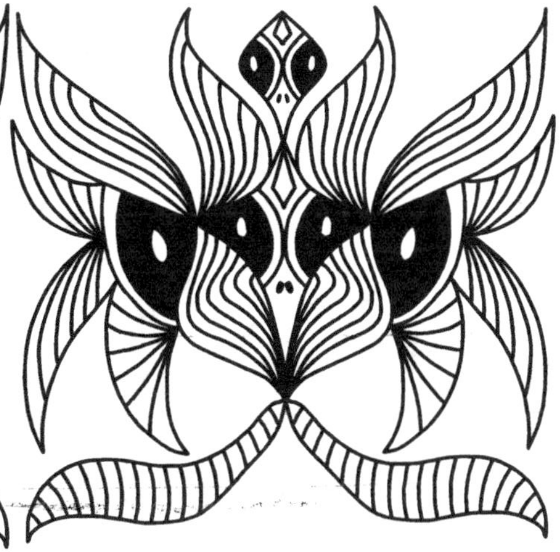

FATLINER WEIRDIES
VOLUME 3

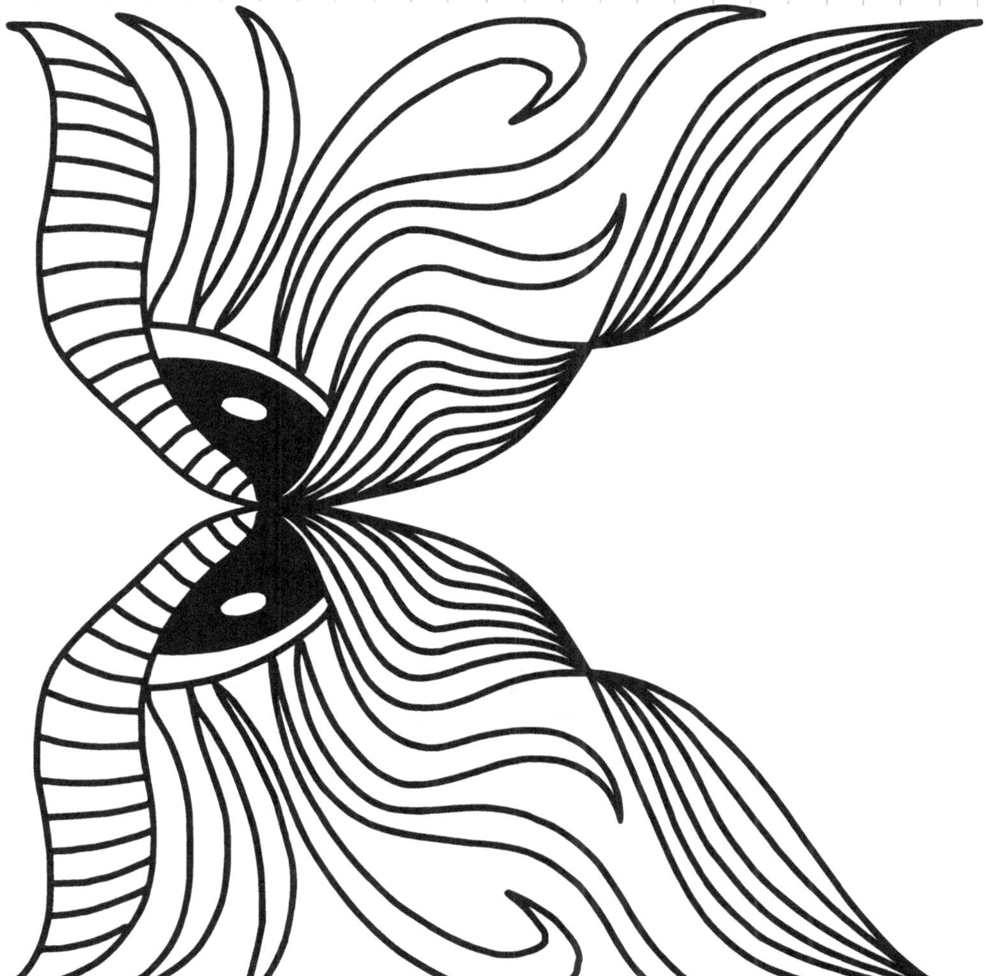

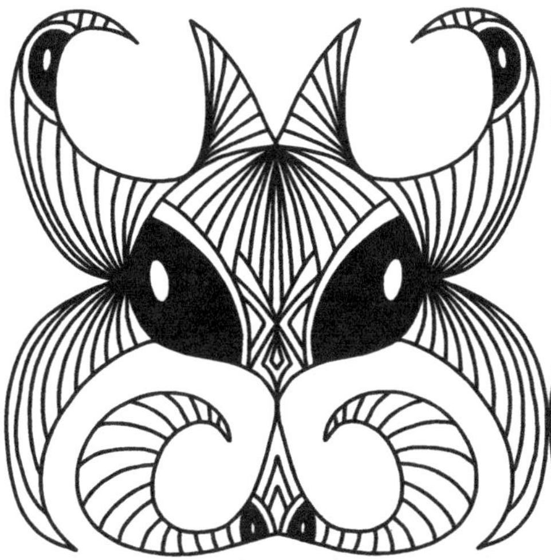

FATLINER WEIRDIES
VOLUME 1

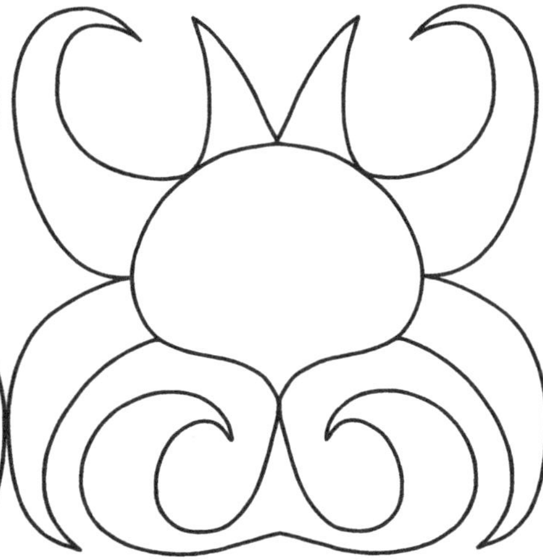

FATLINER WEIRDIES
THE TEMPLATES 1

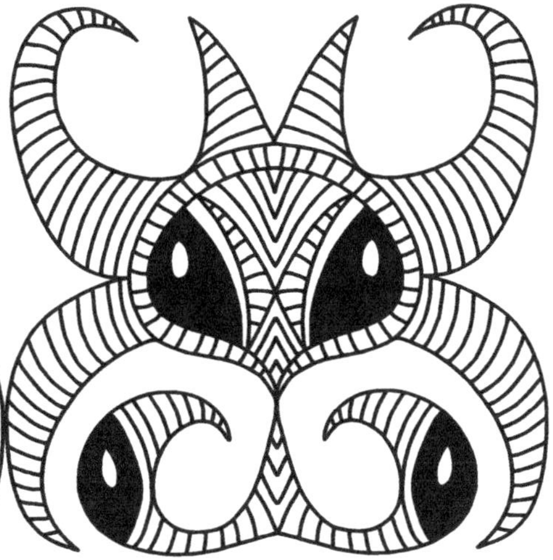

FATLINER WEIRDIES
VOLUME 3

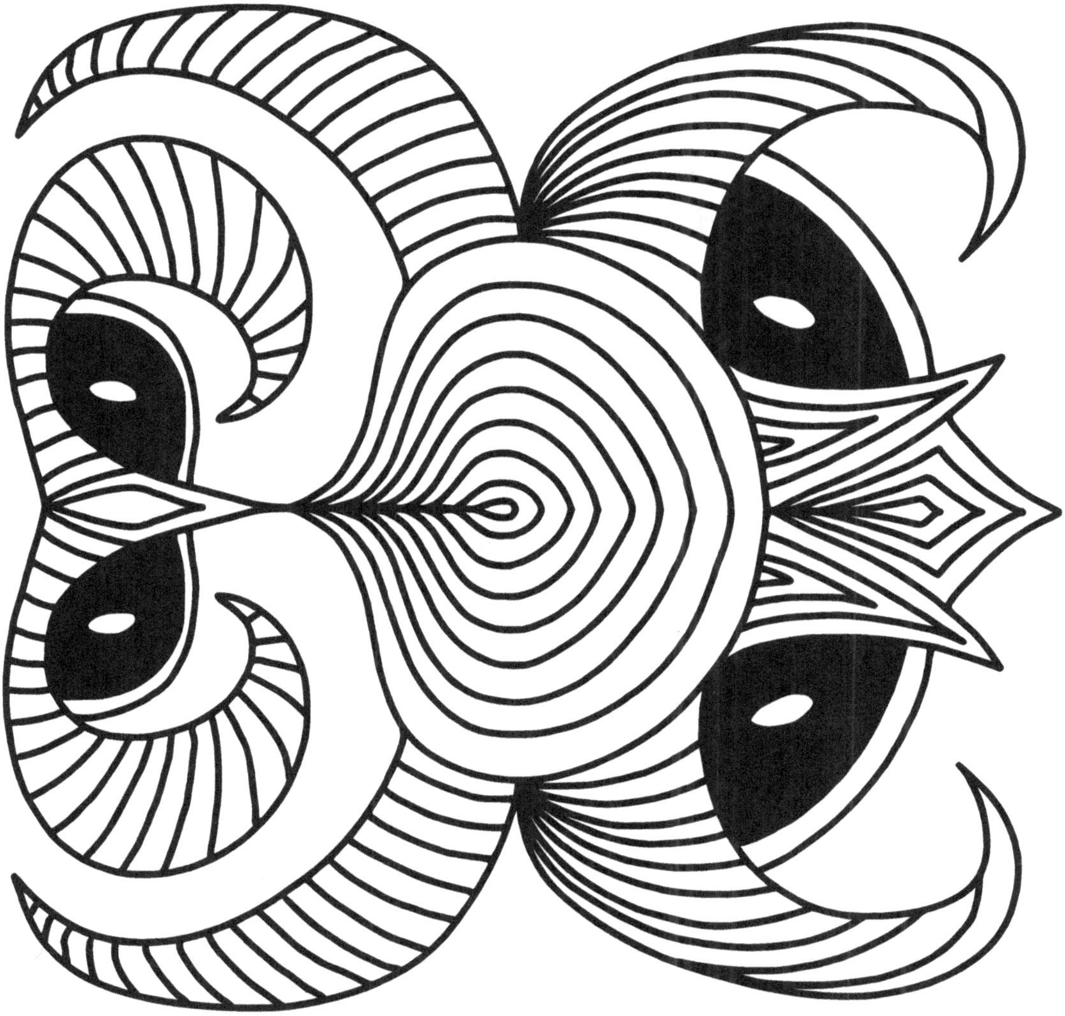

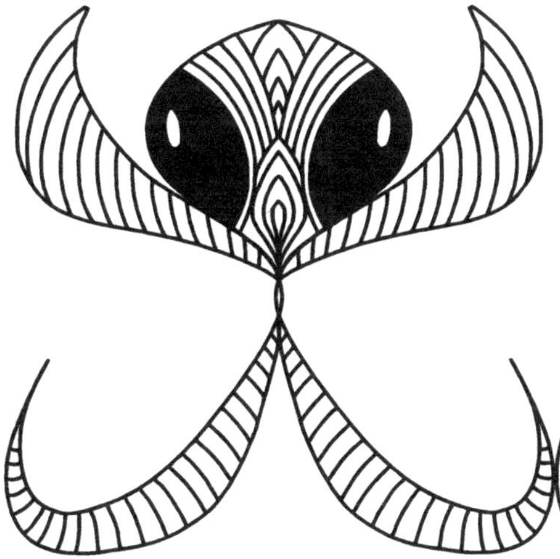

FATLINER WEIRDIES
VOLUME 1

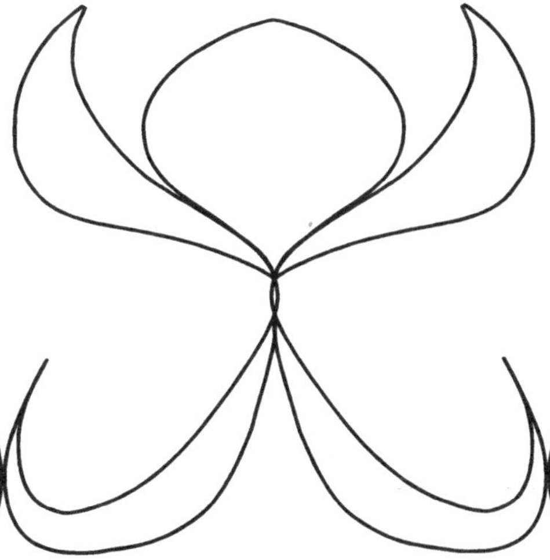

FATLINER WEIRDIES
THE TEMPLATES 1

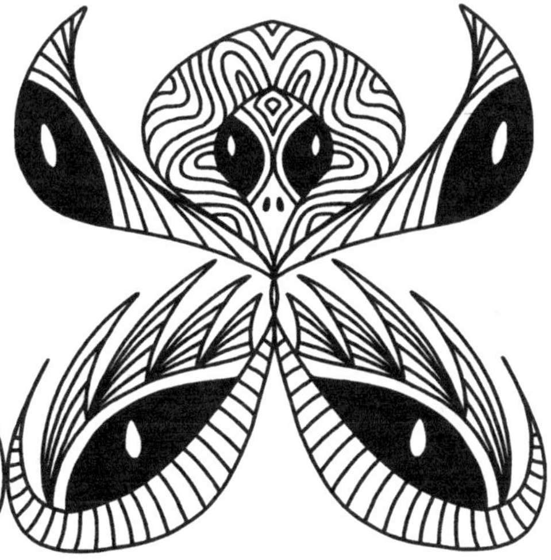

FATLINER WEIRDIES
VOLUME 3

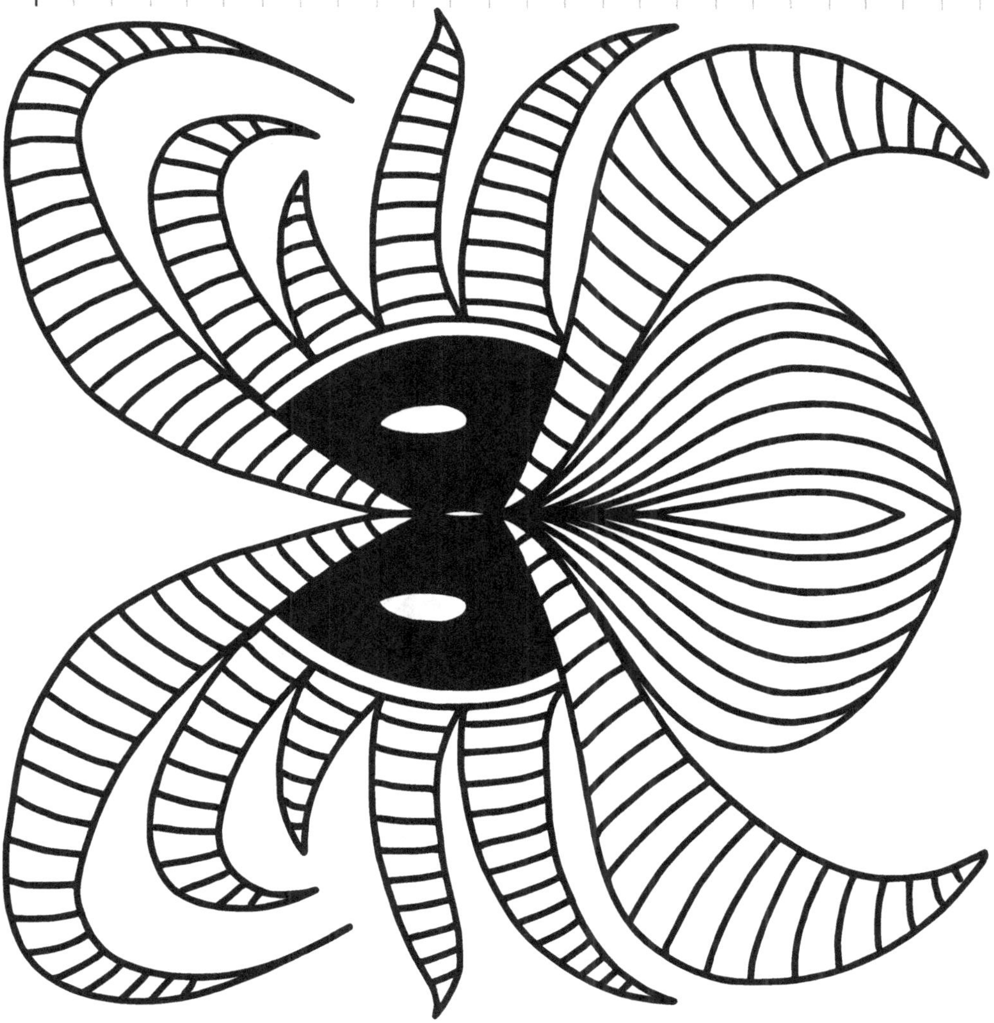

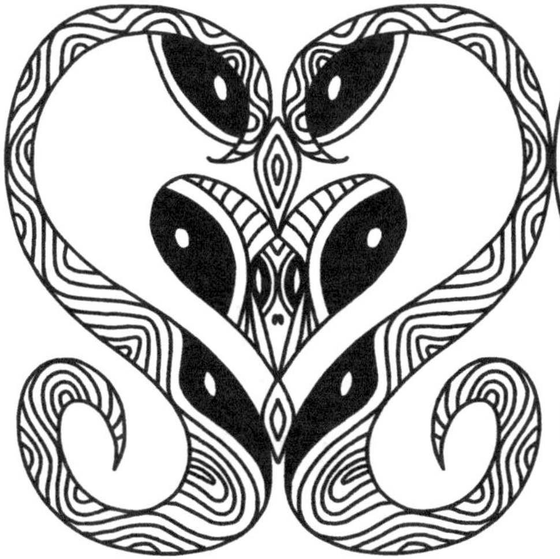

FATLINER WEIRDIES
VOLUME 1

FATLINER WEIRDIES
THE TEMPLATES 1

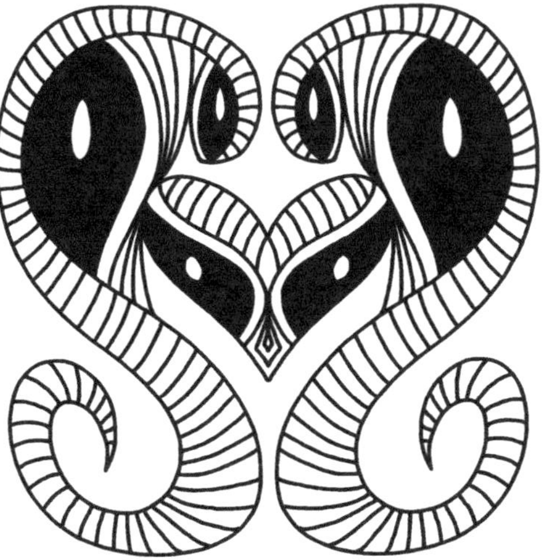

FATLINER WEIRDIES
VOLUME 3

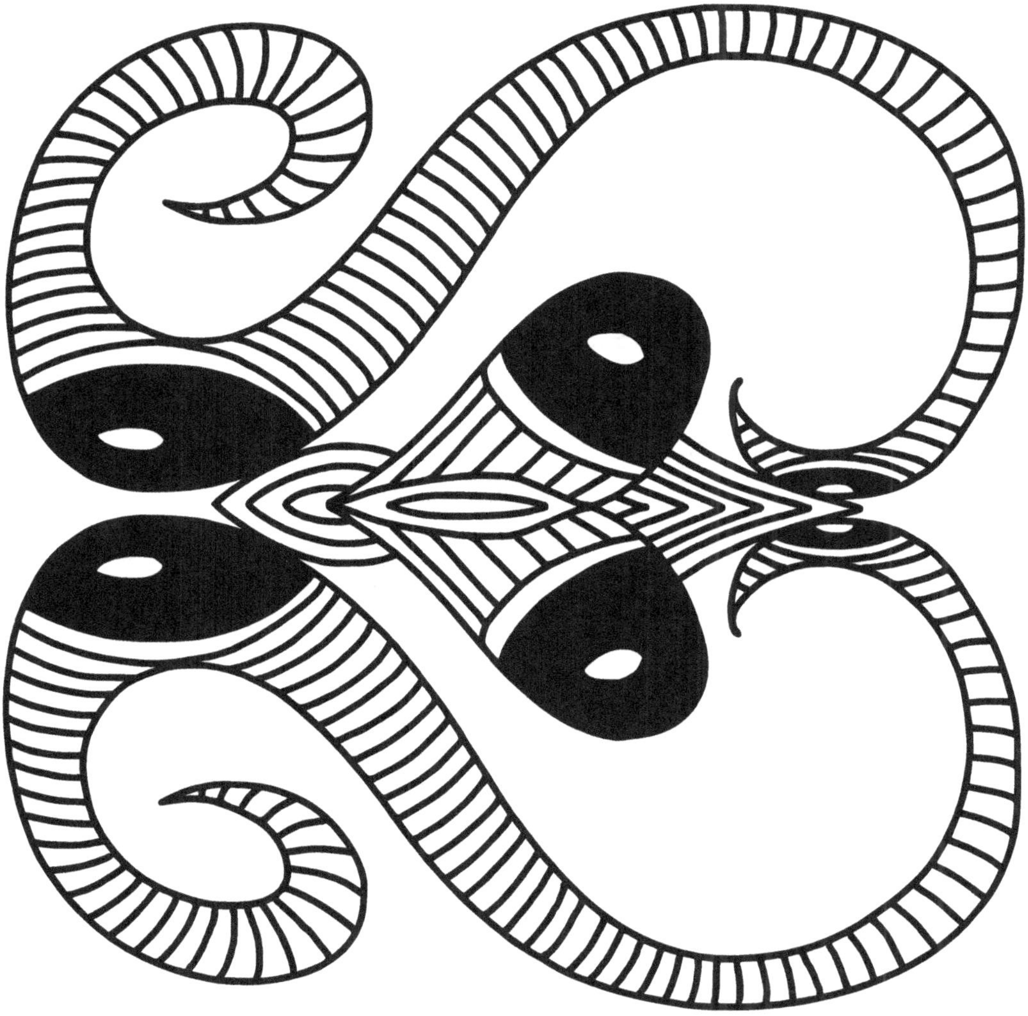

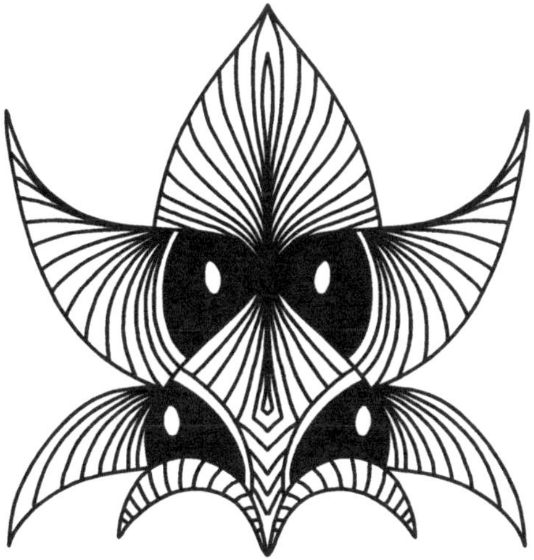
FATLINER WEIRDIES
VOLUME 1

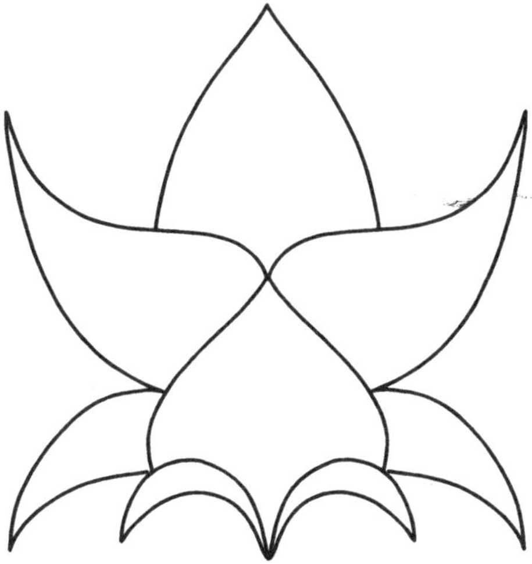
FATLINER WEIRDIES
THE TEMPLATES 1

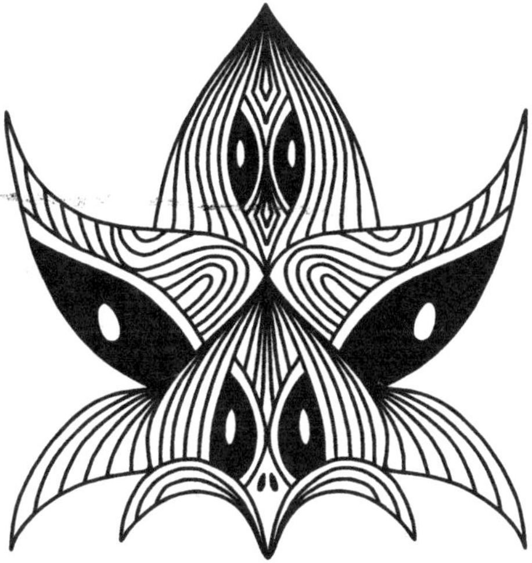
FATLINER WEIRDIES
VOLUME 3

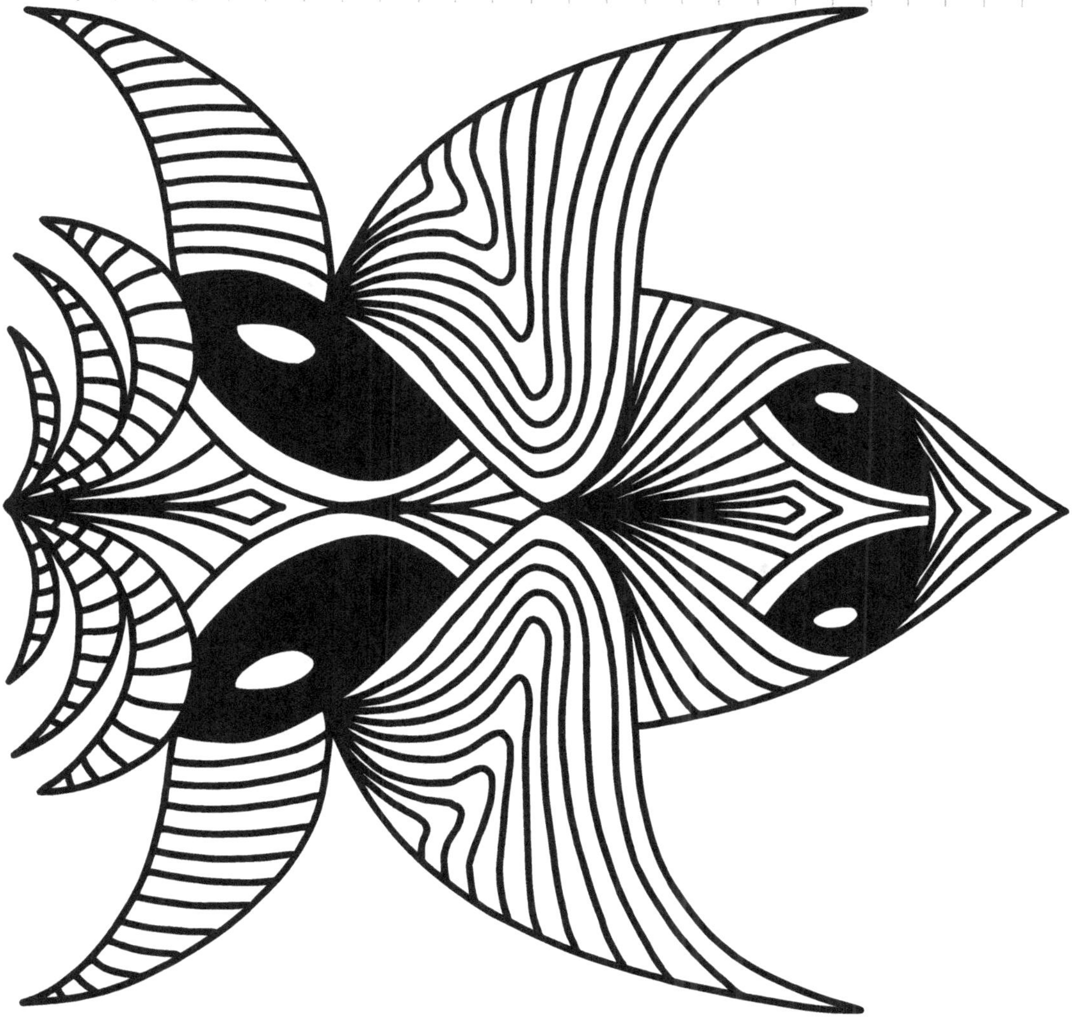

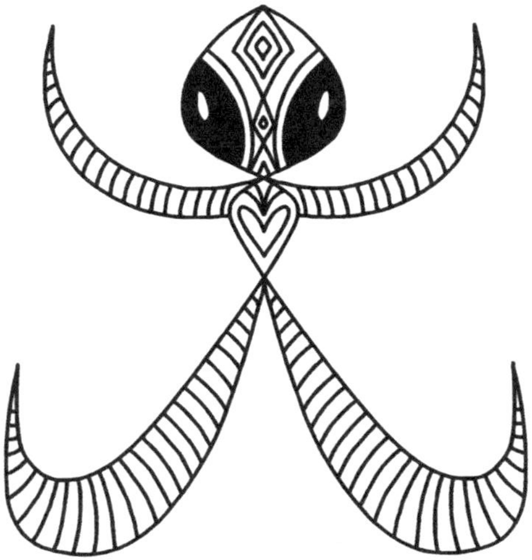

FATLINER WEIRDIES
VOLUME 1

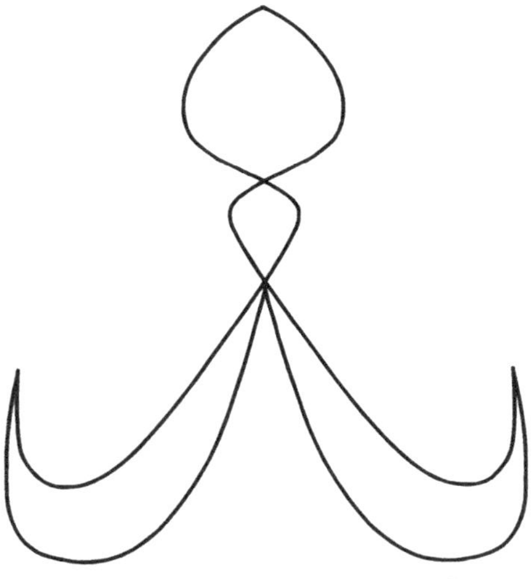

FATLINER WEIRDIES
THE TEMPLATES 1

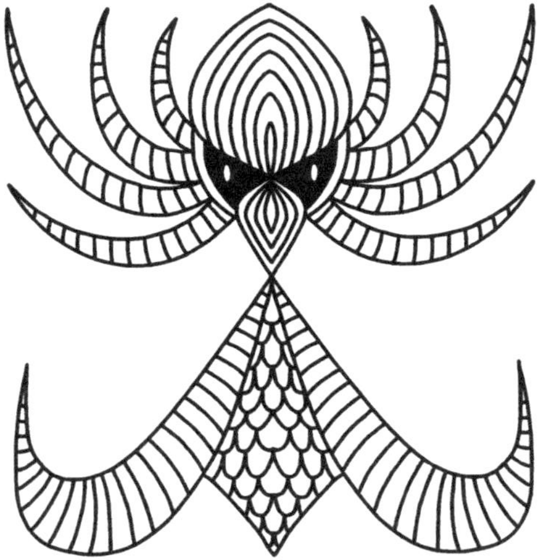

FATLINER WEIRDIES
VOLUME 3

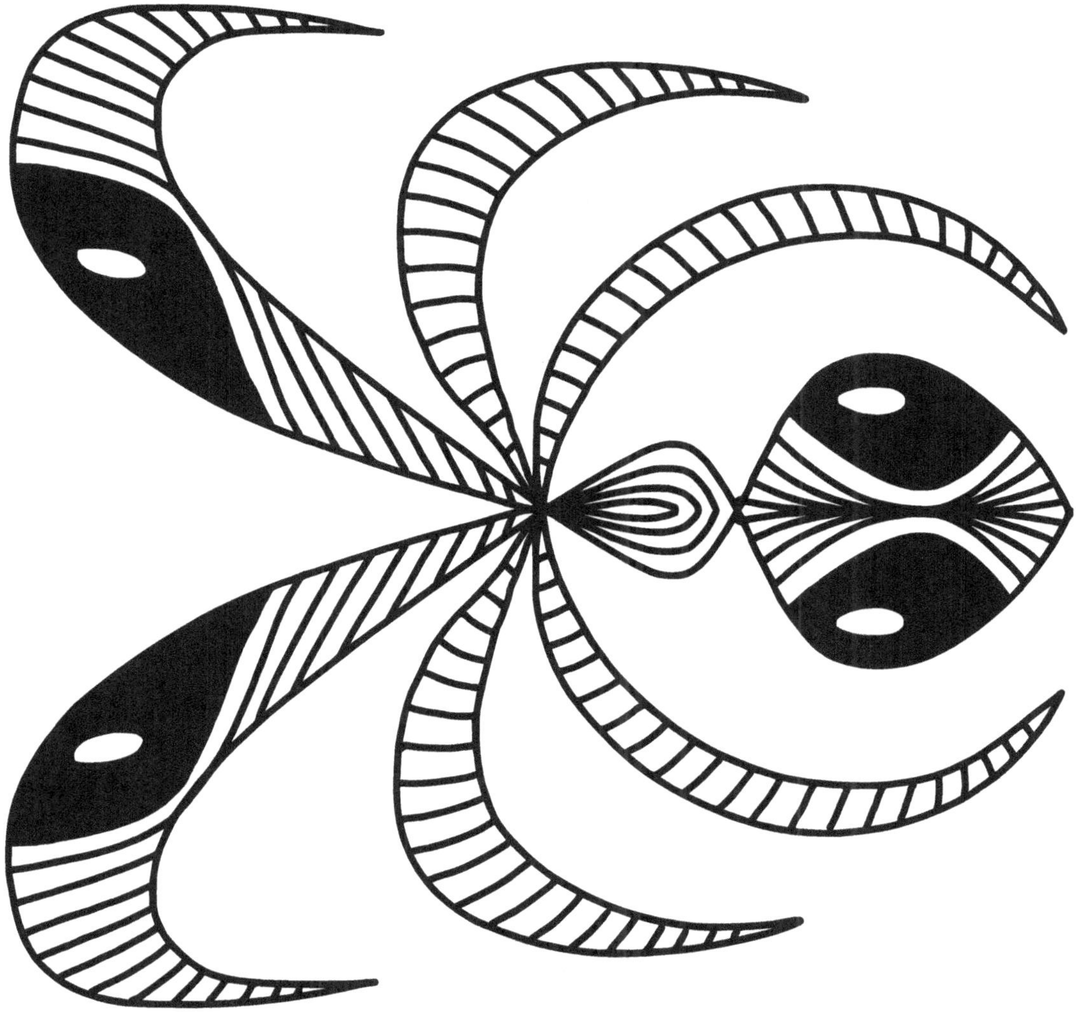

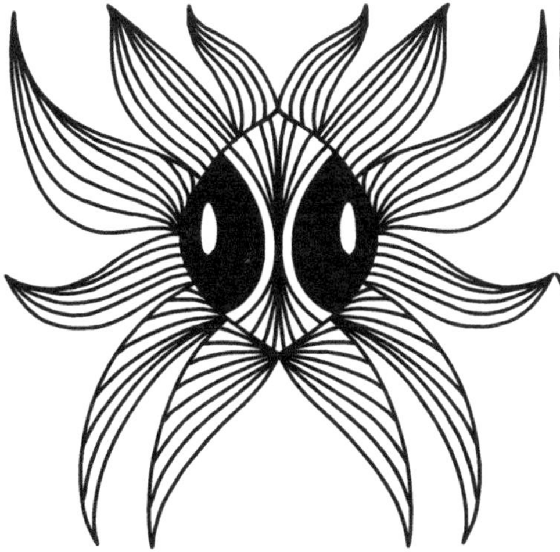

FATLINER WEIRDIES
VOLUME 1

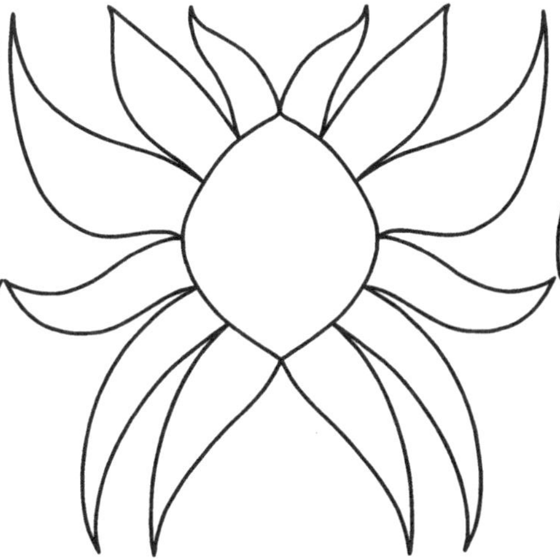

FATLINER WEIRDIES
THE TEMPLATES 1

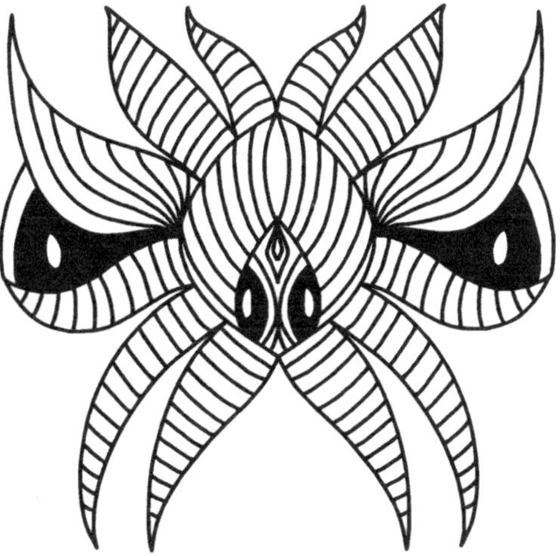

FATLINER WEIRDIES
VOLUME 3

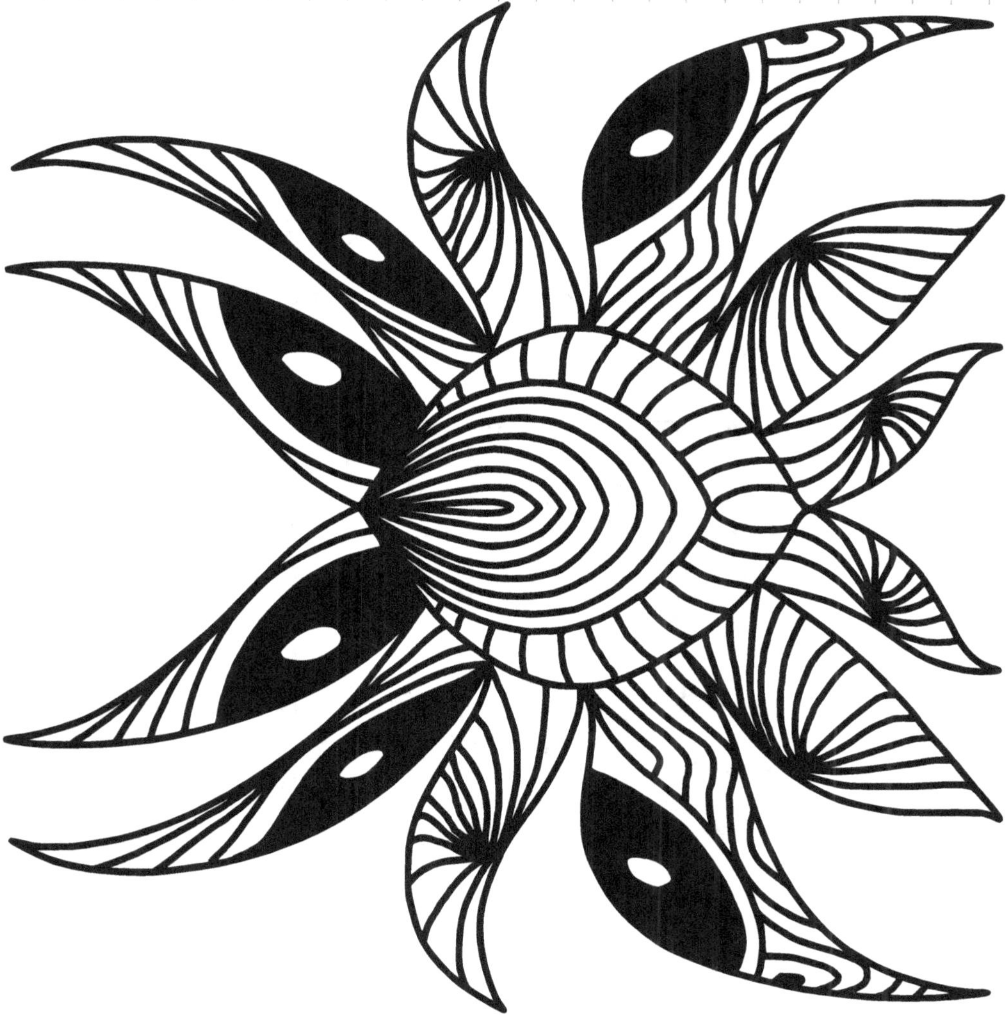

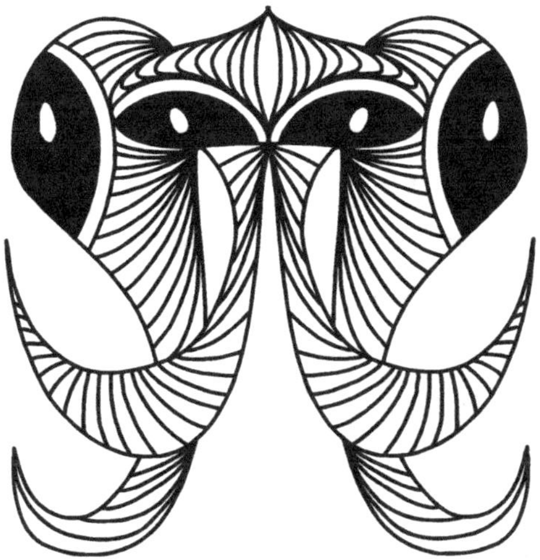

FATLINER WEIRDIES
VOLUME 1

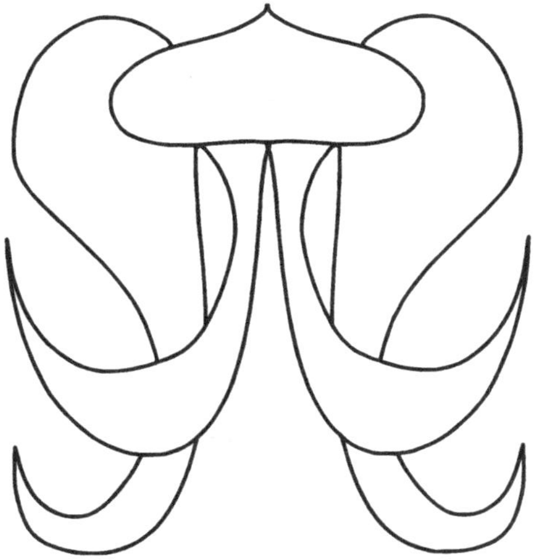

FATLINER WEIRDIES
THE TEMPLATES 1

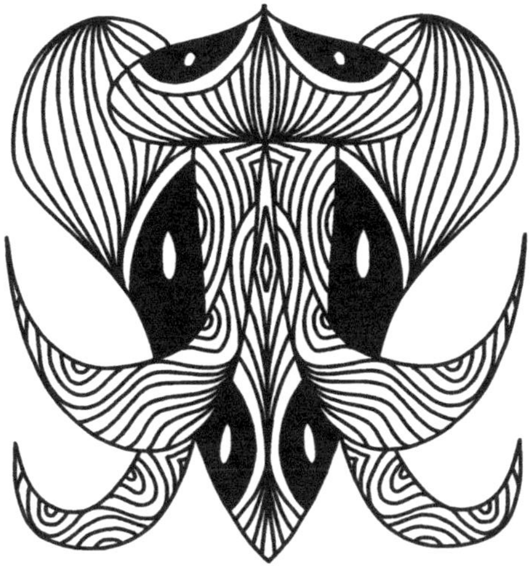

FATLINER WEIRDIES
VOLUME 3

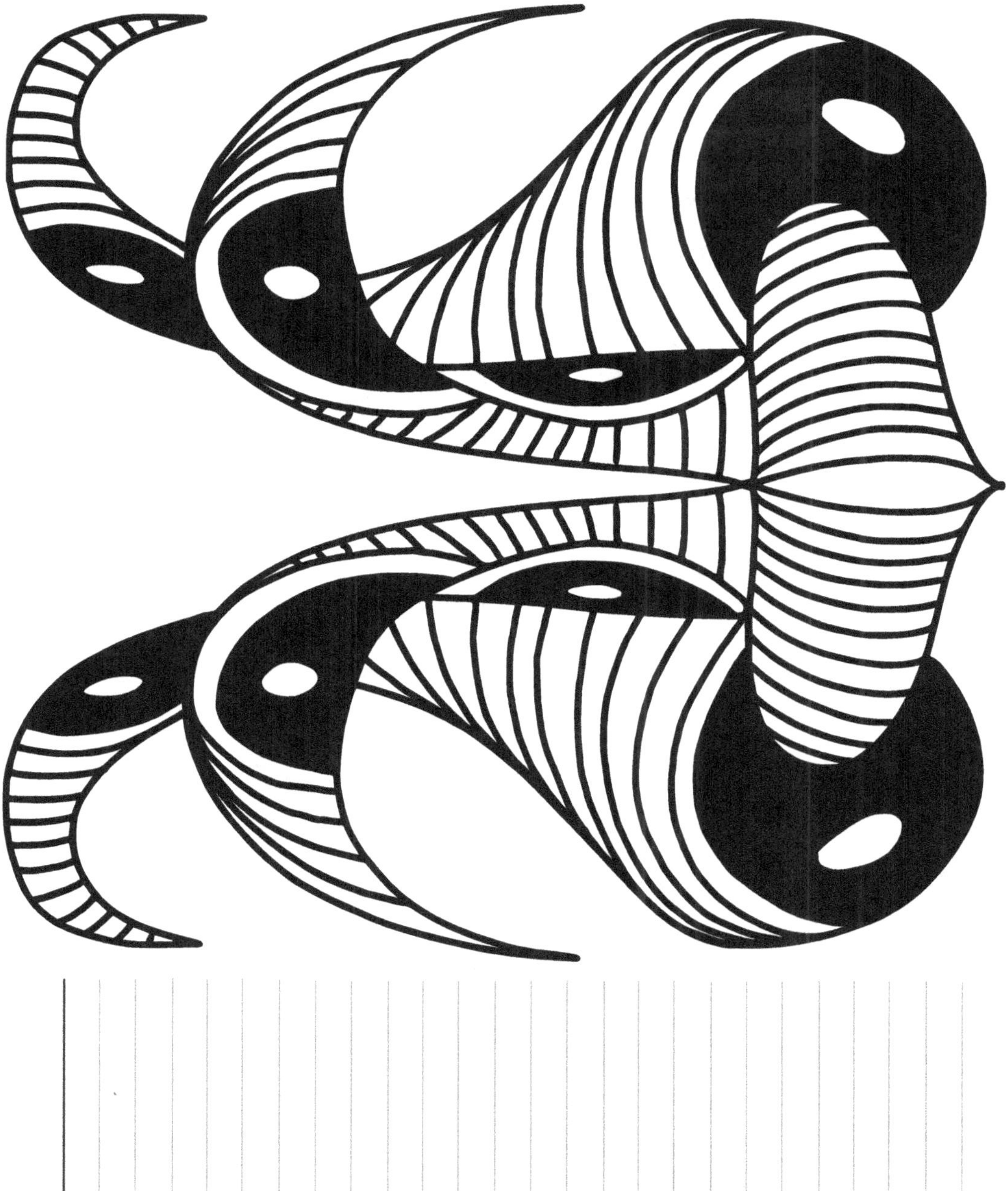

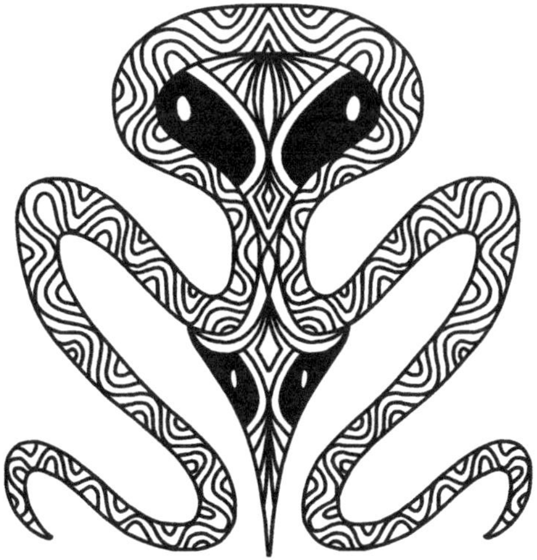

FATLINER WEIRDIES
VOLUME 1

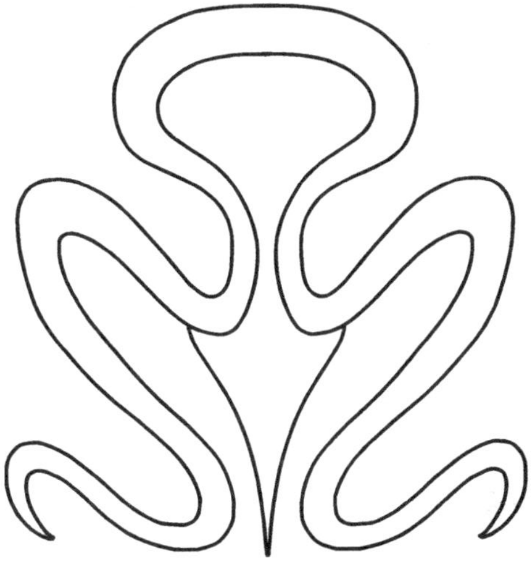

FATLINER WEIRDIES
THE TEMPLATES 1

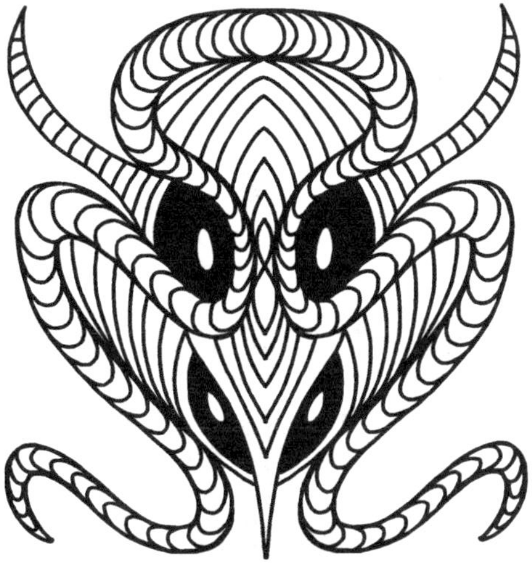

FATLINER WEIRDIES
VOLUME 3

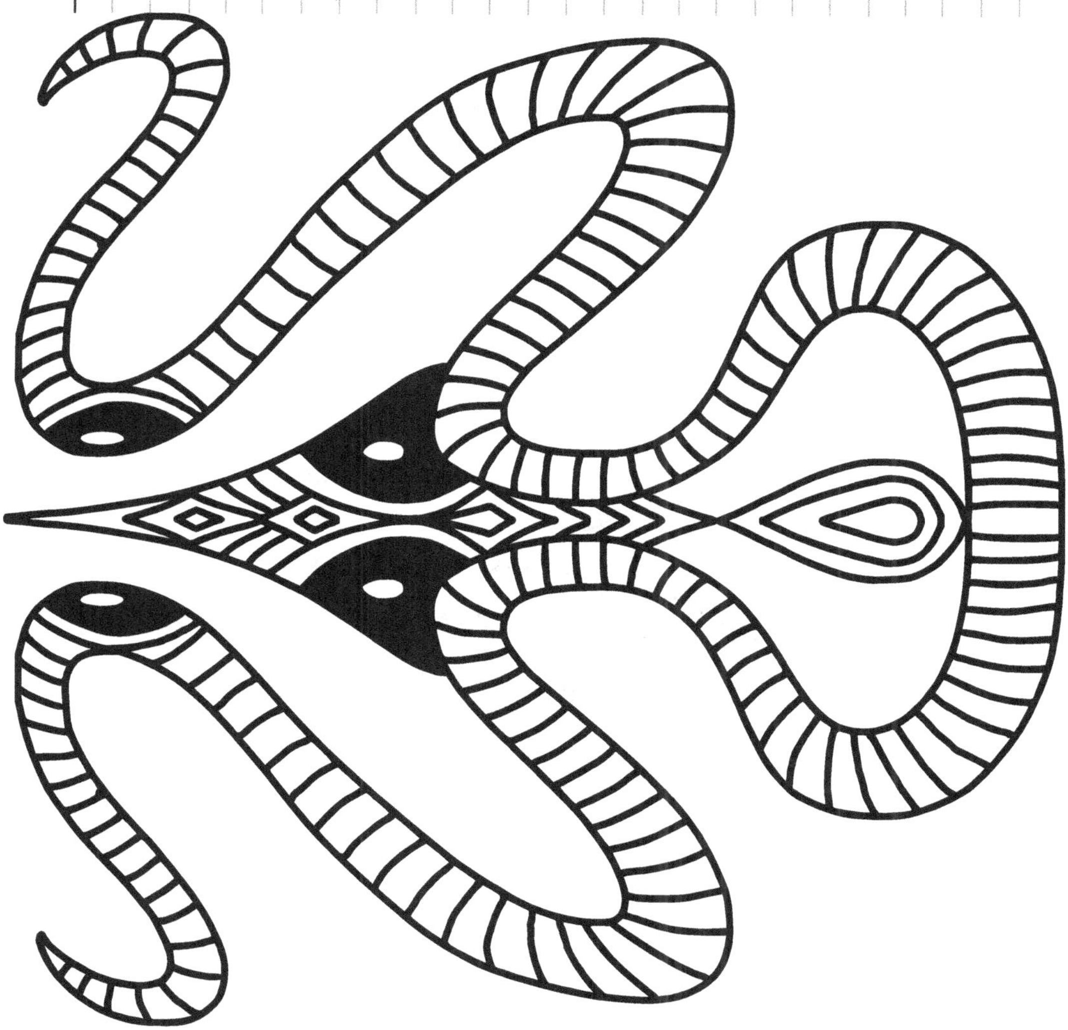

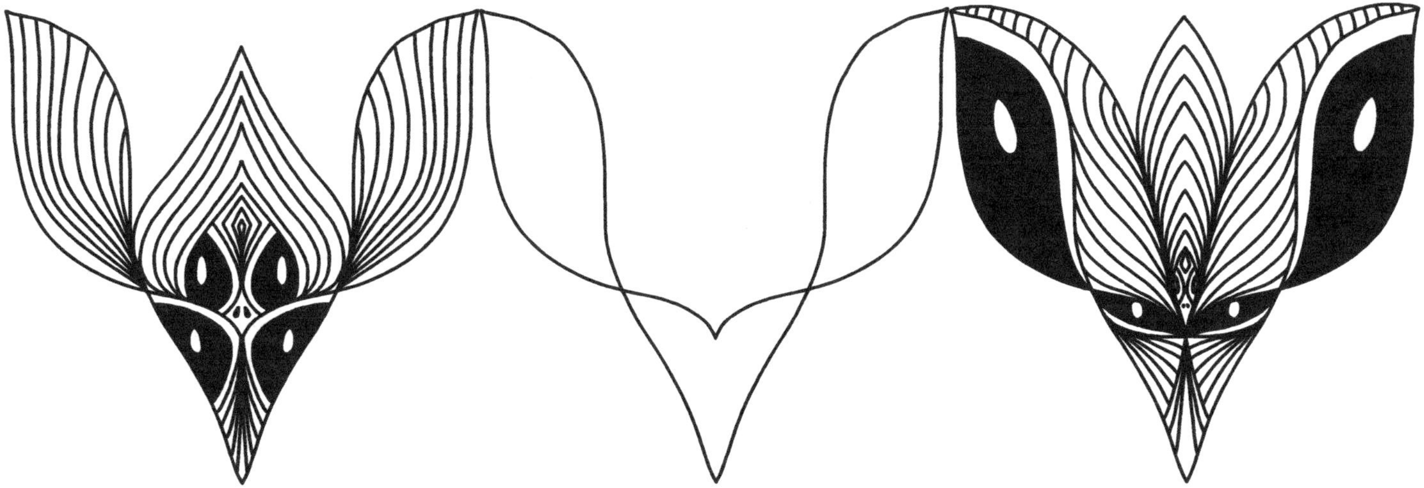

FATLINER WEIRDIES
VOLUME 1

FATLINER WEIRDIES
THE TEMPLATES 1

FATLINER WEIRDIES
VOLUME 3

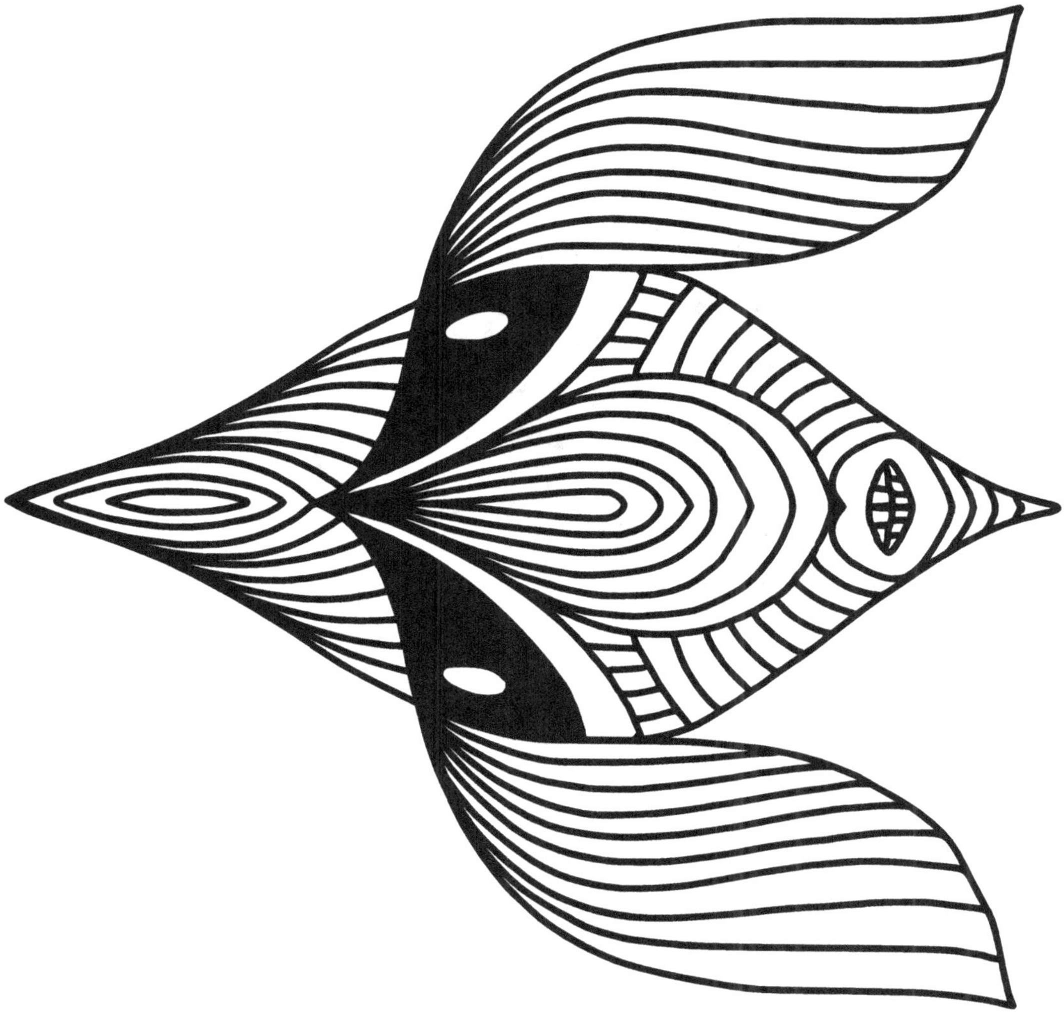

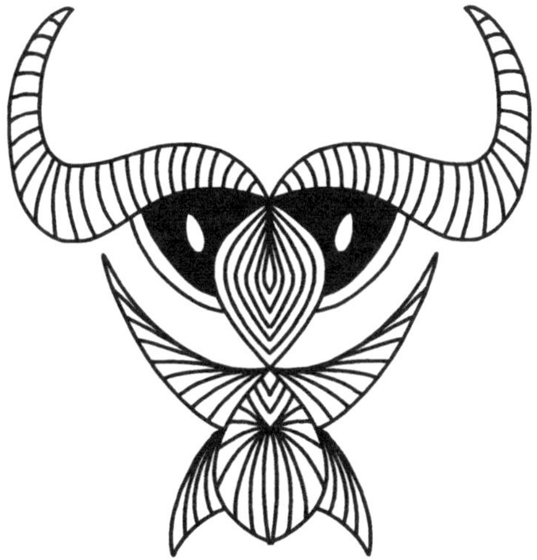

FATLINER WEIRDIES
VOLUME 1

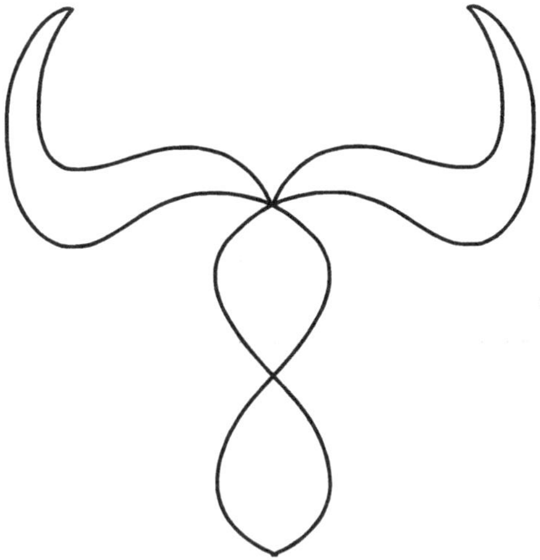

FATLINER WEIRDIES
THE TEMPLATES 1

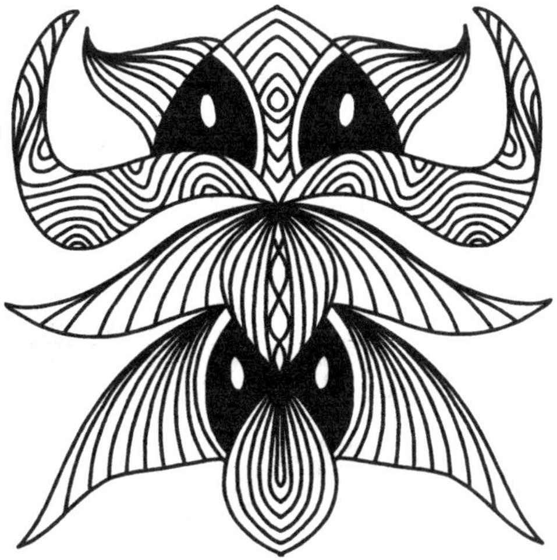

FATLINER WEIRDIES
VOLUME 3

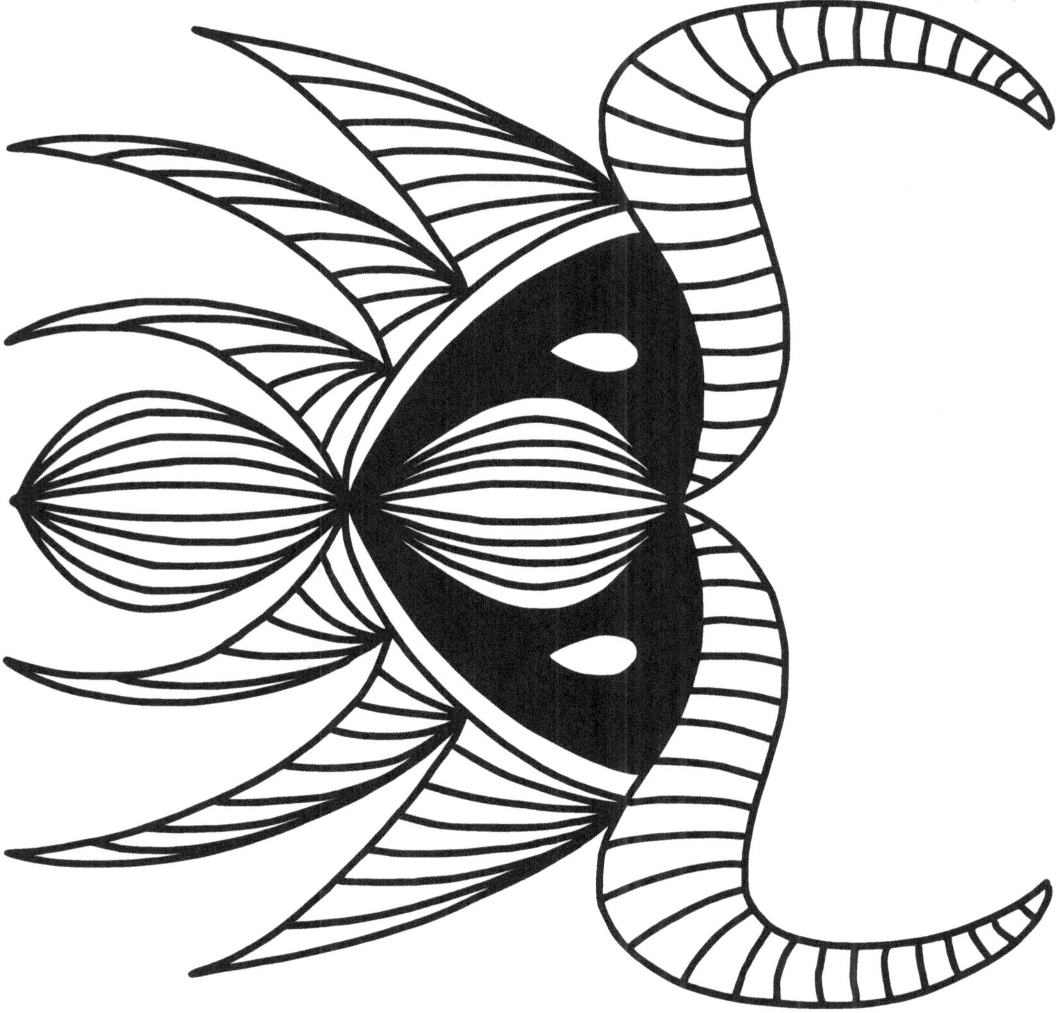

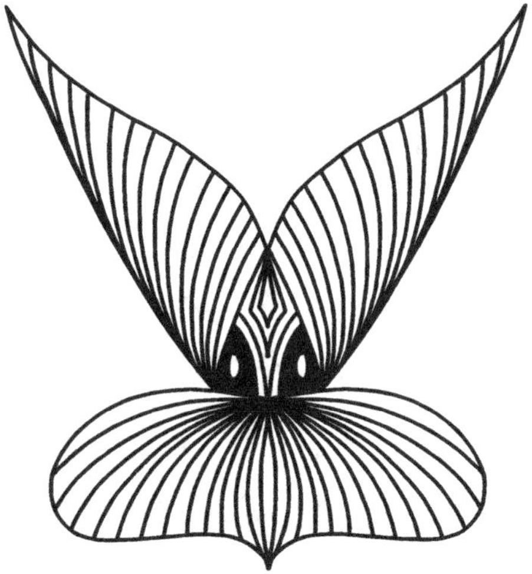

FATLINER WEIRDIES
VOLUME 1

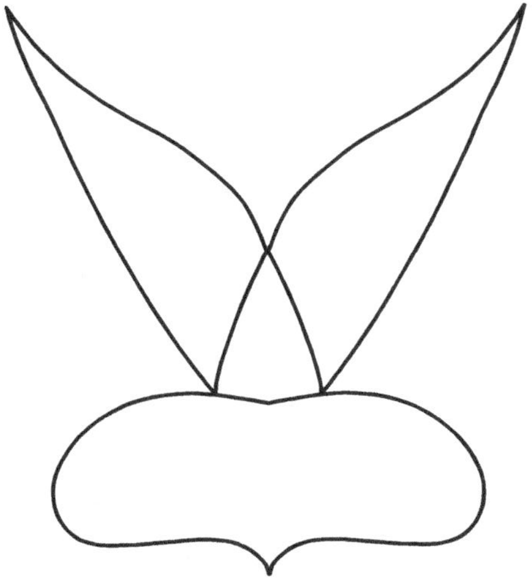

FATLINER WEIRDIES
THE TEMPLATES 1

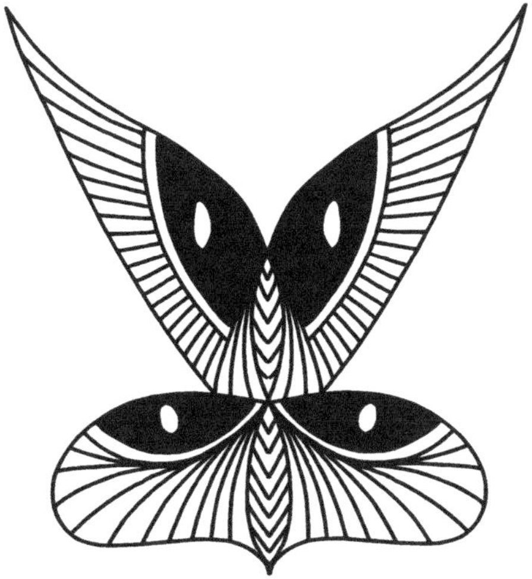

FATLINER WEIRDIES
VOLUME 3

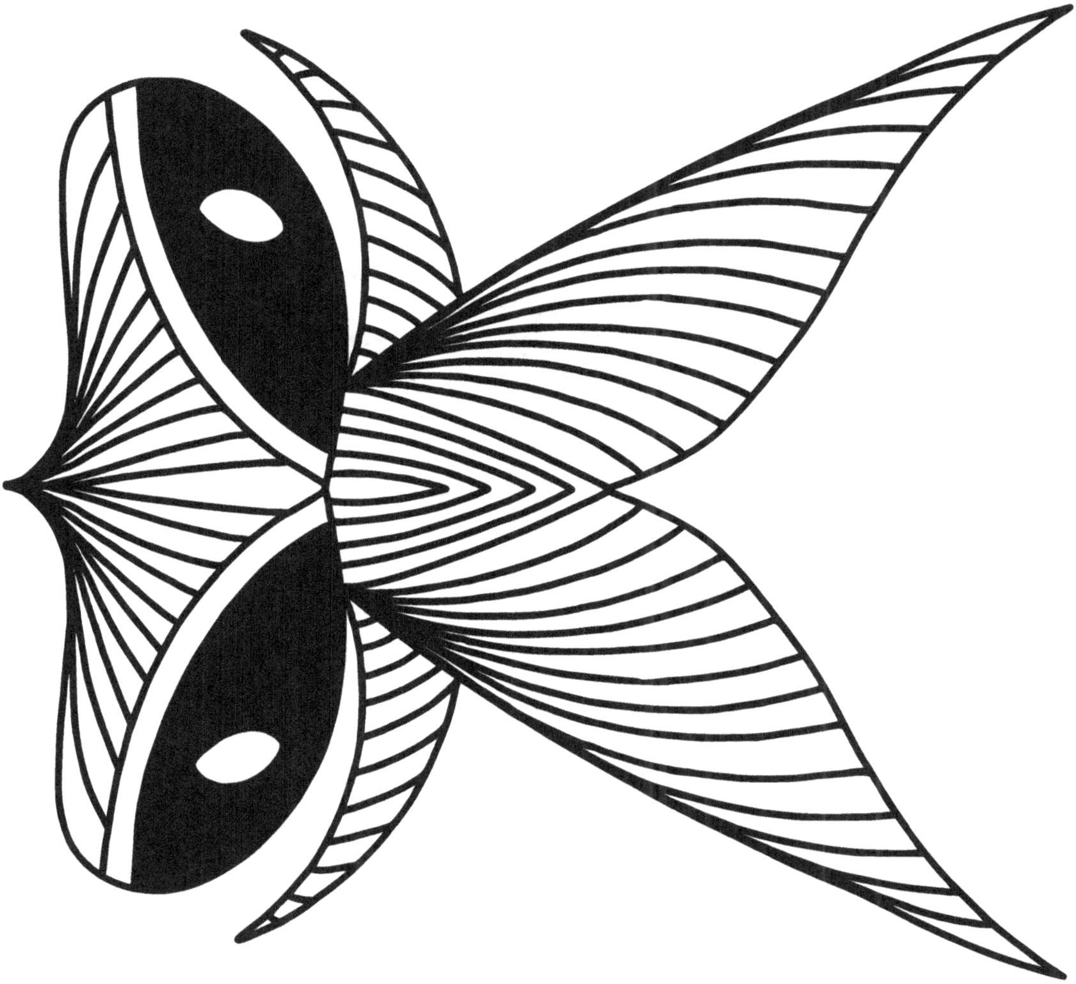

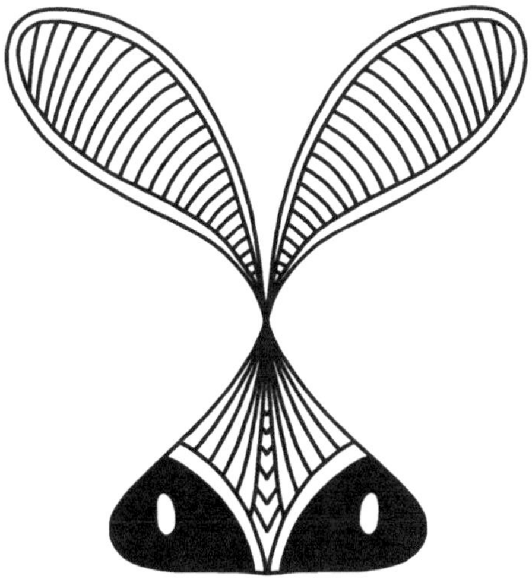

FATLINER WEIRDIES
VOLUME 1

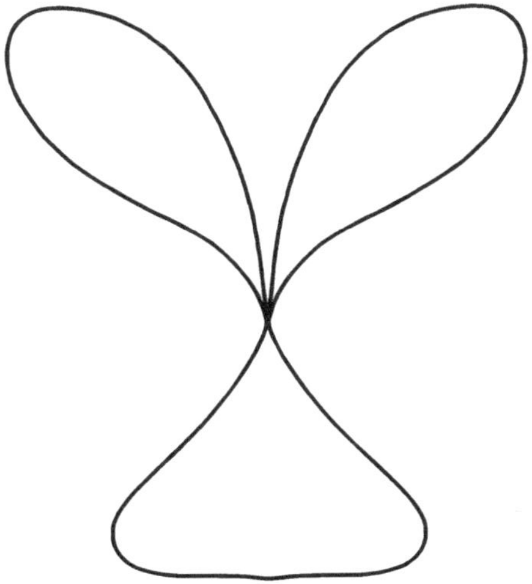

FATLINER WEIRDIES
THE TEMPLATES 1

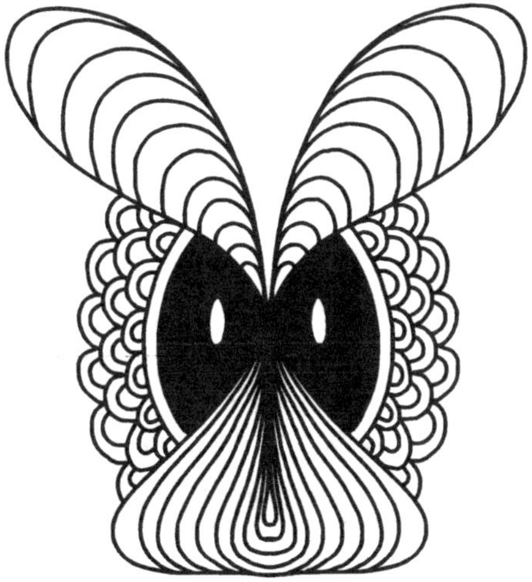

FATLINER WEIRDIES
VOLUME 3

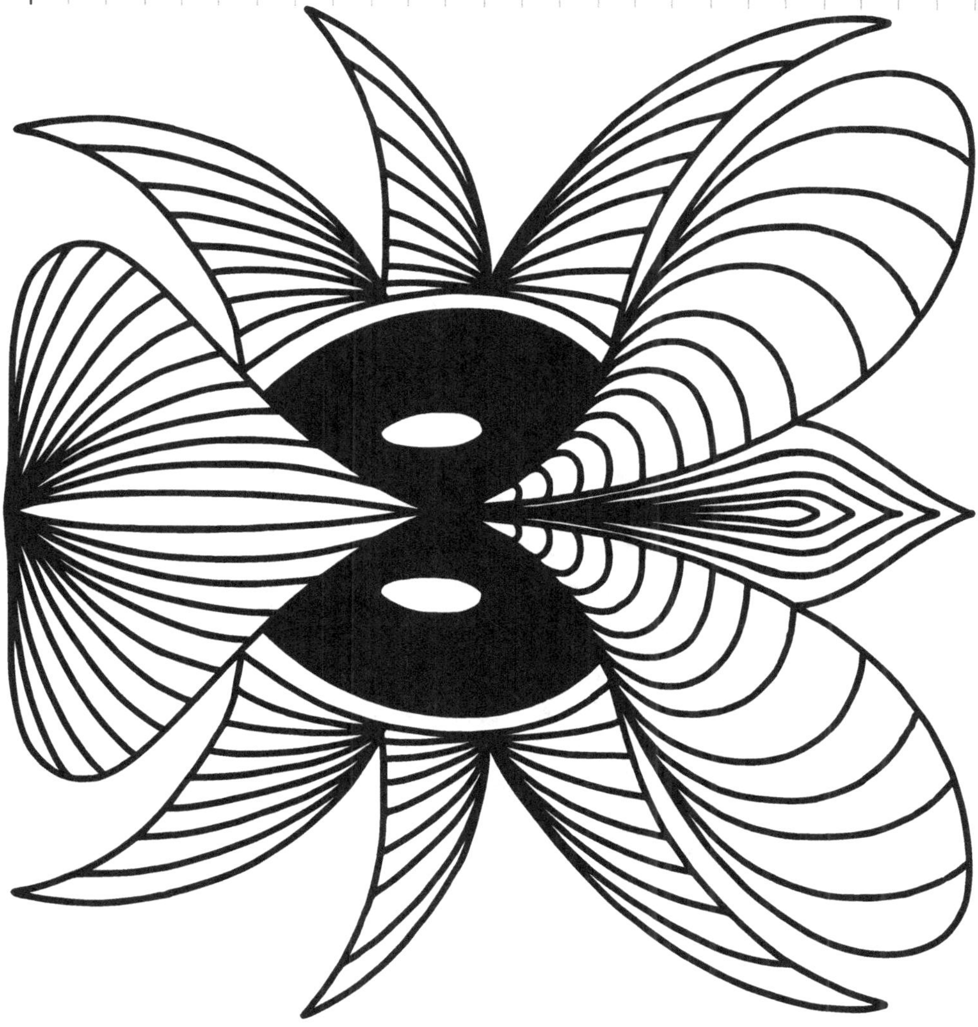

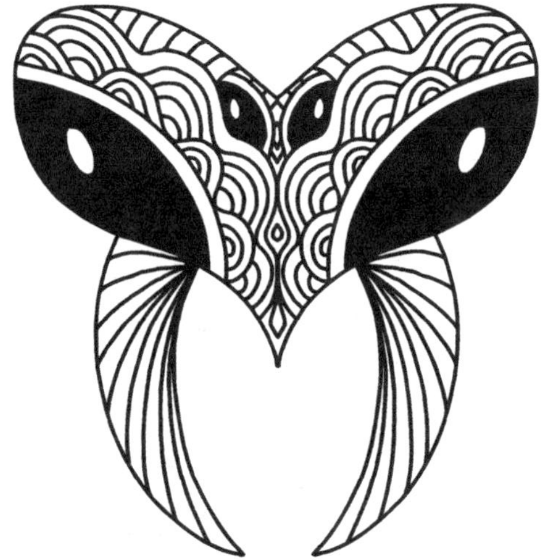

FATLINER WEIRDIES
VOLUME 1

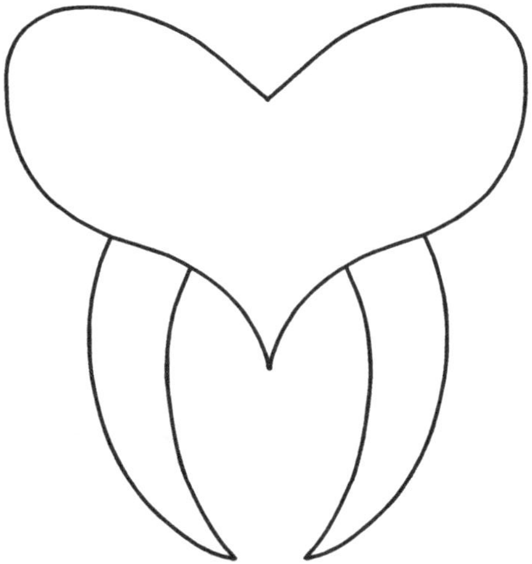

FATLINER WEIRDIES
THE TEMPLATES 1

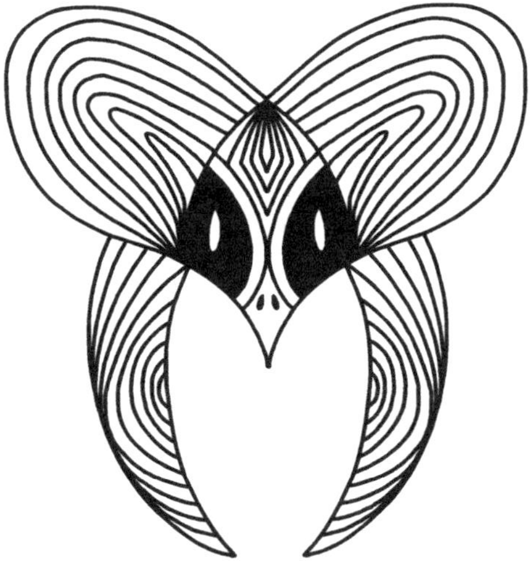

FATLINER WEIRDIES
VOLUME 3

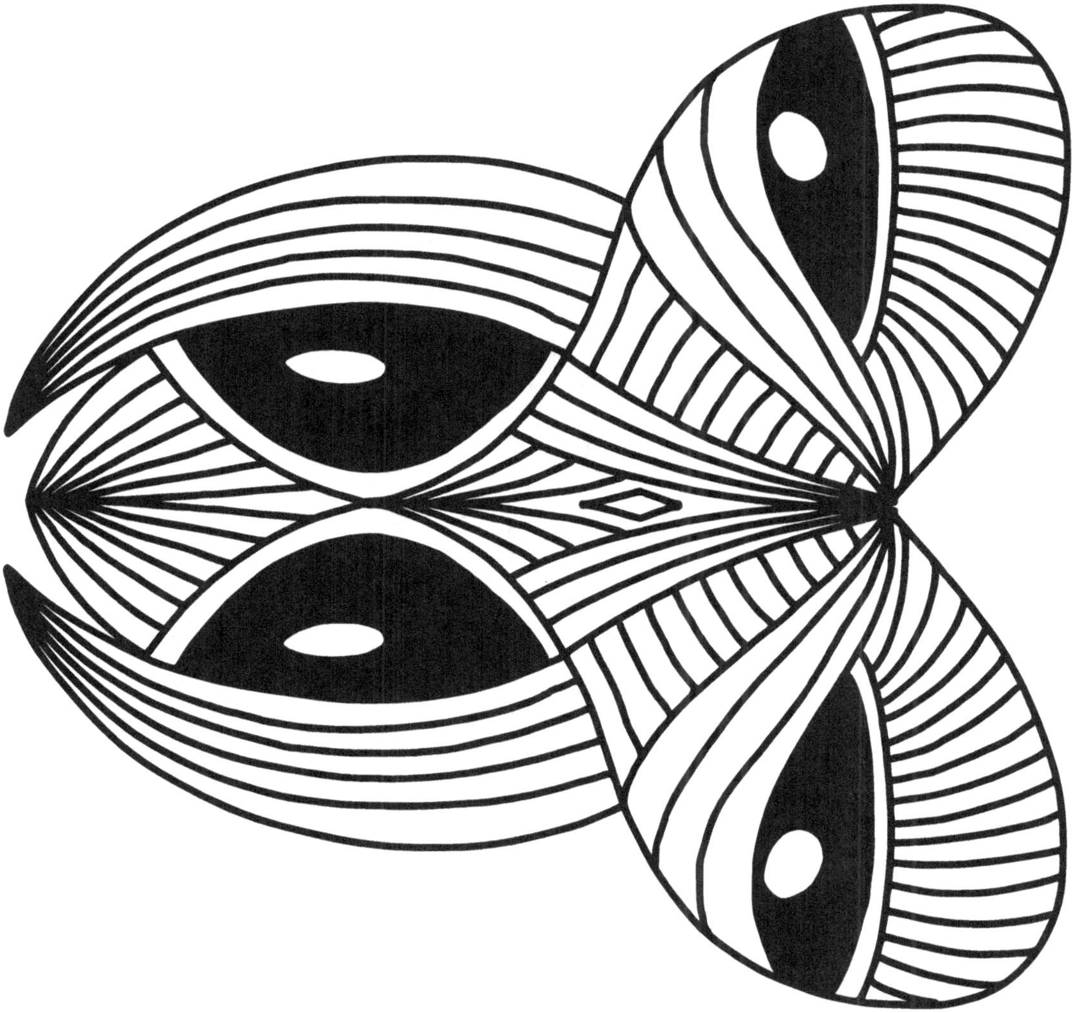

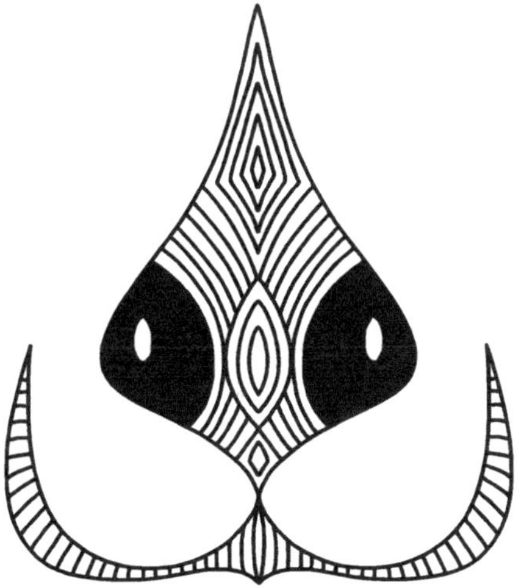
FATLINER WEIRDIES
VOLUME 1

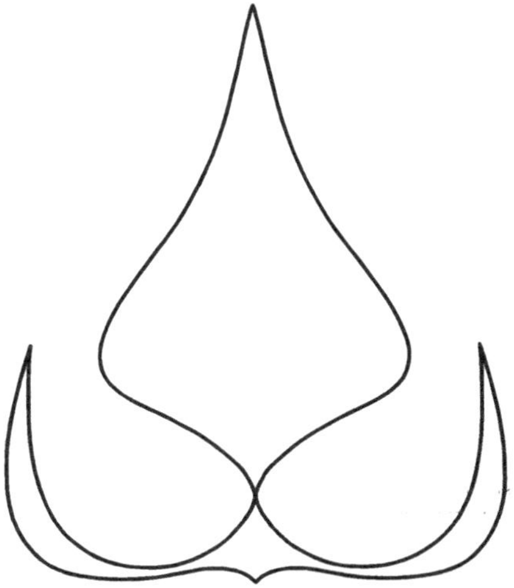
FATLINER WEIRDIES
THE TEMPLATES 1

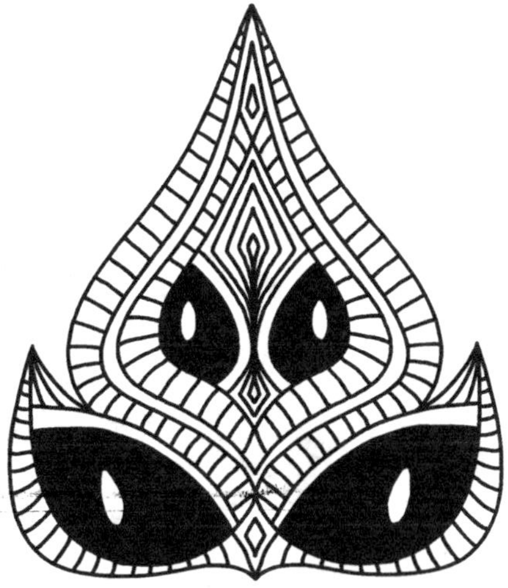
FATLINER WEIRDIES
VOLUME 3

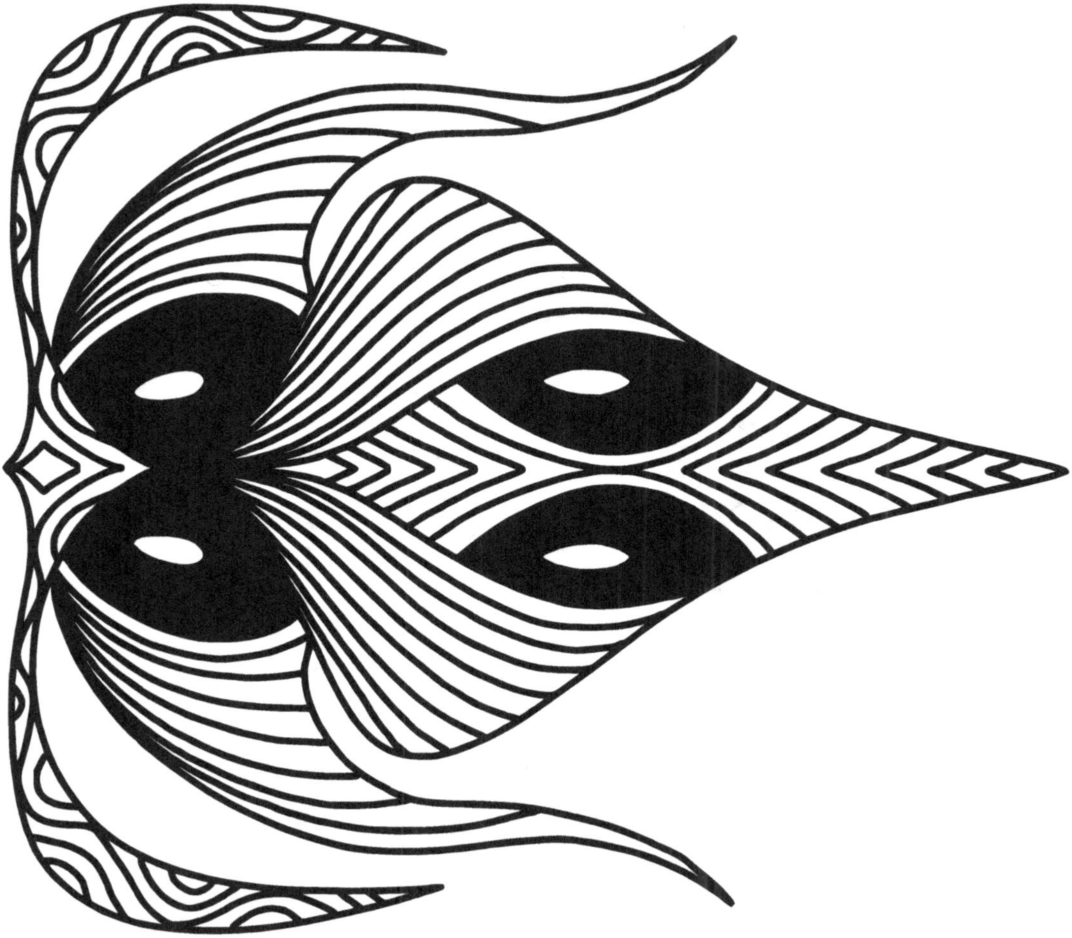

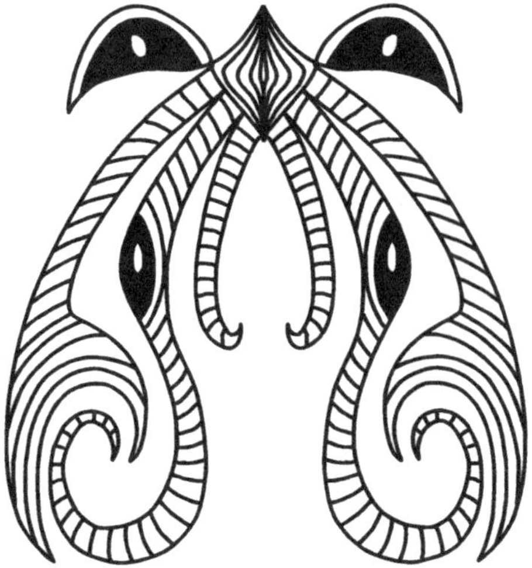
FATLINER WEIRDIES
VOLUME 1

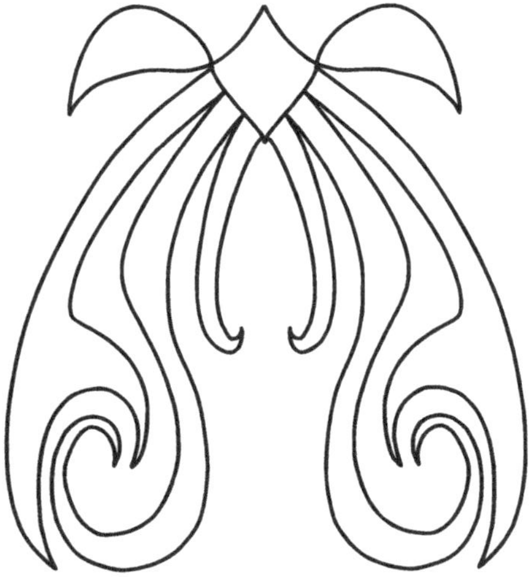
FATLINER WEIRDIES
THE TEMPLATES 1

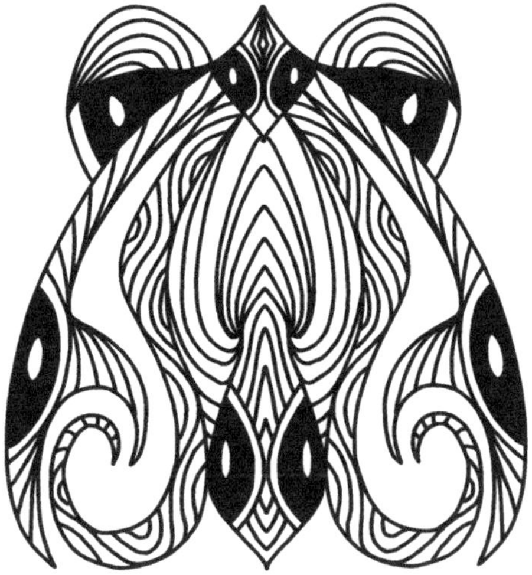
FATLINER WEIRDIES
VOLUME 3

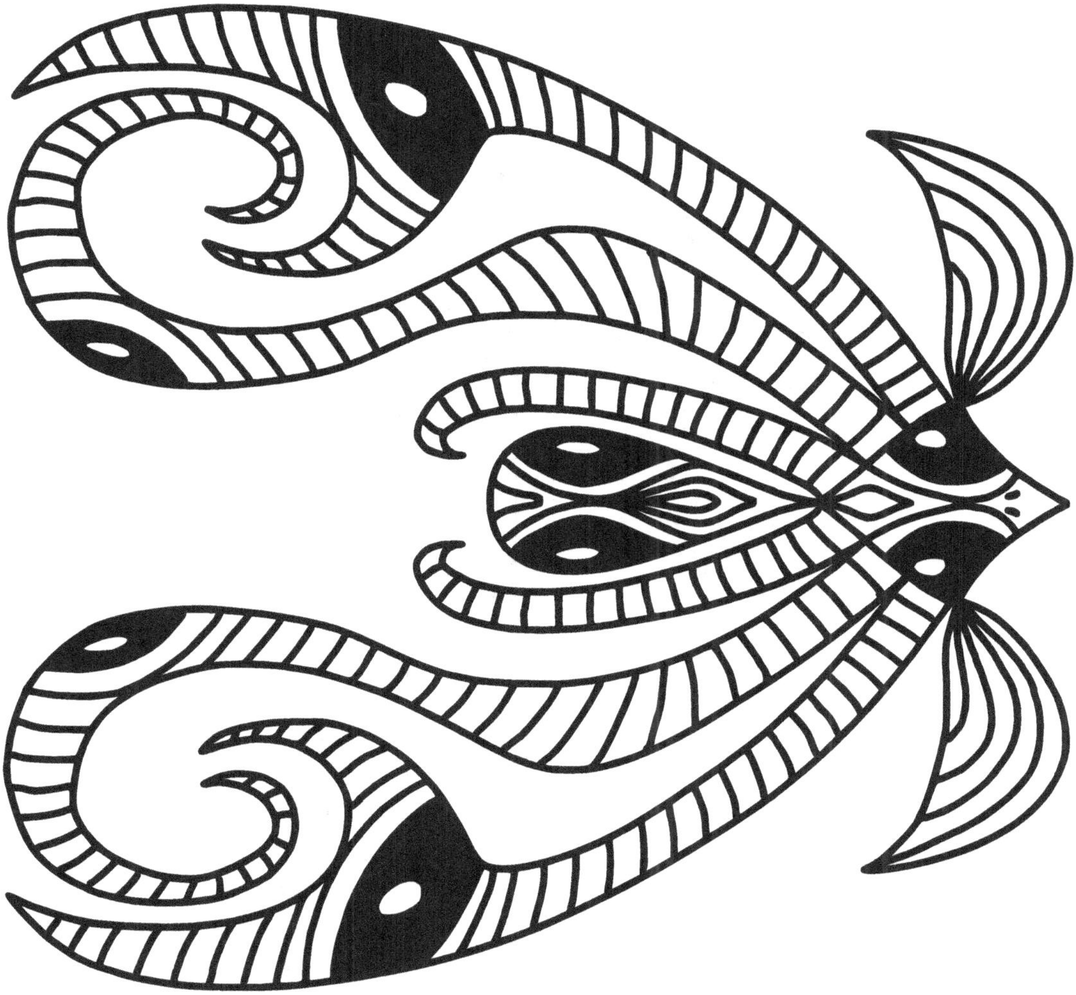

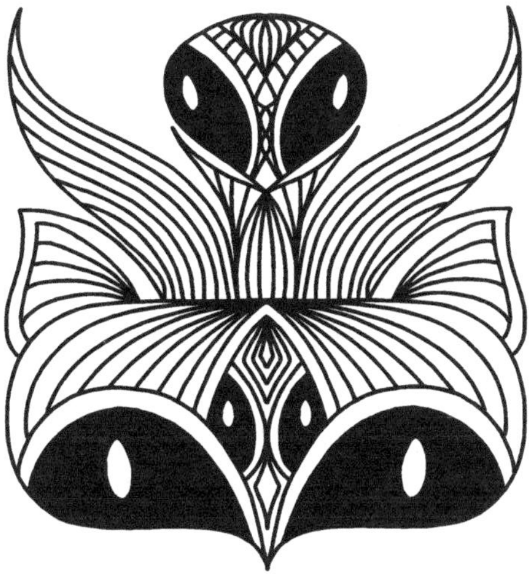

FATLINER WEIRDIES
VOLUME 1

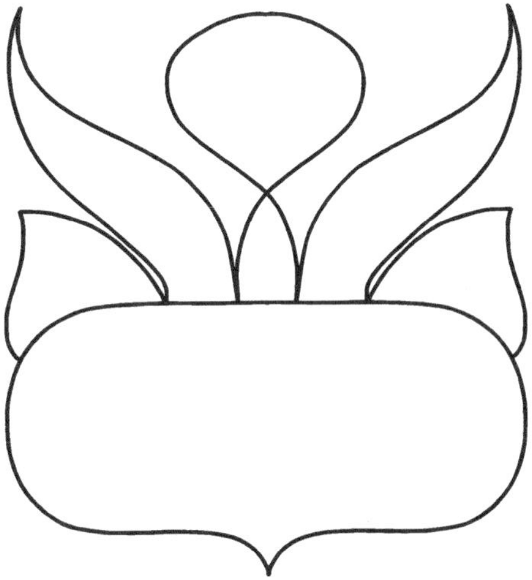

FATLINER WEIRDIES
THE TEMPLATES 1

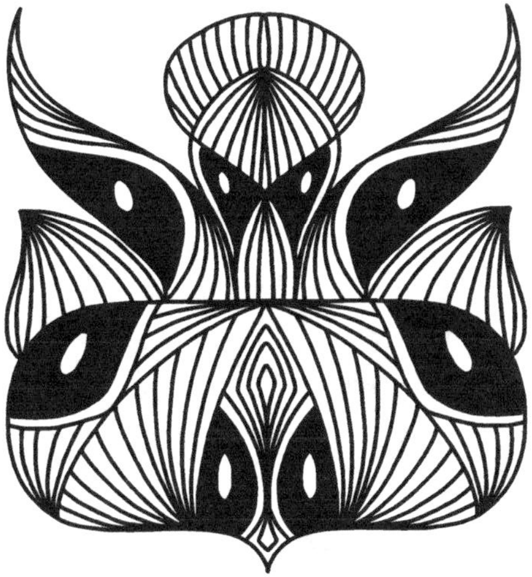

FATLINER WEIRDIES
VOLUME 3

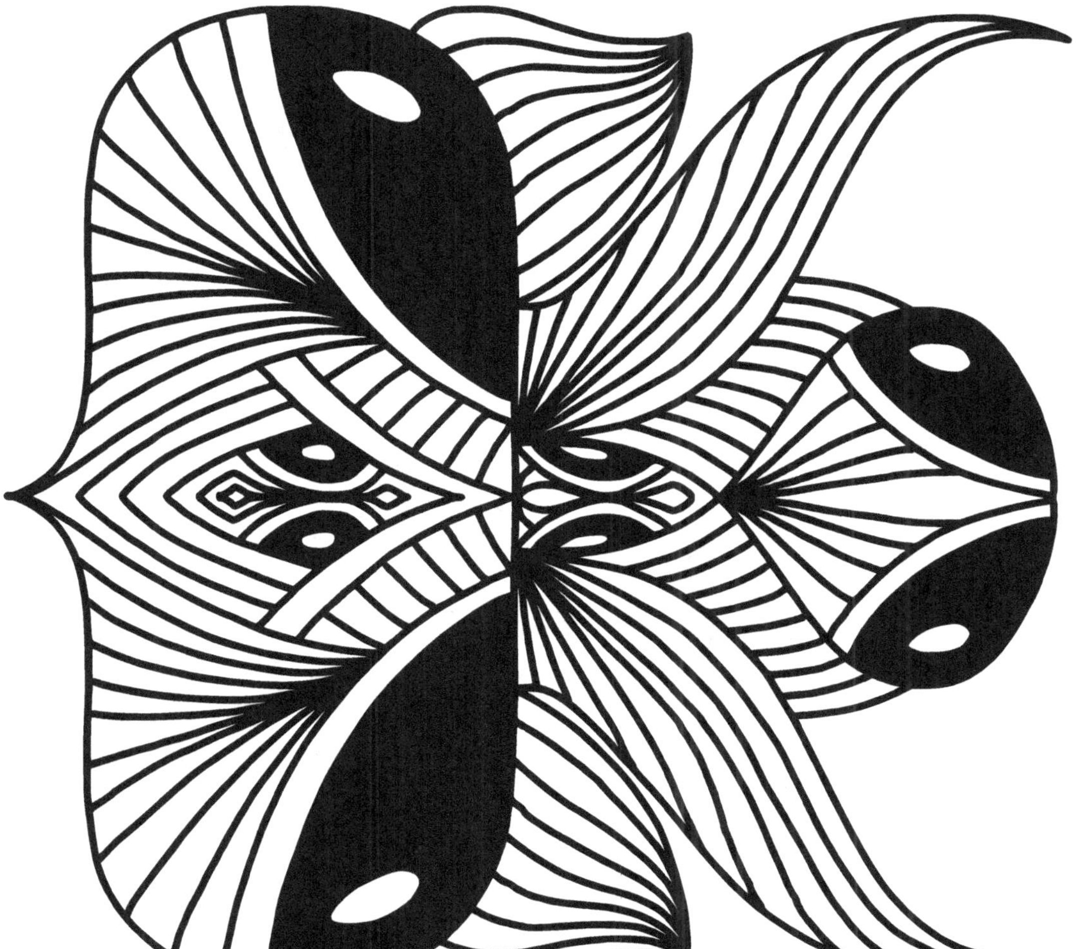

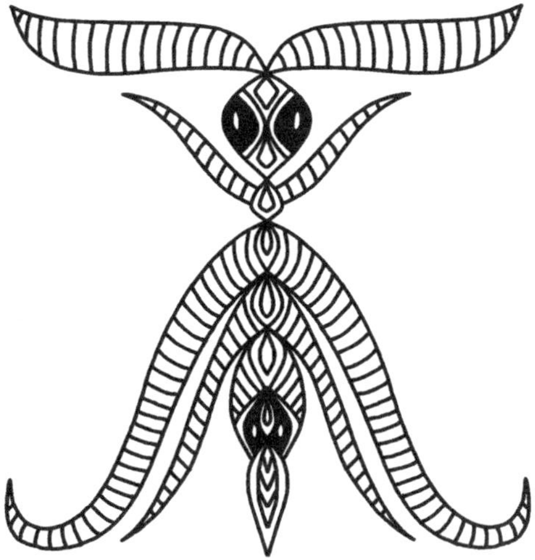

FATLINER WEIRDIES
VOLUME 1

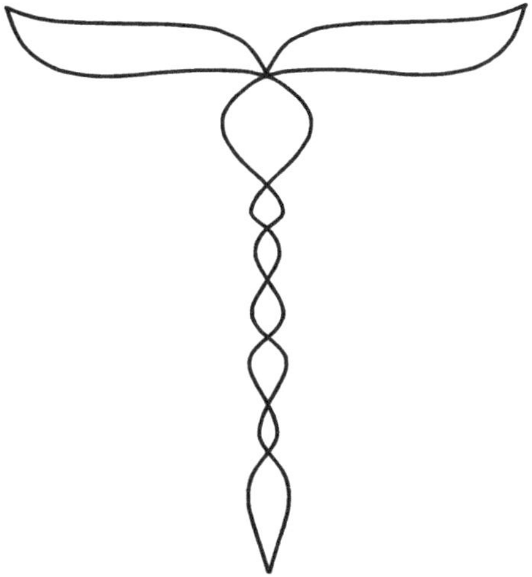

FATLINER WEIRDIES
THE TEMPLATES 1

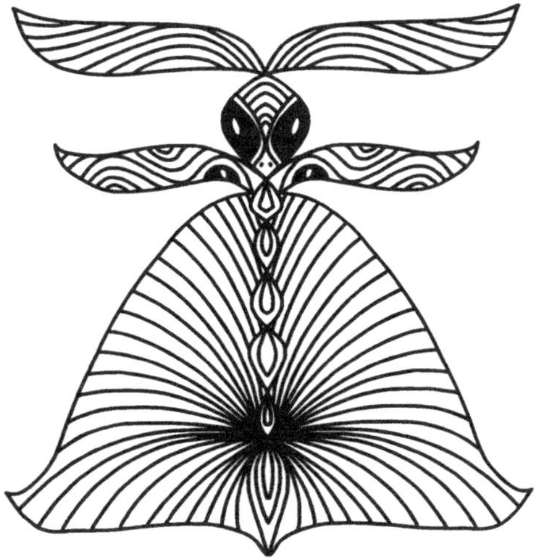

FATLINER WEIRDIES
VOLUME 3

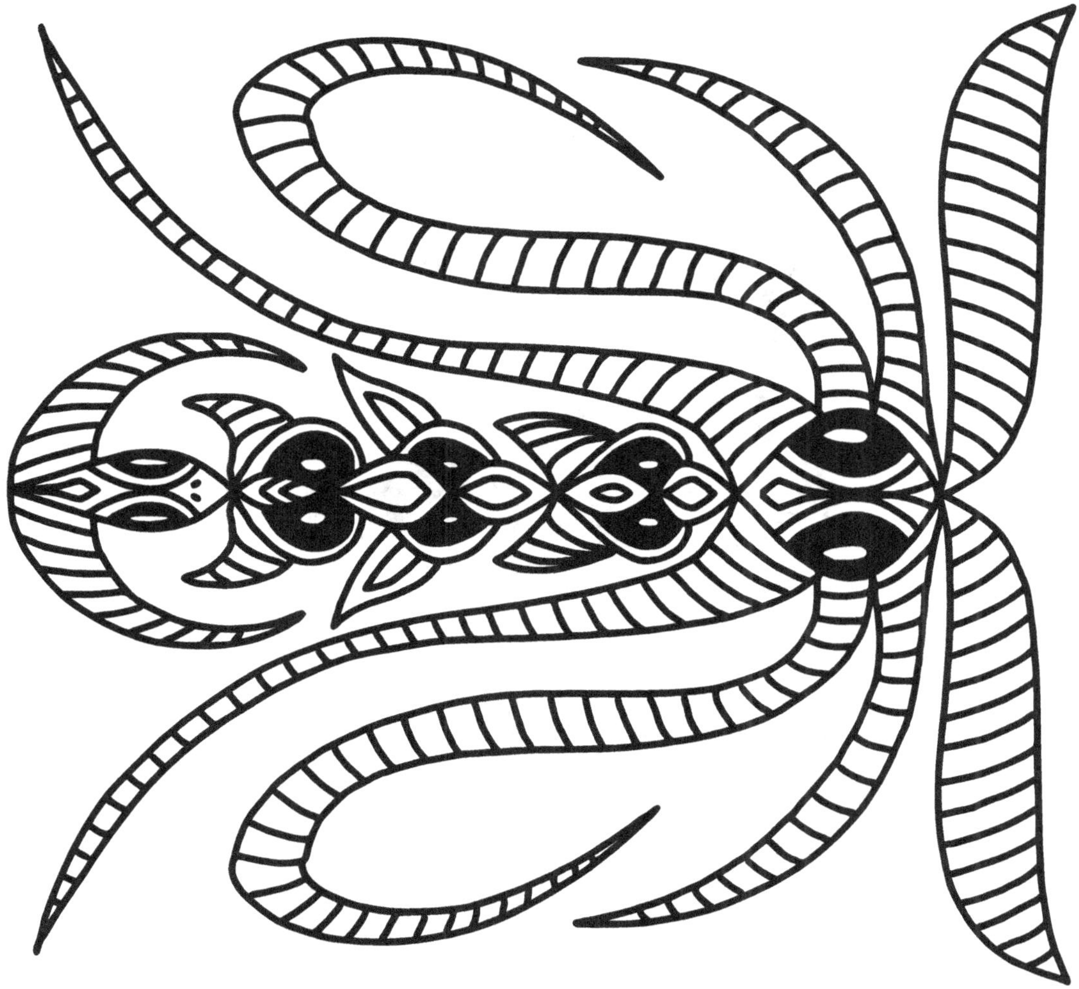

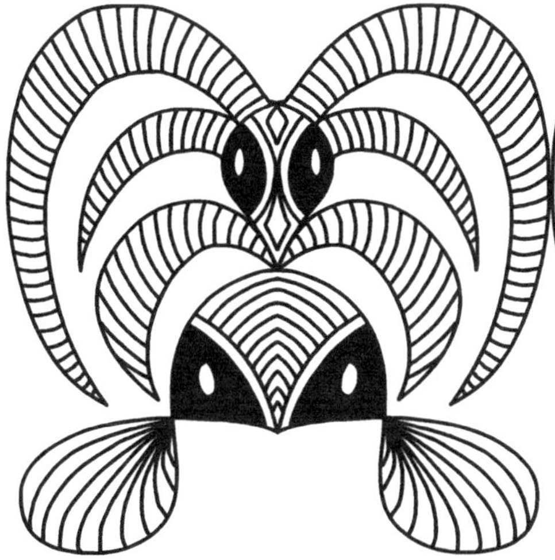

FATLINER WEIRDIES
VOLUME 1

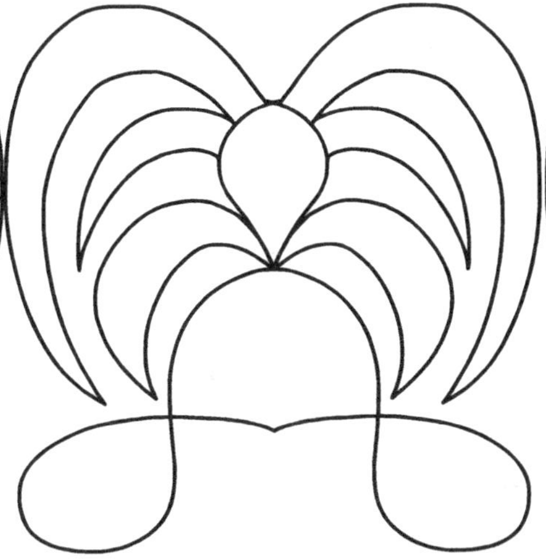

FATLINER WEIRDIES
THE TEMPLATES 1

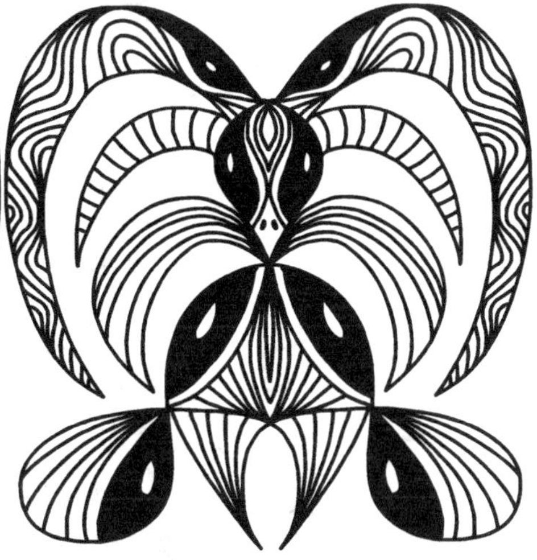

FATLINER WEIRDIES
VOLUME 3

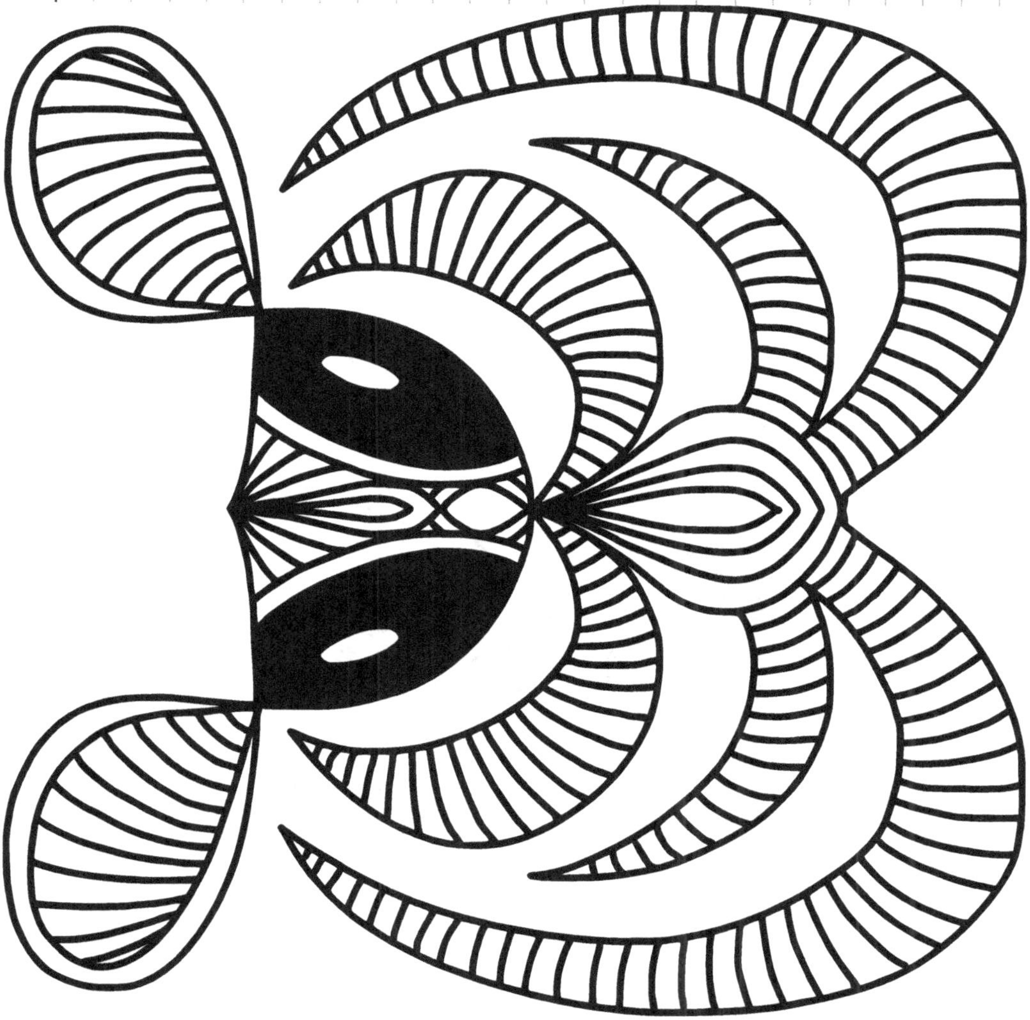

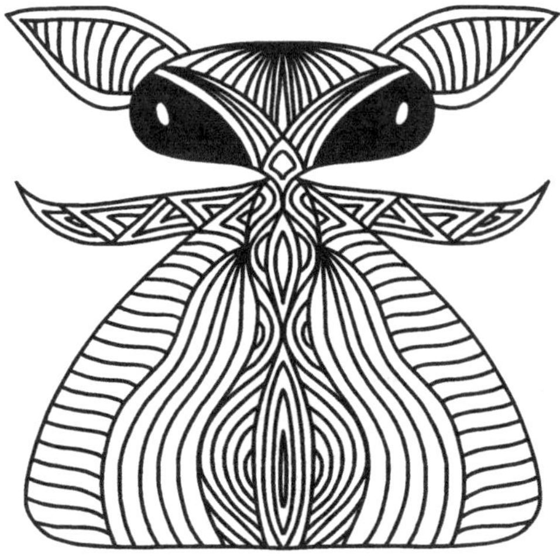

FATLINER WEIRDIES
VOLUME 1

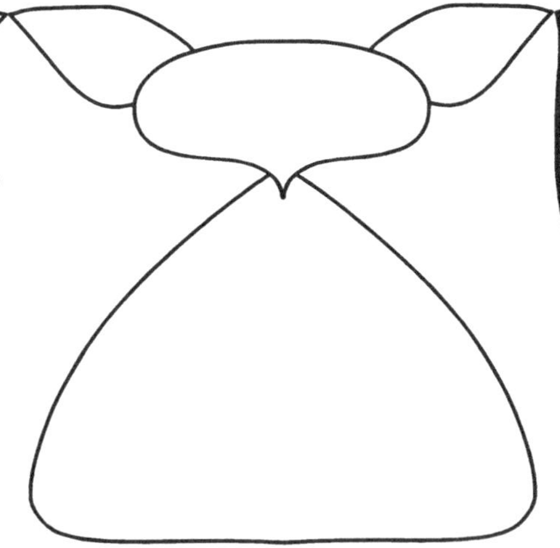

FATLINER WEIRDIES
THE TEMPLATES 1

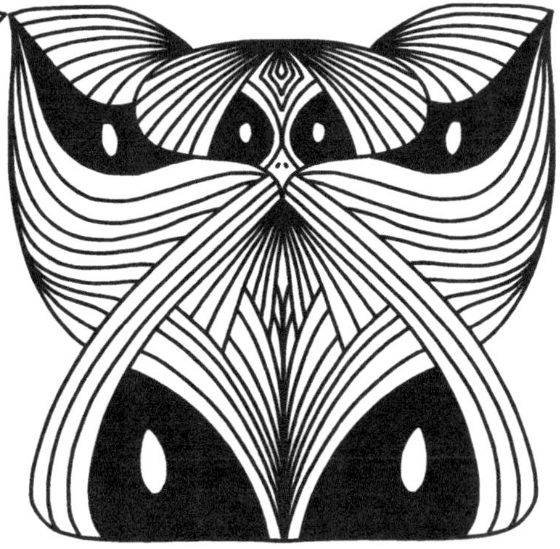

FATLINER WEIRDIES
VOLUME 3

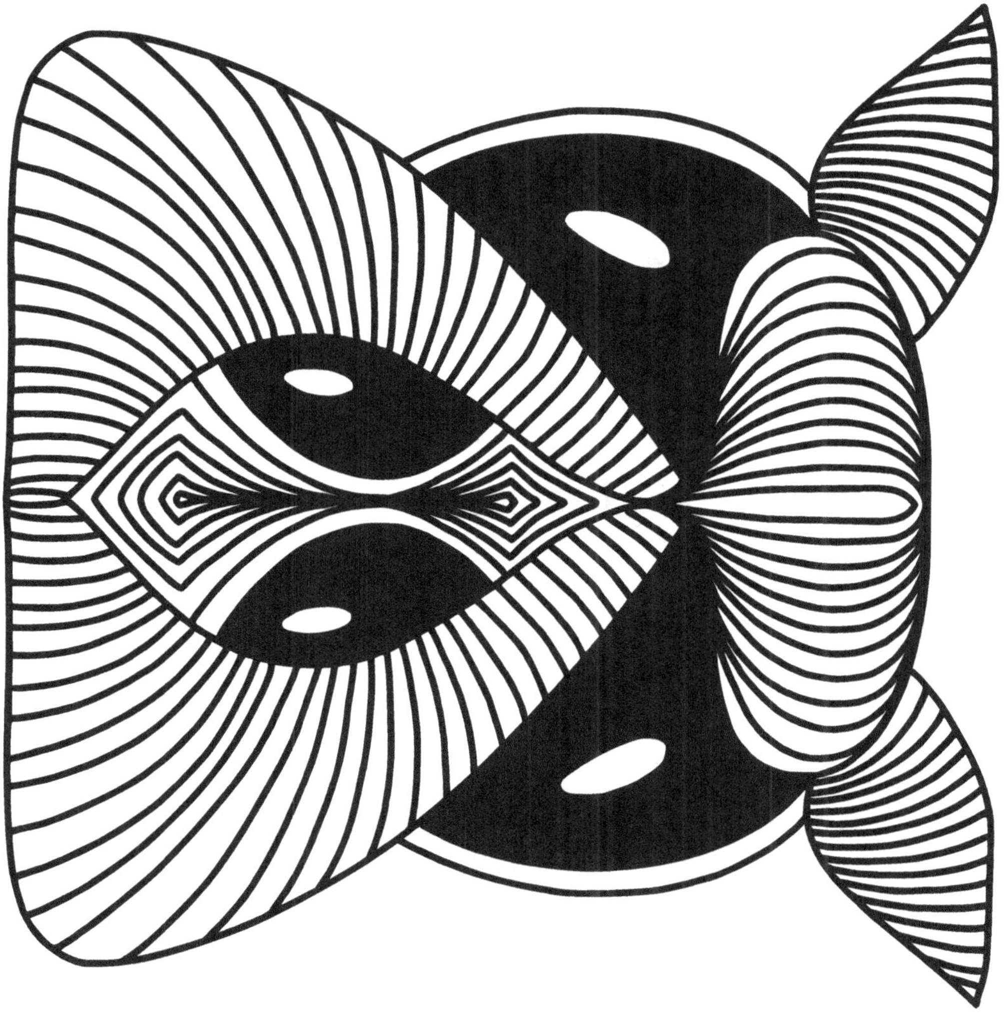

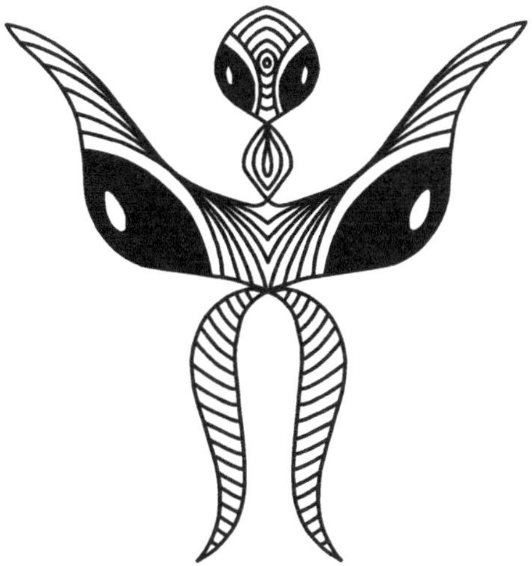

FATLINER WEIRDIES
VOLUME 1

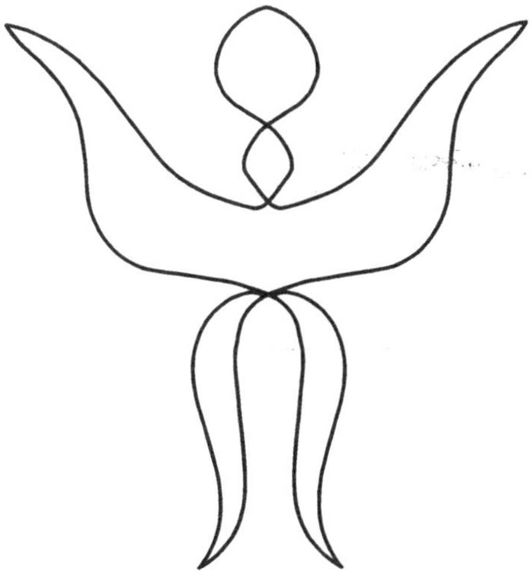

FATLINER WEIRDIES
THE TEMPLATES 1

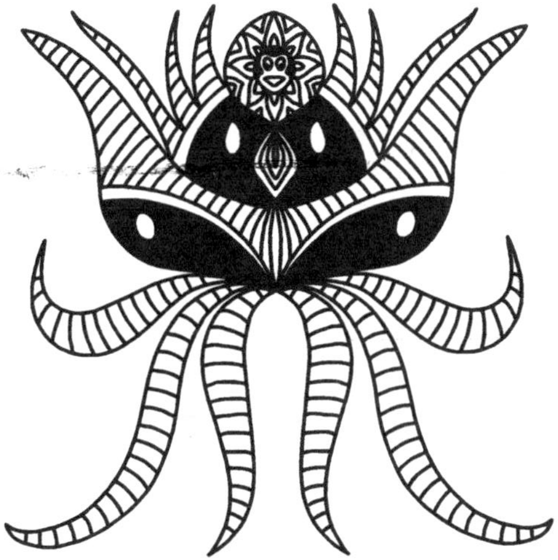

FATLINER WEIRDIES
VOLUME 3

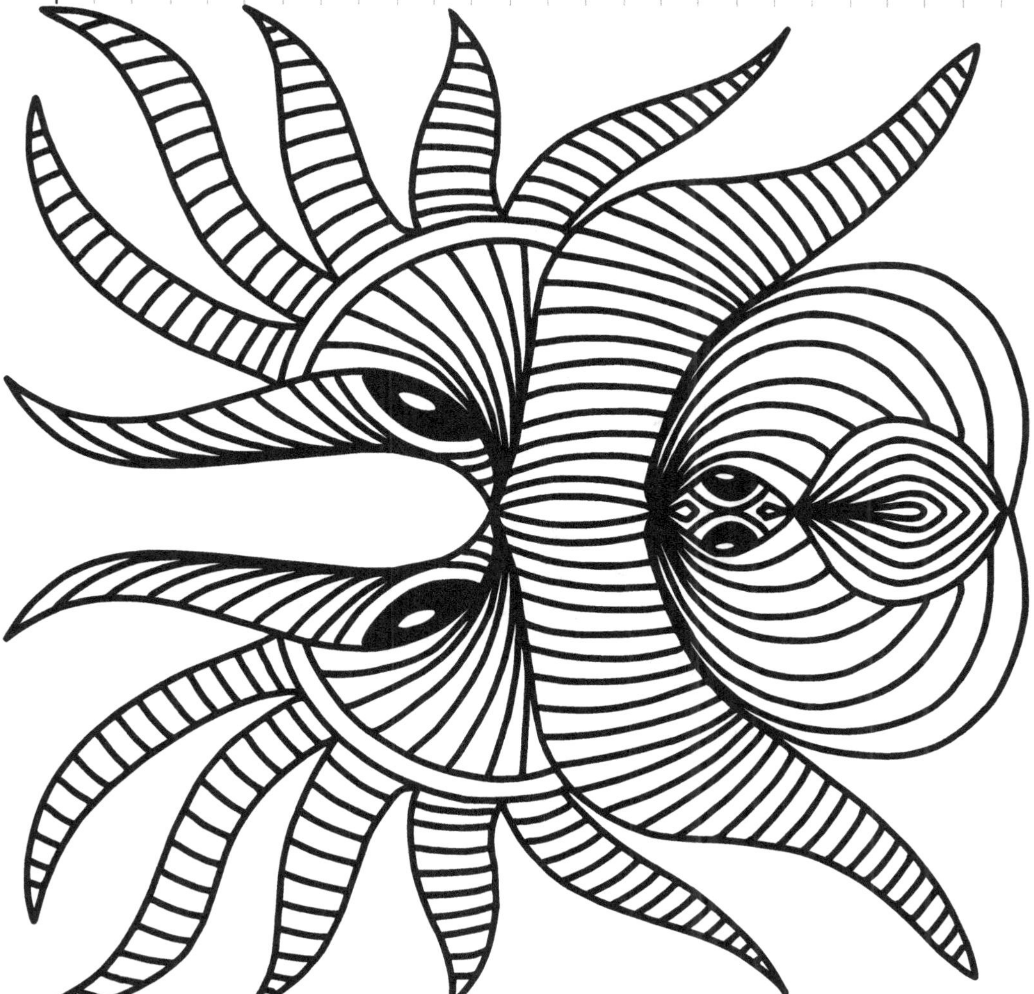

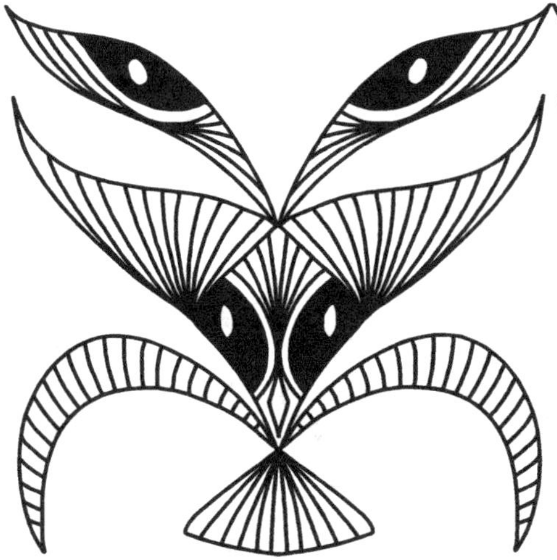

FATLINER WEIRDIES
VOLUME 1

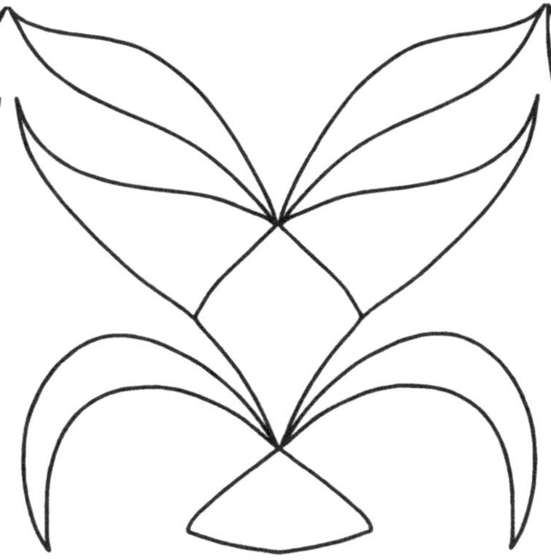

FATLINER WEIRDIES
THE TEMPLATES 1

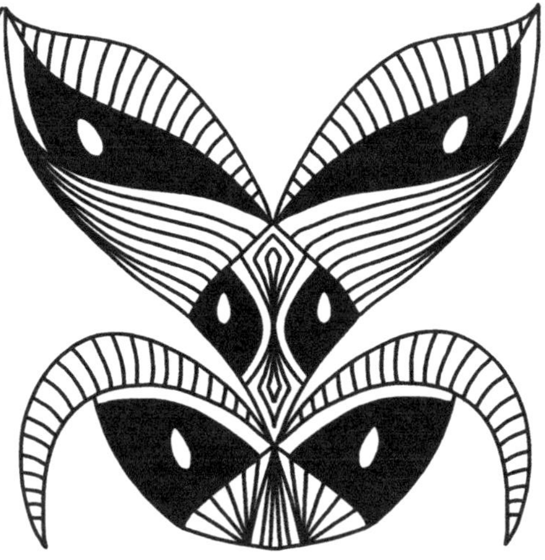

FATLINER WEIRDIES
VOLUME 3

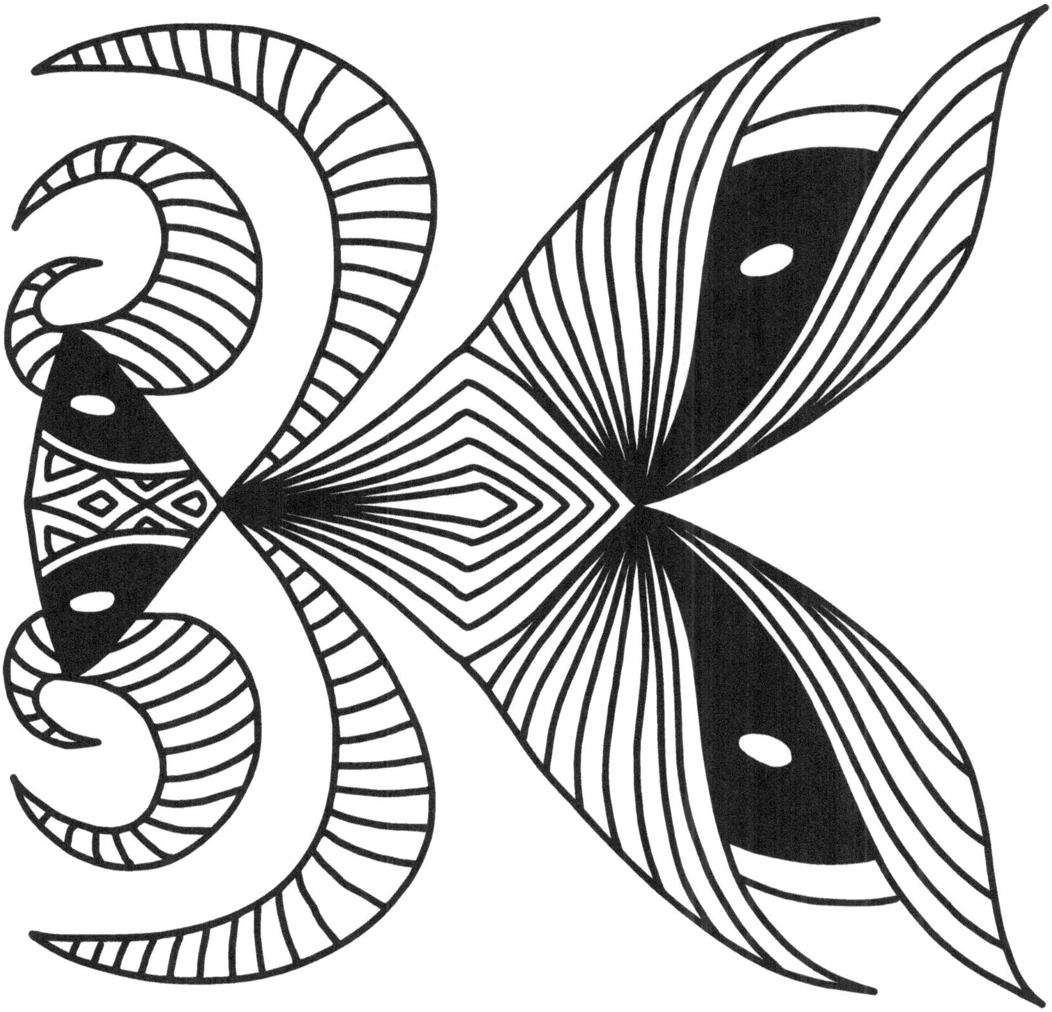

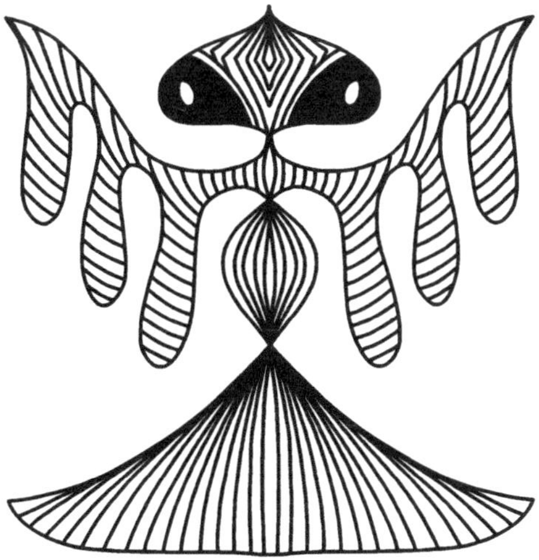
FATLINER WEIRDIES
VOLUME 1

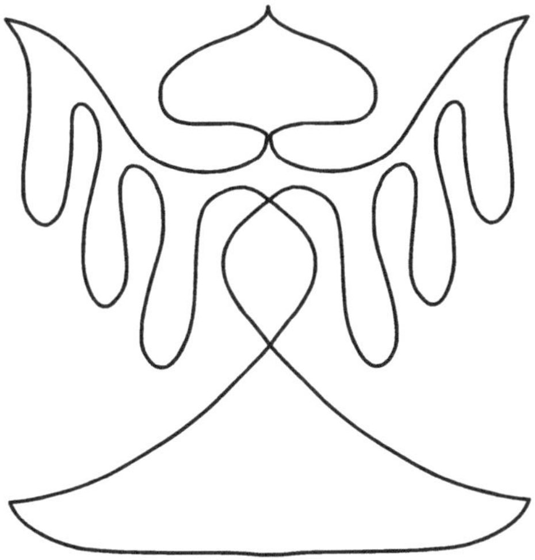
FATLINER WEIRDIES
THE TEMPLATES 1

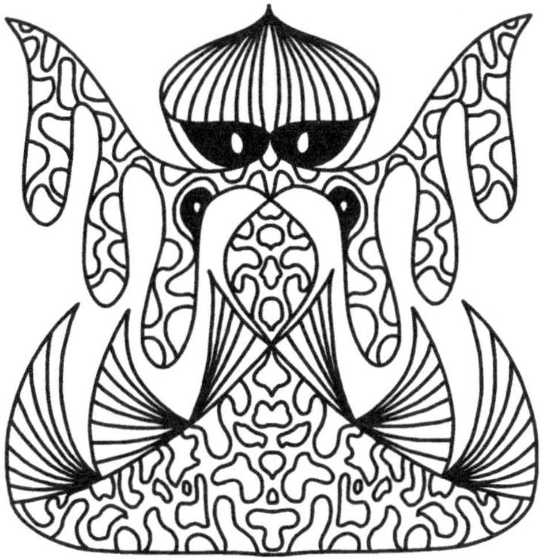
FATLINER WEIRDIES
VOLUME 3

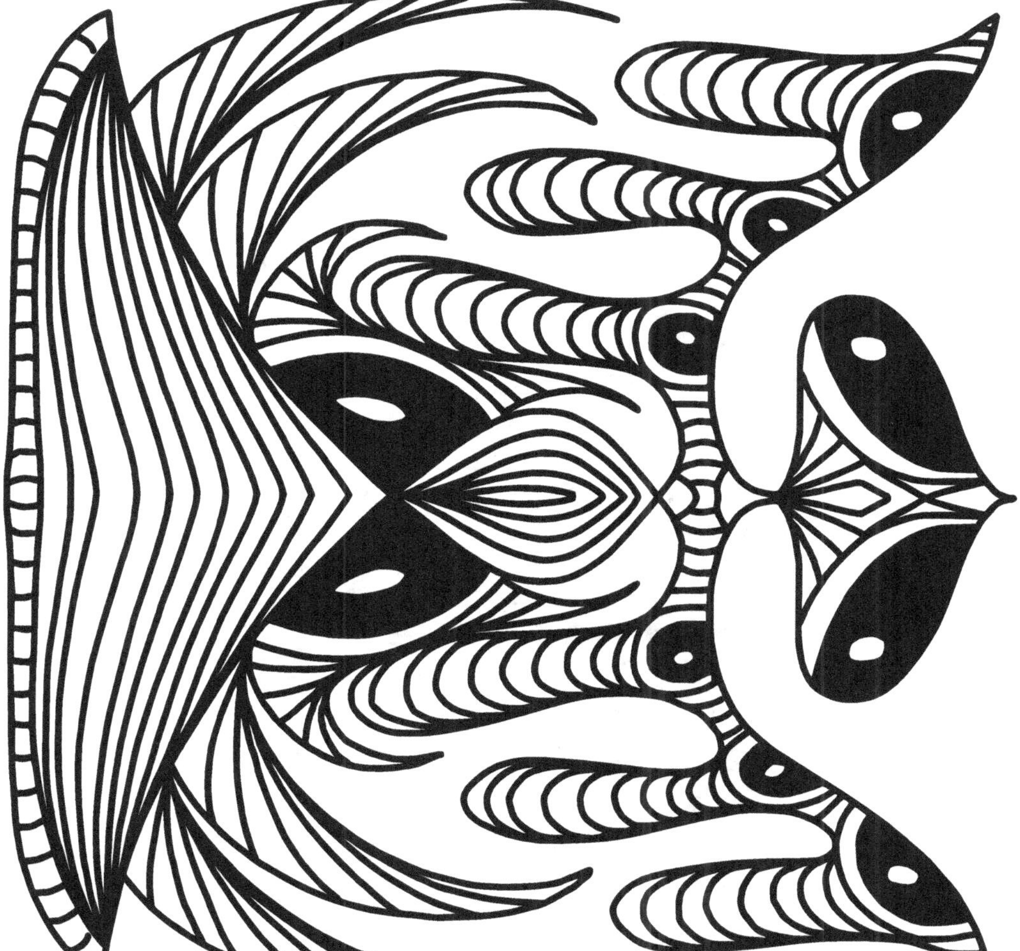

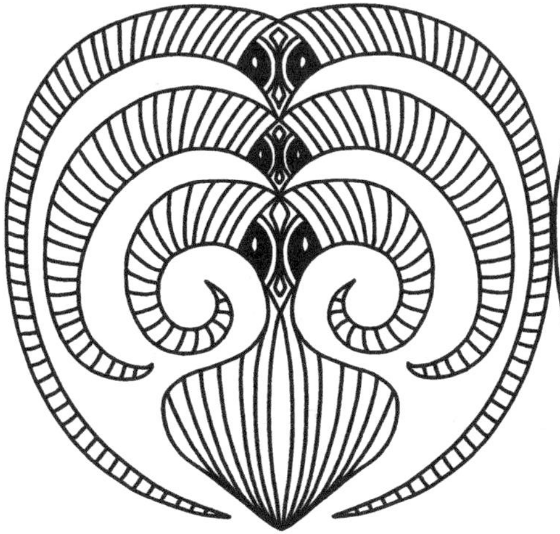
FATLINER WEIRDIES
VOLUME 1

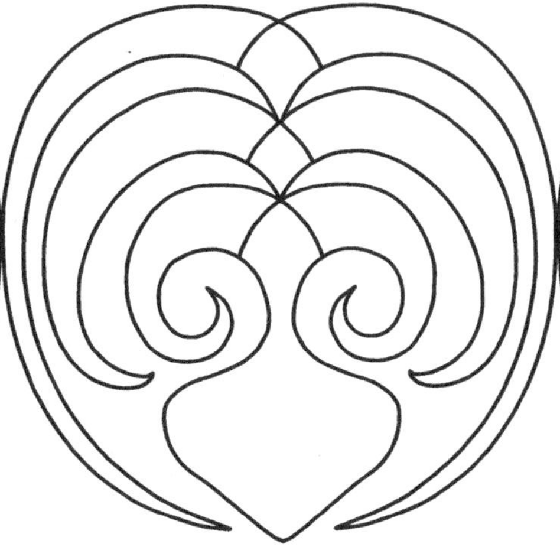
FATLINER WEIRDIES
THE TEMPLATES 1

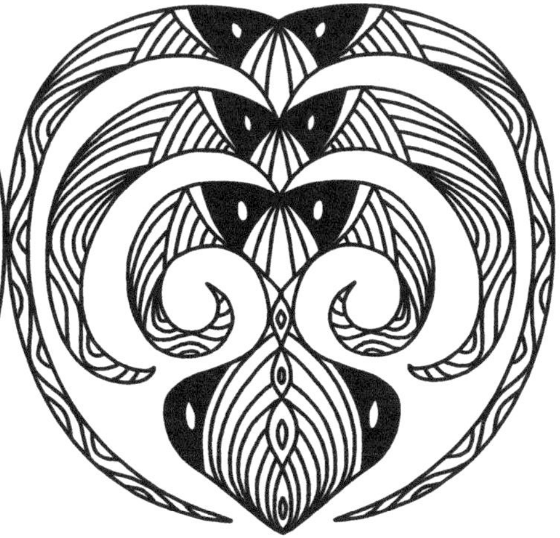
FATLINER WEIRDIES
VOLUME 3

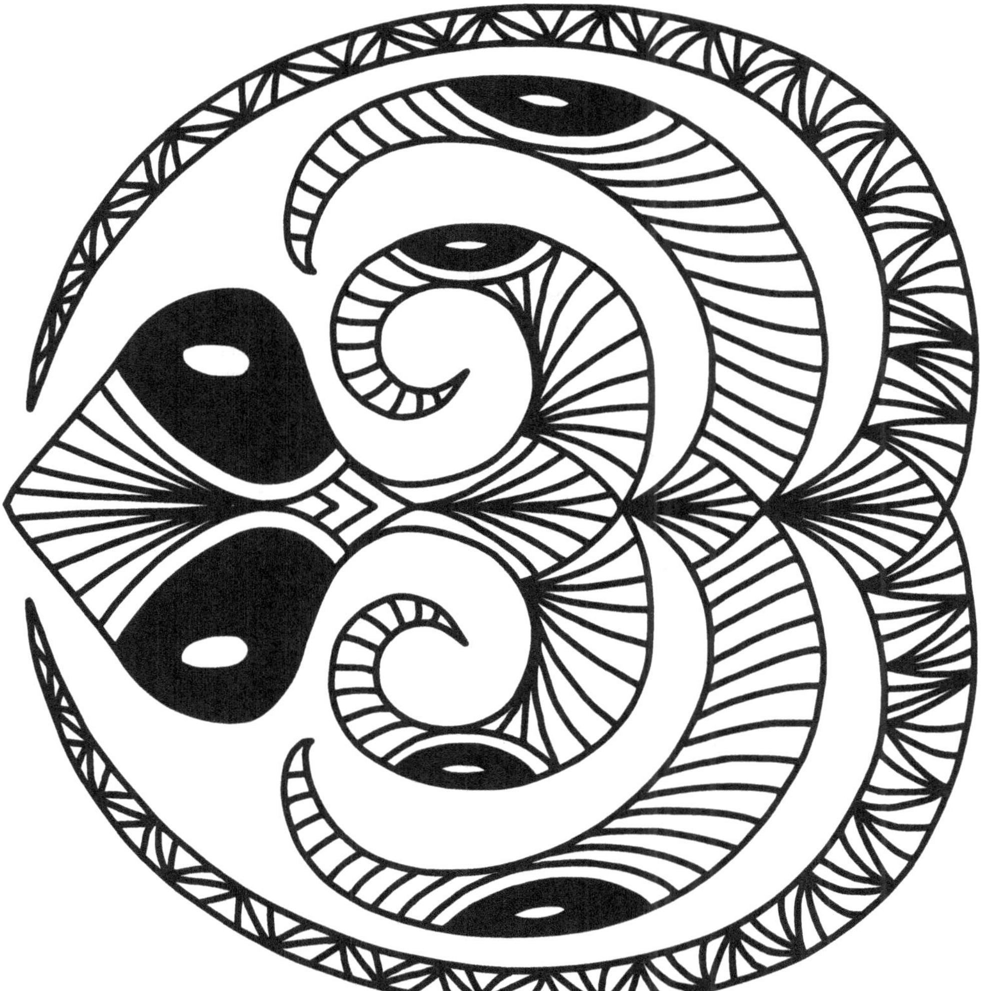

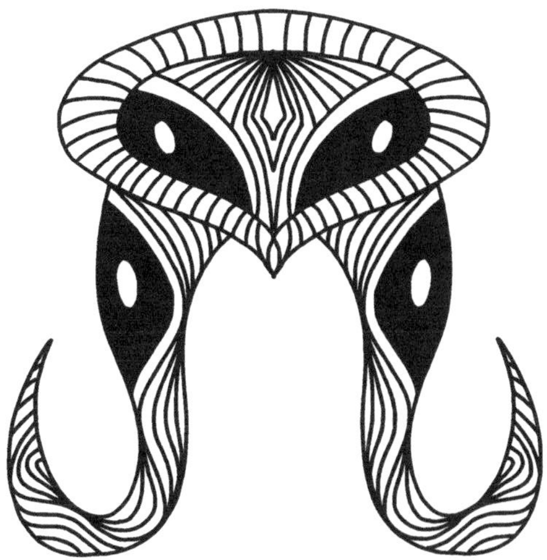

FATLINER WEIRDIES
VOLUME 1

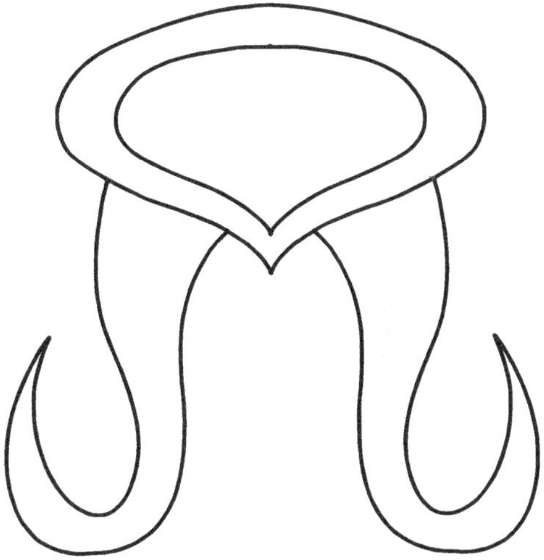

FATLINER WEIRDIES
THE TEMPLATES 1

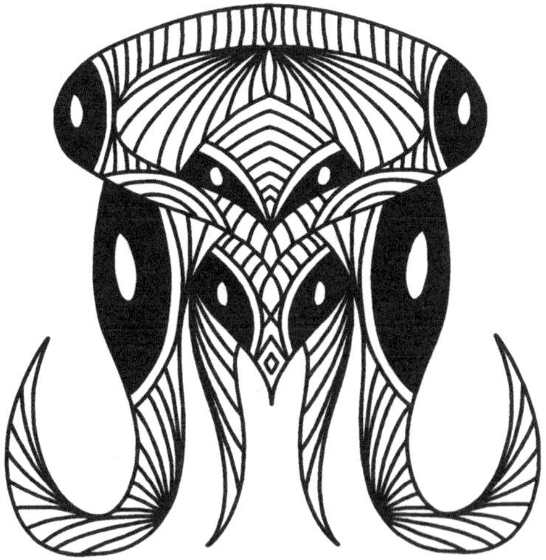

FATLINER WEIRDIES
VOLUME 3

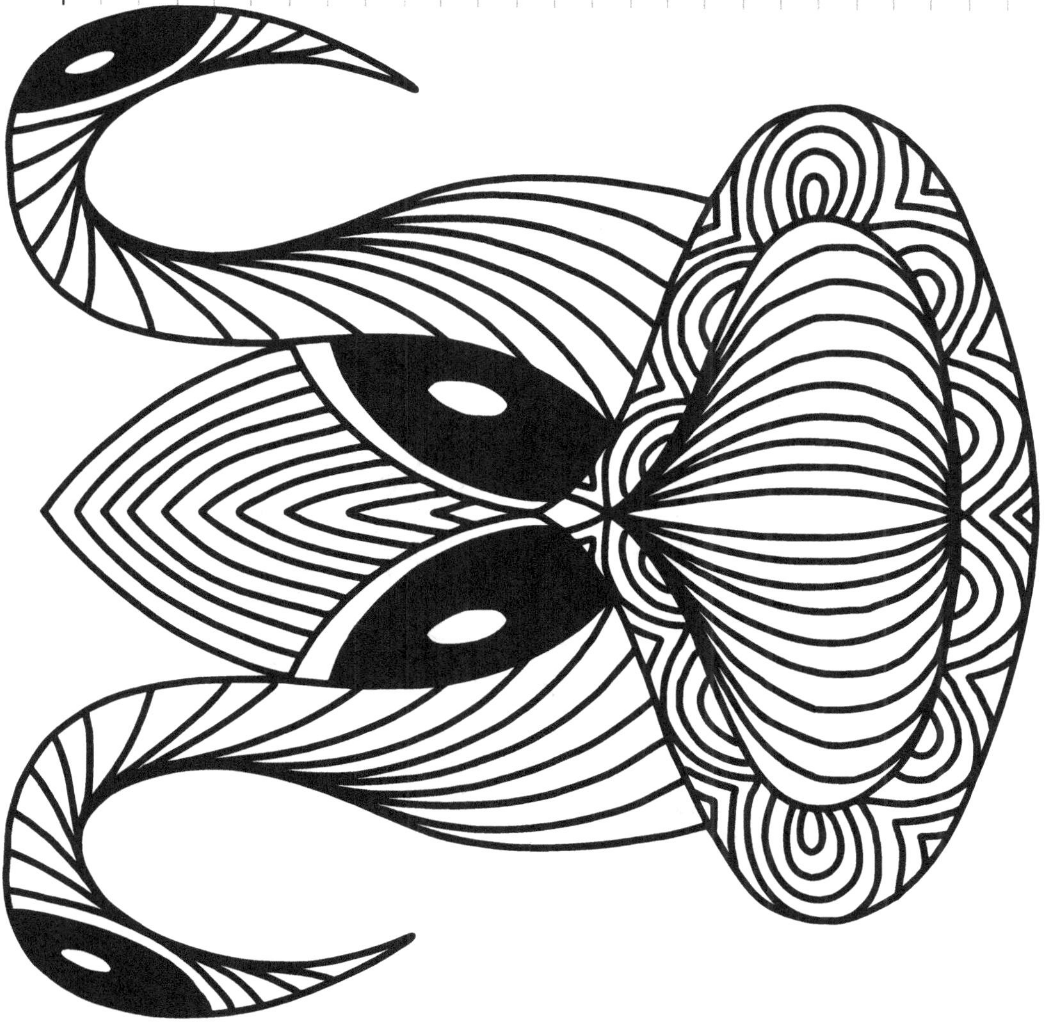

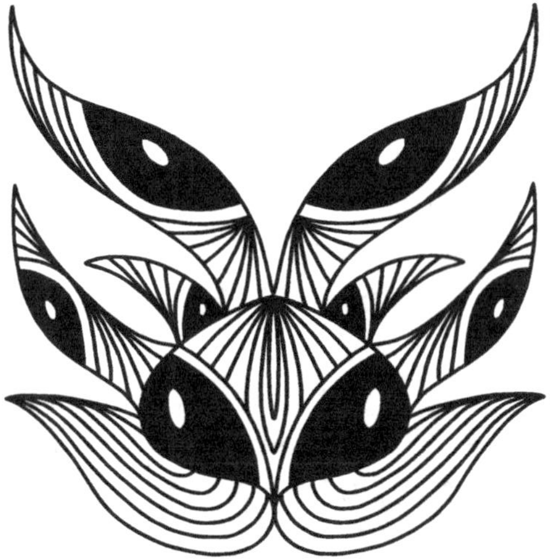

FATLINER WEIRDIES
VOLUME 1

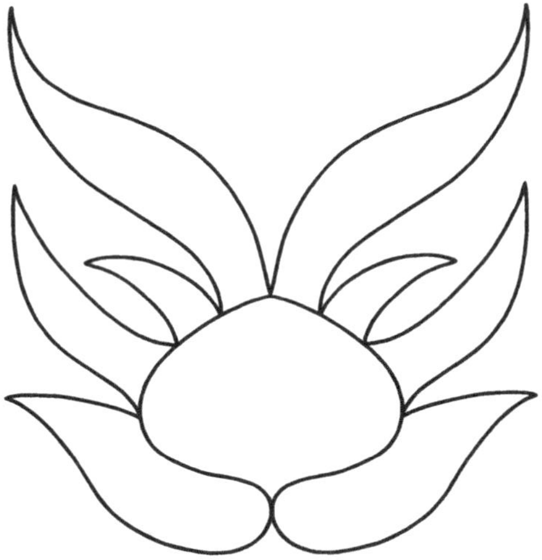

FATLINER WEIRDIES
THE TEMPLATES 1

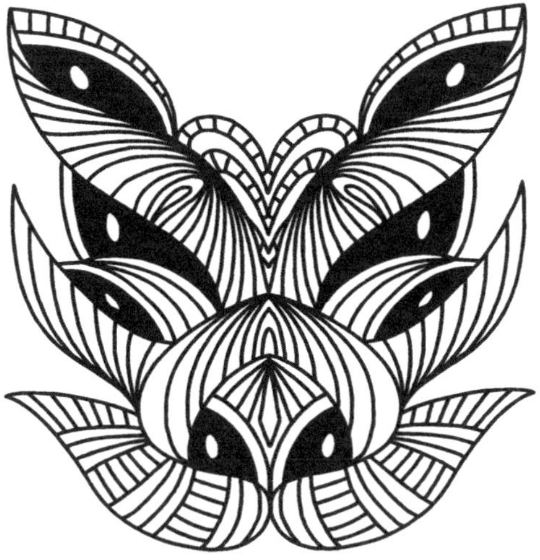

FATLINER WEIRDIES
VOLUME 3

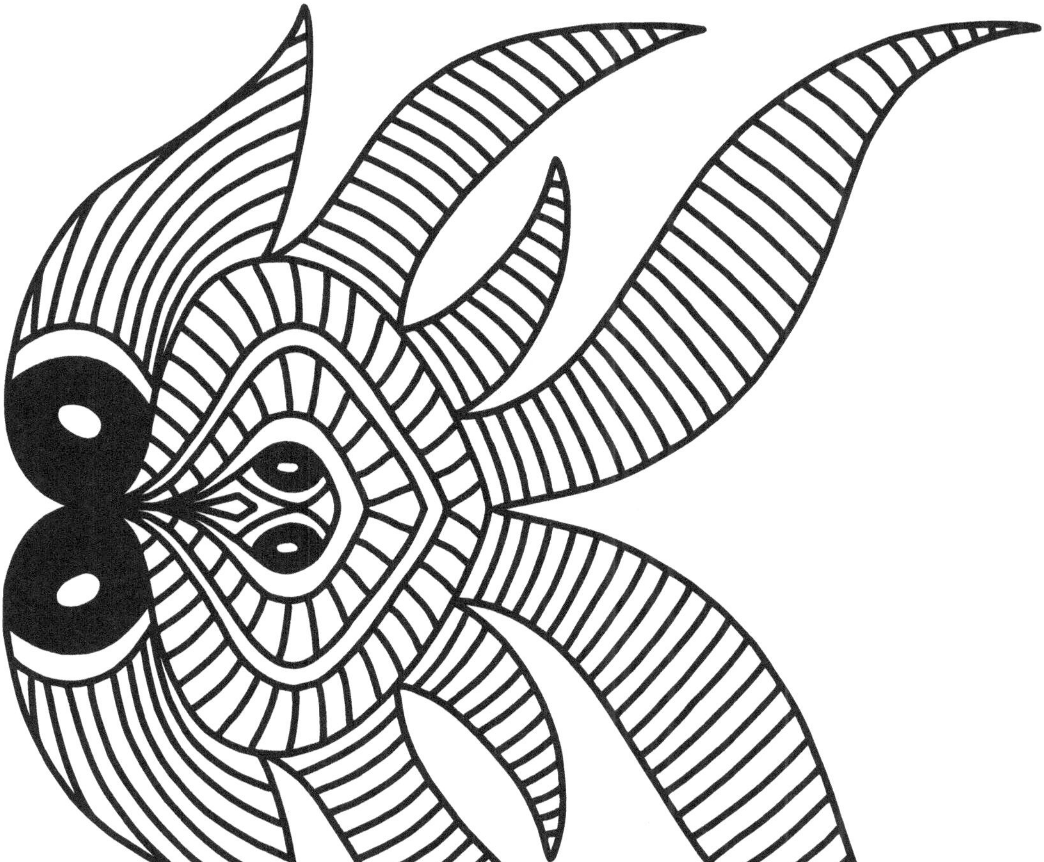

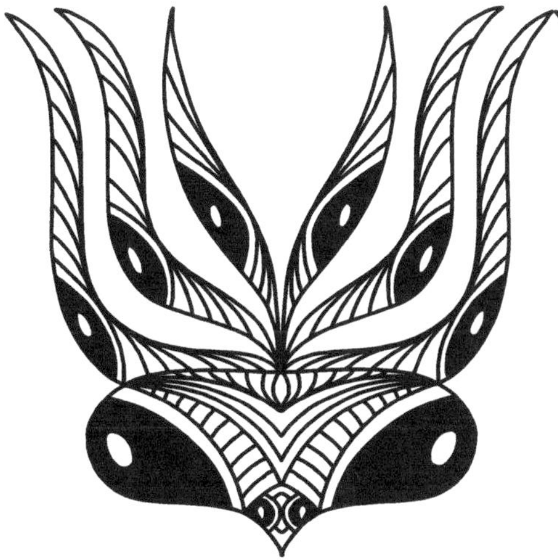

FATLINER WEIRDIES
VOLUME 1

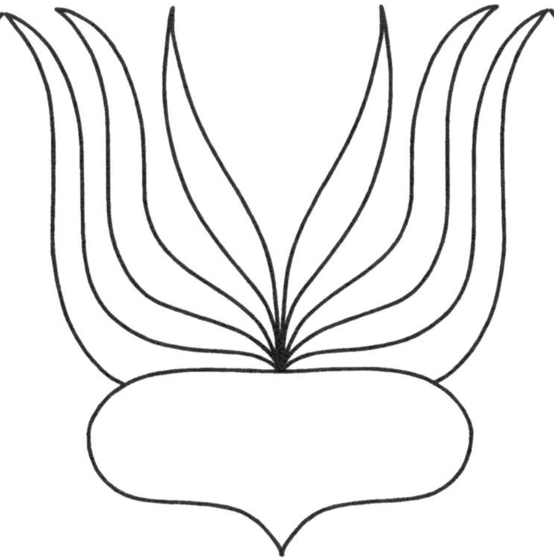

FATLINER WEIRDIES
THE TEMPLATES 1

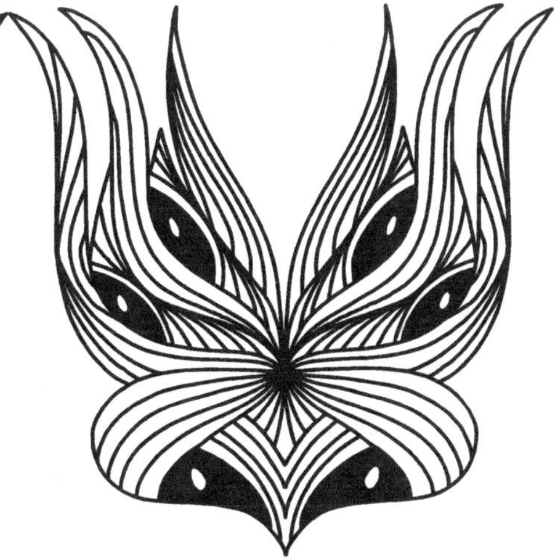

FATLINER WEIRDIES
VOLUME 3

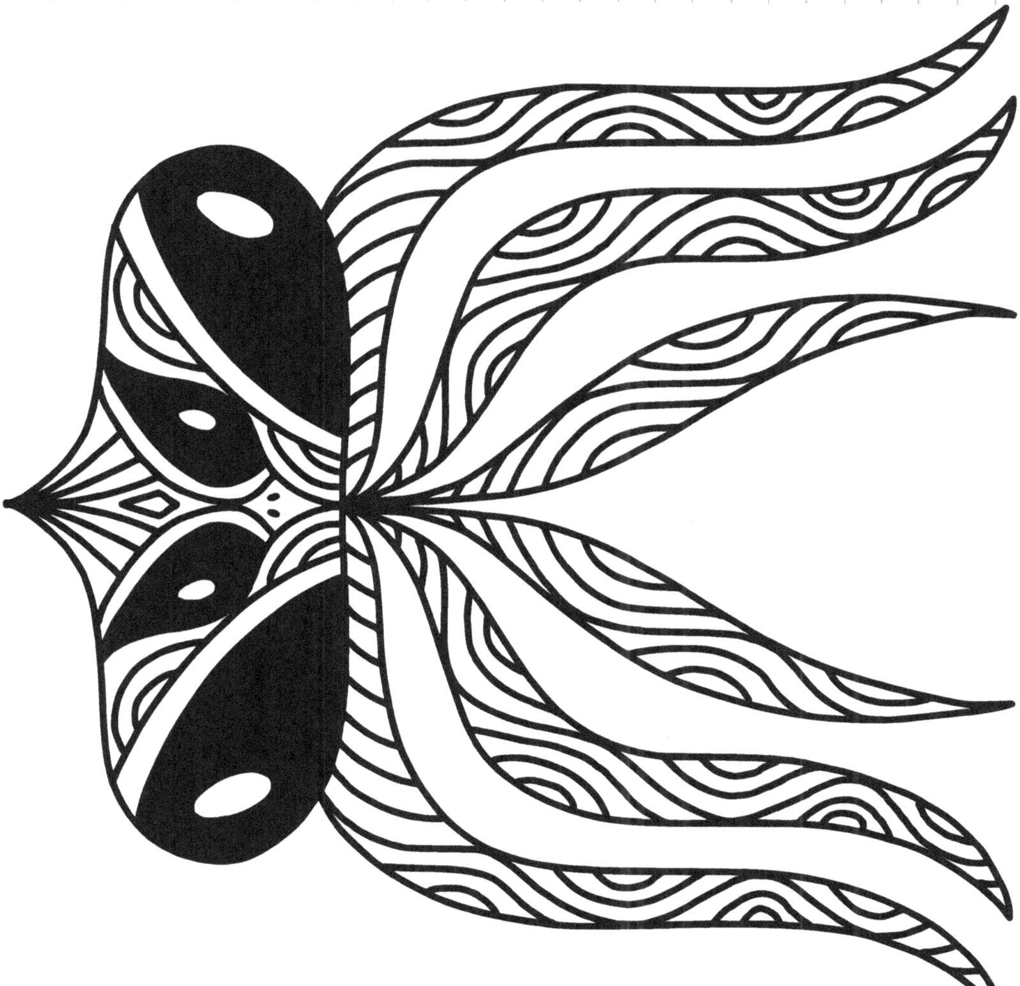

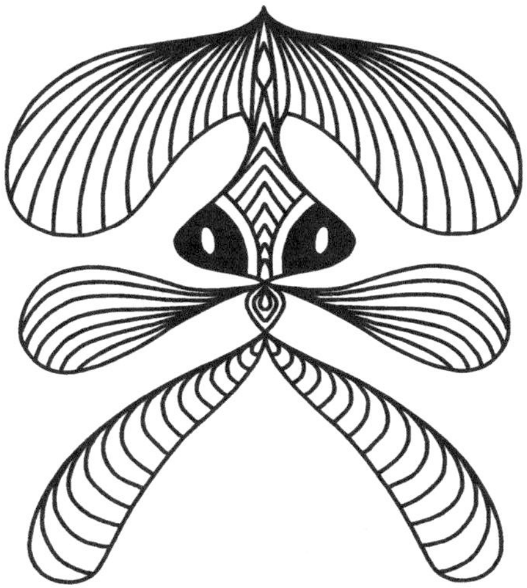
FATLINER WEIRDIES
VOLUME 1

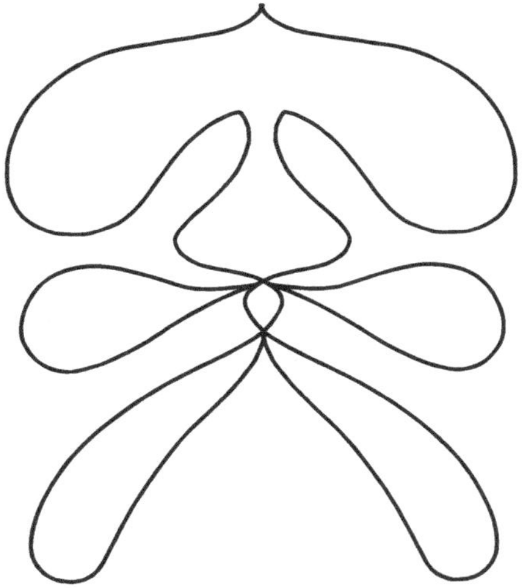
FATLINER WEIRDIES
THE TEMPLATES 1

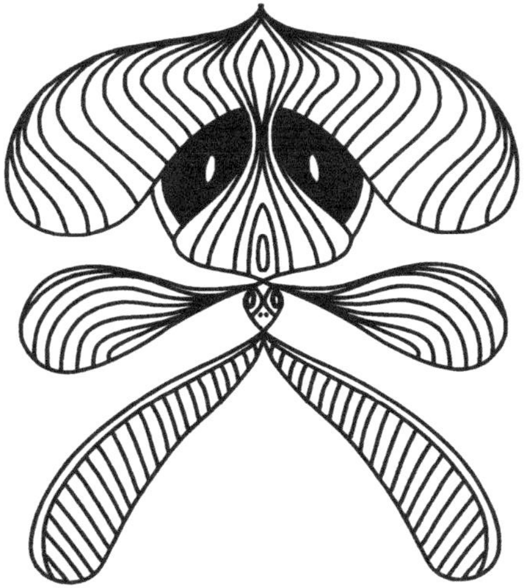
FATLINER WEIRDIES
VOLUME 3

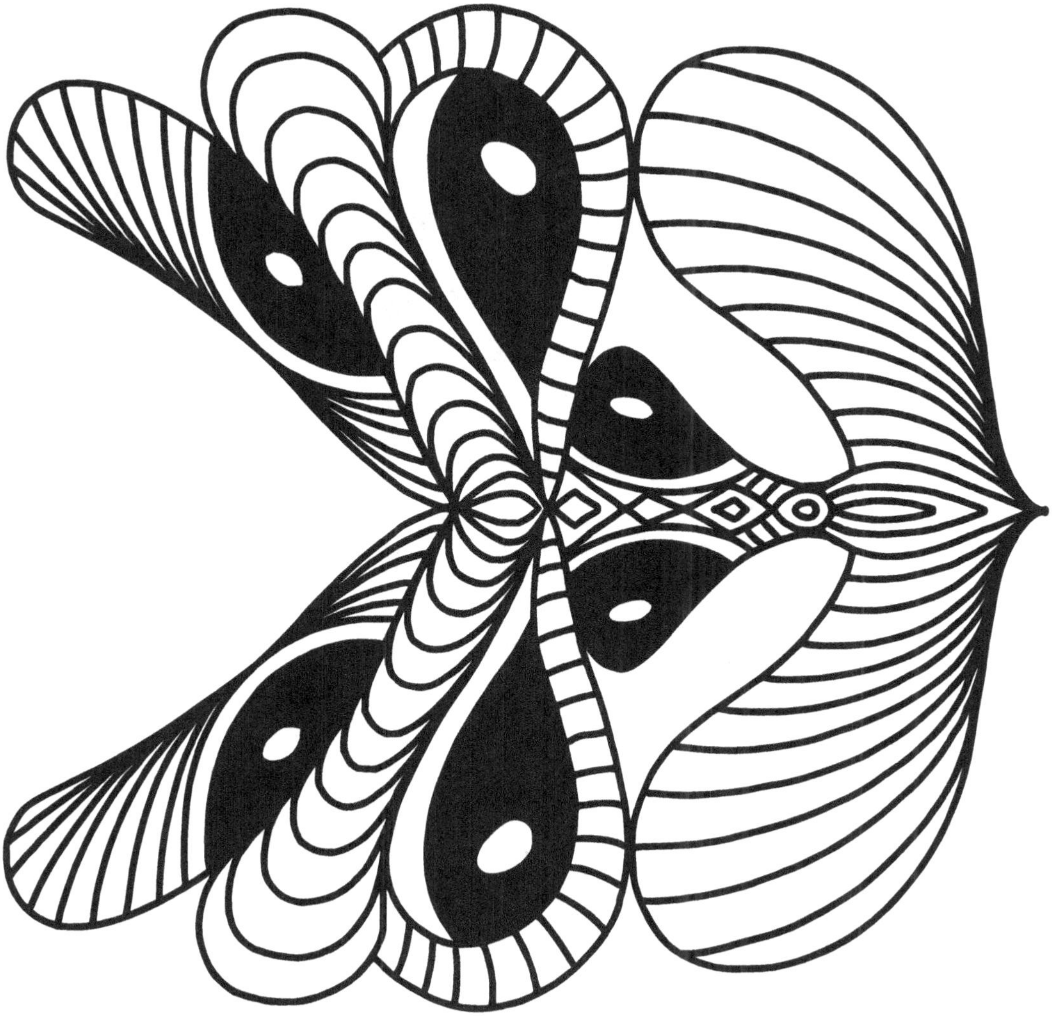

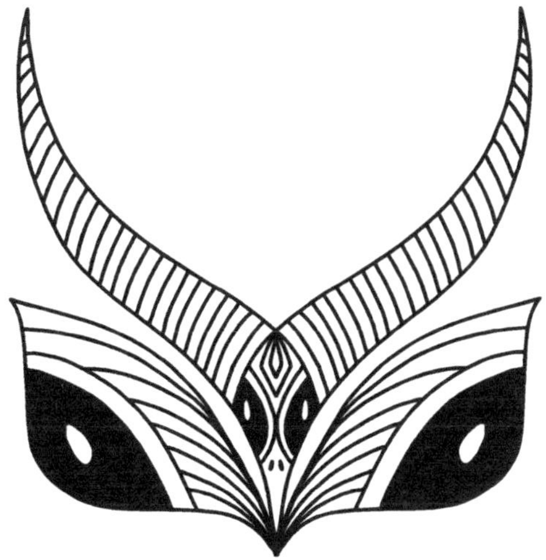

FATLINER WEIRDIES
VOLUME 1

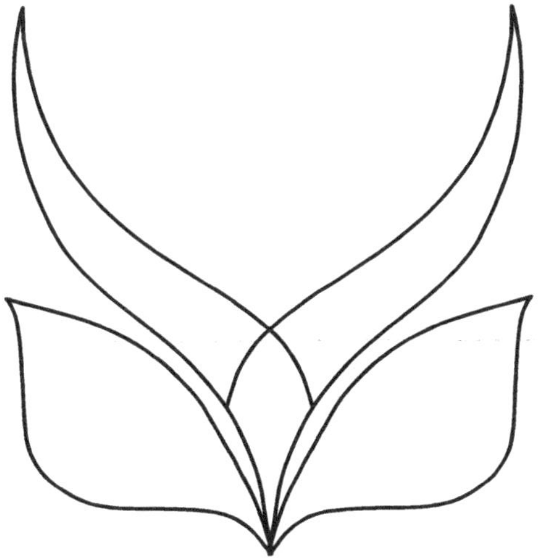

FATLINER WEIRDIES
THE TEMPLATES 1

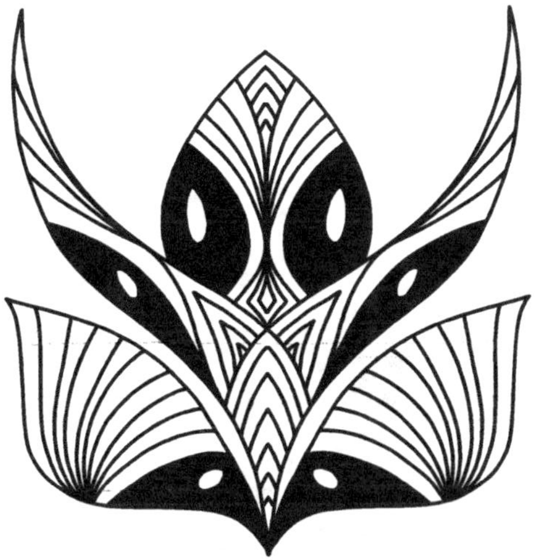

FATLINER WEIRDIES
VOLUME 3

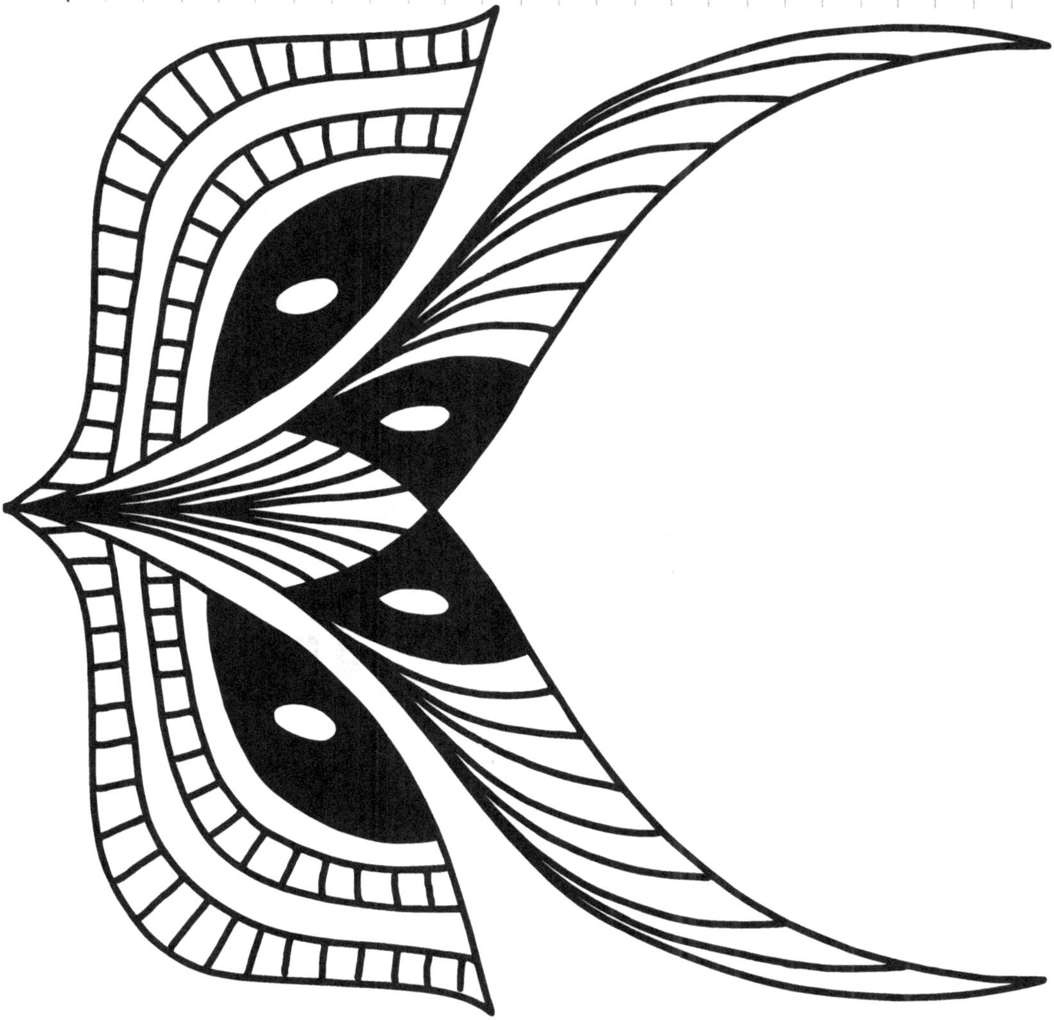

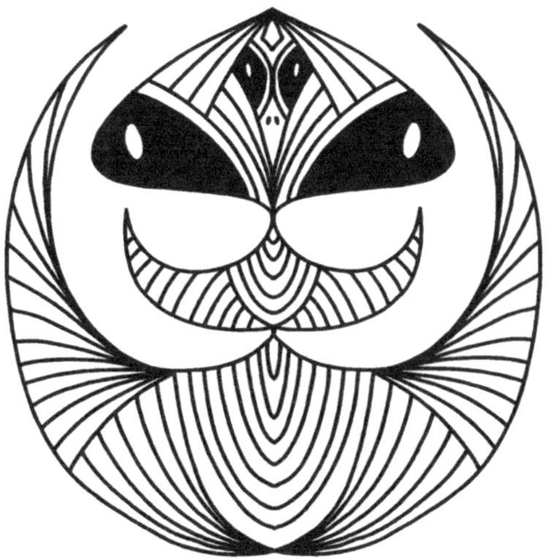

FATLINER WEIRDIES
VOLUME 1

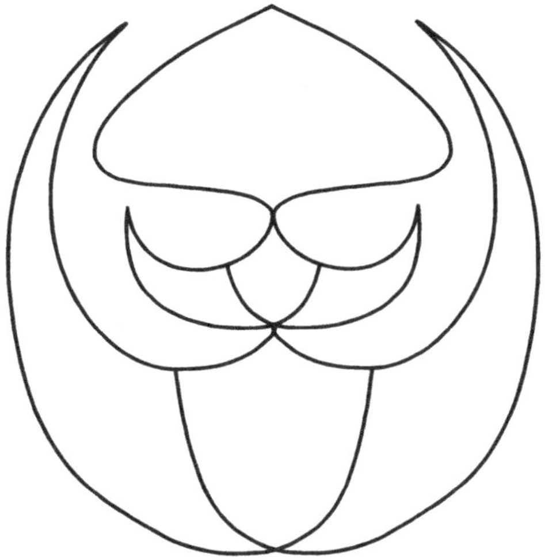

FATLINER WEIRDIES
THE TEMPLATES 1

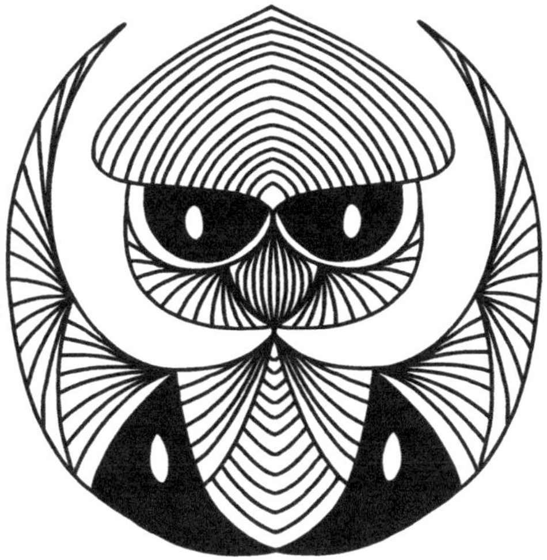

FATLINER WEIRDIES
VOLUME 3

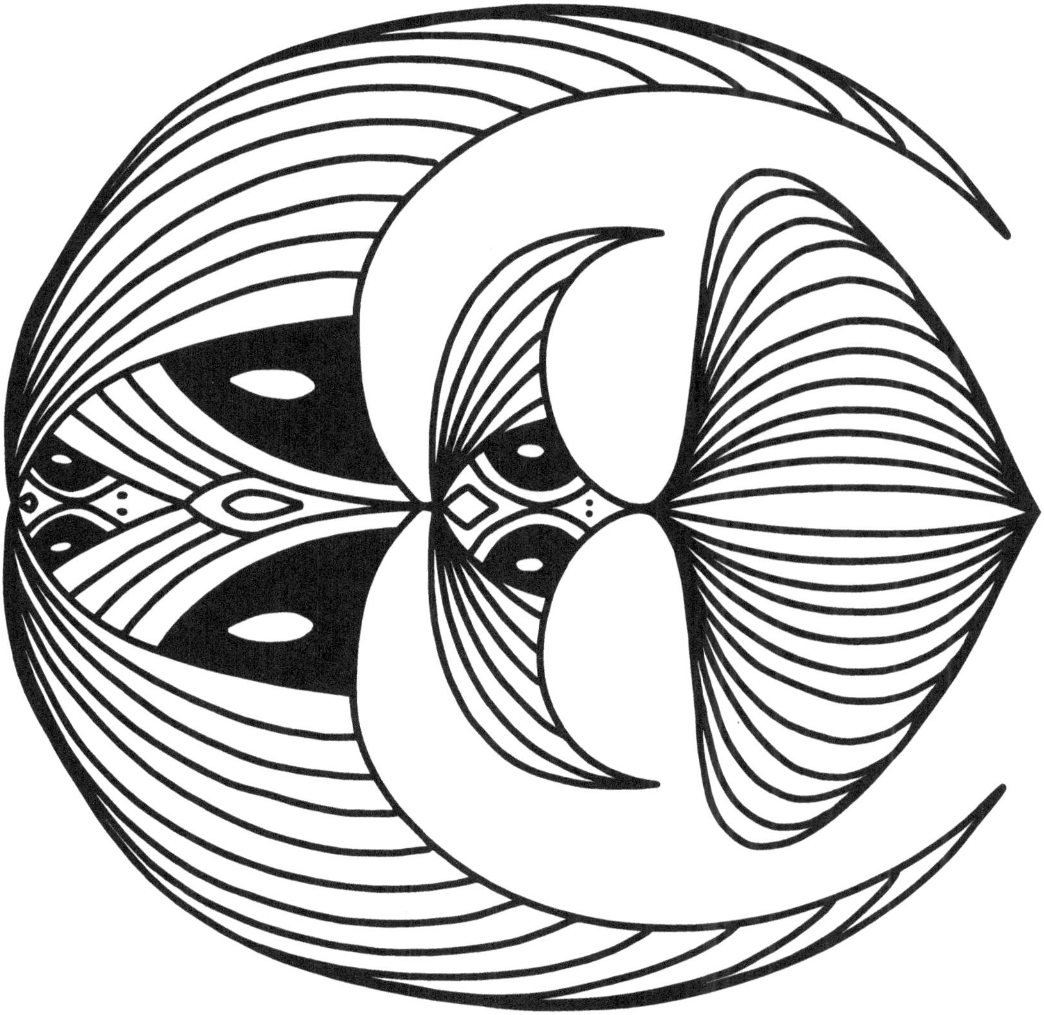

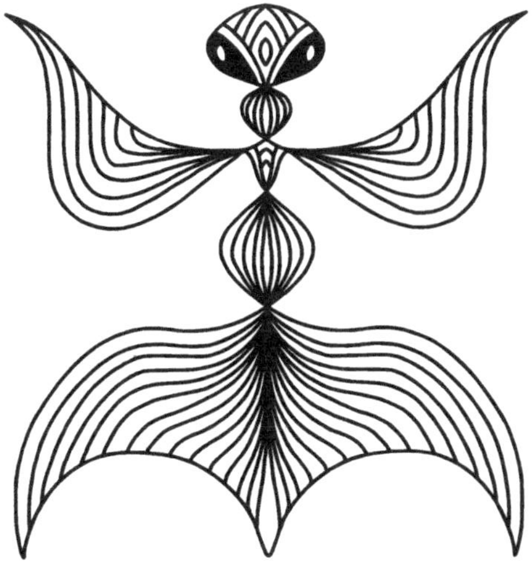

FATLINER WEIRDIES
VOLUME 1

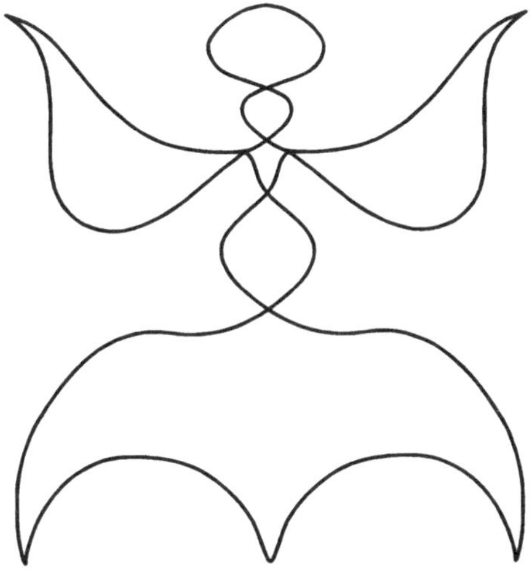

FATLINER WEIRDIES
THE TEMPLATES 1

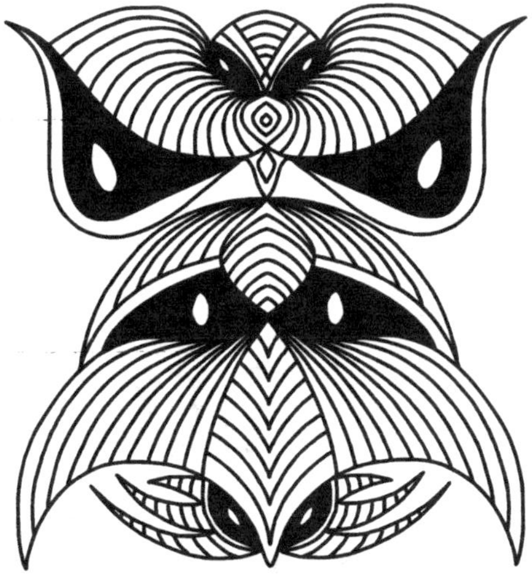

FATLINER WEIRDIES
VOLUME 3

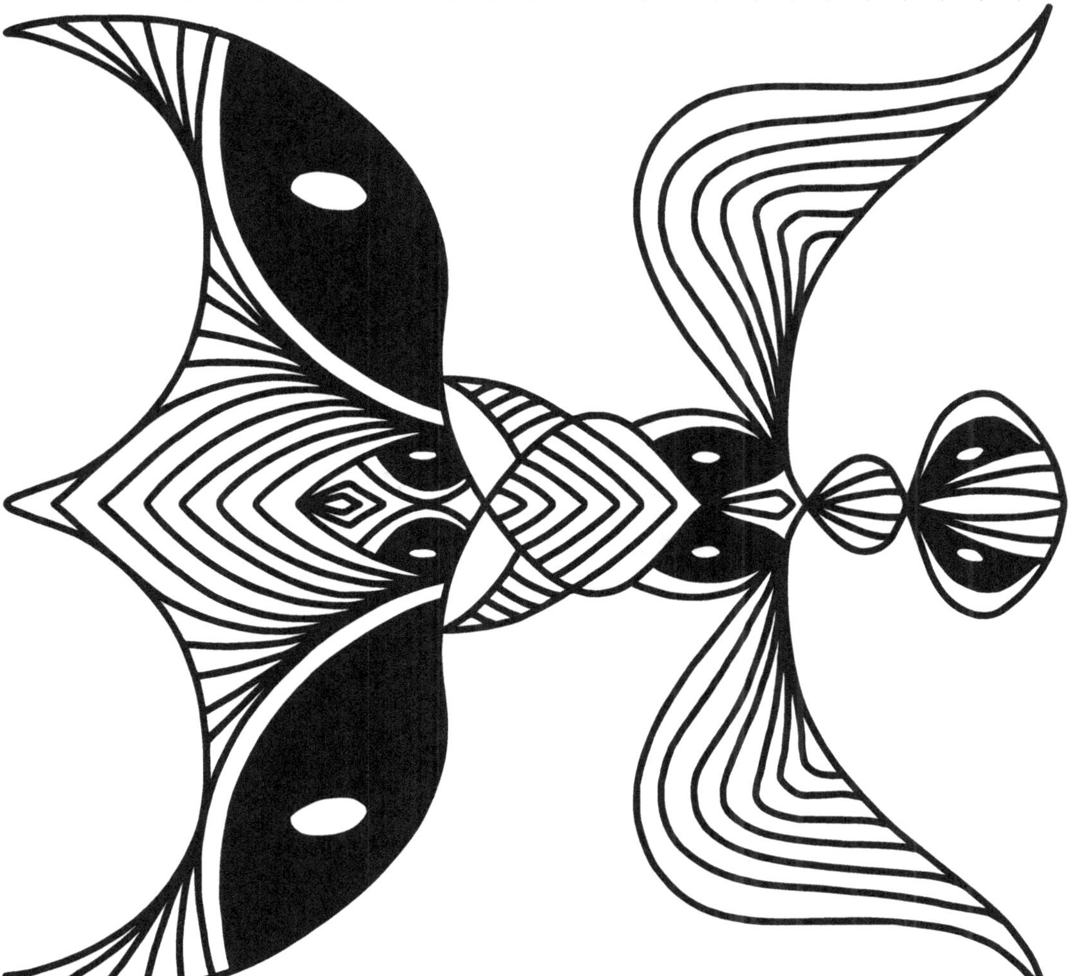

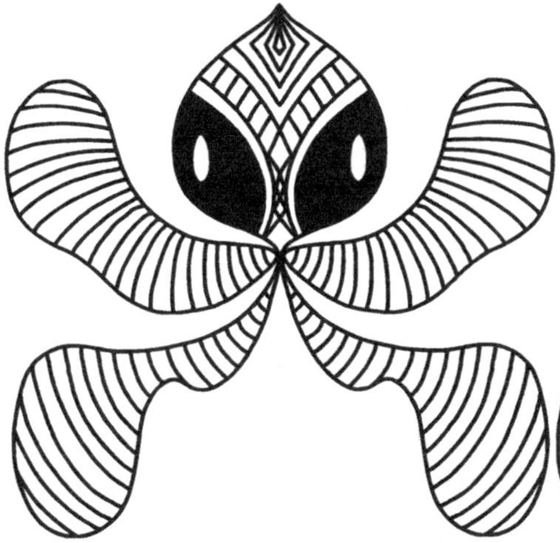

FATLINER WEIRDIES
VOLUME 1

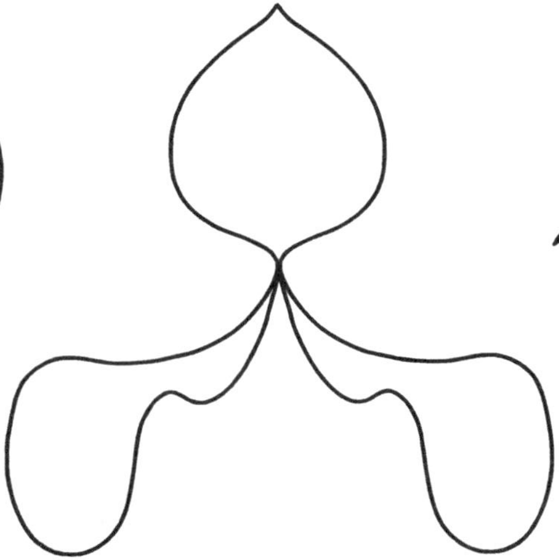

FATLINER WEIRDIES
THE TEMPLATES 1

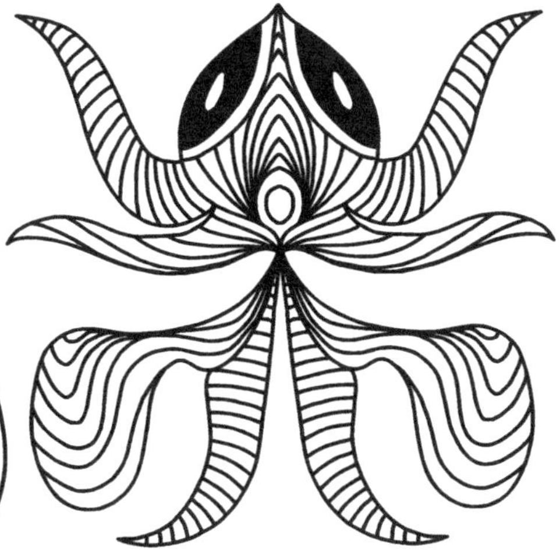

FATLINER WEIRDIES
VOLUME 3

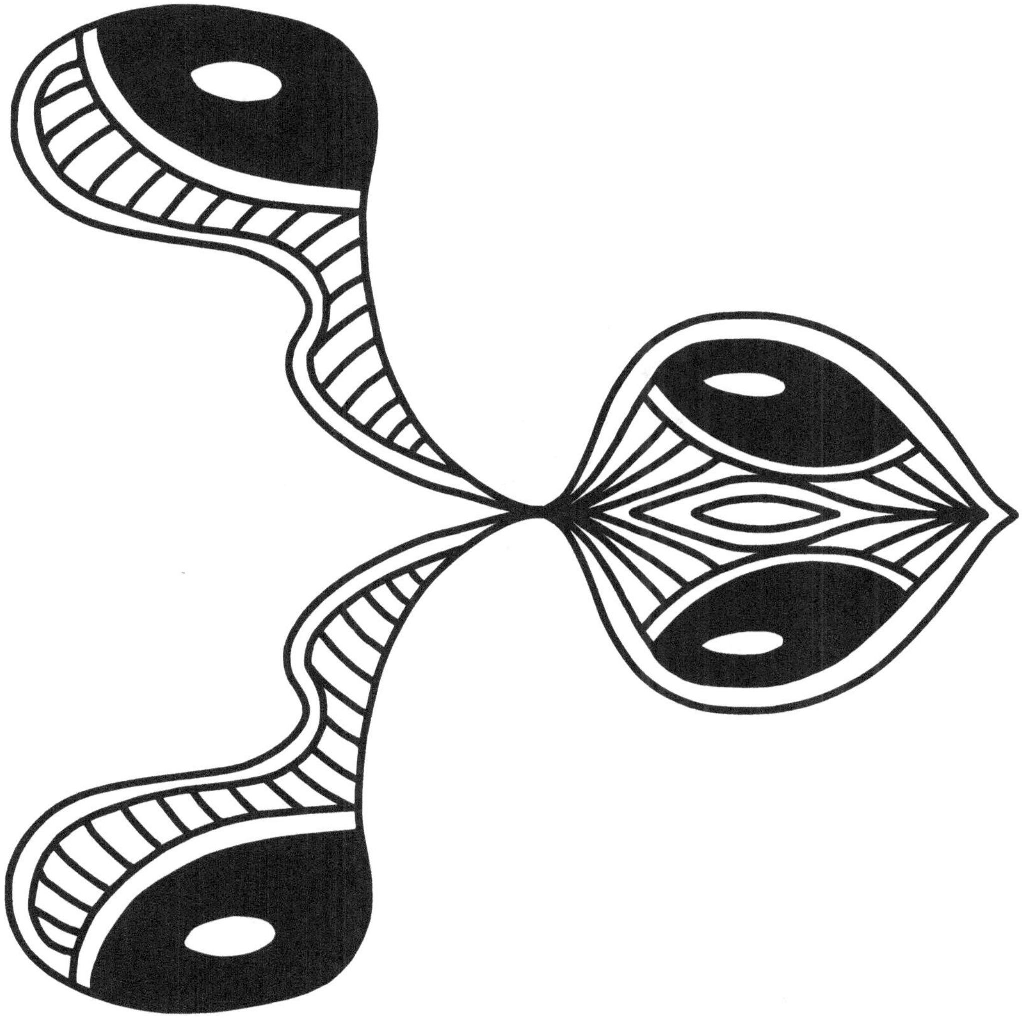

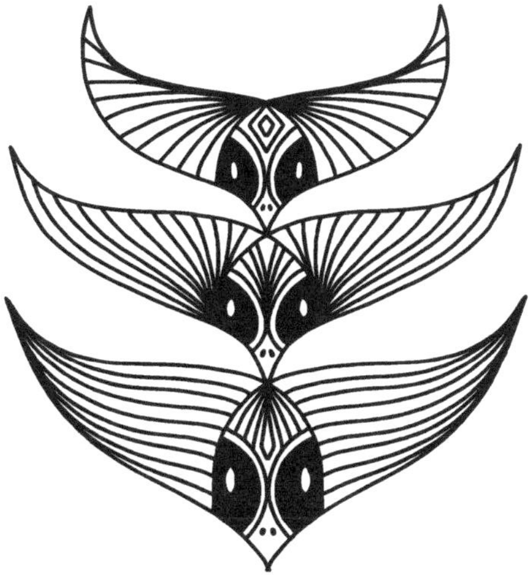

FATLINER WEIRDIES
VOLUME 1

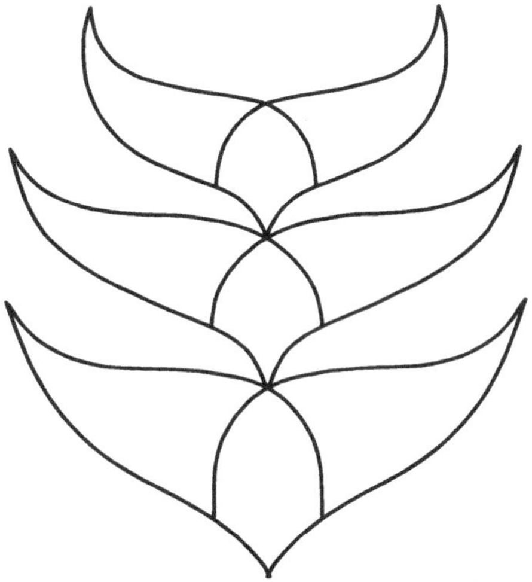

FATLINER WEIRDIES
THE TEMPLATES 1

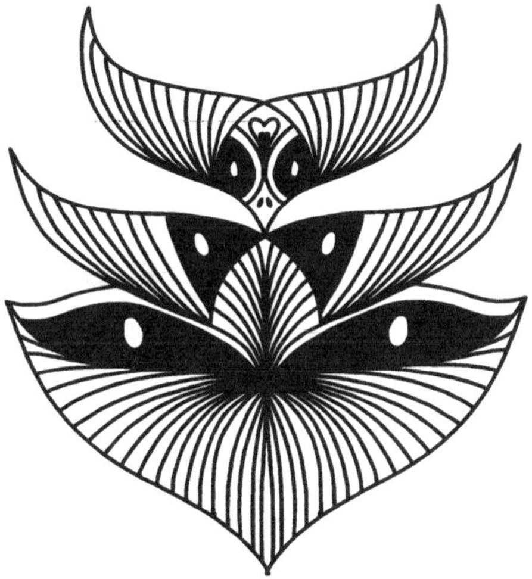

FATLINER WEIRDIES
VOLUME 3

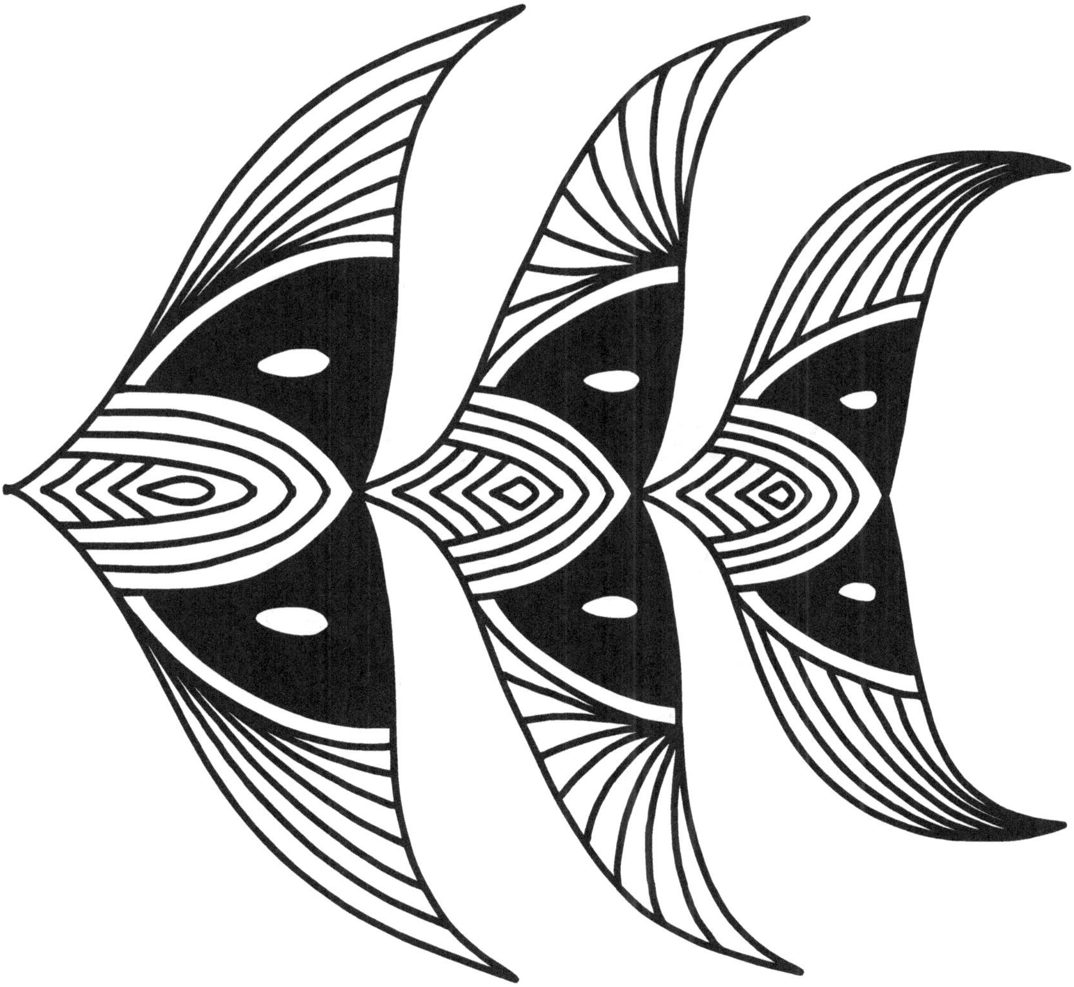

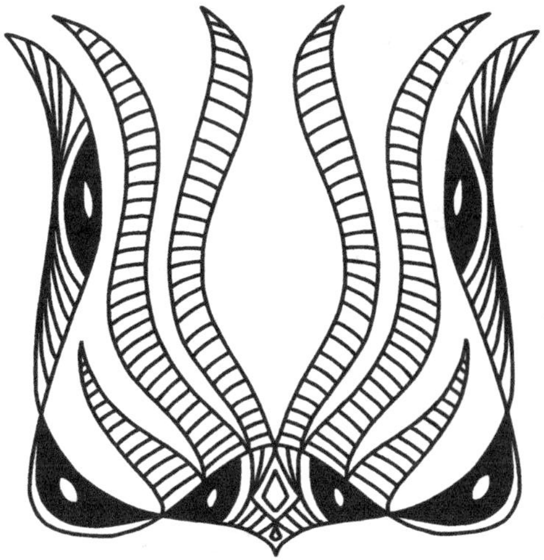

FATLINER WEIRDIES
VOLUME 1

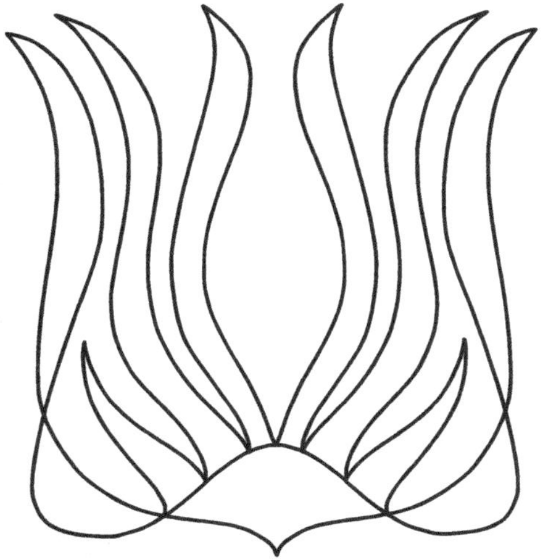

FATLINER WEIRDIES
THE TEMPLATES 1

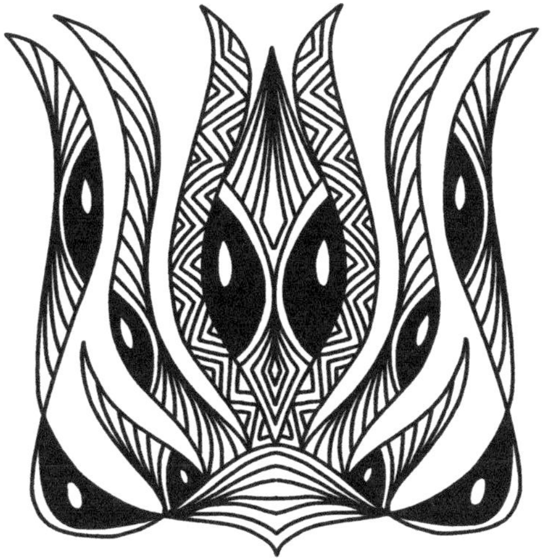

FATLINER WEIRDIES
VOLUME 3

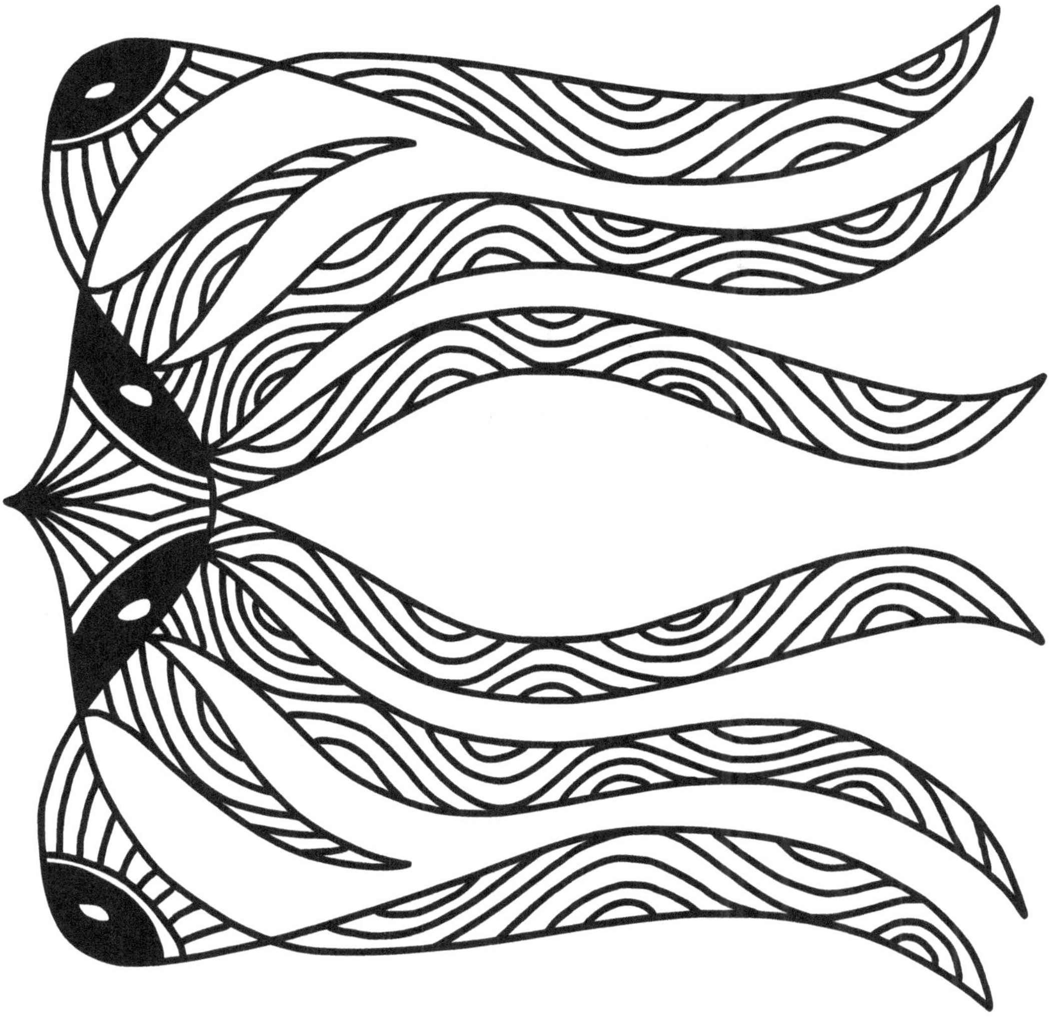

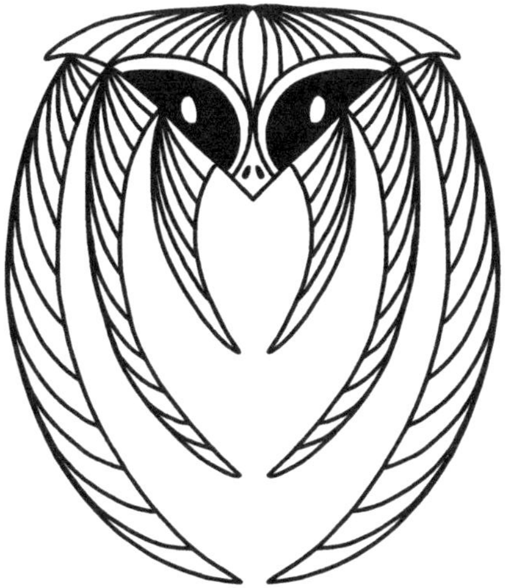

FATLINER WEIRDIES
VOLUME 1

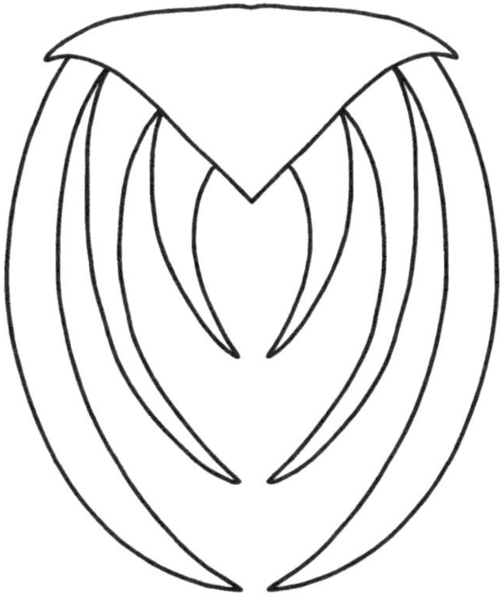

FATLINER WEIRDIES
THE TEMPLATES 1

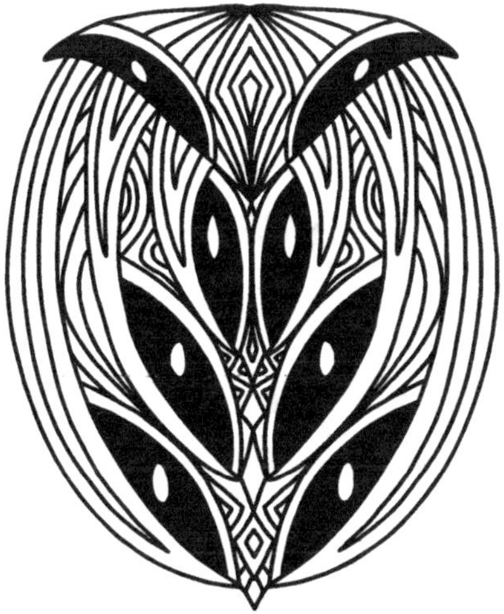

FATLINER WEIRDIES
VOLUME 3

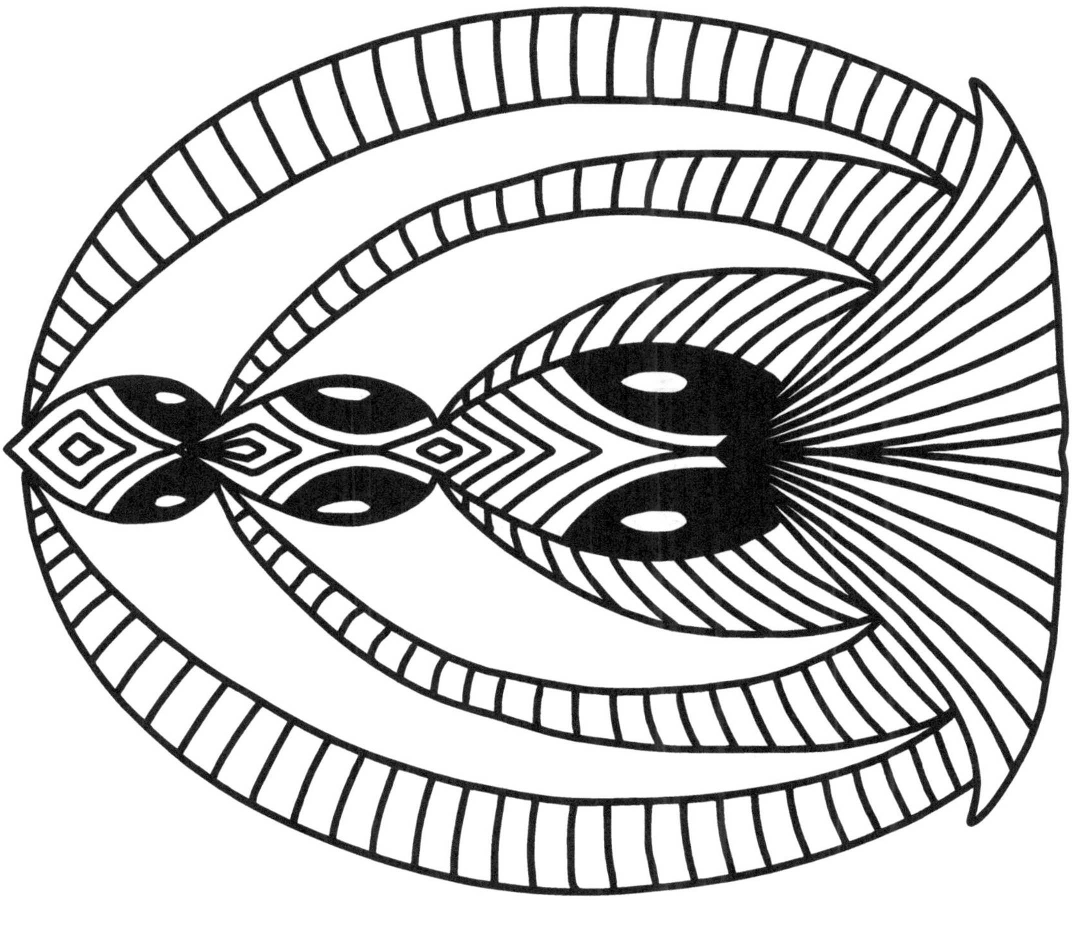

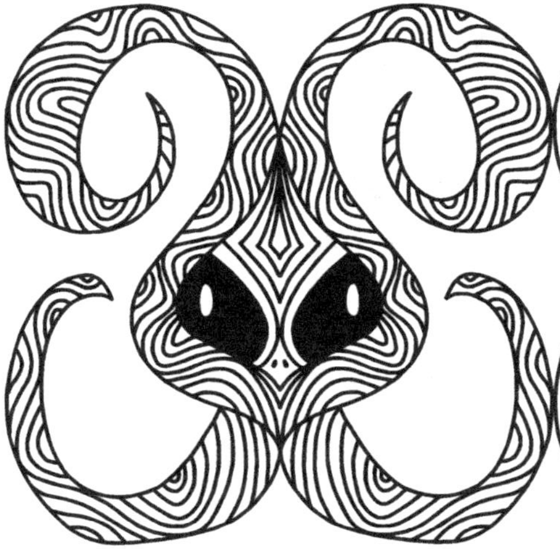

FATLINER WEIRDIES
VOLUME 1

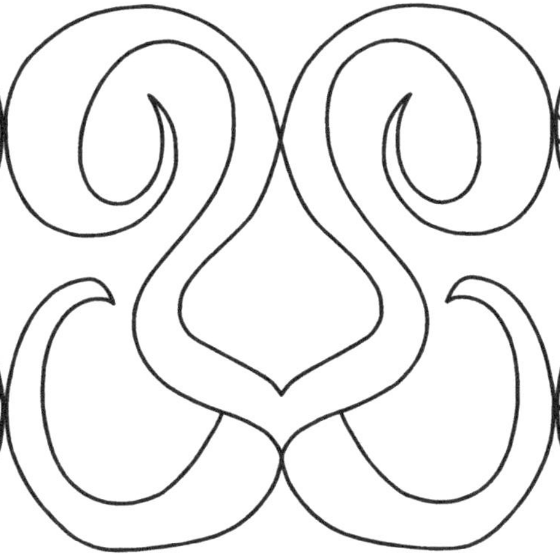

FATLINER WEIRDIES
THE TEMPLATES 1

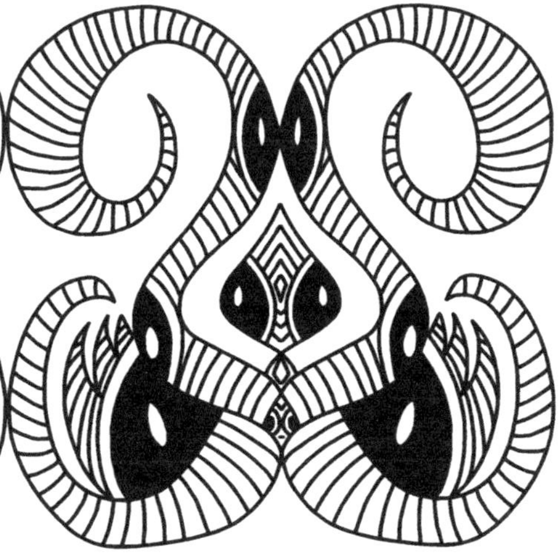

FATLINER WEIRDIES
VOLUME 3

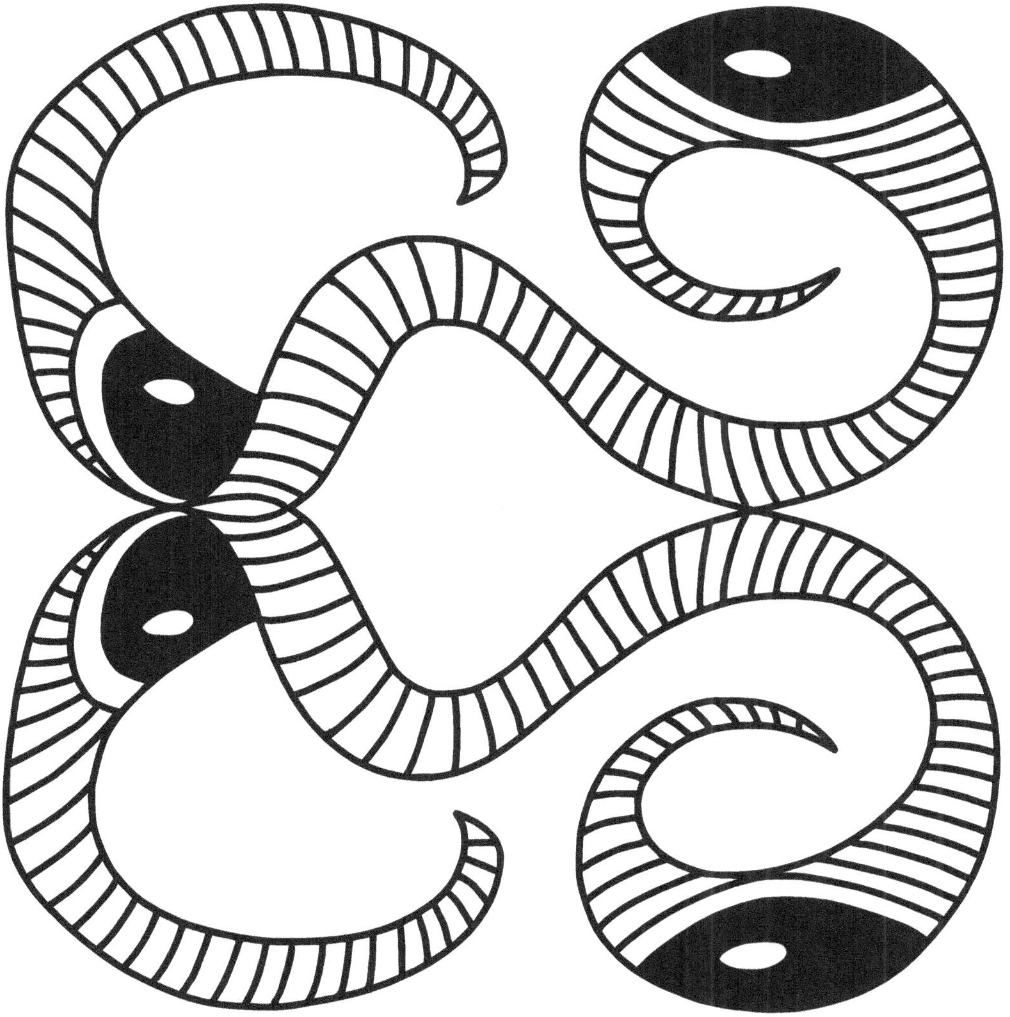

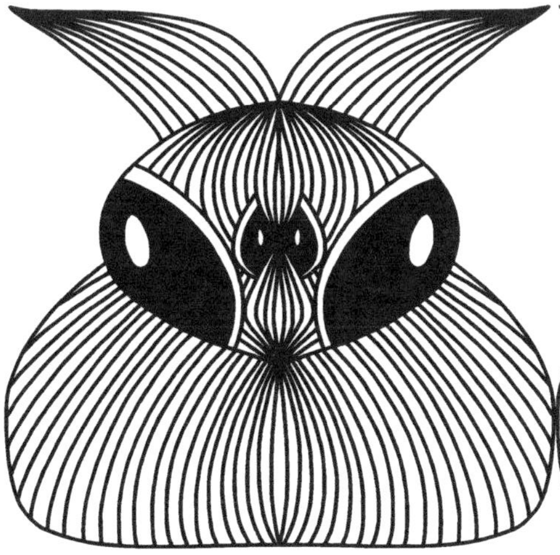
FATLINER WEIRDIES
VOLUME 1

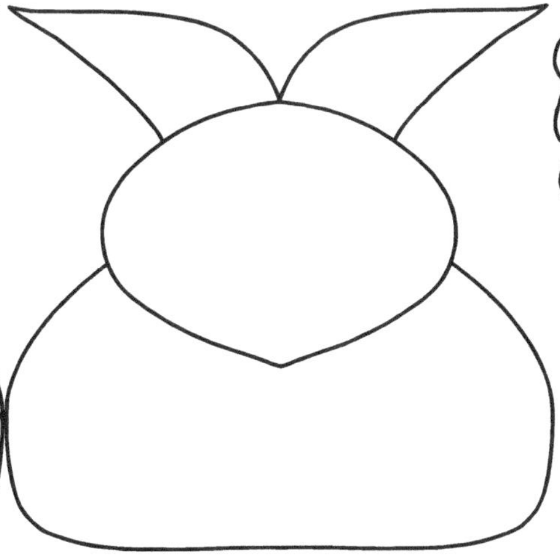
FATLINER WEIRDIES
THE TEMPLATES 1

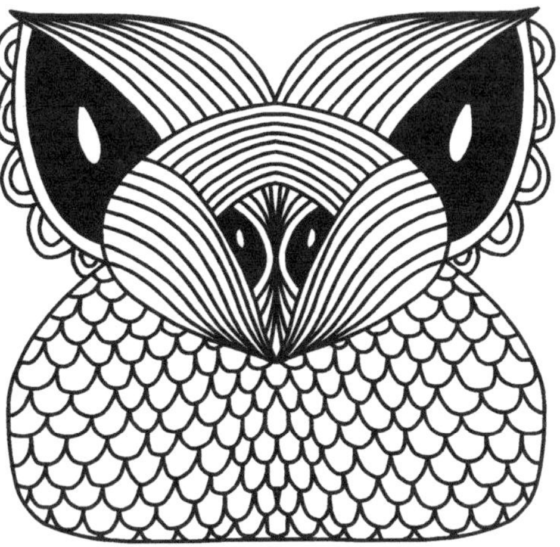
FATLINER WEIRDIES
VOLUME 3

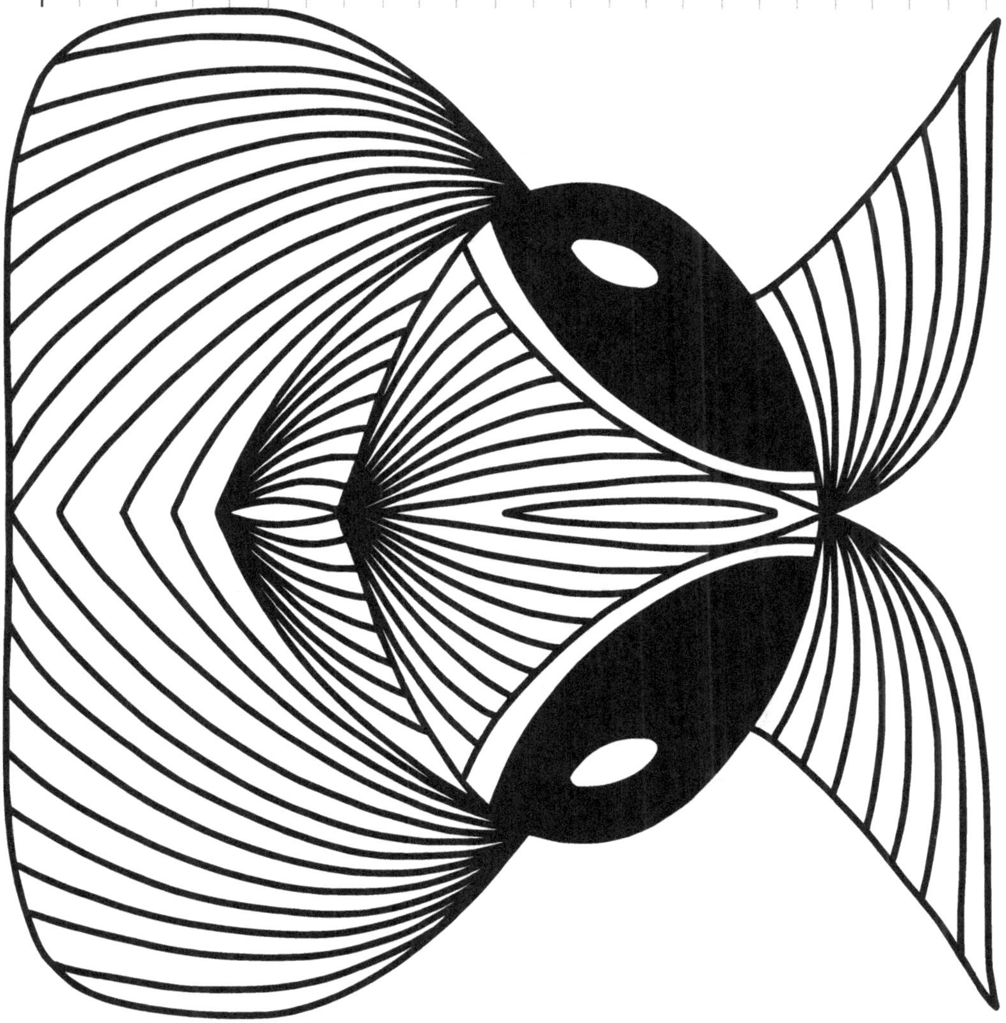

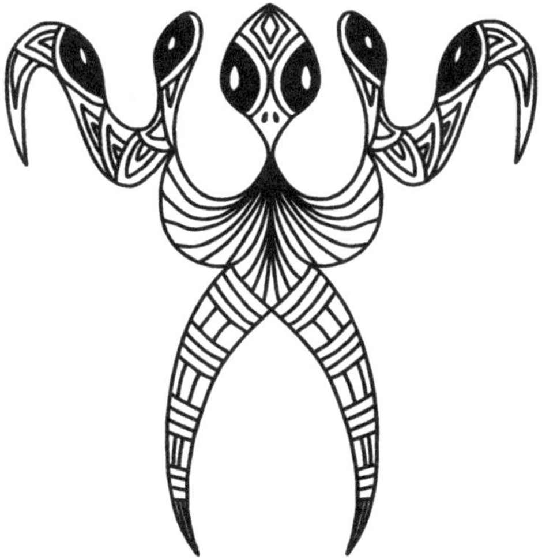

FATLINER WEIRDIES
VOLUME 1

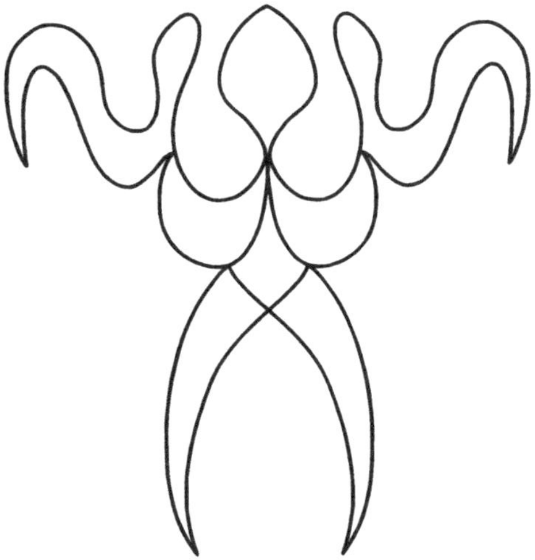

FATLINER WEIRDIES
THE TEMPLATES 1

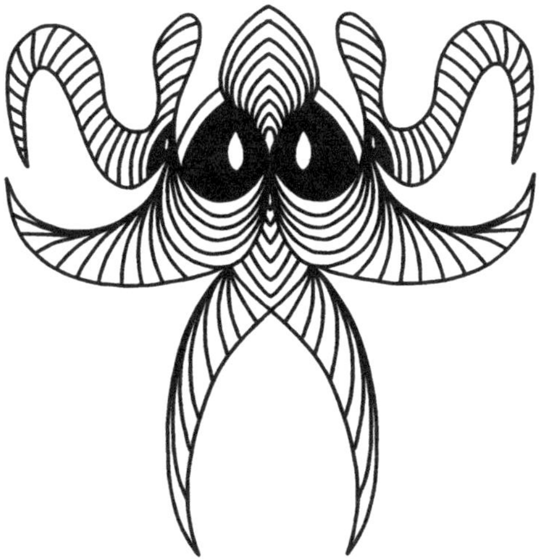

FATLINER WEIRDIES
VOLUME 3

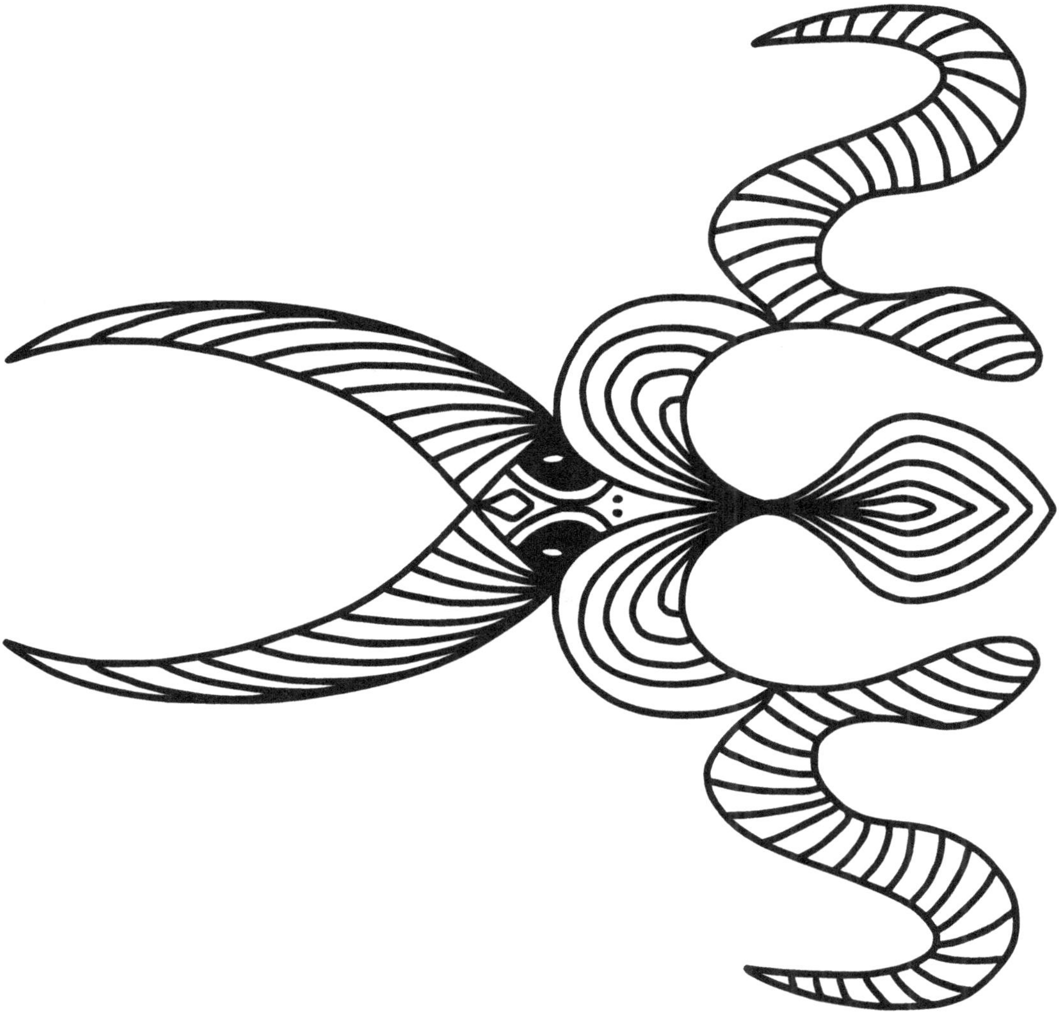

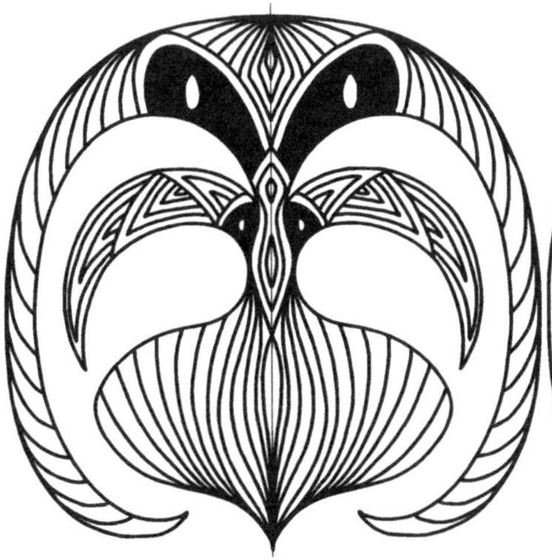

FATLINER WEIRDIES
VOLUME 1

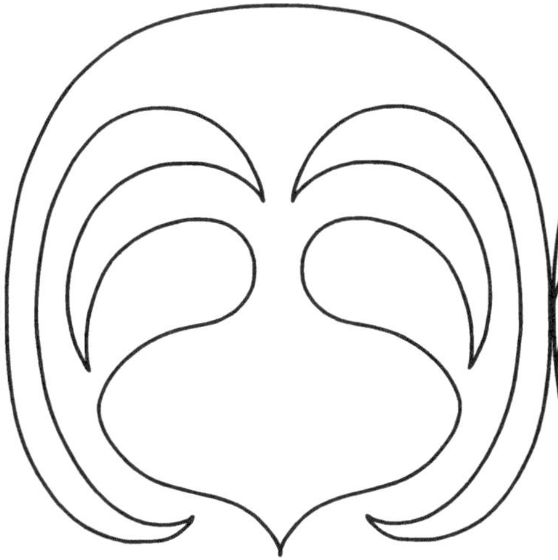

FATLINER WEIRDIES
THE TEMPLATES 1

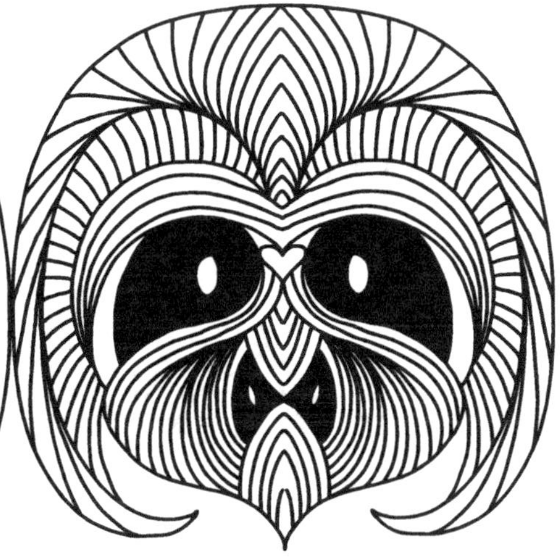

FATLINER WEIRDIES
VOLUME 3

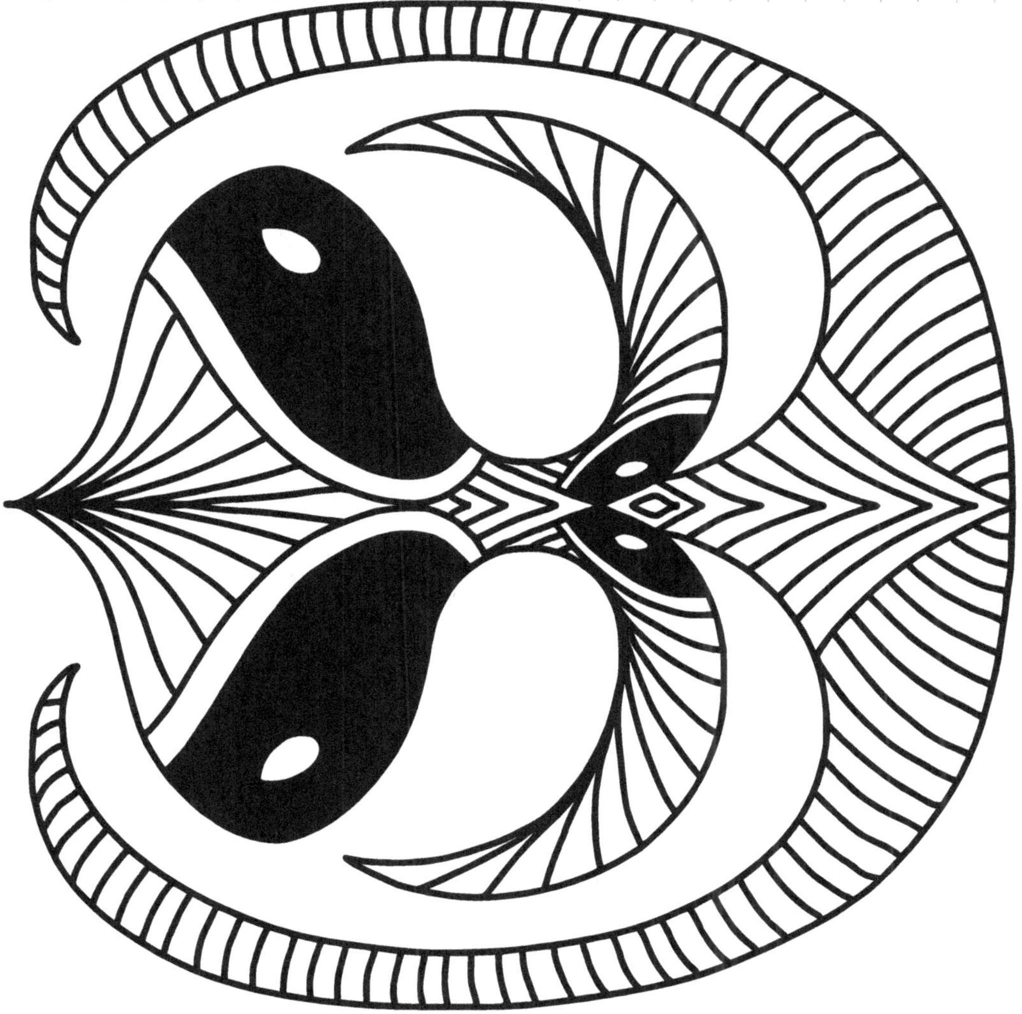

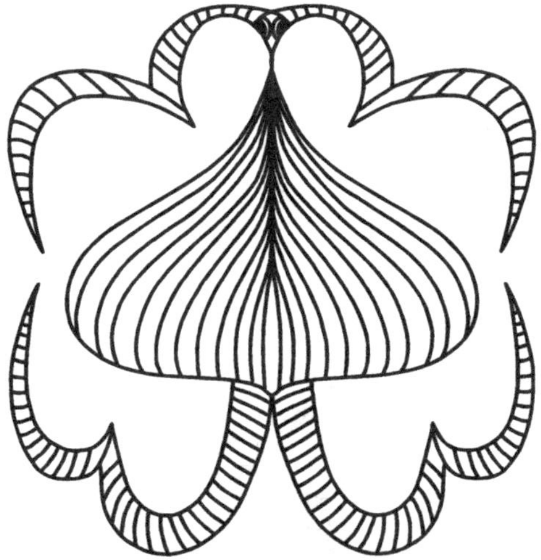

FATLINER WEIRDIES
VOLUME 1

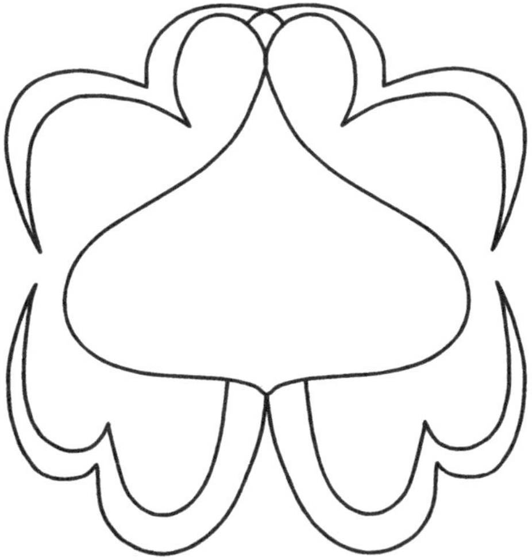

FATLINER WEIRDIES
THE TEMPLATES 1

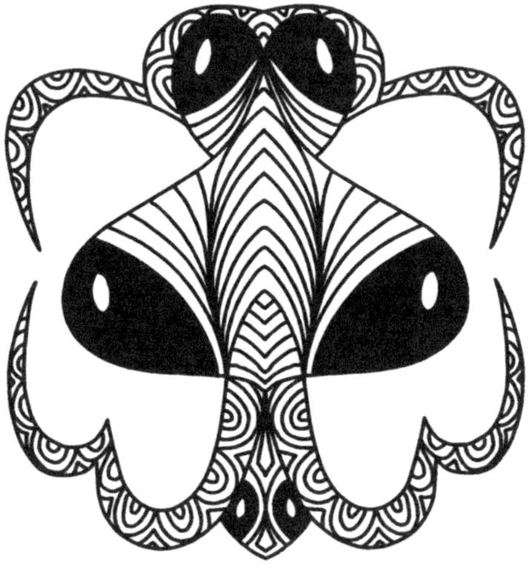

FATLINER WEIRDIES
VOLUME 3

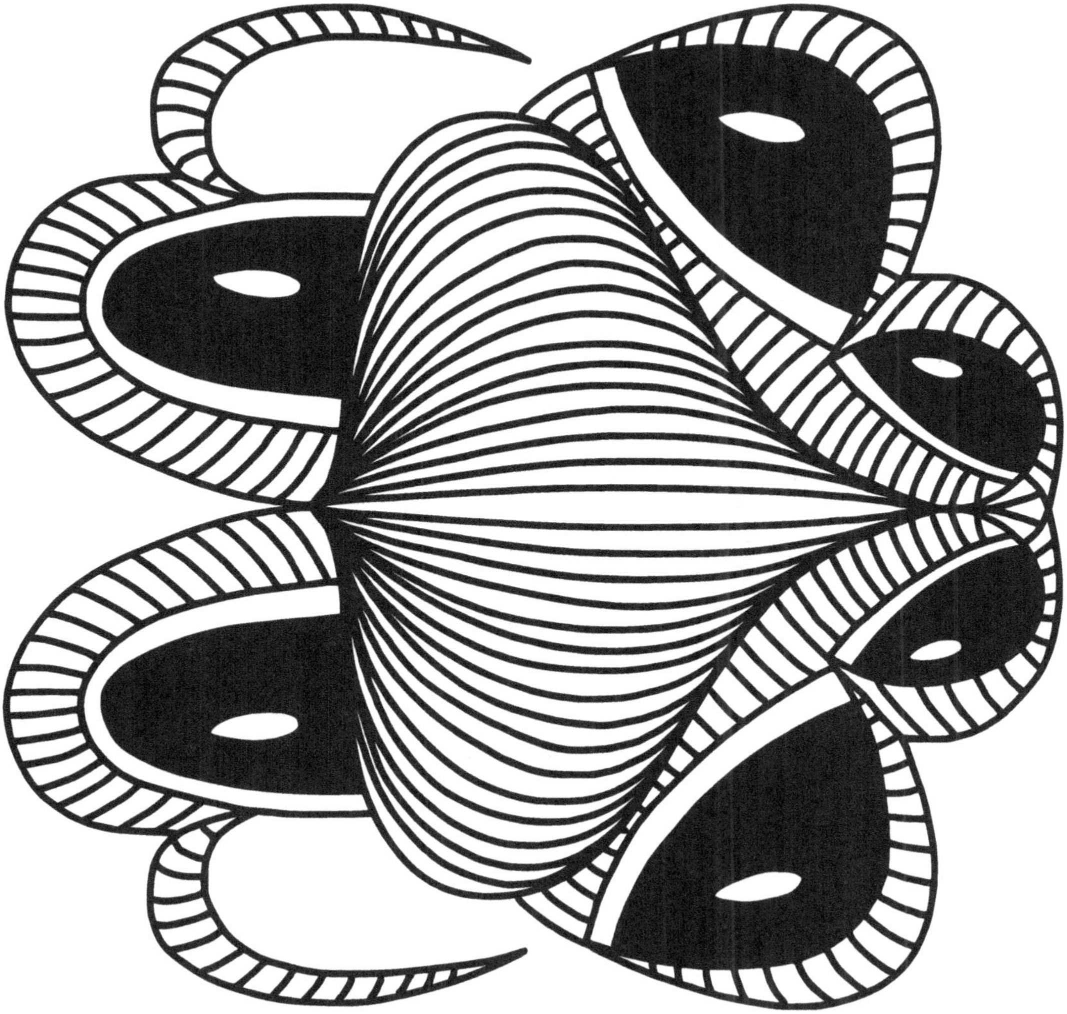

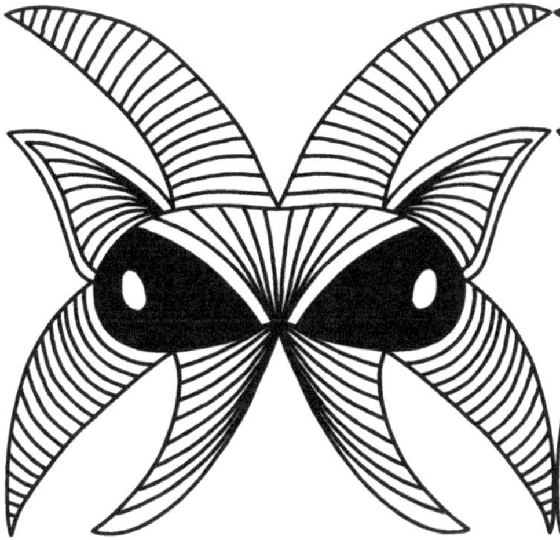

FATLINER WEIRDIES
VOLUME 1

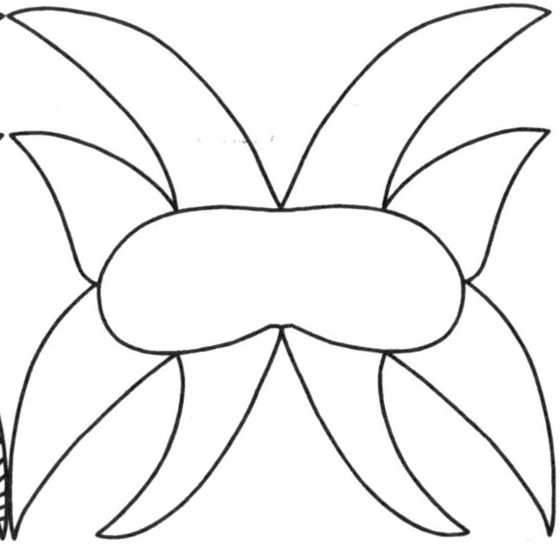

FATLINER WEIRDIES
THE TEMPLATES 1

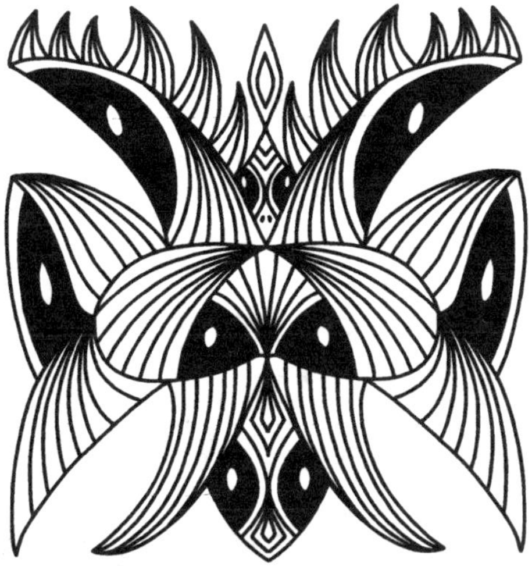

FATLINER WEIRDIES
VOLUME 3

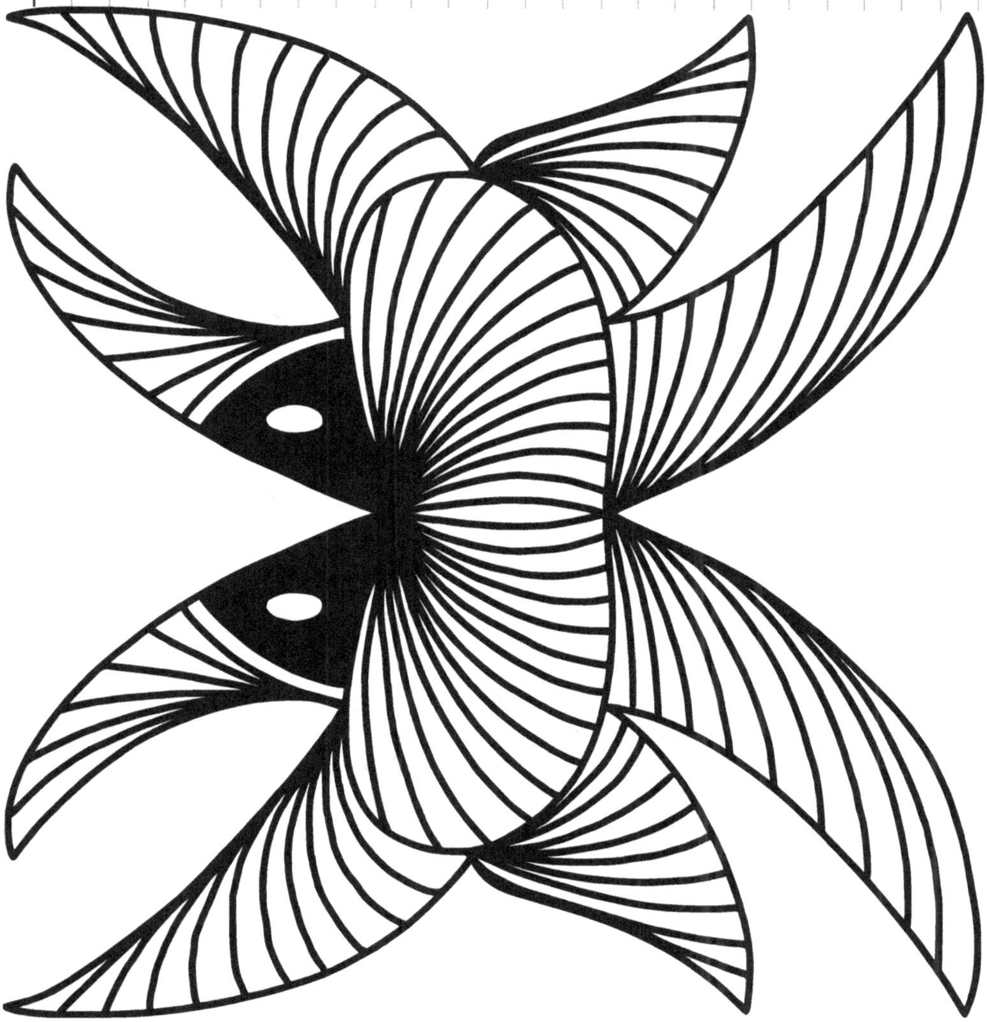

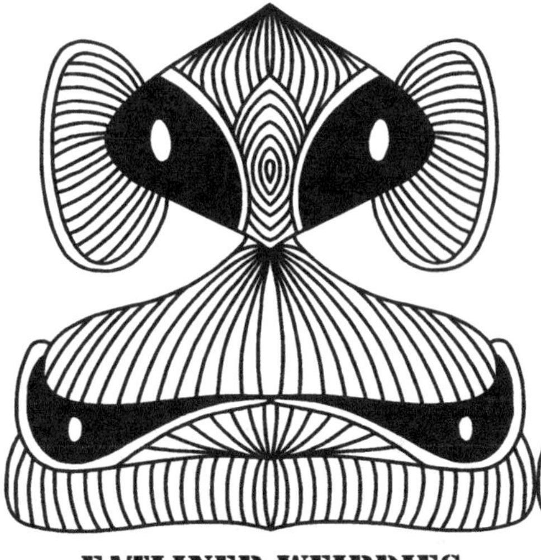

FATLINER WEIRDIES
VOLUME 1

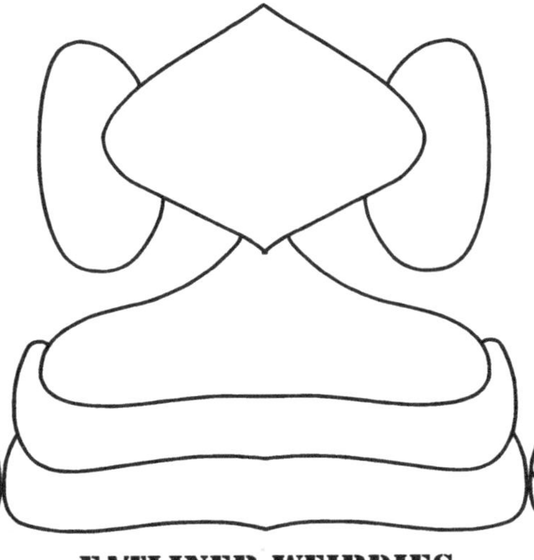

FATLINER WEIRDIES
THE TEMPLATES 1

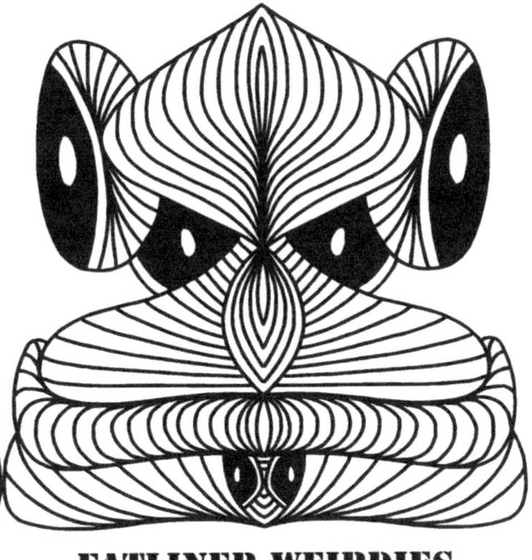

FATLINER WEIRDIES
VOLUME 3

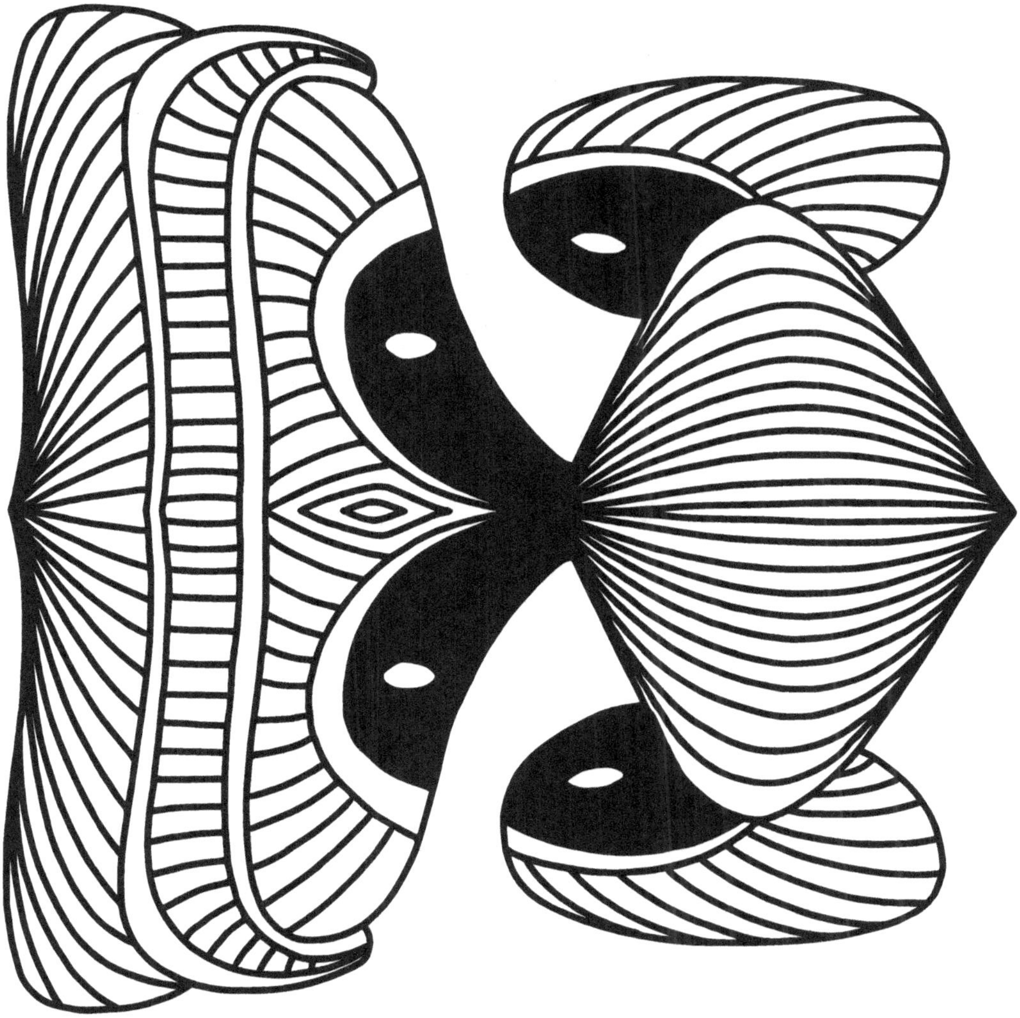

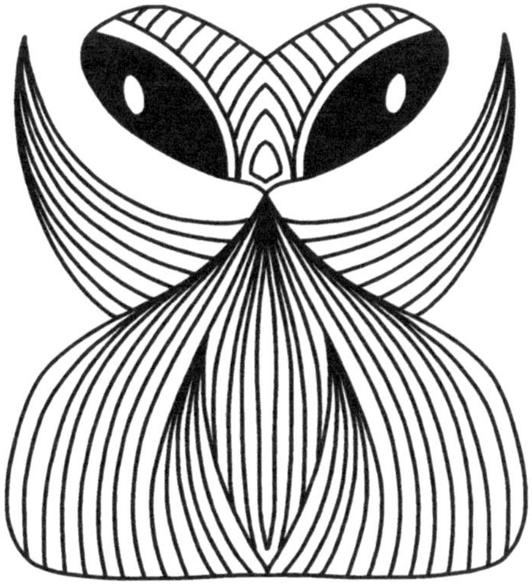

FATLINER WEIRDIES
VOLUME 1

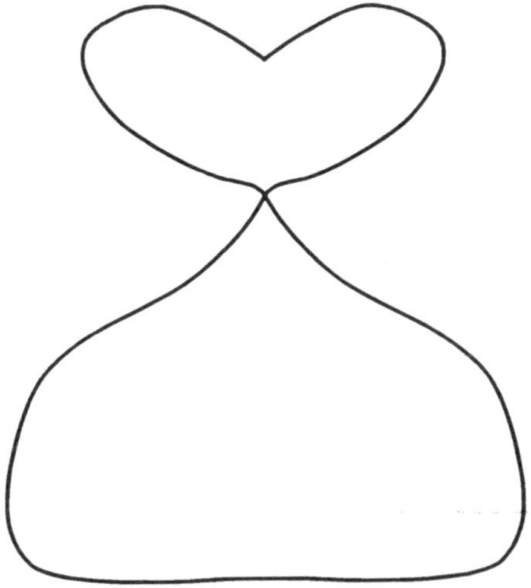

FATLINER WEIRDIES
THE TEMPLATES 1

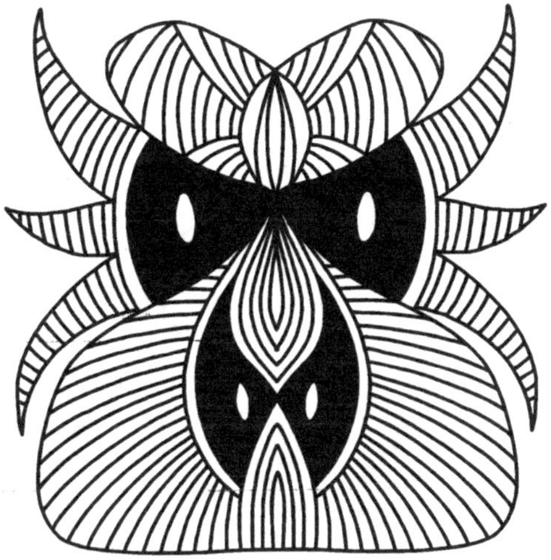

FATLINER WEIRDIES
VOLUME 3

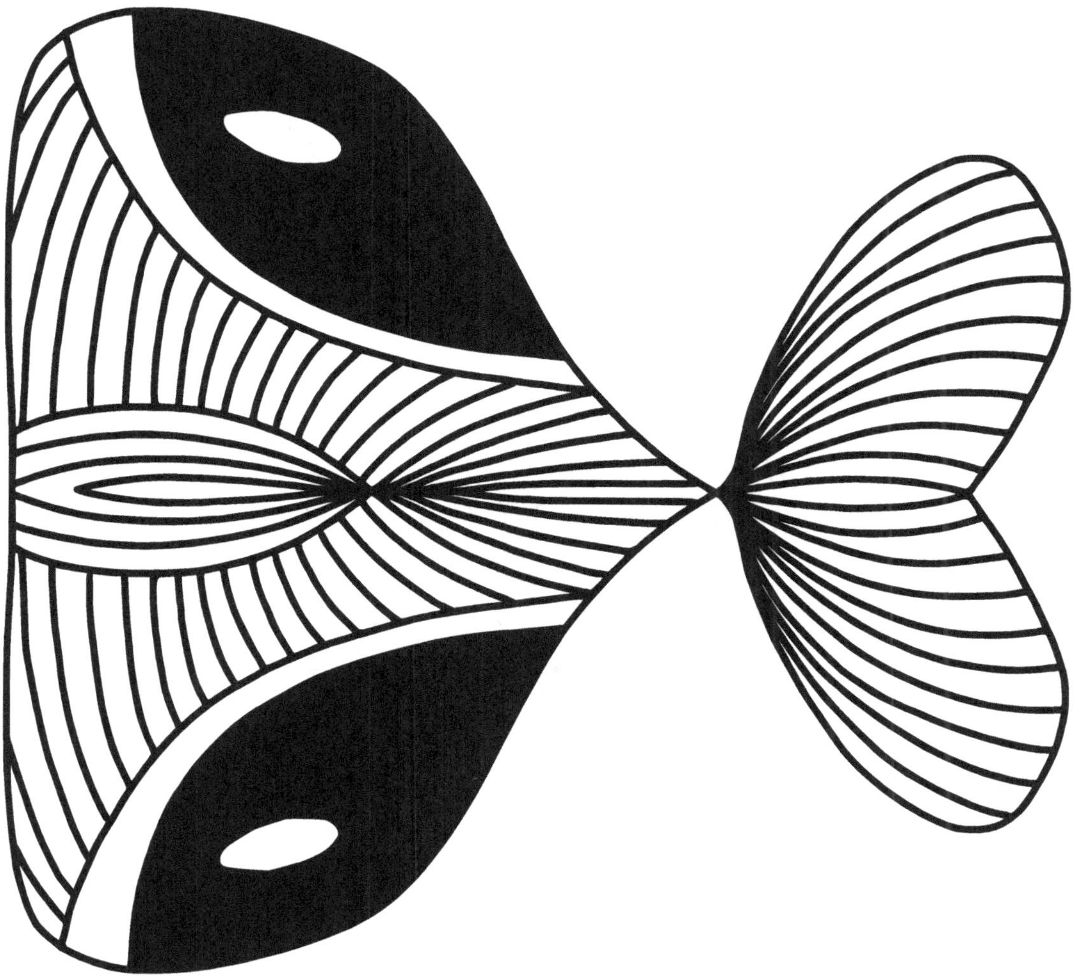

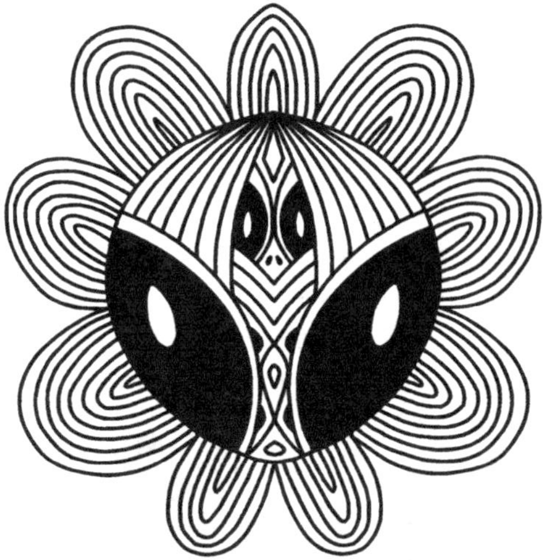

FATLINER WEIRDIES
VOLUME 1

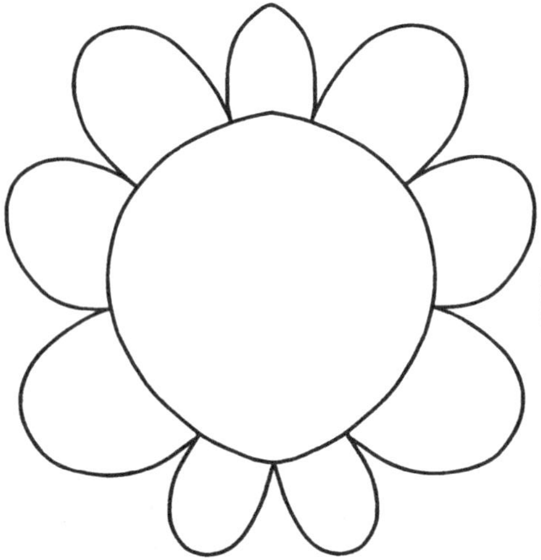

FATLINER WEIRDIES
THE TEMPLATES 1

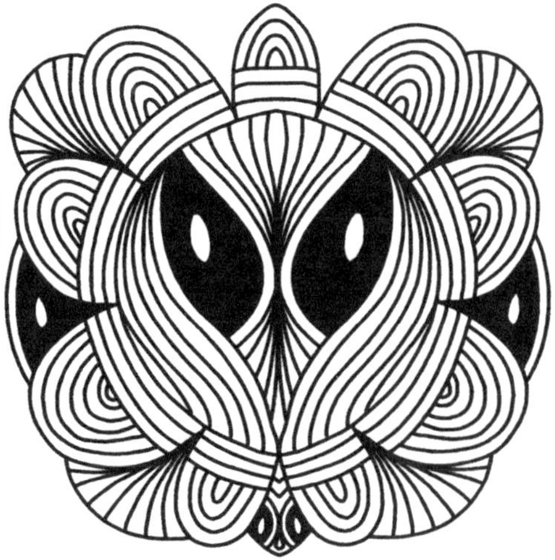

FATLINER WEIRDIES
VOLUME 3

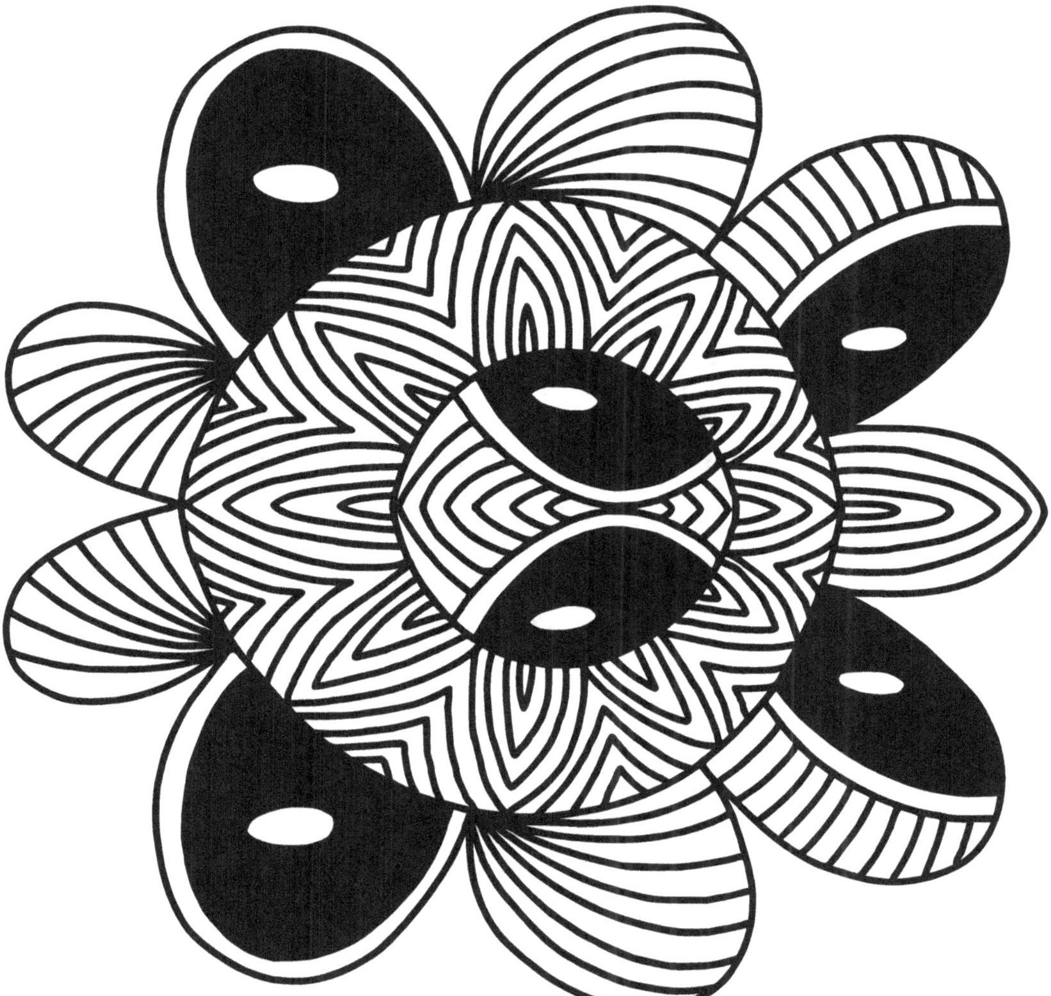

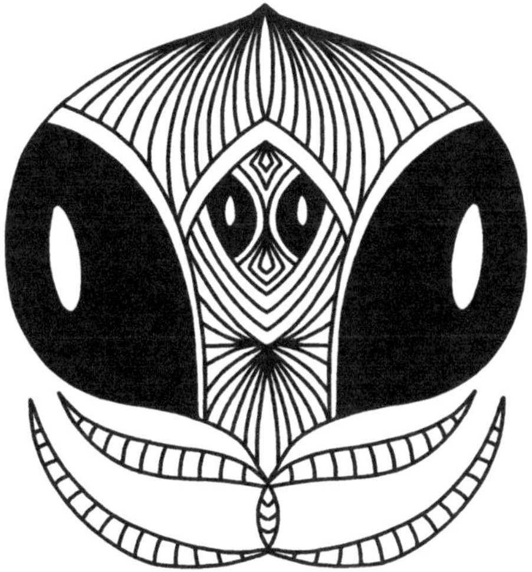

FATLINER WEIRDIES
VOLUME 1

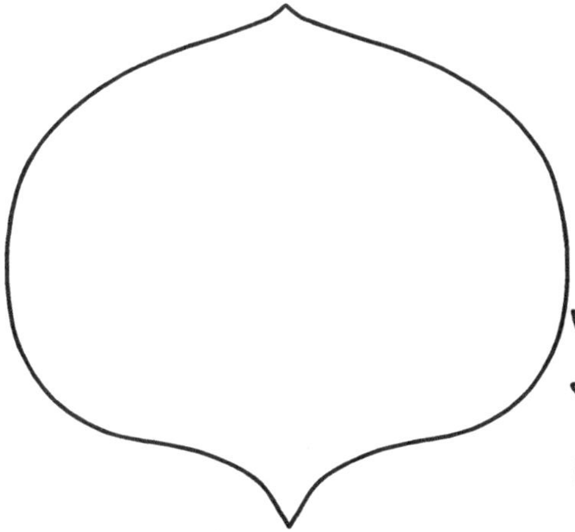

FATLINER WEIRDIES
THE TEMPLATES 1

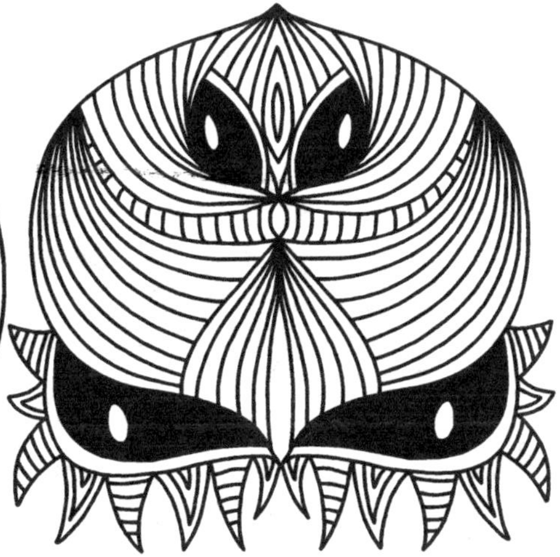

FATLINER WEIRDIES
VOLUME 3

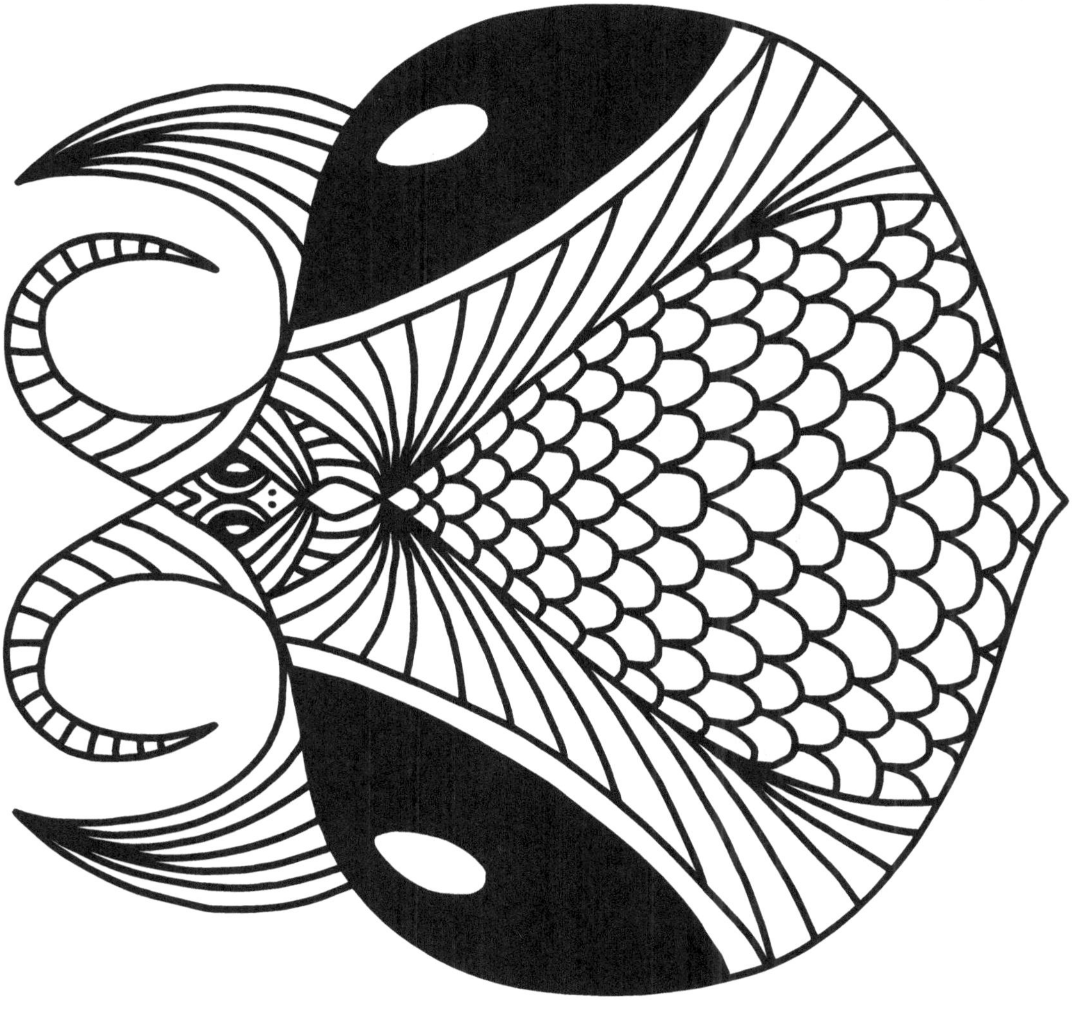

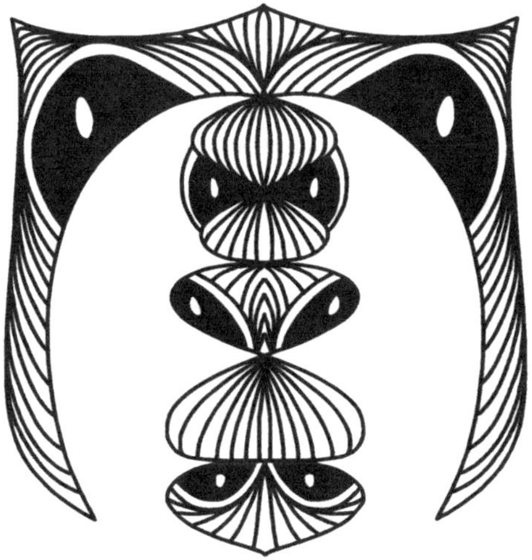

FATLINER WEIRDIES
VOLUME 1

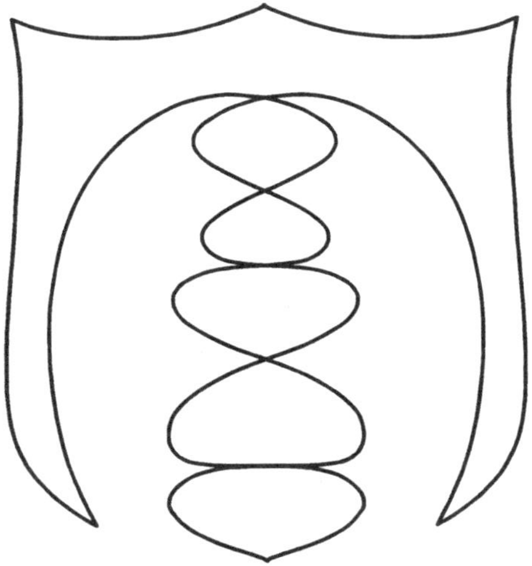

FATLINER WEIRDIES
THE TEMPLATES 1

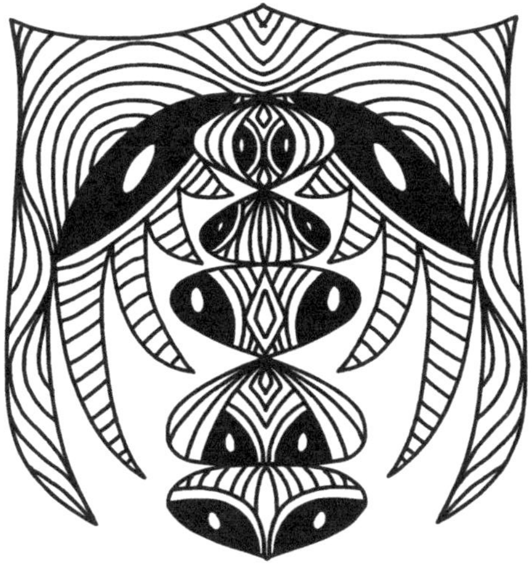

FATLINER WEIRDIES
VOLUME 3

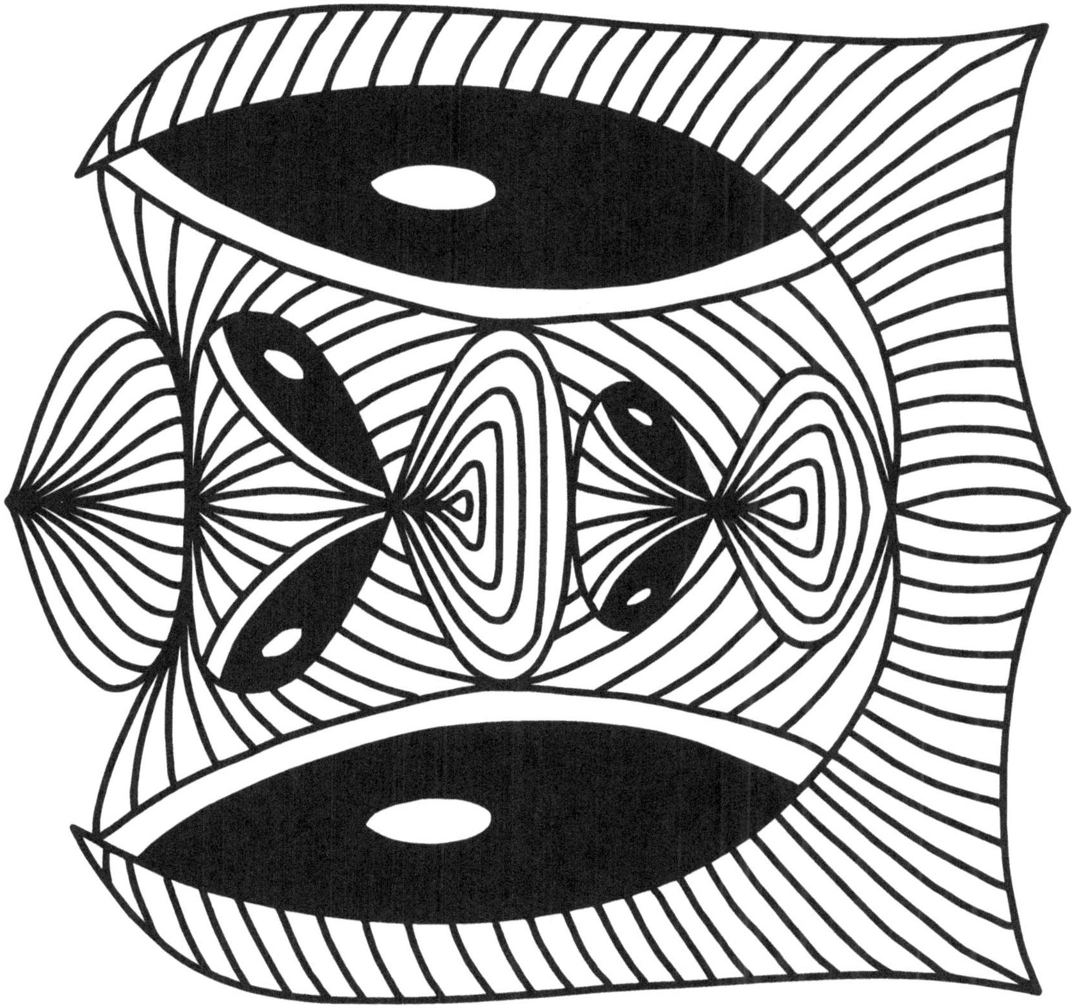

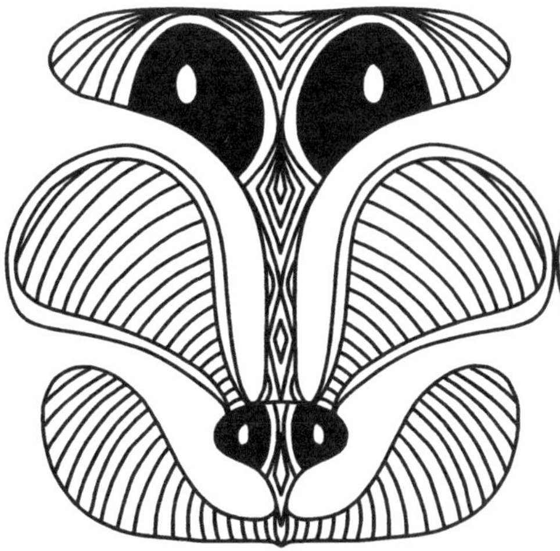

FATLINER WEIRDIES
VOLUME 1

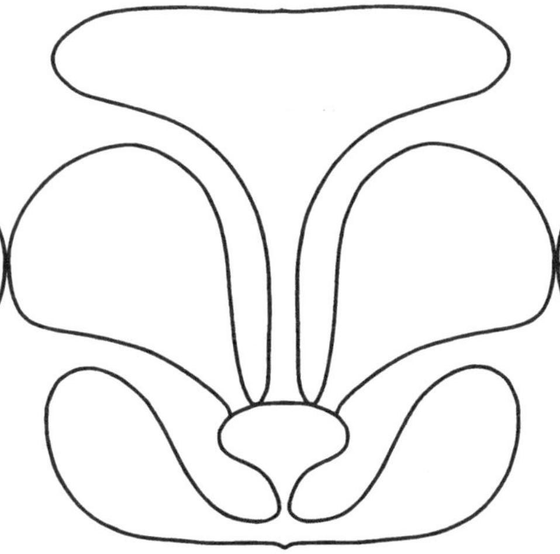

FATLINER WEIRDIES
THE TEMPLATES 1

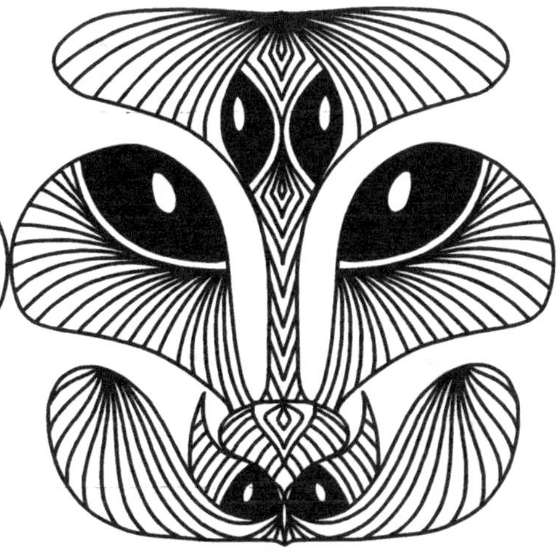

FATLINER WEIRDIES
VOLUME 3

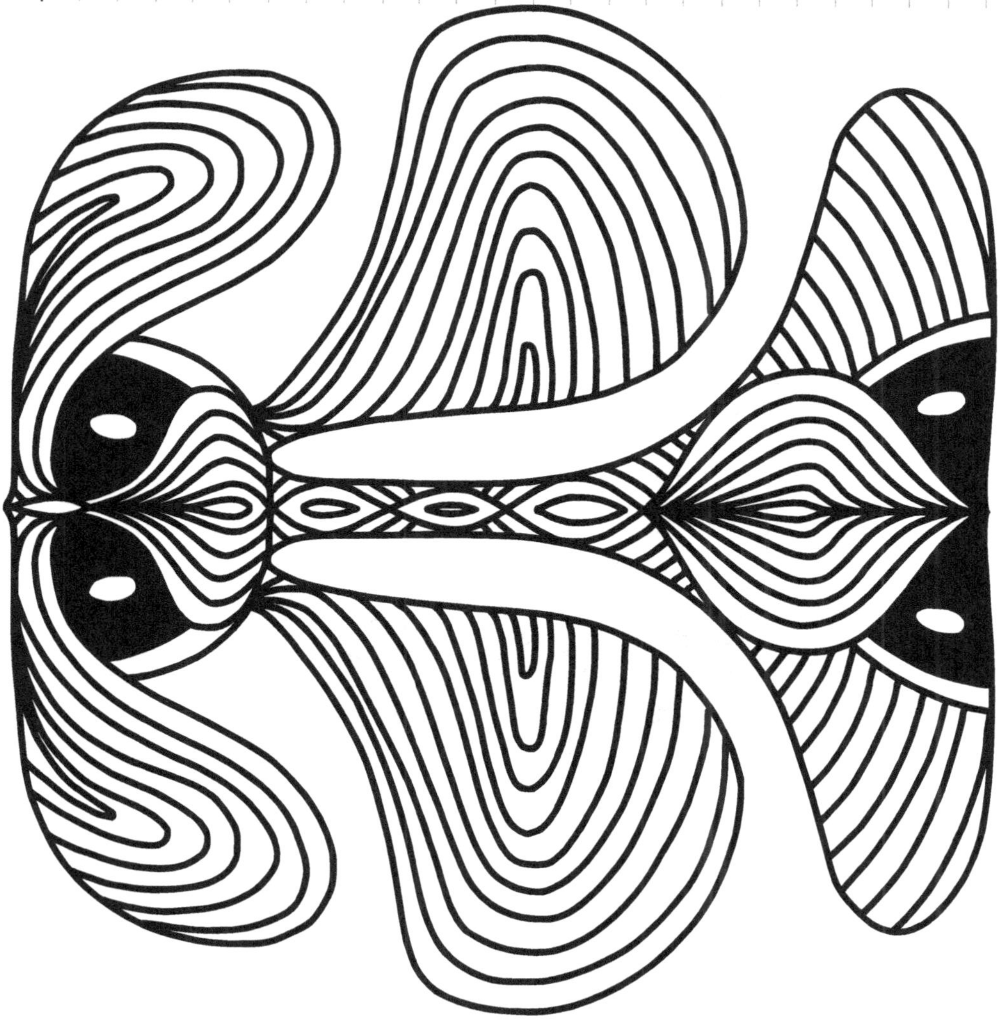

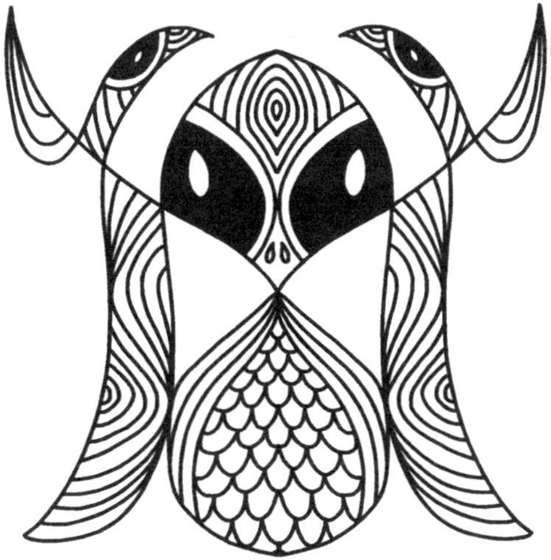

FATLINER WEIRDIES
VOLUME 1

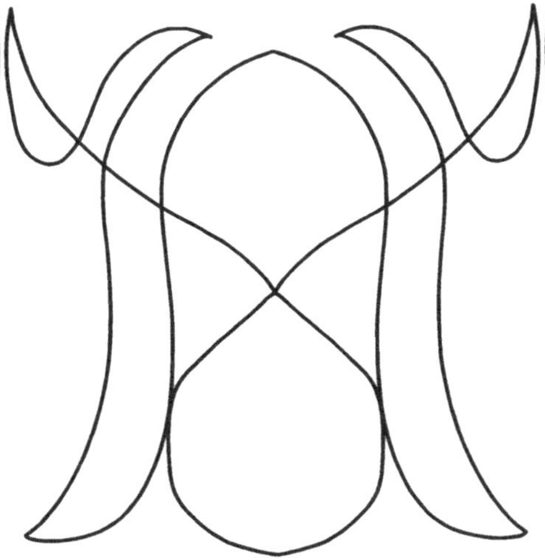

FATLINER WEIRDIES
THE TEMPLATES 1

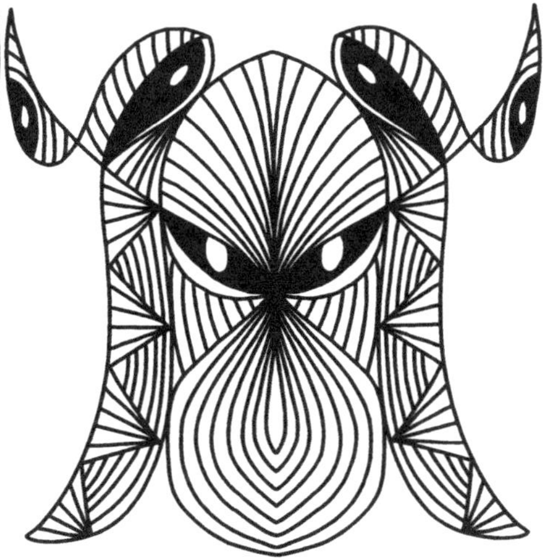

FATLINER WEIRDIES
VOLUME 3

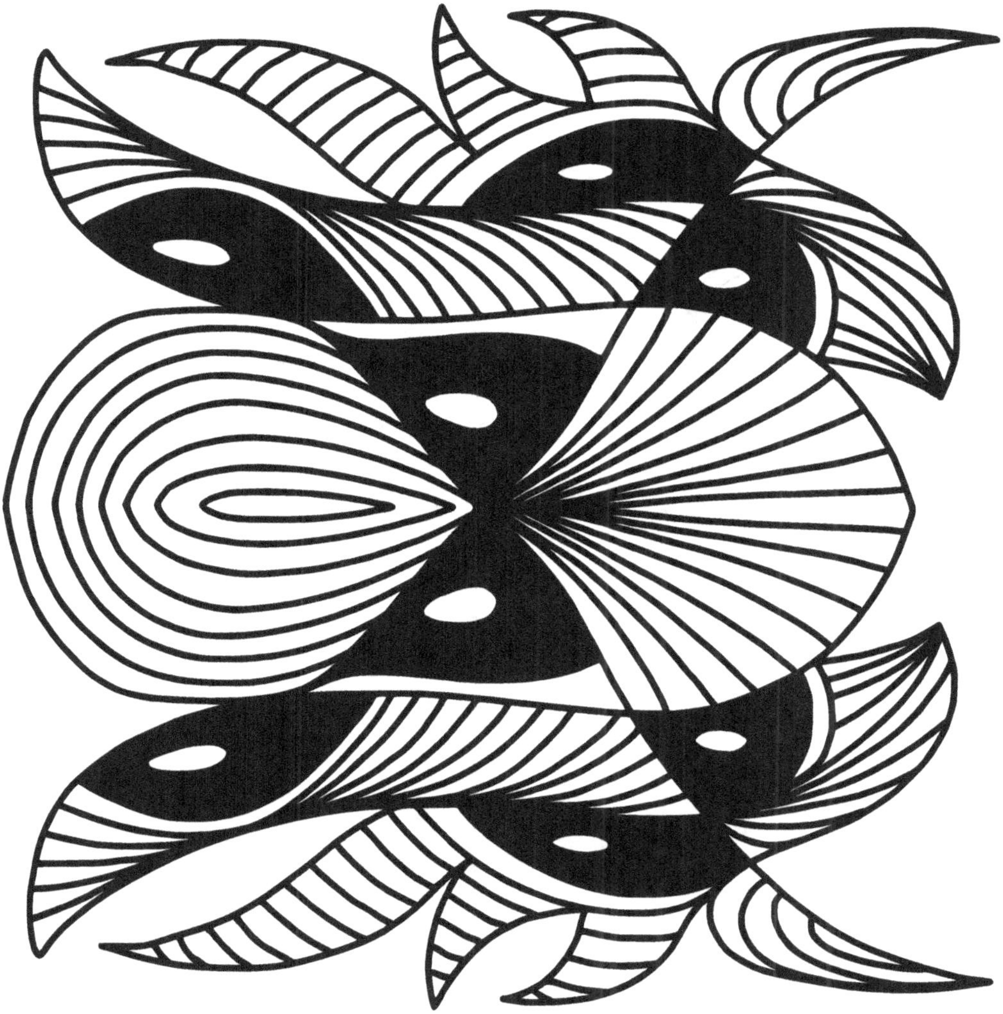

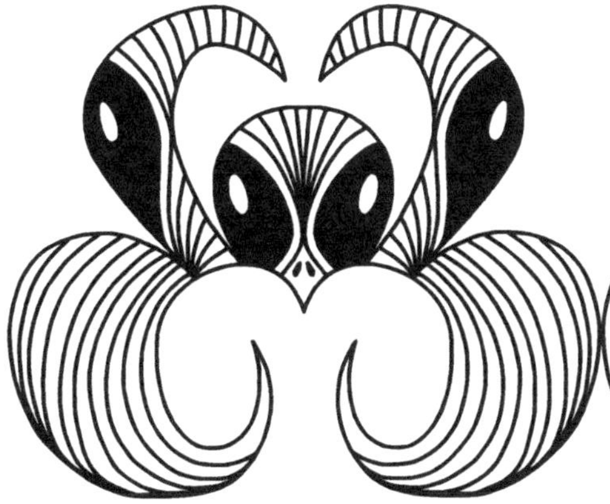

FATLINER WEIRDIES
VOLUME 1

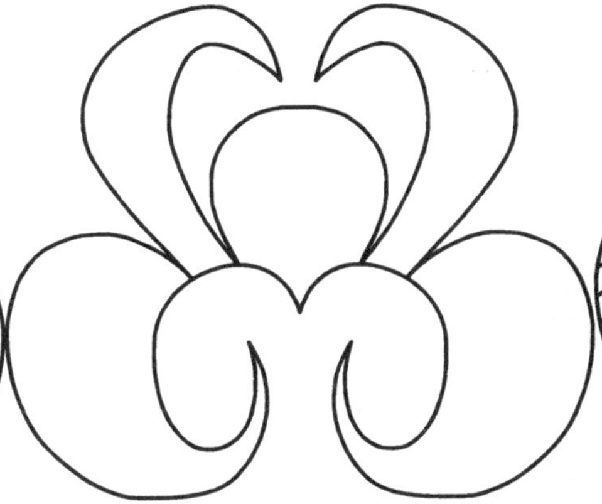

FATLINER WEIRDIES
THE TEMPLATES 1

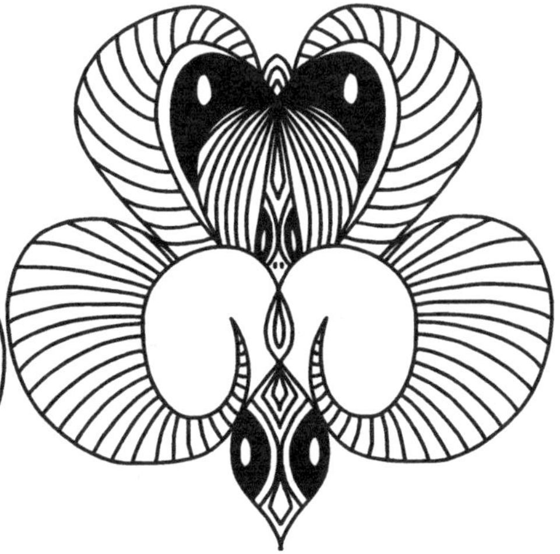

FATLINER WEIRDIES
VOLUME 3

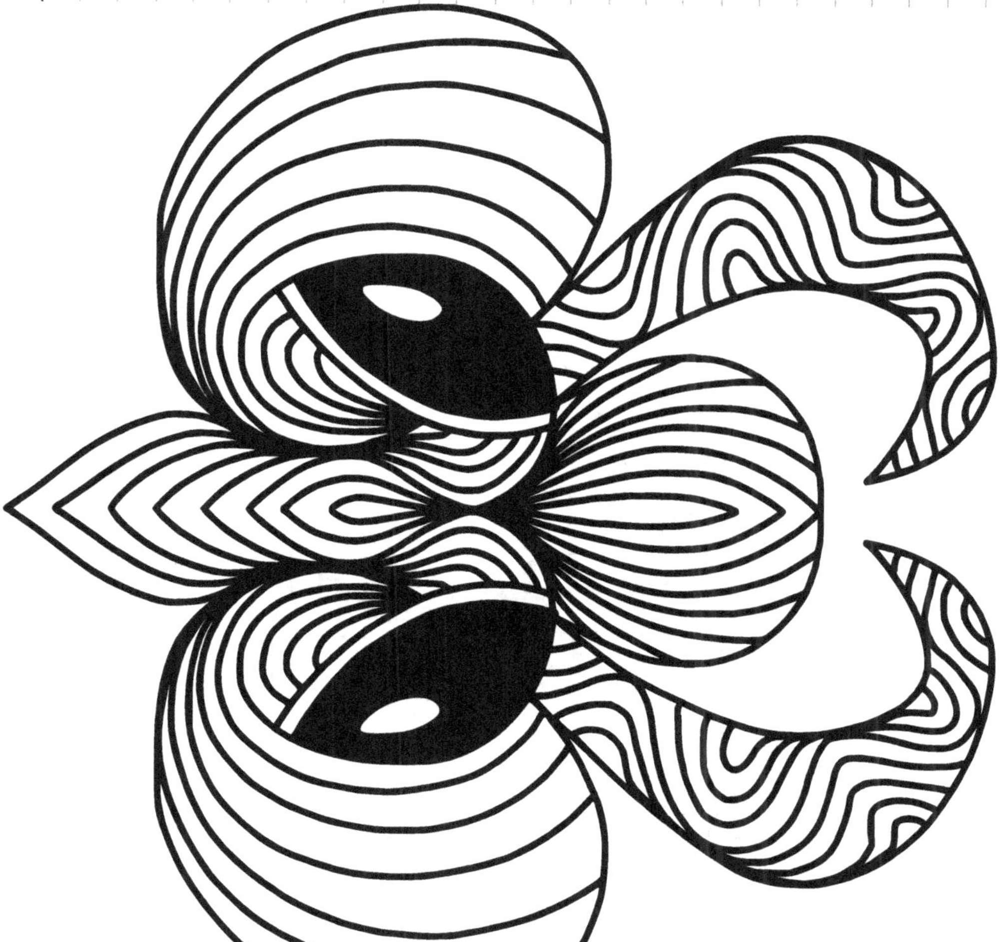

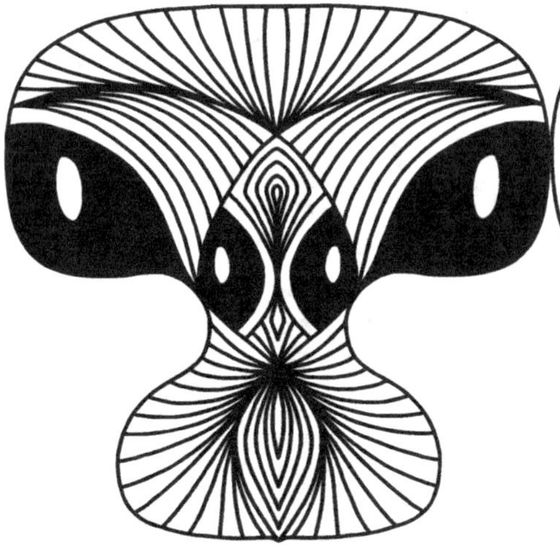

FATLINER WEIRDIES
VOLUME 1

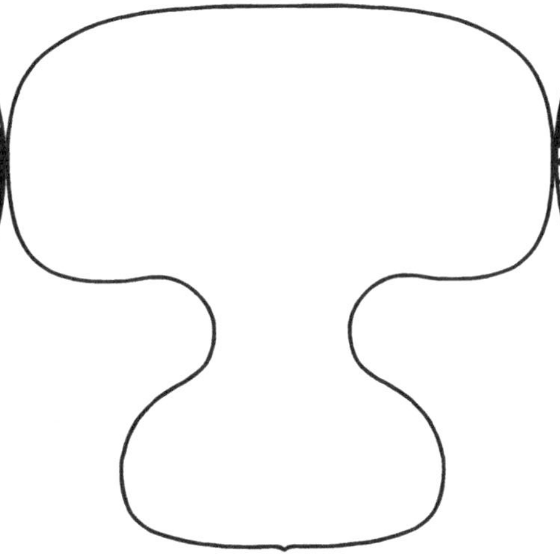

FATLINER WEIRDIES
THE TEMPLATES 1

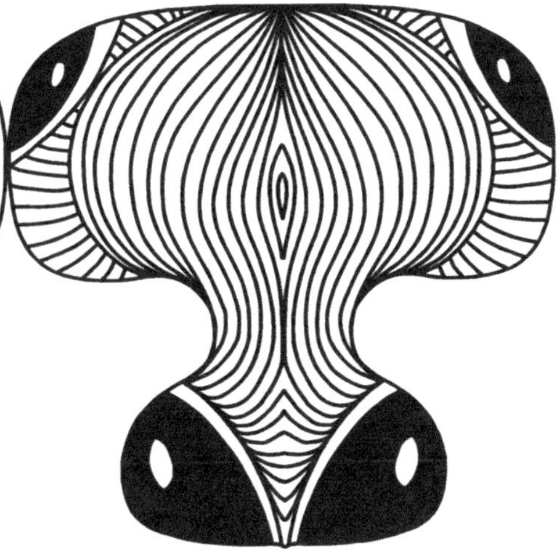

FATLINER WEIRDIES
VOLUME 3

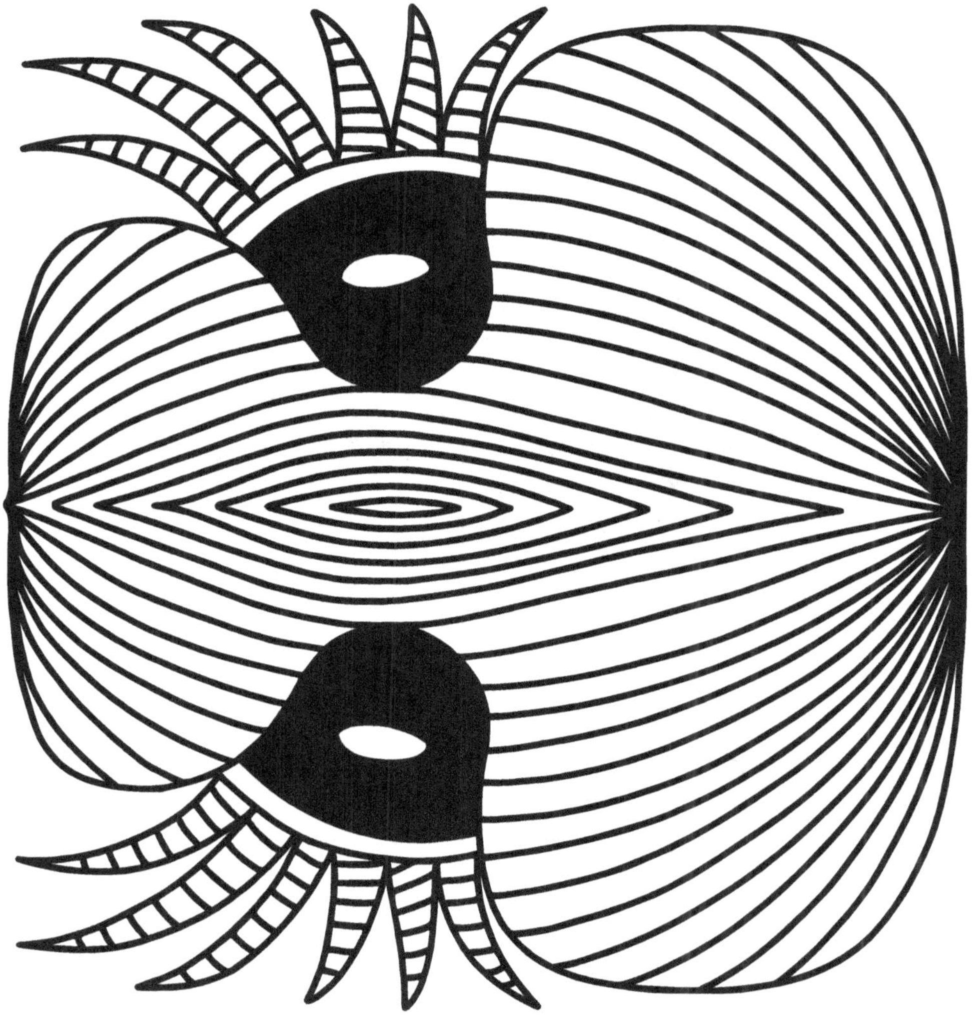

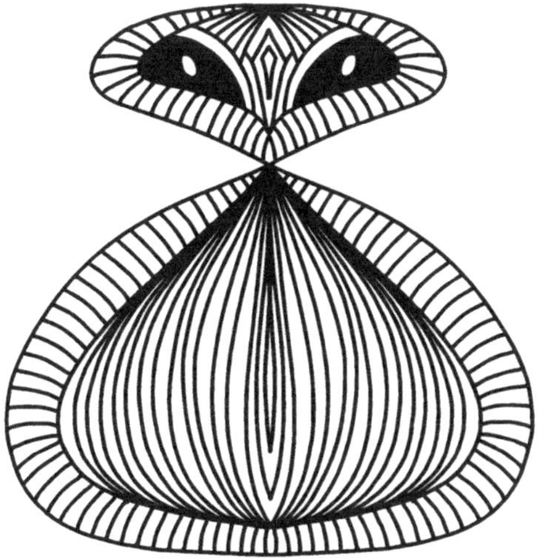

FATLINER WEIRDIES
VOLUME 1

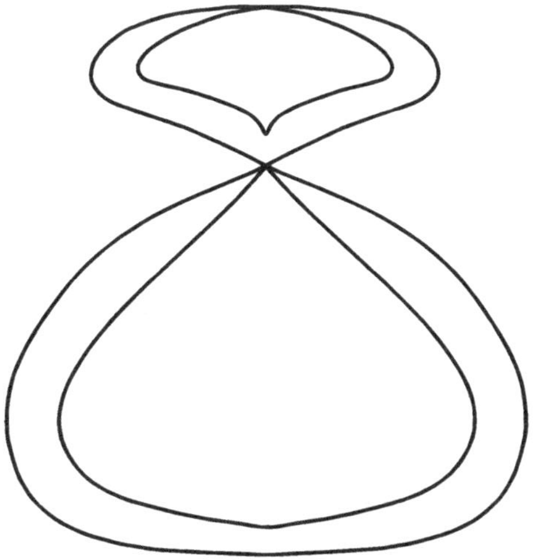

FATLINER WEIRDIES
THE TEMPLATES 1

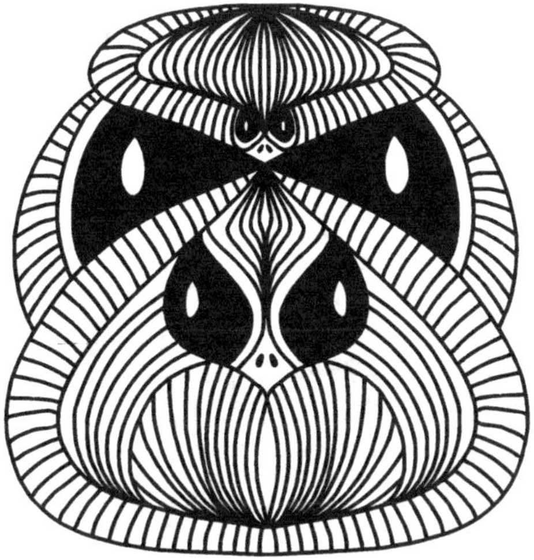

FATLINER WEIRDIES
VOLUME 3

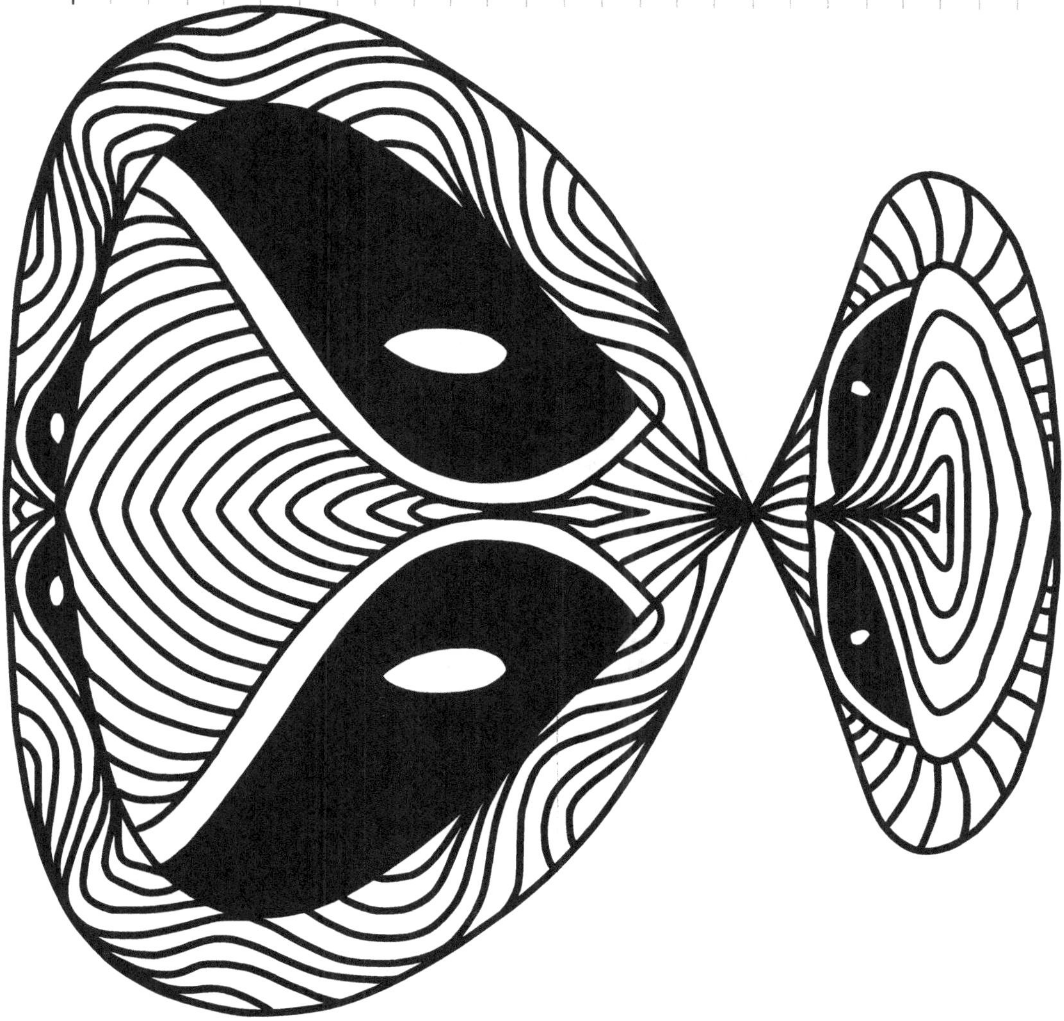

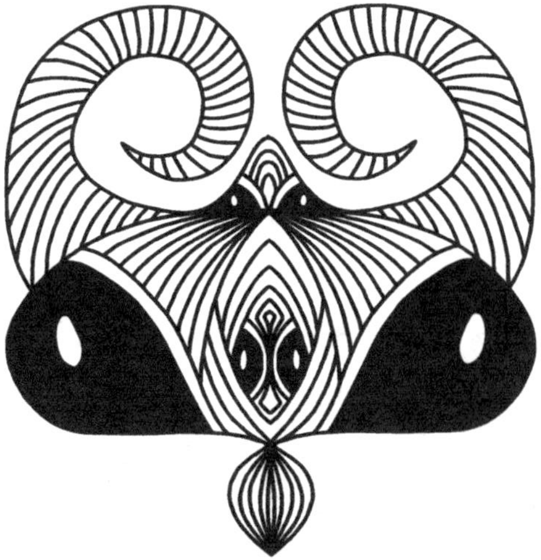

FATLINER WEIRDIES
VOLUME 1

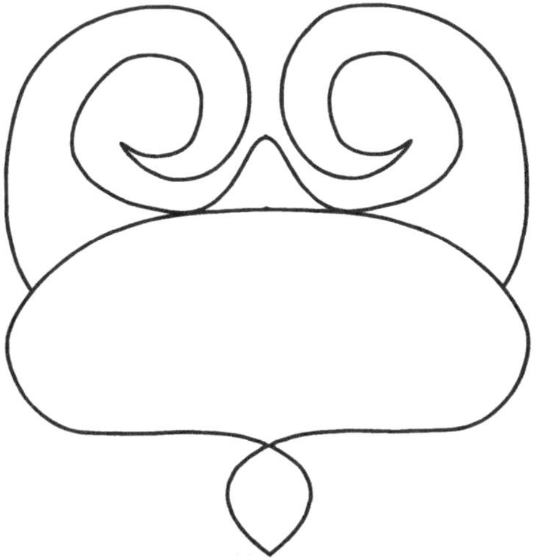

FATLINER WEIRDIES
THE TEMPLATES 1

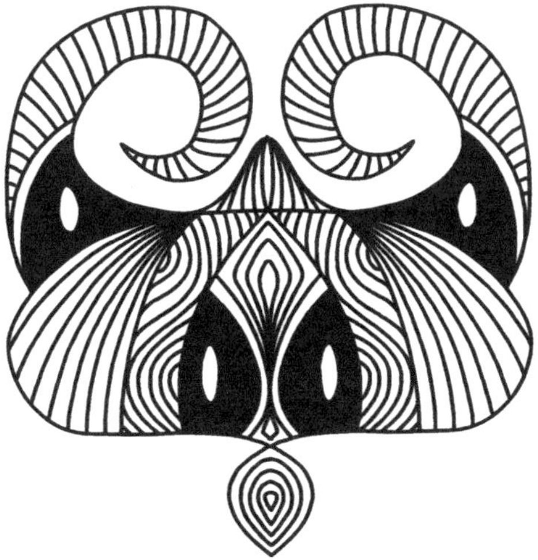

FATLINER WEIRDIES
VOLUME 3

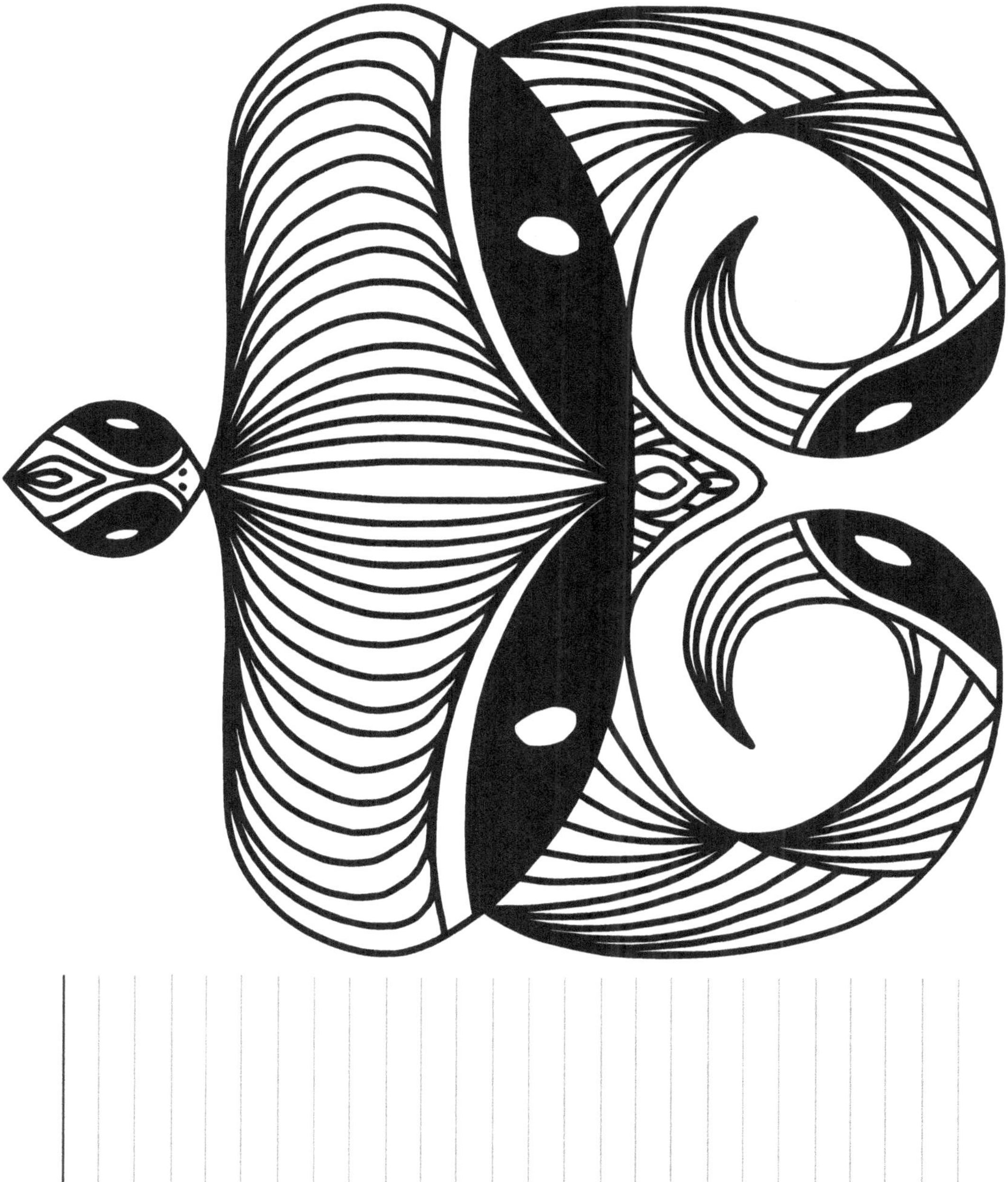

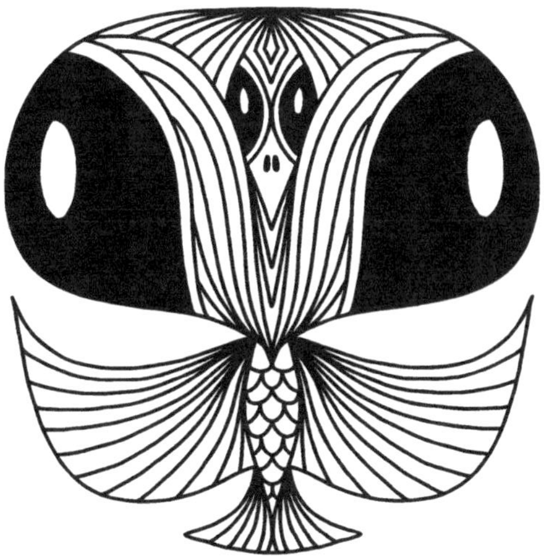

FATLINER WEIRDIES
VOLUME 1

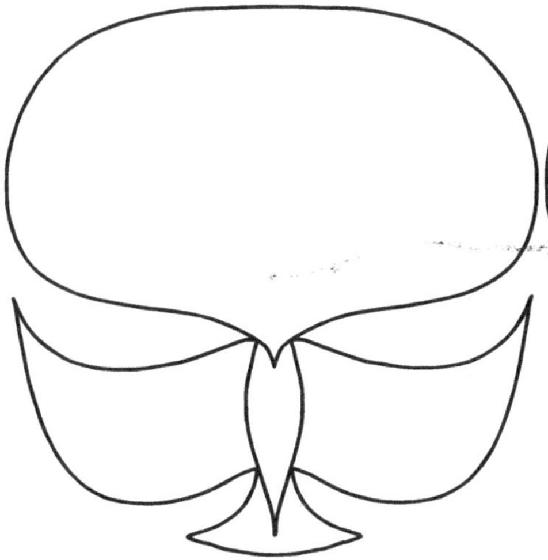

FATLINER WEIRDIES
THE TEMPLATES 1

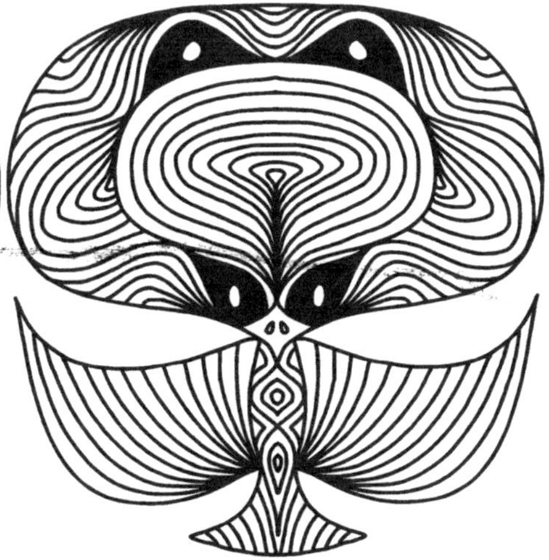

FATLINER WEIRDIES
VOLUME 3

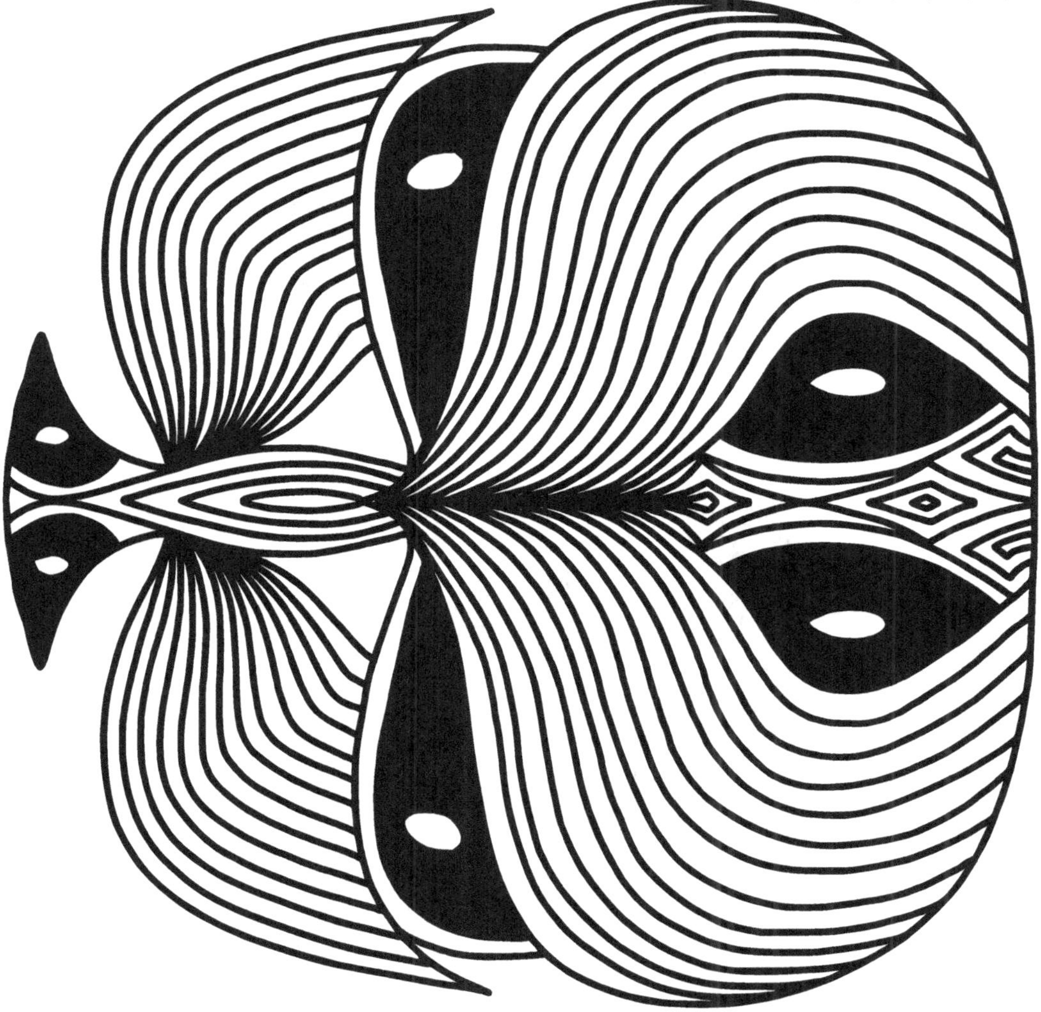

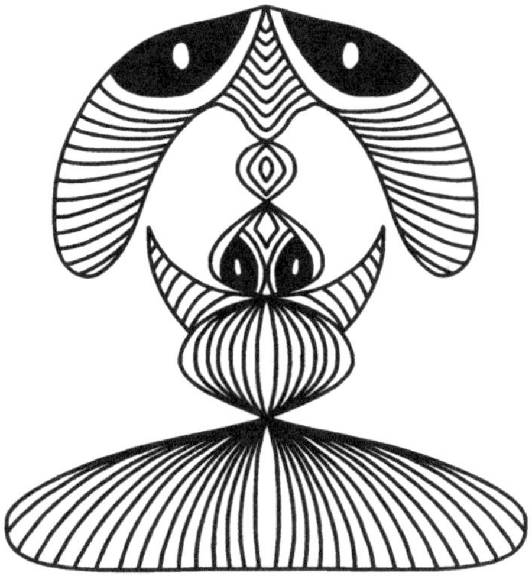

FATLINER WEIRDIES
VOLUME 1

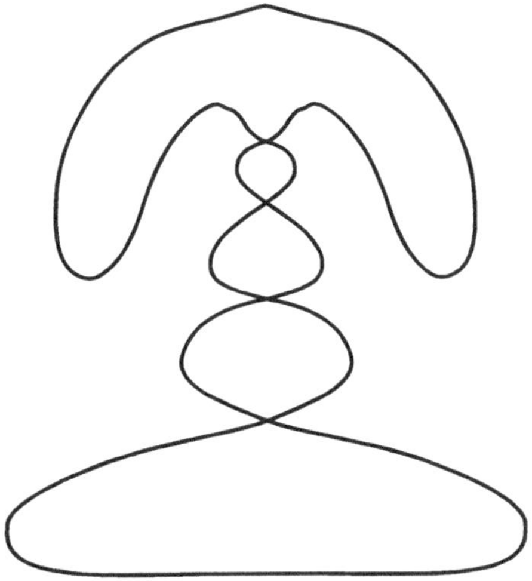

FATLINER WEIRDIES
THE TEMPLATES 1

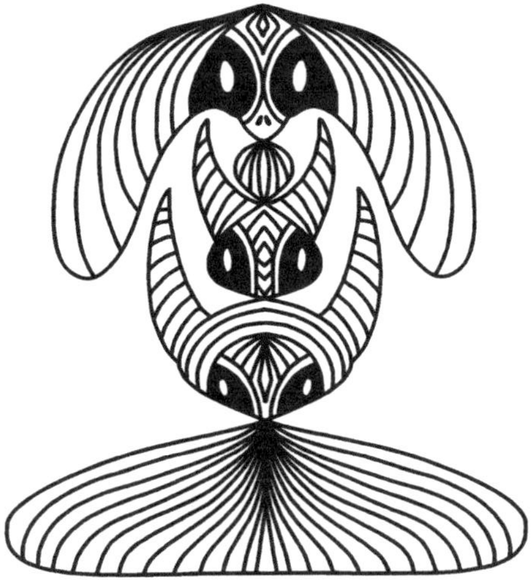

FATLINER WEIRDIES
VOLUME 3

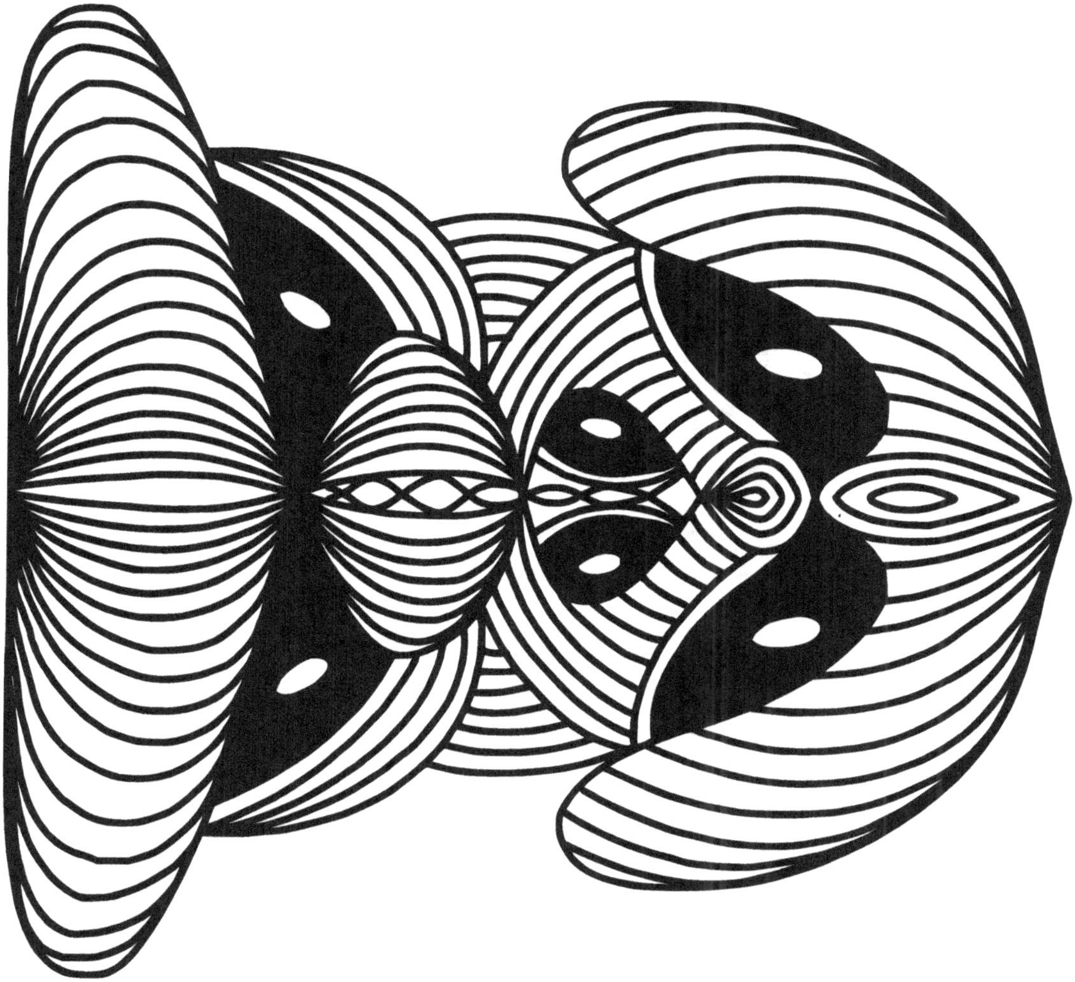

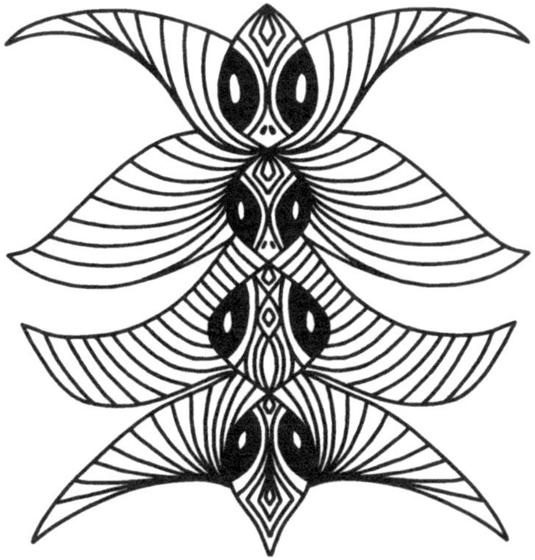

FATLINER WEIRDIES
VOLUME 1

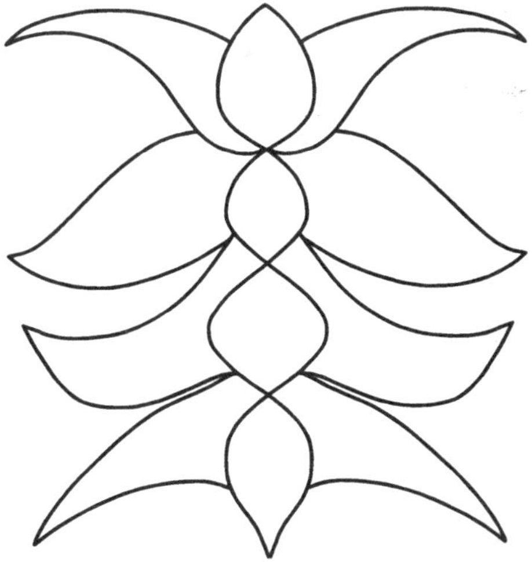

FATLINER WEIRDIES
THE TEMPLATES 1

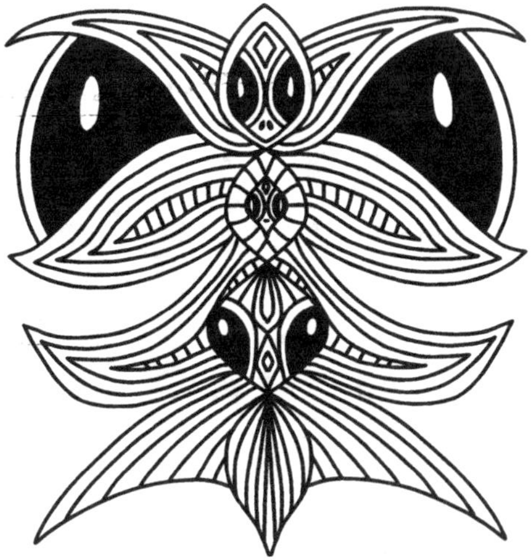

FATLINER WEIRDIES
VOLUME 3

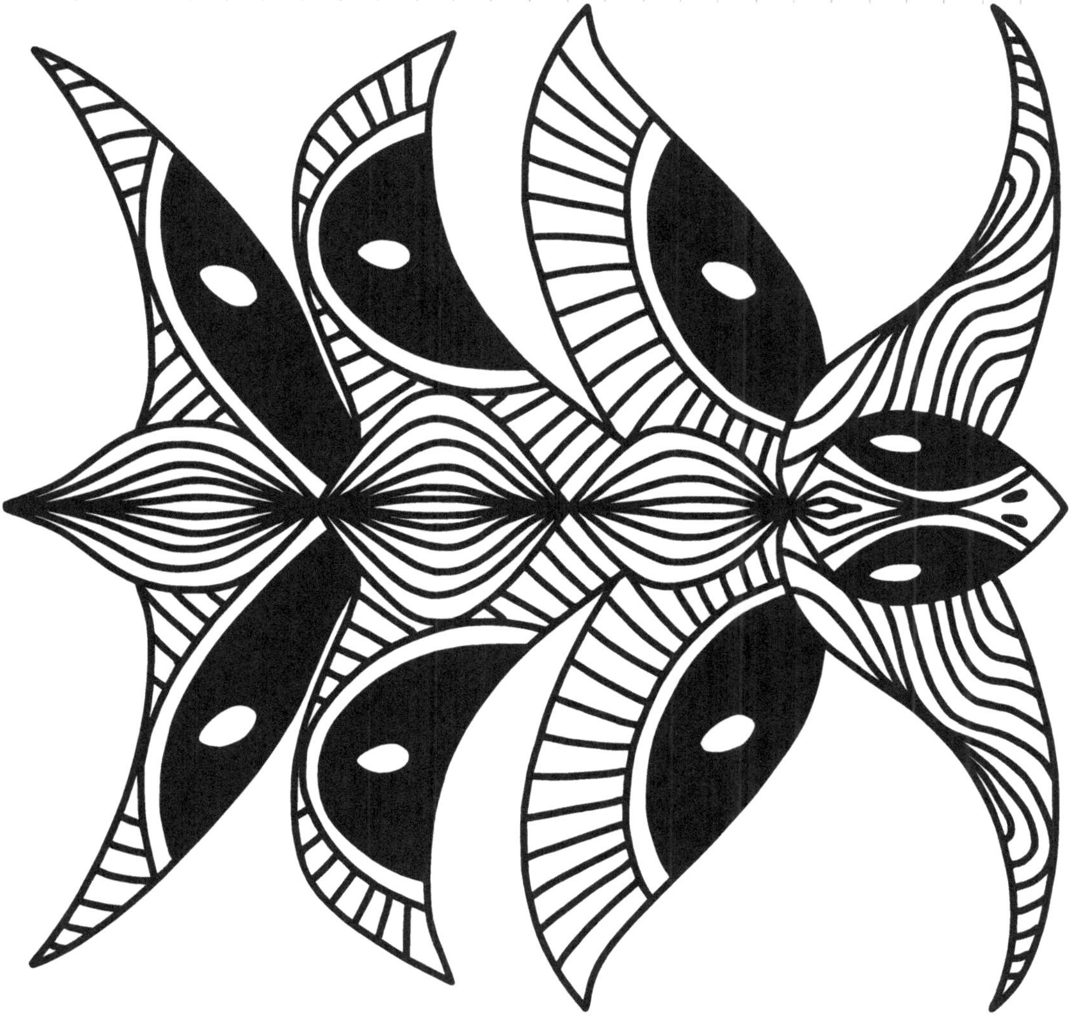

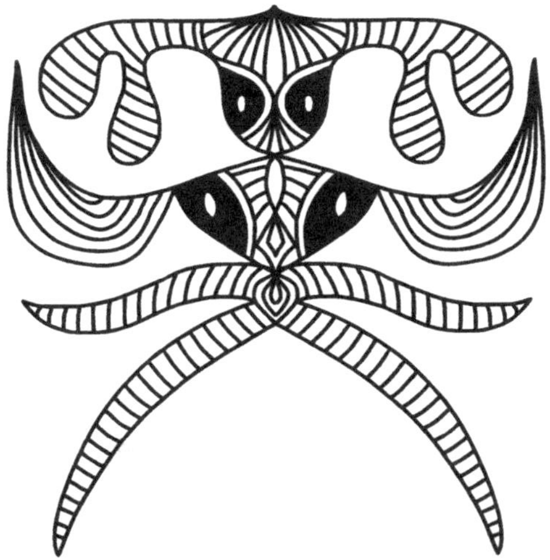

FATLINER WEIRDIES
VOLUME 1

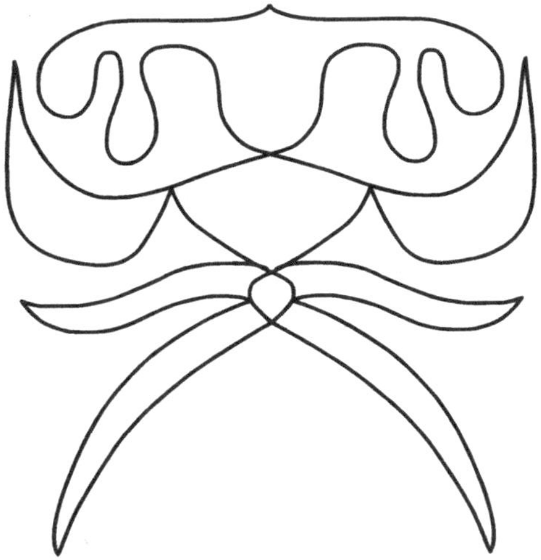

FATLINER WEIRDIES
THE TEMPLATES 1

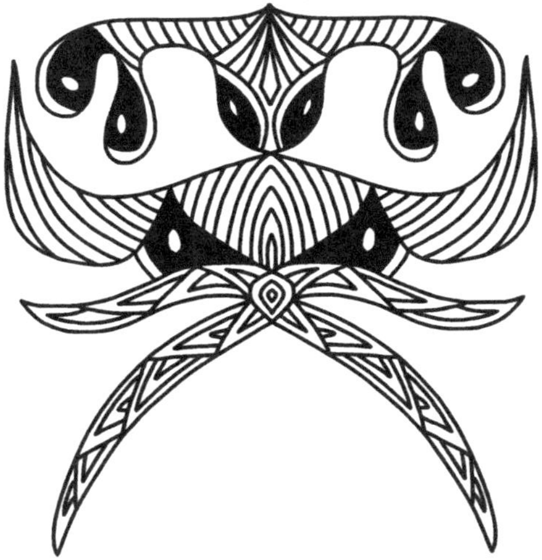

FATLINER WEIRDIES
VOLUME 3

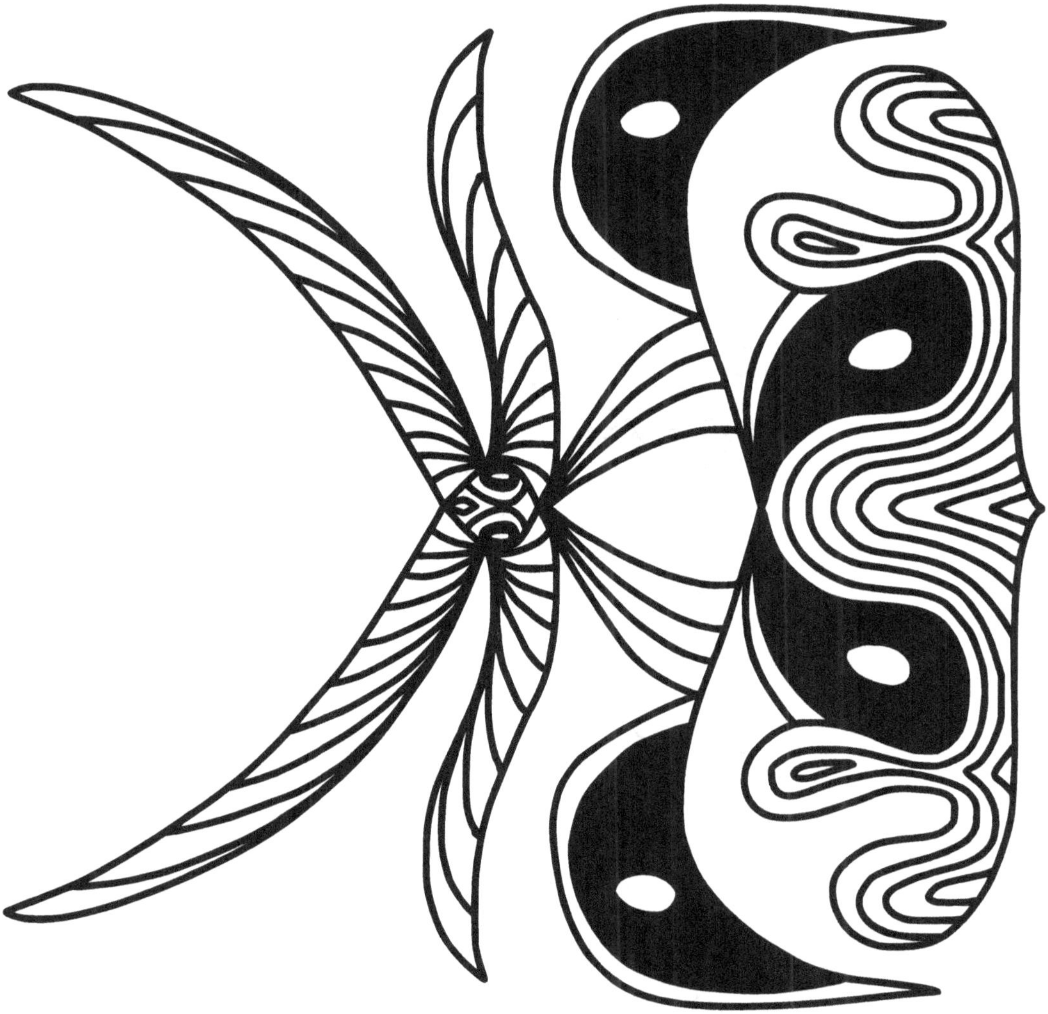

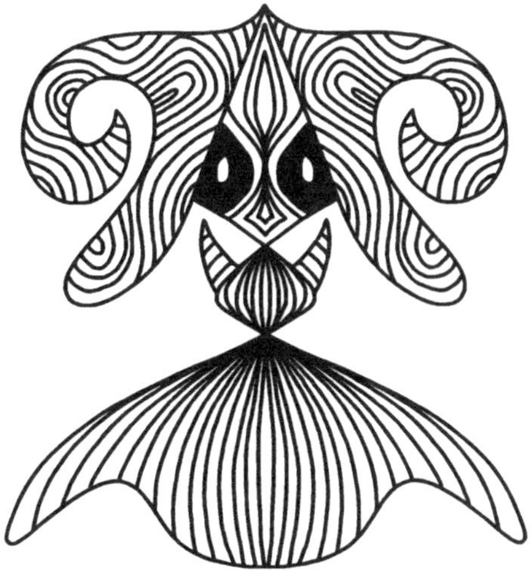

FATLINER WEIRDIES
VOLUME 1

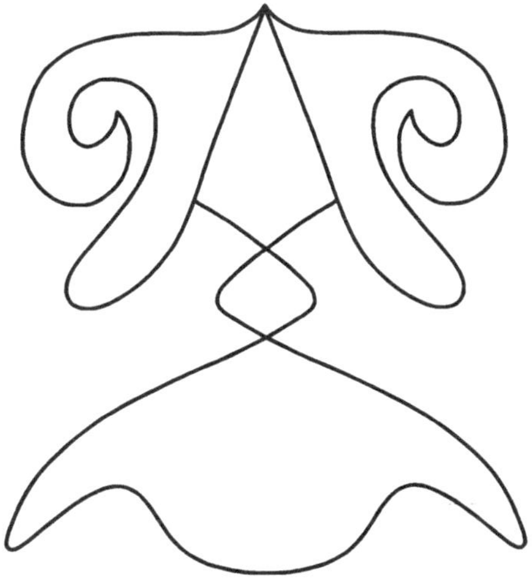

FATLINER WEIRDIES
THE TEMPLATES 1

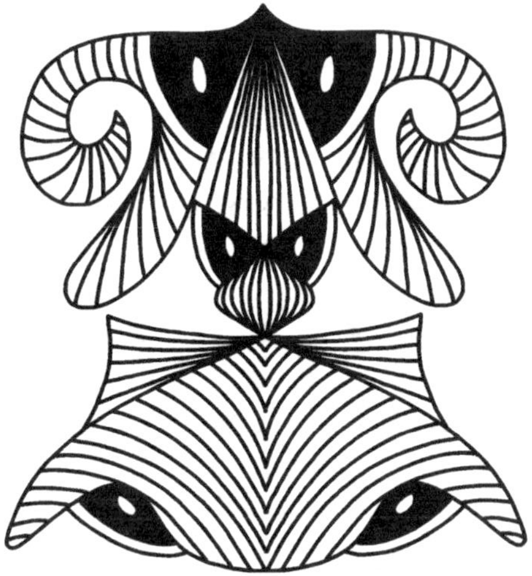

FATLINER WEIRDIES
VOLUME 3

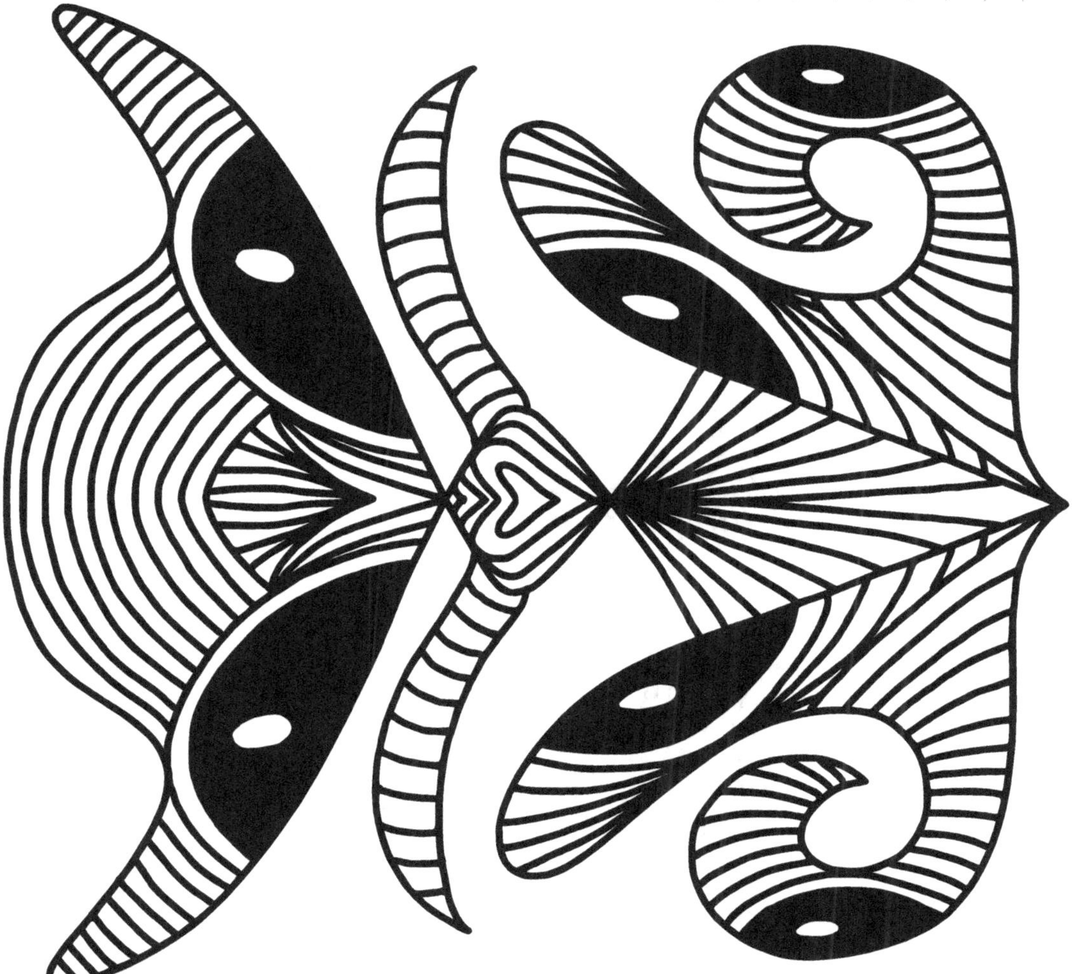

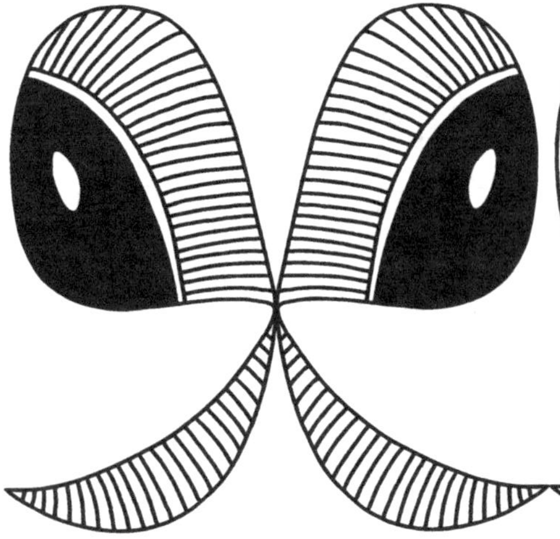

FATLINER WEIRDIES
VOLUME 1

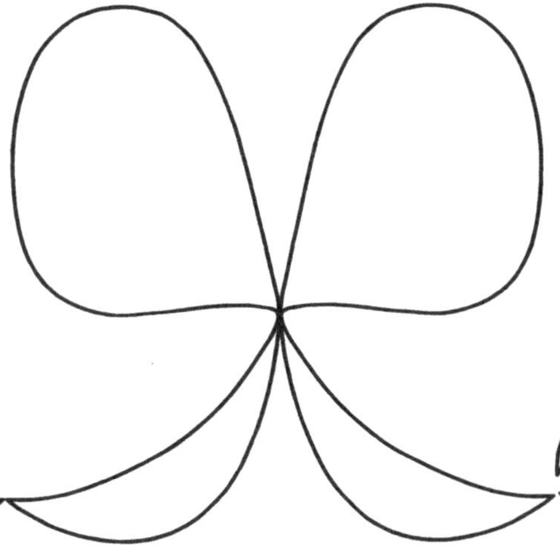

FATLINER WEIRDIES
THE TEMPLATES 1

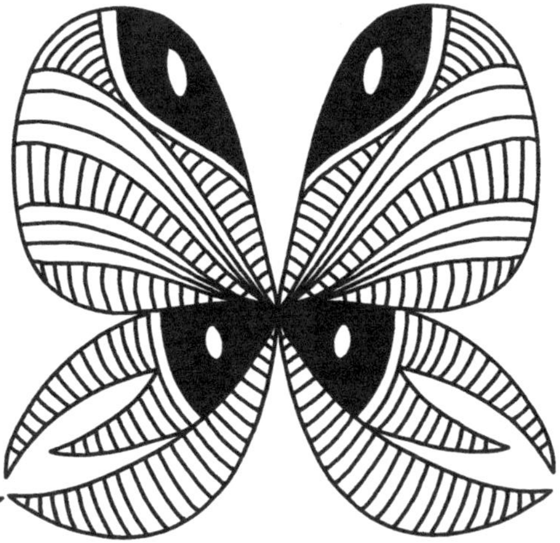

FATLINER WEIRDIES
VOLUME 3

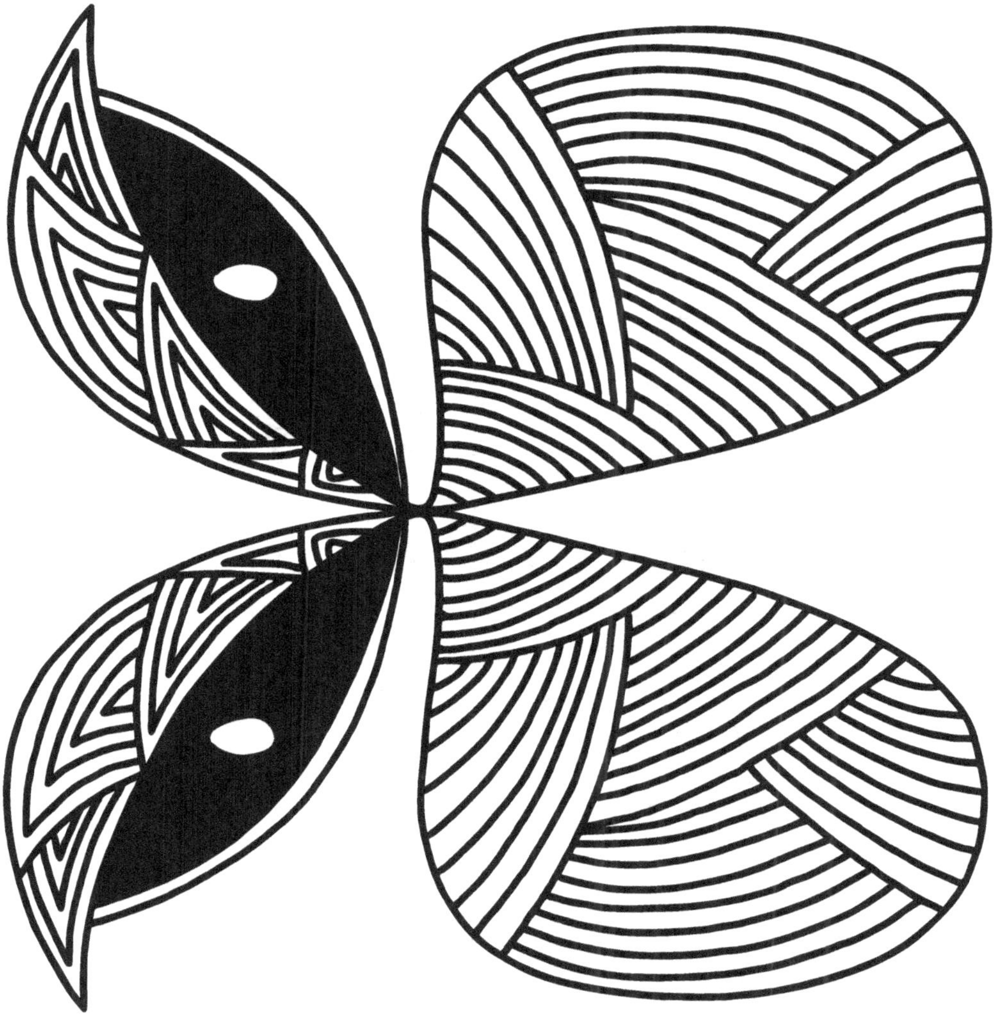

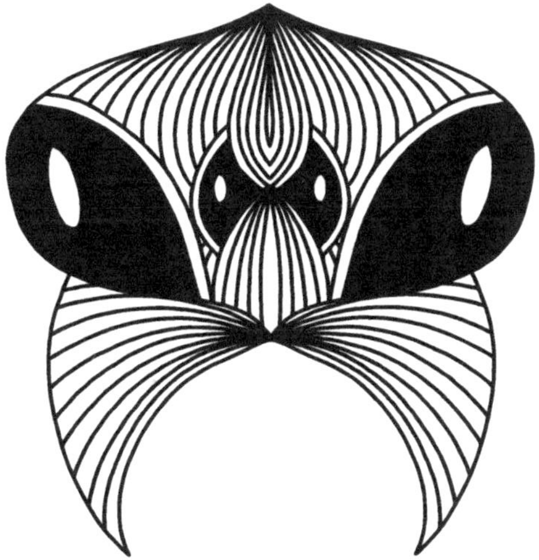

FATLINER WEIRDIES
VOLUME 1

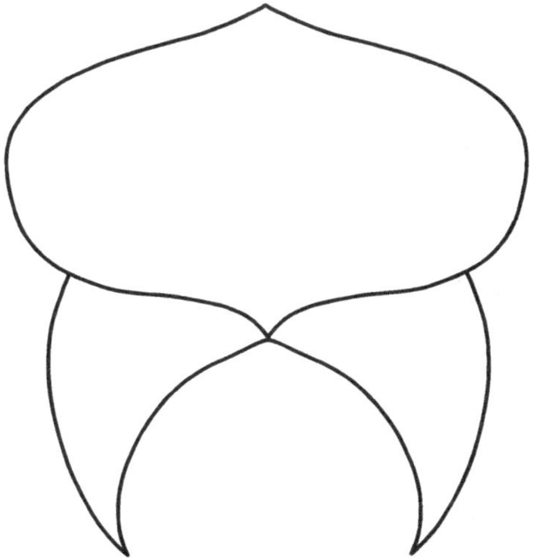

FATLINER WEIRDIES
THE TEMPLATES 1

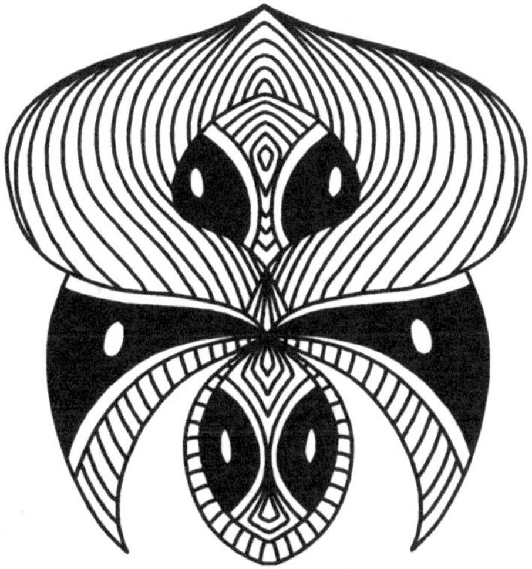

FATLINER WEIRDIES
VOLUME 3

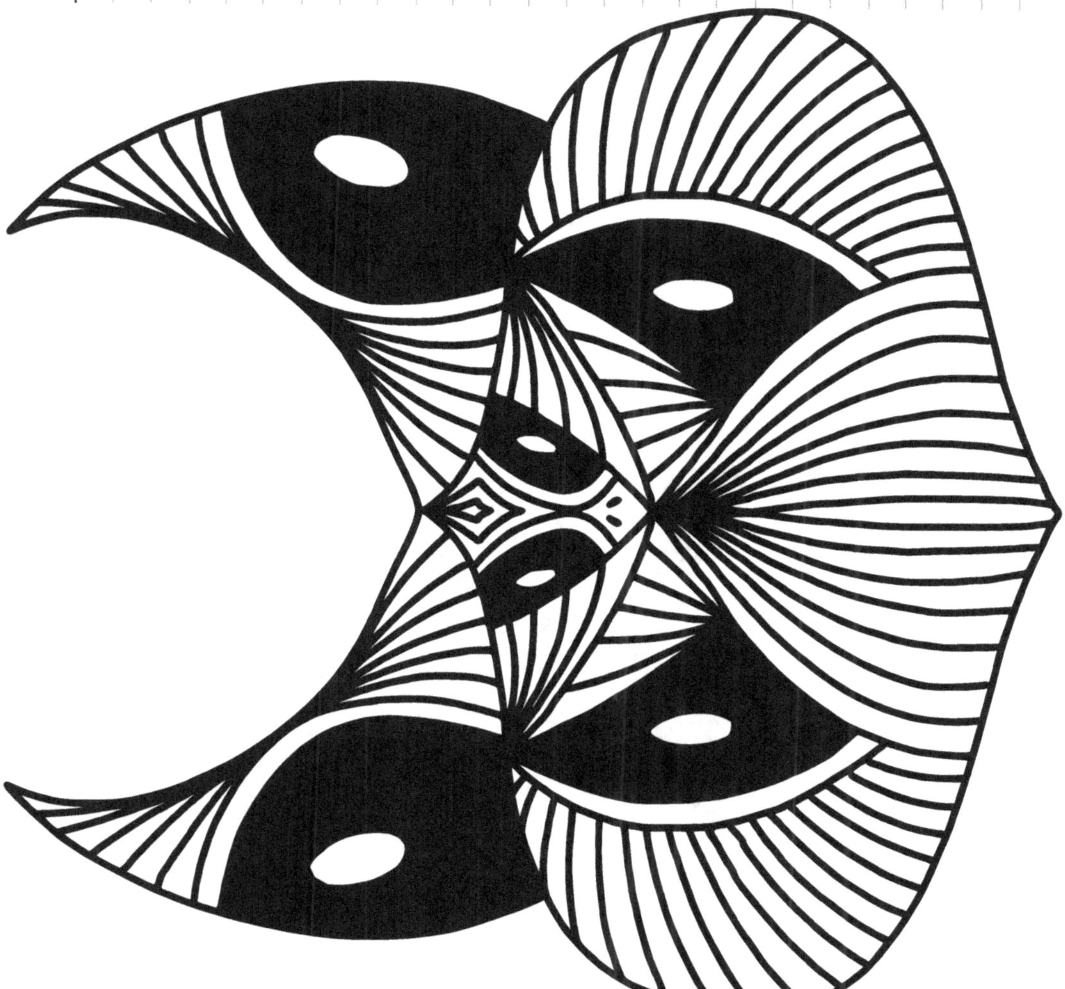

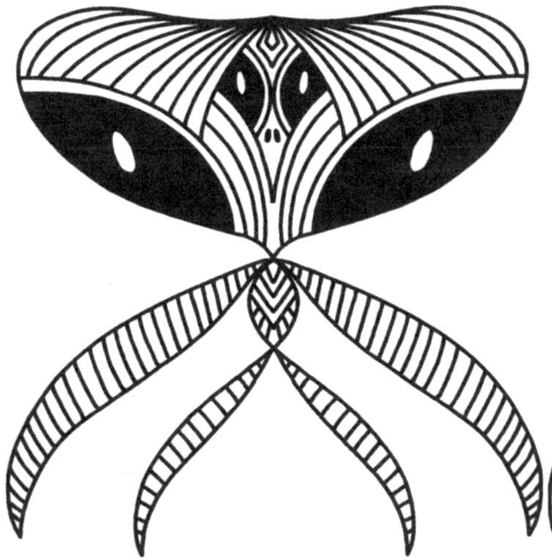

FATLINER WEIRDIES
VOLUME 1

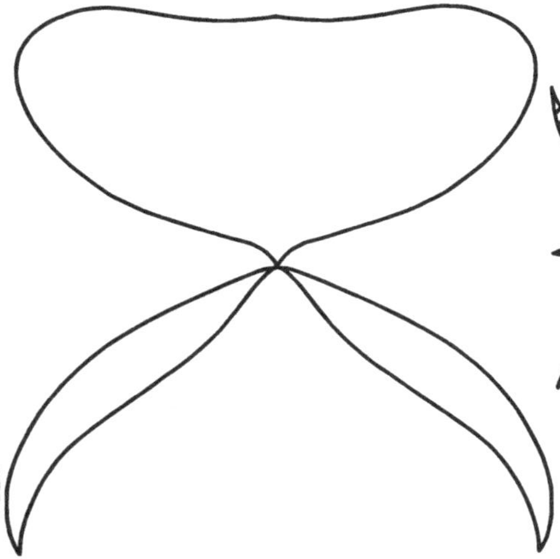

FATLINER WEIRDIES
THE TEMPLATES 1

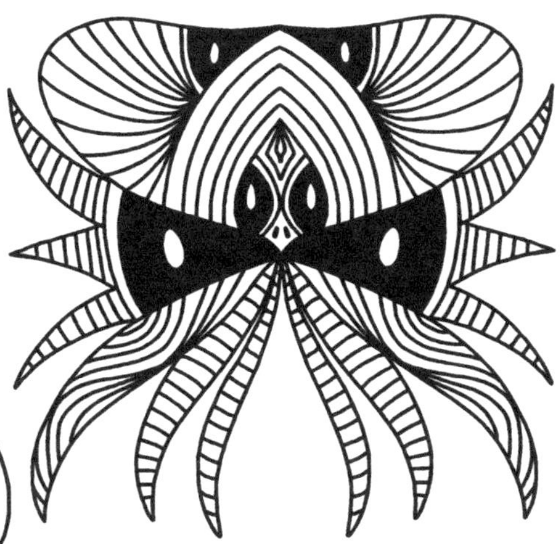

FATLINER WEIRDIES
VOLUME 3

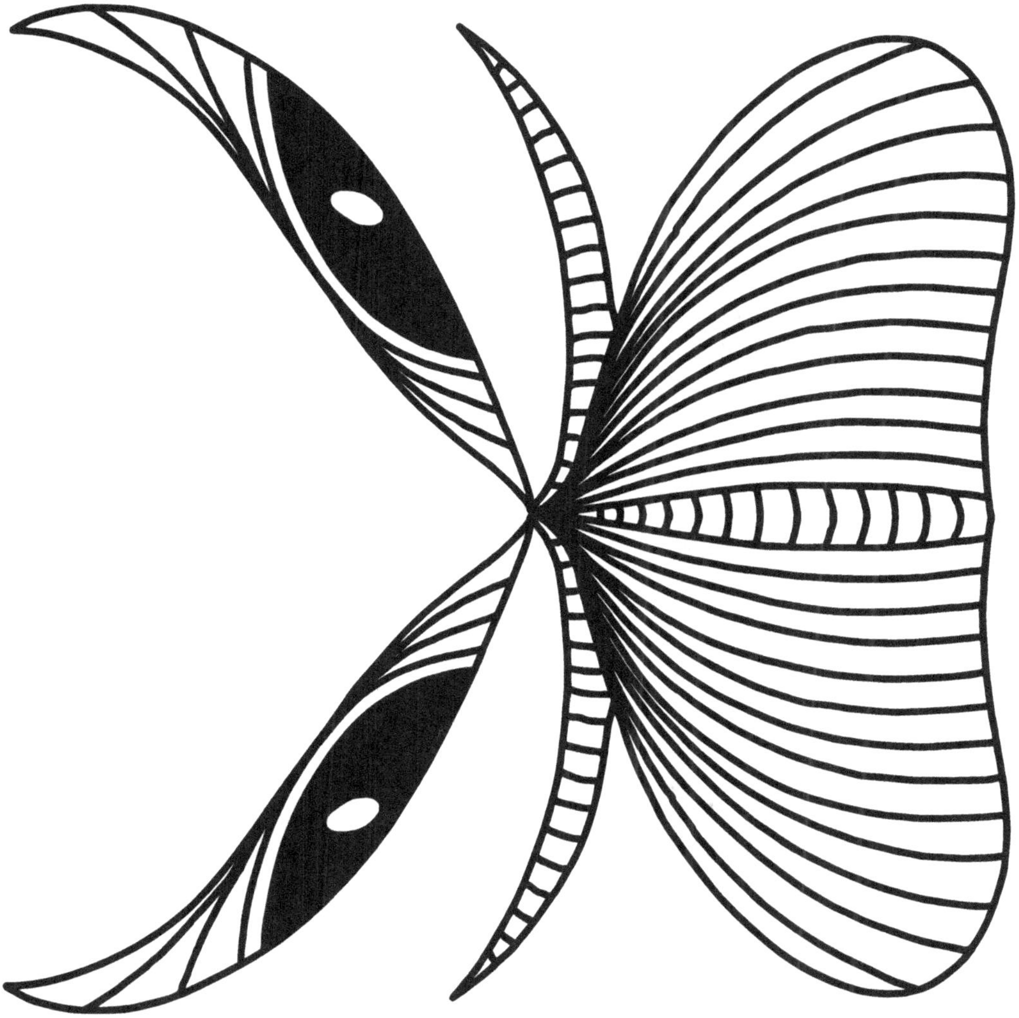

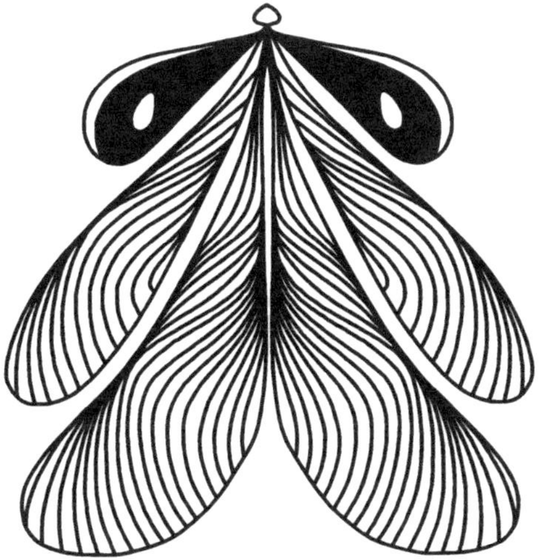

FATLINER WEIRDIES
VOLUME 1

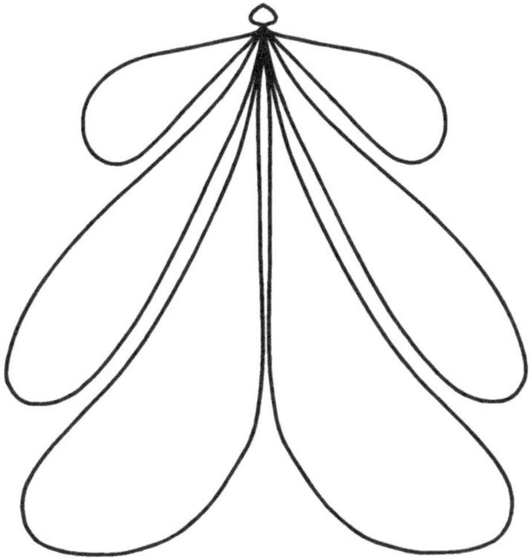

FATLINER WEIRDIES
THE TEMPLATES 1

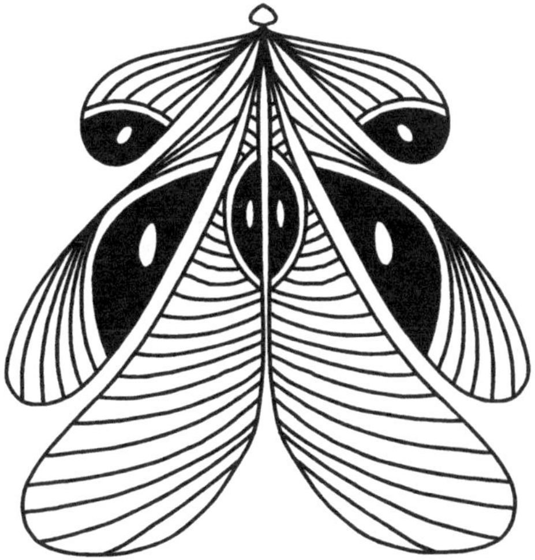

FATLINER WEIRDIES
VOLUME 3

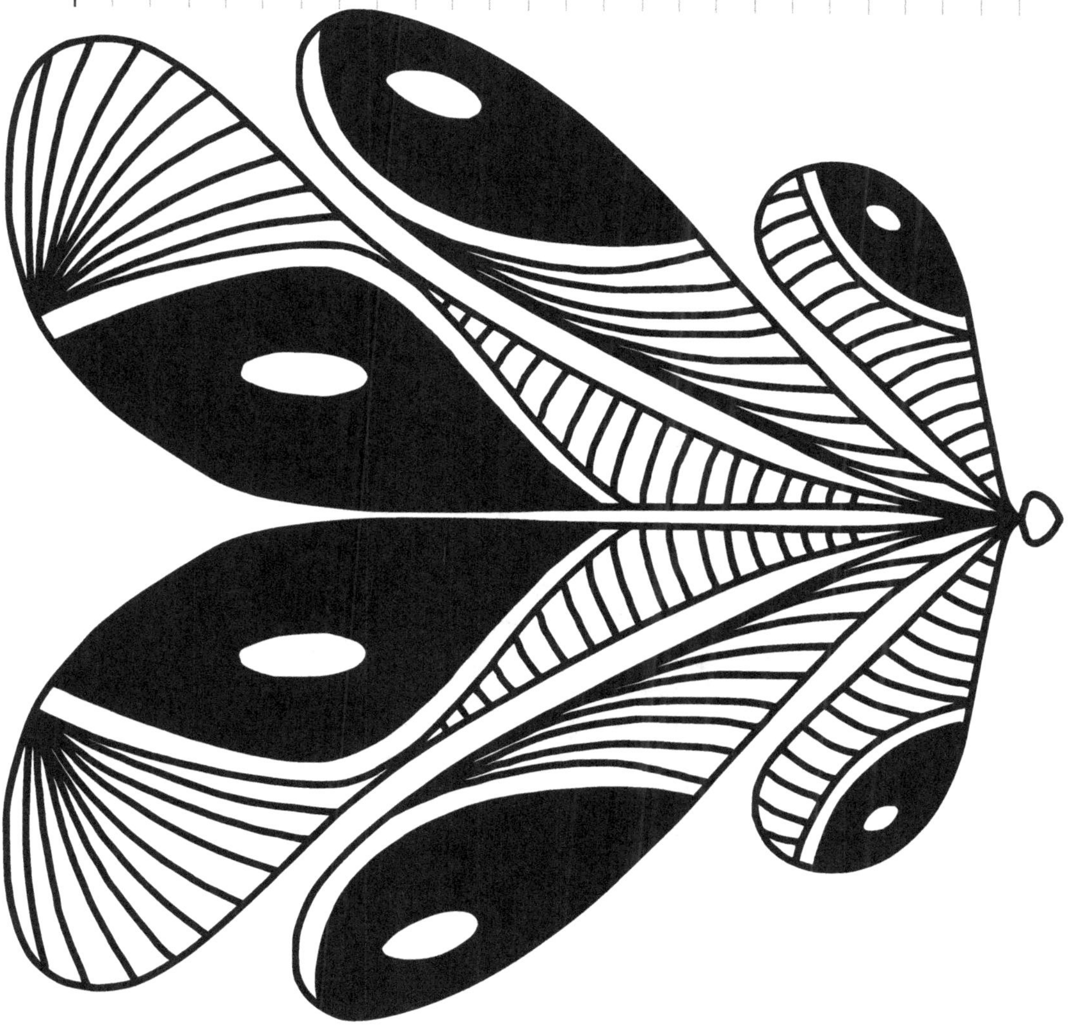

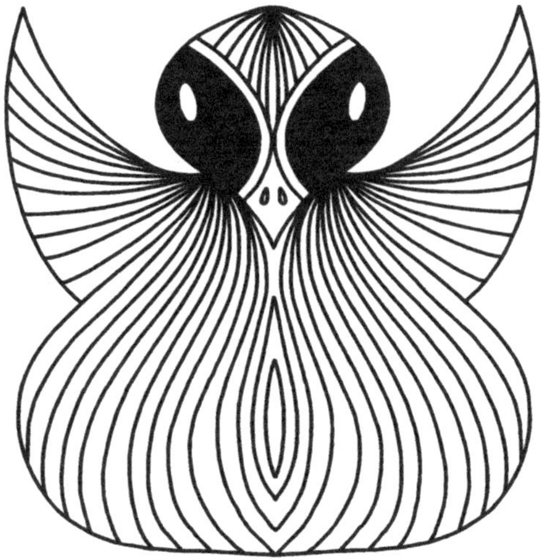

FATLINER WEIRDIES
VOLUME 1

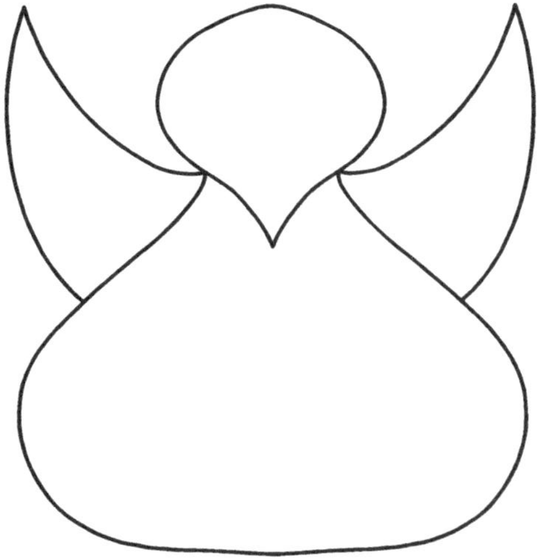

FATLINER WEIRDIES
THE TEMPLATES 1

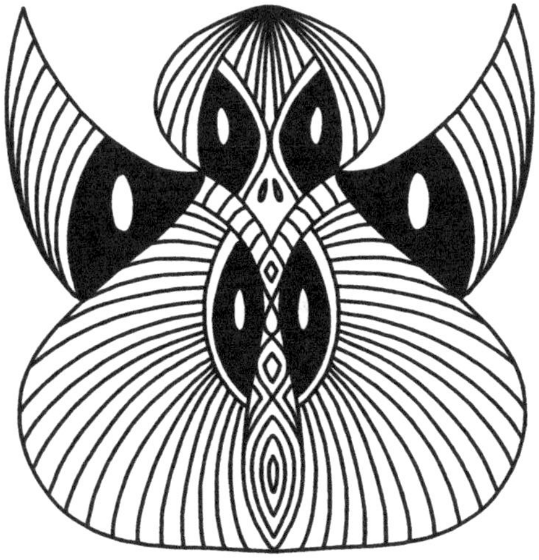

FATLINER WEIRDIES
VOLUME 3

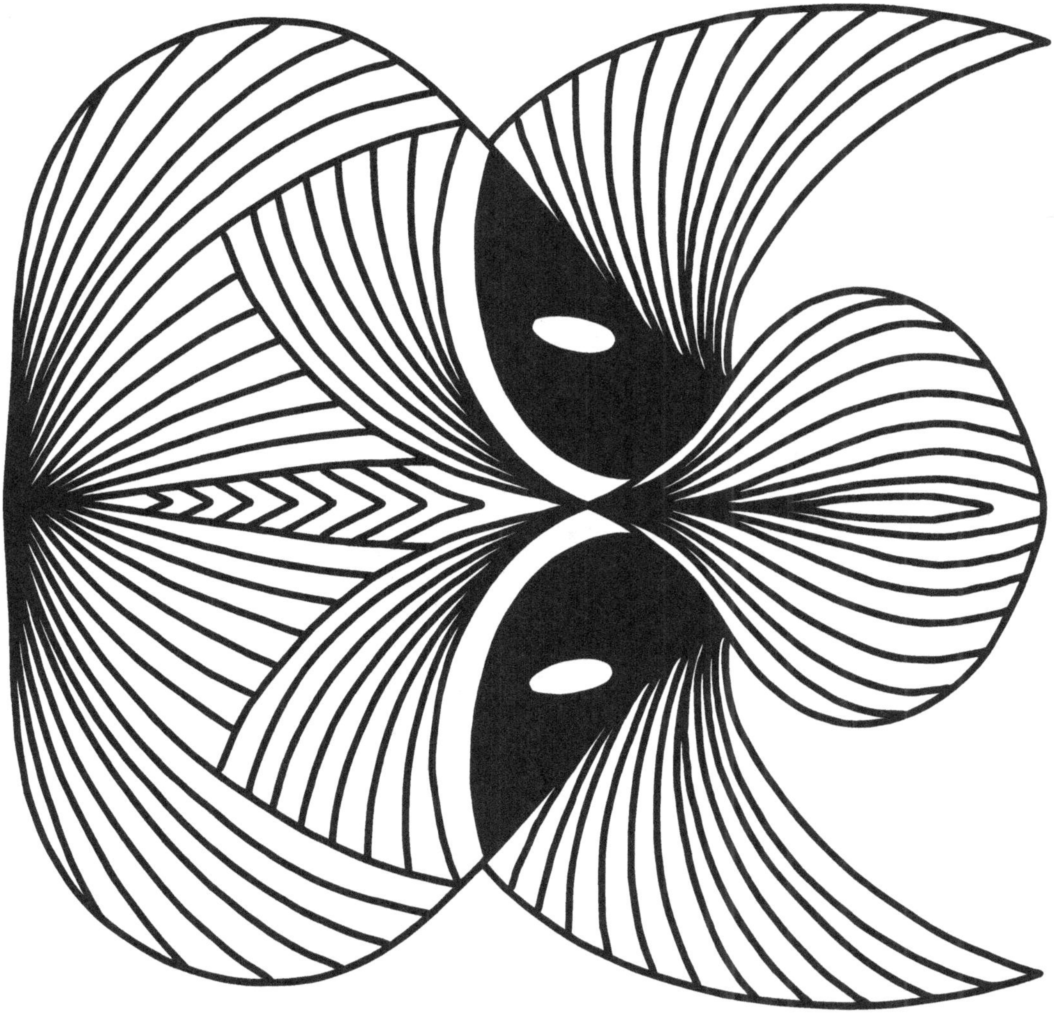

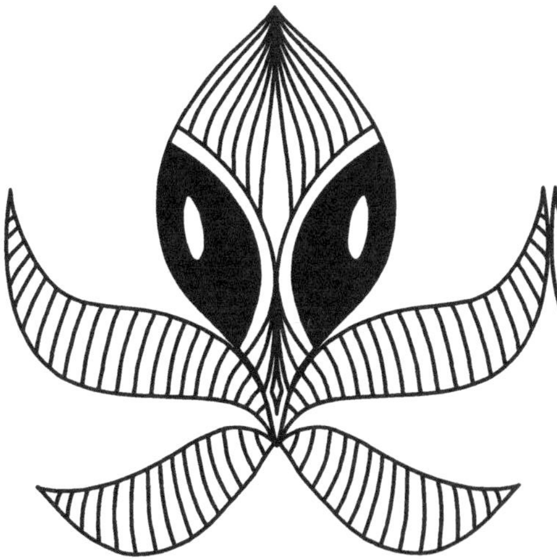

FATLINER WEIRDIES
VOLUME 1

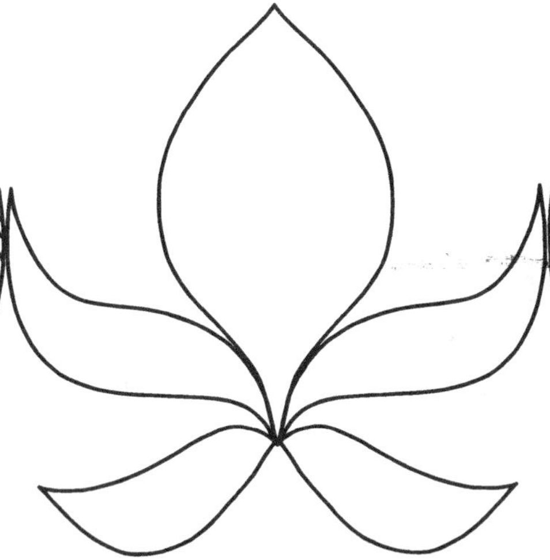

FATLINER WEIRDIES
THE TEMPLATES 1

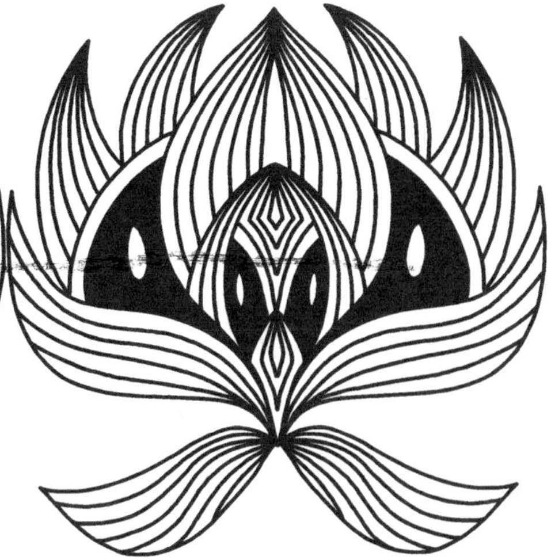

FATLINER WEIRDIES
VOLUME 3

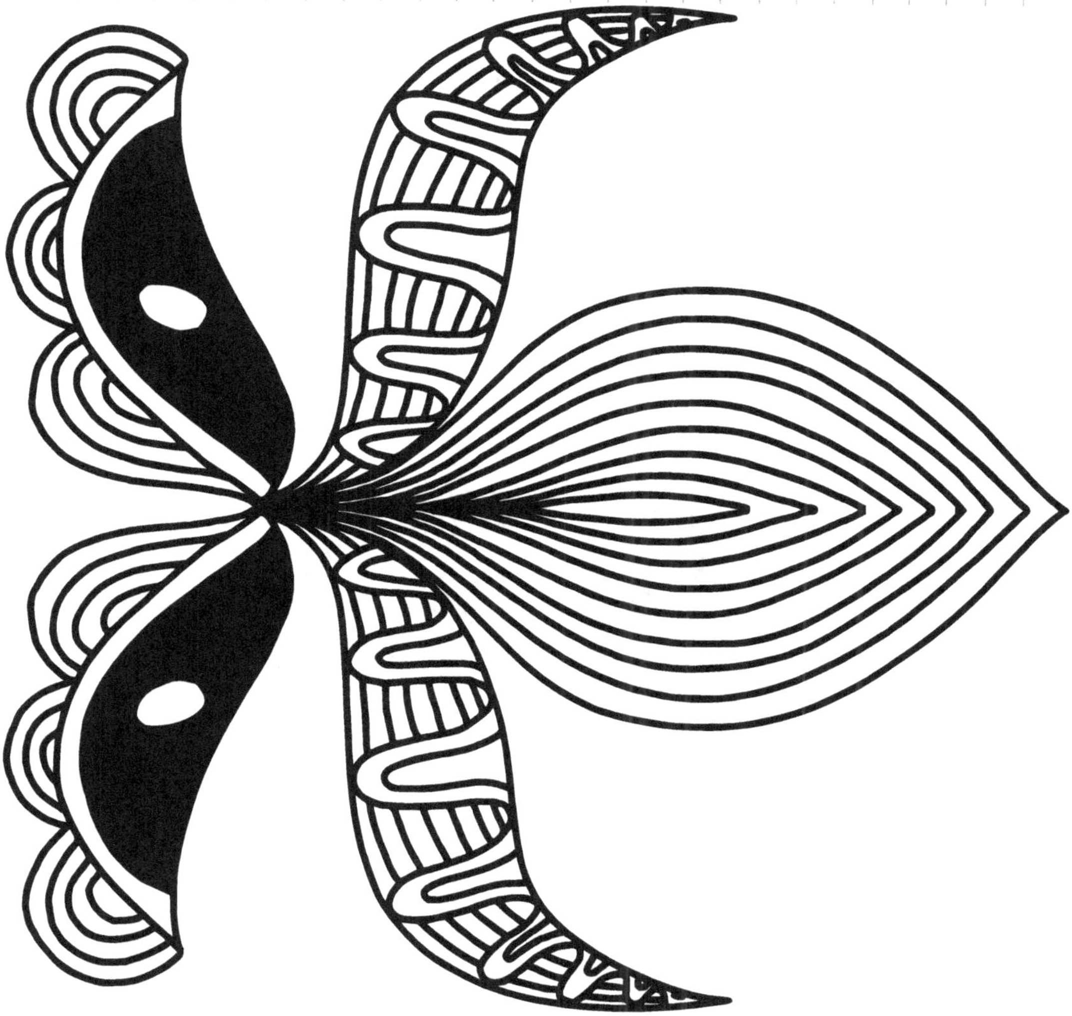

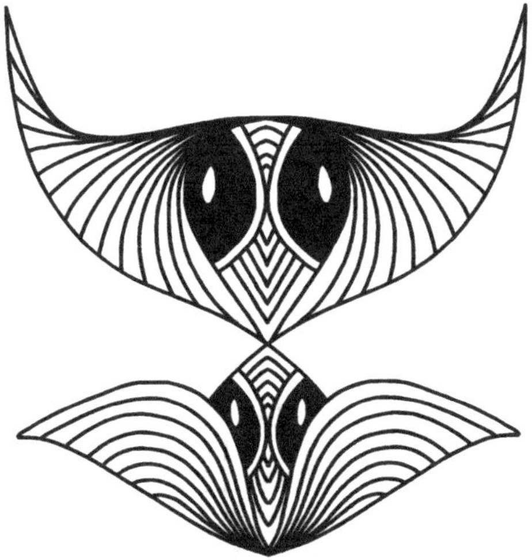

FATLINER WEIRDIES
VOLUME 1

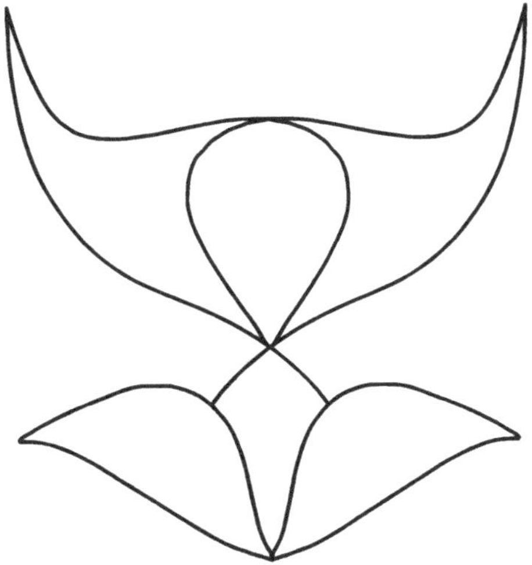

FATLINER WEIRDIES
THE TEMPLATES 1

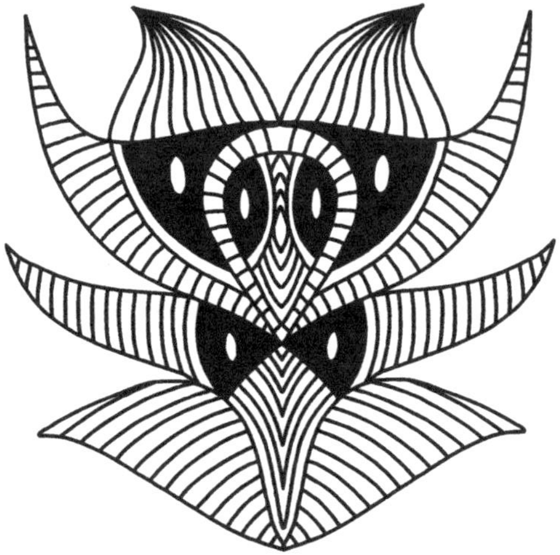

FATLINER WEIRDIES
VOLUME 3

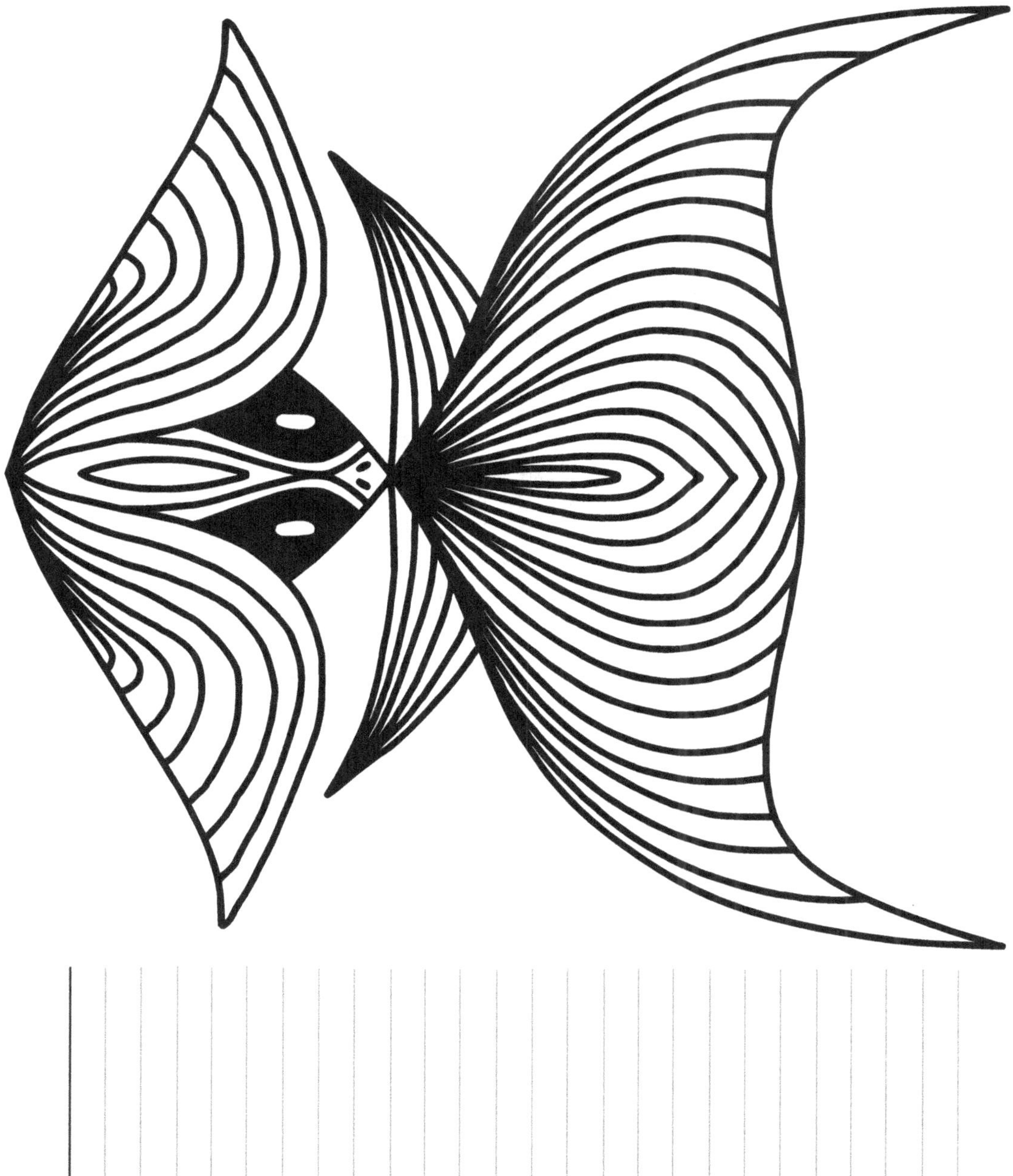

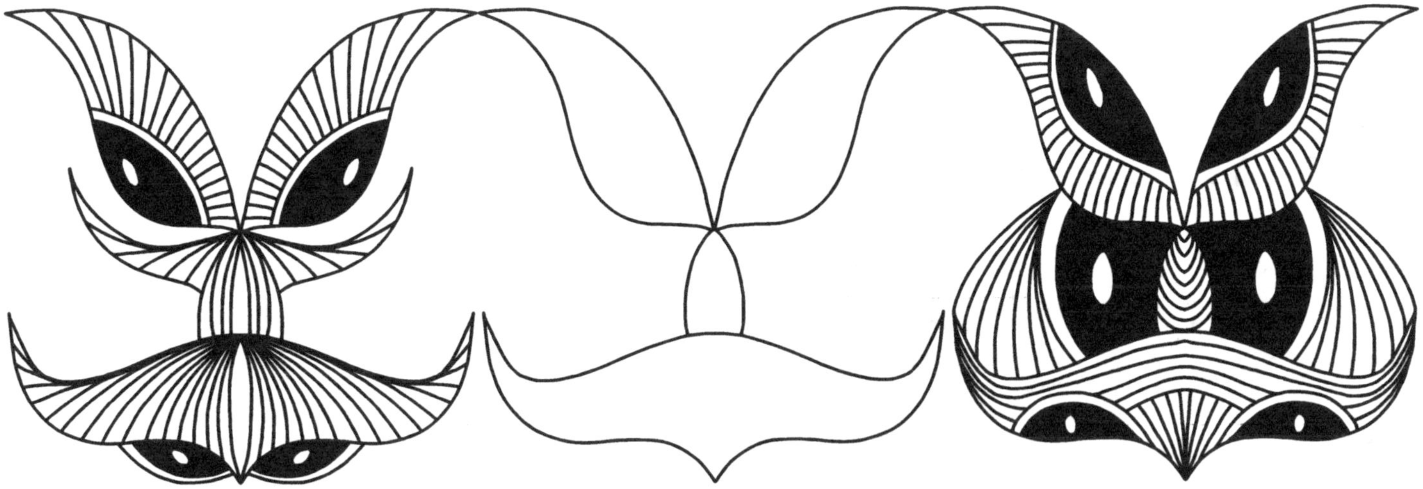

FATLINER WEIRDIES
VOLUME 1

FATLINER WEIRDIES
THE TEMPLATES 1

FATLINER WEIRDIES
VOLUME 3

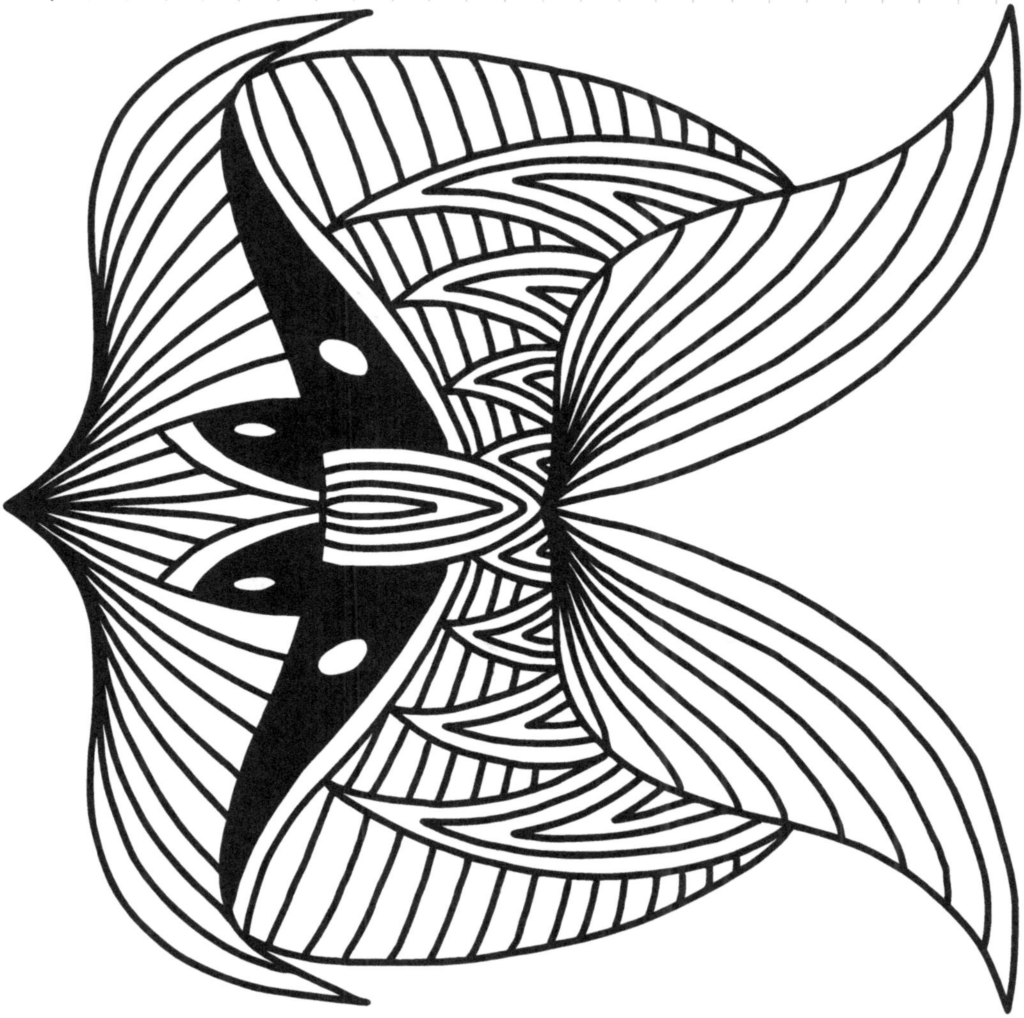

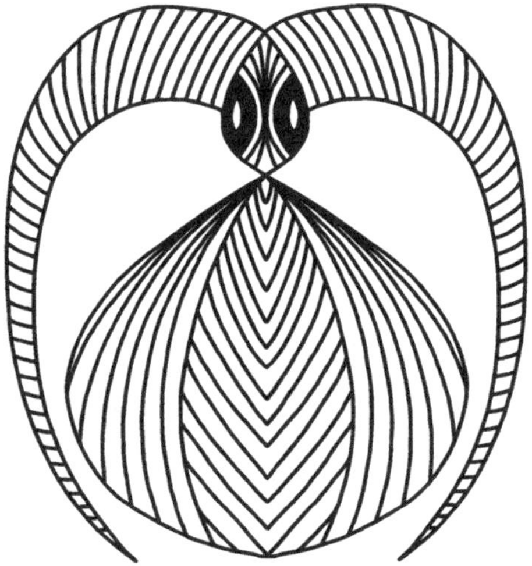

FATLINER WEIRDIES
VOLUME 1

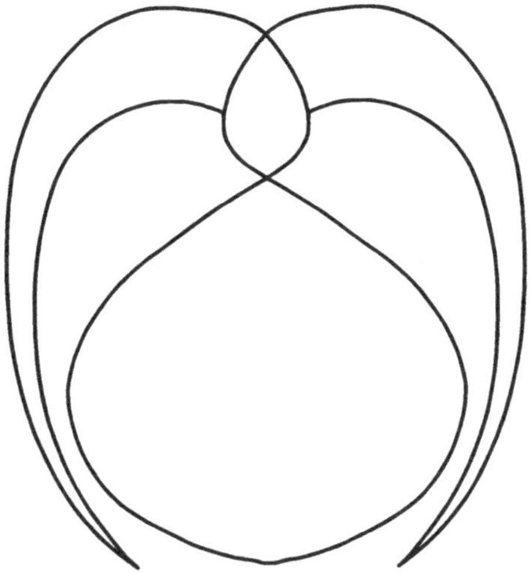

FATLINER WEIRDIES
THE TEMPLATES 1

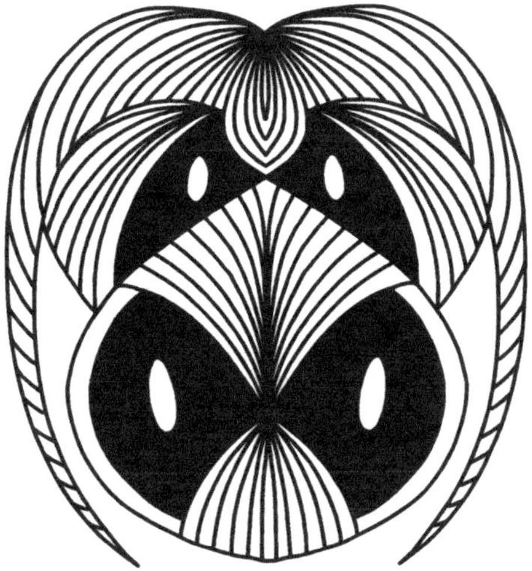

FATLINER WEIRDIES
VOLUME 3

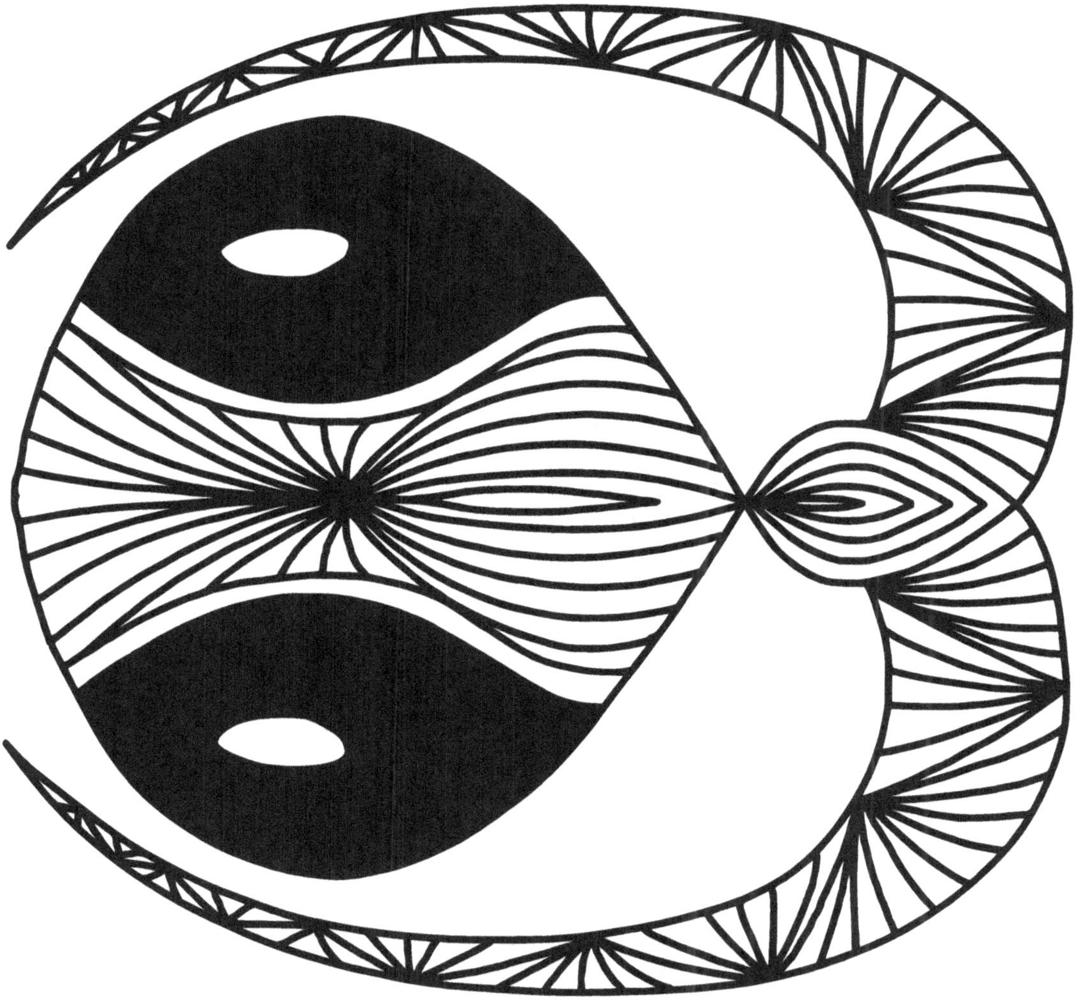

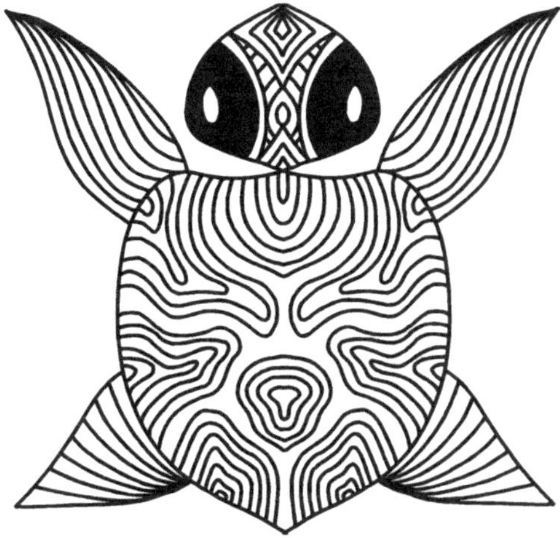

FATLINER WEIRDIES
VOLUME 1

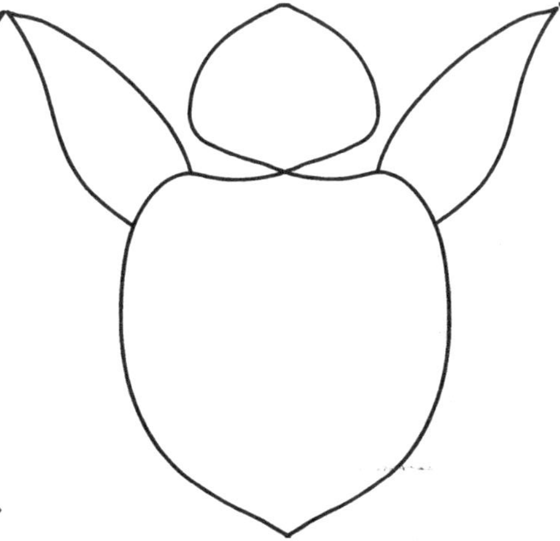

FATLINER WEIRDIES
THE TEMPLATES 1

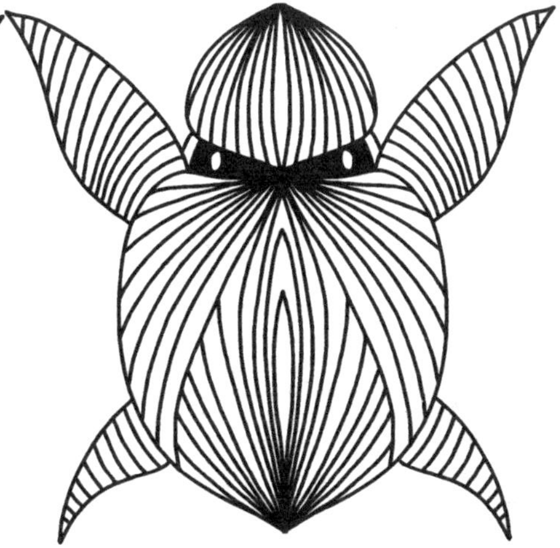

FATLINER WEIRDIES
VOLUME 3

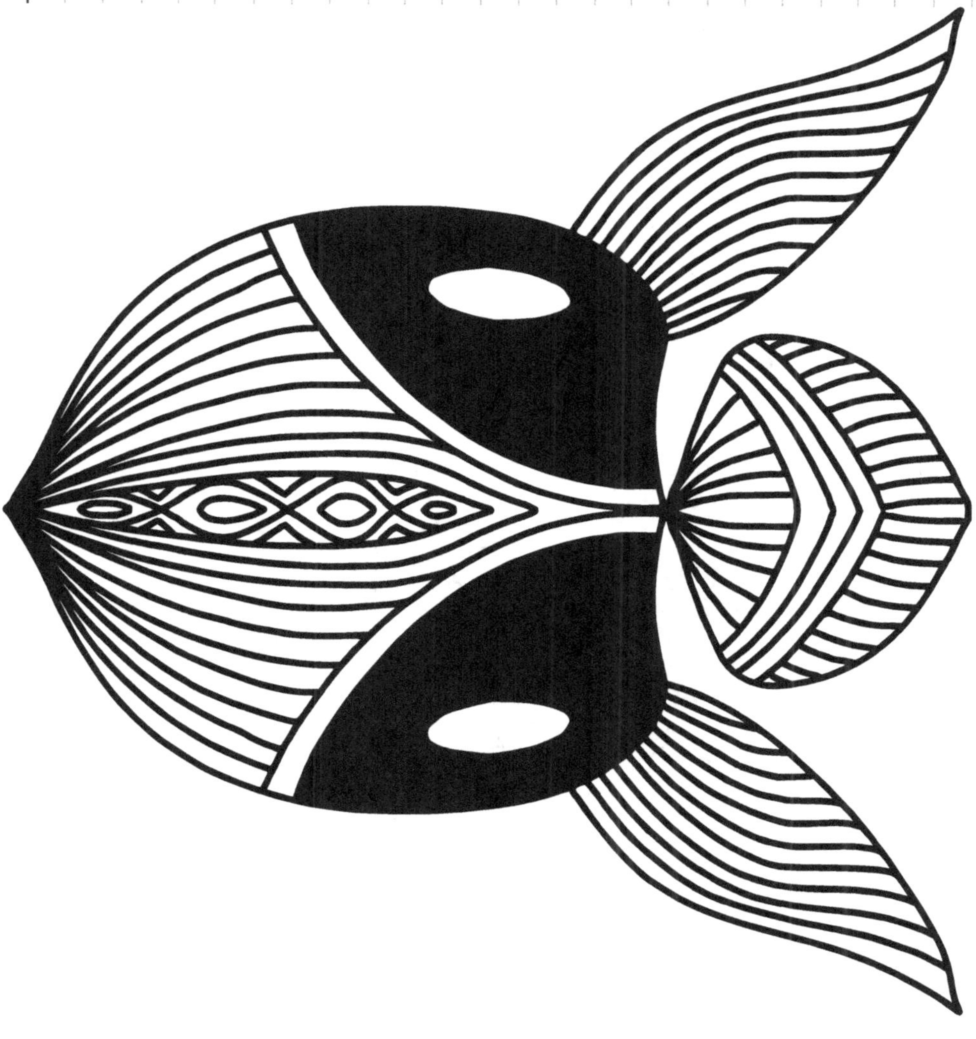

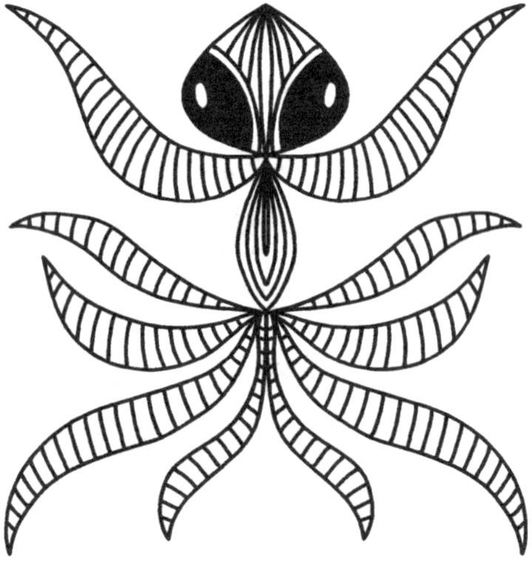

FATLINER WEIRDIES
VOLUME 1

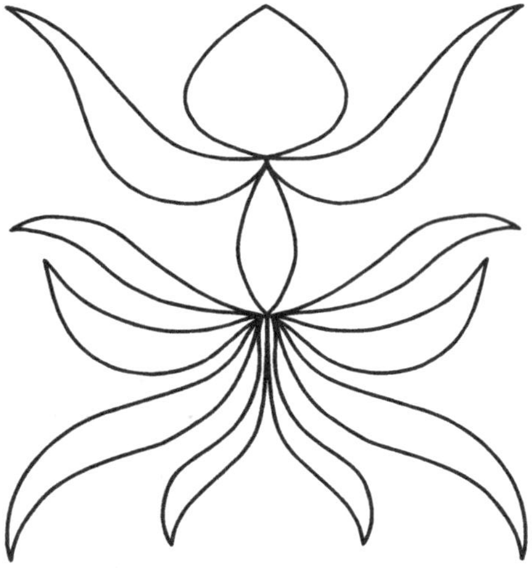

FATLINER WEIRDIES
THE TEMPLATES 1

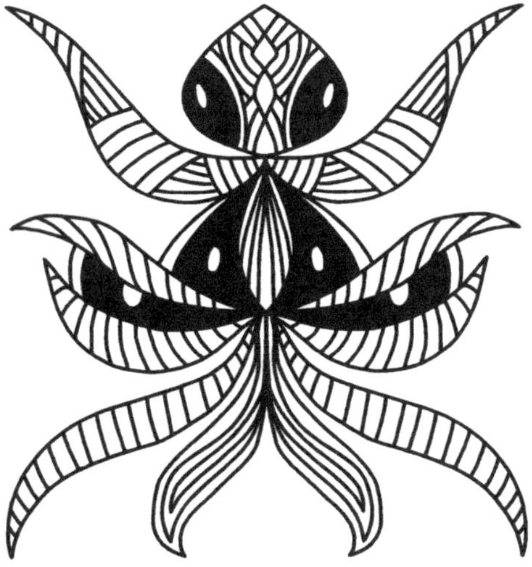

FATLINER WEIRDIES
VOLUME 3

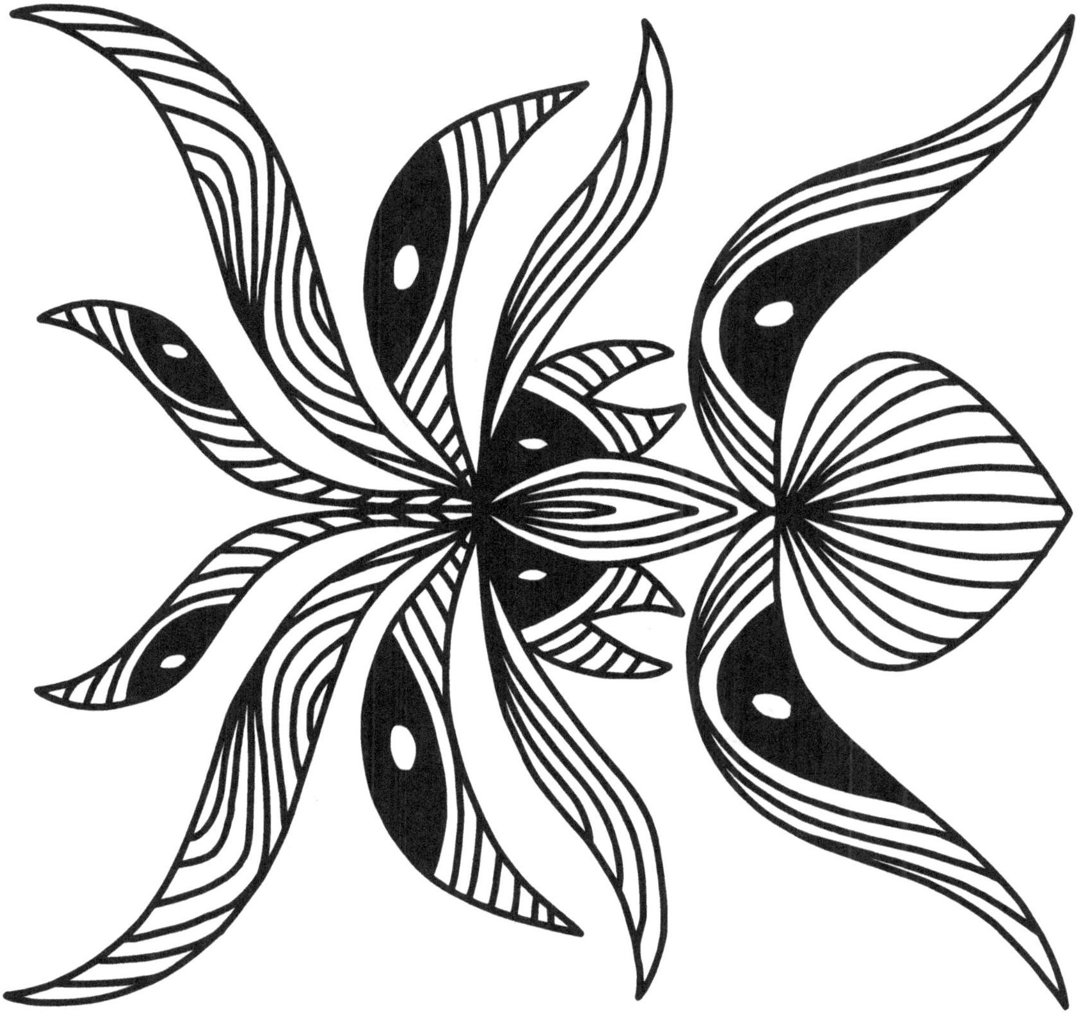

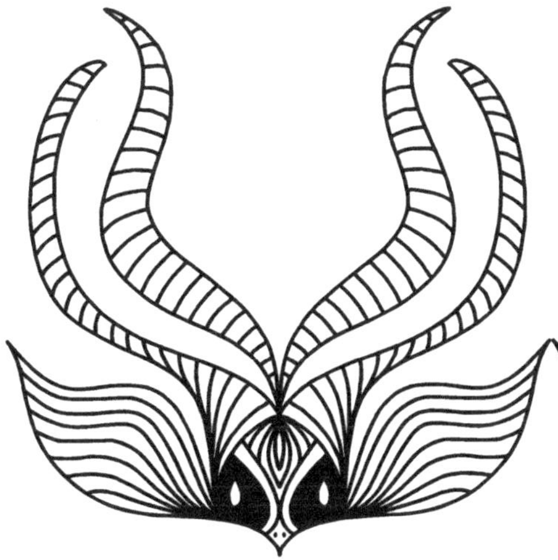

FATLINER WEIRDIES
VOLUME 1

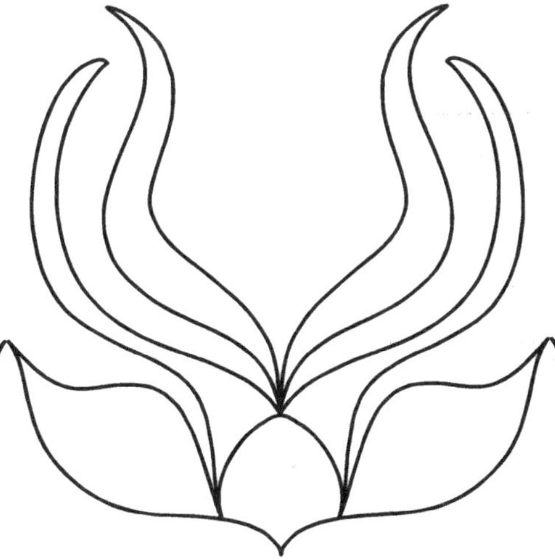

FATLINER WEIRDIES
THE TEMPLATES 1

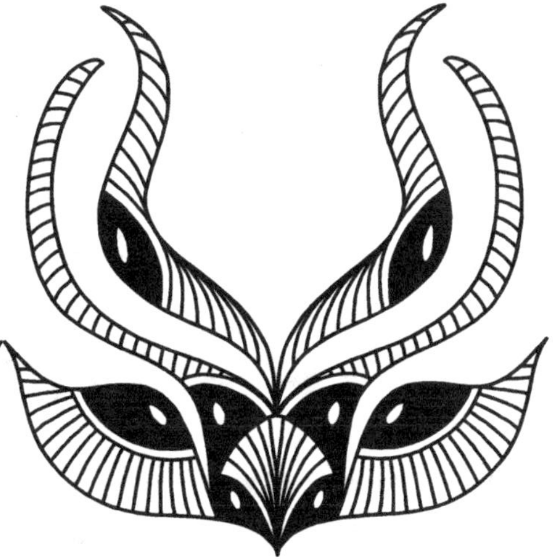

FATLINER WEIRDIES
VOLUME 3

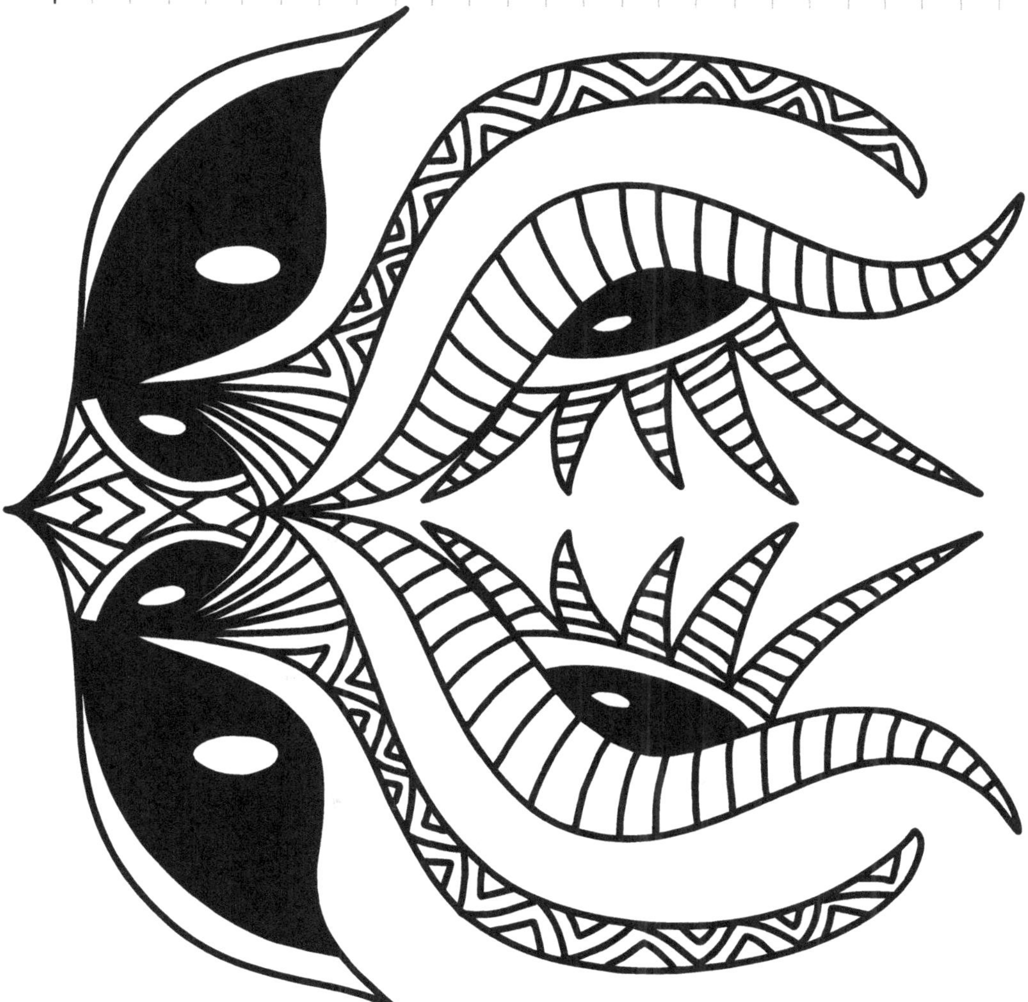

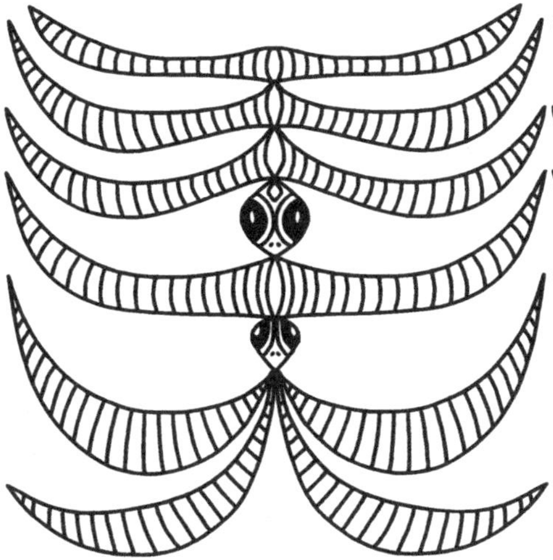

FATLINER WEIRDIES
VOLUME 1

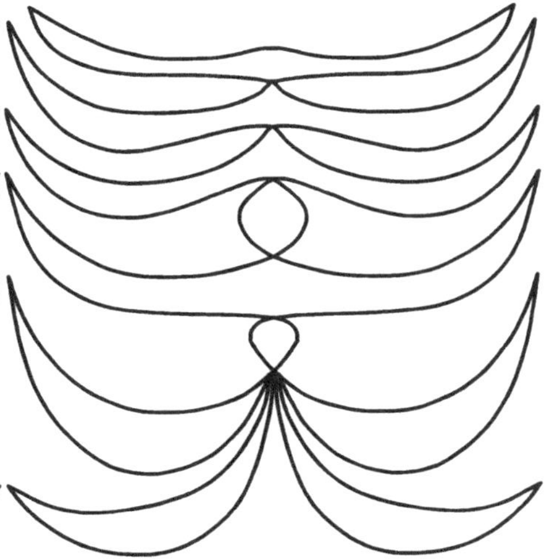

FATLINER WEIRDIES
THE TEMPLATES 1

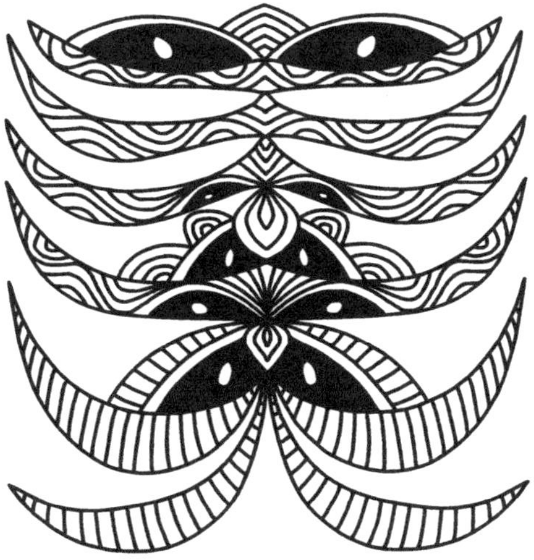

FATLINER WEIRDIES
VOLUME 3

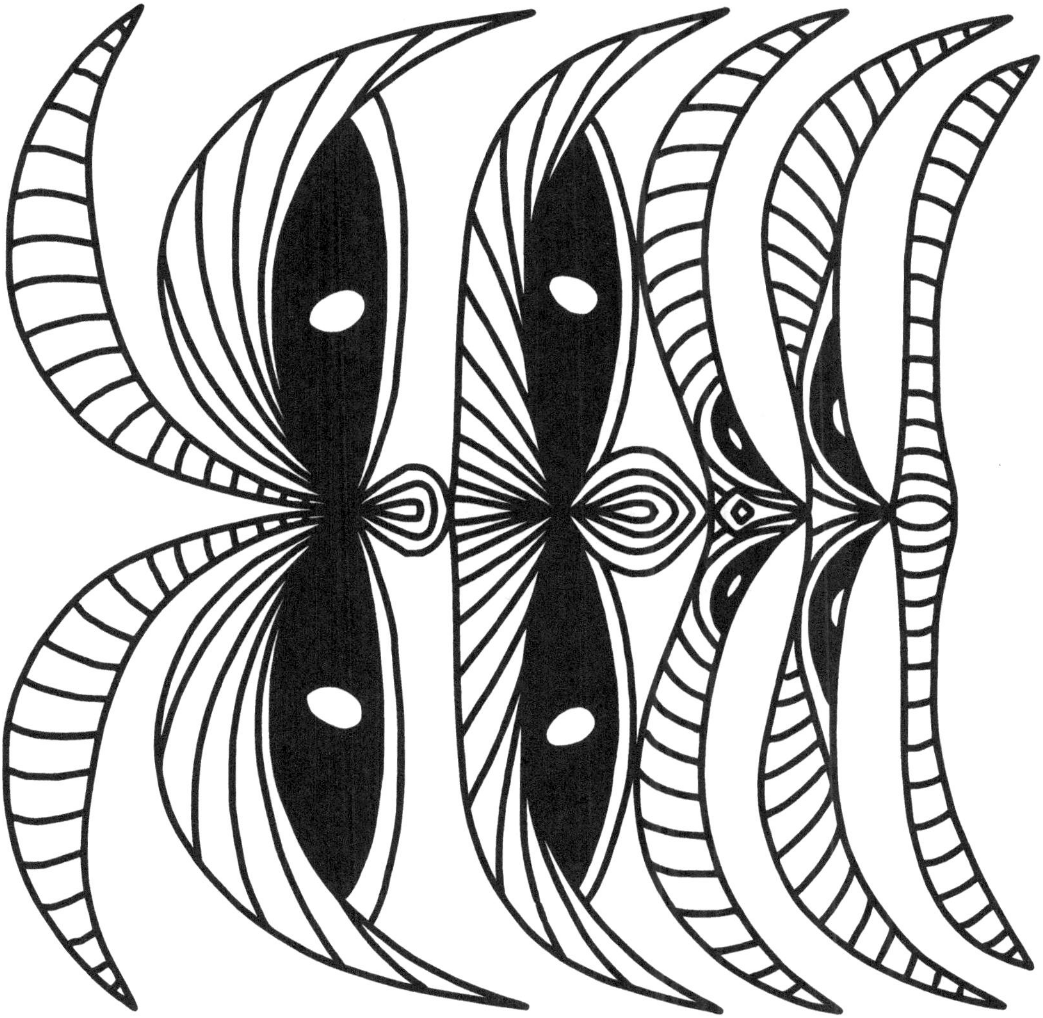

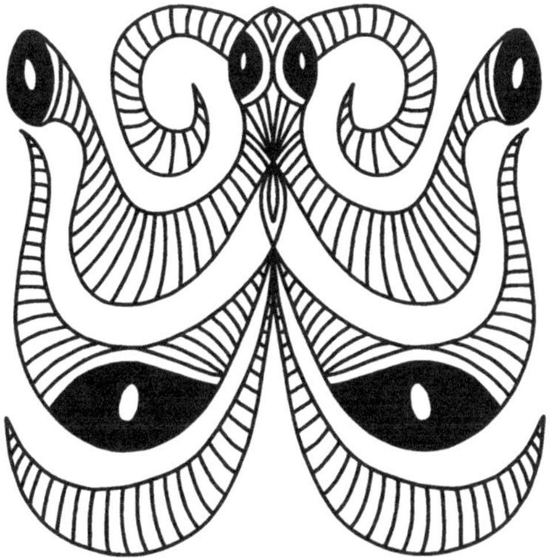

FATLINER WEIRDIES
VOLUME 1

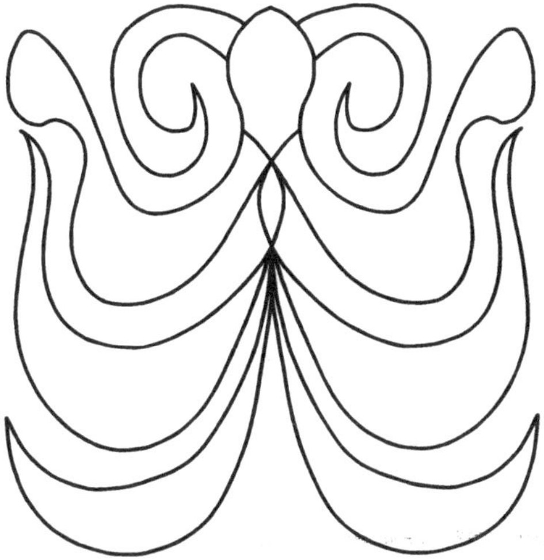

FATLINER WEIRDIES
THE TEMPLATES 1

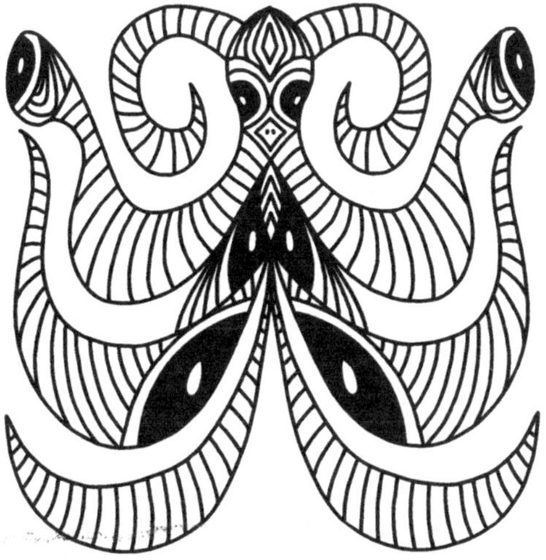

FATLINER WEIRDIES
VOLUME 3

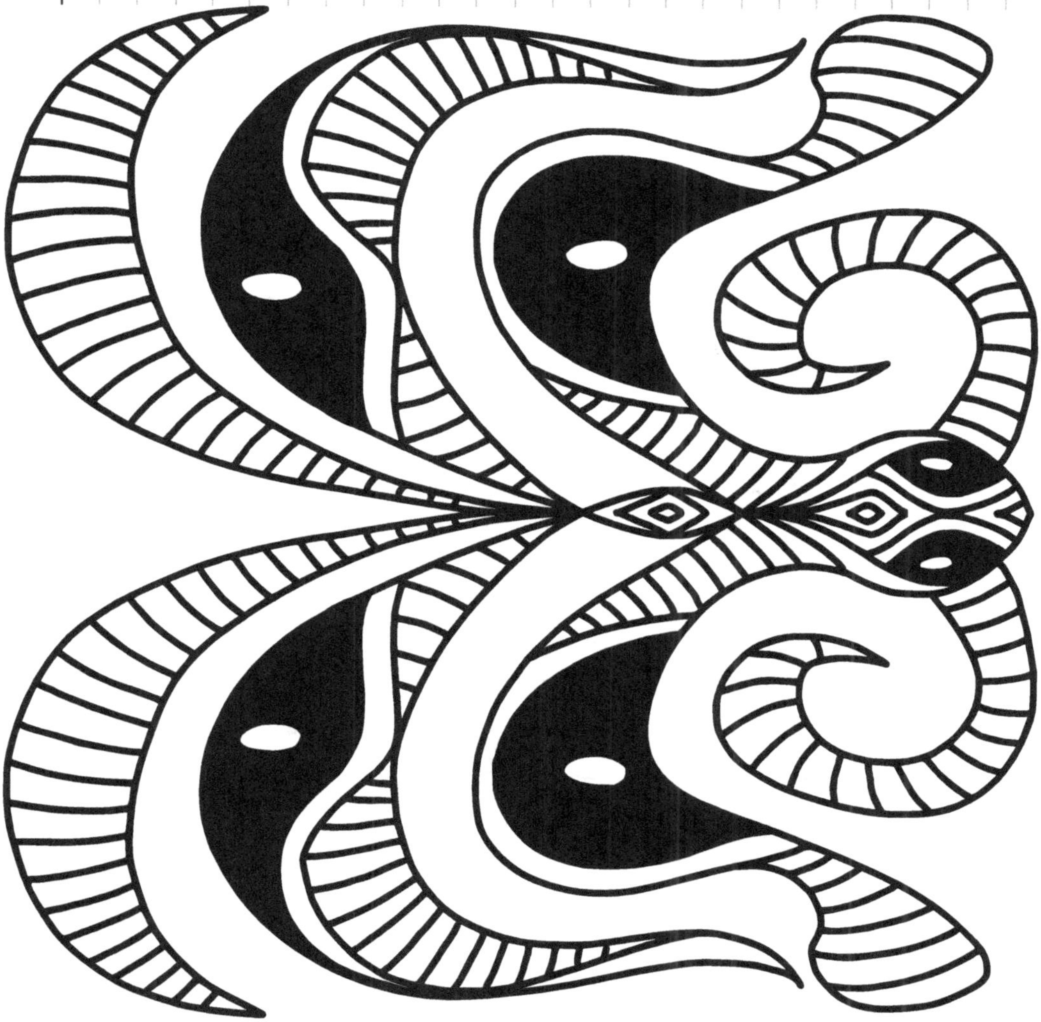

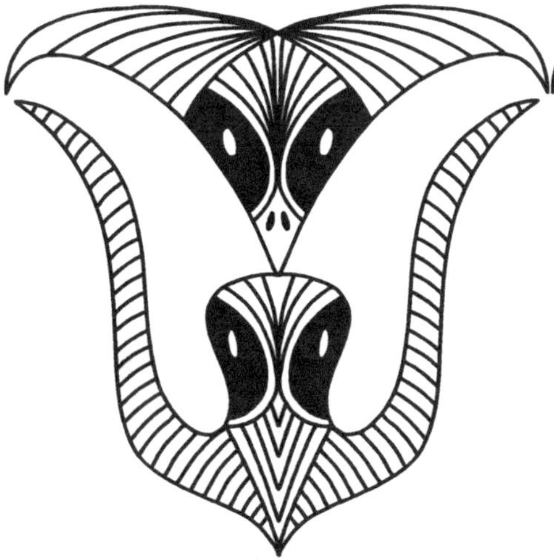

FATLINER WEIRDIES
VOLUME 1

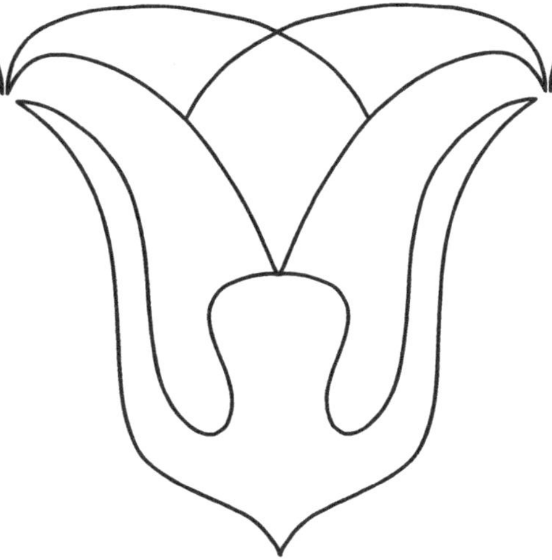

FATLINER WEIRDIES
THE TEMPLATES 1

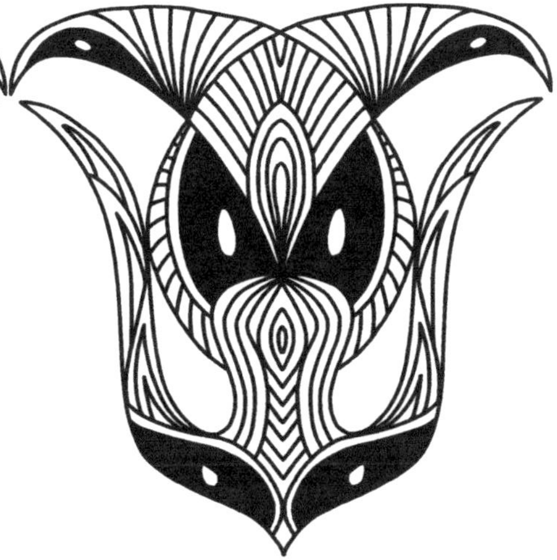

FATLINER WEIRDIES
VOLUME 3

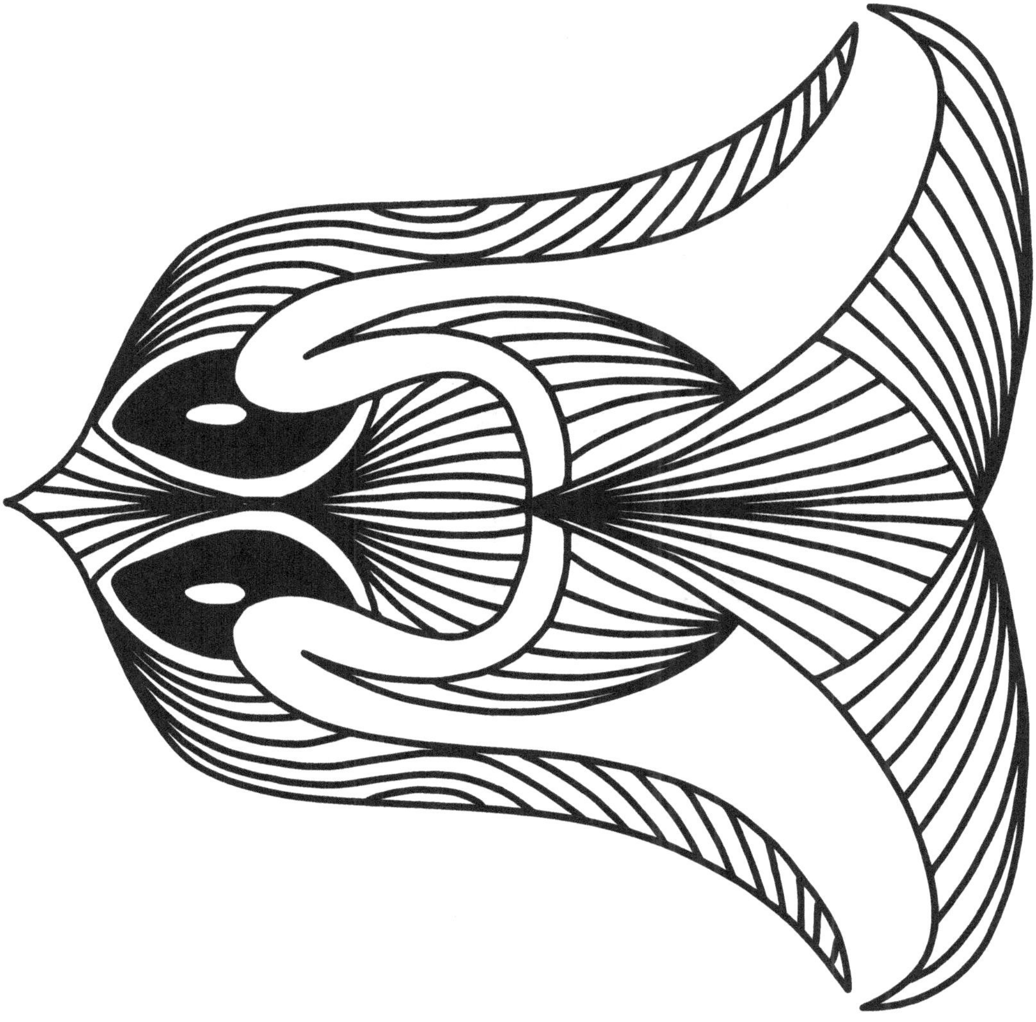

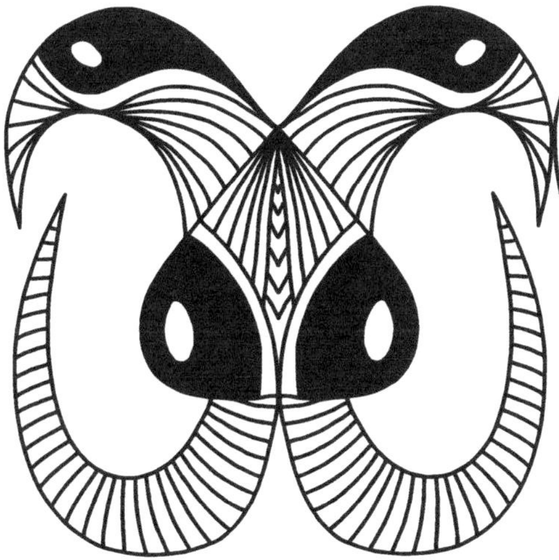

FATLINER WEIRDIES
VOLUME 1

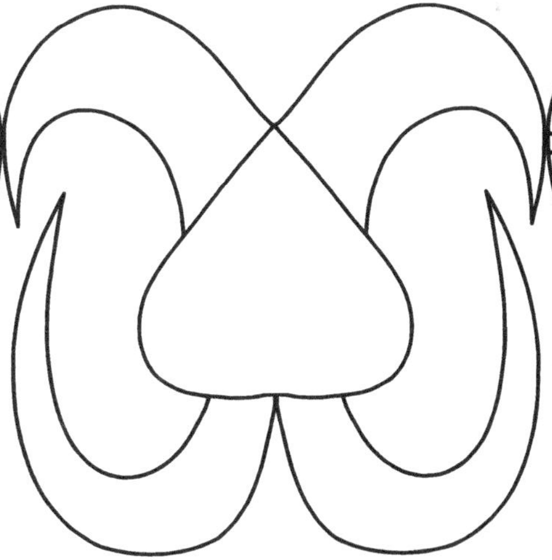

FATLINER WEIRDIES
THE TEMPLATES 1

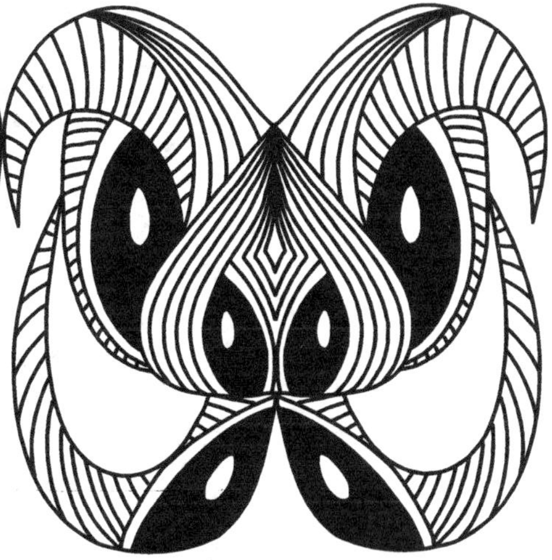

FATLINER WEIRDIES
VOLUME 3

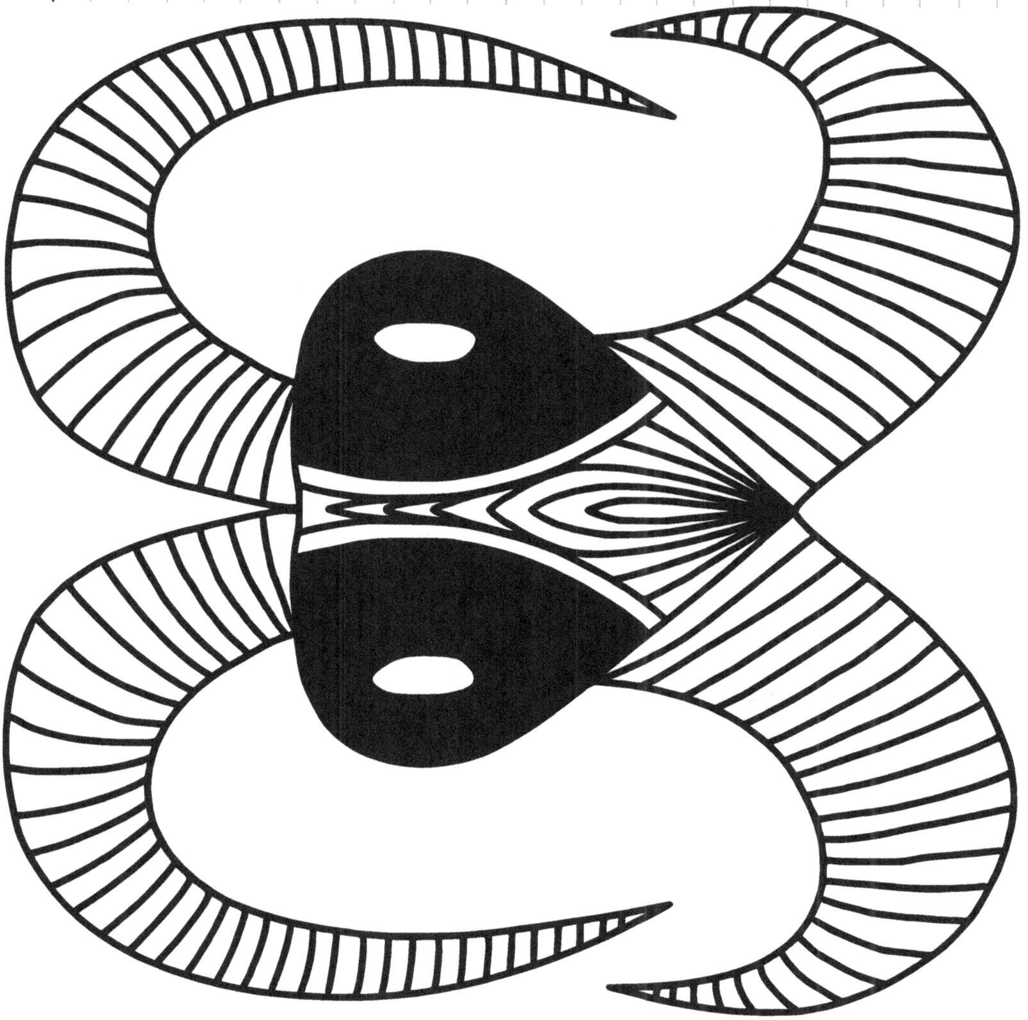

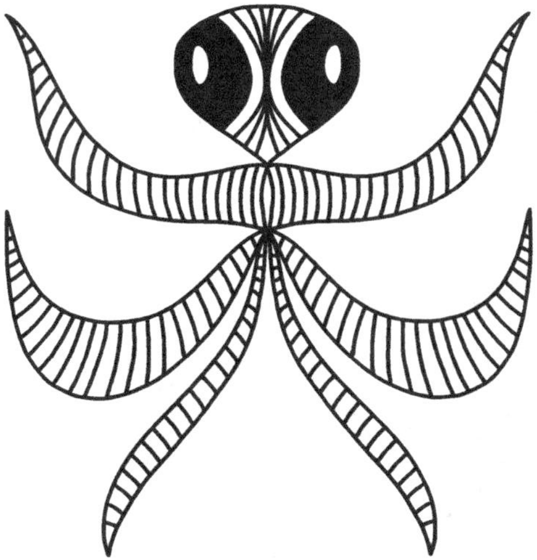
FATLINER WEIRDIES
VOLUME 1

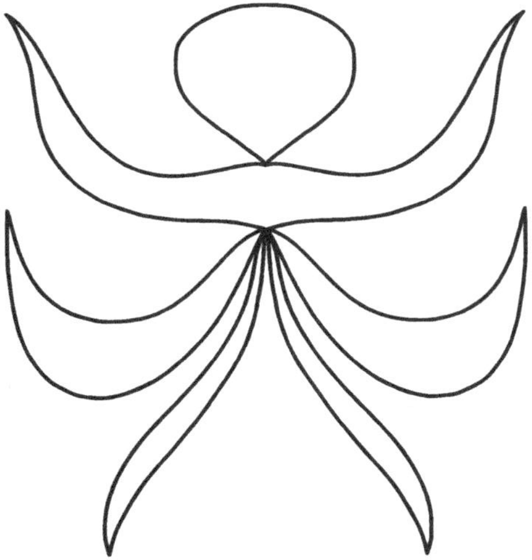
FATLINER WEIRDIES
THE TEMPLATES 1

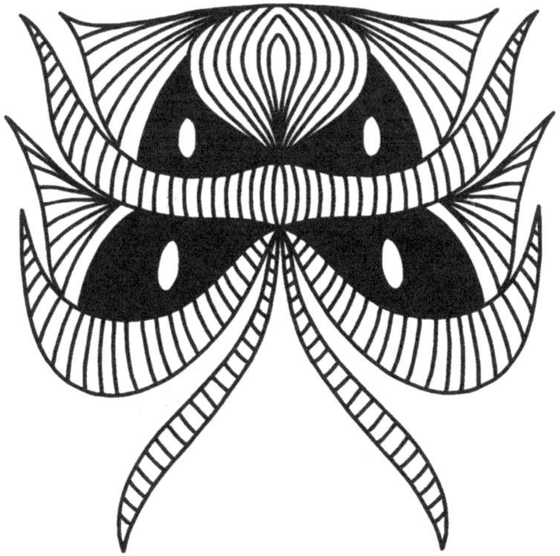
FATLINER WEIRDIES
VOLUME 3

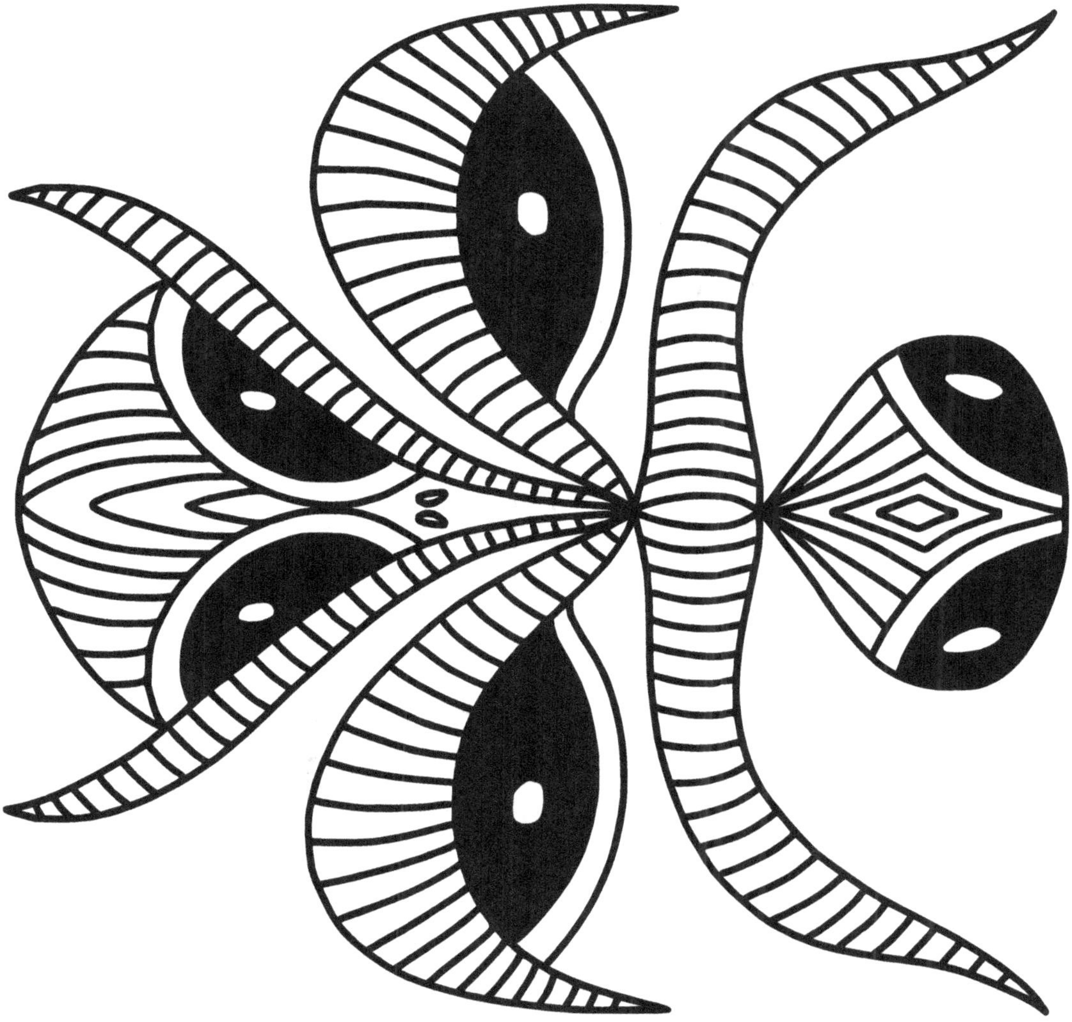

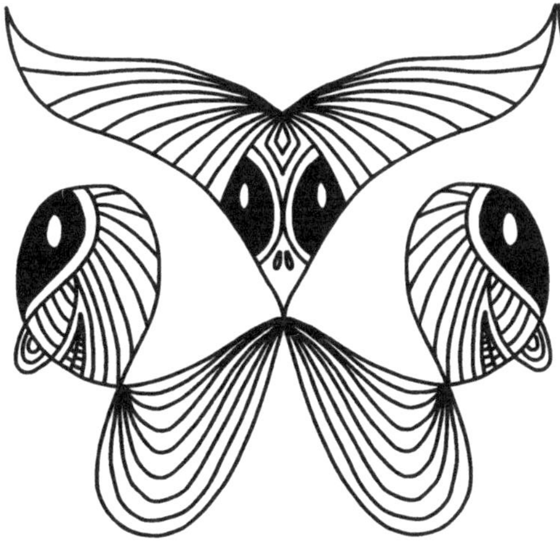
FATLINER WEIRDIES
VOLUME 1

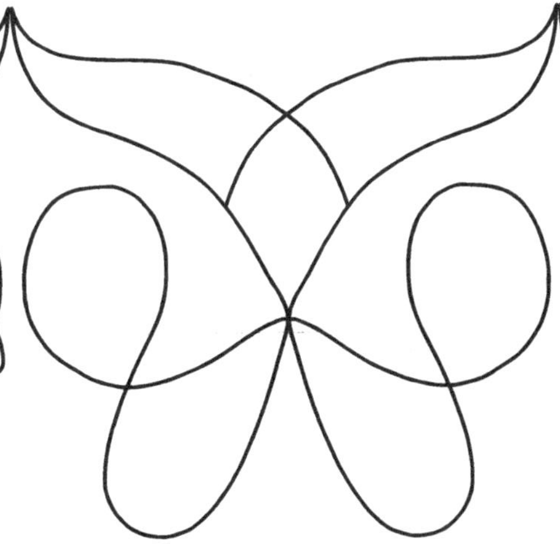
FATLINER WEIRDIES
THE TEMPLATES 1

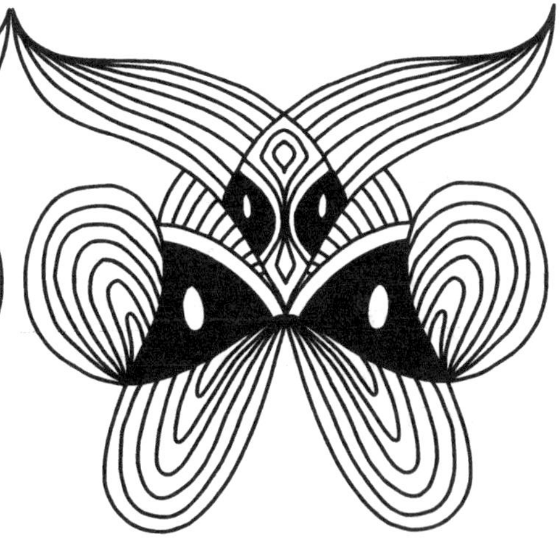
FATLINER WEIRDIES
VOLUME 3

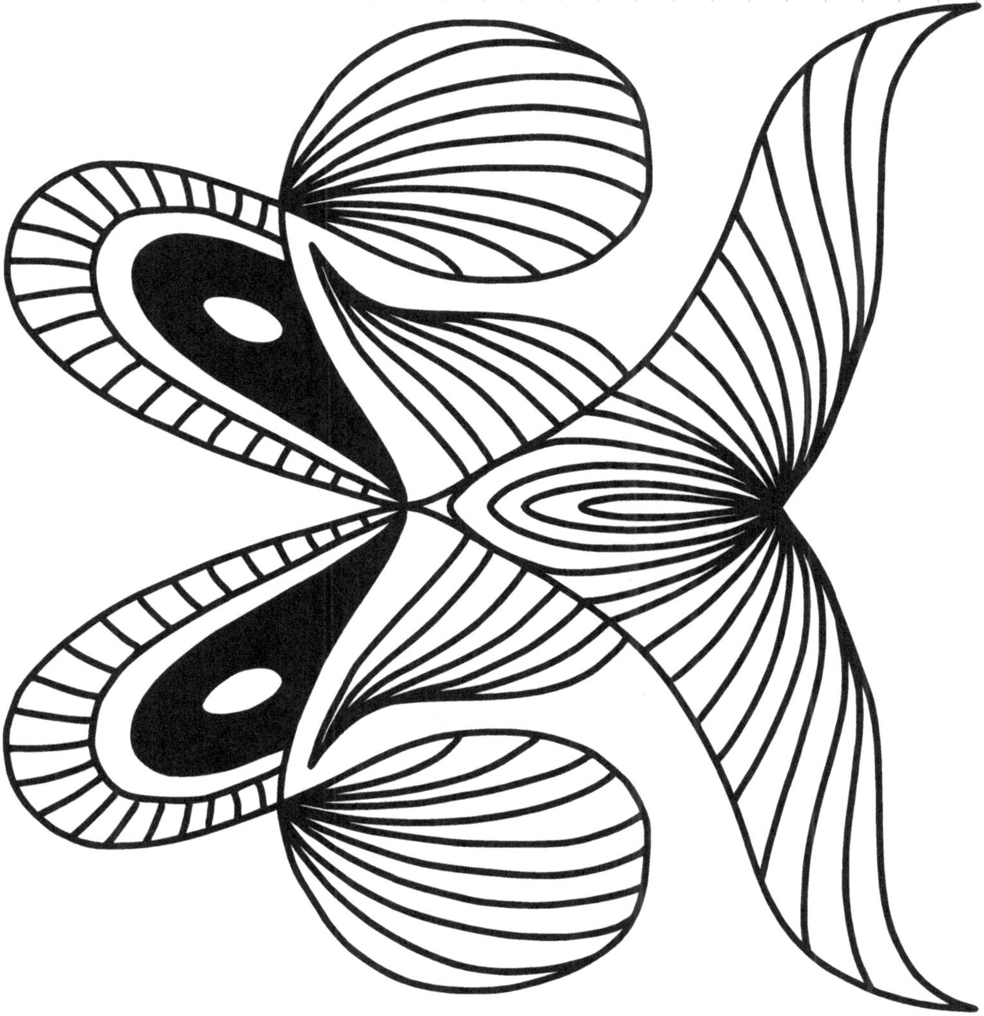

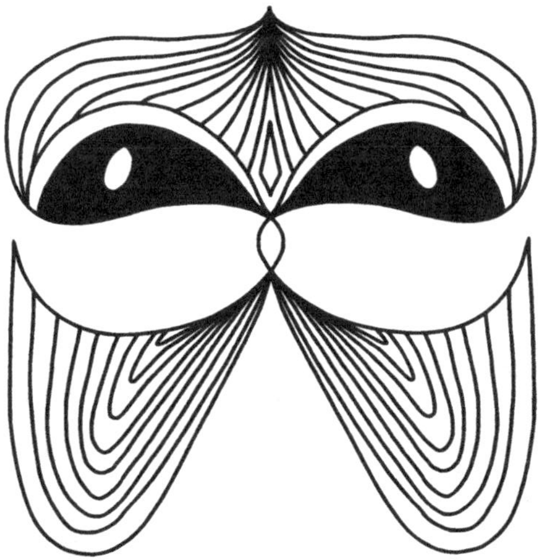

FATLINER WEIRDIES
VOLUME 1

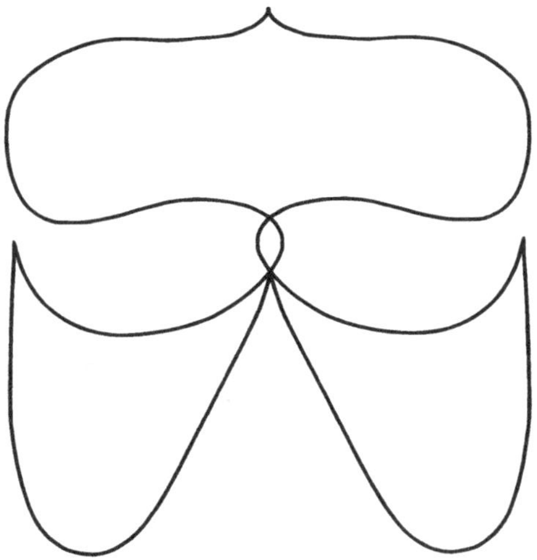

FATLINER WEIRDIES
THE TEMPLATES 1

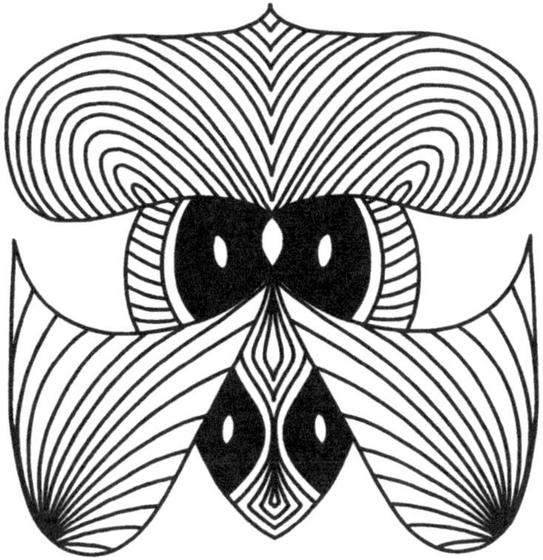

FATLINER WEIRDIES
VOLUME 3

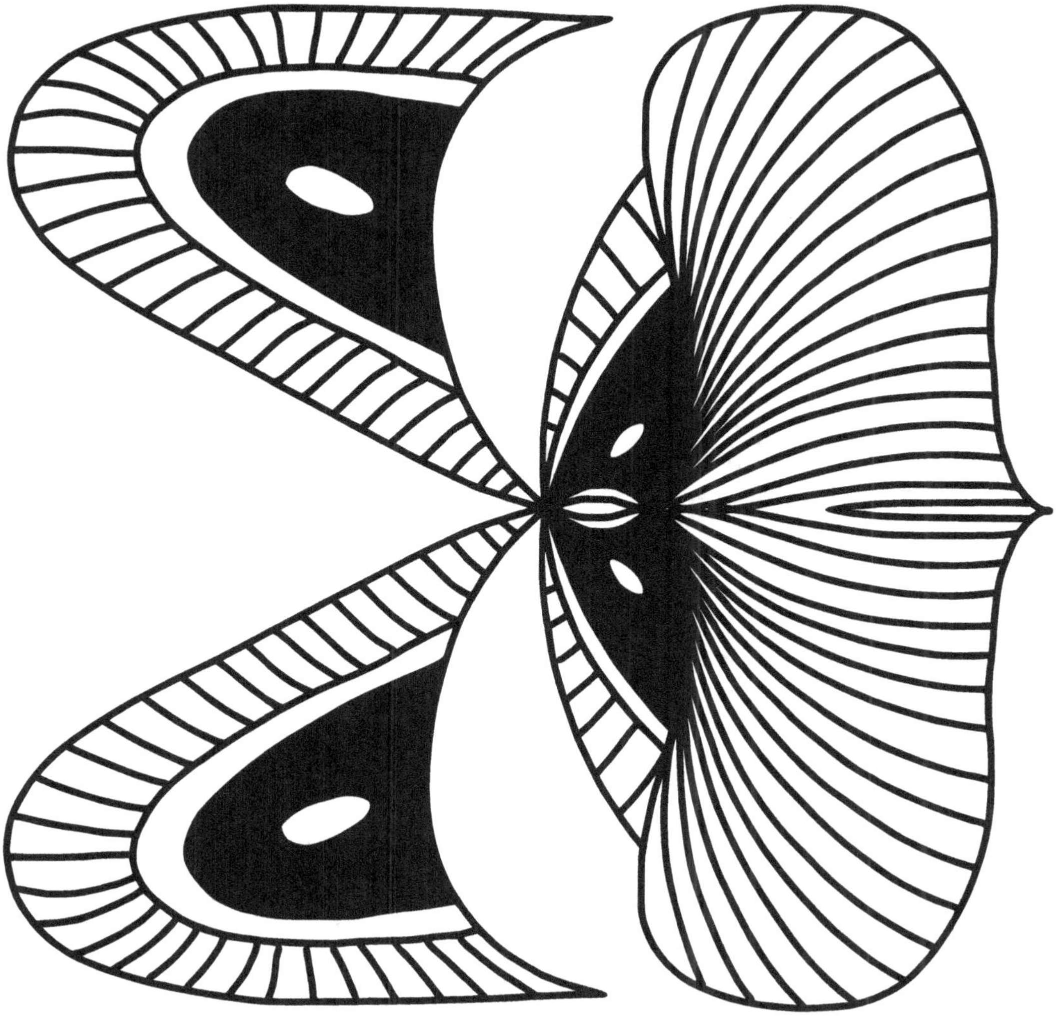

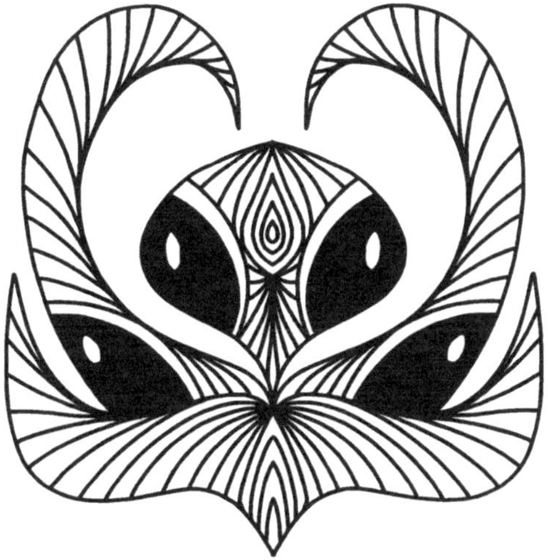

FATLINER WEIRDIES
VOLUME 1

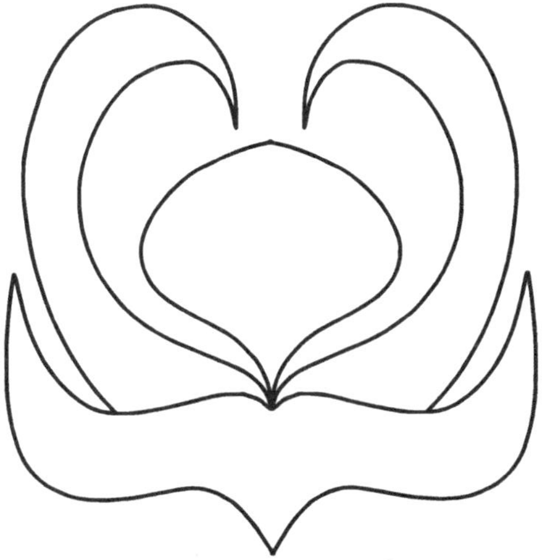

FATLINER WEIRDIES
THE TEMPLATES 1

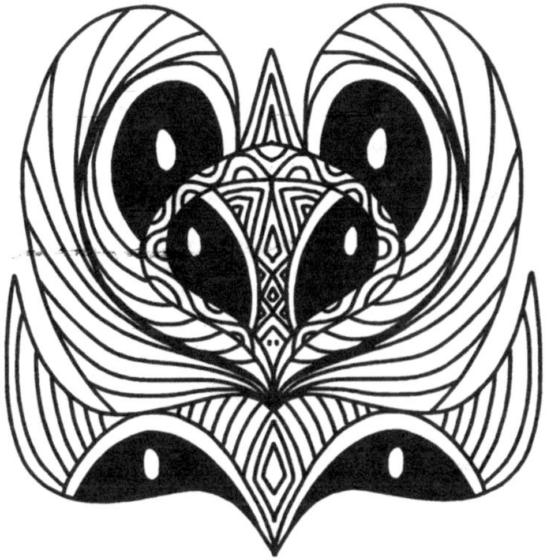

FATLINER WEIRDIES
VOLUME 3

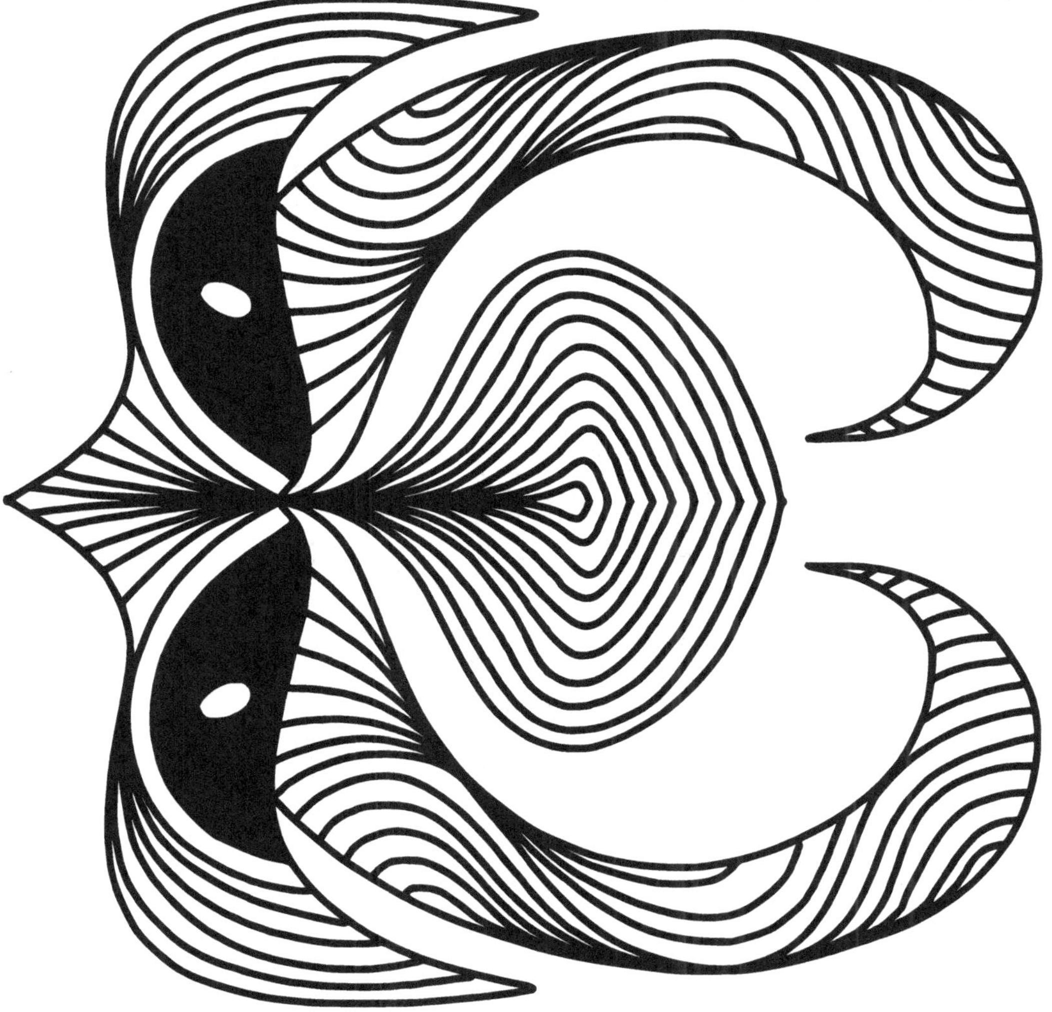

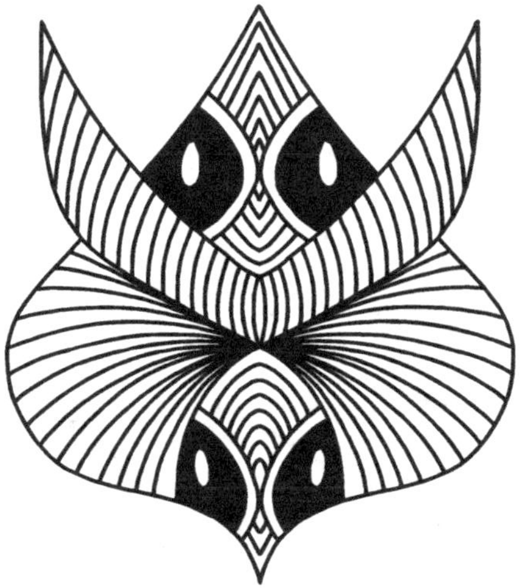

FATLINER WEIRDIES
VOLUME 1

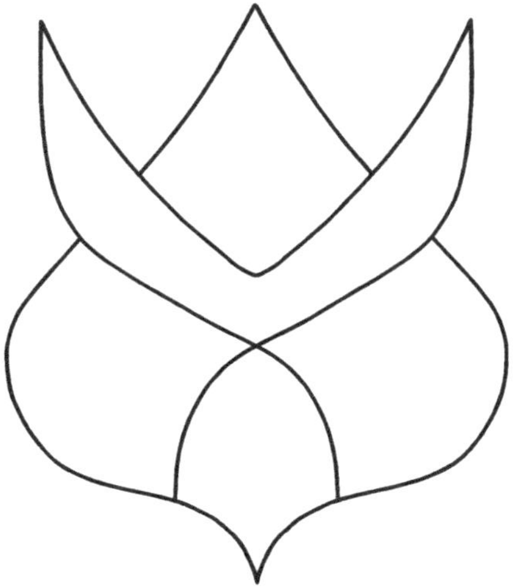

FATLINER WEIRDIES
THE TEMPLATES 1

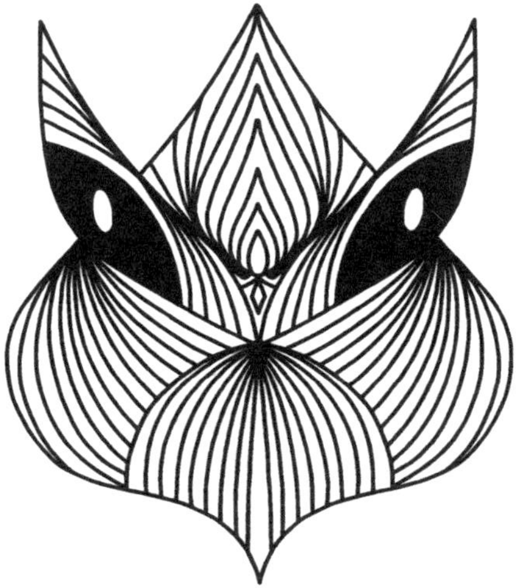

FATLINER WEIRDIES
VOLUME 3

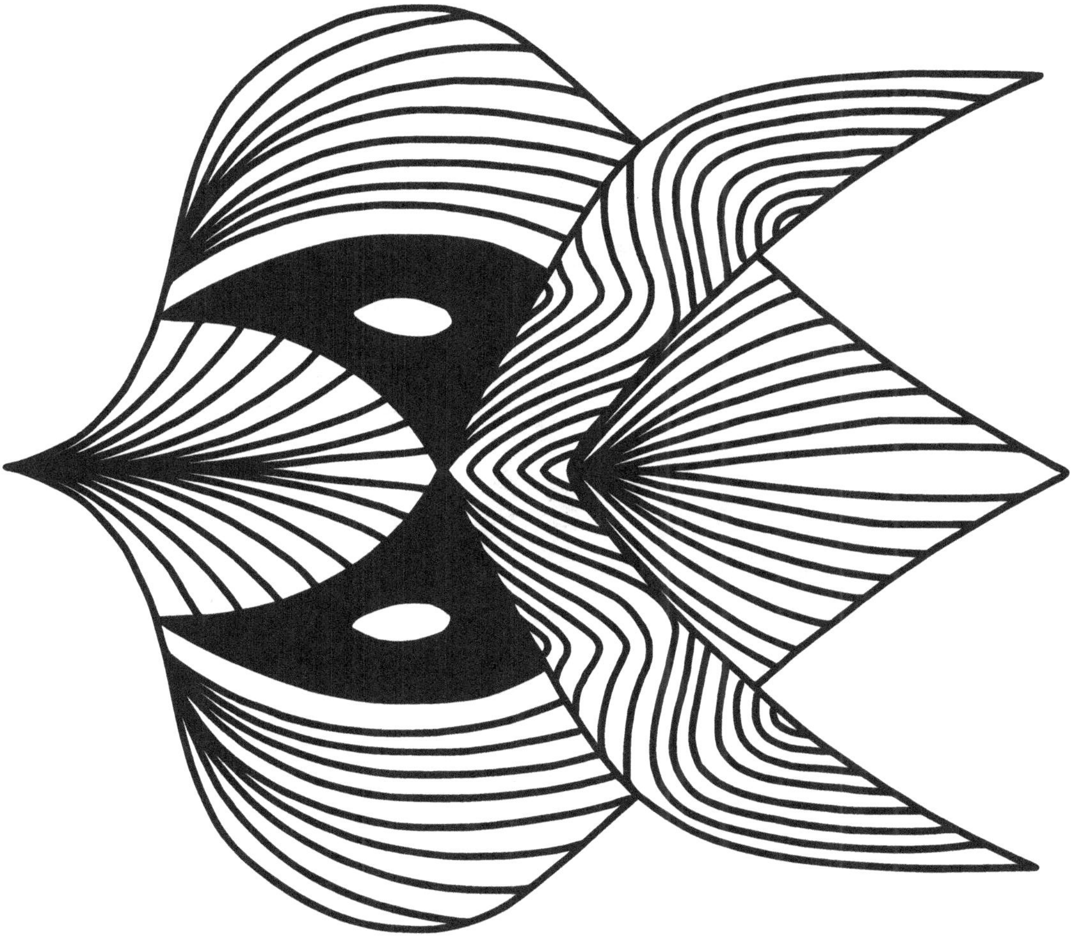

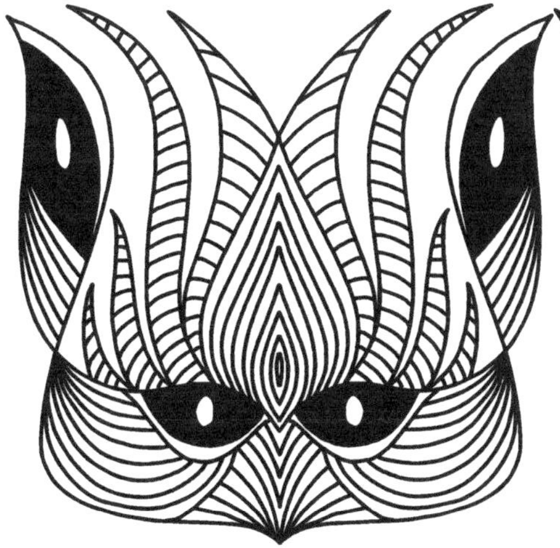

FATLINER WEIRDIES
VOLUME 1

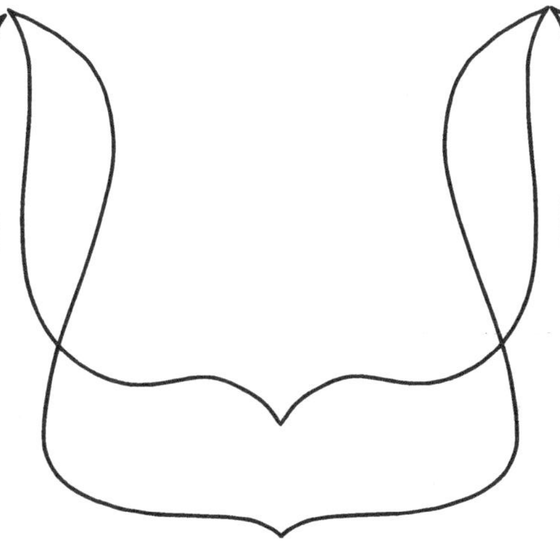

FATLINER WEIRDIES
THE TEMPLATES 1

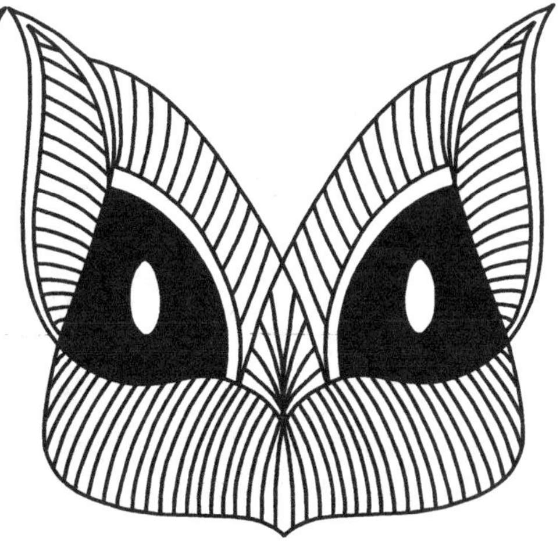

FATLINER WEIRDIES
VOLUME 3

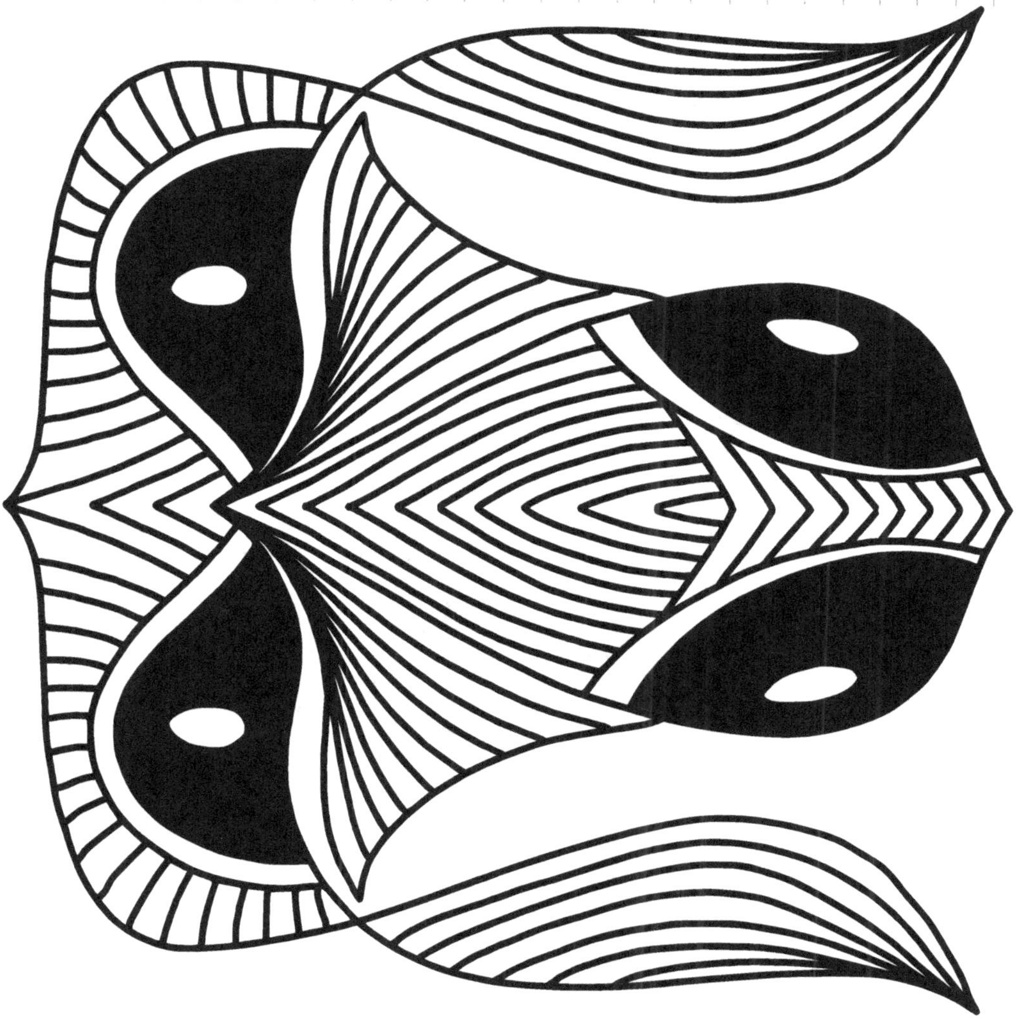

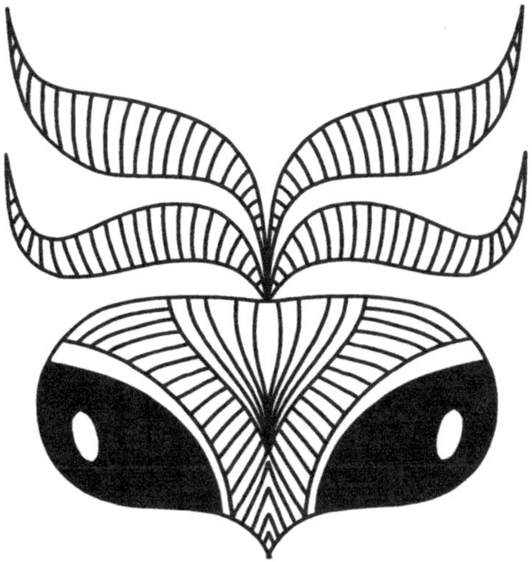

FATLINER WEIRDIES
VOLUME 1

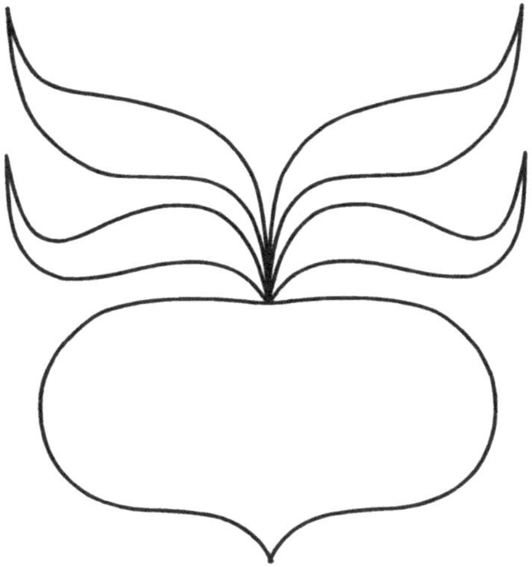

FATLINER WEIRDIES
THE TEMPLATES 1

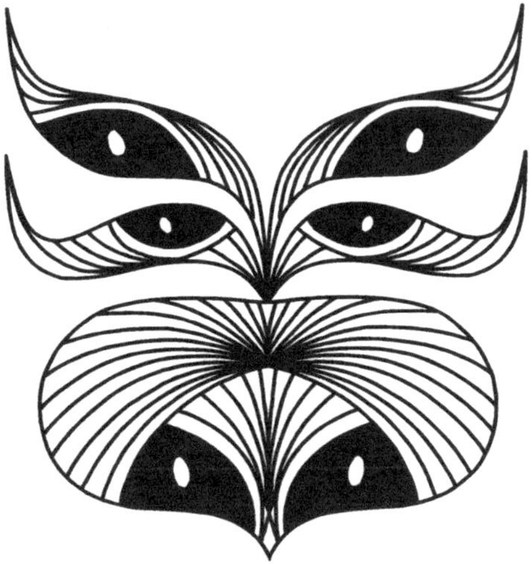

FATLINER WEIRDIES
VOLUME 3

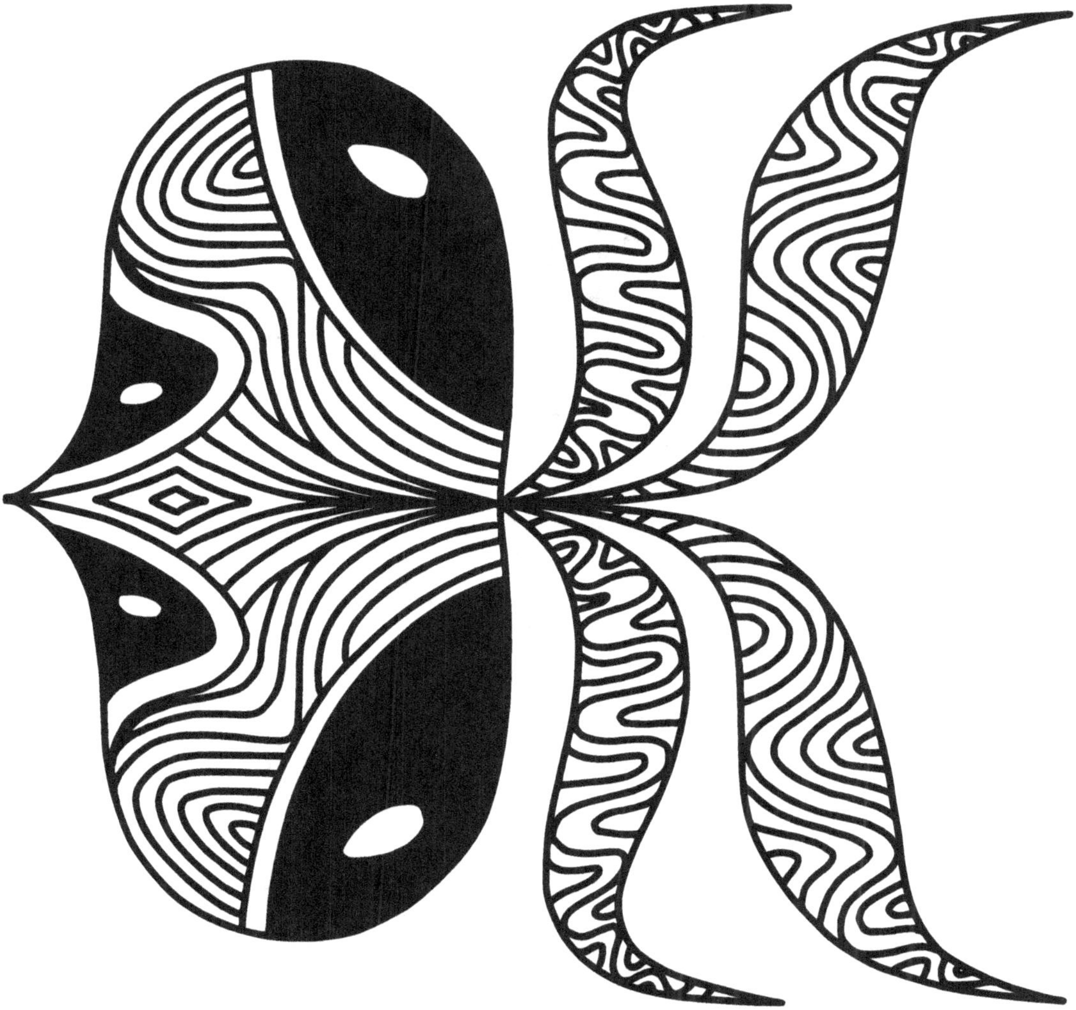

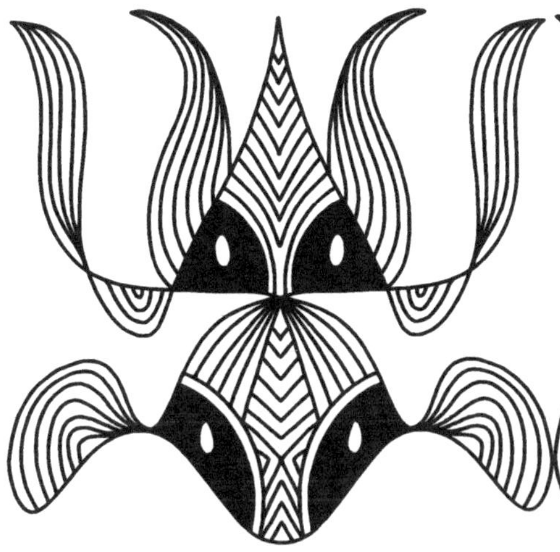
FATLINER WEIRDIES
VOLUME 1

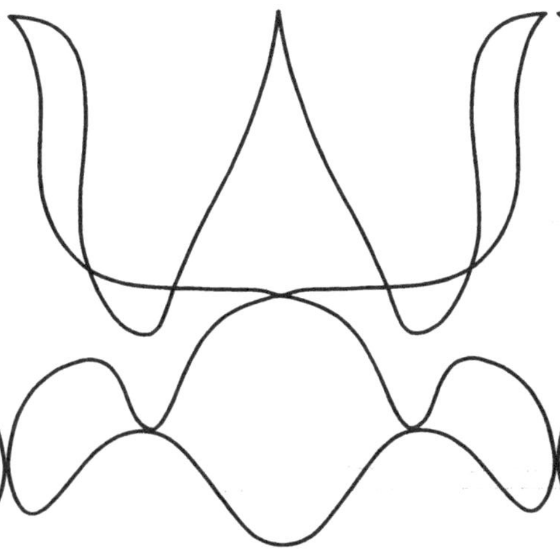
FATLINER WEIRDIES
THE TEMPLATES 1

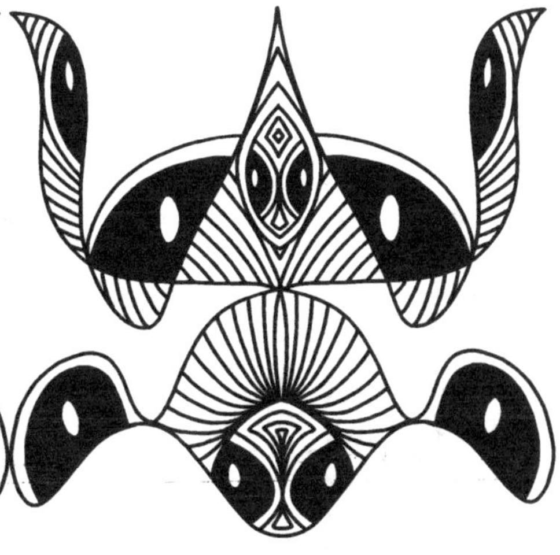
FATLINER WEIRDIES
VOLUME 3

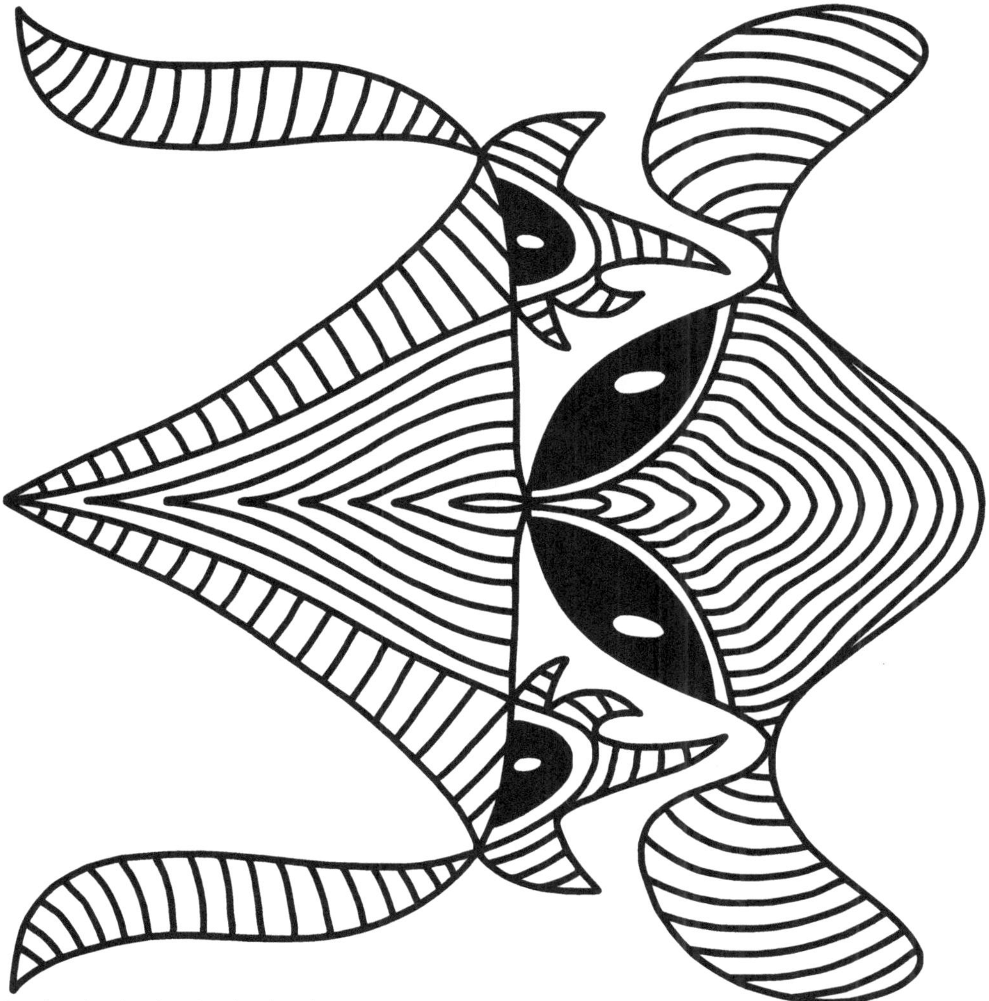

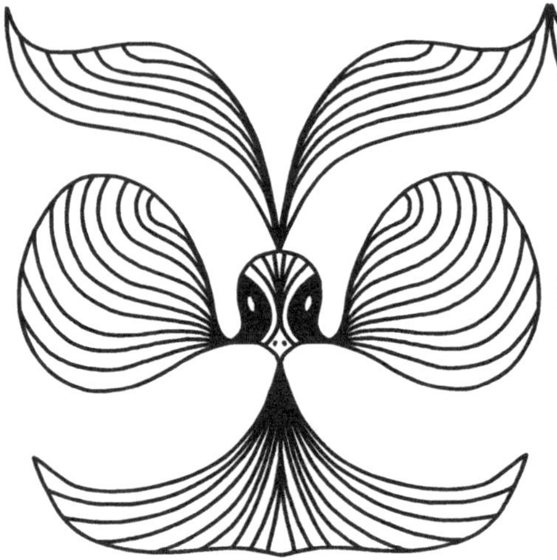

FATLINER WEIRDIES
VOLUME 1

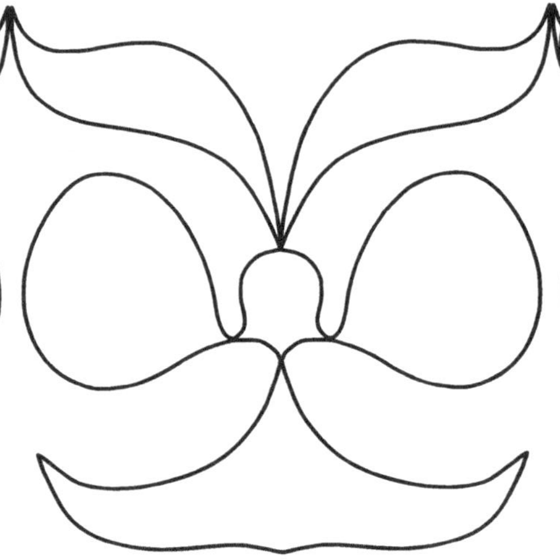

FATLINER WEIRDIES
THE TEMPLATES 1

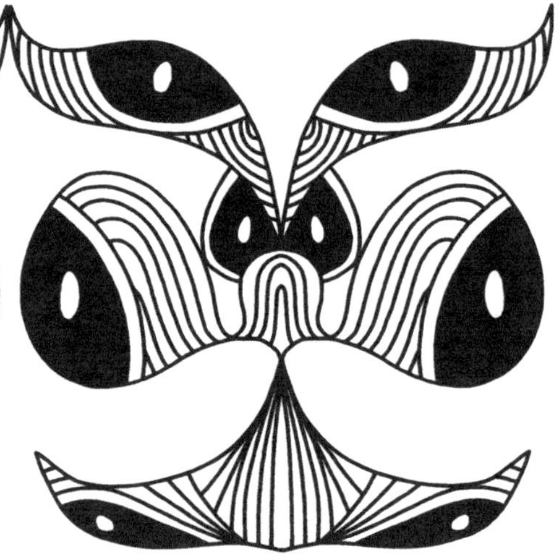

FATLINER WEIRDIES
VOLUME 3

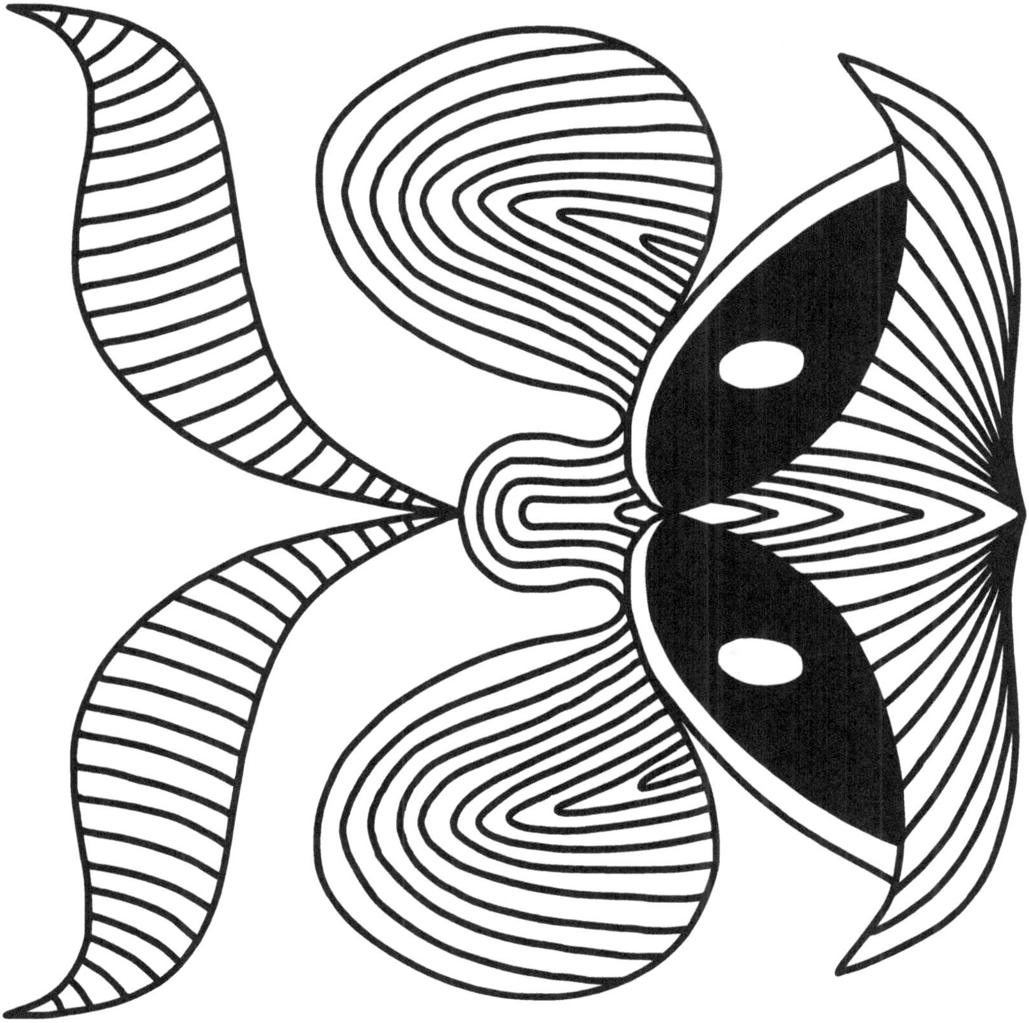

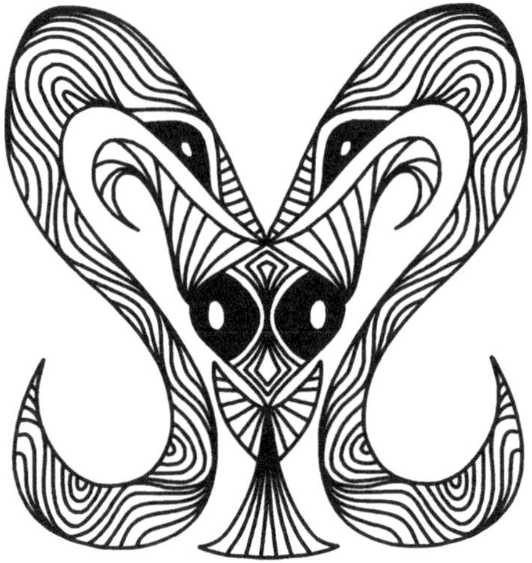

FATLINER WEIRDIES
VOLUME 1

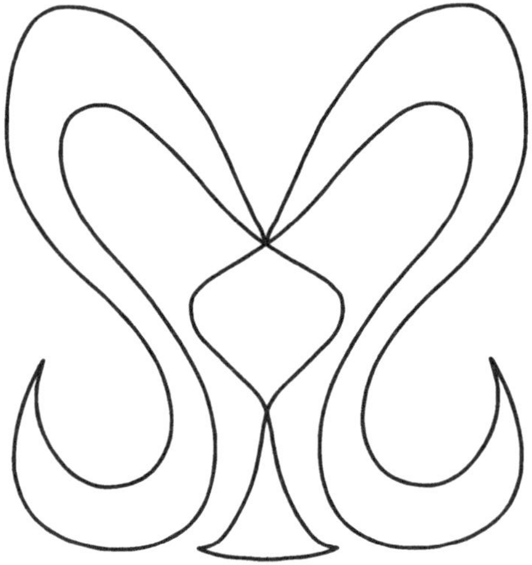

FATLINER WEIRDIES
THE TEMPLATES 1

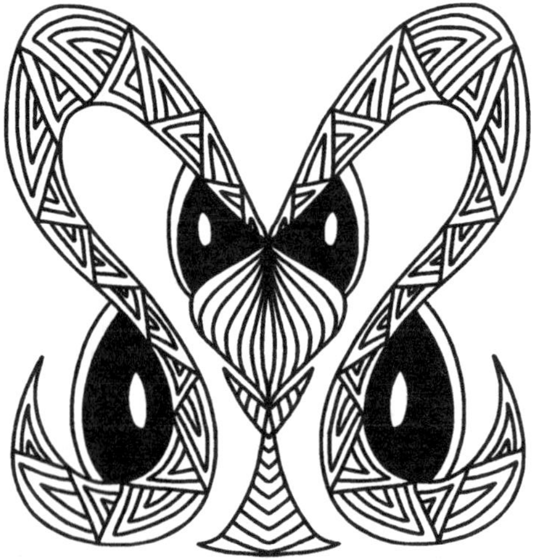

FATLINER WEIRDIES
VOLUME 3

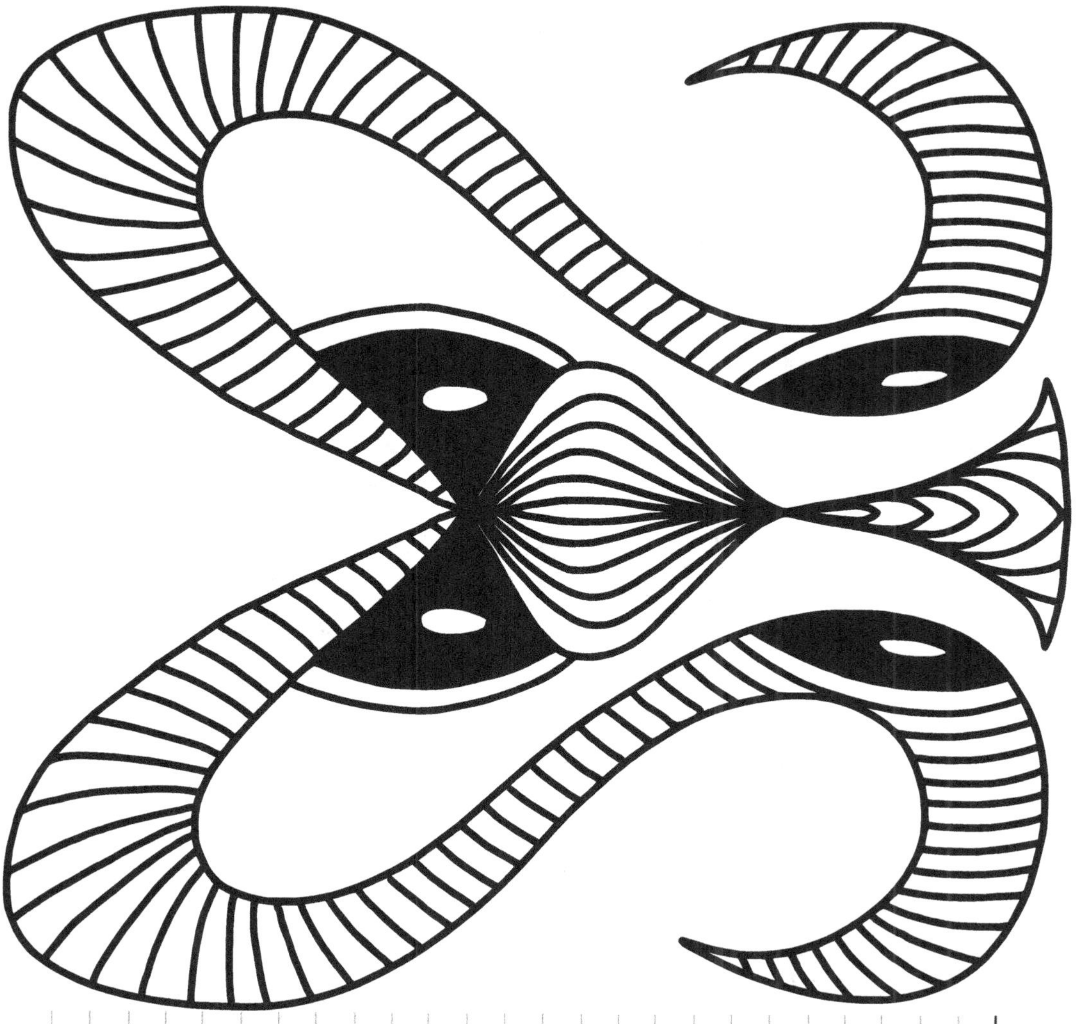

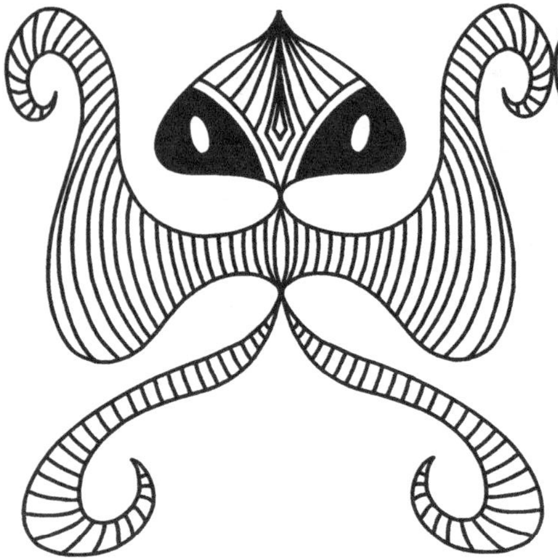
FATLINER WEIRDIES
VOLUME 1

FATLINER WEIRDIES
THE TEMPLATES 1

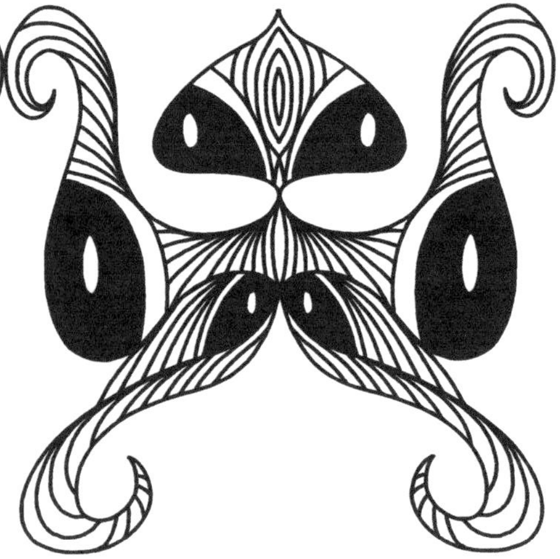
FATLINER WEIRDIES
VOLUME 3

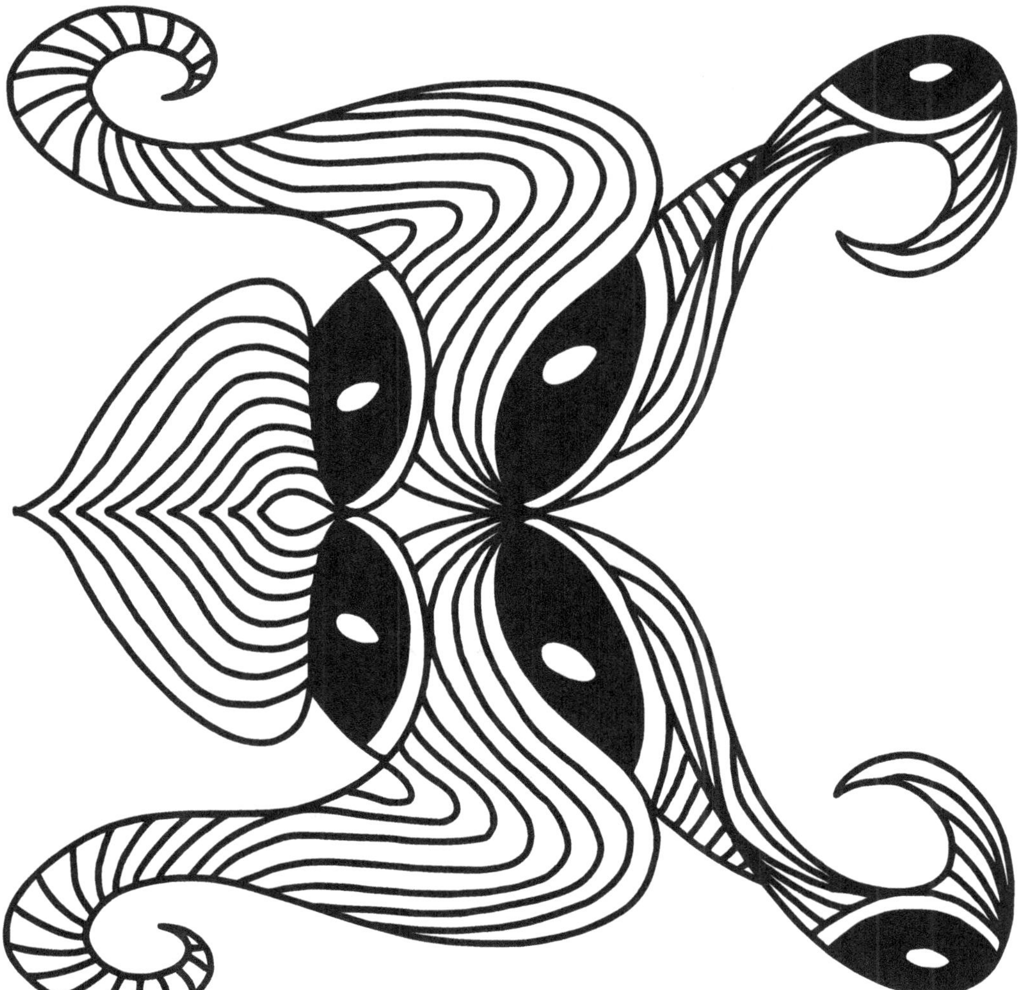

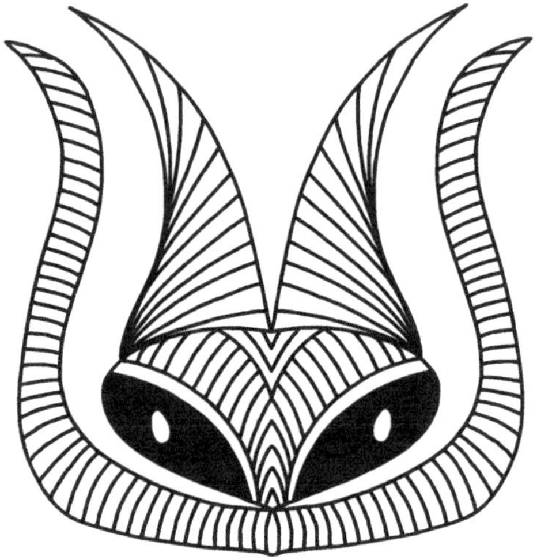

FATLINER WEIRDIES
VOLUME 1

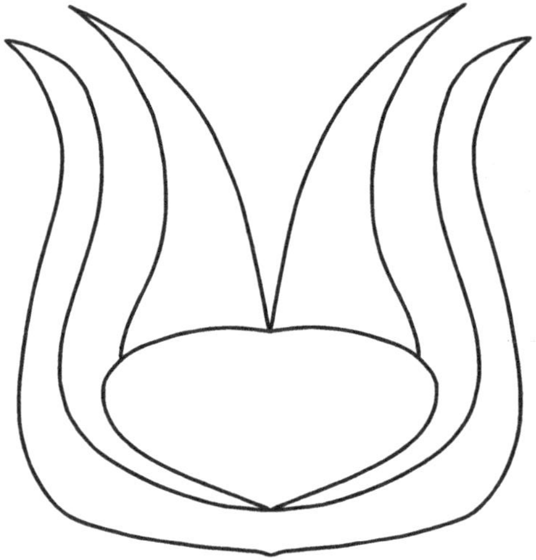

FATLINER WEIRDIES
THE TEMPLATES 1

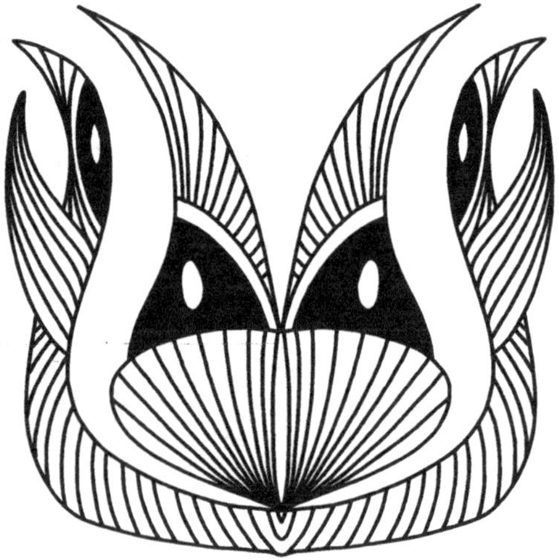

FATLINER WEIRDIES
VOLUME 3

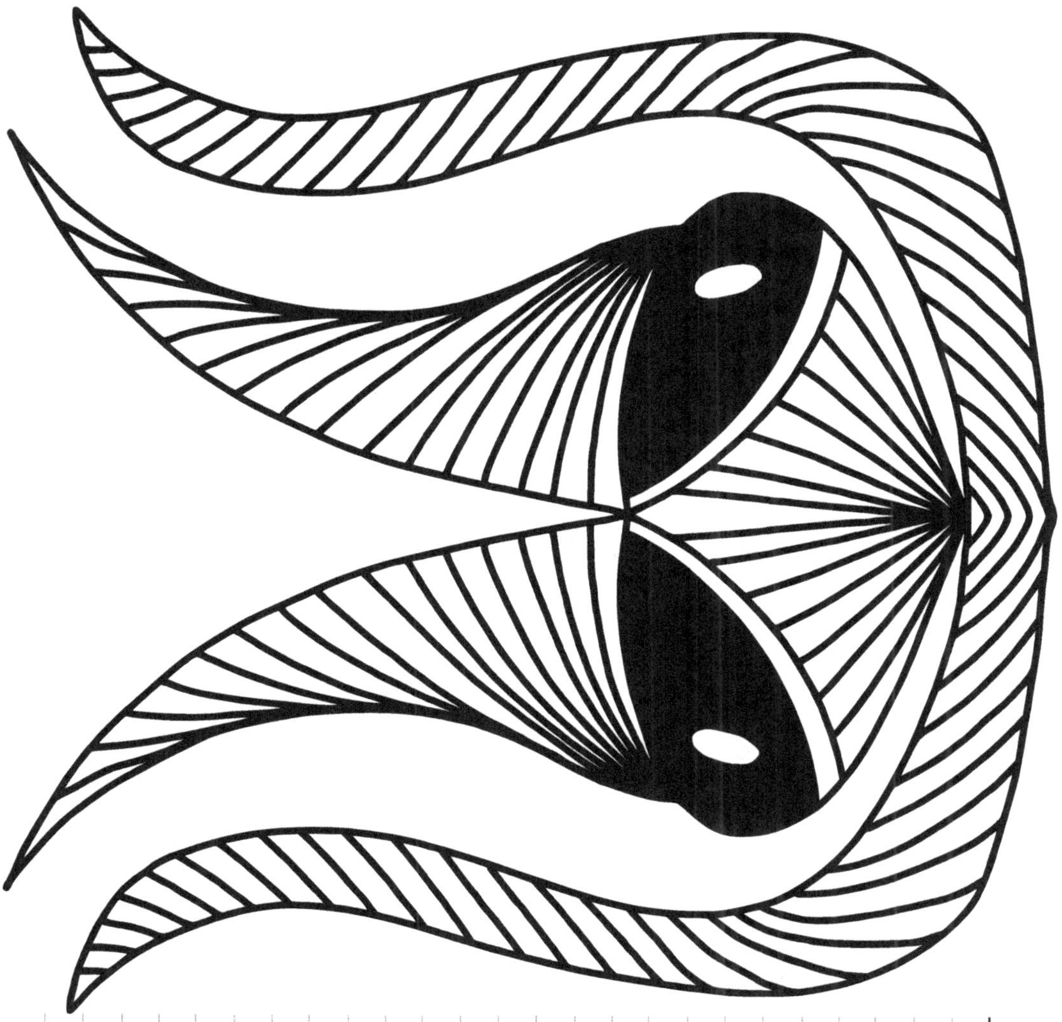

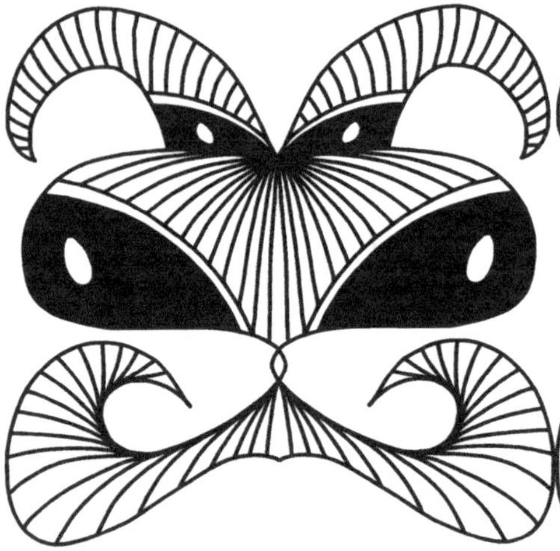

FATLINER WEIRDIES
VOLUME 1

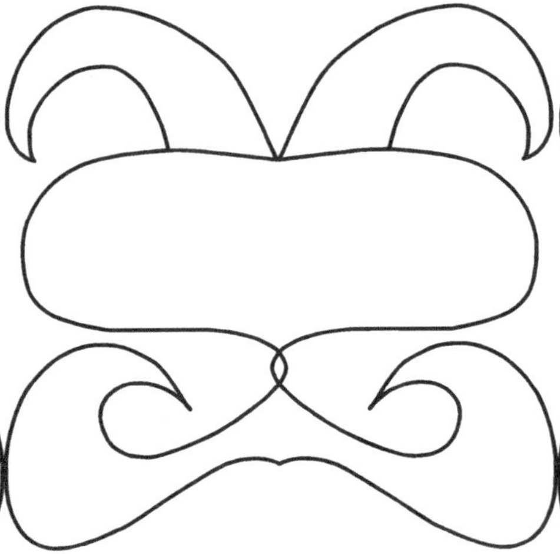

FATLINER WEIRDIES
THE TEMPLATES 1

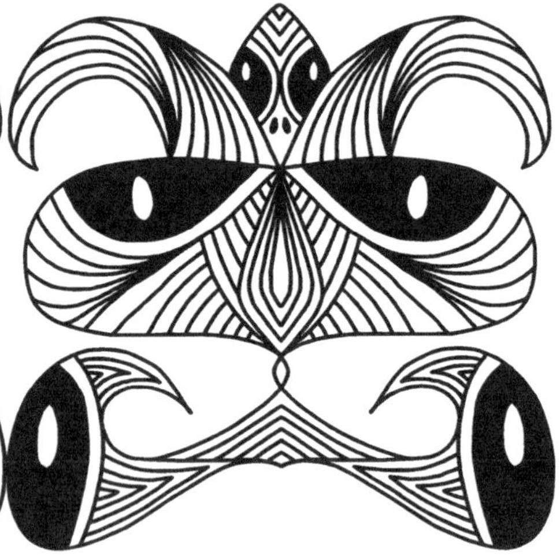

FATLINER WEIRDIES
VOLUME 3

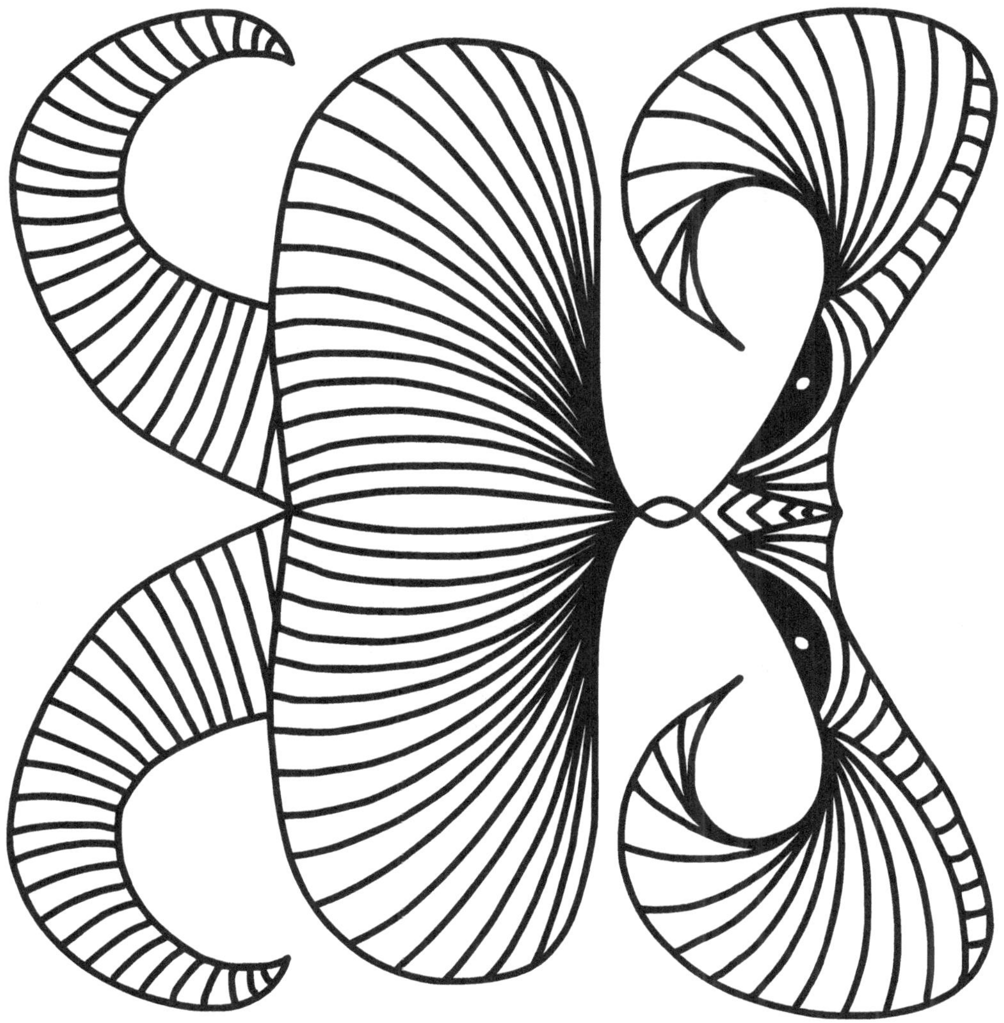

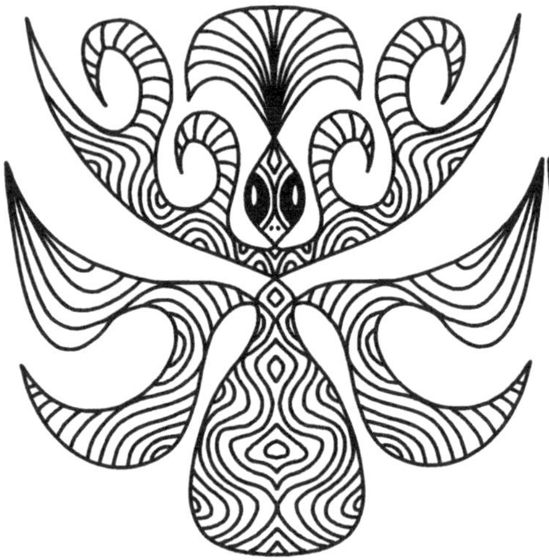

FATLINER WEIRDIES
VOLUME 1

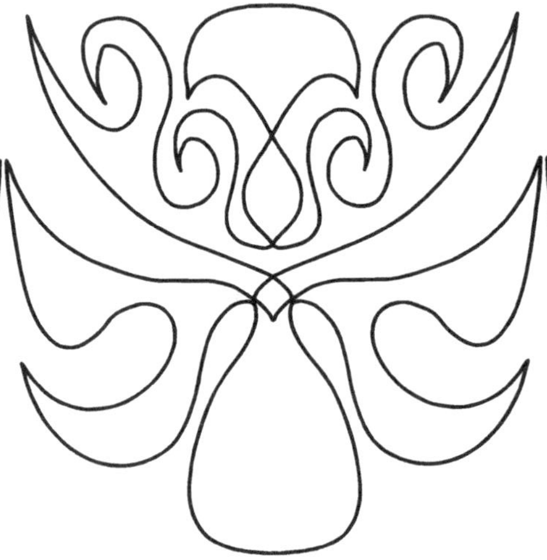

FATLINER WEIRDIES
THE TEMPLATES 1

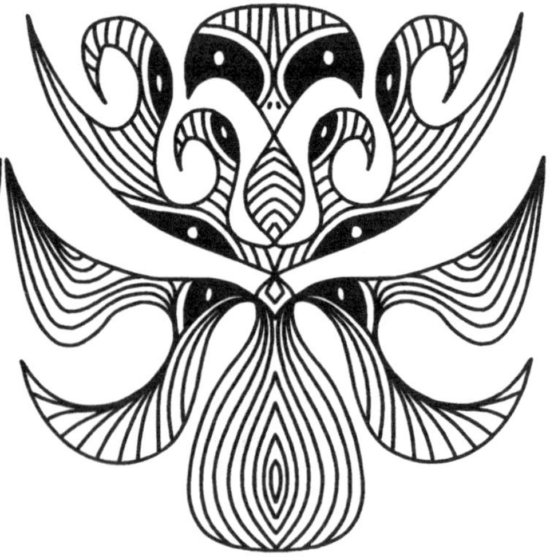

FATLINER WEIRDIES
VOLUME 3

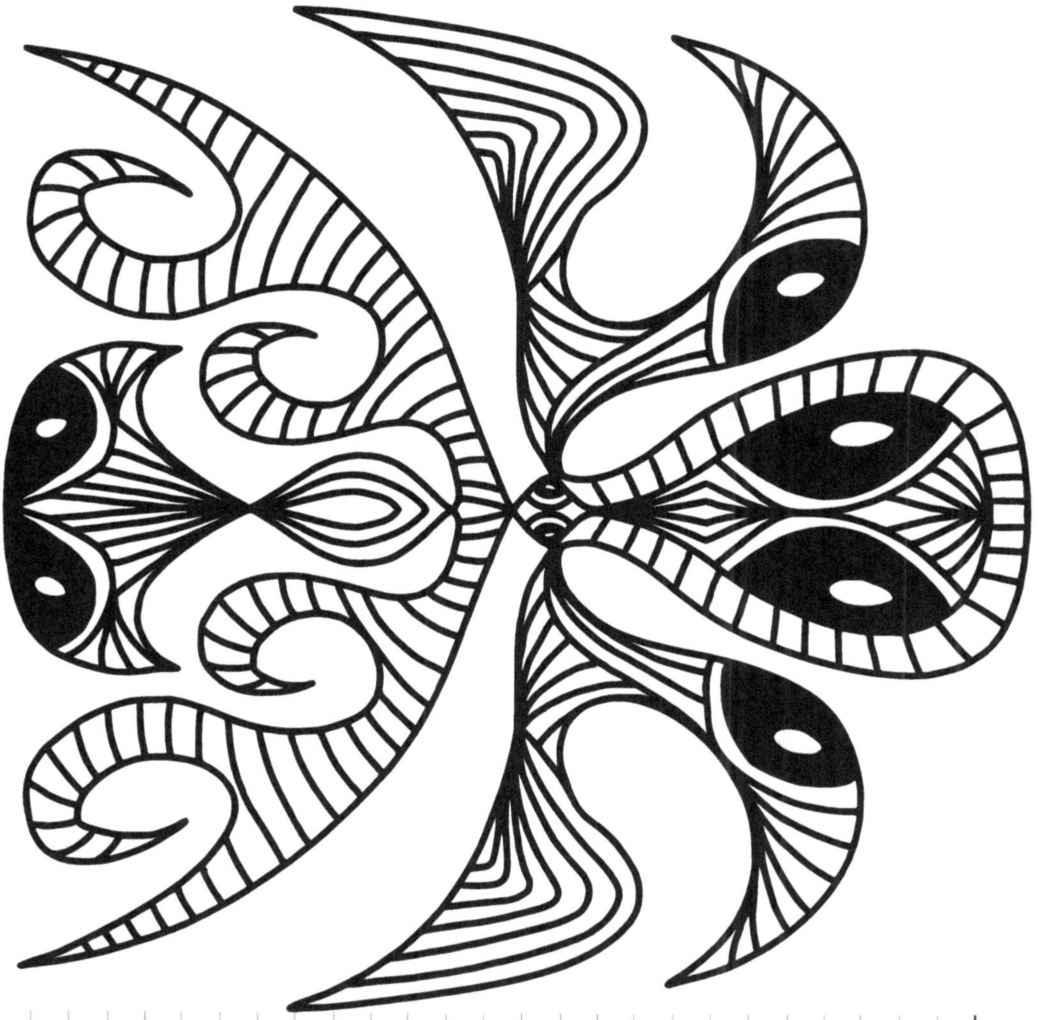

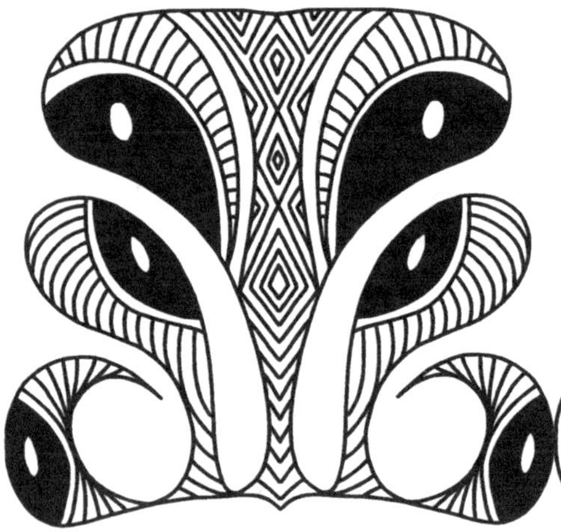
FATLINER WEIRDIES
VOLUME 1

FATLINER WEIRDIES
THE TEMPLATES 1

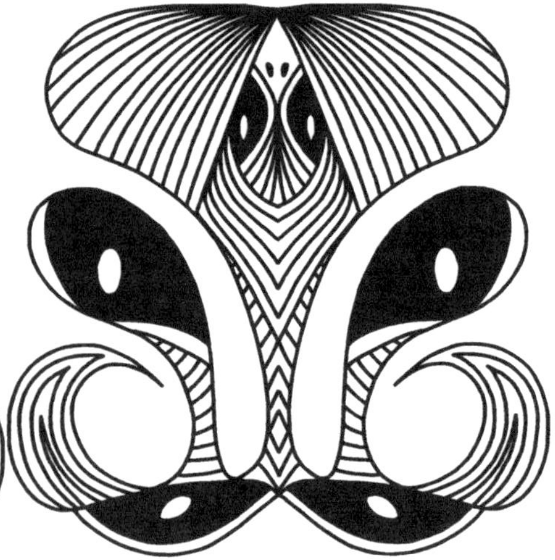
FATLINER WEIRDIES
VOLUME 3

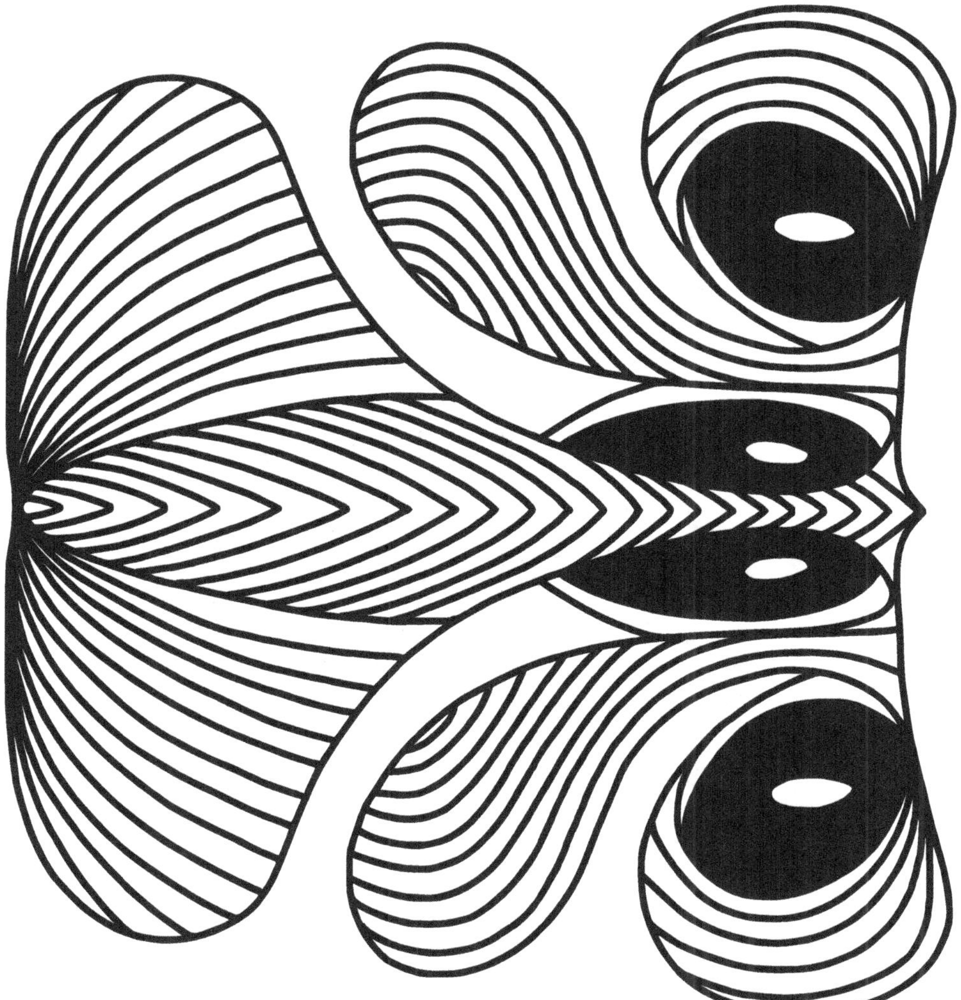

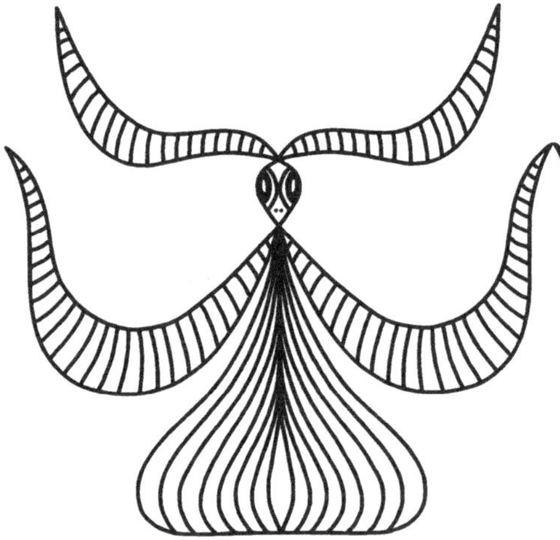

FATLINER WEIRDIES
VOLUME 1

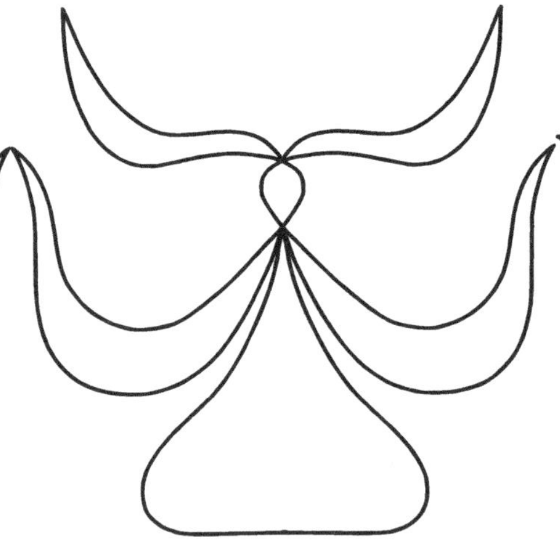

FATLINER WEIRDIES
THE TEMPLATES 1

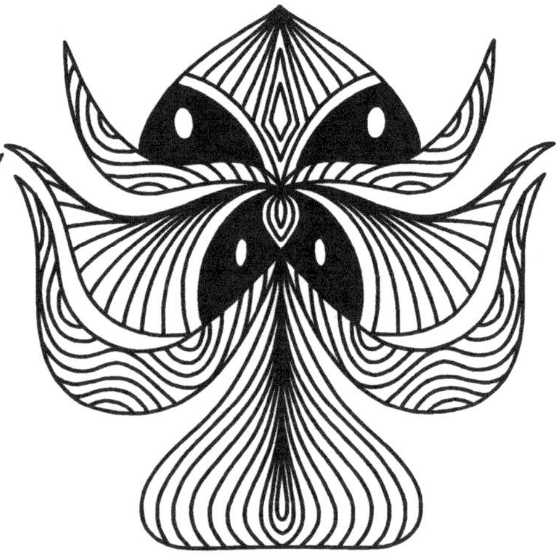

FATLINER WEIRDIES
VOLUME 3

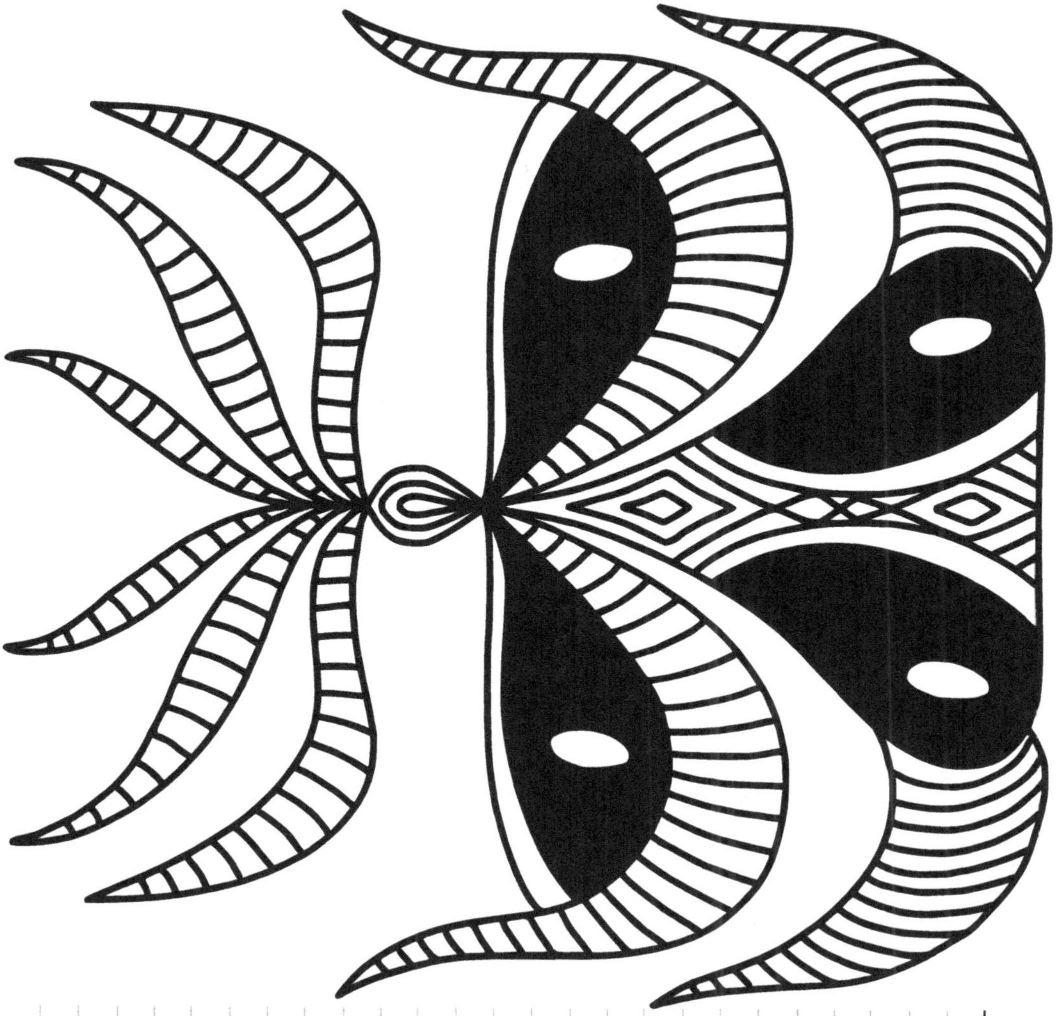

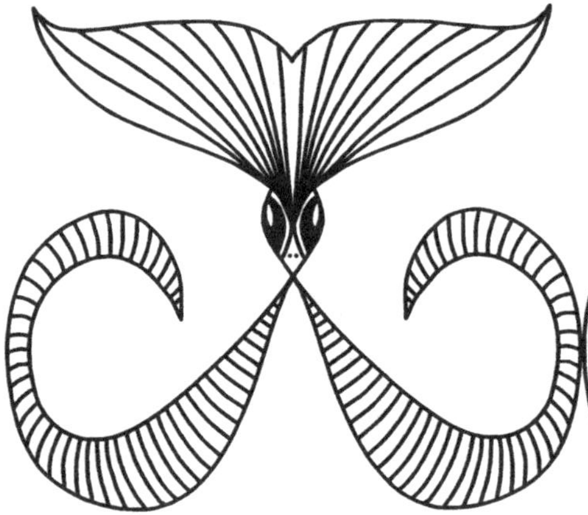

FATLINER WEIRDIES
VOLUME 1

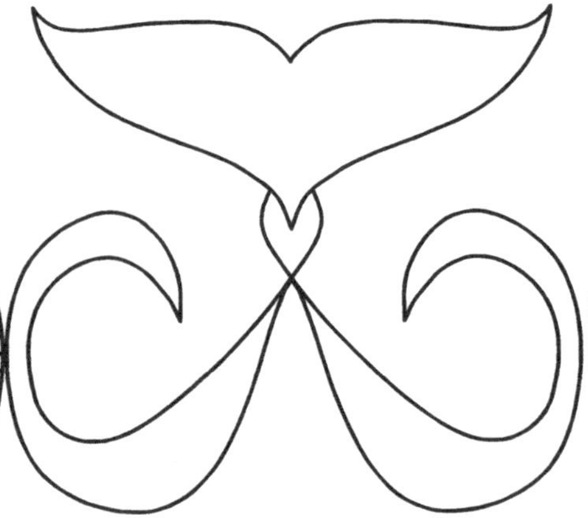

FATLINER WEIRDIES
THE TEMPLATES 1

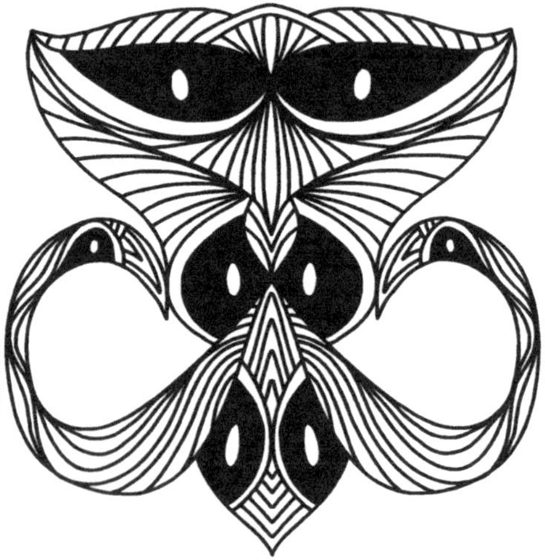

FATLINER WEIRDIES
VOLUME 3

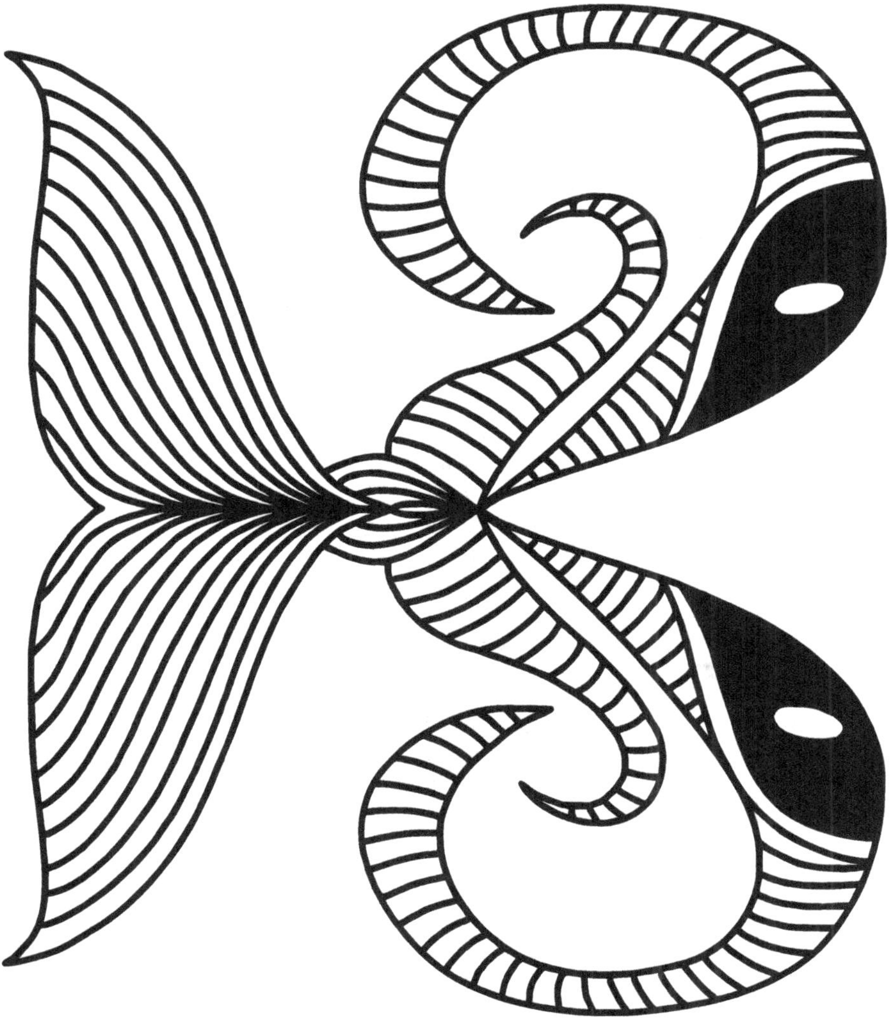

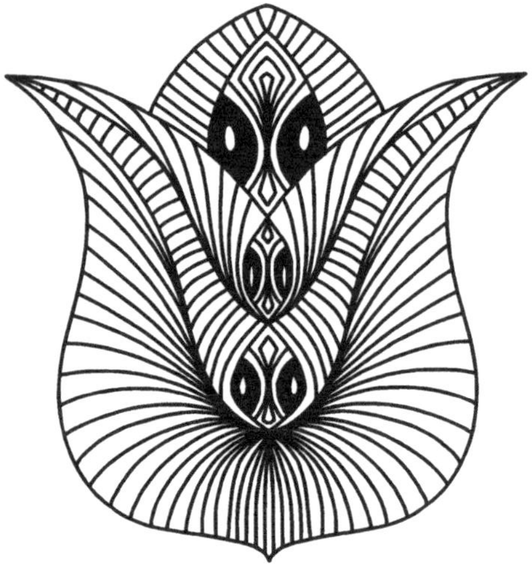

FATLINER WEIRDIES
VOLUME 1

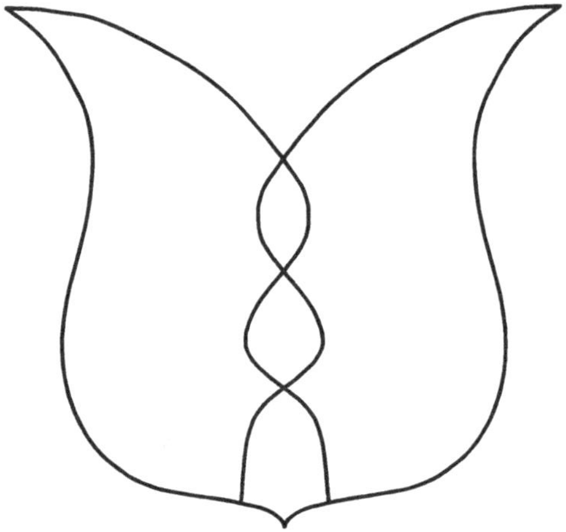

FATLINER WEIRDIES
THE TEMPLATES 1

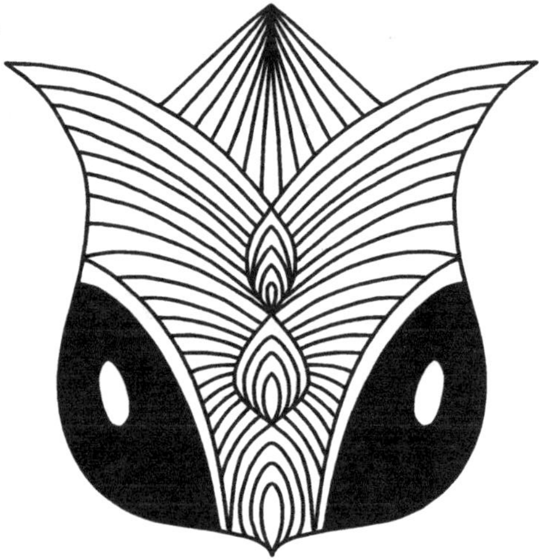

FATLINER WEIRDIES
VOLUME 3

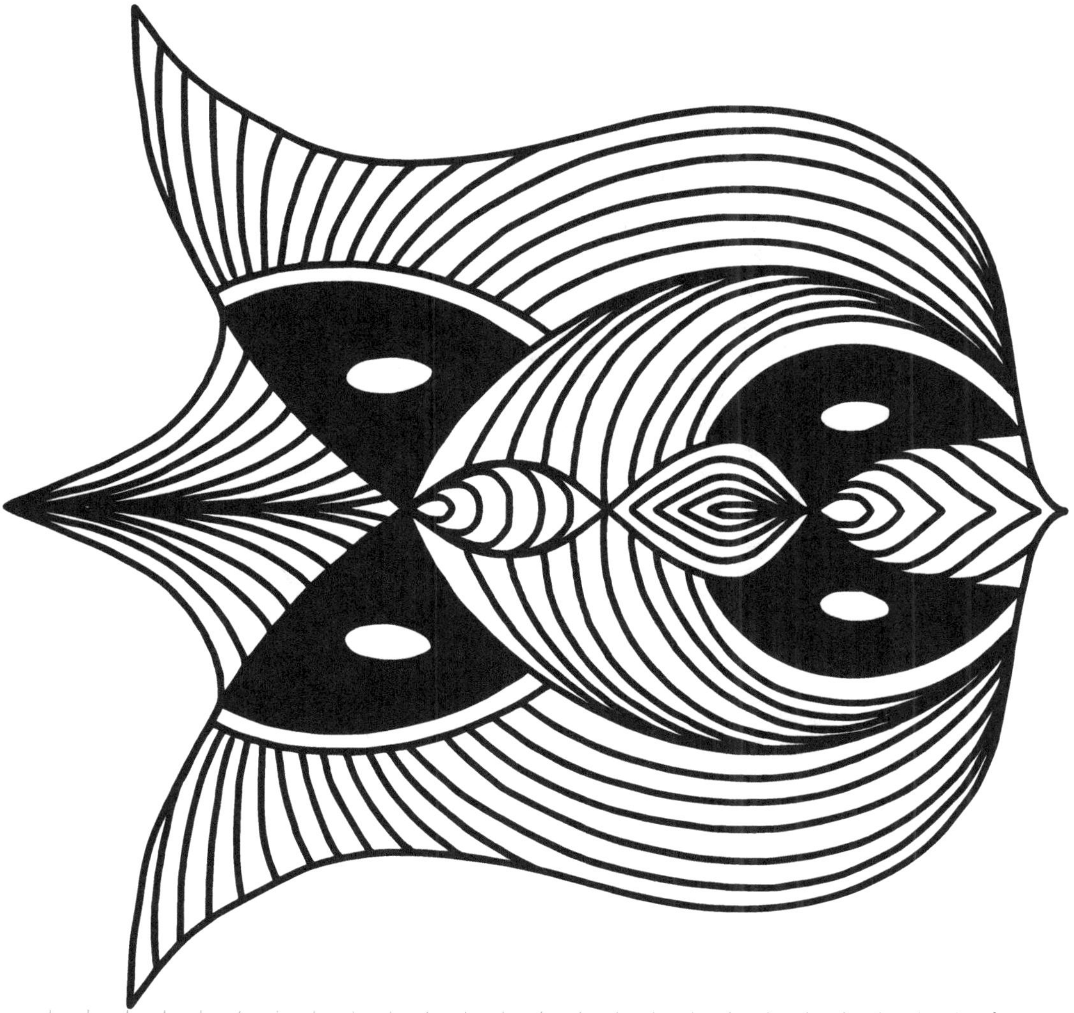

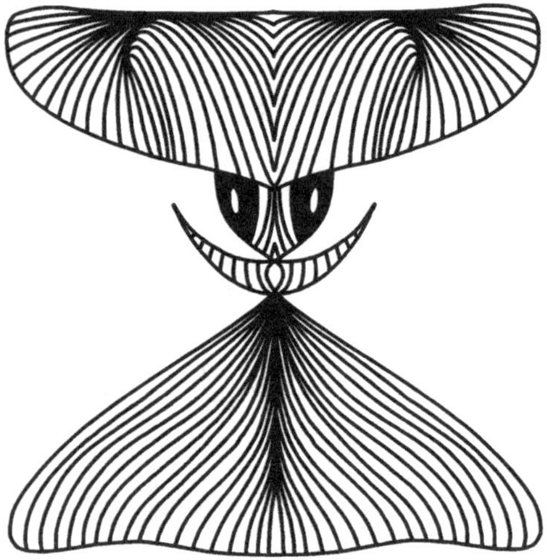

FATLINER WEIRDIES
VOLUME 1

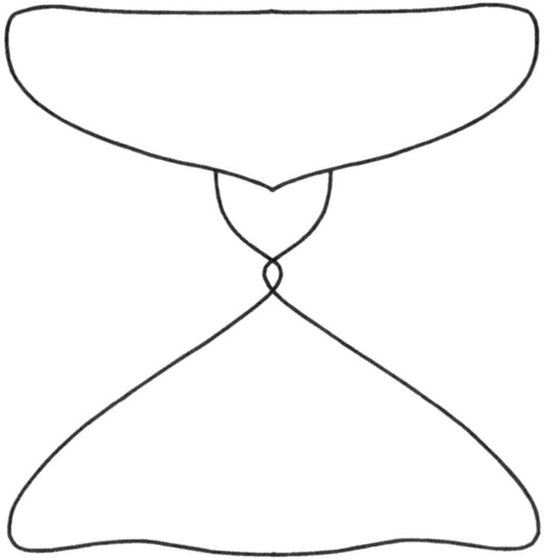

FATLINER WEIRDIES
THE TEMPLATES 1

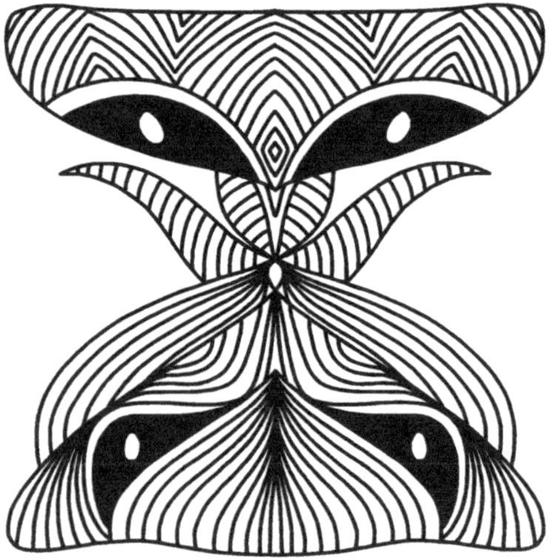

FATLINER WEIRDIES
VOLUME 3

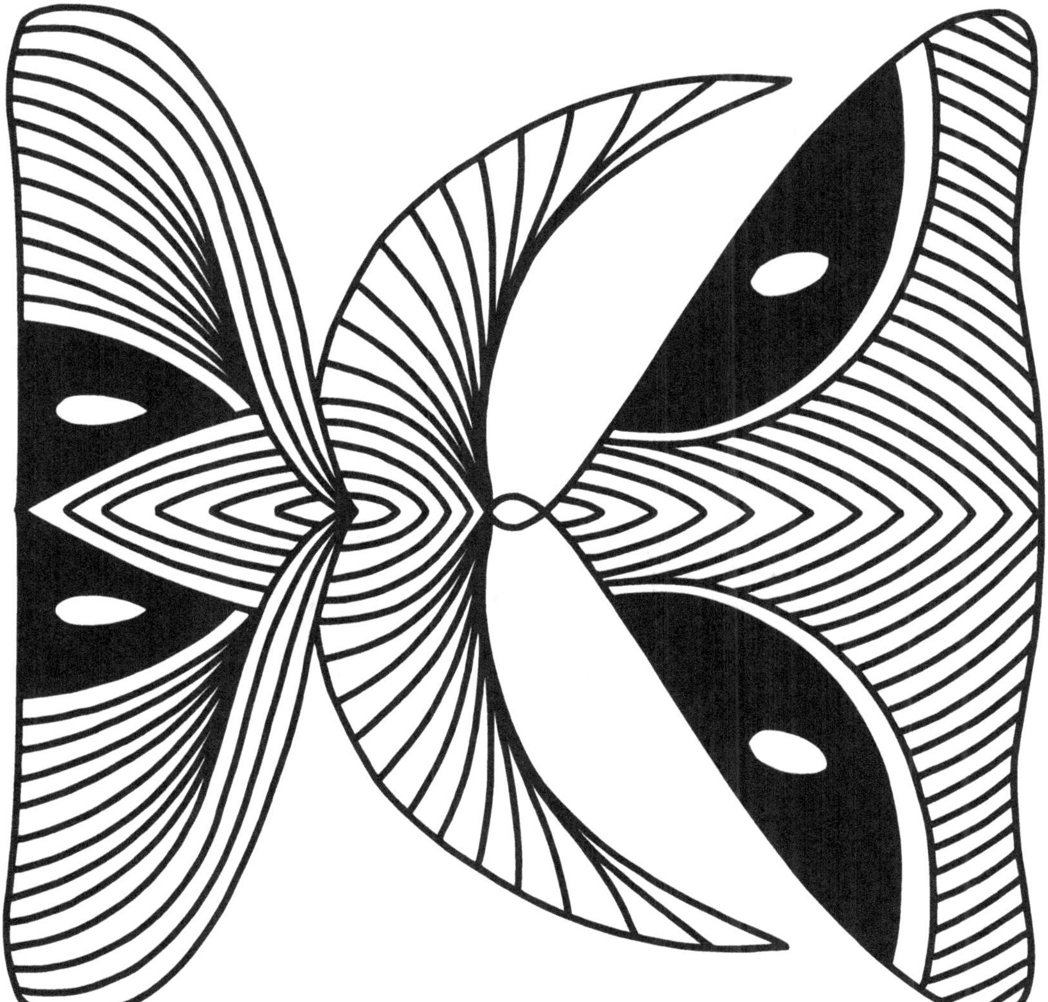

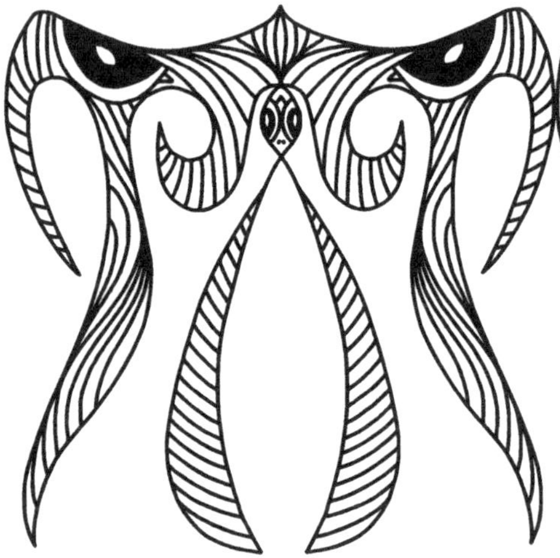

FATLINER WEIRDIES
VOLUME 1

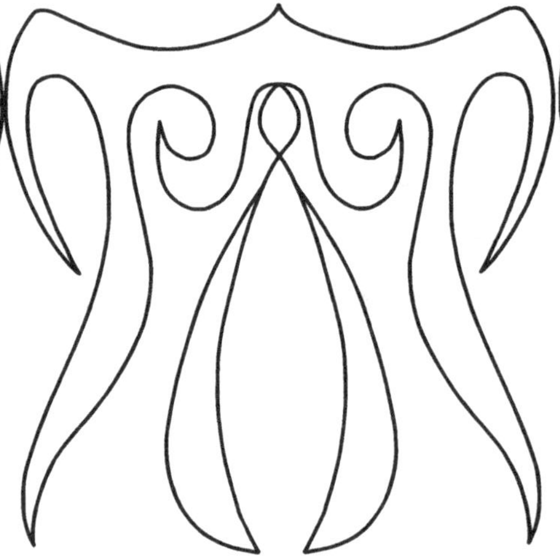

FATLINER WEIRDIES
THE TEMPLATES 1

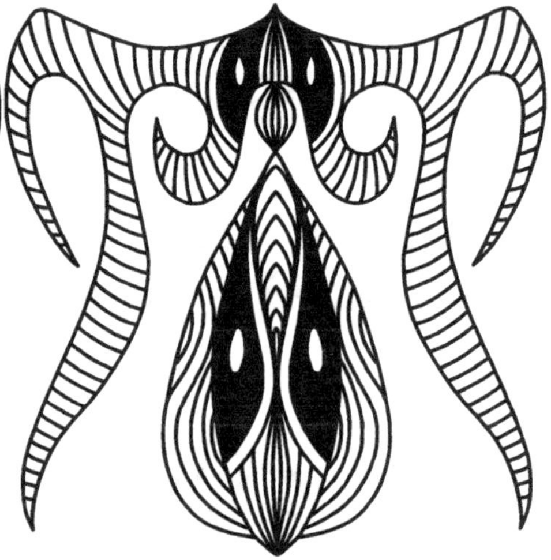

FATLINER WEIRDIES
VOLUME 3

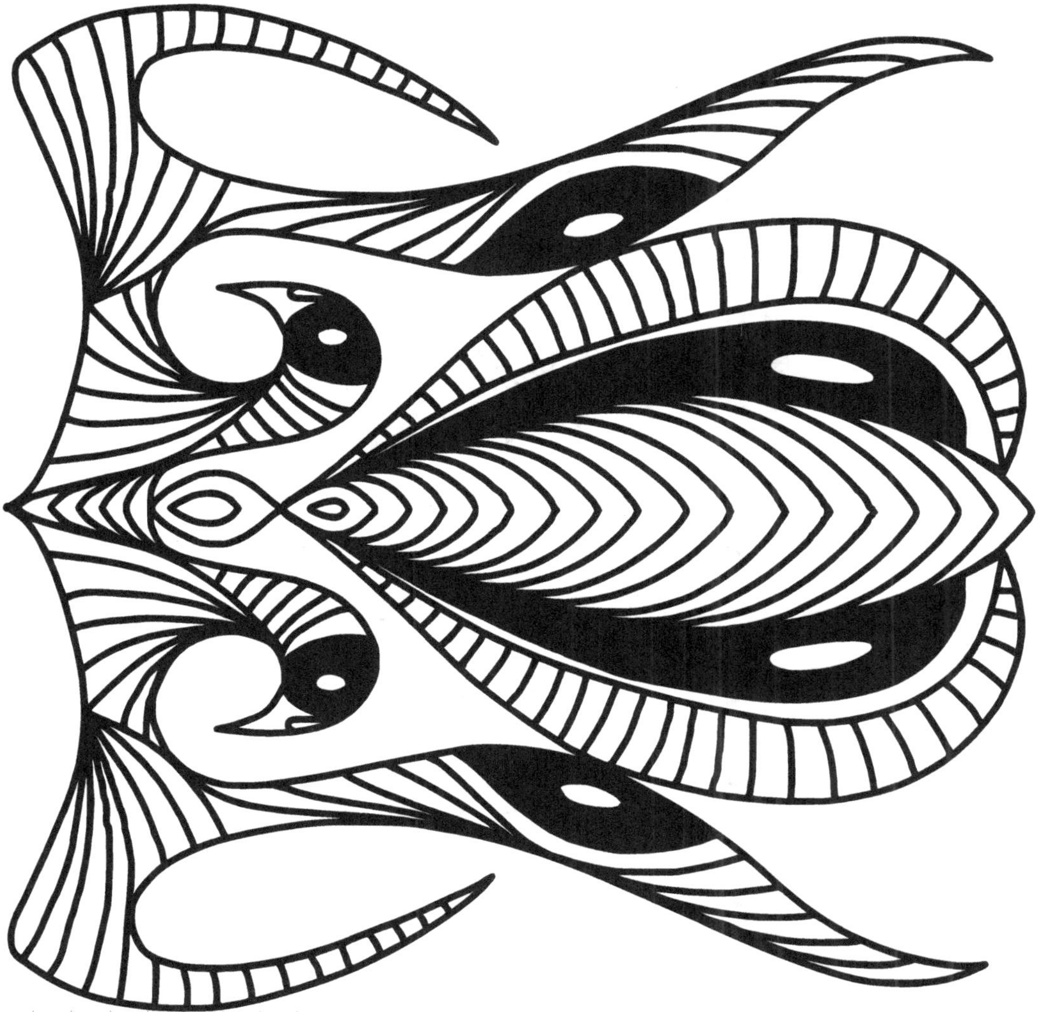

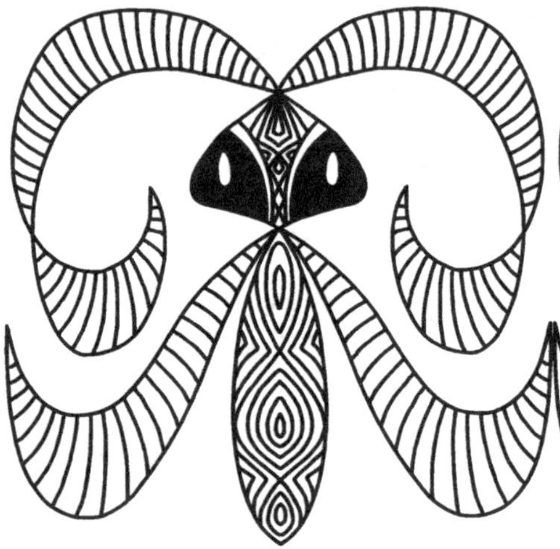

FATLINER WEIRDIES
VOLUME 1

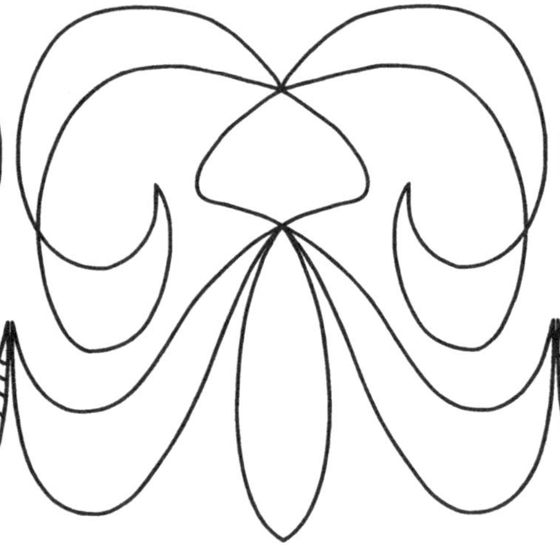

FATLINER WEIRDIES
THE TEMPLATES 1

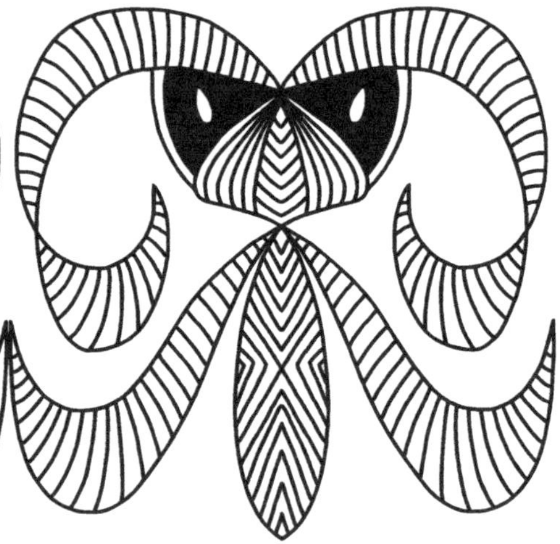

FATLINER WEIRDIES
VOLUME 3

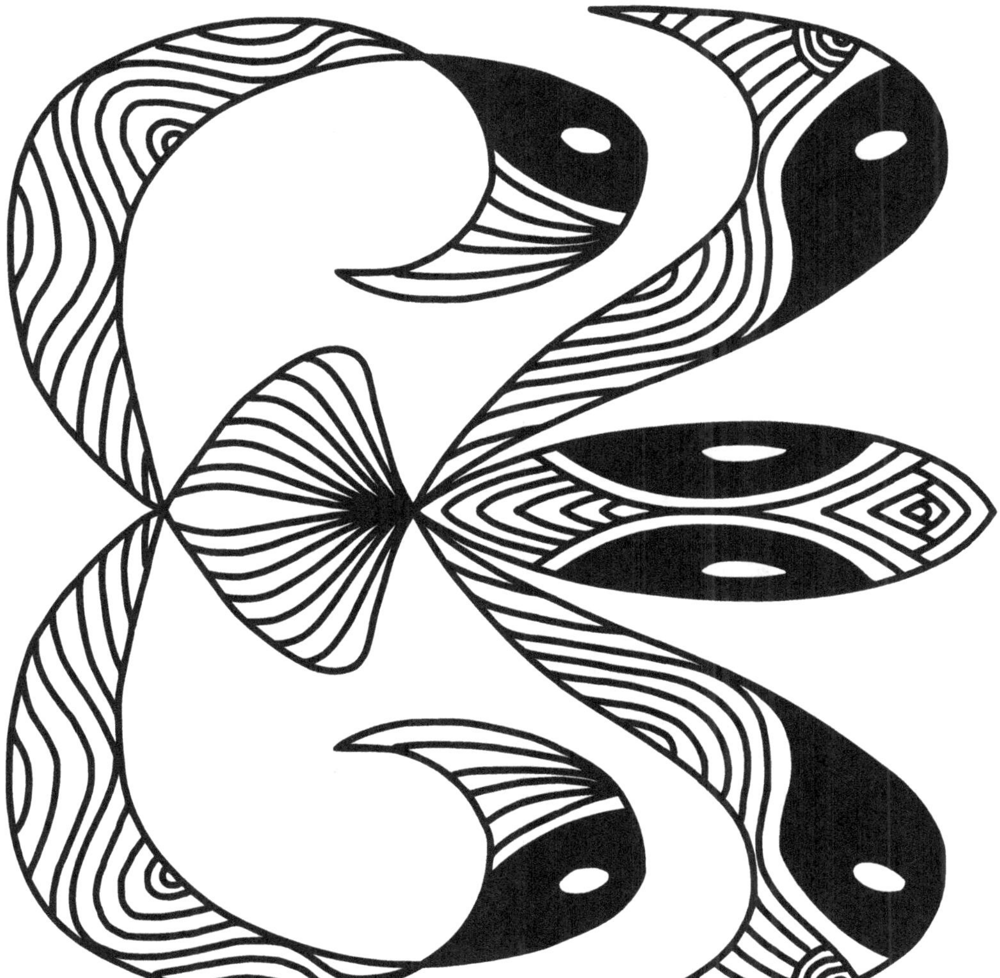

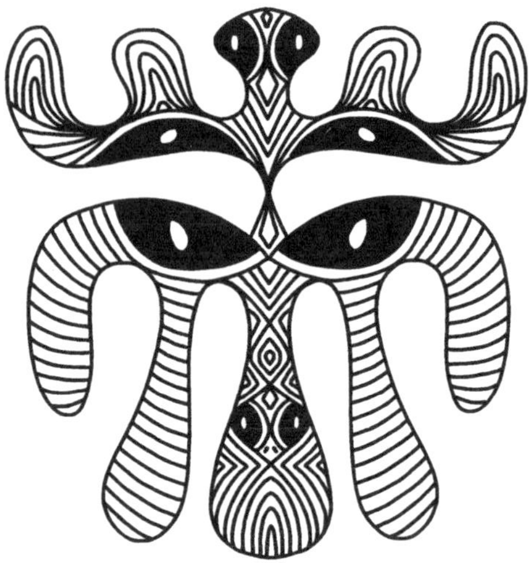

FATLINER WEIRDIES
VOLUME 1

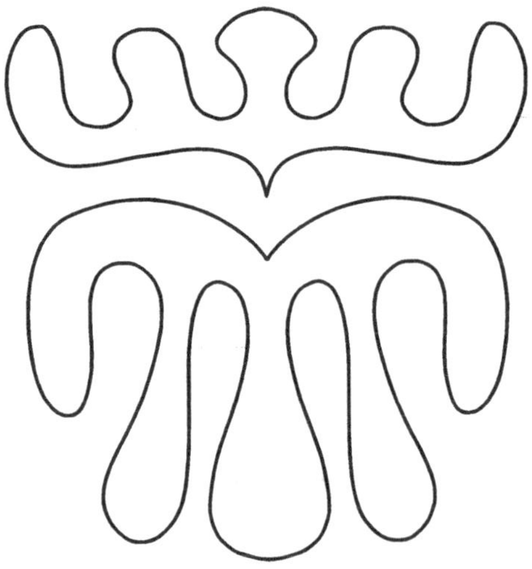

FATLINER WEIRDIES
THE TEMPLATES 1

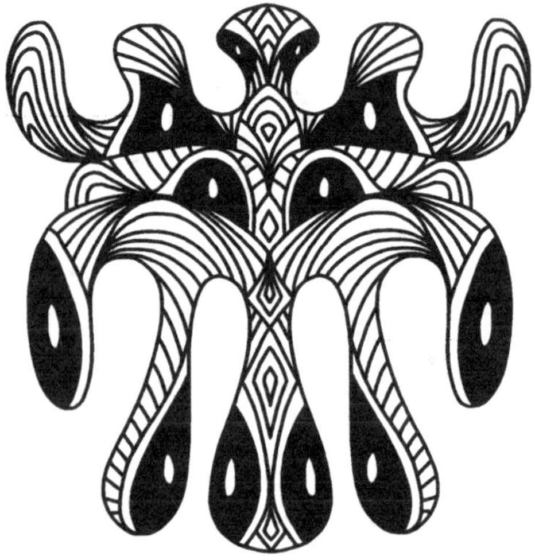

FATLINER WEIRDIES
VOLUME 3

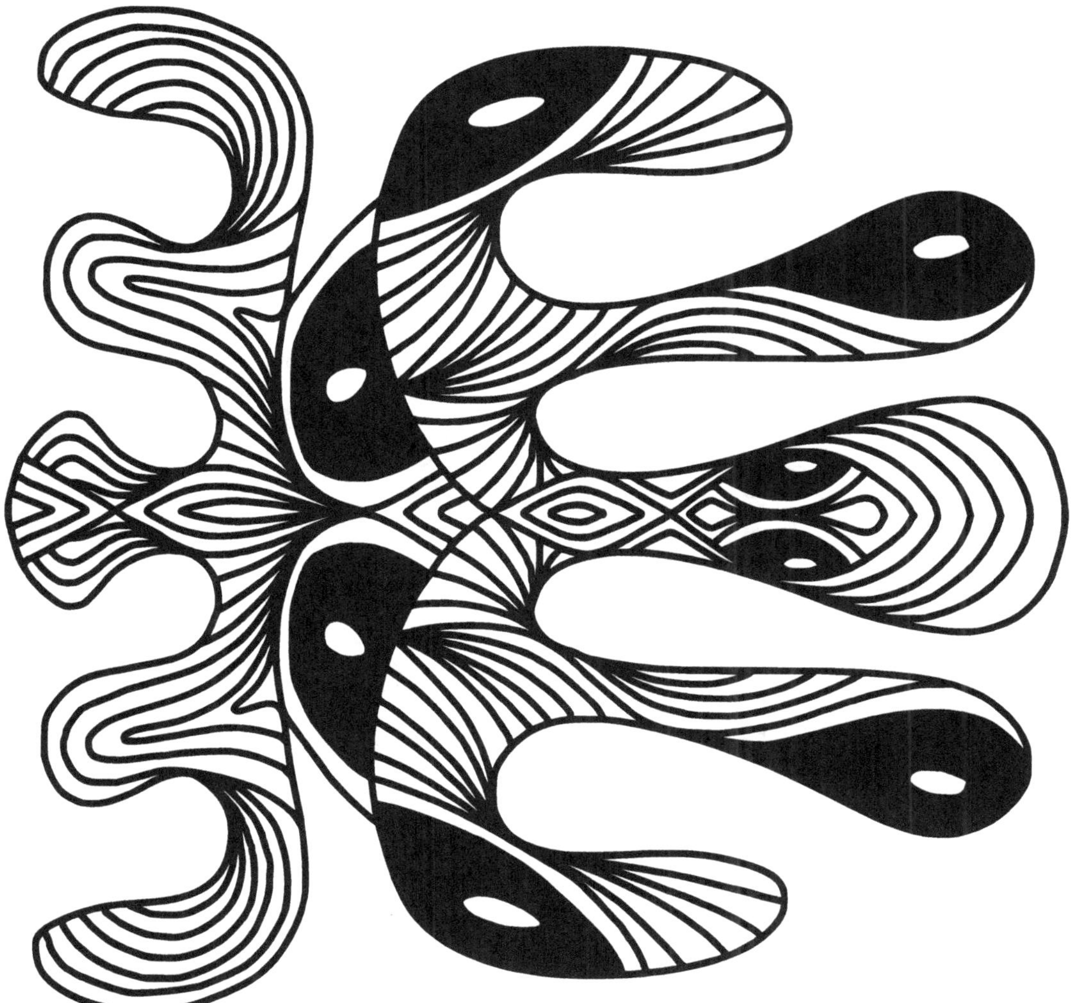

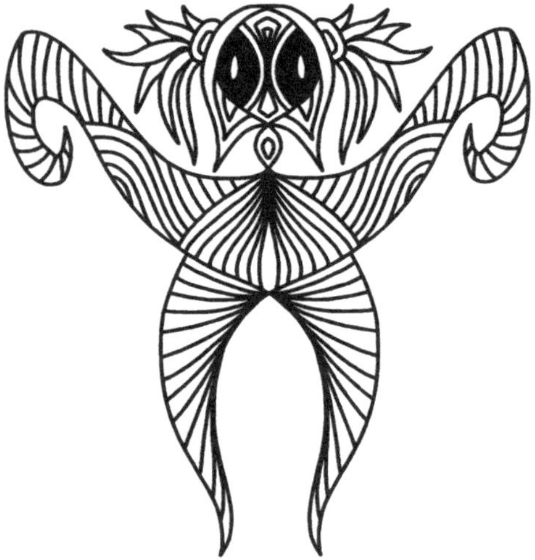

FATLINER WEIRDIES
VOLUME 1

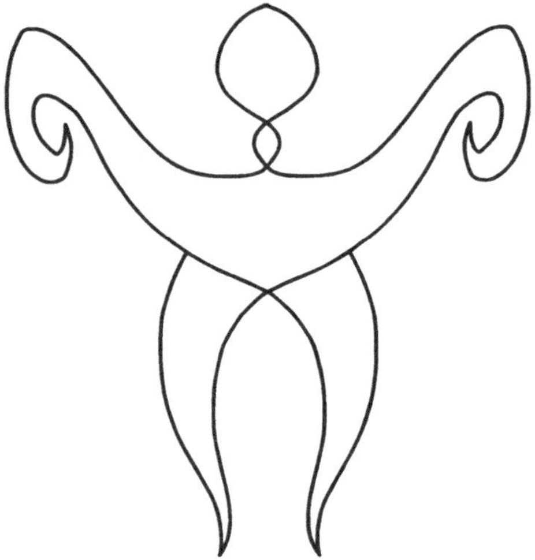

FATLINER WEIRDIES
THE TEMPLATES 1

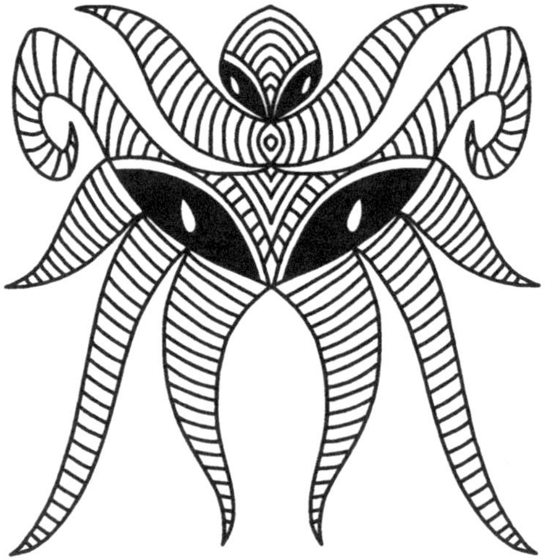

FATLINER WEIRDIES
VOLUME 3

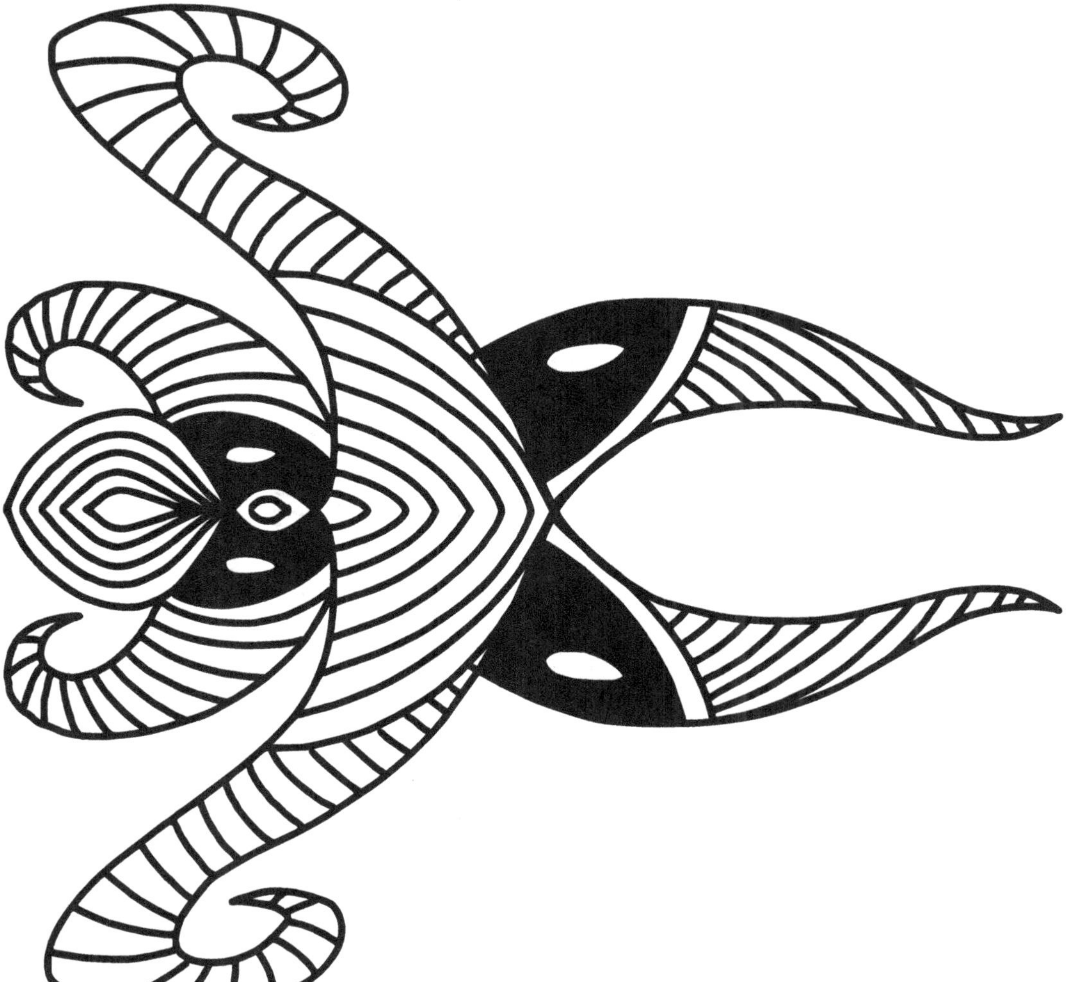

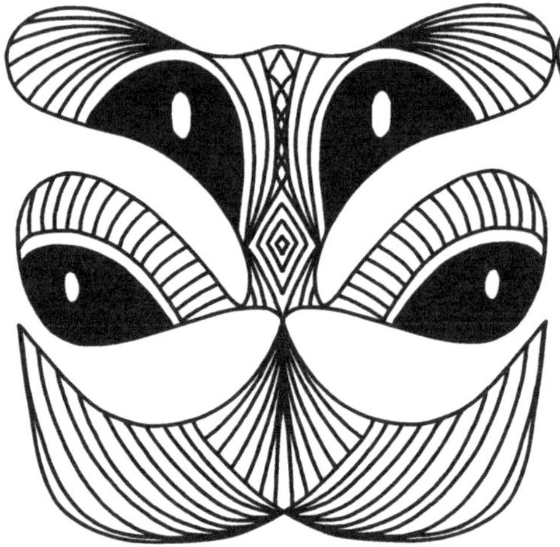

FATLINER WEIRDIES
VOLUME 1

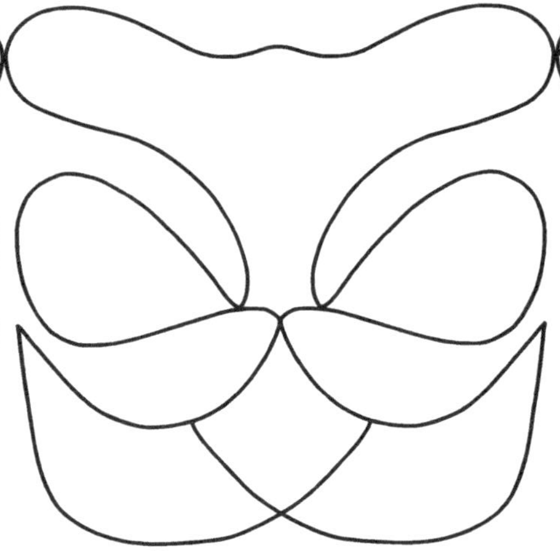

FATLINER WEIRDIES
THE TEMPLATES 1

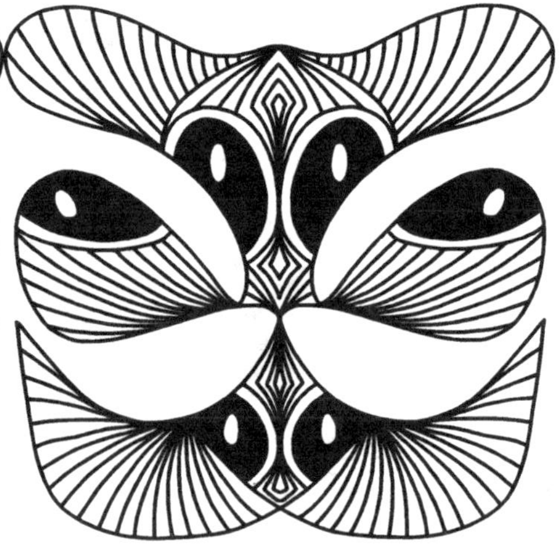

FATLINER WEIRDIES
VOLUME 3

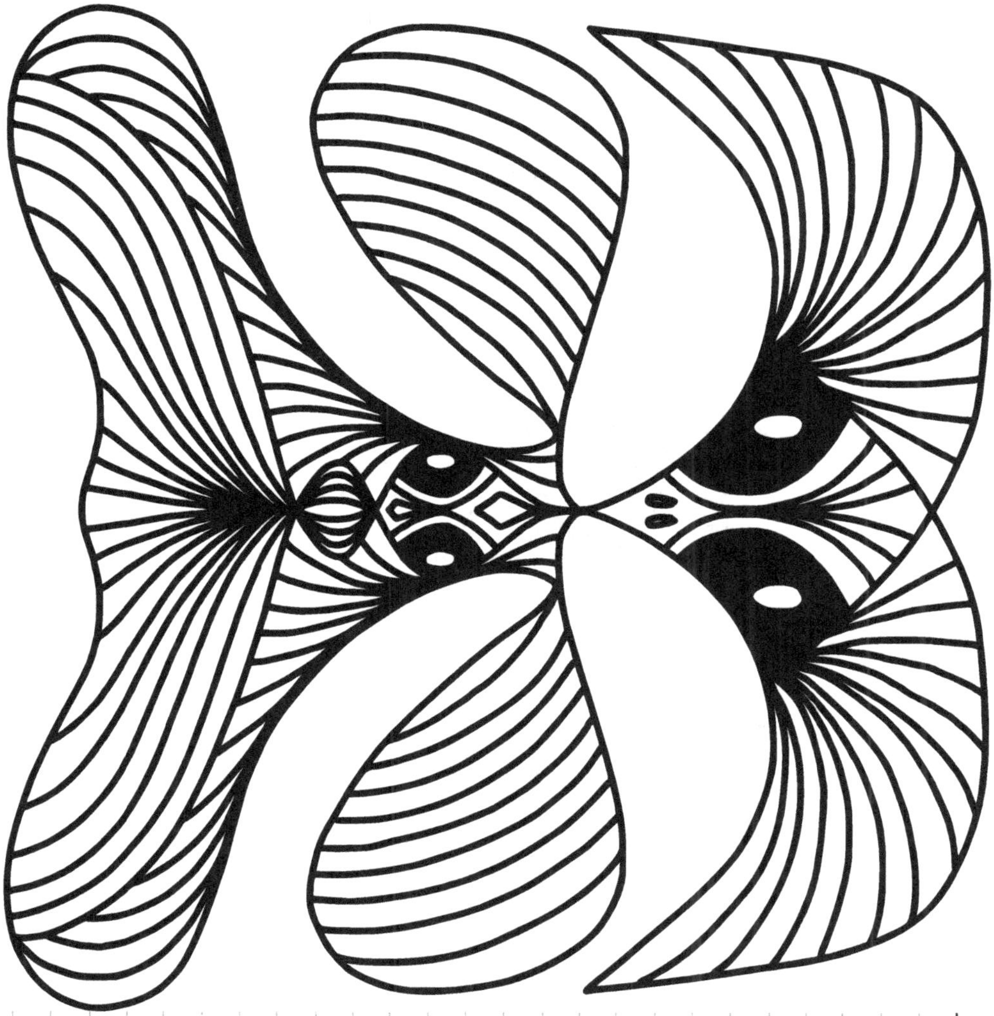

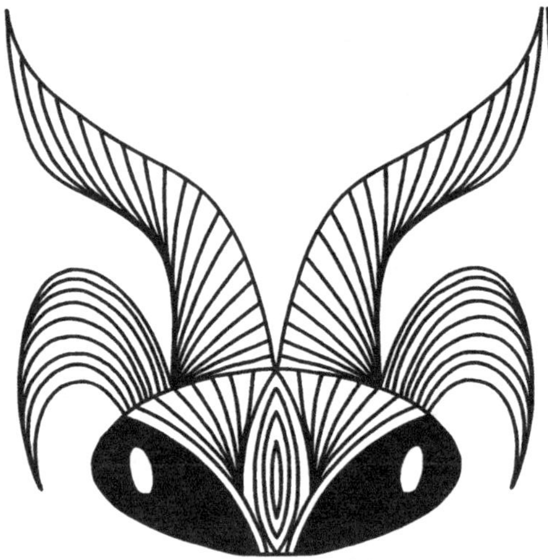

FATLINER WEIRDIES
VOLUME 1

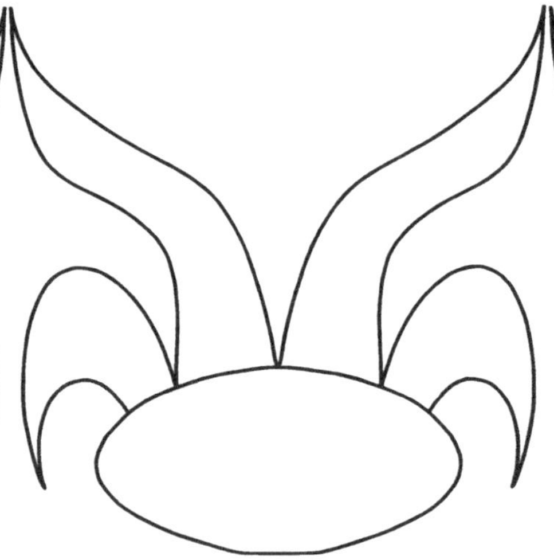

FATLINER WEIRDIES
THE TEMPLATES 1

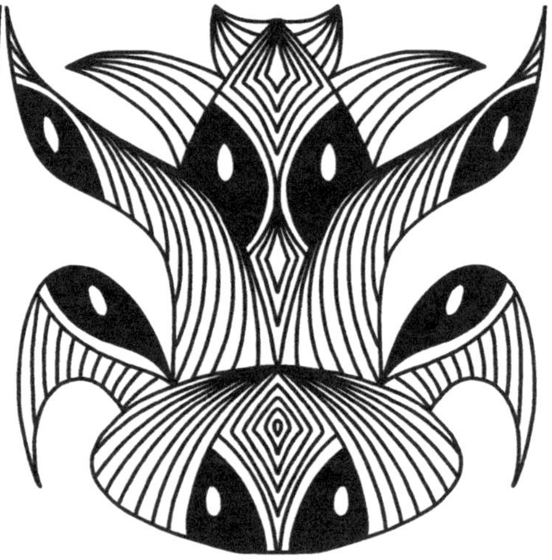

FATLINER WEIRDIES
VOLUME 3

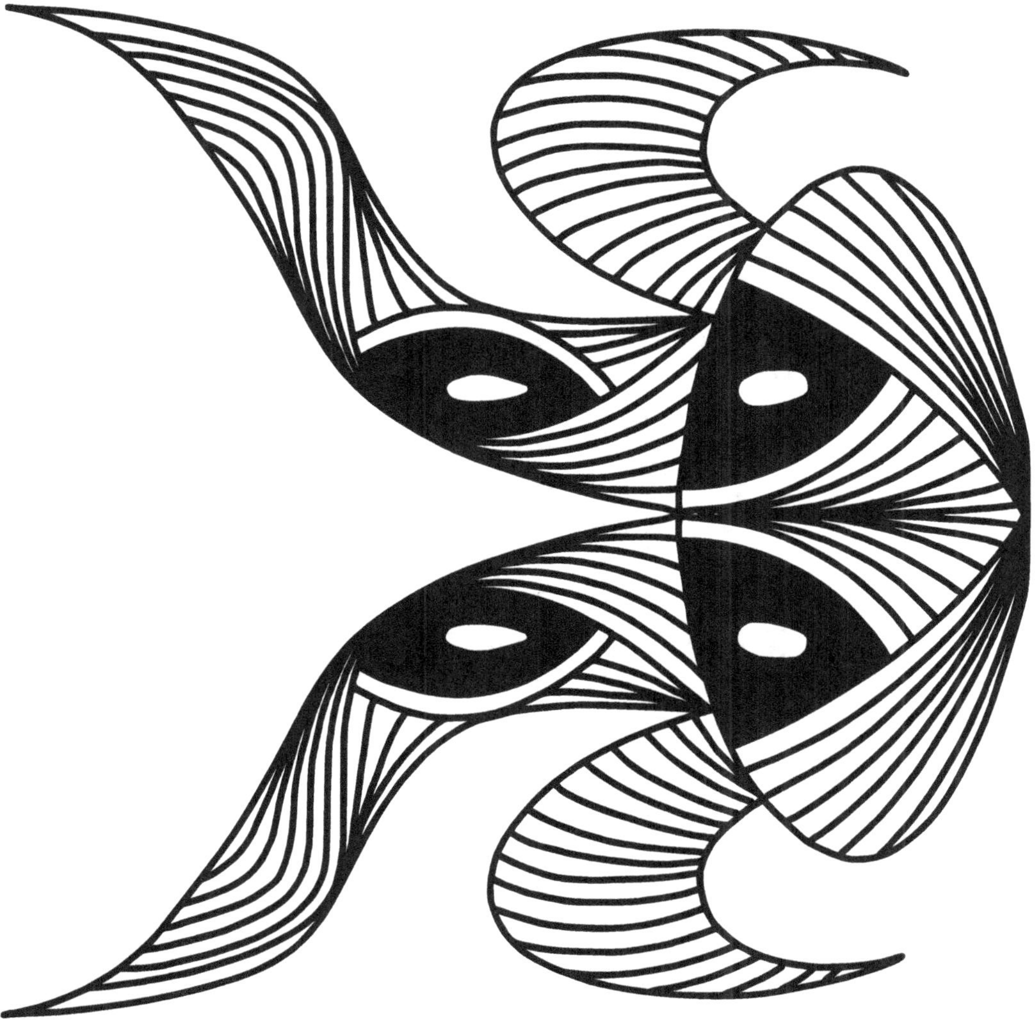

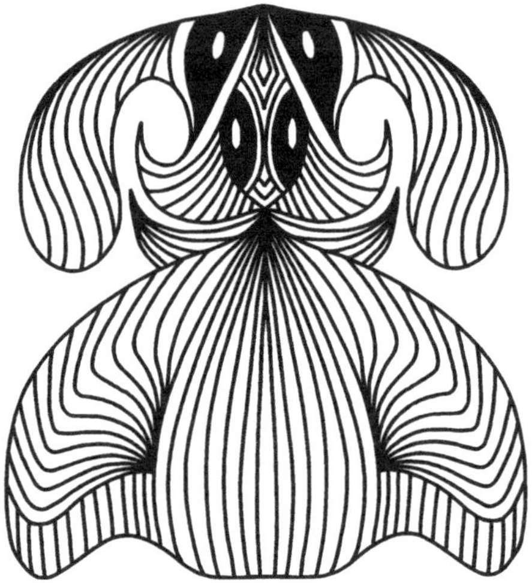

FATLINER WEIRDIES
VOLUME 1

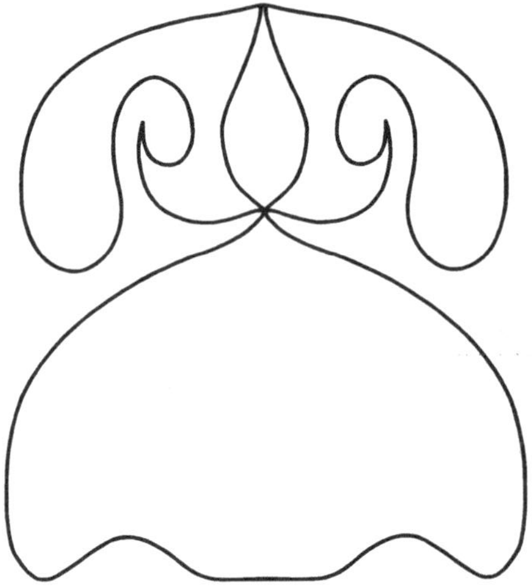

FATLINER WEIRDIES
THE TEMPLATES 1

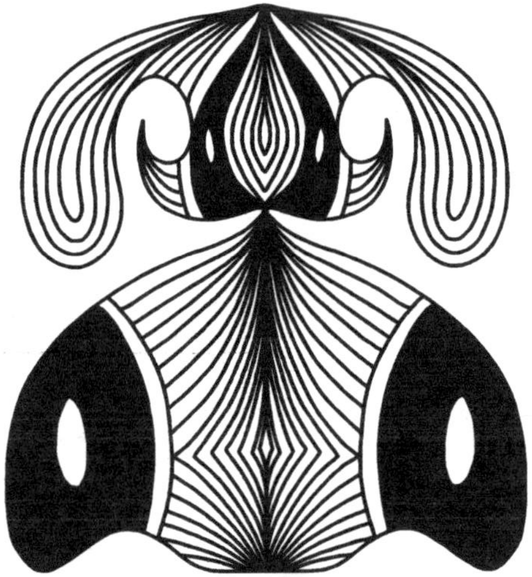

FATLINER WEIRDIES
VOLUME 3

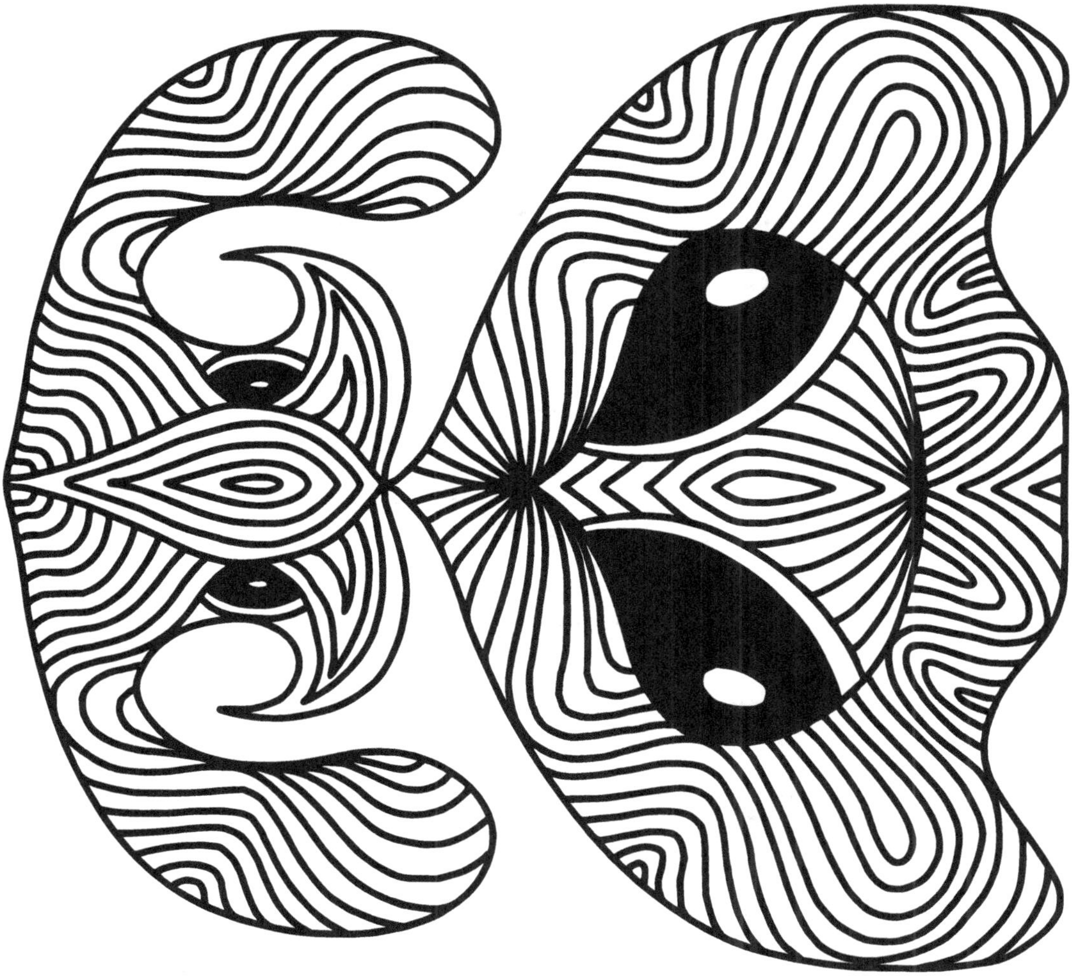

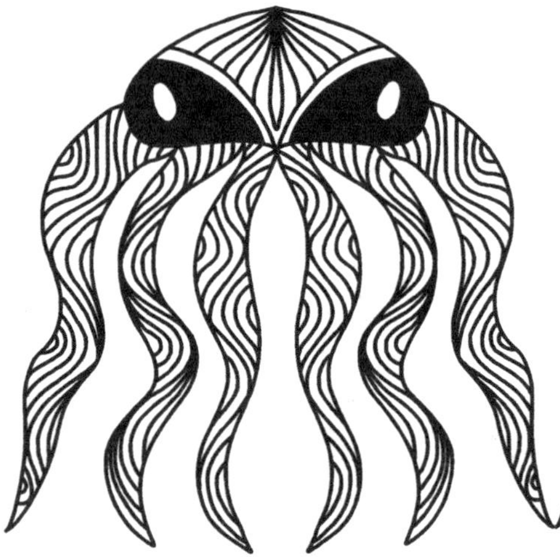

FATLINER WEIRDIES
VOLUME 1

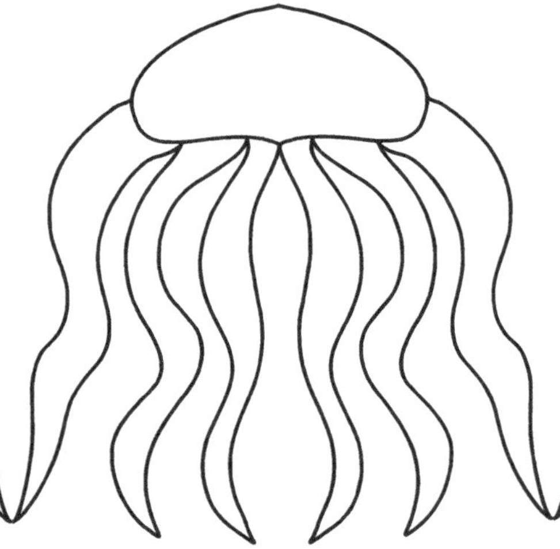

FATLINER WEIRDIES
THE TEMPLATES 1

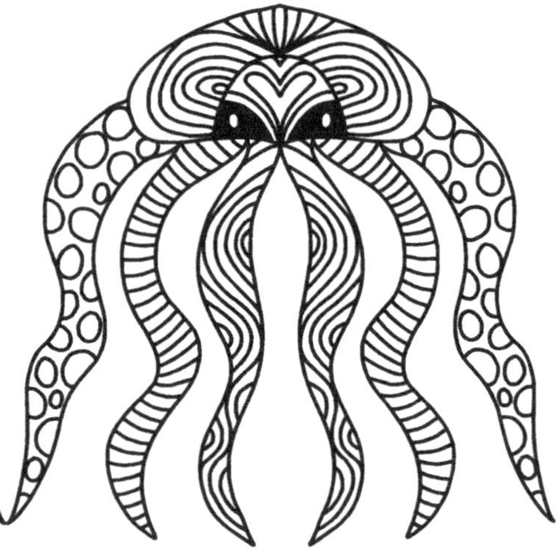

FATLINER WEIRDIES
VOLUME 3

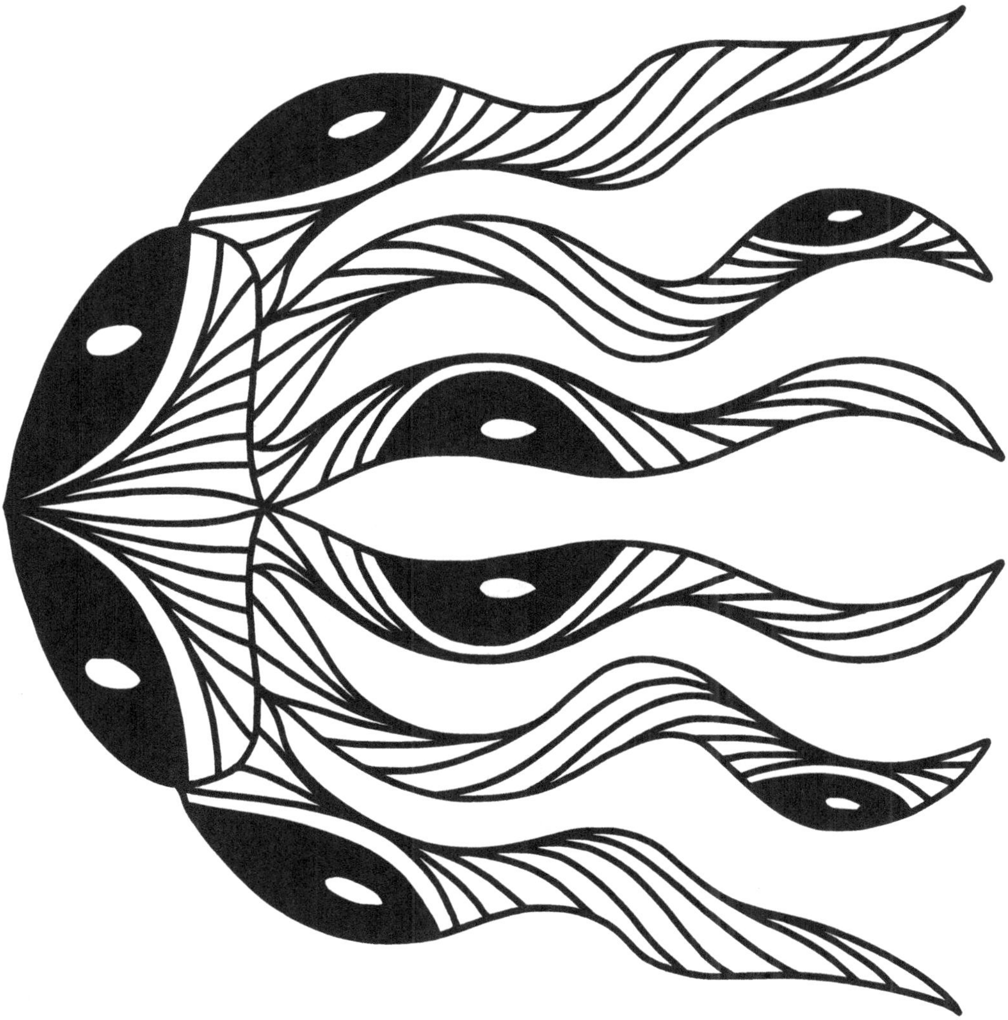

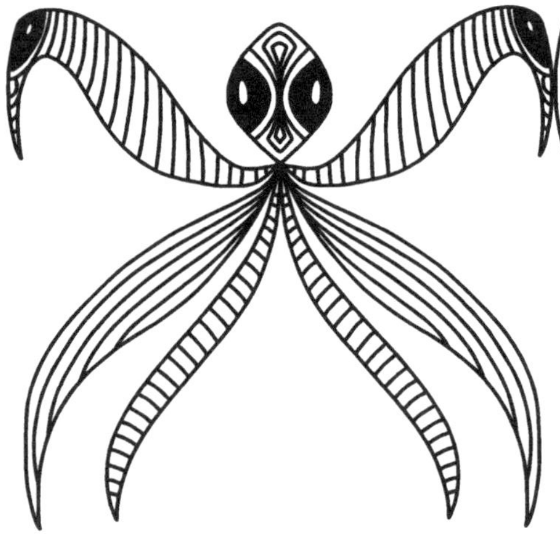

FATLINER WEIRDIES
VOLUME 1

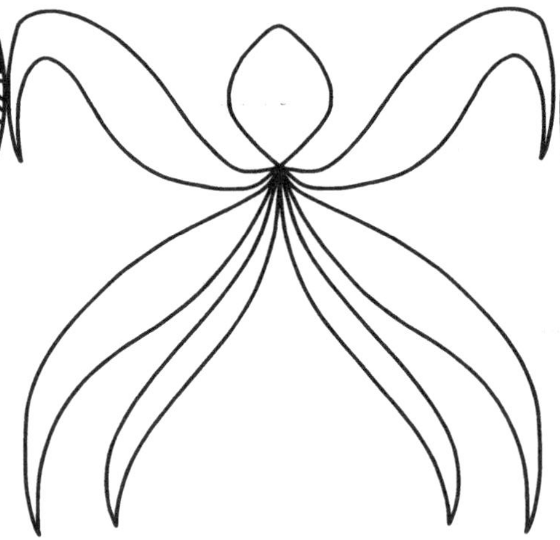

FATLINER WEIRDIES
THE TEMPLATES 1

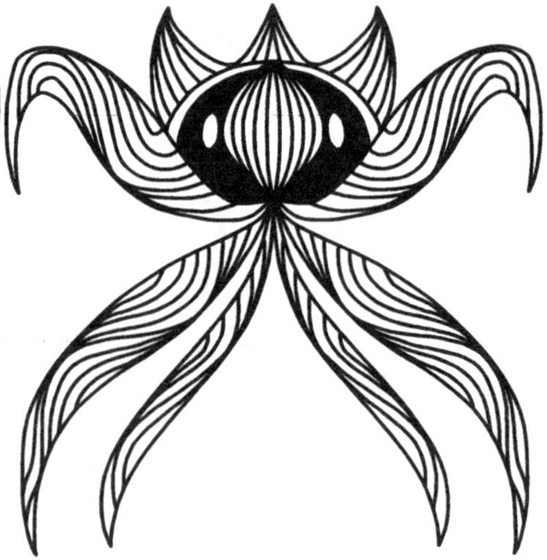

FATLINER WEIRDIES
VOLUME 3

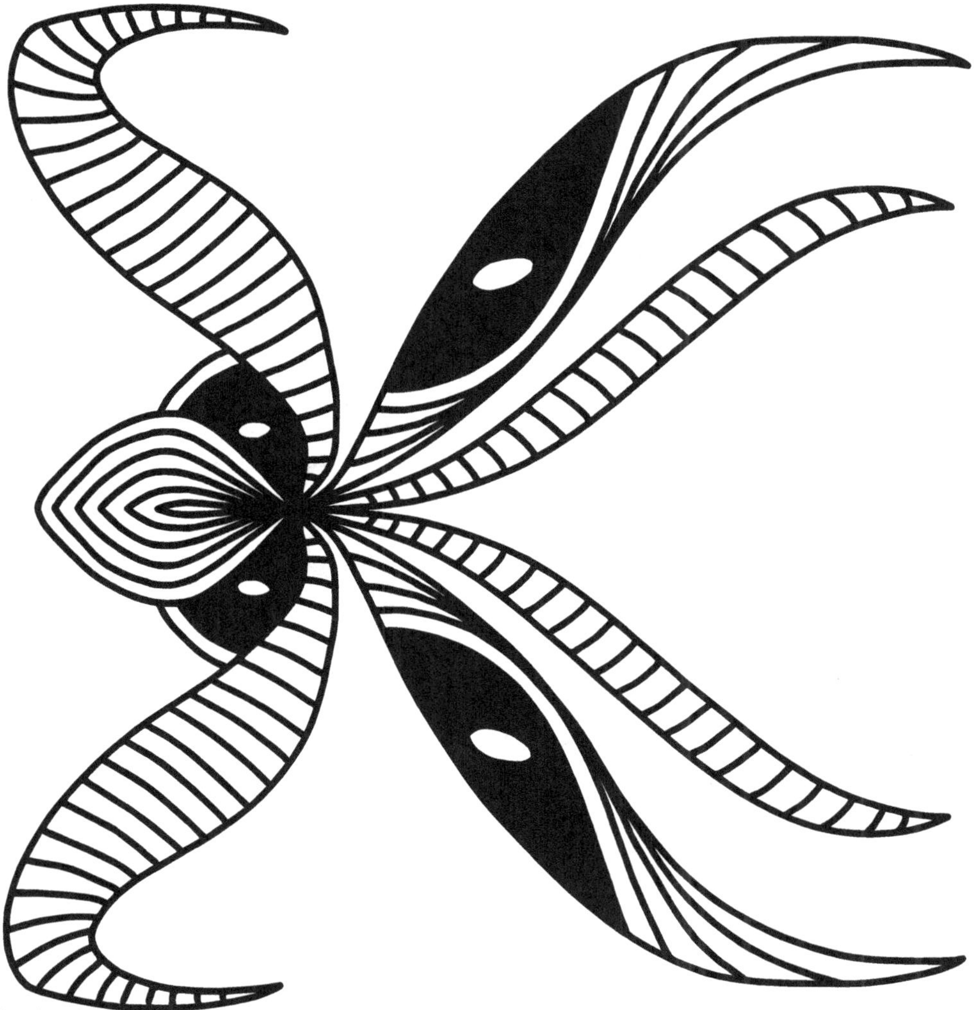

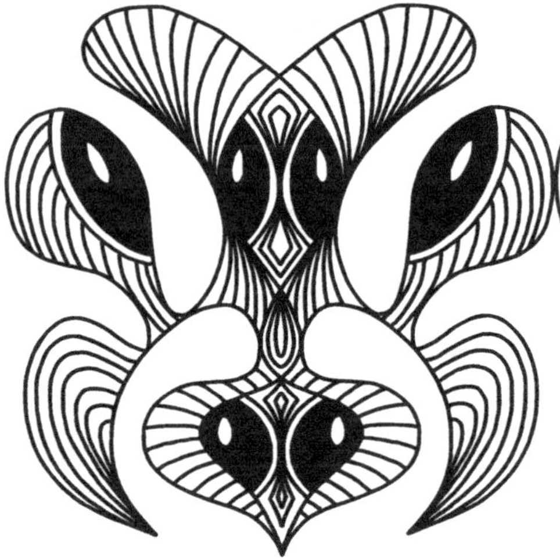

FATLINER WEIRDIES
VOLUME 1

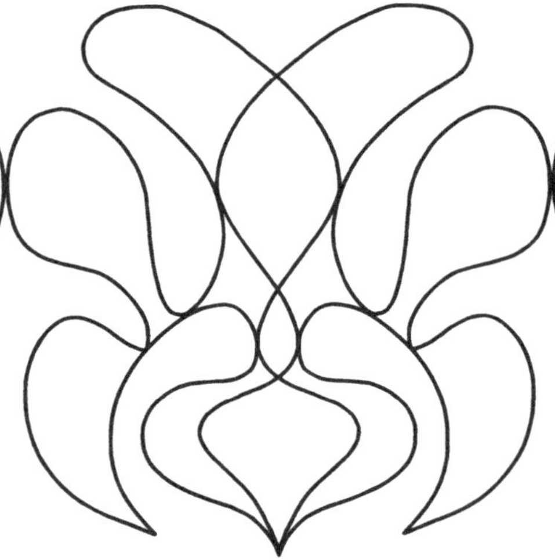

FATLINER WEIRDIES
THE TEMPLATES 1

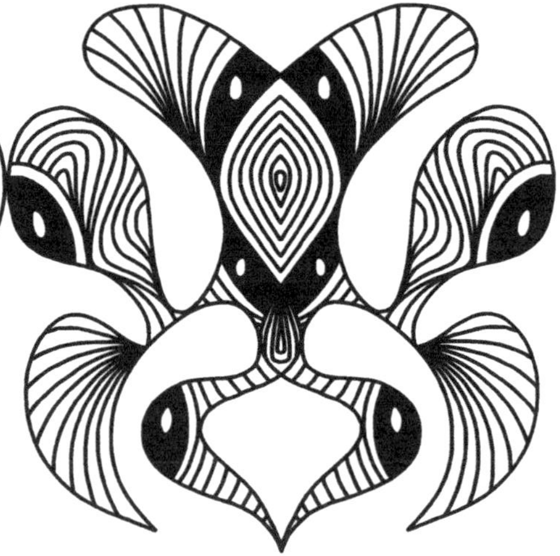

FATLINER WEIRDIES
VOLUME 3

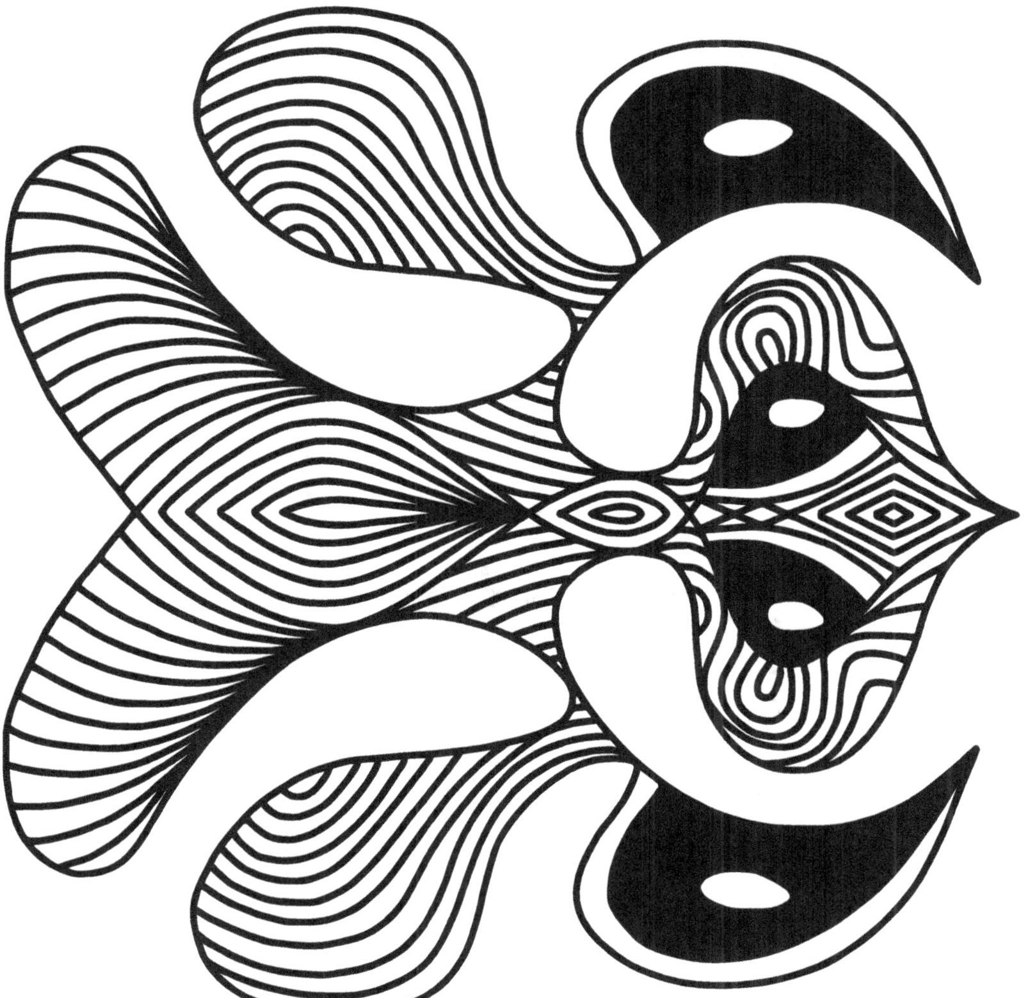

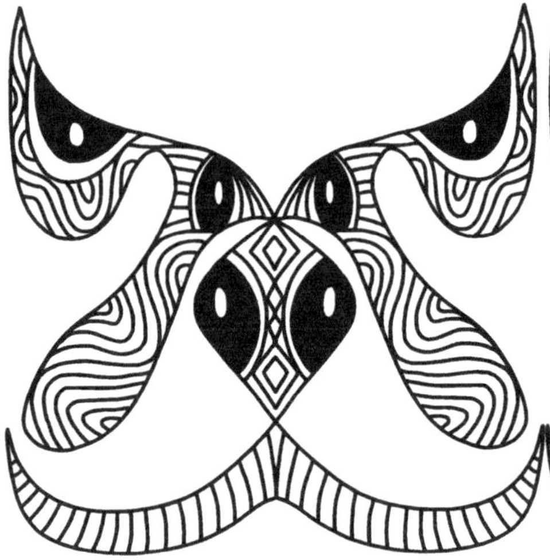

FATLINER WEIRDIES
VOLUME 1

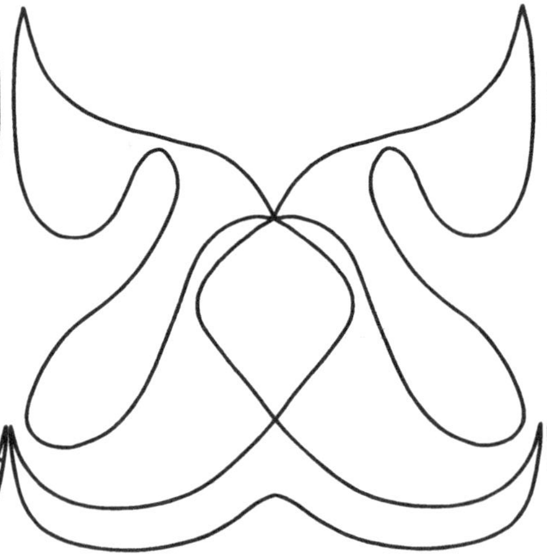

FATLINER WEIRDIES
THE TEMPLATES 1

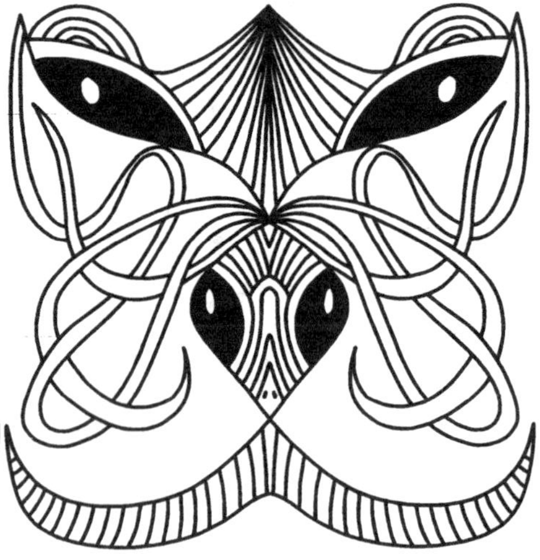

FATLINER WEIRDIES
VOLUME 3

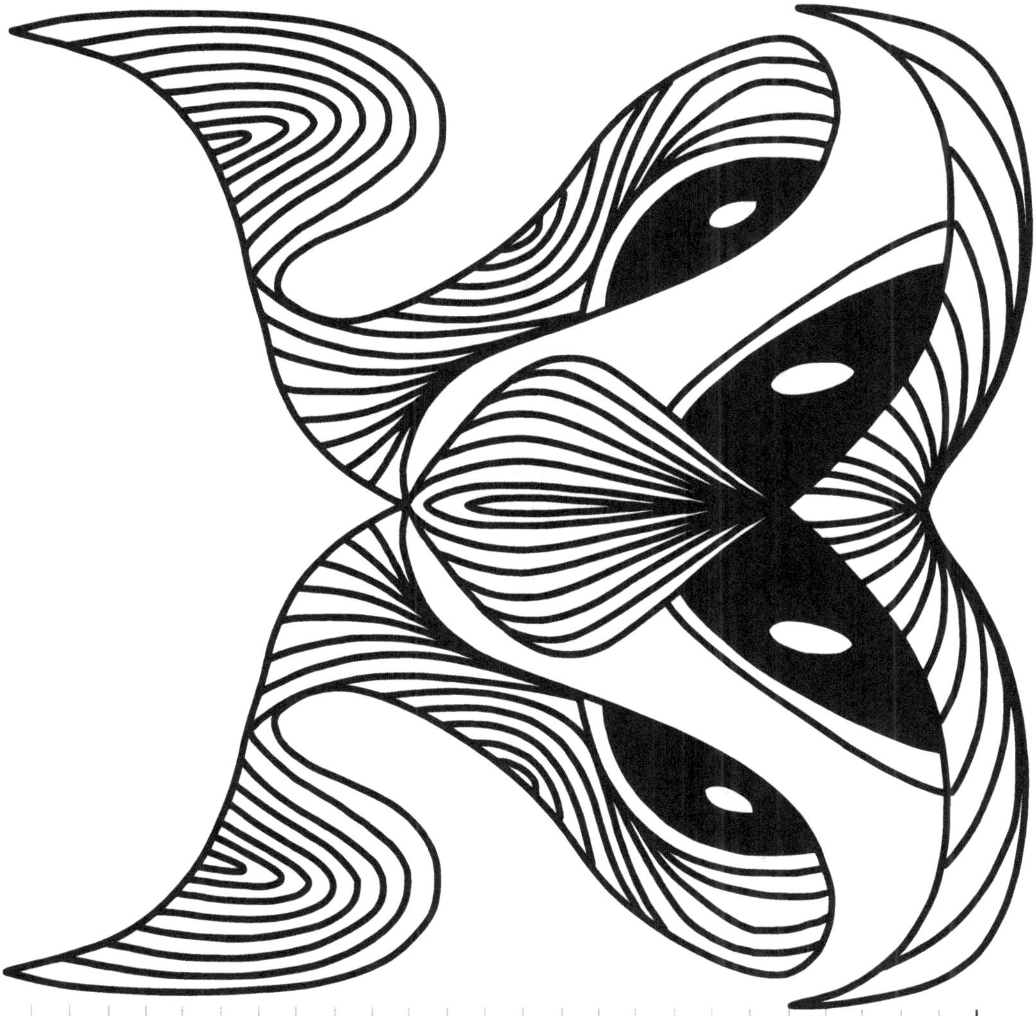

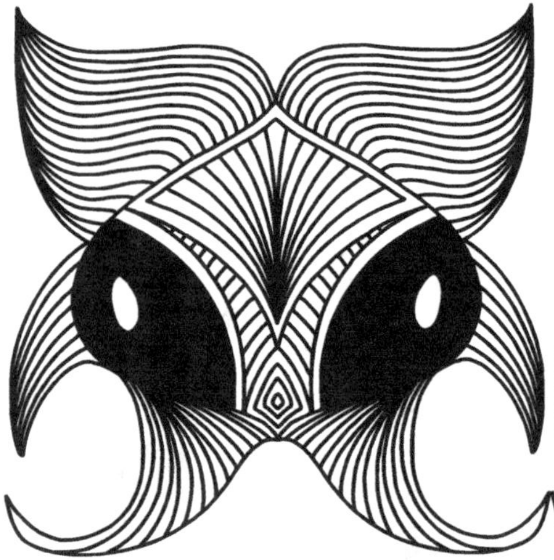

FATLINER WEIRDIES
VOLUME 1

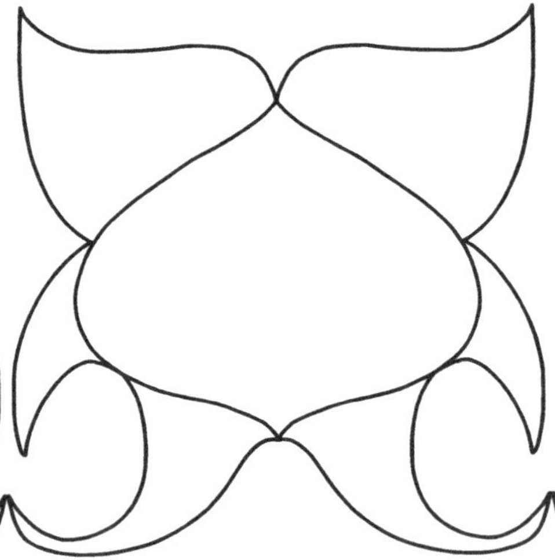

FATLINER WEIRDIES
THE TEMPLATES 1

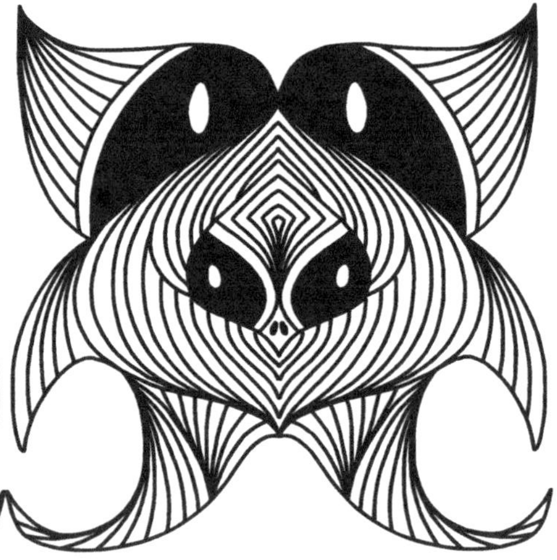

FATLINER WEIRDIES
VOLUME 3

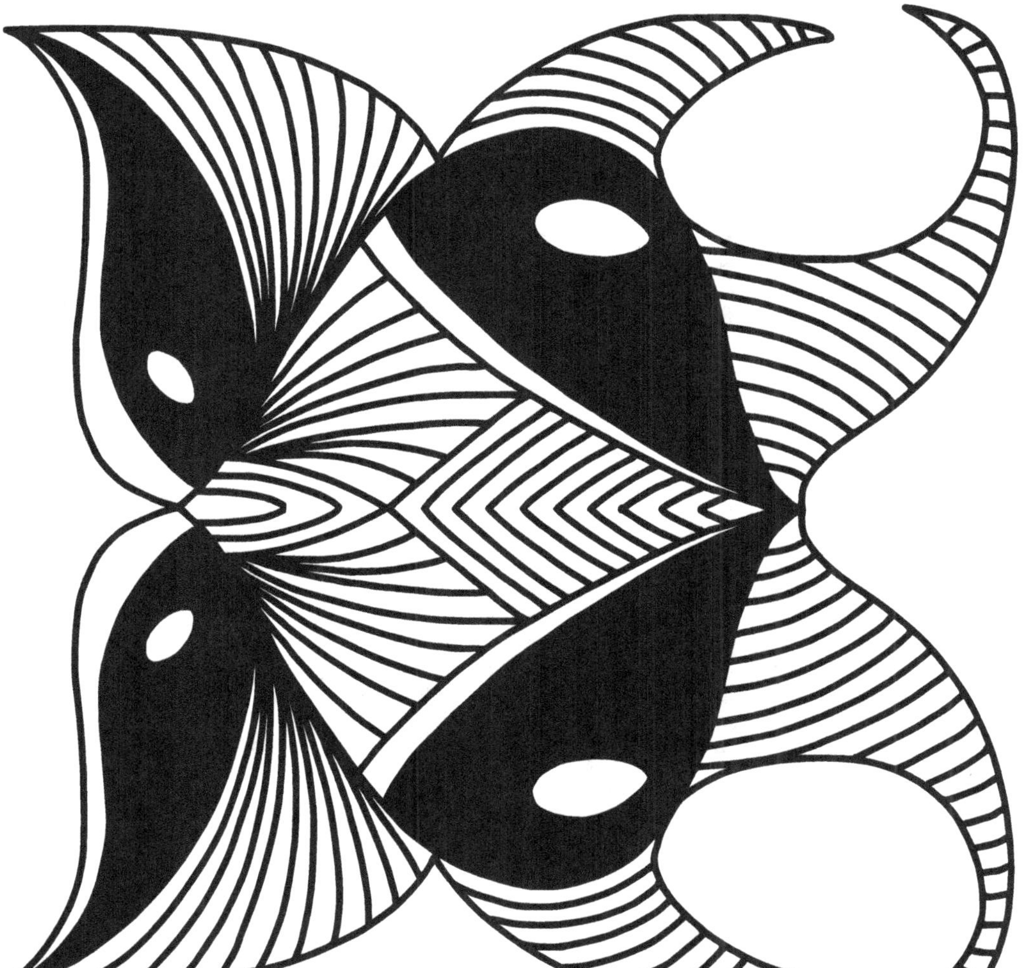

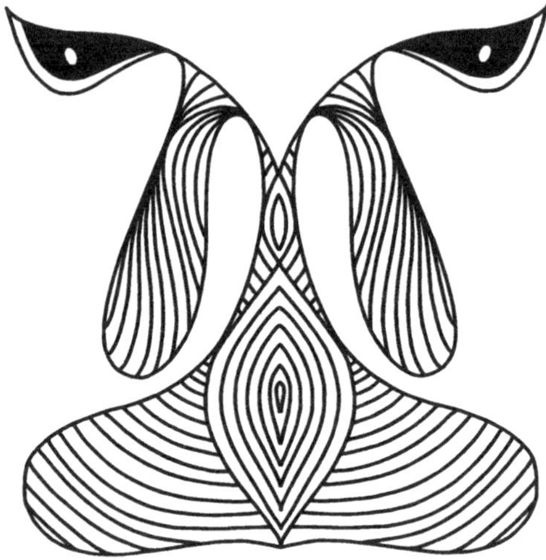

FATLINER WEIRDIES
VOLUME 1

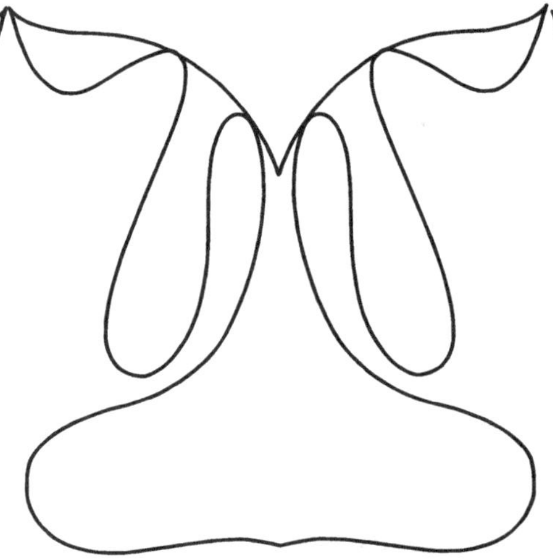

FATLINER WEIRDIES
THE TEMPLATES 1

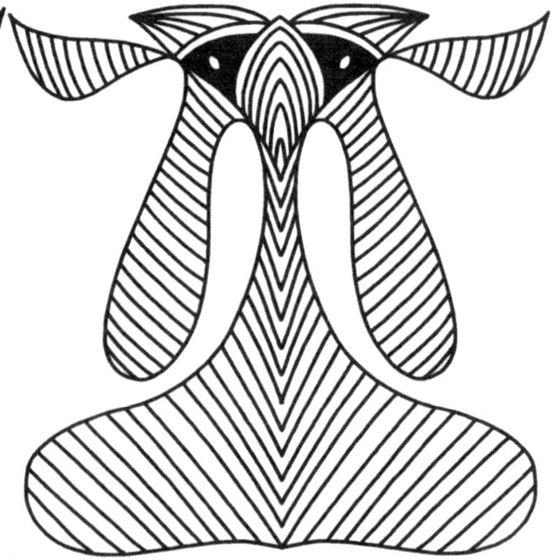

FATLINER WEIRDIES
VOLUME 3

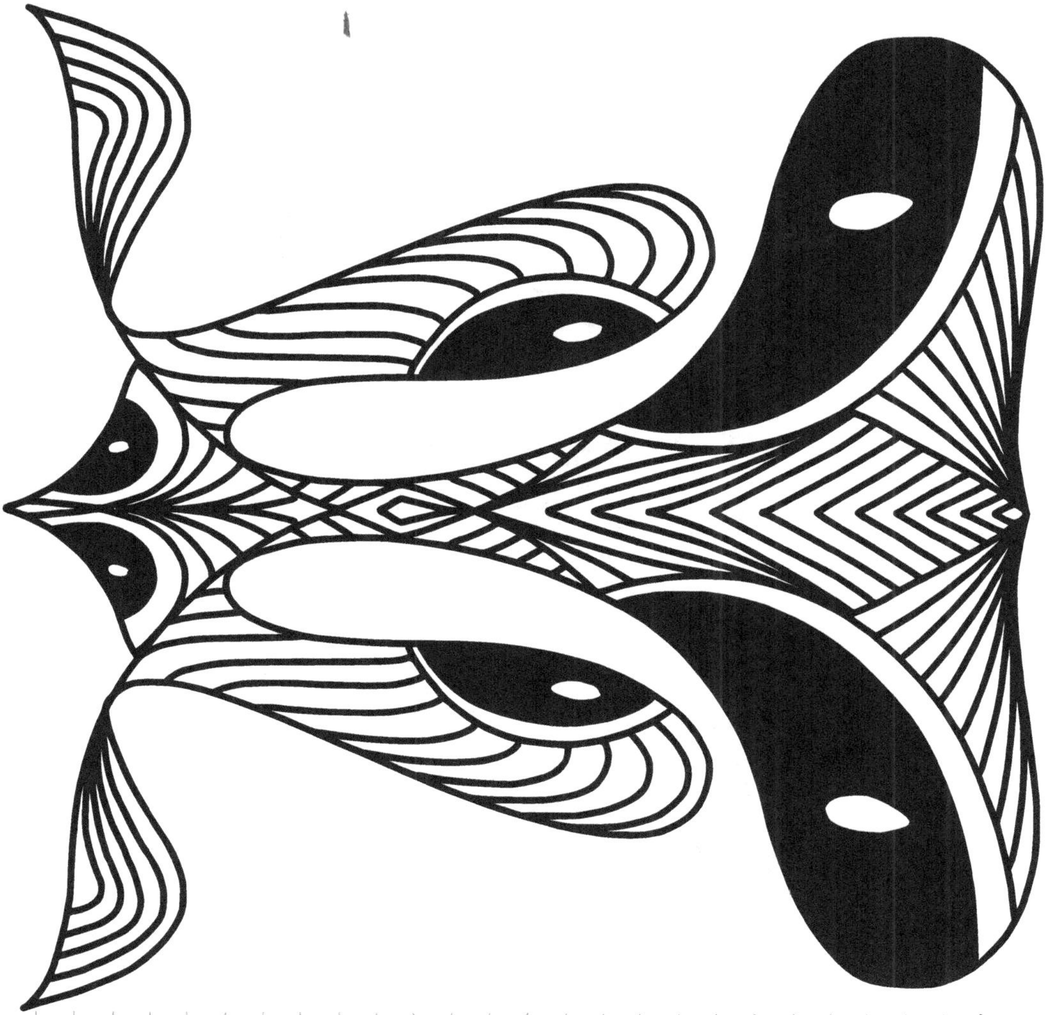

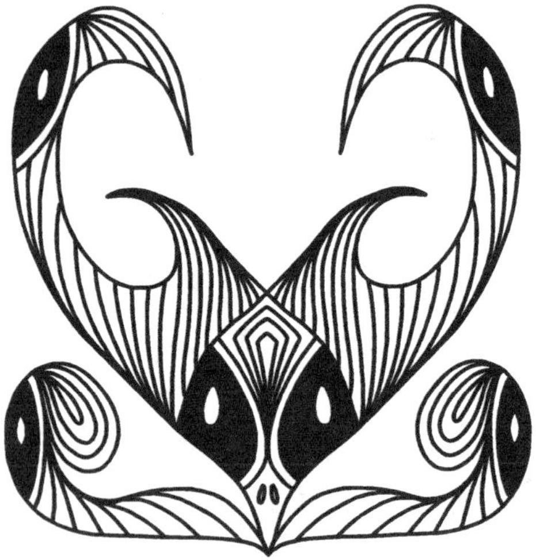

FATLINER WEIRDIES
VOLUME 1

FATLINER WEIRDIES
THE TEMPLATES 1

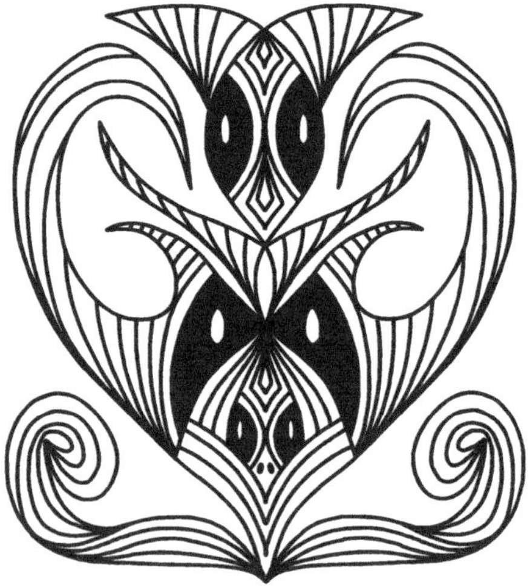

FATLINER WEIRDIES
VOLUME 3

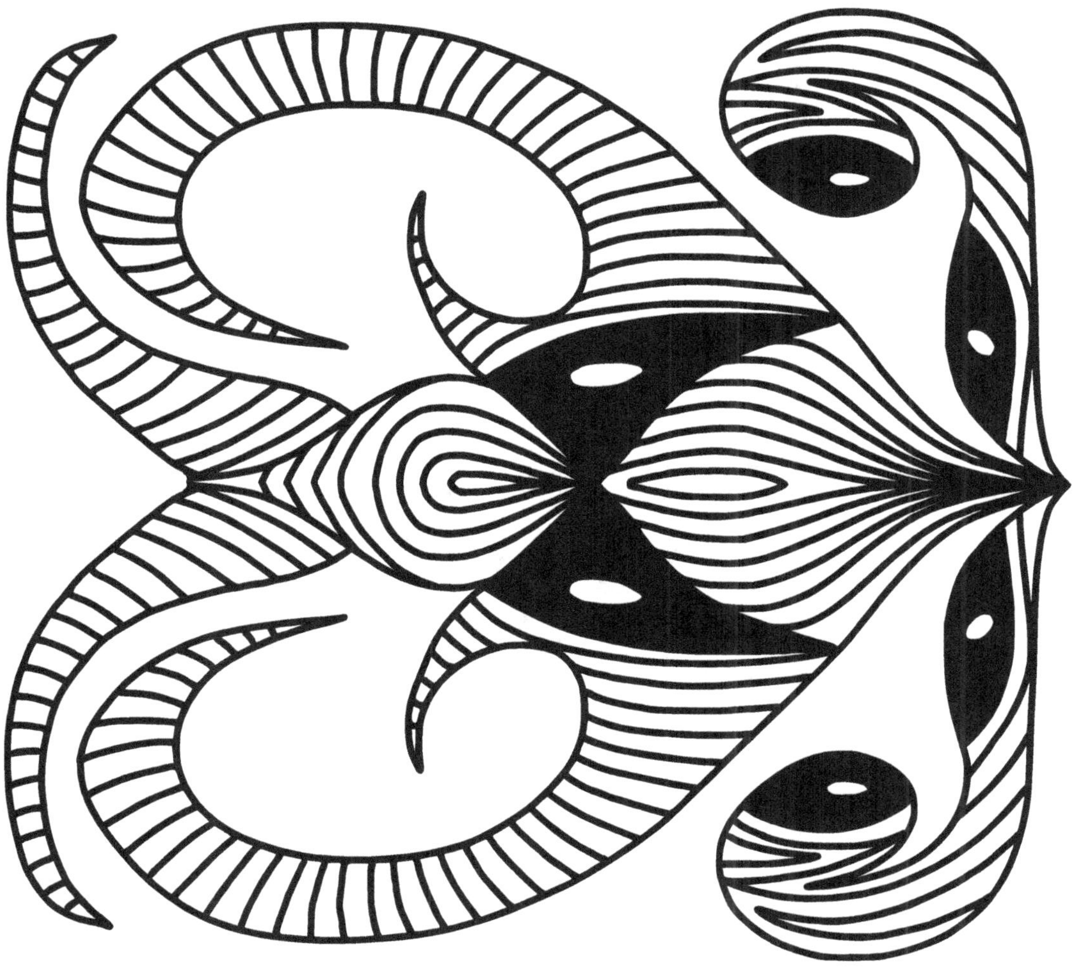

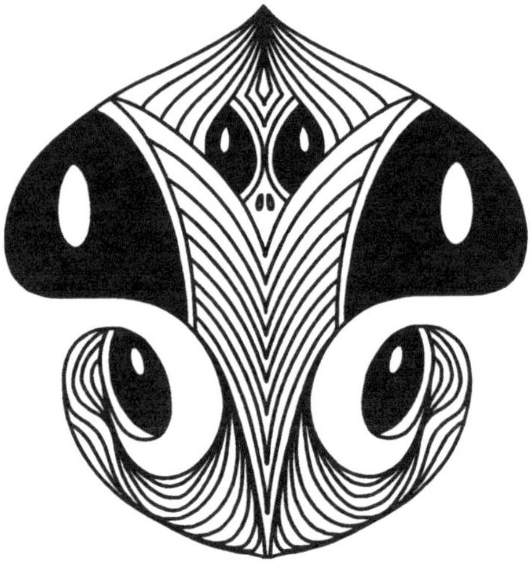

FATLINER WEIRDIES
VOLUME 1

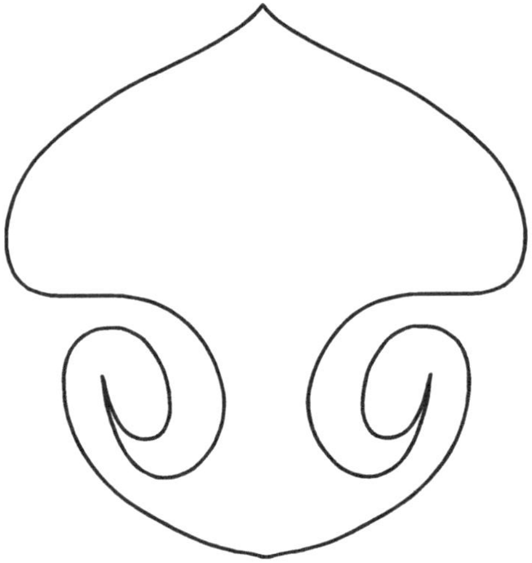

FATLINER WEIRDIES
THE TEMPLATES 1

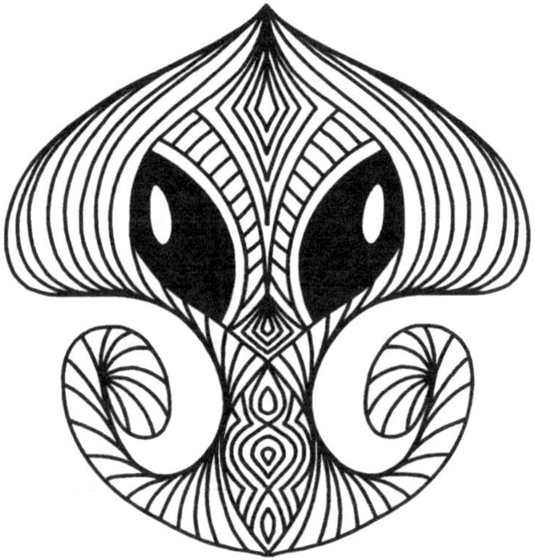

FATLINER WEIRDIES
VOLUME 3

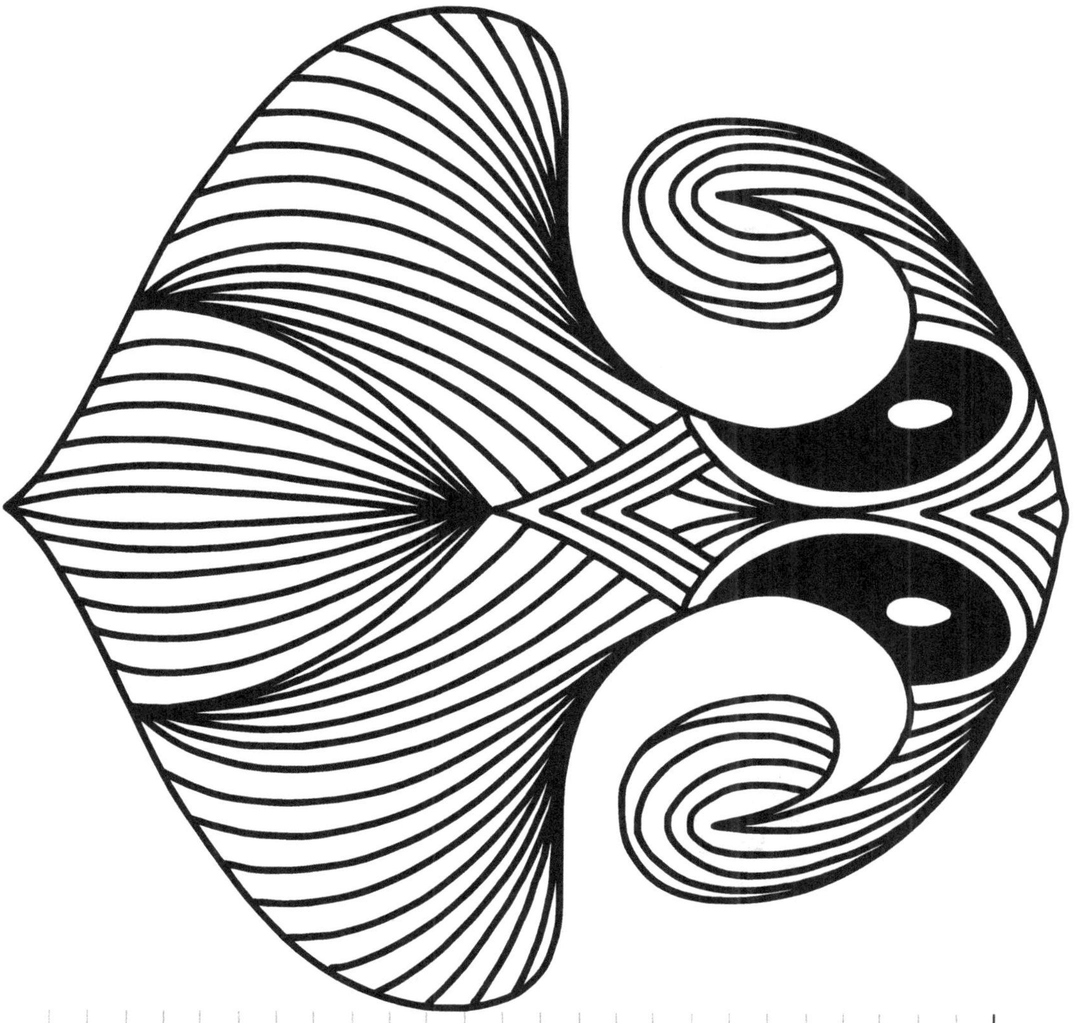

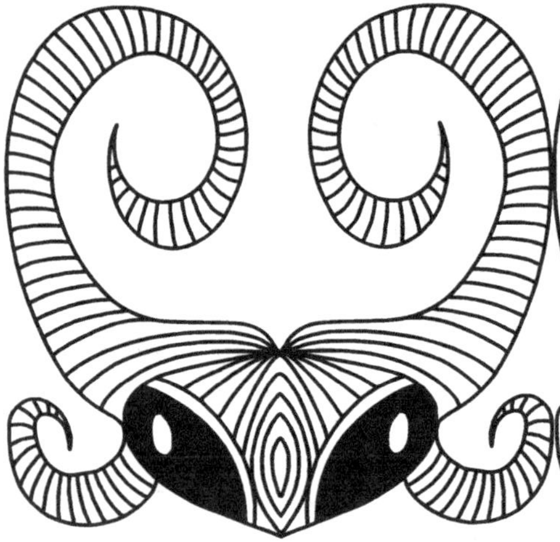

FATLINER WEIRDIES
VOLUME 1

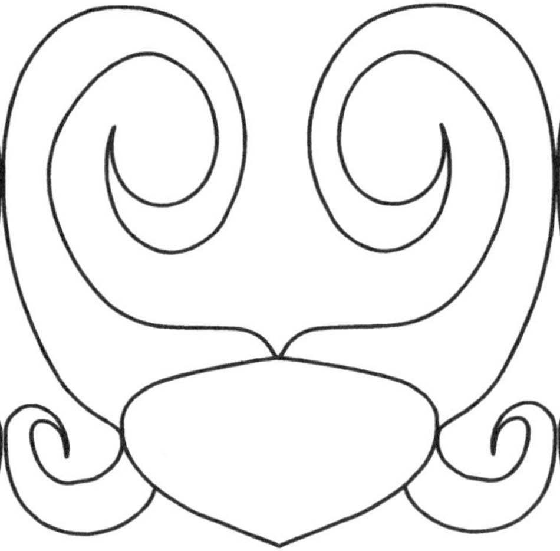

FATLINER WEIRDIES
THE TEMPLATES 1

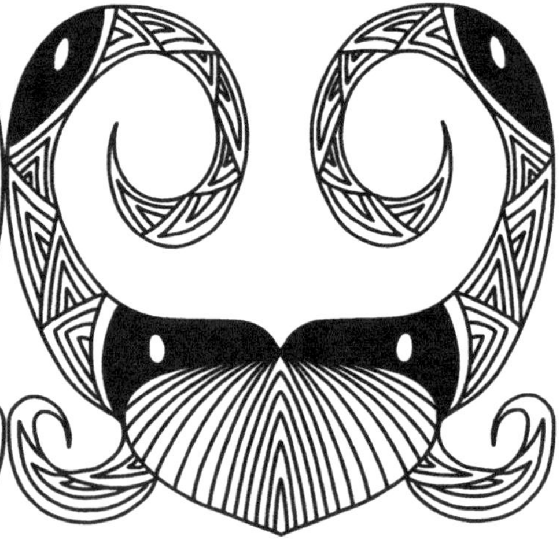

FATLINER WEIRDIES
VOLUME 3

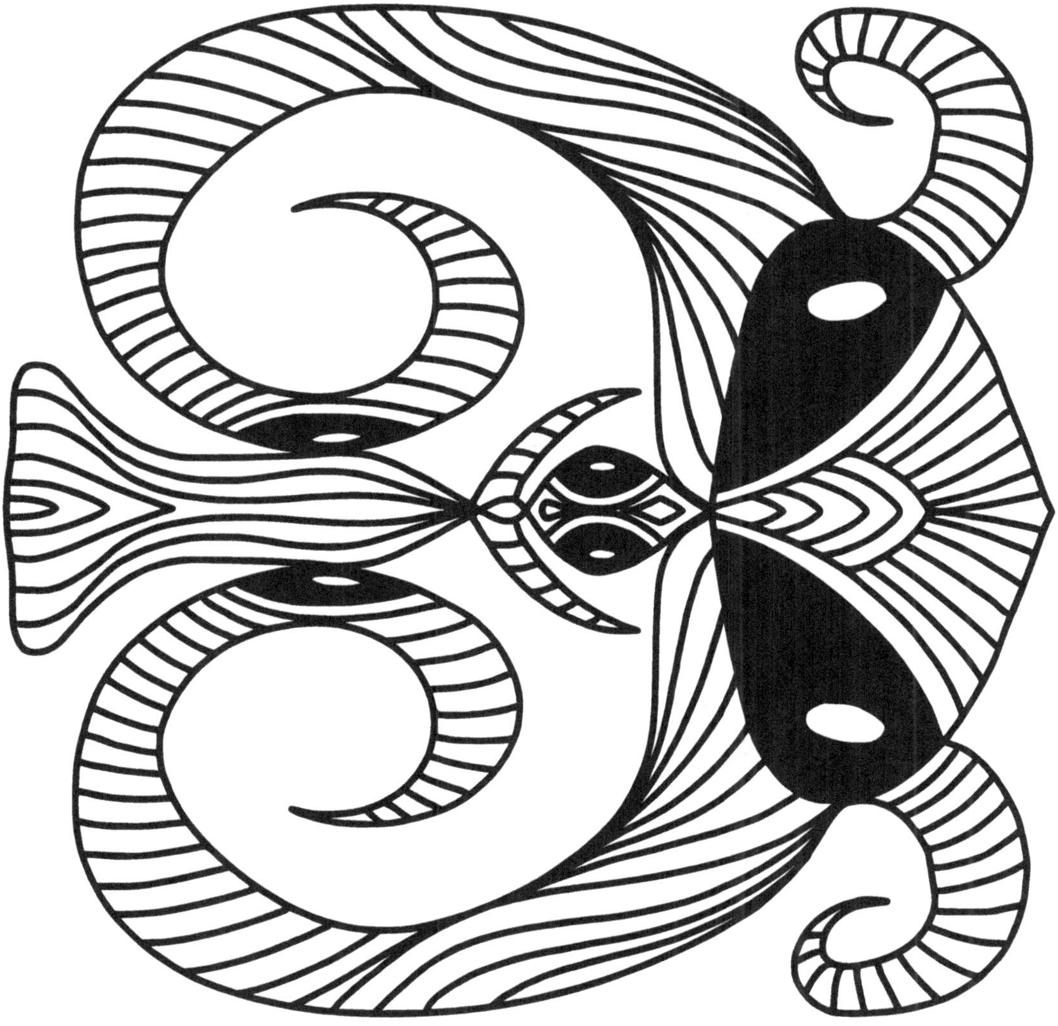

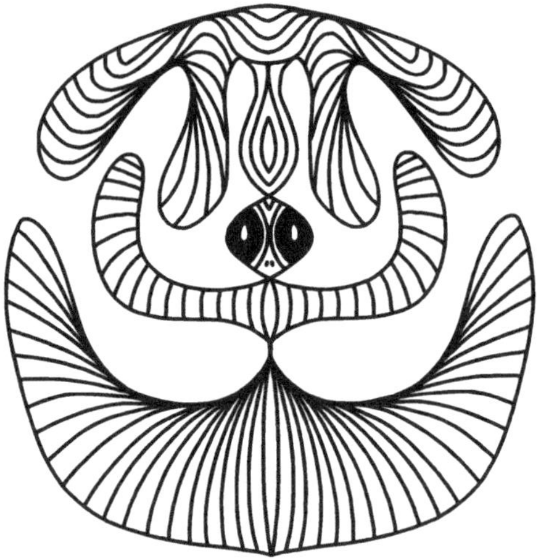

FATLINER WEIRDIES
VOLUME 1

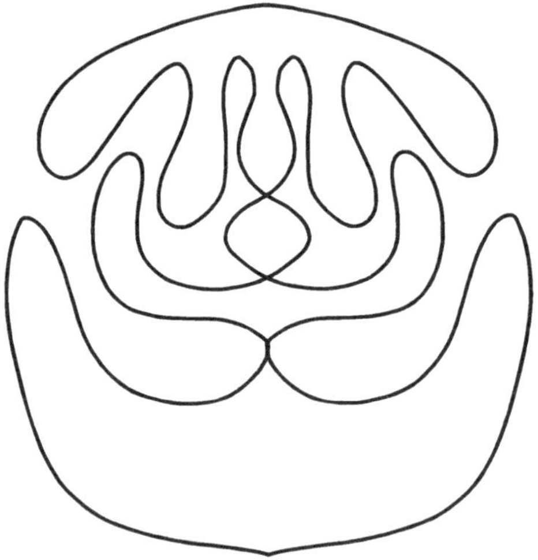

FATLINER WEIRDIES
THE TEMPLATES 1

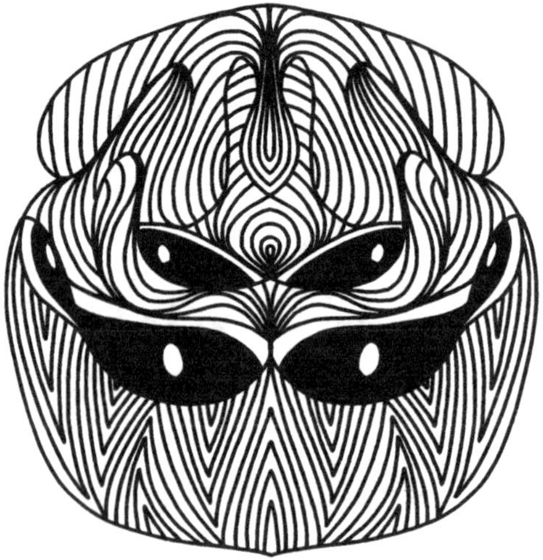

FATLINER WEIRDIES
VOLUME 3

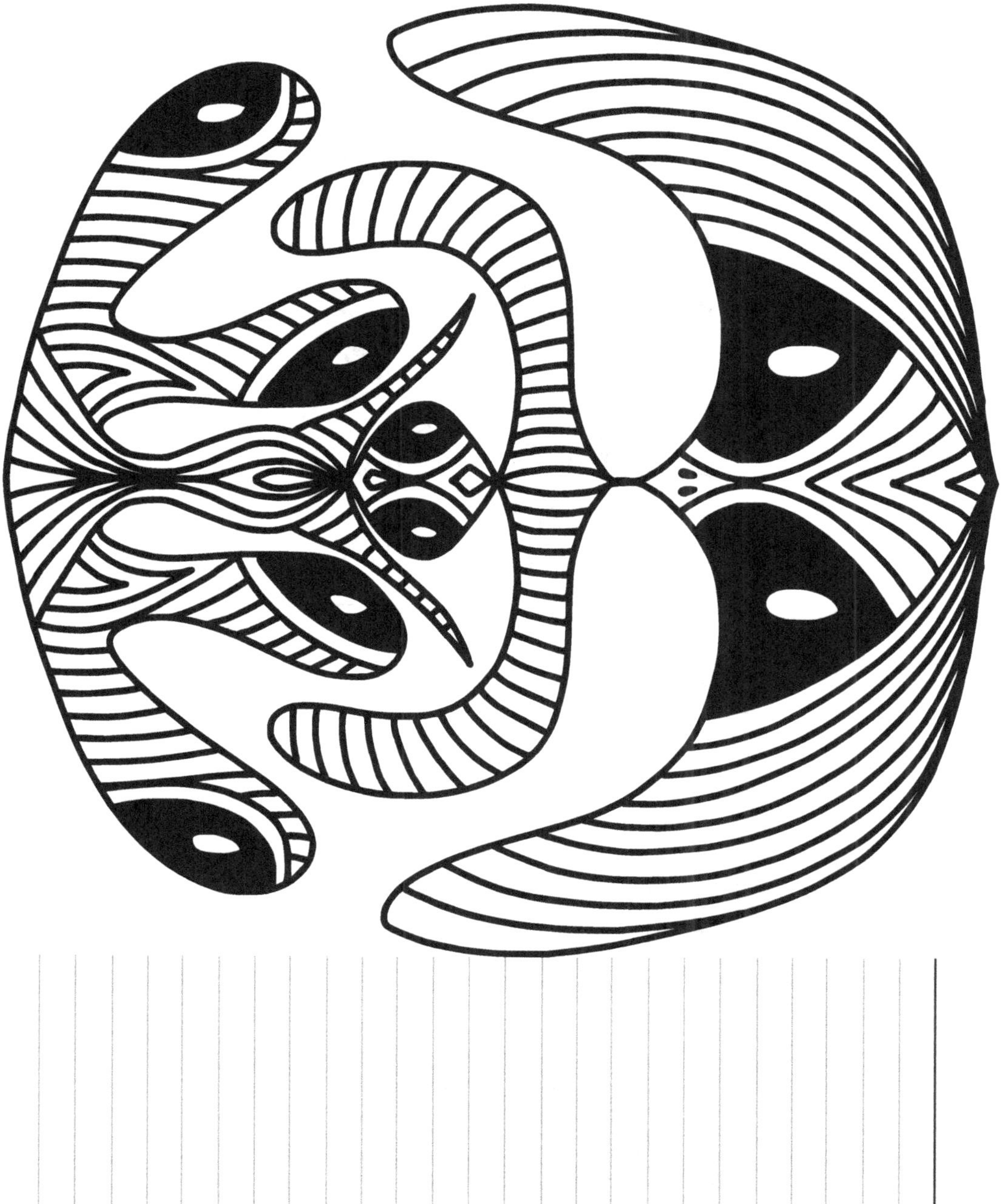

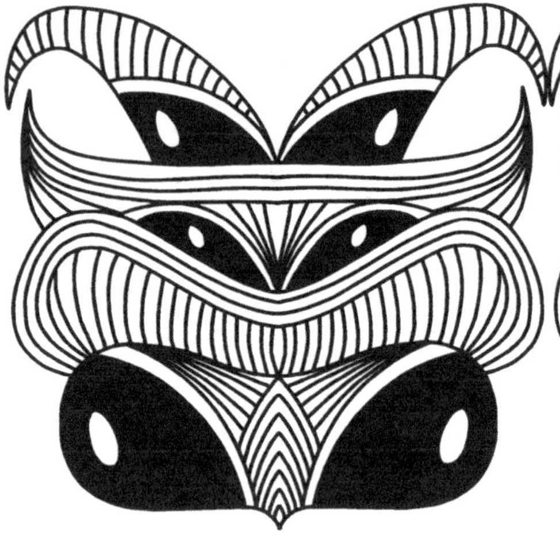

FATLINER WEIRDIES
VOLUME 1

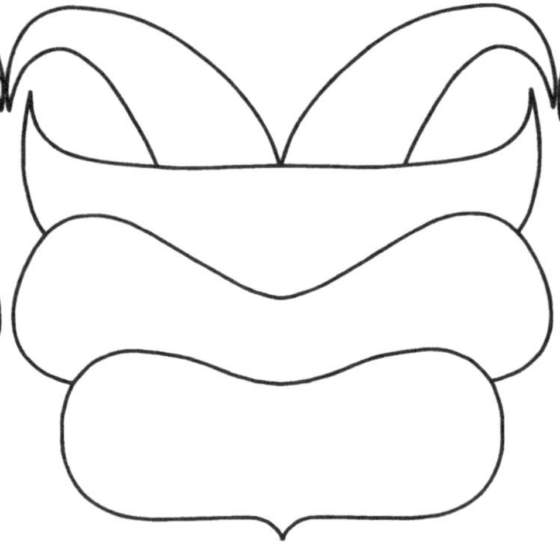

FATLINER WEIRDIES
THE TEMPLATES 1

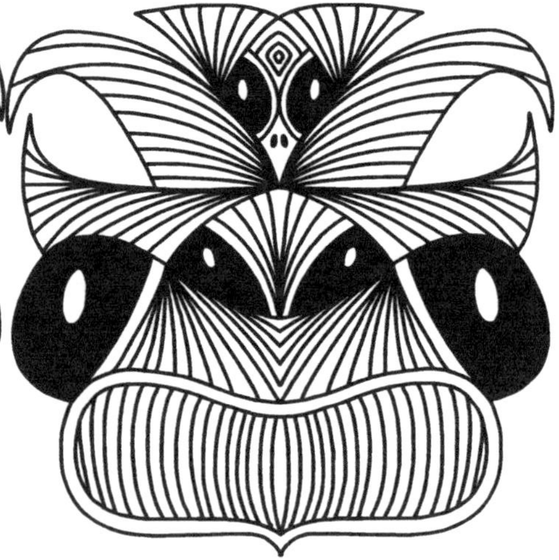

FATLINER WEIRDIES
VOLUME 3

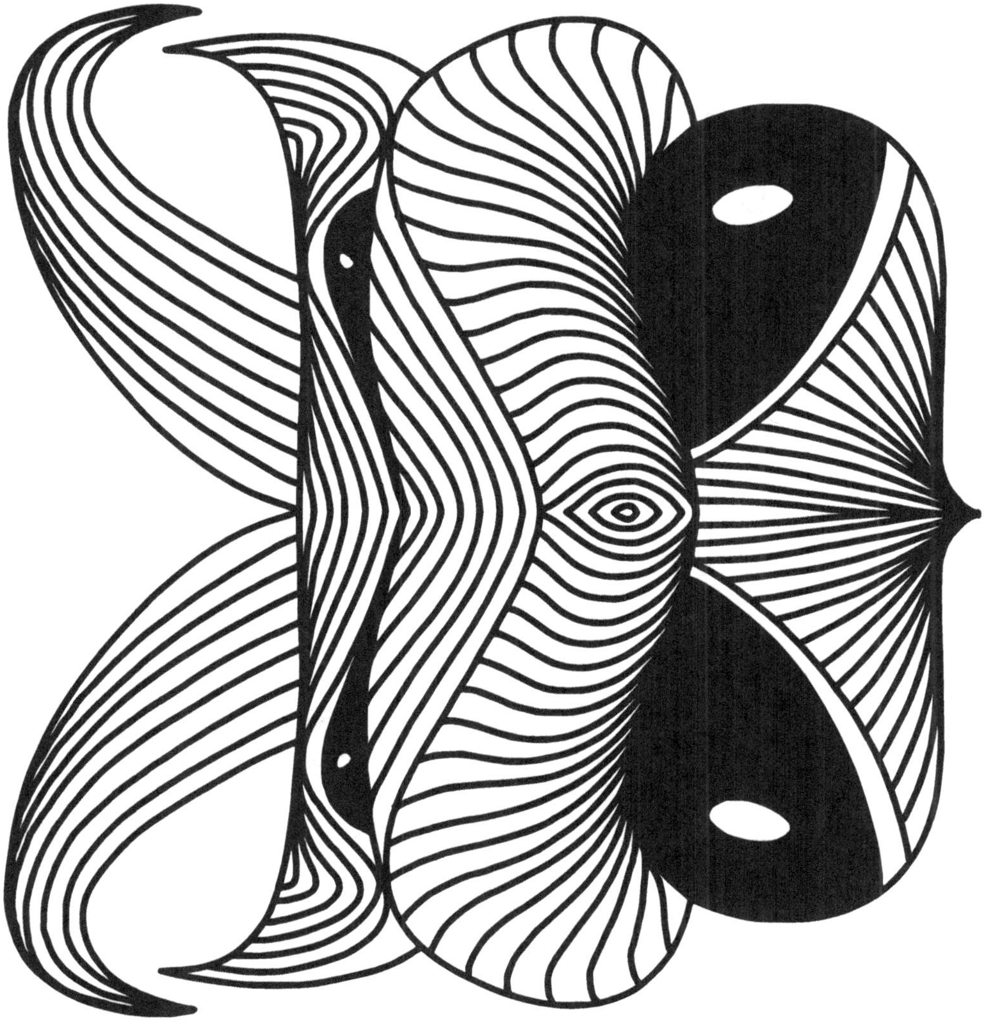

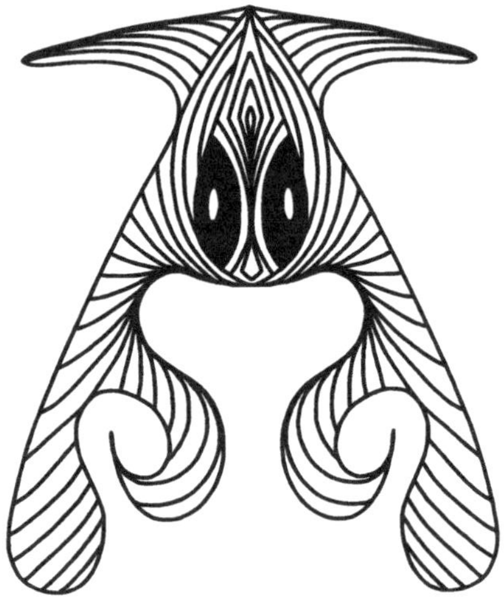

FATLINER WEIRDIES
VOLUME 1

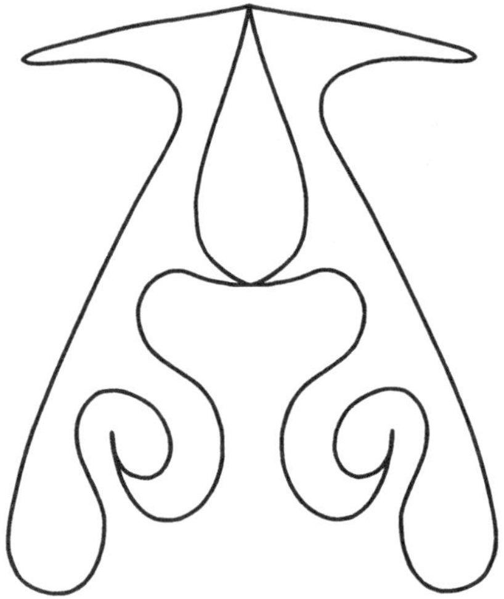

FATLINER WEIRDIES
THE TEMPLATES 1

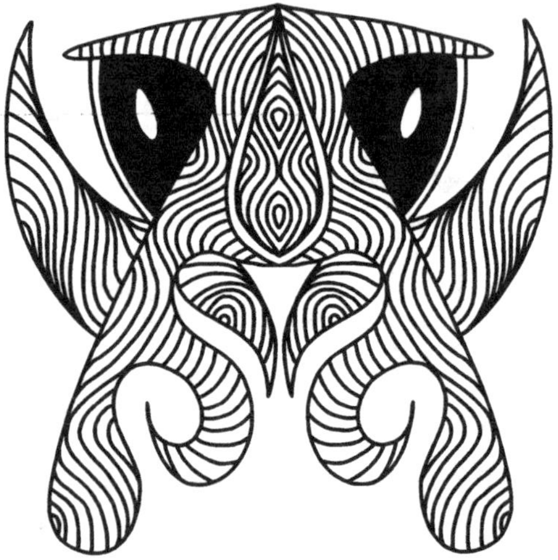

FATLINER WEIRDIES
VOLUME 3

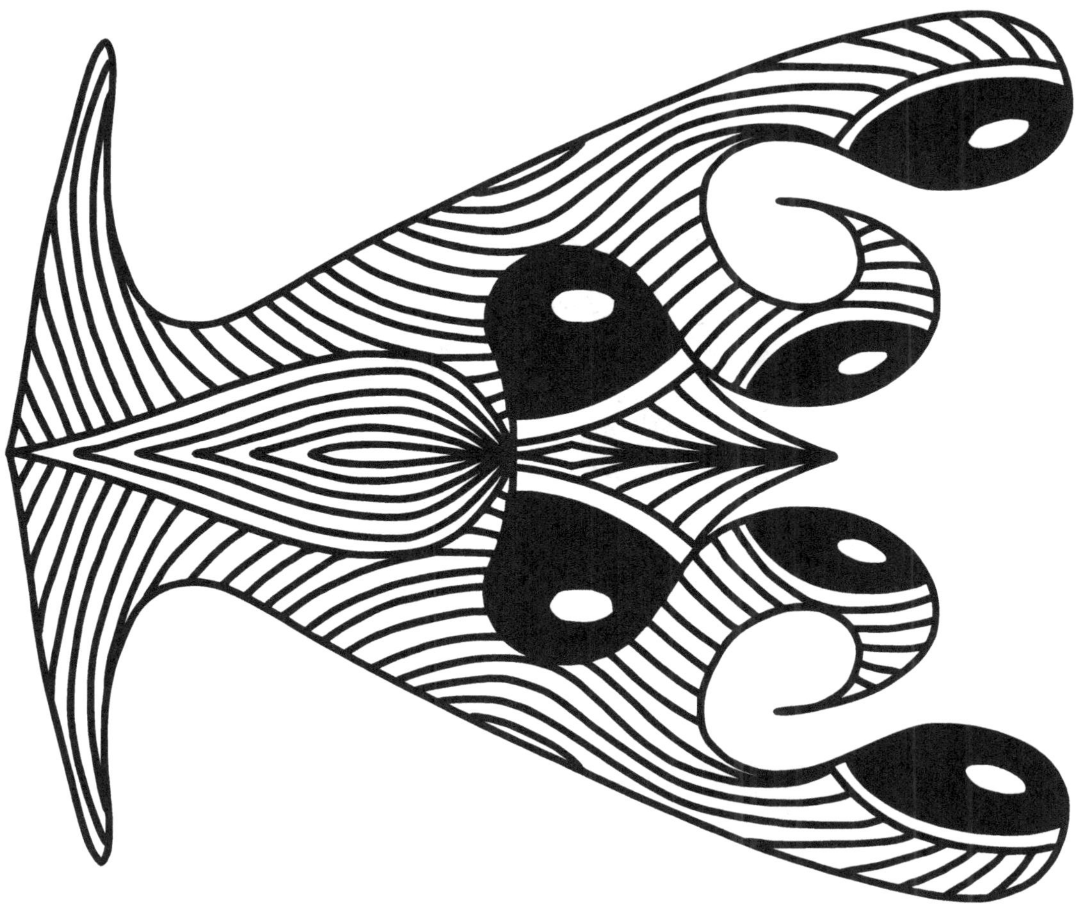

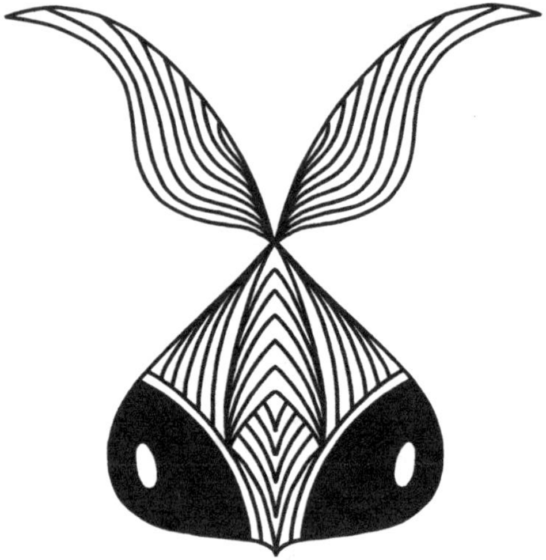

FATLINER WEIRDIES
VOLUME 1

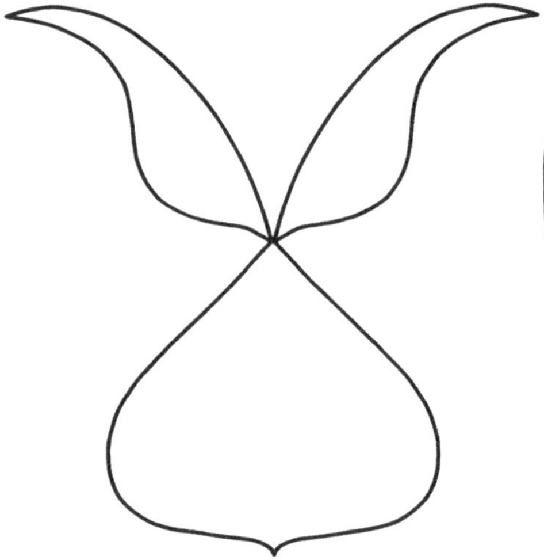

FATLINER WEIRDIES
THE TEMPLATES 1

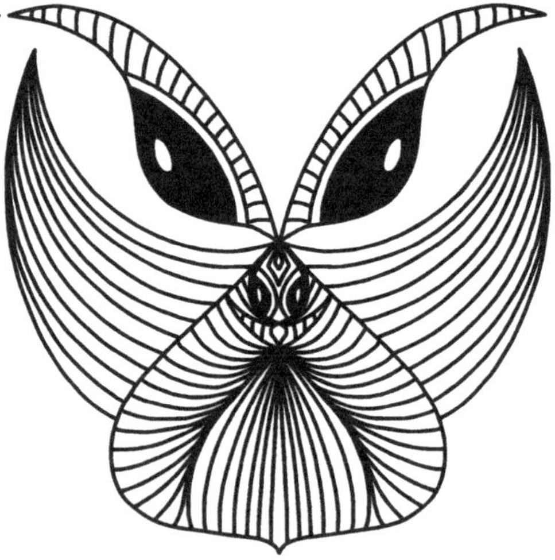

FATLINER WEIRDIES
VOLUME 3

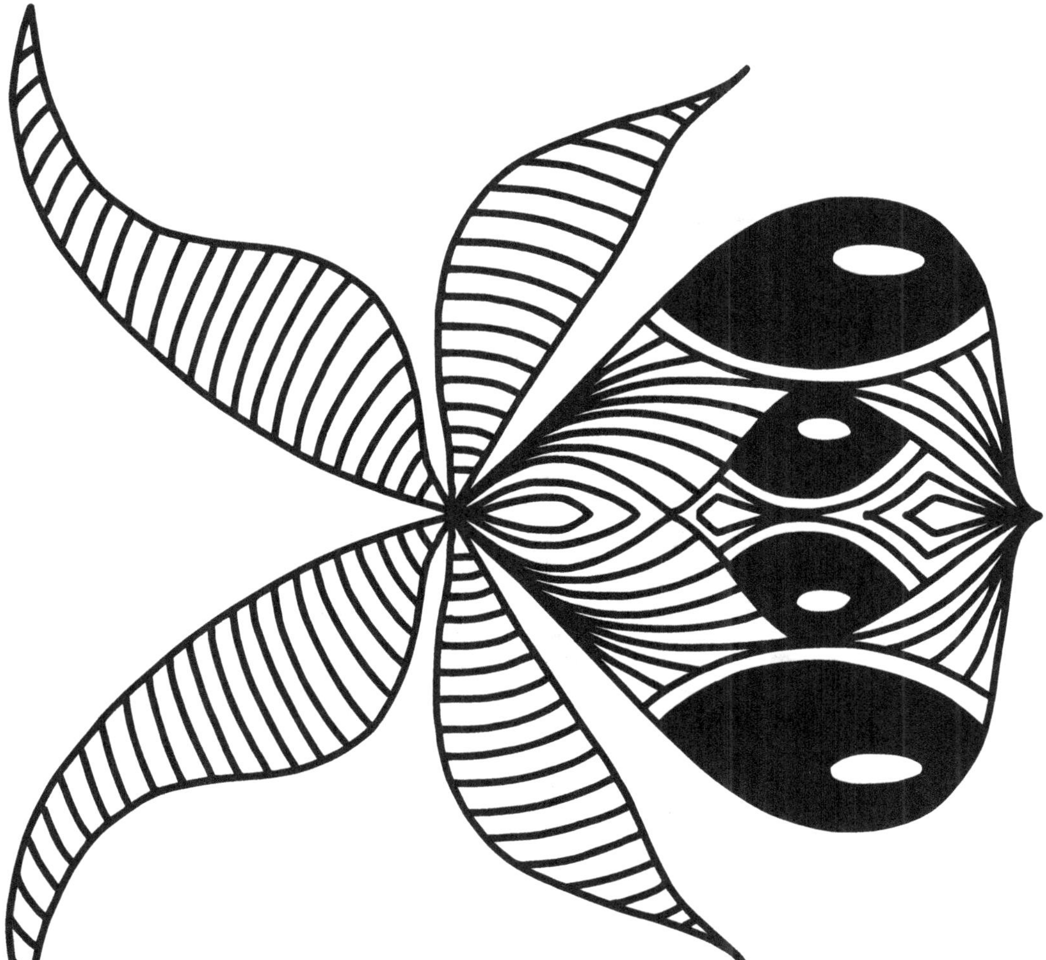

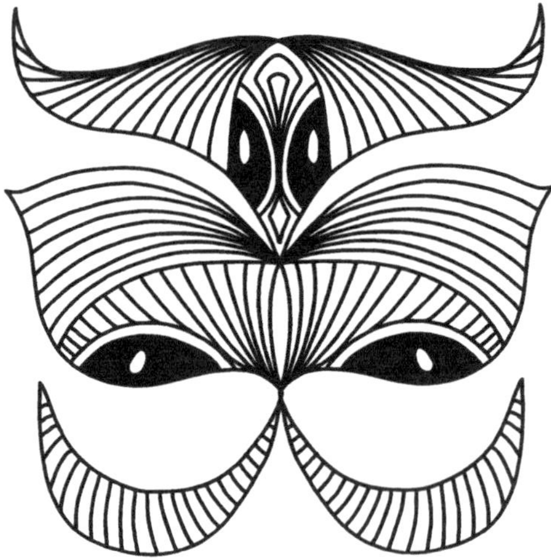

FATLINER WEIRDIES
VOLUME 1

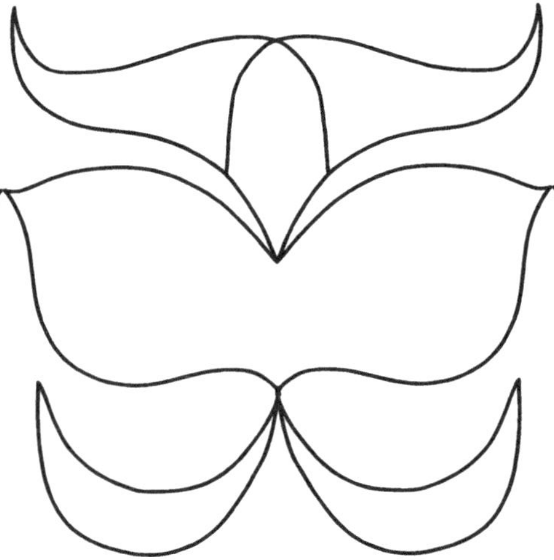

FATLINER WEIRDIES
THE TEMPLATES 1

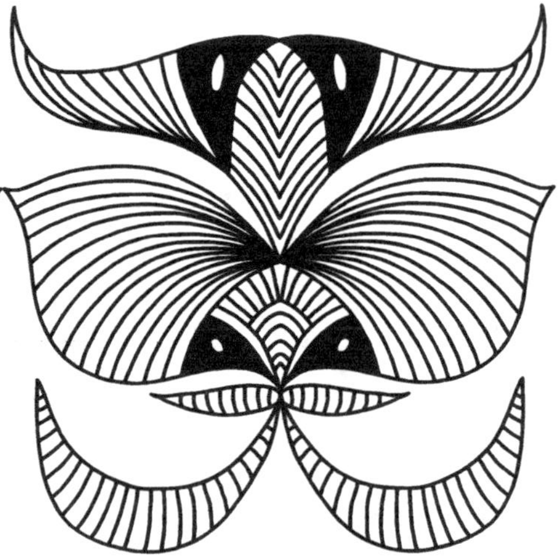

FATLINER WEIRDIES
VOLUME 3

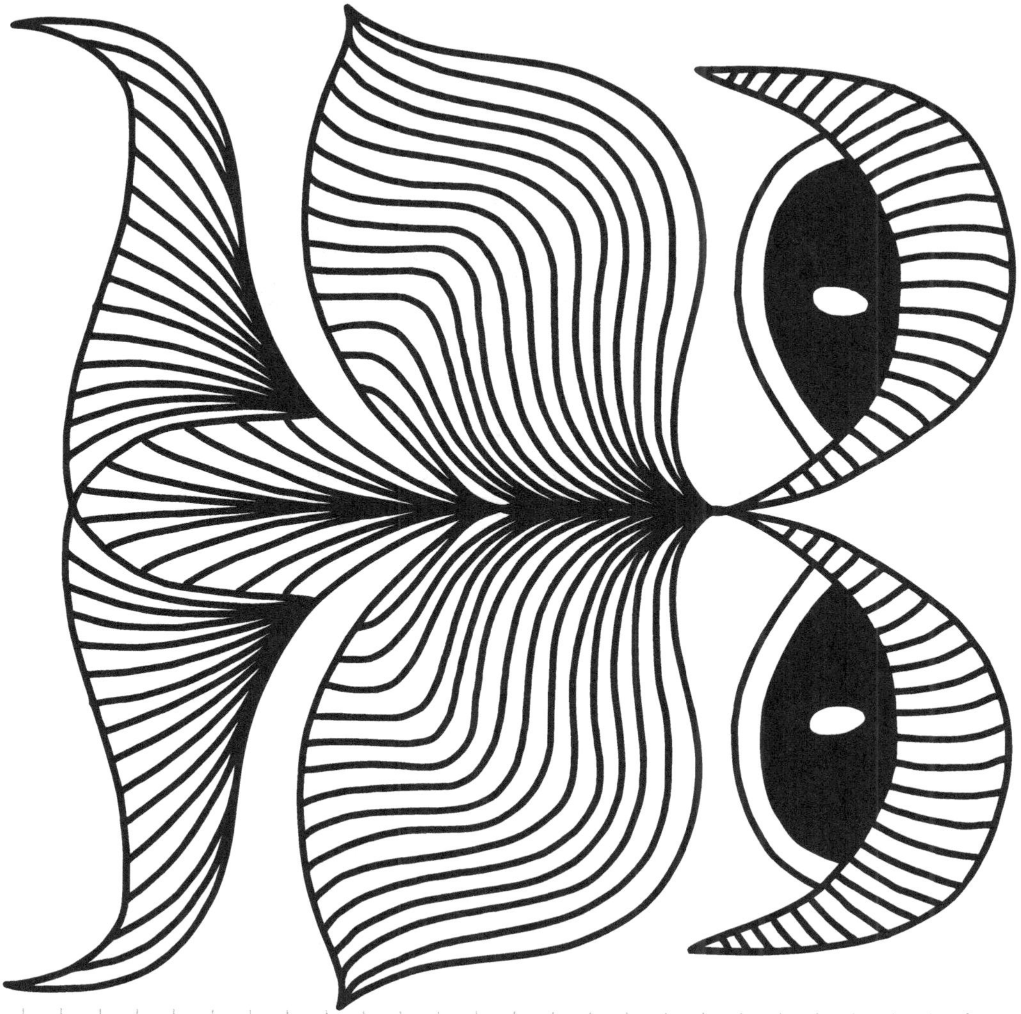

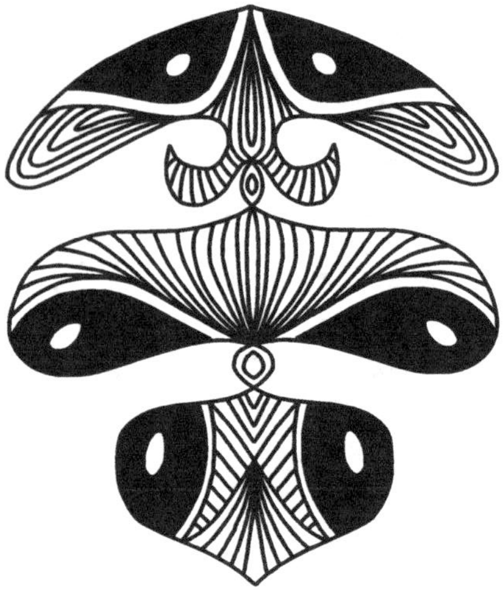

FATLINER WEIRDIES
VOLUME 1

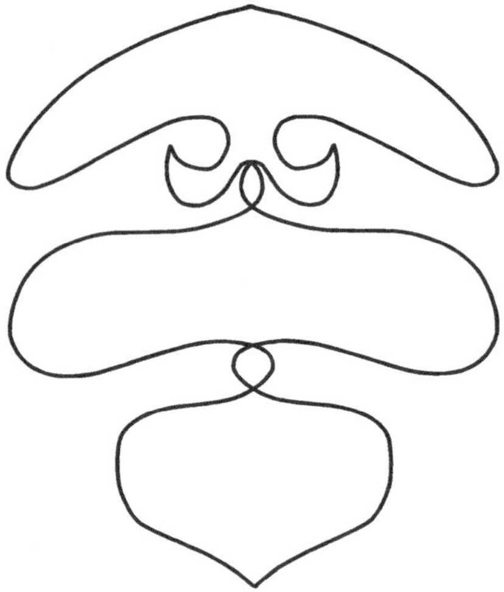

FATLINER WEIRDIES
THE TEMPLATES 1

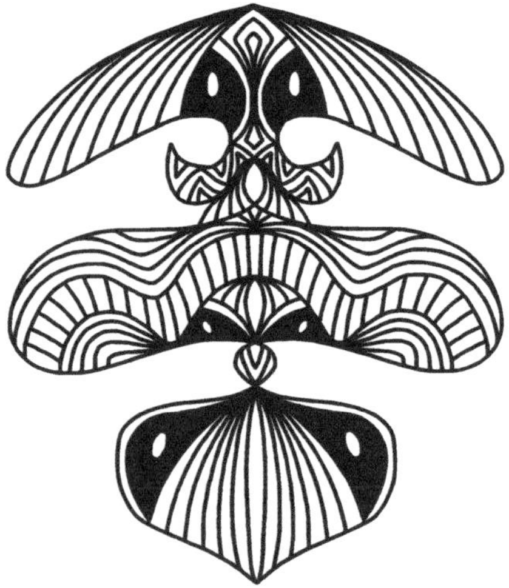

FATLINER WEIRDIES
VOLUME 3

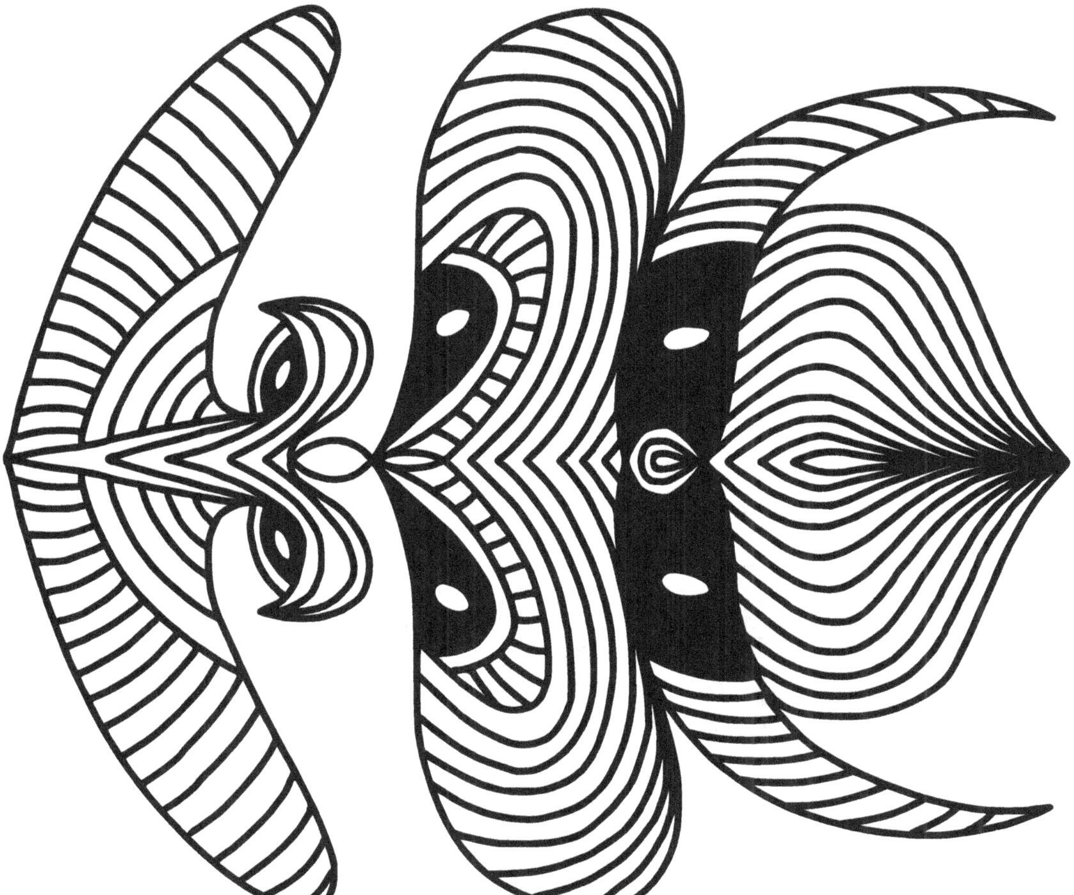

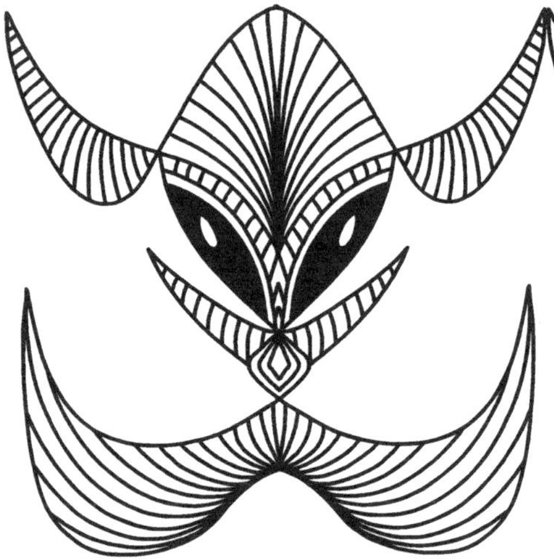

FATLINER WEIRDIES
VOLUME 1

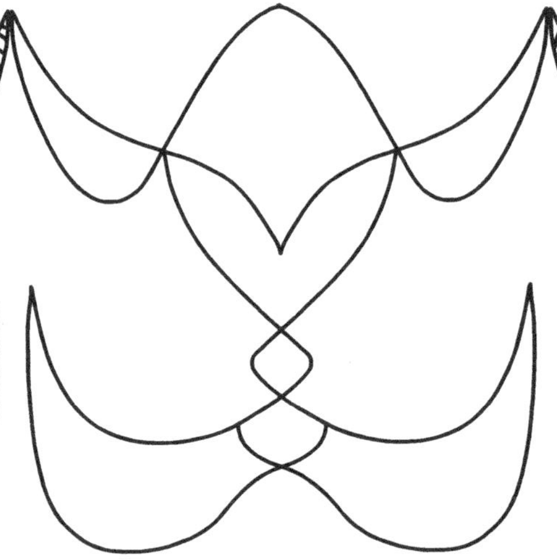

FATLINER WEIRDIES
THE TEMPLATES 1

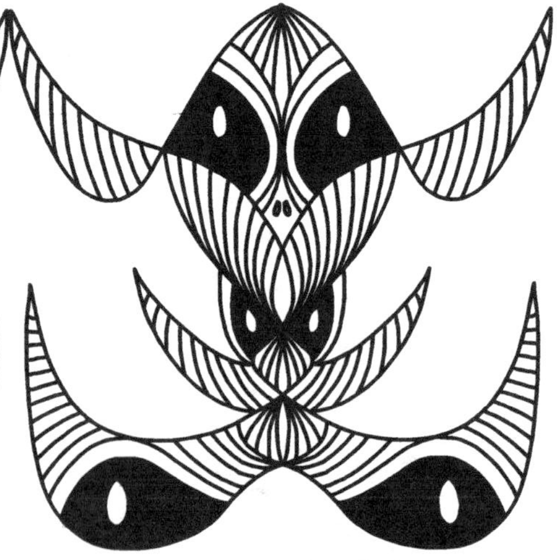

FATLINER WEIRDIES
VOLUME 3

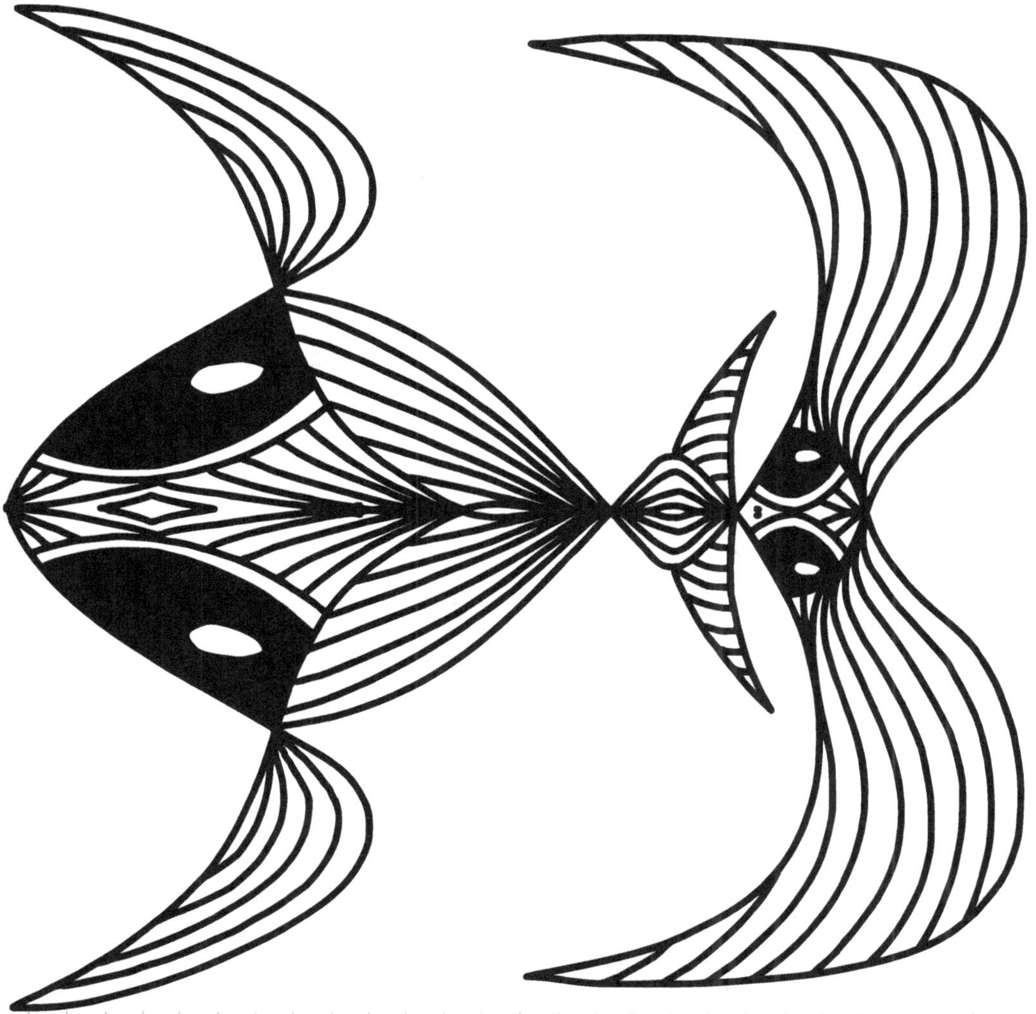

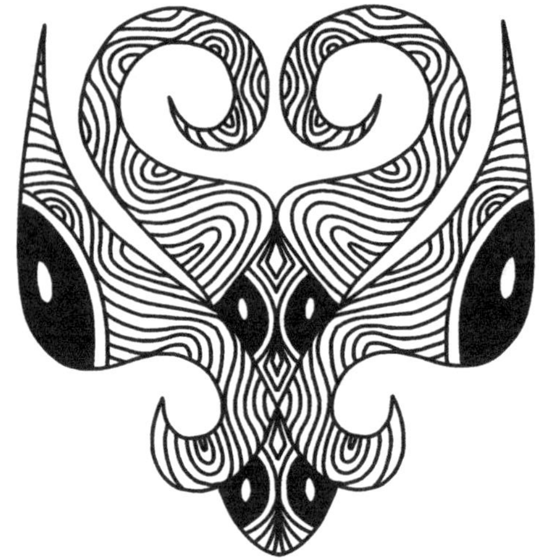
FATLINER WEIRDIES
VOLUME 1

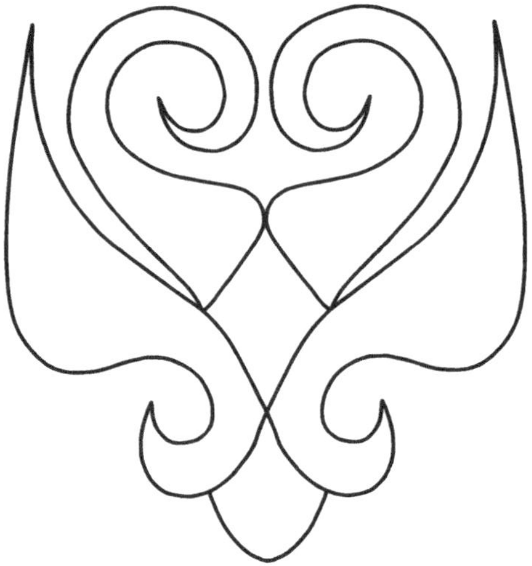
FATLINER WEIRDIES
THE TEMPLATES 1

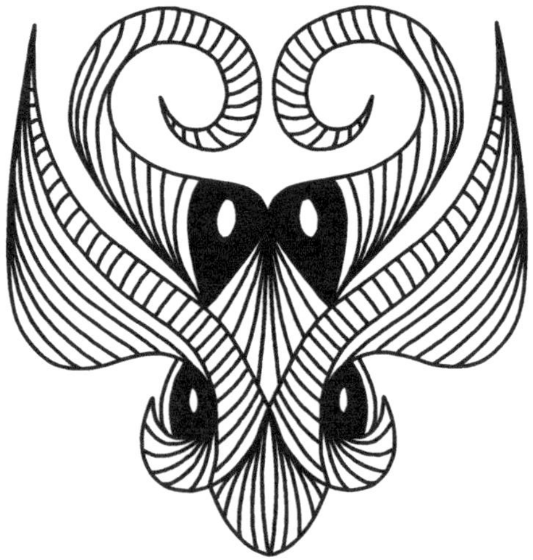
FATLINER WEIRDIES
VOLUME 3

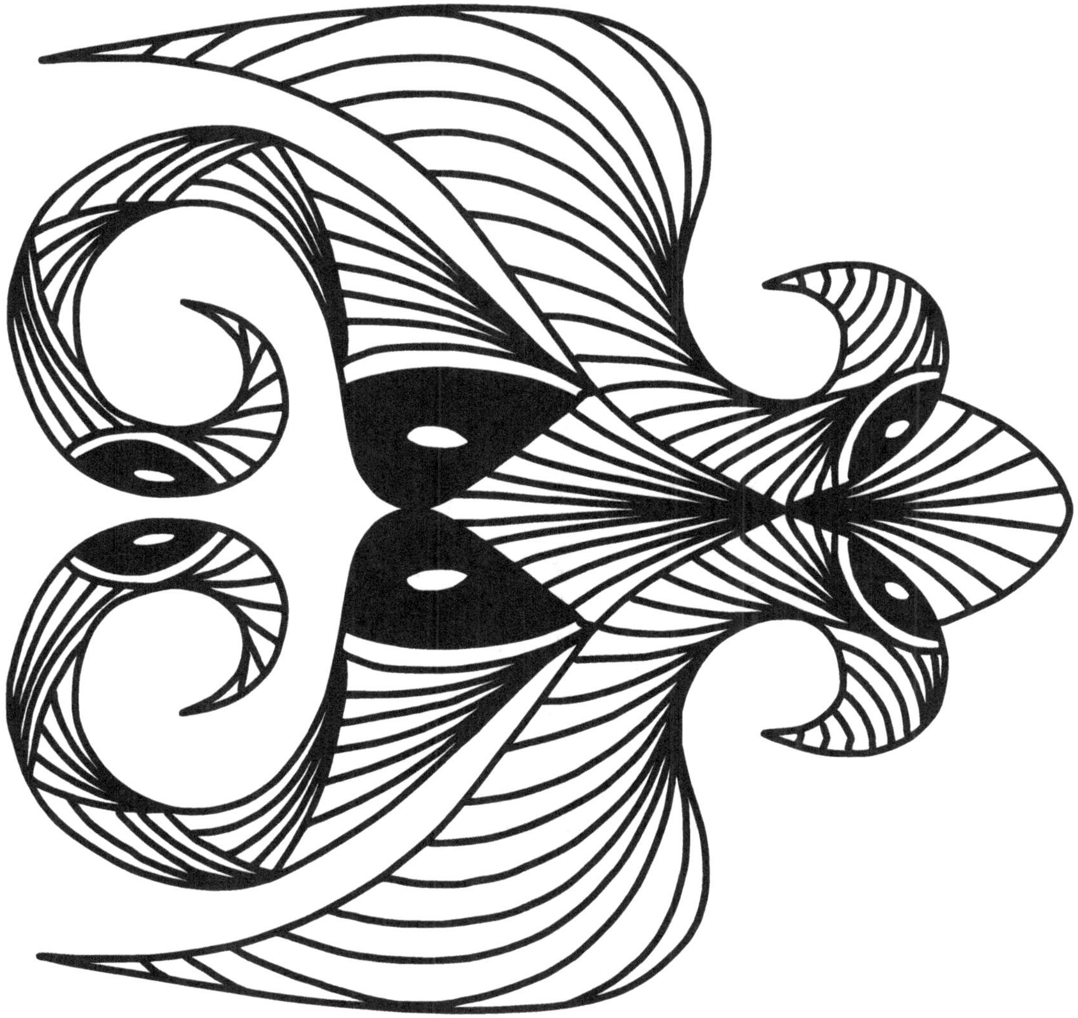

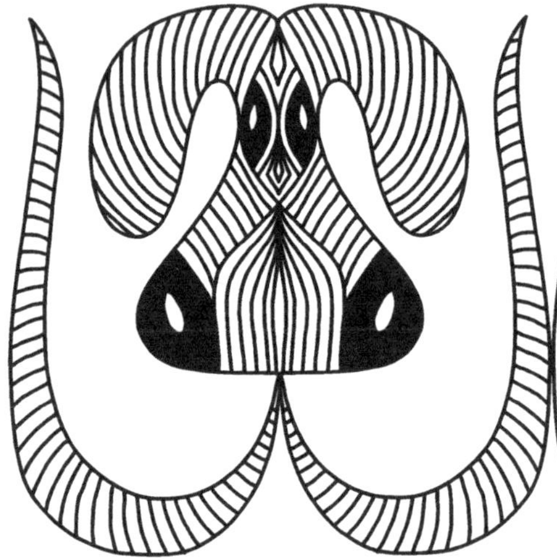
FATLINER WEIRDIES
VOLUME 1

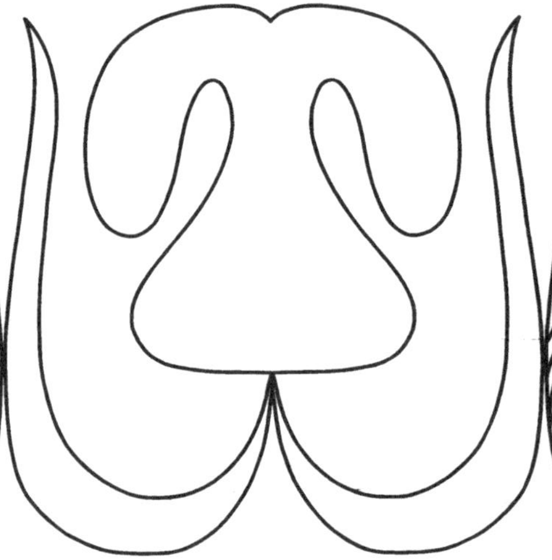
FATLINER WEIRDIES
THE TEMPLATES 1

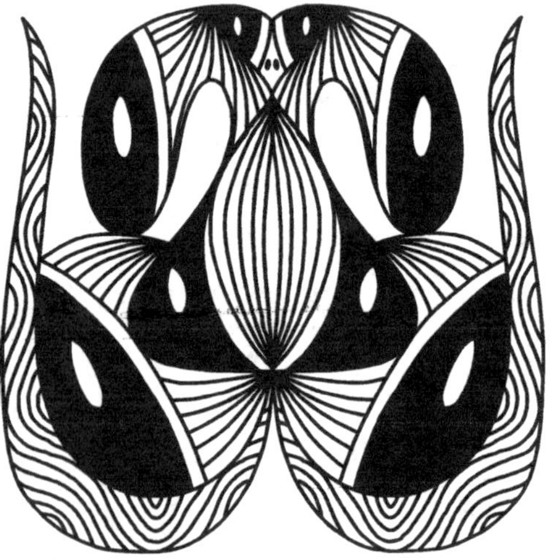
FATLINER WEIRDIES
VOLUME 3

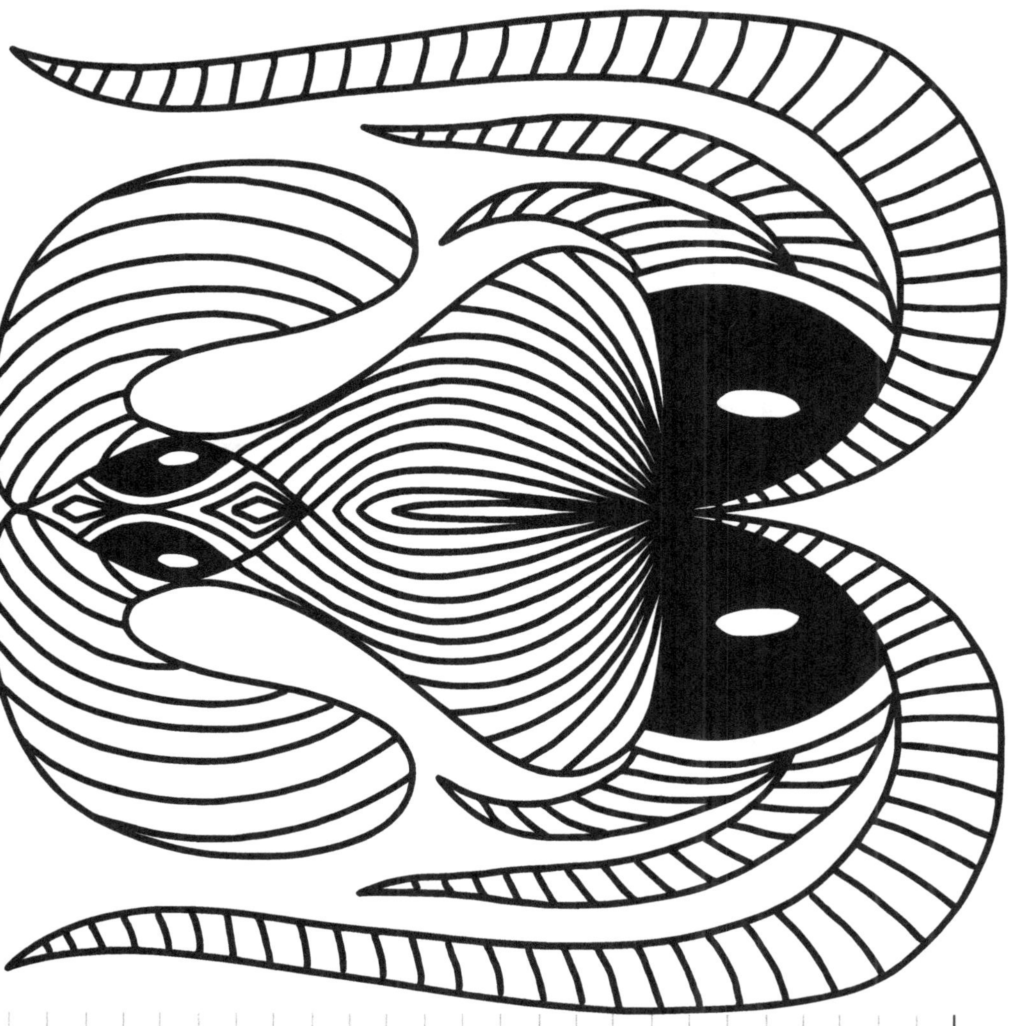

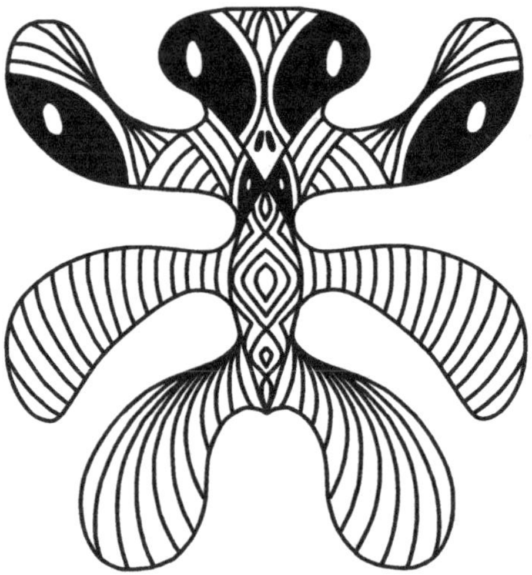

FATLINER WEIRDIES
VOLUME 1

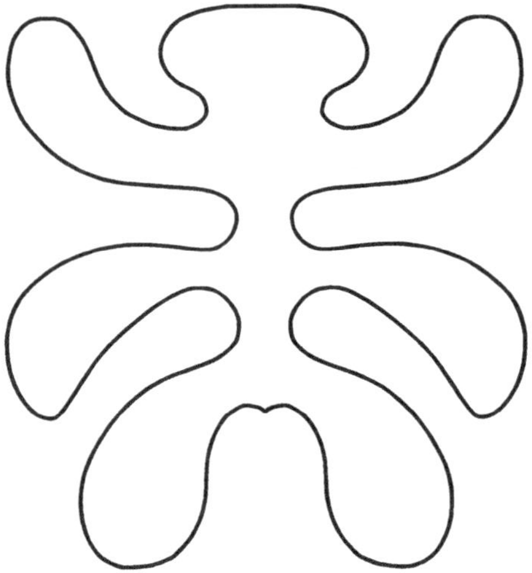

FATLINER WEIRDIES
THE TEMPLATES 1

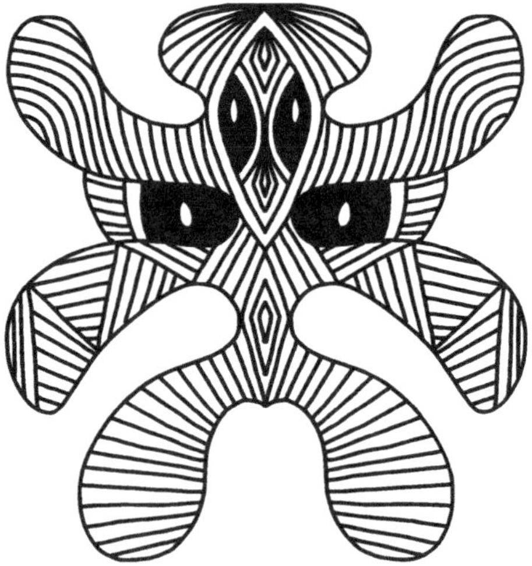

FATLINER WEIRDIES
VOLUME 3

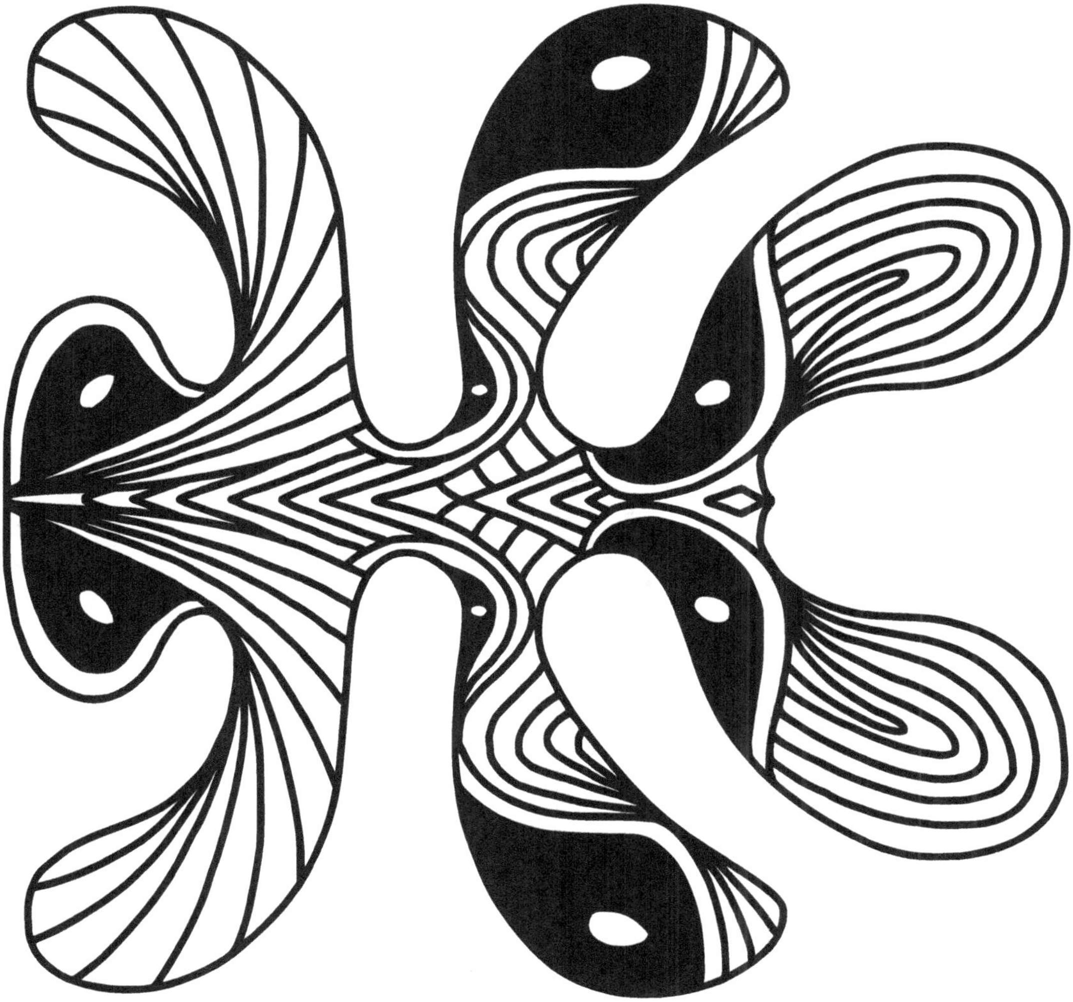

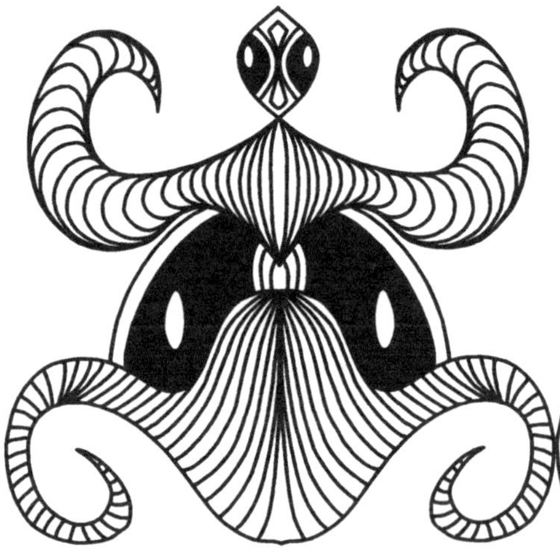

FATLINER WEIRDIES
VOLUME 1

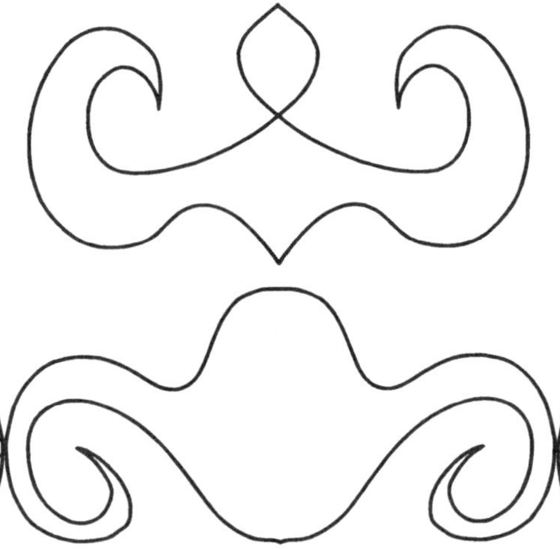

FATLINER WEIRDIES
THE TEMPLATES 1

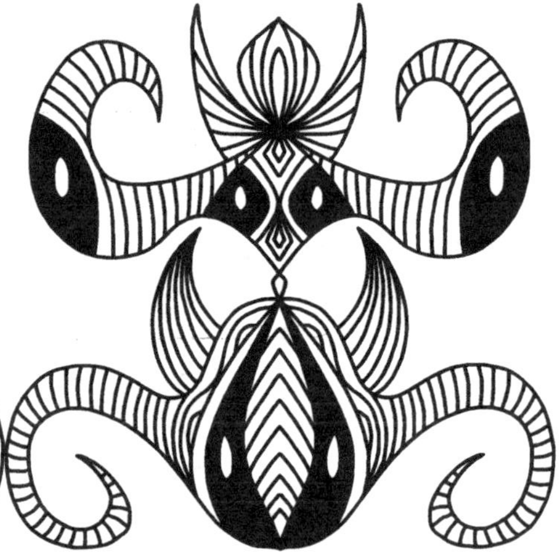

FATLINER WEIRDIES
VOLUME 3

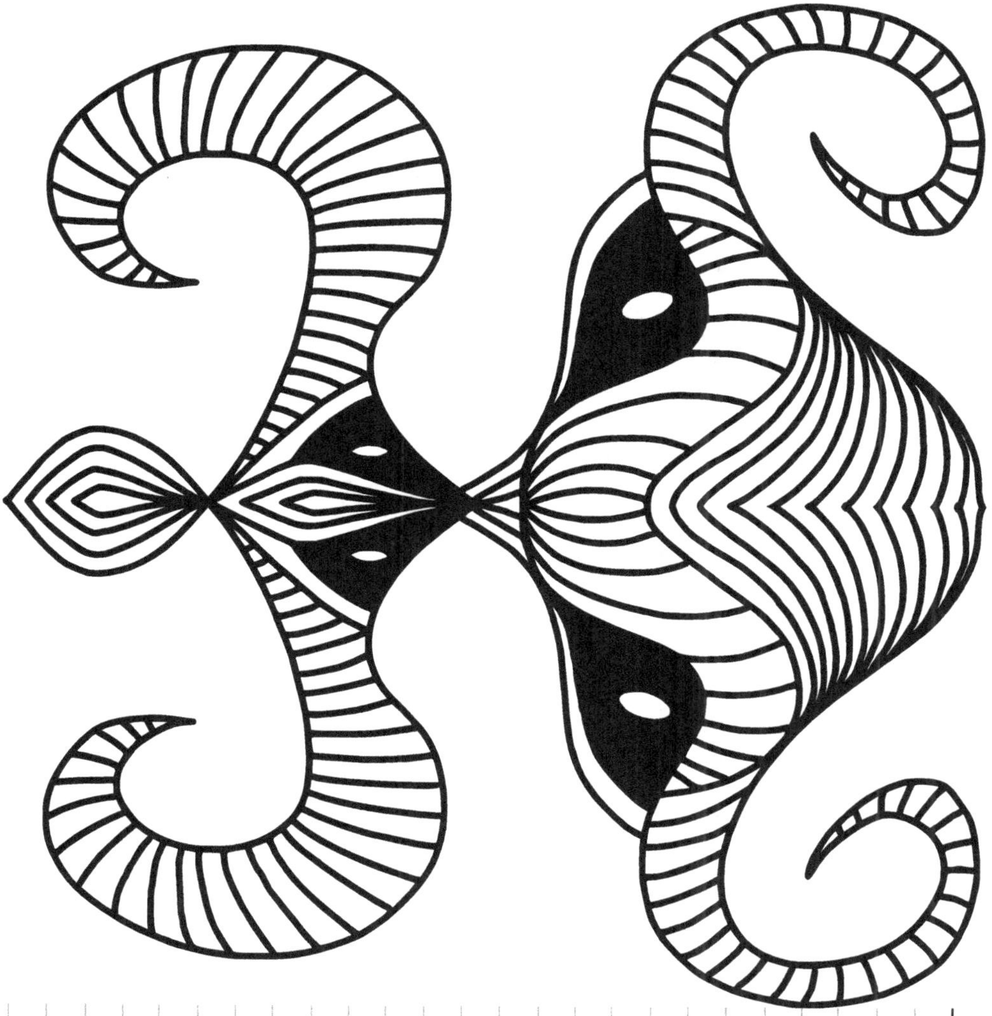

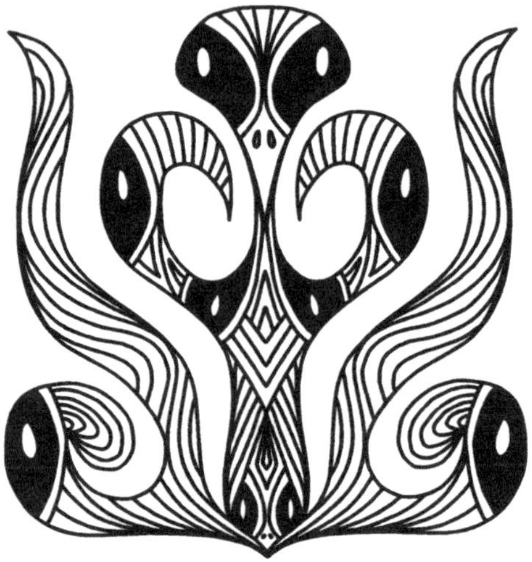

FATLINER WEIRDIES
VOLUME 1

FATLINER WEIRDIES
THE TEMPLATES 1

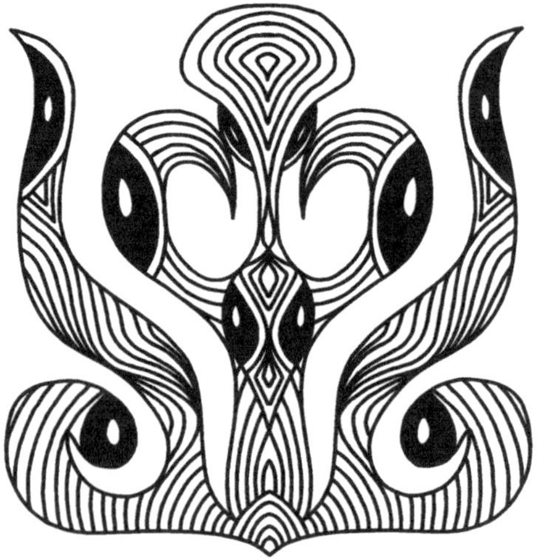

FATLINER WEIRDIES
VOLUME 3

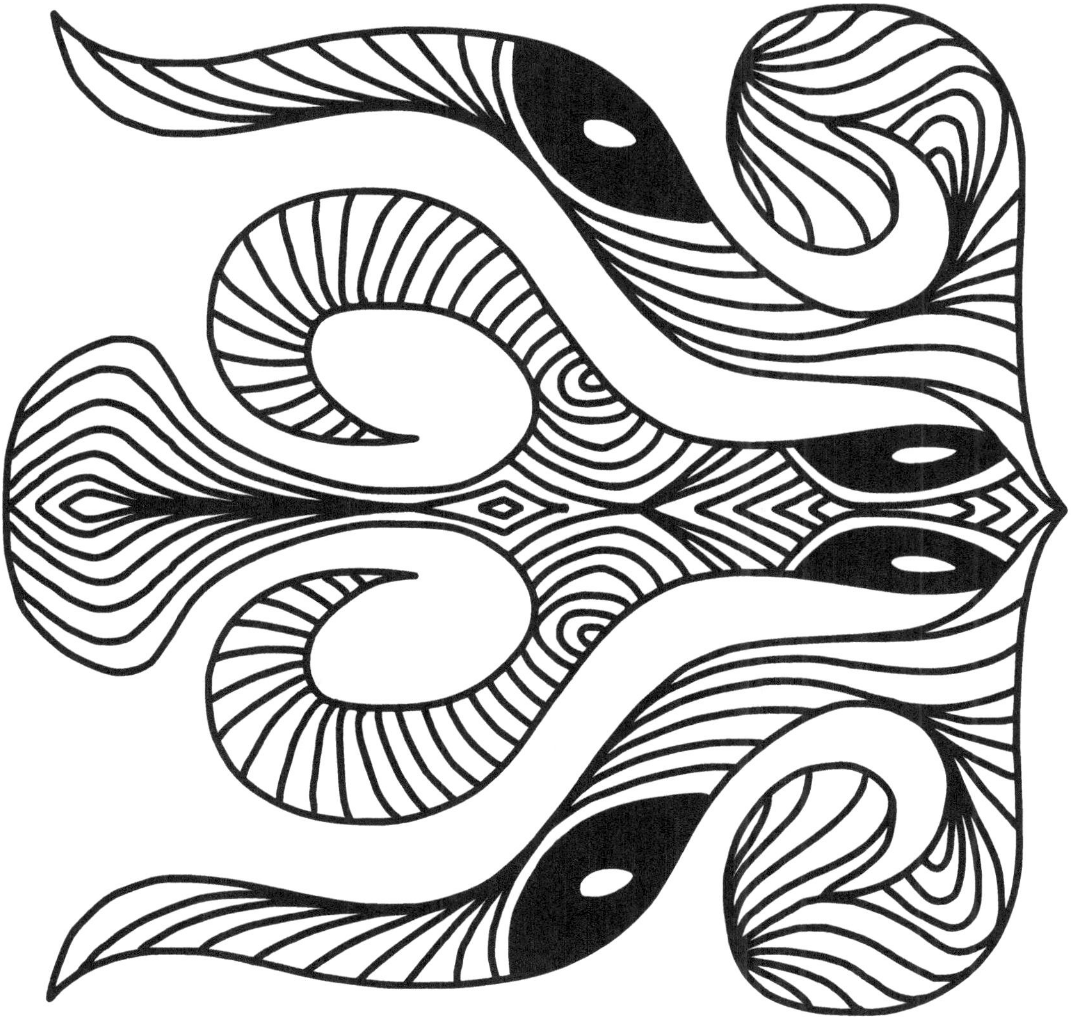

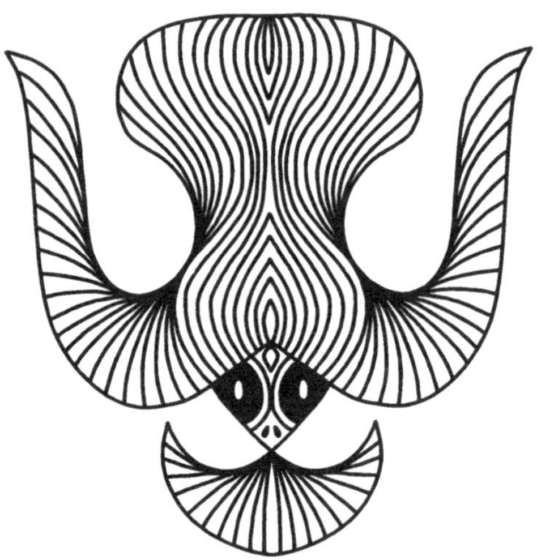

FATLINER WEIRDIES
VOLUME 1

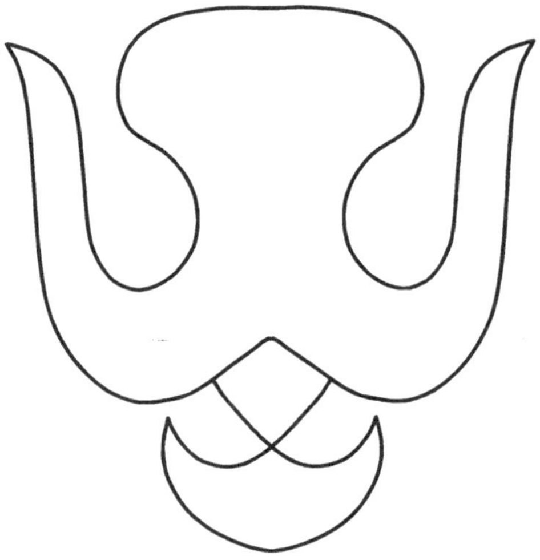

FATLINER WEIRDIES
THE TEMPLATES 1

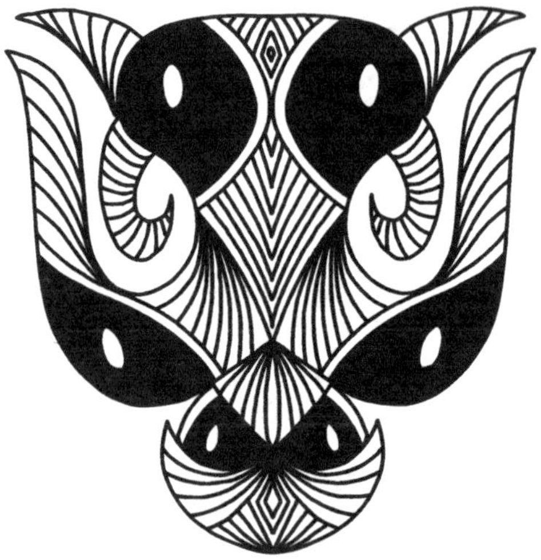

FATLINER WEIRDIES
VOLUME 3

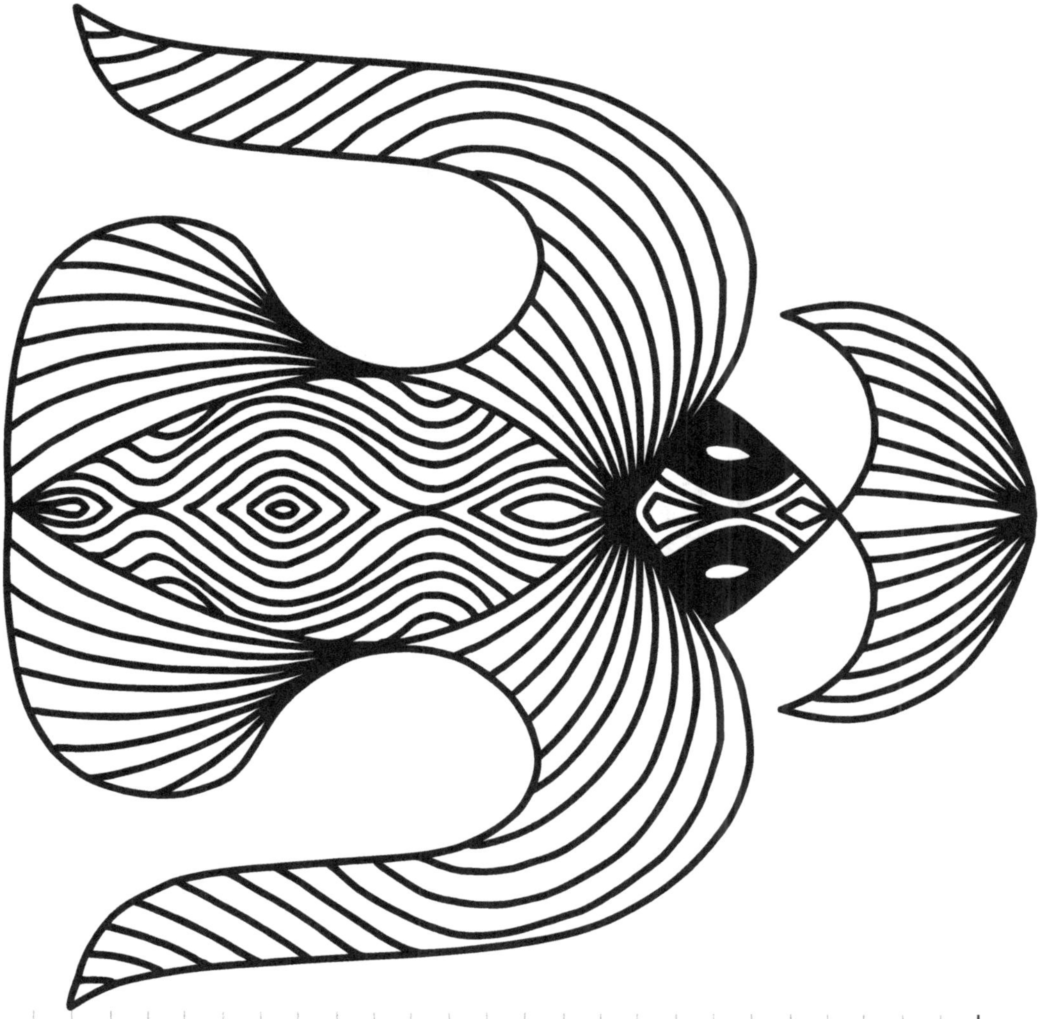

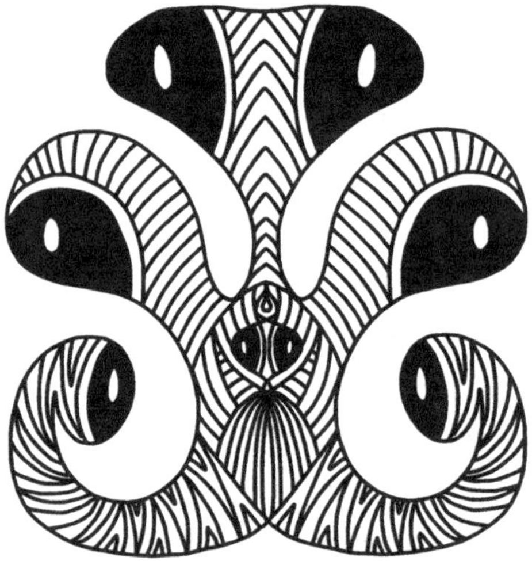

FATLINER WEIRDIES
VOLUME 1

FATLINER WEIRDIES
THE TEMPLATES 1

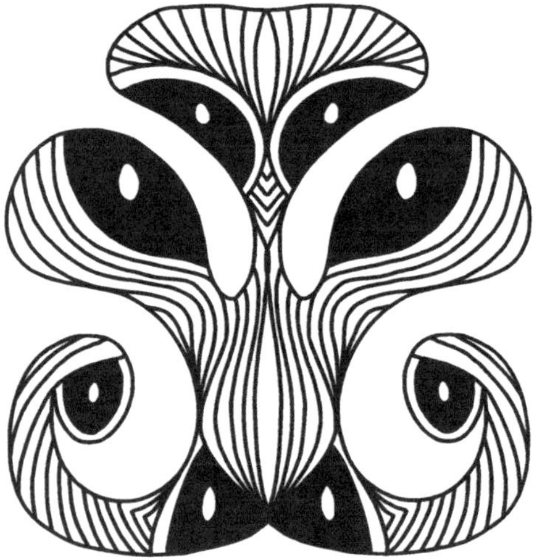

FATLINER WEIRDIES
VOLUME 3

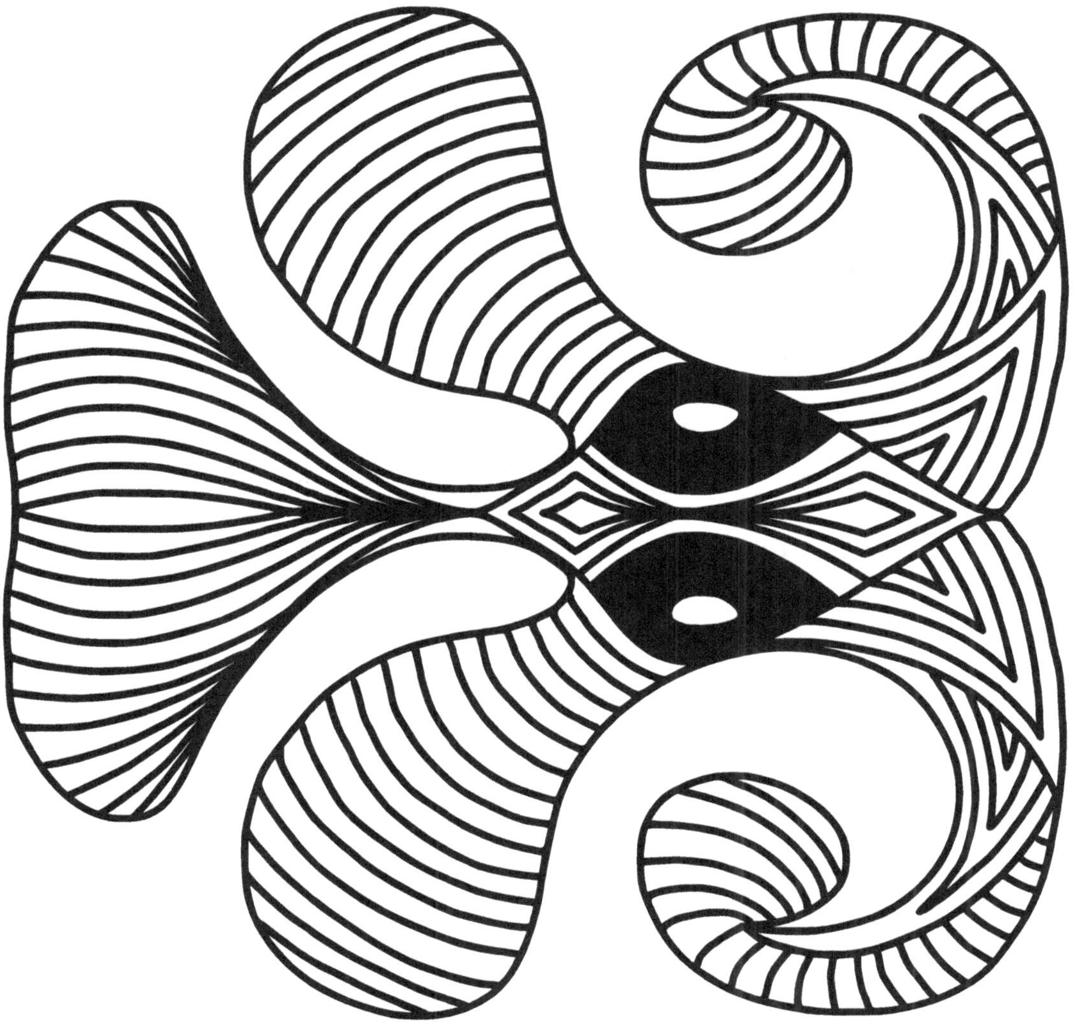

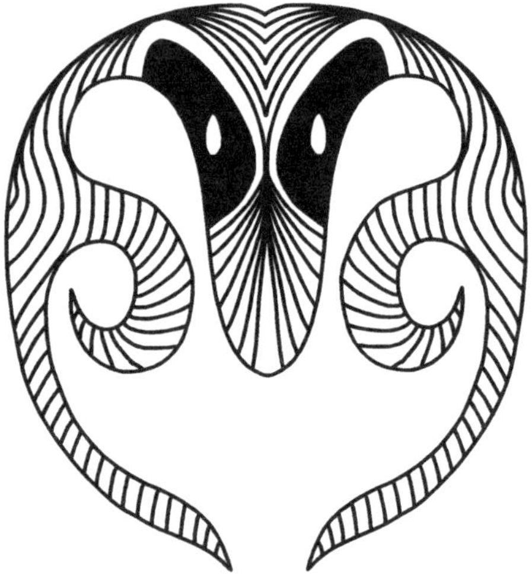

FATLINER WEIRDIES
VOLUME 1

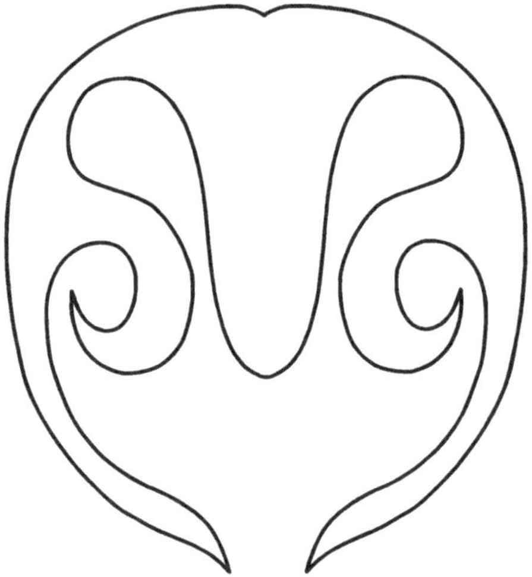

FATLINER WEIRDIES
THE TEMPLATES 1

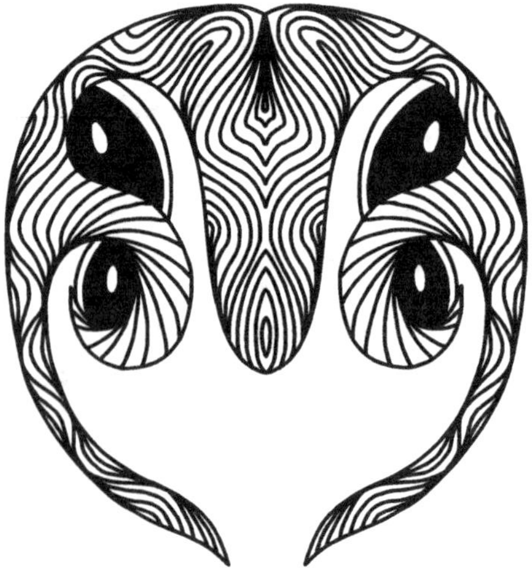

FATLINER WEIRDIES
VOLUME 3

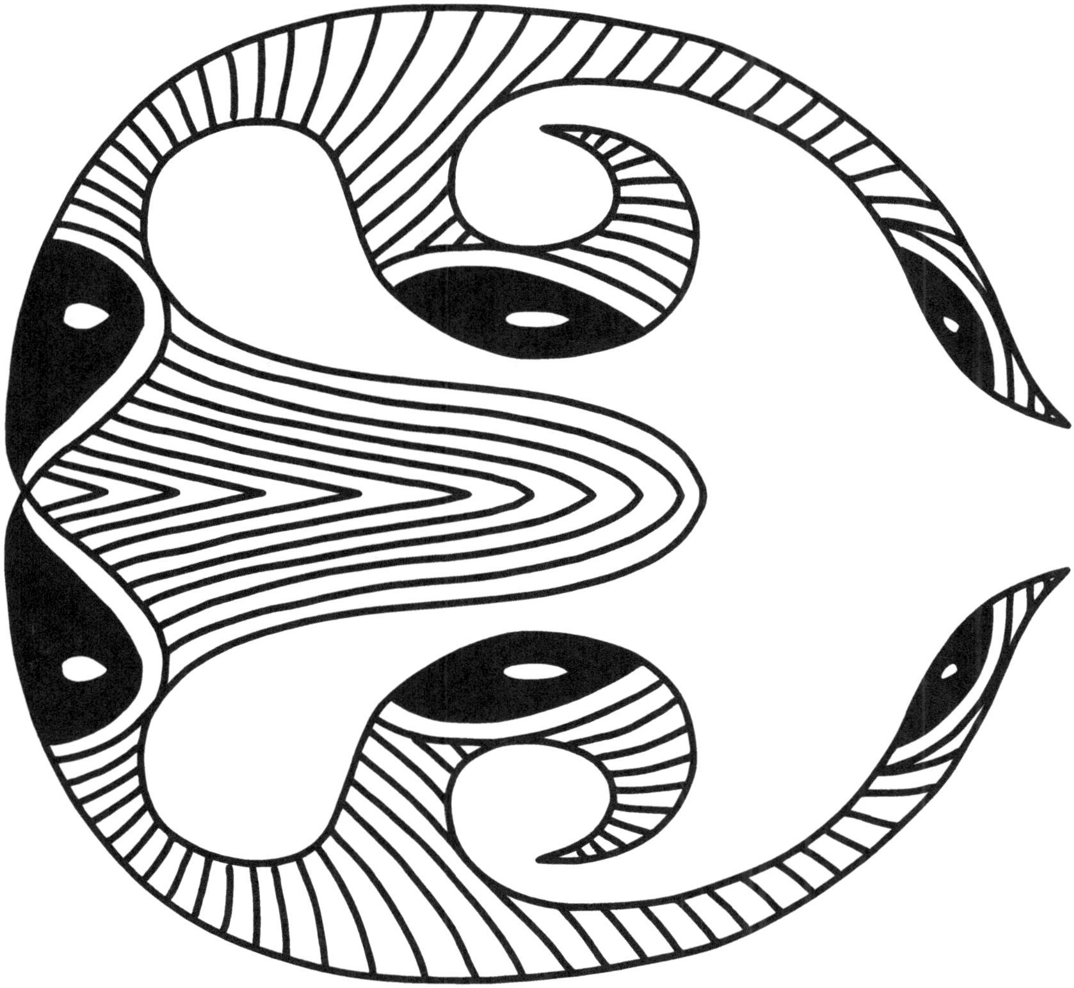

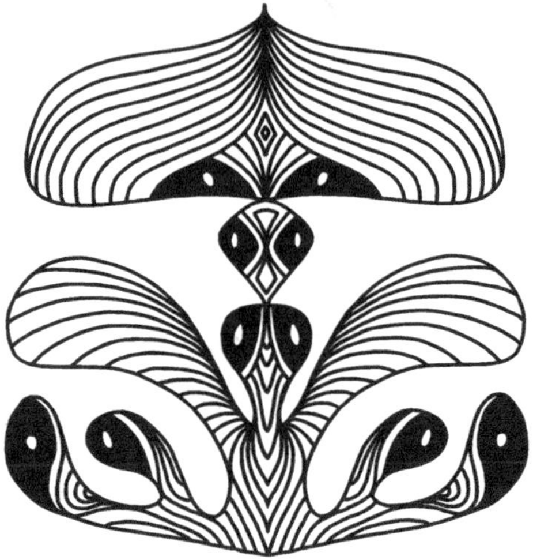

FATLINER WEIRDIES
VOLUME 1

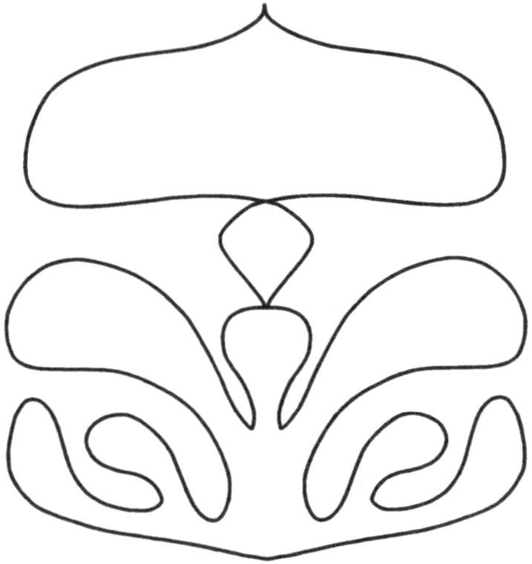

FATLINER WEIRDIES
THE TEMPLATES 1

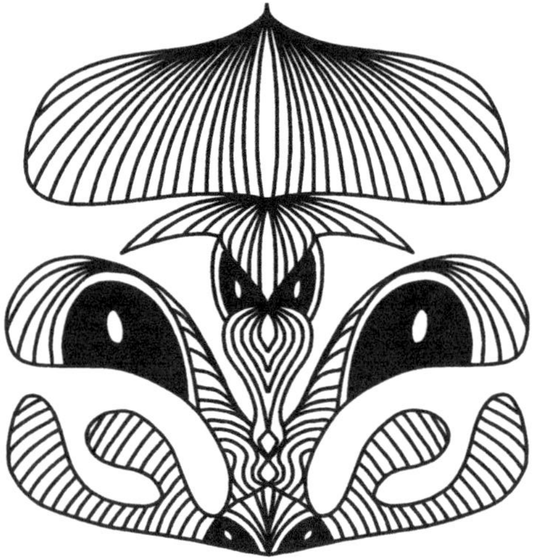

FATLINER WEIRDIES
VOLUME 3

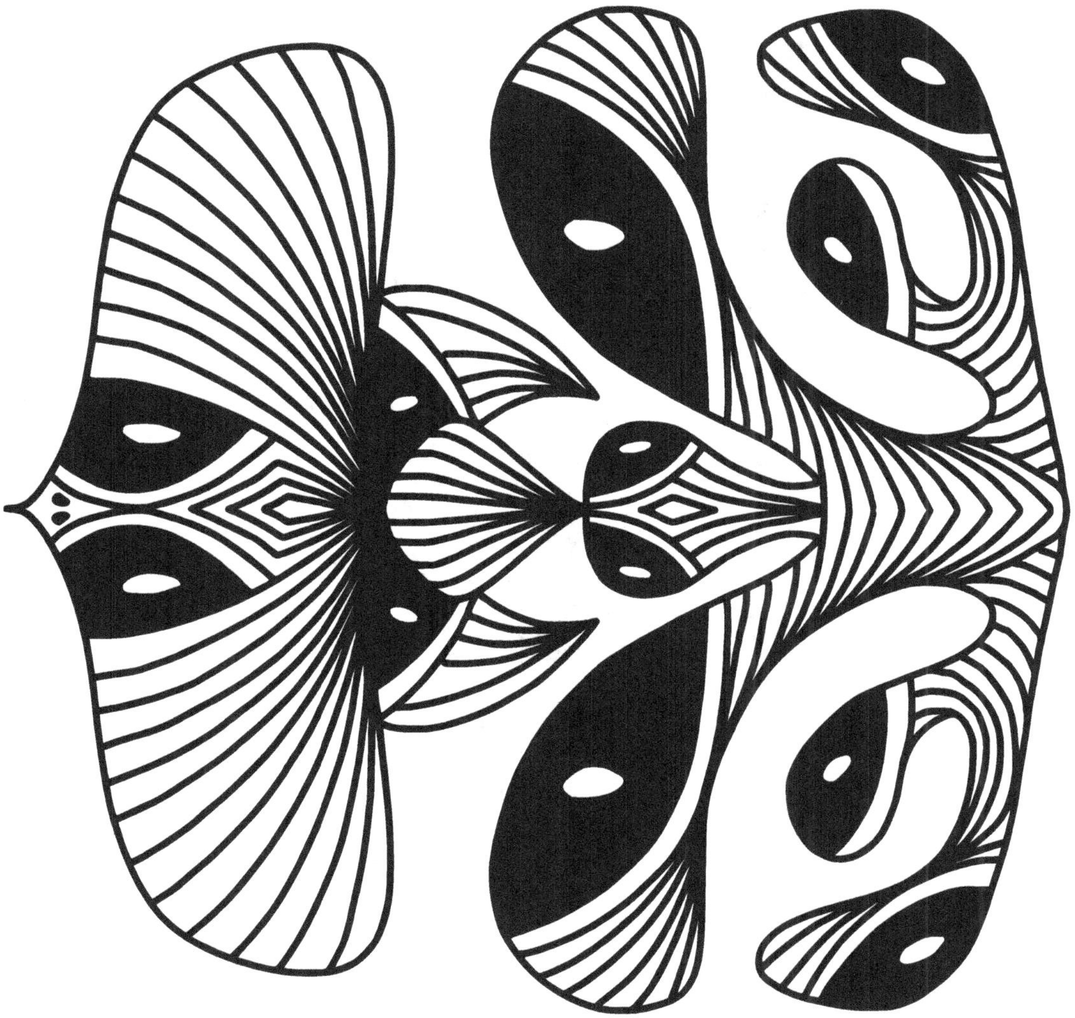

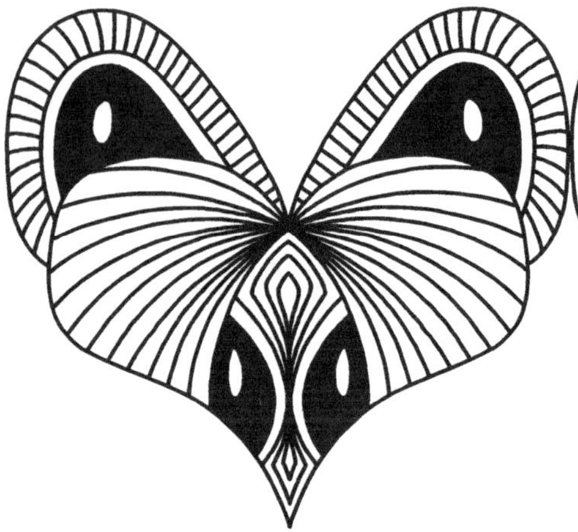

FATLINER WEIRDIES
VOLUME 1

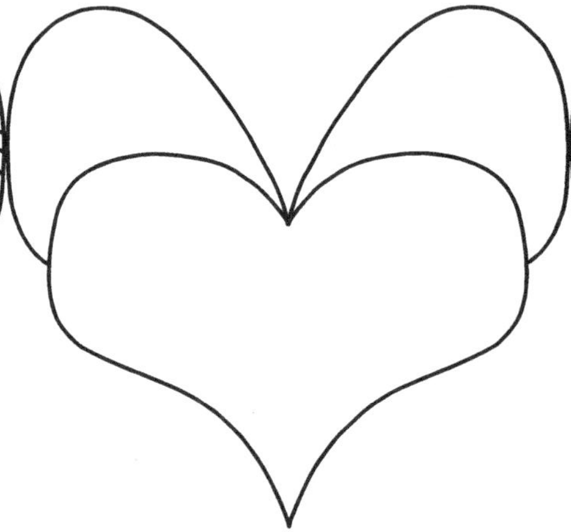

FATLINER WEIRDIES
THE TEMPLATES 1

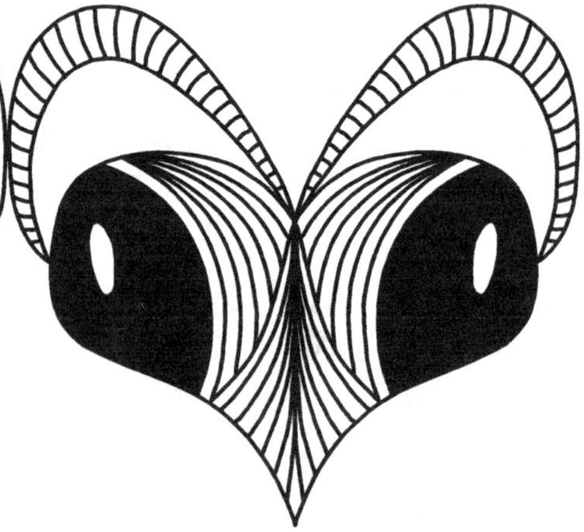

FATLINER WEIRDIES
VOLUME 3

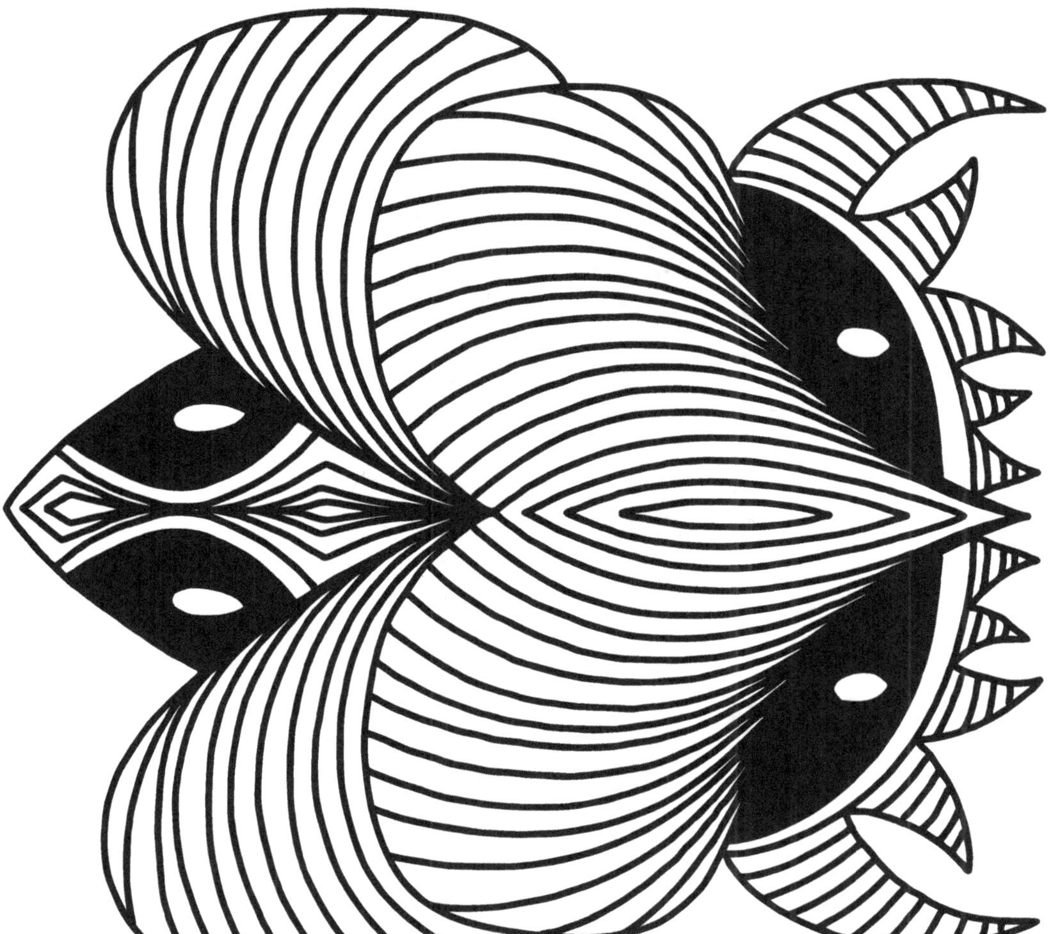

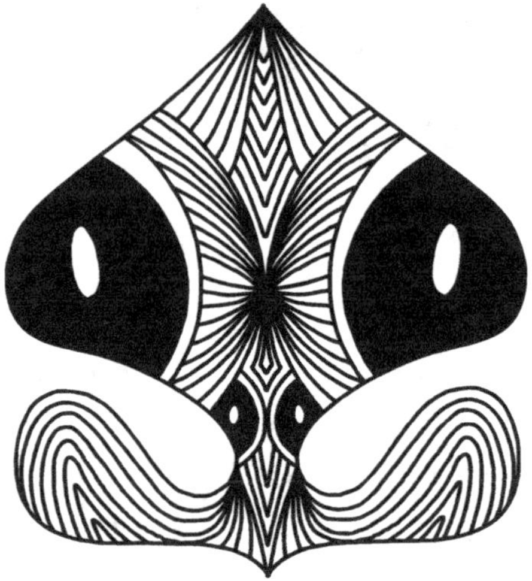

FATLINER WEIRDIES
VOLUME 1

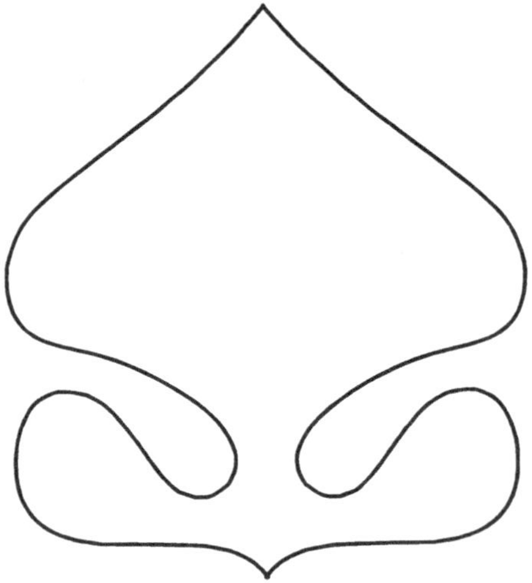

FATLINER WEIRDIES
THE TEMPLATES 1

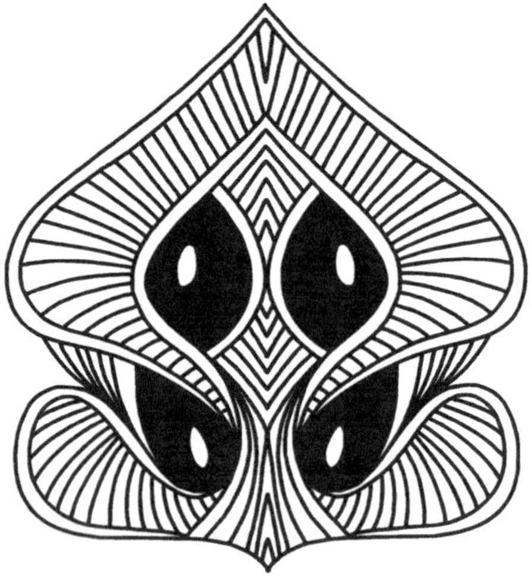

FATLINER WEIRDIES
VOLUME 3

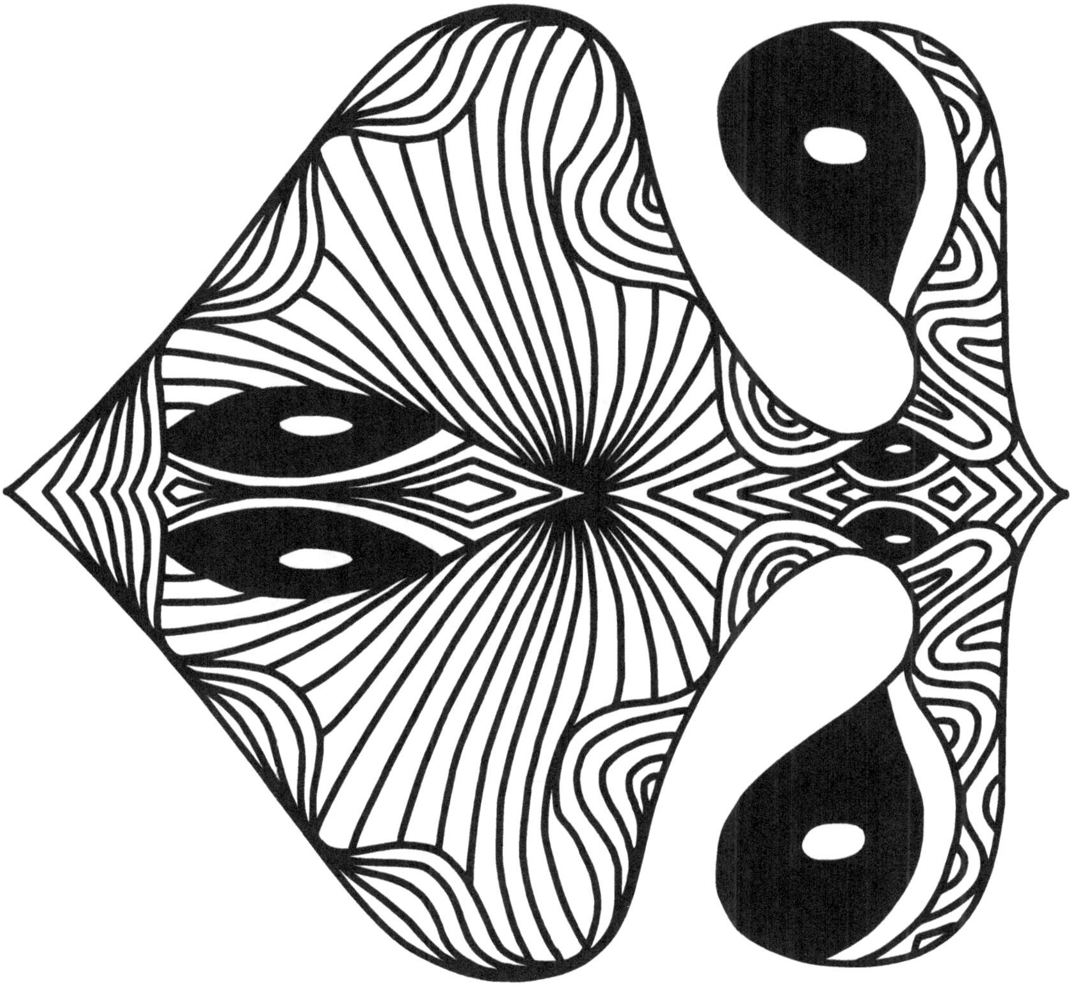

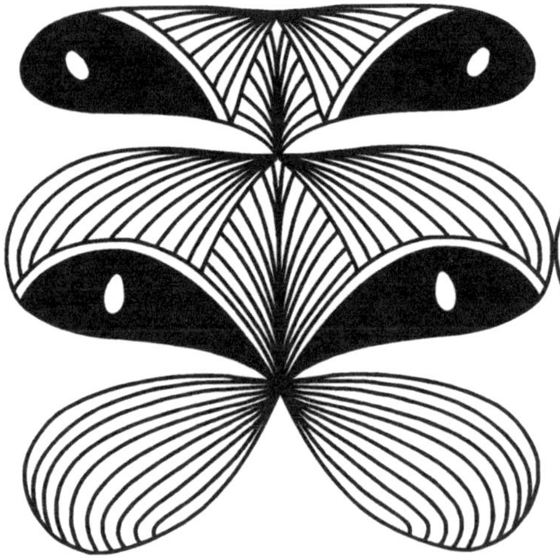

FATLINER WEIRDIES
VOLUME 1

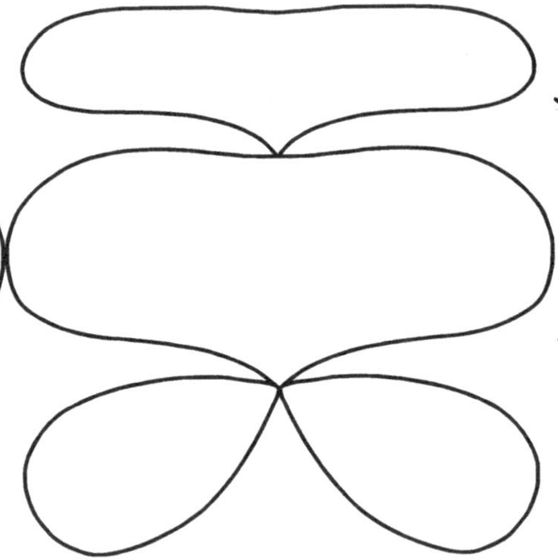

FATLINER WEIRDIES
THE TEMPLATES 1

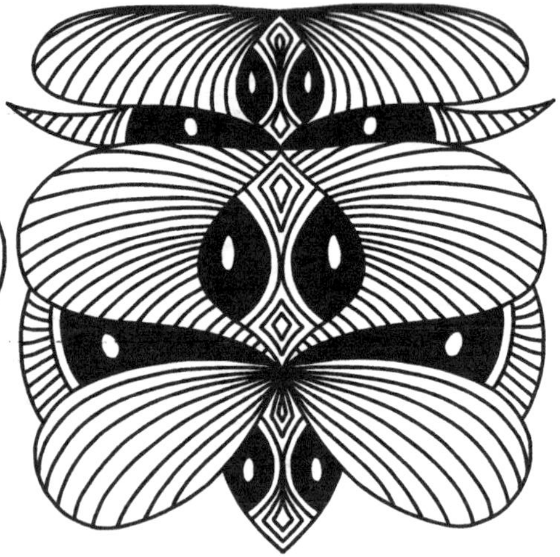

FATLINER WEIRDIES
VOLUME 3

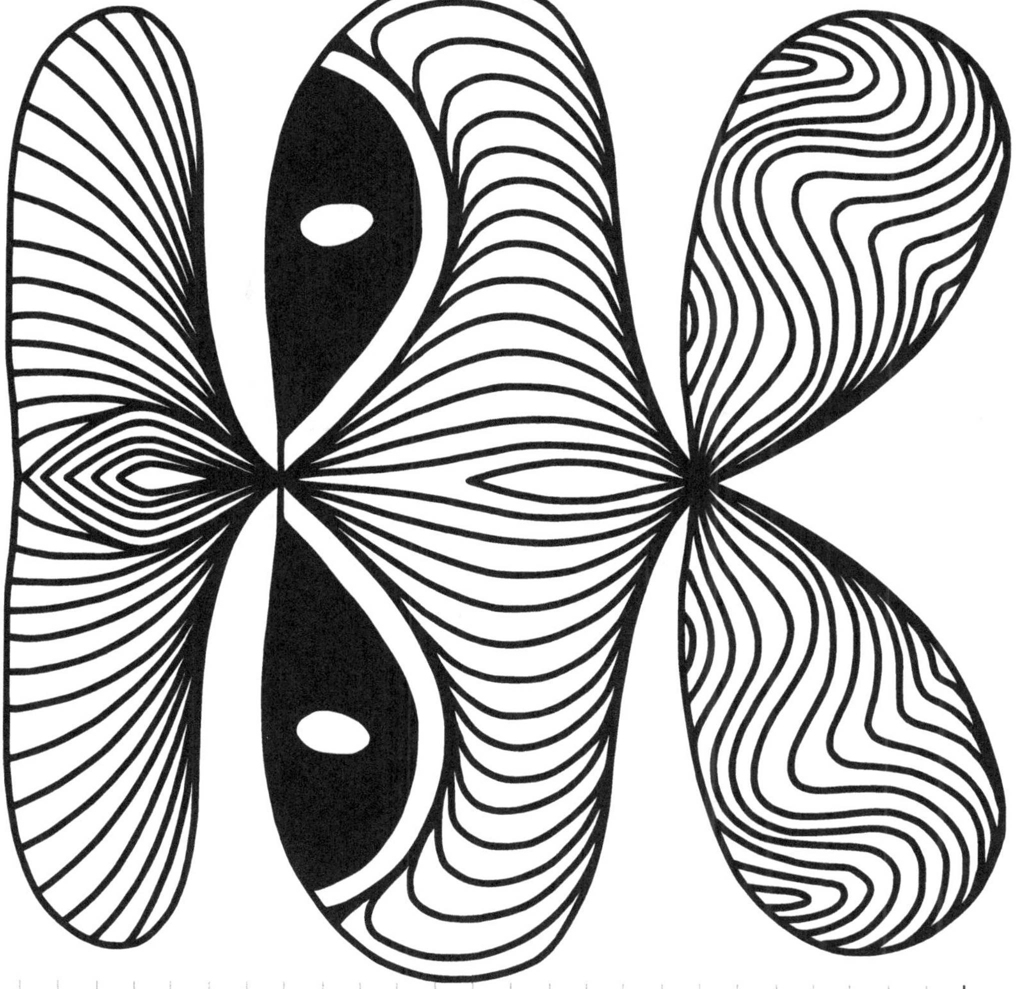

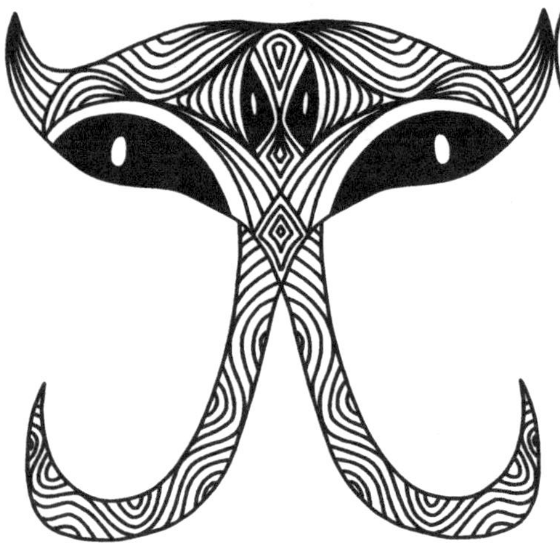

FATLINER WEIRDIES
VOLUME 1

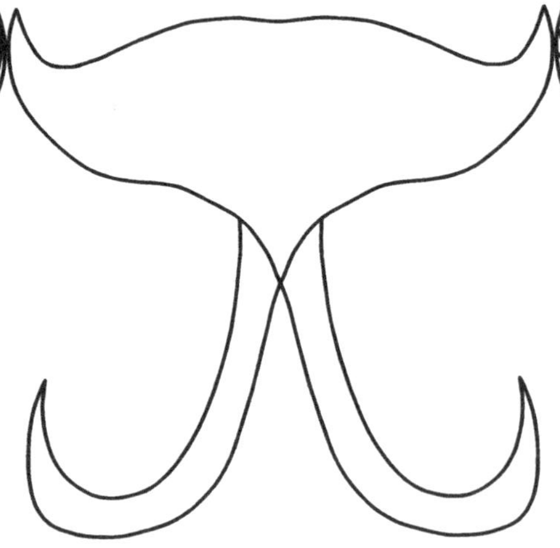

FATLINER WEIRDIES
THE TEMPLATES 1

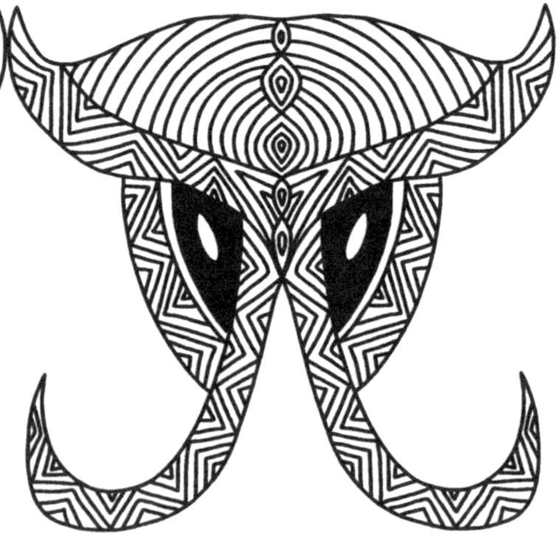

FATLINER WEIRDIES
VOLUME 3

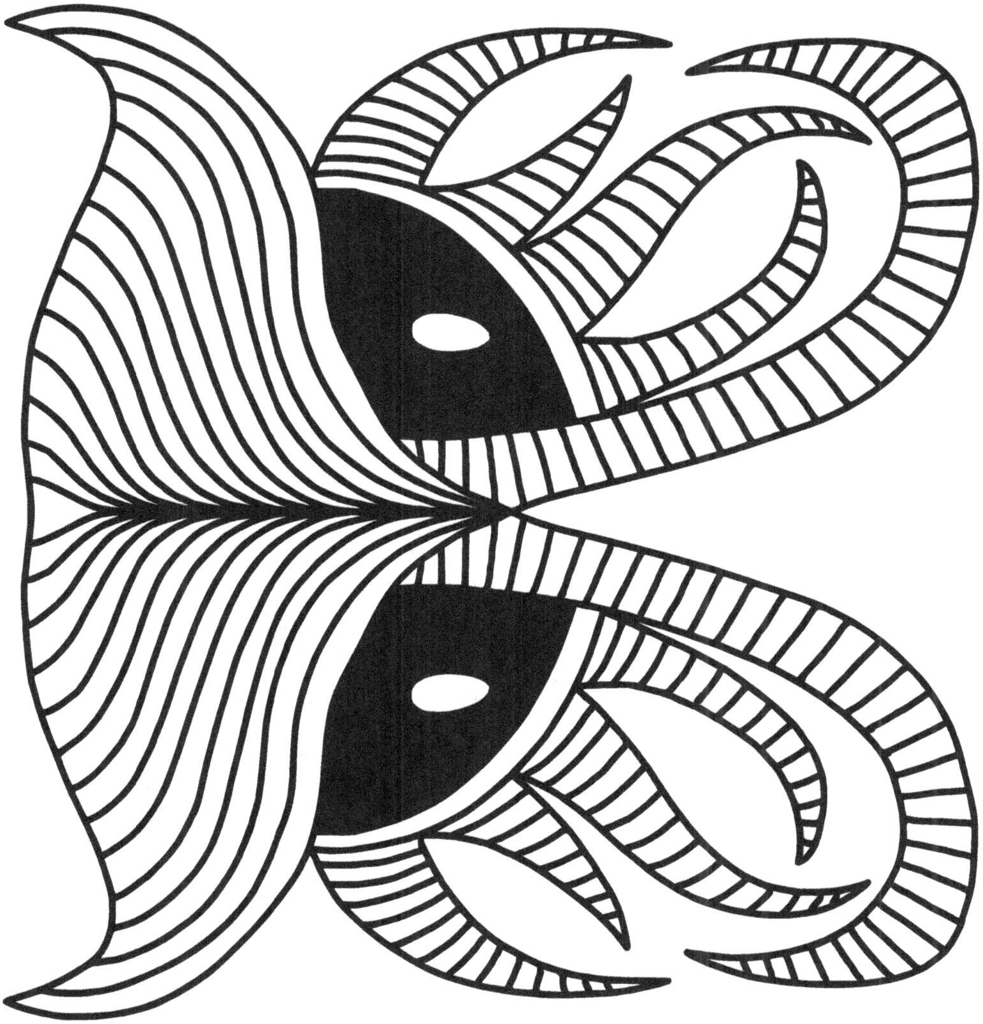

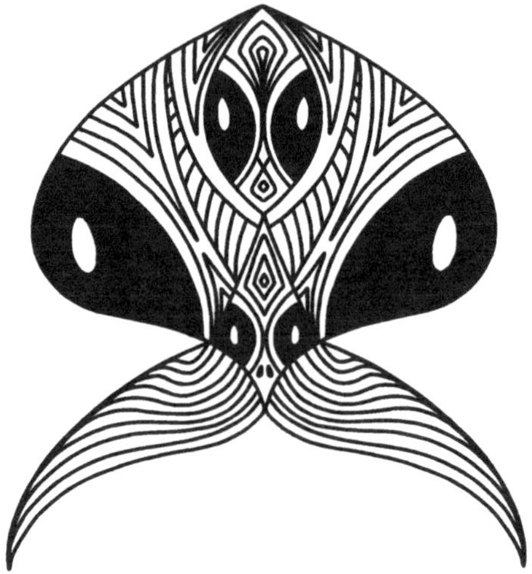

FATLINER WEIRDIES
VOLUME 1

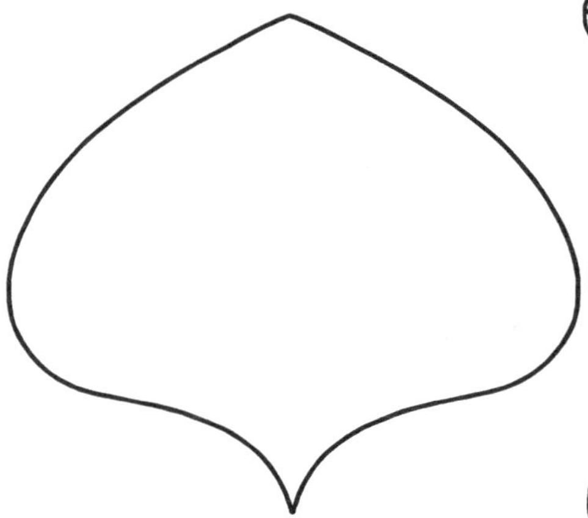

FATLINER WEIRDIES
THE TEMPLATES 1

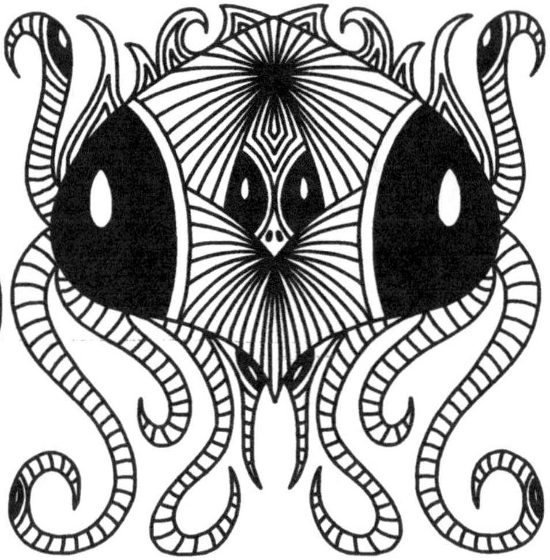

FATLINER WEIRDIES
VOLUME 3

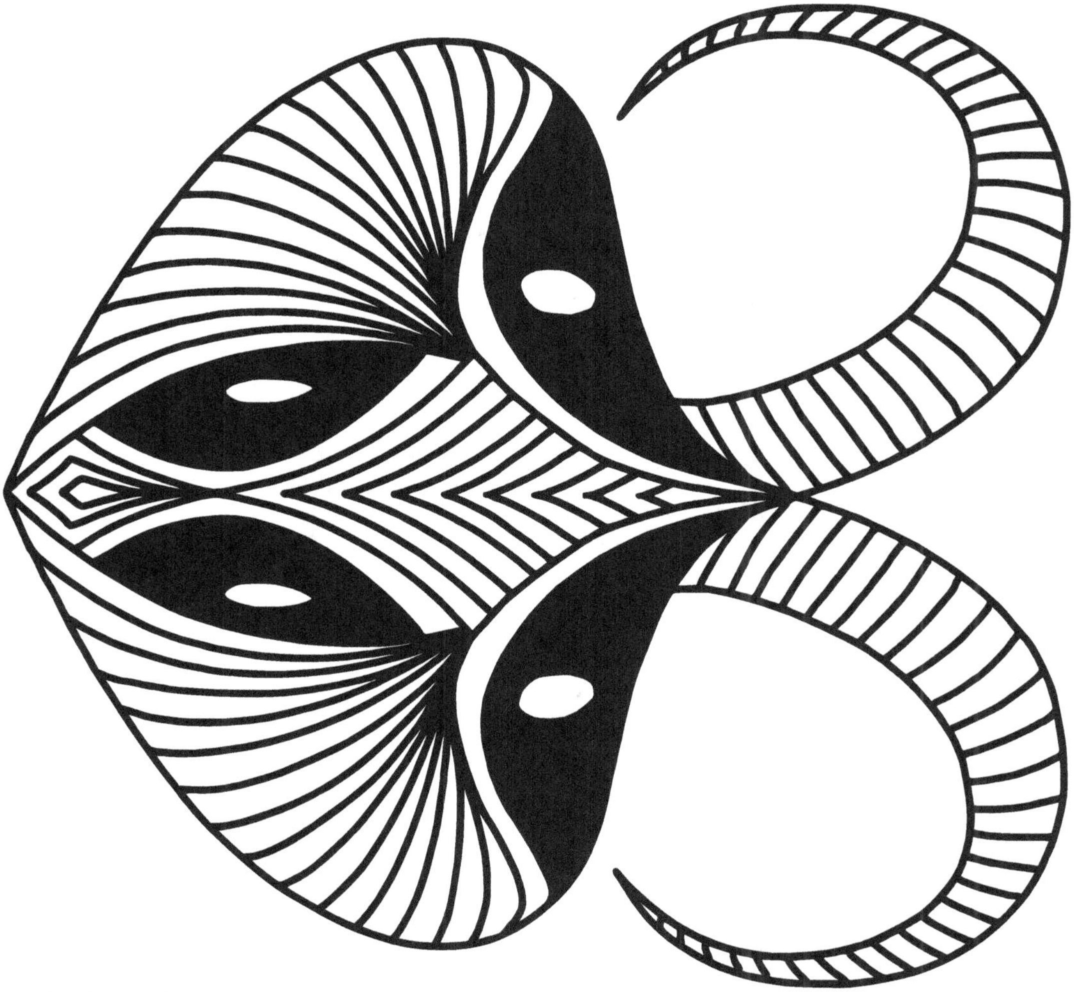

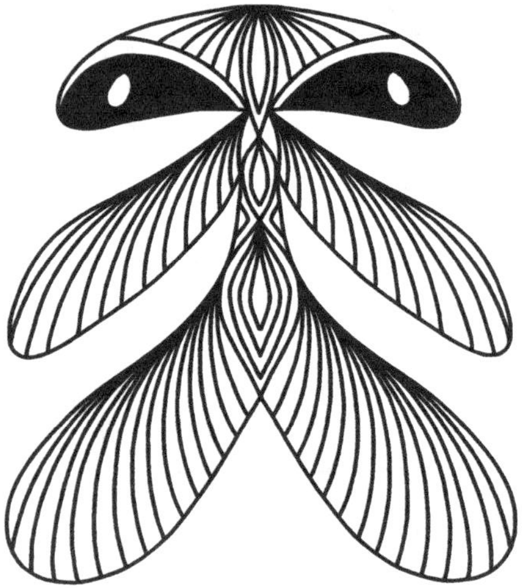

FATLINER WEIRDIES
VOLUME 1

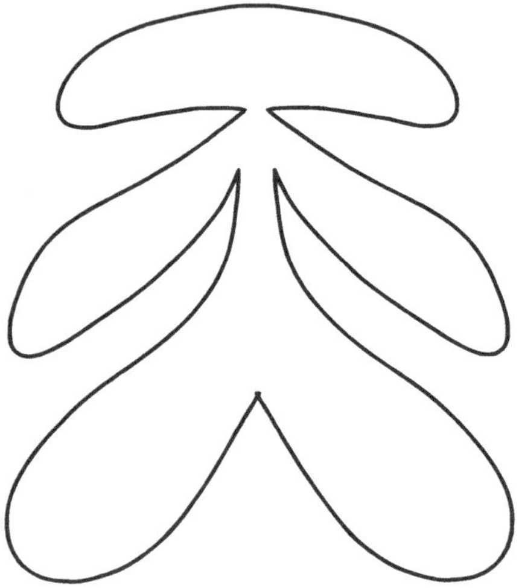

FATLINER WEIRDIES
THE TEMPLATES 1

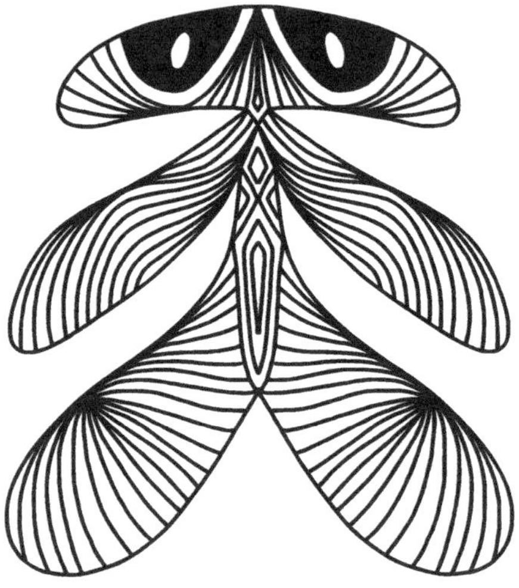

FATLINER WEIRDIES
VOLUME 3

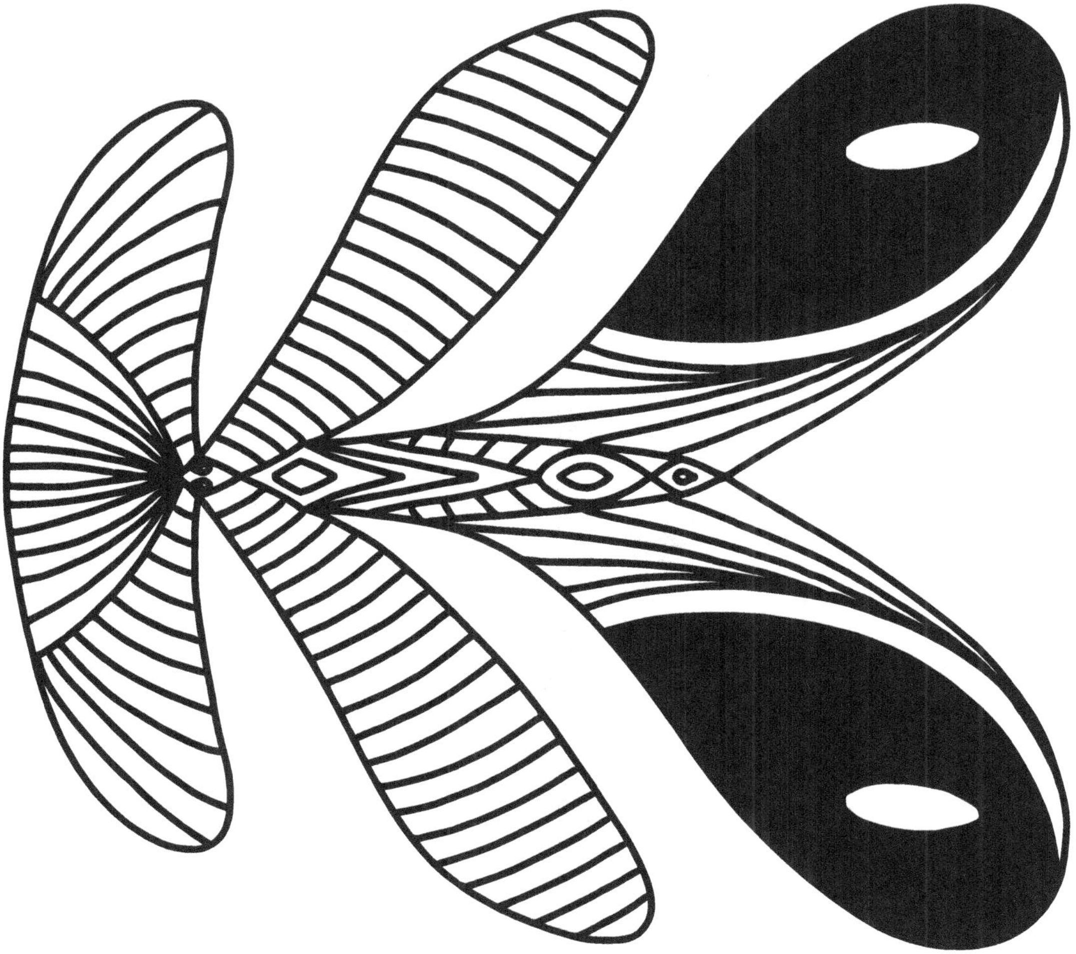

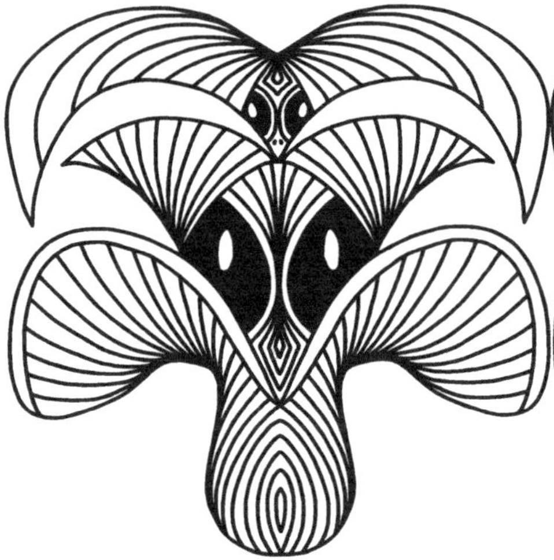

FATLINER WEIRDIES
VOLUME 1

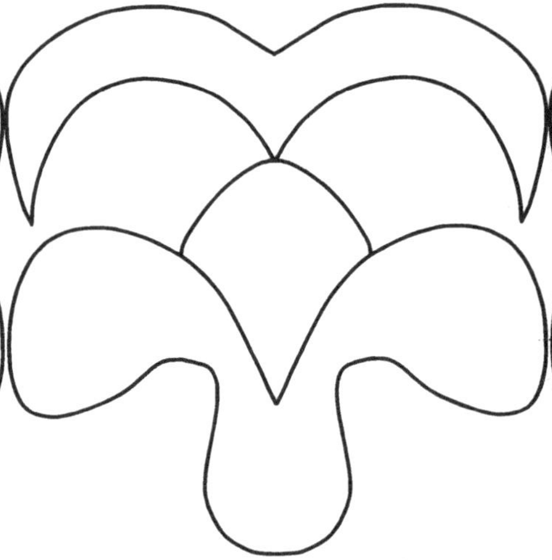

FATLINER WEIRDIES
THE TEMPLATES 1

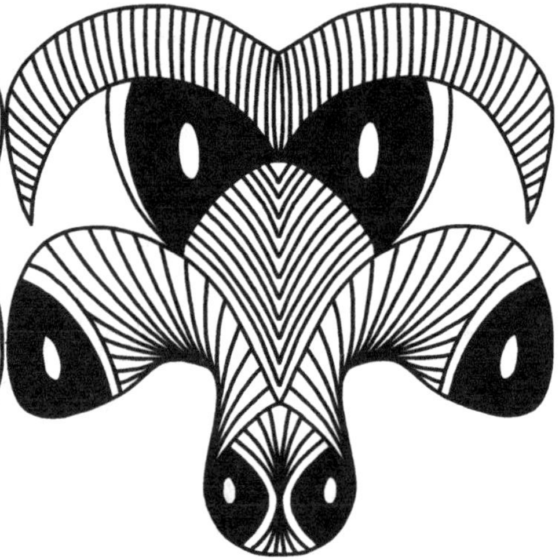

FATLINER WEIRDIES
VOLUME 3

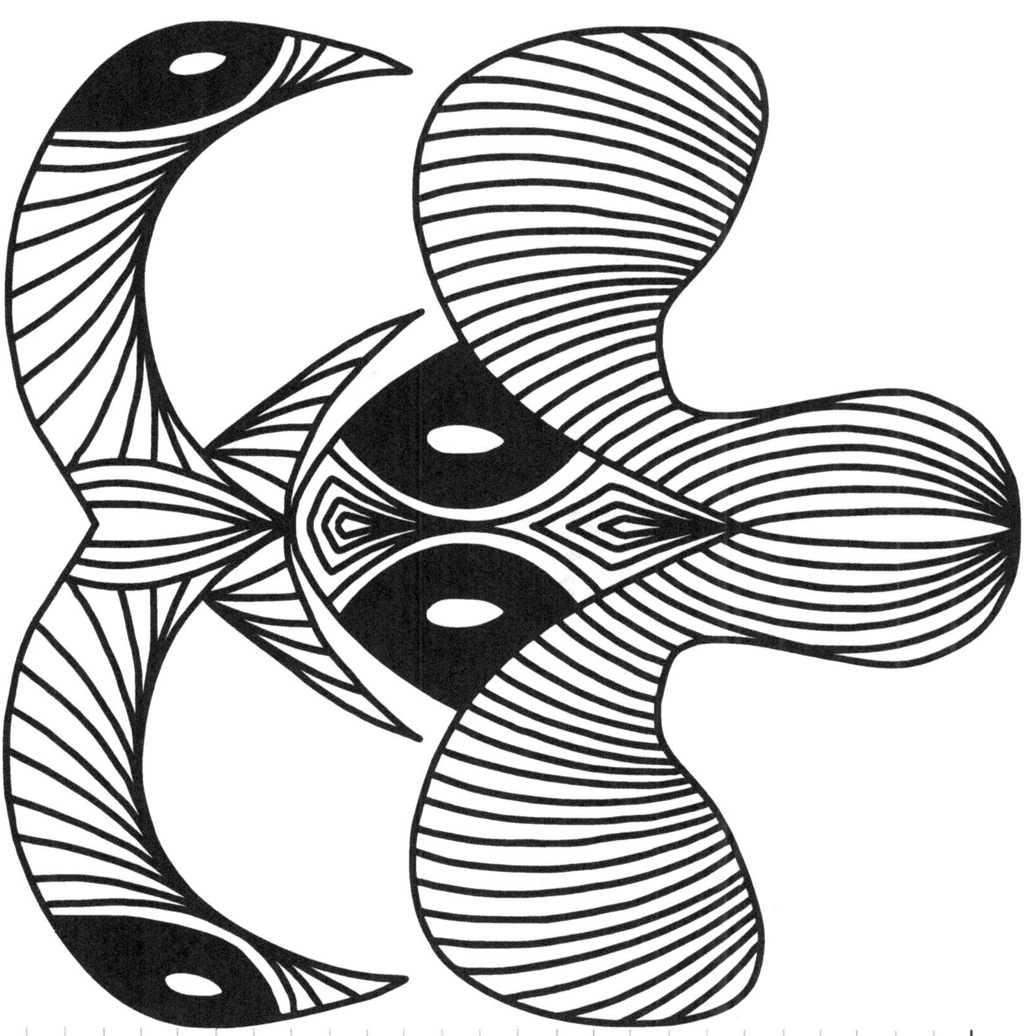

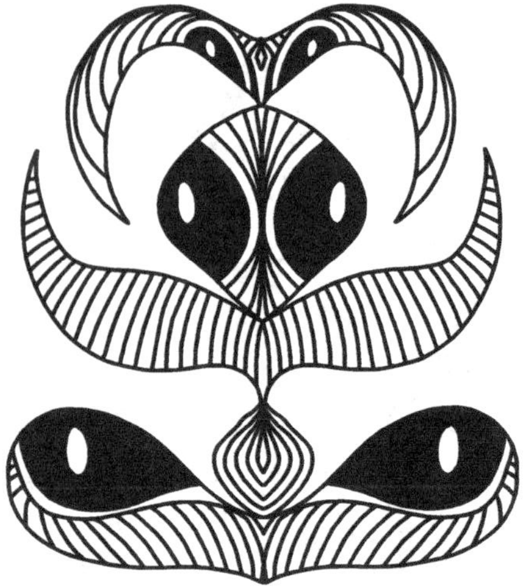

FATLINER WEIRDIES
VOLUME 1

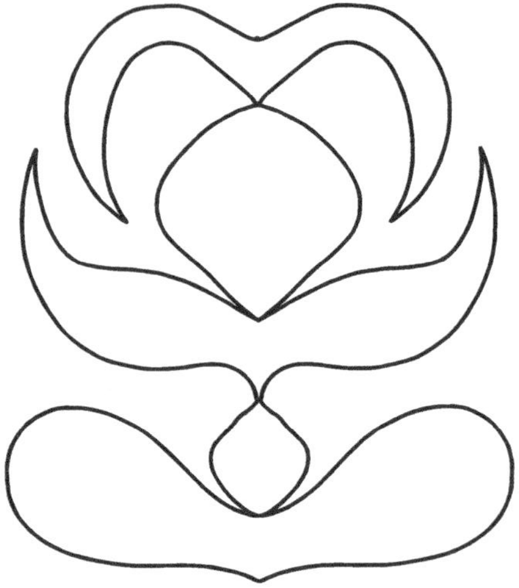

FATLINER WEIRDIES
THE TEMPLATES 1

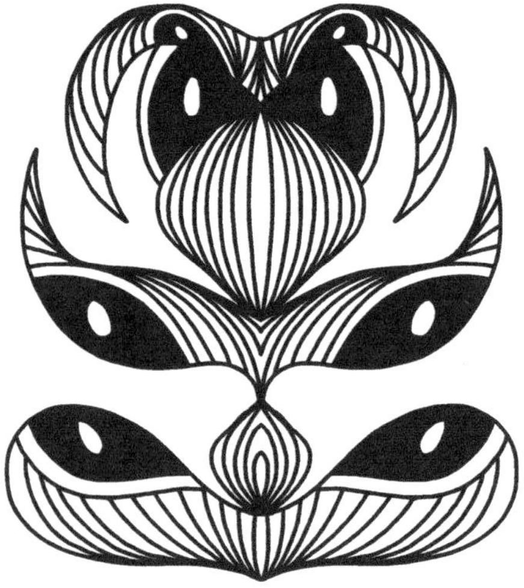

FATLINER WEIRDIES
VOLUME 3

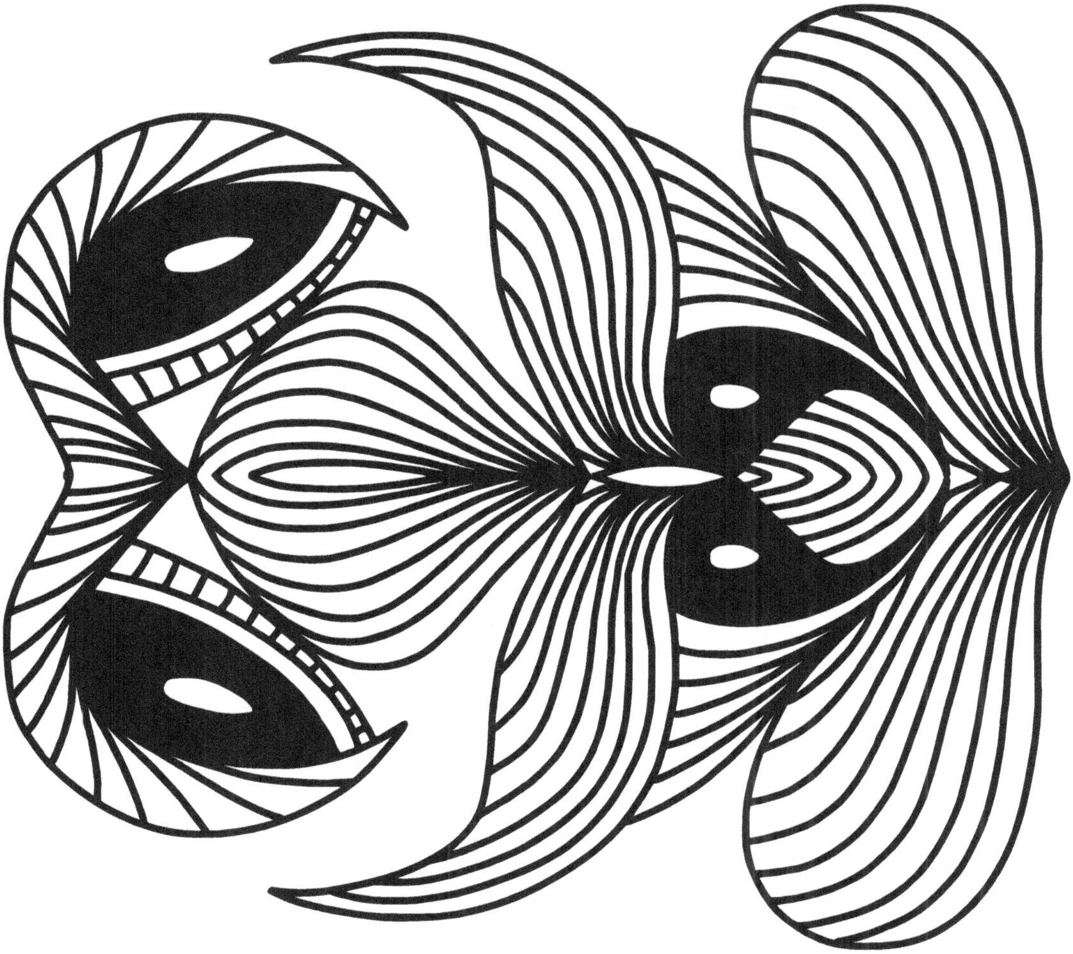

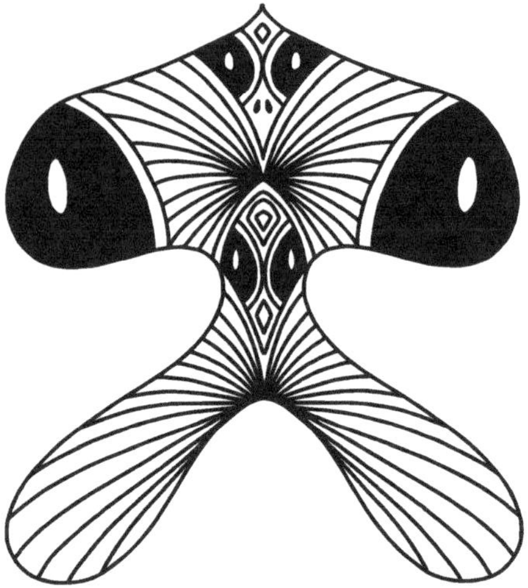

FATLINER WEIRDIES
VOLUME 1

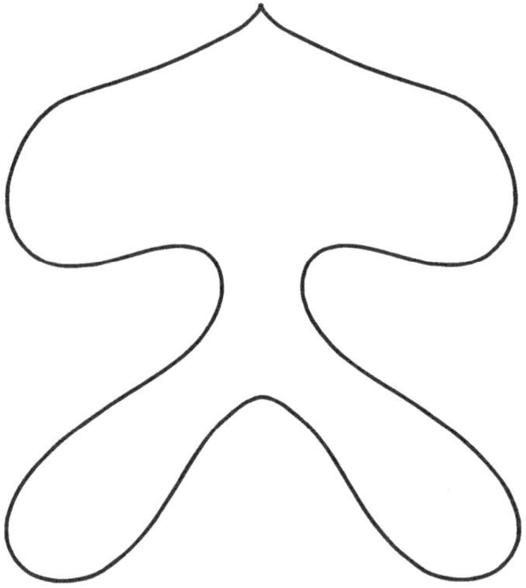

FATLINER WEIRDIES
THE TEMPLATES 1

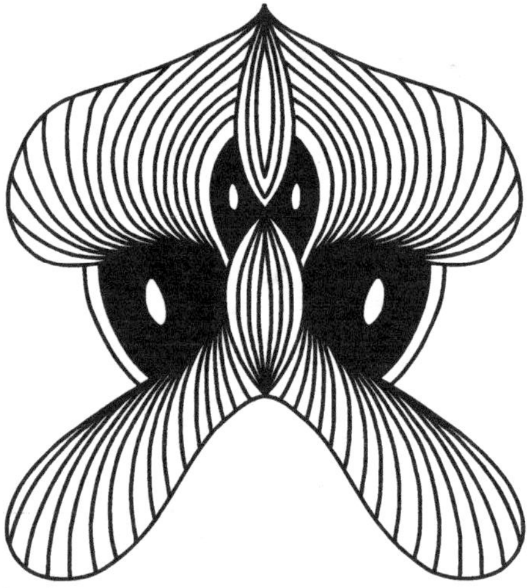

FATLINER WEIRDIES
VOLUME 3

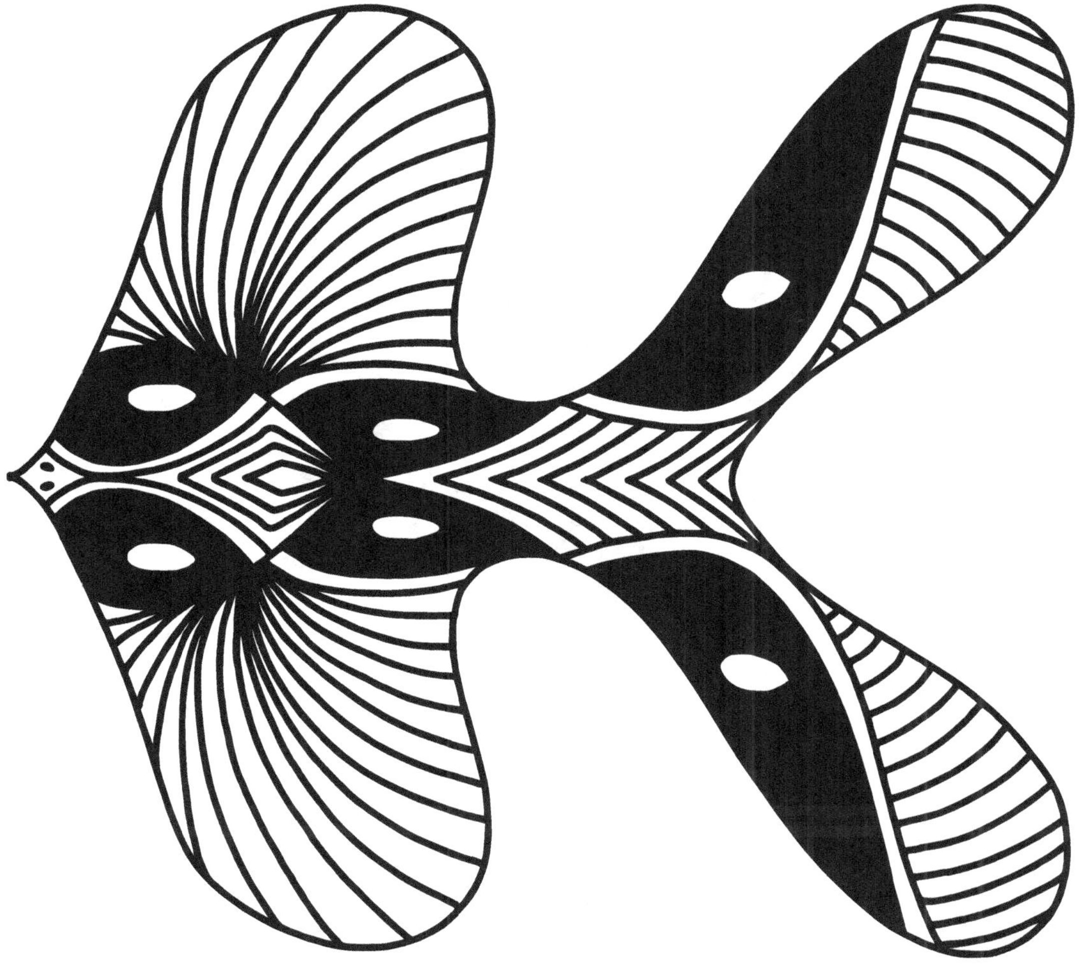

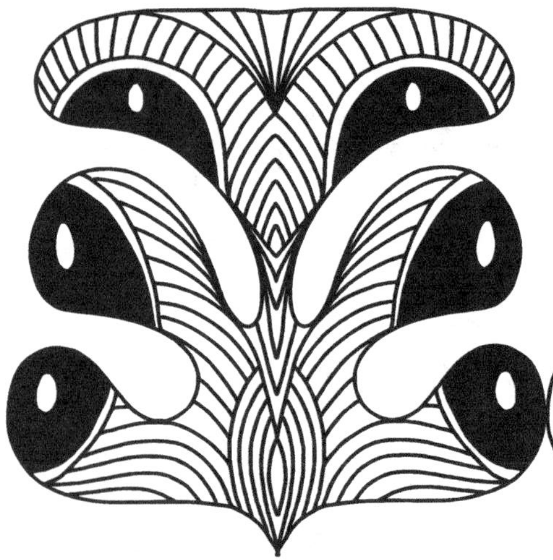

FATLINER WEIRDIES
VOLUME 1

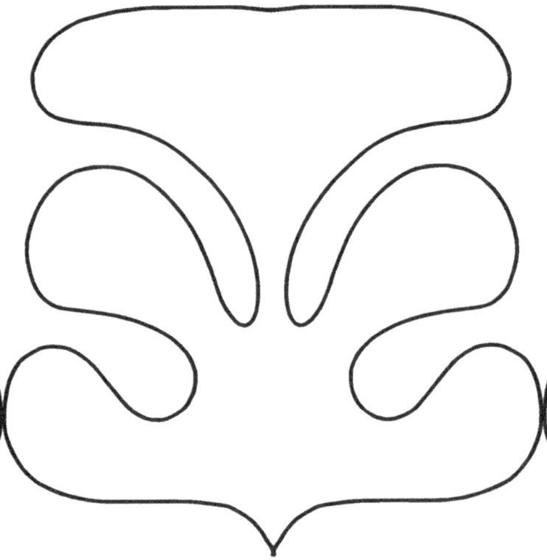

FATLINER WEIRDIES
THE TEMPLATES 1

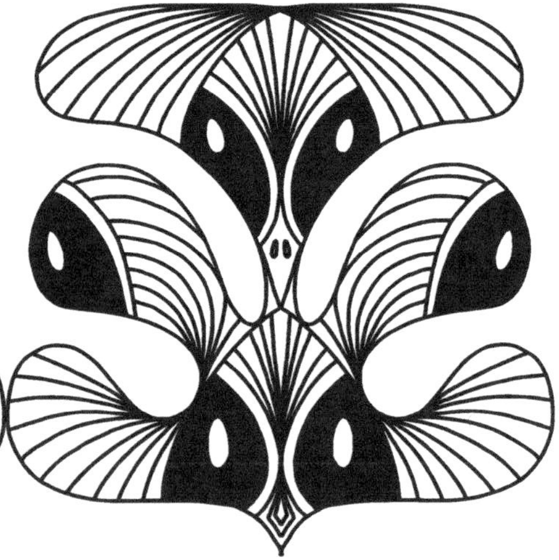

FATLINER WEIRDIES
VOLUME 3

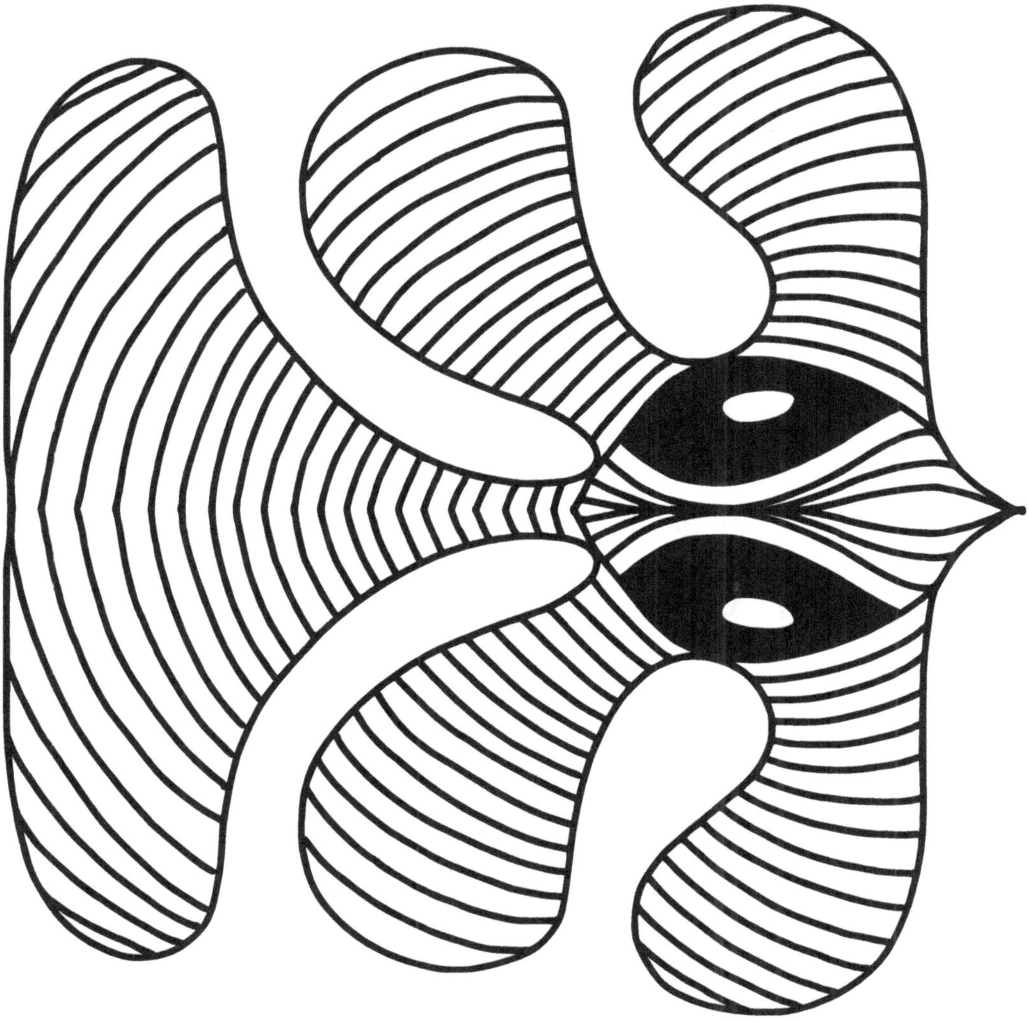

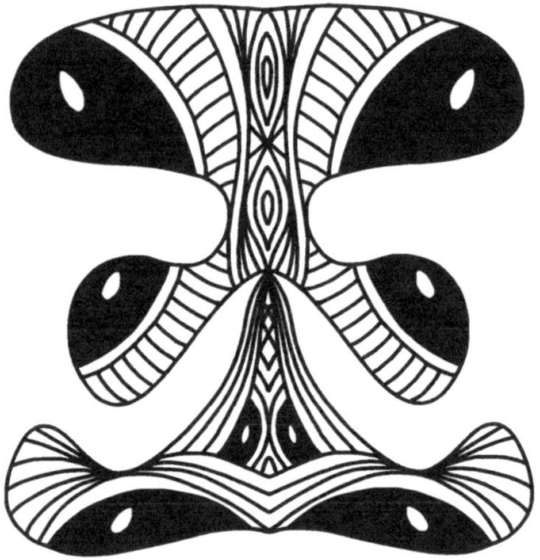
FATLINER WEIRDIES
VOLUME 1

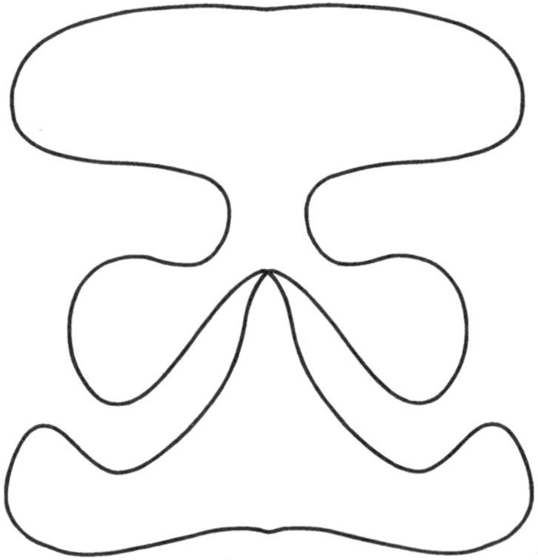
FATLINER WEIRDIES
THE TEMPLATES 1

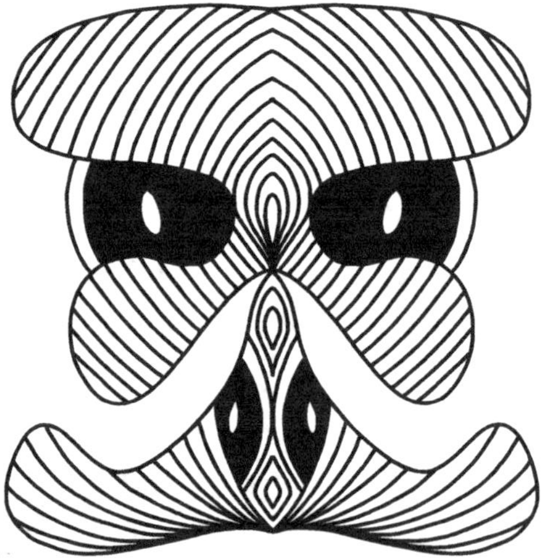
FATLINER WEIRDIES
VOLUME 3

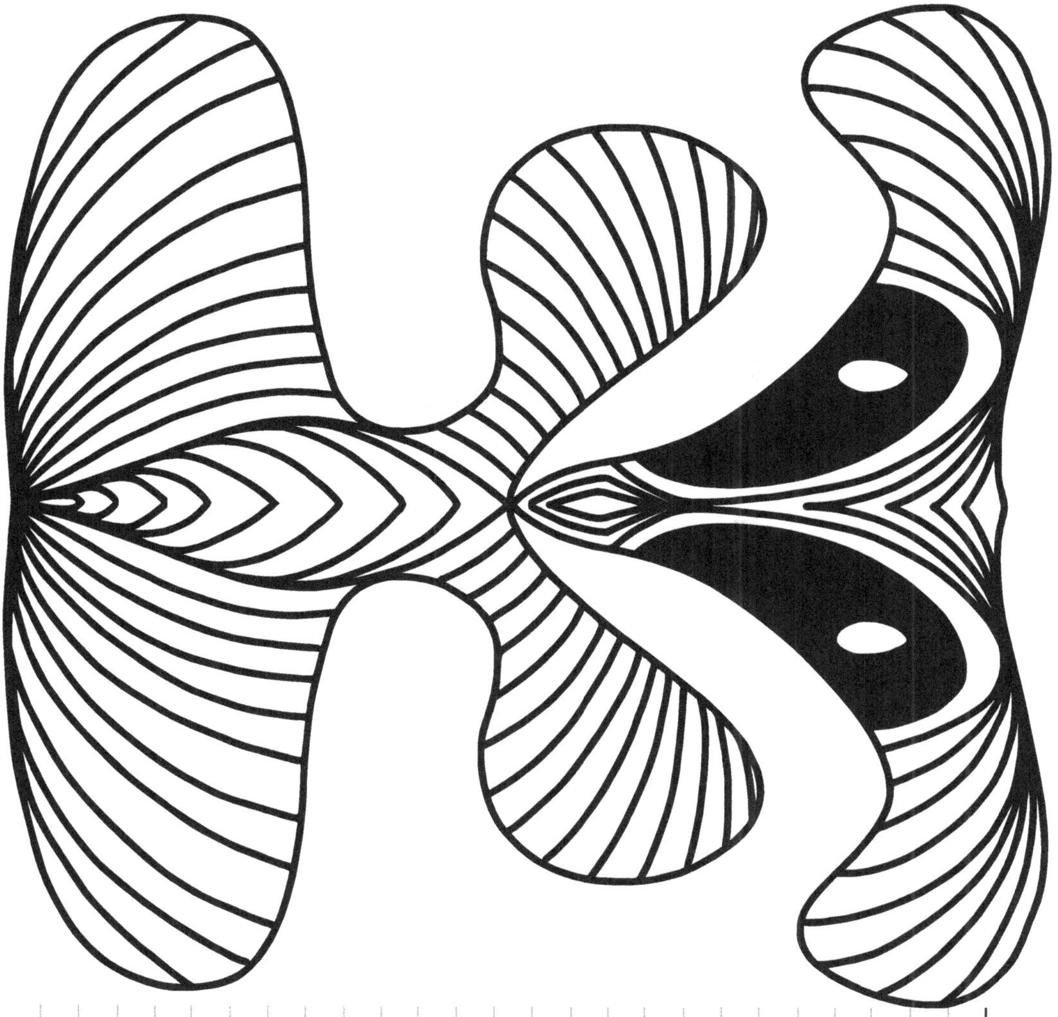

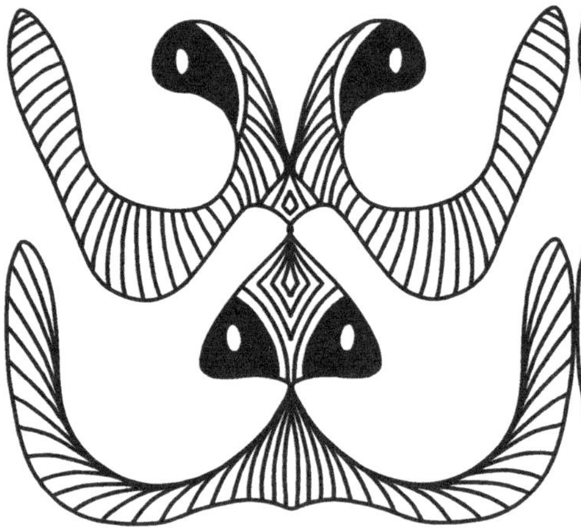

FATLINER WEIRDIES
VOLUME 1

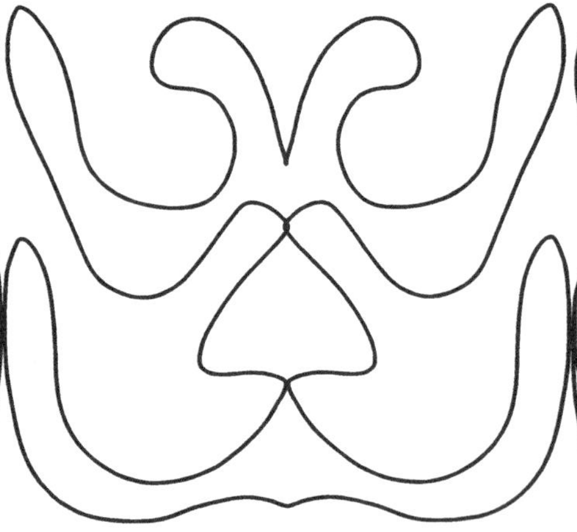

FATLINER WEIRDIES
THE TEMPLATES 1

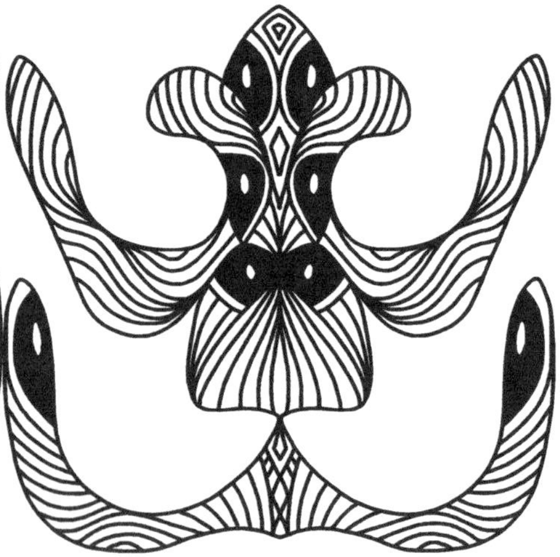

FATLINER WEIRDIES
VOLUME 3

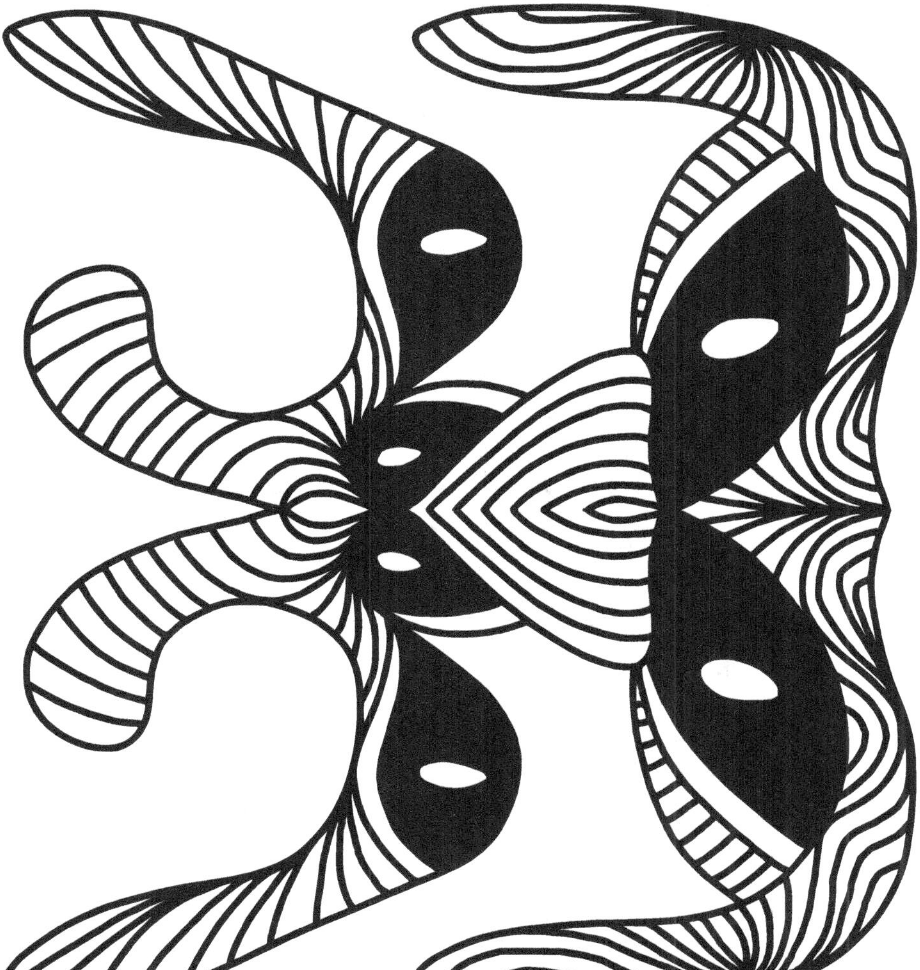

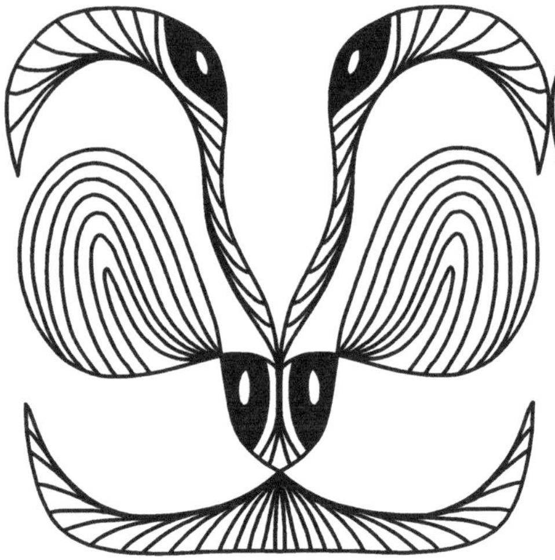

FATLINER WEIRDIES
VOLUME 1

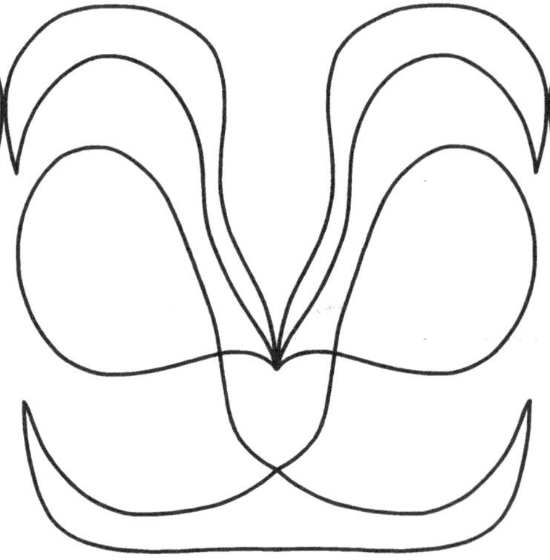

FATLINER WEIRDIES
THE TEMPLATES 1

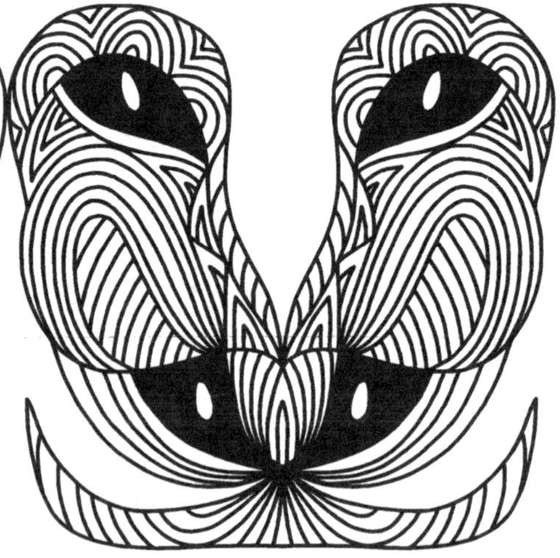

FATLINER WEIRDIES
VOLUME 3

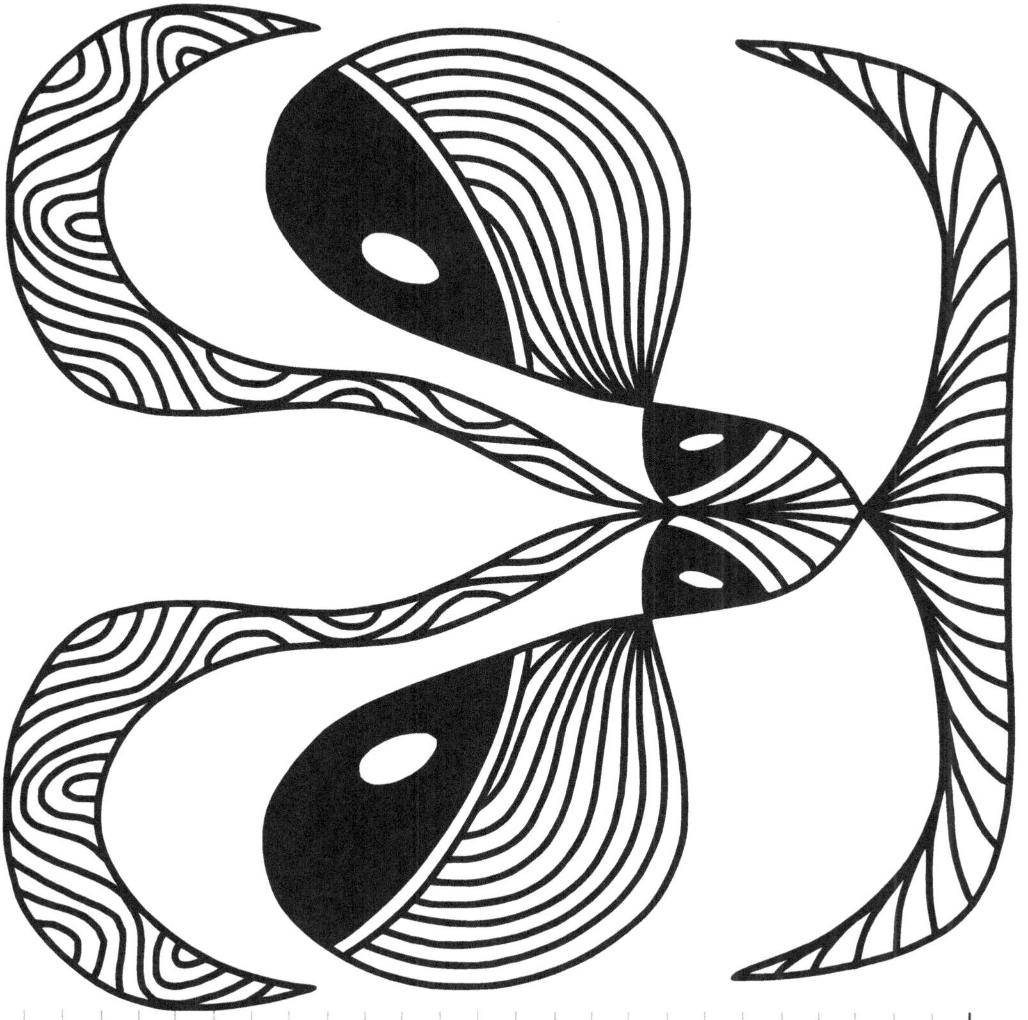

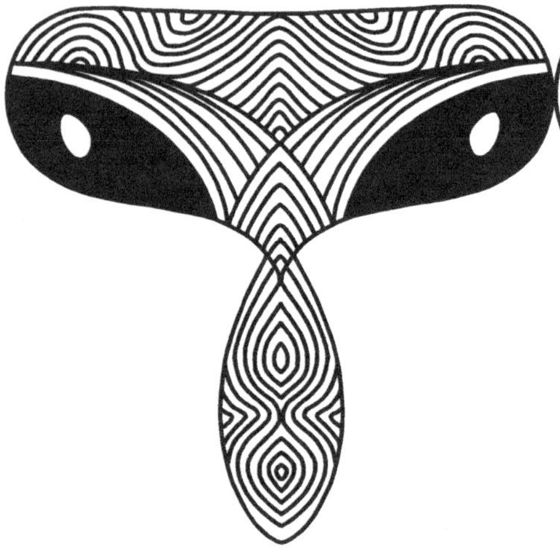

FATLINER WEIRDIES
VOLUME 1

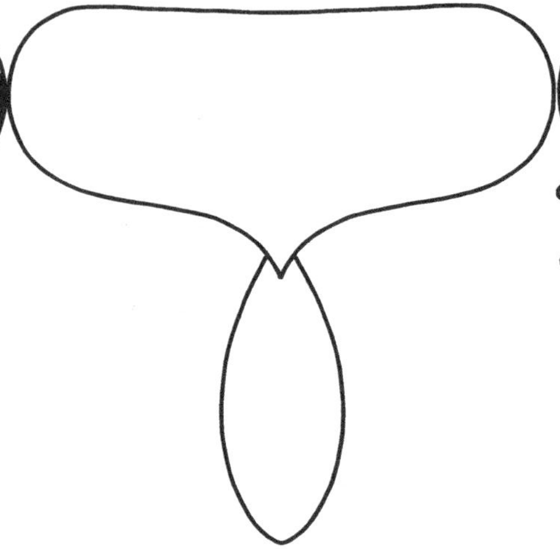

FATLINER WEIRDIES
THE TEMPLATES 1

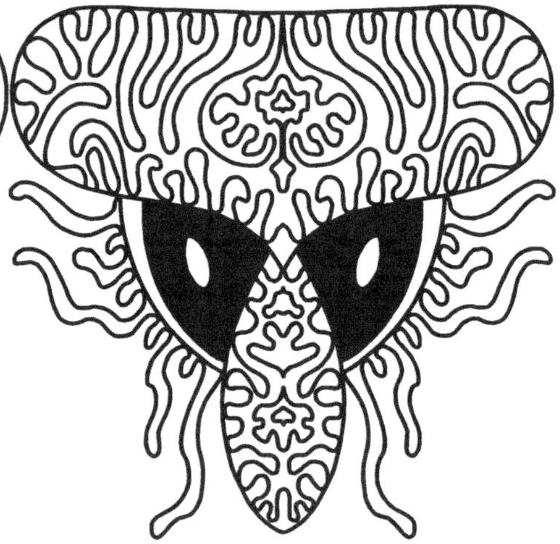

FATLINER WEIRDIES
VOLUME 3

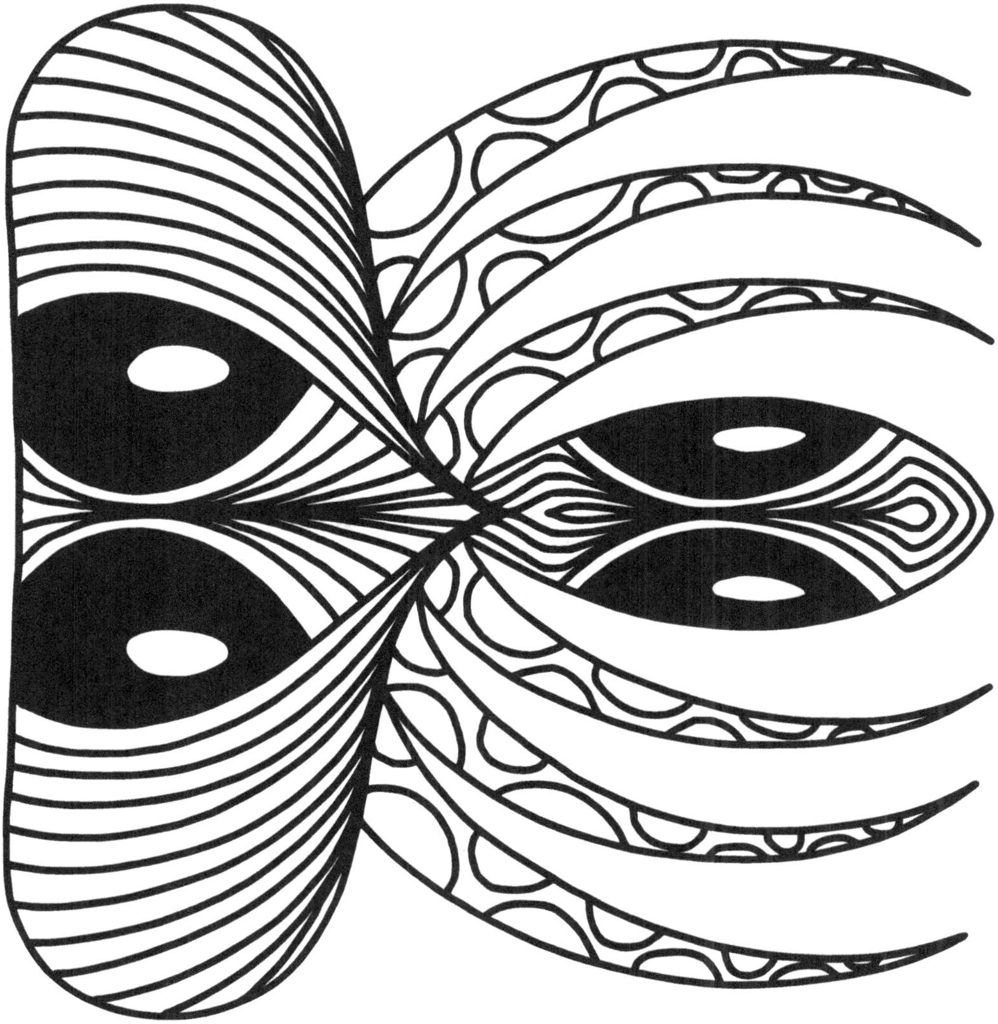

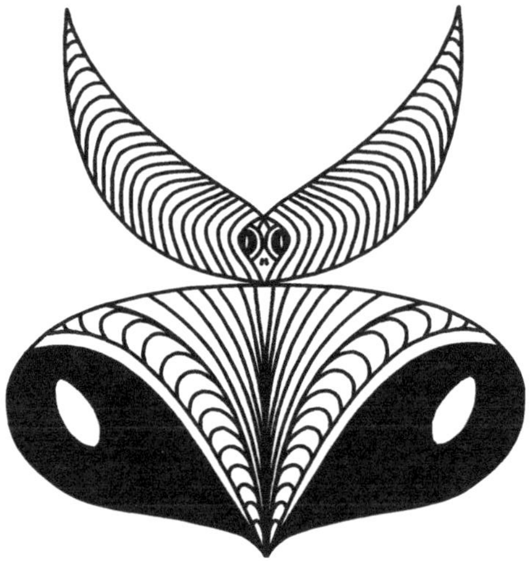

FATLINER WEIRDIES
VOLUME 1

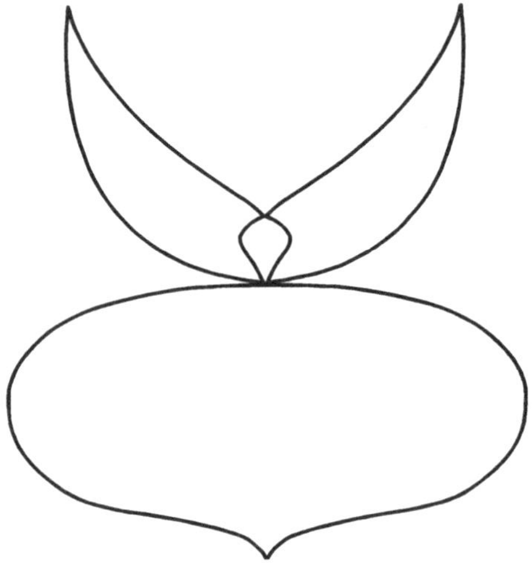

FATLINER WEIRDIES
THE TEMPLATES 1

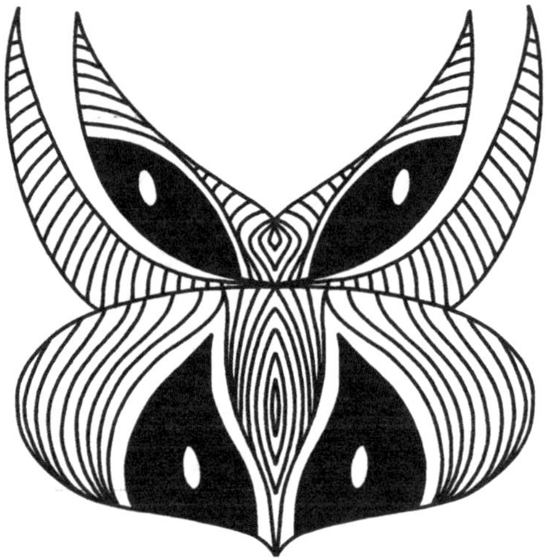

FATLINER WEIRDIES
VOLUME 3

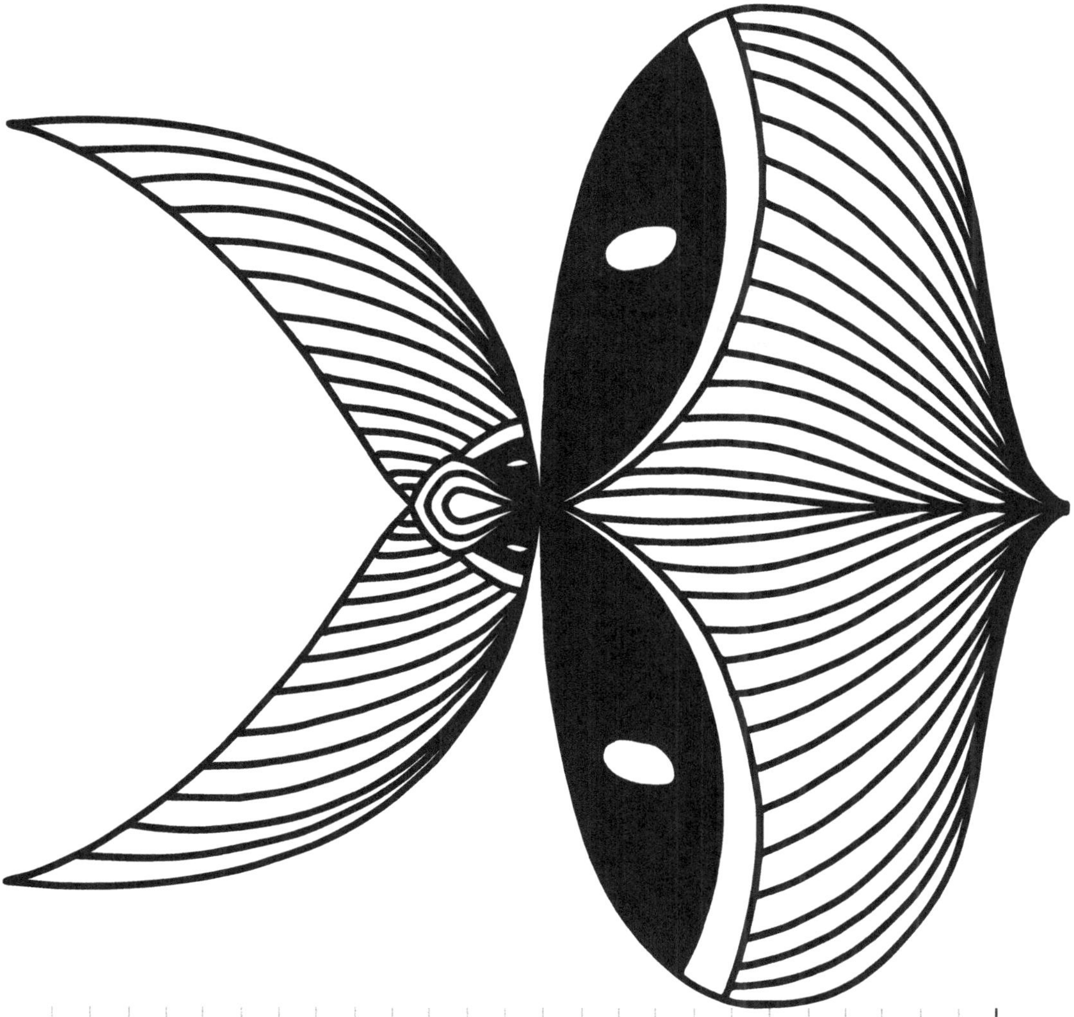

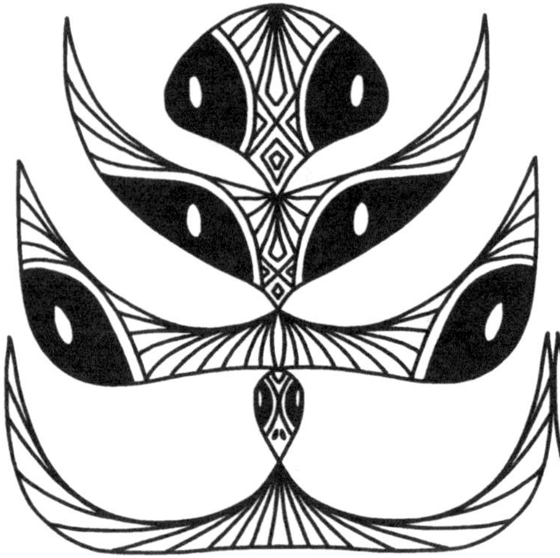

FATLINER WEIRDIES
VOLUME 1

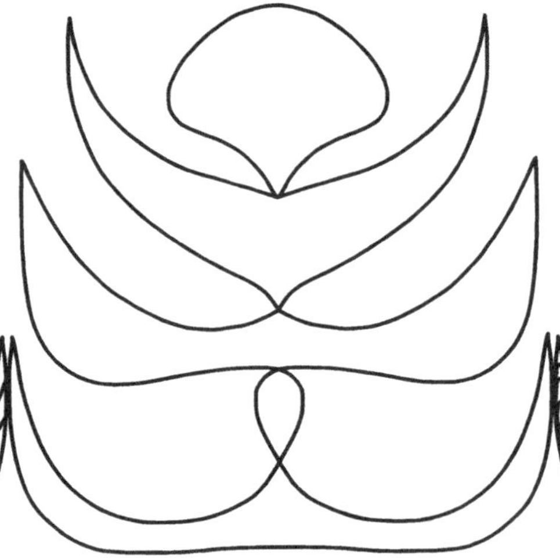

FATLINER WEIRDIES
THE TEMPLATES 1

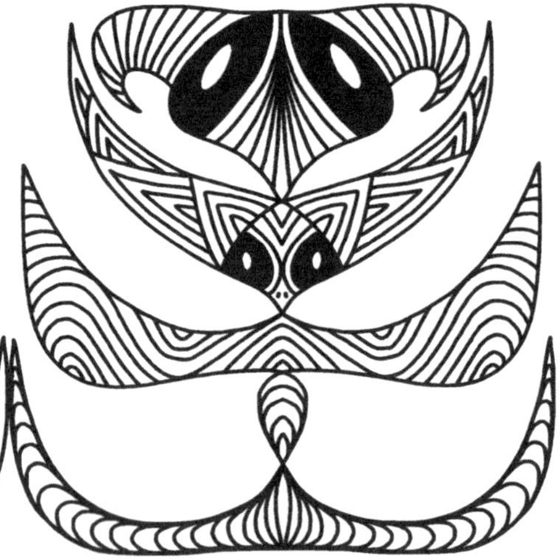

FATLINER WEIRDIES
VOLUME 3

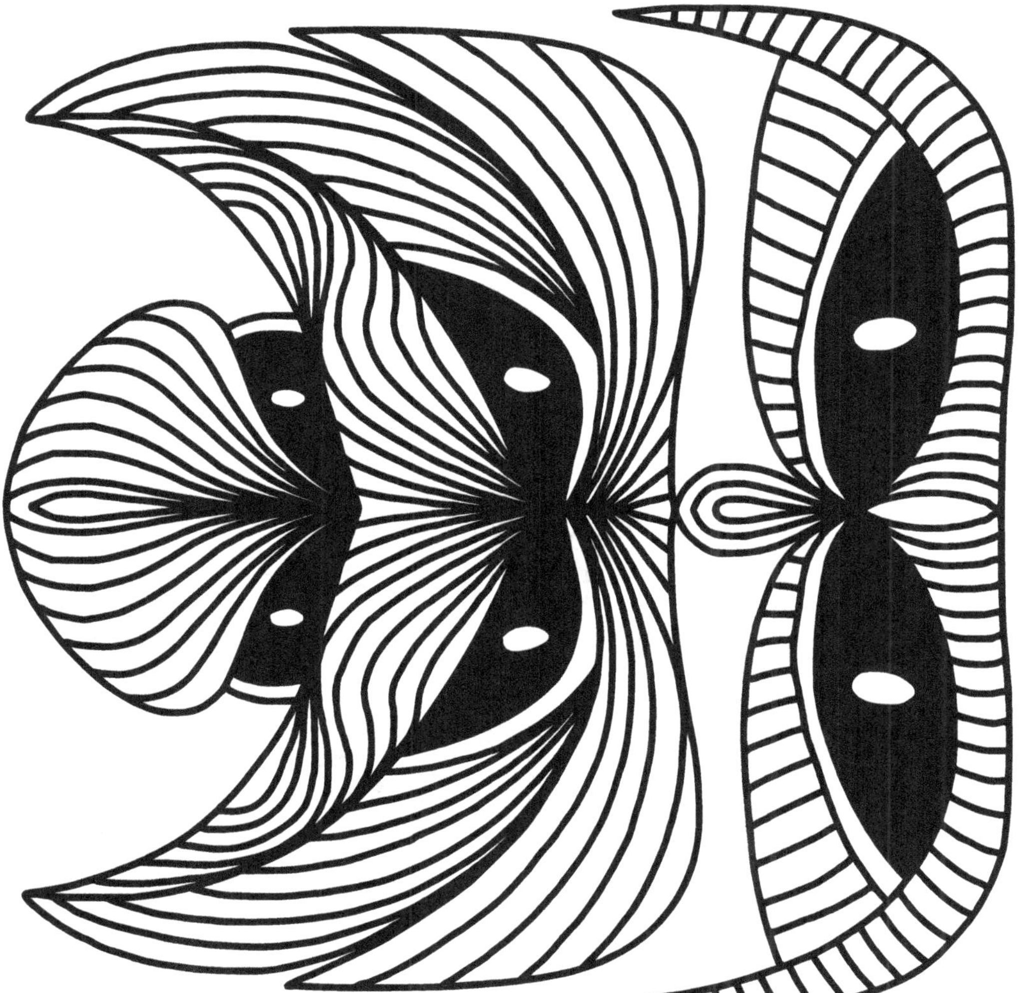

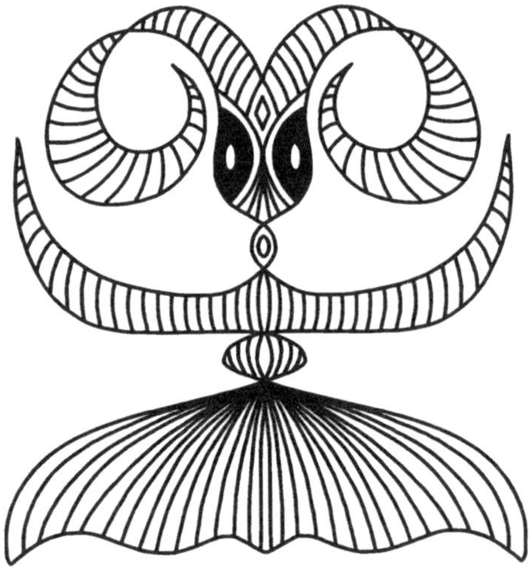

FATLINER WEIRDIES
VOLUME 1

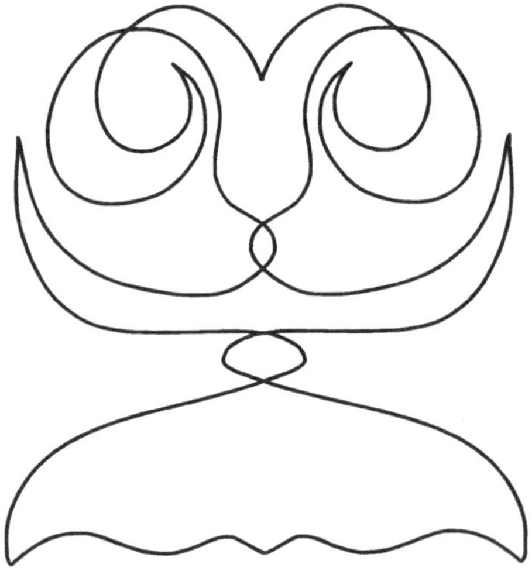

FATLINER WEIRDIES
THE TEMPLATES 1

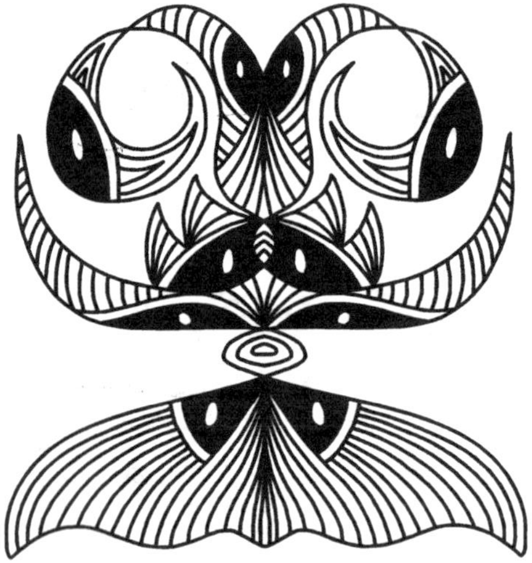

FATLINER WEIRDIES
VOLUME 3

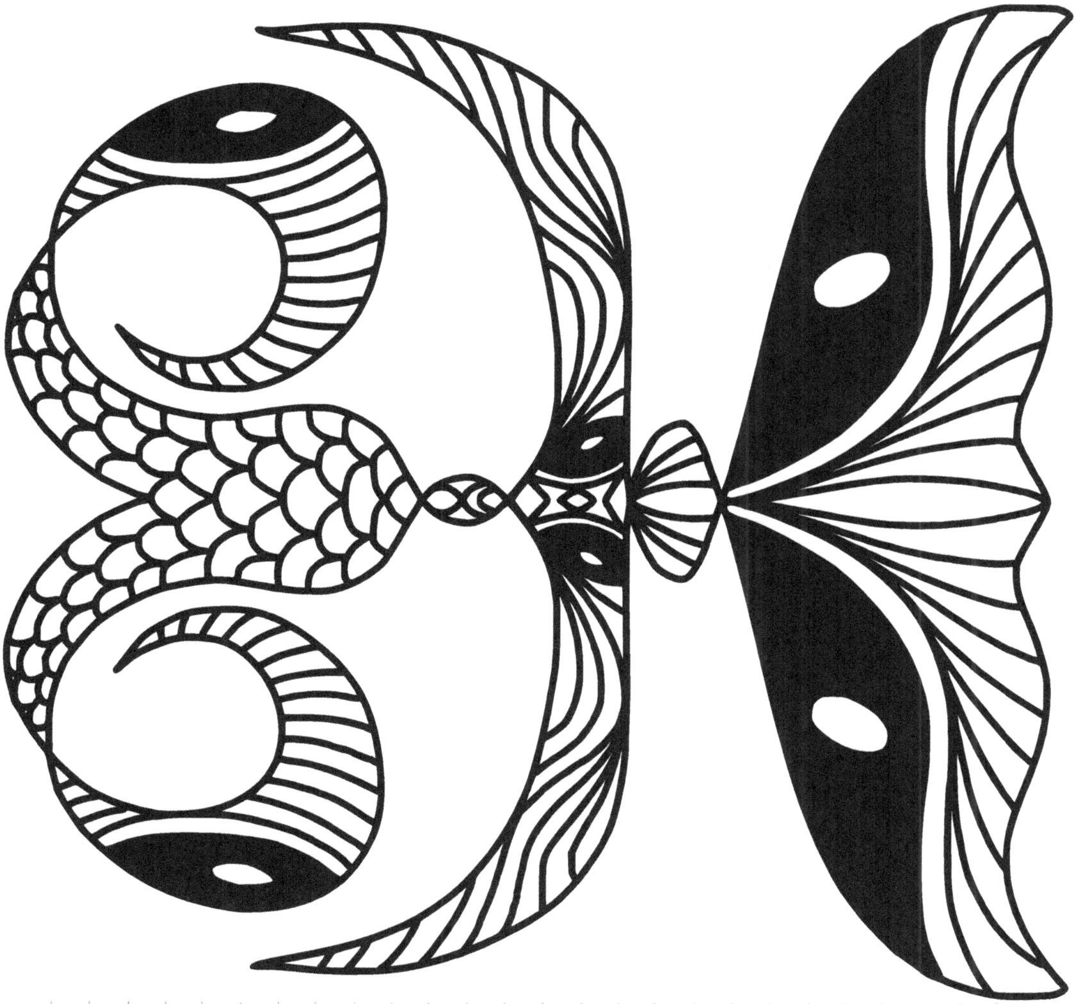

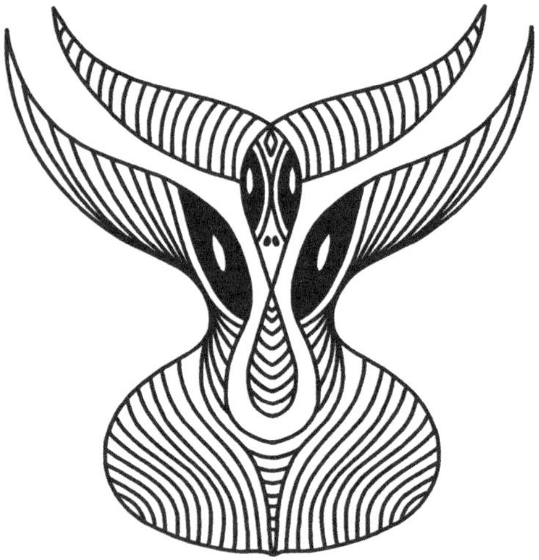

FATLINER WEIRDIES
VOLUME 1

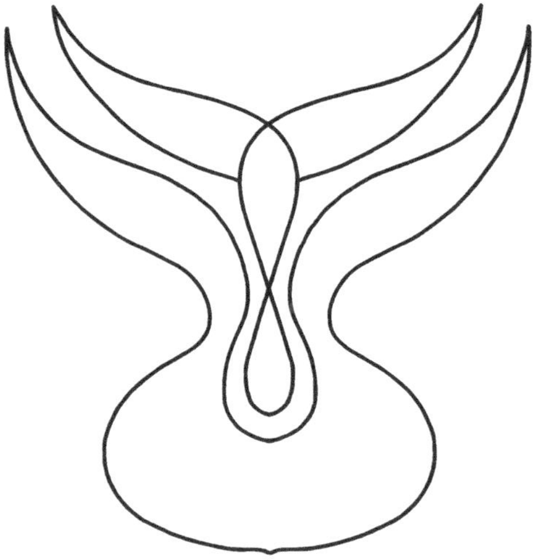

FATLINER WEIRDIES
THE TEMPLATES 1

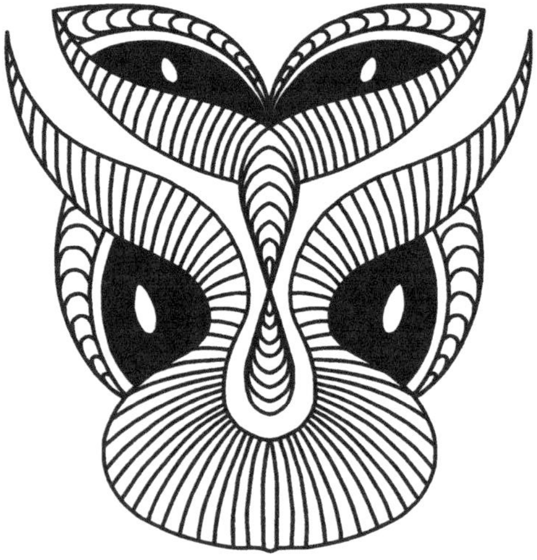

FATLINER WEIRDIES
VOLUME 3

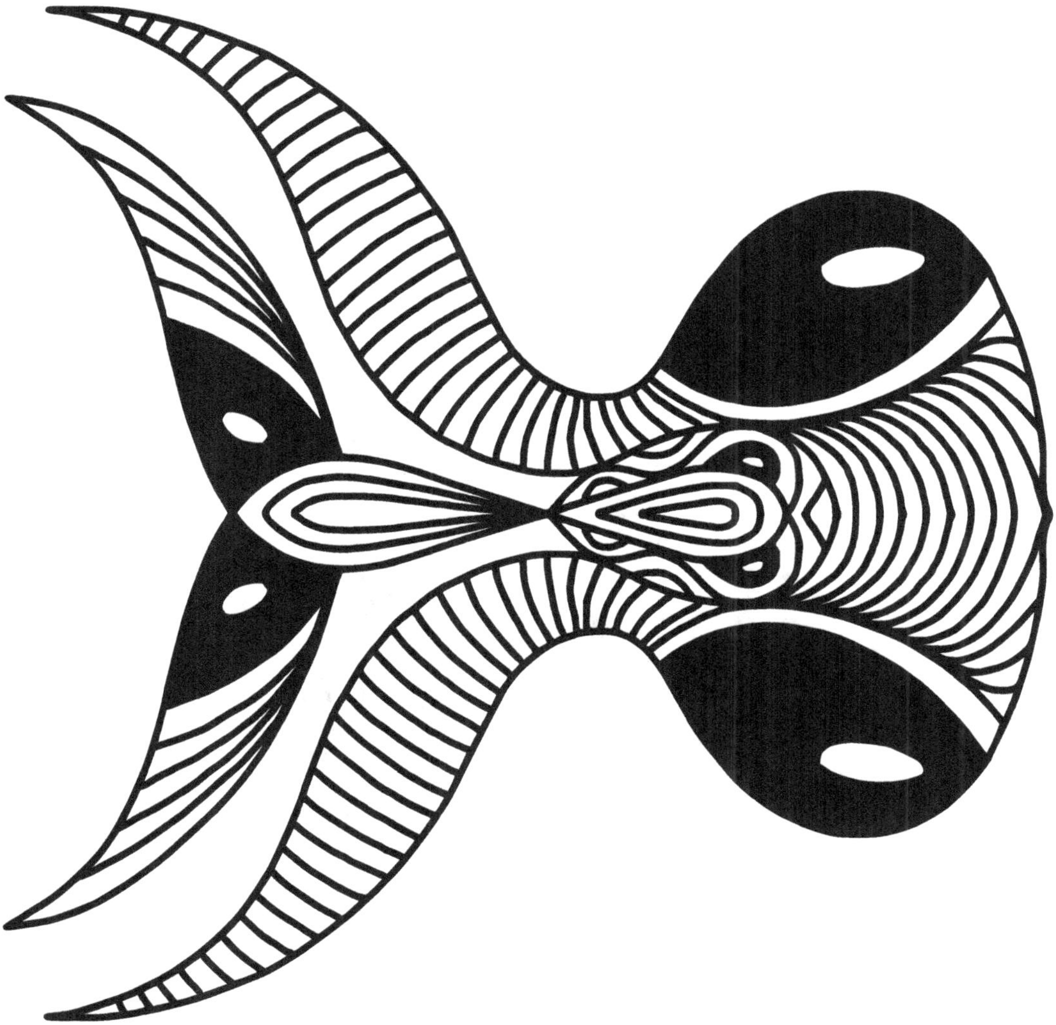

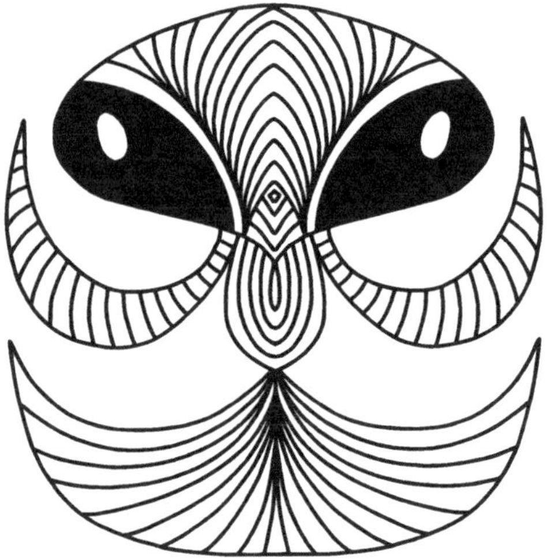

FATLINER WEIRDIES
VOLUME 1

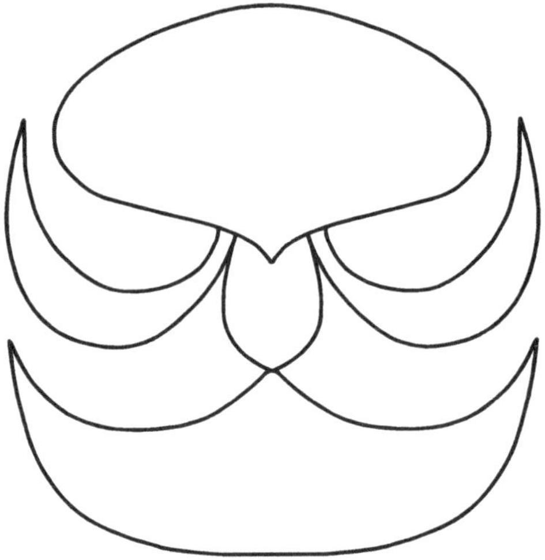

FATLINER WEIRDIES
THE TEMPLATES 1

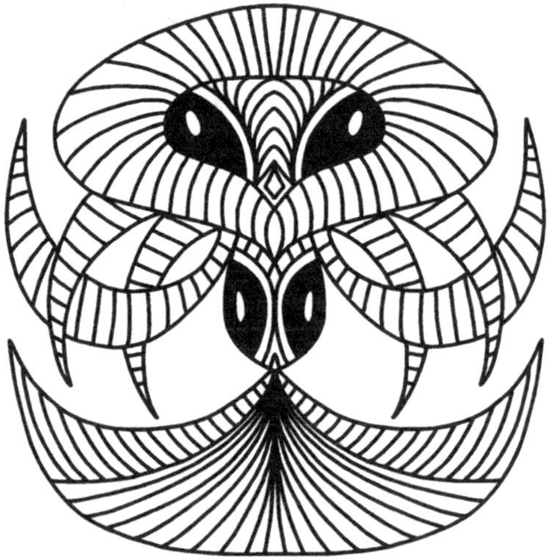

FATLINER WEIRDIES
VOLUME 3

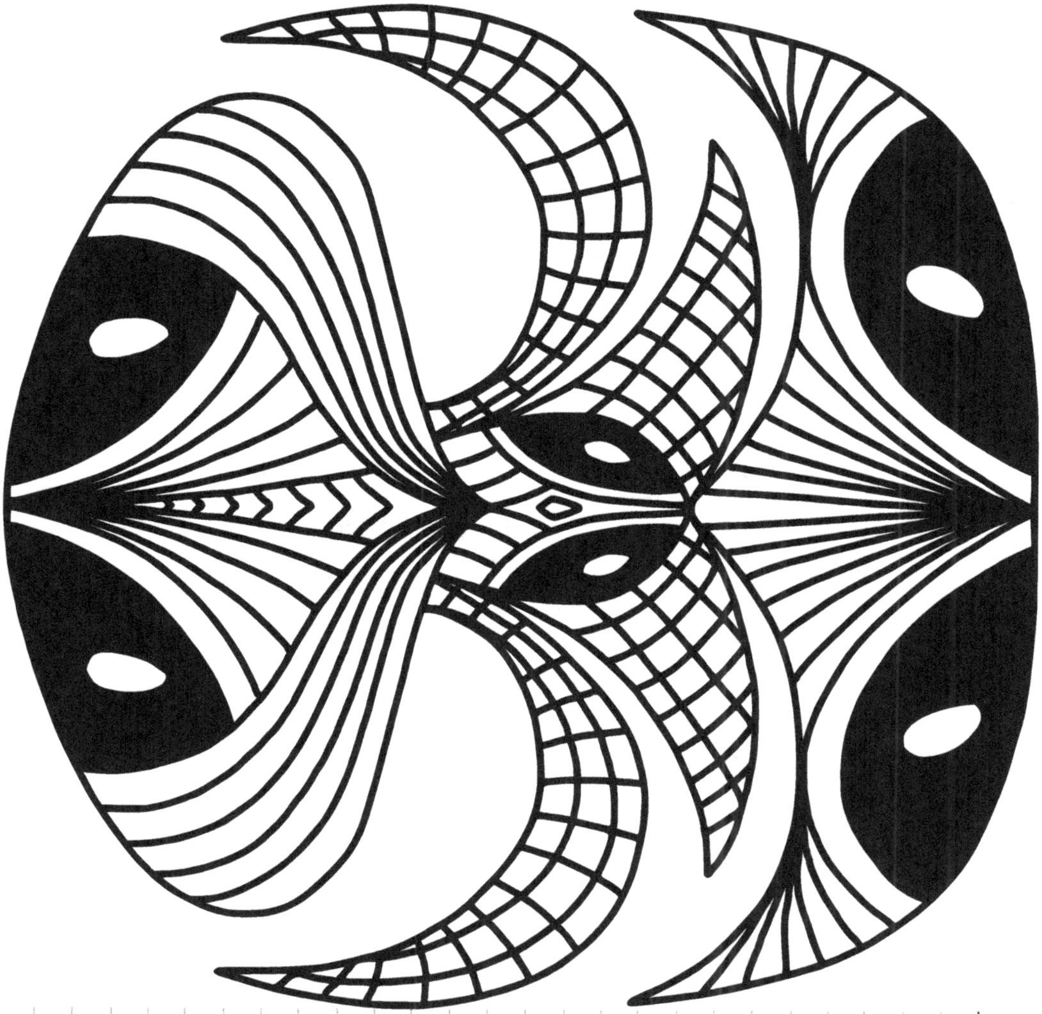

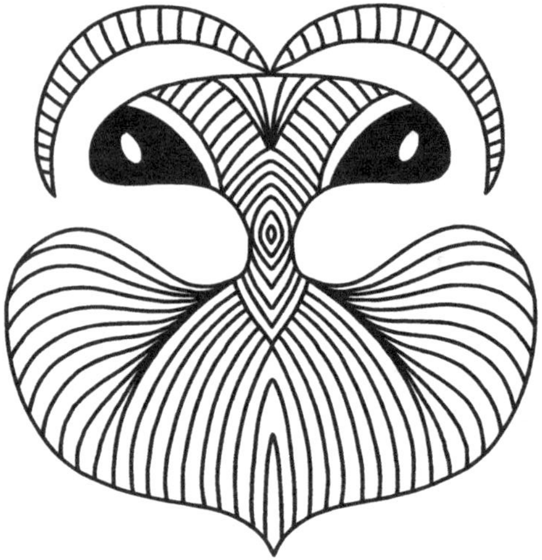

FATLINER WEIRDIES
VOLUME 1

FATLINER WEIRDIES
THE TEMPLATES 1

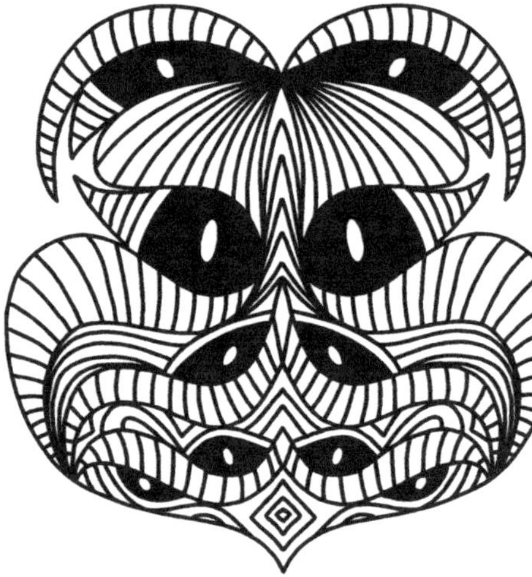

FATLINER WEIRDIES
VOLUME 3

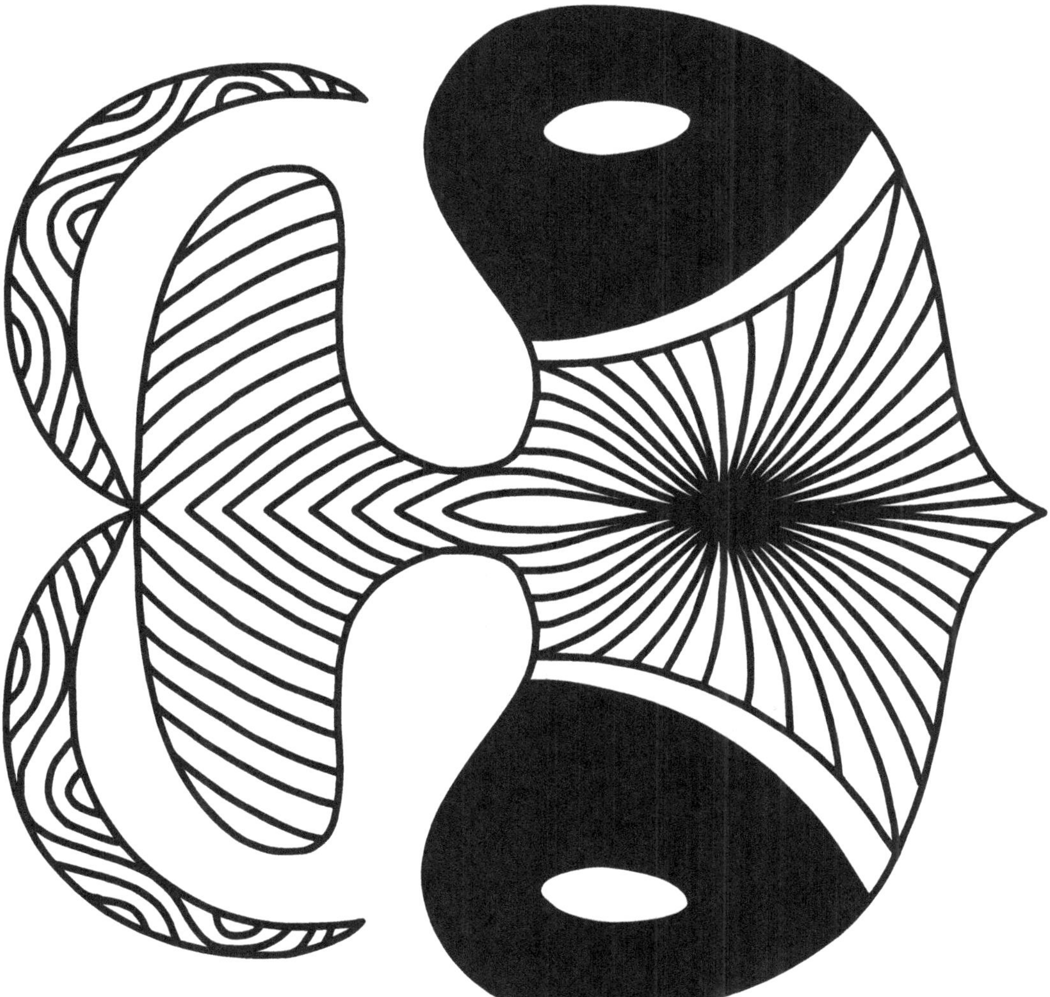

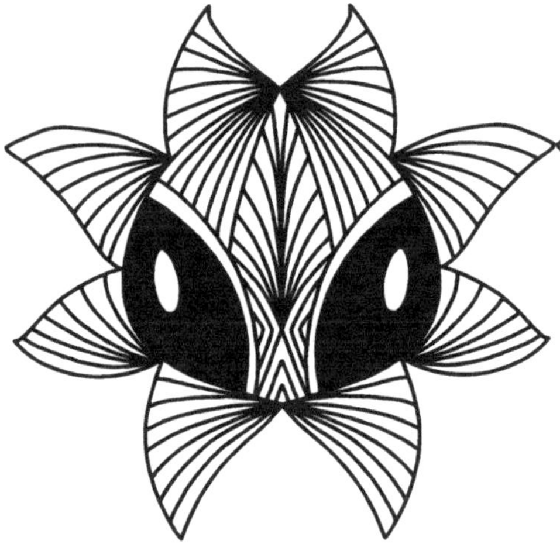

FATLINER WEIRDIES
VOLUME 1

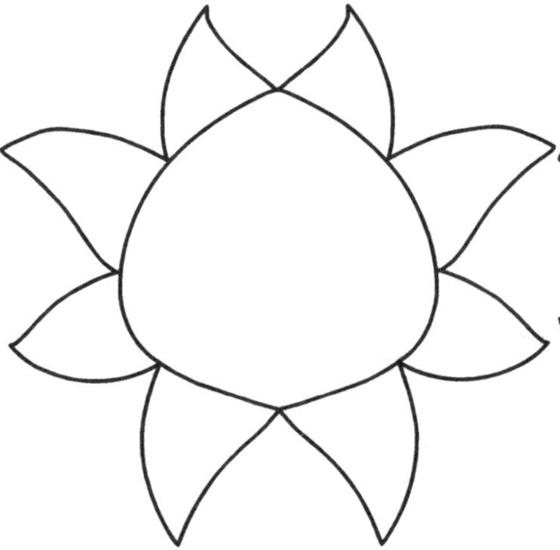

FATLINER WEIRDIES
THE TEMPLATES 1

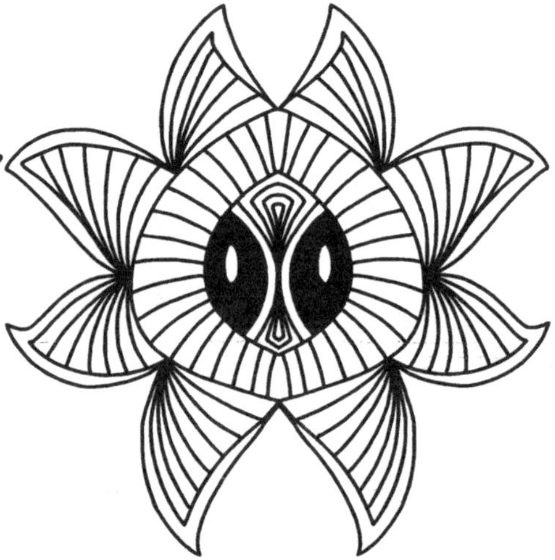

FATLINER WEIRDIES
VOLUME 3

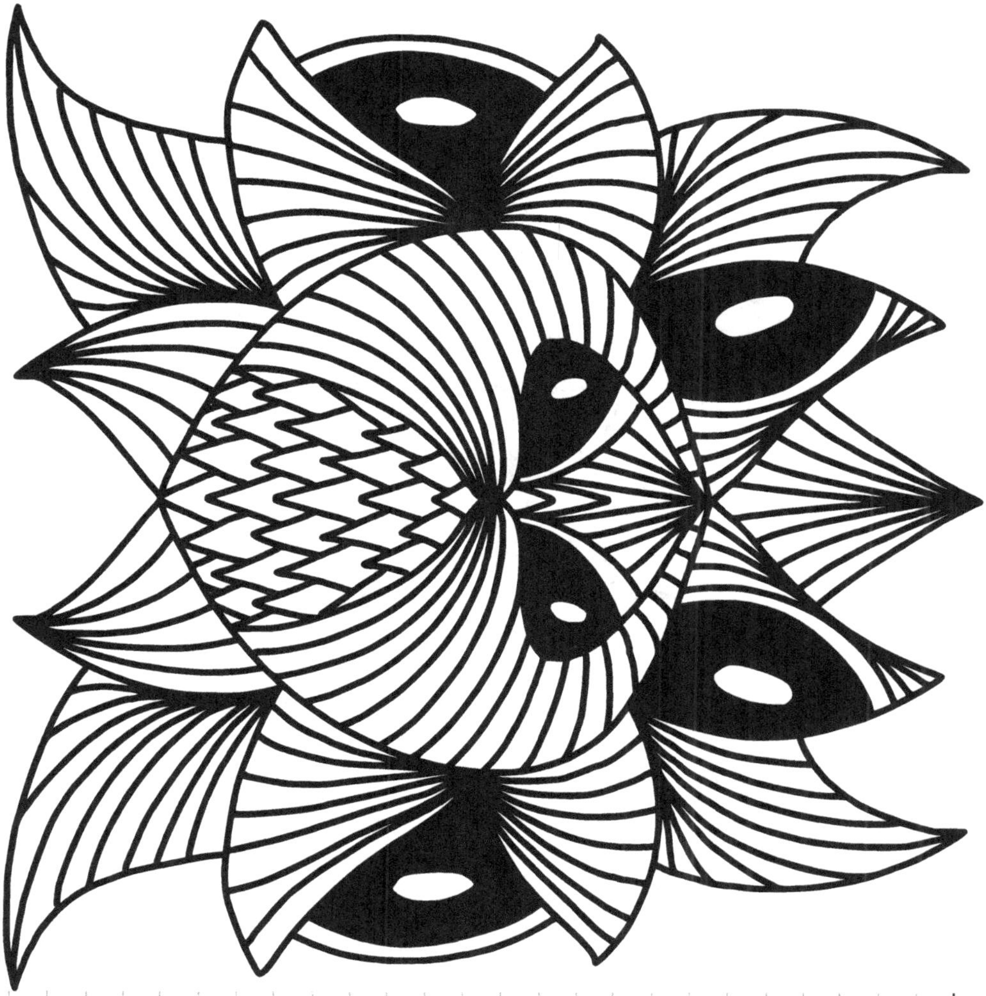

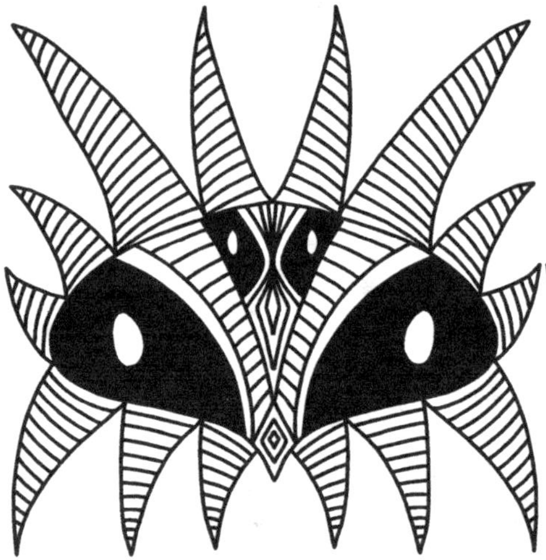

FATLINER WEIRDIES
VOLUME 1

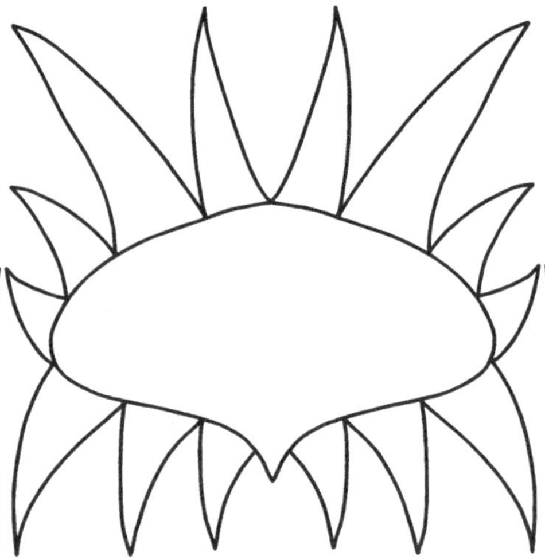

FATLINER WEIRDIES
THE TEMPLATES 1

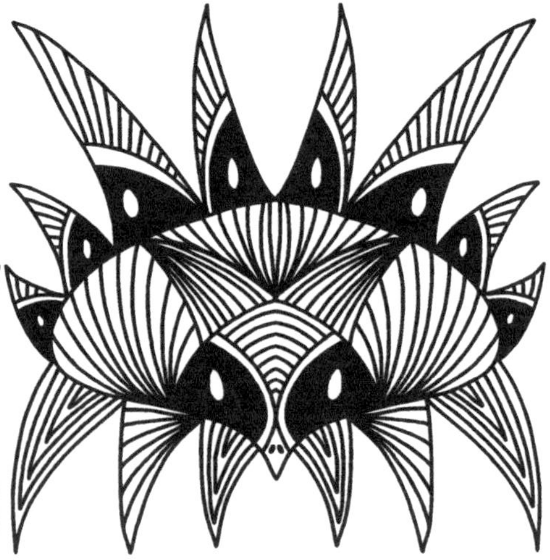

FATLINER WEIRDIES
VOLUME 3

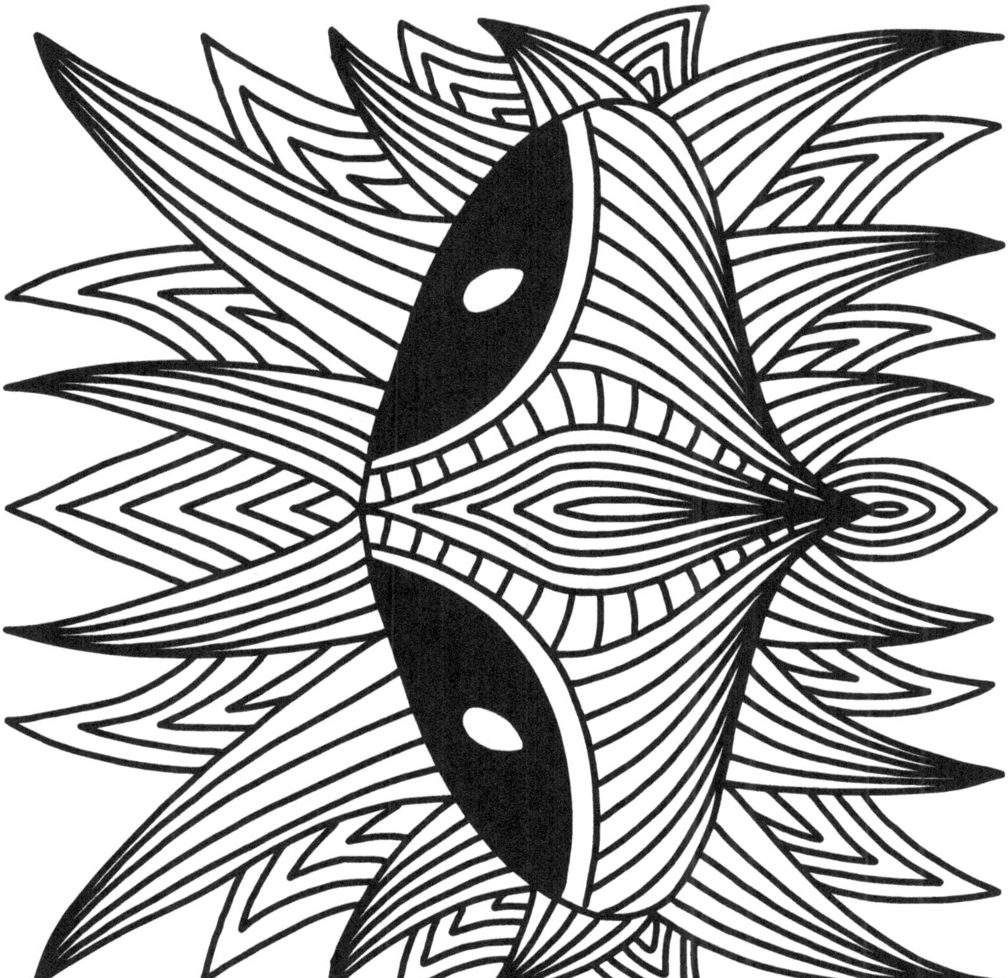

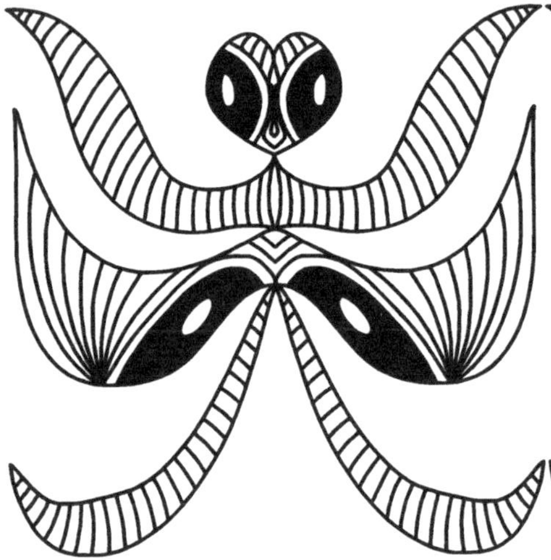

FATLINER WEIRDIES
VOLUME 1

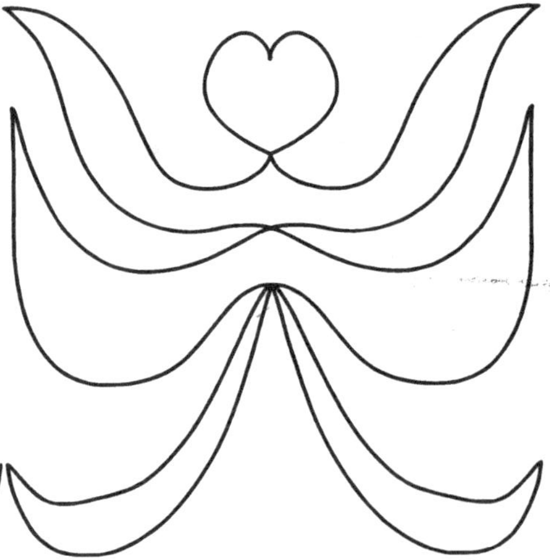

FATLINER WEIRDIES
THE TEMPLATES 1

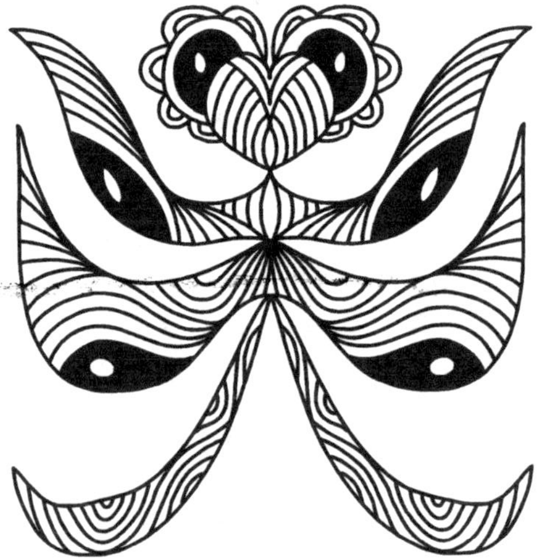

FATLINER WEIRDIES
VOLUME 3

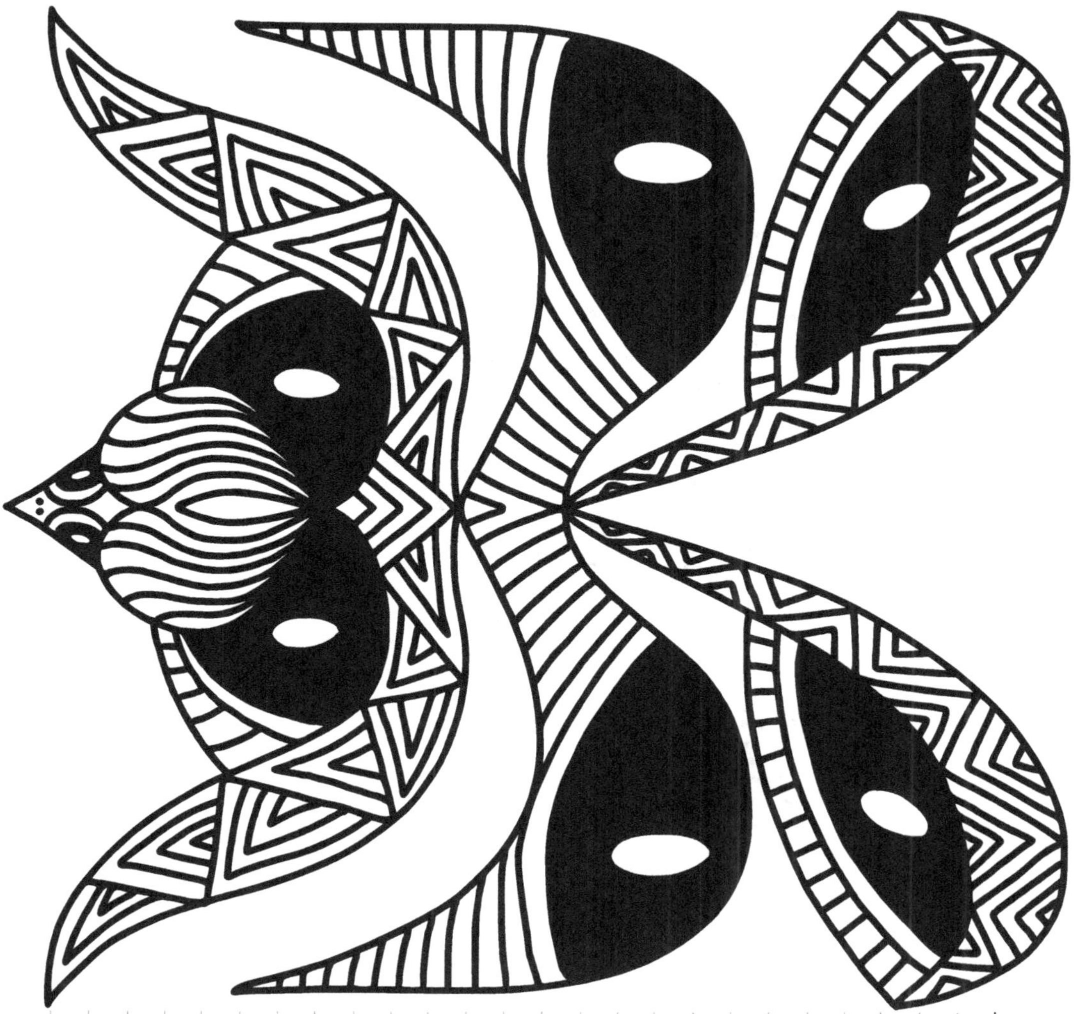

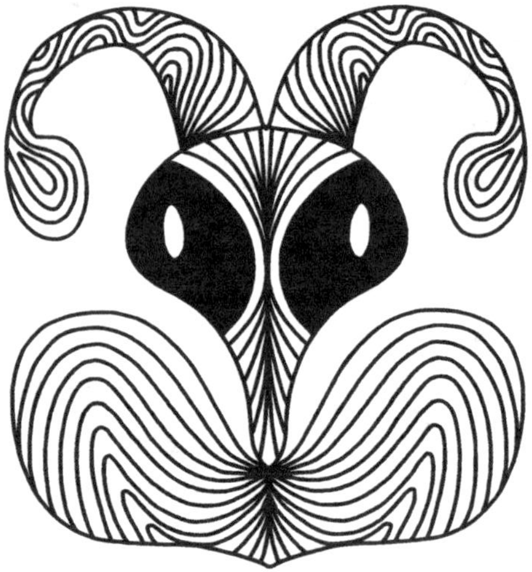

FATLINER WEIRDIES
VOLUME 1

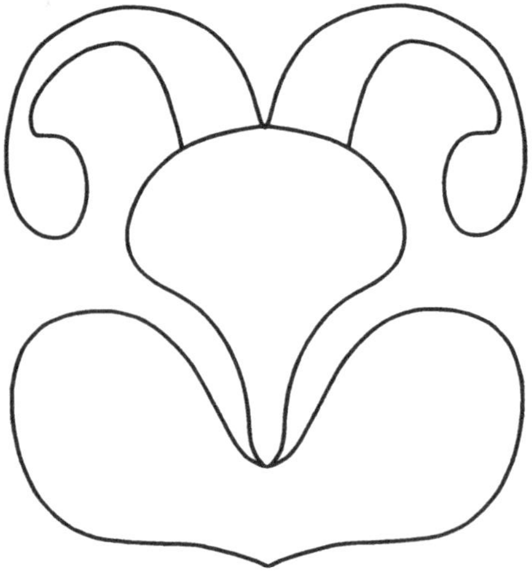

FATLINER WEIRDIES
THE TEMPLATES 1

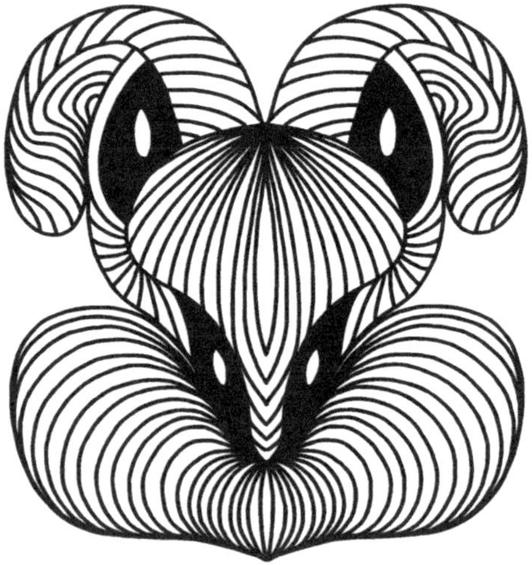

FATLINER WEIRDIES
VOLUME 3

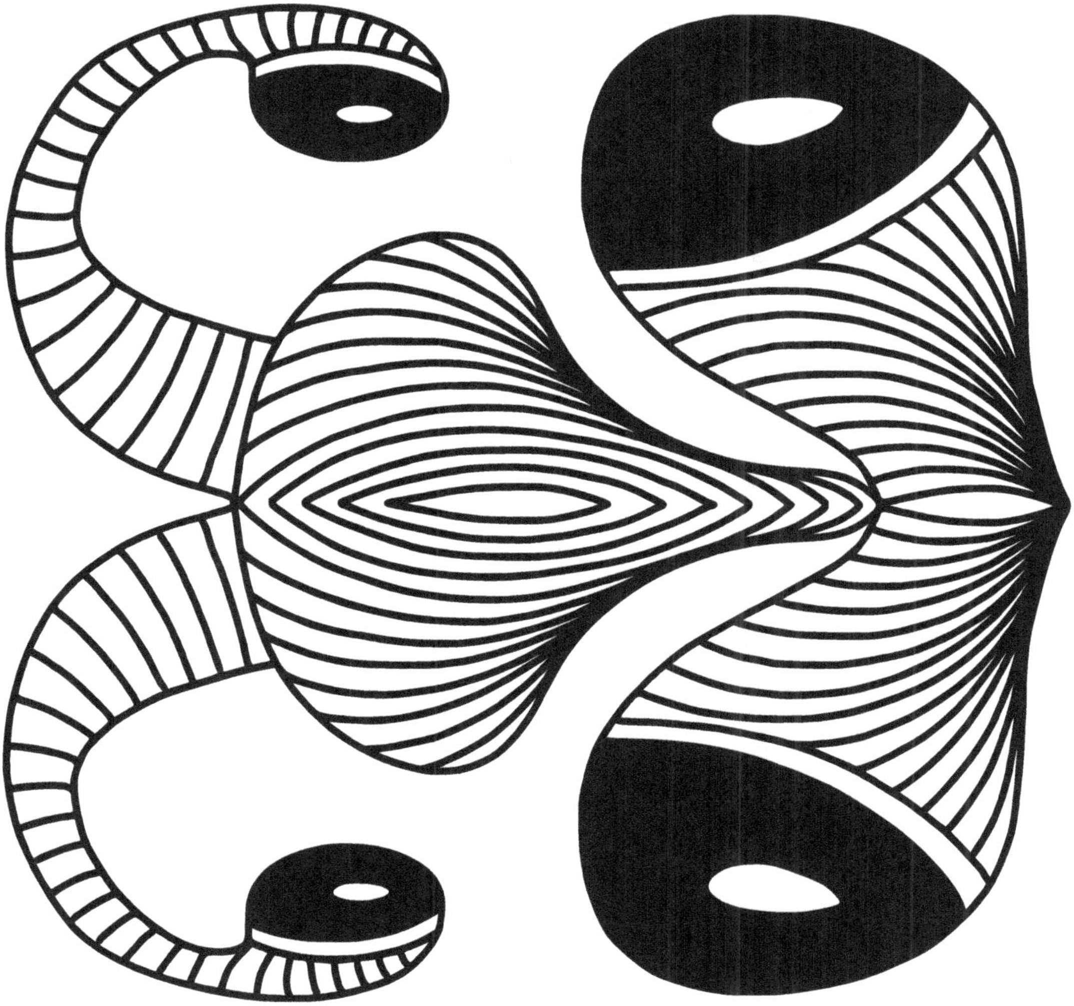

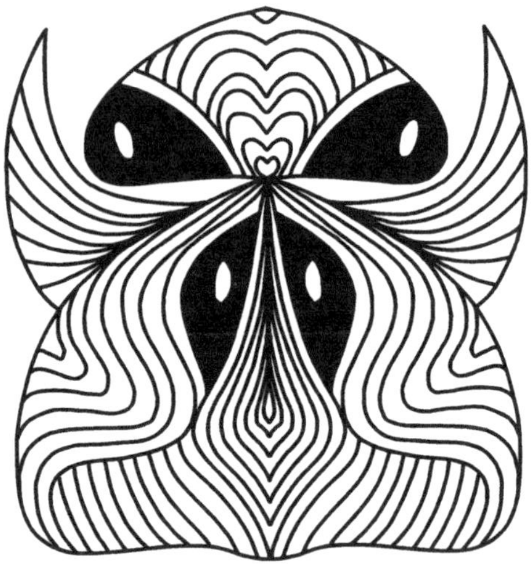

FATLINER WEIRDIES
VOLUME 1

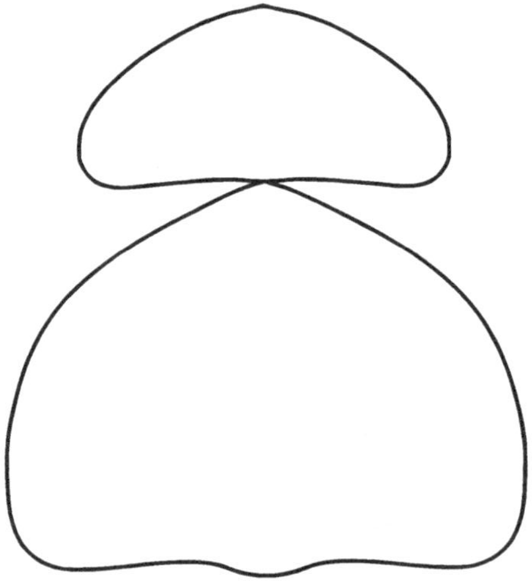

FATLINER WEIRDIES
THE TEMPLATES 1

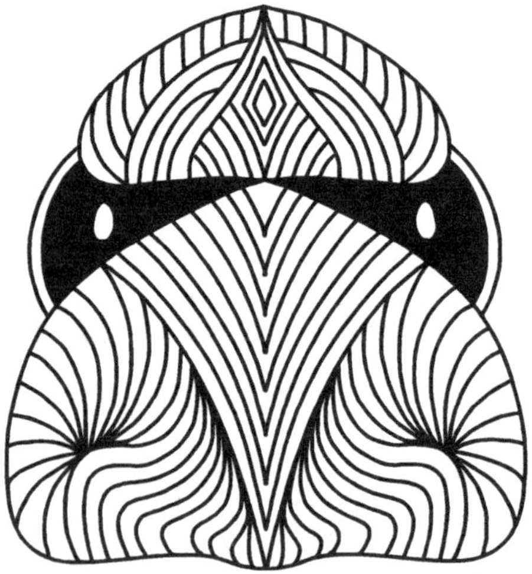

FATLINER WEIRDIES
VOLUME 3

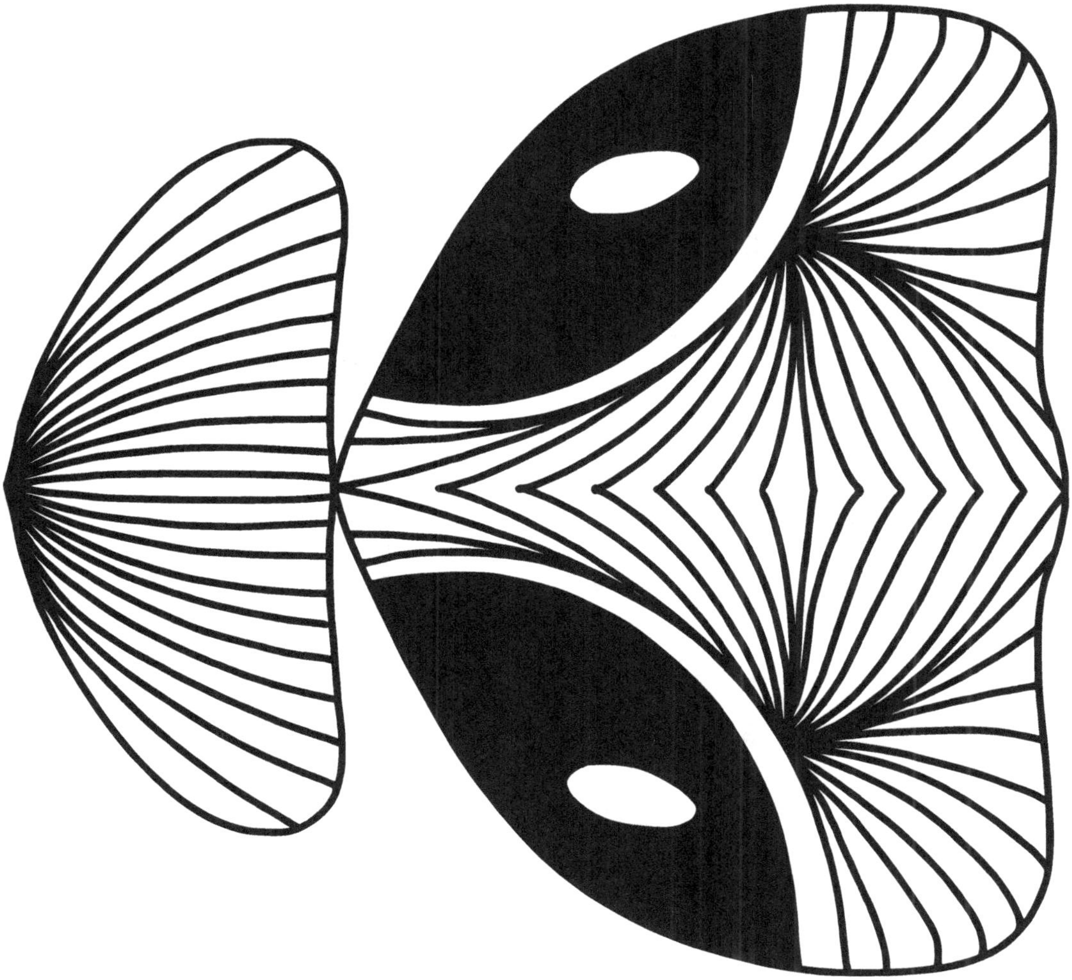

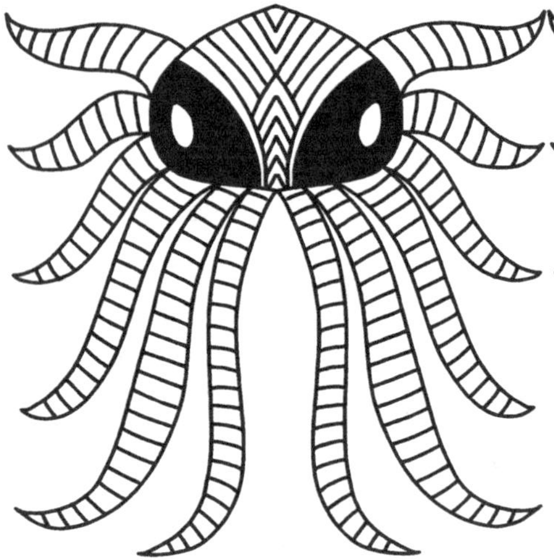

FATLINER WEIRDIES
VOLUME 1

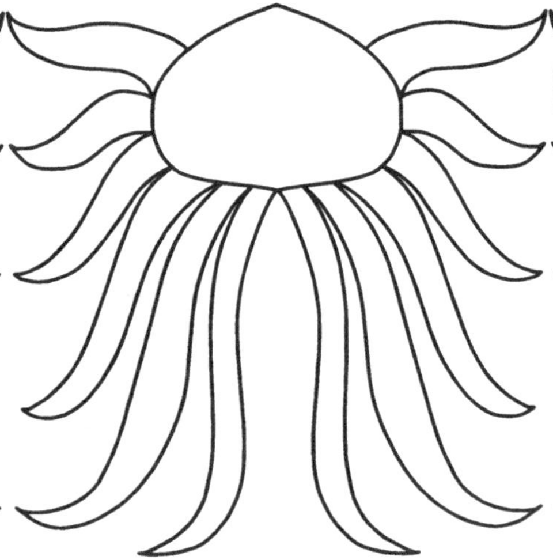

FATLINER WEIRDIES
THE TEMPLATES 1

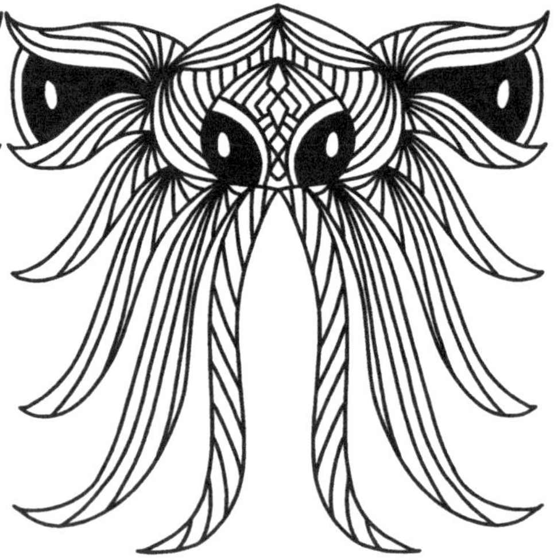

FATLINER WEIRDIES
VOLUME 3

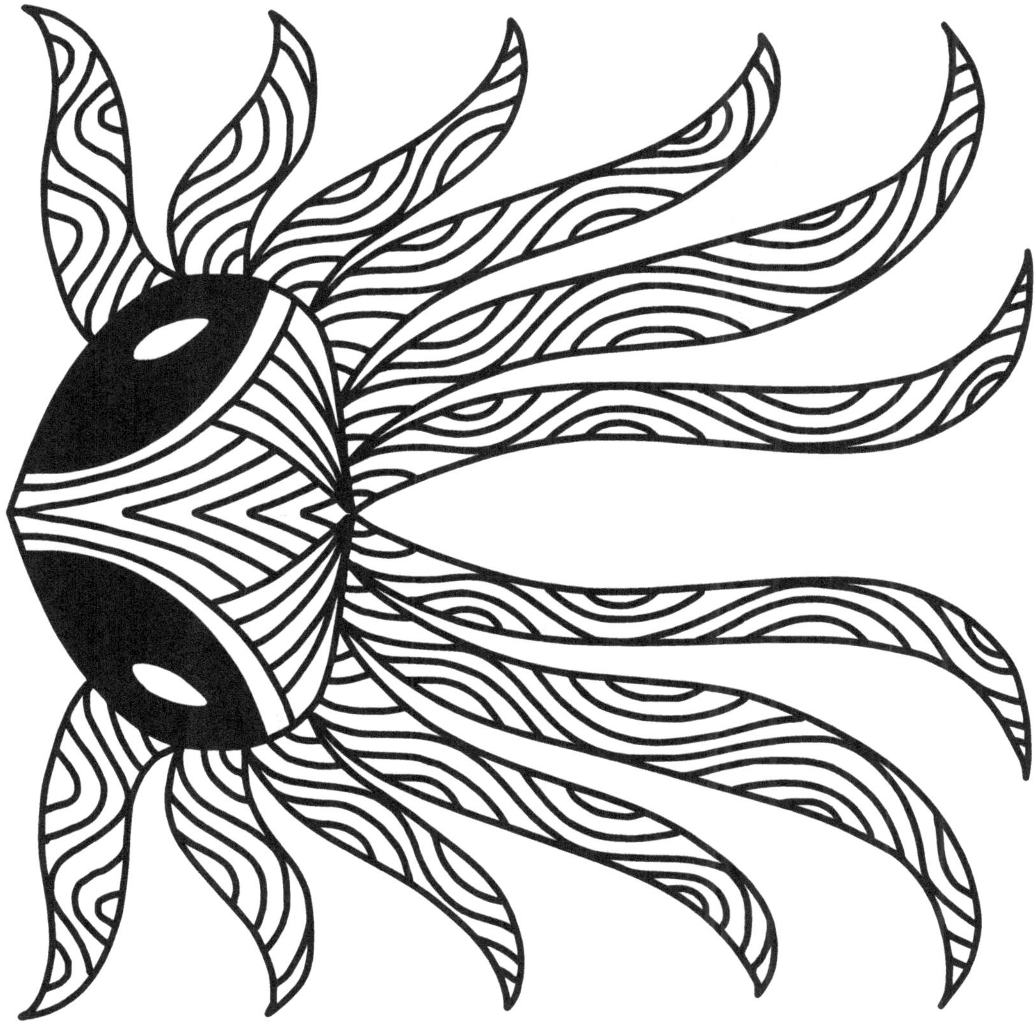

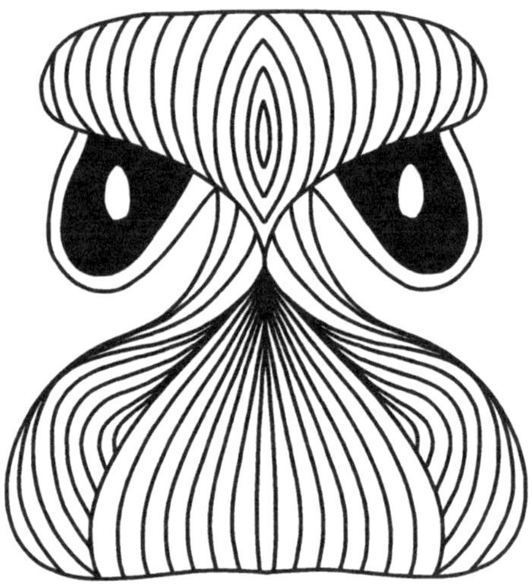

FATLINER WEIRDIES
VOLUME 1

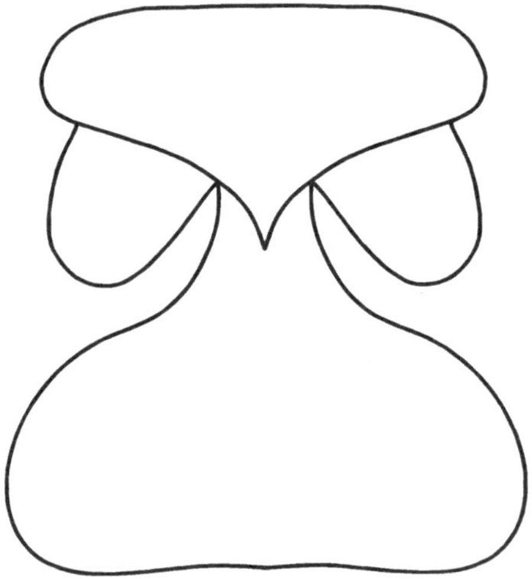

FATLINER WEIRDIES
THE TEMPLATES 1

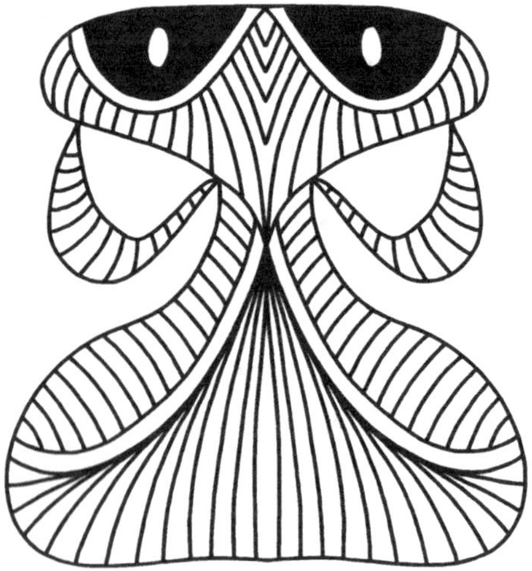

FATLINER WEIRDIES
VOLUME 3

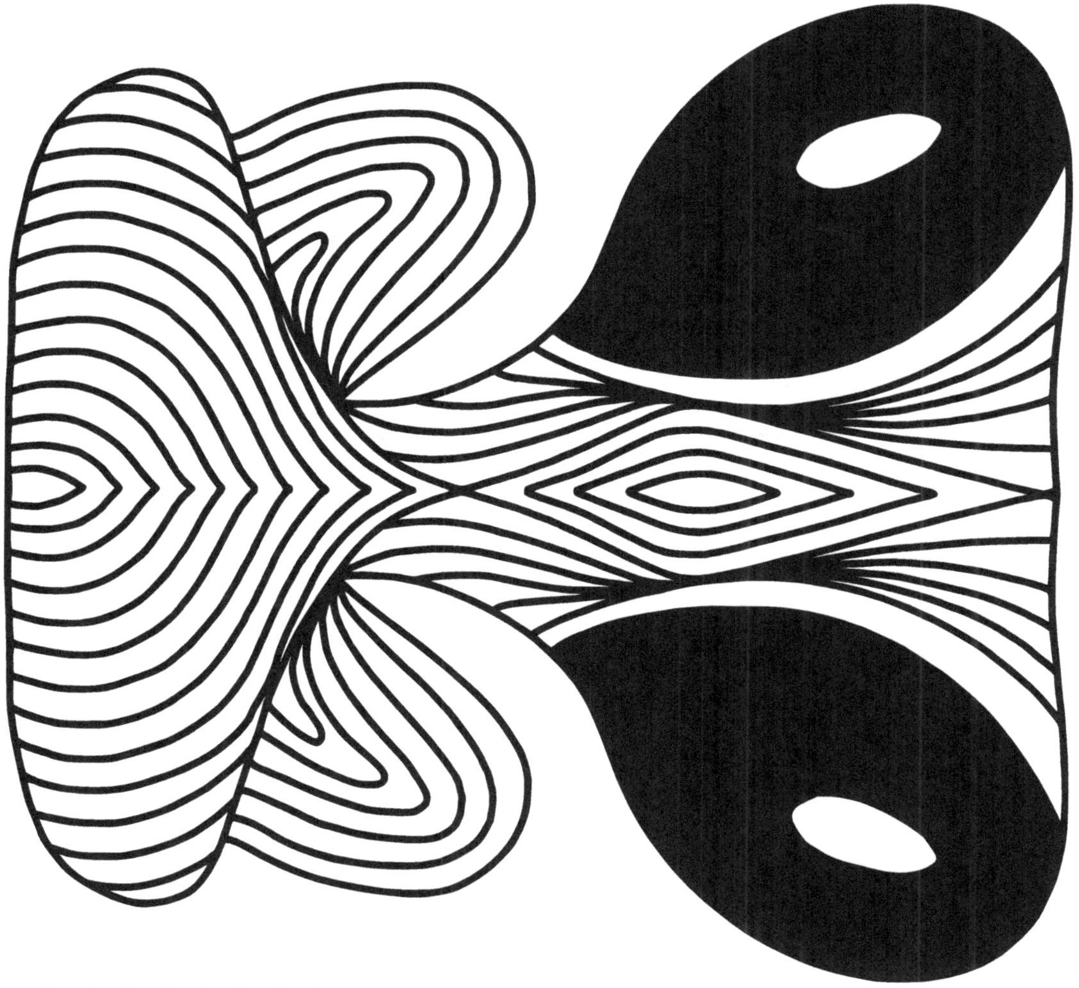

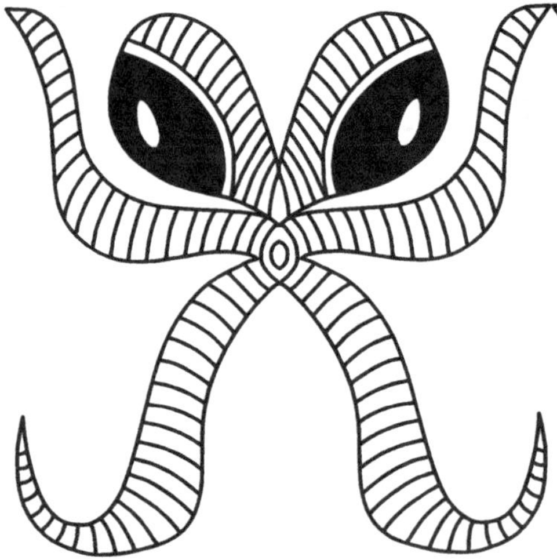

FATLINER WEIRDIES
VOLUME 1

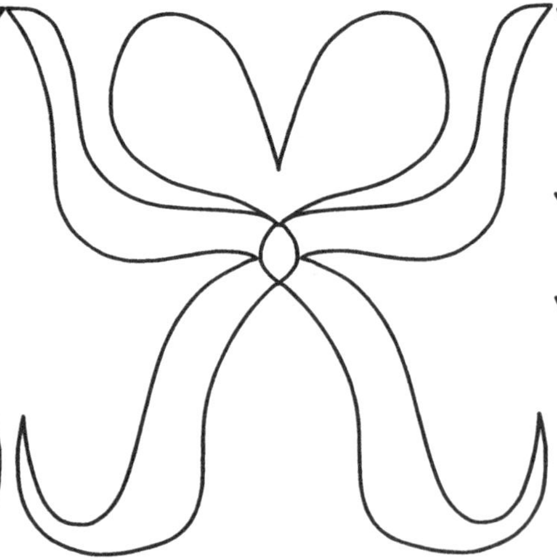

FATLINER WEIRDIES
THE TEMPLATES 1

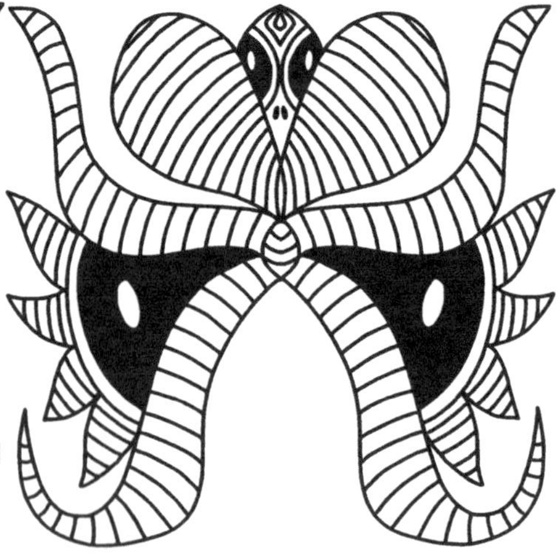

FATLINER WEIRDIES
VOLUME 3

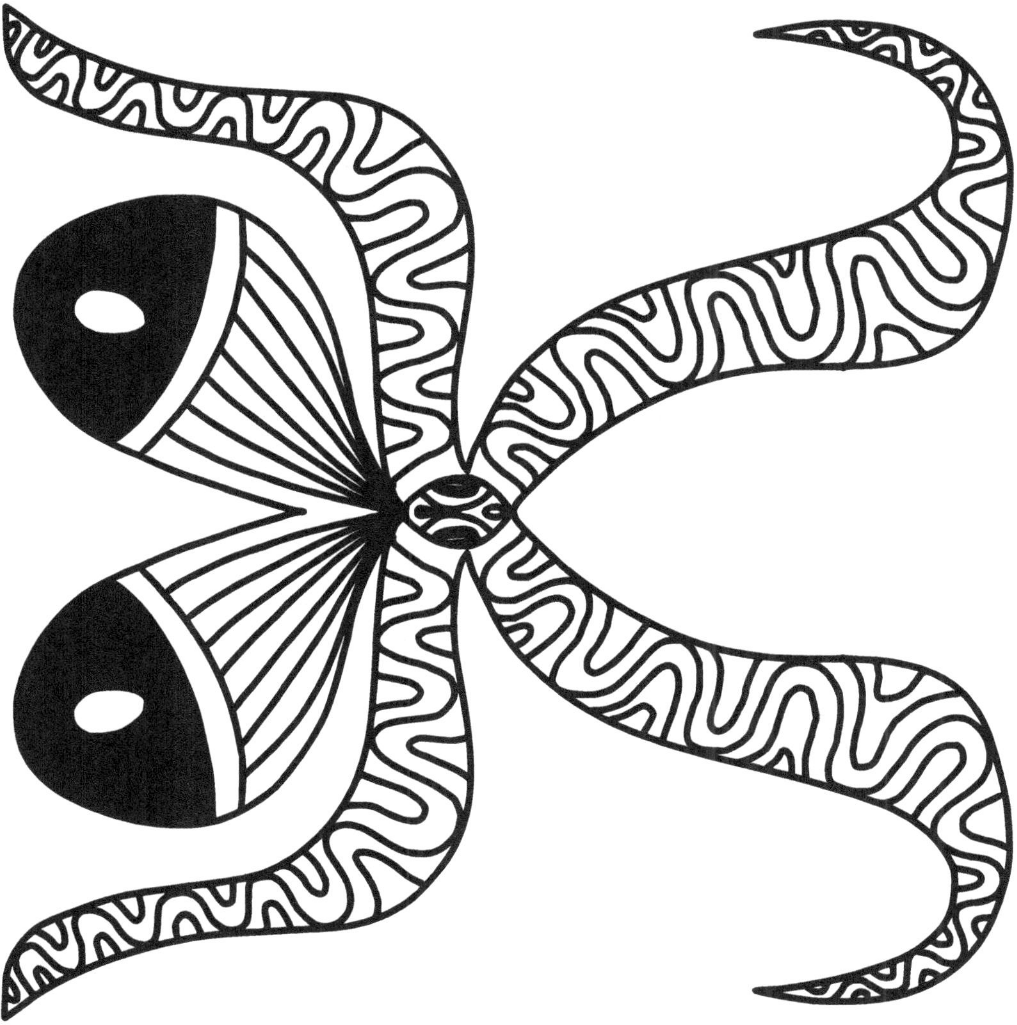

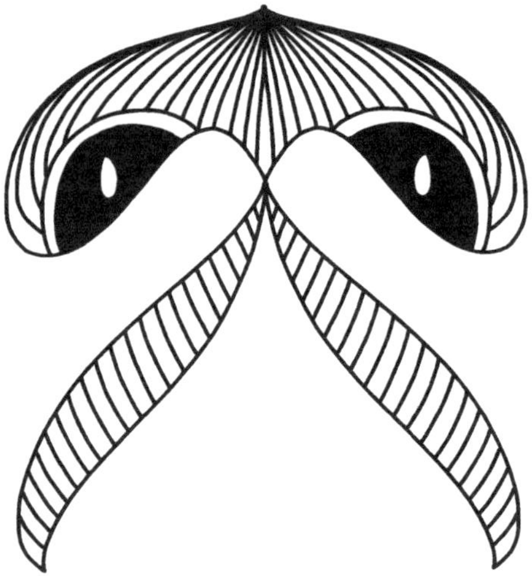
FATLINER WEIRDIES
VOLUME 1

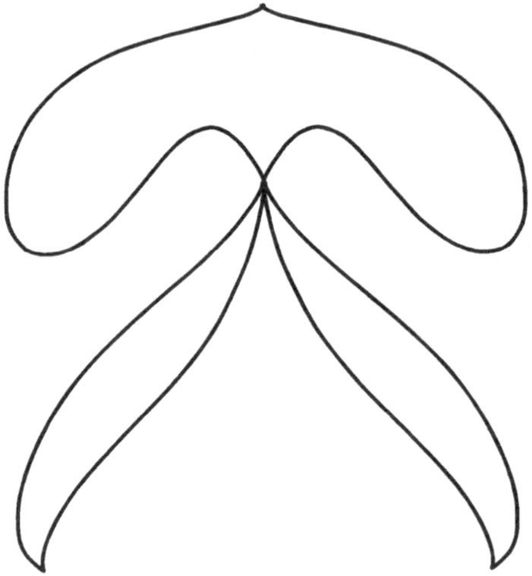
FATLINER WEIRDIES
THE TEMPLATES 1

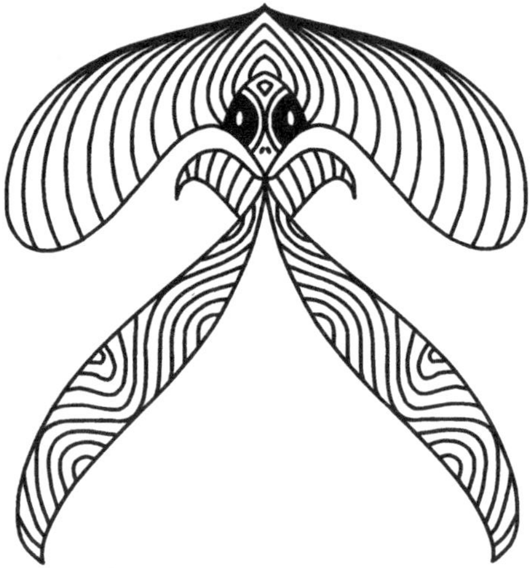
FATLINER WEIRDIES
VOLUME 3

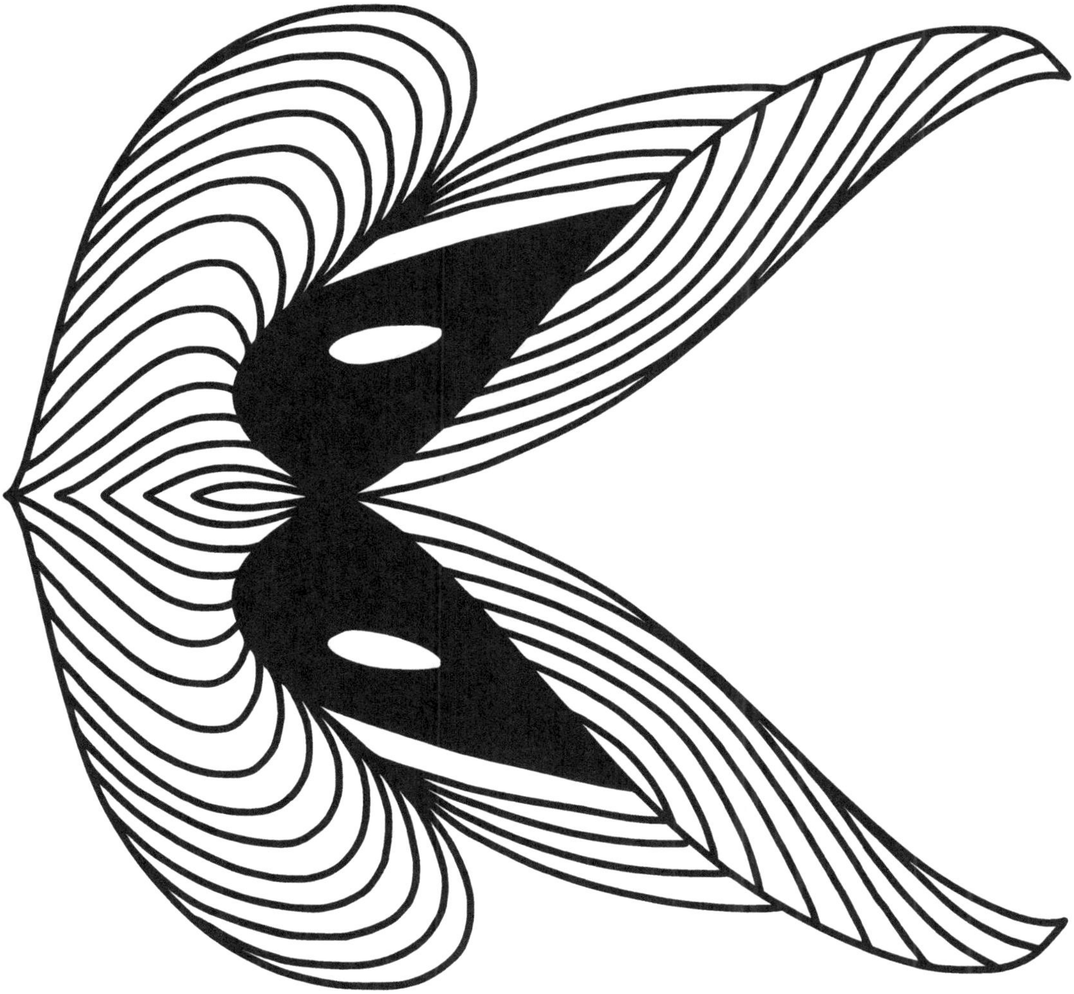

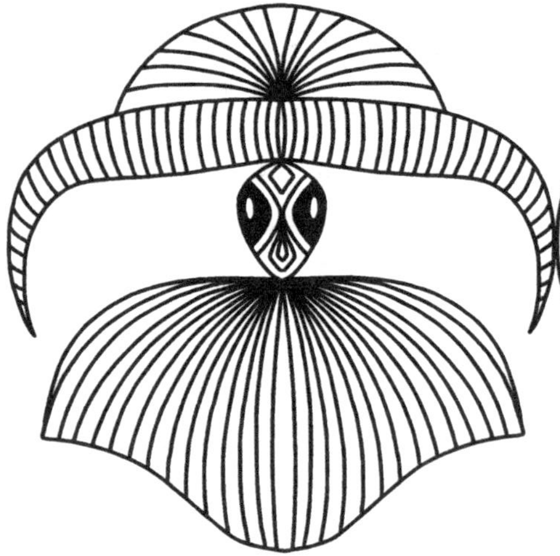

FATLINER WEIRDIES
VOLUME 1

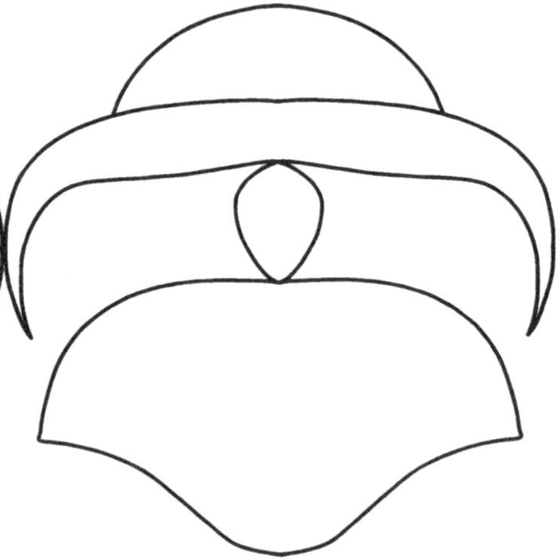

FATLINER WEIRDIES
THE TEMPLATES 1

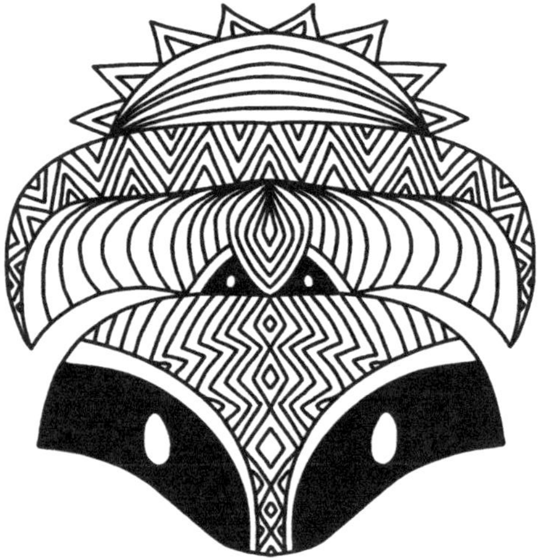

FATLINER WEIRDIES
VOLUME 3

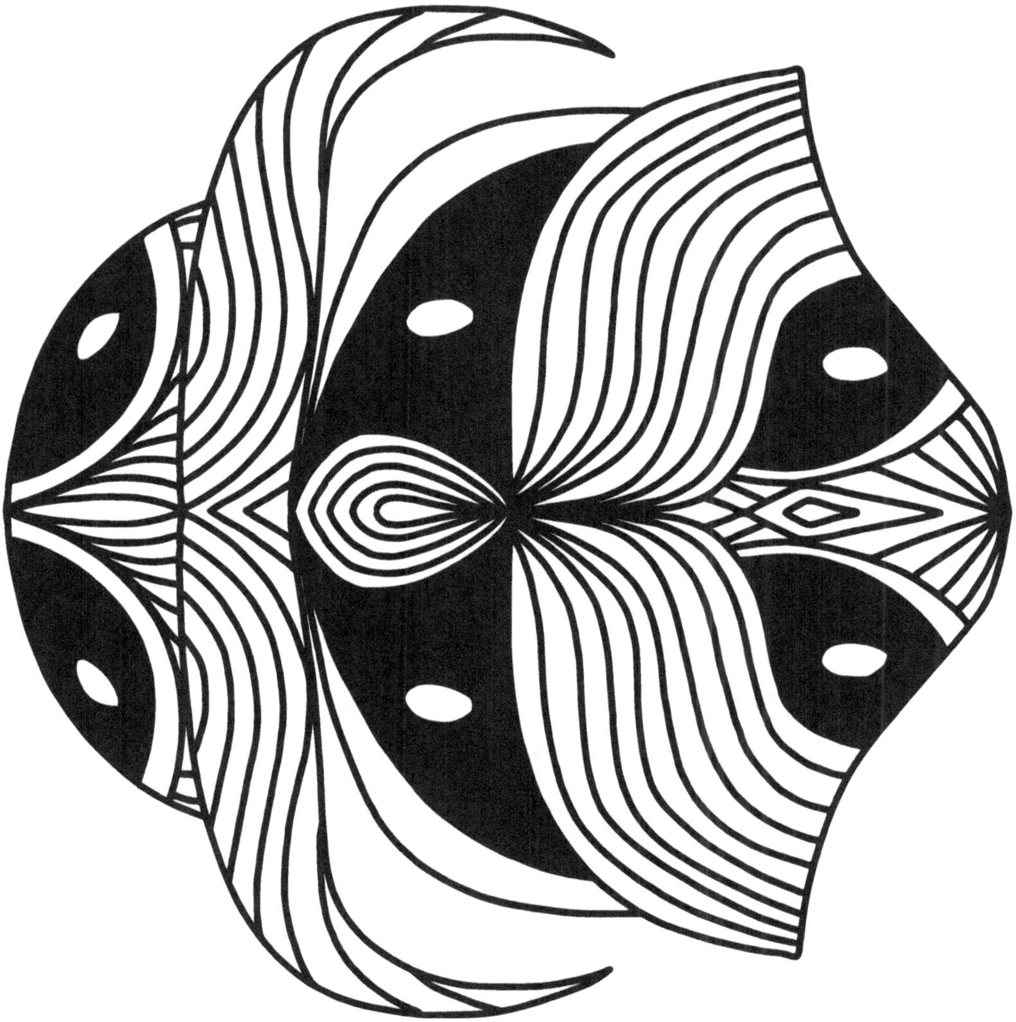

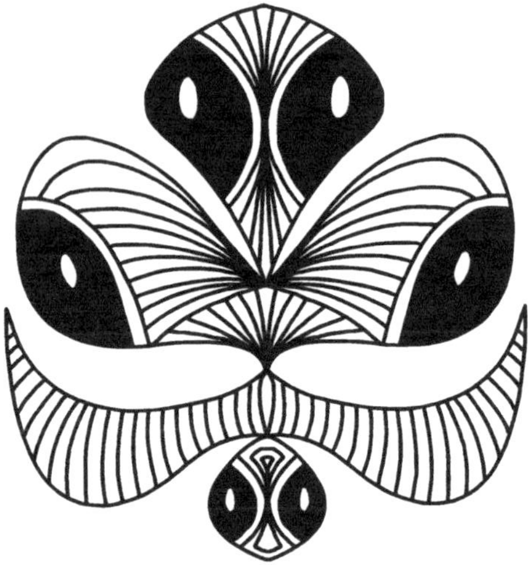

FATLINER WEIRDIES
VOLUME 1

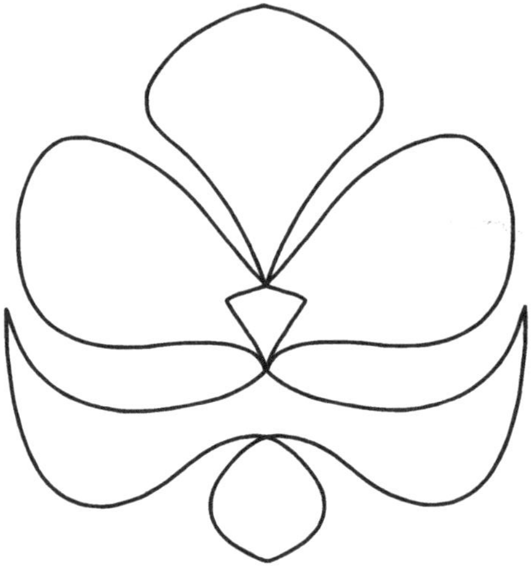

FATLINER WEIRDIES
THE TEMPLATES 1

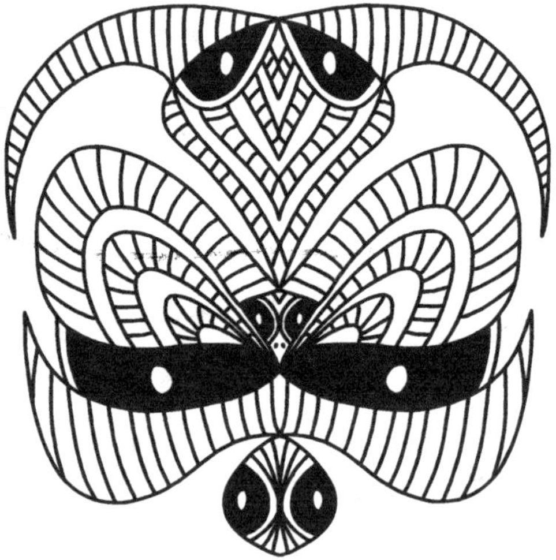

FATLINER WEIRDIES
VOLUME 3

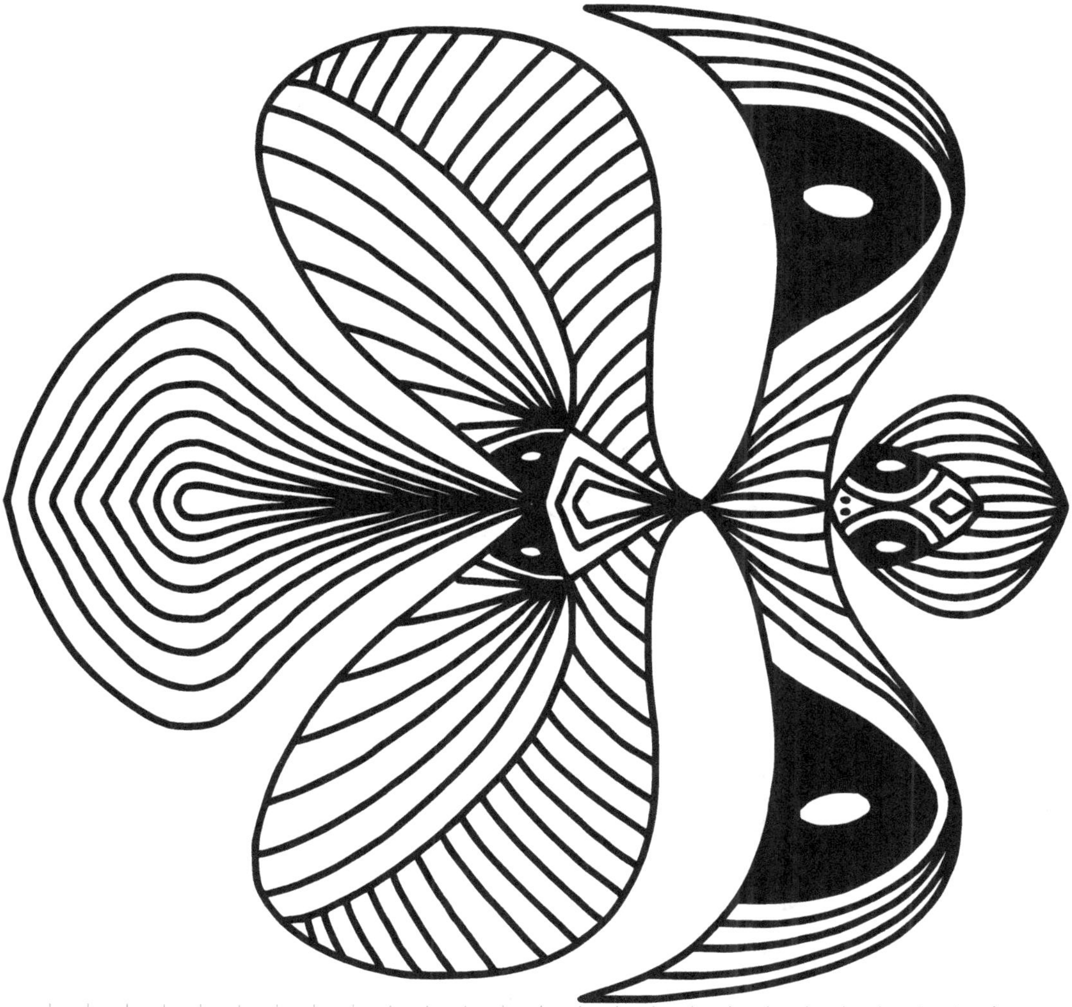

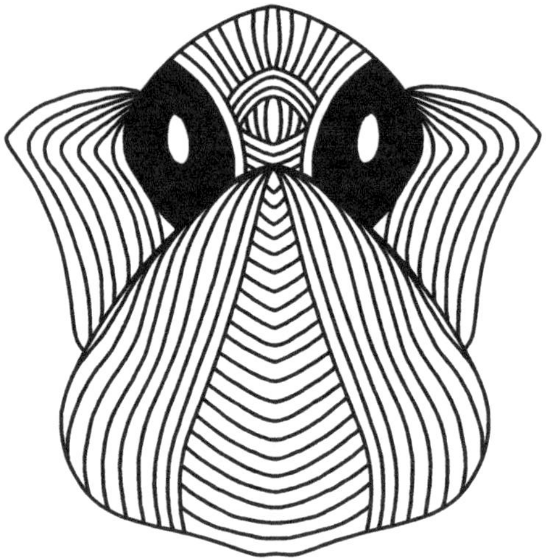

FATLINER WEIRDIES
VOLUME 1

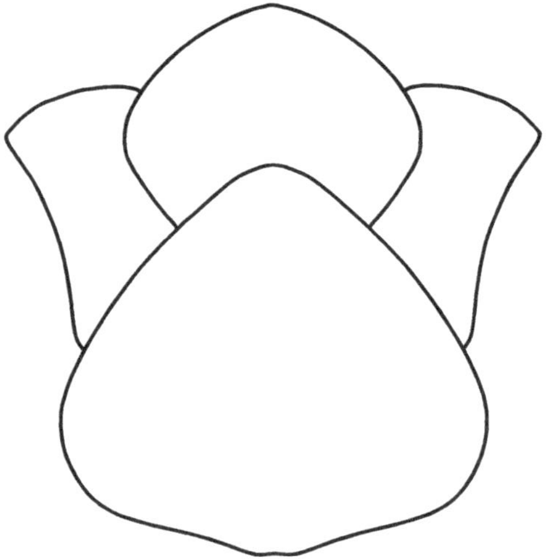

FATLINER WEIRDIES
THE TEMPLATES 1

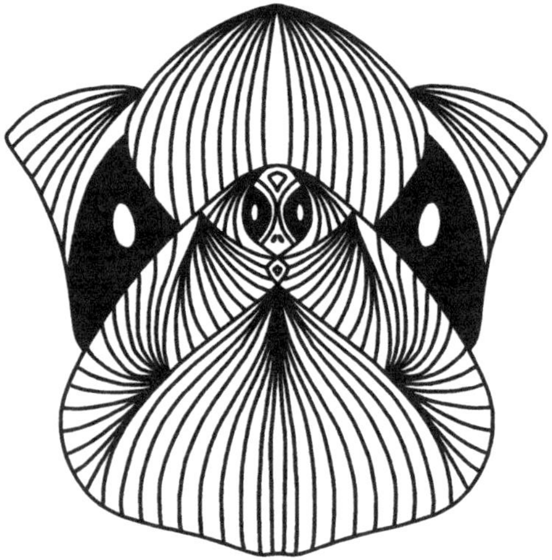

FATLINER WEIRDIES
VOLUME 3

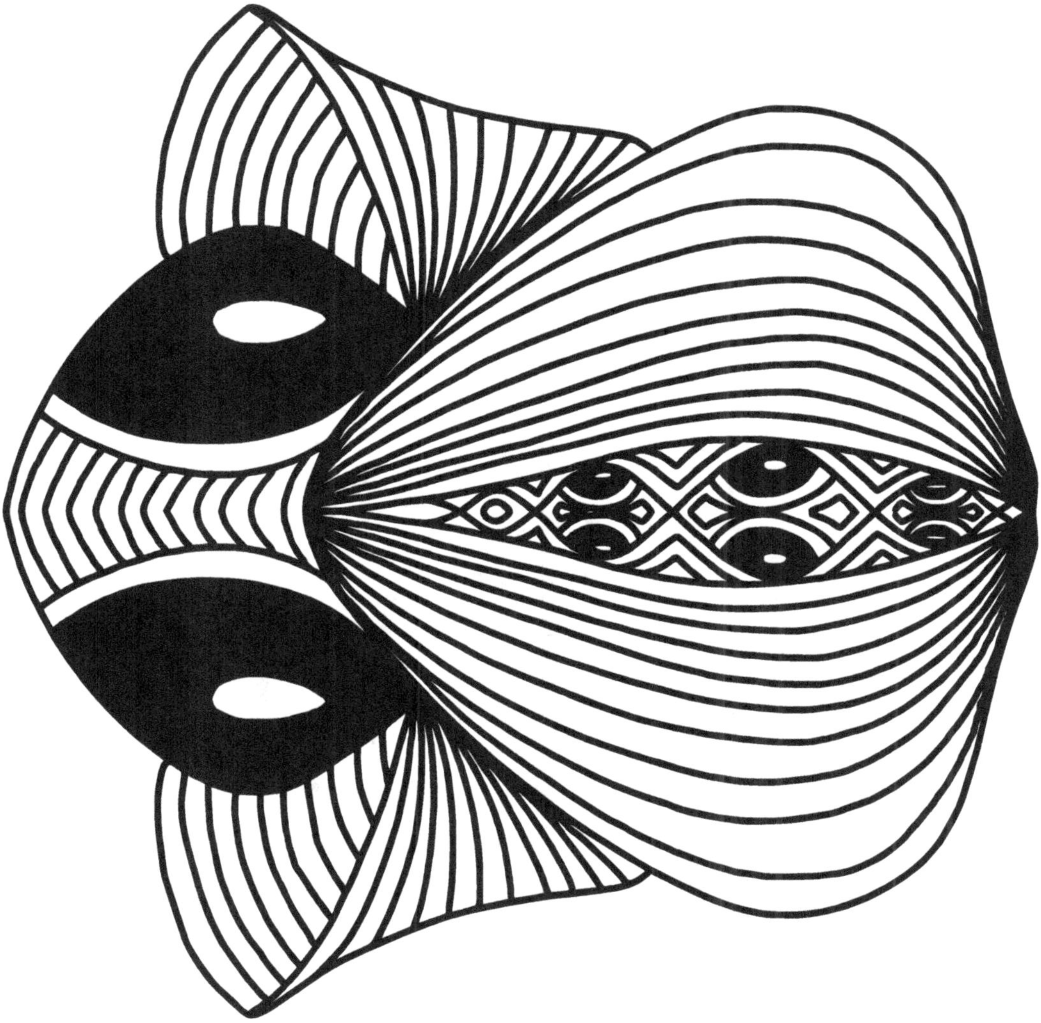

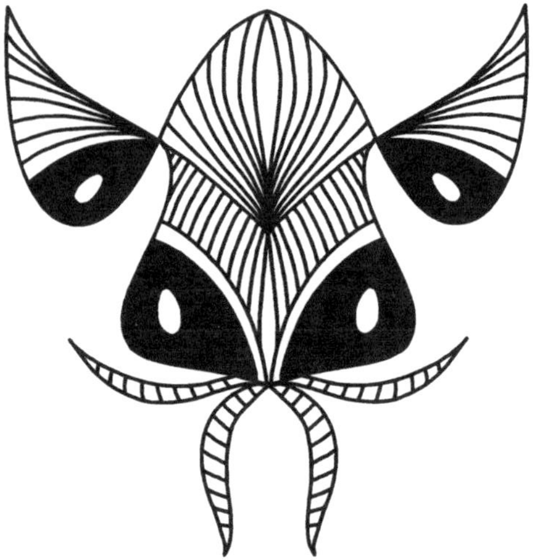

FATLINER WEIRDIES
VOLUME 1

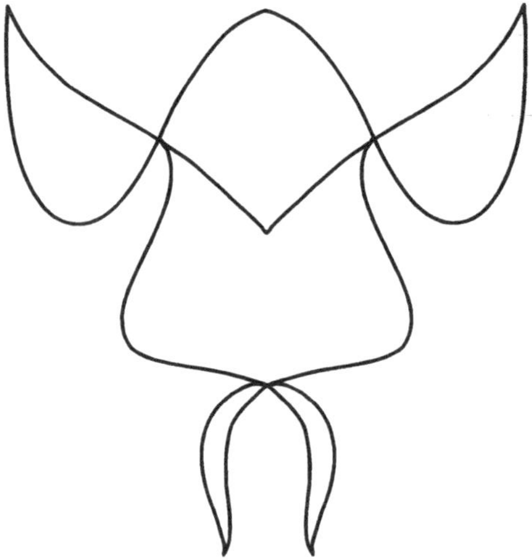

FATLINER WEIRDIES
THE TEMPLATES 1

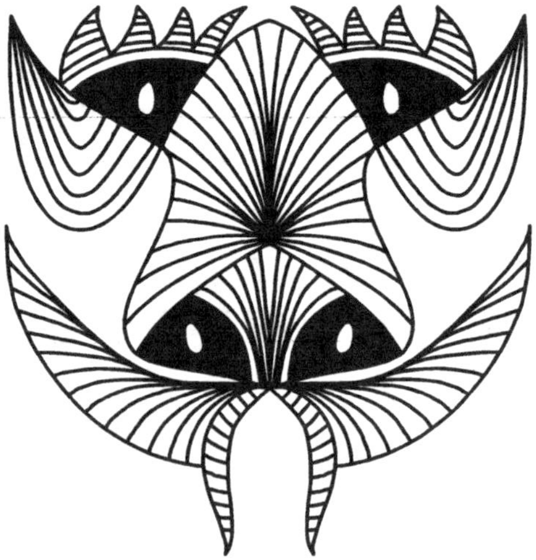

FATLINER WEIRDIES
VOLUME 3

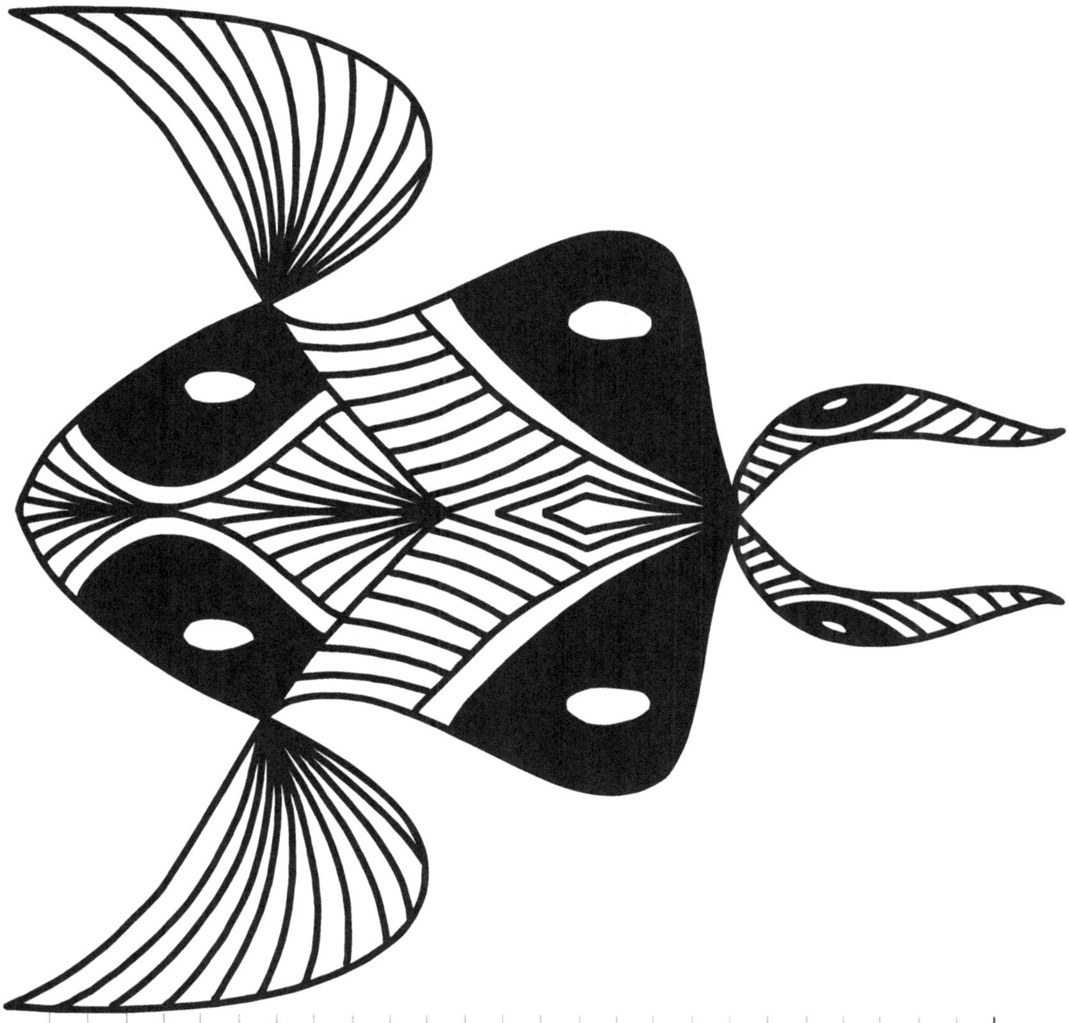

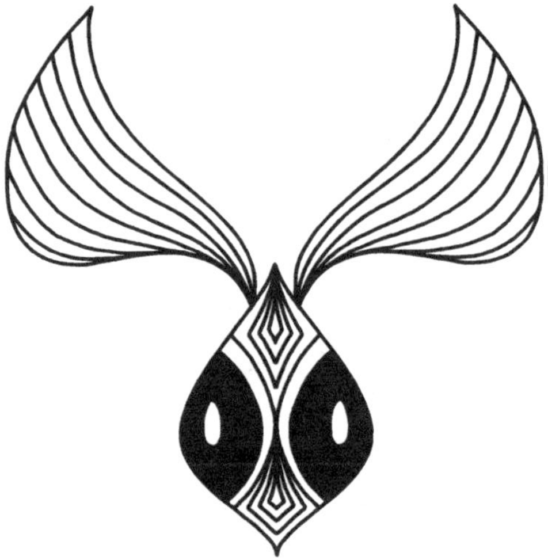

FATLINER WEIRDIES
VOLUME 1

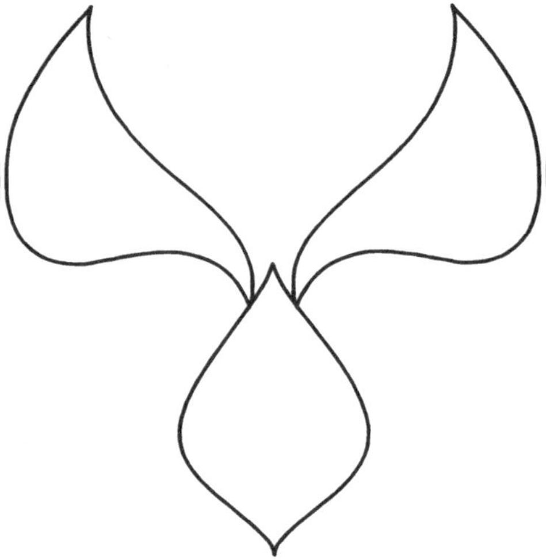

FATLINER WEIRDIES
THE TEMPLATES 1

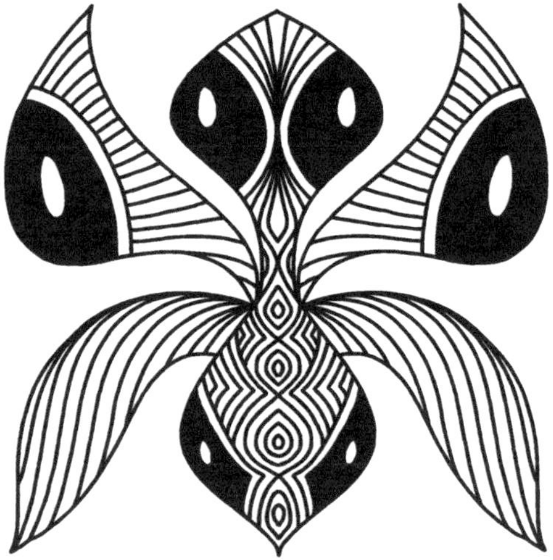

FATLINER WEIRDIES
VOLUME 3

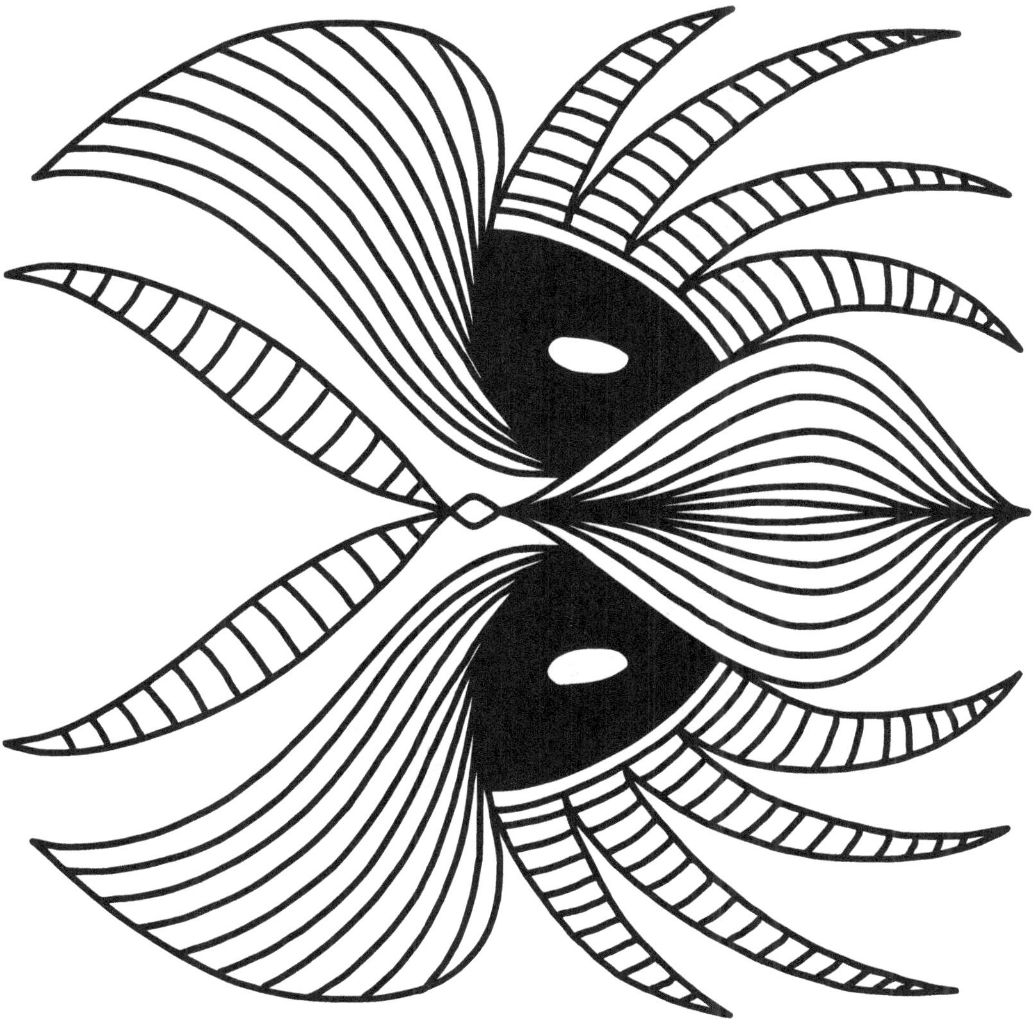

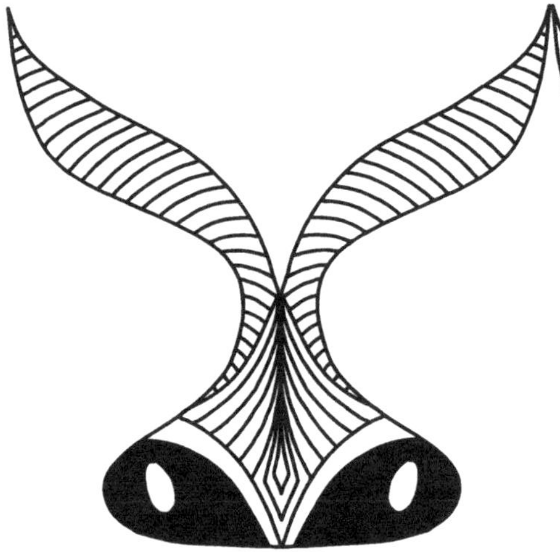

FATLINER WEIRDIES
VOLUME 1

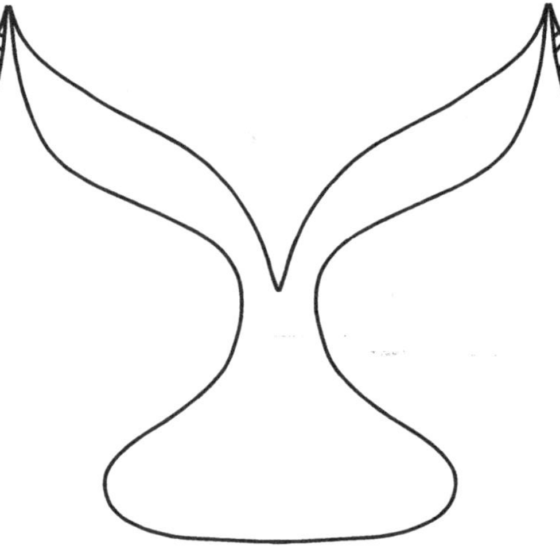

FATLINER WEIRDIES
THE TEMPLATES 1

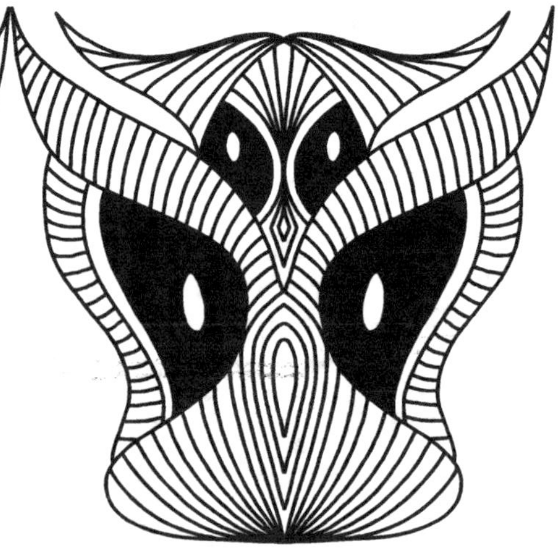

FATLINER WEIRDIES
VOLUME 3

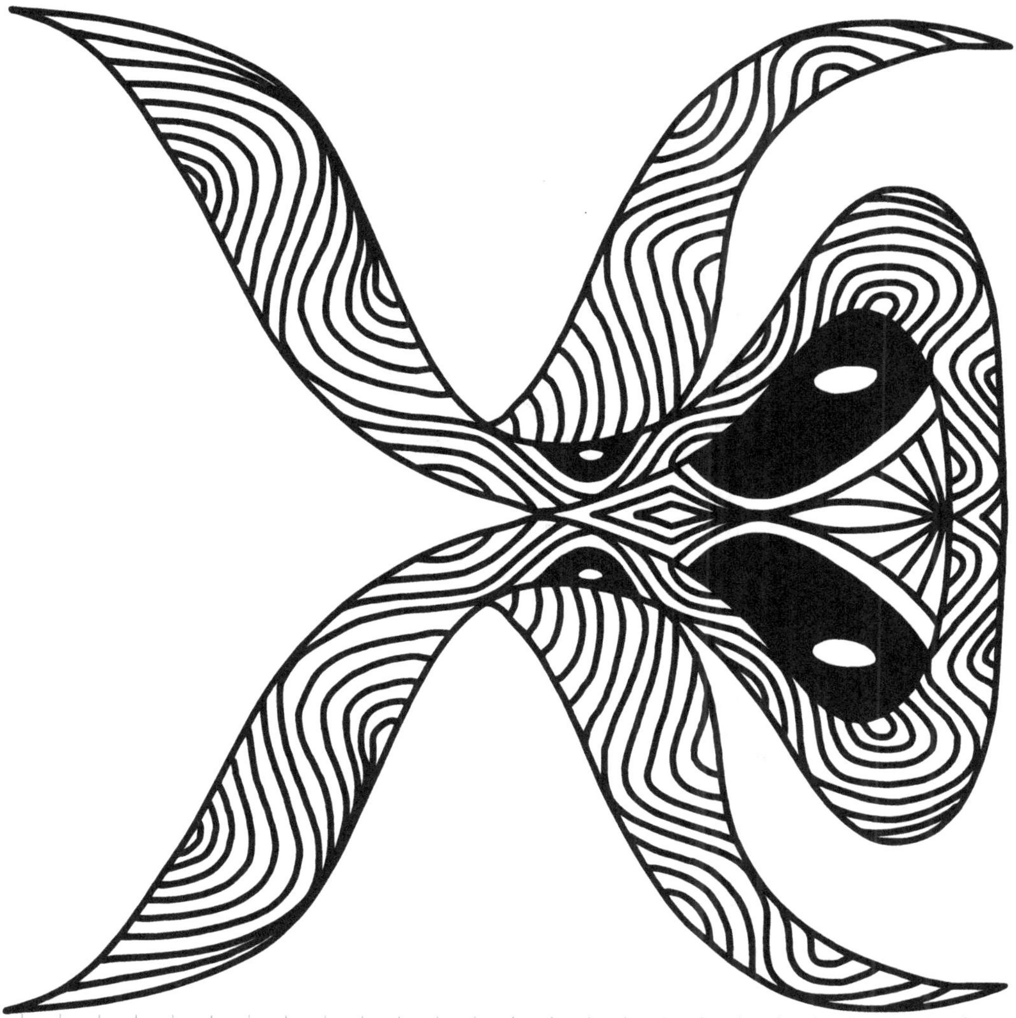

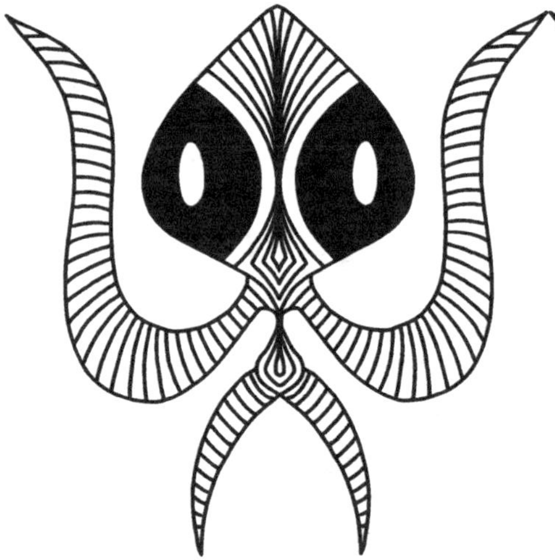

FATLINER WEIRDIES
VOLUME 1

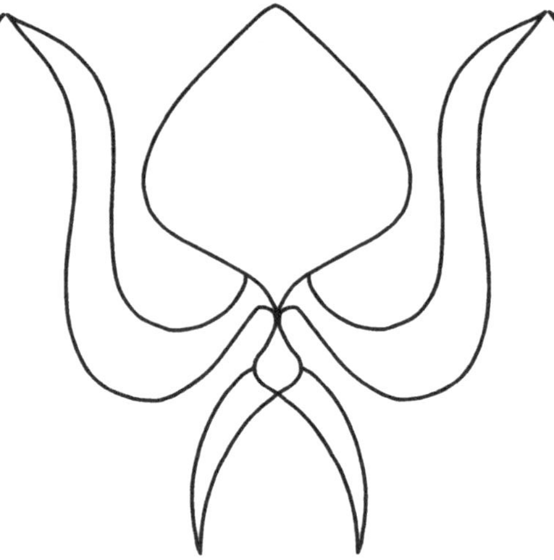

FATLINER WEIRDIES
THE TEMPLATES 1

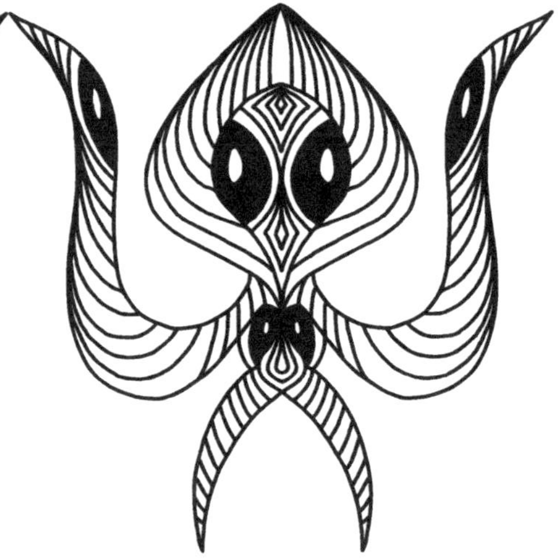

FATLINER WEIRDIES
VOLUME 3

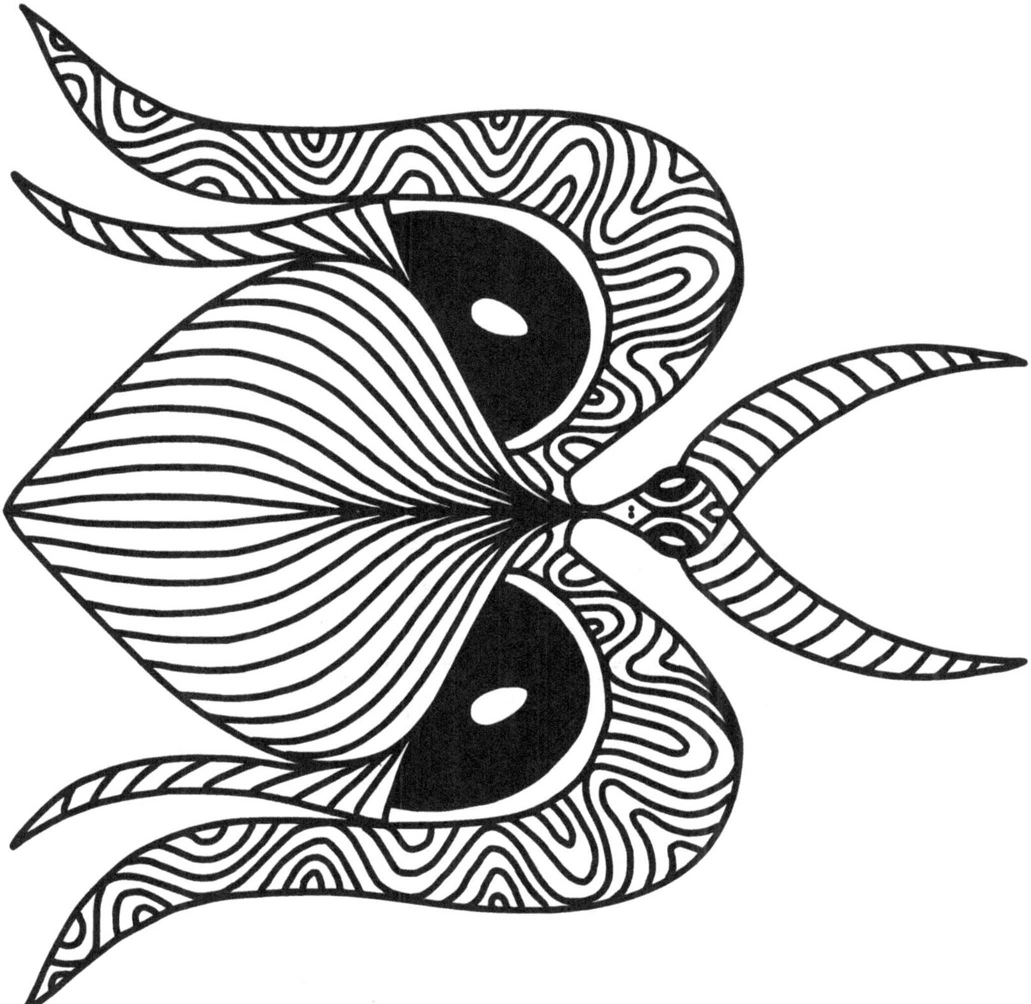

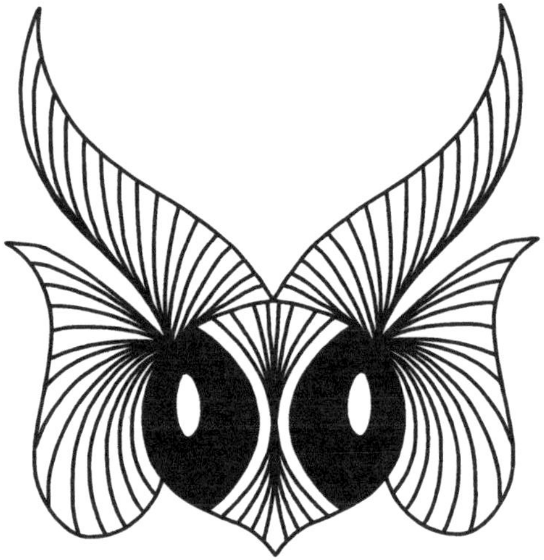
FATLINER WEIRDIES
VOLUME 1

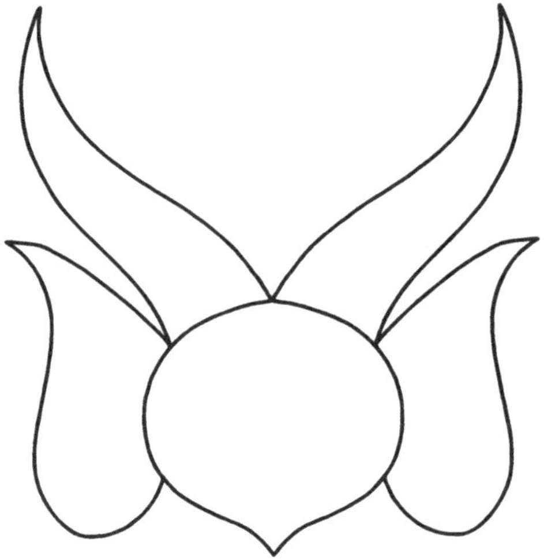
FATLINER WEIRDIES
THE TEMPLATES 1

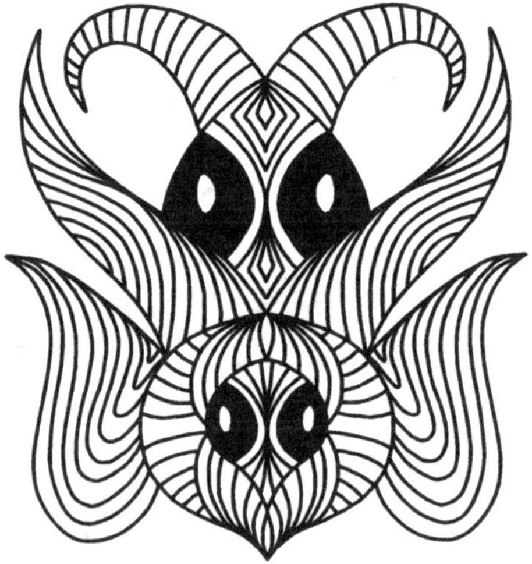
FATLINER WEIRDIES
VOLUME 3

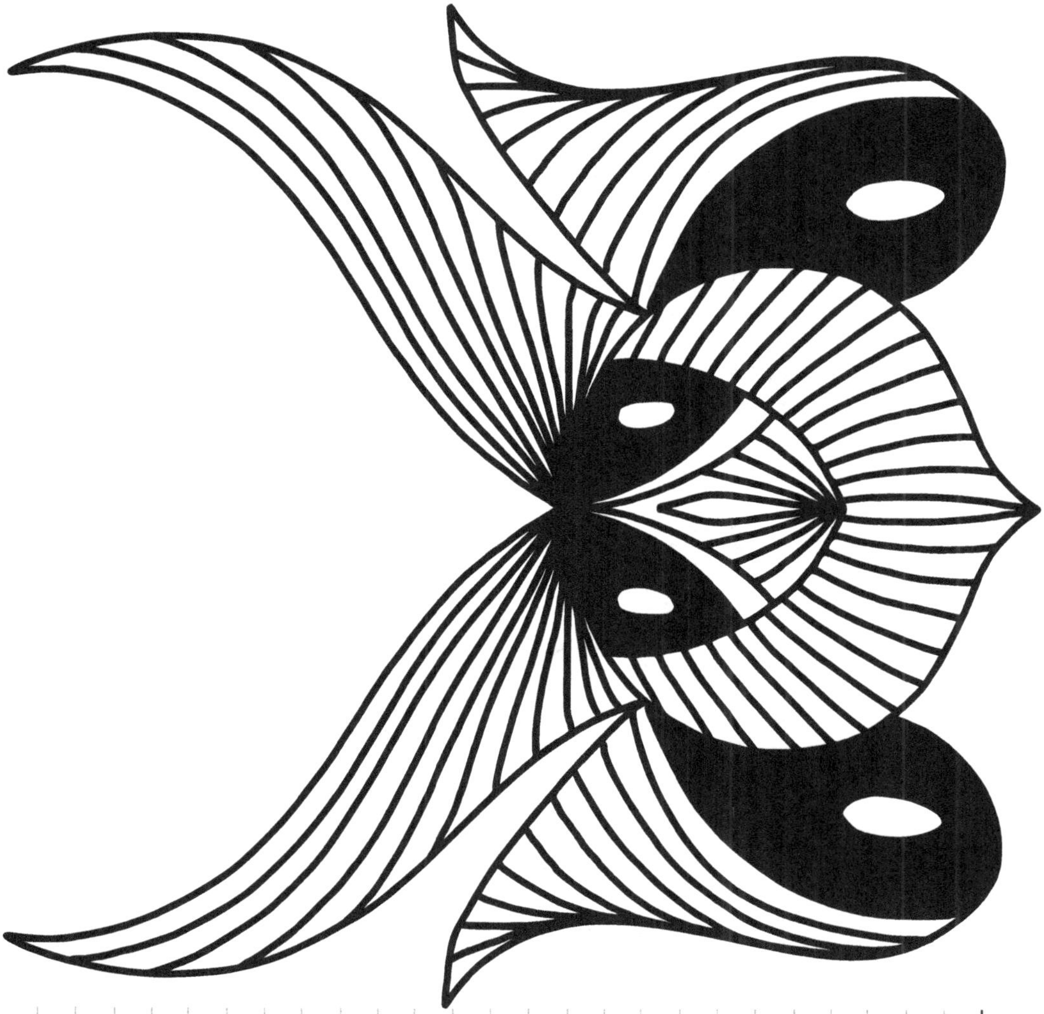

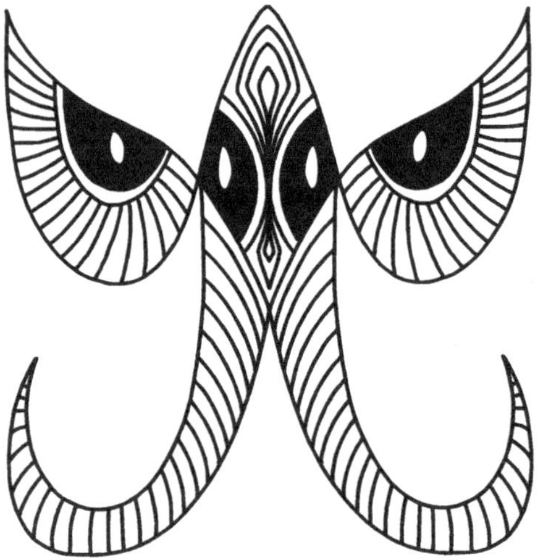

FATLINER WEIRDIES
VOLUME 1

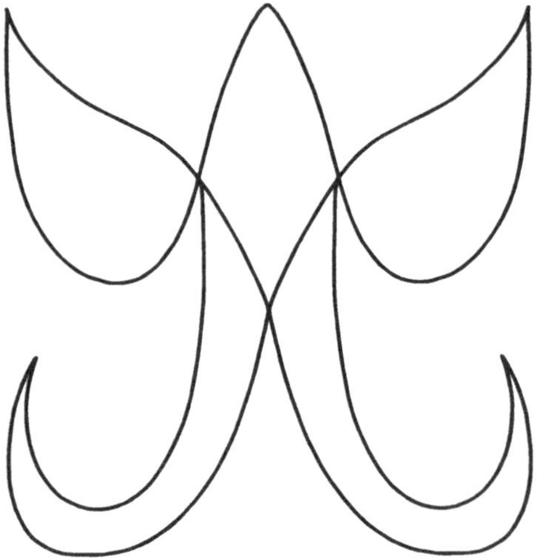

FATLINER WEIRDIES
THE TEMPLATES 1

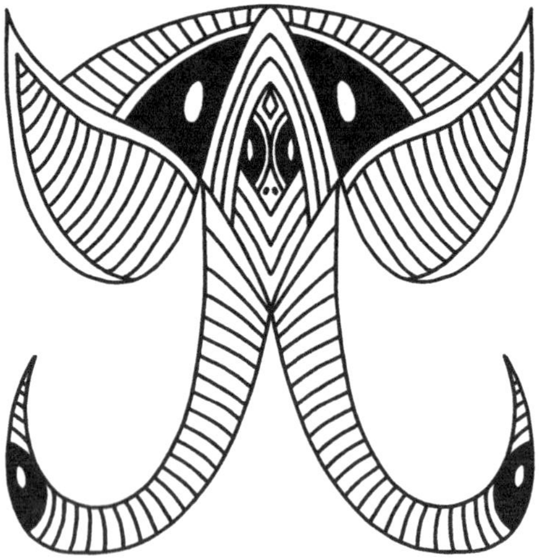

FATLINER WEIRDIES
VOLUME 3

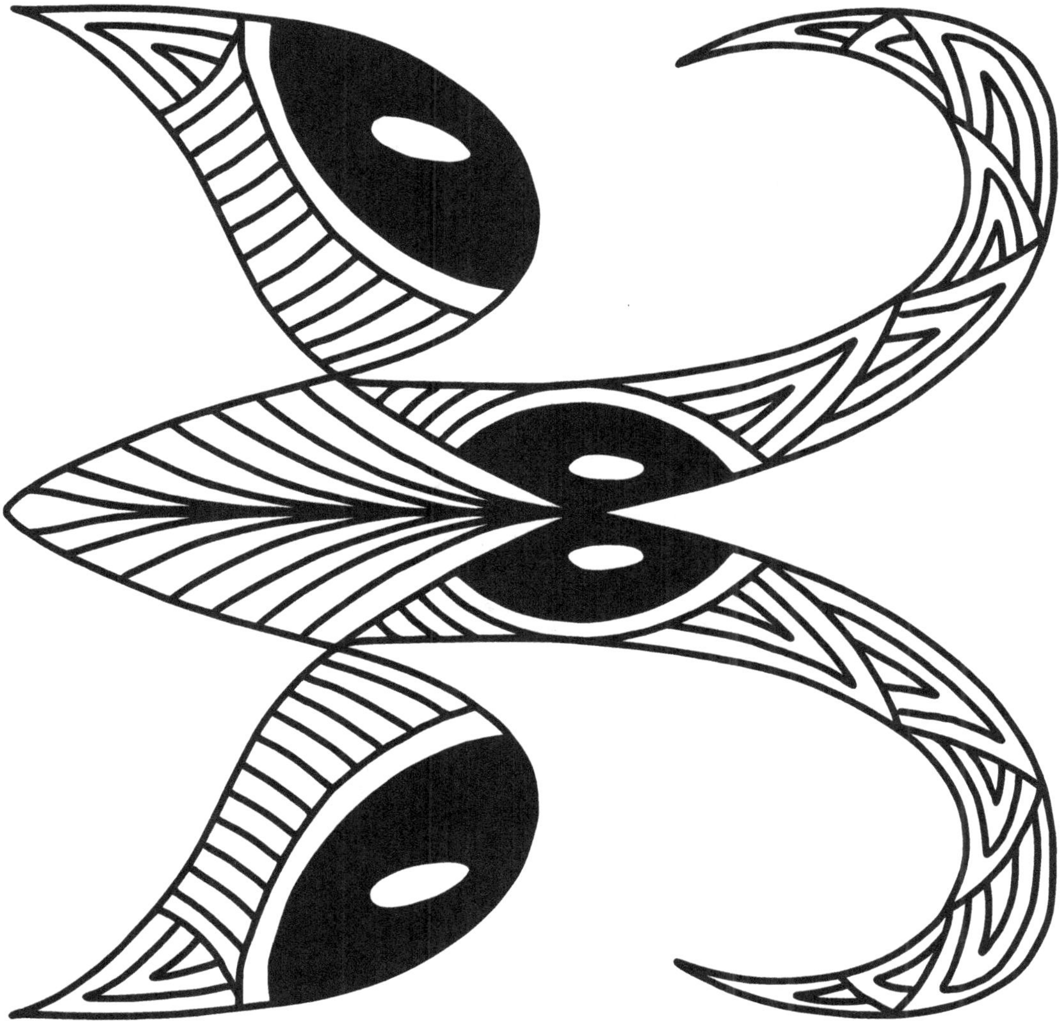

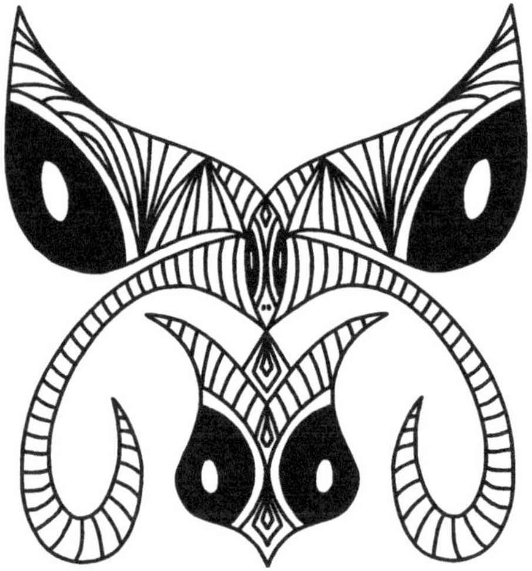

FATLINER WEIRDIES
VOLUME 1

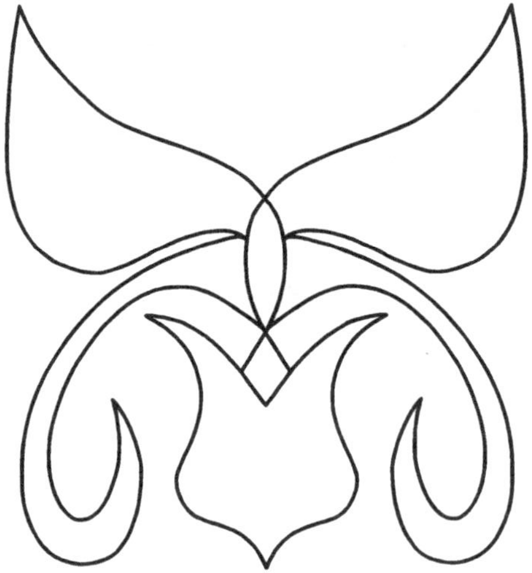

FATLINER WEIRDIES
THE TEMPLATES 1

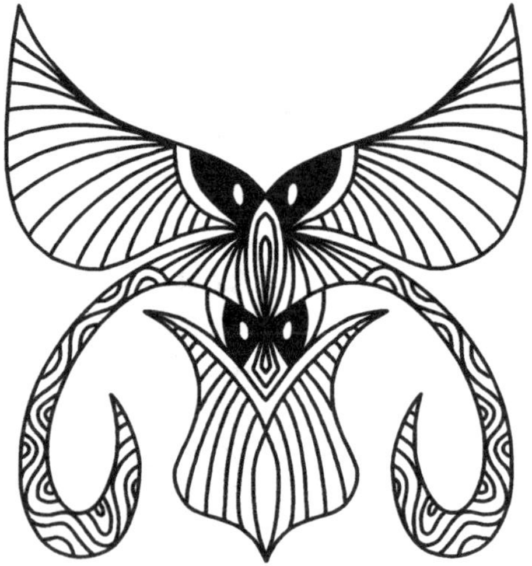

FATLINER WEIRDIES
VOLUME 3

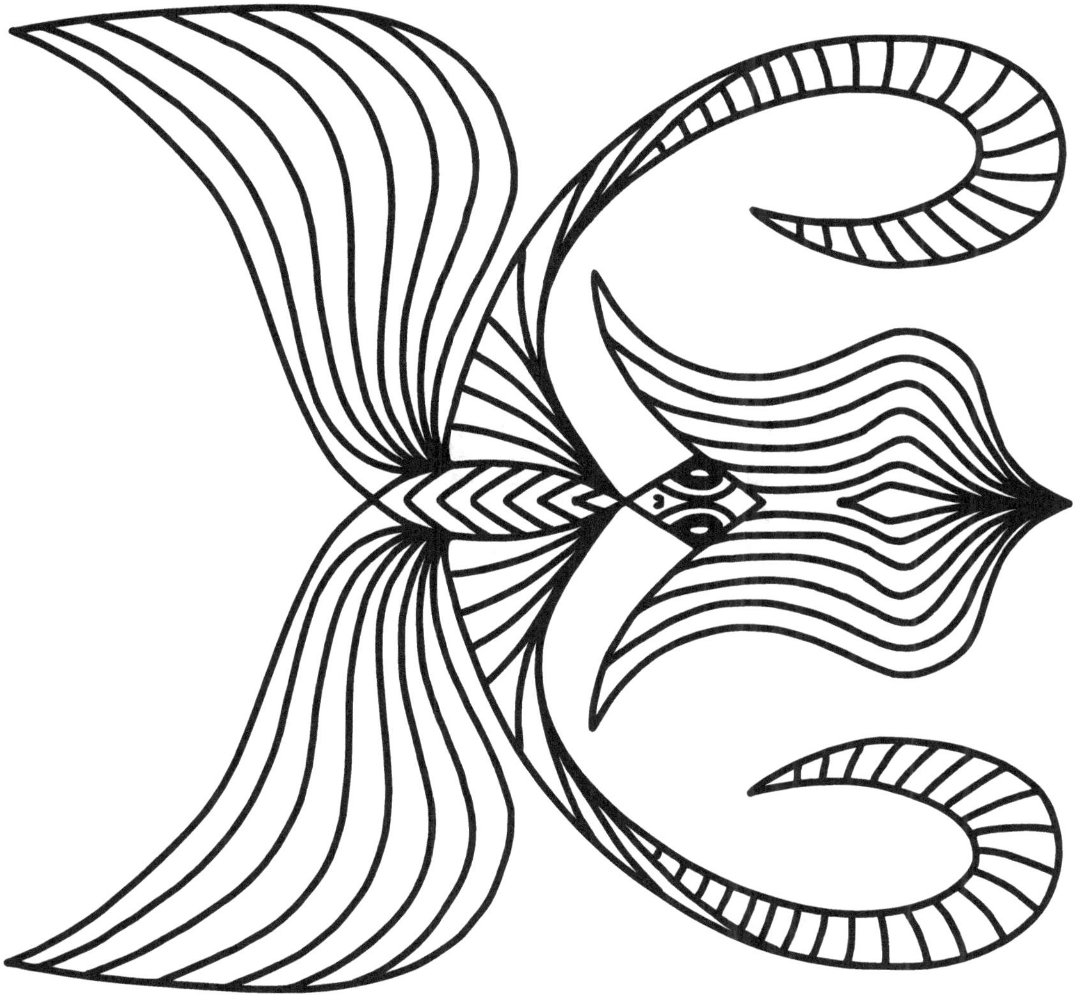

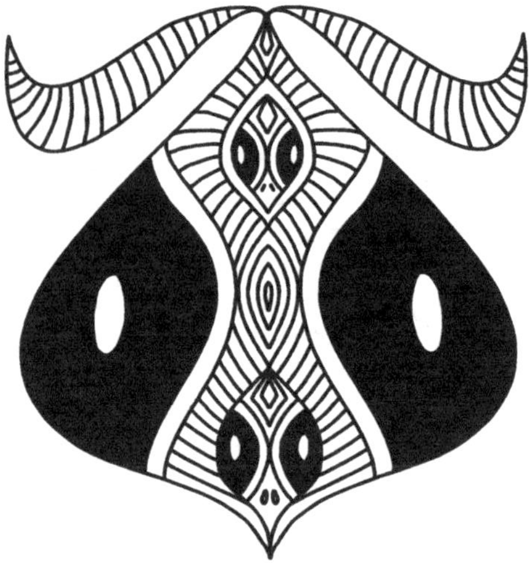

FATLINER WEIRDIES
VOLUME 1

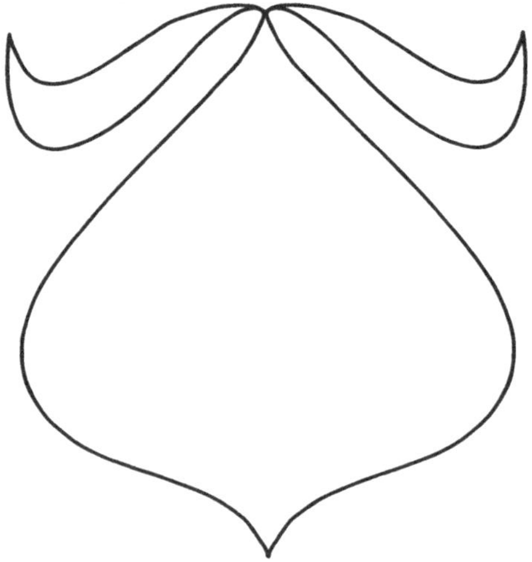

FATLINER WEIRDIES
THE TEMPLATES 1

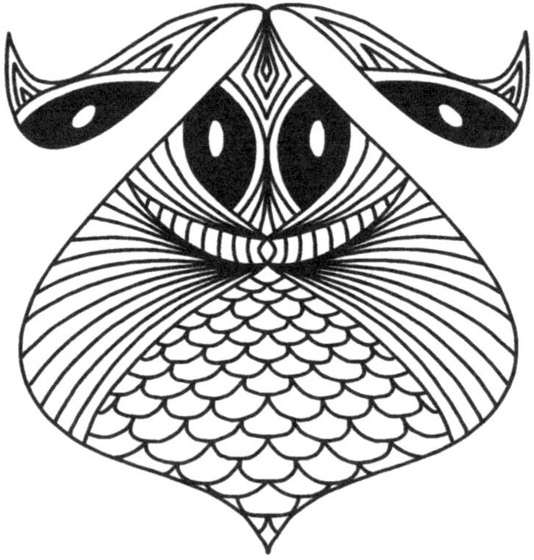

FATLINER WEIRDIES
VOLUME 3

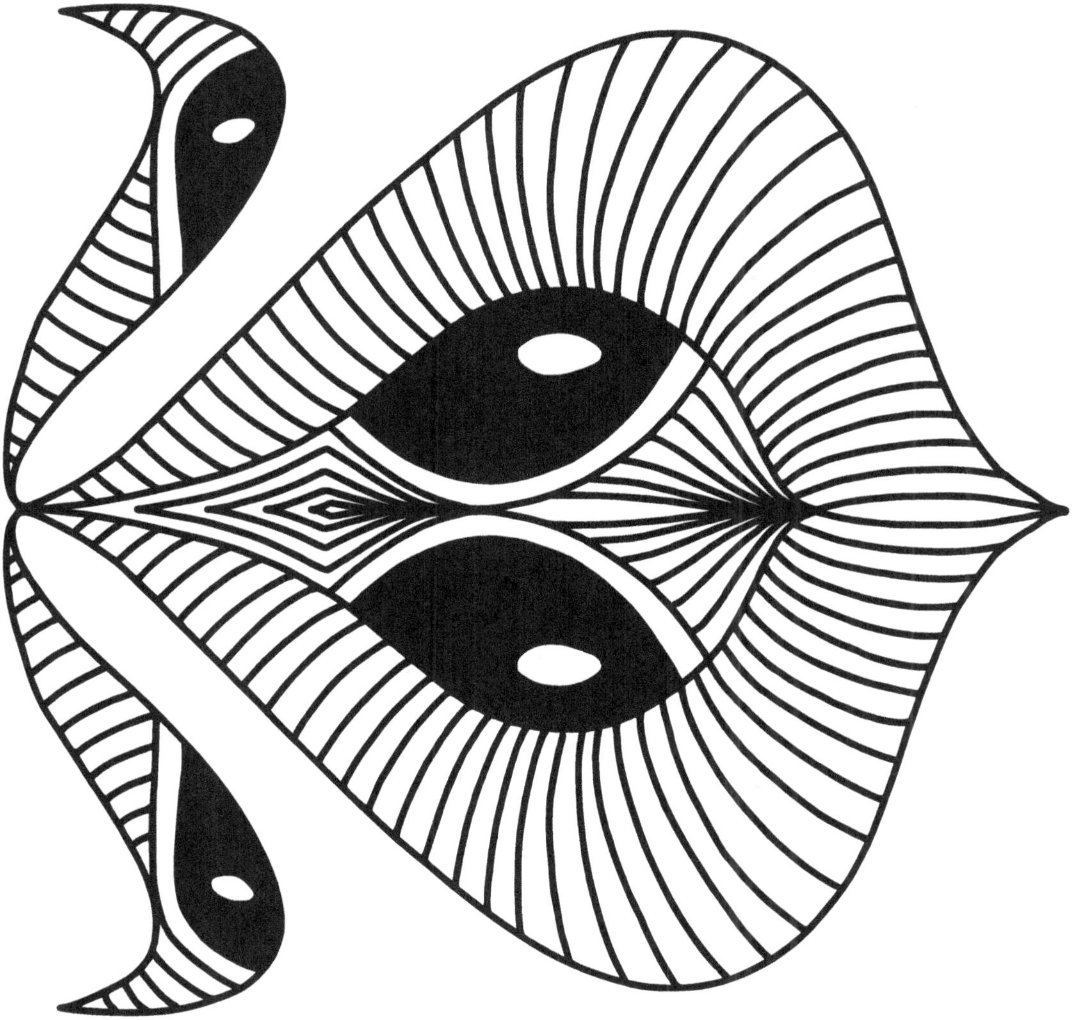

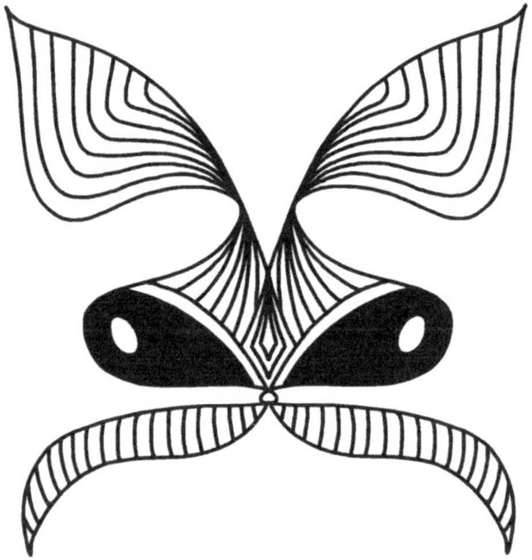

FATLINER WEIRDIES
VOLUME 1

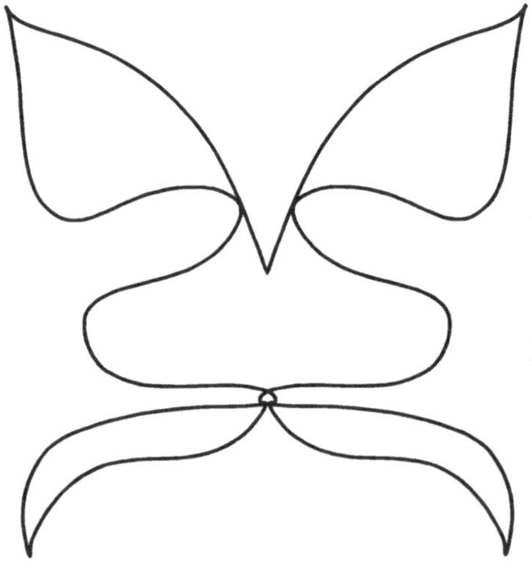

FATLINER WEIRDIES
THE TEMPLATES 1

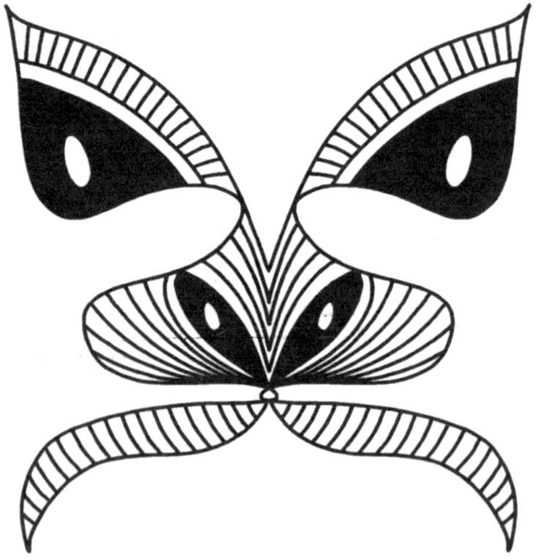

FATLINER WEIRDIES
VOLUME 3

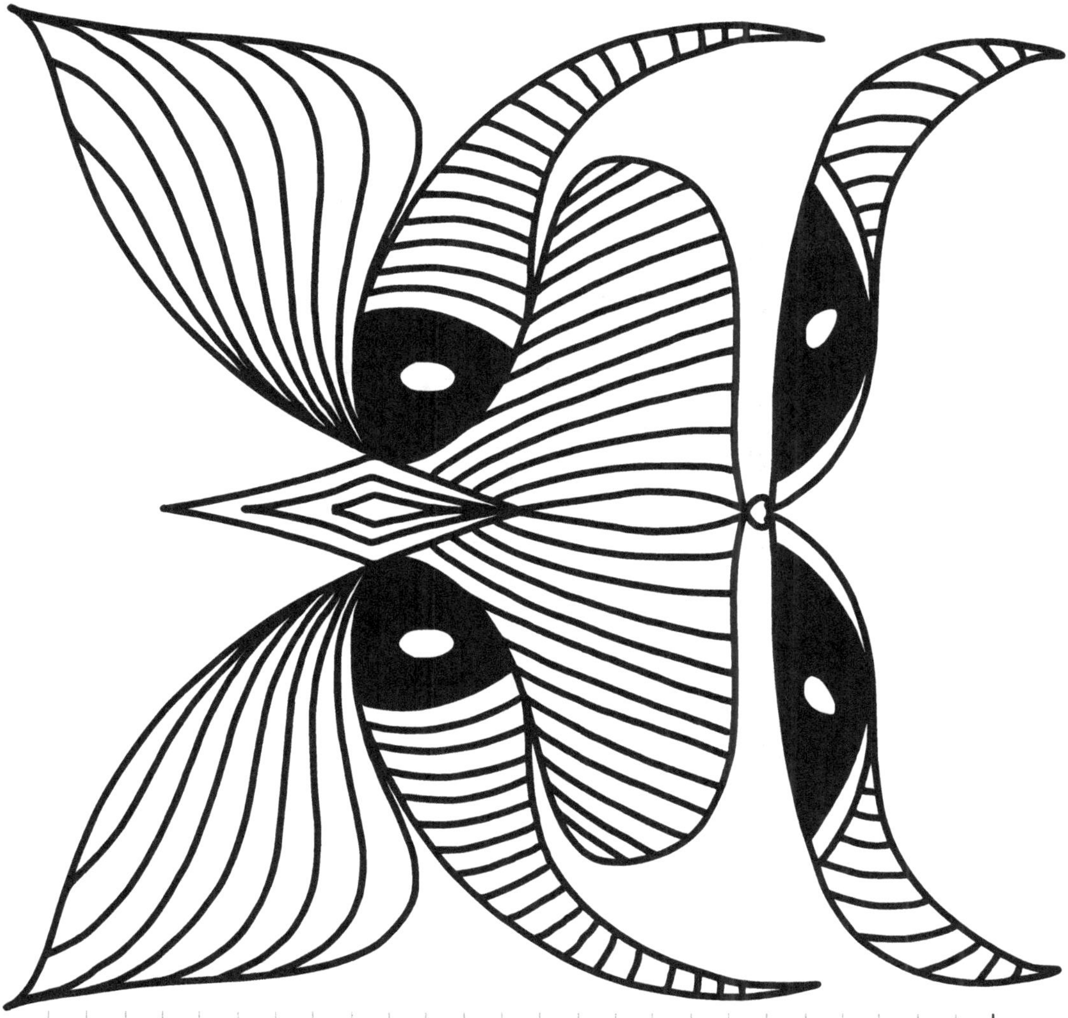

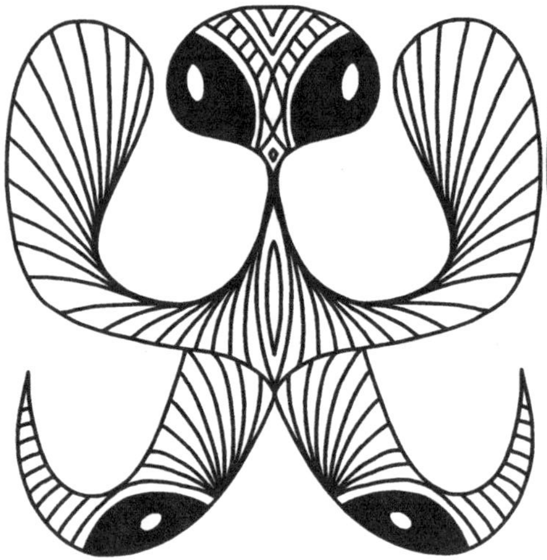

FATLINER WEIRDIES
VOLUME 1

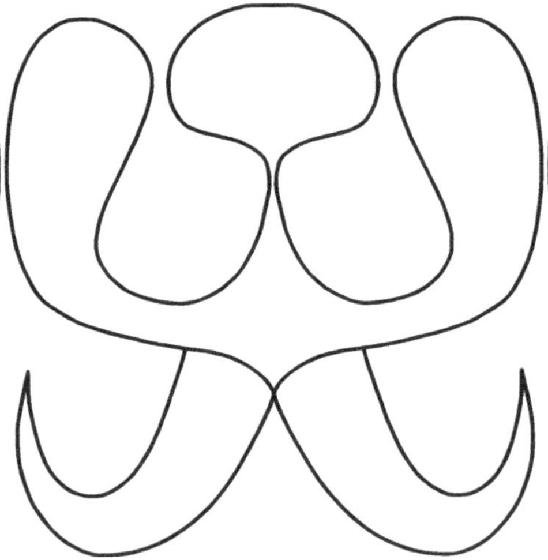

FATLINER WEIRDIES
THE TEMPLATES 1

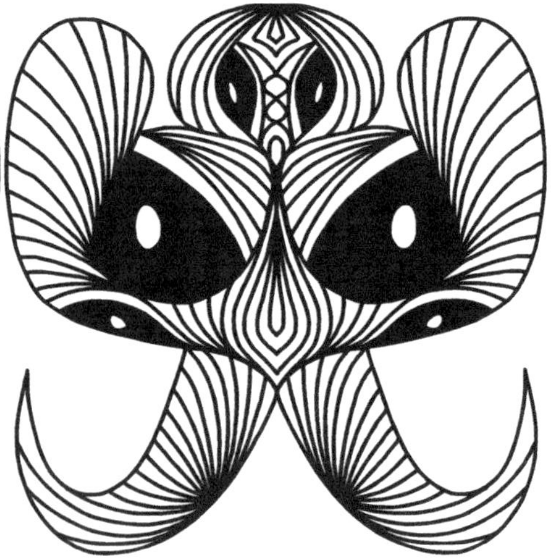

FATLINER WEIRDIES
VOLUME 3

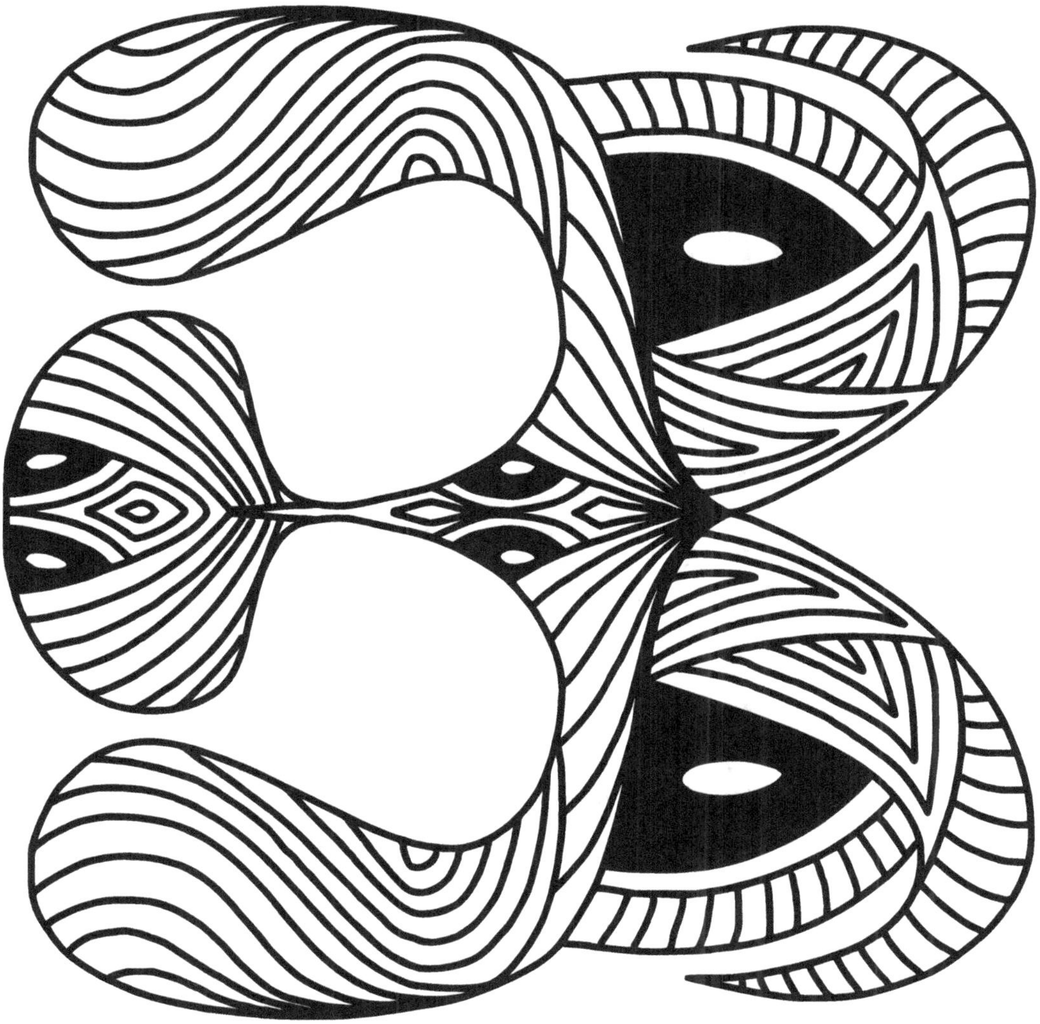

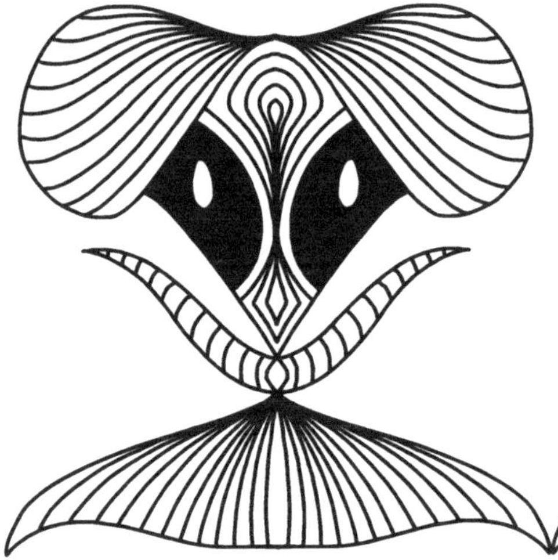

FATLINER WEIRDIES
VOLUME 1

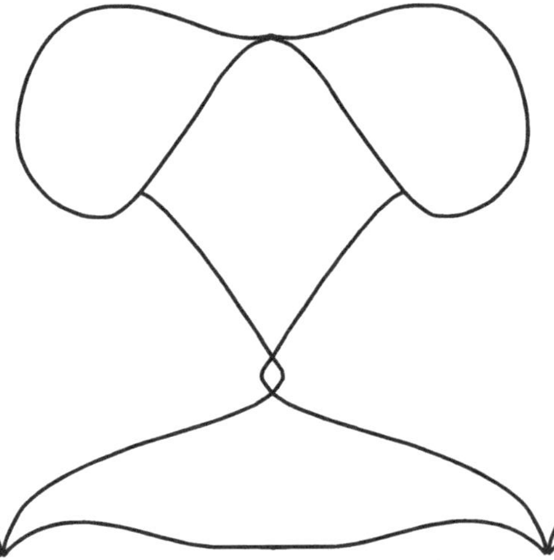

FATLINER WEIRDIES
THE TEMPLATES 1

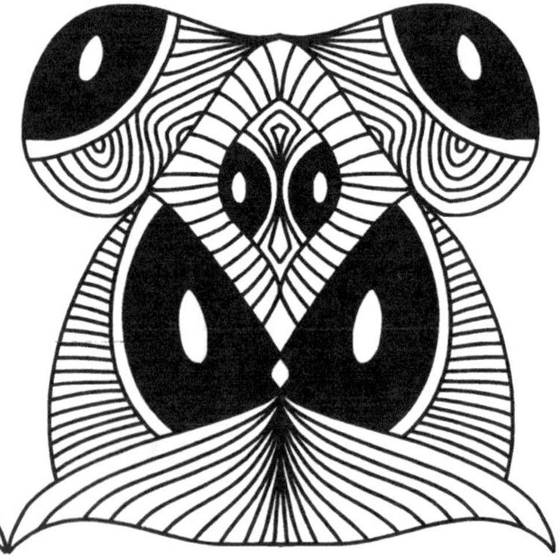

FATLINER WEIRDIES
VOLUME 3

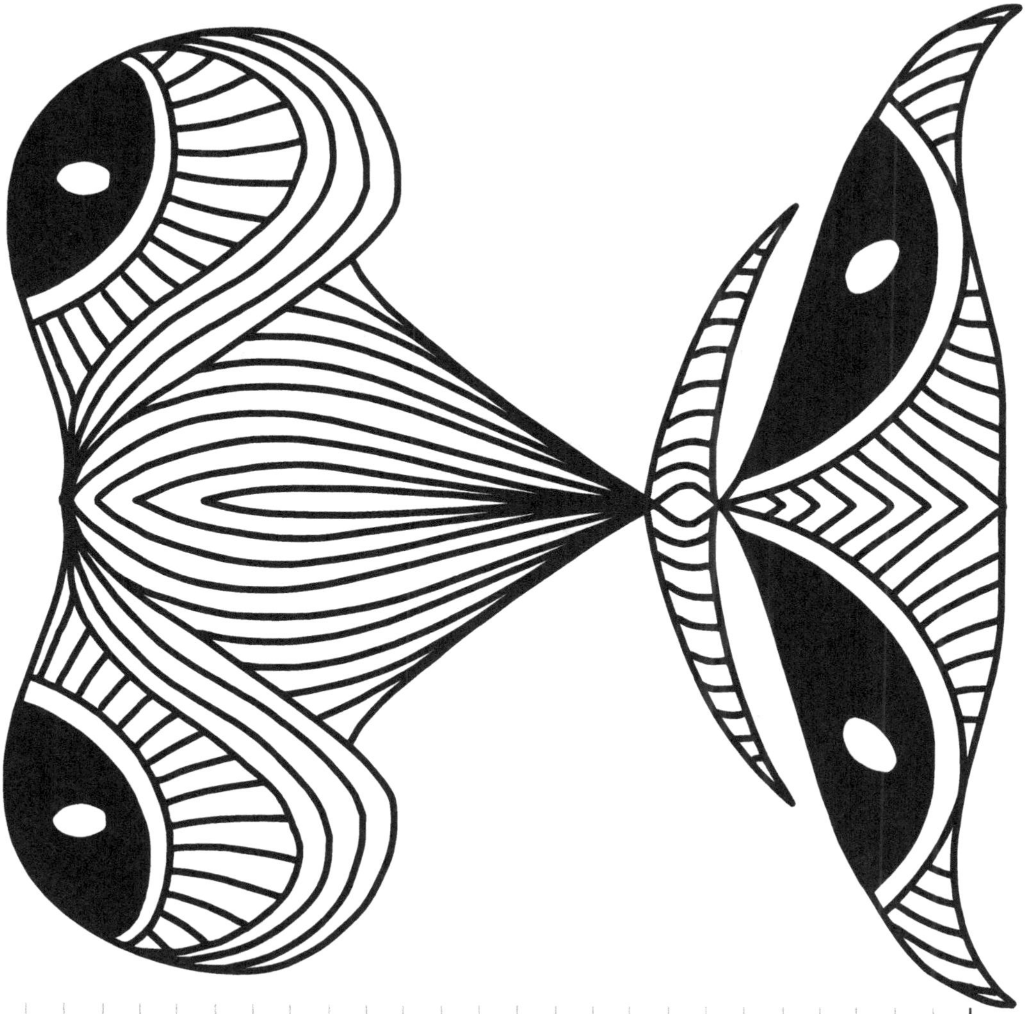

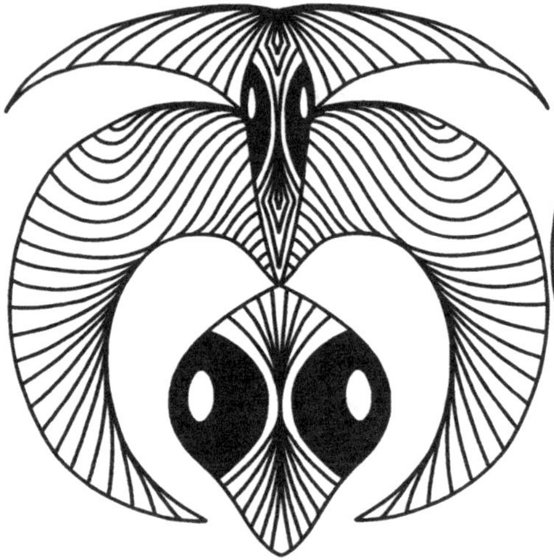

FATLINER WEIRDIES
VOLUME 1

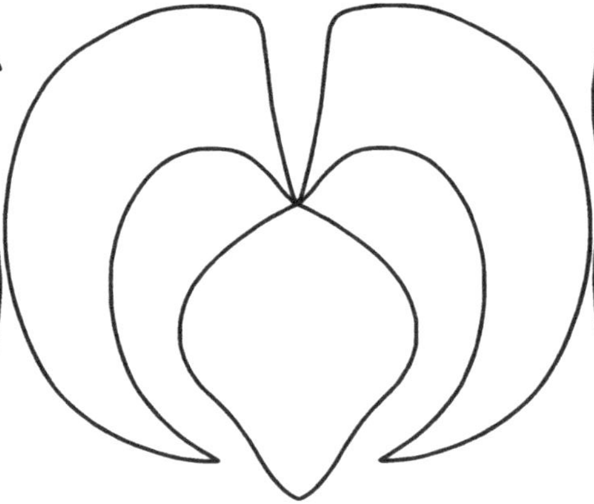

FATLINER WEIRDIES
THE TEMPLATES 1

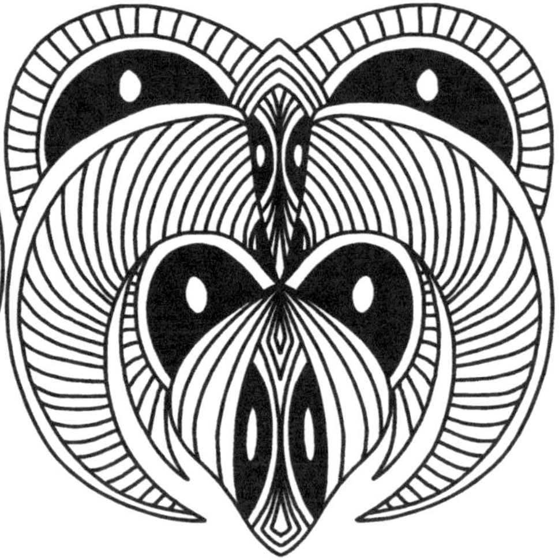

FATLINER WEIRDIES
VOLUME 3

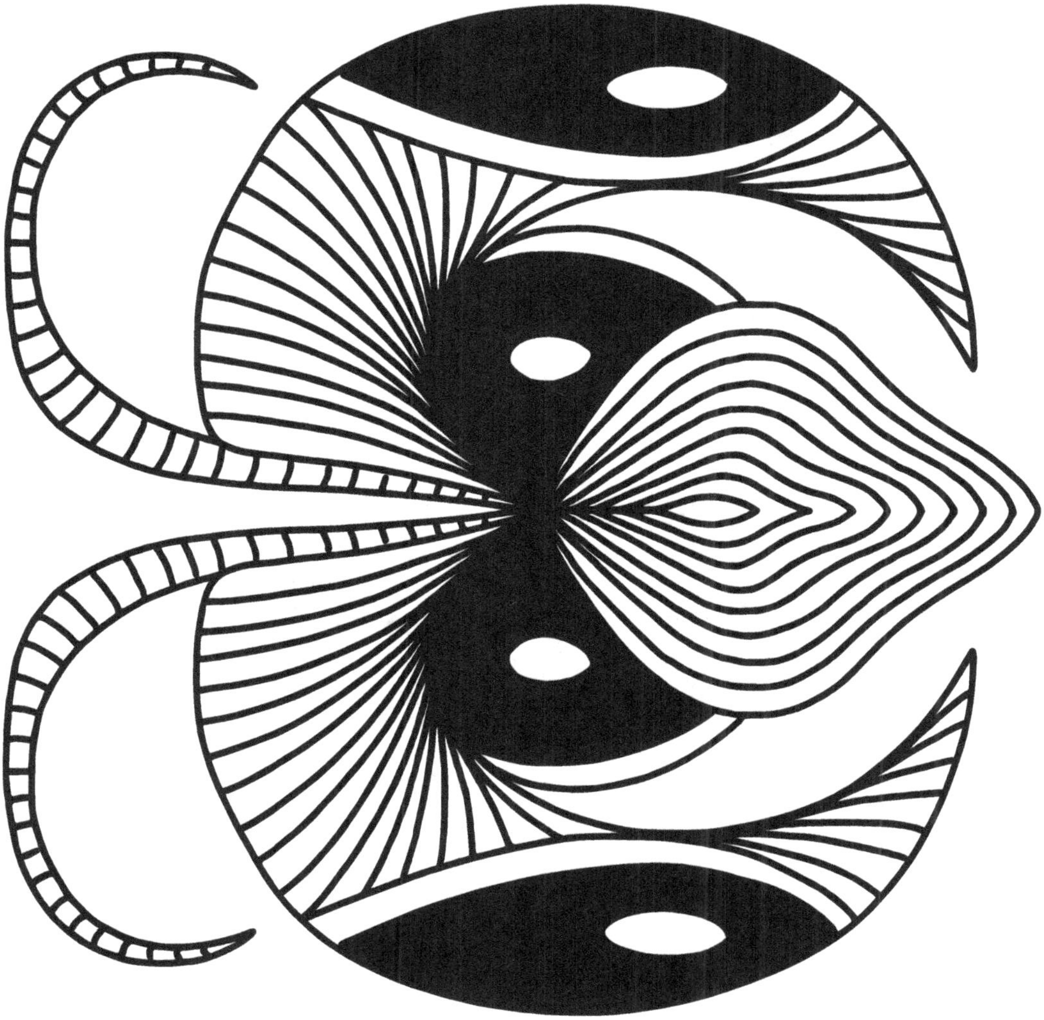

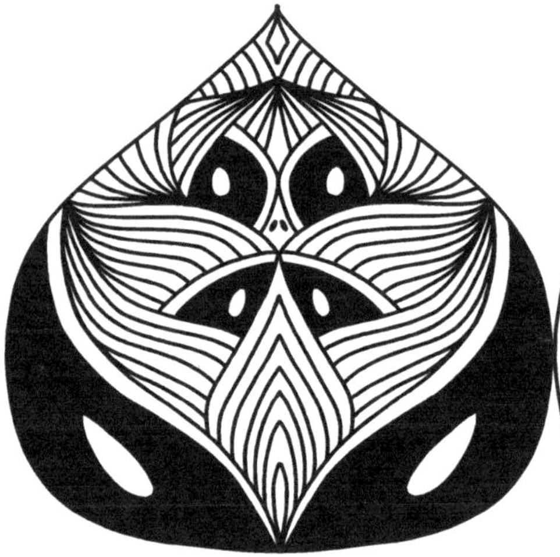

FATLINER WEIRDIES
VOLUME 1

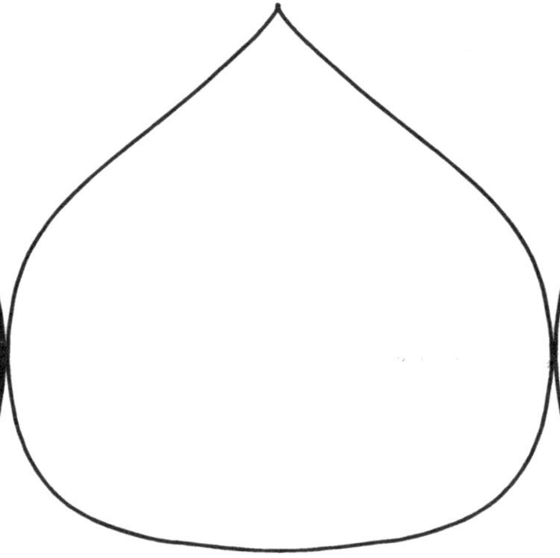

FATLINER WEIRDIES
THE TEMPLATES 1

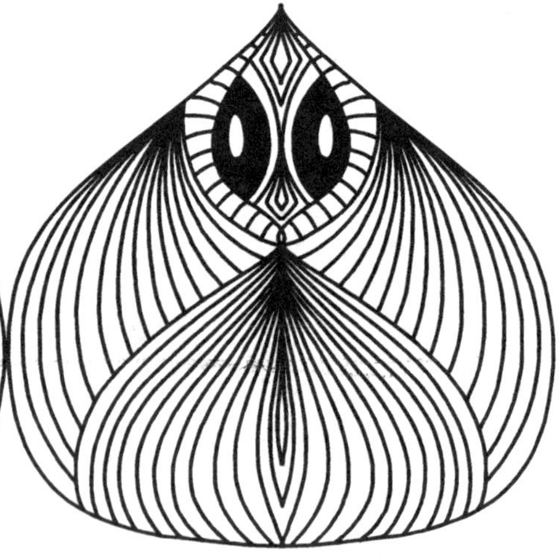

FATLINER WEIRDIES
VOLUME 3

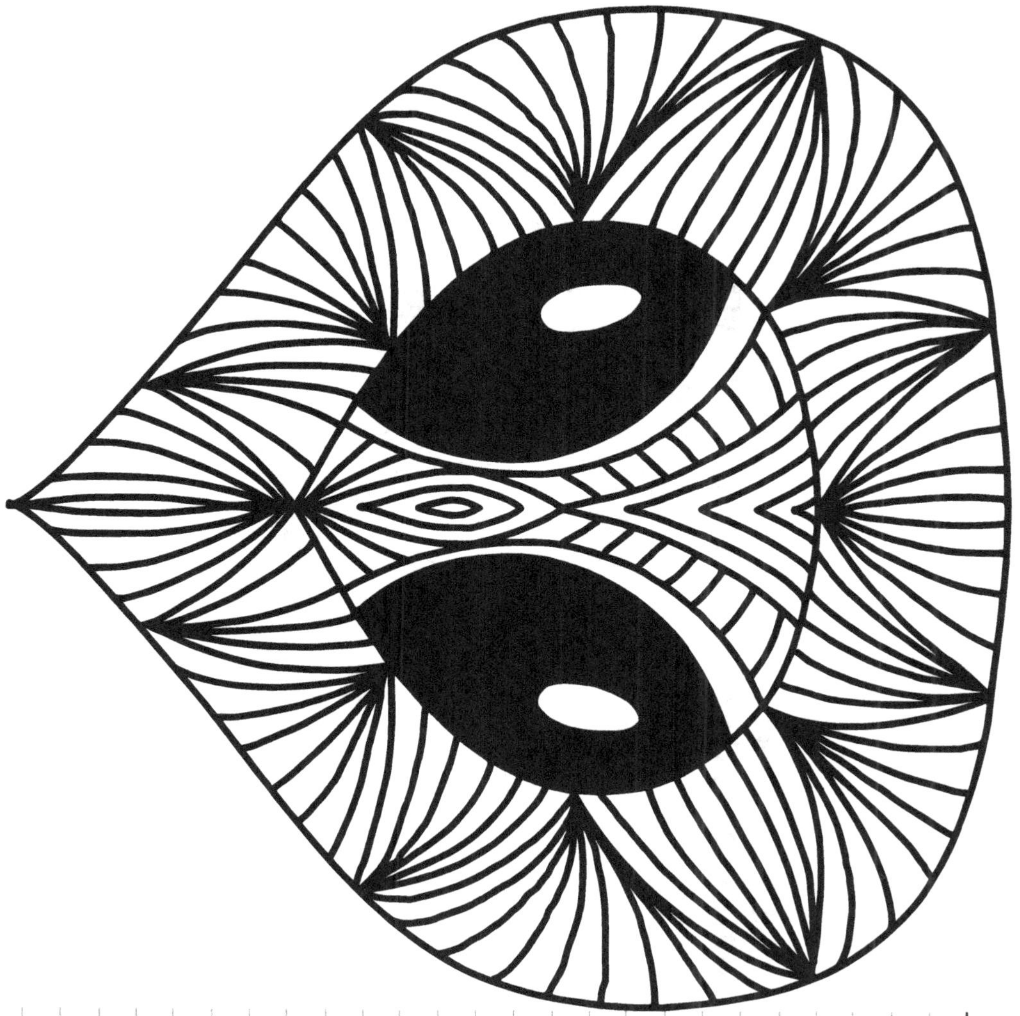

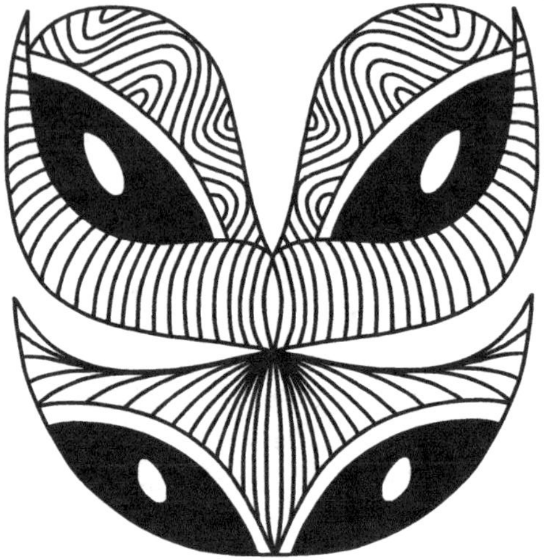

FATLINER WEIRDIES
VOLUME 1

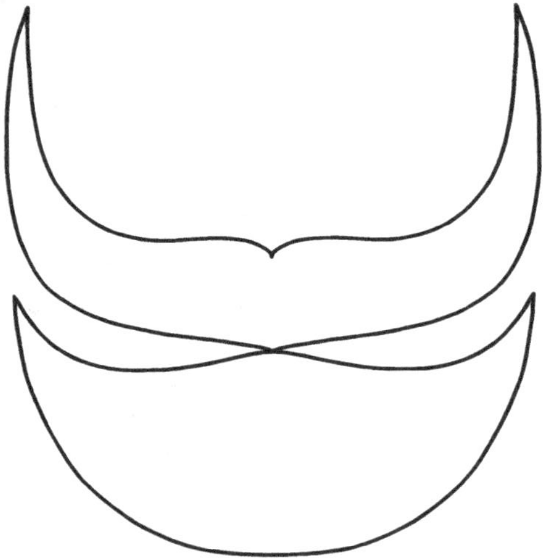

FATLINER WEIRDIES
THE TEMPLATES 1

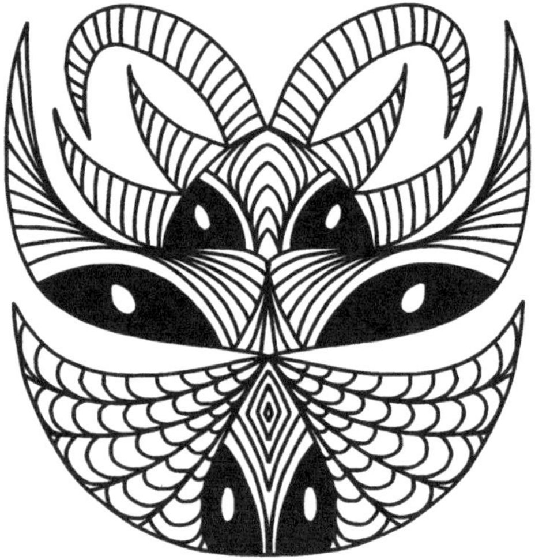

FATLINER WEIRDIES
VOLUME 3

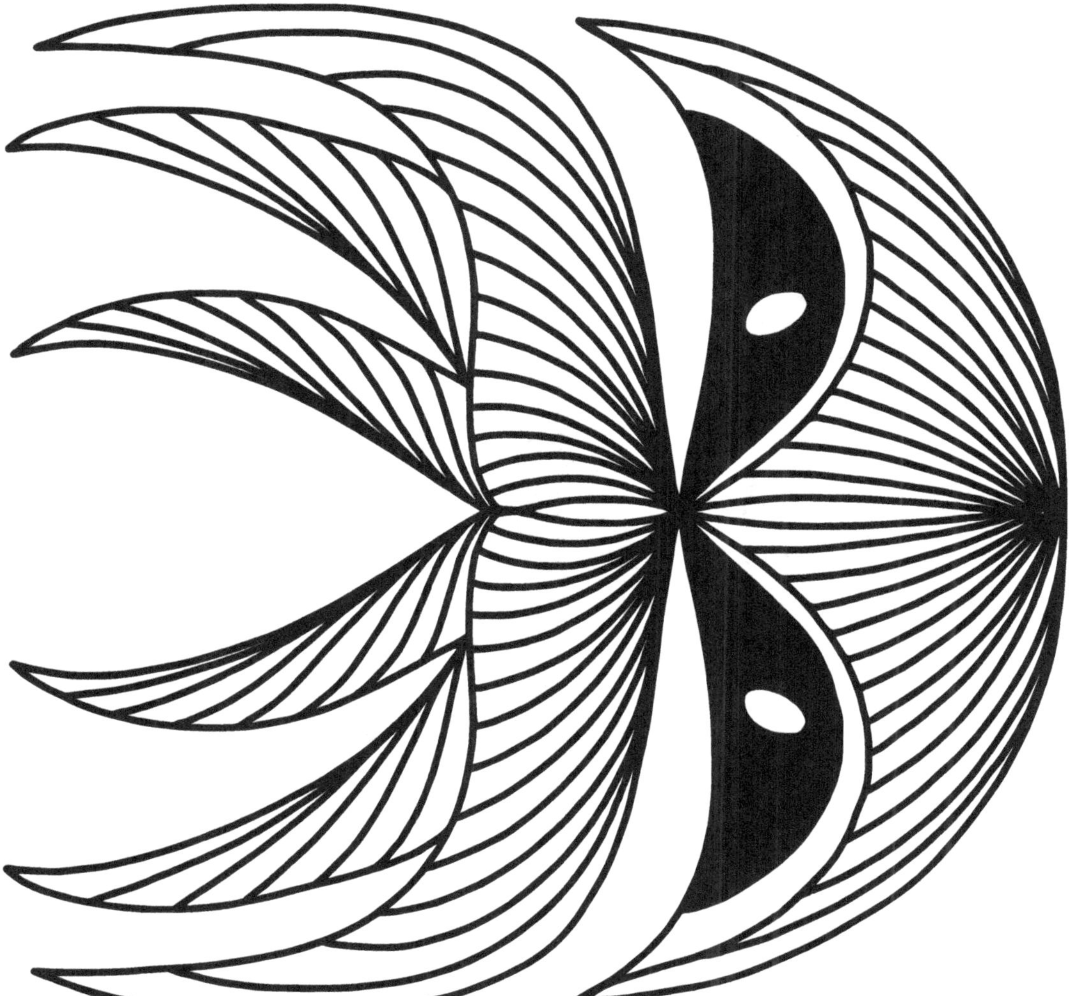

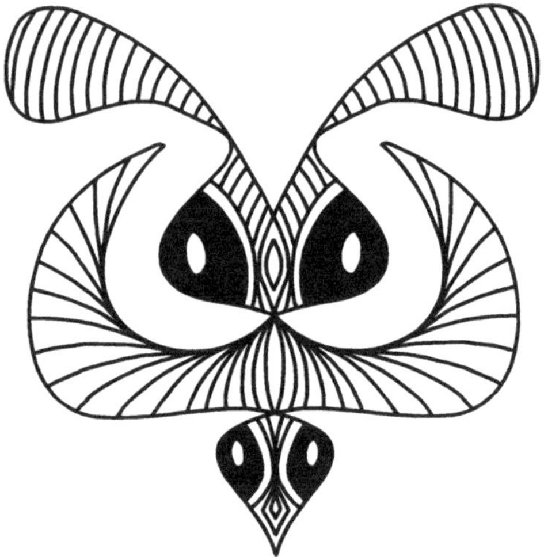

FATLINER WEIRDIES
VOLUME 1

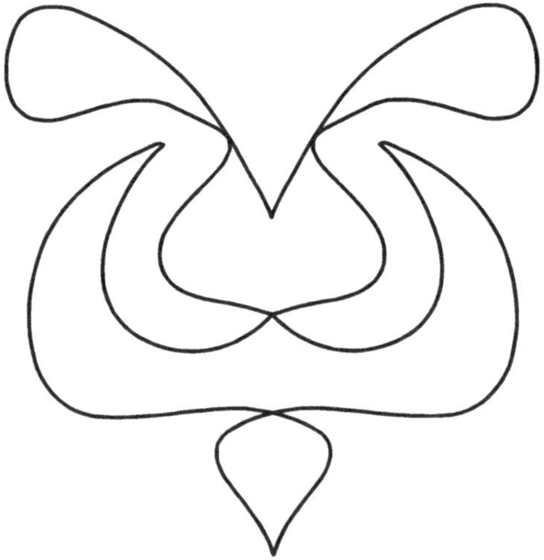

FATLINER WEIRDIES
THE TEMPLATES 1

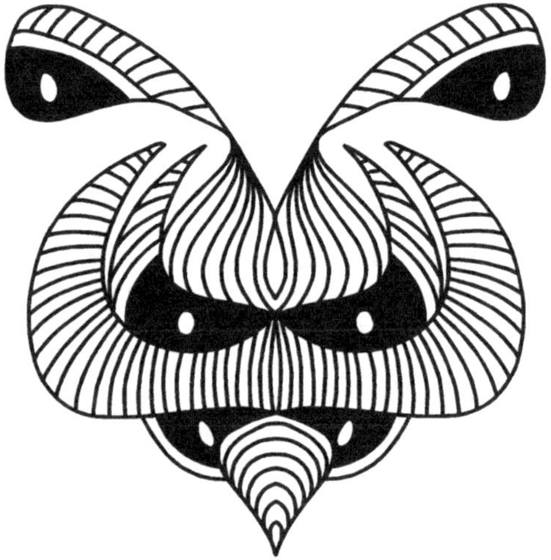

FATLINER WEIRDIES
VOLUME 3

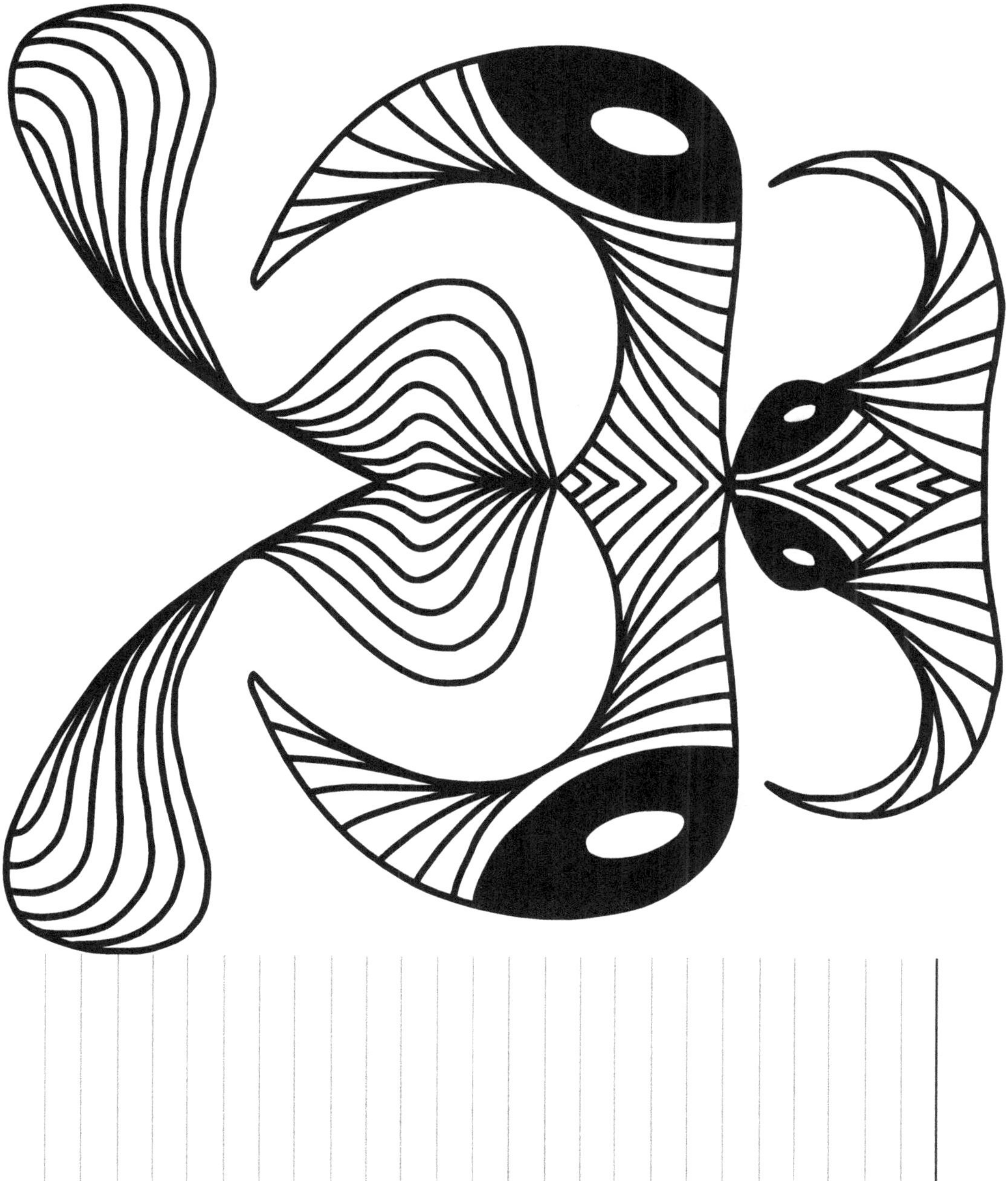

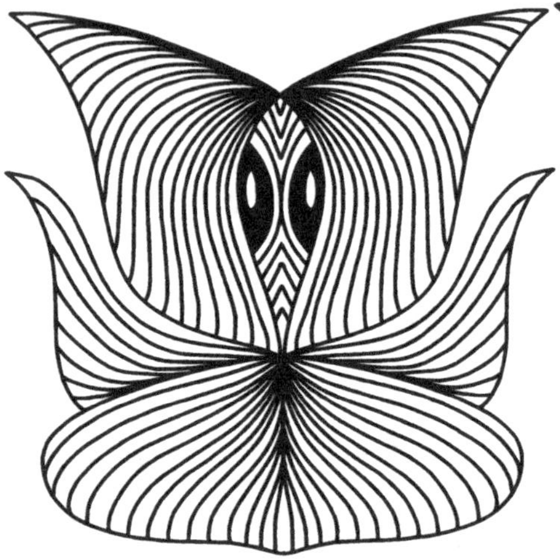

FATLINER WEIRDIES
VOLUME 1

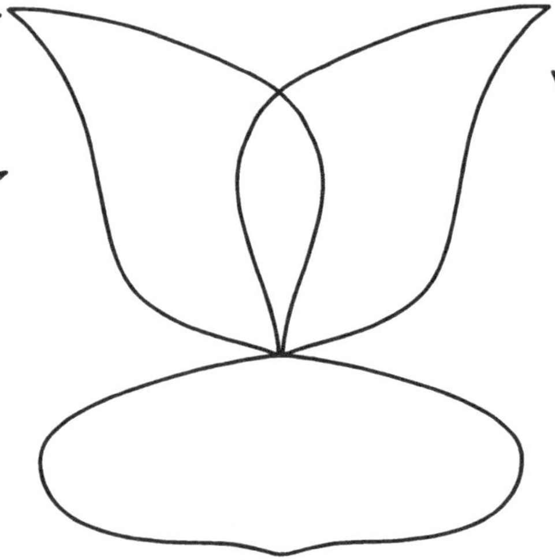

FATLINER WEIRDIES
THE TEMPLATES 1

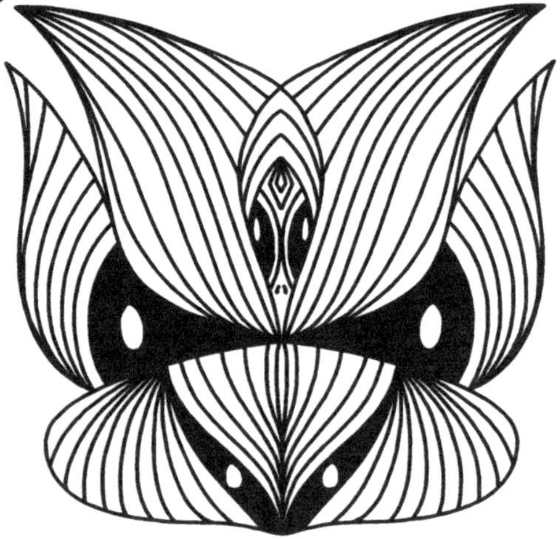

FATLINER WEIRDIES
VOLUME 3

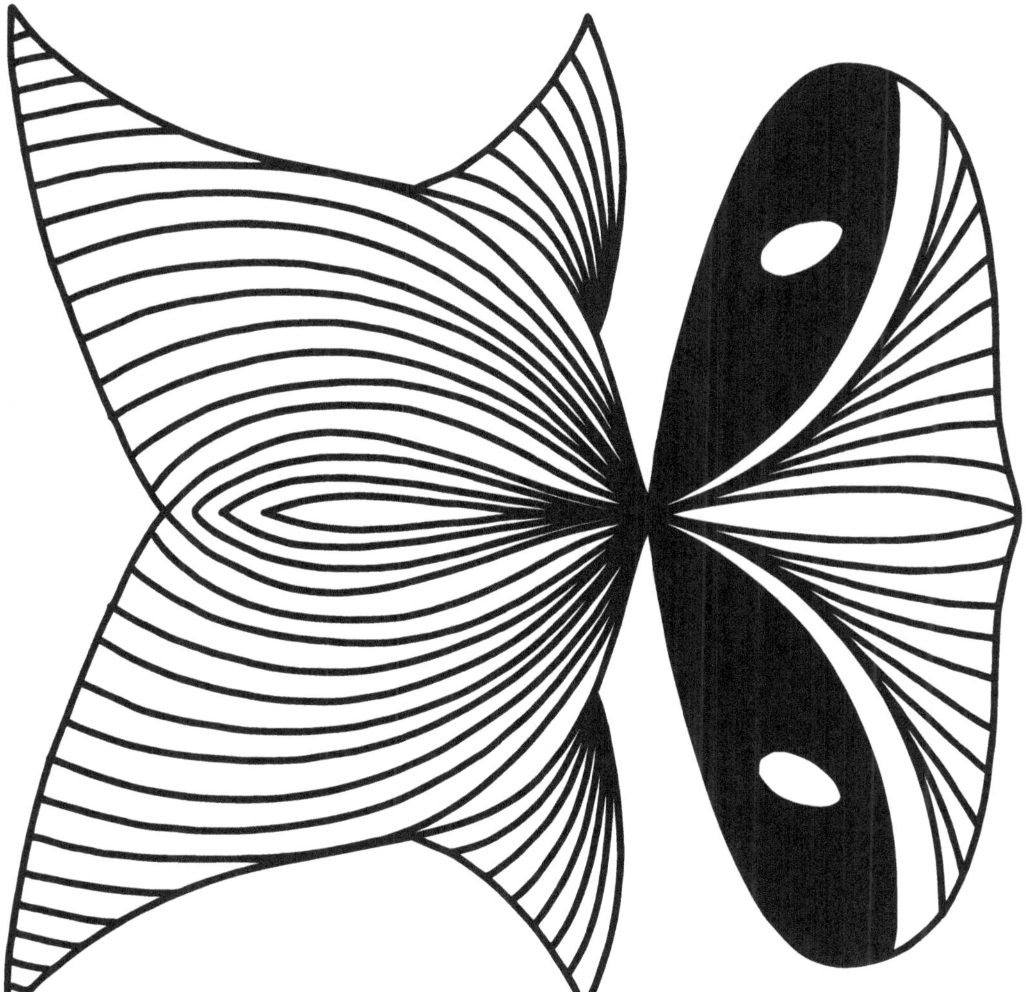

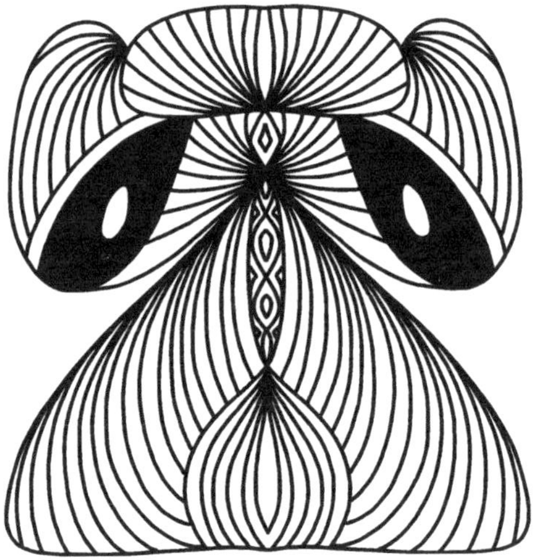

FATLINER WEIRDIES
VOLUME 1

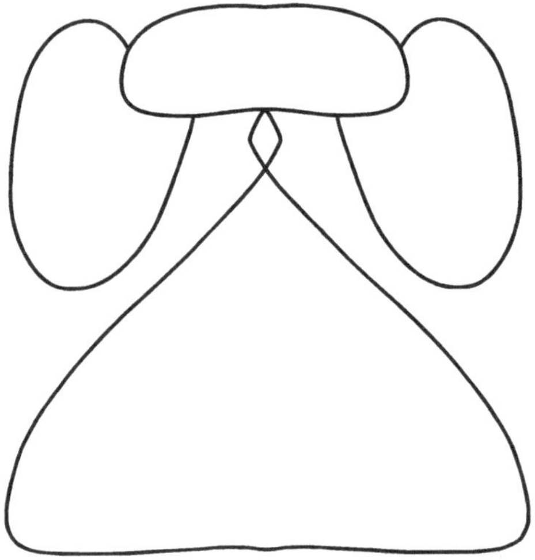

FATLINER WEIRDIES
THE TEMPLATES 1

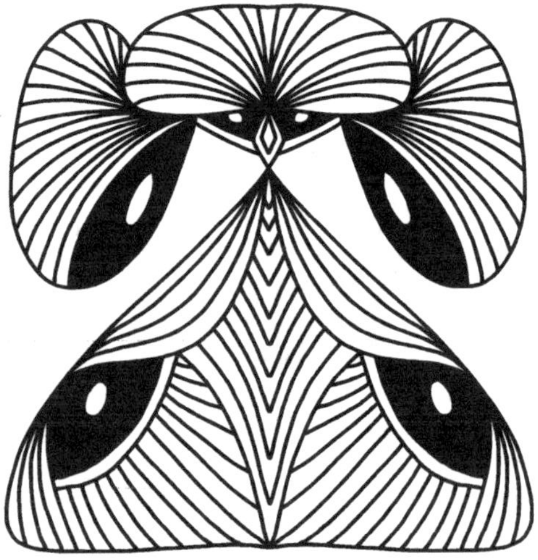

FATLINER WEIRDIES
VOLUME 3

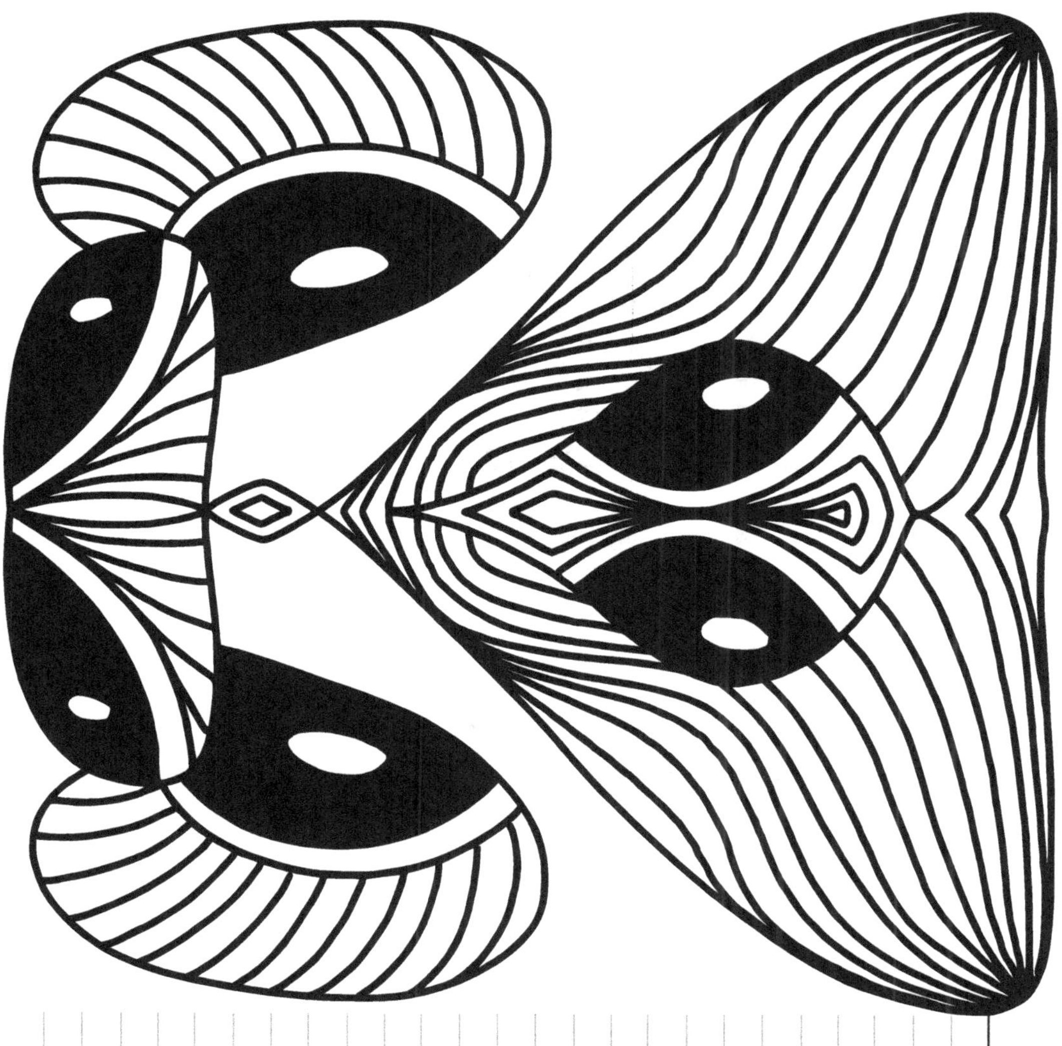

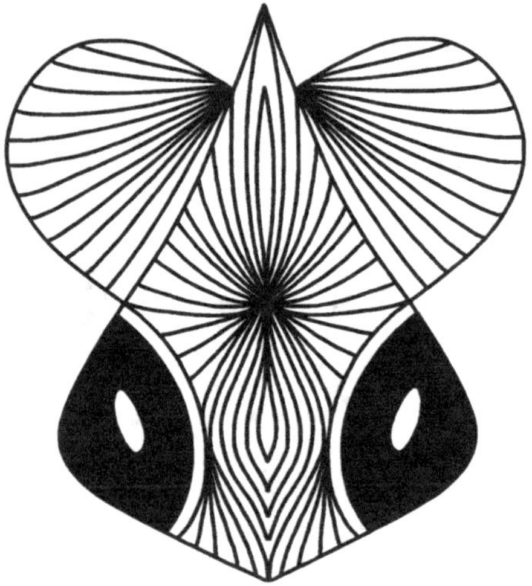

FATLINER WEIRDIES
VOLUME 1

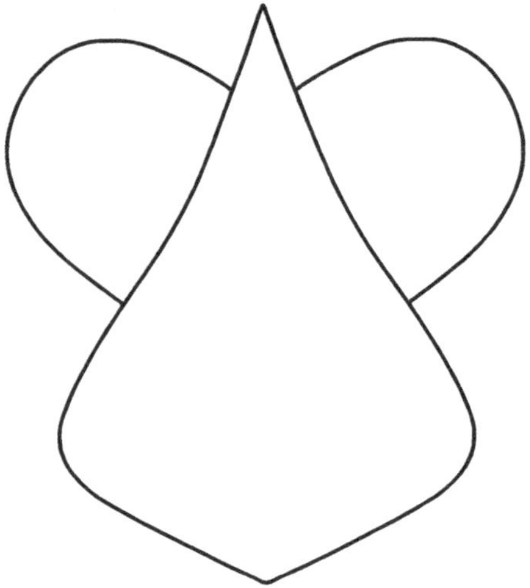

FATLINER WEIRDIES
THE TEMPLATES 1

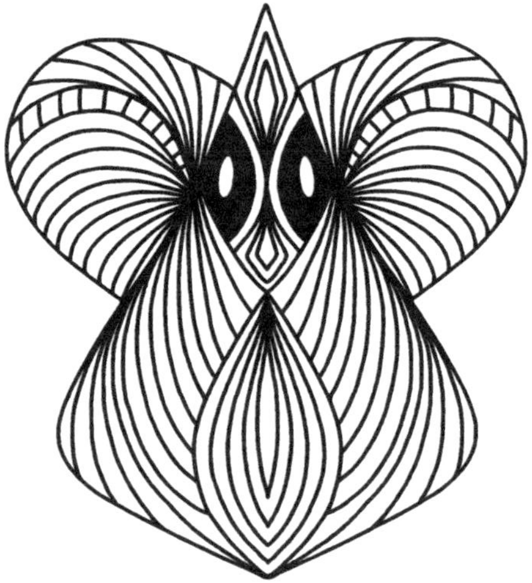

FATLINER WEIRDIES
VOLUME 3

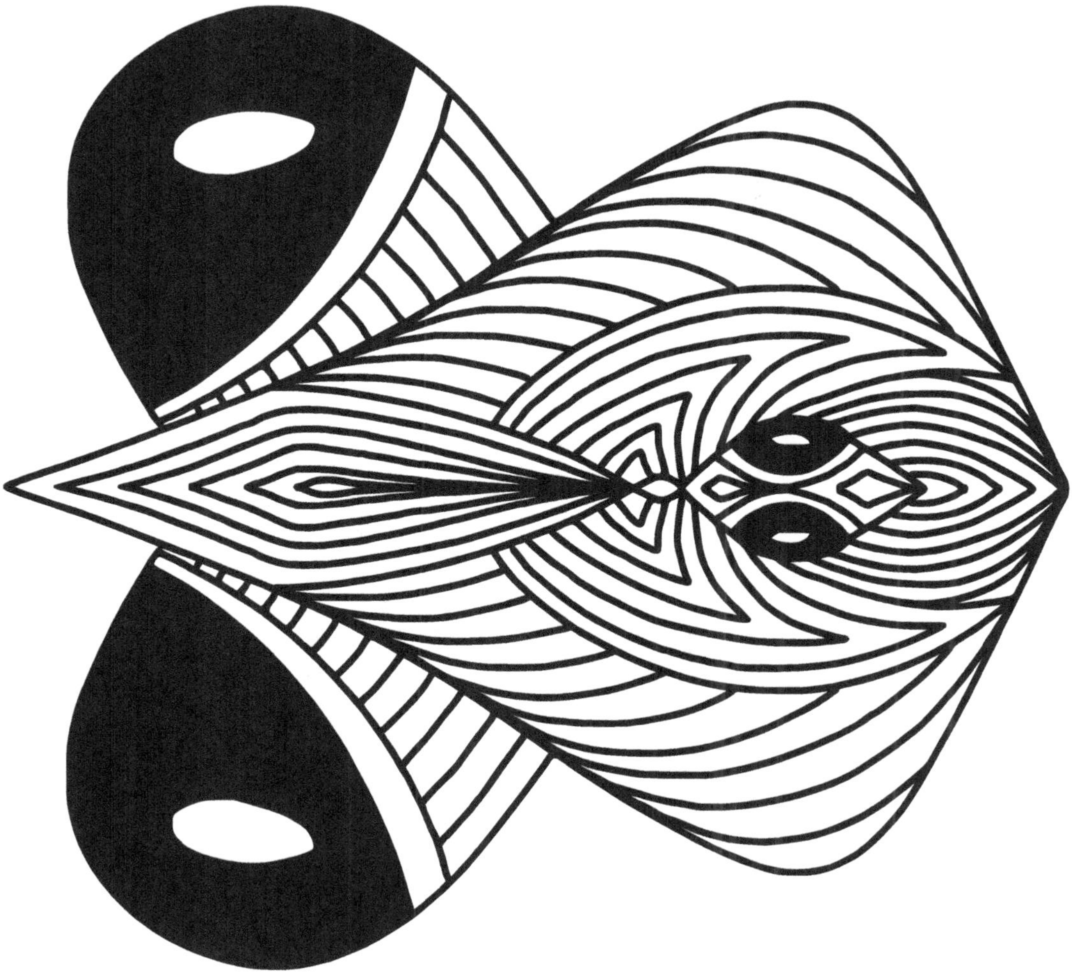

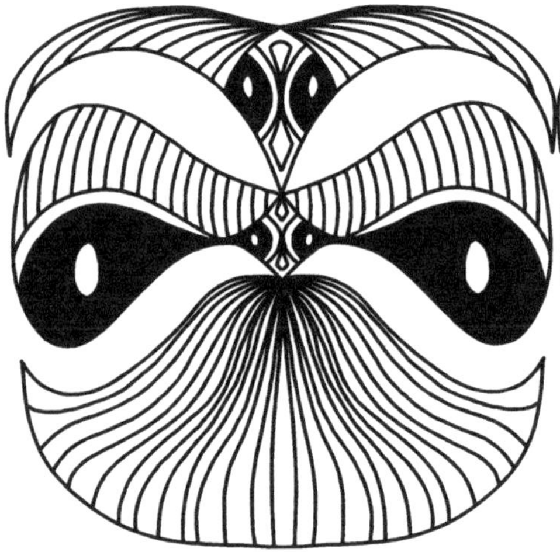

FATLINER WEIRDIES
VOLUME 1

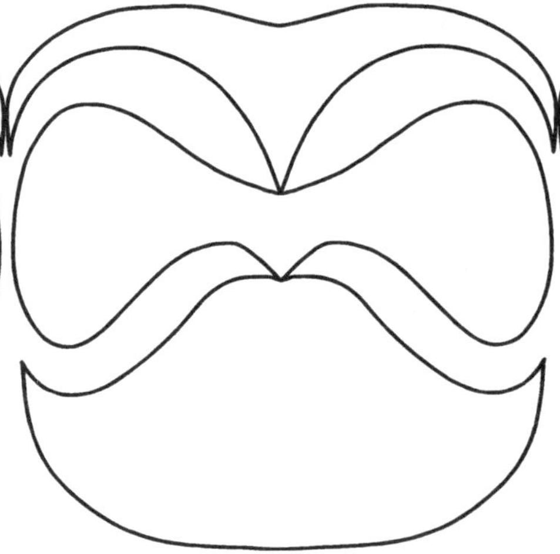

FATLINER WEIRDIES
THE TEMPLATES 1

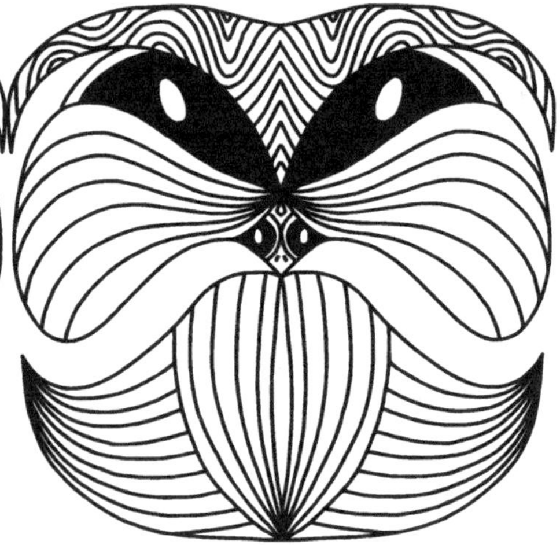

FATLINER WEIRDIES
VOLUME 3

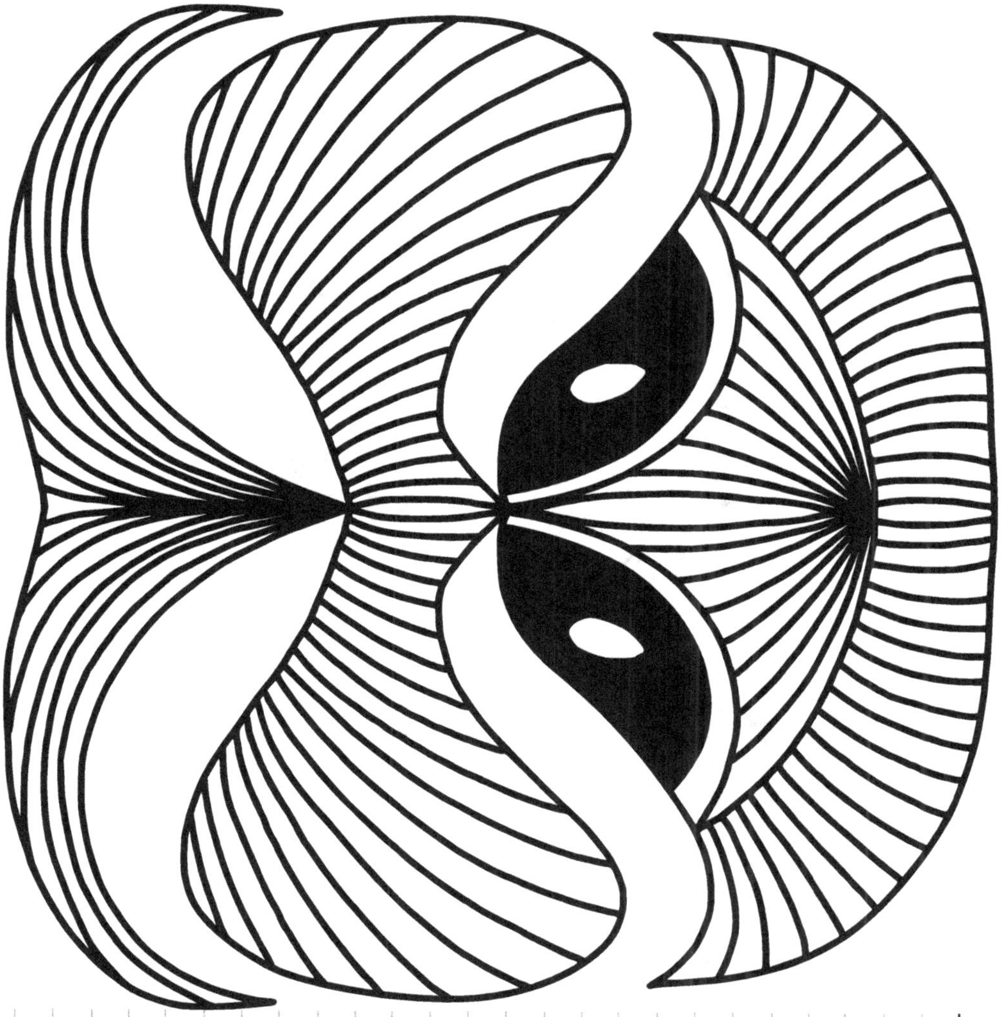

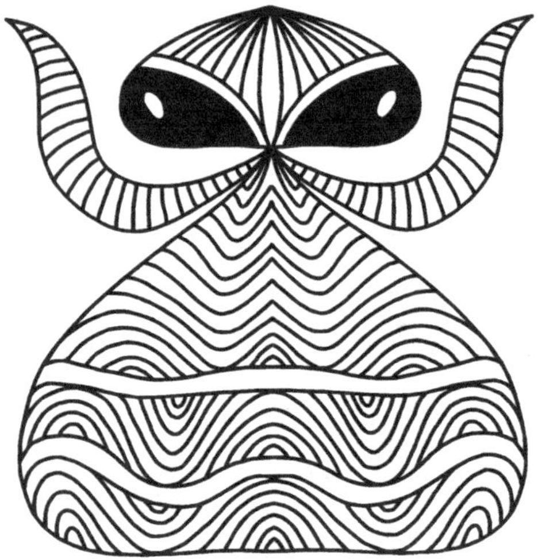

FATLINER WEIRDIES
VOLUME 1

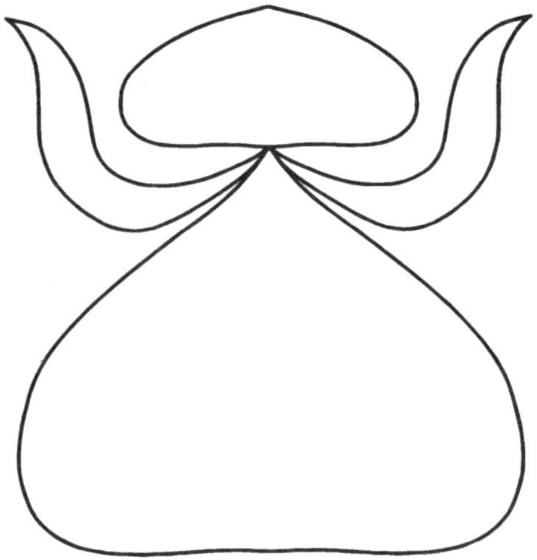

FATLINER WEIRDIES
THE TEMPLATES 1

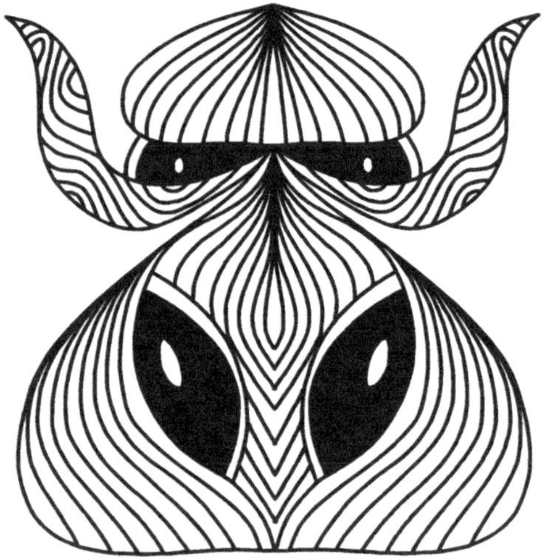

FATLINER WEIRDIES
VOLUME 3

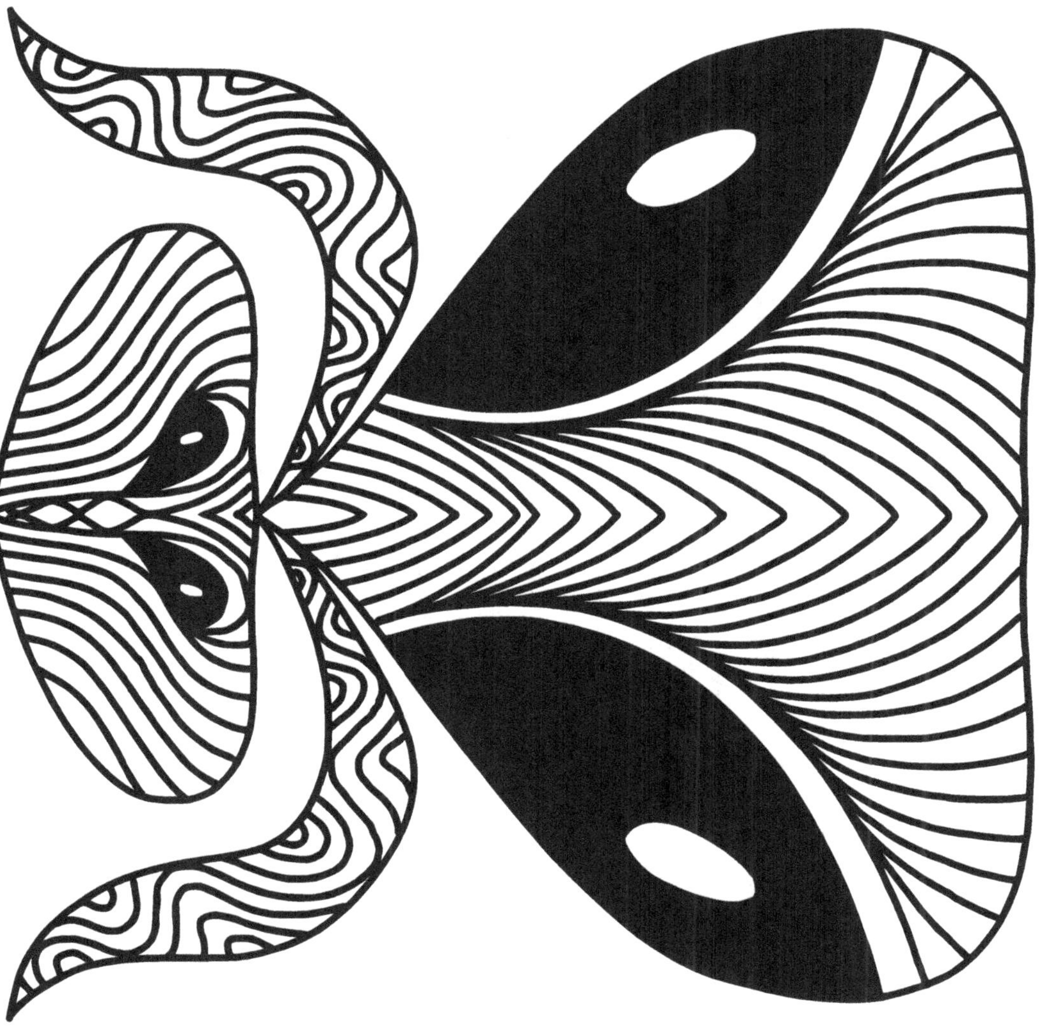

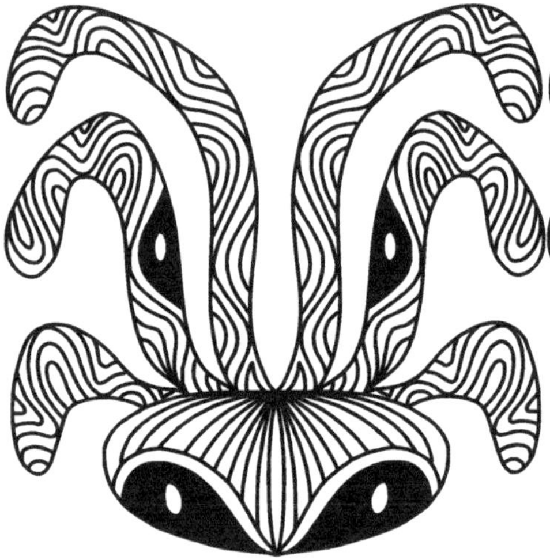

FATLINER WEIRDIES
VOLUME 1

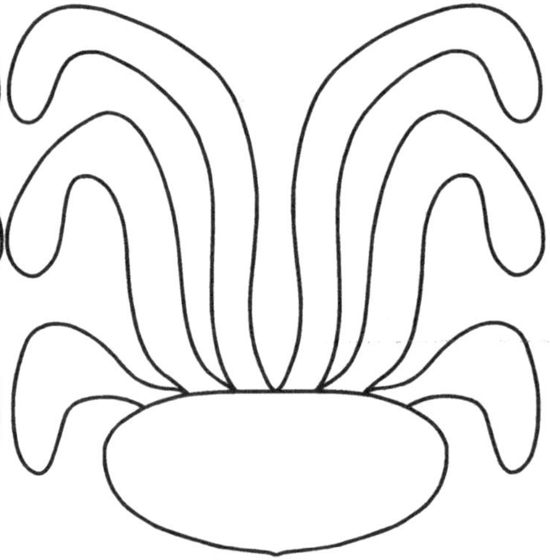

FATLINER WEIRDIES
THE TEMPLATES 1

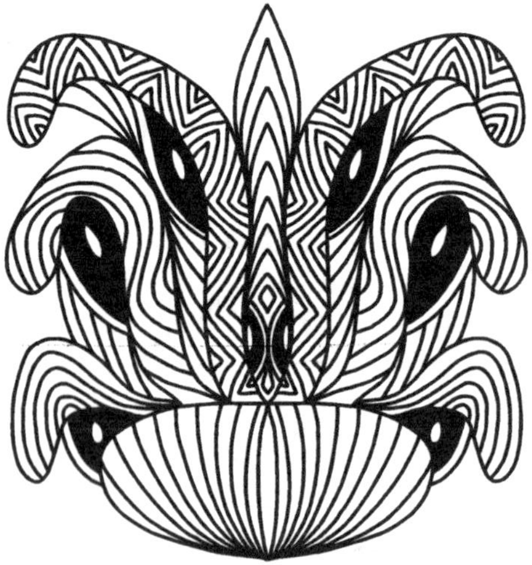

FATLINER WEIRDIES
VOLUME 3

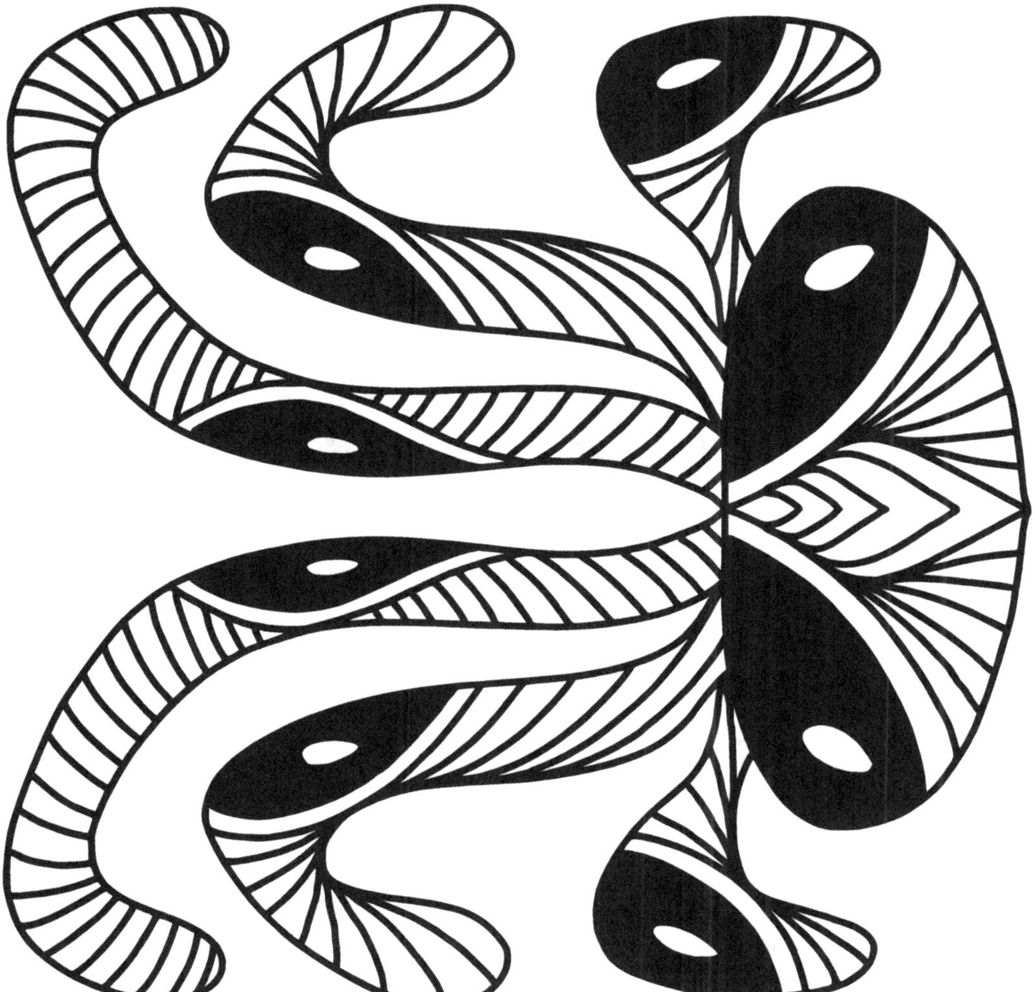

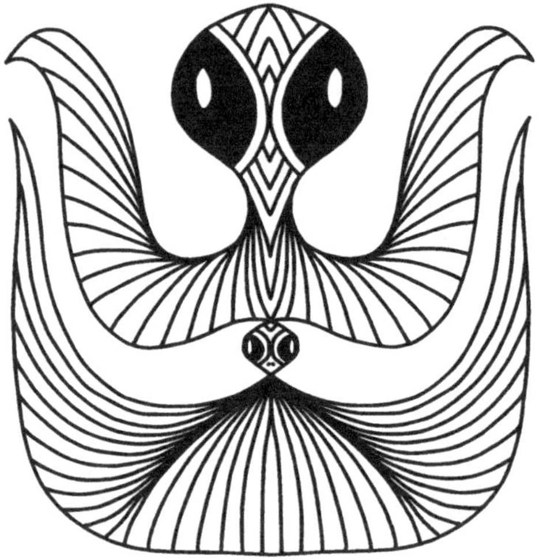

FATLINER WEIRDIES
VOLUME 1

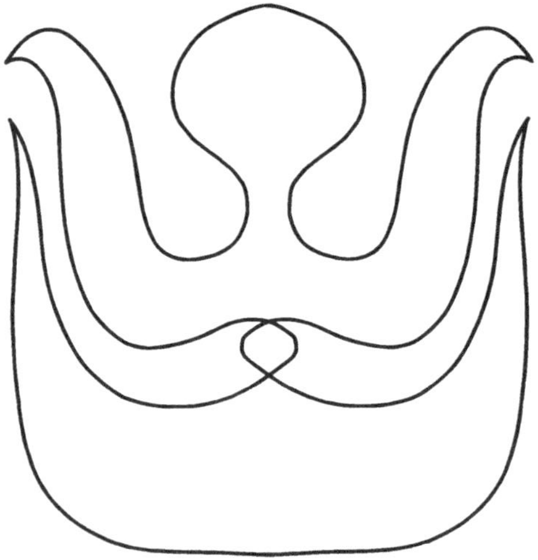

FATLINER WEIRDIES
THE TEMPLATES 1

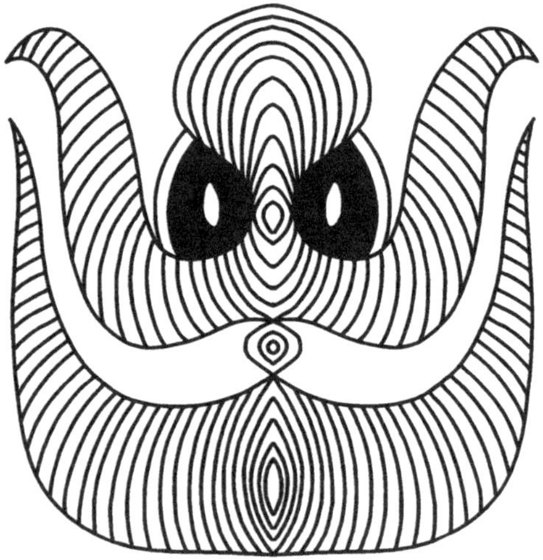

FATLINER WEIRDIES
VOLUME 3

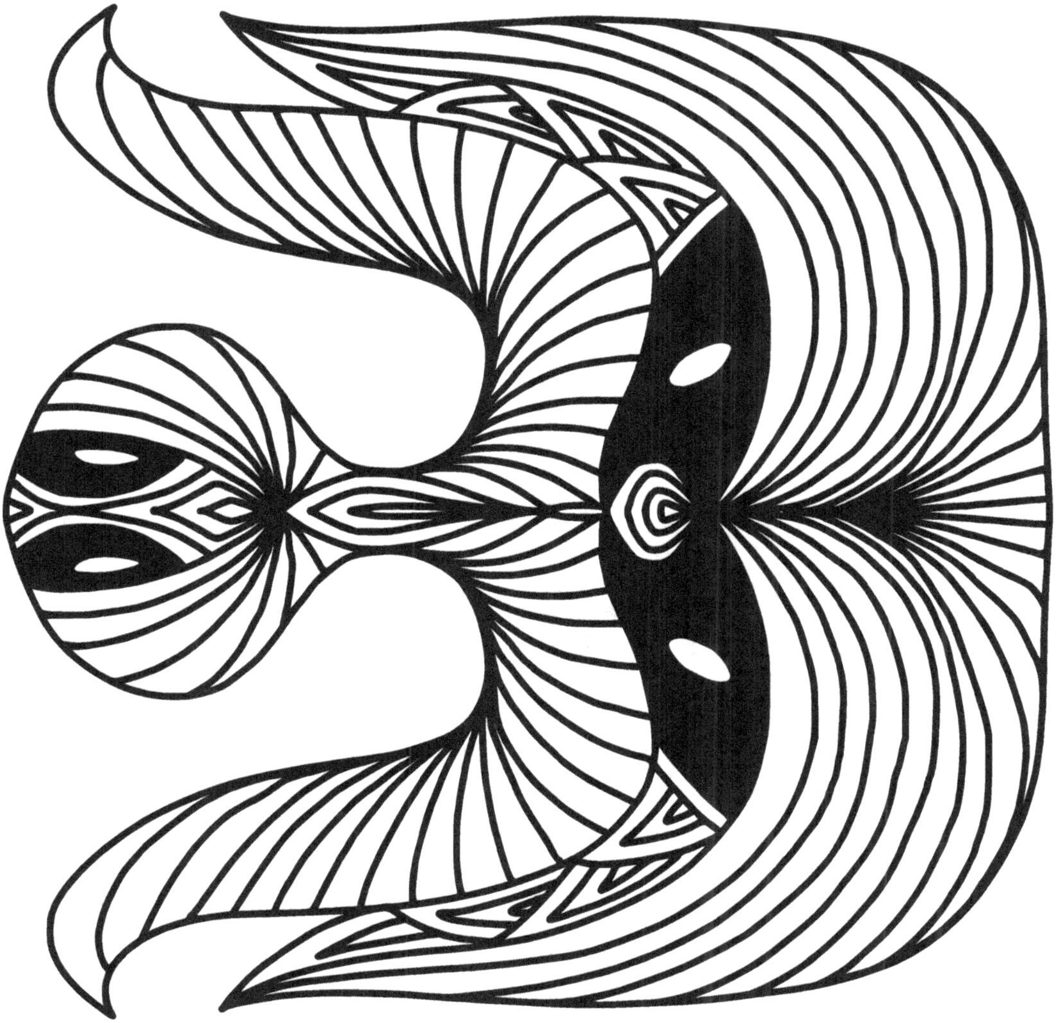

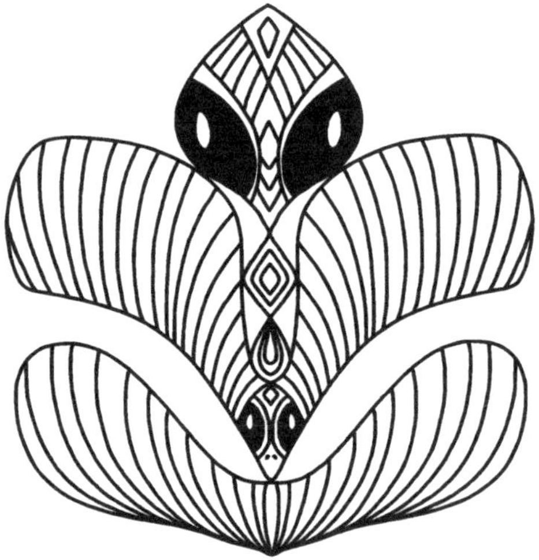

FATLINER WEIRDIES
VOLUME 1

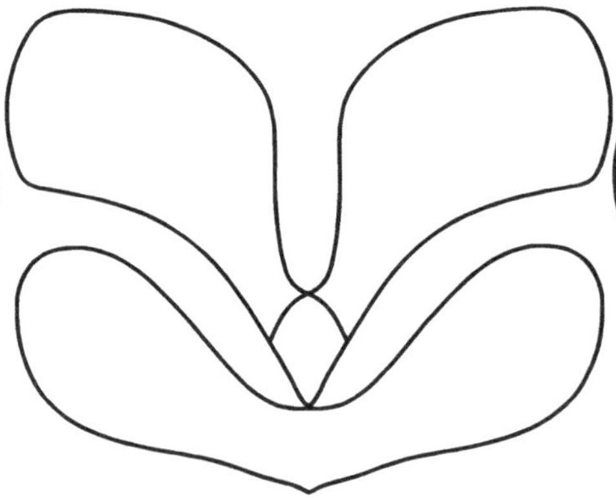

FATLINER WEIRDIES
THE TEMPLATES 1

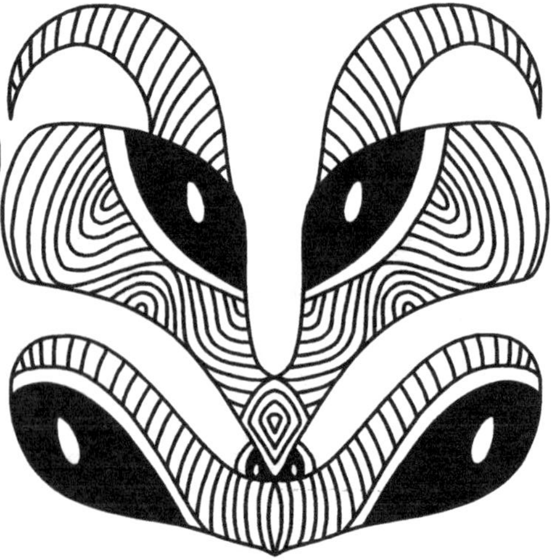

FATLINER WEIRDIES
VOLUME 3

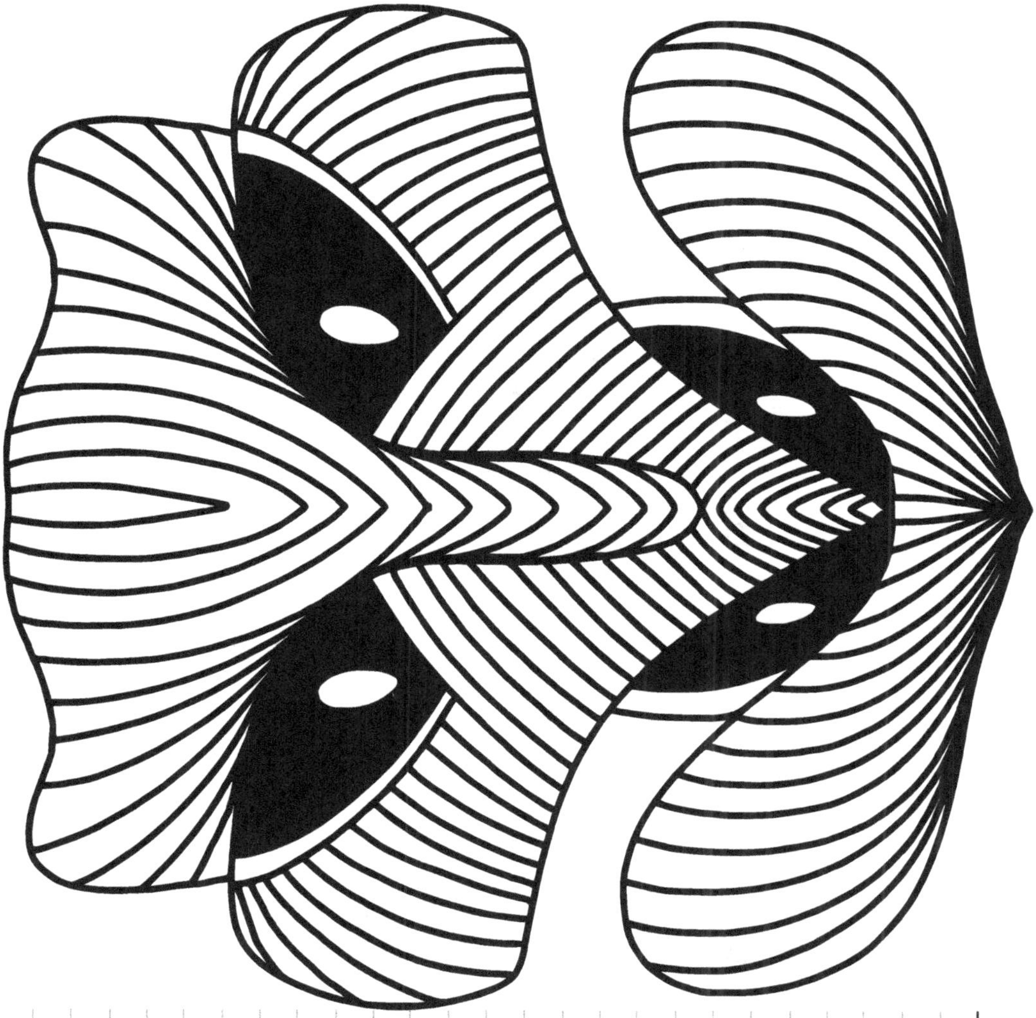

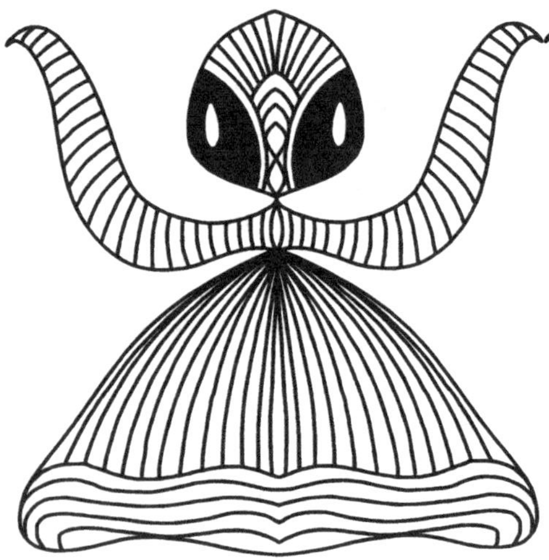

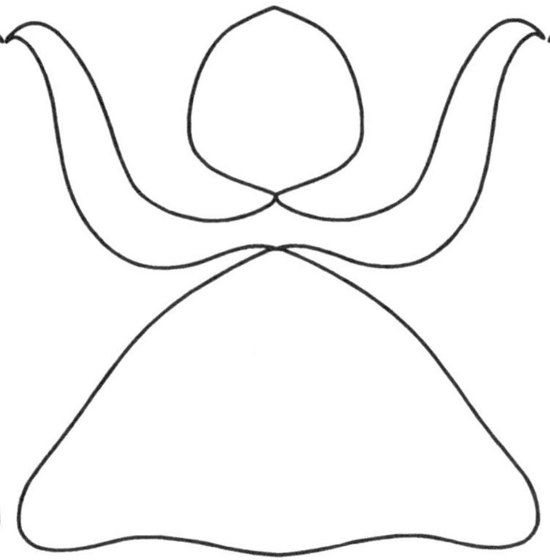

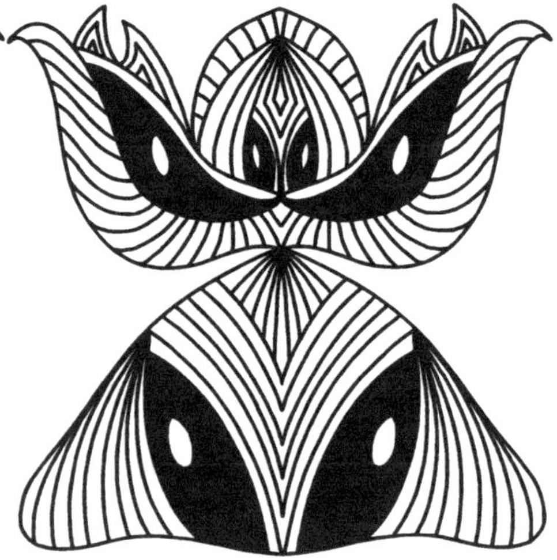

FATLINER WEIRDIES
VOLUME 1

FATLINER WEIRDIES
THE TEMPLATES 1

FATLINER WEIRDIES
VOLUME 3

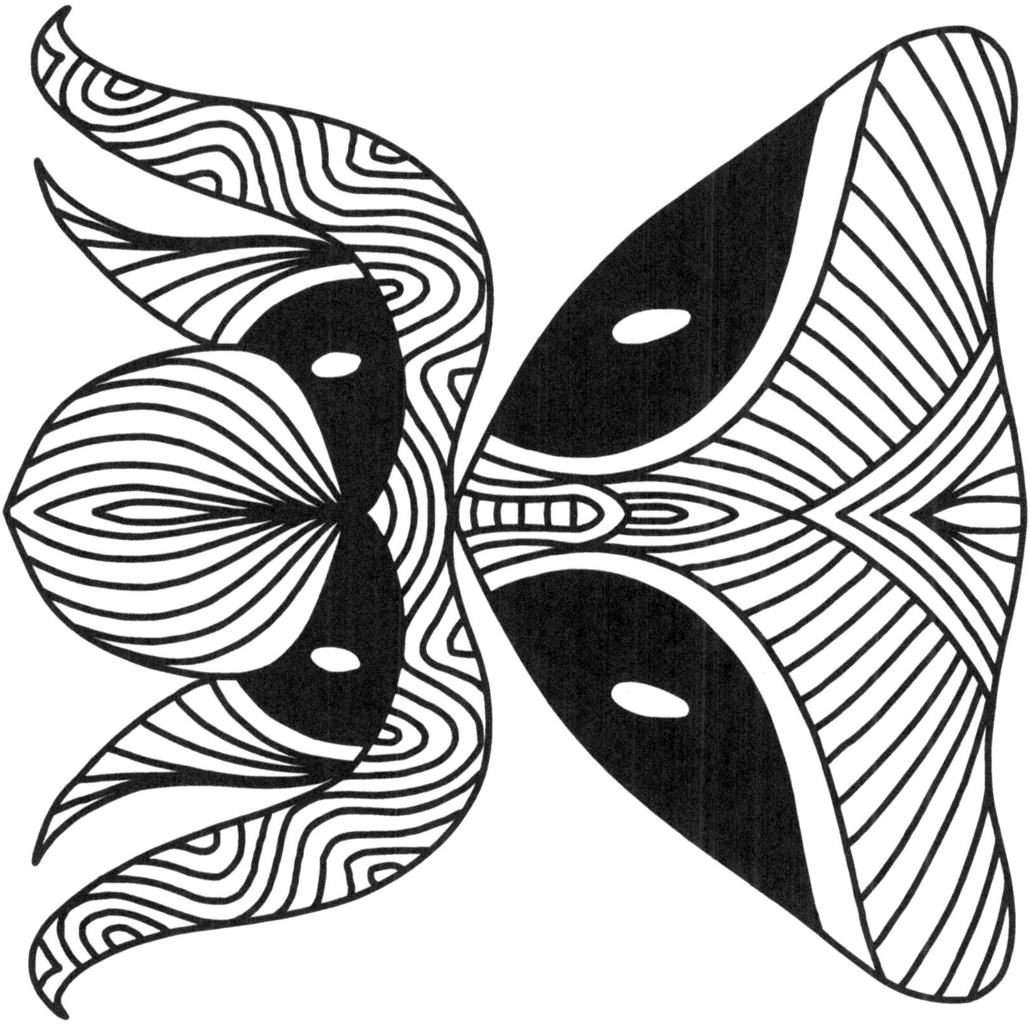

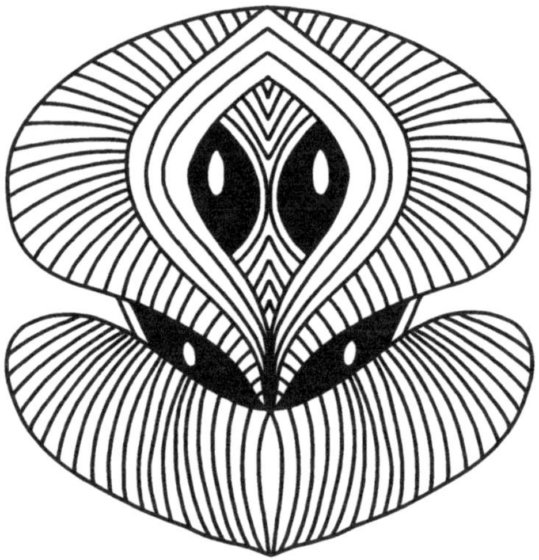

FATLINER WEIRDIES
VOLUME 1

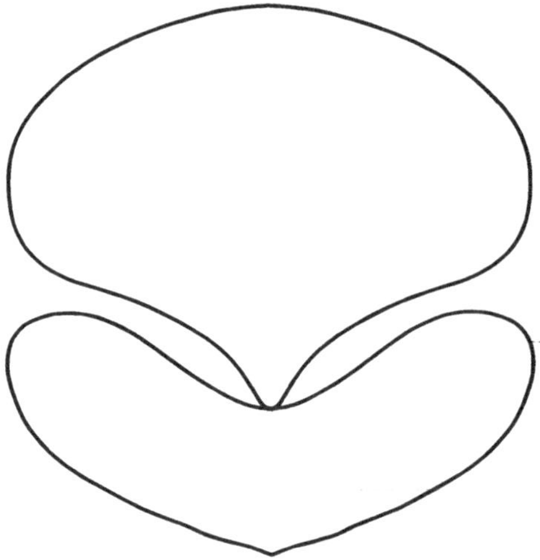

FATLINER WEIRDIES
THE TEMPLATES 1

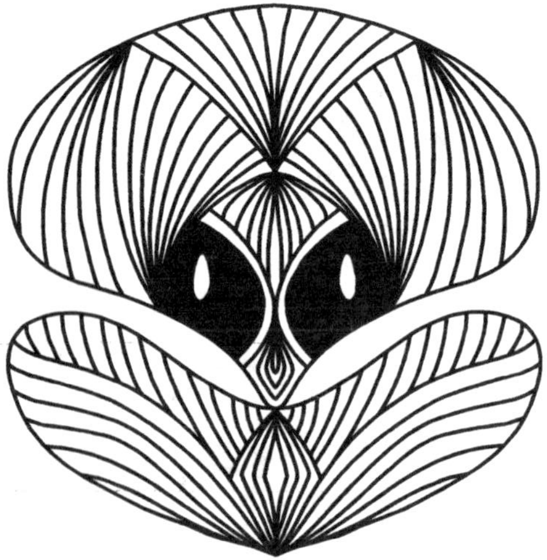

FATLINER WEIRDIES
VOLUME 3

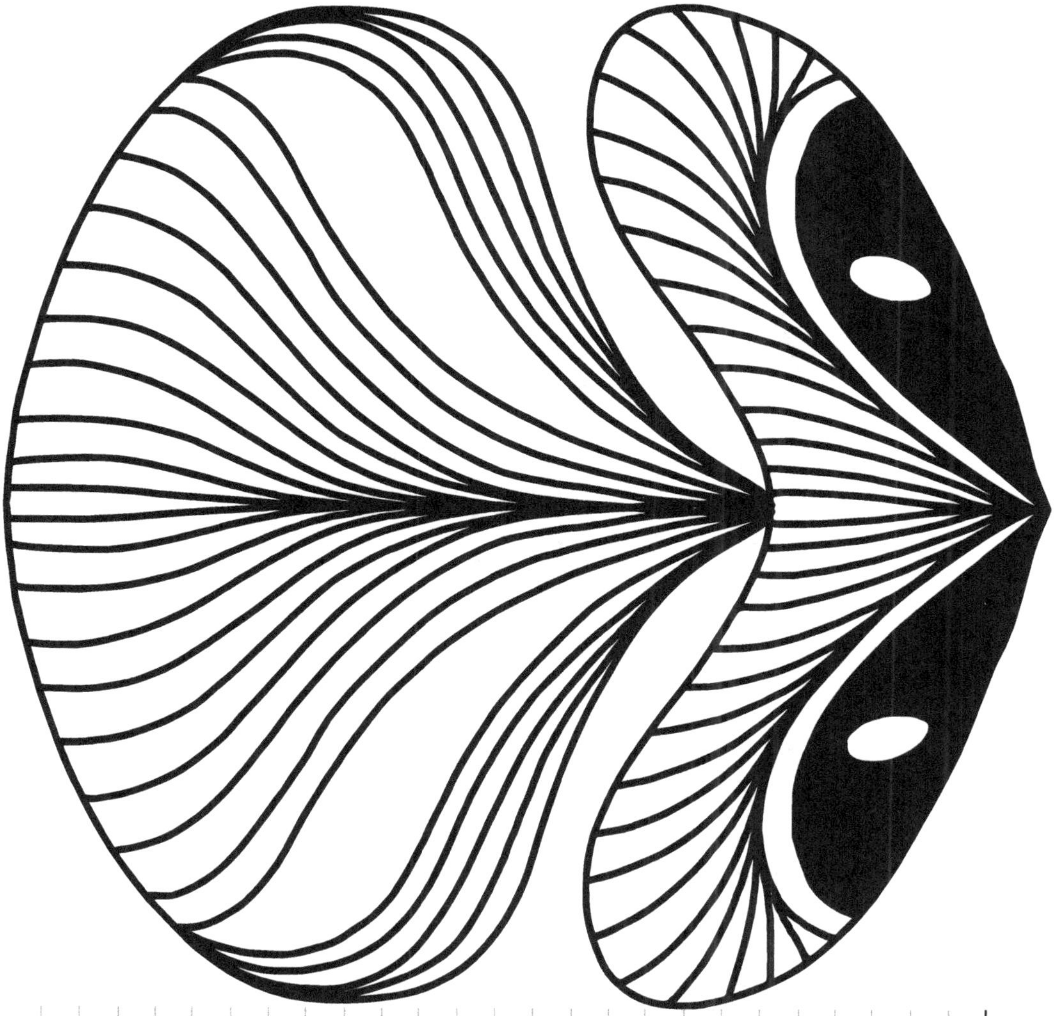

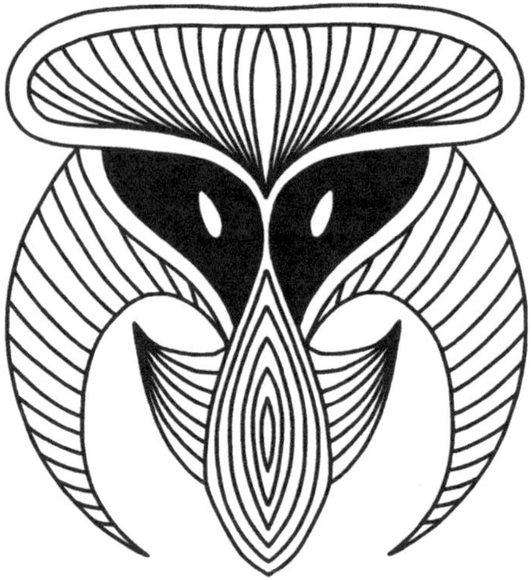

FATLINER WEIRDIES
VOLUME 1

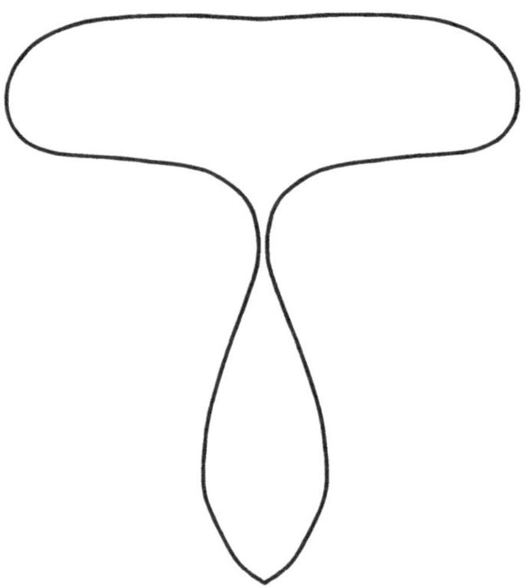

FATLINER WEIRDIES
THE TEMPLATES 1

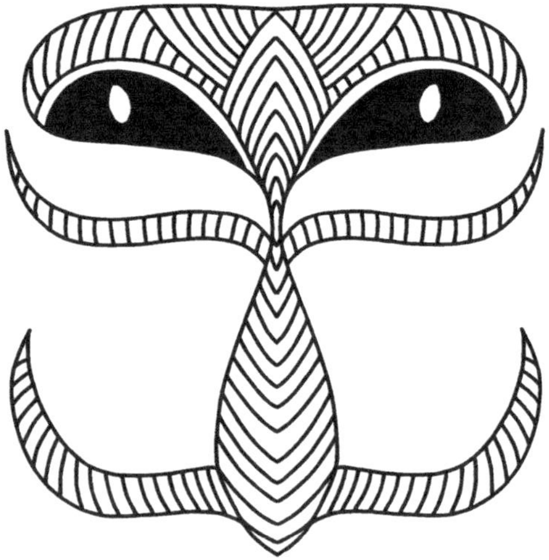

FATLINER WEIRDIES
VOLUME 3

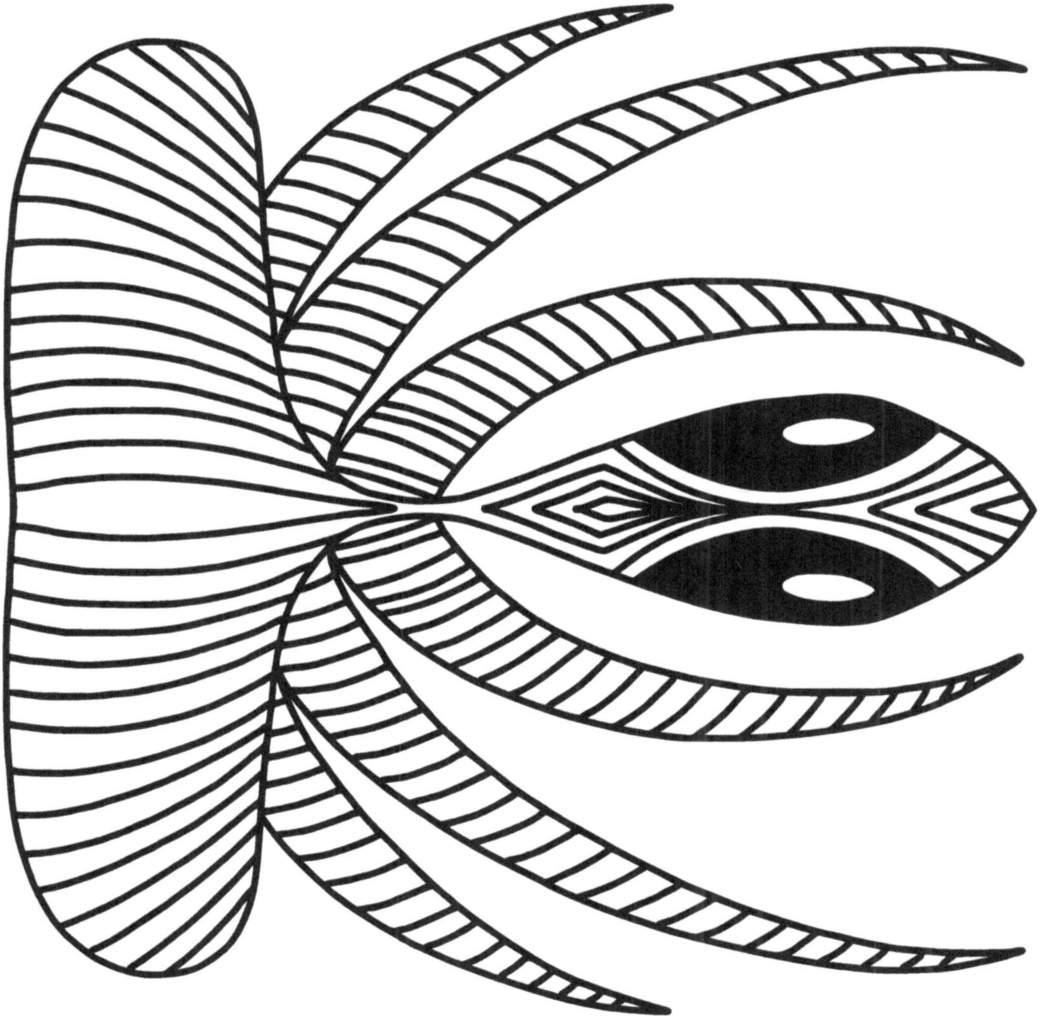

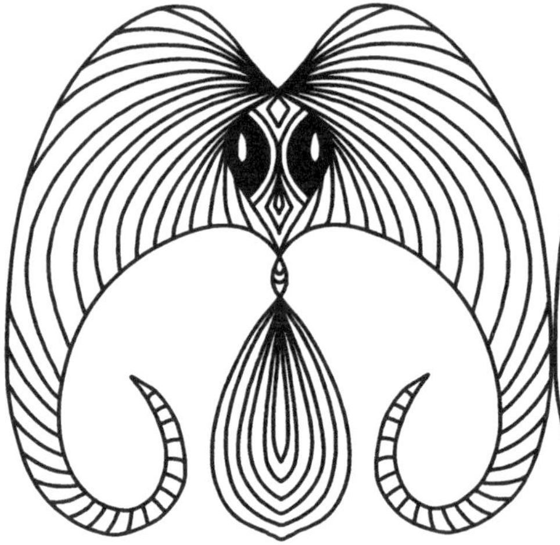

FATLINER WEIRDIES
VOLUME 1

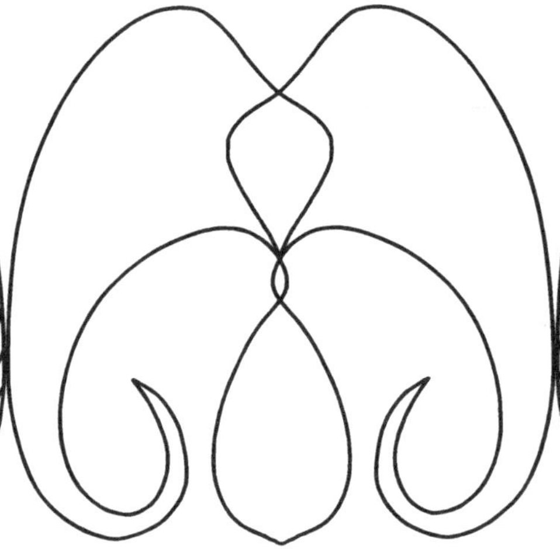

FATLINER WEIRDIES
THE TEMPLATES 1

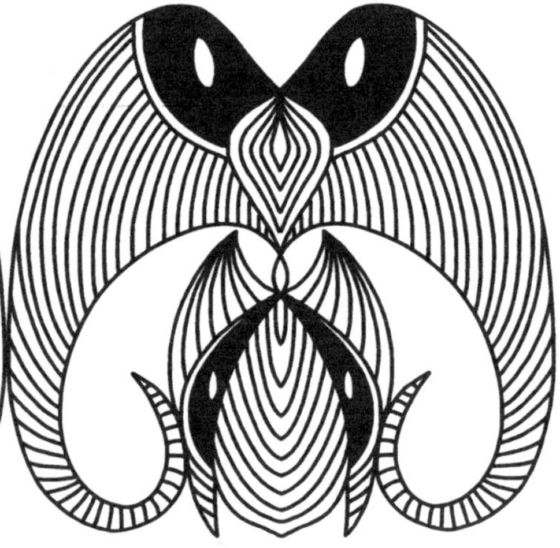

FATLINER WEIRDIES
VOLUME 3

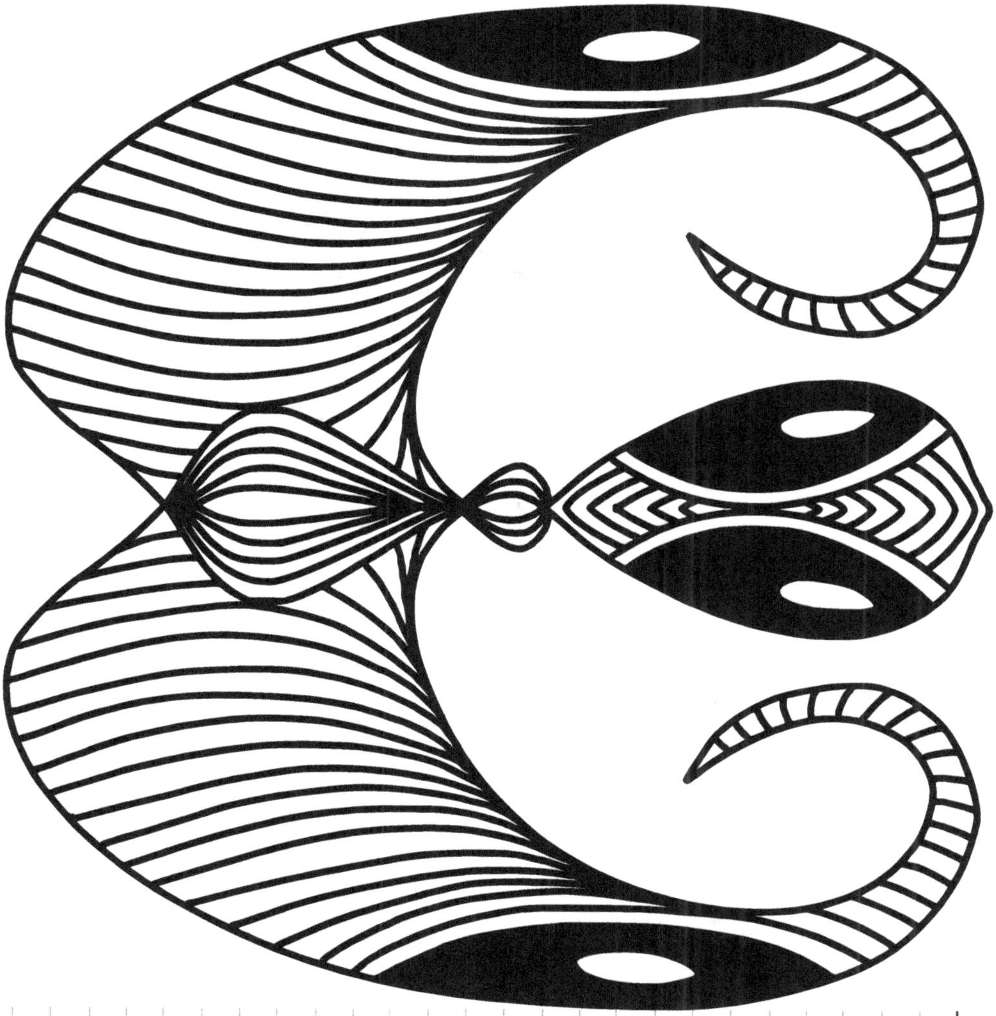

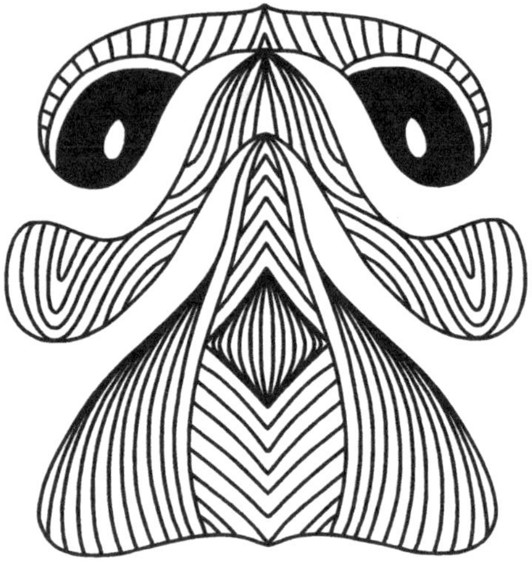

FATLINER WEIRDIES
VOLUME 1

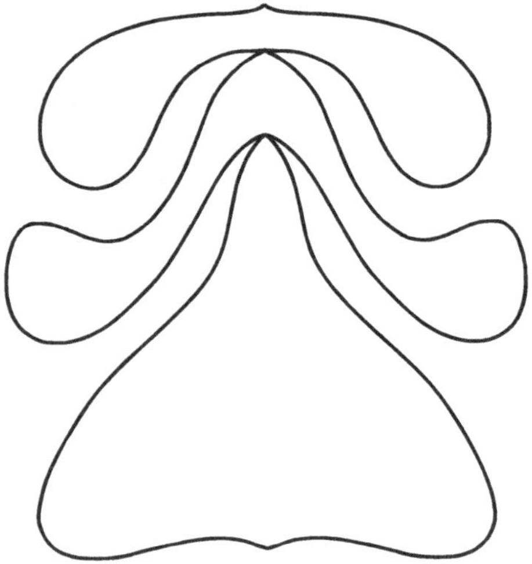

FATLINER WEIRDIES
THE TEMPLATES 1

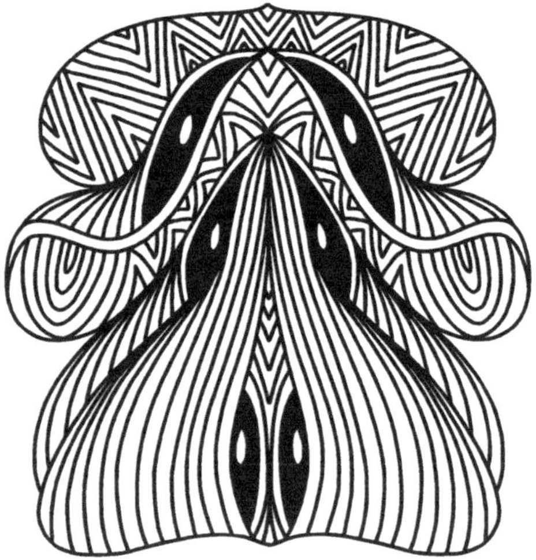

FATLINER WEIRDIES
VOLUME 3

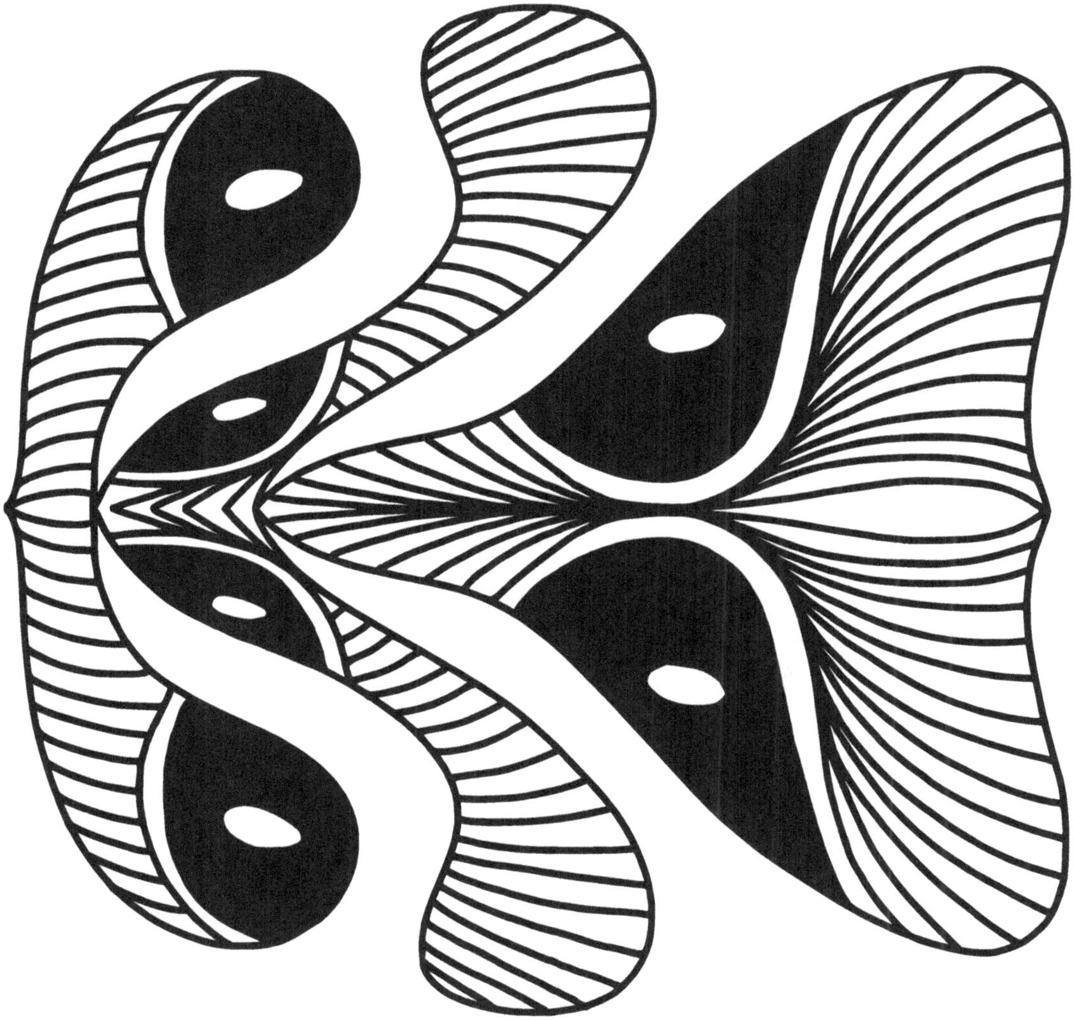

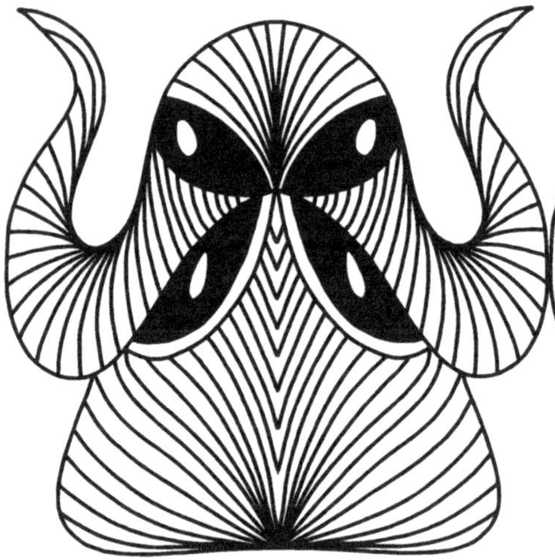

FATLINER WEIRDIES
VOLUME 1

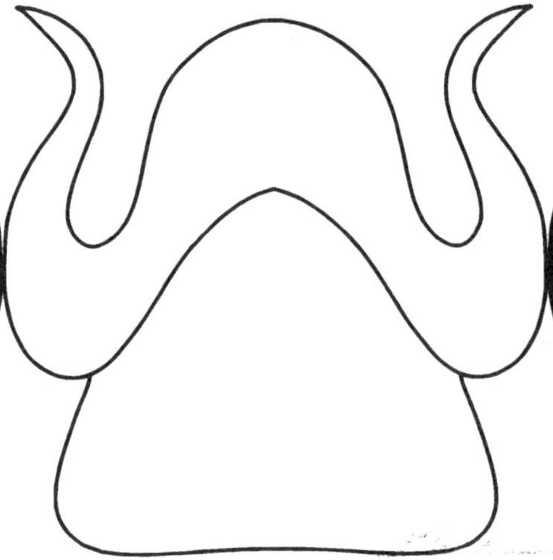

FATLINER WEIRDIES
THE TEMPLATES 1

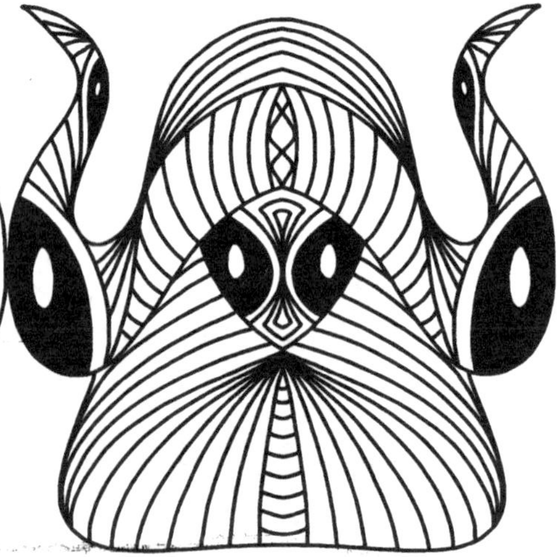

FATLINER WEIRDIES
VOLUME 3

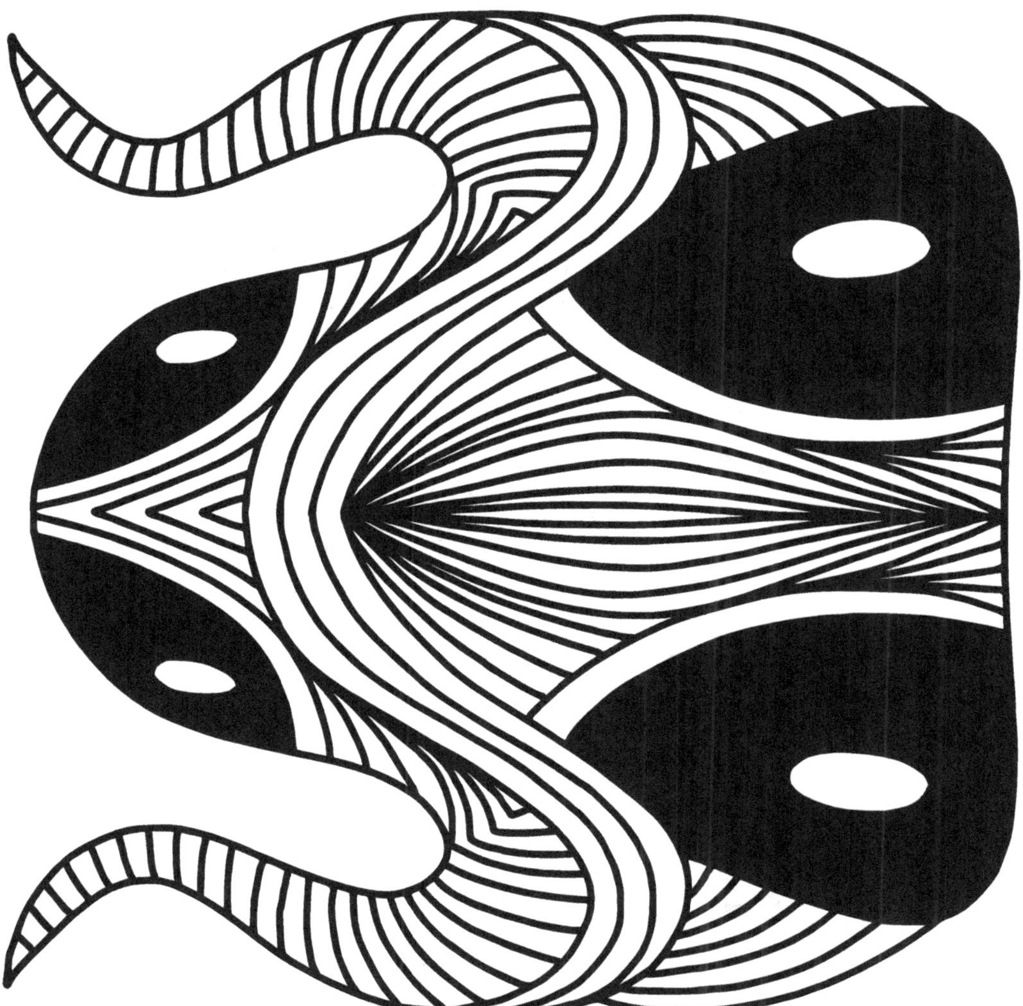

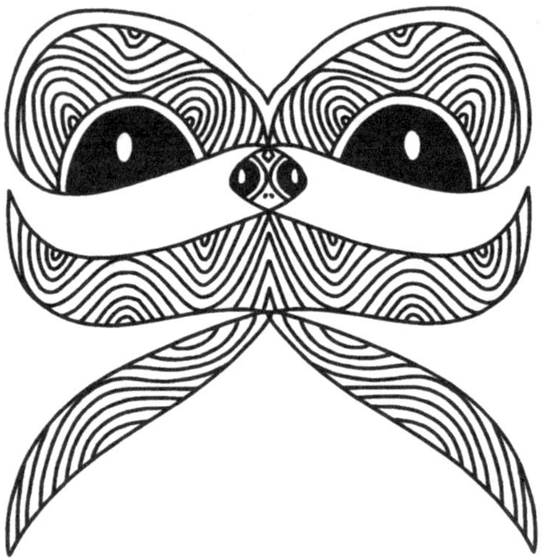

FATLINER WEIRDIES
VOLUME 1

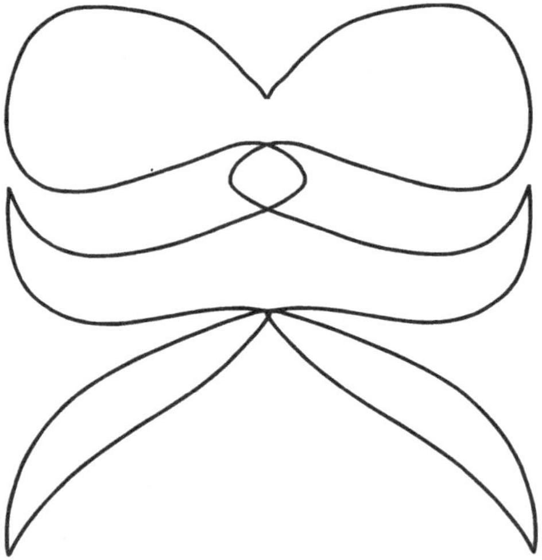

FATLINER WEIRDIES
THE TEMPLATES 1

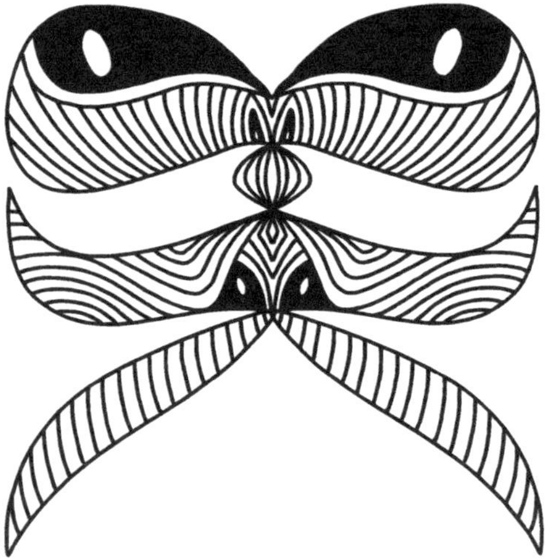

FATLINER WEIRDIES
VOLUME 3

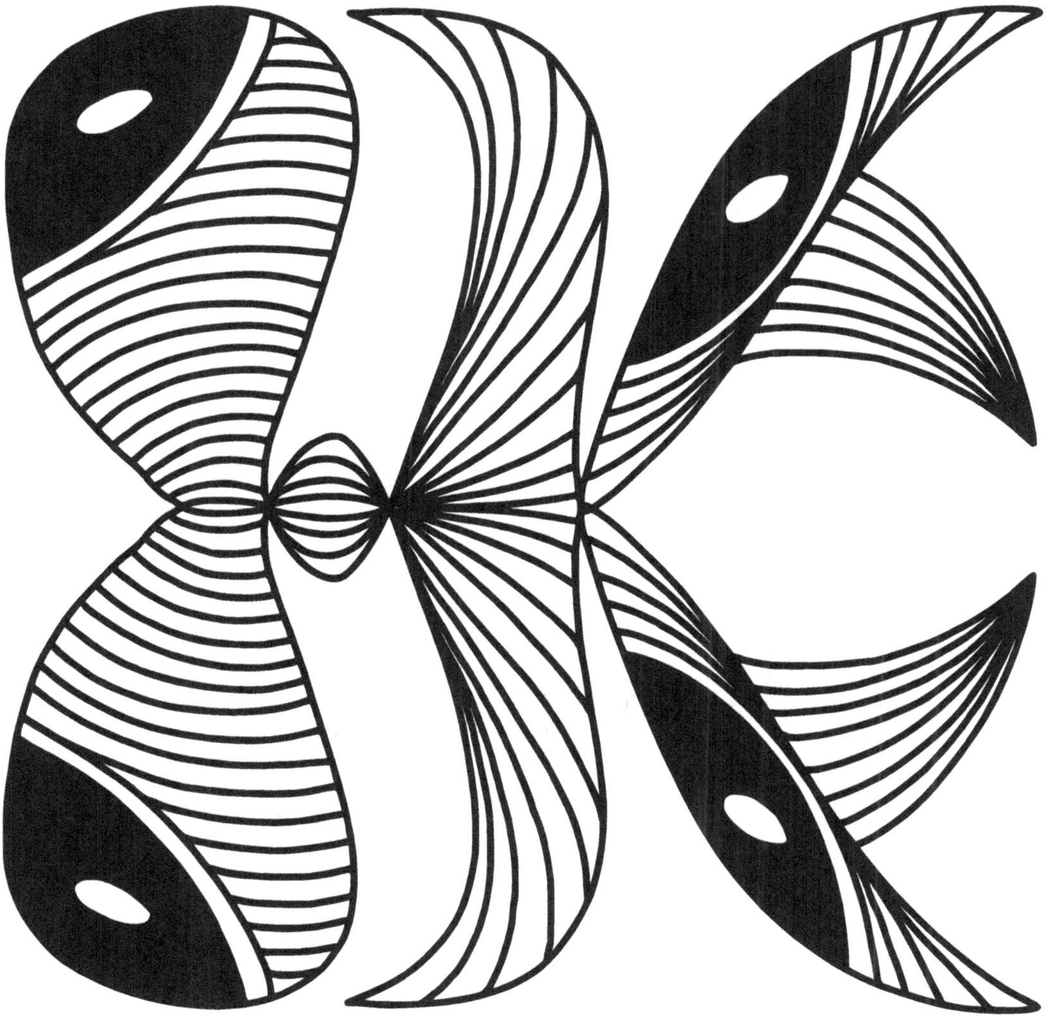

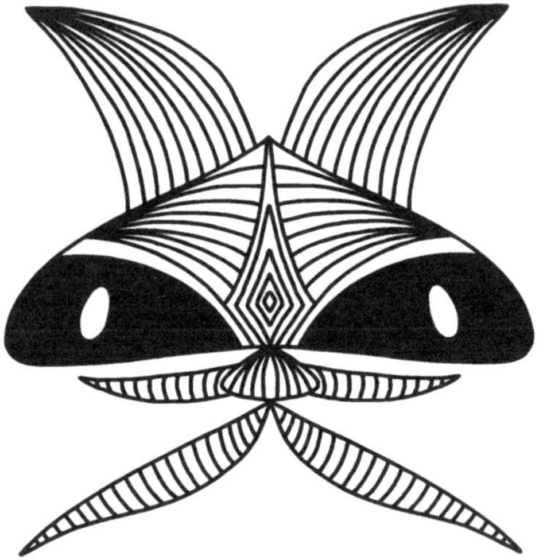

FATLINER WEIRDIES
VOLUME 1

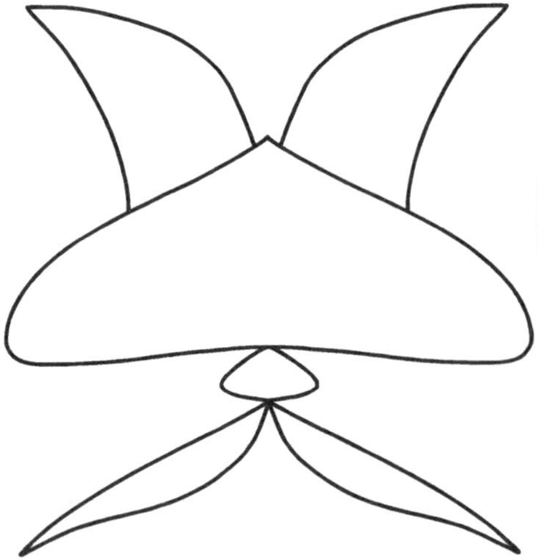

FATLINER WEIRDIES
THE TEMPLATES 1

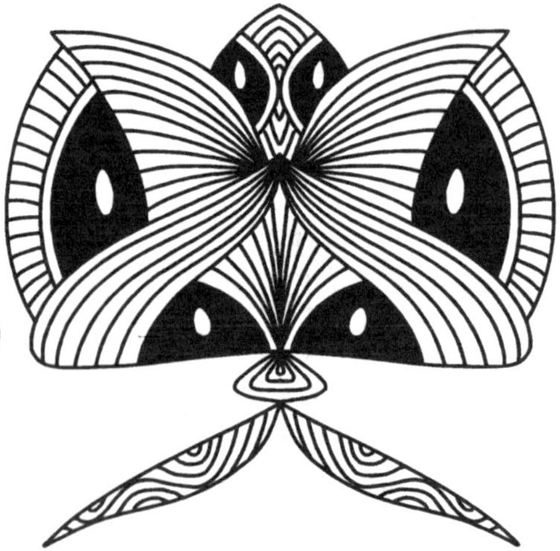

FATLINER WEIRDIES
VOLUME 3

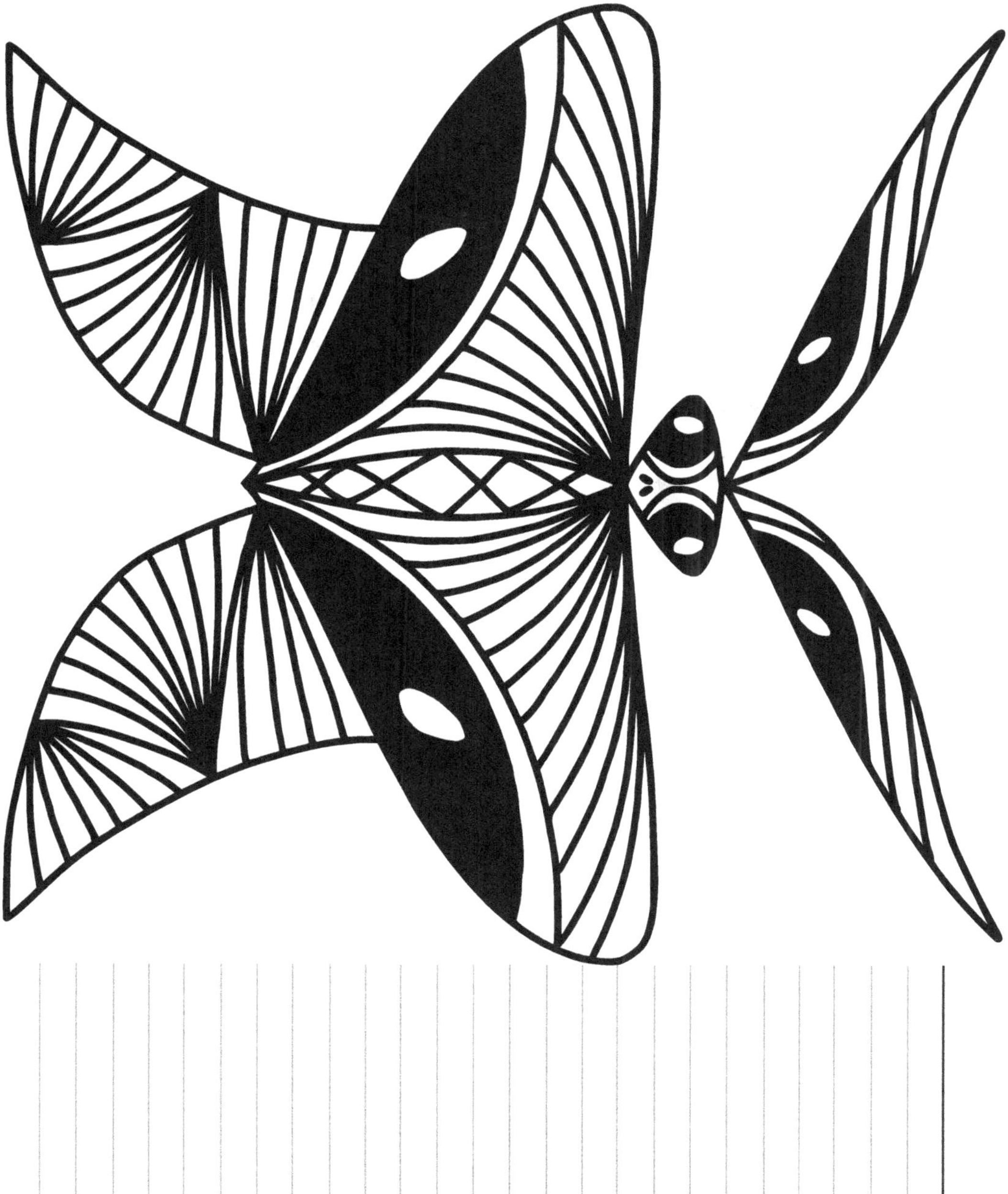

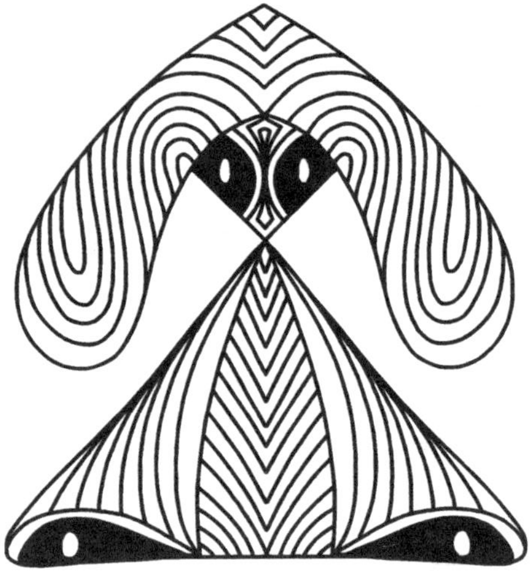

FATLINER WEIRDIES
VOLUME 1

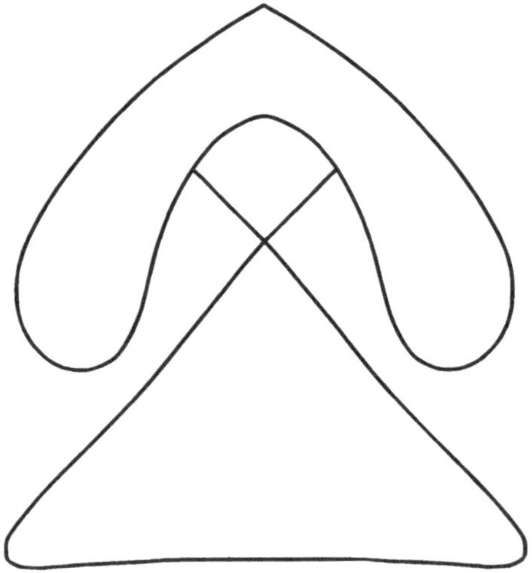

FATLINER WEIRDIES
THE TEMPLATES 1

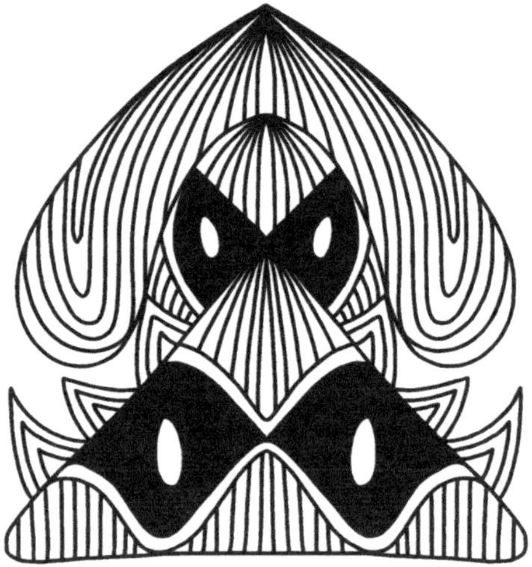

FATLINER WEIRDIES
VOLUME 3

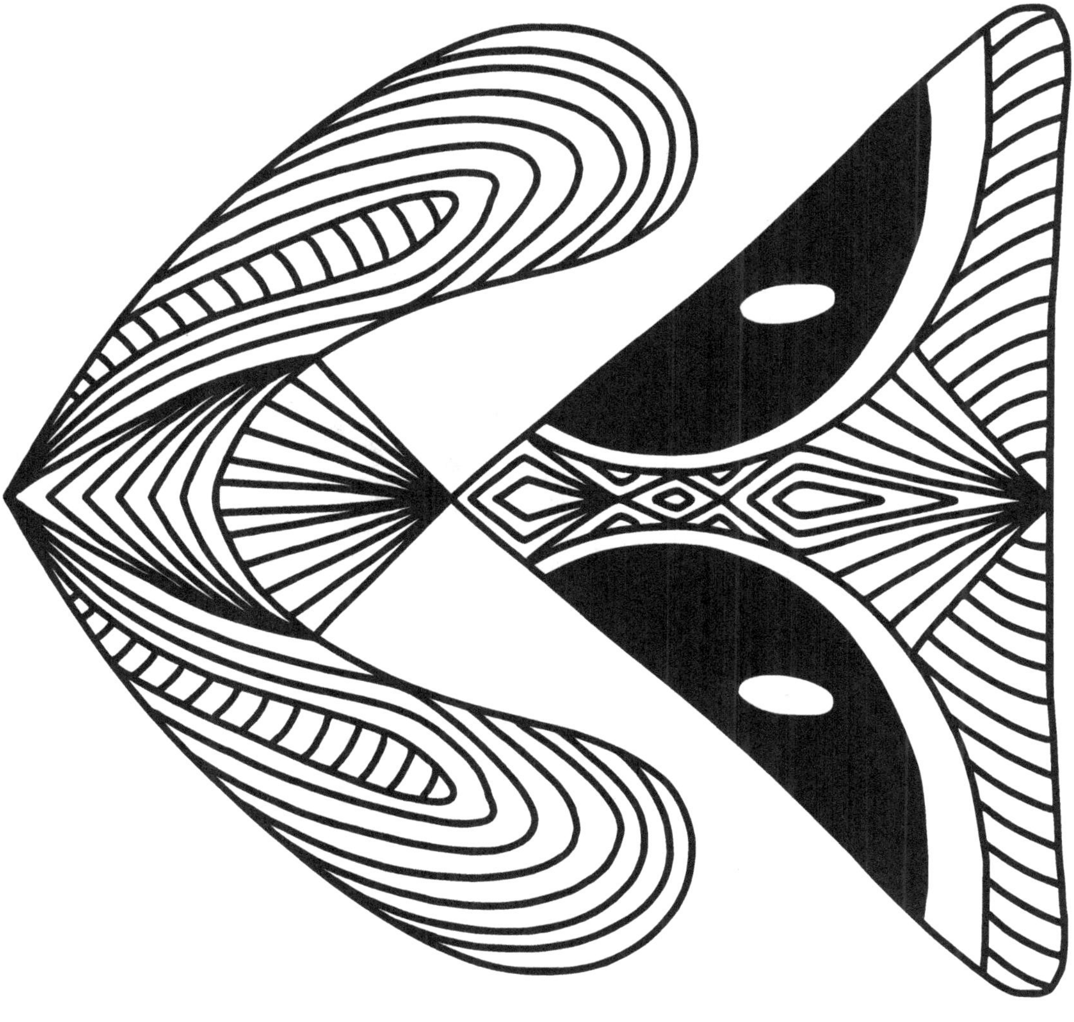

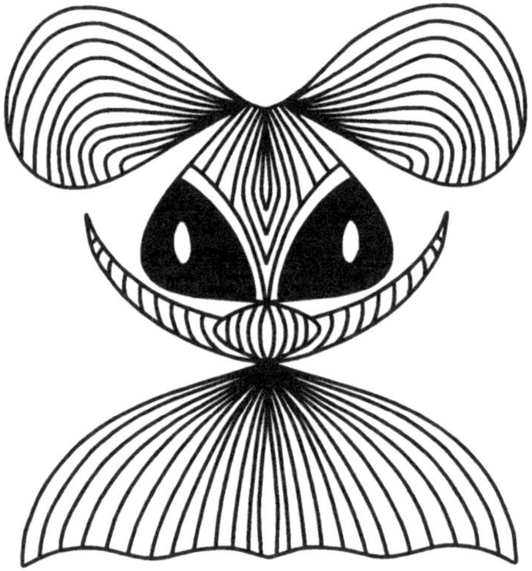

FATLINER WEIRDIES
VOLUME 1

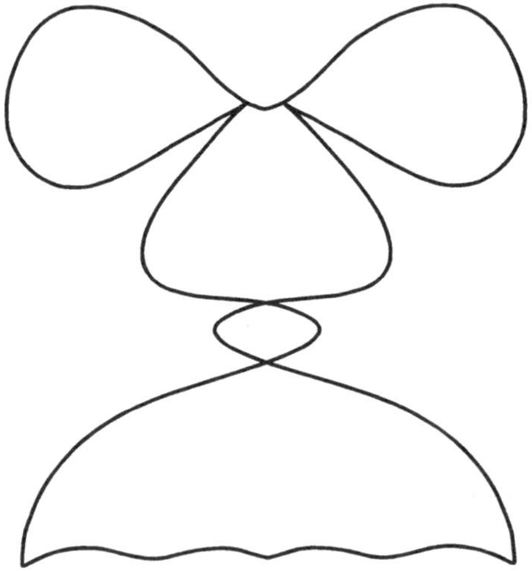

FATLINER WEIRDIES
THE TEMPLATES 1

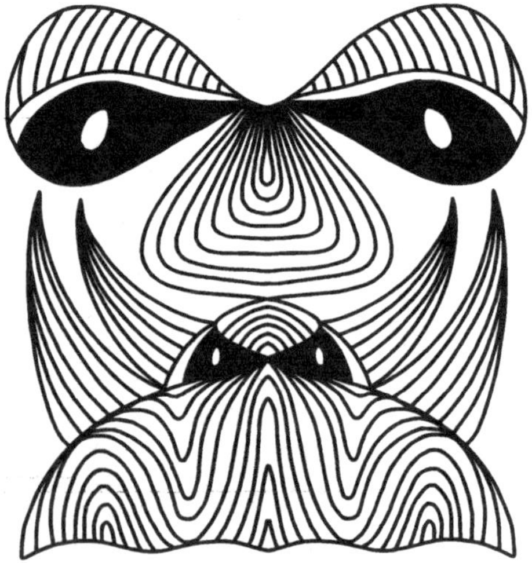

FATLINER WEIRDIES
VOLUME 3

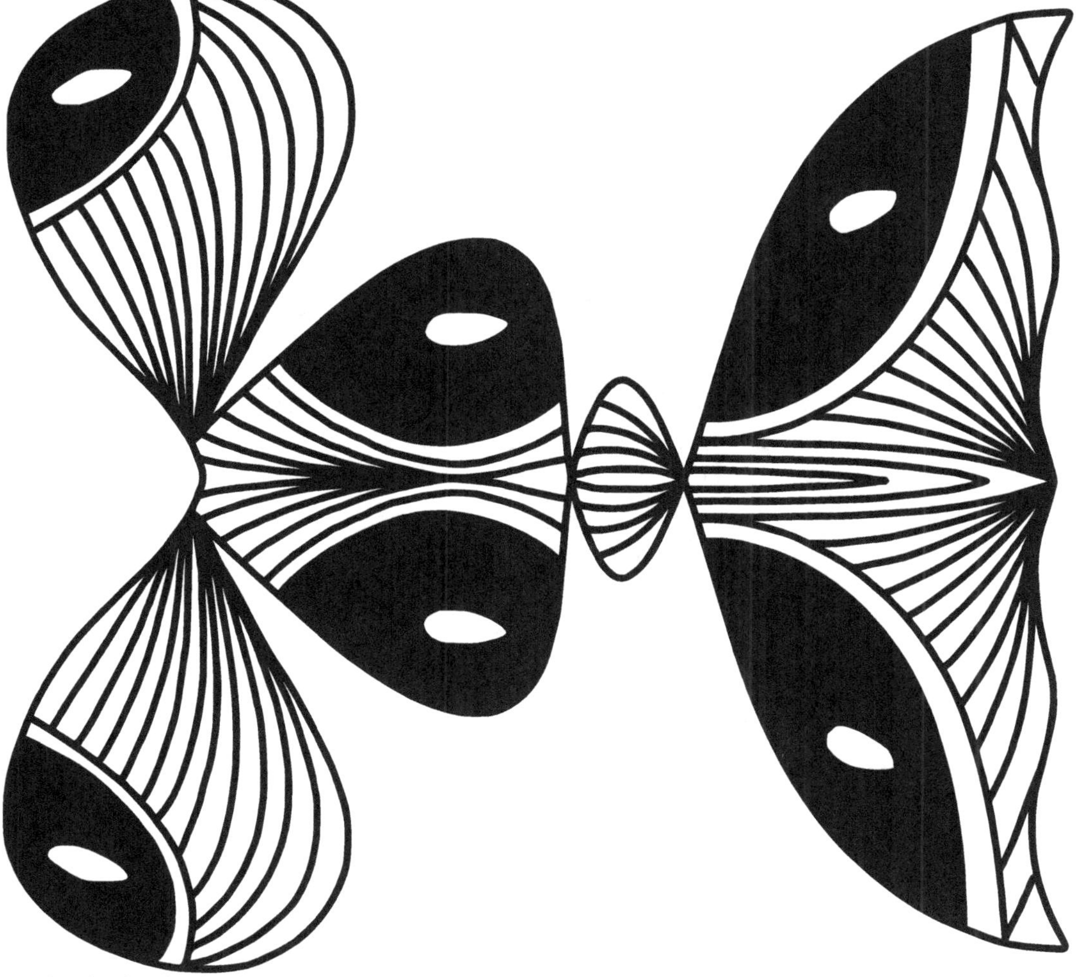

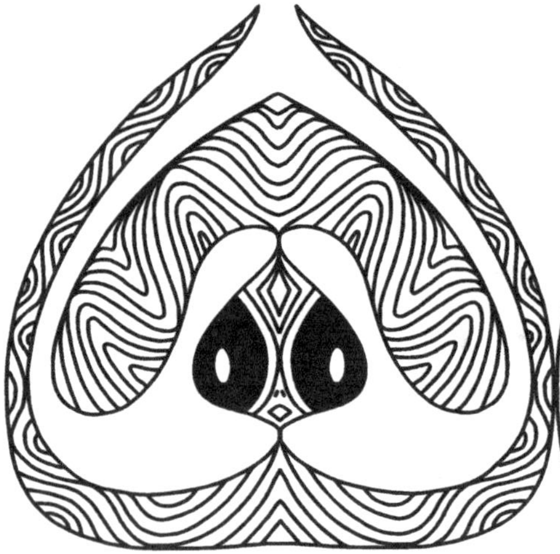

FATLINER WEIRDIES
VOLUME 1

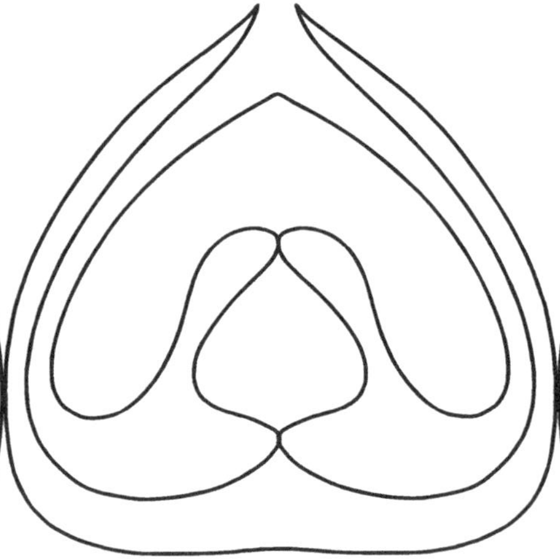

FATLINER WEIRDIES
THE TEMPLATES 1

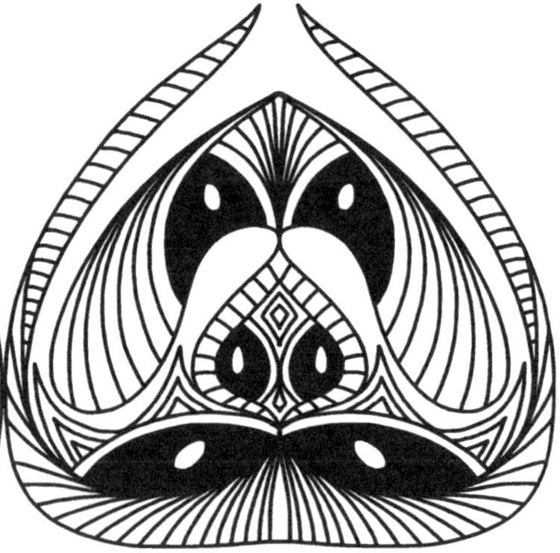

FATLINER WEIRDIES
VOLUME 3

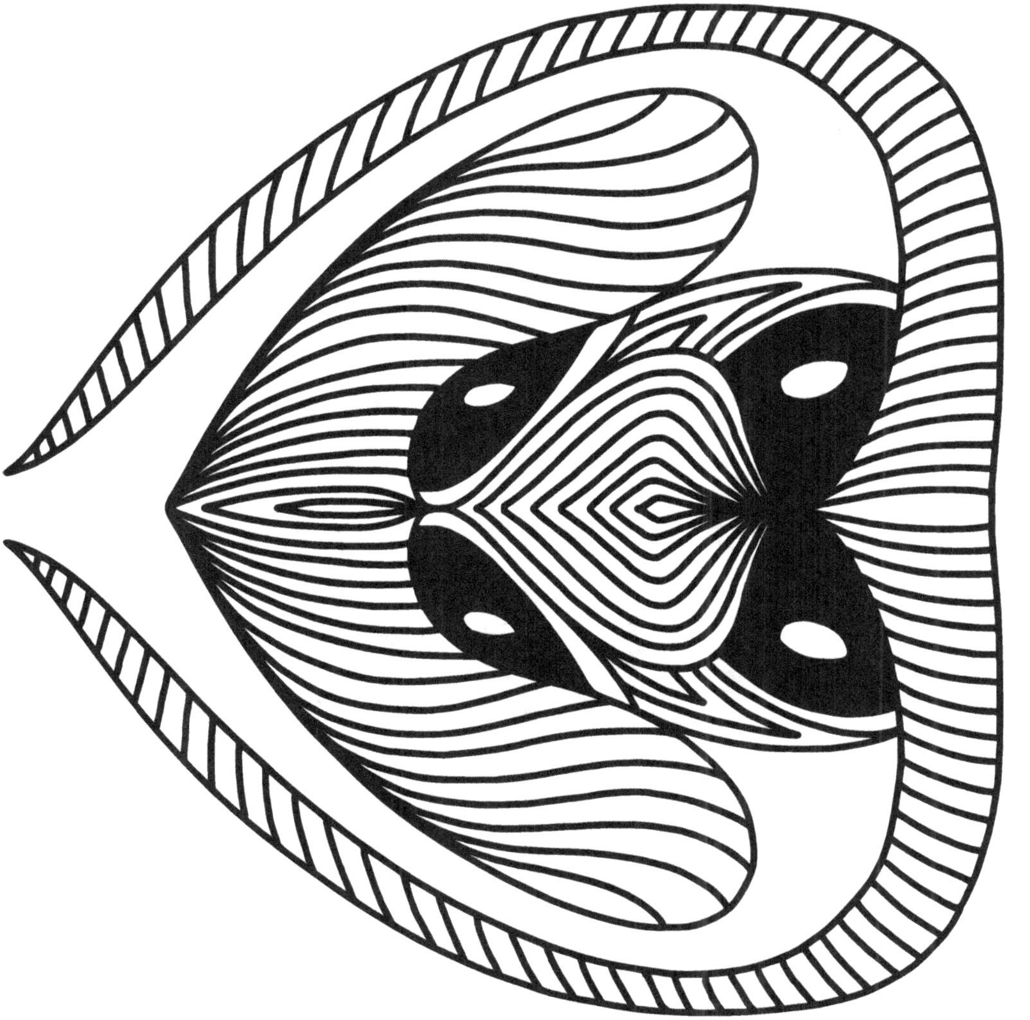

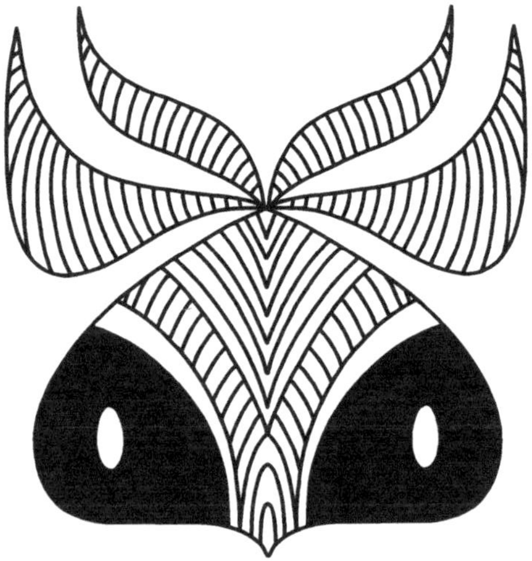

FATLINER WEIRDIES
VOLUME 1

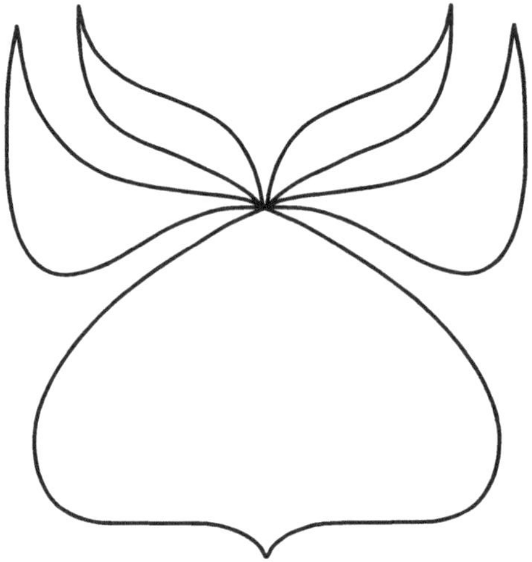

FATLINER WEIRDIES
THE TEMPLATES 1

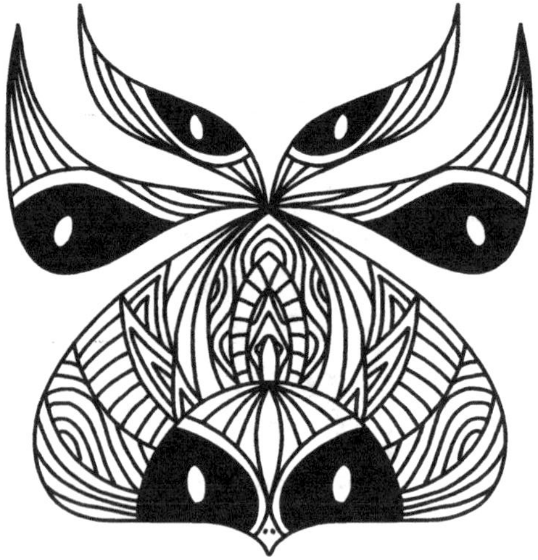

FATLINER WEIRDIES
VOLUME 3

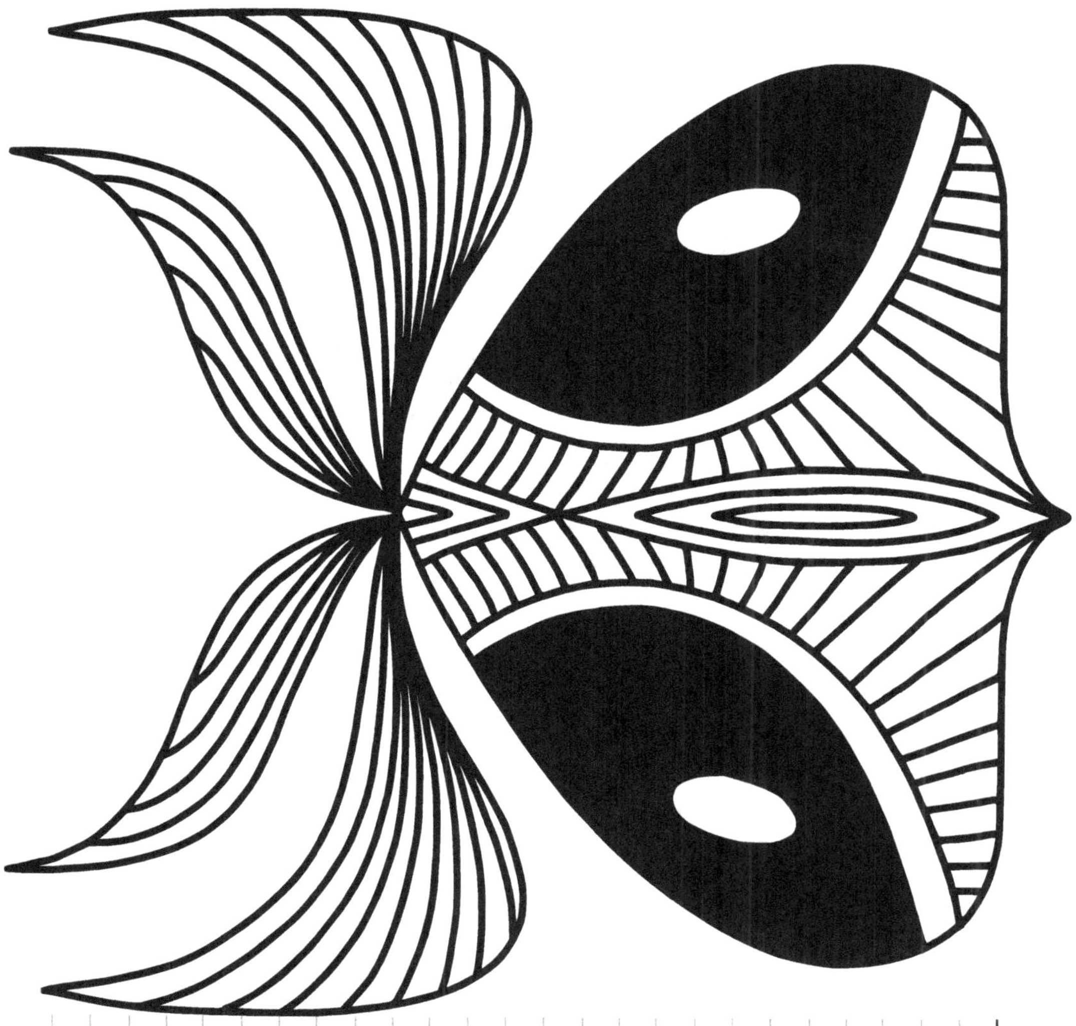

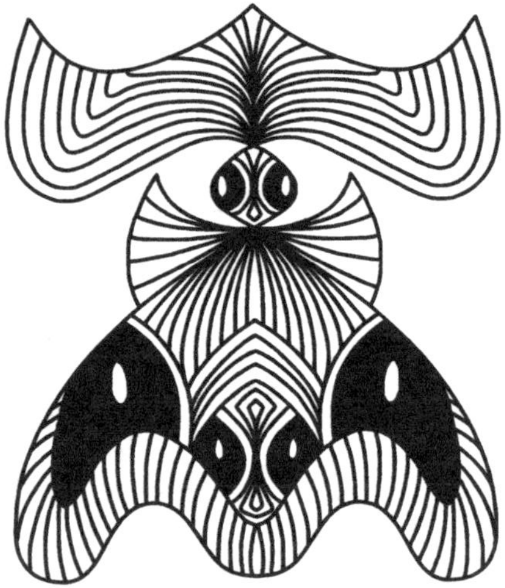

FATLINER WEIRDIES
VOLUME 1

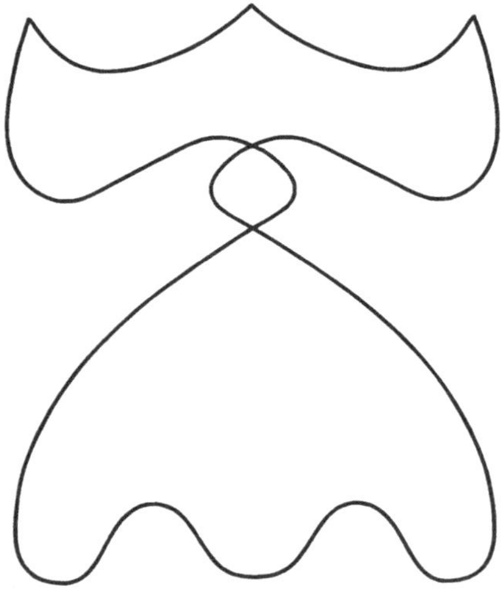

FATLINER WEIRDIES
THE TEMPLATES 1

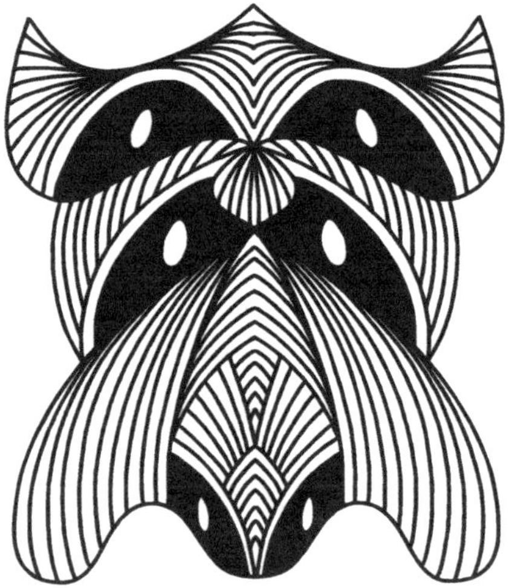

FATLINER WEIRDIES
VOLUME 3

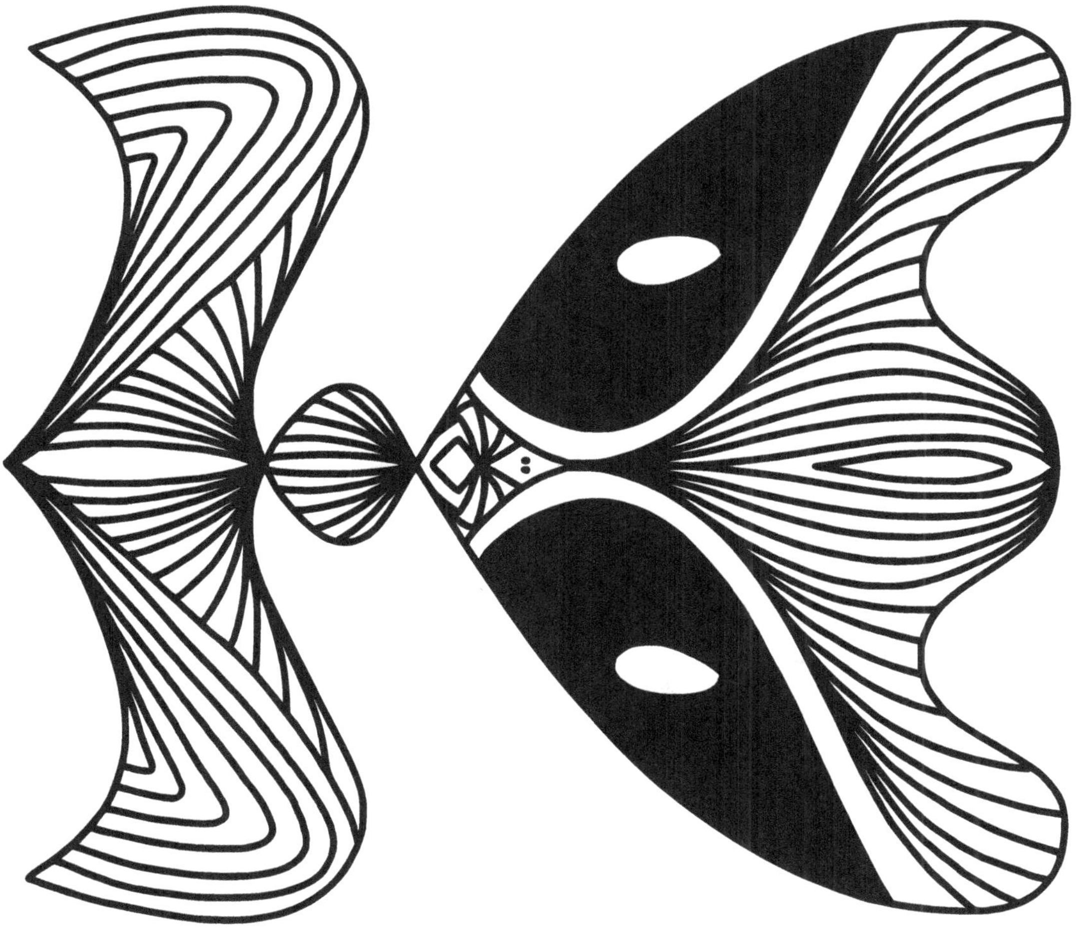

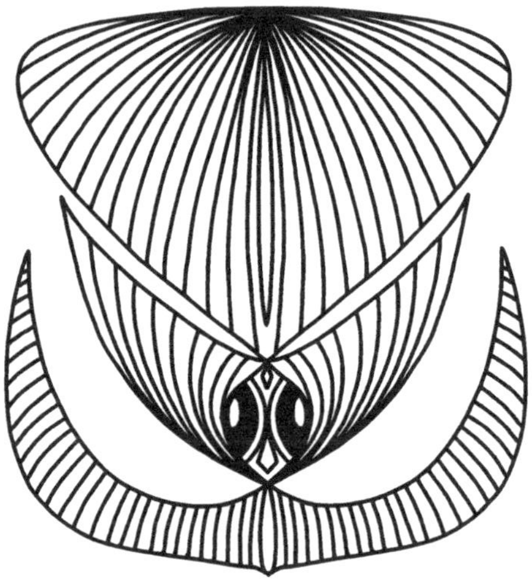

FATLINER WEIRDIES
VOLUME 1

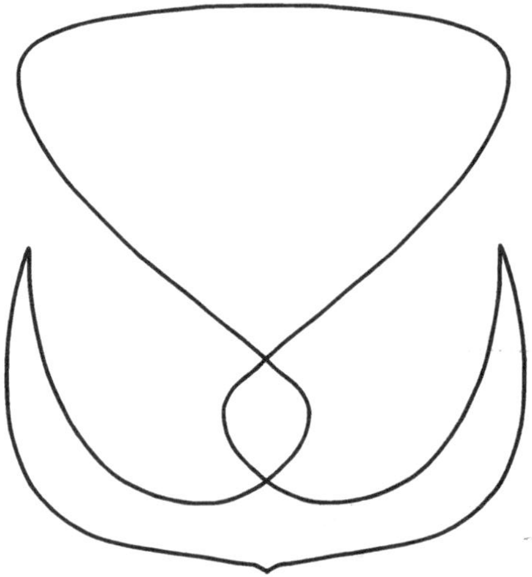

FATLINER WEIRDIES
THE TEMPLATES 1

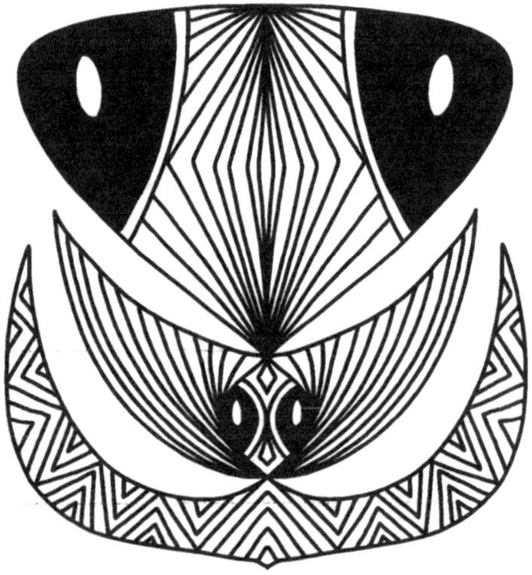

FATLINER WEIRDIES
VOLUME 3

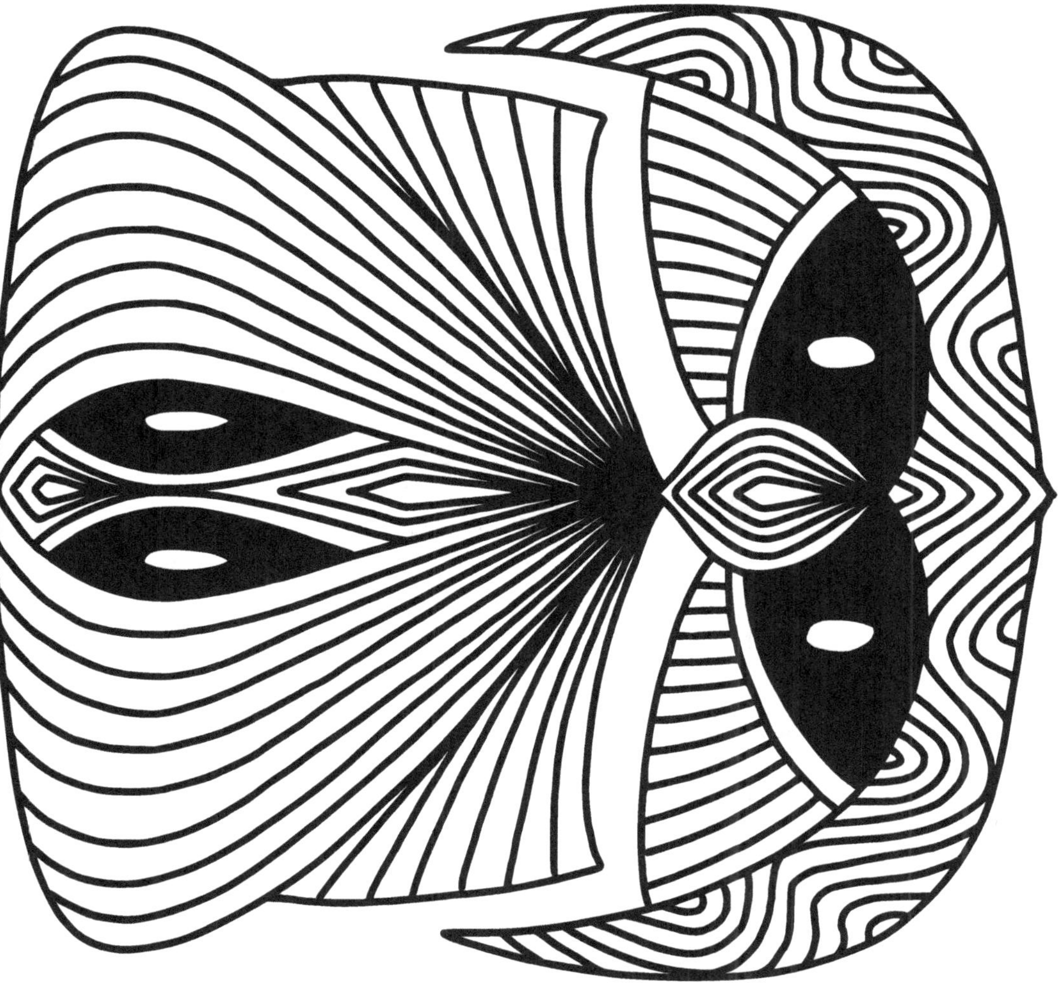

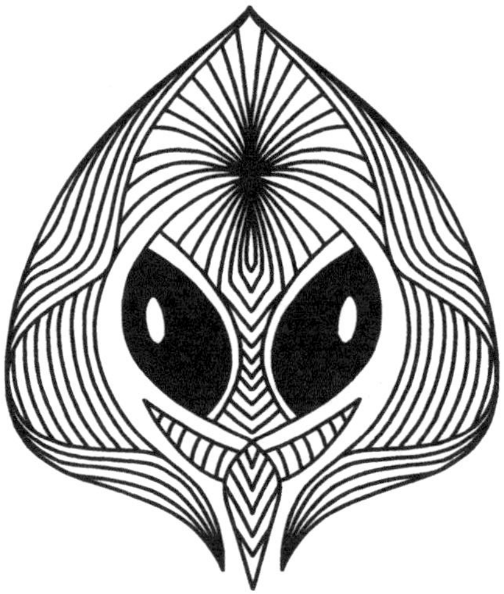

FATLINER WEIRDIES
VOLUME 1

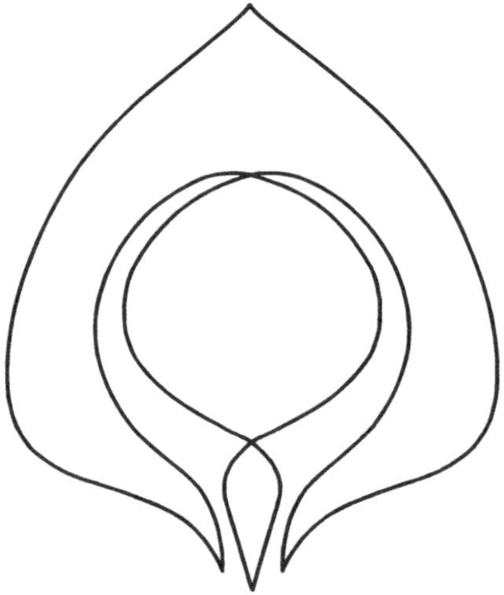

FATLINER WEIRDIES
THE TEMPLATES 1

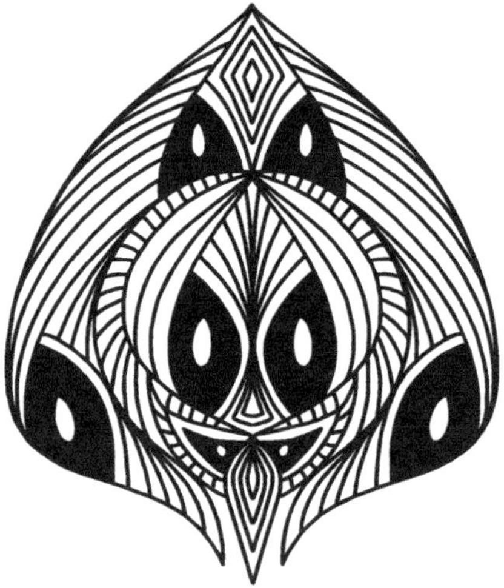

FATLINER WEIRDIES
VOLUME 3

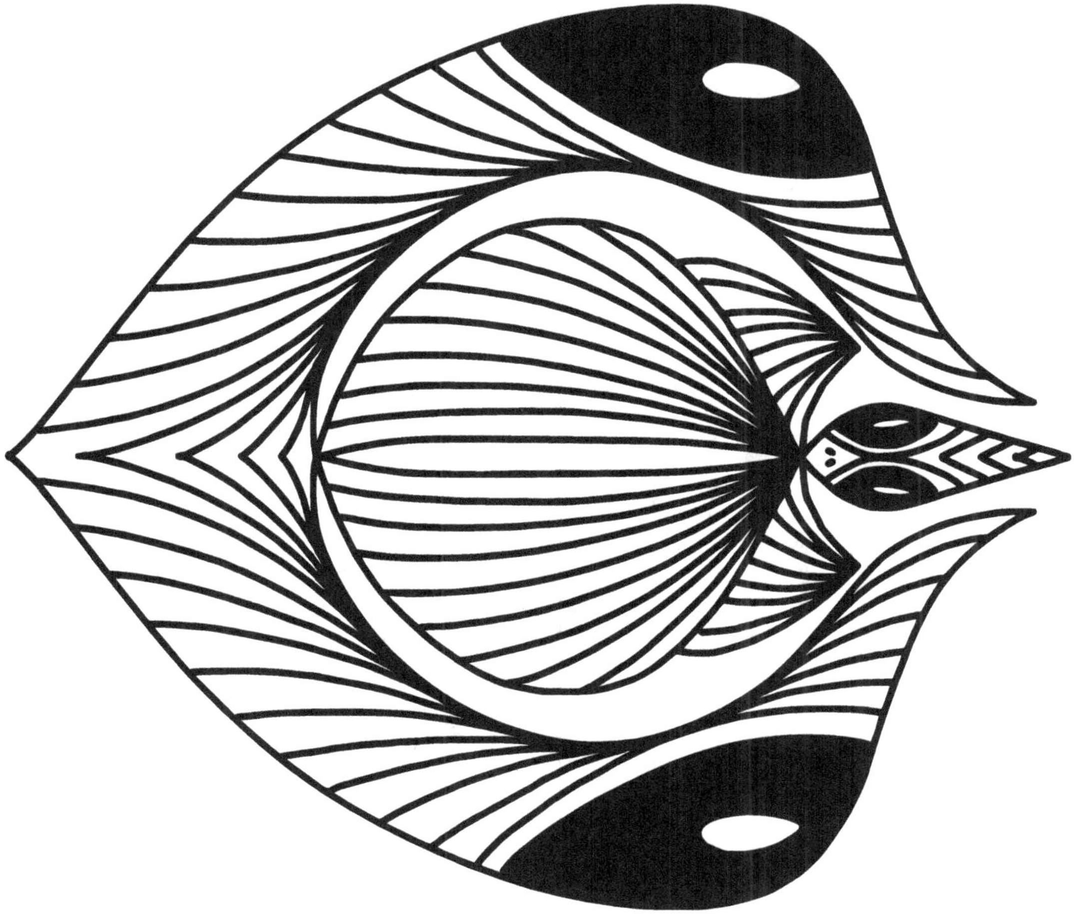

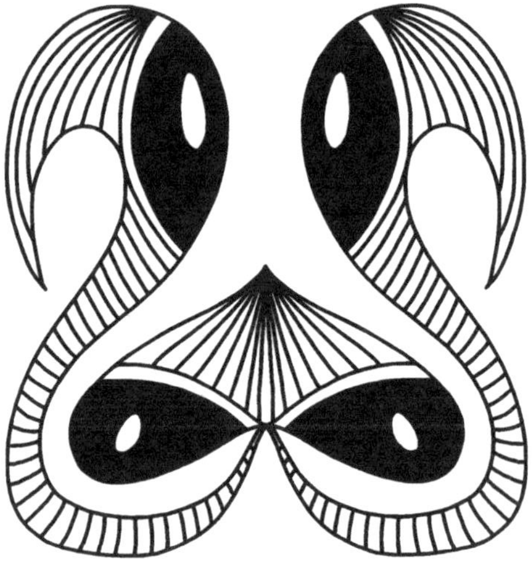

FATLINER WEIRDIES
VOLUME 1

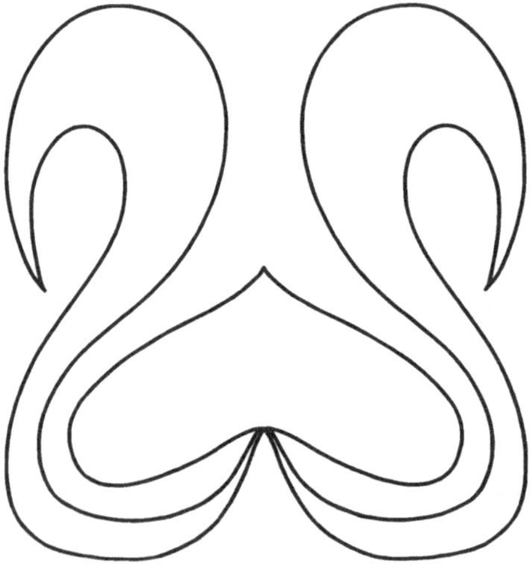

FATLINER WEIRDIES
THE TEMPLATES 1

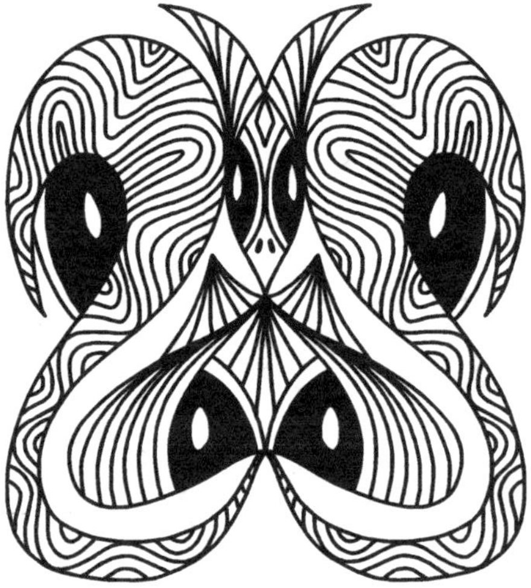

FATLINER WEIRDIES
VOLUME 3

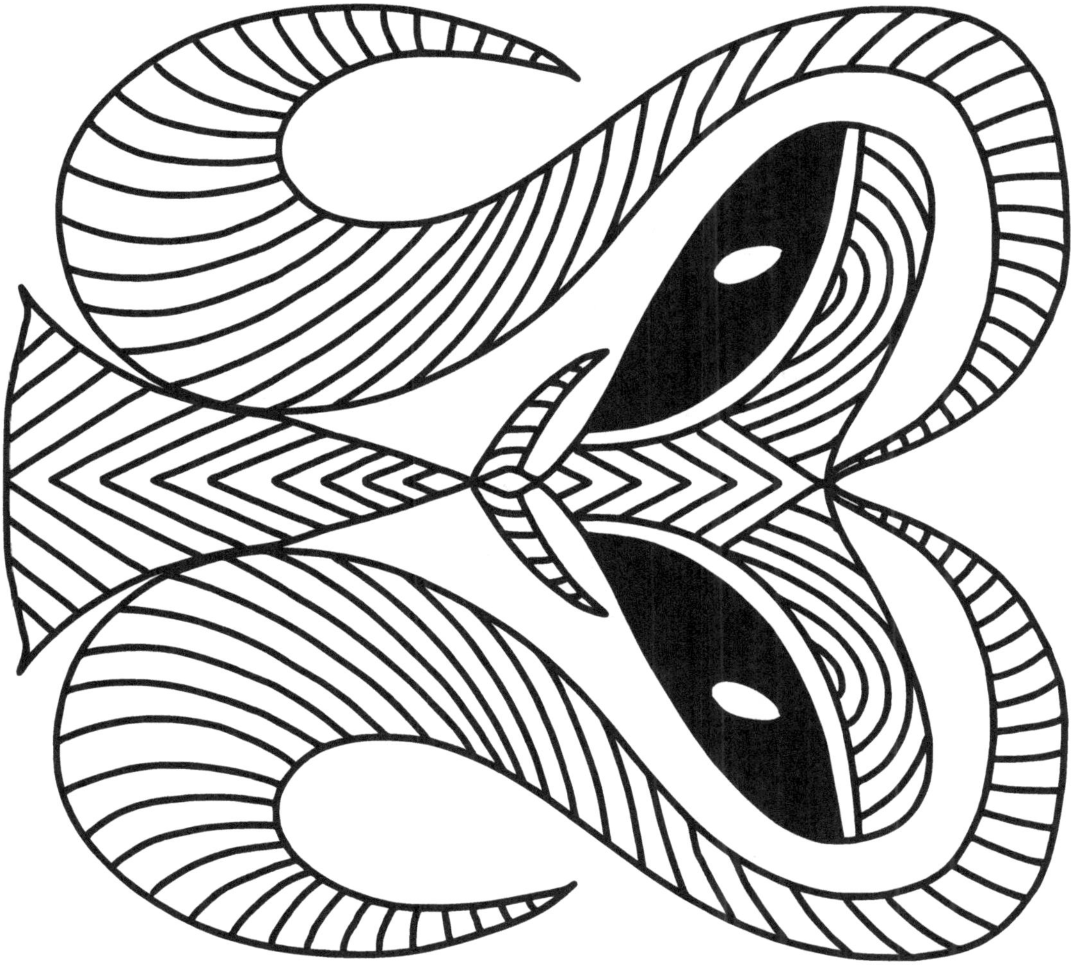

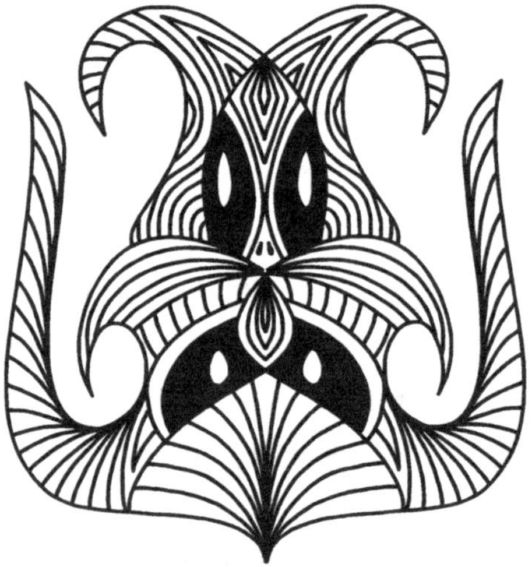

FATLINER WEIRDIES
VOLUME 1

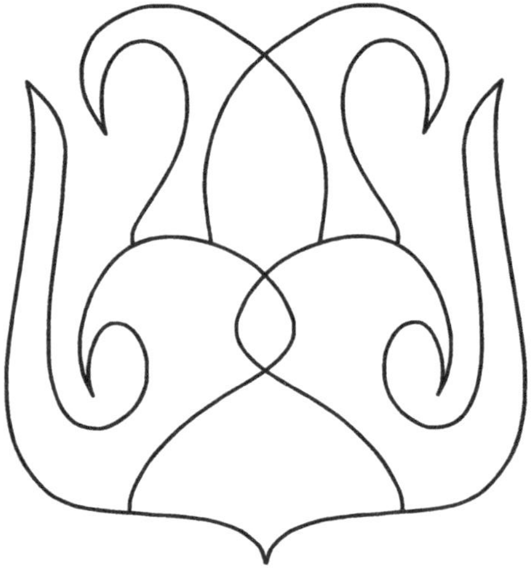

FATLINER WEIRDIES
THE TEMPLATES 1

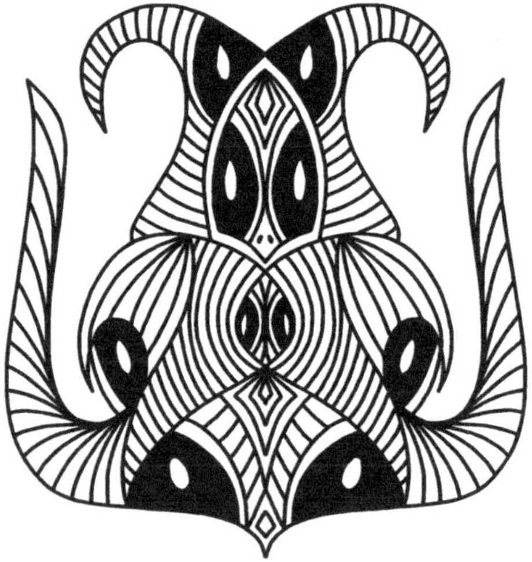

FATLINER WEIRDIES
VOLUME 3

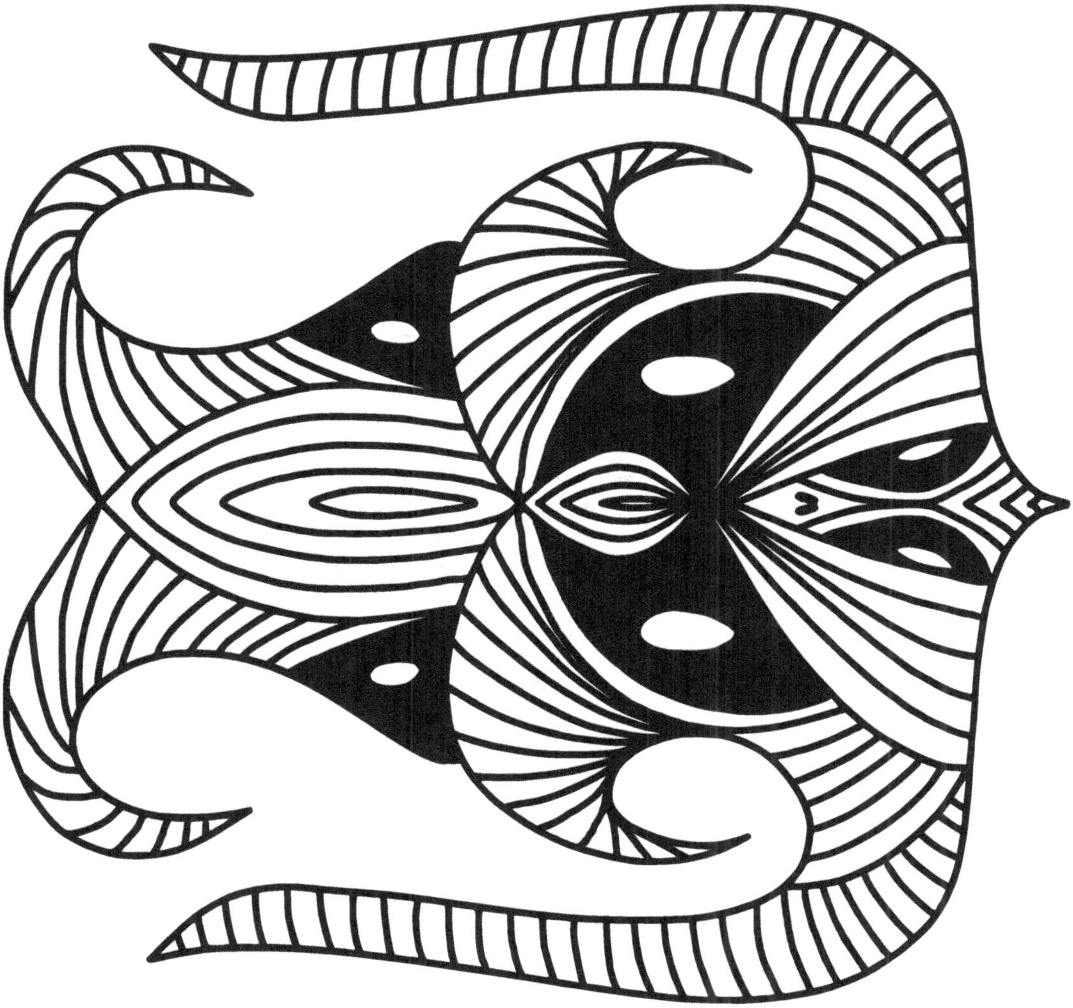

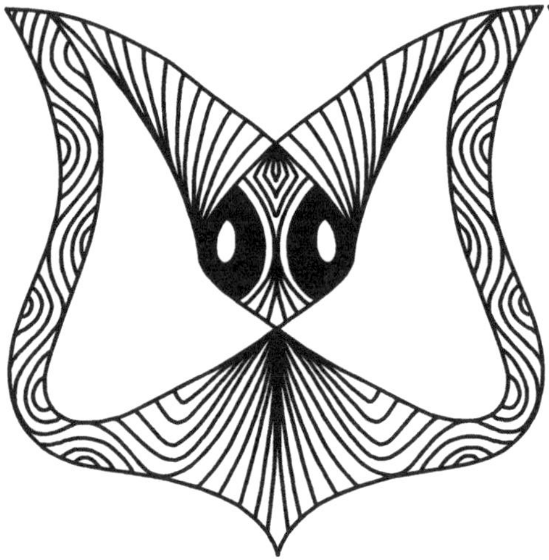

FATLINER WEIRDIES
VOLUME 1

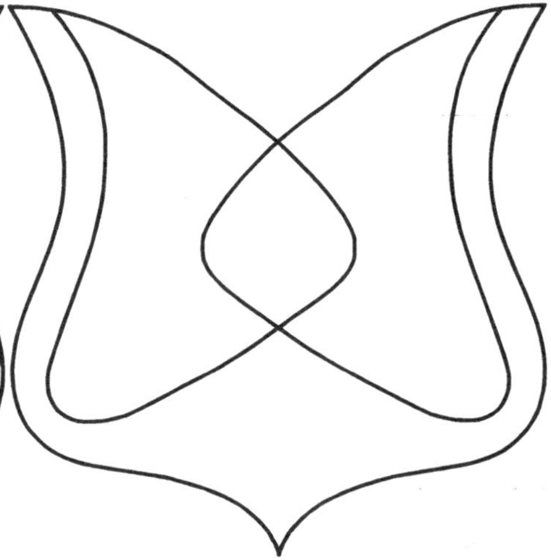

FATLINER WEIRDIES
THE TEMPLATES 1

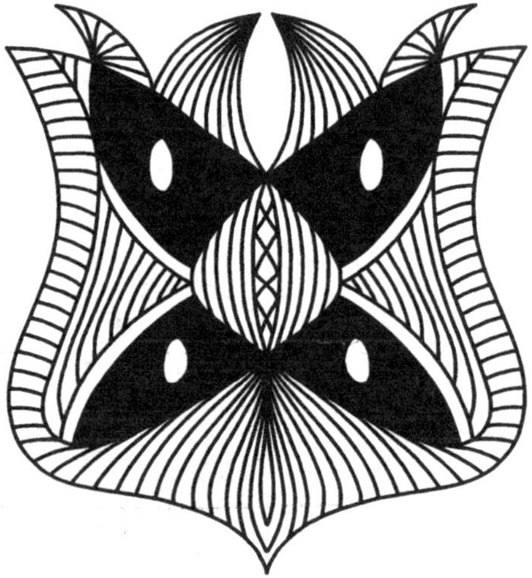

FATLINER WEIRDIES
VOLUME 3

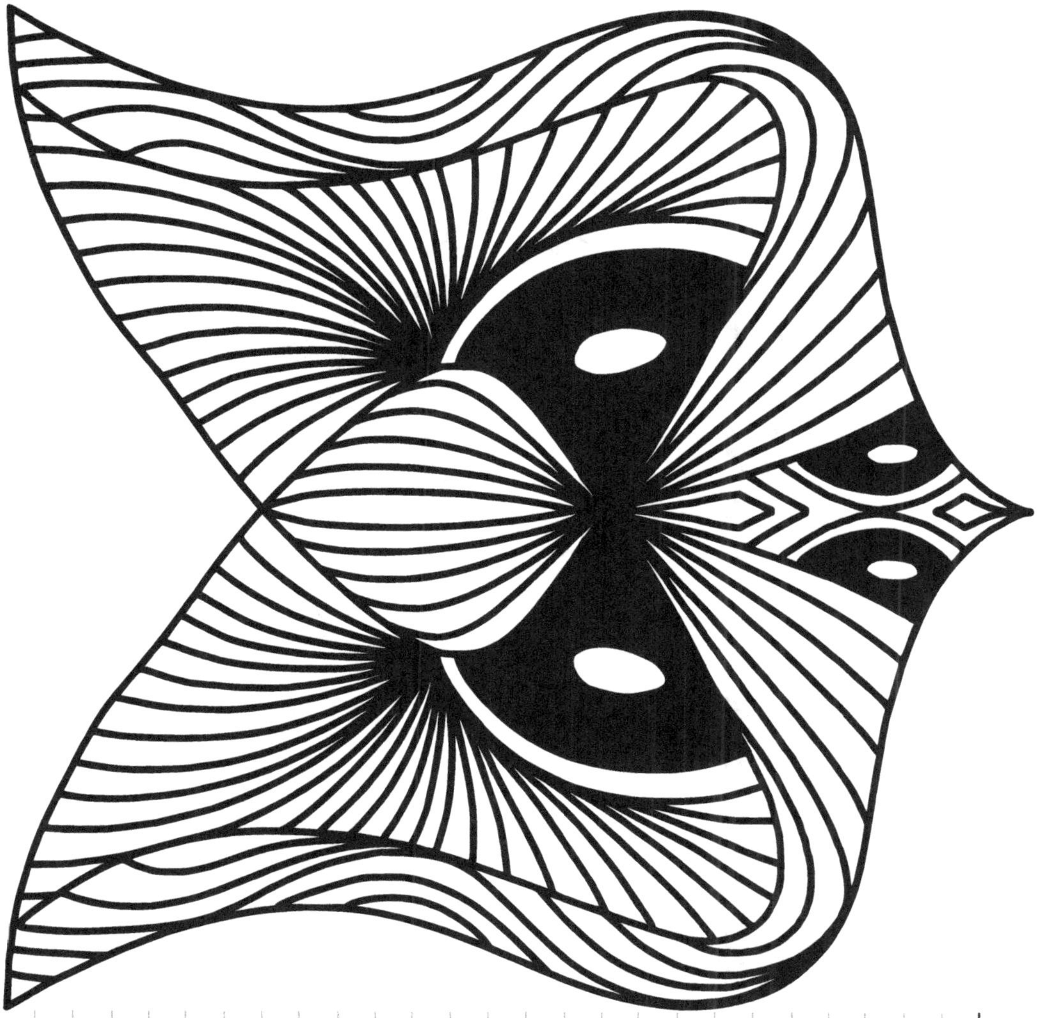

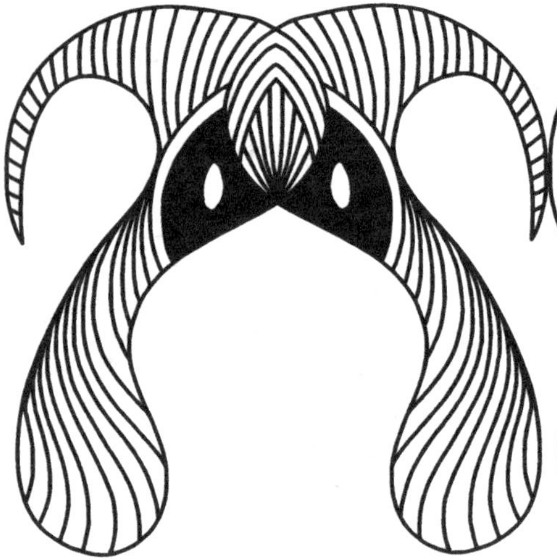

FATLINER WEIRDIES
VOLUME 1

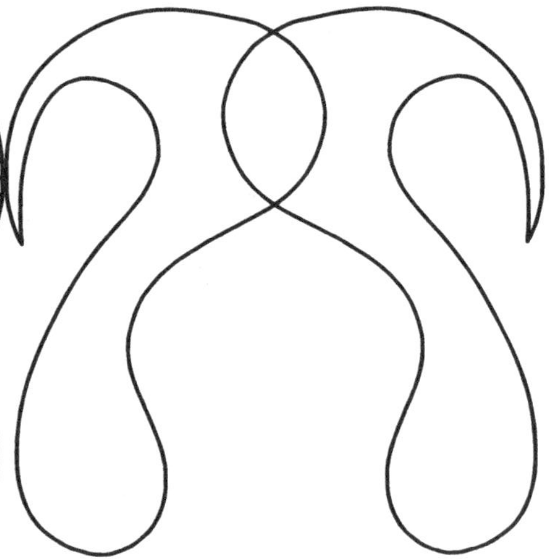

FATLINER WEIRDIES
THE TEMPLATES 1

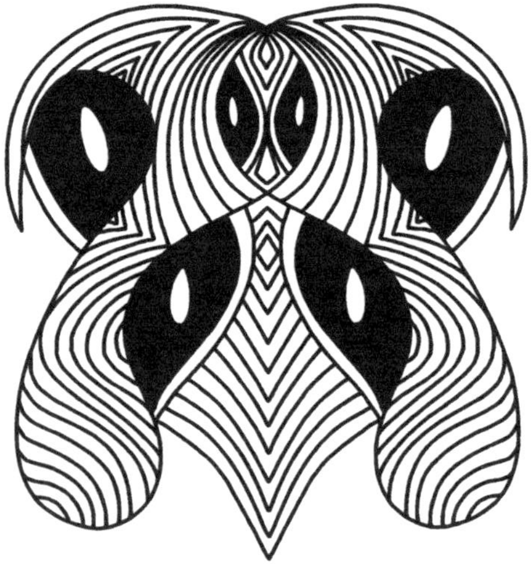

FATLINER WEIRDIES
VOLUME 3

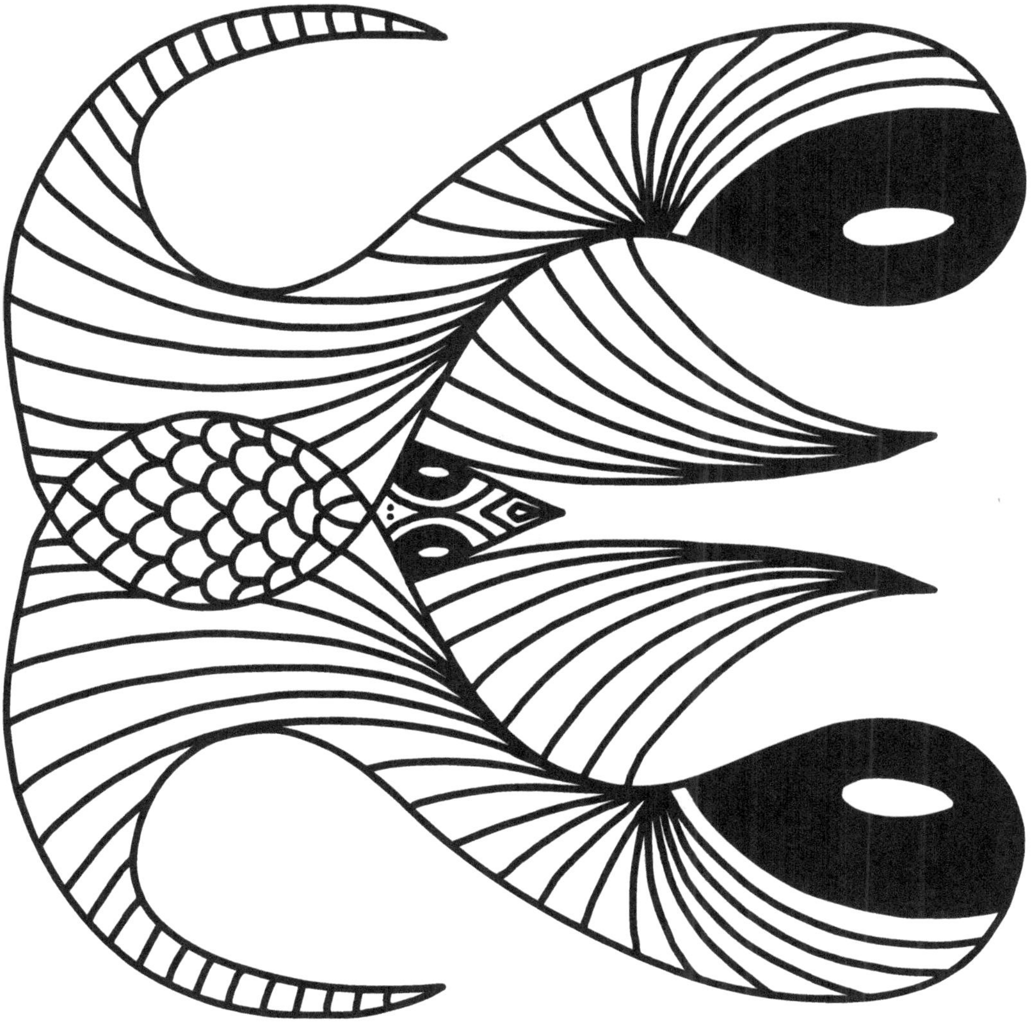

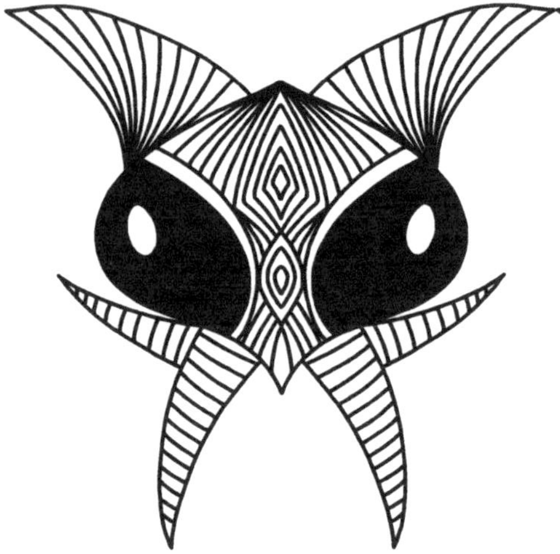

FATLINER WEIRDIES
VOLUME 1

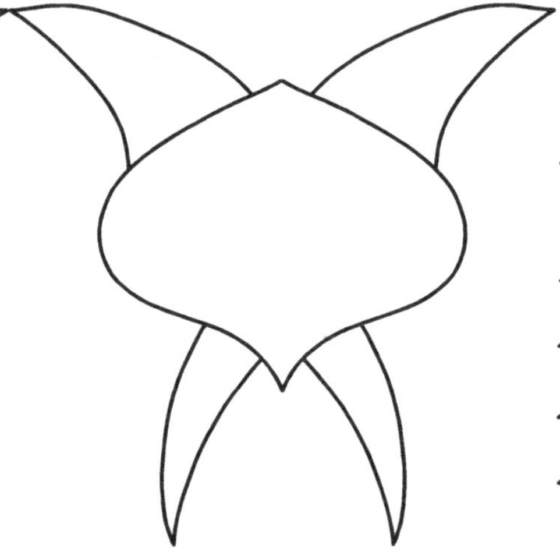

FATLINER WEIRDIES
THE TEMPLATES 1

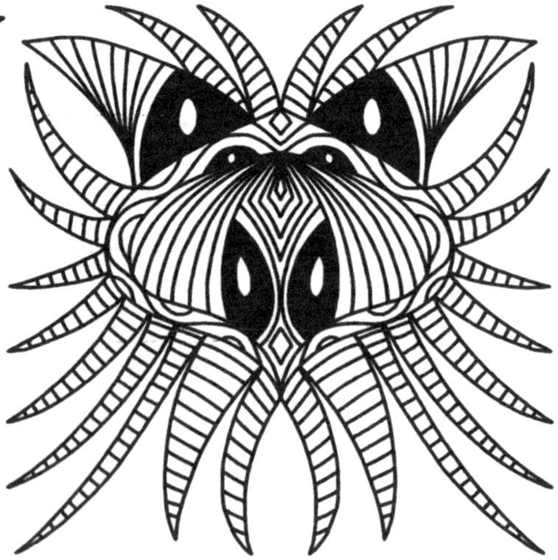

FATLINER WEIRDIES
VOLUME 3

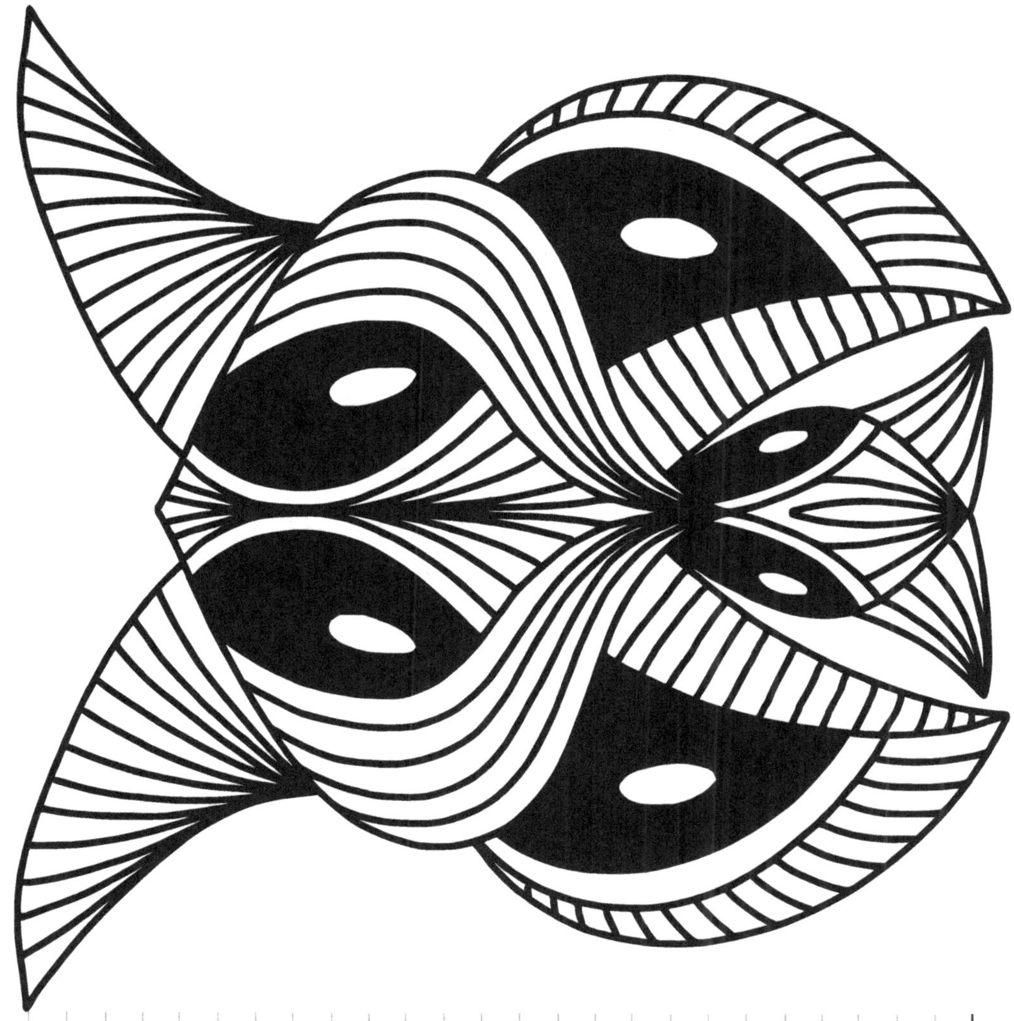

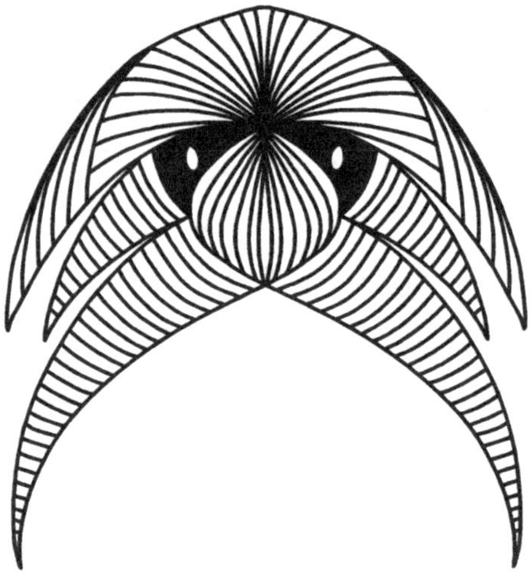

FATLINER WEIRDIES
VOLUME 1

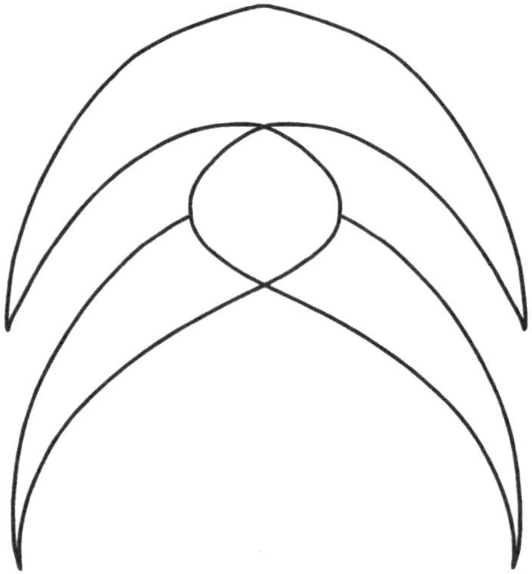

FATLINER WEIRDIES
THE TEMPLATES 1

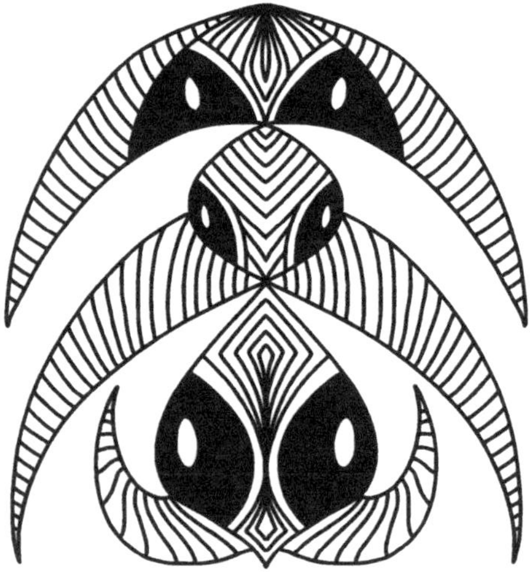

FATLINER WEIRDIES
VOLUME 3

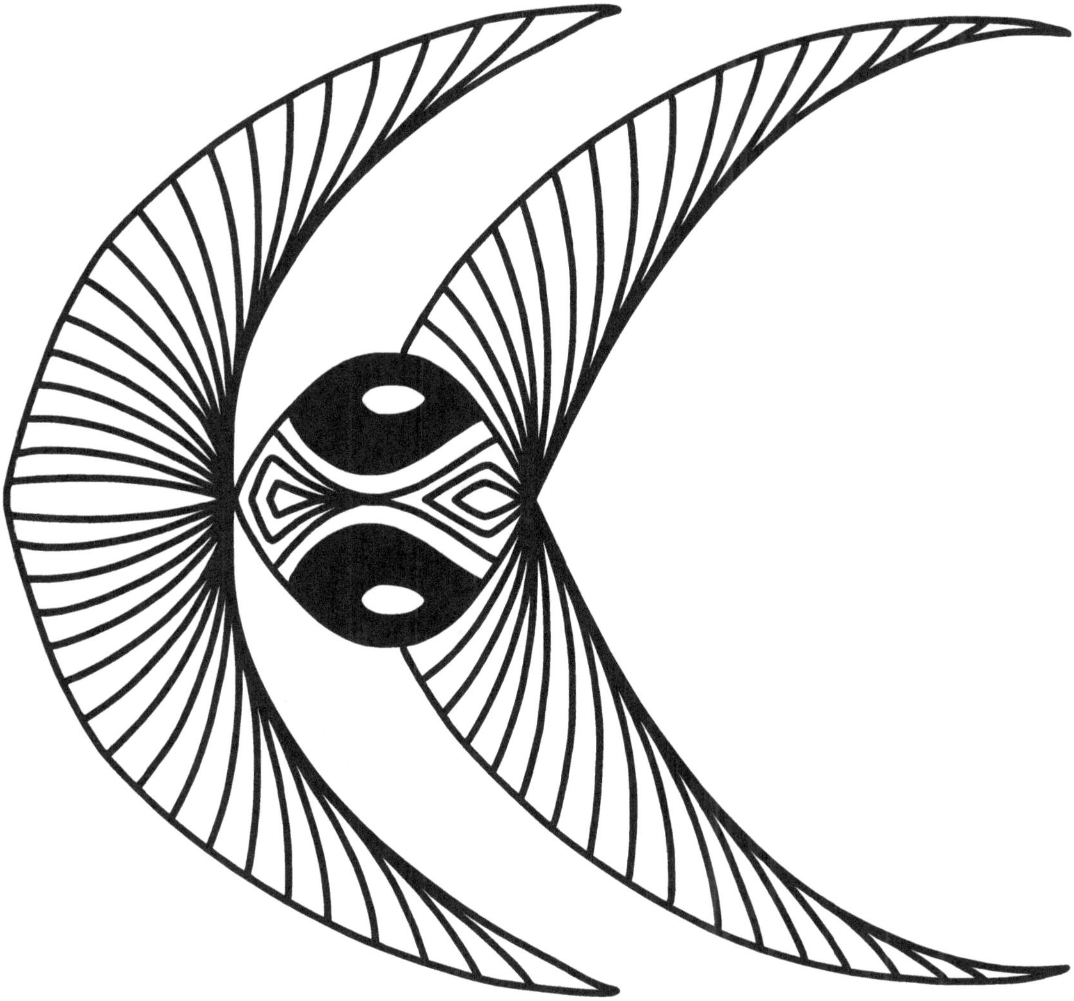

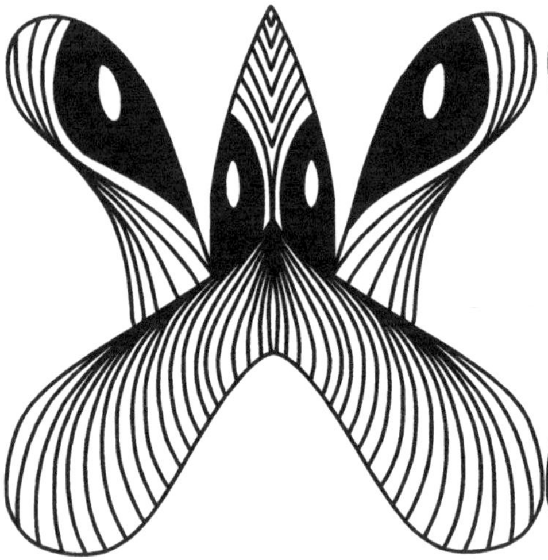

FATLINER WEIRDIES
VOLUME 1

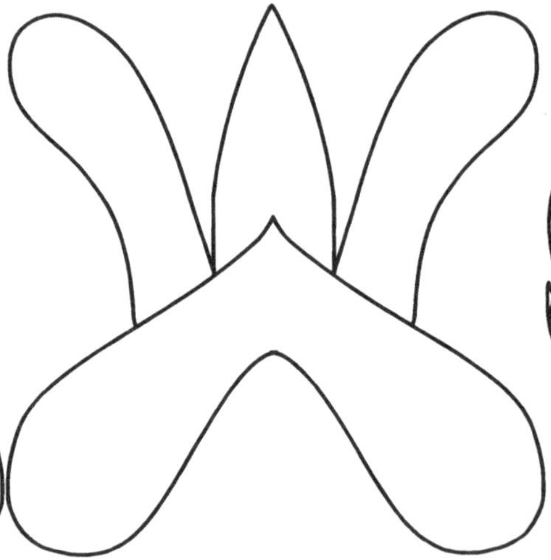

FATLINER WEIRDIES
THE TEMPLATES 1

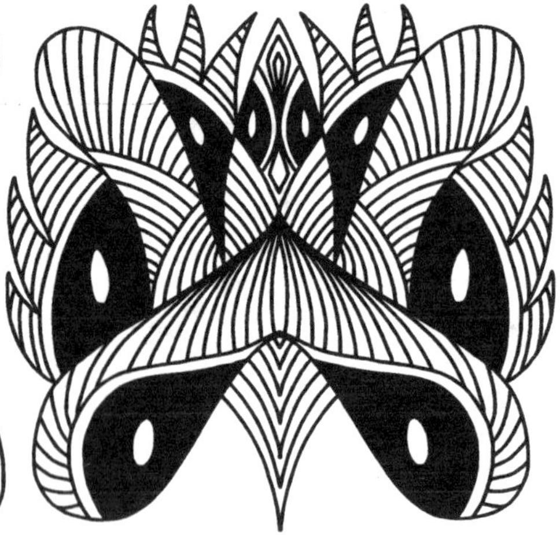

FATLINER WEIRDIES
VOLUME 3

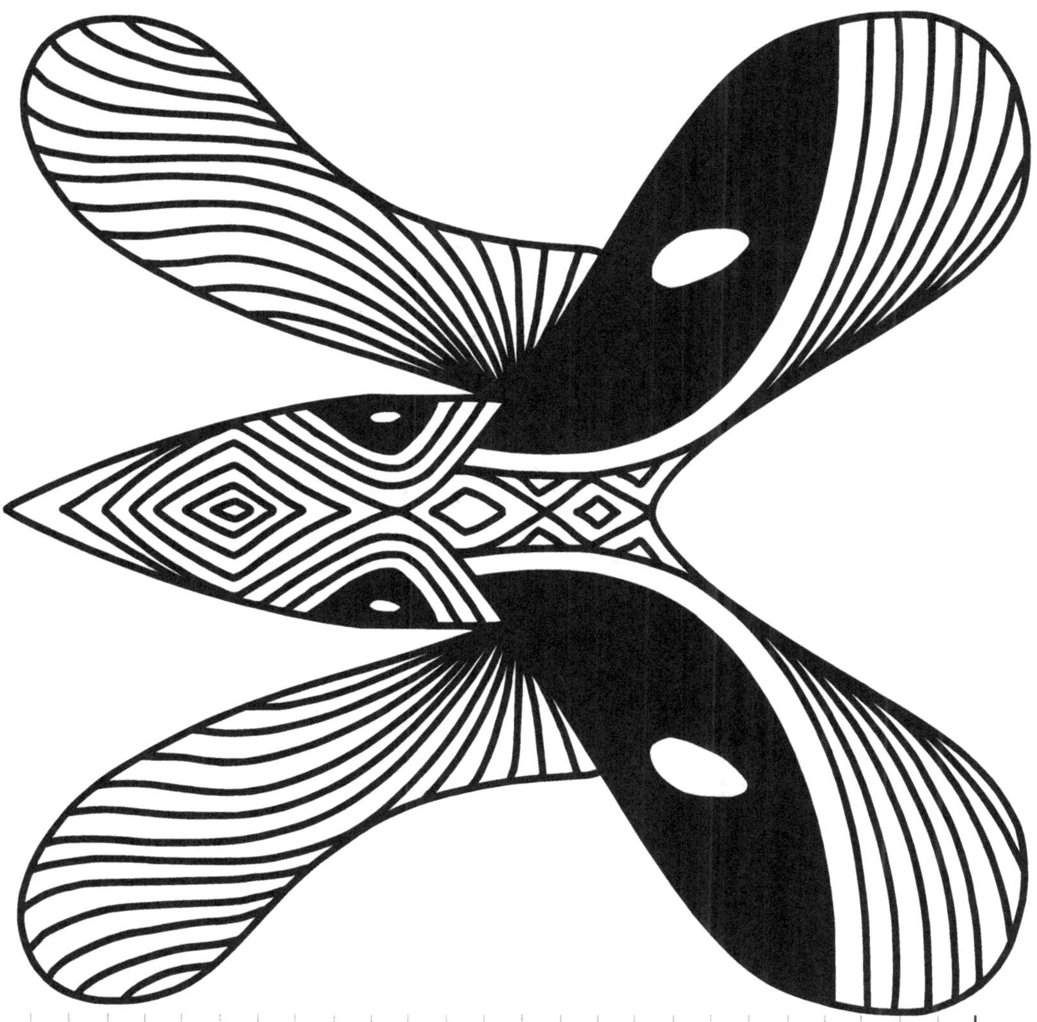

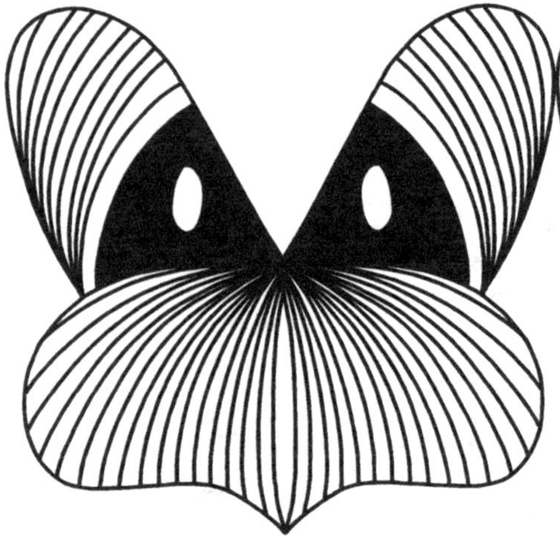

FATLINER WEIRDIES
VOLUME 1

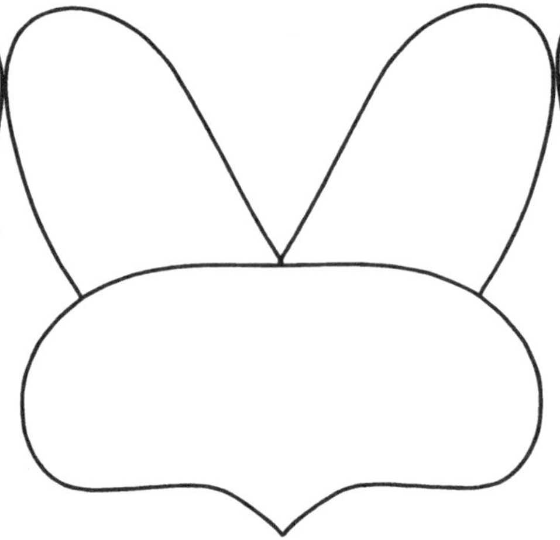

FATLINER WEIRDIES
THE TEMPLATES 1

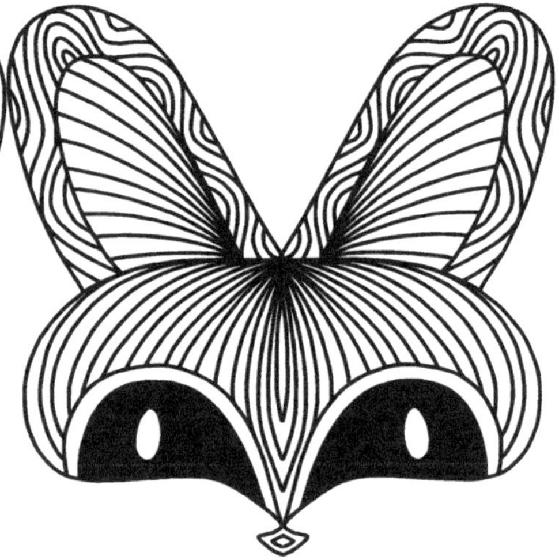

FATLINER WEIRDIES
VOLUME 3

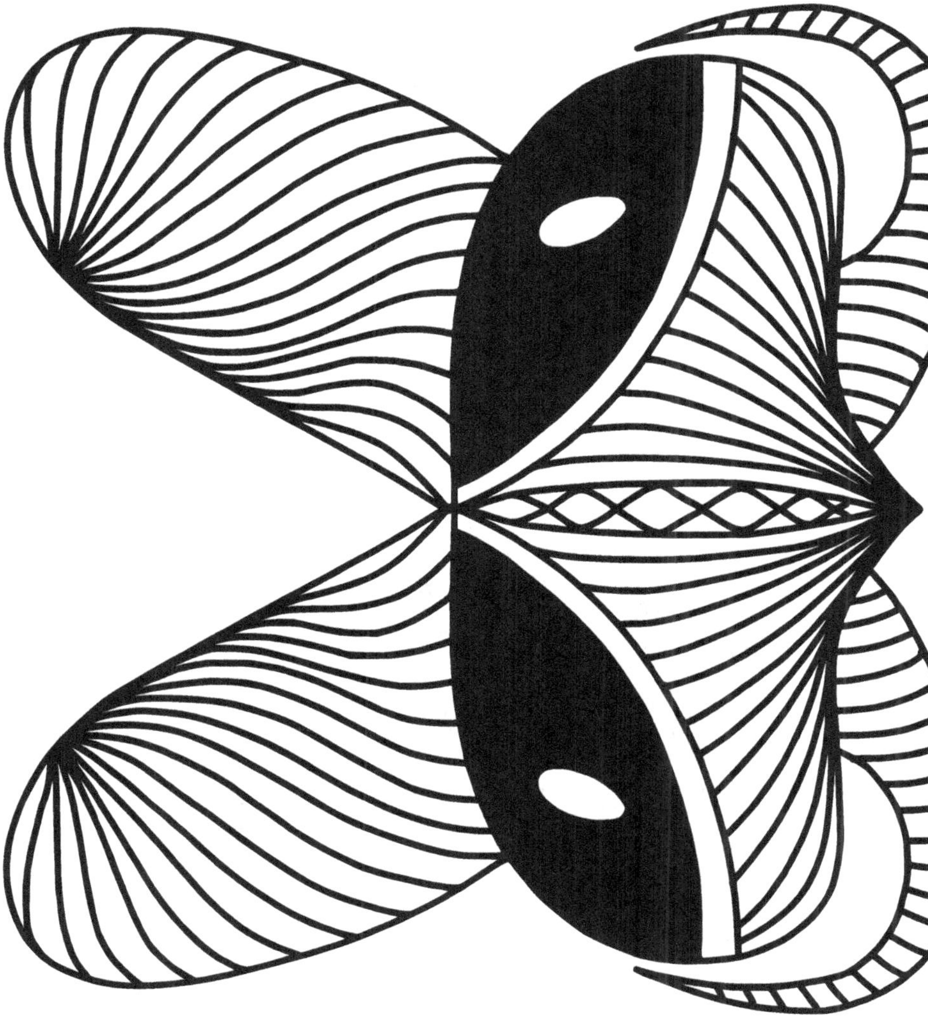

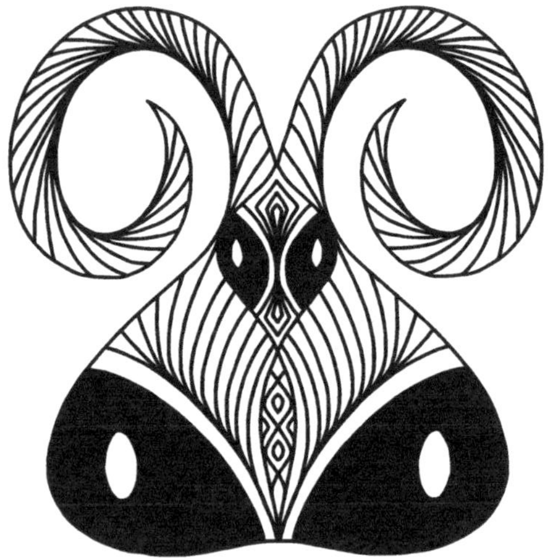

FATLINER WEIRDIES
VOLUME 1

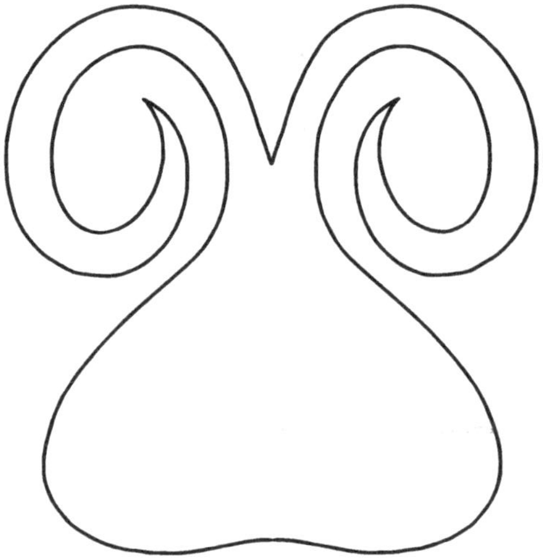

FATLINER WEIRDIES
THE TEMPLATES 1

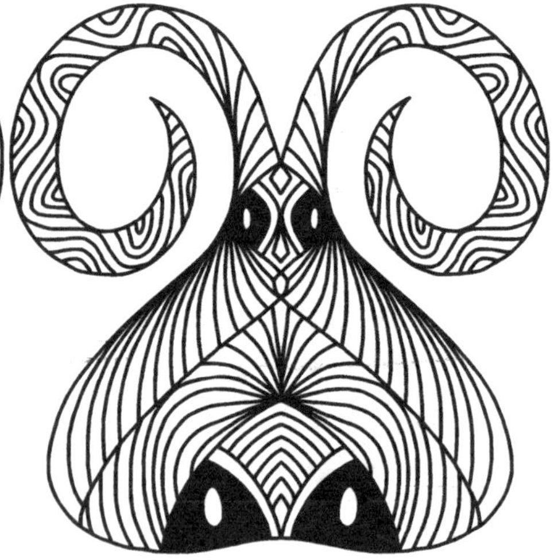

FATLINER WEIRDIES
VOLUME 3

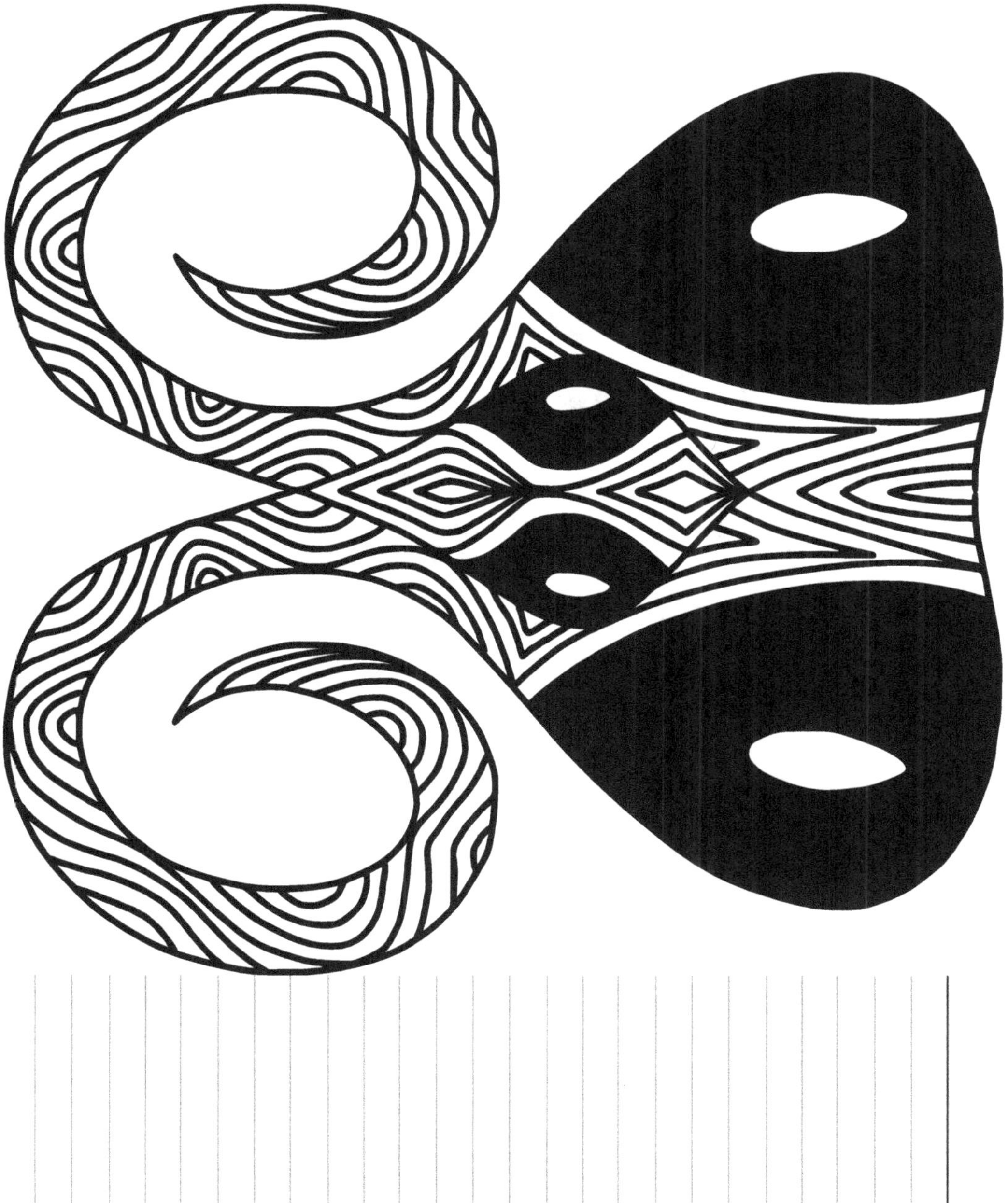

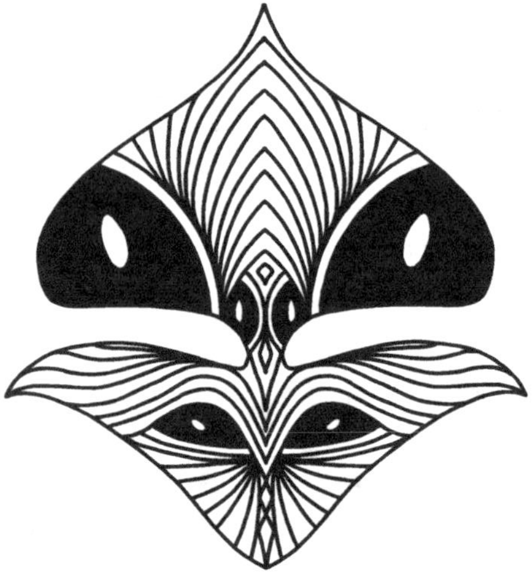

FATLINER WEIRDIES
VOLUME 1

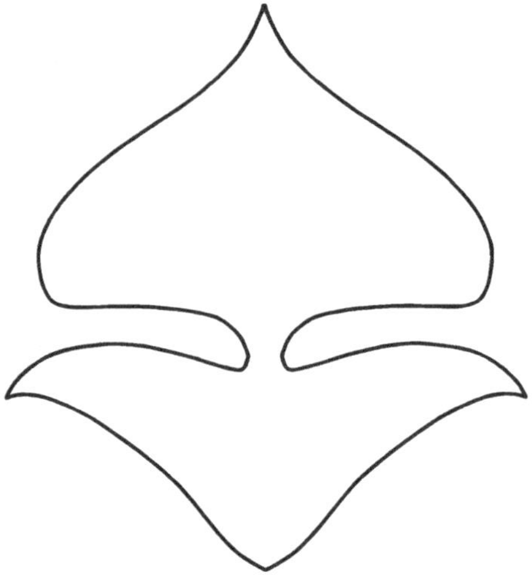

FATLINER WEIRDIES
THE TEMPLATES 1

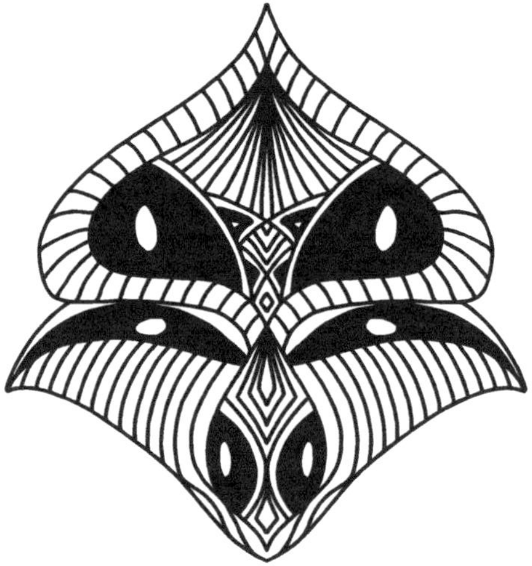

FATLINER WEIRDIES
VOLUME 3

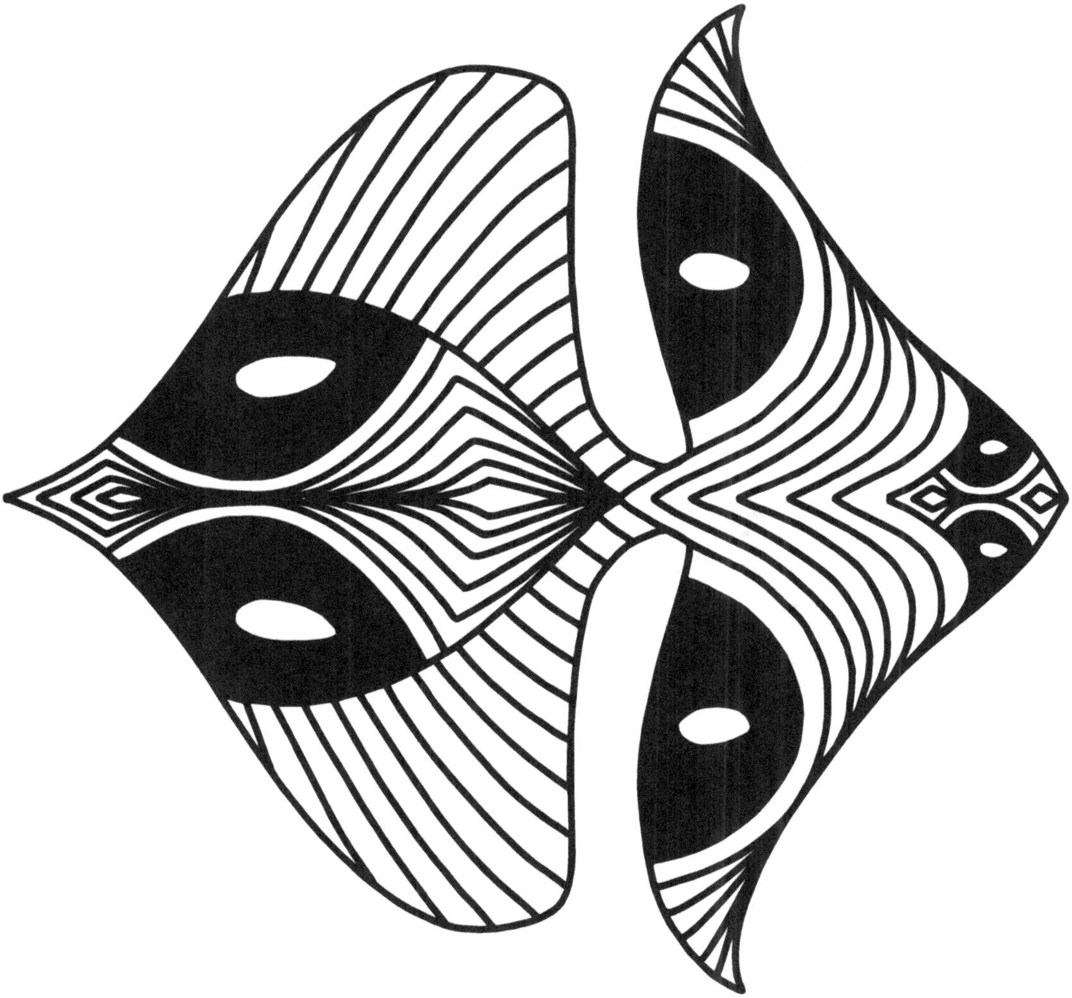

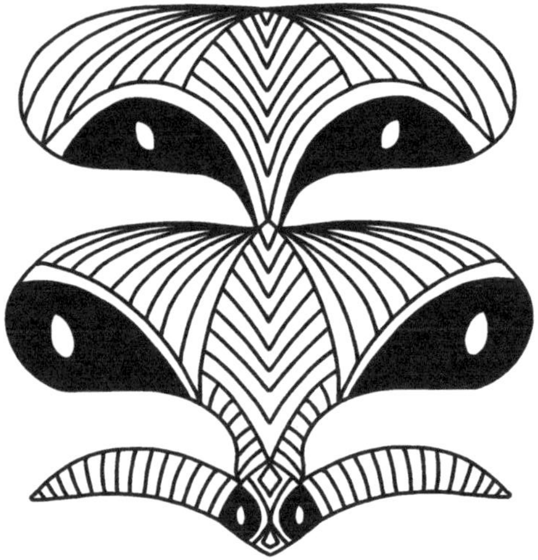

FATLINER WEIRDIES
VOLUME 1

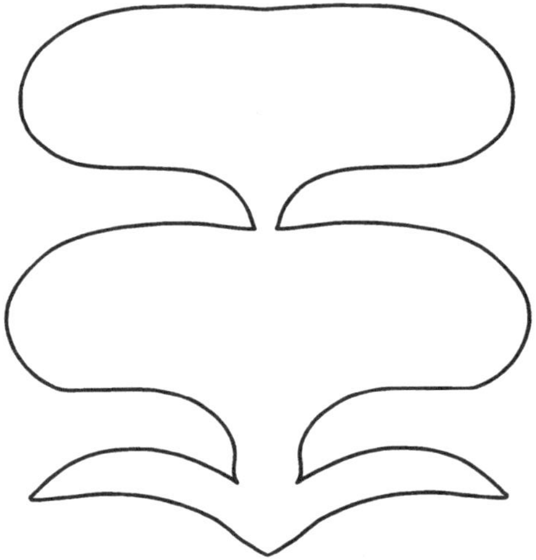

FATLINER WEIRDIES
THE TEMPLATES 1

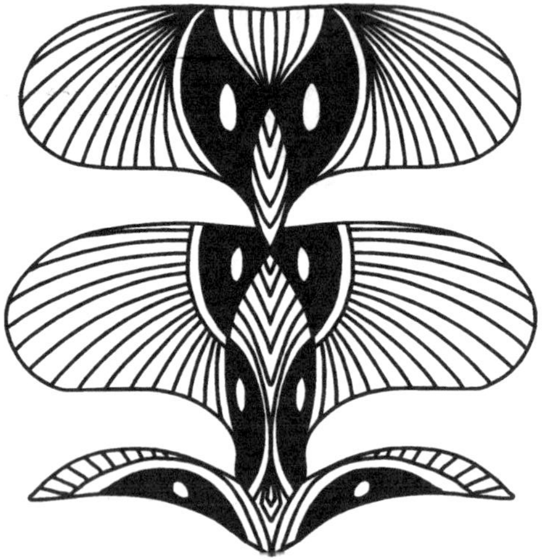

FATLINER WEIRDIES
VOLUME 3

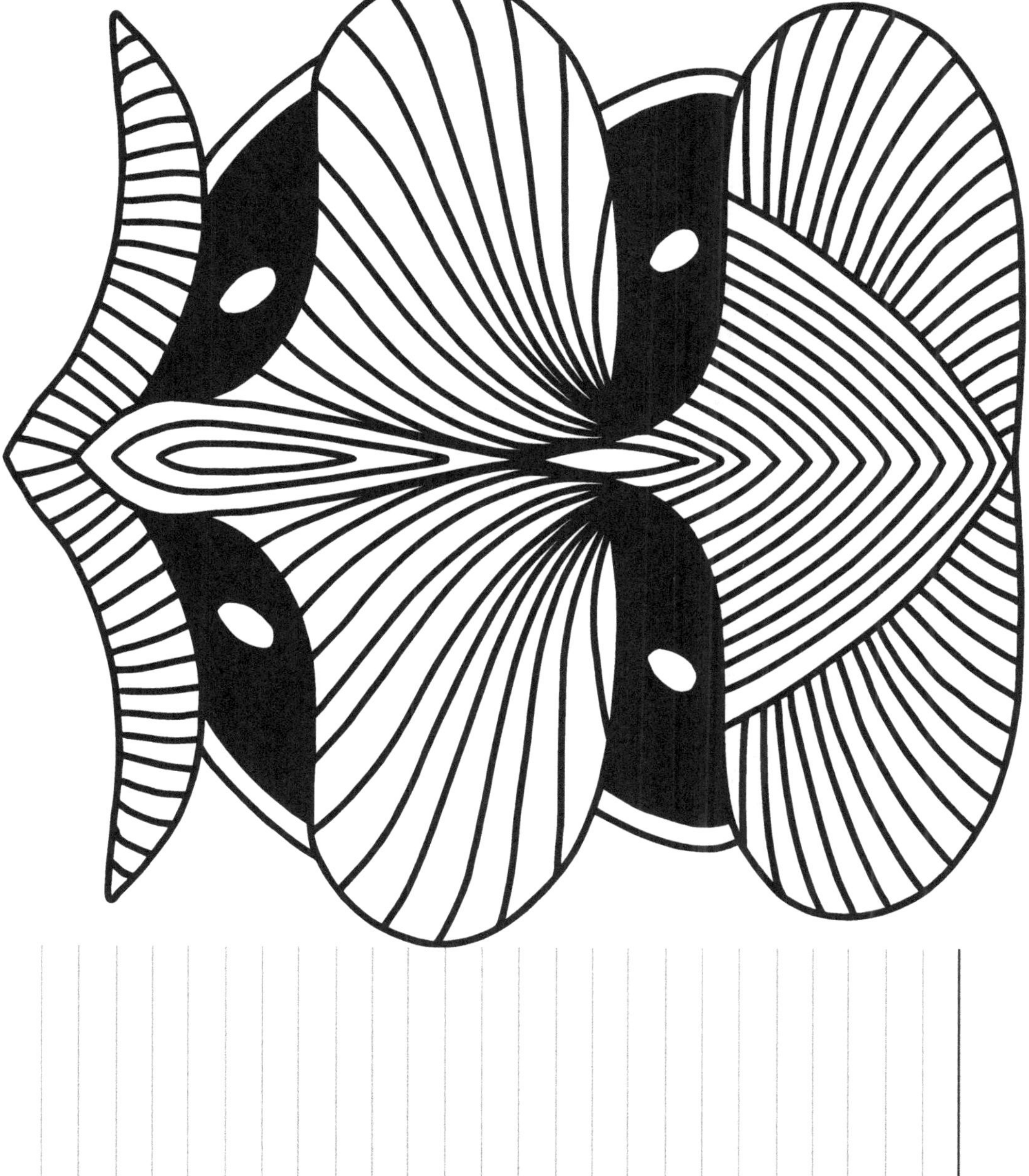

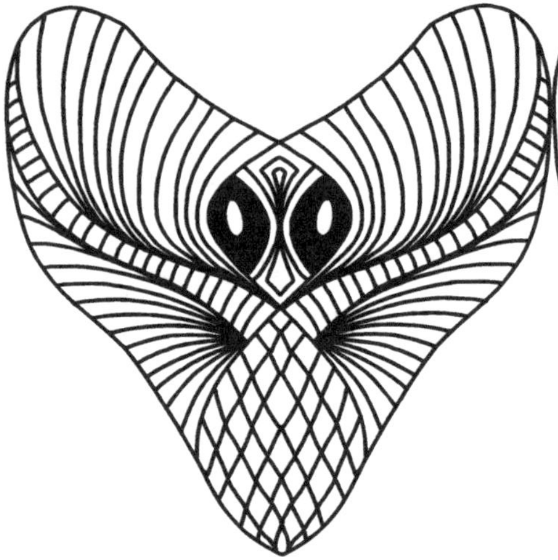

FATLINER WEIRDIES
VOLUME 1

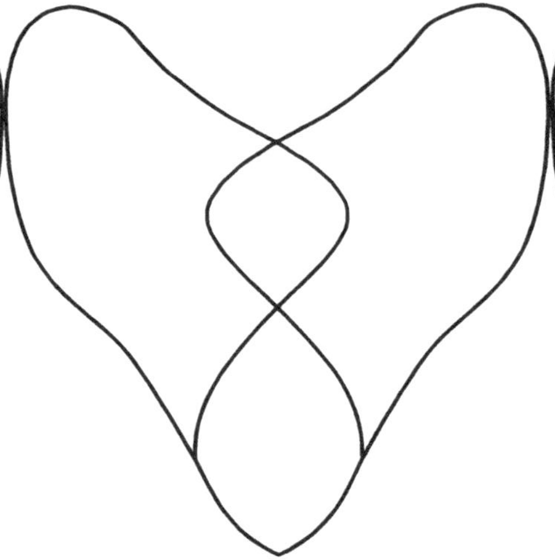

FATLINER WEIRDIES
THE TEMPLATES 1

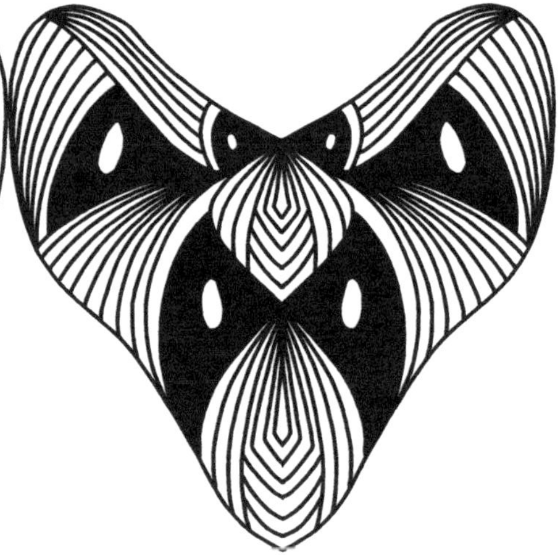

FATLINER WEIRDIES
VOLUME 3

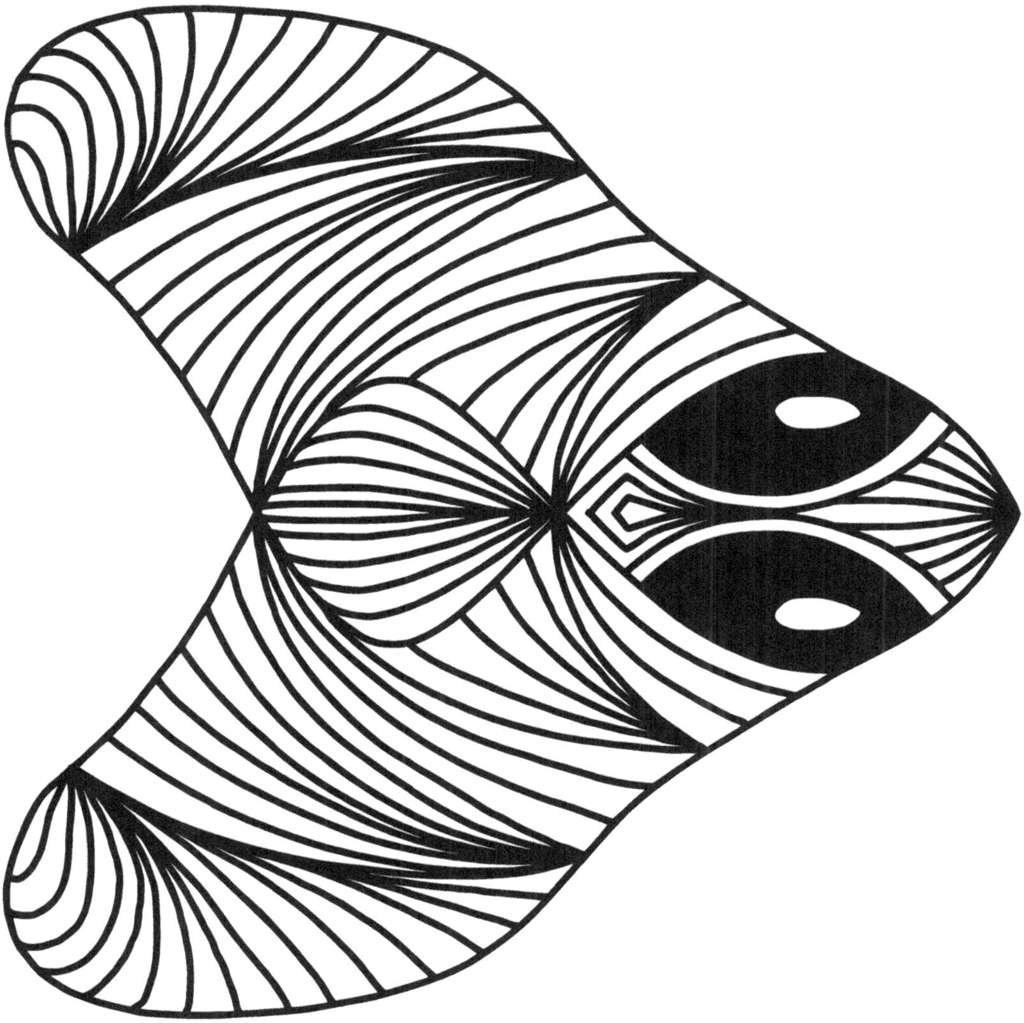

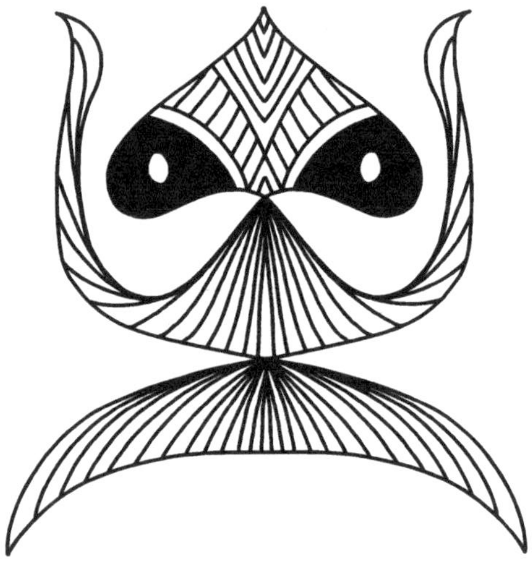

FATLINER WEIRDIES
VOLUME 1

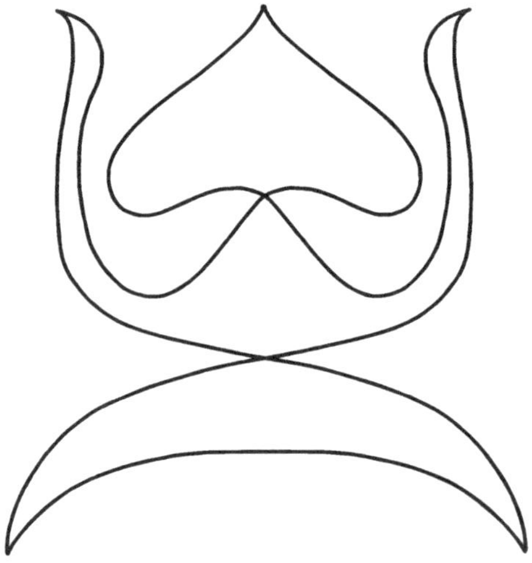

FATLINER WEIRDIES
THE TEMPLATES 1

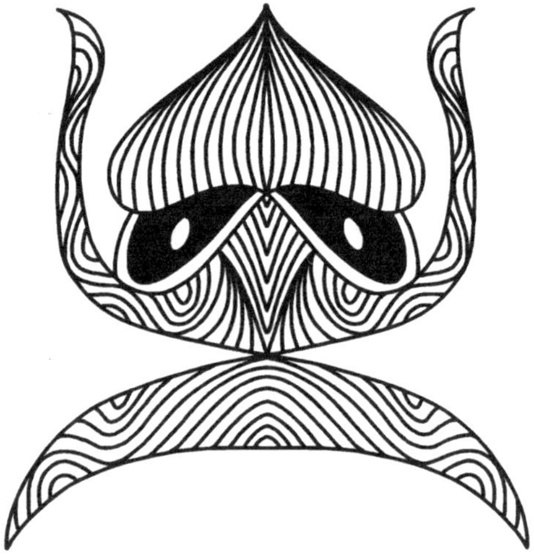

FATLINER WEIRDIES
VOLUME 3

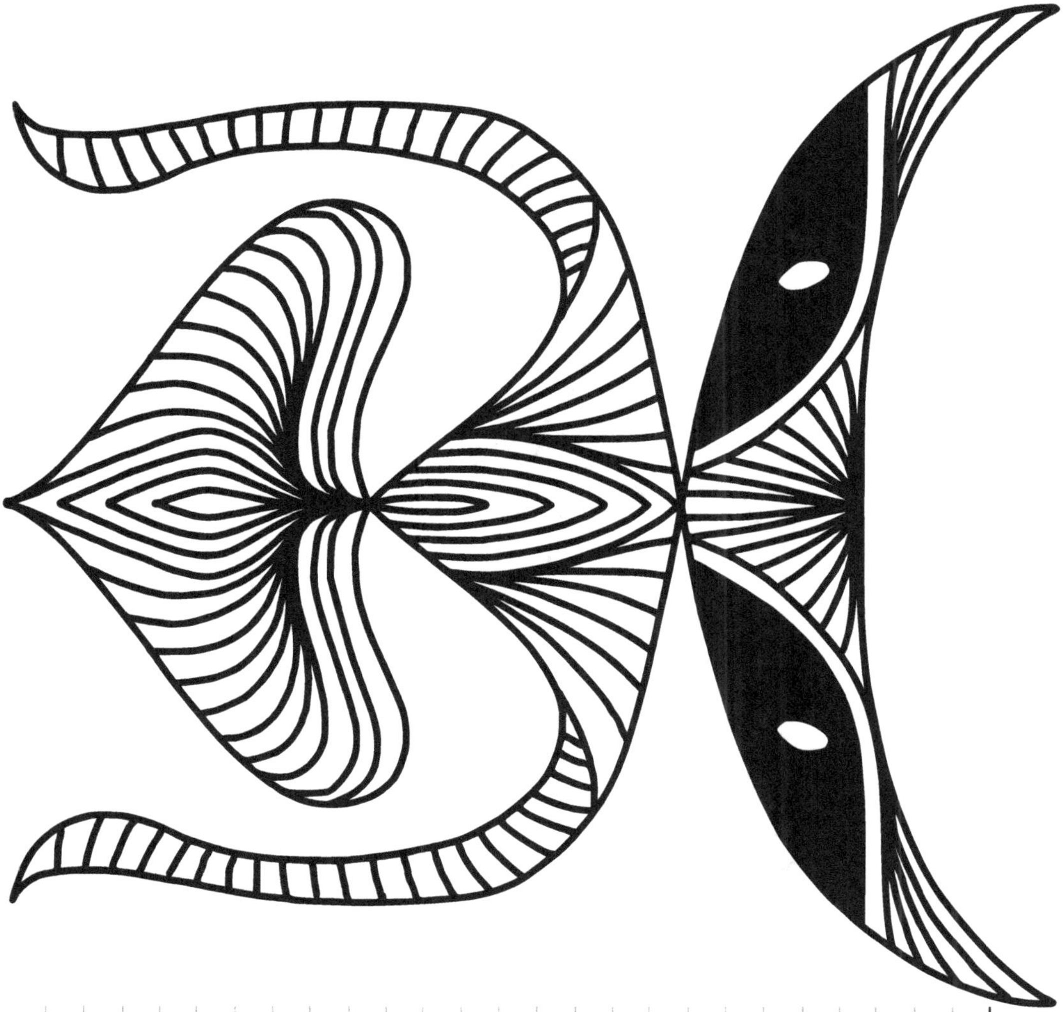

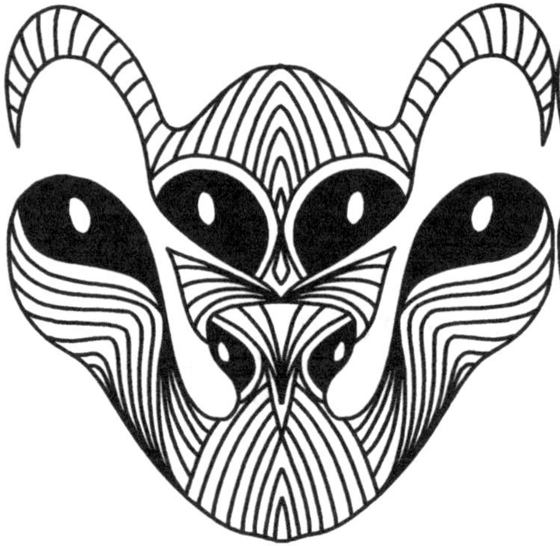

FATLINER WEIRDIES
VOLUME 1

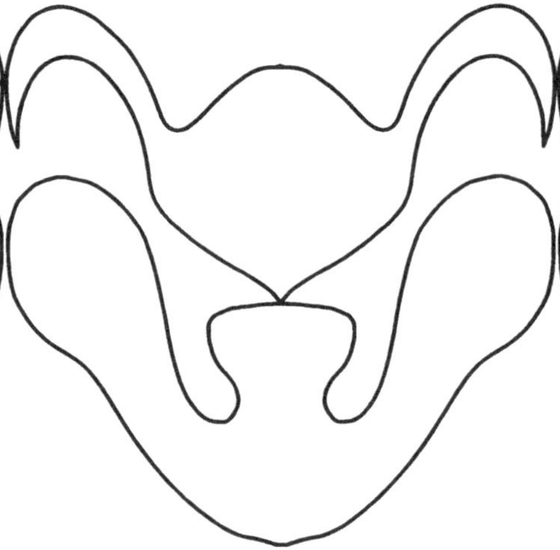

FATLINER WEIRDIES
THE TEMPLATES 1

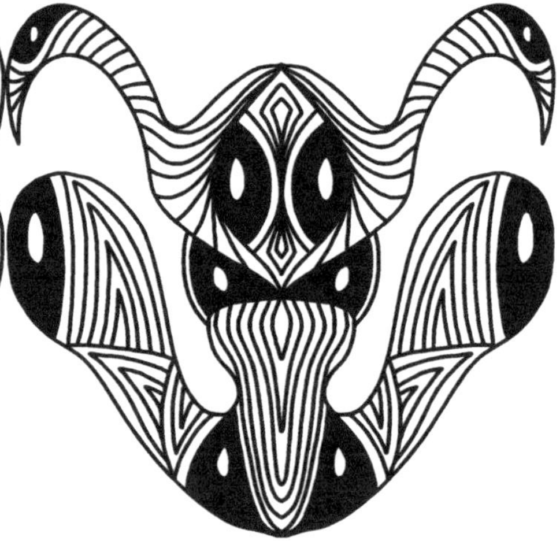

FATLINER WEIRDIES
VOLUME 3

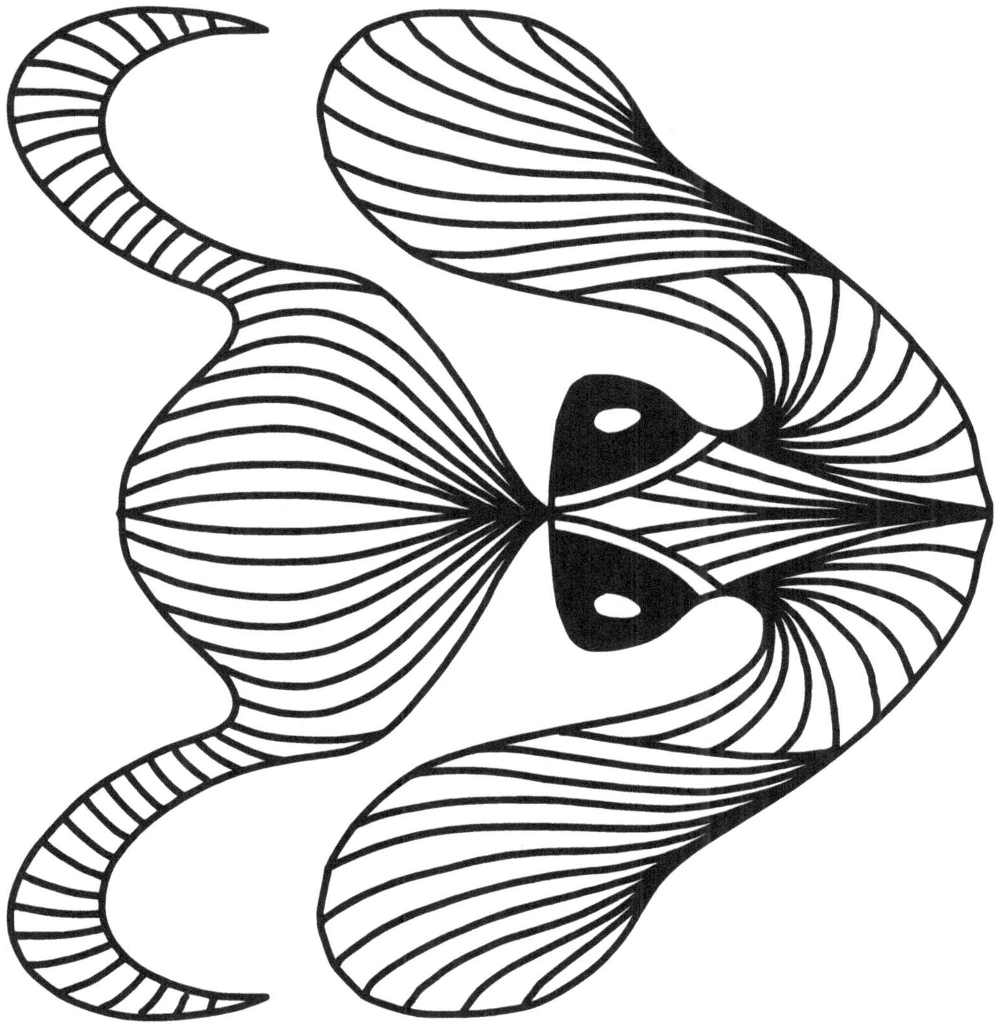

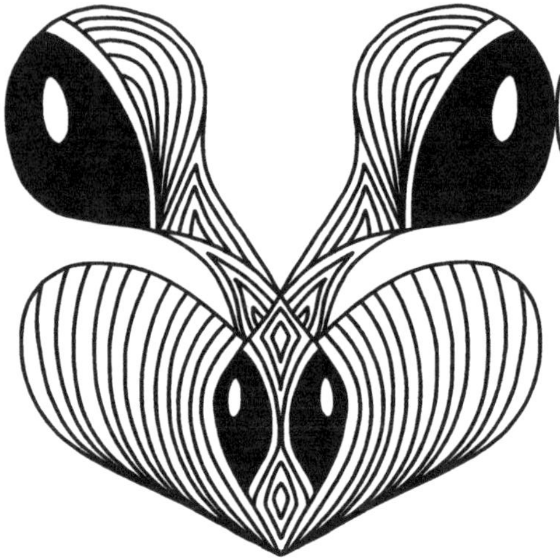

FATLINER WEIRDIES
VOLUME 1

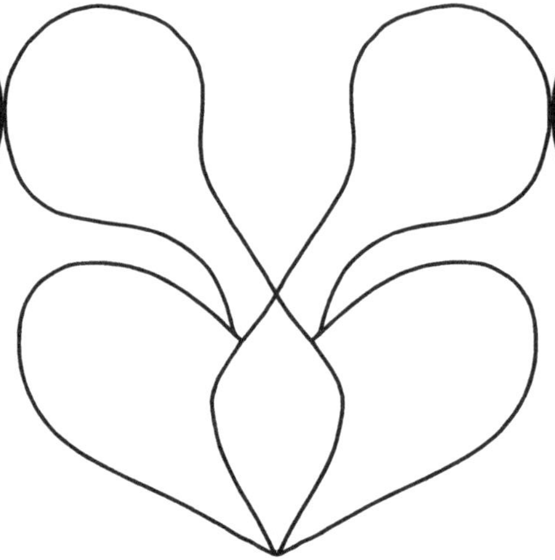

FATLINER WEIRDIES
THE TEMPLATES 1

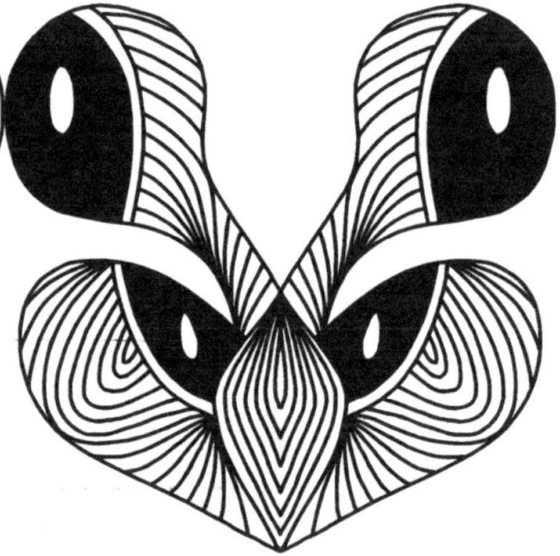

FATLINER WEIRDIES
VOLUME 3

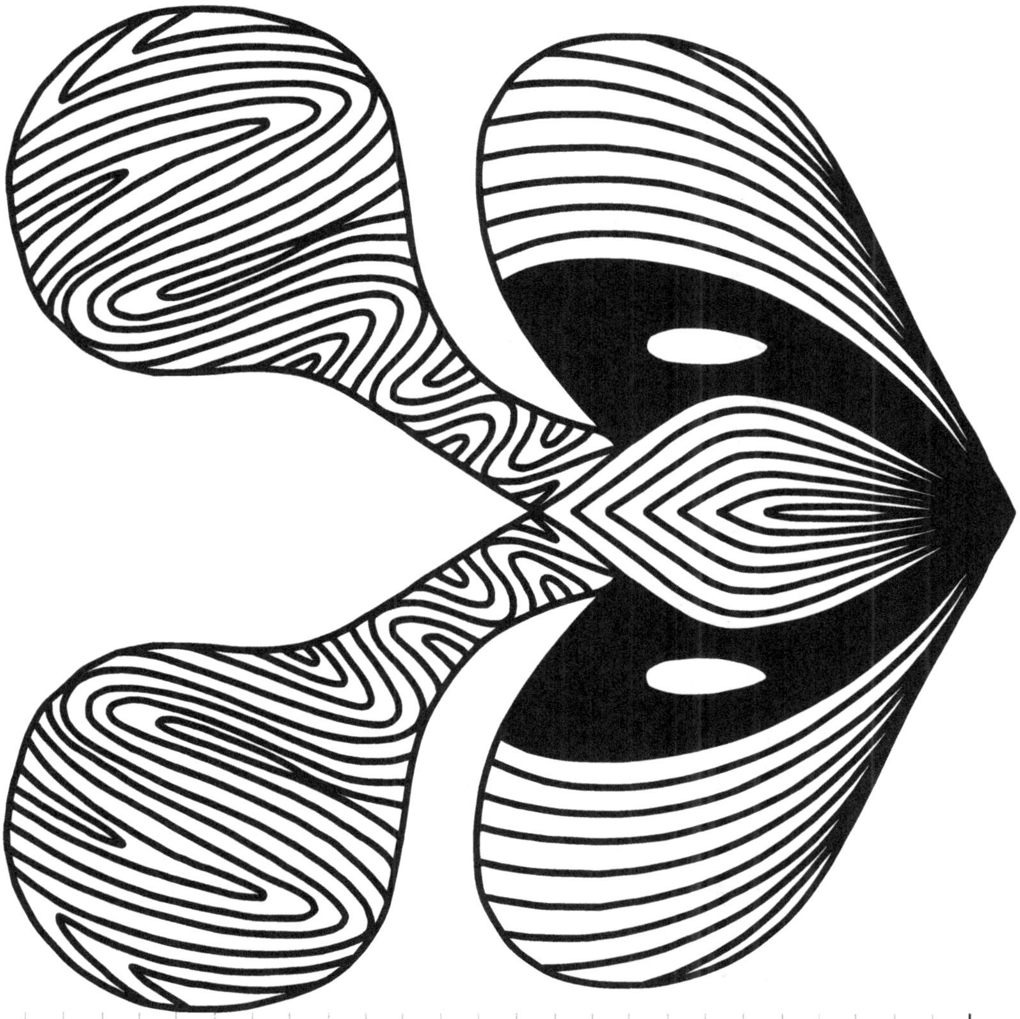

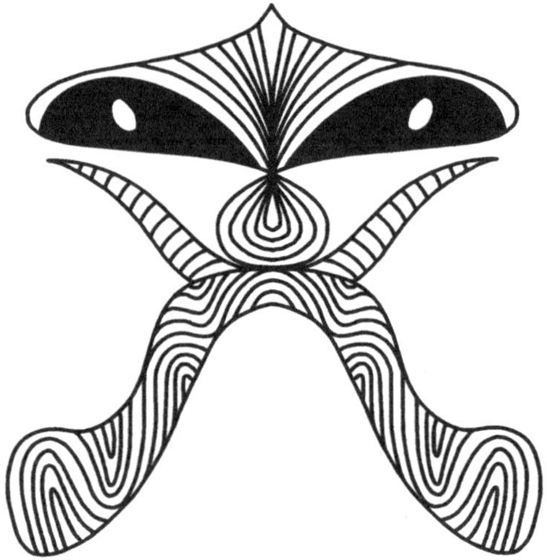

FATLINER WEIRDIES
VOLUME 1

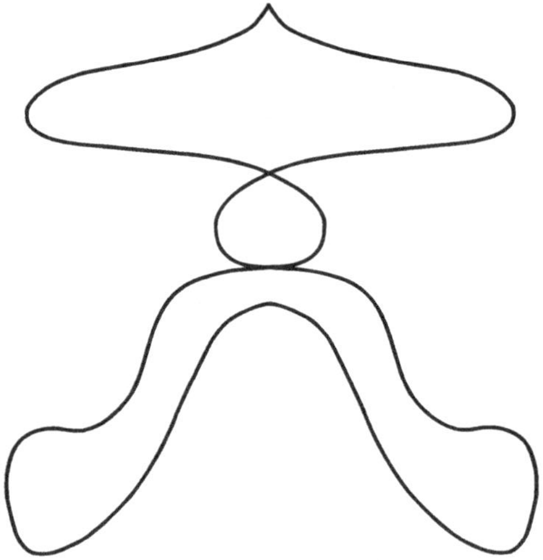

FATLINER WEIRDIES
THE TEMPLATES 1

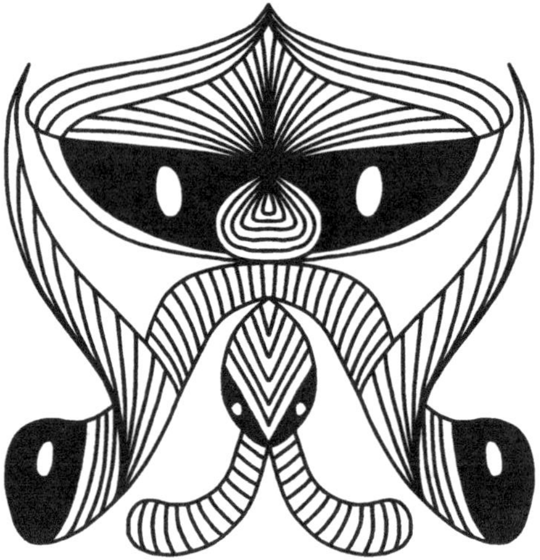

FATLINER WEIRDIES
VOLUME 3

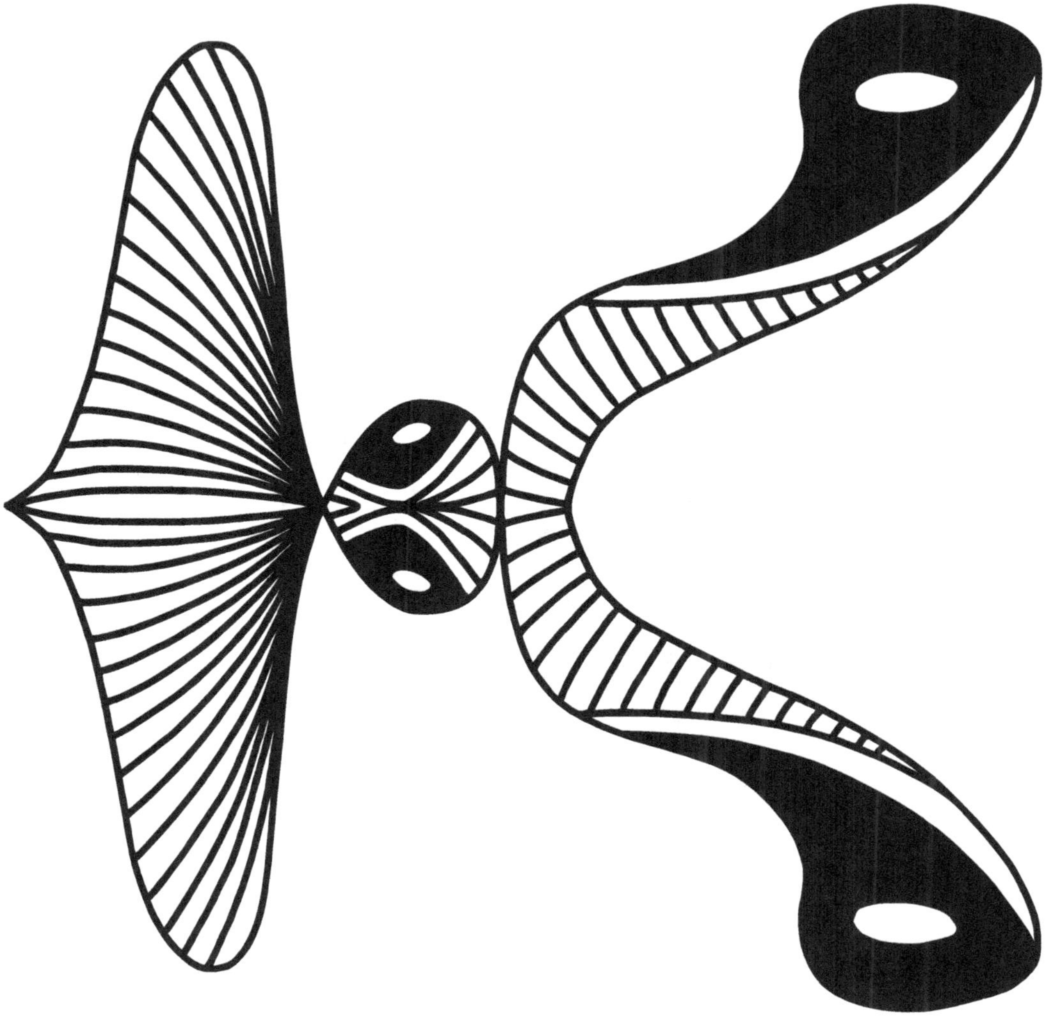

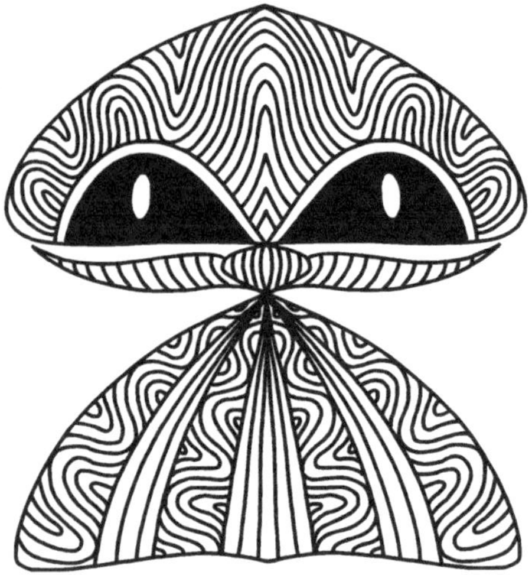

FATLINER WEIRDIES
VOLUME 1

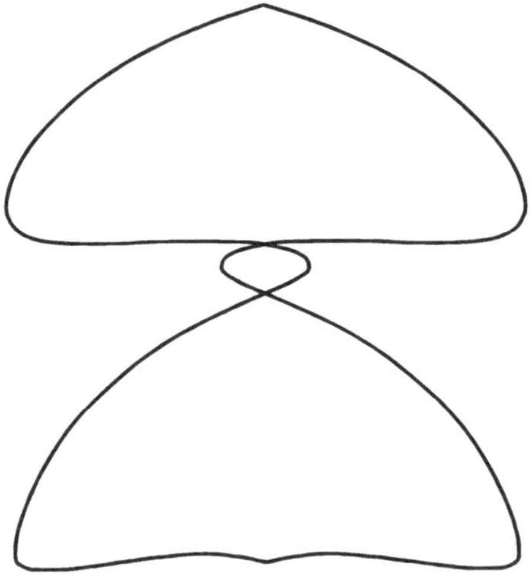

FATLINER WEIRDIES
THE TEMPLATES 1

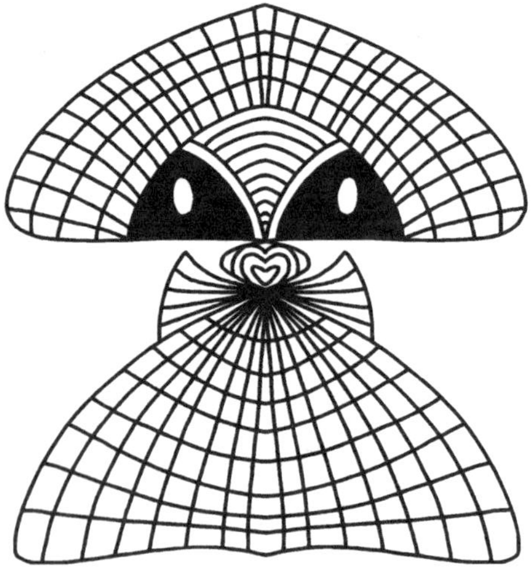

FATLINER WEIRDIES
VOLUME 3

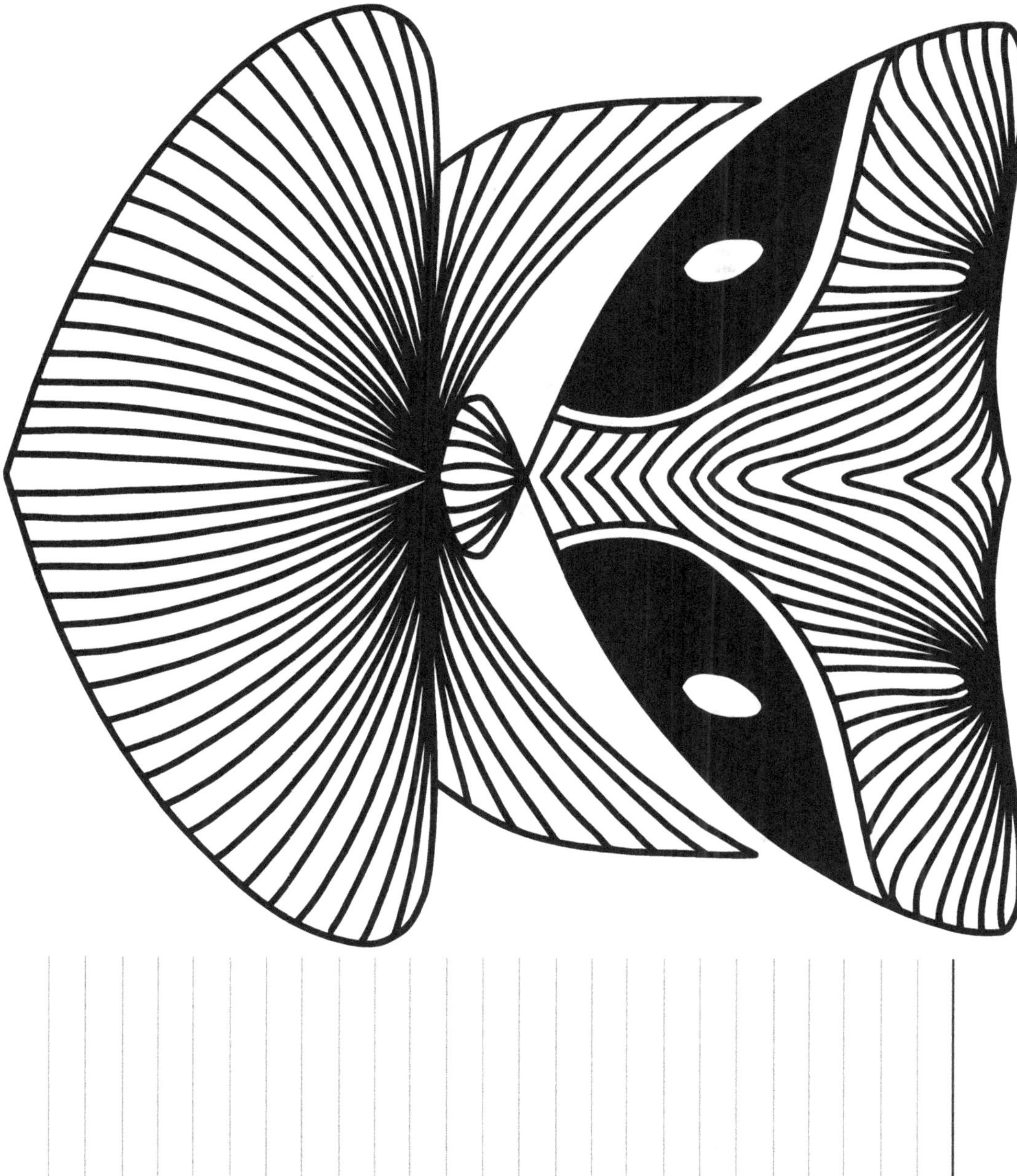

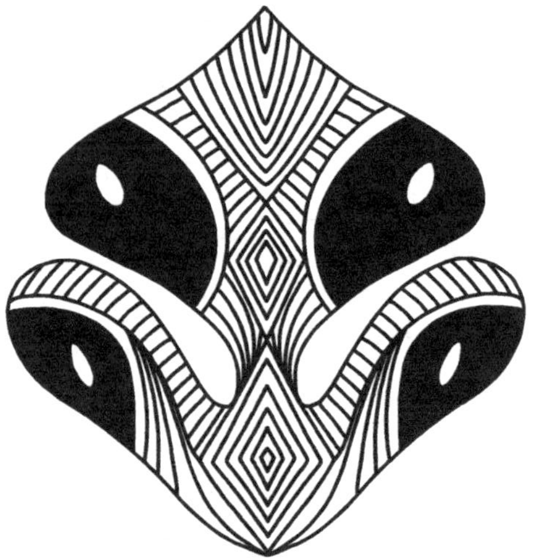

FATLINER WEIRDIES
VOLUME 1

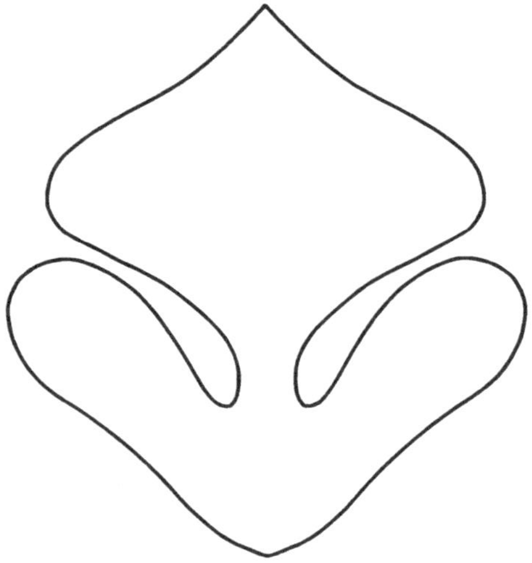

FATLINER WEIRDIES
THE TEMPLATES 1

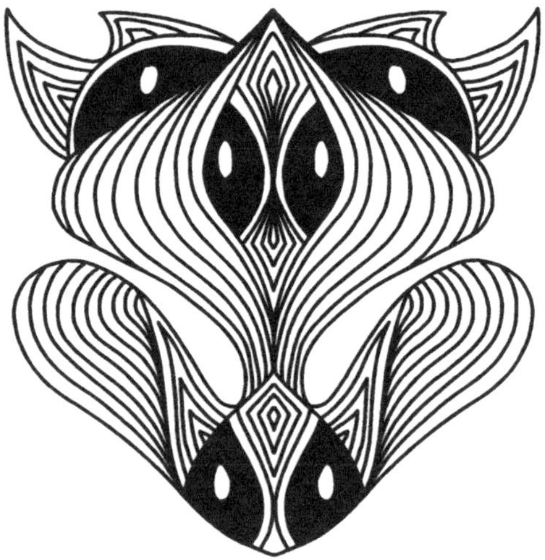

FATLINER WEIRDIES
VOLUME 3

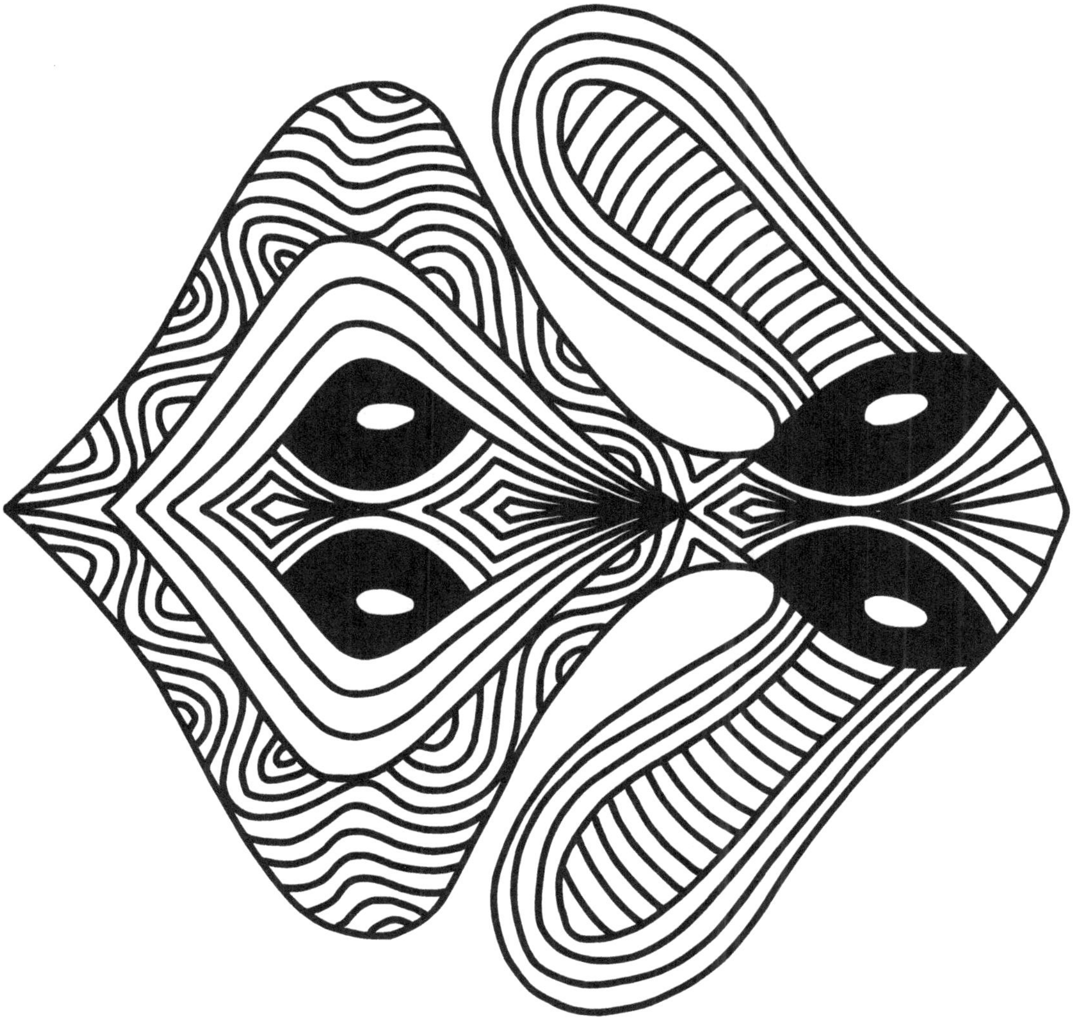

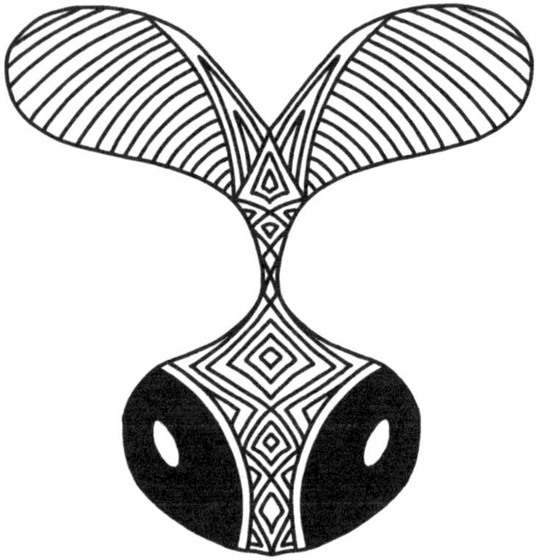

FATLINER WEIRDIES
VOLUME 1

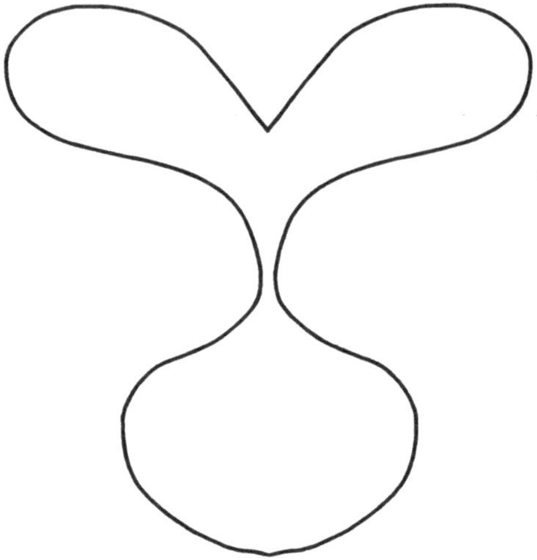

FATLINER WEIRDIES
THE TEMPLATES 1

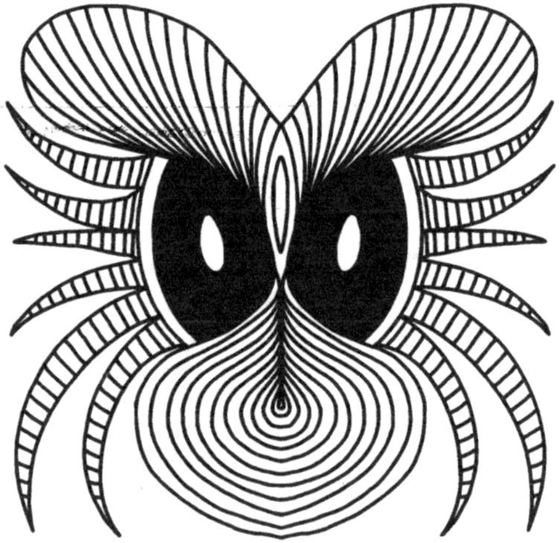

FATLINER WEIRDIES
VOLUME 3

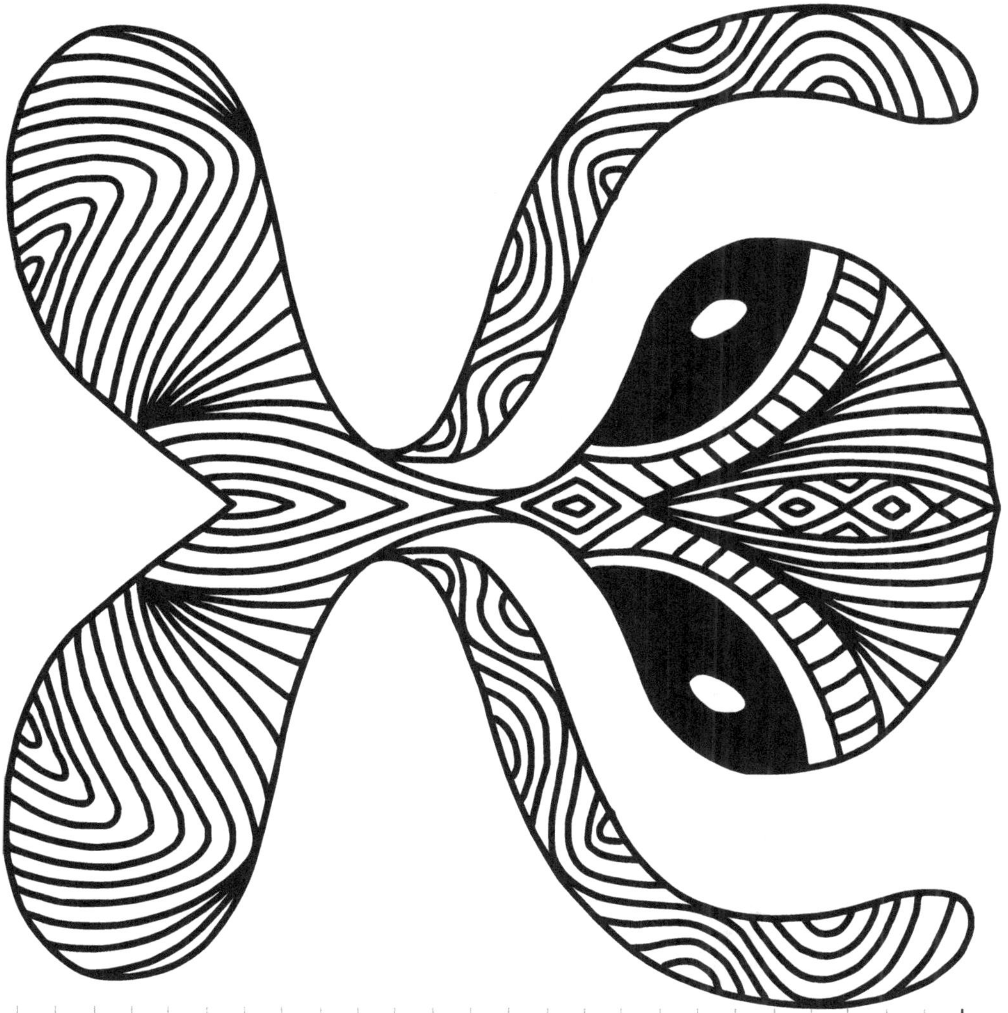

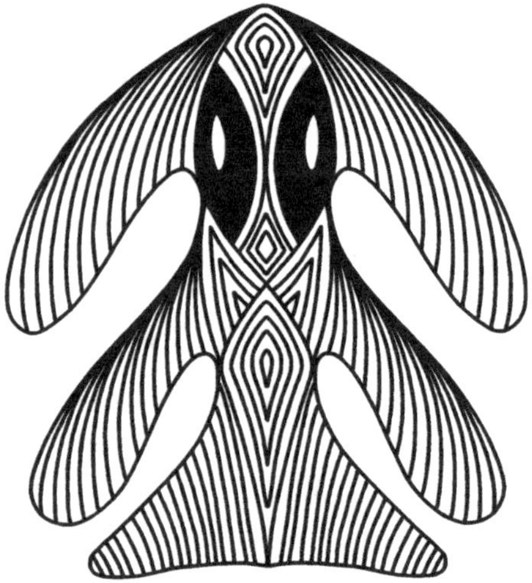

FATLINER WEIRDIES
VOLUME 1

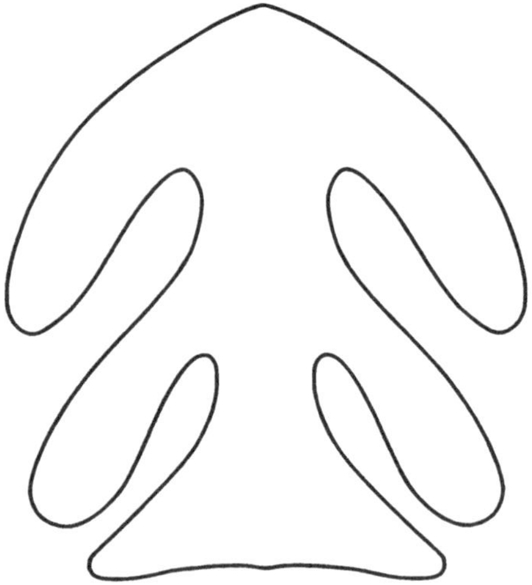

FATLINER WEIRDIES
THE TEMPLATES 1

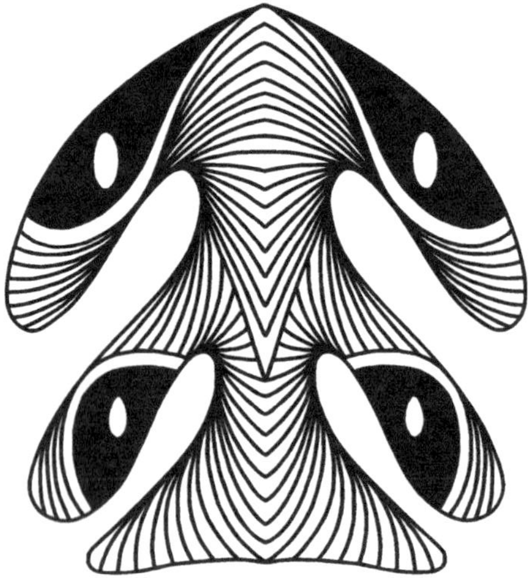

FATLINER WEIRDIES
VOLUME 3

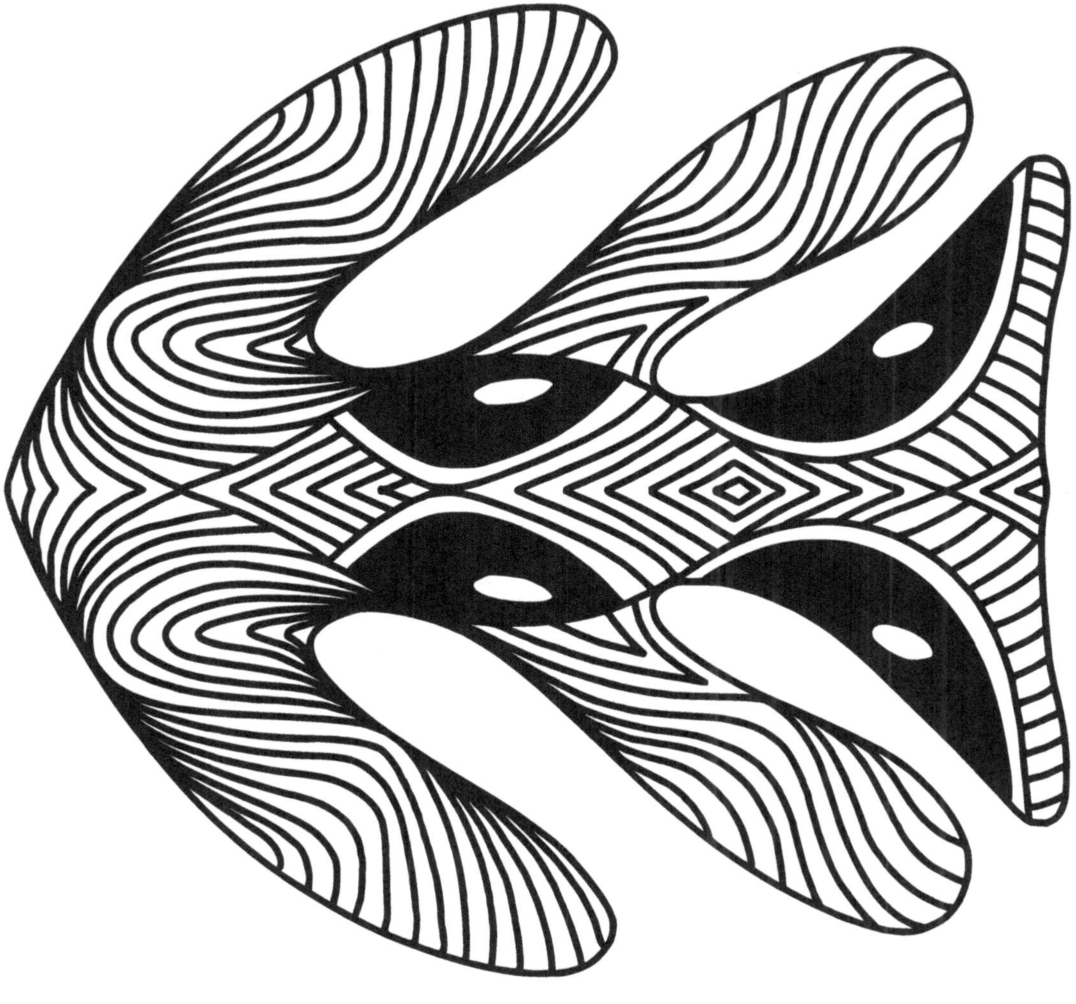

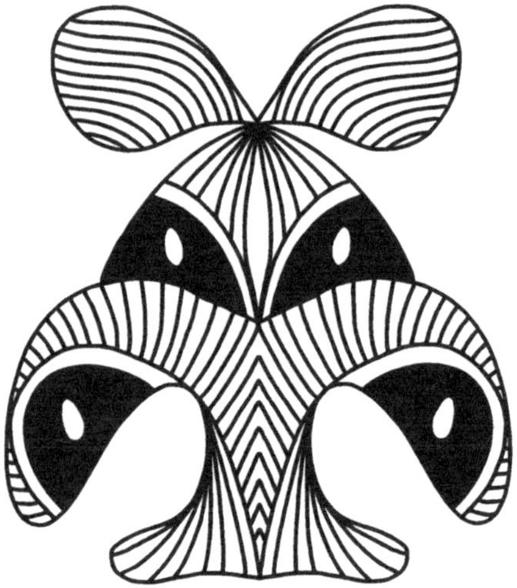

FATLINER WEIRDIES
VOLUME 1

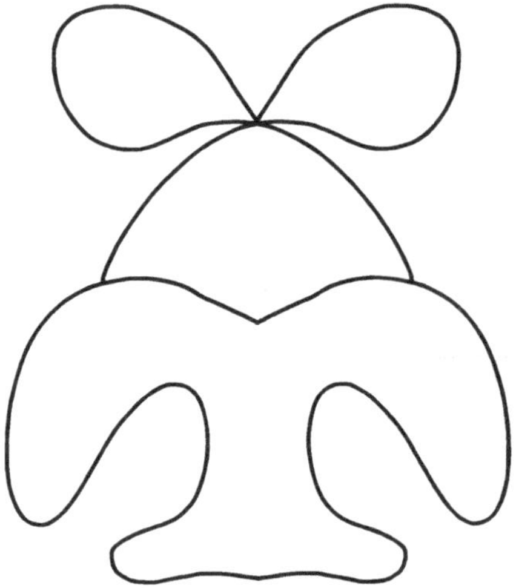

FATLINER WEIRDIES
THE TEMPLATES 1

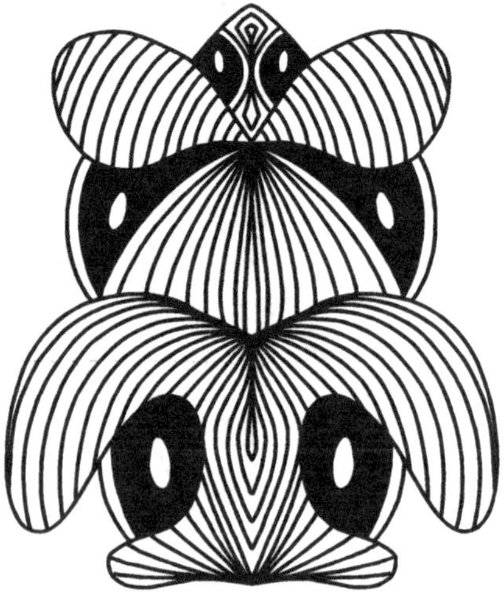

FATLINER WEIRDIES
VOLUME 3

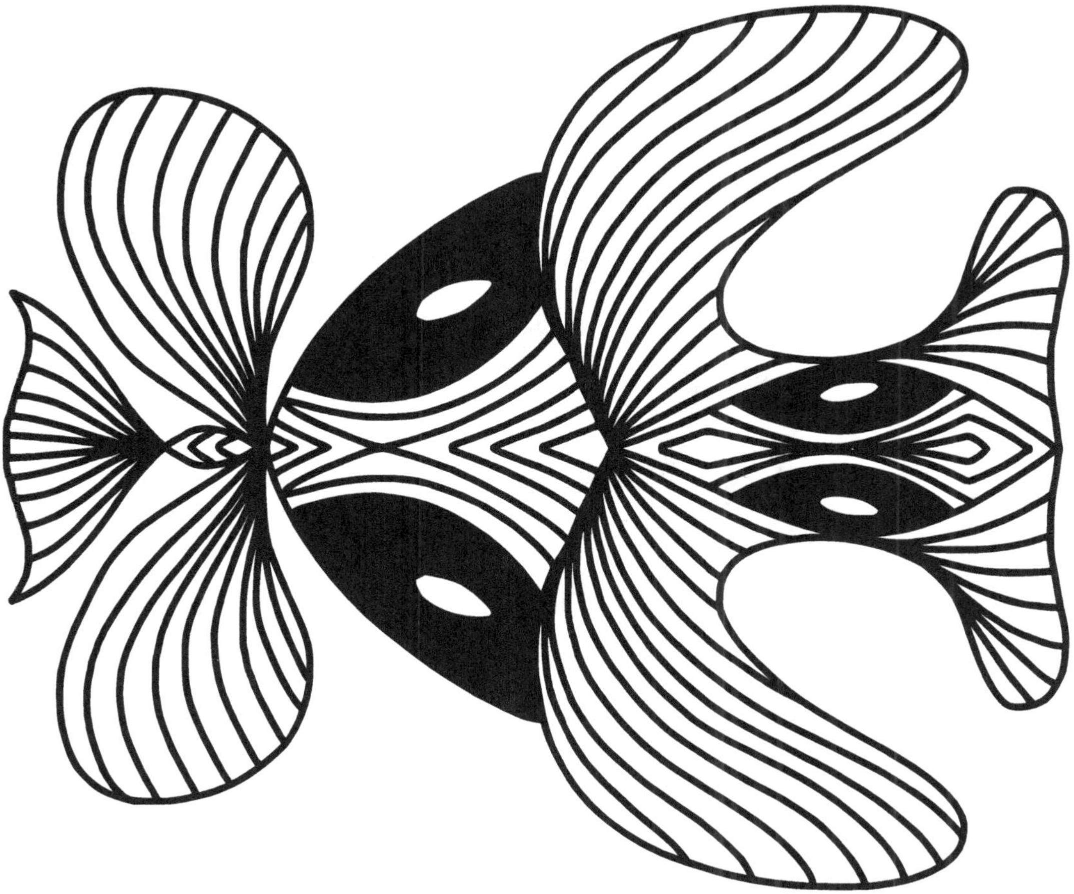

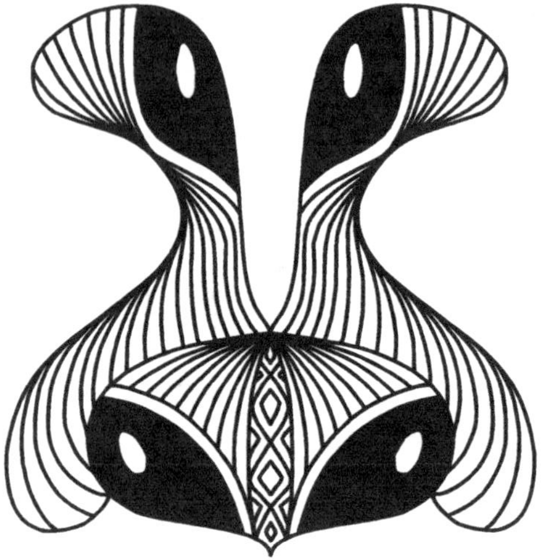

FATLINER WEIRDIES
VOLUME 1

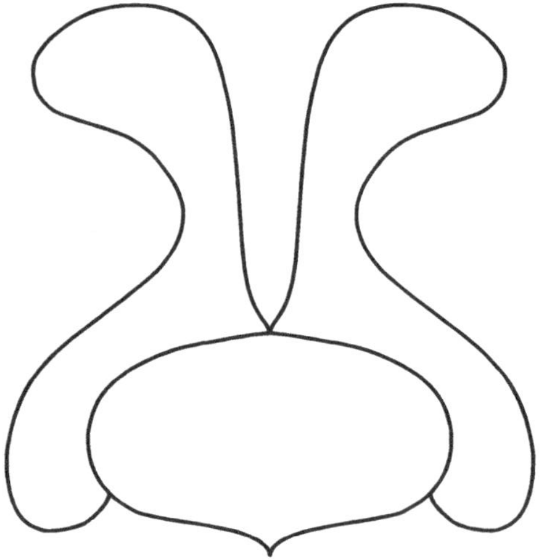

FATLINER WEIRDIES
THE TEMPLATES 1

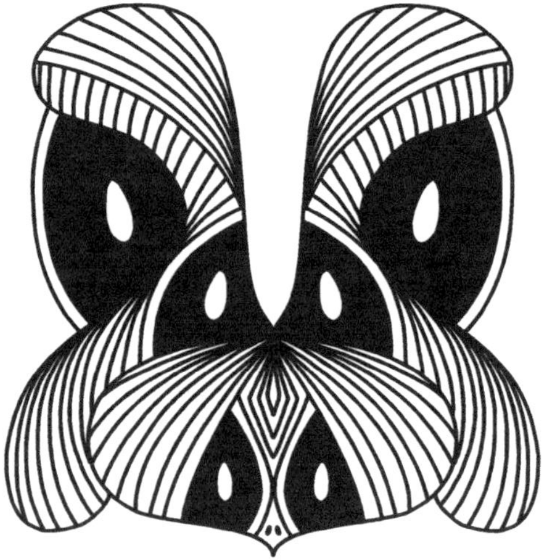

FATLINER WEIRDIES
VOLUME 3

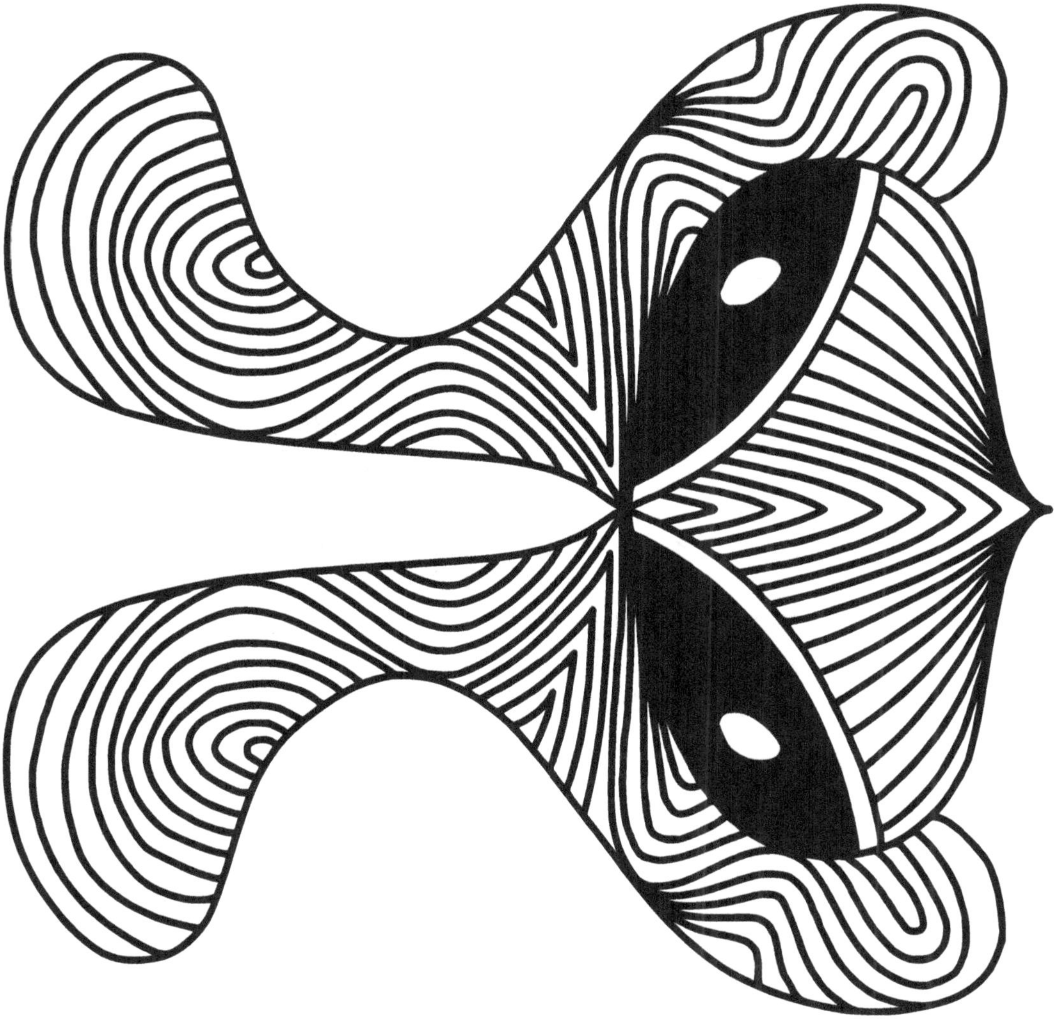

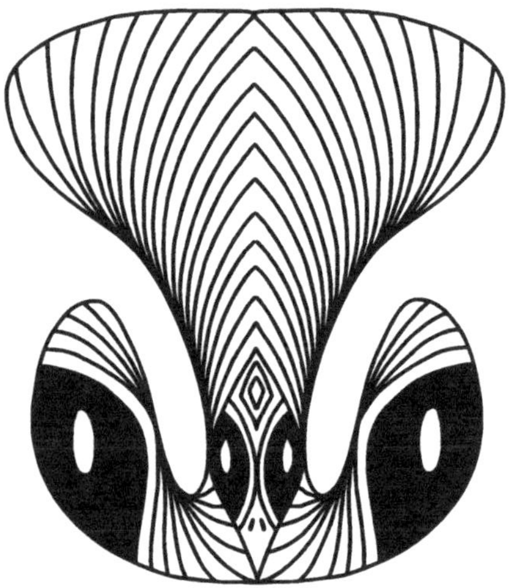

FATLINER WEIRDIES
VOLUME 1

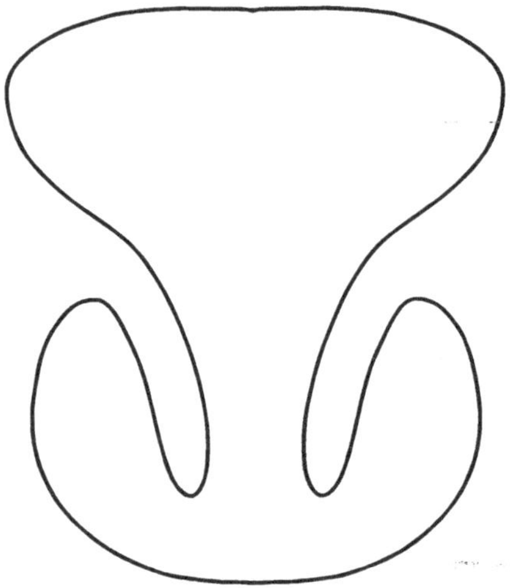

FATLINER WEIRDIES
THE TEMPLATES 1

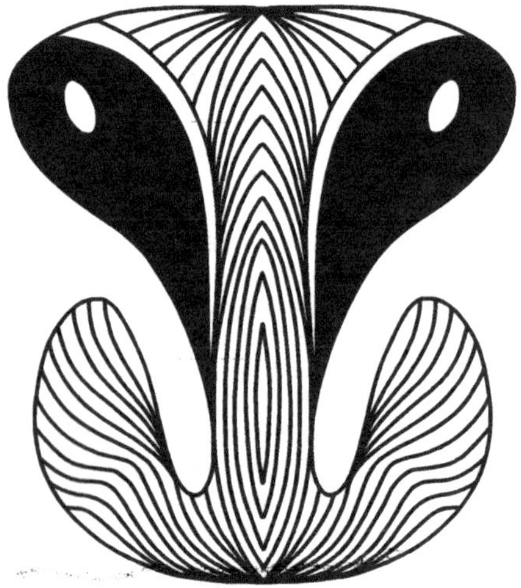

FATLINER WEIRDIES
VOLUME 3

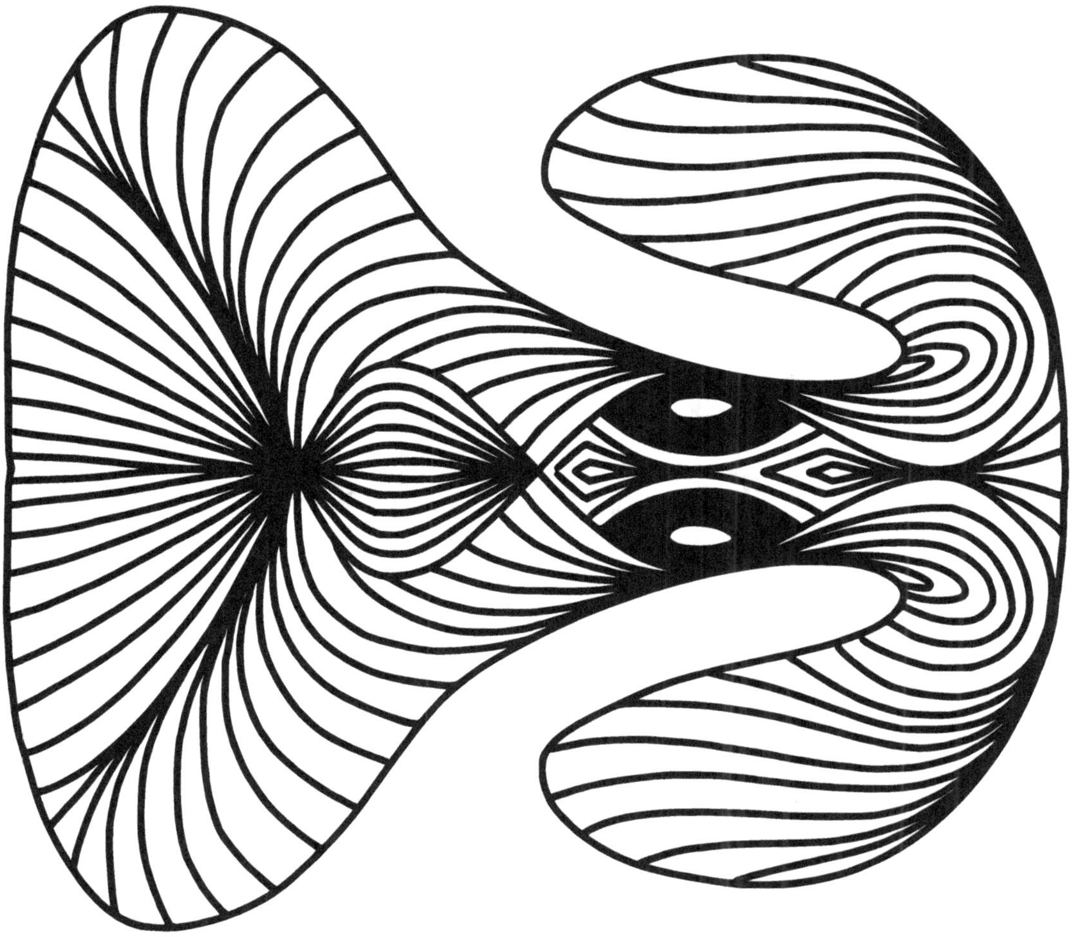

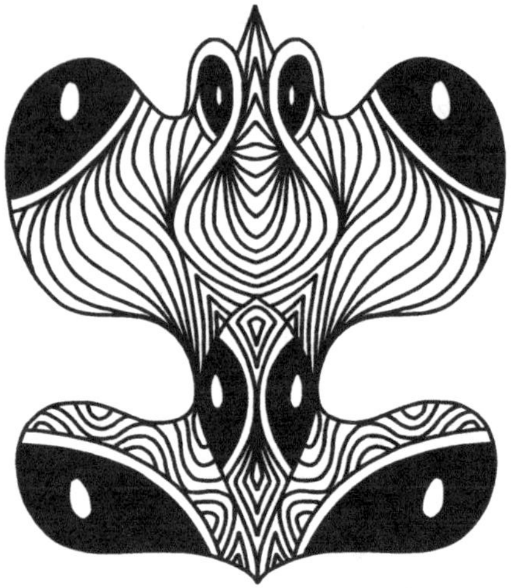

FATLINER WEIRDIES
VOLUME 1

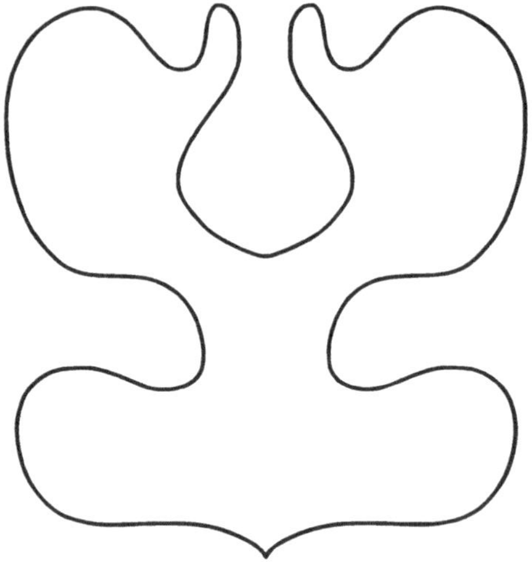

FATLINER WEIRDIES
THE TEMPLATES 1

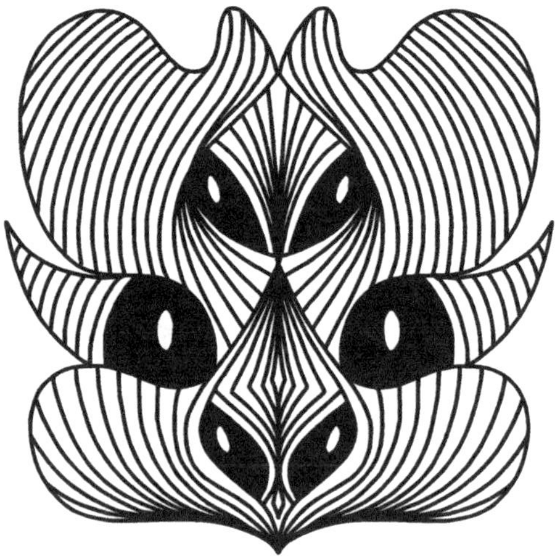

FATLINER WEIRDIES
VOLUME 3

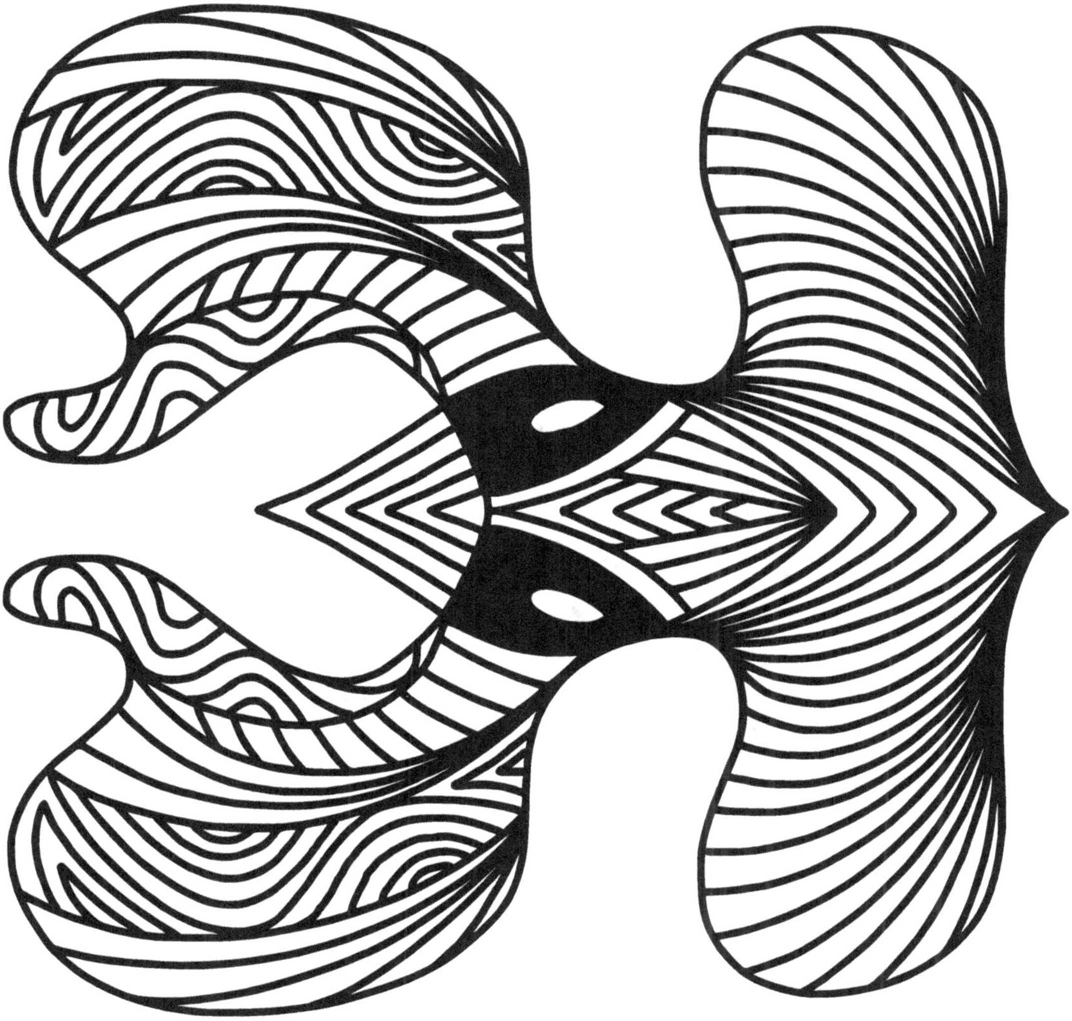

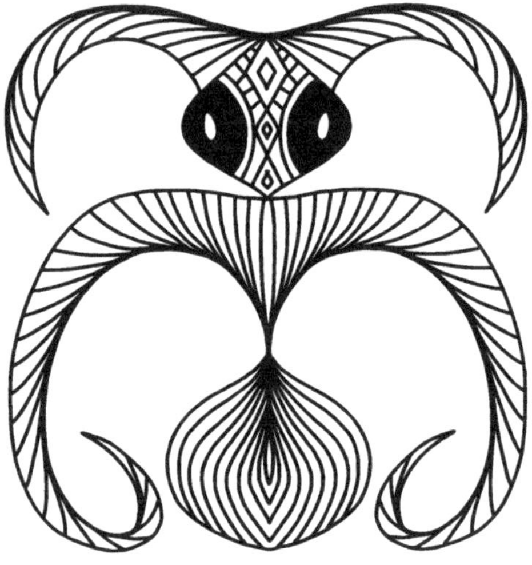

FATLINER WEIRDIES
VOLUME 1

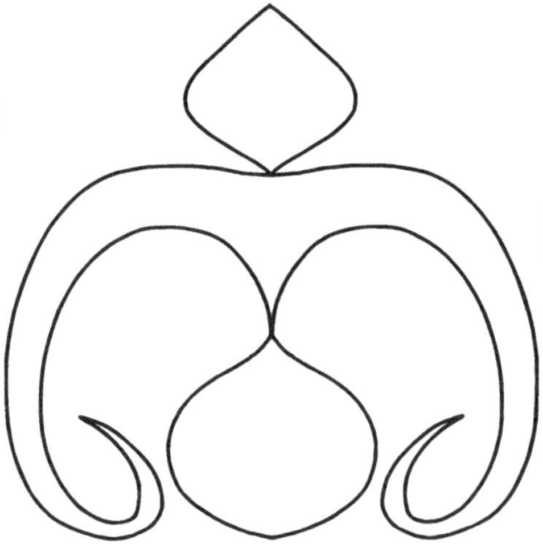

FATLINER WEIRDIES
THE TEMPLATES 1

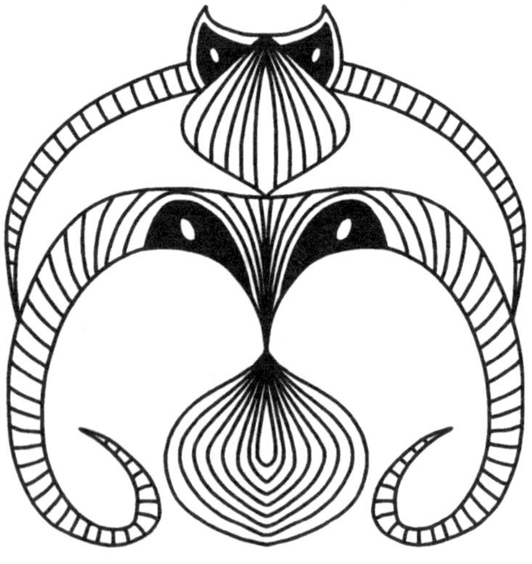

FATLINER WEIRDIES
VOLUME 3

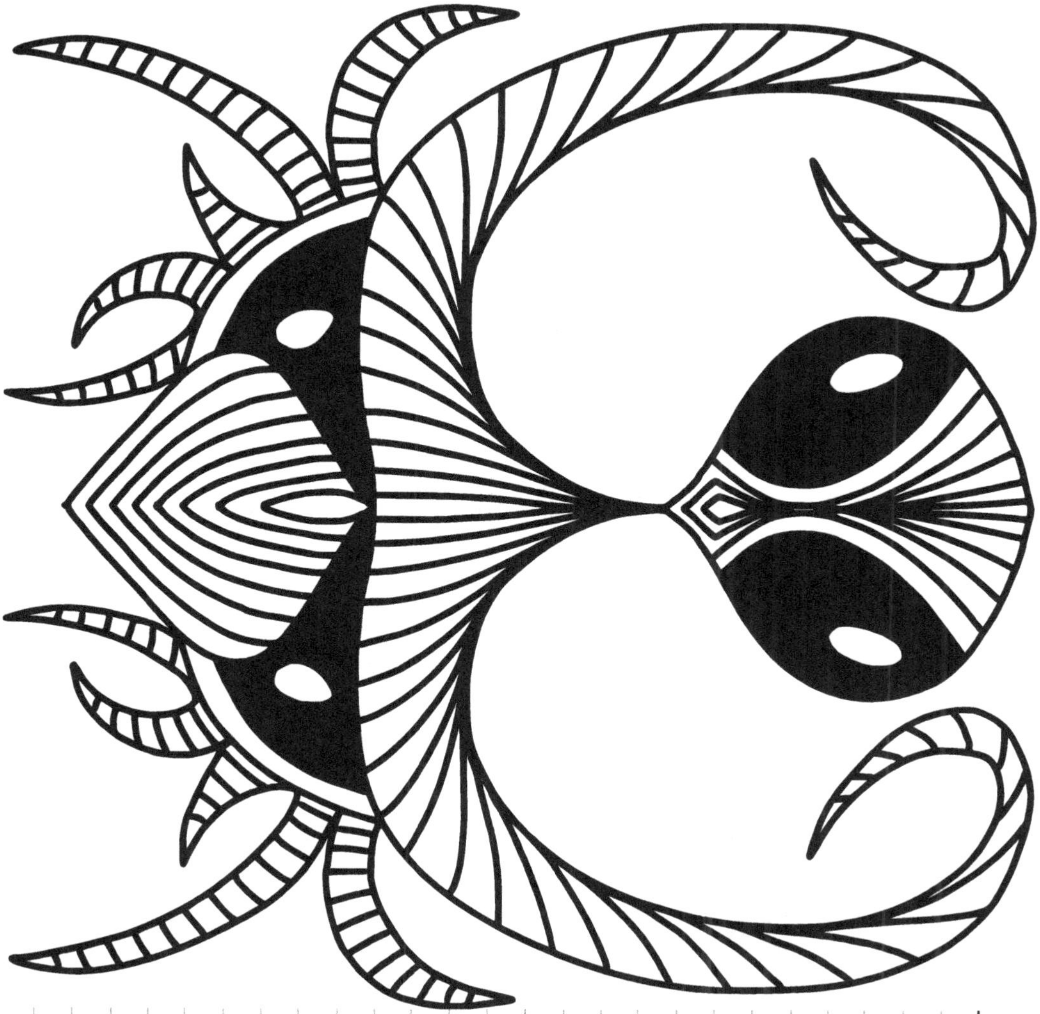

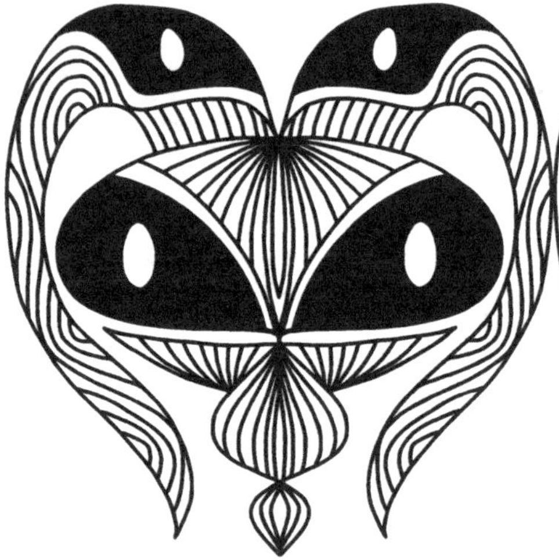
FATLINER WEIRDIES
VOLUME 1

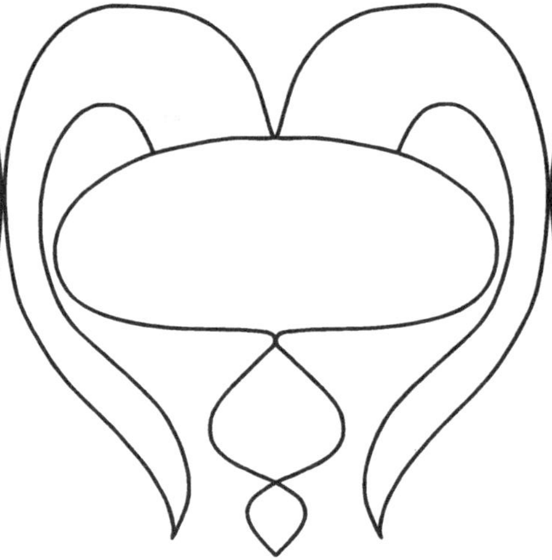
FATLINER WEIRDIES
THE TEMPLATES 1

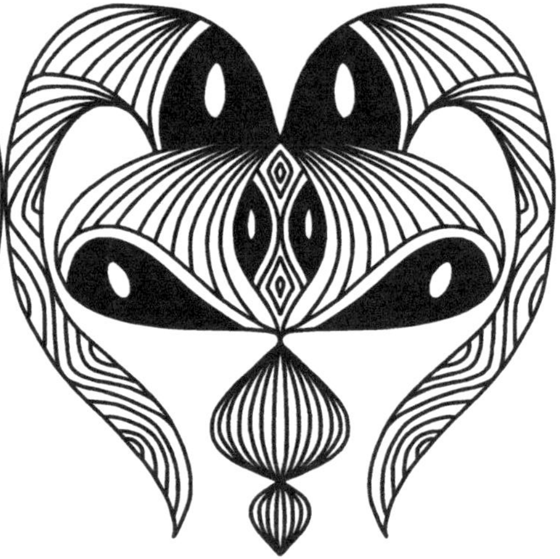
FATLINER WEIRDIES
VOLUME 3

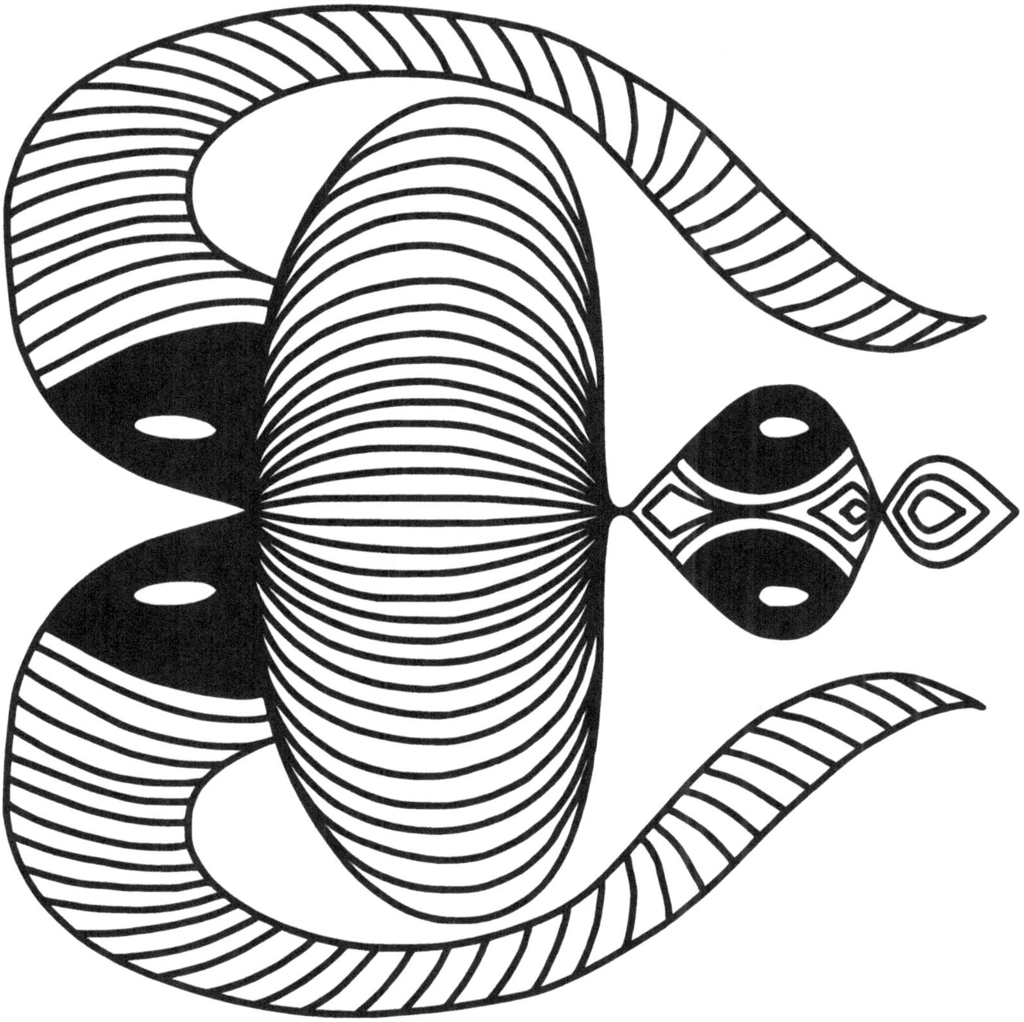

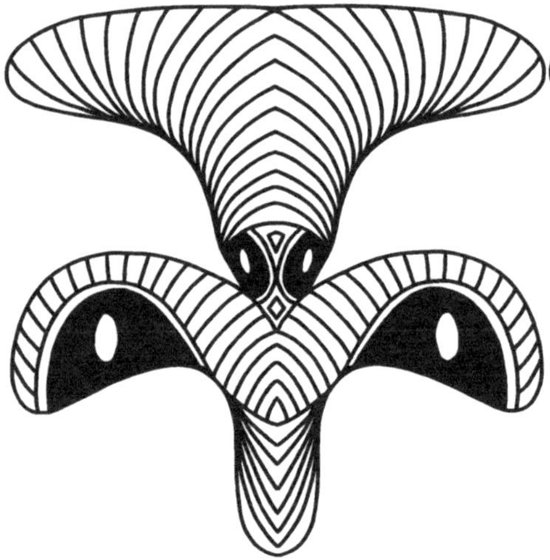

FATLINER WEIRDIES
VOLUME 1

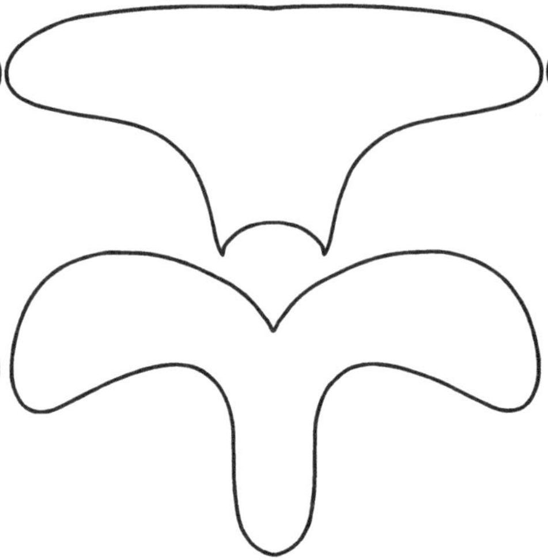

FATLINER WEIRDIES
THE TEMPLATES 1

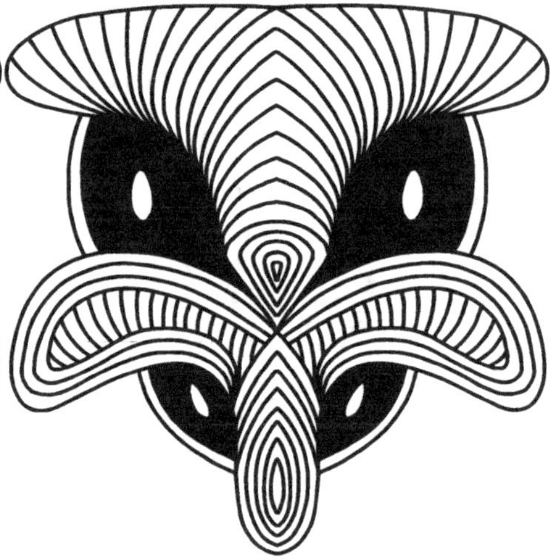

FATLINER WEIRDIES
VOLUME 3

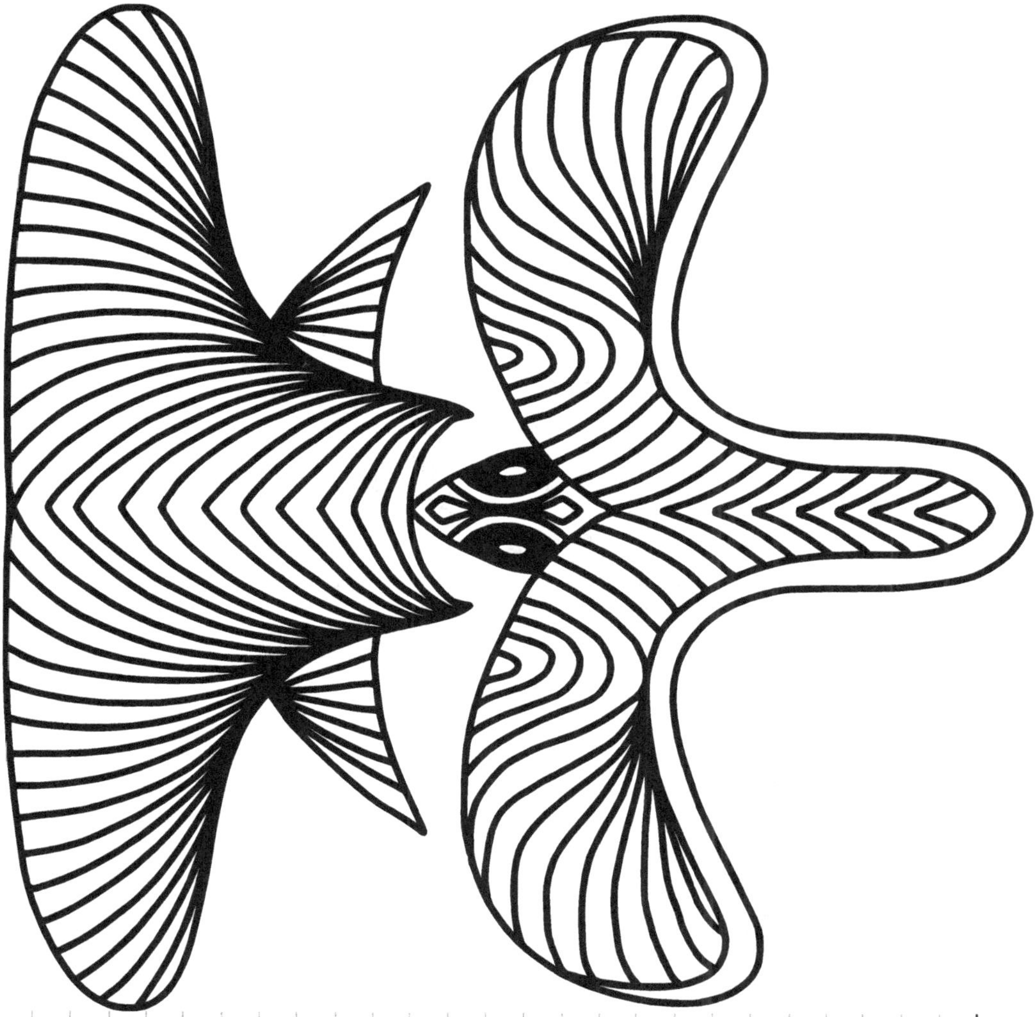

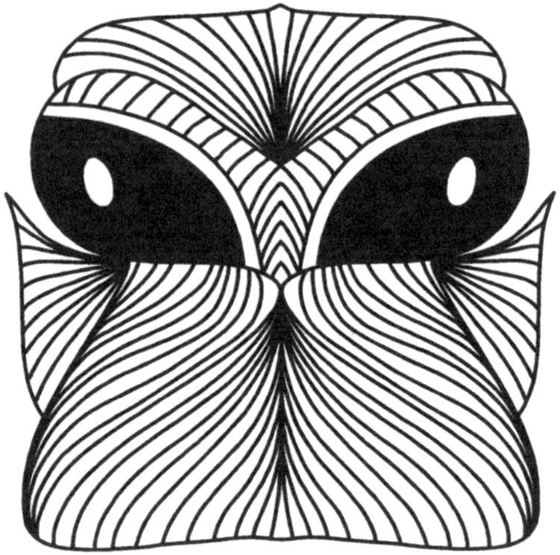

FATLINER WEIRDIES
VOLUME 1

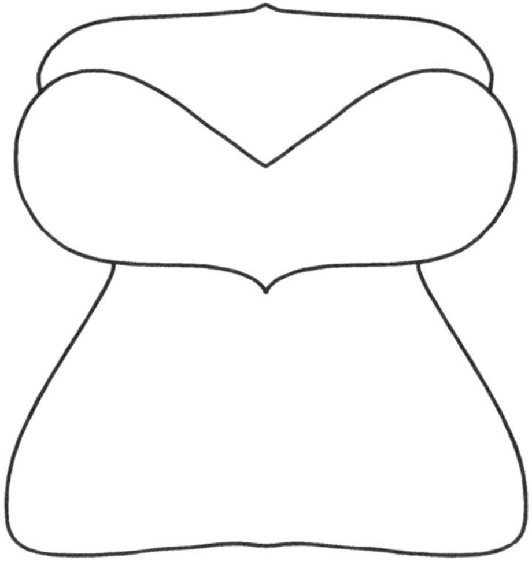

FATLINER WEIRDIES
THE TEMPLATES 1

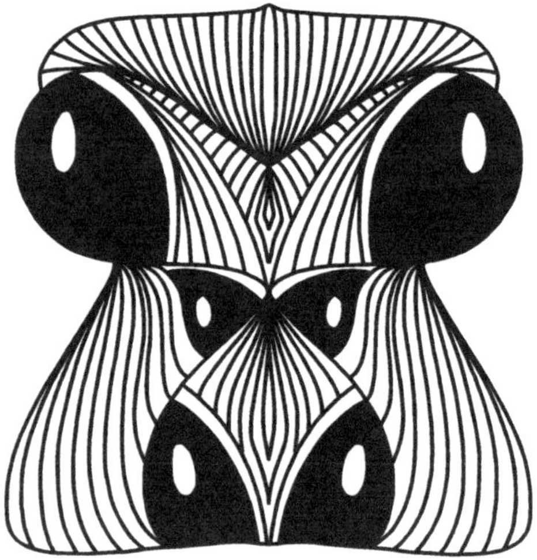

FATLINER WEIRDIES
VOLUME 3

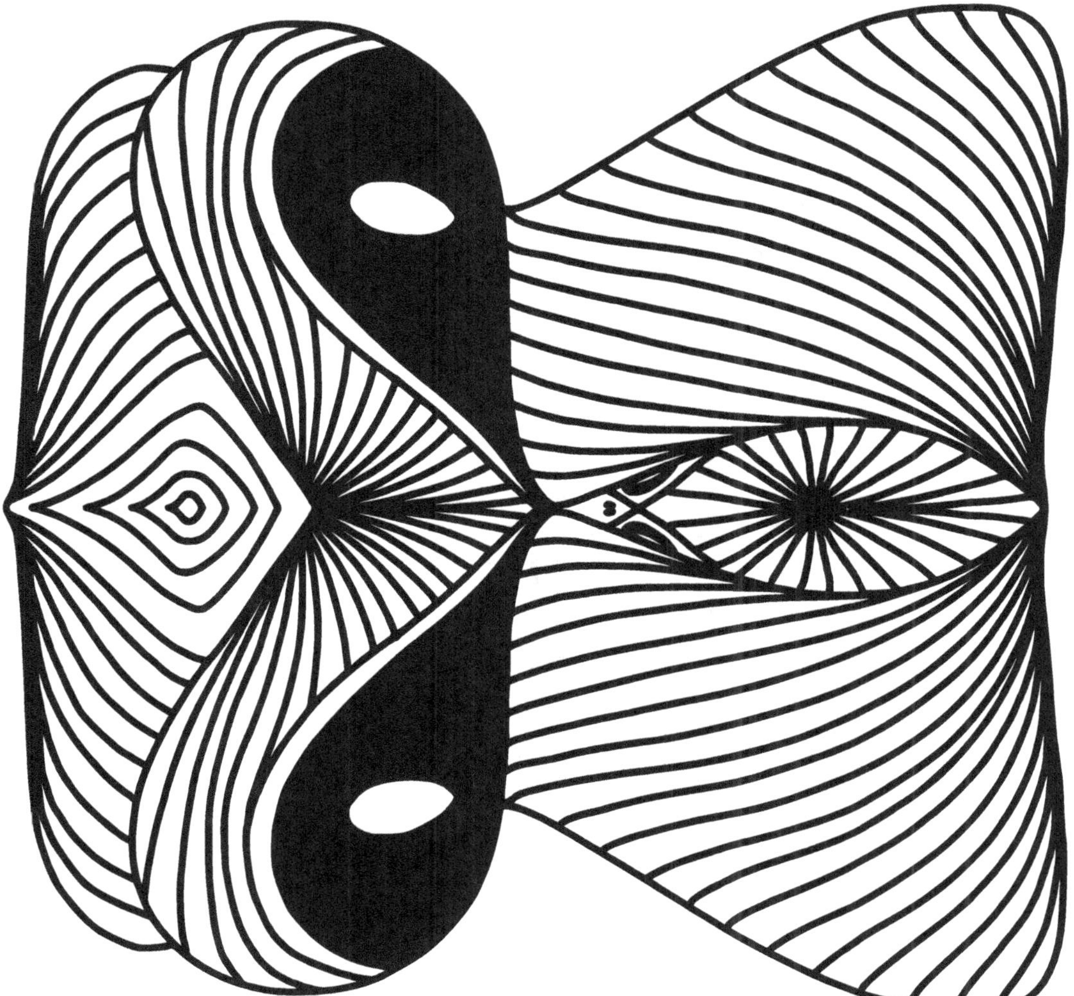

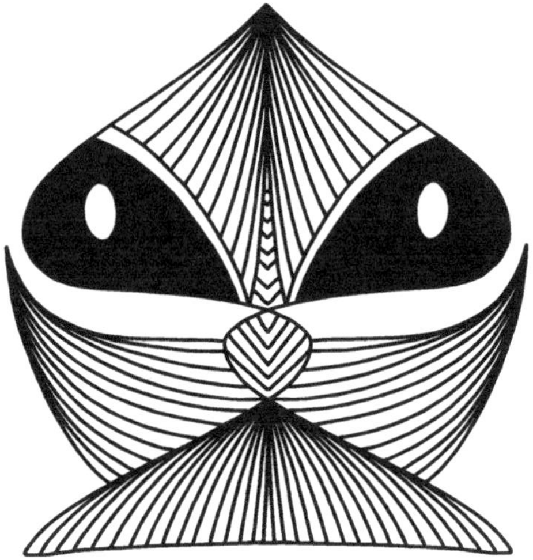

FATLINER WEIRDIES
VOLUME 1

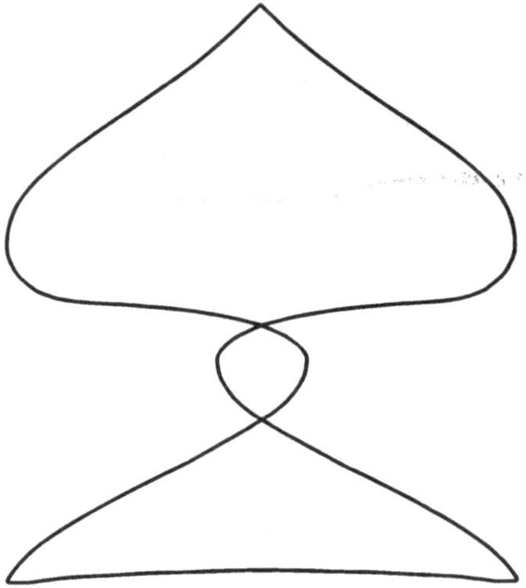

FATLINER WEIRDIES
THE TEMPLATES 1

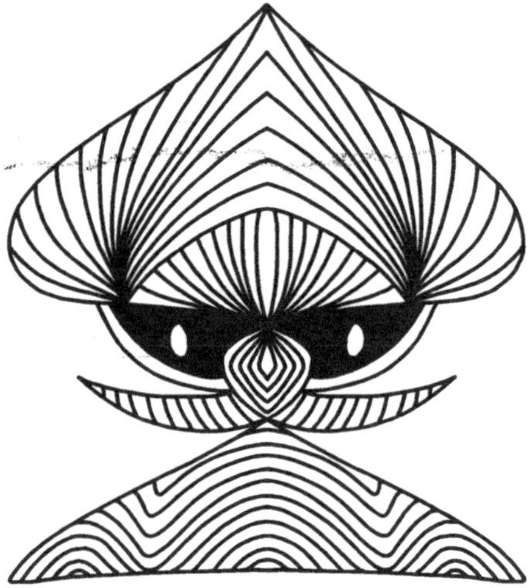

FATLINER WEIRDIES
VOLUME 3

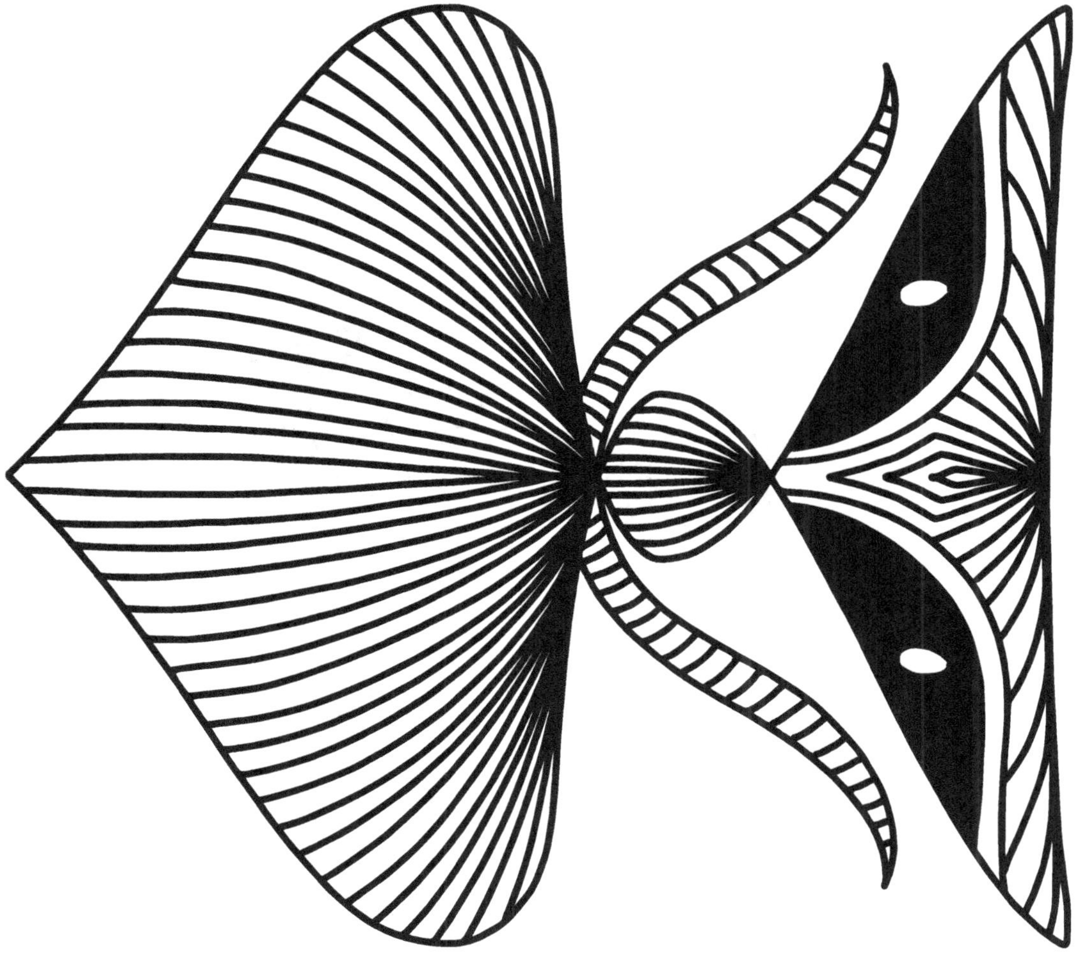

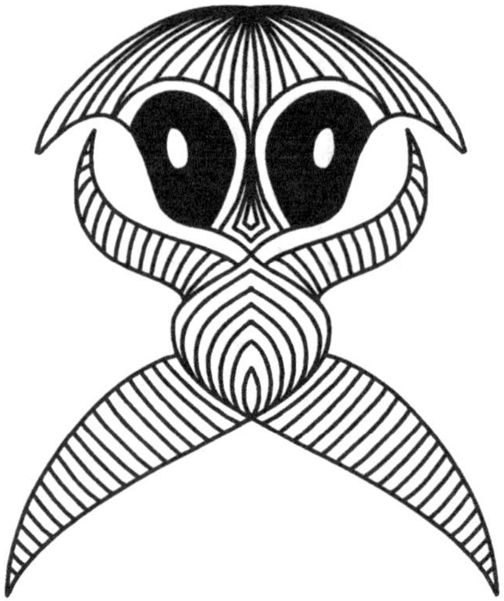

FATLINER WEIRDIES
VOLUME 1

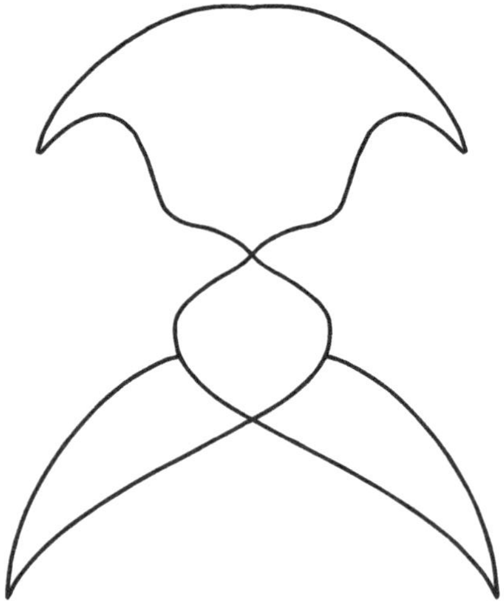

FATLINER WEIRDIES
THE TEMPLATES 1

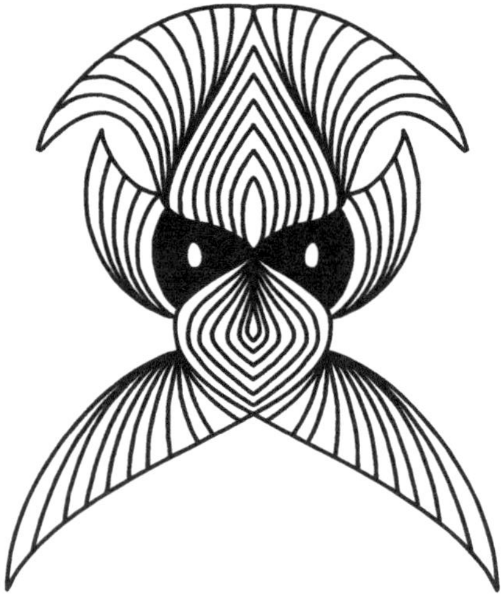

FATLINER WEIRDIES
VOLUME 3

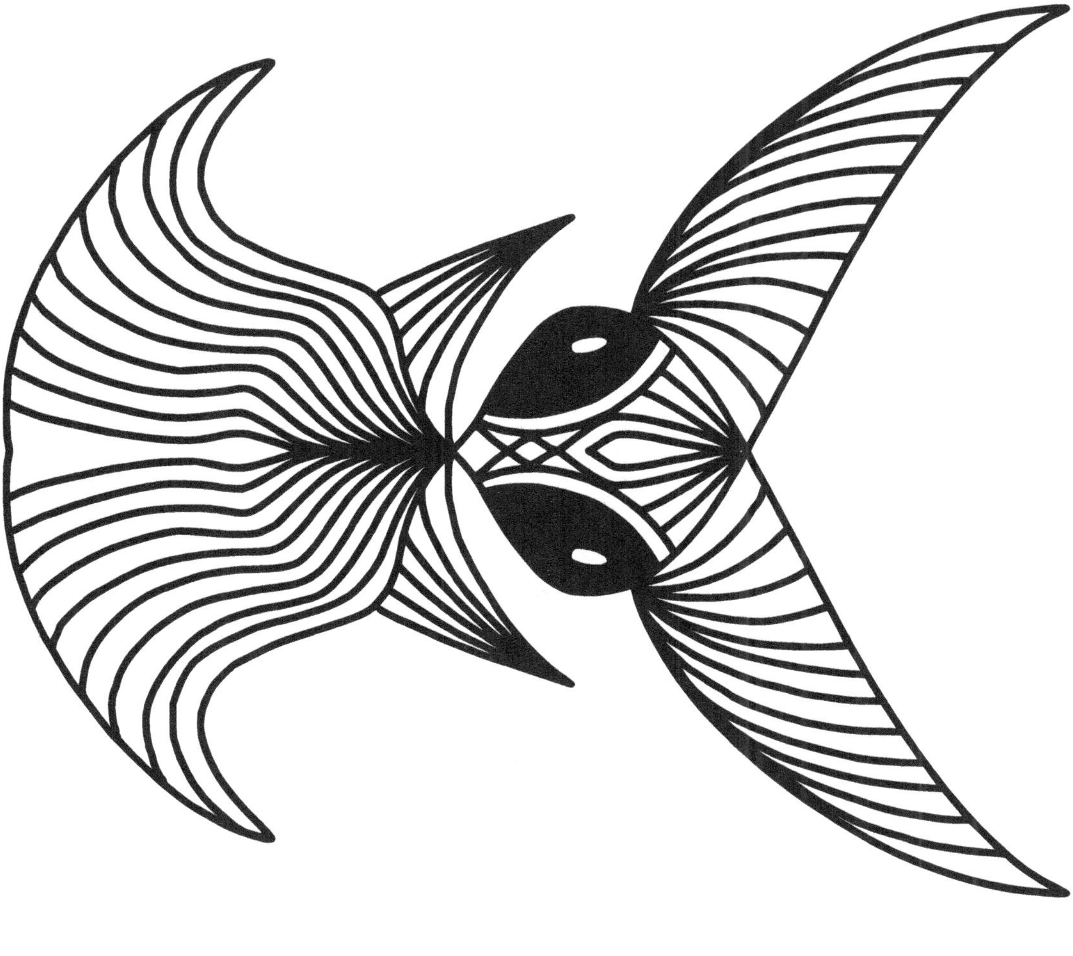

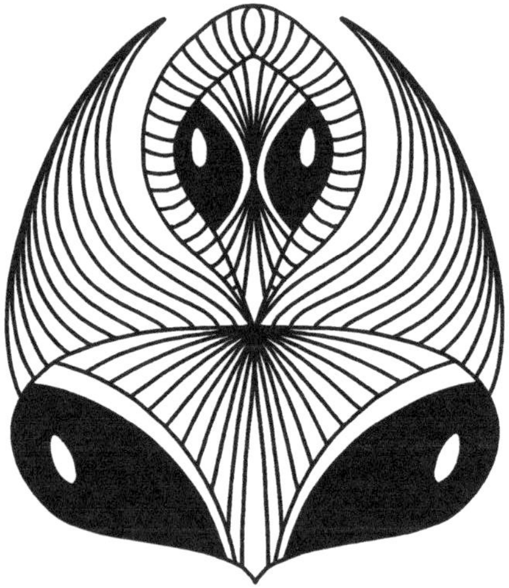

FATLINER WEIRDIES
VOLUME 1

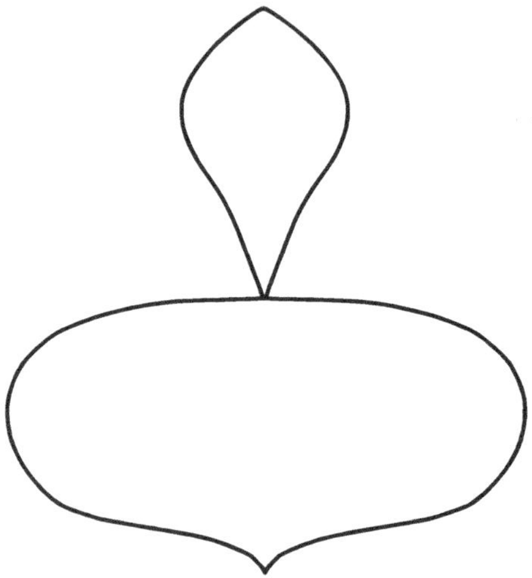

FATLINER WEIRDIES
THE TEMPLATES 1

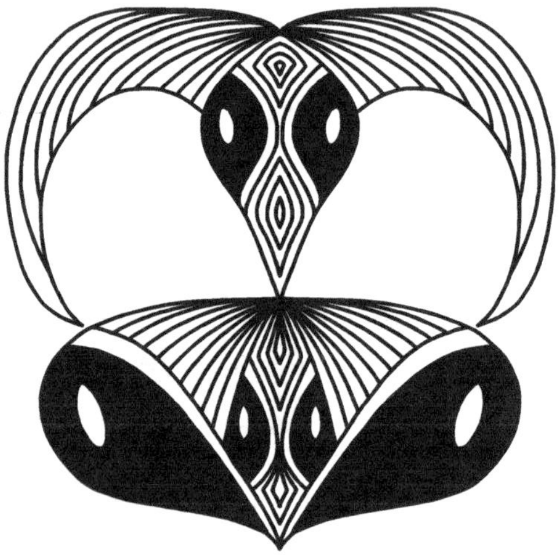

FATLINER WEIRDIES
VOLUME 3

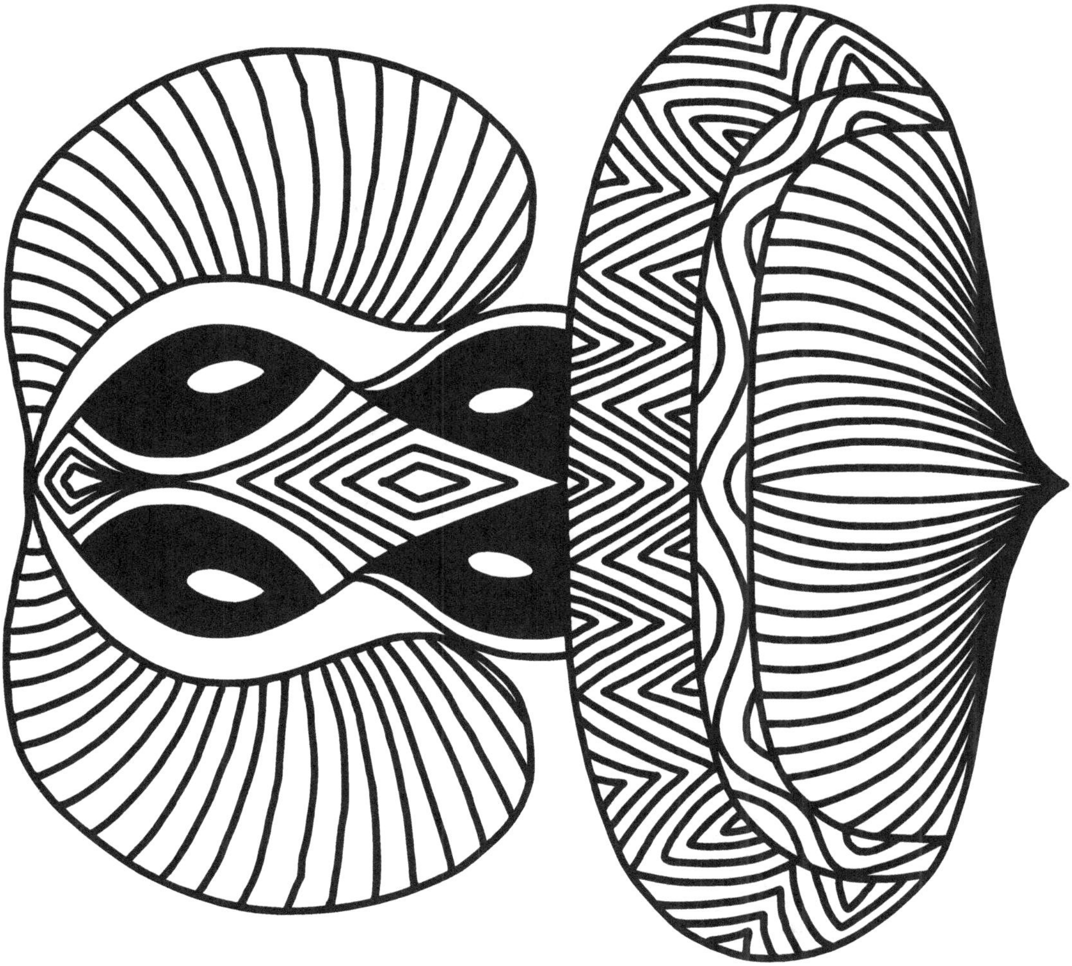

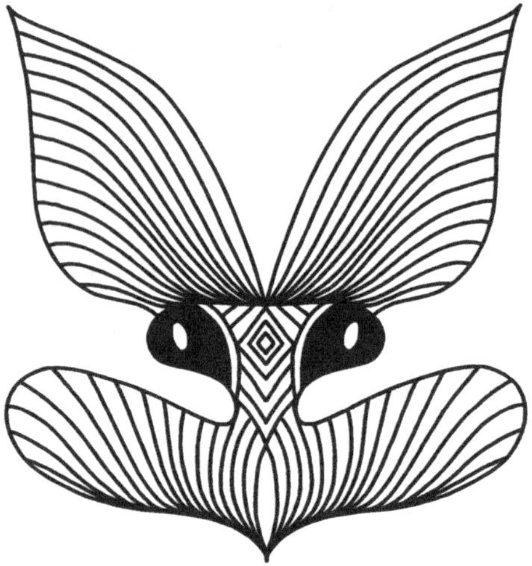

FATLINER WEIRDIES
VOLUME 1

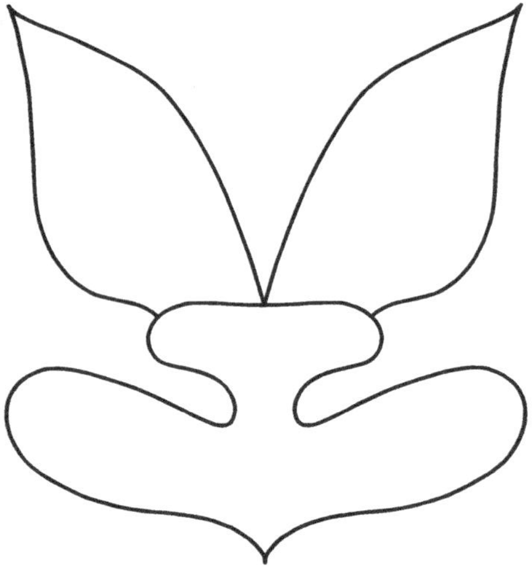

FATLINER WEIRDIES
THE TEMPLATES 1

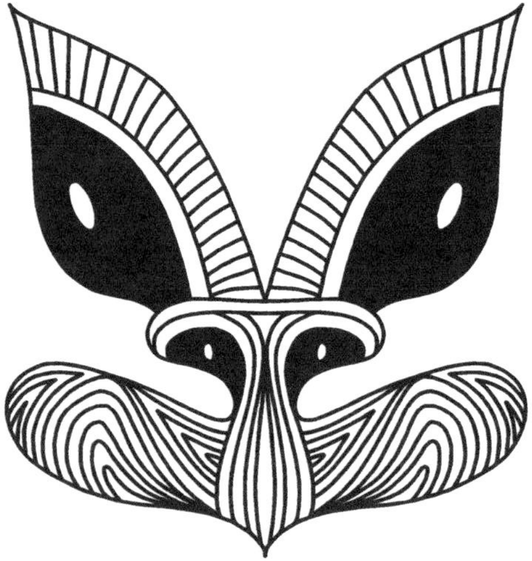

FATLINER WEIRDIES
VOLUME 3

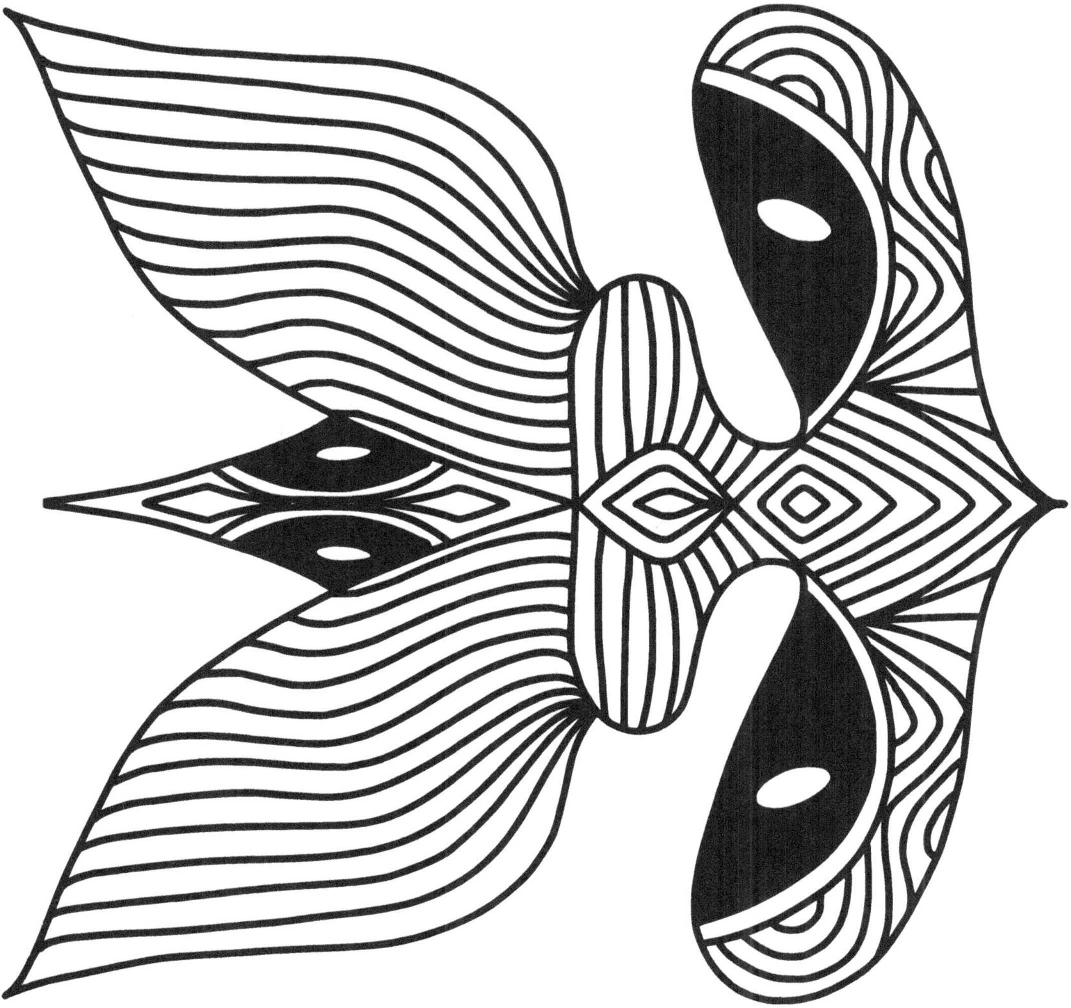

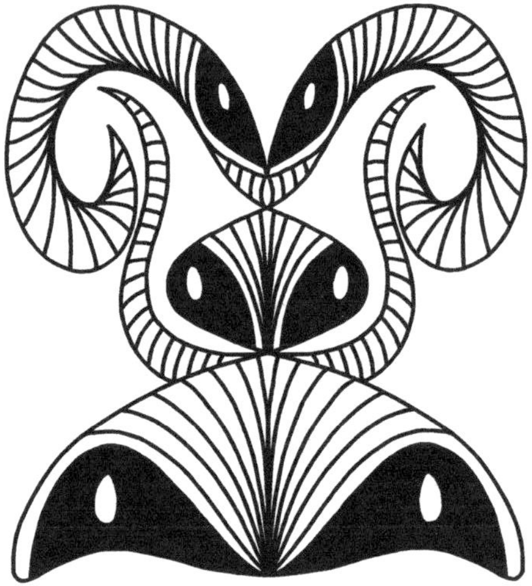

FATLINER WEIRDIES
VOLUME 1

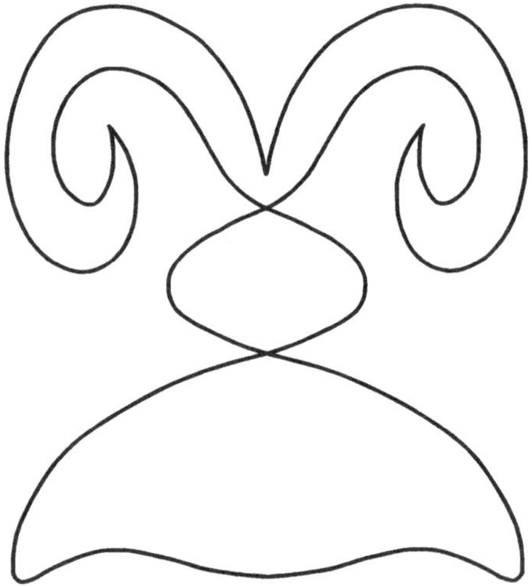

FATLINER WEIRDIES
THE TEMPLATES 1

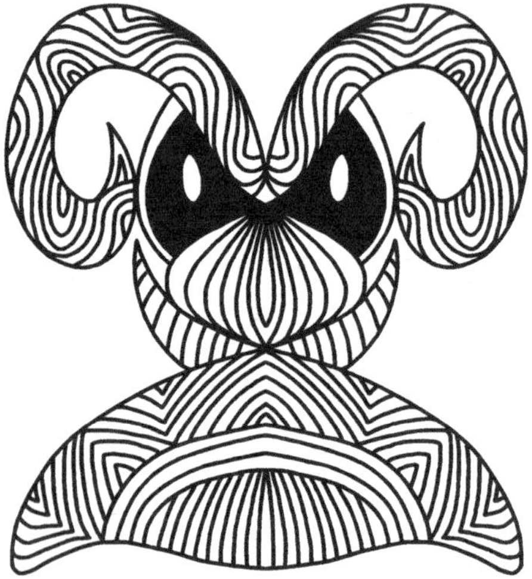

FATLINER WEIRDIES
VOLUME 3

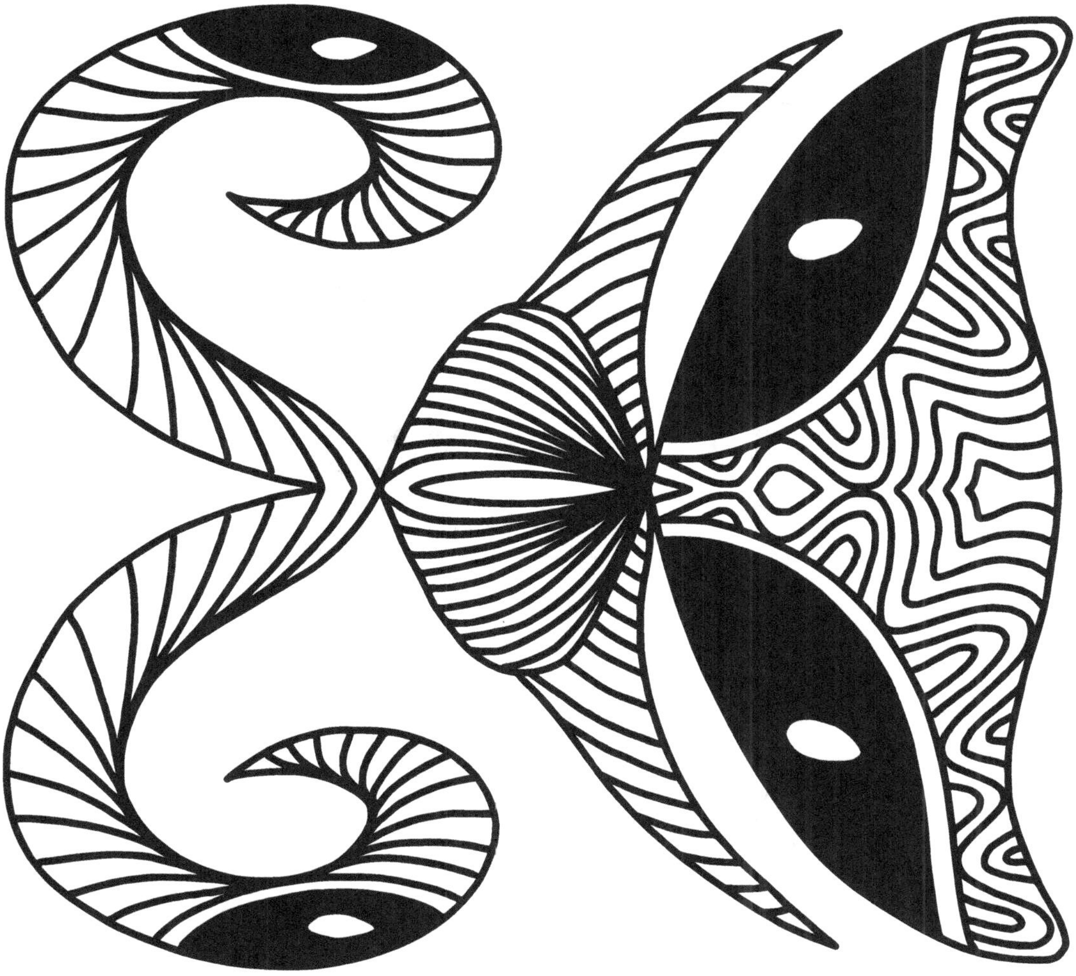

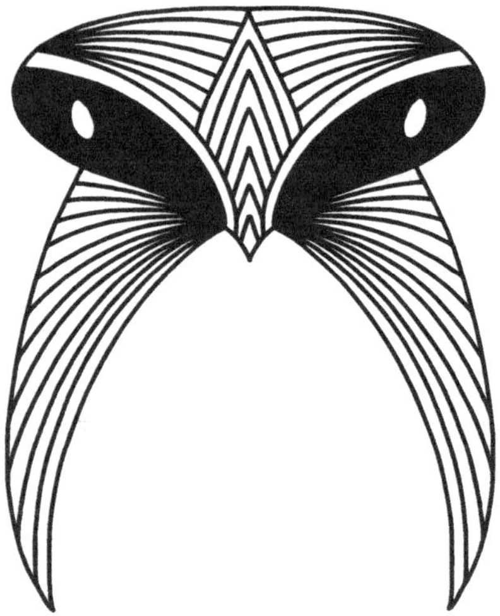

FATLINER WEIRDIES
VOLUME 1

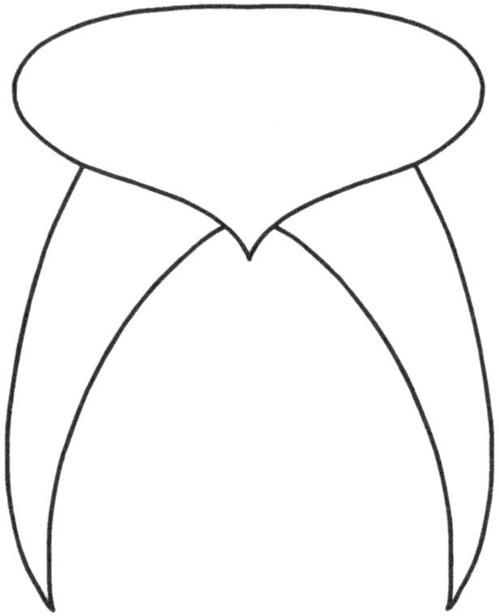

FATLINER WEIRDIES
THE TEMPLATES 1

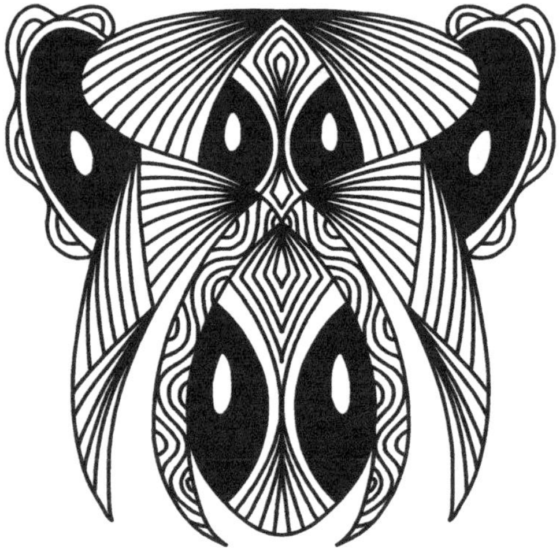

FATLINER WEIRDIES
VOLUME 3

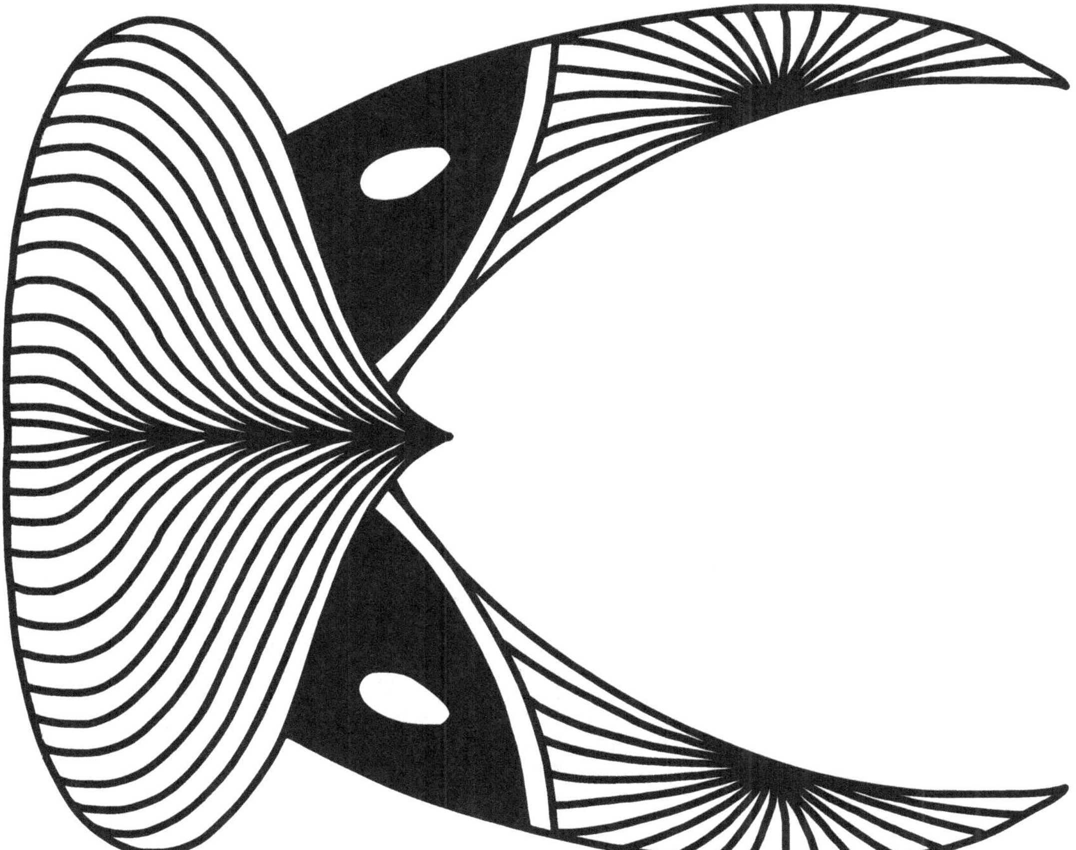

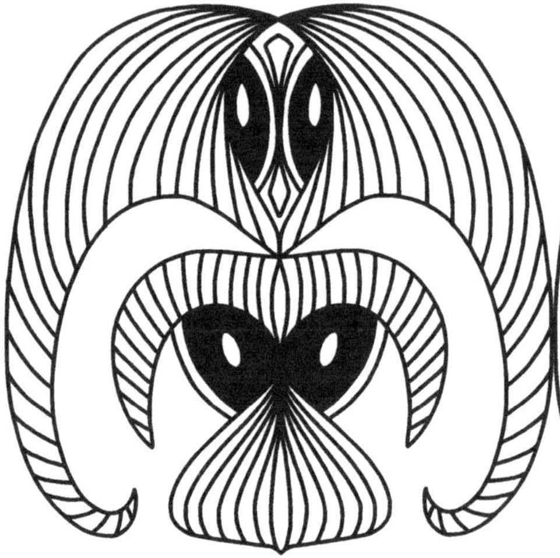

FATLINER WEIRDIES
VOLUME 1

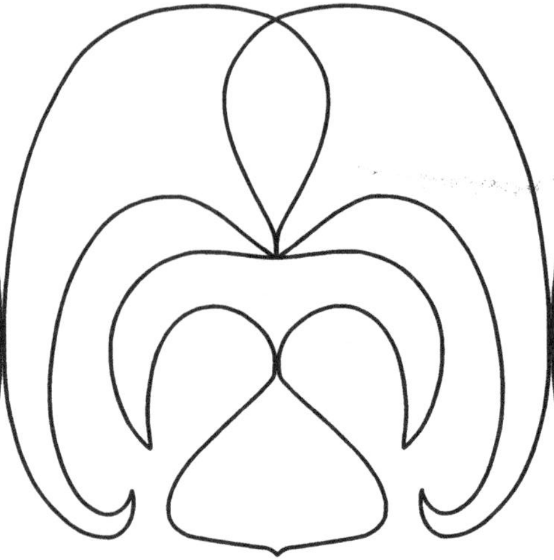

FATLINER WEIRDIES
THE TEMPLATES 1

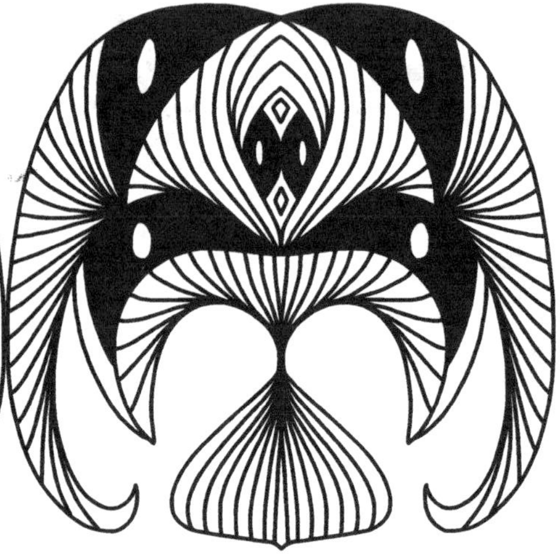

FATLINER WEIRDIES
VOLUME 3

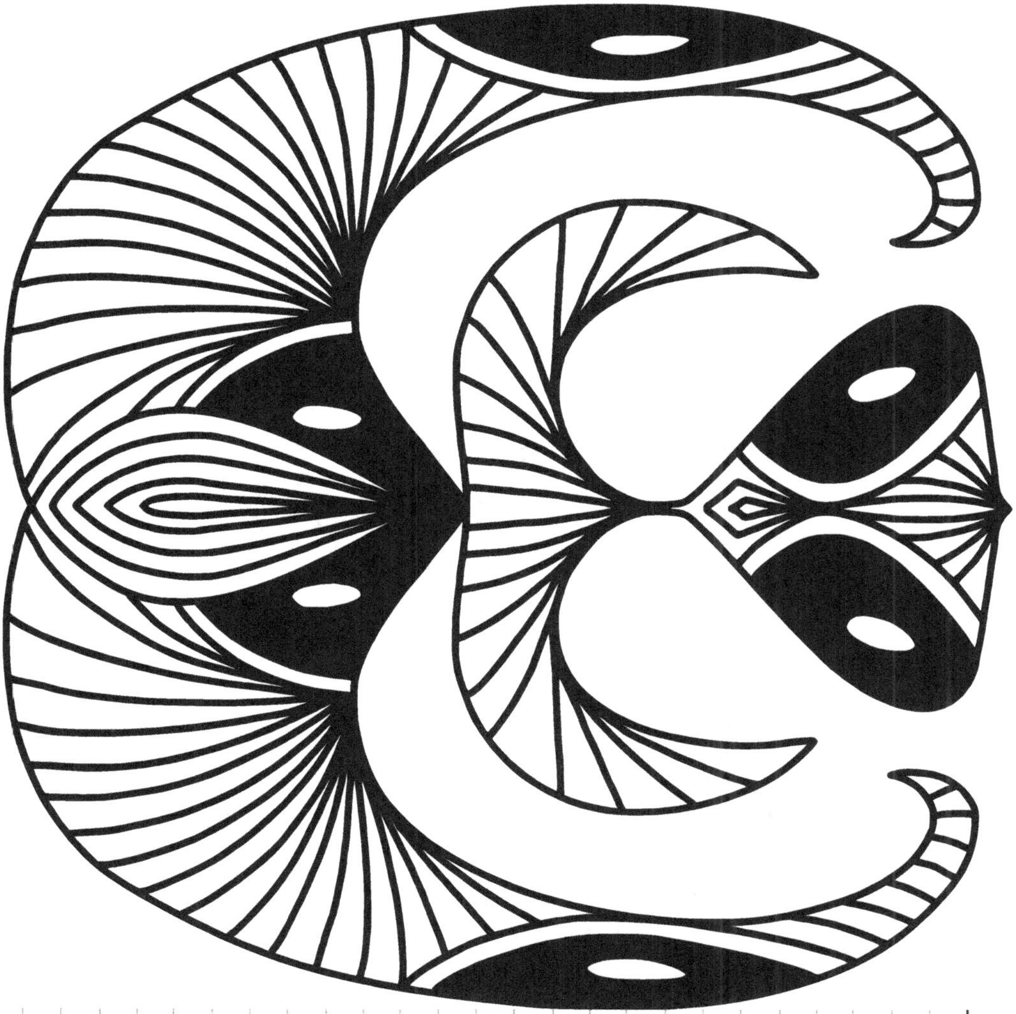

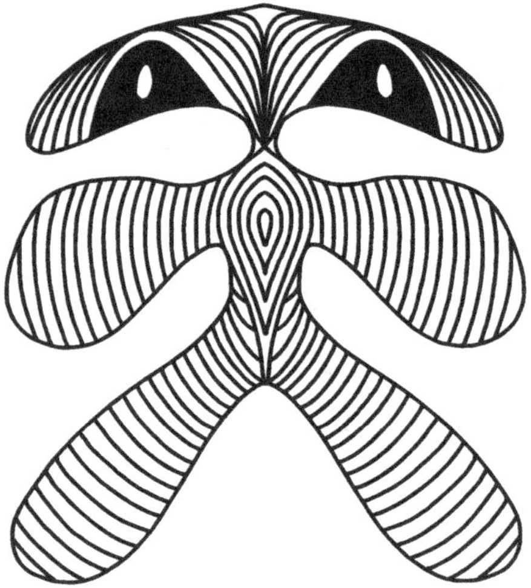

FATLINER WEIRDIES
VOLUME 1

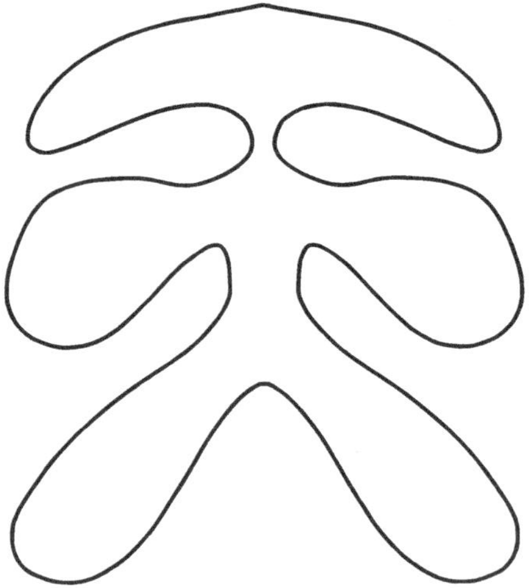

FATLINER WEIRDIES
THE TEMPLATES 1

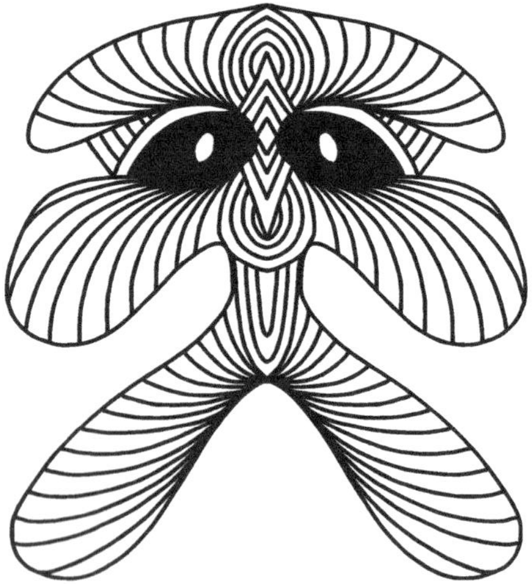

FATLINER WEIRDIES
VOLUME 3

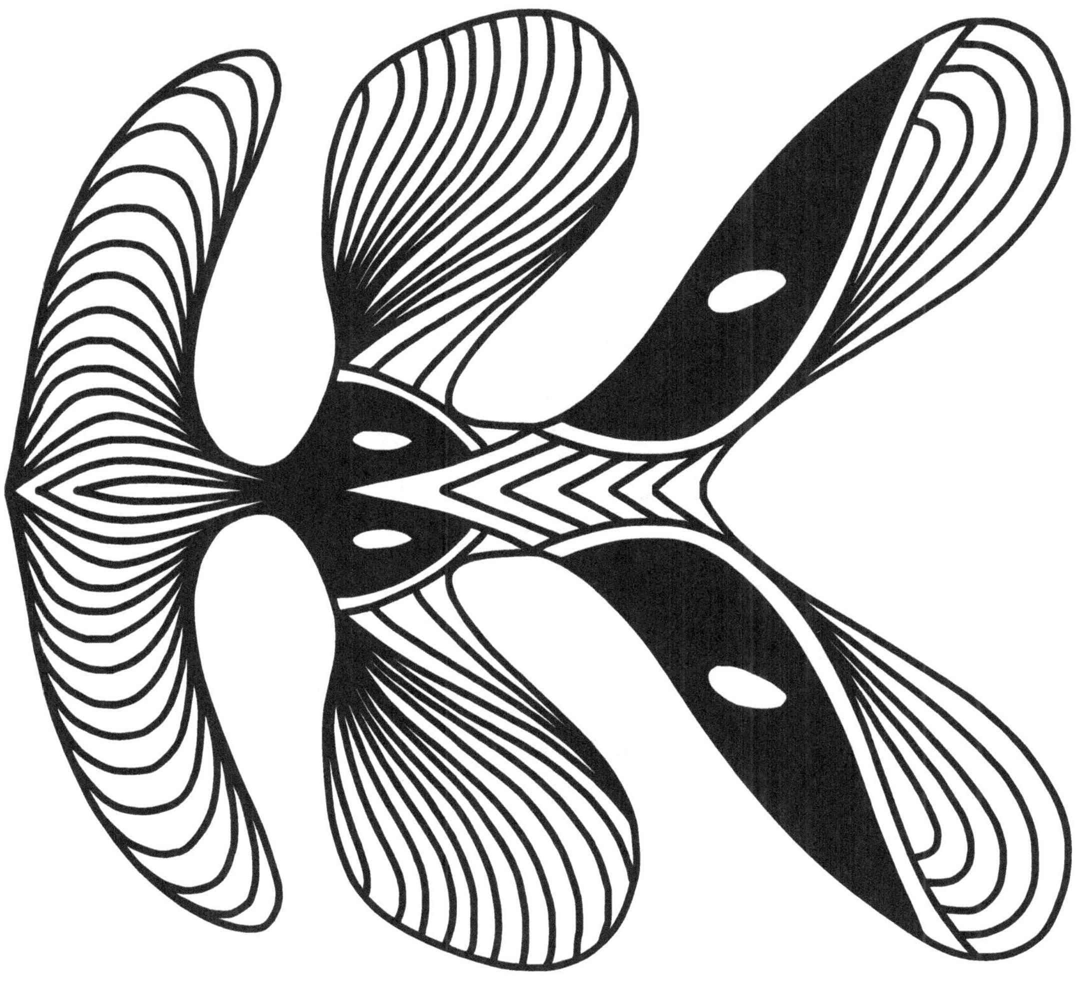

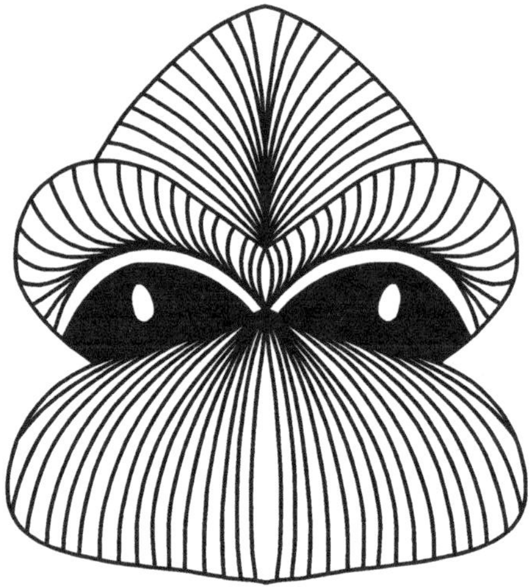

FATLINER WEIRDIES
VOLUME 1

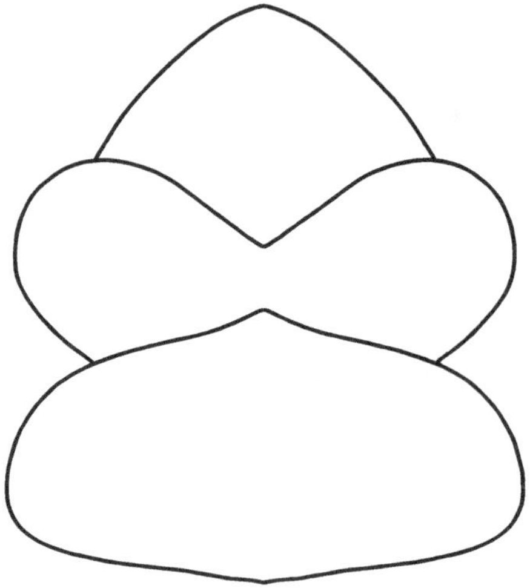

FATLINER WEIRDIES
THE TEMPLATES 1

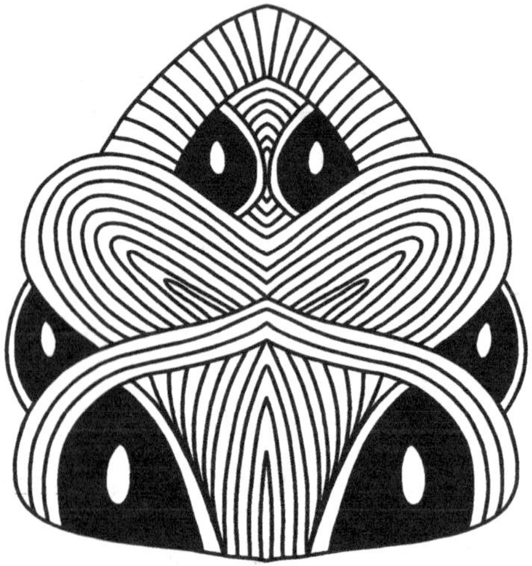

FATLINER WEIRDIES
VOLUME 3

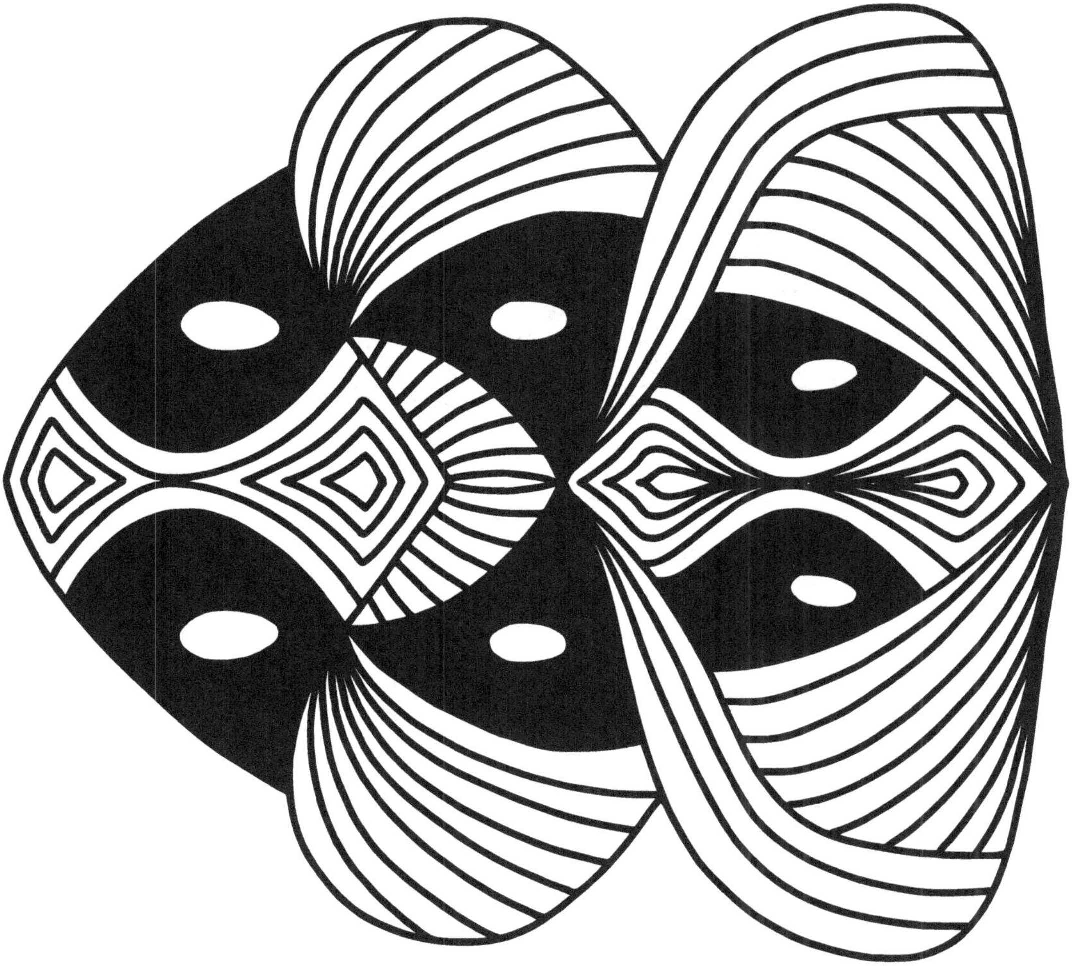

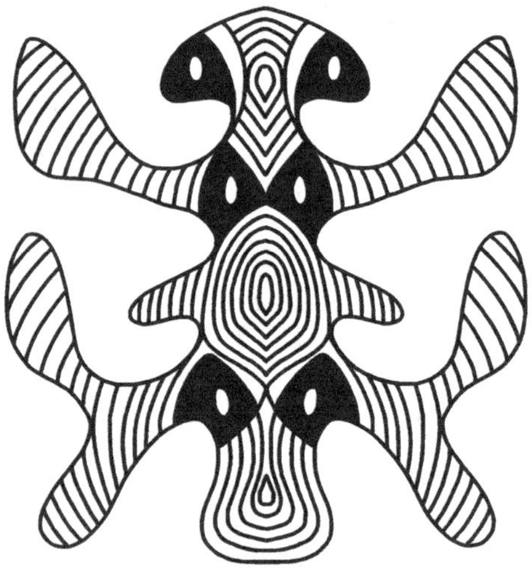

FATLINER WEIRDIES
VOLUME 1

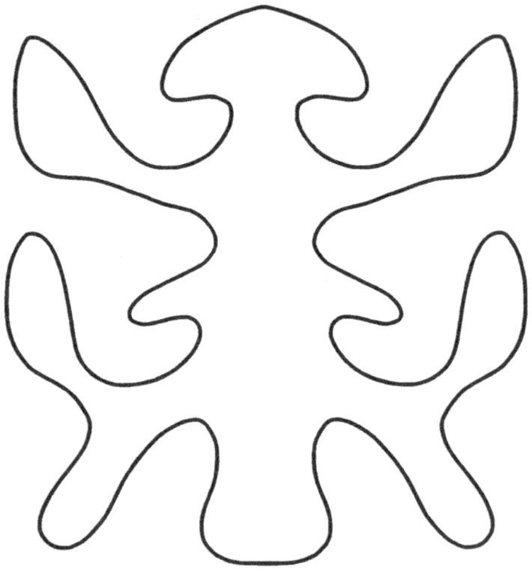

FATLINER WEIRDIES
THE TEMPLATES 1

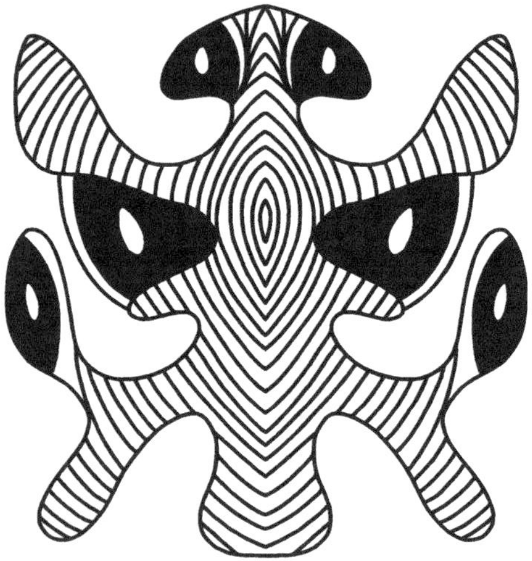

FATLINER WEIRDIES
VOLUME 3

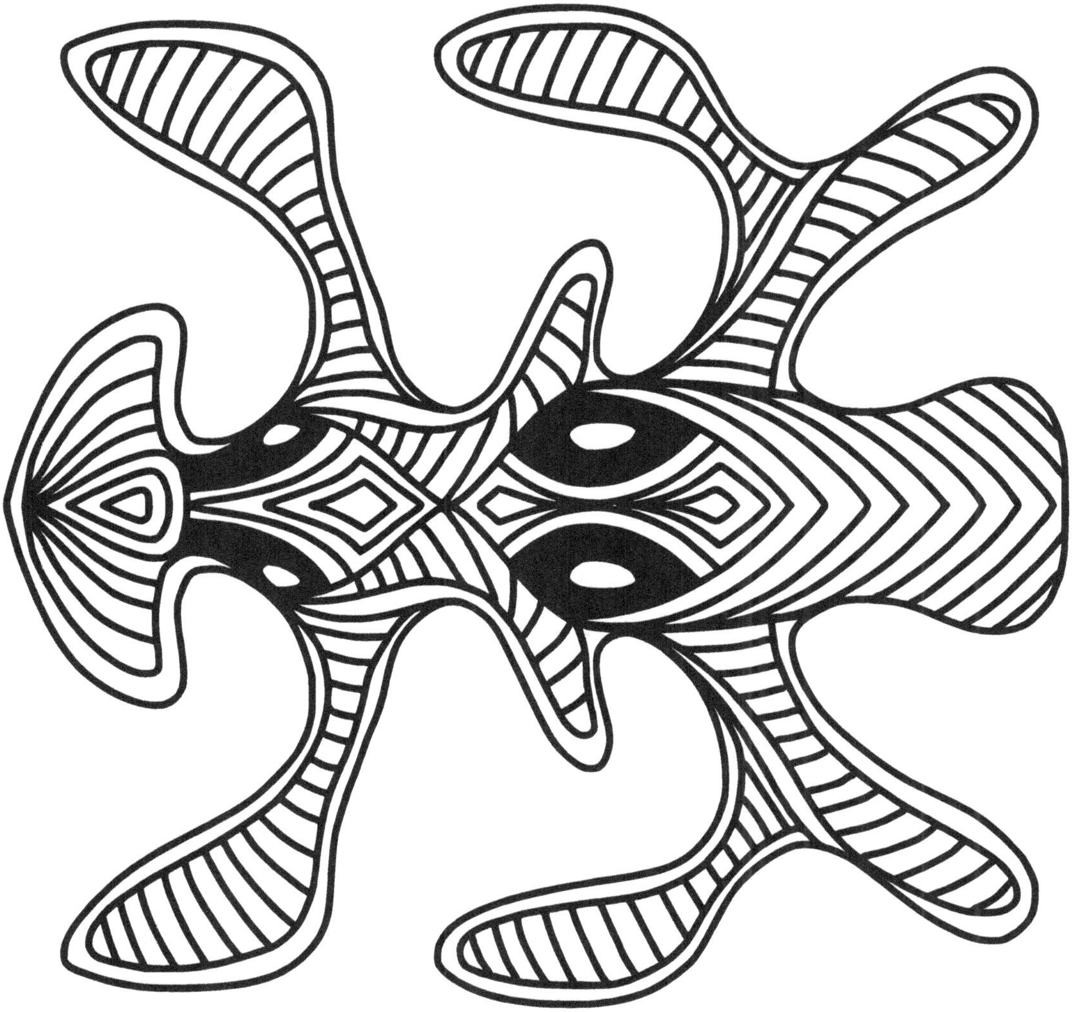

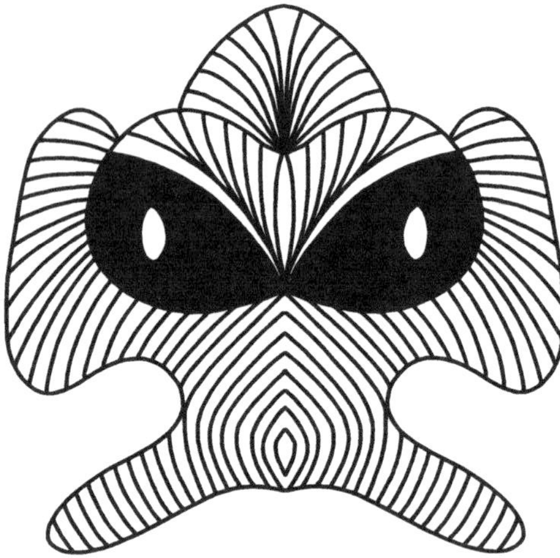

FATLINER WEIRDIES
VOLUME 1

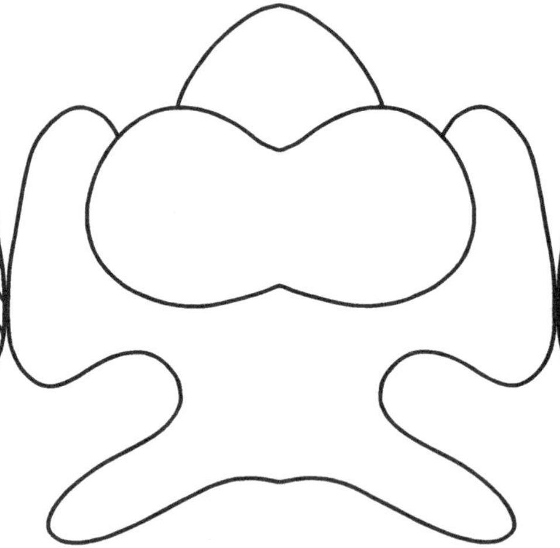

FATLINER WEIRDIES
THE TEMPLATES 1

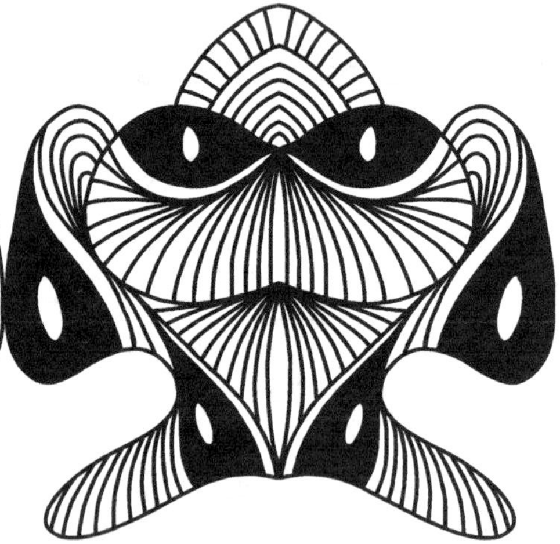

FATLINER WEIRDIES
VOLUME 3

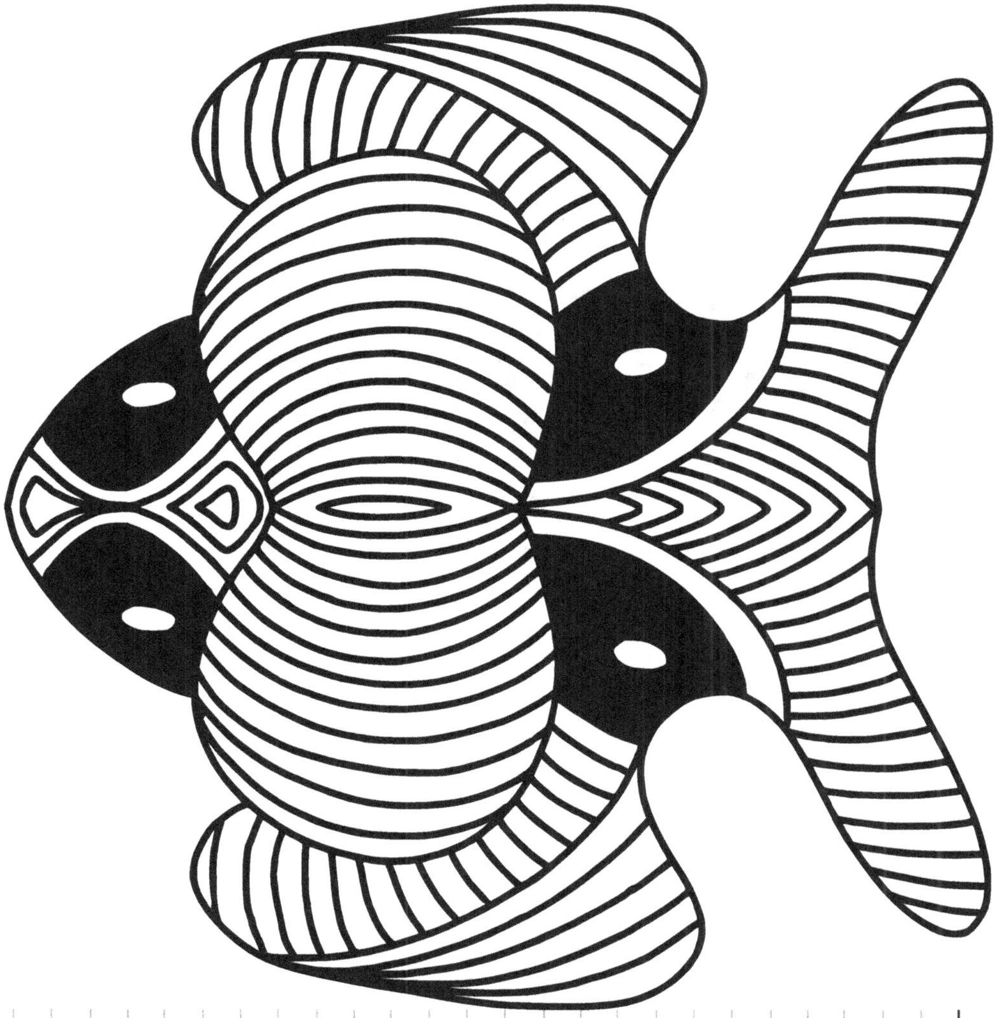

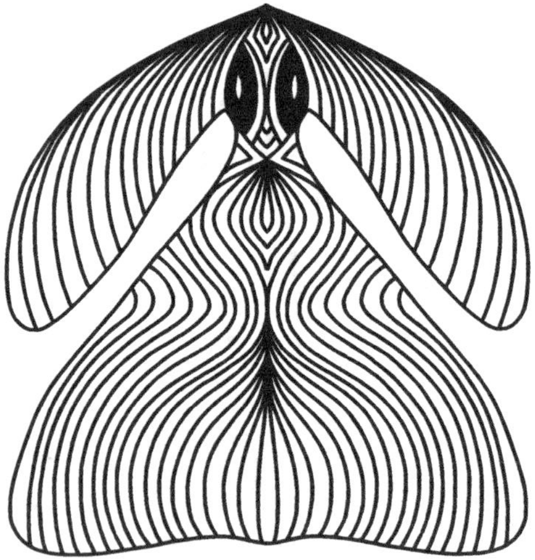

FATLINER WEIRDIES
VOLUME 1

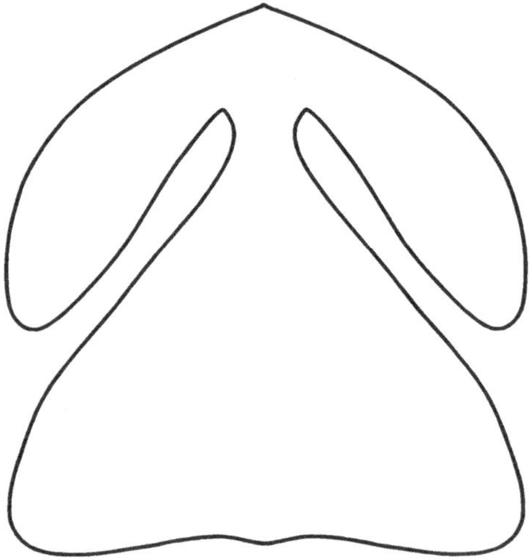

FATLINER WEIRDIES
THE TEMPLATES 1

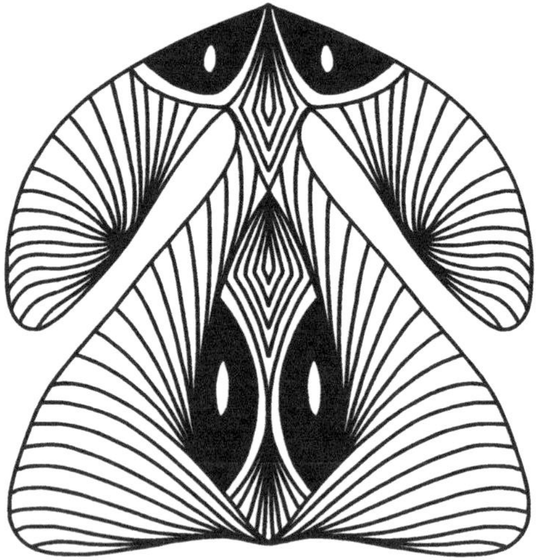

FATLINER WEIRDIES
VOLUME 3

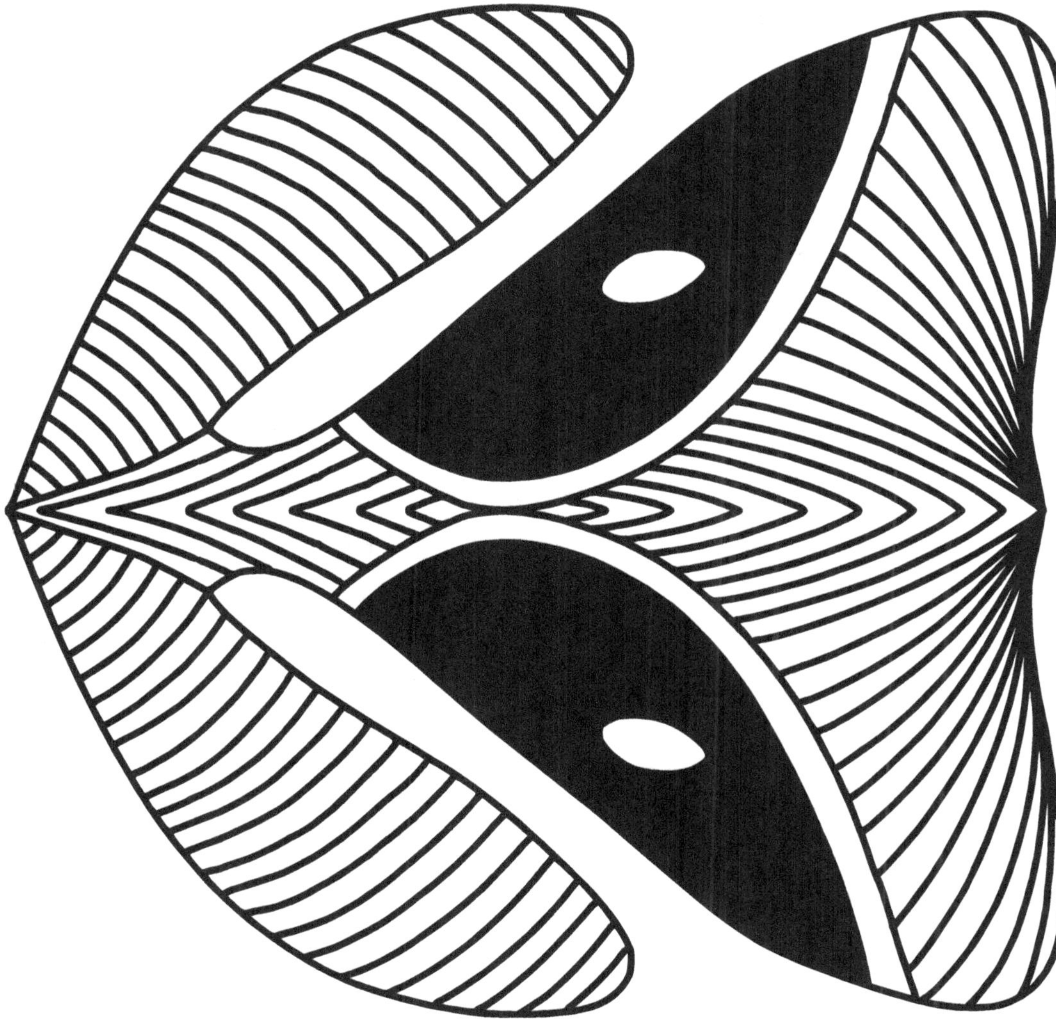

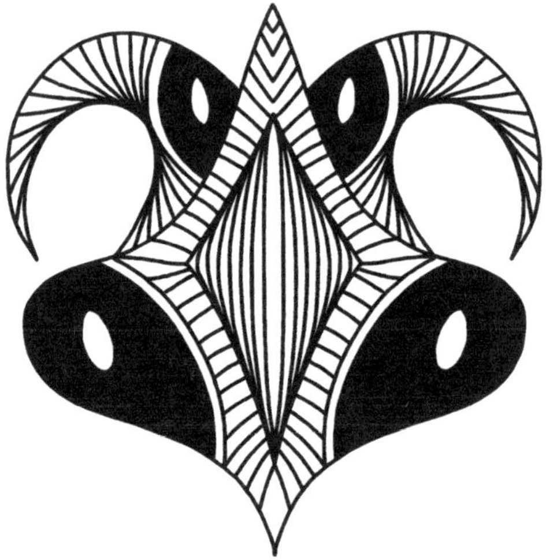

FATLINER WEIRDIES
VOLUME 1

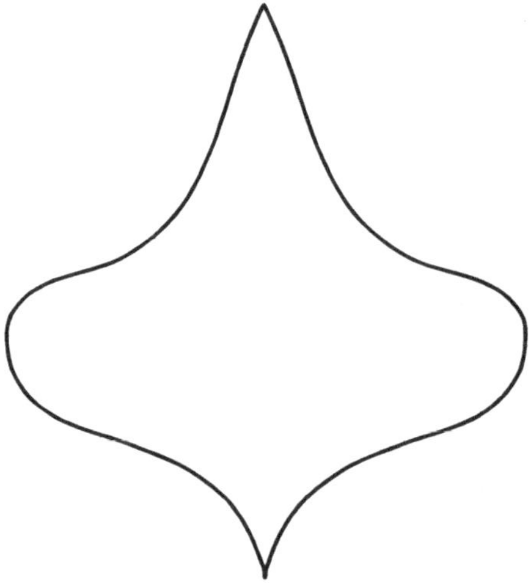

FATLINER WEIRDIES
THE TEMPLATES 1

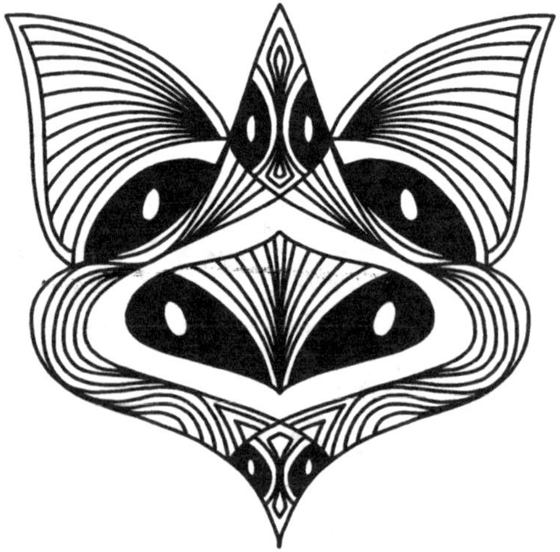

FATLINER WEIRDIES
VOLUME 3

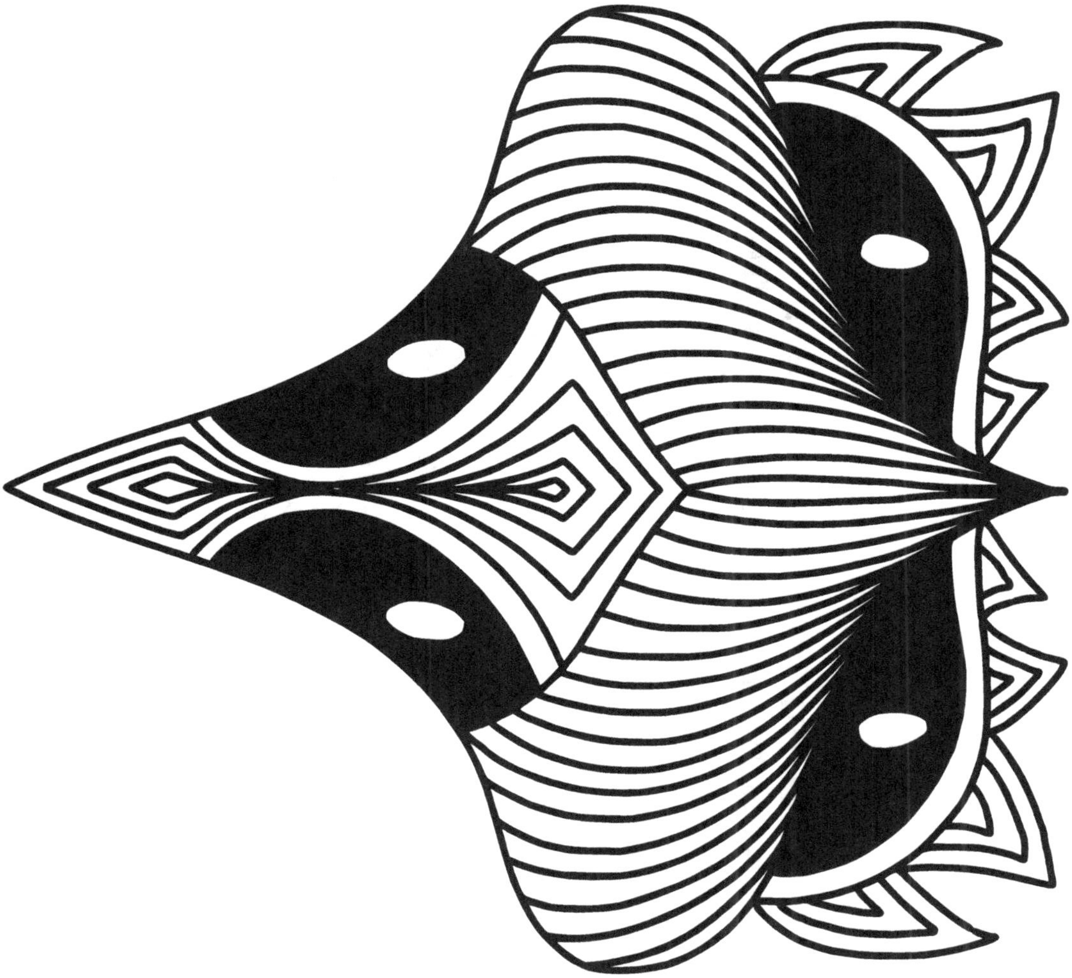

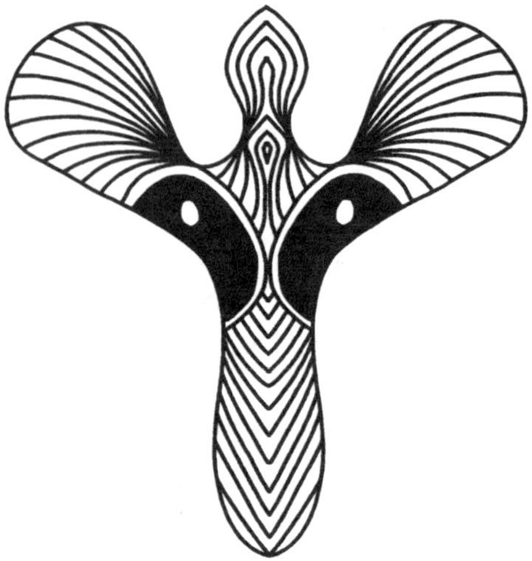

FATLINER WEIRDIES
VOLUME 1

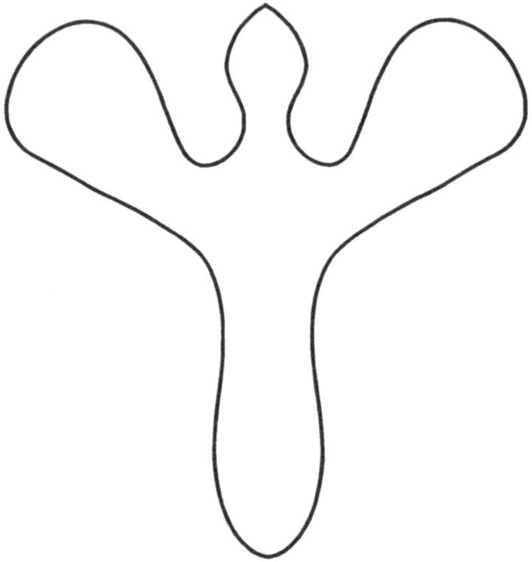

FATLINER WEIRDIES
THE TEMPLATES 1

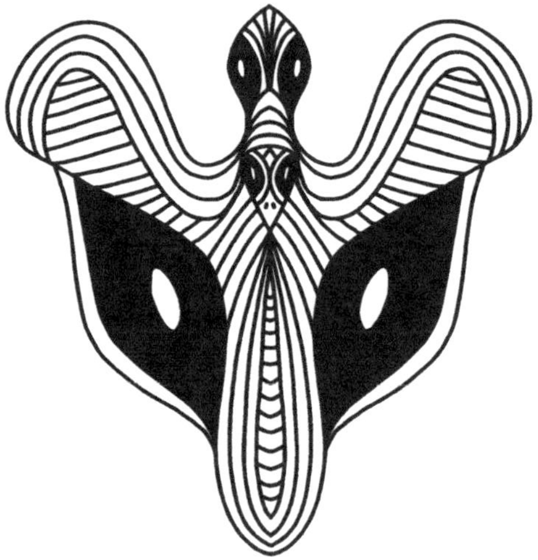

FATLINER WEIRDIES
VOLUME 3

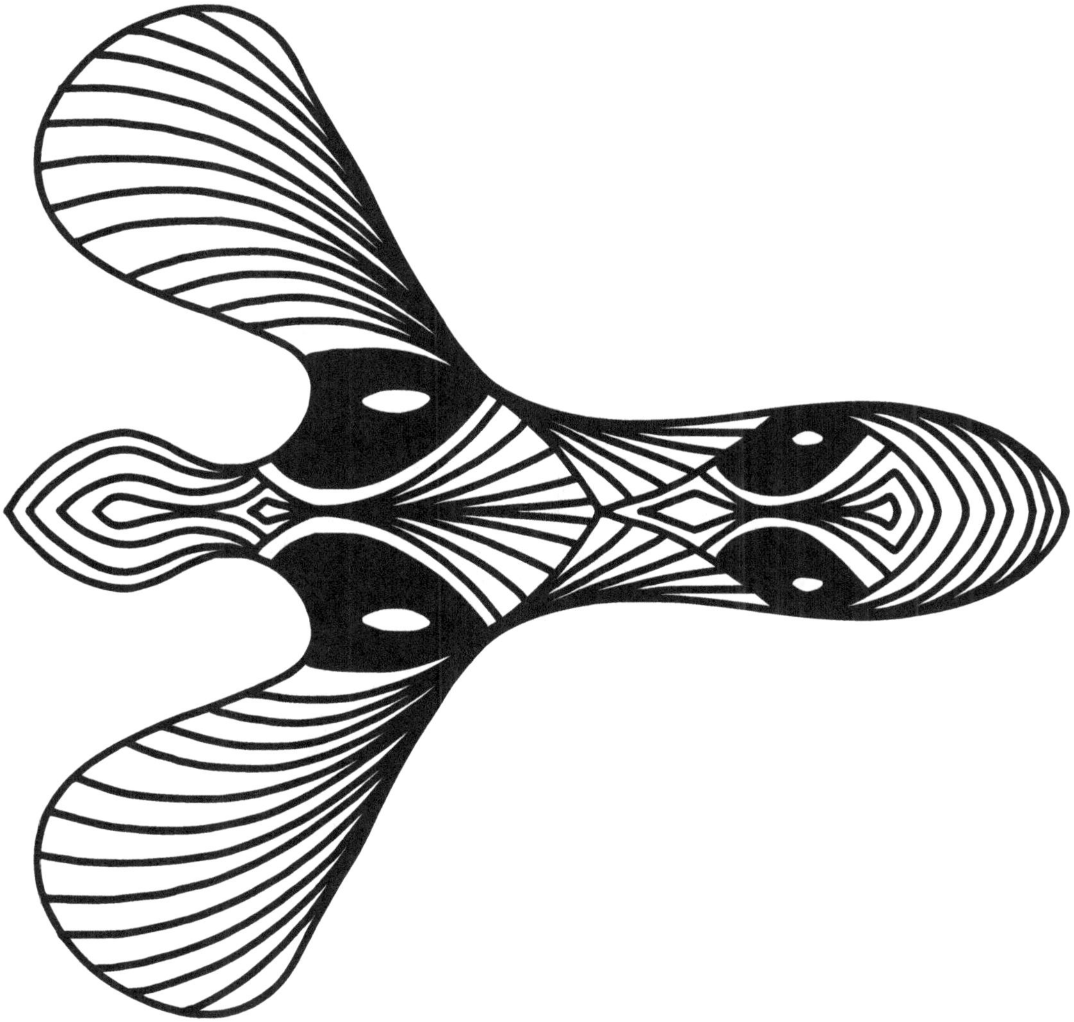

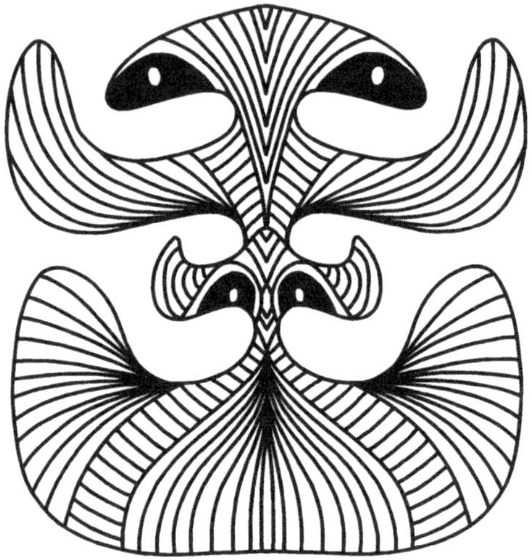

FATLINER WEIRDIES
VOLUME 1

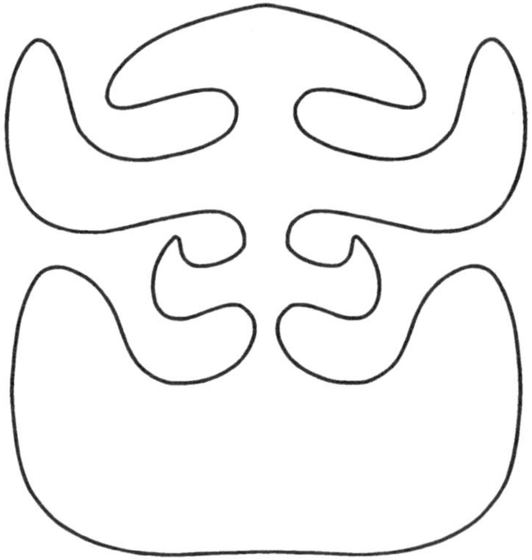

FATLINER WEIRDIES
THE TEMPLATES 1

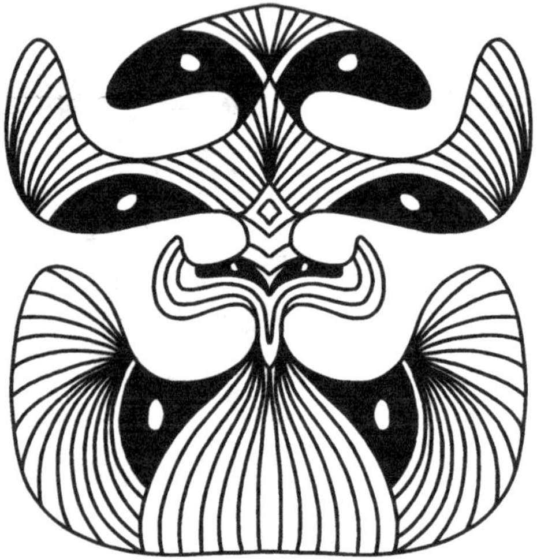

FATLINER WEIRDIES
VOLUME 3

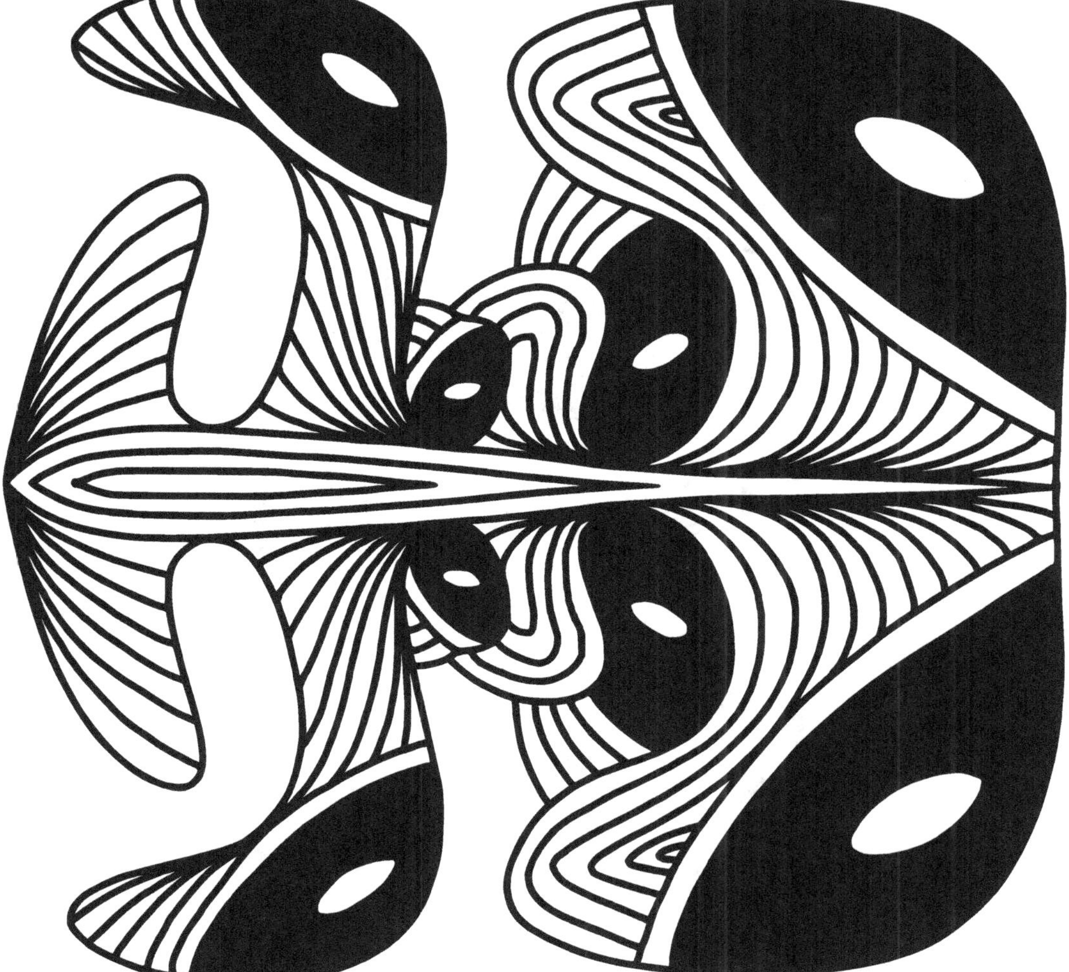

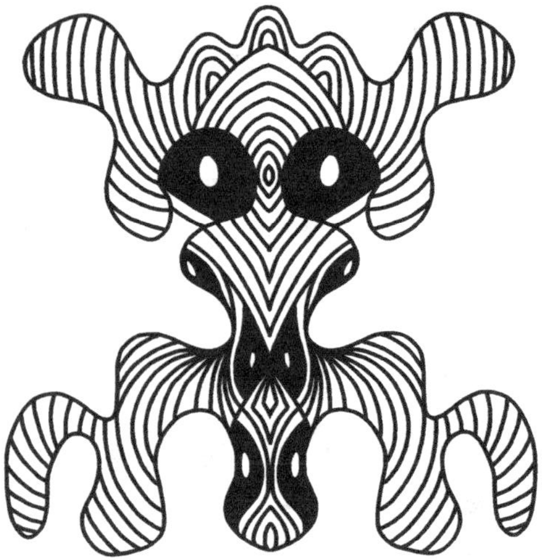

FATLINER WEIRDIES
VOLUME 1

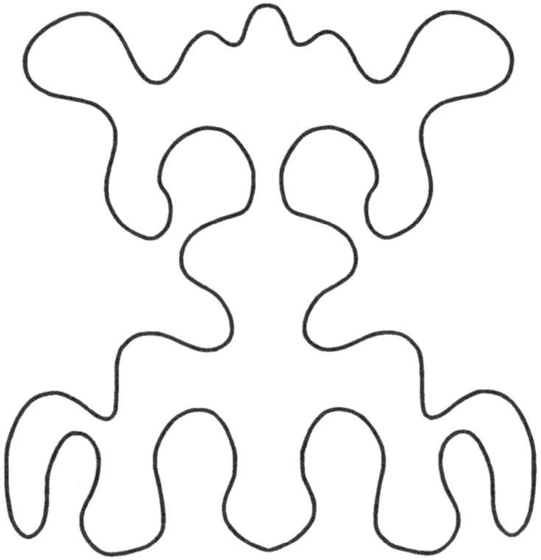

FATLINER WEIRDIES
THE TEMPLATES 1

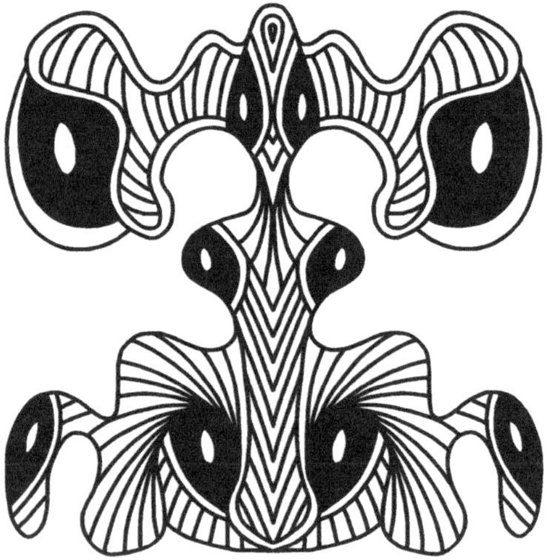

FATLINER WEIRDIES
VOLUME 3

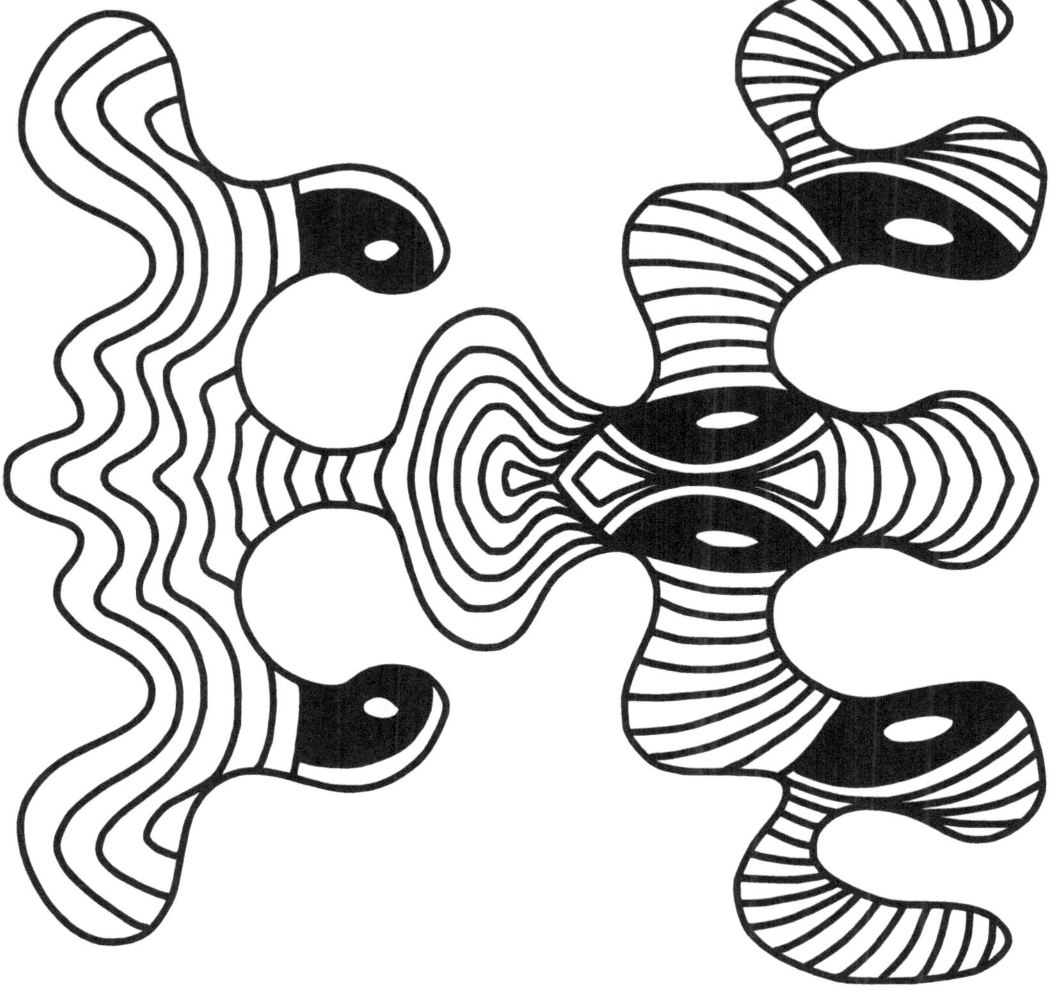

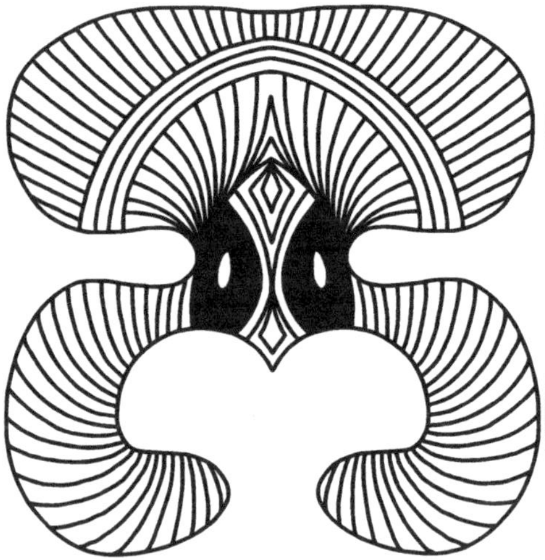

FATLINER WEIRDIES
VOLUME 1

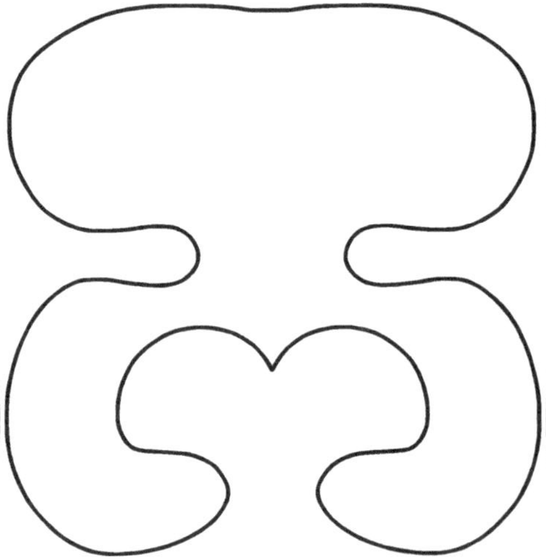

FATLINER WEIRDIES
THE TEMPLATES 1

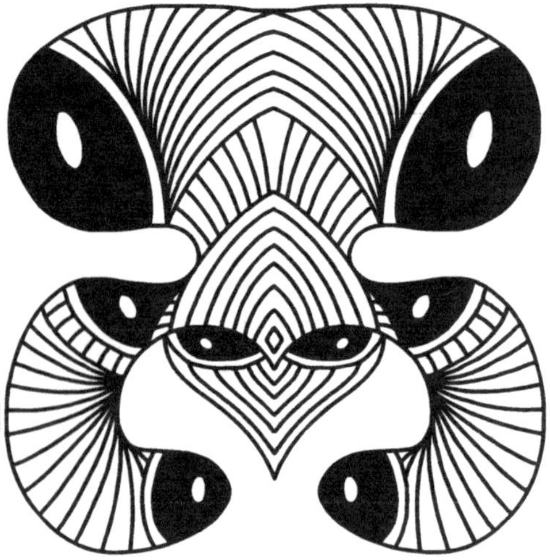

FATLINER WEIRDIES
VOLUME 3

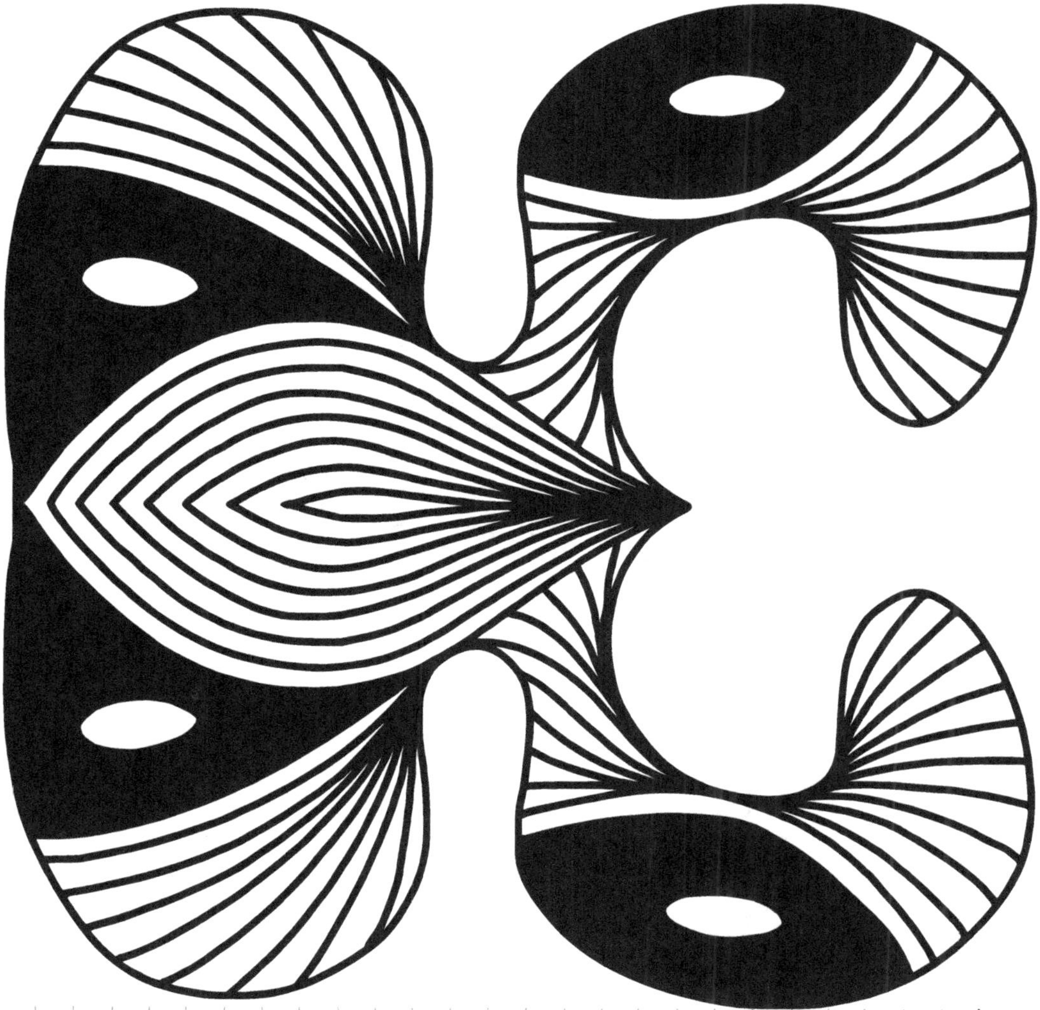

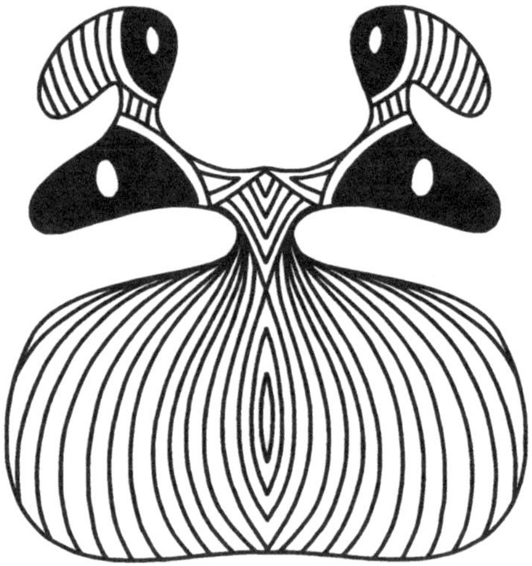
FATLINER WEIRDIES
VOLUME 1

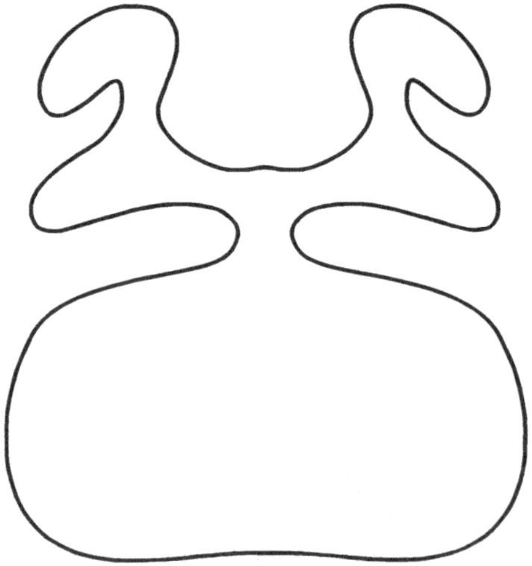
FATLINER WEIRDIES
THE TEMPLATES 1

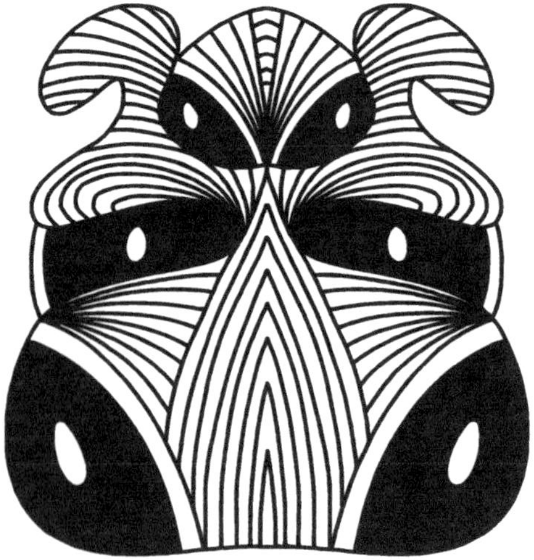
FATLINER WEIRDIES
VOLUME 3

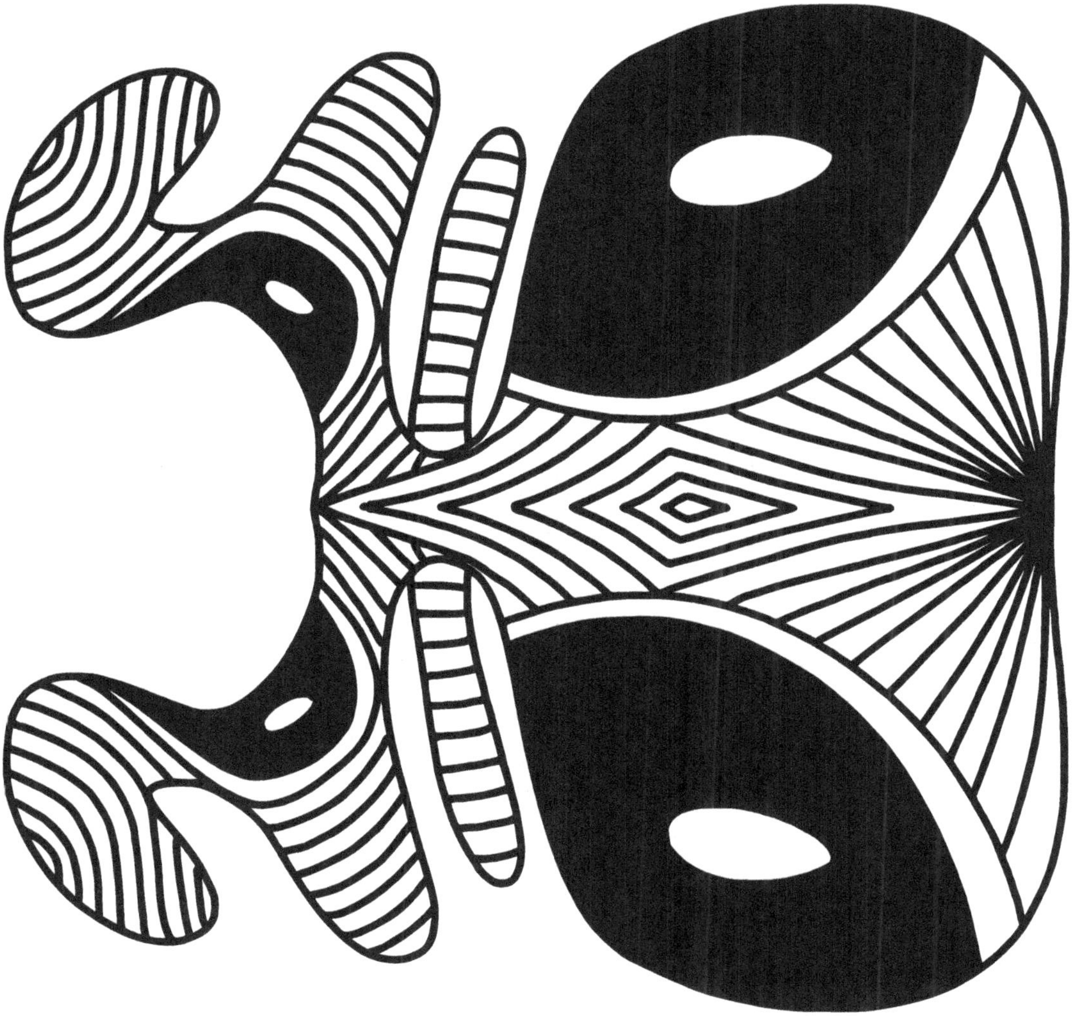

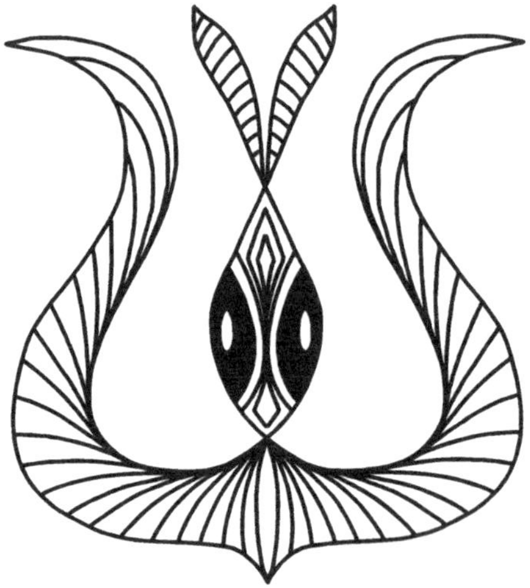

FATLINER WEIRDIES
VOLUME 1

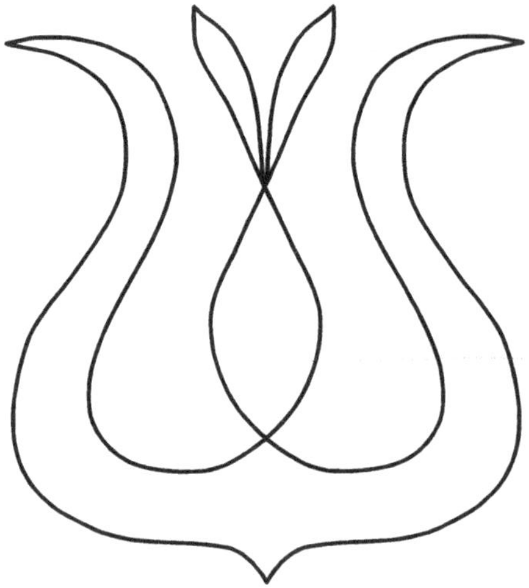

FATLINER WEIRDIES
THE TEMPLATES 1

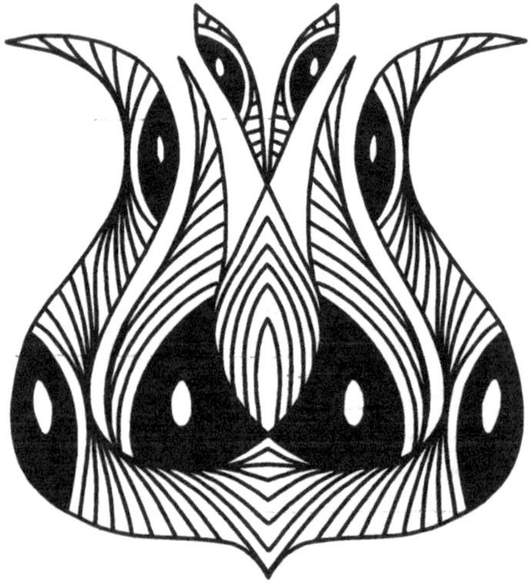

FATLINER WEIRDIES
VOLUME 3

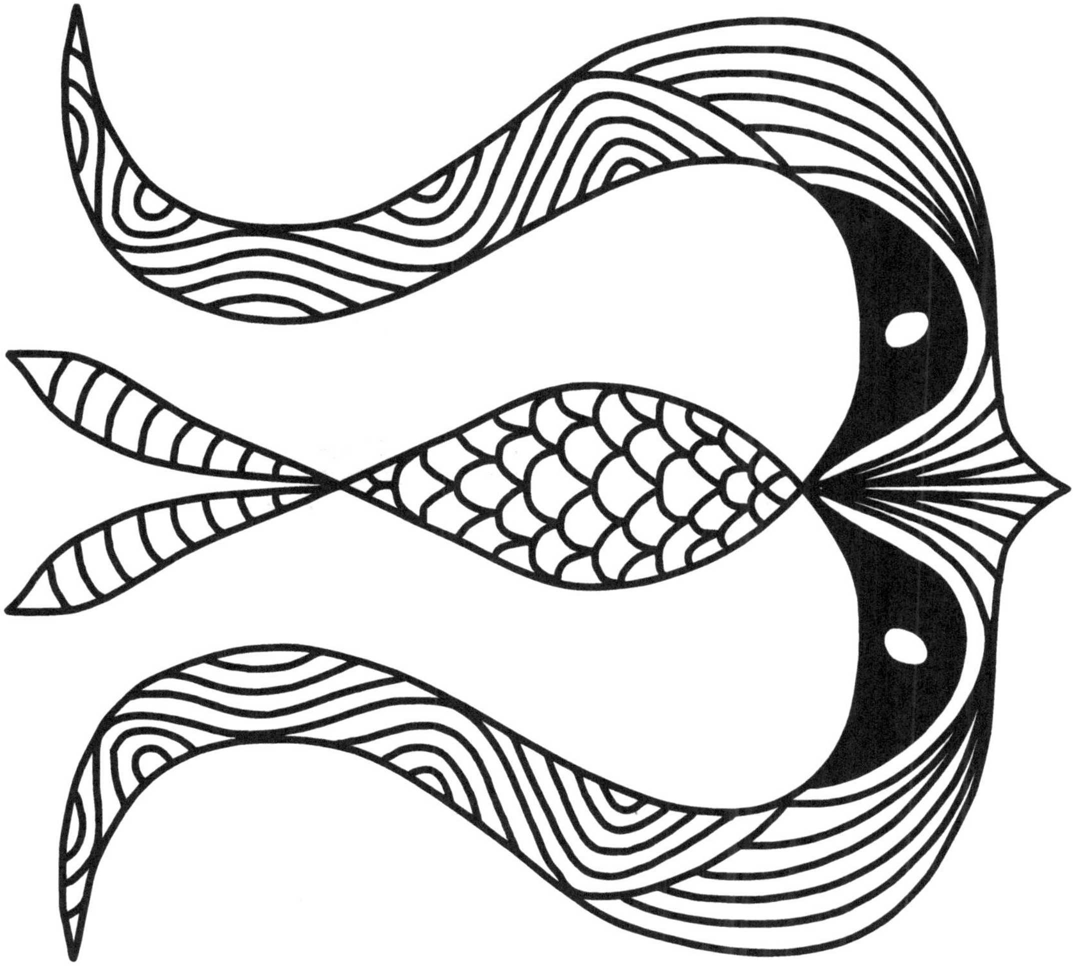

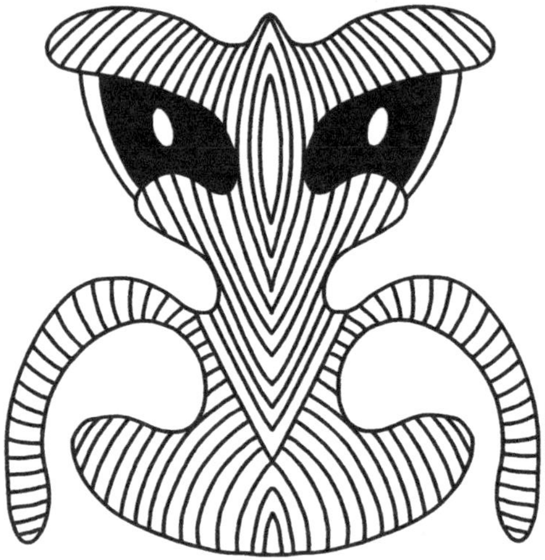

FATLINER WEIRDIES
VOLUME 1

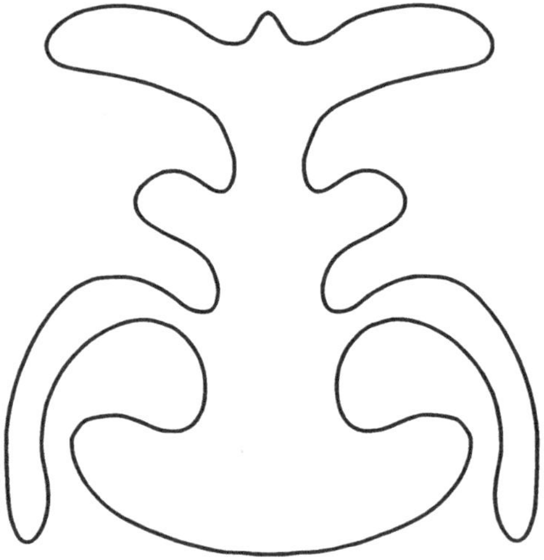

FATLINER WEIRDIES
THE TEMPLATES 1

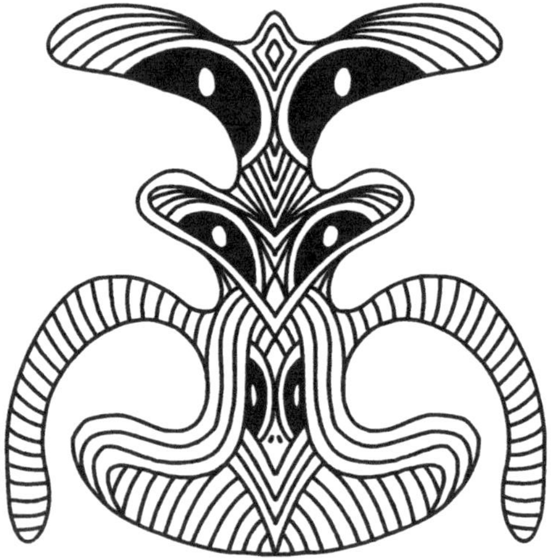

FATLINER WEIRDIES
VOLUME 3

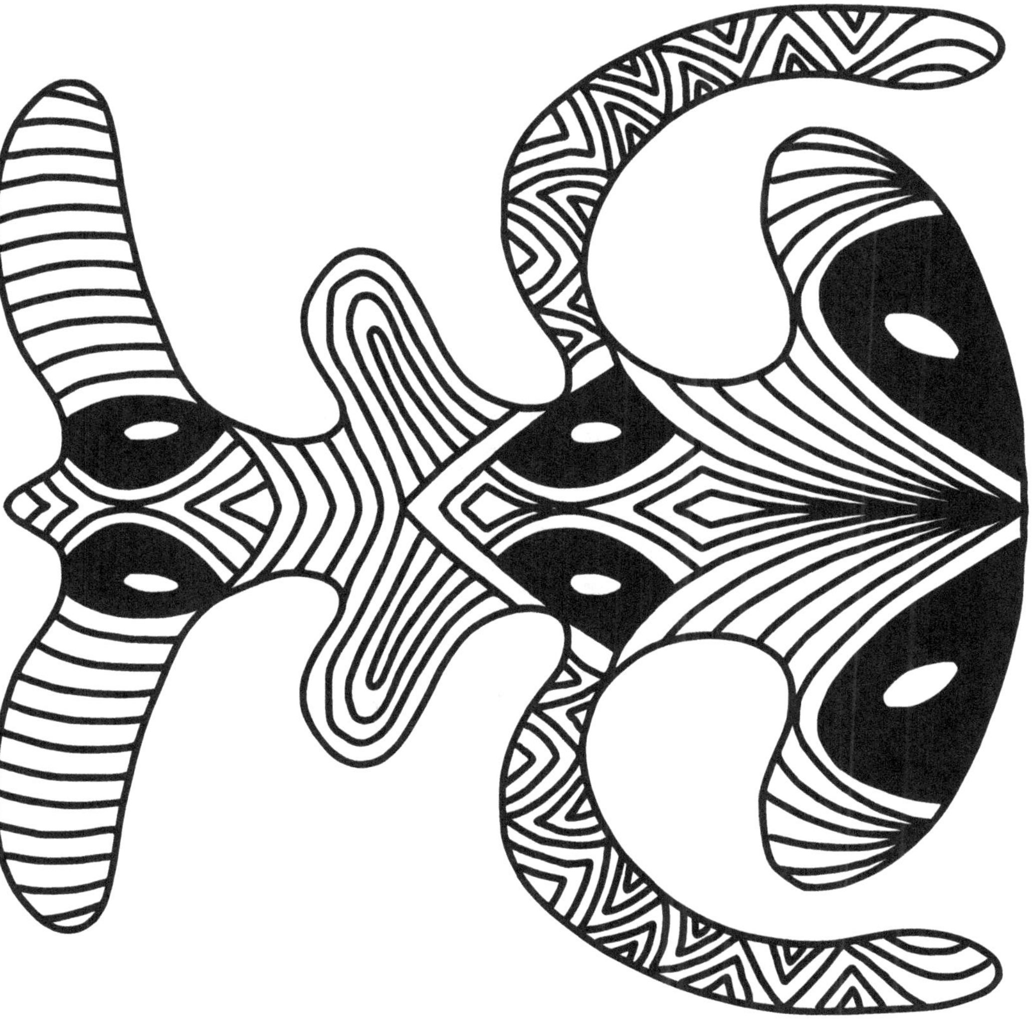

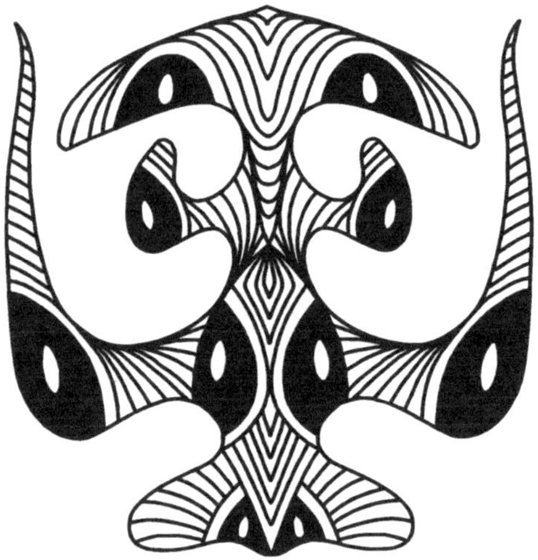

FATLINER WEIRDIES
VOLUME 1

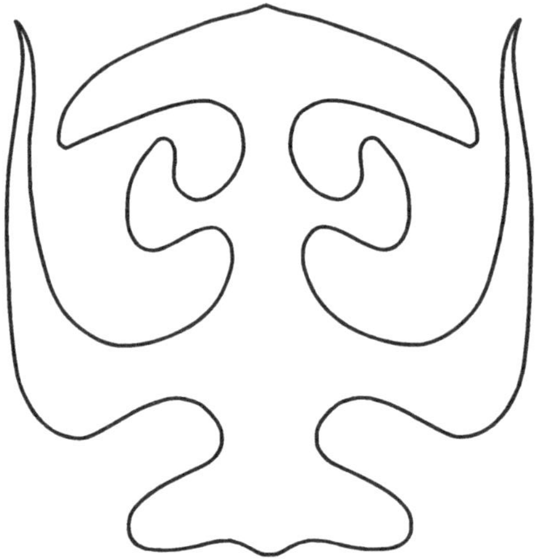

FATLINER WEIRDIES
THE TEMPLATES 1

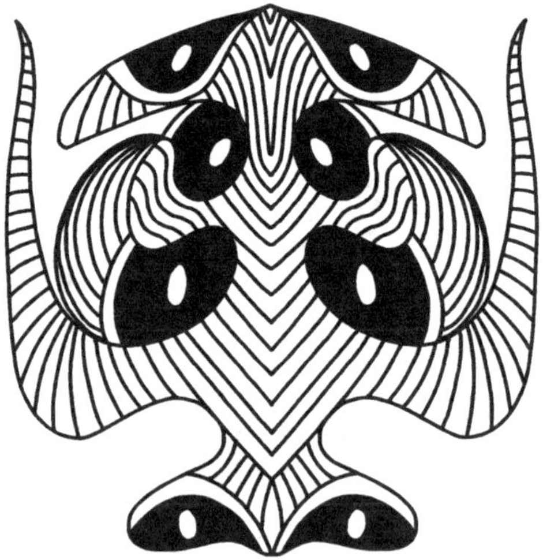

FATLINER WEIRDIES
VOLUME 3

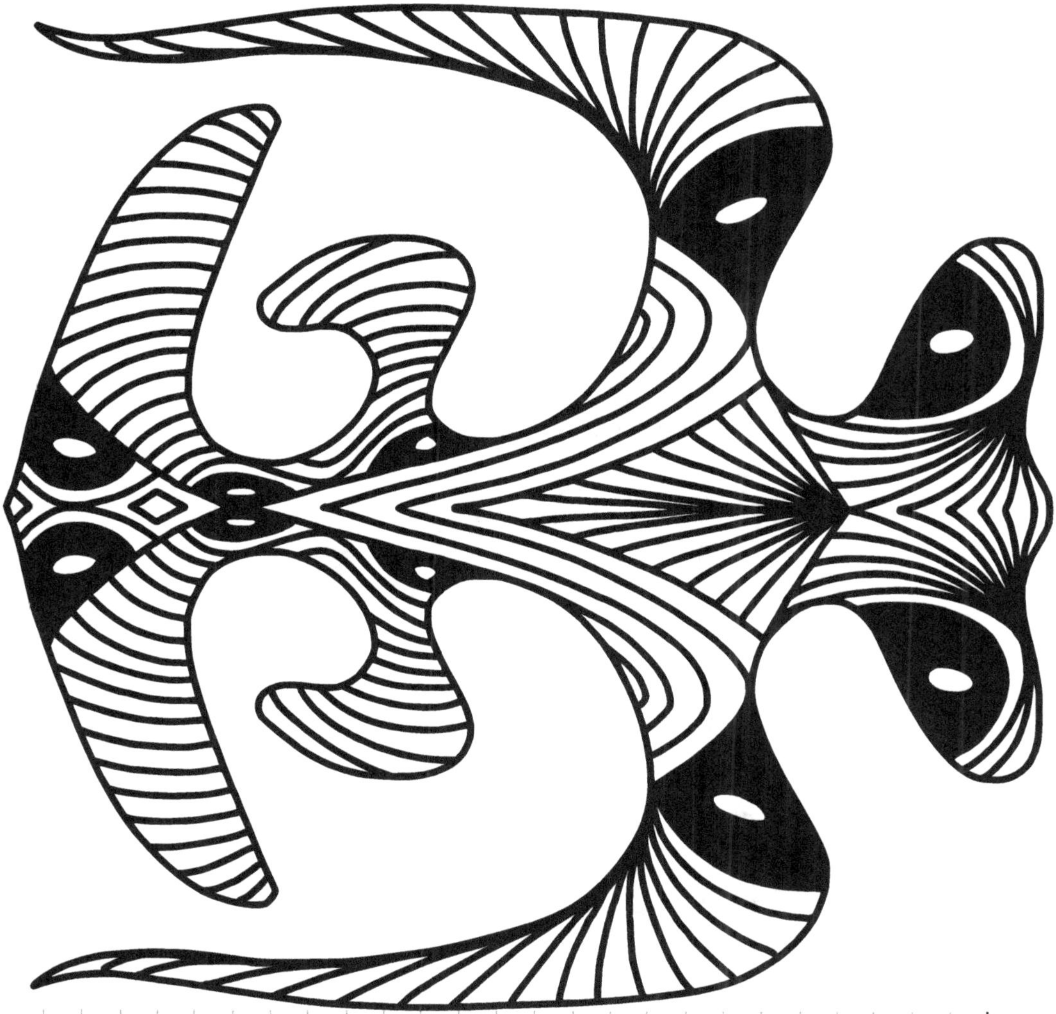

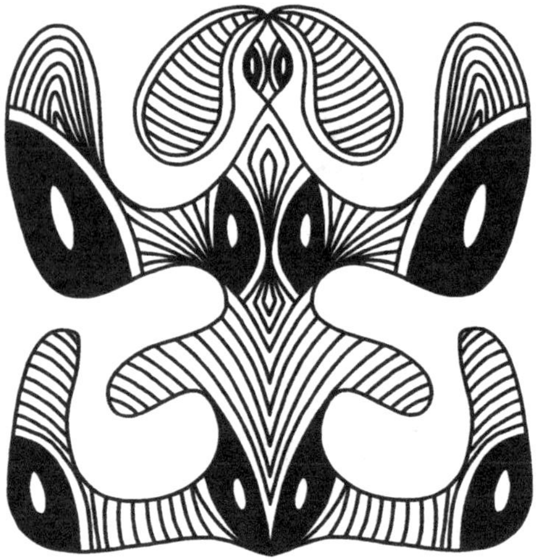

FATLINER WEIRDIES
VOLUME 1

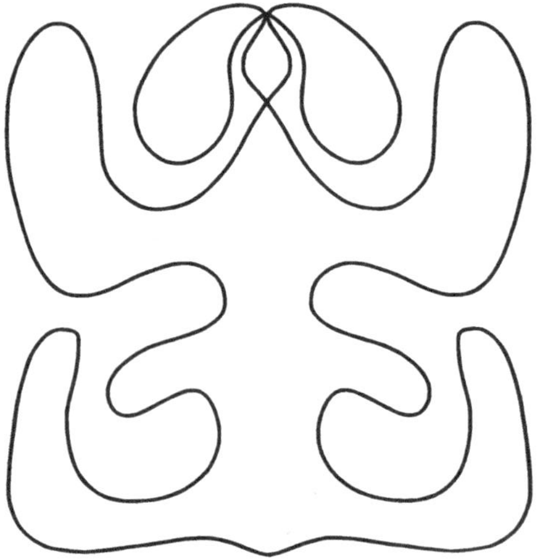

FATLINER WEIRDIES
THE TEMPLATES 1

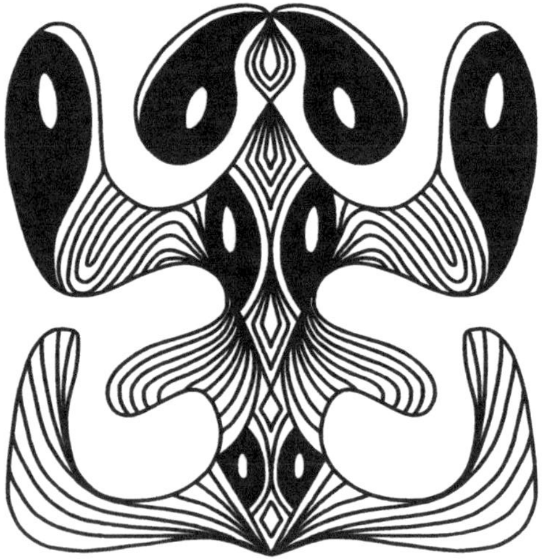

FATLINER WEIRDIES
VOLUME 3

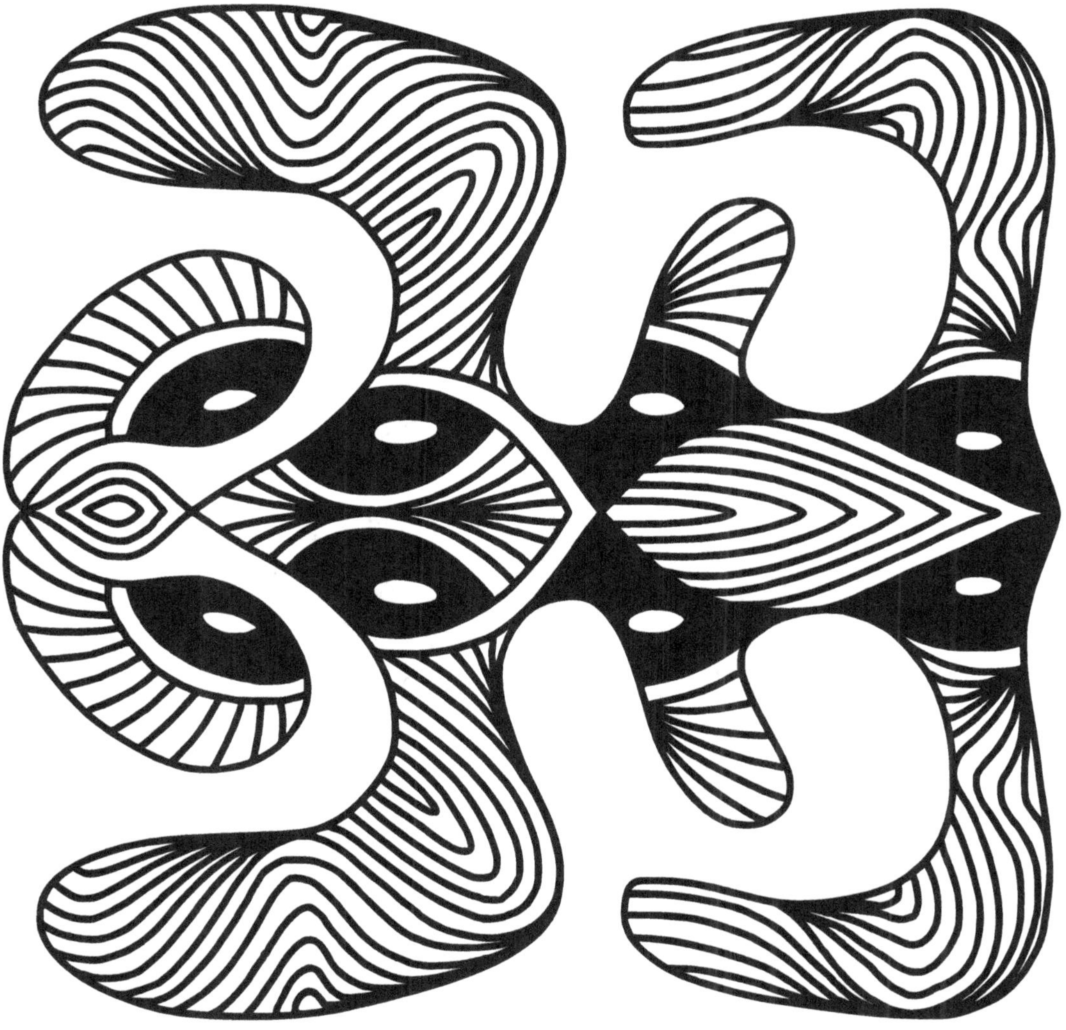

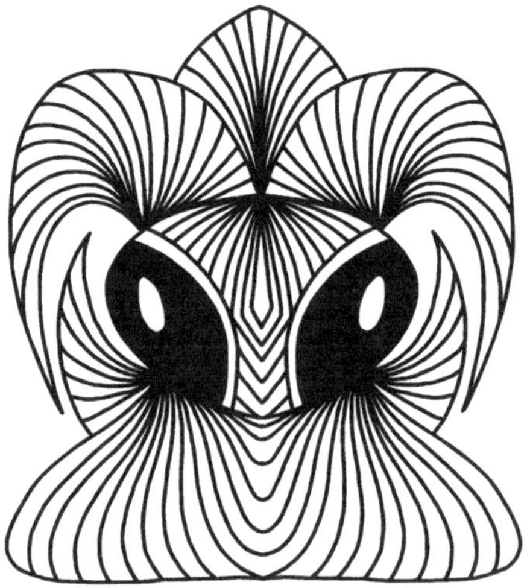

FATLINER WEIRDIES
VOLUME 1

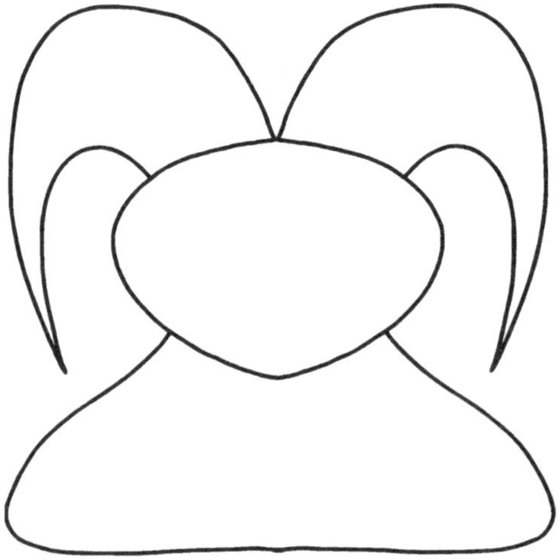

FATLINER WEIRDIES
THE TEMPLATES 1

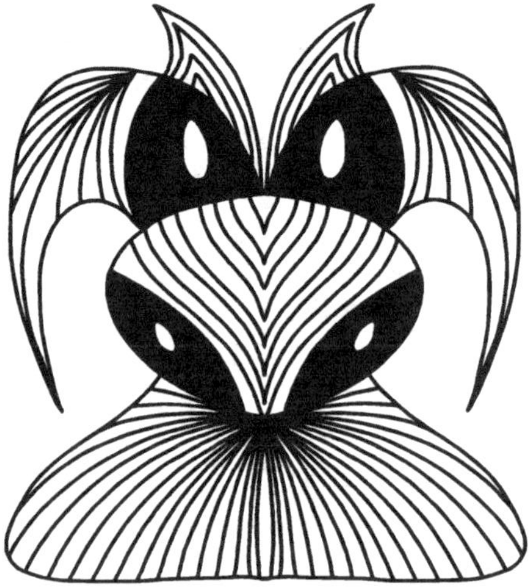

FATLINER WEIRDIES
VOLUME 3

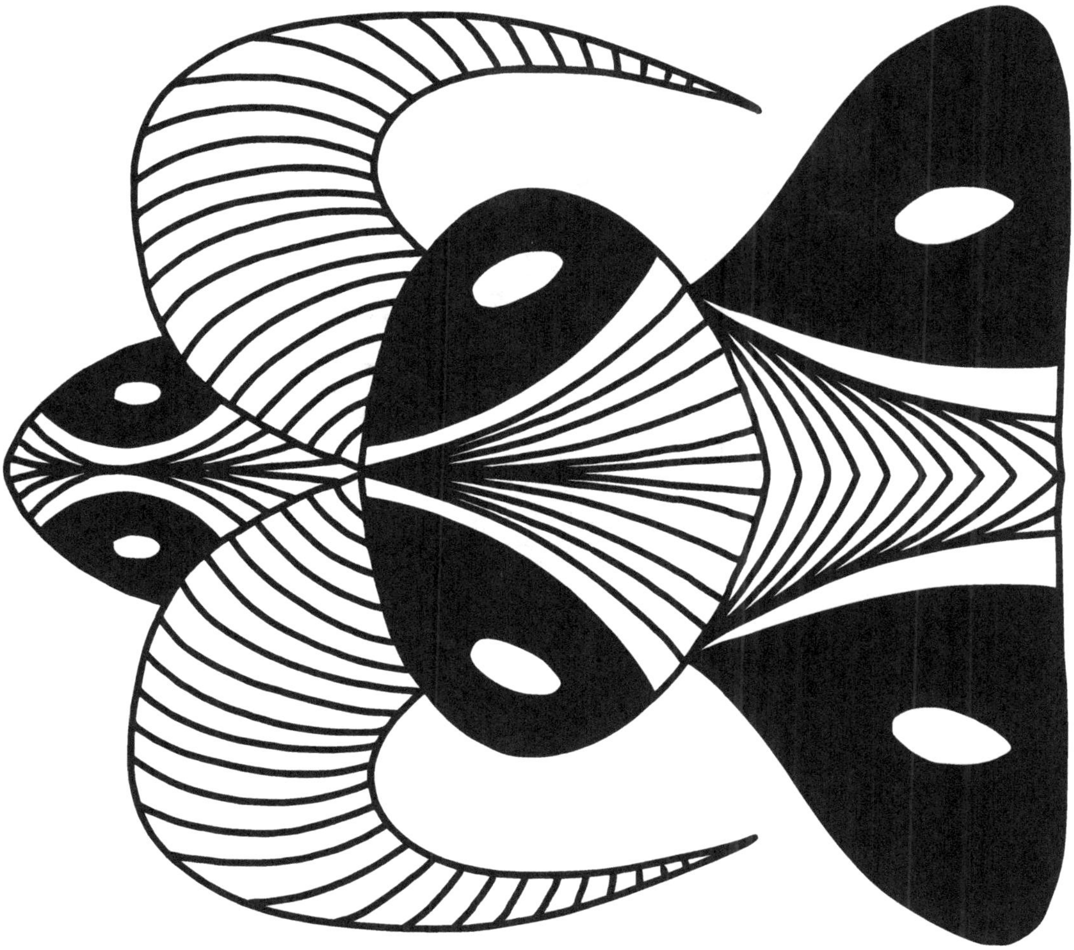

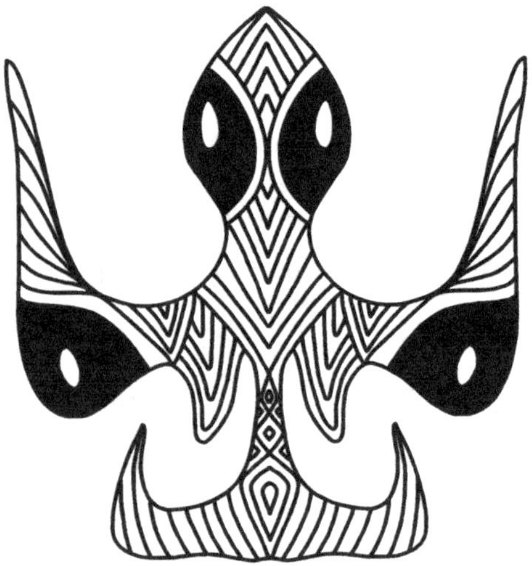

FATLINER WEIRDIES
VOLUME 1

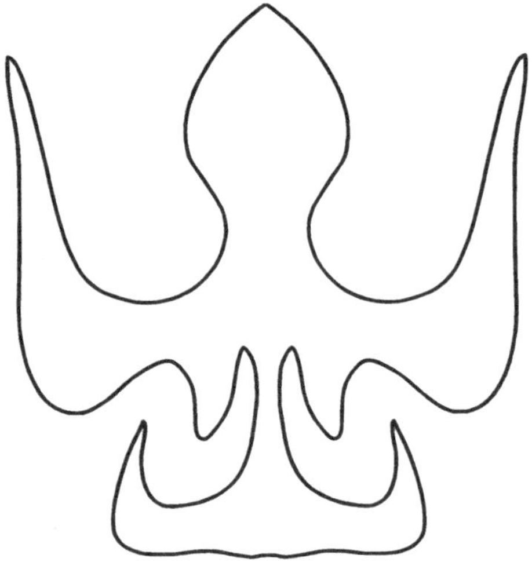

FATLINER WEIRDIES
THE TEMPLATES 1

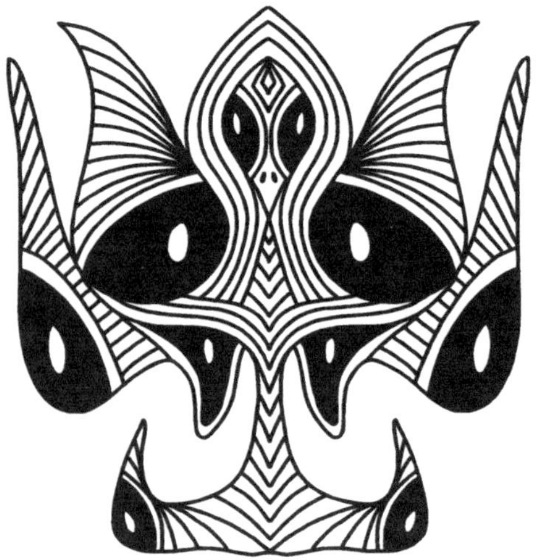

FATLINER WEIRDIES
VOLUME 3

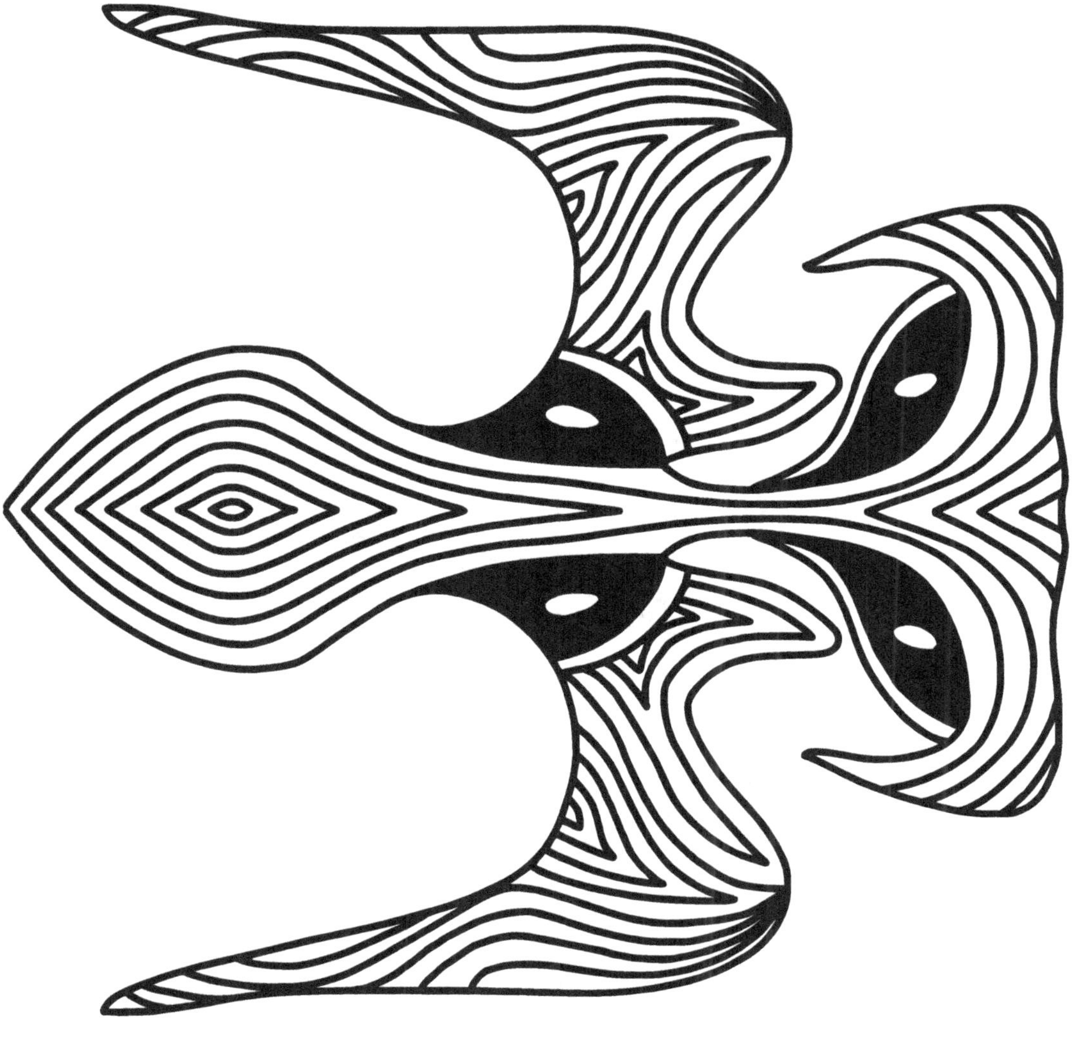

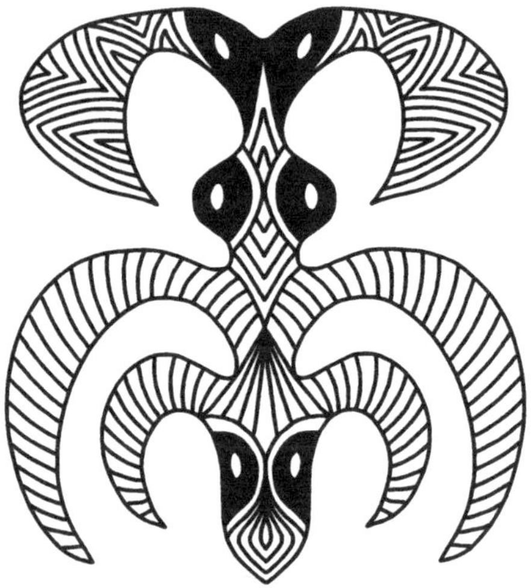

FATLINER WEIRDIES
VOLUME 1

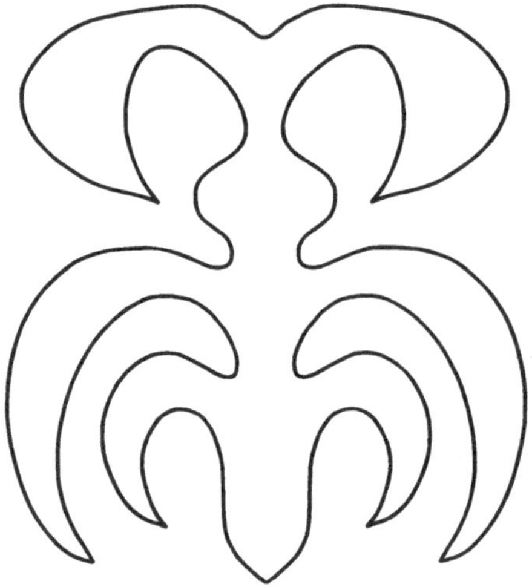

FATLINER WEIRDIES
THE TEMPLATES 1

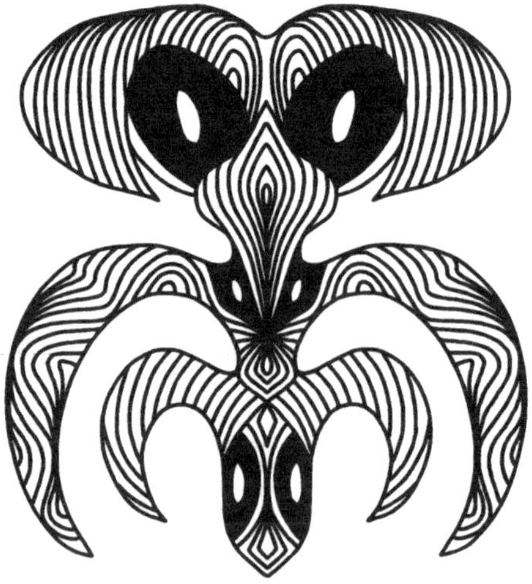

FATLINER WEIRDIES
VOLUME 3

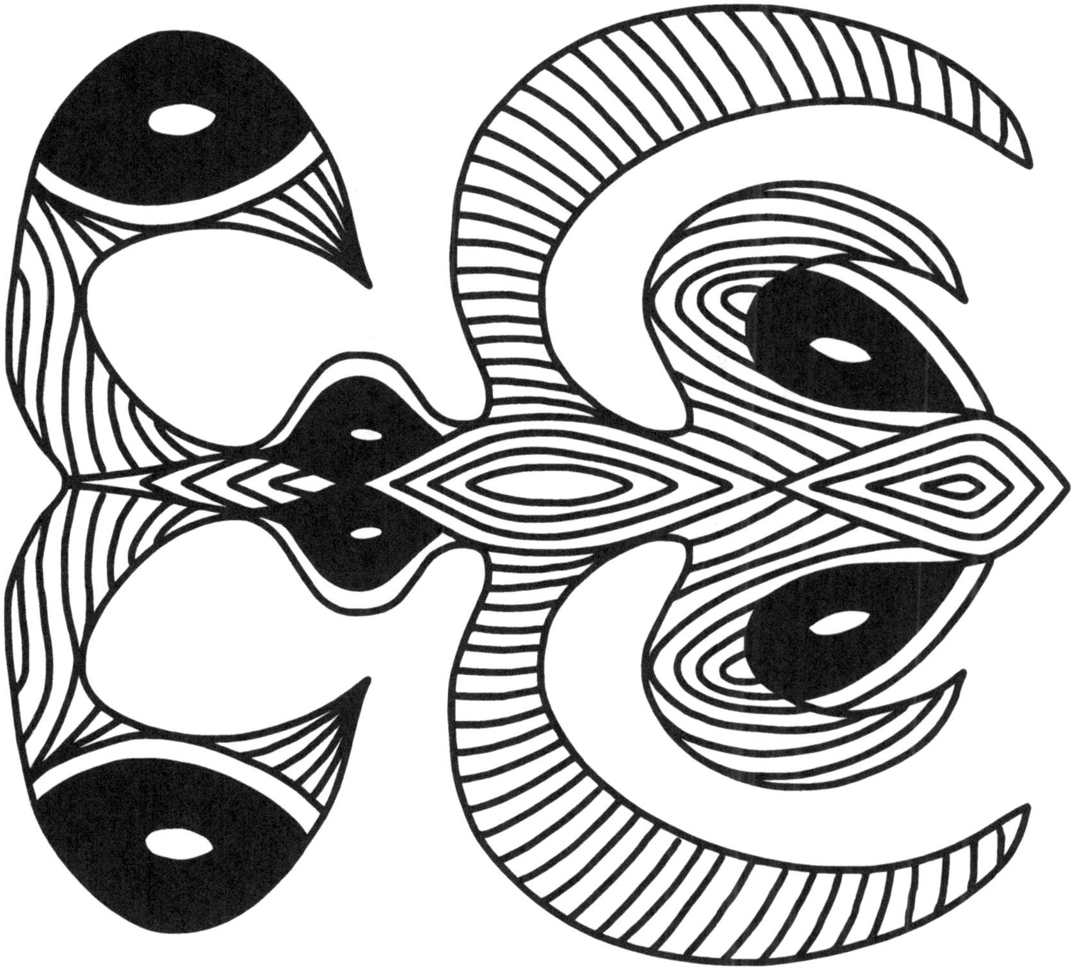

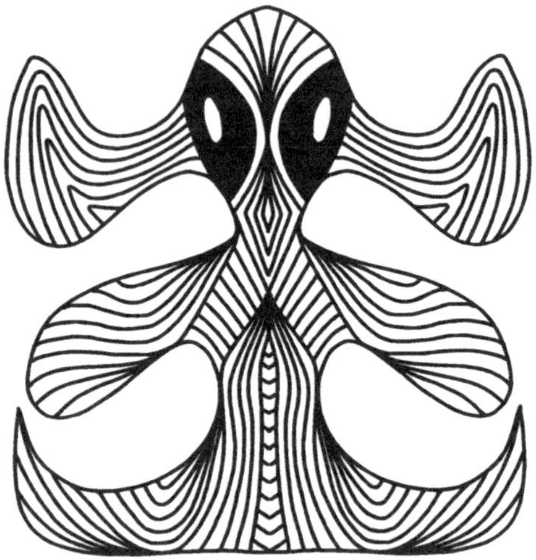

FATLINER WEIRDIES
VOLUME 1

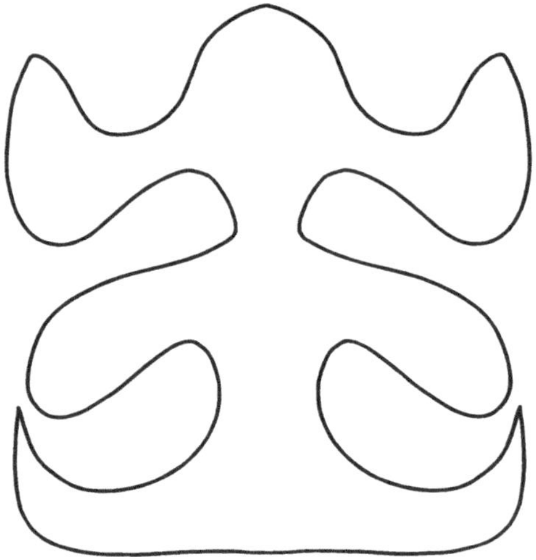

FATLINER WEIRDIES
THE TEMPLATES 1

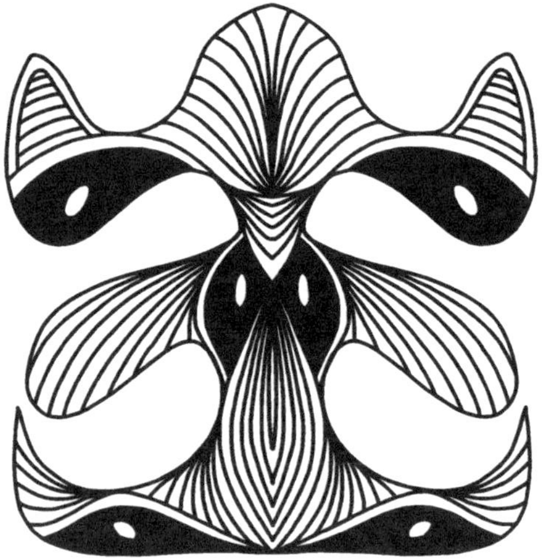

FATLINER WEIRDIES
VOLUME 3

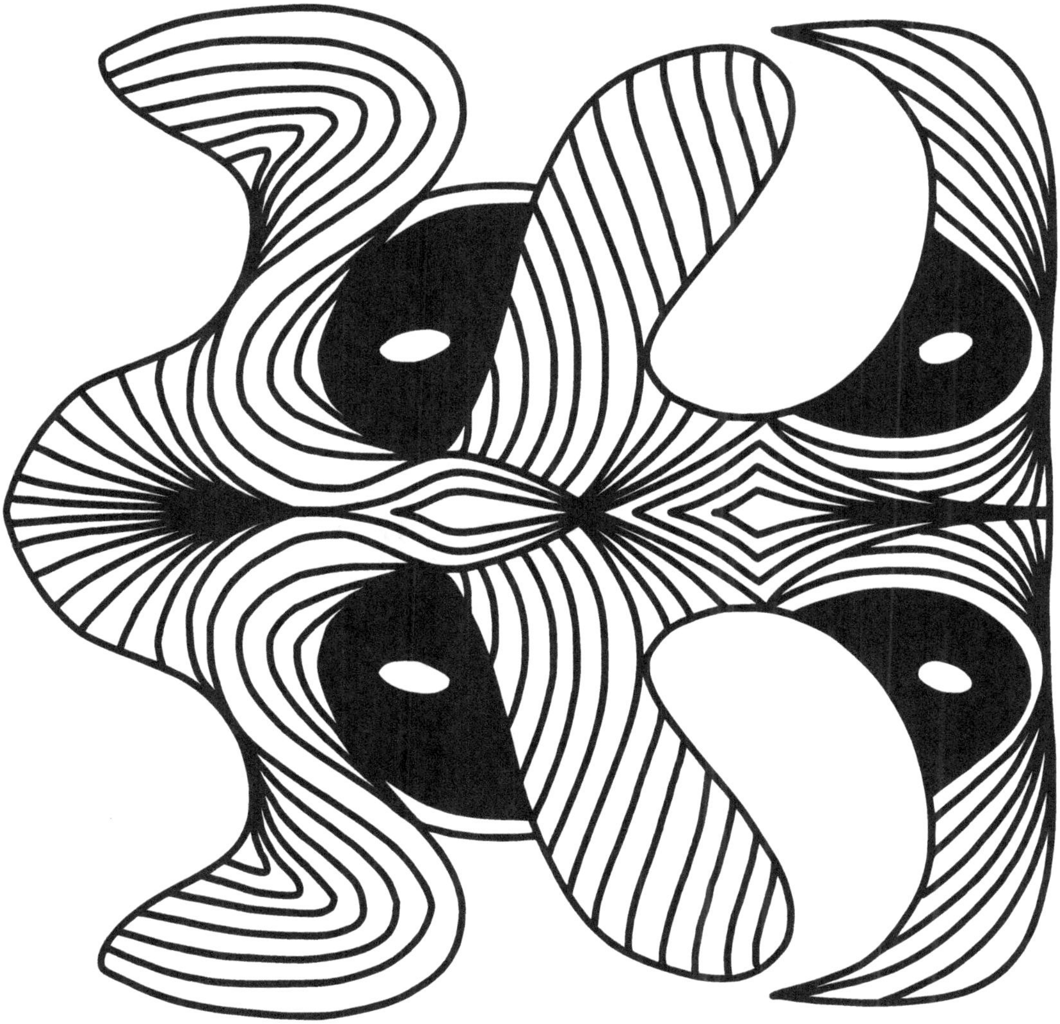

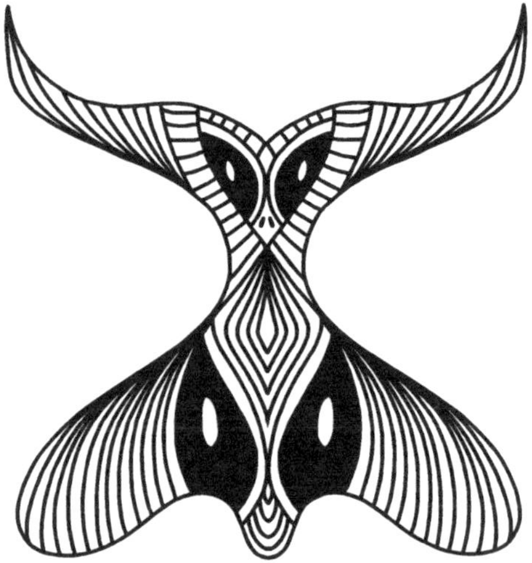

FATLINER WEIRDIES
VOLUME 1

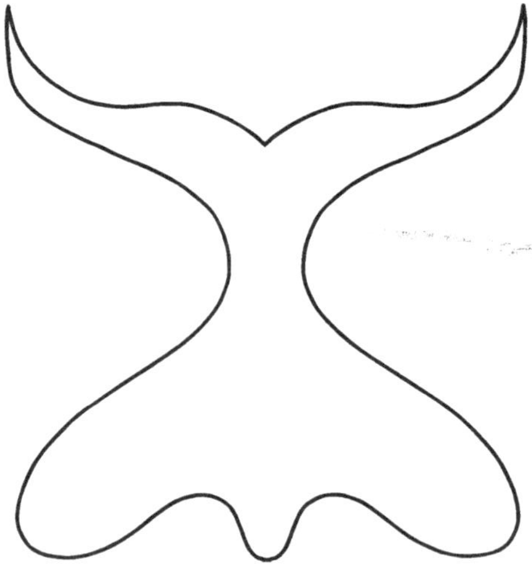

FATLINER WEIRDIES
THE TEMPLATES 1

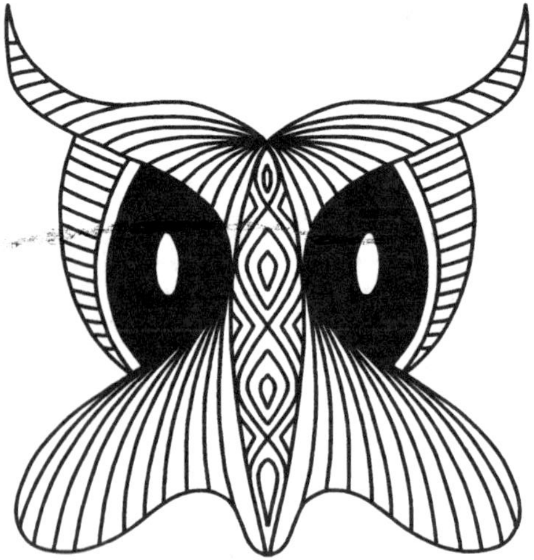

FATLINER WEIRDIES
VOLUME 3

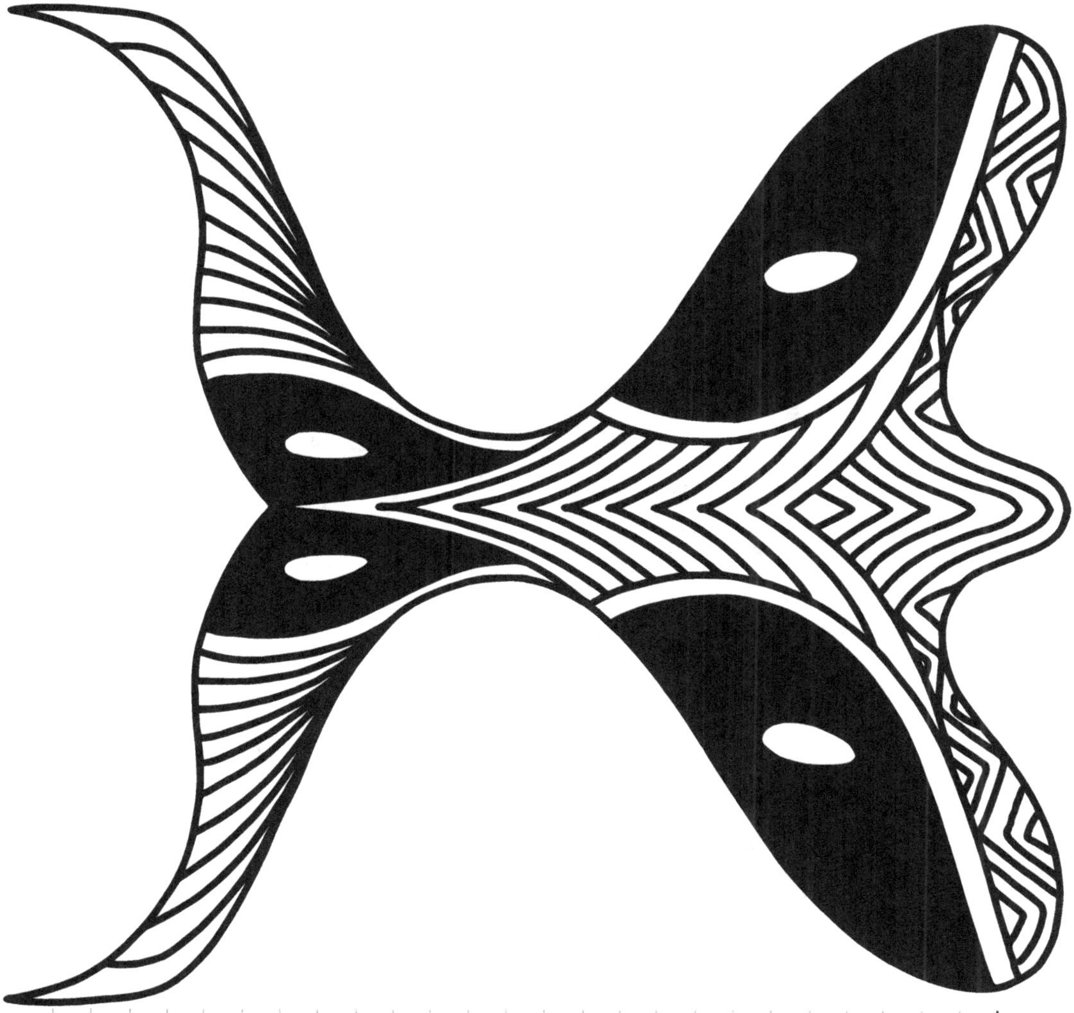

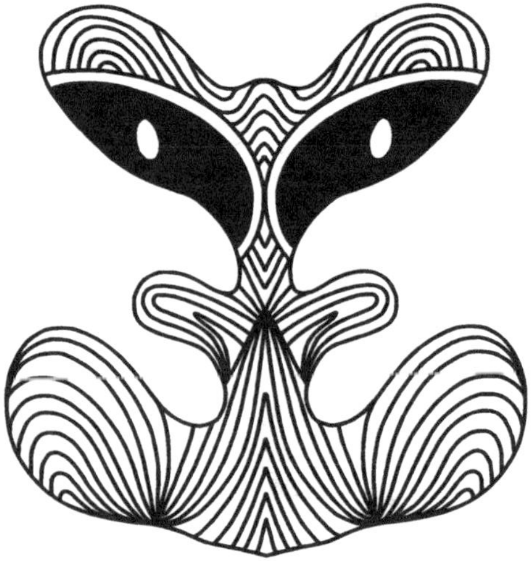
FATLINER WEIRDIES
VOLUME 1

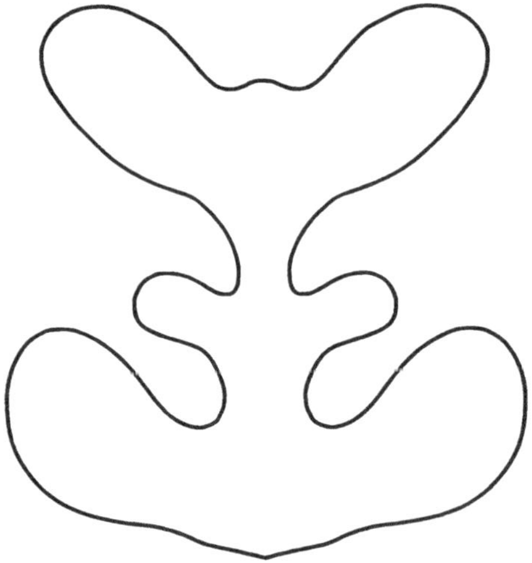
FATLINER WEIRDIES
THE TEMPLATES 1

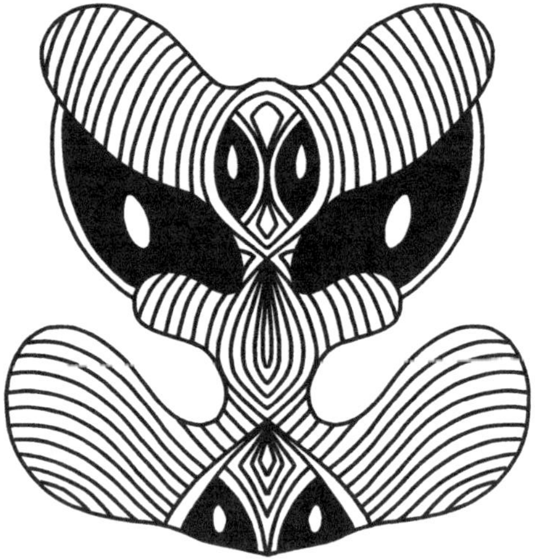
FATLINER WEIRDIES
VOLUME 3

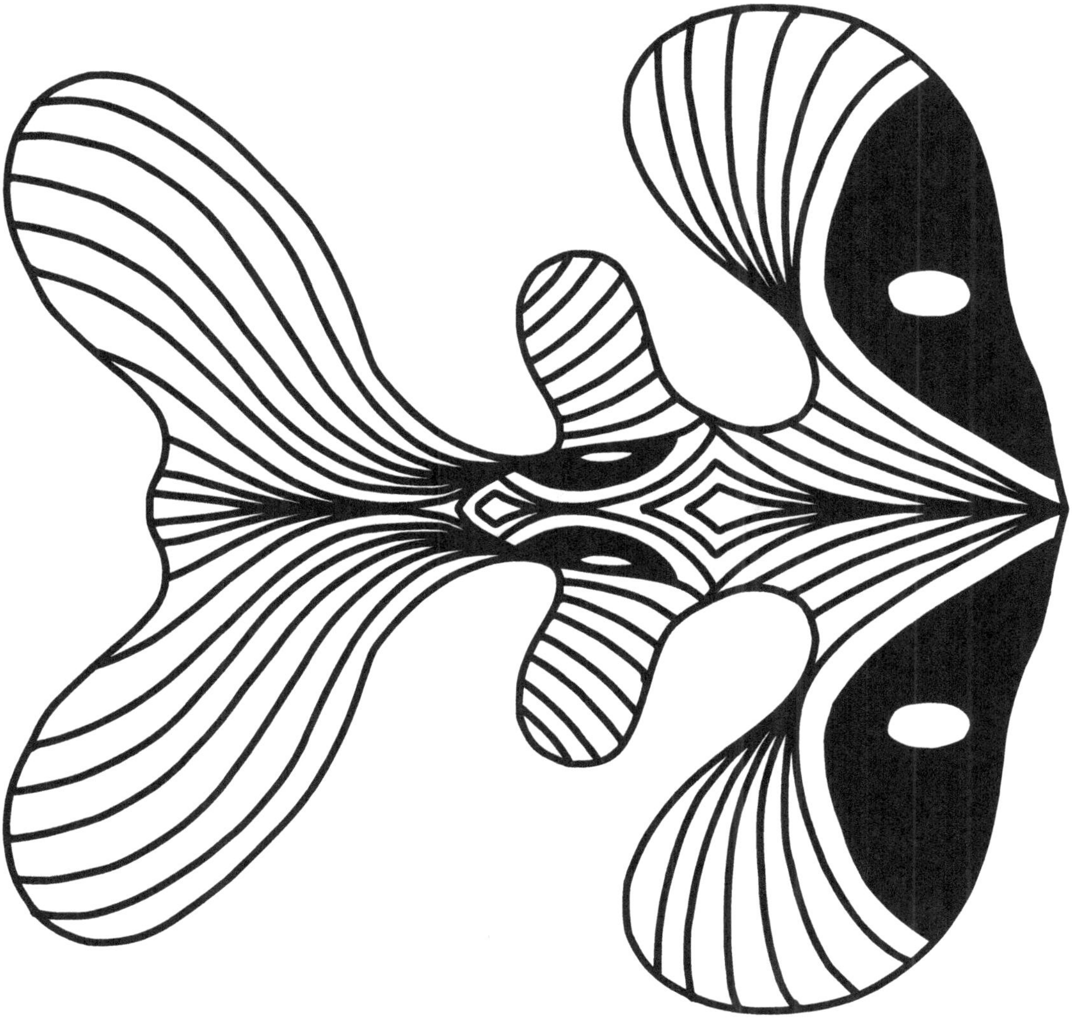

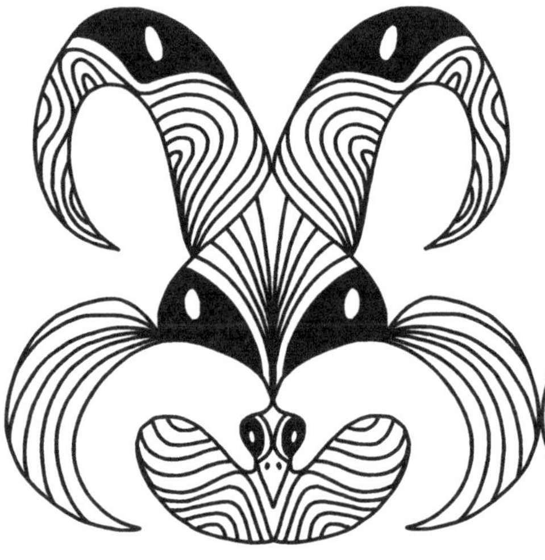

FATLINER WEIRDIES
VOLUME 1

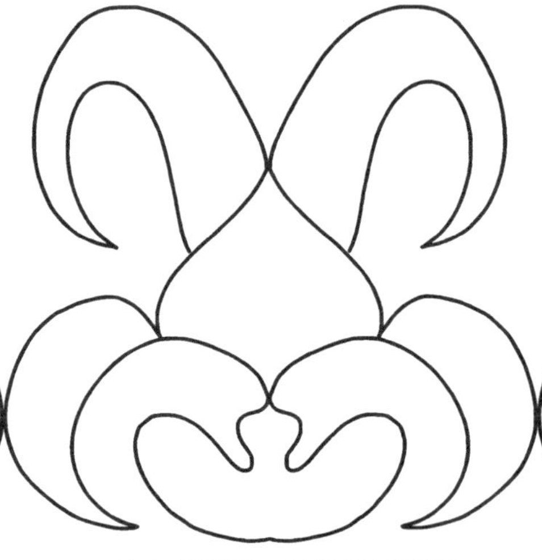

FATLINER WEIRDIES
THE TEMPLATES 1

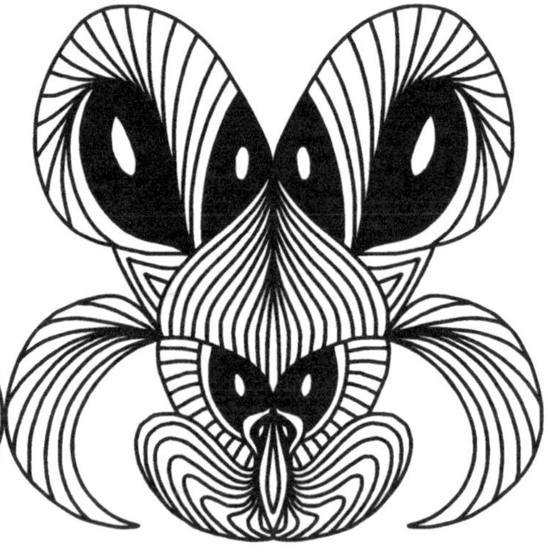

FATLINER WEIRDIES
VOLUME 3

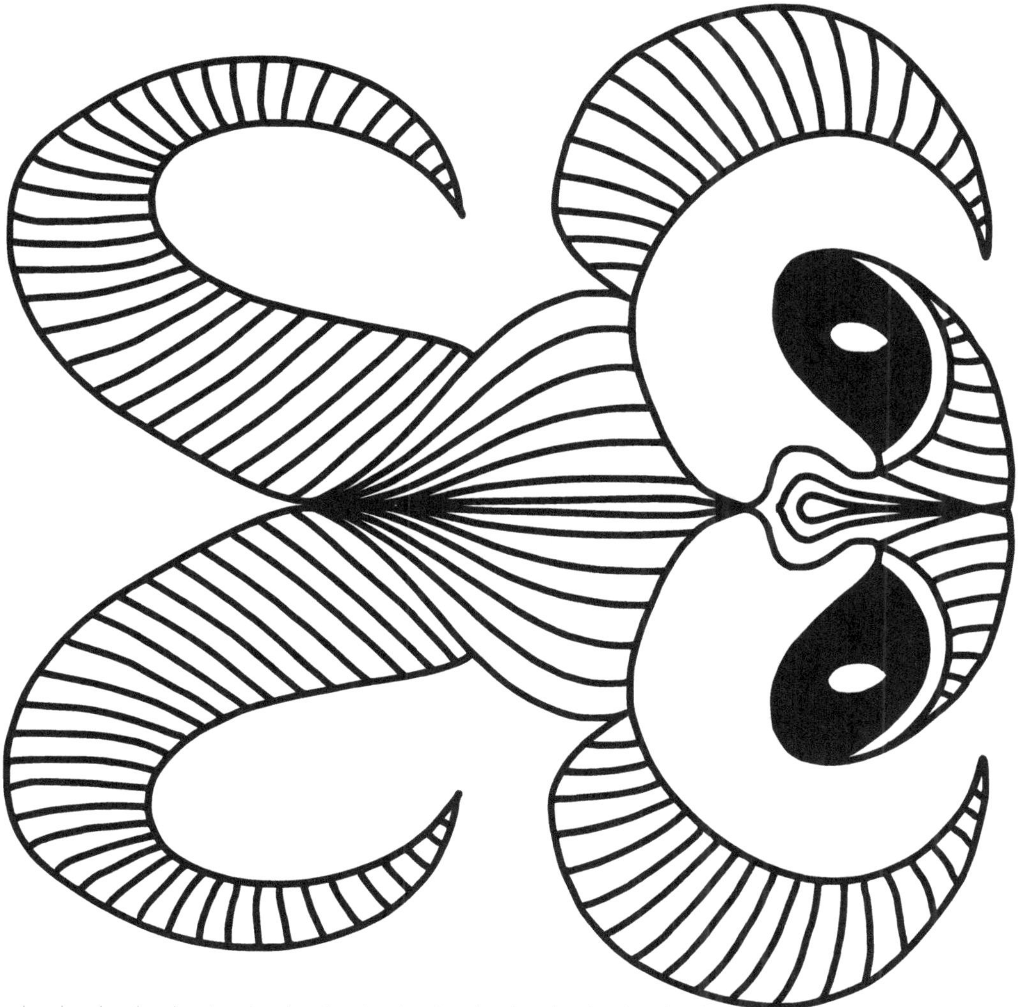

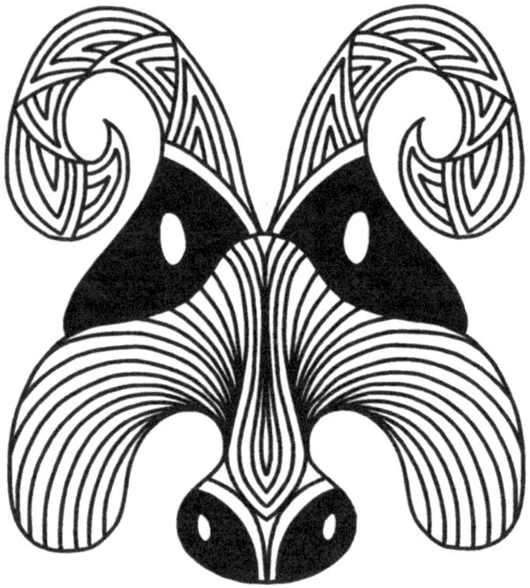

FATLINER WEIRDIES
VOLUME 1

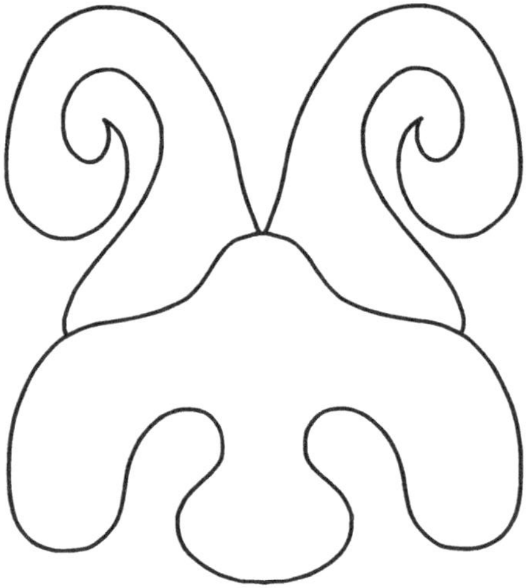

FATLINER WEIRDIES
THE TEMPLATES 1

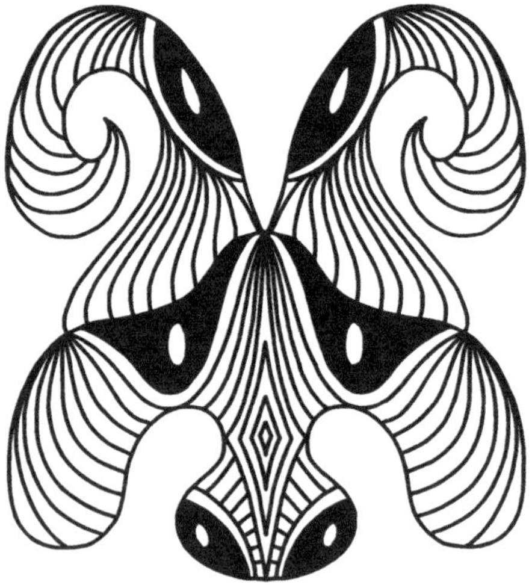

FATLINER WEIRDIES
VOLUME 3

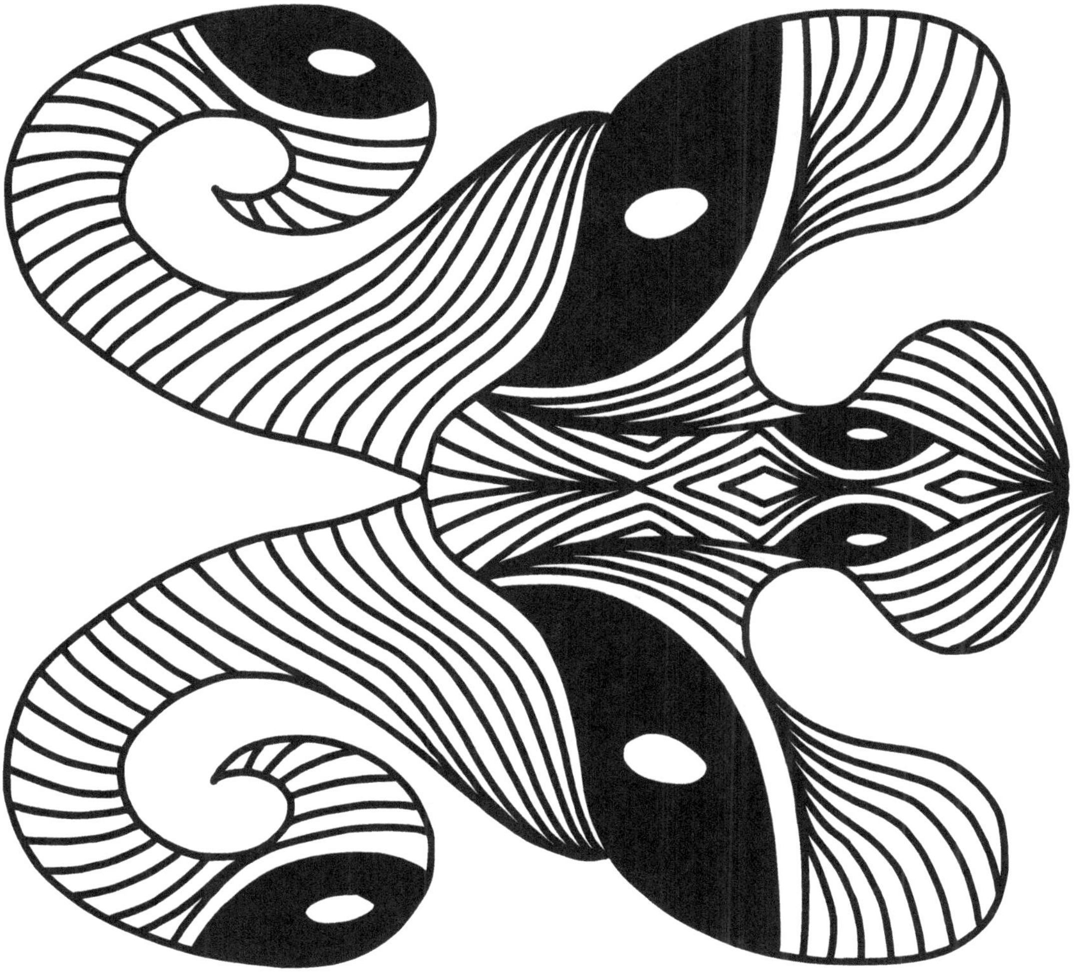

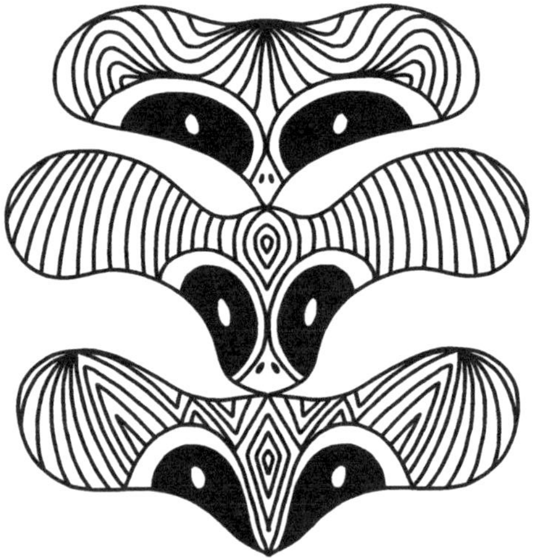

FATLINER WEIRDIES
VOLUME 1

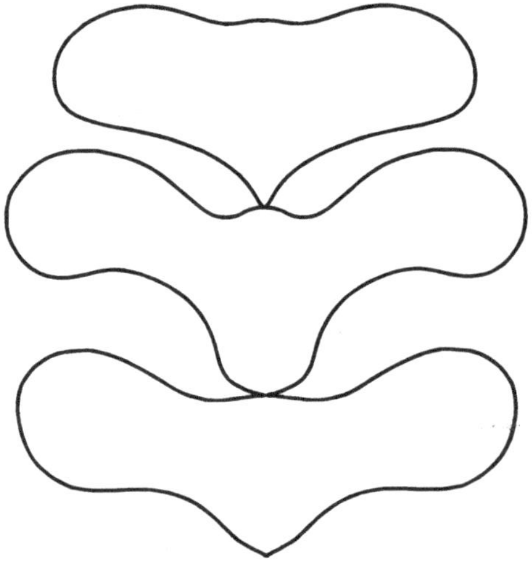

FATLINER WEIRDIES
THE TEMPLATES 1

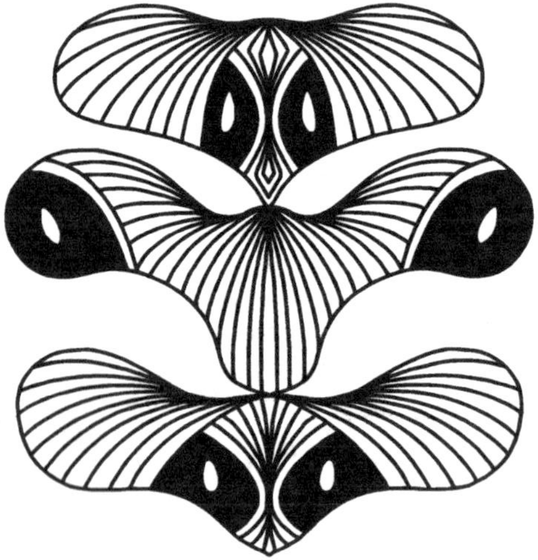

FATLINER WEIRDIES
VOLUME 3

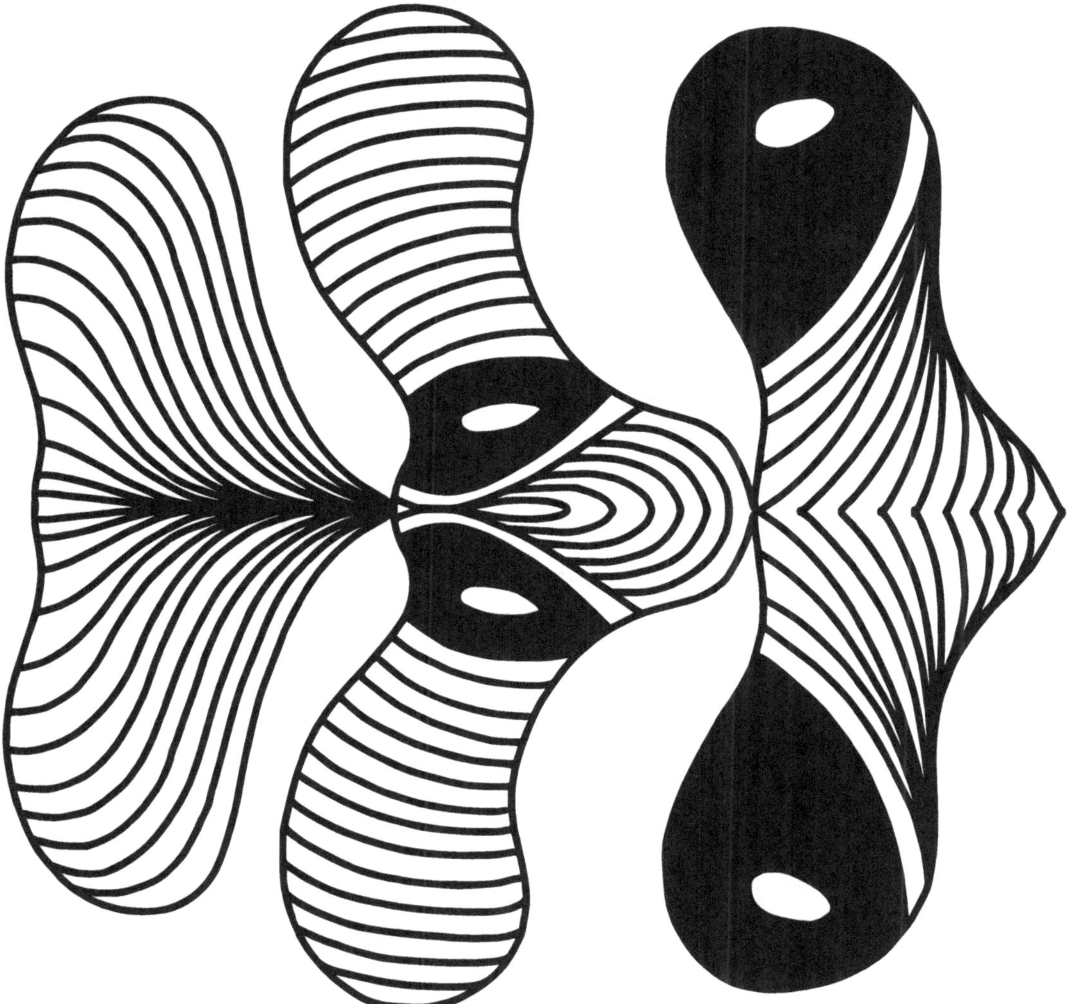

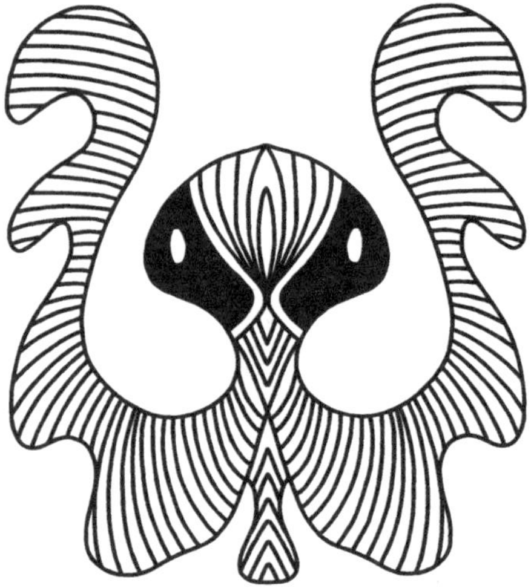

FATLINER WEIRDIES
VOLUME 1

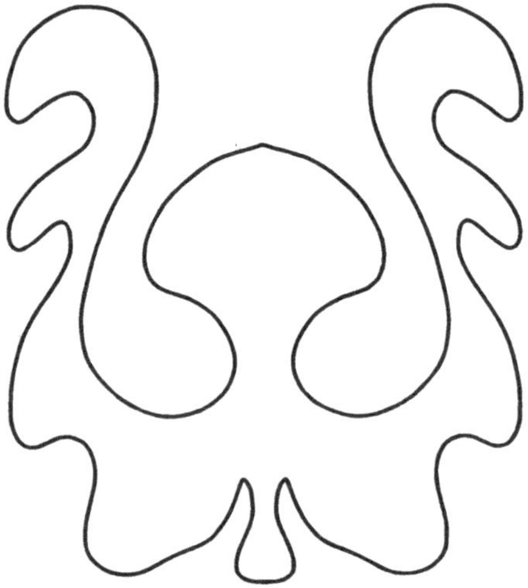

FATLINER WEIRDIES
THE TEMPLATES 1

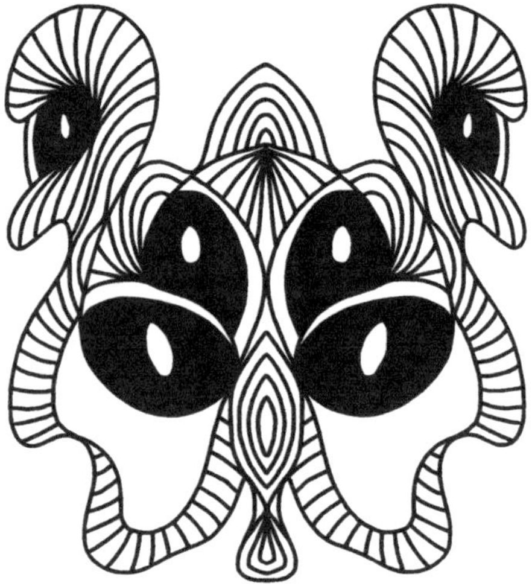

FATLINER WEIRDIES
VOLUME 3

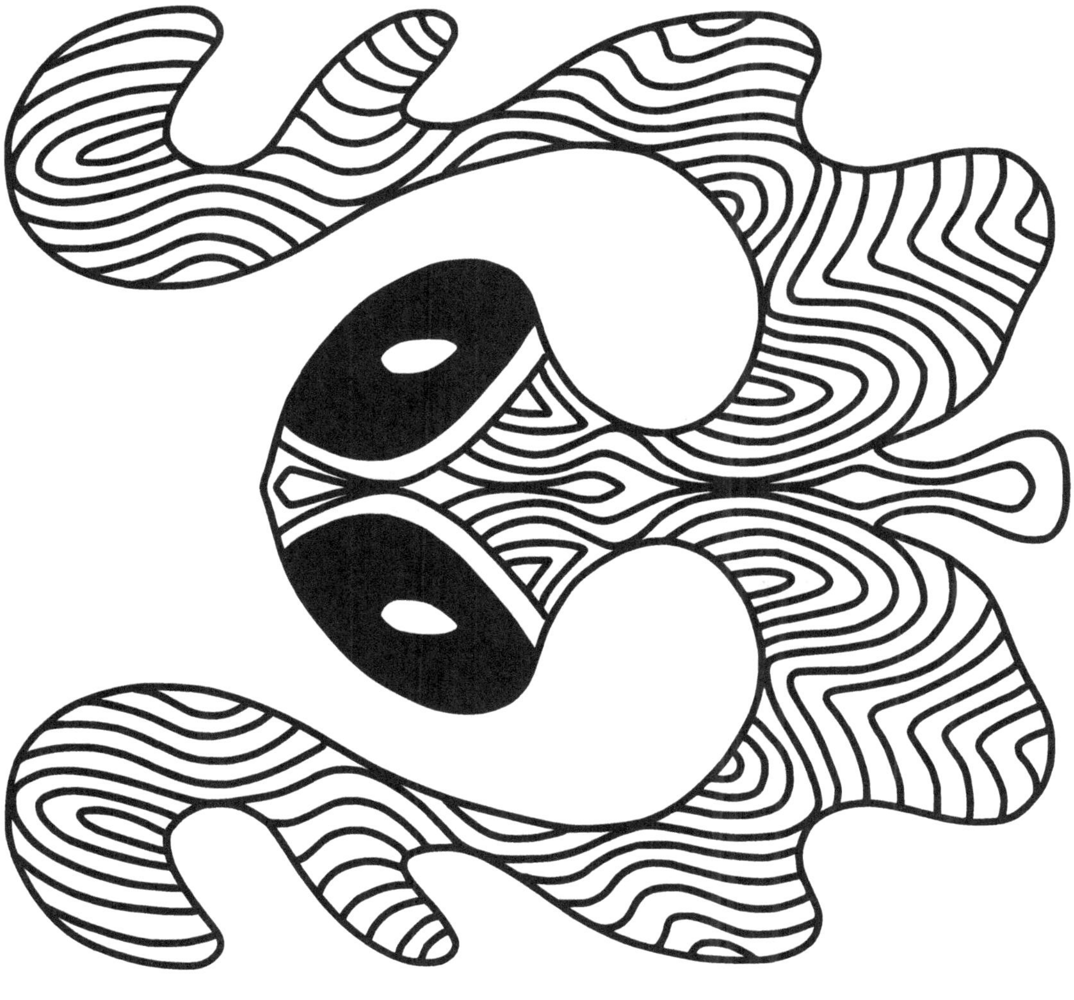

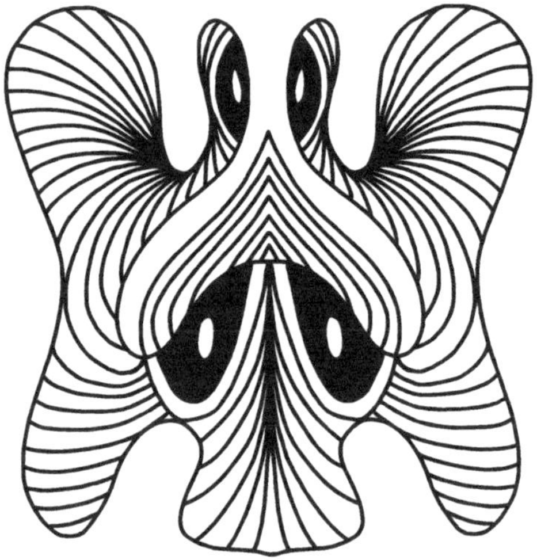

FATLINER WEIRDIES
VOLUME 1

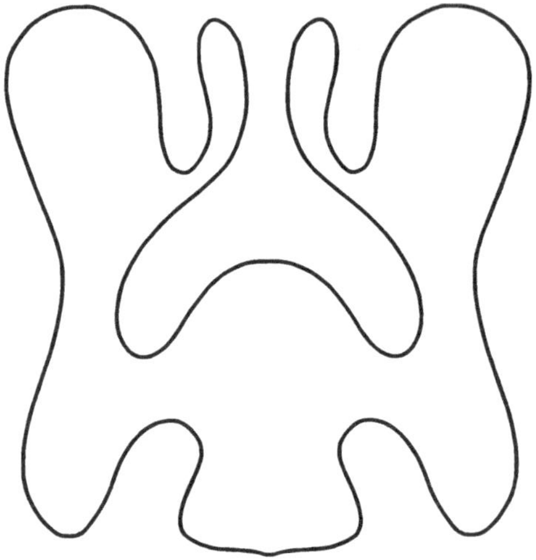

FATLINER WEIRDIES
THE TEMPLATES 1

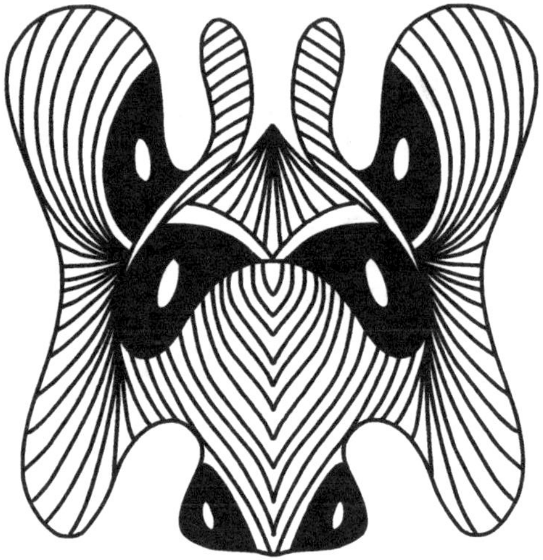

FATLINER WEIRDIES
VOLUME 3

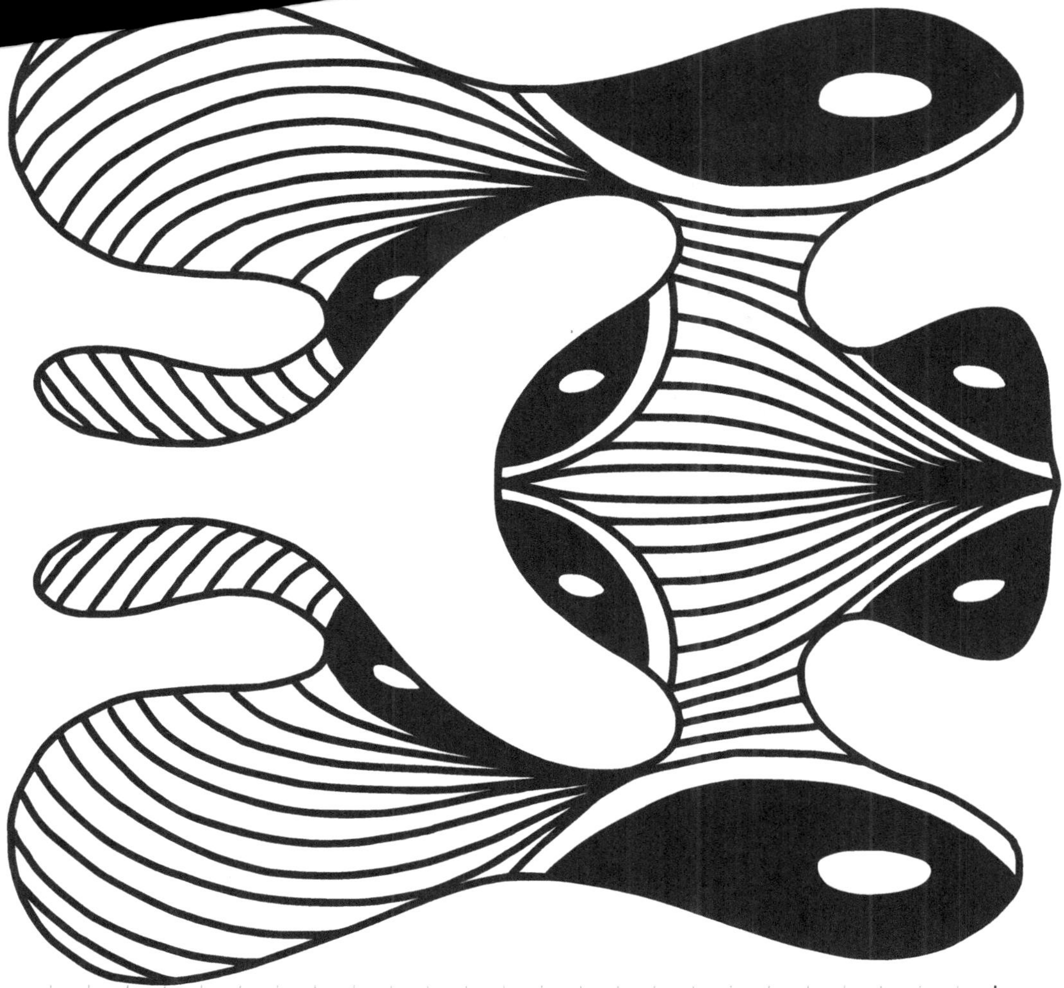

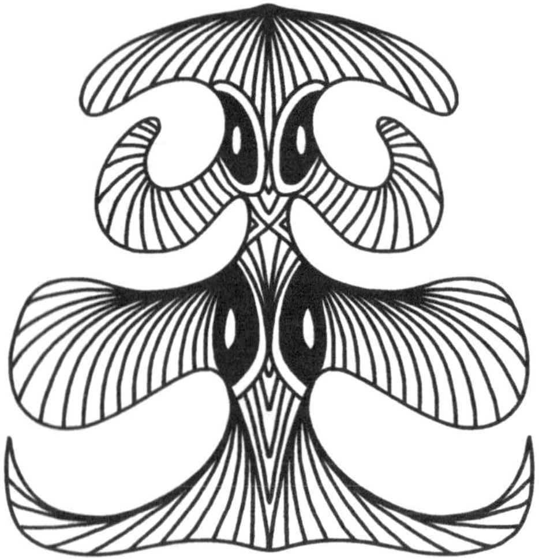

FATLINER WEIRDIES
VOLUME 1

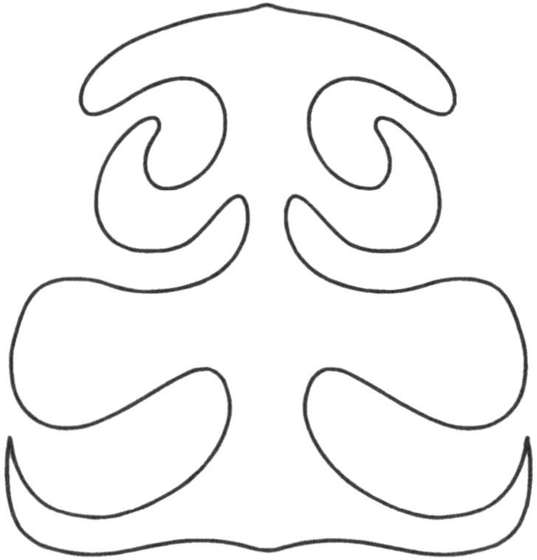

FATLINER WEIRDIES
THE TEMPLATES 1

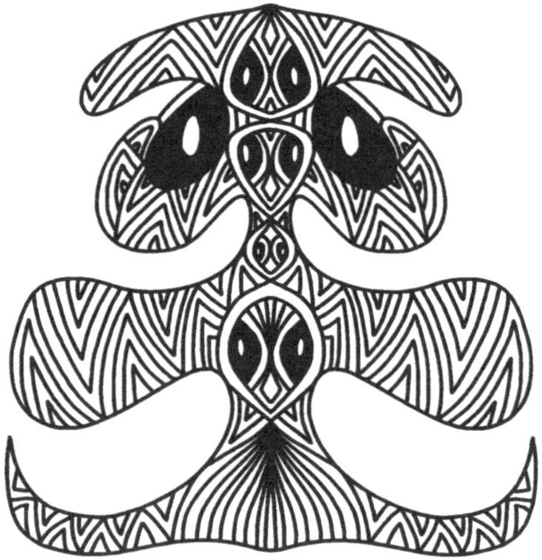

FATLINER WEIRDIES
VOLUME 3

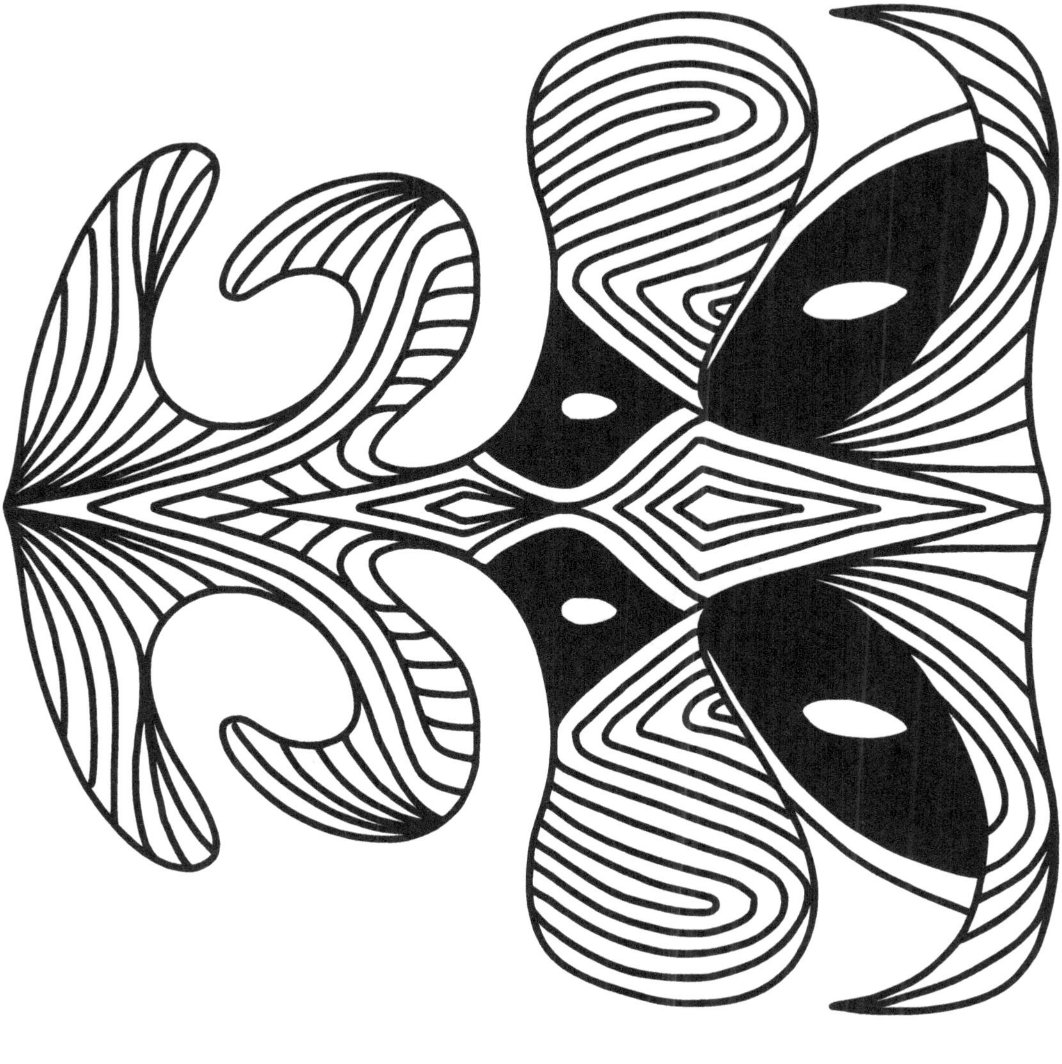

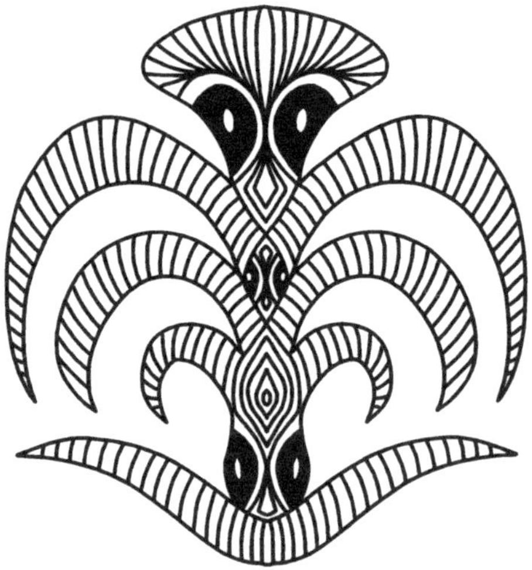

FATLINER WEIRDIES
VOLUME 1

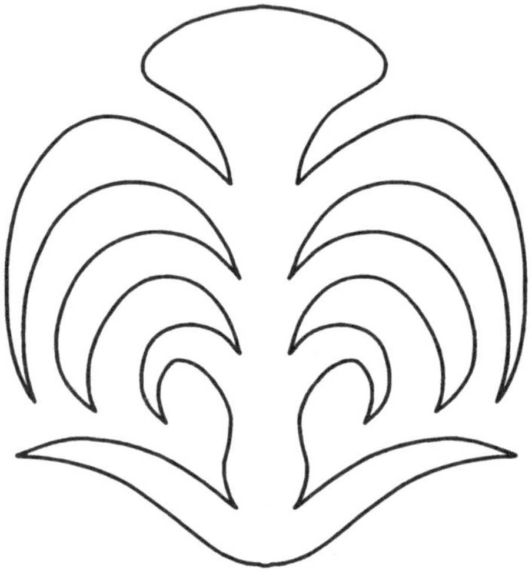

FATLINER WEIRDIES
THE TEMPLATES 1

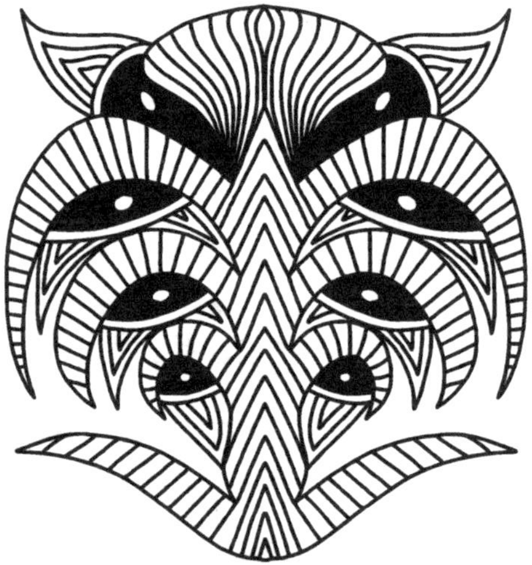

FATLINER WEIRDIES
VOLUME 3

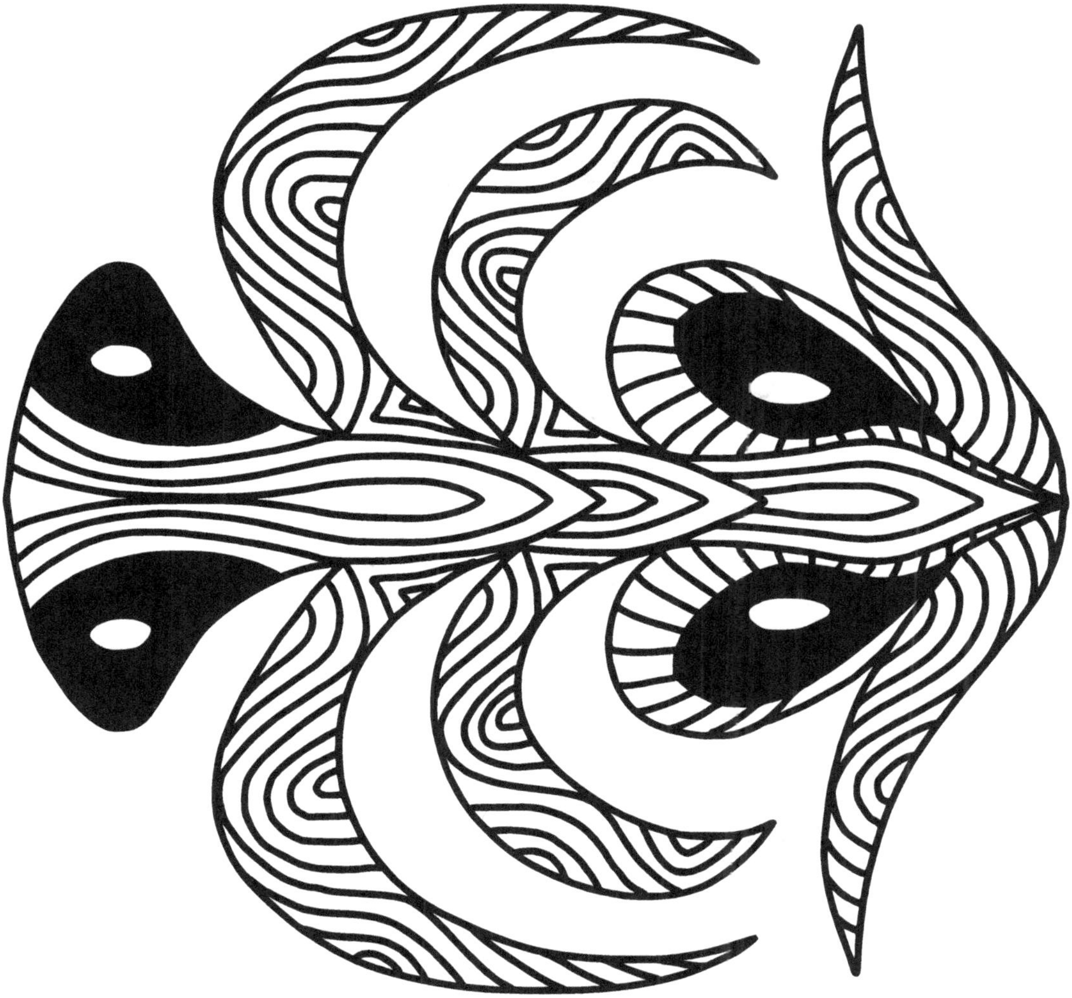

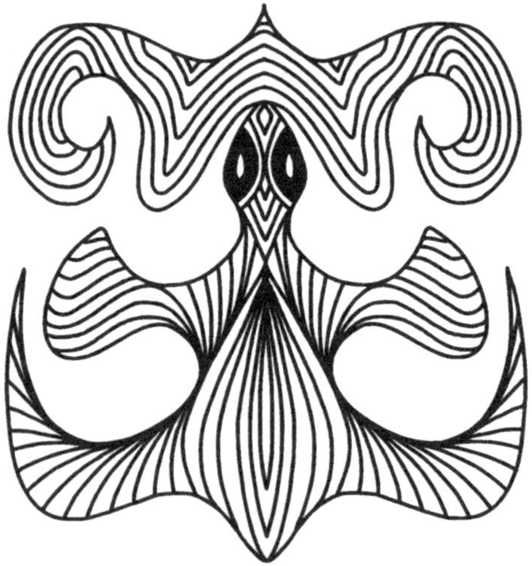

FATLINER WEIRDIES
VOLUME 1

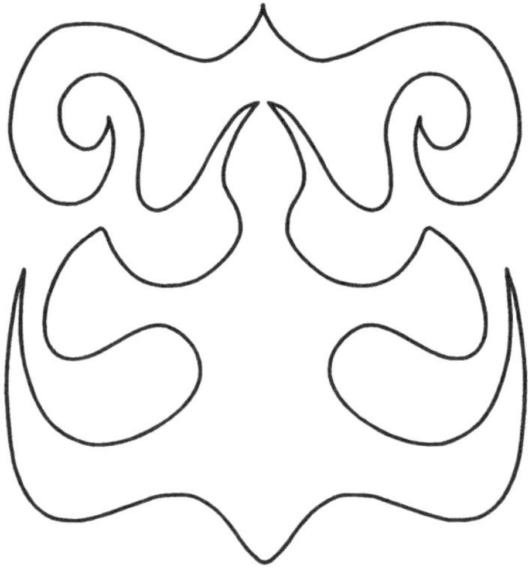

FATLINER WEIRDIES
THE TEMPLATES 1

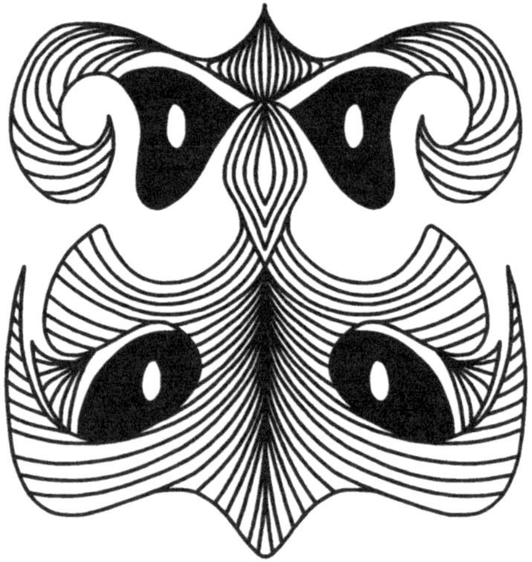

FATLINER WEIRDIES
VOLUME 3

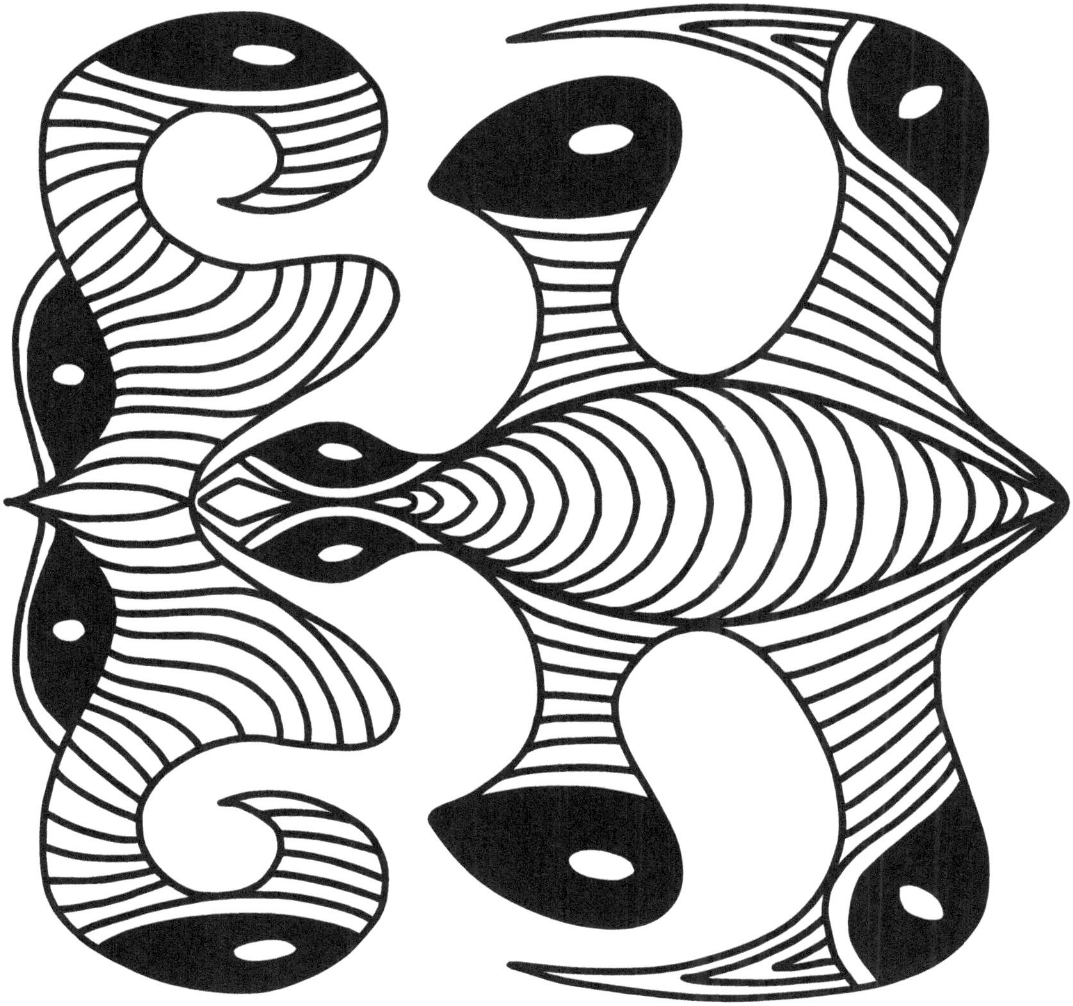

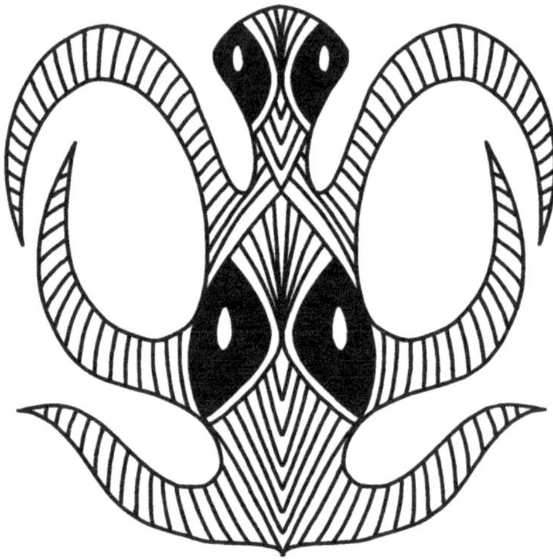

FATLINER WEIRDIES
VOLUME 1

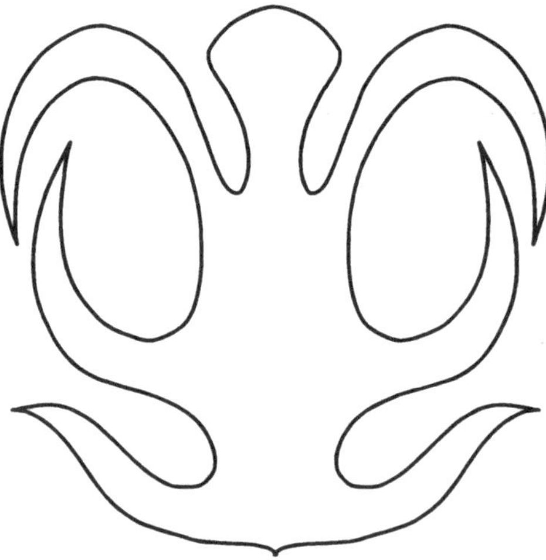

FATLINER WEIRDIES
THE TEMPLATES 1

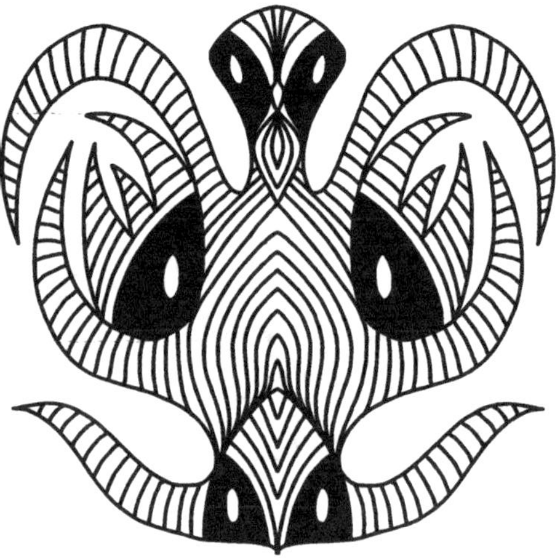

FATLINER WEIRDIES
VOLUME 3

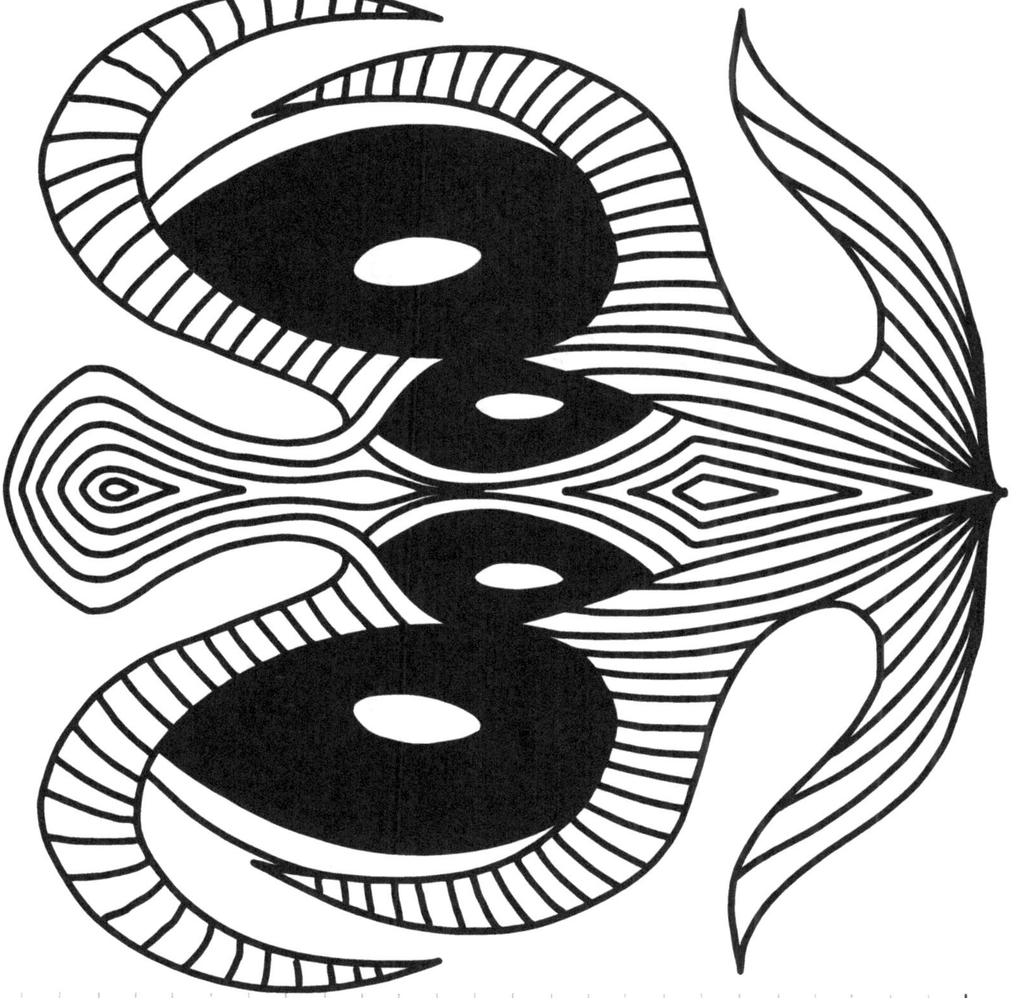

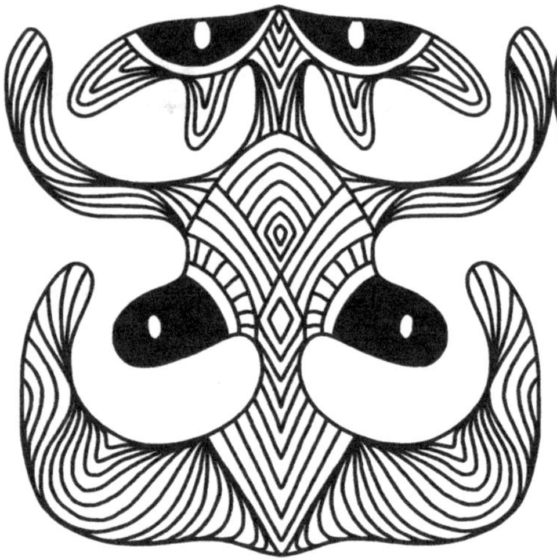

FATLINER WEIRDIES
VOLUME 1

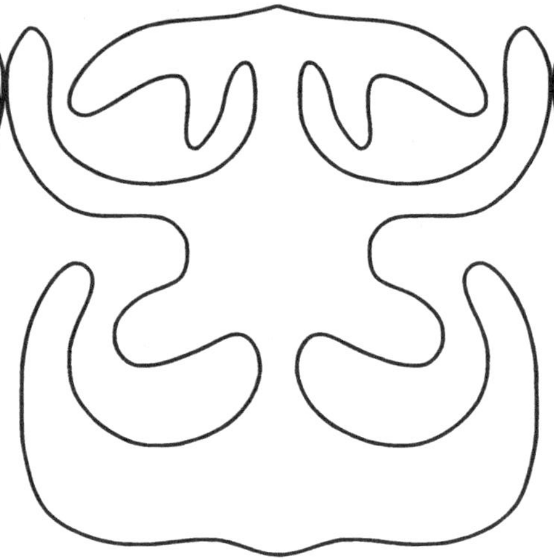

FATLINER WEIRDIES
THE TEMPLATES 1

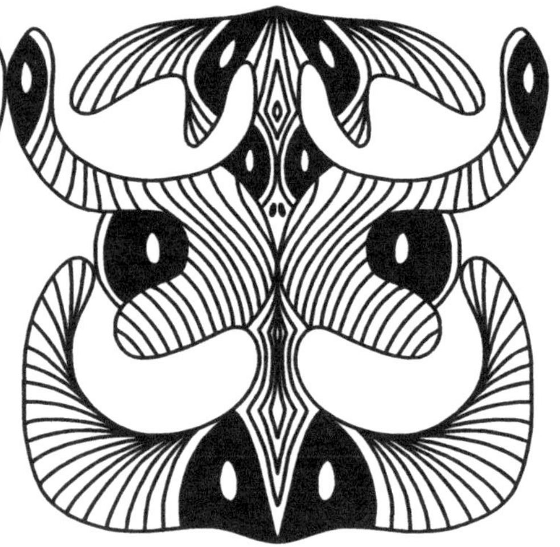

FATLINER WEIRDIES
VOLUME 3

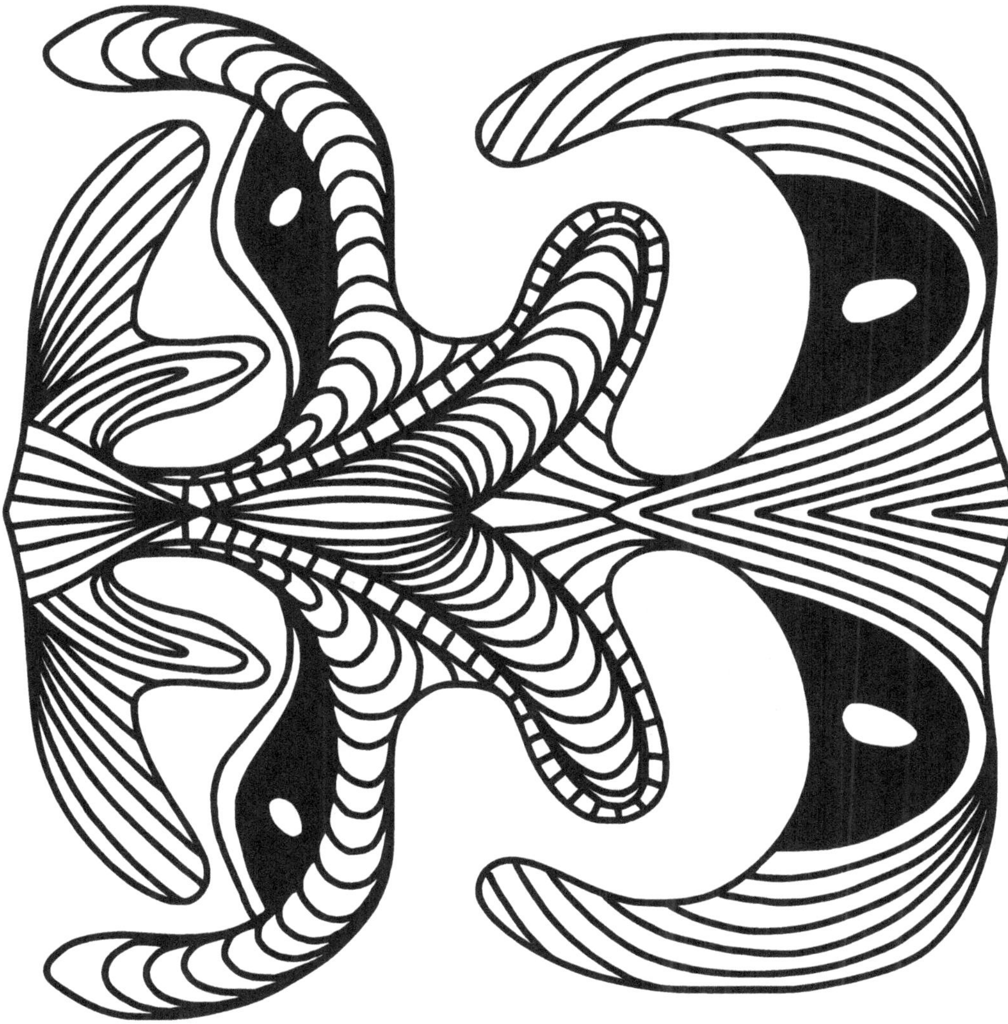

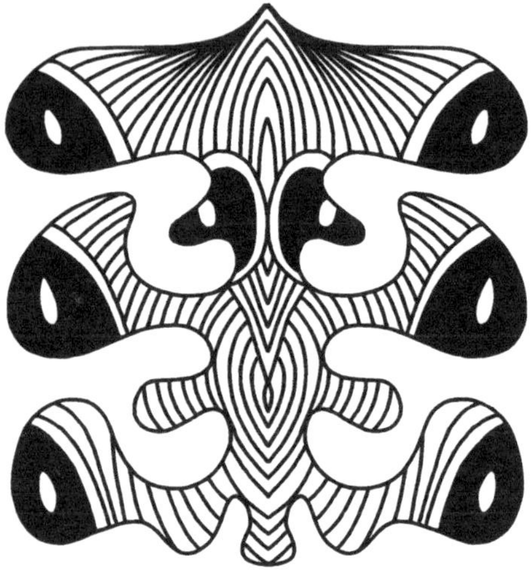
FATLINER WEIRDIES
VOLUME 1

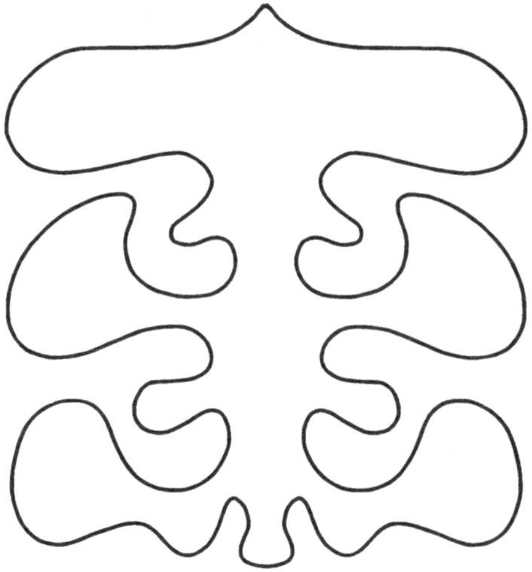
FATLINER WEIRDIES
THE TEMPLATES 1

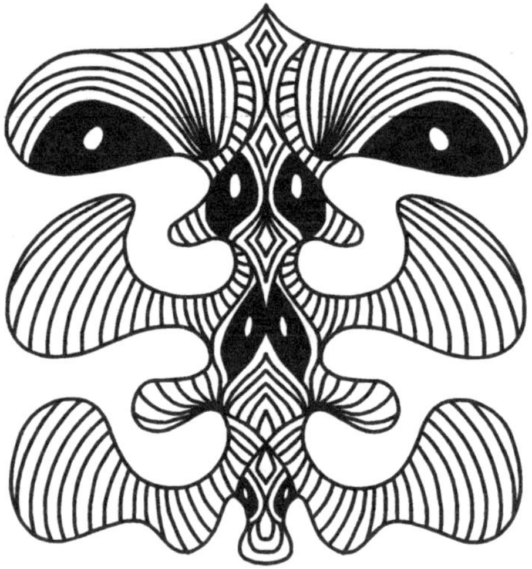
FATLINER WEIRDIES
VOLUME 3

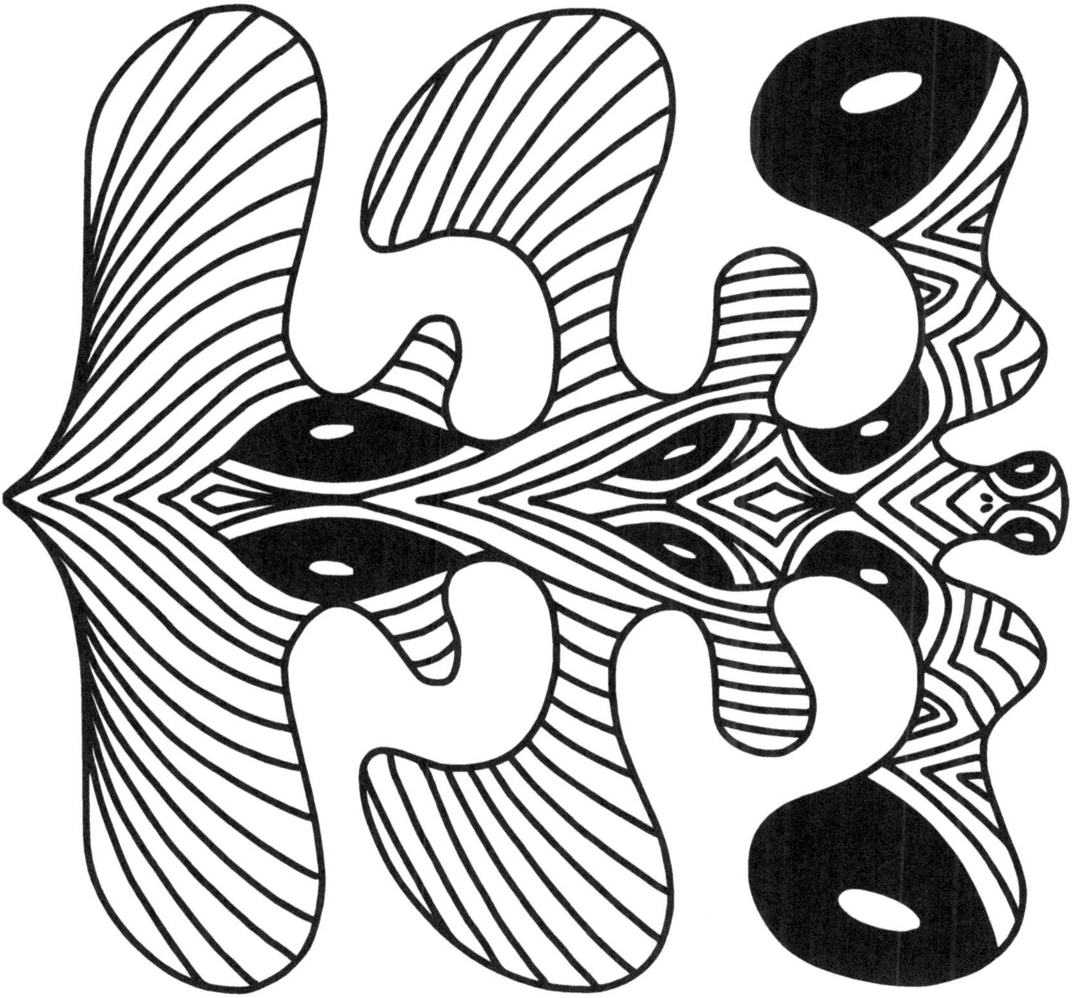

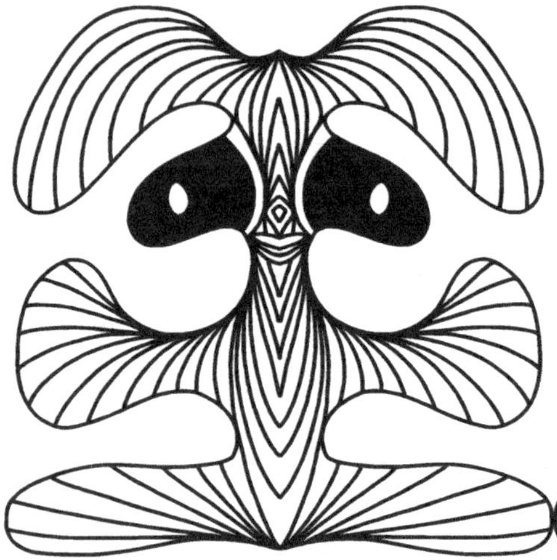

FATLINER WEIRDIES
VOLUME 1

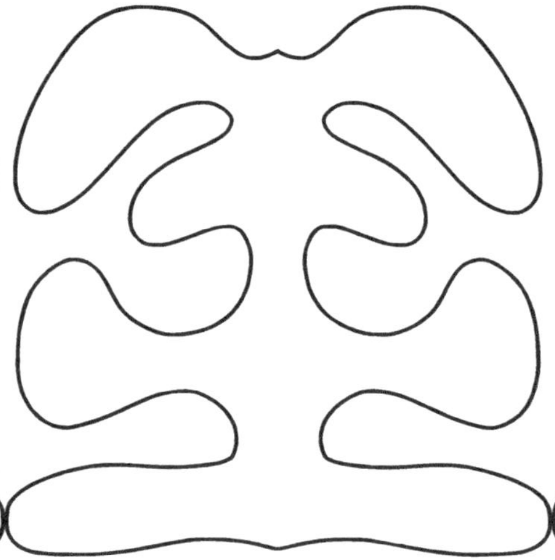

FATLINER WEIRDIES
THE TEMPLATES 1

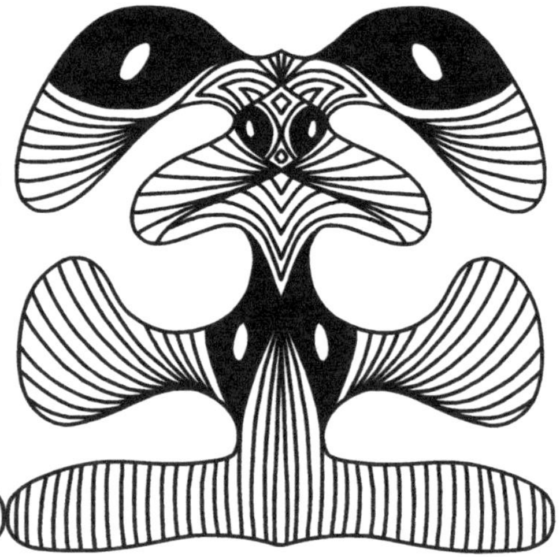

FATLINER WEIRDIES
VOLUME 3

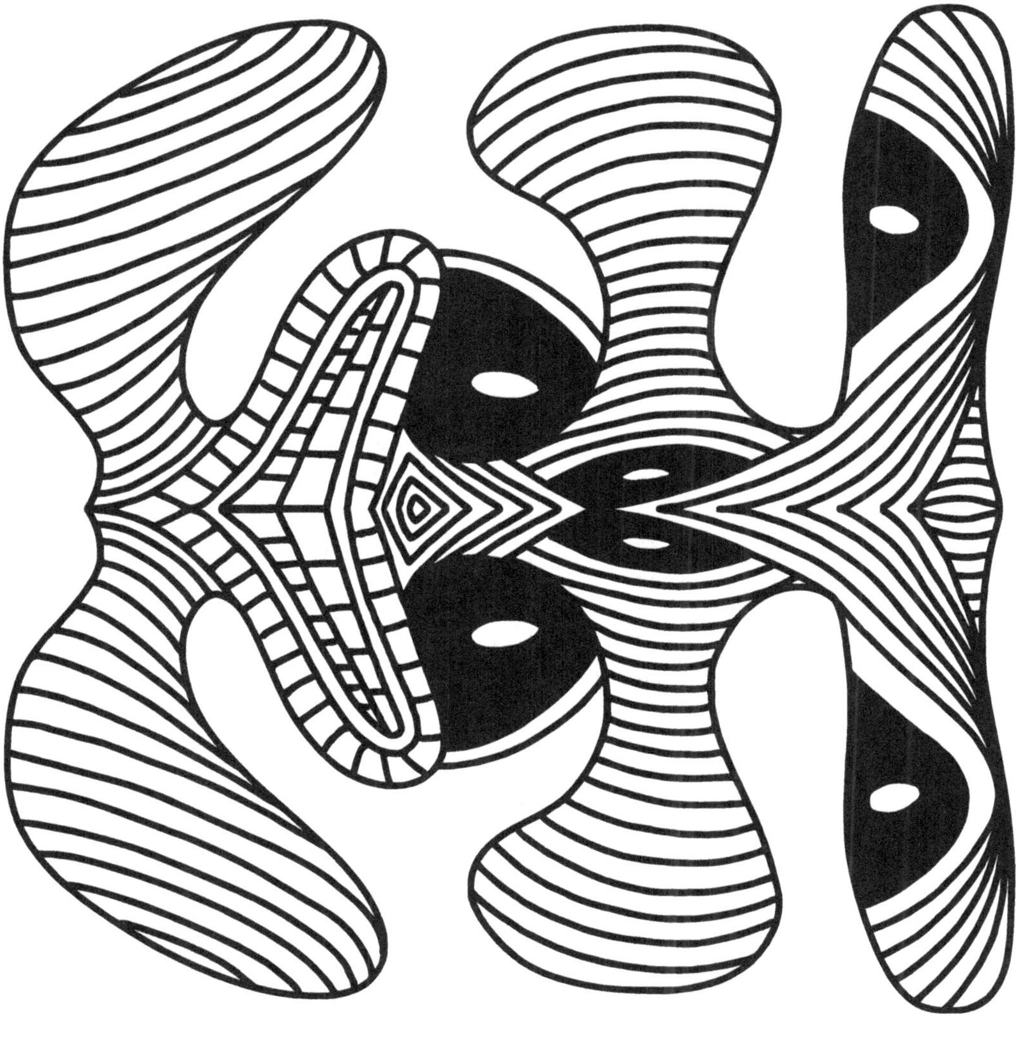

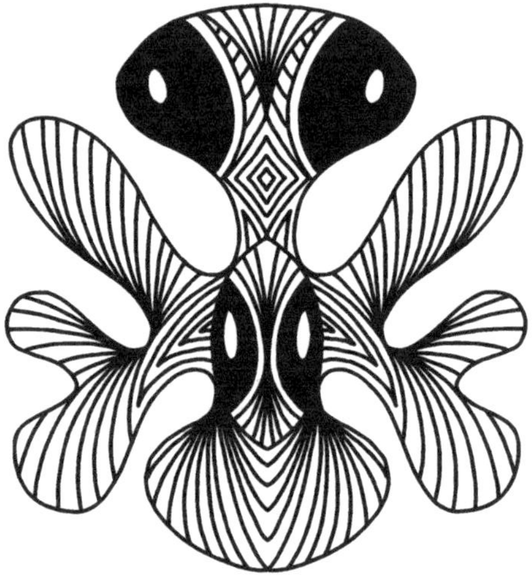

FATLINER WEIRDIES
VOLUME 1

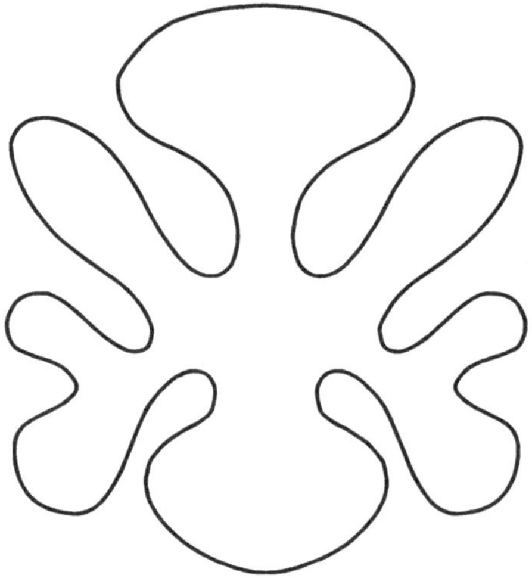

FATLINER WEIRDIES
THE TEMPLATES 1

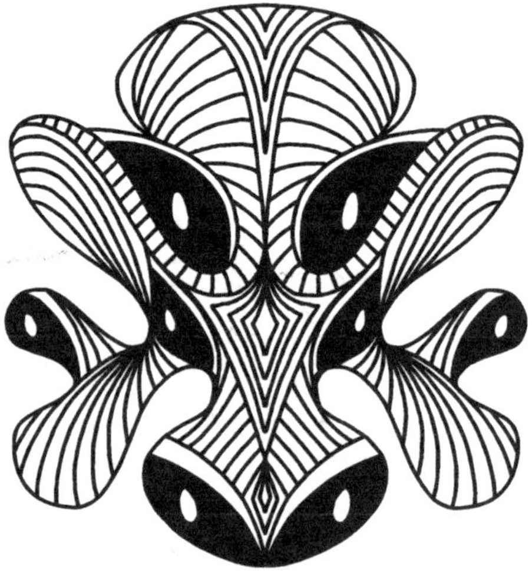

FATLINER WEIRDIES
VOLUME 3

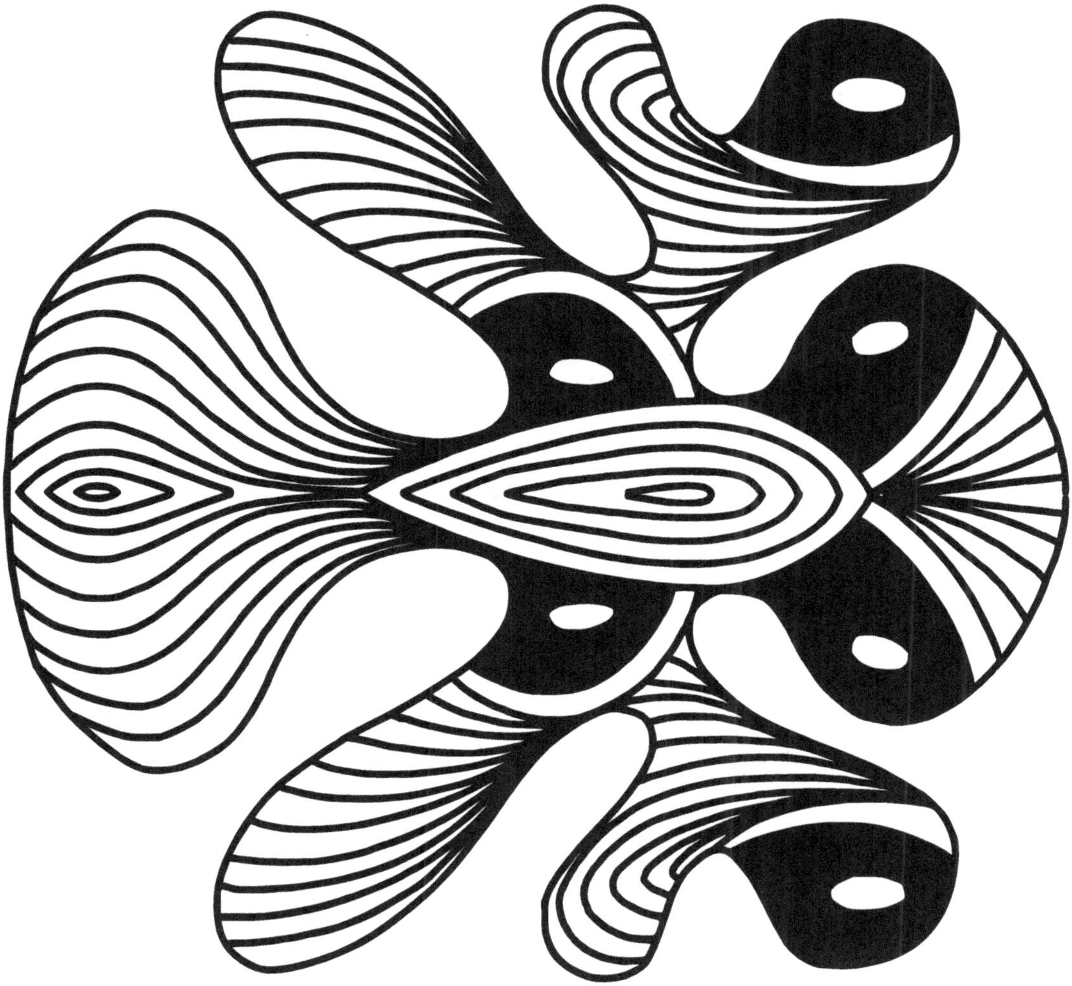

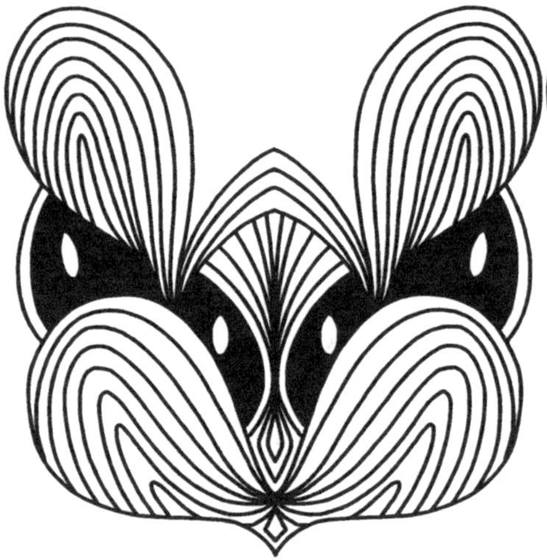

FATLINER WEIRDIES
VOLUME 1

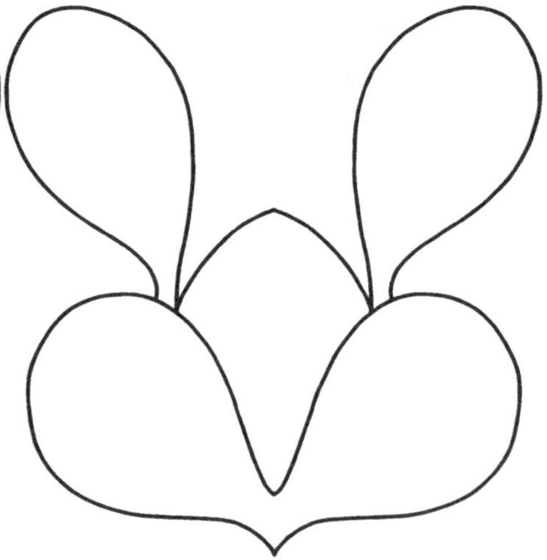

FATLINER WEIRDIES
THE TEMPLATES 1

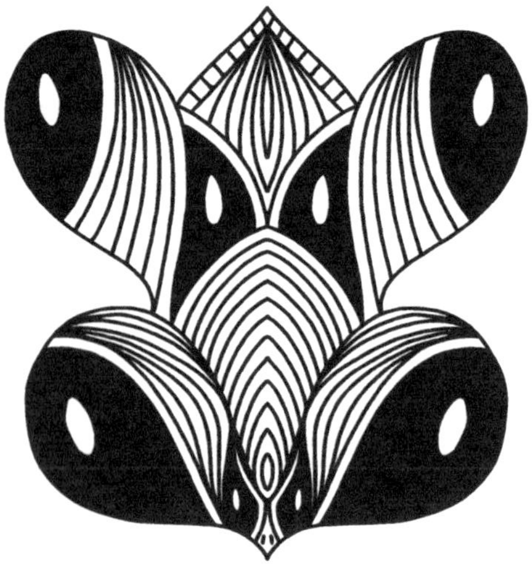

FATLINER WEIRDIES
VOLUME 3

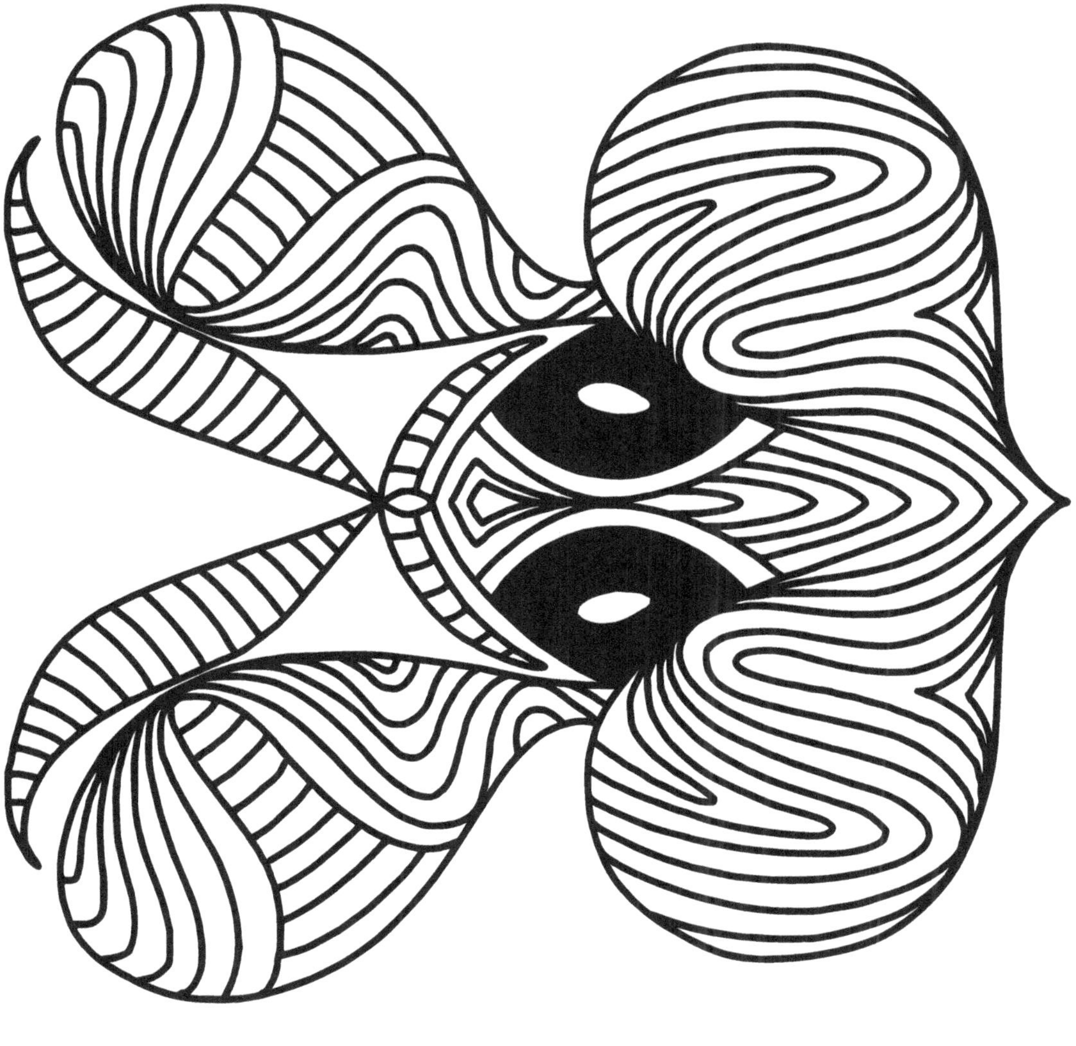

www.ingramcontent.com/pod-product-compliance
Lightning Source LLC
Chambersburg PA
CBHW082318220526
45470CB00008B/2344
9788772012032